W9-AWO-961

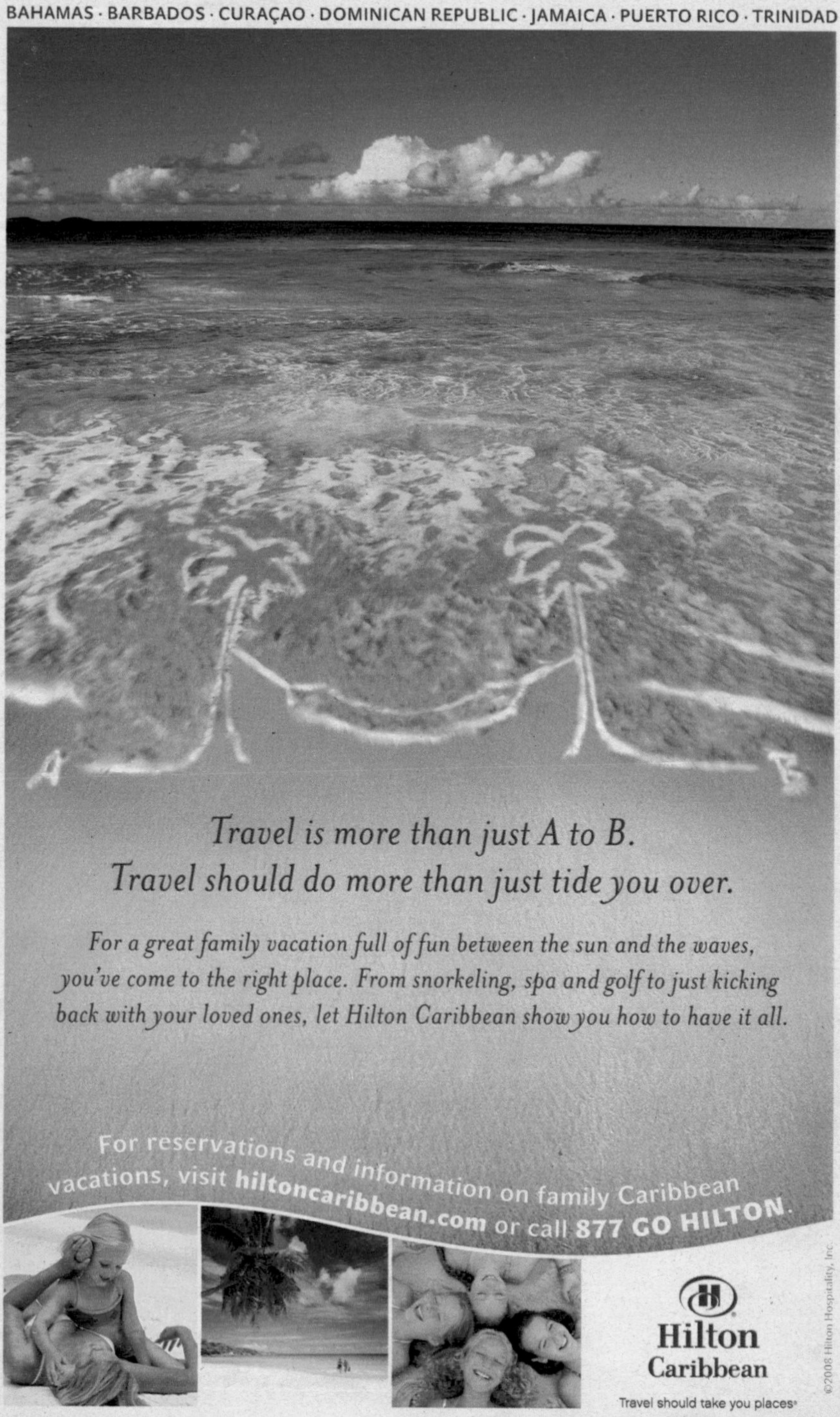

BAHAMAS · BARBADOS · CURAÇAO · DOMINICAN REPUBLIC · JAMAICA · PUERTO RICO · TRINIDAD

Travel is more than just A to B.
Travel should do more than just tide you over.

For a great family vacation full of fun between the sun and the waves, you've come to the right place. From snorkeling, spa and golf to just kicking back with your loved ones, let Hilton Caribbean show you how to have it all.

For reservations and information on family Caribbean vacations, visit **hiltoncaribbean.com** or call **877 GO HILTON**.

Travel should take you places®

Caribbean

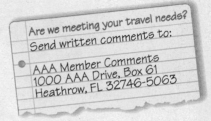

Are we meeting your travel needs?
Send written comments to:

AAA Member Comments
1000 AAA Drive, Box 61
Heathrow, FL 32746-5063

Published by AAA Publishing
1000 AAA Drive
Heathrow, FL 32746-5063

Advertising Rate and Circulation Information: (407) 444-8280

Printed in the USA by Quebecor World, Buffalo, NY

Photo Credit: (Cover & Title Page)
Petit Piton, Soufrière, St. Lucia
© Angelo Cavalli / age fotostock

Printed on recyclable paper.
Please recycle whenever possible.

Stock #1002

Caribbean

MAPS

Featured Information

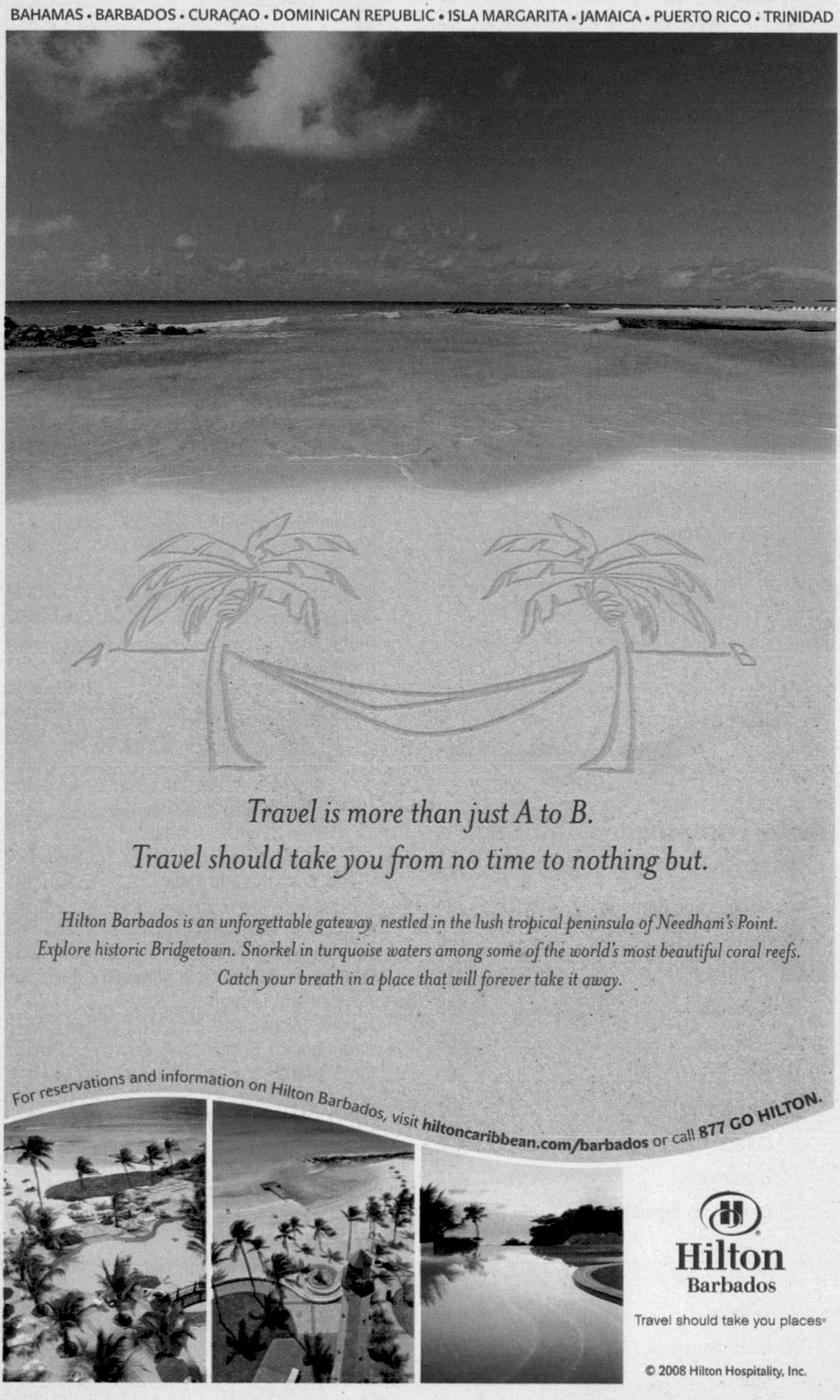

BAHAMAS • BARBADOS • CURAÇAO • DOMINICAN REPUBLIC • ISLA MARGARITA • JAMAICA • PUERTO RICO • TRINIDAD

Travel is more than just A to B.
Travel should take you from no time to nothing but.

Hilton Barbados is an unforgettable gateway nestled in the lush tropical peninsula of Needham's Point. Explore historic Bridgetown. Snorkel in turquoise waters among some of the world's most beautiful coral reefs. Catch your breath in a place that will forever take it away.

Tips for AAA.com's

Quick tips for using TripTik® Travel Planner's enhanced features.

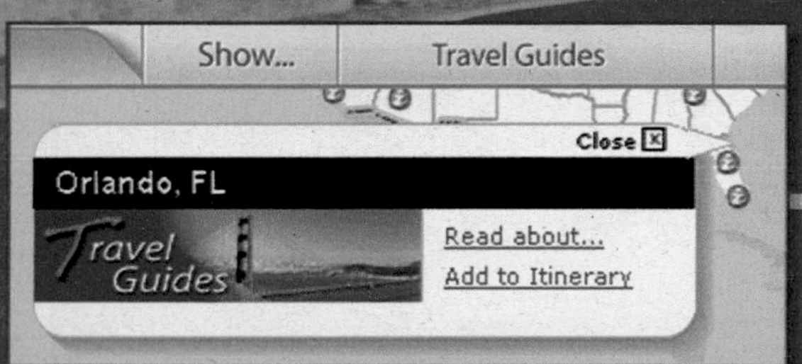

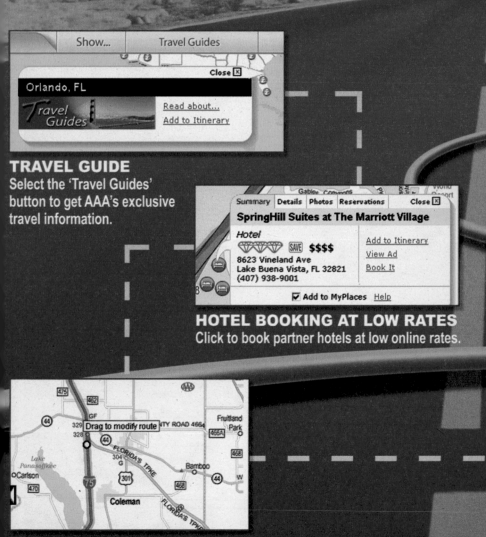

TRAVEL GUIDE
Select the 'Travel Guides' button to get AAA's exclusive travel information.

HOTEL BOOKING AT LOW RATES
Click to book partner hotels at low online rates.

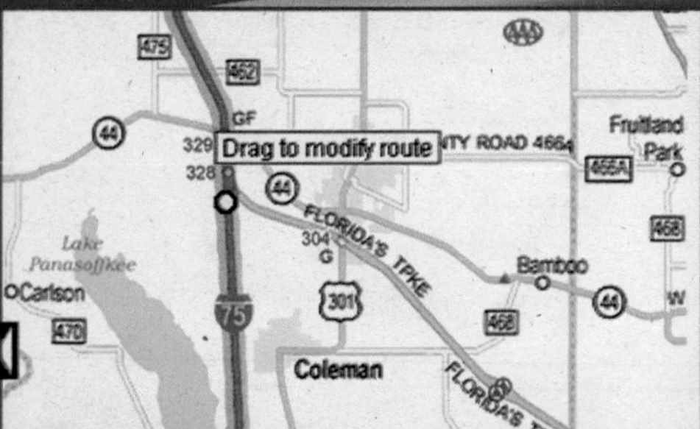

CLICK AND DRAG ROUTE MODIFICATION
Click and drag the route to the roads you prefer to travel.

THE ISLANDS OF THE
bahamas
Grand Bahama Island

USING YOUR GUIDE

Attractions, lodgings and restaurants are listed on the basis of merit alone after careful evaluation and approval by one of AAA/CAA's full-time, professionally trained inspectors. Evaluations are unannounced to ensure that we see an establishment just as you would see it.

An establishment's decision to advertise in the TourBook guide has no bearing on its evaluation or rating. Advertising for services or products does not imply AAA endorsement.

Information in this guide was believed accurate at the time of publication. However, since changes inevitably occur between annual editions, we suggest you work with your AAA travel professional or check on AAA.com to confirm prices and schedules.

How the TourBook Guide is Organized

The TourBook guide is organized into three distinct sections.

The **Points of Interest** section helps you plan daily activities and sightseeing excursions and provides details about the city or attraction you are visiting.

The **Lodgings and Restaurants** section helps you select AAA Approved accommodations and dining facilities meeting your specific needs and expectations.

The **Reference** section provides indexes for locating information within this guide and items to aid the trip planning process.

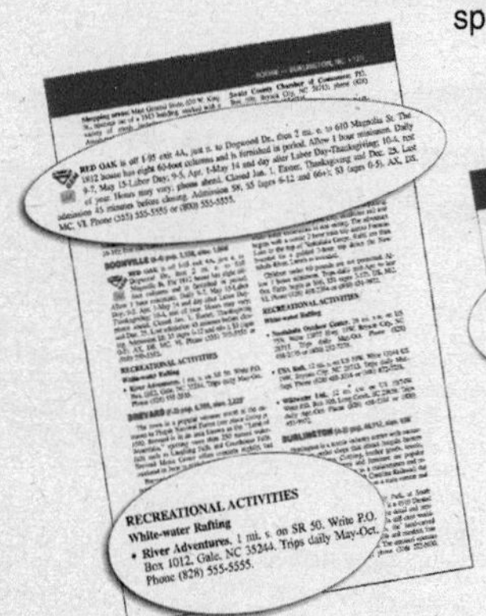
RECREATIONAL ACTIVITIES
White-water Rafting
• River Adventures, 1 mi. s. on SR 50. Write P.O. Box 1012, Gale, NC 35244. Trips daily May-Oct. Phone (828) 555-5555.

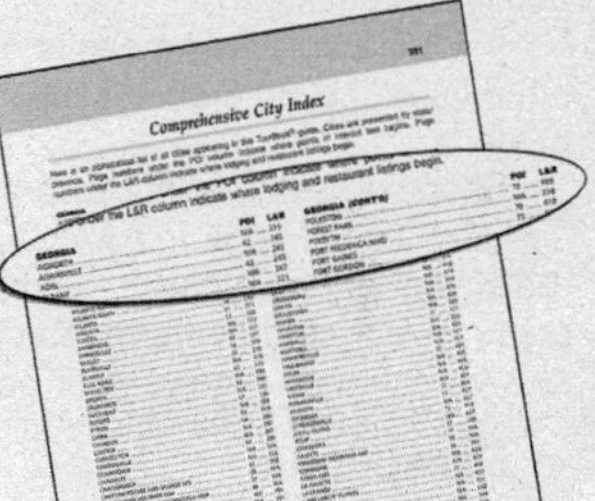
Comprehensive City Index

Locating the Attractions, Lodgings and Restaurants

Attractions, lodgings and restaurants are listed under the city in which they physically are located - or in some cases under the nearest recognized city. Most listings are alphabetically organized by state, province, region or island, then by city and establishment name.

A color is assigned to each state or province so that you can match the color bars at the top of the page to switch from the **Points of Interest** section to the **Lodgings and Restaurants** section.

Spotting maps help you physically locate points of interest, lodgings and restaurants in the major destinations.

The Comprehensive City Index located in the **Reference** section contains an A-to-Z list of cities.

Destination Cities and Destination Areas

Destination cities, established based on government models and local expertise, include metropolitan areas plus nearby vicinity cities. **Destination areas** are regions with broad tourist appeal; several cities will comprise the area.

If a city falls within a destination's vicinity, the city name will appear at its alphabetical location in the book, and a cross reference will give you the exact page on which listings for that city begin.

An orientation map appears at the beginning of each destination section to familiarize you with that destination.

Understanding the Points of Interest Listing

GEM Designation

A GEM icon indicates the attraction has been rated a AAA GEM, a "must see" point of interest that offers a *Great Experience for Members®*. These attractions have been judged to be of exceptional interest and quality by AAA Inspectors.

A GEM listing page with a brief description of individual GEM attractions follows the Orientation map near the beginning of each state or province Points of Interest section. Cross-references guide the reader to the attraction's listing page.

Discount Savings

The SAVE icon denotes those attractions offering AAA/CAA, AAA MasterCard, AAA VISA or international Show Your Card & Save discount cardholders a discount off the attraction's standard admission. Present your card at the attraction's admission desk.

A list of participating points of interest appears in the Reference section of this guide.

Shopping establishments preceded by a SAVE icon also provide to AAA/CAA members a discount and/or gift with purchase; present your card at the mall's customer service center to receive your benefit.

Exceptions

- Members should inquire in advance concerning the validity of the discount for special rates.
- The SAVE discount may not be used in conjunction with other discounts.
- Attractions that already provide a reduced senior or child rate may not honor the SAVE discount for those age groups.
- All offers are subject to change and may not apply during special events, particular days or seasons or for the entire validity period of the TourBook guide.

Adventure Travel

There are inherent risks with adventure travel activities like air tours, hiking, skiing and white-water rafting. For your own safety, please read and adhere to all safety instructions. Mentions of these activities are for information only and do **not** imply endorsement by AAA.

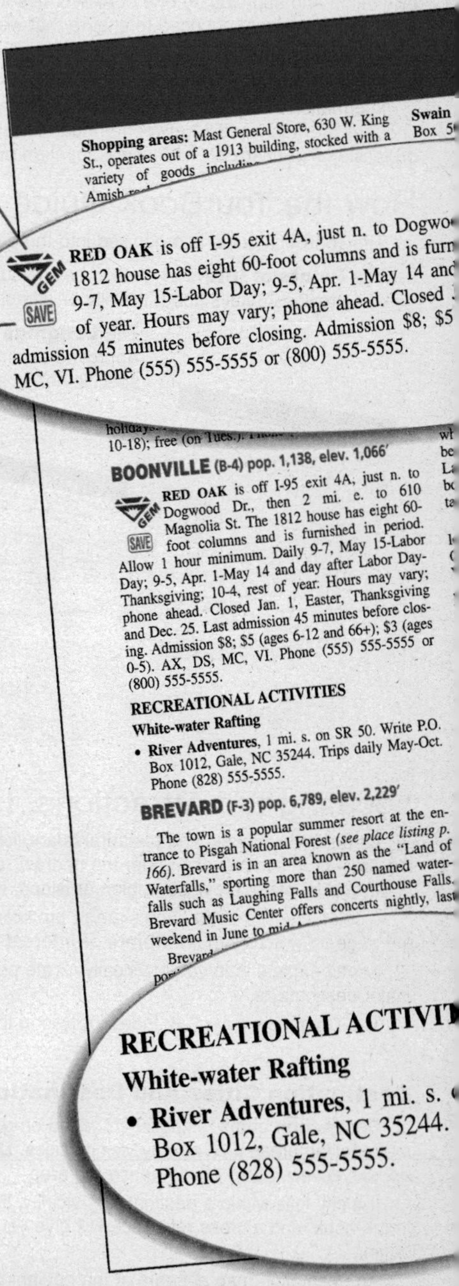

BOONVILLE (B-4) pop. 1,138, elev. 1,066′

RED OAK is off I-95 exit 4A, just n. to Dogwood Dr., then 2 mi. e. to 610 Magnolia St. The 1812 house has eight 60-foot columns and is furnished in period. Allow 1 hour minimum. Daily 9-7, May 15-Labor Day; 9-5, Apr. 1-May 14 and day after Labor Day-Thanksgiving; 10-4, rest of year. Hours may vary; phone ahead. Closed Jan. 1, Easter, Thanksgiving and Dec. 25. Last admission 45 minutes before closing. Admission $8; $5 (ages 6-12 and 66+); $3 (ages 0-5). AX, DS, MC, VI. Phone (555) 555-5555 or (800) 555-5555.

RECREATIONAL ACTIVITIES

White-water Rafting

- **River Adventures**, 1 mi. s. on SR 50. Write P.O. Box 1012, Gale, NC 35244. Trips daily May-Oct. Phone (828) 555-5555.

BREVARD (F-3) pop. 6,789, elev. 2,229′

The town is a popular summer resort at the entrance to Pisgah National Forest *(see place listing p. 166)*. Brevard is in an area known as the "Land of Waterfalls," sporting more than 250 named waterfalls such as Laughing Falls and Courthouse Falls. Brevard Music Center offers concerts nightly, last weekend in June to mid-...

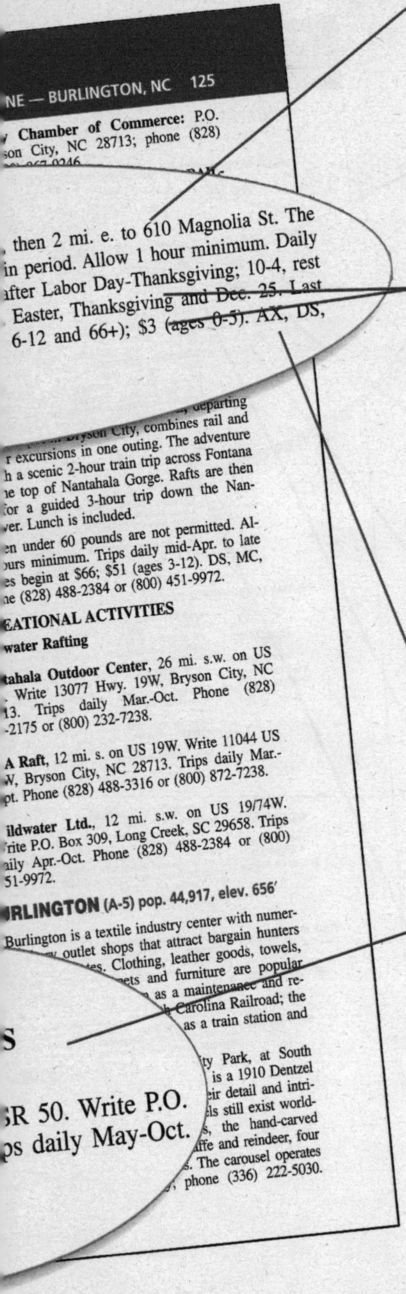

Directions

Unless otherwise specified, directions are given from the center of town, using the following highway designations:

I=interstate highway
SR=state route
FM=farm to market
Mex.=Mexican highway
US=federal highway
CR=county road
FR=forest road
Hwy.=Canadian or Caribbean highway

Prices and Dates of Operations

Admission prices are quoted without sales tax. Children under the lowest age specified are admitted free when accompanied by an adult. Days, months and age groups written with a hyphen are inclusive.

Prices pertaining to points of interest in the United States are quoted in U.S. dollars; points of interest in Canada are quoted in Canadian dollars; prices for points of interest in Mexico and the Caribbean are quoted as an approximate U.S. dollar equivalent.

Schedules and admission rates may change throughout the validity period of this guide. Check AAA.com for the most current information.

Credit Cards Accepted

AX=American Express
CB=Carte Blanche
DC=Diners Club
DS=Discover
JC=Japan Credit Bureau
MC=MasterCard
VI=VISA

Bulleted Listings

Gambling establishments within hotels are presented for member information regardless of whether the lodging is AAA Approved.

Recreational activities of a participatory nature (requiring physical exertion or special skills) are not inspected.

Wineries are inspected by AAA Inspectors to ensure they meet listing requirements and offer tours.

All are presented in an abbreviated bulleted format for informational purposes.

Understanding the Lodging Listing

Local Member Value

AAA or CAA and SAVE identify hotels that offer members a rate guarantee and up to two free special amenities as part of their Official Appointment partnership with AAA. Rate guarantee: Discounted standard room rate (usually based on last standard room availability) or the lowest public rate available at time of booking for dates of stay. Free special amenity options are included in the listing and could be either: breakfast, local telephone calls, newspaper, room upgrade, preferred room, or high-speed Internet.

Diamond Rating

The number of Diamonds informs you of the overall complexity of a lodging's amenities and service. Red indicates an Official Appointment lodging. An fyi in place of Diamonds indicates the property has not been rated but is included as an "information only" service. A detailed description of each rating level appears on page 20.

Classification

All Diamond Rated lodgings are classified using three key elements: style of operation, overall concept and service level. See pages 22-23 for details on our classifications.

Rates

The property's standard 2-person rates and effective dates are shown.

Rates are provided to AAA by each lodging and represent the publicly available rate or ranges for a standard room. Rates are rounded to the nearest dollar and do not include taxes. U.S., Mexican and Caribbean rates are in U.S. dollars; rates for Canadian lodgings are in Canadian dollars.

Information about cancellation and minimum stay policies is provided in the **Terms** section of the property's listing.

Online Reservations

This notation indicates AAA/CAA members can conveniently check room availability, validate room rates and make reservations for this property in a secure online environment at AAA.com.

Service Availability

Unit types, amenities and room features preceded by the word "Some" indicate the item is available on a limited basis, potentially within only one unit. The term "Fee" appearing to the left of an amenity icon indicates an extra charge applies.

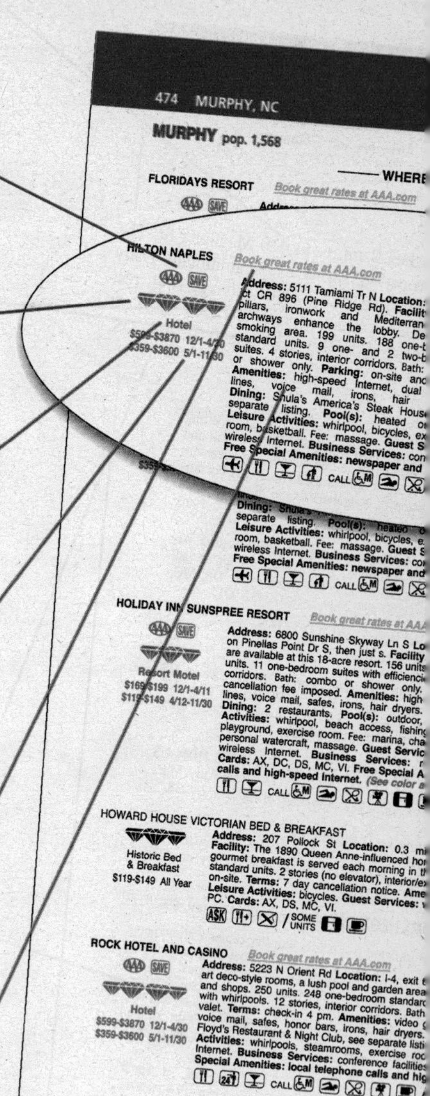

Nationwide Member Value

The blue box in the listing identifies hotel brands that offer an everyday member benefit at all AAA Approved locations. (See page 19 for additional program benefits.)

Spotting Symbol

Black ovals with white numbers are used to locate, or "spot," lodgings on maps we provide for larger cities.

Credit Cards Accepted

AX=American Express
CB=Carte Blanche
DC=Diners Club
DS=Discover
JC=Japan Credit Bureau
MC=MasterCard
VI=VISA

Some properties accept cash but require a credit card at registration. If you plan to pay in cash, call in advance for restrictions.

Icons

Lodging icons represent some of the member values, services and facilities offered.

Discounts

- ASK May offer discount

Member Services

- Airport transportation
- Pets allowed (call property for restrictions and fees)
- Restaurant on premises
- Restaurant off premises (walking distance)
- 24-hour room service
- Full bar
- Child care
- Accessible features (call property for available services and amenities)

Leisure Activities

- Full-service casino
- Pool
- Health club on premises
- Health club off premises
- Recreational activities

In-Room Amenities

- Designated non-smoking rooms
- VCR
- Movies
- Refrigerator
- Microwave
- Coffee maker
- No air conditioning
- No TV
- No cable TV
- No telephones

Safety Features

(see page 24)
(Mexico and Caribbean only)

- S Sprinklers
- D Smoke detectors

Understanding the Restaurant Listing

Official Appointment

[AAA] or [CAA] indicates Official Appointment (OA) restaurants. The OA program permits restaurants to display and advertise the AAA or CAA emblem. These establishments are highlighted in red to help you quickly identify them. The AAA or CAA Approved sign helps traveling members find restaurants that want member business.

Local Member Value

[SAVE] identifies restaurants that offer a Show Your Card & Save® discount to AAA/CAA members.

Diamond Rating

The number of Diamonds informs you of the overall complexity of food, presentation, service and ambience. Red indicates an Official Appointment restaurant. A detailed description of each Diamond level appears on page 21.

Cuisine Type

The cuisine type helps you select a dining facility that caters to your individual taste. AAA currently recognizes more than 120 different cuisine types.

Prices

Rates shown represent the minimum and maximum entree cost per person. Exceptions may include one-of-a-kind or special market priced items. Rates are rounded to the nearest dollar and do not include taxes. U.S., Mexican and Caribbean rates are in U.S. dollars; rates for Canadian restaurants are in Canadian dollars.

Icons

Icons provide additional information about services and facilities.

[AC] No air-conditioning

[&M] Accessible features offered (call property for available services and amenities)

[smoking icon] Designated smoking section available

Menus

This notation indicates AAA/CAA members can conveniently view the restaurant's menu in a secure online environment at AAA.com.

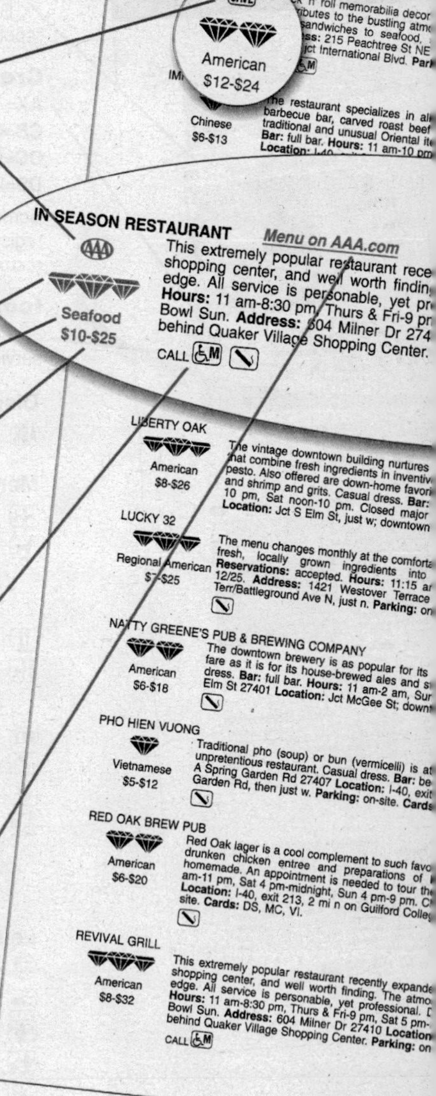

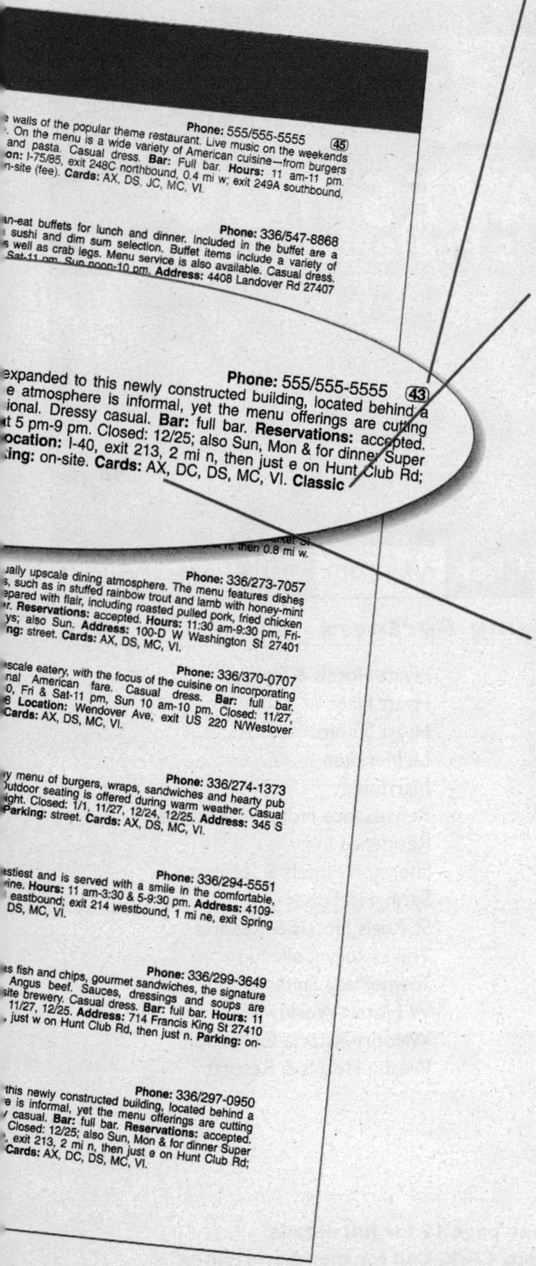

Spotting Symbol

White ovals with black numbers serve as restaurant locators and are used to locate, or "spot," restaurants on maps for larger cities.

Classifications

If applicable, a restaurant may be defined as:

Classic - renowned and/or landmark restaurant in business longer than 25 years, known for unique style and ambience.

Historic - establishments must meet one of the following criteria:

- Listed on the National Register of Historic Places
- Designated a National Historic Landmark
- Located in a National Register Historic District

Separate criteria designate historic properties in Canada, Mexico and the Caribbean.

Credit Cards Accepted

AX=American Express
CB=Carte Blanche
DC=Diners Club
DS=Discover
JC=Japan Credit Bureau
MC=MasterCard
VI=VISA

AAA/CAA members can generally expect to pay no more than the maximum regular rate printed in the TourBook guide in each rate range for a standard room. On rare occasions AAA receives or inadvertently publishes incorrect rates.

Obtain current AAA/CAA member rates and make reservations at AAA.com. Rates may vary within the range, depending on season and room type. Listed rates are usually based on last standard room availability.

Discounts

Member discounts, when offered, will apply to rates quoted within the rate range and are applicable at the time of booking. Special rates used in advertising, as well as special short-term promotional rates lower than the lowest listed rate in the range, are not subject to additional member discounts.

Exceptions

Rates for properties operating as concessionaires for the U.S. National Park Service are not guaranteed due to governing regulations. Rates in the Mexico TourBook are not guaranteed and may fluctuate based on the exchange rate of the peso.

Lodgings may temporarily increase room rates, not recognize discounts or modify pricing policies during special events. Examples of special events range from Mardi Gras and the Kentucky Derby (including pre-Derby events) to college football games, holidays, holiday periods and state fairs. Although some special events are listed in AAA/CAA TourBook guides and on AAA.com, it is always wise to check in advance with AAA travel professionals for specific dates.

Get the Room You Reserved

When making your reservation, identify yourself as a AAA or CAA member and request written confirmation to guarantee: type of room, rate, dates of stay, and cancellation and refund policies. At registration, show your membership card.

When you find your room is not as specified, and you have written confirmation of reservations for a certain type of accommodation, you should be given the option of choosing a different room or finding one elsewhere. Should you choose to go elsewhere and a refund is refused or resisted, submit the matter to AAA/CAA within 30 days, along with complete documentation, including your reasons for refusing the room and copies of your written confirmation and any receipts or canceled checks associated with this problem.

If you are charged more than the maximum rate listed in the TourBook guide for a standard room, question the additional charge. If management refuses to adhere to the published rate, pay for the room and submit your receipt and membership number to AAA/CAA within 30 days. Include all pertinent information: dates of stay, rate paid, itemized paid receipts, number of persons in your party and the room number you occupied, and list any extra room equipment used. A refund of the amount paid in excess of the stated maximum will be made if our investigation indicates that unjustified charging occurred.

Deposit, Refund and Cancellation Policies

Most establishments give full deposit refunds if they have been notified at least 48 hours before the normal check-in time. Listing prose will note if more than 48 hours' notice is required for cancellation. Some properties may charge a cancellation or handling fee. When this applies, "cancellation fee imposed" will appear in the listing. If you cancel too late, you have little recourse if a refund is denied.

When an establishment requires full or partial payment in advance and your trip is cut short, a refund may not be given.

When canceling a reservation, phone the lodging immediately. Make a note of the date and time you called, the cancellation number if there is one, and the name of the person who handled the cancellation. If your AAA/CAA club made your reservation, allow them to make the cancellation for you as well, so you will have proof of cancellation.

Check-in and Check-out Times

Check-in and check-out times are shown in the lodging listings, under Terms, only if they are before 3 p.m. or after 10 a.m. respectively.

Members Save With Our Partners

AAA Show Your Card & Save®

These National Show Your Card & Save® partners provide the listed member benefits. Visit AAA.com/Save to discover all the great Show Your Card & Save® discounts in your area. Admission tickets that offer greater discounts may be available for purchase at the local AAA/CAA club. A maximum of six attraction tickets is available at the discount price at the gate; six discounted tickets is also the maximum for Amtrak and Gray Line.

SeaWorld, Busch Gardens, Sesame Place
AAA.com/SeaWorld, AAA.com/BuschGardens, AAA.com/SesamePlace

- Save on admission at the gate, at participating offices, or online

- Save 10% on up-close dining; visit Guest Relations for details

Six Flags AAA.com/SixFlags

- Save on admission at the gate, at participating offices, or online
- Save 10% on merchandise purchases of $15 or more at in-park stores

Universal Orlando Resort and Universal Studios Hollywood
AAA.com/Universal

- Save on admission at the gate, at participating offices, or online

- Save 10% at select food and merchandise venues in-park and at Universal CityWalk®

Restaurant Partner
Savings applies to AAA/CAA members and up to five guests.

Joe's Crab Shack

- Save 10% on food, non-alcoholic beverages and merchandise

Landry's Seafood House, The Crab House, Chart House, Muer Seafood Restaurants, and Aquarium and Downtown Aquarium Restaurants

- Save 10% on food and non-alcoholic beverages at all of the above restaurants

- Save 10% on merchandise at Aquarium and Downtown Aquarium restaurants

Hard Rock Cafe

- Save 10% on food, non-alcoholic beverages and merchandise at all U.S. and select Canadian and international locations

Tanger Outlet Centers www.tangeroutlet.com

- Save up to 20% on total purchase at select merchants with AAA/CAA coupon booklet
- Member BONUS: FREE $5 gift card for each additional Tanger Outlet Center visited after first within same calendar year
- Show membership card and register at the AAA customer service desk when you visit

Amtrak

- 10% discount on rail fare when booked at least 3 days in advance of travel date

AMTRAK

Grand Canyon Railway

- Save up to 20% on rail fare, hotel accommodations, restaurant and gift shop purchases sold outside of Grand Canyon National Park

Gray Line
AAA.com/GrayLine

- Save 10% on sightseeing tours of 1 day or less worldwide

AAA Preferred Lodging Partners

EXPECT SAVINGS, SELECTION, AND SATISFACTION

- **Best AAA/CAA member rates for your dates of stay.** Provide valid membership number when placing reservation and show your card at hotel check-in.
- **Satisfaction guarantee.** Notify the property if you are dissatisfied with any part of your stay. If the matter cannot be resolved, you may be entitled to compensation (see page 17).
- **Seasonal promotions and special member offers.** Visit AAA.com to view current offers.
- **Everyday member benefit.*** Look for the blue boxes in the TourBook listings for everyday values offered at all AAA Approved locations.

**Offer good at time of publication: Chains and offers may change without notice. Preferred Hotel Partner discounts may vary in Mexico and the Caribbean.*

10% Off Best Available Rates
Best Western International

5% or more Off Best Available Rates
Conrad, Doubletree, Embassy Suites, Hampton, Hilton, Hilton Garden Inn, Hilton Grand Vacations, Homewood Suites, and Waldorf=Astoria Collection

10% Off Best Available Rates
Andaz, Grand Hyatt, Hyatt Place, Hyatt Regency, Hyatt Summerfield Suites, and Park Hyatt

5% or more Off Best Available Rates
Courtyard, Fairfield Inn, JW Marriott, Marriott, Renaissance Hotels & Resorts, Residence Inn, SpringHill Suites, and TownePlace Suites

5-15% Off Best Available Rates
aloft, element, Four Points, Le Meridien, Sheraton, St. Regis, The Luxury Collection, Westin, and W Hotels

Understanding the Diamond Ratings

AAA/CAA inspectors have evaluated and rated each of the 58,000 lodging and restaurant establishments in the TourBook series to ensure quality travel information for our members. All properties must meet AAA's minimum requirements (for lodgings) concerning cleanliness, comfort and security - or - AAA's minimum requirements (for restaurants) pertaining to cleanliness, food preparation and service.

Eligible applicants receive an unannounced evaluation by a AAA/CAA inspector that includes two distinct components:

- **AAA Approval:** The inspector first must determine whether the property meets the criteria required to be AAA Approved. Every establishment that meets these strict guidelines offers AAA members the assurance that, regardless of the Diamond Rating, it provides acceptable quality, cleanliness, service and value.
- **AAA Diamond Rating:** Once an establishment becomes AAA Approved, it is then assigned a rating of one to five Diamonds, indicating the extensiveness of its facilities, amenities and services, from basic to moderate to luxury. These Diamond Ratings guide members in selecting establishments appropriately matched to their needs and expectations.

LODGINGS

1 Diamond

One Diamond lodgings typically appeal to the budget-minded traveler. They provide essential, no-frills accommodations and basic comfort and hospitality.

2 Diamond

Two Diamond lodgings appeal to family travelers seeking affordable yet more than the basic accommodations. Facilities, decor and amenities are modestly enhanced.

3 Diamond

Three Diamond lodgings offer a distinguished style. Properties are multi-faceted, with marked upgrades in physical attributes, amenities and guest comforts.

4 Diamond

Four Diamond lodgings are refined and stylish. Physical attributes are upscale. The fundamental hallmarks at this level include an extensive array of amenities combined with a high degree of hospitality, service and attention to detail.

5 Diamond

Five Diamond lodgings provide the ultimate in luxury and sophistication. Physical attributes are extraordinary in every manner. Service is meticulous, exceeding guest expectations and maintaining impeccable standards of excellence. Extensive personalized services and amenities provide first-class comfort.

fyi The lodging listings with **fyi** in place of Diamonds are included as an *information only* service for members. The icon indicates that a property has not been rated for one or more of the following reasons: too new to rate, under construction, under major renovation, not evaluated, may not meet all AAA requirements.

A property not meeting all AAA requirements is included for either its member value or because it may be the only accommodation available in the area. Listing prose will give insight as to why the **fyi** designation was assigned.

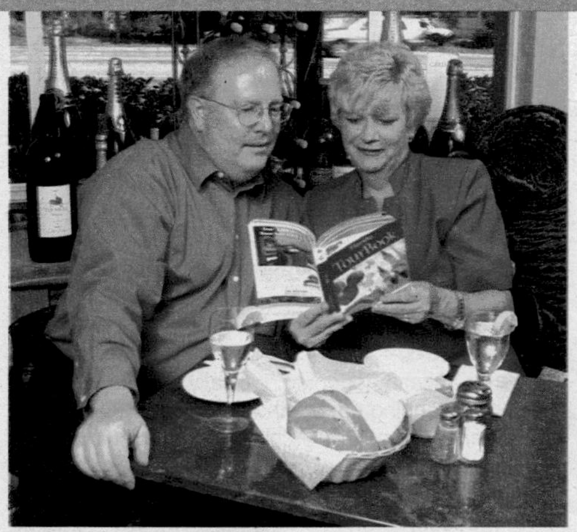

RESTAURANTS

1 Diamond

One Diamond restaurants provide simple, familiar specialty food (such as burgers, chicken, pizza or tacos) at an economical price. Often self-service, basic surroundings complement a no-nonsense approach.

2 Diamond

Two Diamond restaurants offer a familiar, family-oriented experience. Menu selection includes home-style foods and family favorites, often cooked to order, modestly enhanced and reasonably priced. Service is accommodating yet relaxed, a perfect complement to casual surroundings.

3 Diamond

Three Diamond restaurants convey an entry into fine dining and are often positioned as adult-oriented experiences. The atypical menu may feature the latest cooking trends and/or traditional cuisine. Expanded beverage offerings complement the menu. The ambience is well coordinated, comfortable and enhanced by a professional service staff.

4 Diamond

Four Diamond restaurants provide a distinctive fine-dining experience that is typically expensive. Surroundings are highly refined with upscale enhancements throughout. Highly creative chefs use imaginative presentations to augment fresh, top-quality ingredients. A proficient service staff meets or exceeds guest expectations. A wine steward may offer menu-specific knowledge to guide selection.

5 Diamond

Five Diamond restaurants are luxurious and renowned for consistently providing a world-class experience. Highly acclaimed chefs offer artistic menu selections that are imaginative and unique, using only the finest ingredients available. A maitre d' leads an expert service staff in exceeding guest expectations, attending to every detail in an effortless and unobtrusive manner.

fyi The restaurants with **fyi** in place of Diamonds are included as an *information only* service for members. These listings provide additional dining choices but have not yet been evaluated.

Understanding the Lodging Classifications

To ensure that your lodging needs and preferences are met, we recommend that you consider an establishment's classification when making your travel choices. While the quality and comfort at properties with the same Diamond Rating should be consistent (regardless of the classification), there are differences in typical decor/theme elements, range of facilities and service levels.

Lodging Classifications

Bed & Breakfast

Typically smaller scale properties emphasizing a high degree of personal touches that provide guests an "at home" feeling. Guest units tend to be individually decorated. Rooms may not include some modern amenities such as televisions and telephones, and may have a shared bathroom. Usually owner-operated with a common room or parlor separate from the innkeeper's living quarters, where guests and operators can interact during evening and breakfast hours. Evening office closures are normal. A continental or full, hot breakfast is served and is included in the room rate.

1884 Paxton House Inn
Thomasville, GA

Cabin

Vacation-oriented, typically smaller scale, freestanding units of simple construction—roughly finished logs or stone—and basic design or décor. Often located in wooded, rural, or waterfront locations. As a rule, basic cleaning supplies, kitchen utensils, and complete bed and bath linens are supplied. The guest registration area may be located off site.

Greenbrier Valley Resorts
Gatlinburg, TN

Condominium

Vacation-oriented—commonly for extended-stay purposes—apartment-style accommodations of varying design or décor. Routinely available for rent through a management company, units often contain one or more bedrooms, a living room, full kitchen, and an eating area. Studio-type models combine the sleeping and living areas into one room. As a rule, basic cleaning supplies, kitchen utensils, and complete bed and bath linens are supplied. The guest registration area may be located off site.

Sands of Kahana
Kahana, Maui, HI

Cottage

Vacation-oriented, typically smaller scale, freestanding units with home style enhancements in architectural design and interior décor. Often located in wooded, rural, or waterfront locations. Units may vary in design and décor. As a rule, basic cleaning supplies, kitchen utensils, and complete bed and bath linens are supplied. The guest registration area may be located off site.

Paradise Villas, Little Cayman Island

Country Inn

Although similar in definition to a bed and breakfast, country inns are usually larger in scale with spacious public areas and offer a dining facility that serves—at a minimum—breakfast and dinner.

Greenville Inn, Greenville, ME

Hotel

Commonly, a multistory establishment with interior room entrances offering a variety of guest unit styles. The magnitude of the public areas is determined by the overall theme, location and service level, but may include a variety of facilities such as a restaurant, shops, fitness center, spa, business center, and/or meeting rooms.

The Grand America Hotel
Salt Lake City, UT

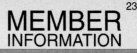

Motel

Commonly, a one- or two-story establishment with exterior room entrances and drive up parking. Typically, guest units have one bedroom with a bathroom of similar décor and design. Public areas and facilities are often limited in size and/or availability.

Best Western Deltona Inn, Deltona, FL

Ranch

Typically a working ranch with an obvious rustic, Western theme featuring equestrian-related activities and a variety of guest unit styles.

Lost Valley Ranch, Deckers, CO

Vacation Rental House

Vacation-oriented—commonly for extended-stay purposes—typically larger scale, freestanding, and of varying design or décor. Routinely available for rent through a management company, houses often contain two or more bedrooms, a living room, full kitchen, dining room, and multiple bathrooms. As a rule, basic cleaning supplies, kitchen utensils, and complete bed and bath linens are supplied. The guest registration area may be located off site.

ResortQuest, Hilton Head Island, SC

Lodging Sub-classifications

The following are sub-classifications that may appear along with the classifications listed previously to provide a more specific description of the lodging.

Boutique

Often thematic and typically an informal, yet highly personalized experience; may have a luxurious or quirky style which is fashionable or unique.

Casino

Extensive gambling facilities are available, such as: blackjack, craps, keno, and slot machines. **Note:** This sub-classification will not appear beneath its Diamond Rating in the listing. It will be indicated by a icon and will be included in the row of icons immediately below the lodging listing.

Classic

Renowned and landmark properties, older than 50 years, well-known for their unique style and ambience.

Contemporary

Overall design and theme reflects characteristics of the present era's mainstream tastes and style.

Extended Stay

Offers a predominance of long-term accommodations with a designated full-service kitchen area within each unit.

Historic

These properties are typically over 75 years of age and exhibit many features of a historic nature with respect to architecture, design, furnishings, public record, or acclaim. Properties must meet one of the following criteria:

- Maintained the integrity of the historical nature
- Listed on the National Register of Historic Places
- National Historic Landmark or located in a National Register Historic District

Separate criteria designate historic properties in Canada, Mexico and the Caribbean.

Resort

Recreation-oriented, geared to vacation travelers seeking a specific destination experience. Travel packages, meal plans, themed entertainment, and social and recreational programs are typically available. Recreational facilities are extensive and may include spa treatments, golf, tennis, skiing, fishing, or water sports. Larger resorts may offer a variety of guest accommodations.

Retro

Overall design and theme reflect a contemporary design reinterpreting styles from a bygone era.

Vacation Rental

Typically houses, condos, cottages or cabins; these properties are a "home away from home" offering more room and greater value for the money. In general, they provide the conveniences of home, such as full kitchens and washers/dryers. Located in resort or popular destination areas within close proximity to major points of interest, attractions, or recreation areas, these properties may require a pre-arranged reservation and check-in at an off-site location. Housekeeping services may be limited or not included.

Vintage

Offers a window to the past and provides an experience reflecting a predominance of traits associated with the era of their origin.

Guest Safety

Room Security

In order to be approved for listing in AAA/CAA TourBook guides for the United States and Canada, accommodations must have dead bolt locks on all guest room entry doors and connecting room doors.

If the area outside the guest room door is not visible from inside the room through a window or door panel, viewports must be installed on all guest room entry doors. Bed and breakfast properties and country inns are not required to have viewports. Ground floor and easily accessible sliding doors must be equipped with some type of secondary security locks.

Even with those approval requirements, AAA cannot guarantee guest safety. AAA Inspectors view a percentage of rooms at each property since it is not feasible to evaluate every room in every lodging establishment. Therefore, AAA cannot guarantee that there are working locks on all doors and windows in all guest rooms.

Fire Safety

Because of the highly specialized skills needed to conduct professional fire safety inspections, AAA/CAA Inspectors cannot assess fire safety.

Properties must meet all federal, state/province and local fire codes. Each guest unit in all U.S. and Canadian lodging properties must be equipped with an operational, single-station smoke detector. A AAA/CAA Inspector has evaluated a sampling of the rooms to verify this equipment is in place.

Mexico and the Caribbean

Requirements for some features, such as door locks and smoke detectors/sprinkler systems, differ in Mexico and the Caribbean. If a property met AAA's security requirements at the time of the evaluation, the phrase "Meets AAA guest room security requirements" appears in the listing.

Service Animals

The Americans with Disabilities Act (ADA) prohibits U.S. businesses that serve the public from discriminating against persons with disabilities. Some businesses have mistakenly denied access to persons who use service animals. Businesses must permit entry to guests and their service animals, as well as allow service animals to accompany guests to all public areas of a property.

A property is permitted to ask whether the animal is a service animal or a pet, and whether the guest has a disability. The property may not, however, ask questions about the nature of the disability, the service provided by the animal, or require proof of a disability or certification that the animal is a service animal. These regulations may not apply in Canada, Mexico or the Caribbean.

No fees or deposits, even those normally charged for pets, may be charged for service animals. Service animals fulfill a critical need for their owners—they are not pets.

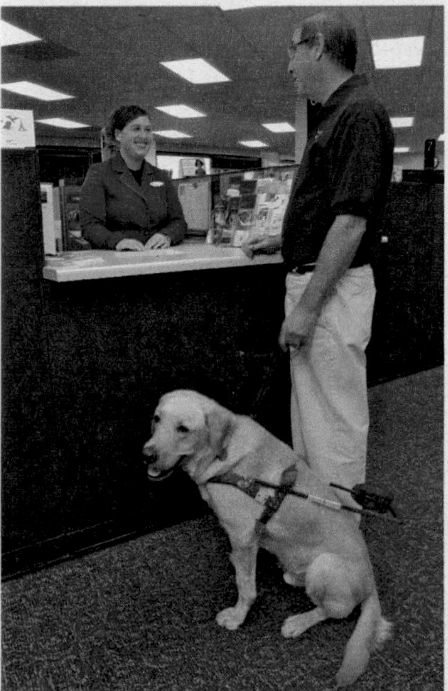

Frank Frand with his seeing eye dog, Cardinal.

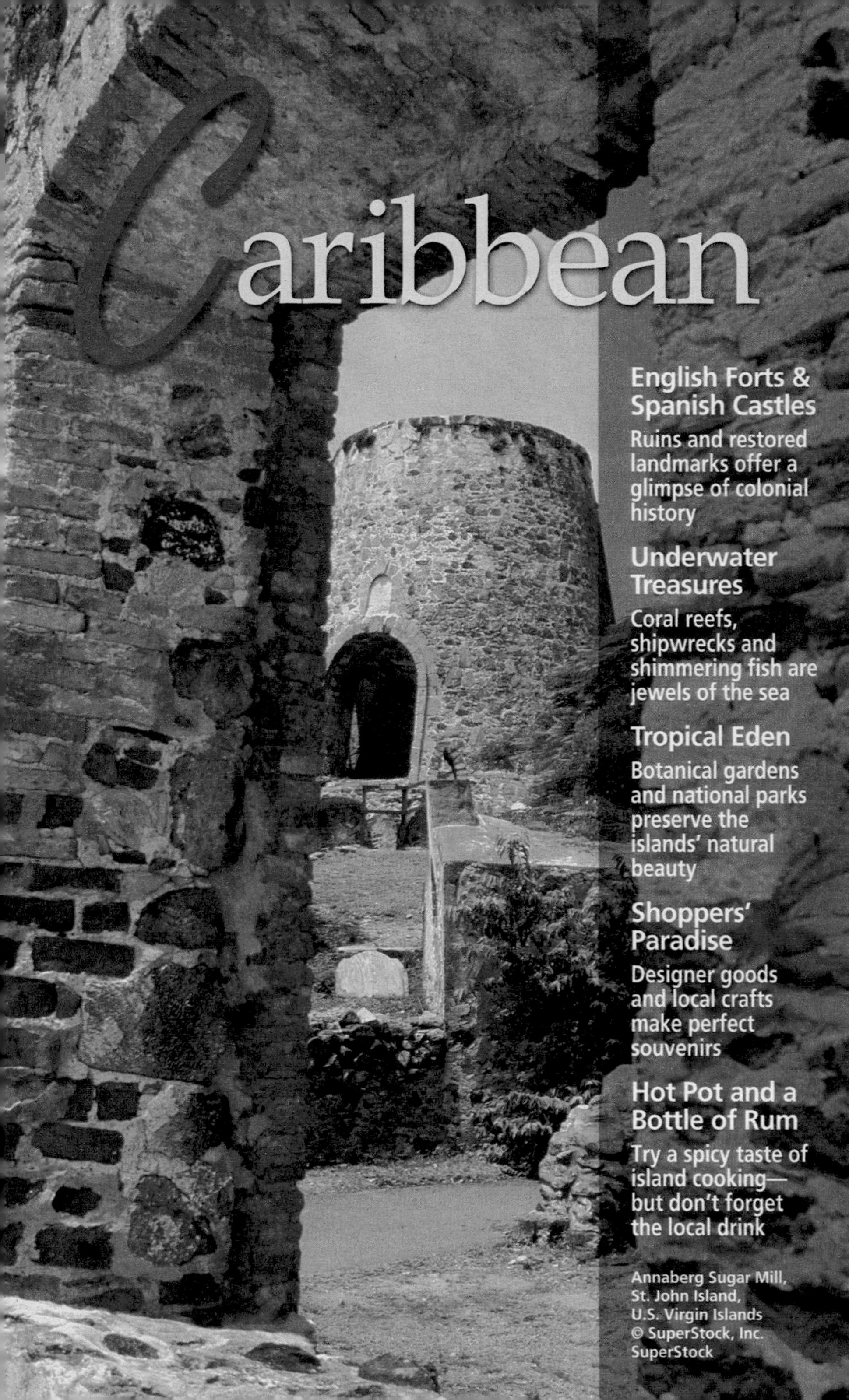

Caribbean
English Forts & Spanish Castles
Ruins and restored landmarks offer a glimpse of colonial history
Underwater Treasures
Coral reefs, shipwrecks and shimmering fish are jewels of the sea
Tropical Eden
Botanical gardens and national parks preserve the islands' natural beauty
Shoppers' Paradise
Designer goods and local crafts make perfect souvenirs
Hot Pot and a Bottle of Rum
Try a spicy taste of island cooking—but don't forget the local drink

Annaberg Sugar Mill, St. John Island, U.S. Virgin Islands

Fort San Felipe del Morro, San Juan, Puerto Rico / © Bob Gevinski / Danita Delimont Stock Photography

Like beads in a coral necklace strung between the Atlantic Ocean and the Caribbean Sea, the islands of the West Indies stretch east and south from the Gulf of Mexico and Florida to the northern coast of South America—a span of more than 2,000 miles.

The Caribbean islands' diversity of races and traditions generates an aura of romance and mystery. The Arawak, Taíno and Carib Indians were the first to arrive, migrating to the Antilles some 2,000 years before Columbus landed in 1492. Spanish, French, Dutch and American settlers would follow, bringing with them African slaves to work the gold mines and sugar mills that flourished on the islands until the late 19th century.

Explorers, pirates, settlers and slaves—all would carry their own customs to the archipelago Columbus called "the most beautiful land that human eyes have seen."

Today, tourism is the lifeblood of the islands, bringing a new influx of travelers from across the seas. Cruise ships have replaced three-masted schooners as the best way to get there, and lying in the sun with an umbrella drink may be all some visitors do once they arrive. For the more energetic, there's sightseeing, shopping, fishing, sailing, scuba diving, horseback riding, tennis and golf.

The lush islands of the Caribbean, The Bahamas and Bermuda offer enough natural beauty and cultural variety to please any visitor's tastes.

The hundreds of islands in the Caribbean archipelago are divided into The Bahamas and the Greater and Lesser Antilles. The Antilles were named after *Antillia*, a mythical island sought by Spanish explorers. The Greater Antilles include the largest islands: Cuba, Jamaica, Puerto Rico and the island of Hispaniola, which contains Haiti and the Dominican Republic.

The Lesser Antilles encompass the remaining arc of smaller isles as well as several islands off the coast of Venezuela. Major groupings within the Lesser Antilles include the Virgin Islands and the Windward and Leeward Islands. Bermuda is not a Caribbean island at all, but is located in the Atlantic Ocean, 650 miles due east of Cape Hatteras, N.C.

According to geologists the Caribbean archipelago is a portion of a once unbroken bridge that joined North and South America. Through unknown events some of the land sank, and what remains are the peaks of a submarine volcanic mountain range. A few of the Caribbean islands, as well as Bermuda, are coral formations.

The easterly trade winds that maintain the region's even temperatures were responsible for depositing Columbus at what he thought was the "back door" to India—probably San Salvador in The Bahamas. Columbus continued onward to Cuba and Hispaniola. Although the great golden treasures he envisioned never fully materialized, he did meet the Arawaks and the Caribs, whom he mistook for East Indians. His return to Spain with charts, a small amount of gold and tales of great fortune gained him financing for three more visits.

On the heels of Columbus came such *conquistadores* as Hernando Cortés and Francisco Pizarro seeking their share of land and gold. European investors built mining operations and sugar plantations, using native Indians as laborers. As the local work force declined, a license was arranged permitting the importation of African slaves—an agreement that was to have far-reaching effects on the New World.

Ships with holds laden with the produce of the Caribbean opened the door on yet another occupation. Buccaneers, pirates, smugglers and freebooters proliferated, using the islands' numerous caves and inlets for shelter and ambush. The result was many years of terror, bloodshed and territorial feuding. As Spanish supremacy in the region weakened, England, France, the Netherlands and the United States all added their cultural marks to the Caribbean.

Caribbean Historical Timeline

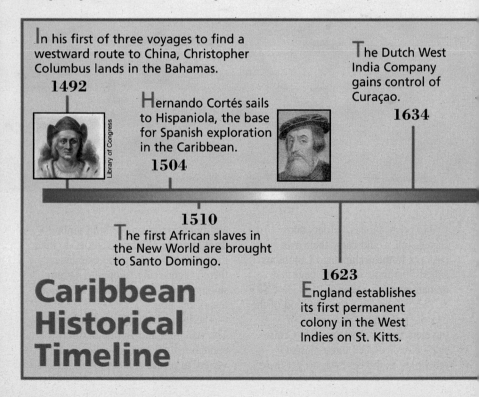

1492 In his first of three voyages to find a westward route to China, Christopher Columbus lands in the Bahamas.

Library of Congress

1504 Hernando Cortés sails to Hispaniola, the base for Spanish exploration in the Caribbean.

1510 The first African slaves in the New World are brought to Santo Domingo.

1623 England establishes its first permanent colony in the West Indies on St. Kitts.

1634 The Dutch West India Company gains control of Curaçao.

Today's island groups reflect this heritage among sovereign states, overseas departments and dependencies. The French West Indies include Guadeloupe, Martinique, St. Barthélemy and St. Martin. The Dutch islands of the Netherlands Antilles are Aruba, Bonaire, Curaçao, St. Eustatius and Saba and St. Maarten. The British West Indies encompass Anguilla, the Cayman Islands, the British Virgin Islands and Turks and Caicos Islands. The American flag flies over the U.S. Virgin Islands and Puerto Rico.

Hundreds of Hideaways

With so many islands to visit, choosing one can be a daunting task. If language barriers are a concern, keep in mind that English is spoken at most large resorts and in most shops and restaurants.

Consider your priorities and interests: If you do not care for water sports, sunbathing or having lots of time on your hands, choose one of the more developed islands that offers plenty of shopping, sightseeing, dining and nightlife. On the other hand, if you want to "get away from it all," there are still some islands that have yet to be "discovered" and commercialized. On such islands modern conveniences might be rather sparse but privacy is abundant.

The local currency exchange rate also might influence your decision. *Check Fast Facts for the governing rates at press time.* Exchange rates can fluctuate significantly, so you should always check them with a financial institution prior to departure.

Because of the varying economic conditions on most islands, the contrast between luxury resorts and poverty-ridden villages can be a harsh reality. You might want to investigate the political and social climate of an island before planning your trip.

Tropical Seasons

Much of The Bahamas and all of the Caribbean islands lie below the Tropic of Cancer, the northern limit of the tropics, and therefore enjoy a mild climate year round. The main season varies from island to island and hotel to hotel but generally runs from mid-December to mid-April. The off-season is late spring, summer and fall, except in Bermuda, which is much farther north, where the off-season spans November to mid-March. Most islands are subject to a rainy season between June and November, which coincides with hurricane season.

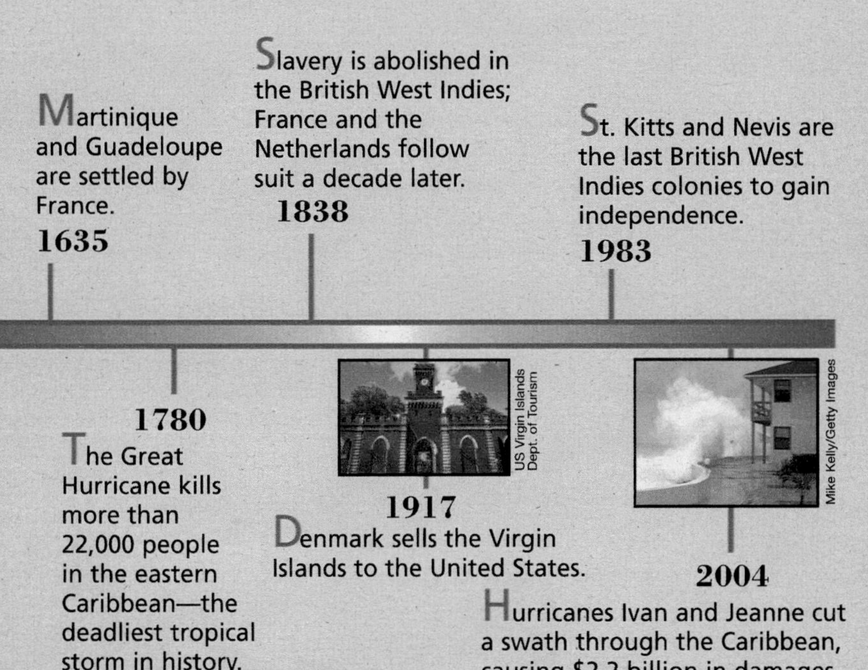

Martinique and Guadeloupe are settled by France.
1635
Slavery is abolished in the British West Indies; France and the Netherlands follow suit a decade later.
1838
St. Kitts and Nevis are the last British West Indies colonies to gain independence.
1983
1780
The Great Hurricane kills more than 22,000 people in the eastern Caribbean—the deadliest tropical storm in history.
US Virgin Islands Dept. of Tourism
1917
Denmark sells the Virgin Islands to the United States.
Mike Kelly/Getty Images
2004
Hurricanes Ivan and Jeanne cut a swath through the Caribbean, causing $2.2 billion in damages.

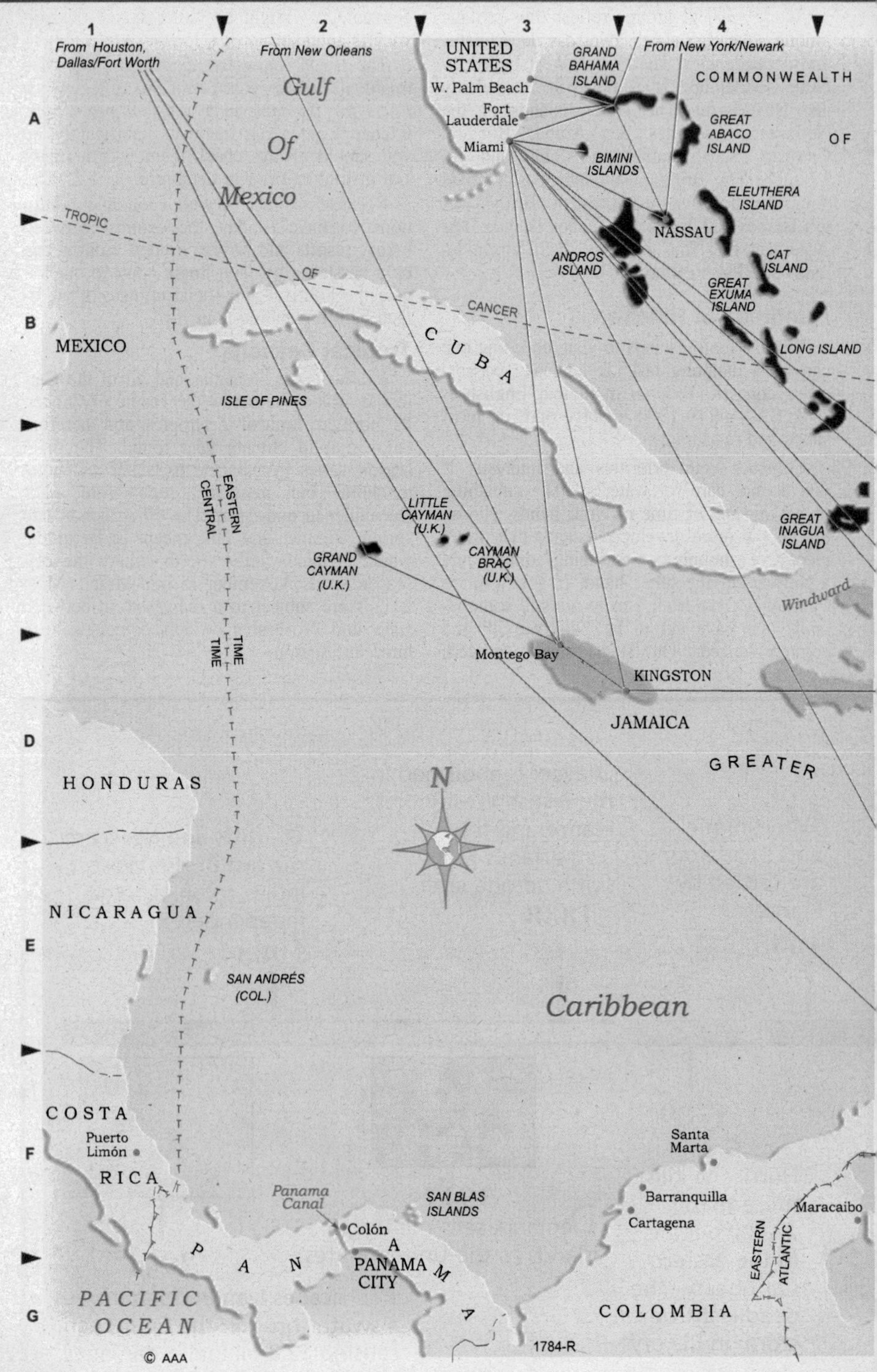

1
2
3
4
A
B
C
D
E
F
G
From Houston, Dallas/Fort Worth
From New Orleans
From New York/Newark
UNITED STATES
W. Palm Beach
Fort Lauderdale
Miami
GRAND BAHAMA ISLAND
COMMONWEALTH OF
GREAT ABACO ISLAND
BIMINI ISLANDS
ELEUTHERA ISLAND
NASSAU
ANDROS ISLAND
CAT ISLAND
GREAT EXUMA ISLAND
LONG ISLAND
Gulf Of Mexico
TROPIC OF CANCER
MEXICO
CUBA
ISLE OF PINES
EASTERN CENTRAL TIME
LITTLE CAYMAN (U.K.)
CAYMAN BRAC (U.K.)
GRAND CAYMAN (U.K.)
GREAT INAGUA ISLAND
Windward
Montego Bay
KINGSTON
JAMAICA
GREATER
HONDURAS
N
NICARAGUA
SAN ANDRÉS (COL.)
Caribbean
COSTA RICA
Puerto Limón
Santa Marta
Barranquilla
Cartagena
Maracaibo
EASTERN ATLANTIC
Panama Canal
SAN BLAS ISLANDS
Colón
PANAMA
PANAMA CITY
PACIFIC OCEAN
COLOMBIA
1784-R
© AAA

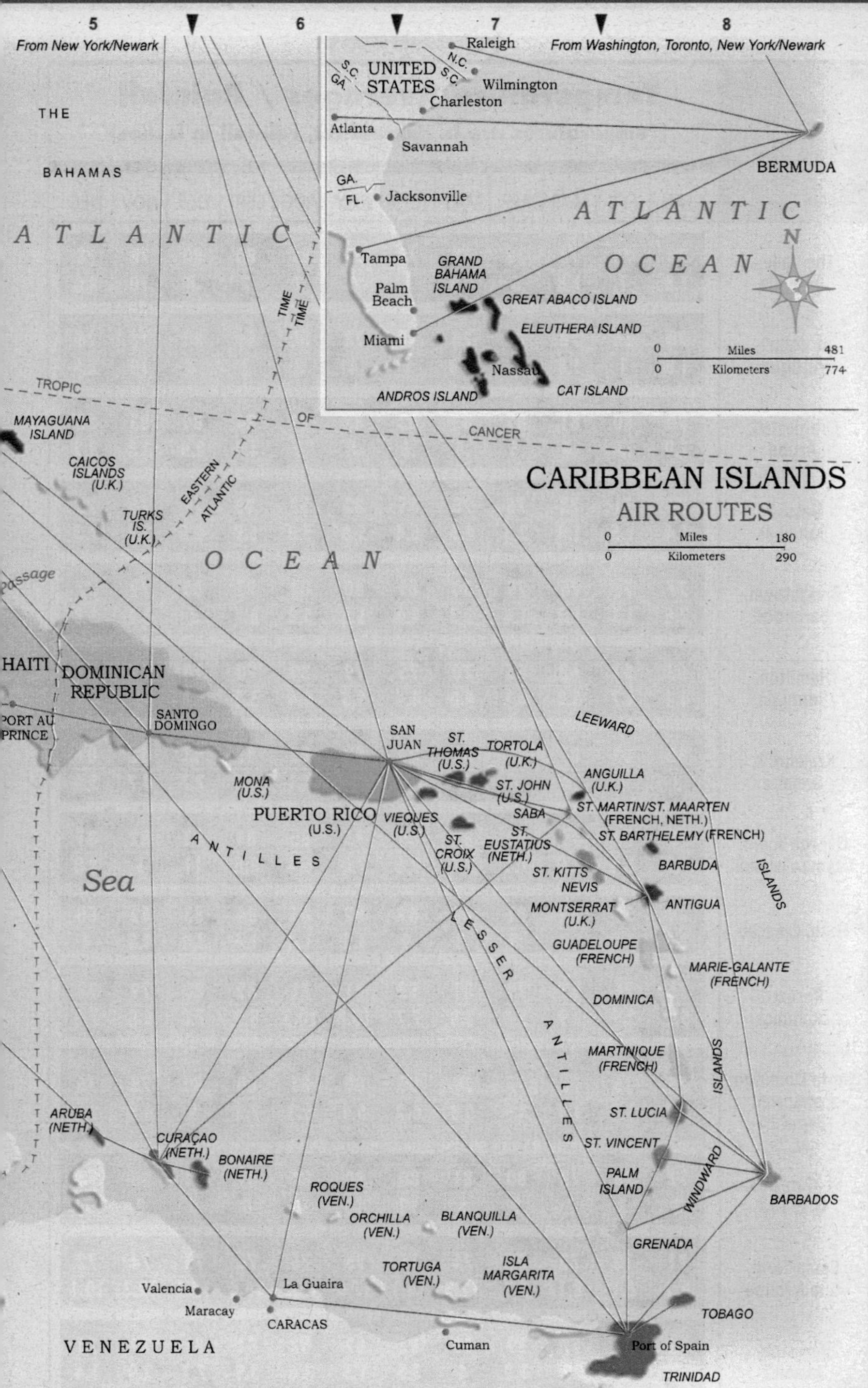

CARIBBEAN ISLANDS
AIR ROUTES
From New York/Newark
From Washington, Toronto, New York/Newark
5
6
7
8
UNITED STATES
Raleigh
Wilmington
Charleston
Atlanta
Savannah
Jacksonville
Tampa
Palm Beach
Miami
BERMUDA
ATLANTIC OCEAN
GRAND BAHAMA ISLAND
GREAT ABACO ISLAND
ELEUTHERA ISLAND
Nassau
ANDROS ISLAND
CAT ISLAND
THE BAHAMAS
MAYAGUANA ISLAND
CAICOS ISLANDS (U.K.)
TURKS IS. (U.K.)
TROPIC OF CANCER
EASTERN ATLANTIC TIME
HAITI
DOMINICAN REPUBLIC
PORT AU PRINCE
SANTO DOMINGO
SAN JUAN
PUERTO RICO (U.S.)
MONA (U.S.)
VIEQUES (U.S.)
ST. THOMAS (U.S.)
ST. JOHN (U.S.)
TORTOLA (U.K.)
ST. CROIX (U.S.)
ANGUILLA (U.K.)
ST. MARTIN/ST. MAARTEN (FRENCH, NETH.)
SABA
ST. EUSTATIUS (NETH.)
ST. BARTHELEMY (FRENCH)
BARBUDA
ST. KITTS
NEVIS
ANTIGUA
MONTSERRAT (U.K.)
GUADELOUPE (FRENCH)
MARIE-GALANTE (FRENCH)
DOMINICA
MARTINIQUE (FRENCH)
ST. LUCIA
ST. VINCENT
PALM ISLAND
BARBADOS
GRENADA
TOBAGO
TRINIDAD
Port of Spain
LEEWARD ISLANDS
WINDWARD ISLANDS
LESSER ANTILLES
ANTILLES
Sea
ARUBA (NETH.)
CURAÇAO (NETH.)
BONAIRE (NETH.)
ROQUES (VEN.)
ORCHILLA (VEN.)
BLANQUILLA (VEN.)
TORTUGA (VEN.)
ISLA MARGARITA (VEN.)
La Guaira
Valencia
Maracay
CARACAS
Cuman
VENEZUELA
0 Miles 180
0 Kilometers 290
0 Miles 481
0 Kilometers 774

Temperature Averages / Rainfall

(Temperatures are in Fahrenheit, rainfall in inches)

	JAN	FEB	MAR	APR	MAY	JUNE	JULY	AUG	SEPT	OCT	NOV	DEC
The Valley, Anguilla	78 / 1.8	76 / 1	78 / 1.8	78 / 5	78 / 4.8	78 / 1	78 / 4	80 / 2	80 / 2	80 / .8	78 / 10	78 / 2.6
St. John's, Antigua	78 / 1.8	76 / 1	78 / 1.8	78 / 5	78 / 4.8	78 / 1	78 / 4	80 / 2	80 / 2	80 / .8	78 / 10	78 / 2.6
Oranjestad, Aruba	80 / 1.9	80 / .7	81 / .4	82 / .5	83 / .5	83 / .6	83 / .8	84 / .7	84 / 1.1	84 / 2.6	83 / 3.8	80 / 3.2
Nassau, Bahamas	71 / 1.4	71 / 1.5	73 / 1.4	75 / 2.5	78 / 4.6	81 / 6.4	82 / 5.8	83 / 5.3	82 / 6.9	79 / 6.5	76 / 2.8	73 / 1.3
Bridgetown, Barbados	77 / 2.6	76 / 1.1	78 / 1.3	79 / 1.4	80 / 2.3	81 / 4.4	80 / 5.8	81 / 5.8	81 / 6.7	80 / 7	79 / 8.1	77 / 3.8
Hamilton, Bermuda	63 / 4.4	63 / 4.7	63 / 4.8	65 / 4.1	70 / 4.6	75 / 4.4	79 / 4.5	80 / 5.4	78 / 5.2	74 / 5.8	69 / 5	65 / 4.7
Kralendijk, Bonaire	80 / 2	80 / 1	81 / .8	81 / .6	82 / .7	82 / .7	82 / 1	83 / 1.1	83 / 1.3	83 / 2.7	82 / 4.7	81 / 3.5
George Town, Cayman Islands	78 / 1.8	78 / 1.4	79 / 1.0	80 / 1.6	83 / 7.4	85 / 9.6	85 / 7.0	85 / 6.4	84 / 8.8	83 / 11	82 / 5	81 / 2.8
Hato, Curaçao	79 / 2.3	79 / 1.2	80 / .7	81 / .8	82 / .8	82 / .9	82 / 1.2	83 / 1.4	84 / 1.4	83 / 3.4	82 / 4.8	80 / 4
Roseau, Dominica	76 / 5.2	76 / 2.9	78 / 2.9	79 / 2.4	81 / 3.8	82 / 7.7	81 / 10.8	81 / 10.3	82 / 8.9	80 / 7.8	79 / 8.8	78 / 7.8
Santo Domingo, Dominican Republic	75 / 2.4	76 / 1.4	76 / 1.9	77 / 3.9	79 / 6.8	80 / 6.2	80 / 6.4	81 / 6.3	80 / 7.3	80 / 6	78 / 4.8	76 / 2.4
St. George's, Grenada	77 / 3	78 / 3	78 / 1	80 / 2	81 / 6	80 / 12	80 / 10	80 / 10	81 / 6	81 / 6	80 / 8	78 / 7
Basse-Terre, Guadeloupe	71 / 9.2	70 / 6.1	70 / 8.1	72 / 7.3	74 / 11.5	75 / 14.1	75 / 17.6	76 / 15.3	76 / 16.4	75 / 12.4	74 / 12.3	72 / 10.1
Kingston, Jamaica	77 / .9	77 / .6	77 / .9	79 / 1.2	80 / 4	82 / 3.5	82 / 1.5	82 / 3.6	81 / 3.9	81 / 7.1	79 / 2.9	78 / 1.4

Temperature Averages / Rainfall

(Temperatures are in Fahrenheit, rainfall in inches)

	JAN	FEB	MAR	APR	MAY	JUNE	JULY	AUG	SEPT	OCT	NOV	DEC
Fort-de-France, Martinique	76 / 4.7	77 / 4.3	77 / 2.9	79 / 3.9	80 / 4.7	80 / 7.4	80 / 9.4	81 / 10.3	81 / 9.3	80 / 9.7	79 / 7.9	78 / 5.9
San Juan, Puerto Rico	75 / 4.3	75 / 2.7	76 / 2.9	77 / 4.1	79 / 5.9	80 / 5.4	80 / 5.7	81 / 6.3	81 / 6.2	80 / 5.6	79 / 6.3	77 / 5.4
Gustavia, St. Barthélemy	73 / 9.6	72 / 6	71 / 8.4	72 / 7	73 / 11.2	75 / 10.2	75 / 18	76 / 15	75 / 16	75 / 12.8	74 / 12.8	73 / 10.2
Oranjestad, St. Eustatius	77 / 2.7	78 / 1.8	78 / 1.9	80 / 2.1	81 / 3.6	82 / 3.4	82 / 4	82 / 4.6	82 / 5.3	81 / 4.8	80 / 5.2	78 / 3.5
Basseterre, St. Kitts	76 / 4.1	76 / 2	77 / 2.3	78 / 2.3	80 / 3.8	81 / 3.6	81 / 4.4	81 / 5.2	81 / 6	80 / 5.4	79 / 7.3	78 / 4.5
Soufrière, St. Lucia	76 / 5.3	76 / 3.6	77 / 3.8	79 / 3.4	81 / 5.9	81 / 8.6	81 / 9.3	81 / 10.6	81 / 9.9	80 / 9.3	78 / 9.1	77 / 7.8
Philipsburg, St. Maarten	77 / 2.6	77 / 1.8	78 / 1.6	79 / 2.4	81 / 4	83 / 3.1	83 / 3.2	83 / 4.3	82 / 5.5	82 / 5	80 / 5.5	78 / 3.3
Kingstown, St. Vincent	76 / 5	77 / 4	78 / 4	78 / 3	78 / .6	78 / 9	78 / 9	78 / 11	78 / 10	77 / 9	76 / 9	76 / 8
Port of Spain, Trinidad	76 / 2.3	77 / 1.2	77 / 1.4	79 / 1.3	80 / 2.8	79 / 6.4	79 / 7.8	79 / 7.6	80 / 6.9	80 / 5.6	79 / 6.5	78 / 4.7
Grand Turk, Turks & Caicos Islands	77 / 2.2	77 / 1.6	78 / 1.0	78 / 1.6	80 / 2.8	81 / 1.8	82 / 1.8	84 / 2	83 / 3.2	82 / 4	82 / 4.6	81 / 2.8
Road Town, Virgin Islands, British	78 / 4	78 / 3	78 / 3	80 / 4	82 / 6	82 / 5.2	82 / 6	82 / 6	82 / 6	82 / 6	80 / 6	78 / 5
Charlotte Amalie, Virgin Islands, U.S.	76 / 1.5	77 / 1.9	77 / 2.2	78 / 2.6	80 / 4.1	82 / 2.8	82 / 3.2	82 / 5.5	81 / 7.6	81 / 7.1	79 / 7.5	77 / 2.9

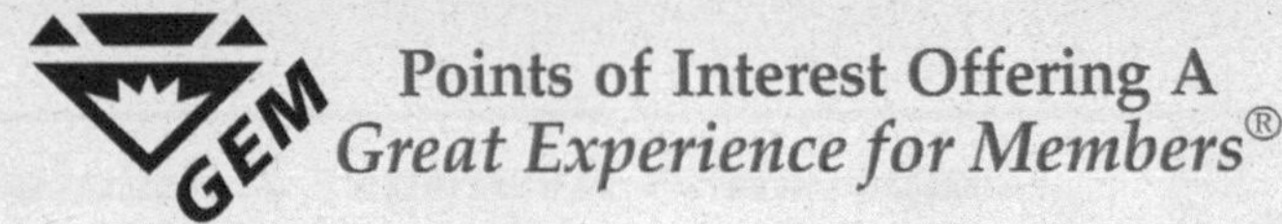

GEM
Points of Interest Offering A
Great Experience for Members®

Antigua

NELSON'S DOCKYARD NATIONAL PARK—The only existing Georgian dockyard was the home port of the British Fleet during the Napoleonic Wars. See p. 53.

Aruba

***ATLANTIS* SUBMARINE EXPEDITION**—Cruises aboard this 65-foot-long, 48-passenger submarine offer excellent views of Barcadera Reef. See p. 63.

Bahamas

DOLPHIN ENCOUNTERS AT BLUE LAGOON ISLAND—A high-speed catamaran takes visitors to this cay off Nassau to swim with inquisitive marine mammals. See p. 76.

Barbados

***ATLANTIS* SUBMARINE EXPEDITION**—Coral formations, marine life and a sunken ship are among the sights on this submarine cruise. See p. 86.

Bermuda

BERMUDA AQUARIUM, MUSEUM AND ZOO—The island's marine life is featured, along with tropical birds, lemurs, golden tamarins, seals and alligators. See p. 95.

Bonaire

BONAIRE NATIONAL MARINE PARK—Scuba diving and snorkeling are the best ways to explore this unique environment. See p. 104.

Cayman Islands

***ATLANTIS* SUBMARINE EXPEDITION**—The underwater vessel cruises along the Cayman Wall at a maximum depth of 100 feet. See p. 115.

BOATSWAIN'S BEACH—Swim or snorkel in a lagoon and visit ponds where you can see and touch turtles. See p. 115.

Dominican Republic

ALTOS DE CHAVON—This re-created 16th-century artisans' village showcases Dominican and international cultural activities. See p. 136.

COLONIAL SANTO DOMINGO (ZONA COLONIAL)—The New World's first fortress, church, hospital and government palace were built here after Columbus' arrival in 1492. See p. 139.

COLUMBUS LIGHTHOUSE MONUMENT (FARO A COLÓN)—The tomb of Christopher Columbus is at the heart of this seven-story monument, which commemorates the 500th anniversary of the explorer's landing. See p. 140.

OCEAN WORLD—Swim with dolphins and play with sea lions at this beachfront marine park. See p. 137.

Jamaica

BRIMMER HALL—Jitney tours explore this large plantation that produces bananas, cocoa, sugarcane and pineapple. See p. 167.

DOLPHIN COVE AT TREASURE REEF—Visitors can splash, swim and dance with bottlenose dolphins in a natural cove. See p. 165.

PROSPECT PLANTATION—A comprehensive tour takes visitors through a working plantation. See p. 166.

RÍO GRANDE RAFTING—Bamboo rafts carry passengers on a memorable trip down the Río Grande River. See p. 166.

Puerto Rico

ARECIBO OBSERVATORY—This massive telescope is used by scientists from around the world to study deep-space objects. See p. 189.

FORT SAN CRISTÓBAL—San Juan's land defense, this 27-acre fortress remains a monument to military engineering. See p. 200.

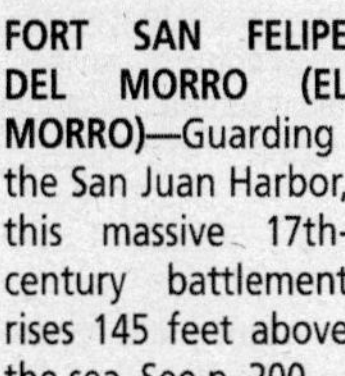

FORT SAN FELIPE DEL MORRO (EL MORRO)—Guarding the San Juan Harbor, this massive 17th-century battlement rises 145 feet above the sea. See p. 200.

PONCE MUSEUM OF ART—The collection of paintings and sculpture from Europe and the Americas spans the 13th through the 20th centuries. See p. 194.

SAN JUAN NATIONAL HISTORIC SITE—This World Heritage Site preserves the largest Spanish fortification in the New World. See p. 199.

St. Kitts

BRIMSTONE HILL FORTRESS NATIONAL PARK—The "Gibraltar of the West Indies" offers a panoramic view of the island and its Caribbean neighbors. See p. 222.

ST. KITTS SCENIC RAILWAY—Historic narration, musical entertainment and spectacular vistas are all part of this "national rail tour." See p. 222.

Virgin Islands, U.S.

***ATLANTIS* SUBMARINE EXPEDITION**—Departing from St. Thomas, an underwater voyage takes visitors to the dramatic Buck Island Reef. See p. 270.

BUCK ISLAND REEF NATIONAL MONUMENT—Two miles off St. Croix, this underwater park protects some 700 acres of barrier reef. See p. 267.

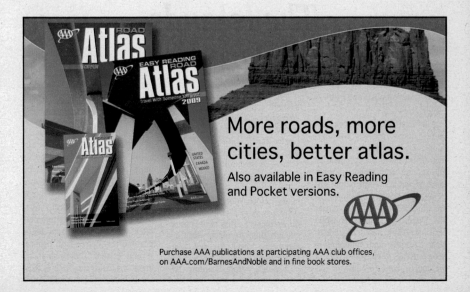

Planning Your Trip

Getting There

Travel to the islands is by plane, cruise ship or charter boat. Planned excursions tailored to fit your schedule and pocketbook are abundant; the mode of transportation you select is a matter of personal preference. However you choose to travel, a AAA travel agent can make all the necessary arrangements.

By Air

Air transportation has made the weekend, 1- or 2-week vacation as practical as it is delightful. Many excursion fares, some with stopovers, are available. Most Caribbean destinations can be reached in a matter of hours from major cities and often in a matter of minutes from Miami. Some islands do not have direct air service; check with a AAA travel agent about access to these smaller destinations. Also consult your travel agent for group fares, special packages, seasonal rates and current schedules. Most offices can make plane reservations and obtain tickets.

Air travel in the Caribbean requires some special considerations. Many island governments require visitors to complete a tourist card and perhaps a customs declaration form before entering their country. These forms are provided by your air carrier and should be completed while en route. Allow about an hour to clear customs and immigration upon arrival. *Keep your copy of the tourist card; it must be returned when you depart.*

Though island travel laws may vary, the U.S. Dept. of Homeland Security requires that all citizens returning from the Caribbean present a valid passport. See your destination's *Fast Facts* box for specific immigration requirements. AAA recommends carrying a passport when traveling anywhere outside the United States, both to expedite your way through customs and to provide identification in case of emergency.

Oranjestad / Aruba Tourism Authority

The Islands of Paradise

For information about the passport application process or an emergency passport, contact the National Passport Information Center at (877) 487-2778. Passport photos are available through your AAA travel office.

On departure day you should arrive at the airport at least 2 hours before your flight leaves. (Check with your airline for local requirements.) This will ensure enough time to obtain seat assignments, check luggage, convert currency and clear security checkpoints before boarding. Allow another hour when you land to claim your luggage and clear customs. Allow at least 90 minutes to make a connecting flight. Schedule similarly for your return home, allowing time to pay departure taxes, convert unspent currency and submit customs declaration forms.

By Sea

Other than owning and operating your own vessel, there are two ways to visit the Caribbean via the bounding main: by charter boat and by cruise ship.

By Air and Sea

Try a combination air *and* sea vacation. Some cruise lines will fly you from their departure point to one of the balmy Caribbean islands where you can relax and unwind for a few days; then you can return by luxury cruise ship—or cruise to the Caribbean and return by air. Many cruise lines will pay part of your airfare to and from their departure point as part of the full cruise package.

Interisland Travel

Island hopping is enjoyable and simple. Although almost all of the Caribbean islands are accessible by air or seaplane, a more exotic way to travel is by sailboat. These leisurely cruises to other islands usually include beverages and a meal. Mail boats, though not as glamorous, often take on passengers for a nominal fee. Ferries also connect several islands. Information on these services is available at most hotels, tourist bureaus and shops.

Intraisland Travel

Driving conditions on the islands range from good to poor. Most roads are not as well maintained as in the United States, and some are narrow and meandering, making it difficult to stay to one side. As well, in some areas domestic animals are known to roam the roads freely. Where road signs exist they are usually in the native tongue, so studying a phrase book or translation dictionary in advance is helpful. On most of the islands driving is on the left side of the road.

Given the confusion of other tourists and the independent driving nature of some locals, defensive driving is a must. It might be best to first monitor the driving conditions on the island before going out on your own. You might decide to leave the driving to the cabbies and bus operators.

Sightseeing Tours

Sunning, swimming, surfing and skin diving are all part of a Caribbean vacation, but to make your pleasure complete add another "S"—sightseeing. Each island has its own scenic attractions, quaint villages and exotic countryside. To miss them is to miss some of the islands' charm and history. For information on self-guiding or guided tours, see *Sightseeing* under the individual islands.

Car rentals are available on the major islands; rental information is listed under *Transportation.* To avoid disappointment, make reservations well in advance through a local AAA club. Arrangements for guided tours can be made through a AAA travel agency, your hotel activities desk or your ship's cruise director.

Climate and Clothing

The best rule to follow when packing for any trip, whether by plane or ship, is to first include everything that seems absolutely indispensable and then repack, taking only half as much as you would have originally planned. Another rule is to not take anything you would hate to lose, such as expensive jewelry or unneeded credit cards. Remember to pack toiletries, film and extra sunglasses, as they are often more expensive on the islands. Be sure to pack prescription medicines, in their original containers, and other essentials in your carry-on luggage.

Keep in mind the climate, the islands you will visit and where you plan to stay. Clothing made from artificial fibers can be uncomfortable in the heat. A good compromise is a cotton-synthetic blend that is both cool and wrinkle free.

Grenada Board of Tourism

In general, colorful, lightweight sport and resort-style clothes are appropriate all year throughout the islands. A lightweight wrap for cool evenings should be added for The Bahamas, Bermuda, the Cayman Islands, the Dominican Republic and Jamaica. In fact, it is always wise to pack a sweater, no matter how tropical the climate. In Bermuda, silks and lightweight woolens are comfortable during the day from mid-December to late March. For the most part, cocktail dresses and jackets and ties are not required for evening wear in the Caribbean except at resorts and large hotels on some of the more developed islands.

When packing for a cruise follow the same general rules. Formal clothes—dinner jackets and long dresses—are suitable for such highlights as the captain's dinner or the captain's cocktail parties. For regular dinners, most passengers change from their daytime attire to more sophisticated garb.

For shore visits or strolling around the deck, any type of vacation or outdoor clothing is appropriate. Swimwear, however, should be worn only at the beach or pool, not in public areas. Bathing *au naturel* or topless is fashionable at some beaches in the French West Indies, but is still an unwelcome trend on most of the other islands. Some of the people in the more conservative countries are offended by revealing clothes, especially if they are worn in the daytime.

Electricity

Typical U.S. electric shavers, hair dryers and travel irons operate on 110- to 120-volt, 60-cycle alternating current. However, some islands use 210-230 volt, 50-cycle AC electricity, which will burn out most U.S. appliances. On other islands, 110- to 127-volt, 50-cycle AC current is used. At 50 cycles U.S. electric appliances operate at slower than normal speeds and damage to an appliance can occur. A converter plug is necessary in the French West Indies, where European plugs are used. Check the *Fast Facts* boxes for the electric current used locally.

While some U.S. department stores do sell electric items for use overseas, be sure to check the voltage requirements before you purchase; do not be misled by a salesperson who offers you an "adapter" that only enables you to plug the appliance into the wall socket. A transformer is needed to convert high-voltage current for use with U.S. appliances.

Barbados Tourism Authority

Health and Safety

The sun's rays are intense in the Caribbean. Just an hour in the Caribbean sun can result in a painful sunburn and even illness to the unwary visitor. Be sure to bring plenty of suntan lotion or sunscreen; the higher the sunscreen rating the more it protects the skin from the most harmful rays. A good pair of sunglasses and a lightweight hat give added protection.

Some other common-sense precautions include taking an extra pair of glasses or contact lenses and extra quantities of prescription medicines, along with a letter from your physician stating the nature of your ailment and the recommended dosage. Keep prescription medicines in their original containers. Persons with physical conditions that might require emergency care should carry a card or tag identifying the condition.

Even the strongest constitution can sometimes be caught off guard by the excitement of travel or by culinary exploration. Reasonable precautions will usually eliminate serious risks, but should they fail, see a doctor. Medical services are generally excellent on the more developed islands, and your hotel desk or travel agent can refer you to a reliable physician or clinic. Emergency medical treatment also is available on cruise ships.

Rain is the main source of fresh water on many islands; sparse rainfall means scarce water. Even on islands where water is distilled from the sea, the supply is limited and should be used sparingly. Tap water and water served in restaurants and bars is generally safe; if in doubt, abstain or drink bottled water, beverages made with boiled water, canned or bottled carbonated beverages, beer or wine. If the water quality is unknown, avoid ice, containers that have held water, and such foods as fruit or vegetables that might have been rinsed in contaminated water.

Where mosquitoes abound, use a repellent, wear clothing that covers your arms and legs and stay in well-screened areas. Mosquitoes bearing malaria, yellow fever and other infections exist in very limited regions. In the Caribbean the risk of malaria is present in Haiti and in rural areas of the Dominican Republic bordering Haiti. Travelers to any of these areas are urged to check with their physician or local health department to determine the advisability of taking a preventative drug.

Cases of dengue (breakbone) fever, also a mosquito-borne infection, have been reported on most Caribbean Islands and throughout northern South America, Central America and Mexico. There are no preventative medical measures other than wearing insect repellent, and treatment is limited to relieving the symptoms. A few cases of yellow fever have occurred in Trinidad and

Tobago. Inoculations for yellow fever are available; most of the islands require vaccination certificates for yellow fever *only* of those travelers arriving from endemic countries.

Hepatitis B is highly prevalent in the Dominican Republic and Haiti. A hepatitis B vaccination is recommended for those traveling to these areas. Hepatitis A is found in rural areas. Schistosomiasis is a parasitic infection contracted in Antigua, the Dominican Republic, Guadeloupe, Martinique, Puerto Rico and St. Lucia. A few cases of poliomyelitis have been reported in the Dominican Republic and Haiti; visitors should consult a physician about the need for immunization.

The Centers for Disease Control and Prevention in Atlanta recommends that before traveling, visitors should make sure that all immunizations are current (the tetanus/diphtheria vaccine should be boosted as needed). It also is recommended that travelers receive either an immune serum globulin or the hepatitis A vaccine if they are planning to visit an area of questionable sanitation. The center's hot line, offering international health requirements and recommendations for foreign travelers, is available daily 24 hours; phone (877) 394-8747.

Carefully assess the risk potential of recreational activities on the islands. Sports equipment that you rent or buy might not meet U.S. safety standards. Unless you are certain that scuba diving equipment, for example, is safe, do not use it. Be especially careful when out on excursions: Should you need it, help might not be readily available.

Many pools and beaches on the islands do not have lifeguards, so take heed when swimming. Undertows can be treacherous; be sure to inquire about such conditions before entering the water. Do not dive into unknown waters; hidden rocks, coral formations and shallow depths can cause serious injury or death.

Familiarize yourself with the local laws and customs of the islands you are visiting; remember, you are subject to *their* laws. It is wise to leave a copy of your travel itinerary with family or friends at home and to phone or register in person with the U.S. embassy or consulate upon your arrival. If you get in trouble, contact the U.S. consulate.

Aruba Tourism Authority

You can take various precautions to avoid being victimized by thieves. Travel light and do not leave luggage unattended in public places. It also is a good idea to leave expensive jewelry, clothing and unnecessary credit cards at home. Be sure not to travel with all of your money, credit cards and travelers checks in one place. Consider leaving valuables in your hotel safe or safe deposit box.

You should be alert at all times, especially in crowds. Secure your wallet carefully, perhaps in a front pocket, or wear a money belt; carry your purse diagonally across your chest. When shopping, keep just a small amount of spending money readily available; do not display the entire contents of your wallet. Try to conceal your camera when not in use. Do not venture into unfamiliar areas, especially when you are alone and certainly not at night.

Visitors are often approached on the street by locals offering a variety of products and services that are best obtained through more reputable outlets. In most cases a polite "No, thank you" will suffice, but the more persistent vendor will require several similar responses. It is best to display a pleasant but assertive manner in such situations. Avoid prolonged discussions and do not answer questions that might reveal where you are staying or what your plans are. Accept rides from only licensed taxi or tour operators.

Travel Advisories

The U.S. Department of State issues Consular Information Sheets, Travel Warnings and Public Announcements concerning serious health or security conditions that might affect U.S. citizens. They can be obtained at U.S. embassies and consulates abroad, regional passport agencies in the United States and from the Overseas Citizens Services; phone (202) 647-5225. The Bureau maintains a Web site at http://travel.state.gov.

Consular Information Sheets provide information about entry requirements, currency regulations, health conditions, security, political disturbances, areas of instability and drug penalties. A Travel Warning is issued when the situation in a country is dangerous enough for the Department of State to recommend that Americans not travel there. Public Announcements are a means of releasing information to travelers about short-term conditions that might pose security risks to Americans traveling abroad.

In addition, travelers are urged to remain abreast of regional events and to contact their AAA travel agent or air or sea carrier for the latest updates.

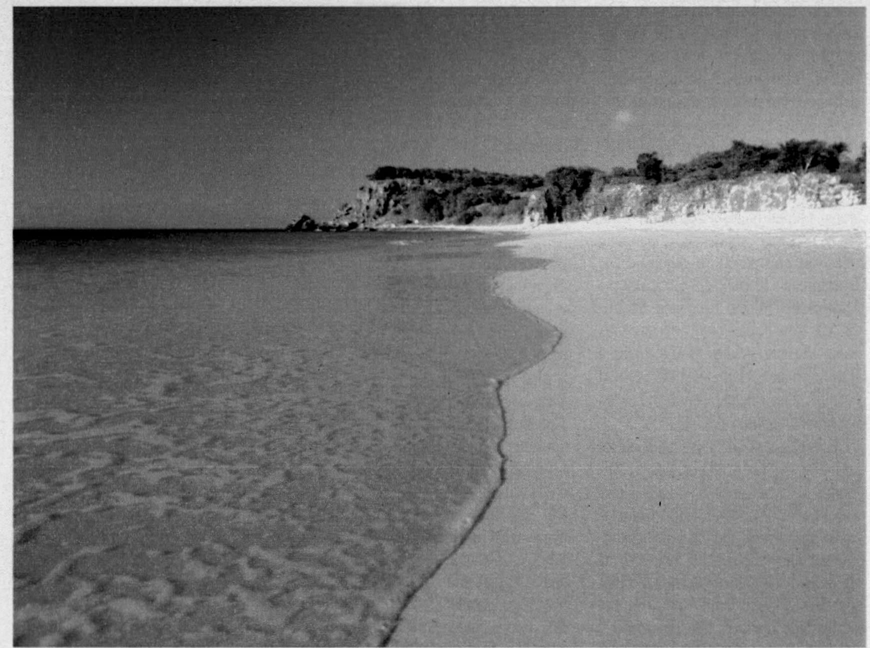

© Sylvain Grandadam / age fotostock

Anguilla

Long and narrow Anguilla (An-GWIL-ah) takes its name from the Spanish word for eel. The island lies about 9 miles (14 km) north of St. Martin and 60 miles (97 km) north of St. Kitts. Unlike the other Leeward Islands, low-lying Anguilla is of coral limestone rather than volcanic formation. Cottages and houses are sprinkled across the island, with concentrations around the capital of The Valley and the villages of South Hill, Stoney Ground, Blowing Point and Island Harbour. Accommodations on Anguilla range from charming cottages to world-class hotel and villa resort properties.

History

Christopher Columbus sighted Anguilla during his second voyage in 1493; it is not known whether he actually visited the island. English settlers from St. Kitts colonized Anguilla in 1650, and the island has remained a British territory ever since. In 1688 the island was attacked by a party of Irishmen who eventually settled there, and such surnames as Smith and Webster are evident among their descendants, particularly around Island Harbour. Anguilla repelled two attacks by the French in the 18th century. The island declared its independence from the Associated State of St. Kitts and Nevis and became a self-governing territory of the British Commonwealth in 1967. After several years of negotiations, Anguilla became a separate British dependent territory on Dec. 19, 1980.

It is said that the first seeds of the highly prized sea island cotton came from Anguilla. Today the island's economy is based on tourism and financial services.

Shopping

Visitors to Anguilla won't find the duty-free shops and open markets common on other islands, but browsing at a resort boutique, an art gallery or a craft shop is still a popular pastime. Local shopping favorites include the Anguilla Arts and Crafts Center in the Brooks Complex in The Valley; Irie Life, overlooking the scenic Road Bay and Sandy Ground; Cheddie's Carving Studio, on the island's west end, containing sculptures and carvings; Malliouhana's, presenting an extensive selection of fine jewelry; Devonish Art Gallery; Le Petit Gift Shop; World Art and Antiques; and La Galleria. Boutiques such as Caribbean Fancy, Janvel's, Kimmy's, Liacia's, Shoes Plus and Something Special feature elegant resort wear, casual summer fashions, shoes and accessories.

Fresh fruits and vegetables are available from the People's Market in The Valley and at roadside stands throughout the island. Shopping hours are generally Mon.-Sat. 8-4; some stores are open on Sundays. Banking hours are Mon.-Thurs. 8-3, Fri. 8-5.

Food and Drink

Fine dining is a specialty in Anguilla, which calls itself the "cuisine capital of the Caribbean." Local restaurants—from casual beachside eateries to elegant five-star establishments—serve sumptuous dishes that reflect the ancestry of island residents: European, African and Caribbean.

Freshly caught lobster, crayfish, whelk, and red and yellowtail snapper are several of the seafood delights that appear on tables in Anguilla. The tantalizing fare includes stuffed crab, conch salad, grilled crayfish and Creole soups.

Sports and Amusements

Nightlife of the classic variety is somewhat limited on Anguilla. Most hotels offer nightly music, and several beach bistros can be found at Sandy Ground and Shoal Bay. Most recreation, however, is related to the island's white coral sand beaches, which offer many opportunities for swimming and shell collecting; swimming and sunbathing *au naturel* are prohibited.

Some of the island's 33 beaches are accessible only by rough dirt roads or paths. The secluded atmosphere of these beaches, however, makes the visit worth the trouble. Popular beaches include those at Meads Bay, Rendezvous Bay and Shoal Bay East. Visitors should note that wearing swimsuits in public places other than the beach is considered inappropriate.

The crystal-clear waters surrounding Anguilla are excellent for snorkeling, scuba diving and fishing. Favorite snorkeling and diving spots are Little Bay, Cove Bay and

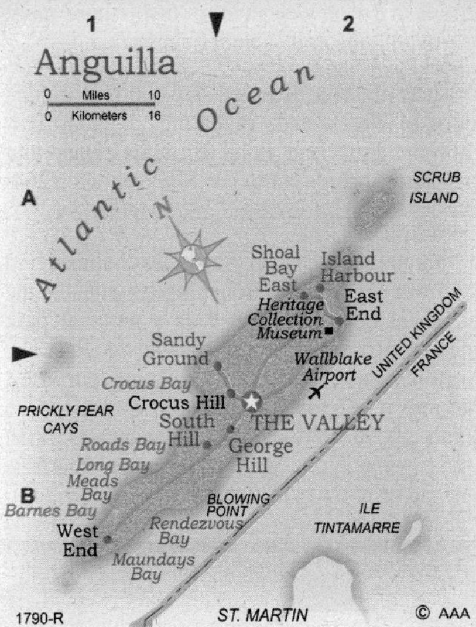

Shoal Bay, the last distinguished by its undersea garden trail. Experienced divers can reach seven shipwreck sites. Shoal Bay Scuba rents snorkeling equipment, while Anguillian Divers can take you to the hottest dive spots on the eastern part of the island. Hooked on Watersports makes arrangements for windsurfing and sailing in Cove Bay. Most hotels rent water sports equipment. Tennis also is popular on the island; most hotels and villas have courts. The Ronald Webster Park Complex in The Valley offers two public courts.

Boats and guides for fishing trips are available for hire at Sandy Ground and Island Harbour. Many islanders are anglers by trade, and you can sample their succulent bounty at any local café or restaurant. Fish soup, sweet and sour conch, and lobster with lime butter are some of the primary delicacies.

Special events are held on Anguilla Day, May 30, and in August during the annual Summer Festival. On both occasions, sailors race boats made in Anguilla. Summer Festival, which begins on the last Friday in July and ends on the first Sunday in August, features calypso contests, street dancing, the coronation of Miss Anguilla (the carnival queen), sailboat races, beach barbecues and the Prince and Princess Show.

Sightseeing

Sightseeing tours can be arranged through Anguilla Travel Services, Bennie's Travel & Tours and Malliouhana Travel & Tours, all in The Valley. Bennie's offers tours of the island and half- and full-day trips to Prickly Pear; Marigot, St. Martin; and Philipsburg, St. Maarten. Sandy Island Enterprises offers fishing trips and excursions to offshore cays, nearby islands and secluded harbors.

The Anguilla National Trust offers guided tours of the island, including stops at Fort Hill, the East End Pond Bird Sanctuary and the Big Spring Heritage Site; phone (264) 497-5297 for information and reservations.

Fountain Cavern in Shoal Bay, considered the most significant archeological site on the island, is being developed as a national park and is currently closed to the public. The Arawaks used this cave for ritual purposes, carving a 12-foot stalagmite statue of the Taíno god Jocahu beside a freshwater pool. Other petroglyphs depict the solar chieftain and the rainbow god, Juluca.

Transportation

Connections to Wallblake Airport are through San Juan, St. Thomas, Antigua, St. Kitts and St. Maarten. Rental cars or taxis are necessary to get around the island, as beaches, stores and various accommodations are not within reasonable walking distance. Taxi rates are fixed, but agree on the fare in advance.

The Blowing Point Ferry runs to Marigot, St. Martin, about every half hour from 7:30 a.m. to 6:15 p.m. The final return from Marigot leaves at 7 p.m. The ferry trip takes about 20 minutes. Travel documents are required, and a $20 U.S. departure tax is collected upon departure from Anguilla (day trippers from Anguilla pay a departure tax of $5 U.S.); departure tax from St. Martin is $5 U.S. One-way fare is $15 U.S.

Fast Facts

POPULATION: 14,254.

AREA: 91 sq km (35 sq mi.).

CAPITAL: The Valley.

HIGHEST POINT: 65 m (213 ft.), Crocus Hill.

LOWEST POINT: Sea level, Caribbean Sea.

TIME ZONE(S): Atlantic Standard.

LANGUAGE: English.

GOVERNMENT: British Overseas Territory.

UNIT OF CURRENCY: Eastern Caribbean (E.C.) dollar. $1 U.S. = 2.7 E.C. dollars. U.S. currency is widely accepted.

ELECTRICITY: 110 volts, 60 cycles AC.

MINIMUM AGE FOR DRIVERS: 21-25, depending on the rental car agency. Temporary local license ($20 U.S.) required, available at rental agencies and issued on presentation of current license from home country; valid for 6 months; drive on left.

SEAT BELT/CHILD RESTRAINT LAWS: Seat belts are not required by law, but are recommended for all passengers.

HELMETS FOR MOTORCYCLISTS: Required.

HOLIDAYS: Jan. 1; Good Friday; Easter Monday; Labour Day, May (1st Mon.); Whit Monday, May or June (8th Mon. after Easter); Anguilla Day, May 30; Queen's Birthday, June (2nd Mon.); August Monday, August Thursday and Constitution Day, (1st Mon. and following Thurs. and Fri.); Separation Day, Dec. 19; Christmas, Dec. 25; Boxing Day, Dec. 26.

TAXES: A 10 percent room tax and 10 percent service charge are added to most hotel bills, plus $1 U.S. per room, per night. A 10 percent service charge is also added to restaurant bills. Departure tax is $20 U.S. by air, or by sea at Blowing Point Ferry Port.

IMMIGRATION REQUIREMENTS: A valid passport and return or onward ticket are required. No visa needed for stays up to 3 months. The U.S. Dept. of Homeland Security requires all U.S. citizens returning from the Caribbean to present a valid passport.

PHONING THE ISLANDS: To call Anguilla from the U.S. or Canada, dial 1 + 264 + the 7-digit local number.

FURTHER INFORMATION FOR VISITORS:

Anguilla Tourist Board New York
246 Central Ave.
White Plains, NY 10606
(914) 287-2400
(877) 426-4845

Anguilla Tourist Board
Coronation Avenue
P. O. Box 1388
The Valley, Anguilla AI-2640
(264) 497-2759
(800) 553-4939

Anguilla Hotel and Tourism Association
Coronation Avenue
P.O. Box 1020
The Valley, Anguilla AI-2640
(264) 497-2944

Points of Interest

EAST END (A-2) pop. 614

The tombstone of Gov. John Richardson, who was buried in the Sandy Hill Cemetery in 1742, is thought to be the oldest on the island. Southwest along the coast are the ruins of Sandy Hill Fort. Here the Anguilla militia held off the second French invasion in 1796.

HERITAGE COLLECTION MUSEUM is next to East End Pond Bird Sanctuary. Artifacts, photographs and archeological relics span the island's history from the Arawak culture to the 1967 revolution. Exhibits highlight Anguilla's fishing and boat-building trades, as well as the salt industry that collapsed in the 1980s. Allow 1 hour minimum. Mon.-Sat. 10-5; closed major holidays. Admission $5; $3 (ages 5-11). Phone (264) 497-4092.

THE VALLEY (B-2) pop. 1,169

Anguilla's tiny capital sits at the center of the coral limestone island. The Valley's oldest building is Wallblake House, the only surviving plantation manor from the 18th century. Other historic structures are found on the road to Crocus Hill, including Ebenezer Methodist Church, built by slaves in 1830. The Warden's Place, former quarters of the magistrate, is now home to the Koal Keel Restaurant. The limestone blocks used to build its high foundation were carved from the cliffs of nearby Crocus Bay.

Farther west at Sandy Ground is the Manse, a three-gabled house recently restored as a center for art studios and shops. The Old Salt Factory and Pumphouse preserves the history of the once-thriving salt industry in Anguilla.

WALLBLAKE HOUSE is on Carter Rey Blvd. next to St. Gerard's Catholic Church. Thought to have been built by sugar planter William Blake in the 1780s, this is the oldest house on the island and one of the last survivors of 18th-century plantation life. The mansion was set ablaze by French soldiers during the 1796 invasion, but the stone walls withstood the fire. Later used as a Catholic rectory, the plantation complex was restored in 2004. It is one of few in the Caribbean to retain all of its original outbuildings, including a bakery, a stone cistern, stables and workers' quarters. Guided tours are offered Mon., Wed. and Fri. 10-2. Admission $5.

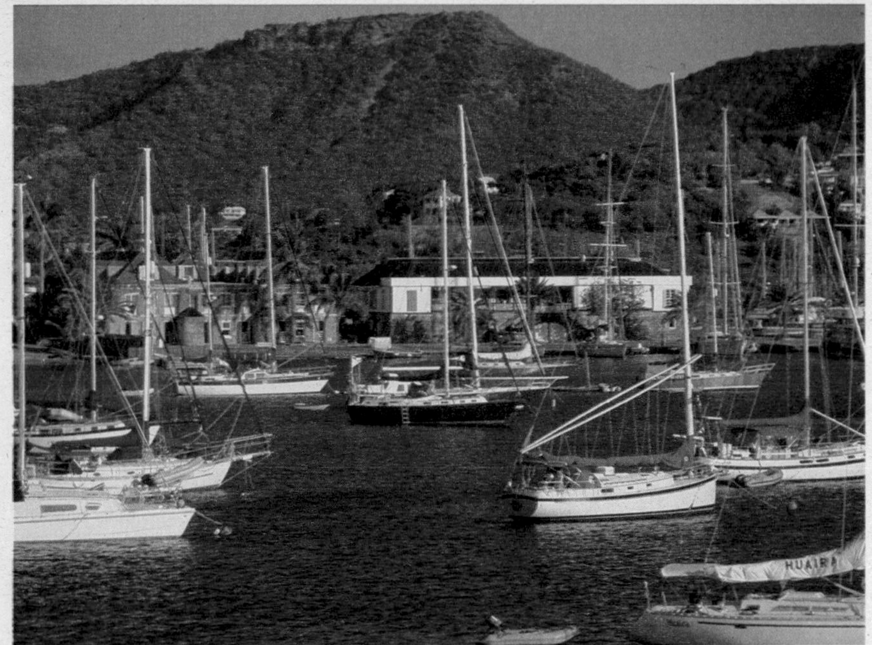

Nelson's Dockyard National Park, English Harbour, Antigua / © age fotostock / SuperStock

Antigua and Barbuda

At the northeastern curve of the West Indies, Antigua (an-TEE-ga) is one of 11 links in the chain of Leeward Islands. Christopher Columbus' first impression adequately describes this tropical paradise: "What beautiful lands the sun lights up in the distance." The seascape alternates rocky coves with white, sunny beaches punctuated by gentle salt breezes. Thirty miles (48 km) north is the tiny coral island of Barbuda (bar-BEW-da), a haven for seabirds. The rocky volcanic islet of Redonda is an uninhabited dependency.

Antiguans are charming people, reserved but cordial. Their expressive English *patois* with its musical intonation enchants visitors. While engaged in daily affairs, the locals form a vivid tableau. Sitting around a *warri* board, taxi drivers play an ancient game while waiting for a fare. Dressed for school in distinctive uniforms that vary according to school and grade, Antiguan children add their smiles and colors to the scene. In equally vivid dress, members of Antigua's many steel bands parade during Carnival in St. John's, where the colorful activities contrast with the more traditionalist English atmosphere of the island's capital.

History

Christopher Columbus sighted Antigua in 1493, naming it after Santa Maria de la Antigua, a church in Seville, Spain. An attempt to colonize the island was not made until almost a century and a half later, perhaps due to the unwelcoming population of Carib Indians.

Antigua became a British possession in 1632, when English planters from nearby St. Kitts successfully settled the area despite Carib resistance. African slaves were imported to clear forests for the planting of tobacco, ginger, cotton and indigo. In 1666 French raiders claimed the island, but the Treaty of Breda in 1667 restored the land to the British.

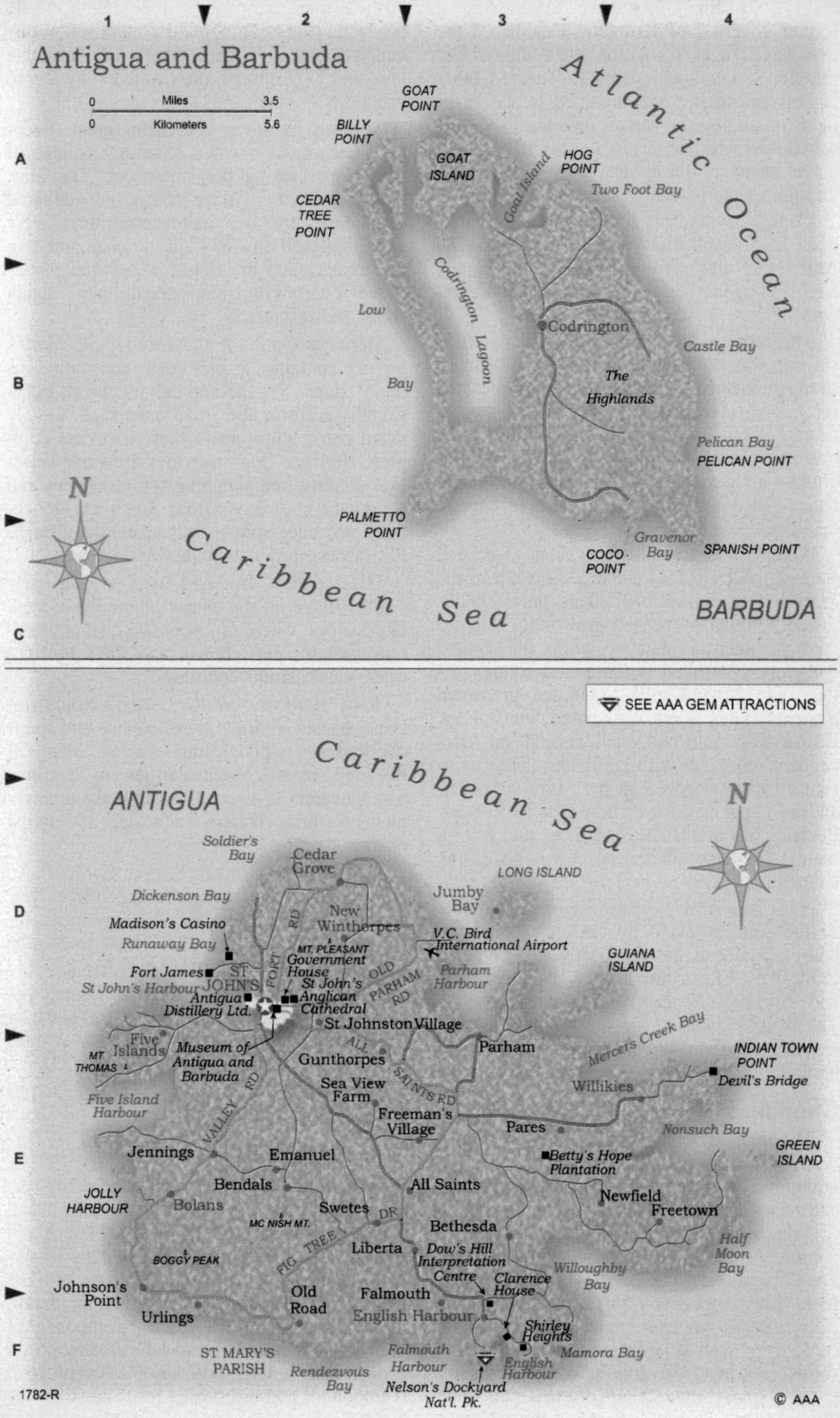

Antigua and Barbuda

1 2 3 4

A B C D E F

0 Miles 3.5
0 Kilometers 5.6

Atlantic Ocean

GOAT POINT
BILLY POINT
GOAT ISLAND
HOG POINT
Goat Island
Two Foot Bay
CEDAR TREE POINT
Codrington Lagoon
Low Bay
Codrington
Castle Bay
The Highlands
Pelican Bay
PELICAN POINT
PALMETTO POINT
Gravenor Bay
COCO POINT
SPANISH POINT
N
Caribbean Sea
BARBUDA

SEE AAA GEM ATTRACTIONS

Caribbean Sea
ANTIGUA
N
Soldier's Bay
Cedar Grove
LONG ISLAND
Dickenson Bay
New Winthorpes
Jumby Bay
Madison's Casino
Runaway Bay
RD
MT. PLEASANT
V.C. Bird International Airport
GUIANA ISLAND
Fort James
Government House
St John's Anglican Cathedral
FORT
OLD PARHAM RD
Parham Harbour
St John's Harbour
ST JOHN'S
Antigua Distillery Ltd.
St Johnston Village
Mercers Creek Bay
Five Islands
Museum of Antigua and Barbuda
ALL SAINTS RD
Parham
INDIAN TOWN POINT
MT THOMAS
Gunthorpes
Willikies
Devil's Bridge
Five Island Harbour
VALLEY RD
Sea View Farm
Freeman's Village
Pares
Nonsuch Bay
Jennings
Emanuel
Betty's Hope Plantation
GREEN ISLAND
JOLLY HARBOUR
Bendals
All Saints
Newfield
Bolans
Swetes
Freetown
MC NISH MT.
DR
Bethesda
FIG TREE
Liberta
Half Moon Bay
BOGGY PEAK
Dow's Hill Interpretation Centre
Willoughby Bay
Clarence House
Johnson's Point
Old Road
Falmouth
Urlings
English Harbour
Shirley Heights
Mamora Bay
ST MARY'S PARISH
Falmouth Harbour
English Harbour
Rendezvous Bay
Nelson's Dockyard Nat'l. Pk.

1782-R

In 1674 Sir Christopher Codrington, a former governor of Barbados, established the first large sugar plantation on Antigua. Codrington's accomplishments encouraged other landowners to become involved in the sugar industry, and by the early 1700s the landscape was dotted with some 170 sugar mills; the ruins of many of these structures can be seen throughout the island.

Codrington and his brother settled on Barbuda four years prior to cultivating sugar on Antigua. Ruins of the Codrington estate, Highland House, are on the island's highest point.

The economy suffered a severe blow when slavery was abolished in 1834, and a labor shortage ensued. Due to mounting pressure for a free trade market, sugar prices steadily declined and forced several plantations out of business. Three natural disasters in the mid-1800s—a hurricane, a fire and an earthquake—also contributed to the economic decline.

Antigua was granted status as an associated state of the United Kingdom as a result of the West Indies Act of 1967. This provision allowed Antigua to be self-governing with regard to internal matters, while the United Kingdom controlled defense and foreign affairs. On Nov. 1, 1981, Antigua graduated from its status as an Associated State of the British Commonwealth and became an independent country with Barbuda. The twin-island nation is governed by a prime minister and an upper and lower house of Parliament. Barbuda has often talked of secession, but remains for now with its own governing council.

Antigua's strategic position in the middle of the Antilles chain, as well as its natural harbors, made it the chief British naval base in the West Indies during the Napoleonic Wars and a prime U.S. base during World War II. The main sources of income for most islanders are tourism, light manufacturing and agriculture.

Shopping

The main shopping district is in St. John's between Redcliffe and Newgate streets, but numerous other shops are concealed in alleys and lanes. Popular buys are imports, straw handicrafts and sea island and silk-screened cottons. Antigua's duty-free shopping includes French perfumes, cashmeres, English tweeds, Irish linen, tobacco, pipes, English bone china, Swiss watches, jewelry, crystal and cameras as well as children's clothing, accessories and toys. St. John's also has several jewelry stores where shoppers can find good buys on their favorite gemstones. Both locally produced rum and imported liquors sell at discounted prices. Cuban cigars are available here, but U.S. citizens are forbidden by law to bring them home.

Situated on lower Redcliffe Street, Redcliffe Quay consists of a charming collage of shops overlooking the waterfront. The area, which was once a slave compound, harbored warehouses for area merchants after slavery was abolished in 1834. Traditional architecture is accented by narrow alleys and picturesque courtyards interspersed with quaint shops and restaurants.

Heritage Quay, at the foot of St. Mary's Street, contains a pier that accommodates cruise ships. Reggae and calypso bands occasionally perform at a small band shell, usually when cruise ships are in port. A modern complex, Heritage Quay provides a diverse selection of duty-free shopping for gemstones and handcrafted jewelry. Other shops feature apparel and accessories, fragrances and cosmetics, tobacco products, liquor and linens.

Local potters live and work at Sea View Farm Village, at the center of the island near Gunthorpes, where products range from primitive cooking pots, bowls and trays to figurines, vases, lamps and mugs.

Jolly Harbour, on the island's southwest coast, boasts an array of restaurants and shops overlooking a picturesque marina. Many of the shops feature beachwear, jewelry, perfume and souvenirs. Visitors also can make arrangements for boat charters, car rentals and diving excursions.

Nelson's Dockyard in English Harbour also accommodates an extensive marketplace. Restaurants and shops are tucked away in the restored buildings of what was once the headquarters of the British Royal Navy.

Some shops have extended hours, but stores are generally open Mon.-Sat. 8-5. Many shops are open on Sundays when cruise ships are in port. Banking hours are Mon.-Thurs. 8-2, Fri. 8-4; the Bank of Antigua also is open Sat. 8-noon.

Food and Drink

West Indian cookery, influenced by the English, graces most tables. Favorite local dishes include salted codfish, curry conch and souse, or pickled pork. *Fungi,* a type of polenta made with cornmeal and okra, is often served with pepperpot stew. Ducana dumplings are a favorite dessert, a mixture of grated sweet potato and coconut steamed in a banana leaf. A large portion of Antiguan food is imported, and resort-area restaurants feature

American, Continental, French and Italian cuisine. Many eateries close during the summer months. In season, lobsters are caught daily off the coast of both Antigua and Barbuda. Locally grown fruits and vegetables include herbs, eddoes, papayas, breadfruit, coconuts, ginger, pumpkins, soursop, okra, sugarcane, sweet potatoes, mangoes and Antigua's famous black pineapples.

Sports and Amusements

Antigua is known as a sailor's paradise, and is a popular mooring spot for a variety of vessels, including luxury yachts. At most hotels and at English Harbour, you can charter yachts and other types of sailing vessels with trained crews for an afternoon or for longer island-hopping excursions. Smaller vessels also are available for rent.

Yachts, schooners and gaffers converge on English Harbour in mid-April for the Antigua Classic Yacht Regatta, a celebration of traditional artisanship. Events include races, a heritage festival and the Concours d'Elegance show and competition. Antigua Sailing Week, considered by some to be *the* world's warm-water sailing regatta, generally is held the last Sunday in April through the first Saturday in May. The island also hosts the 9-day Antigua Charter Yacht Show in early December.

The coastline of Antigua is indented with beautiful bays and some 365 coral beaches, many accessible only by boat. Swimmers, shell collectors and sunbathers need never visit the same beach more than once in a year. Those planning beach outings are advised to carry insect repellent; no-see-ums can be a nuisance on the leeward side of the island, especially at dusk.

The beaches on the northwest coast are frequented by tourists due to the high concentration of resorts in the area. Popular northwest coast beaches include Dickenson Bay, a pretty white-sand beach bordered by several hotels and restaurants. Water sports enthusiasts will appreciate the multitude of operators offering rental equipment for windsurfing. The bay also is a departure point for glass-bottom boat and catamaran excursions.

The gentle surf at Runaway Beach also is perfect for water sports, especially children's activities. Visitors can rent floats, kayaks, windsurfers and sailboats. Water skiing also can be arranged. Landlubbers can explore the area on horseback.

The coral reefs and the remains of shipwrecks, where many multicolored fish gather, make snorkeling and scuba diving popular; many dive operators on the island provide equipment and lessons. In Deep Bay, snorkelers and divers can explore a sunken ship, *The Andes*. The stately ruins of Fort Barrington rise high above the picturesque beach area bordering the bay. A path leads to the top of the fort; the hike can be strenuous, and only those in good physical condition should attempt it. Hikers who make the trek to the top will be rewarded with striking views of St. John's Harbour.

Half Moon Bay, in Half Moon Bay National Park on Antigua's southeast coast, derives its name from the coastline's shape. The crescent-shaped beach, enhanced by azure waters and cool breezes, is perfect for a pleasant stroll. Visitors like to climb the rocks at the north end of the shore. Surf conditions vary due to the bay's shape; visitors can experience crashing waves that present excellent opportunities for body surfing or gentle ripples ideal for swimming.

Darkwood Beach is situated on the island's southwest coast. The white-sand beach, surrounded by a hilly landscape, is punctuated by sailboats docked in crystal-blue water. Beach chairs can be rented at a small snack area, and shelters covered with palm fronds provide respite from the sun. On a clear day, visitors can see the island of Montserrat looming on the horizon. Morris Bay, off Antigua's south coast, is the site of the Curtain Bluff Resort. In this tranquil, secluded setting adorned by sweeping palms, a prominent bluff rises majestically from the sea.

Deep-sea fishing trips for marlin, wahoo, kingfish, shark and barracuda may be chartered out of Falmouth Harbour. Fishing tournaments are held every Labour Day and Whit Monday.

Golf enthusiasts have two 18-hole courses on which to chase birdies: Cedar Valley Golf Club, (268) 462-0161; and Jolly Harbour Golf Course, (268) 480-6950. Tennis courts are available at most hotels, and tournaments held throughout the year attract many professionals. Men's and women's singles and doubles matches take place along with matches that pit amateurs against the pros. Antigua Tennis Week is held at Curtain Bluff in early May and mid-November.

As in other English West Indian islands, cricket is the national obsession, and Antigua is home to some of the world's best cricketers. A stadium for World Cup Cricket is named for one of the island's cricket legends, Sir Vivian Richards. Tournaments between local district teams can be seen across the island on weekends. Spectators also enjoy netball (a women's game similar to basketball, only the hoop has no backboard), basketball, soccer and Thoroughbred racing in season.

Carnival is the island's most spectacular event. Inspired by the splendor of Queen Elizabeth's coronation and the desire for a yearly festival symbolizing freedom, the Antigua and Barbuda Tourist Board instituted the Antigua Carnival. Beginning the last week in July, Carnival commemorates the Antiguan people's emancipation in 1834.

For 10 days, culminating the first Monday and Tuesday in August, Carnival throngs revel from early evening until dawn to the pulsating strains of steel and brass band music. Holiday visitors join the community in the traditional "jump up," a kaleidoscope of singing, dancing and laughter from the early morning hours until the sun is high in the sky. Carnival City, in the Recreation Grounds at St. John's, presents talented entertainers amid magnificent sets.

Shirley Heights Lookout, which offers a spectacular view of English Harbour, is the site of 6 hours of nonstop entertainment on Sunday beginning at 4 p.m. Visitors have the opportunity to mingle with residents, enjoy succulent barbecue and dance to the beat of reggae and steel bands. The island has a few small nightclubs, and year-round nightlife opportunities range from an evening at the theater to gambling in a casino or strolling on a beach.

Sightseeing

Three-hour and all-day sightseeing cruises along Antigua's coast depart from Dickenson Bay and Heritage Quay. Catamaran cruises and eco-tours often include stops for snorkeling and swimming. Many other types of boat trips are available, including cocktail, barbecue and glass-bottom boat cruises. For more information inquire at your hotel, the Antigua and Barbuda Department of Tourism in St. John's at the Government Complex on Queen Elizabeth Highway, or the information booths at V.C. Bird International Airport, St. John's Harbor and Heritage Quay pier.

Fig Tree Drive in southwestern Antigua winds inland through terrain similar to a rain forest and takes about 1 hour to explore by private car. Although this scenic drive is a bit bumpy, visitors are rewarded with views of old sugar mills and lush vegetation. Such tropical fruits as mangoes, oranges, guavas, pineapples, bananas and soursop grow alongside the road. Don't expect to see any figs—in Antigua, fig is the word for banana. Fig Tree Drive residents sell fruits and vegetables from stands in front of their homes. The road leading to Fig Tree Hill provides breathtaking views of fertile valleys and magnificent 1,320-foot (402-m) Boggy Peak.

From Green Castle Hill, south of St. John's between Jennings and Emanuel, visitors can survey the island's interior plain and a volcanic formation.

Allow about a day to drive the coastal routes, taking time along the way to explore Nelson's Dockyard in English Harbour, the small fishing villages and such coastal archeological sites as Indian Creek and Mill Reef.

An excellent opportunity to mingle with Antiguans is at Heritage Market near "The Bridge" on Market Street in southern St. John's. At this open-air market, you can bargain for fresh fish, fruits, vegetables and spices or simply enjoy the stimulating, colorful atmosphere. Local arts and crafts are featured in an adjacent complex. The market is open daily.

Another way to grasp the nature of the island and its people is to watch a game of *warri.* This ancient betting game is played on a board with 14 holes and a handful of seeds. Originally brought from Africa with the slave trade, it has remained a favorite pastime.

Air and sea excursions travel north to Barbuda, a sparsely populated coral island lined with white and pink sand beaches that run for miles. Reefs harbor tropical fish and lobster while hiding nearly 100 sunken wrecks. Barbuda's interior, notable for its wildlife, includes a large natural frigate bird sanctuary, said to be the largest in the Western Hemisphere.

The only monument on Barbuda is the Martello Tower; although its origins are unknown, its design and location suggest that it was a lighthouse. Caves near Two Foot Bay have sheltered Barbudans for centuries—even during the 2004 hurricanes. Dark Cave is home to a species of blind shrimp found in only two places in the world. There are a few guest houses in the main village of Codrington, which is named for the family who leased the island from the British Crown for "one fat pig per year if asked." Today most of the population lives here, leaving the rest of the island unspoiled.

A full-day excursion to Barbuda by air includes a tour of the Frigate Bird Sanctuary and Codrington as well as a picnic lunch with rum punch. Most hotels will make arrangements for the Barbuda day tour, which should be planned at least 24 hours in advance.

Eco-tours to Long Island and the Jumby Bay resort offer a rare glimpse of the hawksbill turtle, one of the most endangered sea turtles in the Caribbean. A stretch of sand known as Hawksbill Beach is one of the largest breeding grounds. Turtle watches are organized during nesting season from May to December.

Flights to Montserrat, the island paradise devastated by volcanic eruptions since 1995, depart four times daily from V.C. Bird International Airport via WINAIR.

Transportation

Direct service to V.C. Bird International Airport, 6 miles (10 km) from St. John's, is provided from Atlanta, New York City and Newark; carriers include American Airlines, Caribbean Airways, Continental Airlines and US Airways. LIAT offers nonstop flights to Antigua from San Juan, Puerto Rico. US Airways and LIAT service other island destinations, with connections to Barbuda's Codrington Airport. Many cruise ships include Antigua on their regular itineraries.

You can drive rented cars over most of Antigua's roads; however, use caution due to left-hand driving. Be on the lookout for the occasional goat wandering across the road. The primary roads are navigable, but potholes are common—and so are "sleeping policemen" (the Antiguan nickname for speed bumps). Although most of the island's roads are not marked, most hotels and the Antigua and Barbuda Department of Tourism provide a map that is easy to follow.

Signs throughout Antigua show arrows pointing toward major resorts and attractions: These can assist in determining direction. If you are planning to drive through St. John's, be sure to obtain a good map; even though most of the streets are well-marked, many of them are one-way.

Presentation of a valid U.S. license and $20 entitles you to a driver's license good for 90 days. Hertz in St. John's offers rental car discounts to AAA members; phone the head office on Carlisle Estate Airport Road, (268) 481-4440; or branch offices at the Jolly Harbour Hotel, (268) 481-4456; the Royal Antiguan Hotel, (268) 481-4457; and the airport, (268) 481-4455. Other car rental agencies and scooter rental agencies are listed in the telephone directory. Taxis are readily available at major resorts and are plentiful throughout St. John's. Fares from the airport to hotels are listed at the airport, and range from $5 to $26 for four passengers and their luggage, depending upon the destination; for all other excursions round-trip fares are charged. Be sure to ask if fares are quoted in U.S. dollars or the local E.C. currency.

Fast Facts

POPULATION: 69,481.

AREA: 280 sq km (108 sq mi.).

CAPITAL: St. John's.

HIGHEST POINT: 405 m (1,320 ft.), Boggy Peak.

LOWEST POINT: Sea level, Caribbean Sea.

TIME ZONE(S): Atlantic Standard.

LANGUAGE: English and an English patois.

GOVERNMENT: Independent. Member of the British Commonwealth of Nations.

UNIT OF CURRENCY: Eastern Caribbean (E.C.) dollar. $1 U.S. = 2.7 E.C. dollars. U.S. currency is widely accepted.

ELECTRICITY: 110 volts AC and 220 volts AC, 60 cycles; voltage and current vary with location.

MINIMUM AGE FOR DRIVERS: 21-25, depending on the rental car agency. Local license ($20 U.S.) required, valid for 90 days; drive on left.

MINIMUM AGE FOR GAMBLING: 18.

SEAT BELT/CHILD RESTRAINT LAWS: Seat belts are required for all passengers. Children under 10 must ride in the back seat.

HOLIDAYS: Jan. 1; Good Friday; Easter Monday; Labour Day, May (1st Mon.); Whit Monday, May or June (8th Mon. after Easter); Carnival, Aug. (1st Mon. and Tues.); Independence Day, Nov. 1; V.C. Bird Day, Dec. 9; Christmas, Dec. 25; Boxing Day, Dec. 26.

TAXES: An 8.5 percent room tax and 10-15 percent service charge are added to most hotel bills. Departure tax is $20 U.S. and is usually included in airline ticket prices.

IMMIGRATION REQUIREMENTS: Passport or proof of U.S. citizenship and a return or onward ticket are required. No visa needed for stays up to 6 months. The U.S. Dept. of Homeland Security requires all U.S. citizens returning from the Caribbean to present a valid passport.

PHONING THE ISLANDS: To call Antigua and Barbuda from the U.S. or Canada, dial 1 + 268 + the 7-digit local number.

FURTHER INFORMATION FOR VISITORS:

Antigua and Barbuda Department of Tourism
3 Dag Hammarskjold Plaza
305 E. 47th St.-6A
New York, NY 10017
(646) 215-6035
(888) 268-4227

Antigua and Barbuda Department of Tourism, St. John's
Government Complex
Queen Elizabeth Highway
St. John's, Antigua
Antigua and Barbuda
(268) 462-0480

Points of Interest

See map page 47.

Antigua

The largest of the British Leeward Islands, Antigua is about 14 miles (22 km) long and 11 miles (35 km) wide. On the hilly southwestern side is Boggy Peak, the island's highest point. Fig Tree Drive offers a magnificent view.

This island stronghold was once guarded by 40 British forts, many of which are still visible. Sites include Fort Barrington at Deep Bay, Fort Berkeley at English Harbour, Fort Charles at Falmouth Harbour, Fort George at Monks Hill, Fort James at St. John's and Fort Shirley at Shirley Heights.

ENGLISH HARBOUR (F-2) pop. 614

English Harbour is 15 miles (24 km) from St. John's on the south side of the island. Once an outfitting center for British warships, this harbor played host to the ships of Horatio Nelson, Sir Francis Drake and Walter Rodney. It suffered from neglect for many years until yachtsmen rediscovered its charm and natural beauty. Restored to its 18th-century appearance, the town is now one of the island's most popular tourist destinations.

DOW'S HILL INTERPRETATION CENTRE is near Shirley Heights. "Reflections of the Sun" is a multimedia show tracing Antigua's history, heritage and culture. Displays include a shell collection and 18th-century artifacts. A guided tour includes a visit to the Belvedere, an observation area that provides a 360-degree panorama of Nelson's Dockyard National Park. In the distance, the islands of Guadeloupe and Martinique are often visible. The remains of a 1780s house and a gun platform also are on the grounds.

Allow 30 minutes minimum. Daily 9-5. Admission (includes Nelson's Dockyard National Park) $5; free (ages 0-11). MC, VI. Phone (268) 481-5022.

GEM **NELSON'S DOCKYARD NATIONAL PARK** extends inland from a line along the southern coastline from Mamora Bay to Carlisle Bay. Built 1743-94, this UNESCO World Heritage Site is reputed to be the only existing Georgian dockyard. It was used by a number of British admirals, including Horatio Nelson, as the home port of the British Fleet during the Napoleonic Wars. The dockyard also was used as a repair and maintenance station for ships. Several buildings have been restored. Fort Berkeley, the original British garrison, was built in 1704 and manned by more than 3,000 troops. Also noteworthy is the dockyard's marketplace.

The park, which covers 15 square miles (39 sq km) of rolling hills, affords memorable views of the dockyard and surrounding countryside. Guided tours are offered daily. Food is available. Allow 1 hour minimum. Dockyard open daily 9-6. Admission (includes Dow's Hill Interpretation Centre and Shirley Heights) $5; free (ages 0-11). MC, VI. Phone (268) 481-5022.

Nelson's Dockyard Museum is on the ground floor of the Admiral's House in Nelson's Dockyard National Park. Displays in the 1855 Victorian building include naval buttons, maps, coins from the 1800s, telescopes, muskets, cannon balls, clay pipes, ships models and belongings of Horatio Nelson. A late 1700s sandbox tree next to the museum produces pods which once were used as ink blotters. Open daily 8-5. Free with park admission. Phone (268) 481-5037.

SHIRLEY HEIGHTS is across the bay from Nelson's Dockyard. This lovely rise, which affords a view of Antigua's southern coast, was named for Gen. Thomas Shirley, who became governor in 1781. Clarence House, the Georgian villa on the road to the Heights, was built 1804-1806 as the residence of the commissioner of the Royal Navy's dockyard. The Heights served as the main lookout post in the days of Nelson. Approximately 60 structures were built here 1781-1825, and visitors can see the remains of Fort Shirley's barracks, officers' quarters and powder magazines.

The Shirley Heights Barbecue, popular with tourists and locals alike, starts every Sunday at 4 and runs late into the night with live music and dancing. Food is available. Heights open daily 24 hours. Free. A fee is charged for the Sunday event.

PARES (E-3)

BETTY'S HOPE PLANTATION is in the rural limestone district. Once the largest sugar plantation on Antigua, the site served as the seat of government 1689-1704. Sir Christopher Codrington assumed ownership in 1674, naming the plantation for his daughter. The estate remained in the Codrington family for nearly 300 years. Most of the buildings lie in ruin, but one of the windmill towers has been restored. Museum exhibits illustrate the history of sugar in the West Indies, and interpretive markers describe the site. Tues.-Sat. 10-4. Admission $2. Phone (268) 462-4930 or (268) 462-1469.

DEVIL'S BRIDGE is about 5 mi. (8 km) e. at Indian Town Point. This natural limestone arch was created by the erosive force of the Atlantic Ocean. Water rushes through crevices in the rock and spouts through blowholes in dramatic bursts. Archeologists have uncovered artifacts at nearby Indian Town, one of the earliest Arawak settlements on the island.

ST. JOHN'S (D-2) pop. 22,342

Antigua's capital, St. John's has quaint shops and colonial homes above a landlocked harbor. Tempering St. John's 19th-century English atmosphere is a progressive spirit symbolized by modern architecture. The man-made harbor, completed in 1968, has made the island an important port of call for passenger and commercial vessels; cruise ships dock at Heritage Quay.

Shops, banks and other businesses line High Street, which runs through the center of the city to the pier. The produce market in the southern part of town is divided into sections for fruits and vegetables, meat and fish. Vendors pay weekly or monthly rent for stalls, except on Saturdays when they pay according to the number of bundles they carry through the gates. Visitors enjoy watching this "weighing-in" process.

St. John's Botanical Garden is near the intersection of Factory Road and Independence Avenue, behind the National Archives building. This small park's shaded benches and gazebo provide a quiet refuge from the bustle of activity in St. John's.

Antigua and Barbuda Department of Tourism: Government Complex, Queen Elizabeth Highway, St. John's, Antigua; phone (268) 462-0480.

ANTIGUA DISTILLERY LTD. is on Friars Hill Road. The only distillery on the island produces nearly 400,000 gallons of rum each year, bottling under two labels, Cavalier and English Harbour. The company was formed in 1934 with the purchase of several old sugar estates and a muscovado molasses factory; copper stills are still used. Daily 8-4. Free. Phone (268) 480-3200.

FORT JAMES is at the northern entrance to St. John's harbor. Built in 1739 to guard the port, Fort James is one of the many installations built by the British in the 18th century. Fear of French invasion prompted its construction. A powder magazine, several cannons and the foundation of the fort's walls remain. Daily 24 hours. Free.

GOVERNMENT HOUSE is on Independence Dr. Originally known as "The Parsonage," the official residence and office of the governor-general of Antigua has dignified colonial lines and is surrounded by beautiful grounds. The grounds are open to the public; the house is closed for ongoing restoration. Phone (268) 462-0003.

MUSEUM OF ANTIGUA & BARBUDA is at Long and Market sts. The Old Court House, built in 1750, contains exhibits tracing the history of early inhabitants, colonists and slaves. Allow 30 minutes minimum. Mon.-Thurs. 8:30-4, Fri. 8:30-3, Sat. 10-2; closed holidays. Admission $3. AX, MC, VI. Phone (268) 462-1469.

ST. JOHN'S ANGLICAN CATHEDRAL is at the intersection of Newgate St. and Church Ln. The Church of St. John the Divine was originally built in 1683 and redone in stone in 1745. An earthquake destroyed it nearly 100 years later, and it had to be reconstructed yet again. Island legend holds that the figures of St. John the Baptist and St. John the Divine at the south gate were taken from the masts of one of Napoleon's ships.

The cathedral is open to the public for tours, except during religious services; renovations are ongoing. Donations. Phone (268) 462-0820.

GAMBLING ESTABLISHMENTS

- **Grand Princess Casino** is at Jolly Harbour. Daily 7 a.m.-5 a.m. Phone (268) 562-9900.
- **King's Casino** is at Heritage Quay. Daily 10 a.m.-4 a.m. Phone (268) 462-1727.
- **Madison's Casino** is at Runaway Bay. Daily 10 a.m.-3 a.m. Phone (268) 562-7874.

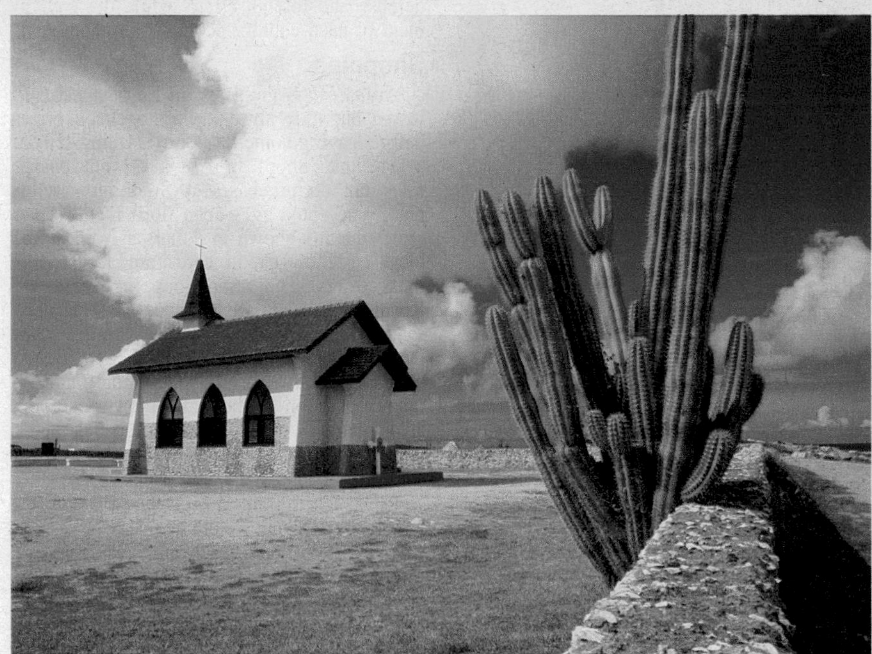

Alto Vista Chapel, Oranjestad / Angelo Cavalli / Getty Images

Aruba

Aruba is the smallest and most westerly of the "ABC" (Aruba, Bonaire and Curaçao) islands. Just 15 miles (24 km) north of Venezuela, it has an exceptionally dry climate that is considered one of the most desirable in the Caribbean. Aruba's arid interior, marked by surreal, wind-bent divi-divi trees, sprawling stands of cactus and aloe vera, and huge boulders strewn like marbles contrasts sharply with the more tropical, palm-lined southwest coast. It is perhaps as much the desert landscape as the active nightlife that gives Aruba the reputation as the Las Vegas of the Caribbean.

History

Assessments of Aruba's worth have varied since 1499, when Alonso de Ojeda claimed the island for Spain. Because the Spaniards considered Aruba worthless, the native Arawak Indians were spared the annihilation their kinfolk faced on islands thought more valuable. The Dutch, who hardly considered the island prime real estate, took over in 1636.

During the Napoleonic Wars the British settled Aruba for a few years, but by 1816 the Dutch had returned to stay. Compared with other Caribbean islands, Aruba had a rather quiet history; the island was fought over only twice and suffered few pirate attacks.

Gold discovered on Aruba in 1824 attracted considerable investment, but a century later the mine was exhausted. A different sort of gold renewed interest in the island in 1924, when the Lago Oil and Transport Co. built a large refinery that brought one of the highest standards of living in the Caribbean.

This prosperity was furthered by the development of tourism, which became Aruba's primary industry when the refinery closed in 1985. (It reopened in 1991.) Because of the focus on tourism and the number of resorts on

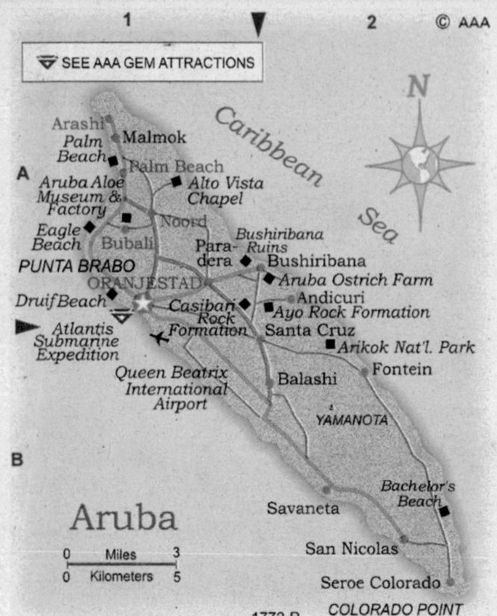

the island, Arubans enjoy a very low unemployment rate. A moratorium on building new hotels or timeshare resorts contributes to sustainable development and a high standard of living on the island. Arubans are proud of their heritage and are concerned that with the importation of additional workers the island's local flavor might be lost.

Aruba's location outside the hurricane belt, its near constant 82 F (28 C) temperature, the ever-present trade winds (which, at times, can be quite gusty) that cool off even the hottest days, its comparatively low humidity and infrequent rainy days combine to make the island a favorite for visitors year-round.

Practically all Arubans are fluent in four languages: English, Dutch and Spanish and Papiamentu, the native language of the three "ABC" islands. A mélange of Dutch, Spanish, Portuguese, African, English and French, Papiamentu is a lilting, melodic language spoken by locals at home and with friends. Arubans, known for their hospitality and their friendly, outgoing nature, treat visitors as important guests and extend a sincere *bon bini* ("welcome"). This conviviality can be traced to a line from the country's national anthem: "The greatness of our people is their great cordiality."

Aruba became a separate entity within the Kingdom of the Netherlands on Jan. 1, 1986; prior to that date it was a member of the Netherlands Antilles. The Kingdom of the Netherlands, which includes the Netherlands, the Netherlands Antilles (Bonaire, Curaçao, St. Eustatius, St. Maarten and Saba) and Aruba, is responsible for the entire kingdom's defense and foreign affairs while the government of each country performs autonomously.

Shopping

Aruba offers the finest in European luxury items, but it is always wise to check prices before leaving home, as not everything sells at a discount. Shops in Aruba do not charge sales tax on purchases. U.S. dollars are as readily accepted as Aruban florins, and prices are frequently shown in dollars as well as the local currency. Credit cards are accepted at most stores. The main shopping areas are Royal Plaza Mall, Renaissance Mall, Renaissance Marketplace, Aventure Mall, Plaza Daniel Leo and the shops along Caya Betico Croes (Main Street) in cosmopolitan Oranjestad. In addition to these downtown shopping areas, many of the larger hotels have shopping arcades that feature branches of the downtown shops.

Royal Plaza Mall on L.G. Smith Boulevard features designer clothing, jewelry and watches. Souvenirs, beachwear and local and foreign music also can be found at the colorful mall built in the Dutch Caribbean style of architecture. Though Cuban cigars are available here, U.S. citizens are expressly forbidden from bringing them home.

Behind the Royal Plaza Mall are a post office; the Setar Teleshop, where travelers can place overseas phone calls; and Botica Kibrahacha, a drugstore and pharmacy. Two ATMs inside the mall offer local currency and U.S. dollars. The Renaissance Mall adjoining the Renaissance Resort has entrances on Havenstraat and L.G. Smith Boulevard. The mall, where visitors can see the hotel's indoor boat lagoon, contains more than 60 shops and designer boutiques.

On Plaza Daniel Leo across from the Seaport Mall are European boutiques, perfumeries and cosmetics shops. The square is recognized by its Dutch Colonial architecture painted in pastels.

Shops along Caya Betico Croes, which starts at Plaza Daniel Leo, offer clothing, perfume and cosmetics, sunglasses, souvenirs and imported items such as Dutch pewter, Delftware and Hummel figurines.

Renaissance Marketplace is on L.G. Smith Boulevard across from the Government Executive Office. Situated on the waterfront next to a marina and the Seaport Casino, the market contains a movie theater, restaurants and souvenir shops.

Most Oranjestad stores are open Mon.-Sat. 9-6. Some stores also are open Sunday mornings and holidays when cruise ships are in port. The port, which can handle up to four ships, is near downtown Oranjestad and convenient to the main shopping areas. Banking hours are Mon.-Fri. 8-4. The Caribbean Mercantile Bank at the airport is open daily 8-4.

Food and Drink

Menus catering to all tastes and budgets can be found in Oranjestad. Signs reading *Aki ta bende kuminda krioyo* mean "local food sold here." Island specialties include *funchi,* a polenta-like cornmeal staple served with meat or fish; *pan bati,* a somewhat sweet Aruban pancake made of cornmeal; and *keri keri,* a mixture of tomatoes, peppers, shredded codfish and herbs.

Other popular Aruban dishes include *keshi yena,* a Dutch cheese stuffed with meat, chicken or fish that is seasoned with raisins, olives, onions and tomatoes; and *pastechi,* pastries filled with cheese, meat, seafood or other ingredients. *Erwten soep* is a thick pea soup cooked with pork, ham and sausage; *stoba* is a stew of vegetables and meat (usually goat); and *soppi di pisca* is fish soup seasoned with *yerbi hole*, a local variety of basil. *Robo porco*, salted pig's tail, is often added to traditional dishes.

Island flavors are evident in fresh caught fish such as wahoo, snapper or grouper simply prepared and served with a *Criollo* (Creole) sauce of tomatoes, onions, garlic and bell peppers. The proximity of the island to South America accounts for the popularity of Argentinian *churrasco* steaks and *churrascarias,* Brazilian steak houses. A popular accompaniment to any Aruban meal is the locally produced Balashi beer, a pilsner-style brew.

Most restaurants automatically add a service charge of 15 percent to the bill, not all of which goes to the server. An additional tip is appreciated, especially when service is exceptional. Dinner reservations are recommended at the island's better restaurants, and the majority accept credit cards.

As for liquid refreshment, sparse rainfall used to make drinking water scarce, but modern technology allows fresh water to be distilled from the sea. In fact, Aruba boasts one of the world's largest desalinization plants; drinking tap water is safe and refreshing.

Sports and Amusements

As on its sister islands, vegetation on Aruba is sparse. The dusty interior contains huge boulders and wind-bent *divi-divi* (watapana) trees. Recreational activities include hiking through Arikok National Park; cave exploring at Fontein, Huliba and Guadirikiri; and horseback riding through the outback.

There is plenty to do along the coast, with beach-related and water activities at the top of the list. Although all of Aruba's beaches are public, beach chairs are reserved for hotel guests. *Palapas,* or thatch-covered beach huts, are so coveted for shade that guests line up early in the morning for reservations.

Seven miles (11 km) of uninterrupted beach stretch from Druif Beach to Eagle Beach and from Palm Beach to Malmok. The best swimming spots are Eagle and Palm beaches, due to the fact that the water is the calmest off the island's southwest coast. These beaches also are where the majority of the island's hotels are concentrated. Banana boats and parasailers being towed behind speed boats are a common sight along Palm Beach. For those in search of expansive stretches of sand, Eagle Beach and nearby Manchebo Beach offer wider strips than can be found at Palm Beach.

Druif Beach, south of Eagle Beach, also is a pleasant place to swim for those not averse to some slight wave action. There are small beach coves on the north coast—Boca Prins, Boca Grandi and Dos Playa. Although the scenery is beautiful, the north coast is not recommended for swimming, due to strong currents and large waves.

The beaches in the southeast section of the island just beyond the oil refinery tend to be less populated than the southwest beaches. Baby Beach, a large, secluded inlet at the island's southeast tip, is so named because it is perfect for small children and inexperienced swimmers. This is because the water remains shallow quite a distance from the shore, achieving depths no greater than 5 feet (1.5 m). It also is a popular beach among the locals for relaxing and picnicking.

At Rodgers Beach, next to Baby Beach, swimmers can enjoy a little more surf and find good swimming and snorkeling opportunities. And although it can be somewhat disconcerting to see the large refinery looming so close by, the water and air at Baby and Rodgers beaches are crystal clear, and the beaches are ideal for a family outing.

Trade winds that blow at a maximum speed of 27 knots (31 mph, 50 km/h) daily, with an average speed of 18 knots (21 mph, 34 km/h), make conditions perfect for windsurfing; the Aruba Hi-Winds Tournament takes place in June. The entire area of coast between Hadicurari and Malmok beaches provides excellent windsurfing opportunities. Hadicurari, locally referred to as "Fishermen's Huts," is one of the most popular spots.

North of Fishermen's Huts, the Malmok Beach area is a great place to learn how to windsurf since the water is only between 2 and 3 feet (.6 and .9 m) deep. There are many small guest houses and day-rental apartments in this area which cater to windsurfers, and windsurfing lessons and equipment rental are readily available. Boca Grandi, just north of Seroe Colorado Point, is an area famous for professional windsurfing.

Visibility in Aruba's clear waters can extend as far as 90 feet (27 m) and the water temperature is never under 70 F (21 C), making the area very desirable for snorkeling and scuba diving. A vessel often explored by divers is the *Antilla,* the wreckage of a World War II German freighter off the coast midway between Arashi and Malmok. One of the largest wrecks in the Caribbean, the ship was purposefully sunk in 1941 in order to avoid capture by Allied forces. Another cement cargo ship, the *Jane Sea,* lies near the Barcadera Reefs.

Arashi Beach, north of Malmok on the southwest coast, is frequented by both scuba divers and snorkelers. Mangel Halto, a reef off the southeast coast halfway between Oranjestad and San Nicolas, is a favorite with divers; snorkeling also is possible in this area. Isla d'Oro, about 1 mile (1.6 km) east of Spanish Lagoon, is another popular dive site. Barcadera Reef is especially recommended for scuba diving.

Snorkeling is a featured activity at De Palm Island, and a beautiful reef is easily accessible off the shallow channel of Baby Beach. Berth Reef, off Rodgers Beach, and the reefs off Bachelor's Beach, on the northeast coast, are favored snorkeling spots for advanced swimmers. Rental equipment for diving, windsurfing and water skiing is available throughout the island.

Fishing for blue and white marlin, kingfish, tuna, bonito and other game fish is best July through October. Also in abundant supply are sailfish, mahi mahi, amberjack, wahoo and barracuda. Boats for deep-sea fishing can be chartered at the Seaport Marina and Oranjestad piers. Some yachts and catamarans offer 2-hour coastal cruises, complete with snacks and beverages. Motorboats, small sailboats, pedalboats and sea jeeps (wave runners) can be rented for shorter periods of time at diverse aquatic facilities.

As for non-aquatic recreation, most hotels and private clubs provide tennis courts and information about horseback riding. Tierra del Sol, (297) 586-7800, features an 18-hole golf course designed by Robert Trent Jones Jr. The Aruba Golf Club, (297) 584-2006, near San Nicolas has a nine-hole golf course.

Regardless which outdoor activity you choose—whether languidly soaking up some sun on the beach or energetically hiking or bicycling through the island's interior—always remember that you are in the tropical Caribbean, and the effects of the sun can be devastating. Keep hydrated, use plenty of high-octane sunscreen and wear a head covering.

In addition to the many activities available during the day, Aruba also has an active nightlife: Hotel casinos and various nightclubs and restaurants offer dancing and after-dinner entertainment. The island's resorts sponsor more than 50 themed events that occur on a weekly basis, including folkloric, limbo and steel-band shows.

Casino gambling is a popular pastime in Aruba, with 11 casinos offering blackjack, roulette, baccarat, craps and slot machines. One of the most common games is Caribbean stud poker, which can be played by table or machine. Visitors to the casinos must be at least 18. Aruba's casinos are not as formal as those in Atlantic City or Las Vegas, and casual attire is acceptable.

Dance revues with a Latin flair can be enjoyed at the Crystal Theatre at the Renaissance Aruba Beach Resort.

Some of the best local entertainment takes place at the Bonbini Festival, held every Tuesday evening at Fort Zoutman in Oranjestad at 6:30 p.m. Offerings include food, music and crafts. Concerts and folkloric shows also are performed at the Cultural Center at Vondellaan 2 in Oranjestad. Movies, usually American, are shown at the drive-in theater at Balashi and at the cinema at the Renaissance Marketplace.

The island version of New Orleans' Mardi Gras, Aruba's Carnival is celebrated during January and February and enlists locals and tourists alike in parades, dances, contests and parties; the Grand Parade takes place the Sunday before Ash Wednesday.

Aruba's three English newspapers—*Aruba Daily, Aruba Today* and *The News*—are available free of charge at most hotels.

Sightseeing

Aruba has good roads, though many are unmarked. However, the government has marked the roads to point the way to the resort areas and specific attractions. You might have to rely on word of mouth or try navigating by the divi-divi trees which always point southwest away from the trade winds; if you are lost, just remember that these trees blow in the direction of the resorts. The island is about 19.6 miles (32 km) long and 6 miles (10 km) wide at its broadest point and most of it can be toured by car.

Jeep tours are a popular way to experience the otherworldly rock-strewn, almost moon-like landscape common to Aruba's interior, and caravans of four-wheel-drive vehicles are a familiar sight along the hilly, bumpy dirt roads of such spots as Arikok National Park. A guide, who rides in the lead vehicle, provides a narration, which can be heard through speakers mounted in each visitor-driven jeep.

For an adventurous excursion, drive into Aruba's *cunucu,* or countryside, where fields of cactuses and aloe vera are punctuated by wandering goats and colorful cottages. Old-style cunucu houses, which appear throughout the island, are characterized by such features as rain tanks, a necessity in the days before desalinization, wooden windows and doors, and chimneys once used for cooking.

Chances are you will find your own Kodak moment—perhaps one of the huge rock formations that mark the area around Casibari and Ayo, from which a road continues northeast to Andicuri. Here was the famed Natural Bridge, a coral limestone formation that collapsed into the sea in 2005. A smaller "daughter" bridge is nearby. With a little further exploration you might discover secluded inlets where crashing waves leap upward above the cliffs.

On J.E. Irausquin Boulevard, the main road leading to the high-rise hotels at Palm Beach, is an Aruban landmark, the Old Dutch Windmill. Built in the Netherlands in 1804, it was moved to Aruba and reconstructed at its present site in 1974. It currently houses a restaurant.

Directly across the road from the windmill is the Bubali Bird Sanctuary. An anomaly in semi-arid Aruba, the lush refuge is a resting and breeding grounds for more than 80 species of migrating waterfowls, including herons, egrets, cormorants, ducks and gulls. There is no charge to walk through the marsh grasses or bird watch from the observation tower.

Visitors can view the entire island at Hooiberg, also nicknamed Haystack Mountain, between Santa Cruz and Ayo. Athletically inclined individuals may choose to climb the more than 600 steps that ascend to the mountain's top, which at 541 feet (165 m) is the island's second highest elevation. Yamanota, to the southeast at the center of the island, is Aruba's highest point at 617 feet (188 m). The panorama from its summit includes Frenchman's Pass on the south coast, where Indians defended their island against the French.

At the island's northern tip, the California Lighthouse, named for the wreck of the passenger ship *California* just offshore, is on a cliff that offers a panorama of Arashi, Malmok, Palm and Eagle beaches. At this point, the difference can be observed between the calm southern coast and the northern coast with waves crashing against the shoreline.

Glass-bottom boats provide views of colorful fish, coral formations and shipwrecks during 90-minute trips to the California Lighthouse. Trimaran and catamaran sailing excursions, which offer snorkeling trips and sunset cocktail cruises, also are available.

Reputable ticket booking establishments include *Atlantis* Submarine, DePalm Tours, Pelican Watersports, Red Sail Sports, Unique Sports of Aruba and Wave Dancer. Both half-day and full-day tours, in various combinations, are available; check with your hotel for details.

Some companies offer tours that cater to such specialized interests as wildlife or history. Information about excursions can be obtained at the Aruba Tourism Authority Public

Relations Department in Oranjestad and at most hotels; phone (297) 582-3777.

Transportation

Queen Beatrix International Airport has direct flights from Atlanta, Baltimore, Boston, Houston, Miami, Newark, New York, Philadelphia, Puerto Rico and Tampa; interisland flights to the other "ABC" islands are available on Dutch Antilles Express. Direct flights from Aruba to Colombia and Venezuela also are available. In addition, Aruba is a popular port of call for cruise ships.

Hotels, by law, are not allowed to provide transportation to and from the airport for their guests. Taxis, however, are readily available at the airport. Cabs are not metered, but fares are set by the government and are based on destination rather than mileage. The fare (per taxi, not per person) from the airport to the downtown area is $13; the fee to the Eagle Beach hotel area is $17; and to the Palm Beach hotel area the cost is $20.

Most American car rental firms have branches on the island, and there also are several local companies. Many rental agencies have outlets across from the main terminal at Queen Beatrix International Airport, though if you prefer to rent a car for just a few days, the larger hotels have rentals available on-site. Hertz—with outlets at the airport, the cruise terminal and at several major hotels—offers discounts to AAA members; phone (297) 582-1845.

Speed limits in Aruba are generally 30 mph (50 km/h) in town and 50 mph (80 km/h) on out-of-town roads. Drivers should be aware that most of the traffic in Oranjestad is one-way, and vehicles approaching from the right have the right of way when there is no road sign posted. Driving is on the right side of the road, and right turns on red are not permitted. "Roundabouts," traffic circles common in Europe, also can be found at major intersections in Aruba.

Traffic in the heart of Oranjestad can be quite congested during peak hours, and parking spaces are often at a premium. The free parking lot near Royal Plaza Mall, adjacent to the main bus station, is a good alternative; from there it's only a short walk to the main shopping areas.

Due to Aruba's European heritage, speed limits and distances on road signs are presented in kilometers, and the international symbols used on the signs may be unfamiliar to drivers accustomed to U.S. signage. Not all of these symbols are self-explanatory; be sure and familiarize yourself with their meanings before setting out.

Part of L.G. Smith Boulevard, which runs in front of the Palm Beach hotels, is known as J.E. Irausquin Boulevard. Some street signs in the stretch of road between the Divi Tamarijn and the Aruba Marriott Resort & Stellaris Casino reflect this name.

Although maps might show street names and highway numbers, once you leave the downtown area in Oranjestad road signs and street markers are few and far between. Also, outside the main commercial and residential areas, and especially if you venture into the countryside *(cunucu)*, roads are not likely to be paved. Even so, it's a small island and not difficult to navigate as long as you remember to ask for directions before heading out.

Use caution when traveling on wet roads; dirt and oil accumulate due to scarce rainfall, resulting in slippery conditions in the rain. If you are planning an excursion through Aruba's interior, a car with four-wheel-drive is a good idea. Make sure your vehicle is in good working order, since repair facilities are not always available.

Scooters and motorcycles also can be rented, but keep in mind that the island is deserted in certain areas and the terrain can be rough and hilly. Taxis also can be hired for sightseeing. If you choose to take a cab, check the fixed taxi rates beforehand. To order a cab phone (297) 582-2116.

An inexpensive transportation option to Oranjestad from the hotels at Eagle and Palm beaches is the regular bus service provided by Arubus. Stops are conveniently located in front of most major lodgings along the road to the downtown area. The main bus terminal is on L.G. Smith Boulevard, exit to Royal Plaza in downtown Oranjestad.

Buses run daily 5:40 a.m.-11:40 p.m. From Monday through Saturday the buses make scheduled stops 20 minutes before the hour, 10 minutes before the hour, on the hour and 25 minutes after the hour; after 7 p.m. buses only stop 20 minutes before the hour. On Sunday buses run on a reduced schedule, stopping 20 minutes before the hour. The fare is $1.15, or $2 for a round-trip.

Since the U.S. Dept. of Homeland Security has officers stationed at Queen Beatrix International Airport, U.S. visitors save time by clearing customs in Aruba before departure rather than at their destination.

Fast Facts

POPULATION: 100,018.

AREA: 181 sq km (70 sq mi.).

CAPITAL: Oranjestad.

HIGHEST POINT: 188 m (617 ft.), Mount Jamanota.

LOWEST POINT: Sea level, Caribbean Sea.

TIME ZONE(S): Atlantic Standard.

LANGUAGE: Dutch and Papiamentu are the official languages, but Spanish and English are widely spoken.

GOVERNMENT: Autonomous member of the Kingdom of the Netherlands.

UNIT OF CURRENCY: Aruba florin divided into 100 cents. $1 U.S. = approx. 1.8 Aruba florin. U.S. currency is widely accepted.

ELECTRICITY: 110-120 volts, 60 cycles AC.

MINIMUM AGE FOR DRIVERS: 21-25, depending on the rental car agency; maximum age 65-70. U.S. license valid; drive on right.

MINIMUM AGE FOR GAMBLING: 18.

SEAT BELT/CHILD RESTRAINT LAWS: Seat belts are required for all passengers. Children under 12 must ride in the back seat. Child restraints are required for under age 5.

HELMETS FOR MOTORCYCLISTS: Required.

HOLIDAYS: Jan. 1; G.F. "Betico" Croes' Day, Jan. 25; Carnival Monday, Feb. (Mon. before Ash Wednesday); National Anthem and Flag Day, Mar. 18; Good Friday; Easter; Easter Monday; Queen's Birthday, Apr. 30; Labour Day, May 1; Ascension Day, May (6th Thurs. after Easter); Christmas, Dec. 25; Boxing Day, Dec. 26.

TAXES: There is no sales tax on purchases, though a 6 percent government tax and 10-12 percent service charge are added to most hotel and restaurant bills. For flights to the United States, a departure tax of $36.75 U.S. and a special facility charge of $3.25 are usually included in airline ticket prices.

IMMIGRATION REQUIREMENTS: Passport or proof of U.S. citizenship and return or onward ticket are required. No visa needed for stays up to 3 months. The U.S. Dept. of Homeland Security requires all U.S. citizens returning from the Caribbean to present a valid passport.

PHONING THE ISLANDS: To call Aruba from the U.S. or Canada, dial 011 + 297 + the 7-digit local number beginning with "5."

FURTHER INFORMATION FOR VISITORS:

Aruba Tourism Authority
100 Plaza Drive, First Floor
Secaucus, NJ 07094
(201) 558-1110
(800) 862-7822

Aruba Tourism Authority, Oranjestad
L.G. Smith Blvd. 172
P.O. Box 1019
Oranjestad, Aruba
Netherlands Antilles
(297) 582-3777
See color ad p. 298.

Points of Interest

See map page 56.

BUSHIRIBANA (A-2)

The castle-like ruins of an old pirate stronghold still stand at Bushiribana, perhaps dating to the 15th century. Here too are the abandoned gold mines that once produced some three million pounds of gold. The rugged north coast is known for its crashing waves and unusual rock formations.

The island's most famous tourist attraction, the Natural Bridge, fell into the sea in 2005. The 100-foot-long coral span, which had survived centuries of the ocean's pounding, was the largest of its kind in the Caribbean.

ARUBA OSTRICH FARM is on Natural Bridge Road at Matividiri 57. Guided tours of the 12-acre (5-hectare) farm provide information about these long-necked birds, raised solely for breeding and educational purposes. Aruba's climate is too humid for eggs to mature on their own; visitors see the incubators where the huge eggs are kept until they hatch. Chicks frequently can be seen and held, and the older birds can be fed.

The birds' life cycle is explained as visitors are led around the complex. Food is available. Allow 30 minutes minimum. Tours daily 9-4, every half-hour. Admission $12; $6 (children). Phone (297) 585-9630.

AYO ROCK FORMATION is 1.9 mi. (3 km) s. of Bushiribana. The origin of this geological mystery has never been determined. Diorite boulders, each weighing several thousand tons, balance precariously on edge or on each other. Indian paintings can be seen on some of the rocks.

BUSHIRIBANA GOLD MINE RUINS is at Boca Mahos. Remains of the Aruba Island Gold Mining Company's smelting works, built in 1872 and used for only a decade, stand in a barren area with desert-like terrain. Some 3 million pounds of gold were produced here. Striking views of the north coast can be seen from the ruins.

CASIBARI ROCK FORMATION is just s. of Paradera. Diorite boulders weighing thousands of tons make up this stone summit. A climb to the top, made possible by ascending steps that wind through the boulders, is rewarded by a panorama of the southwest portion of the island. A rock garden at the base of the formation is accented by beachgrape trees and contains boulders said to resemble certain animals. Only those in good physical condition should attempt the climb. Open daily dawn-dusk.

FONTEIN (B-2)

Aruba's caves first provided shelter to Arawak Indians who left their paintings on the cave walls. According to legend, pirates later stashed their gold in these grottoes along the north coast. Now preserved within Arikok National Park, the caves have become a popular tourist destination.

ARIKOK NATIONAL PARK is w. on Hwy. 7A near San Fuego. The park, which covers nearly 20 percent of the island, abounds with such wildlife as parakeets, goats, donkeys, iguanas and the wara-wara, a red-beaked eagle. Flora includes such rare species of trees as brazilwood, lignum vitae, kibrahacha and the only divi-divi tree that doesn't grow in a characteristically bent shape. Indian symbols can be seen on some of the boulders at Cunucu Arikok. The summit of Mount Jamanota, the island's highest point, offers a sweeping view of the northeast coast and Boca Prins.

Because of its rugged landscape, the park is best experienced in a jeep. A $10 park guide with driving and hiking maps is available at the park office at Piedra Plat 42 in Paradera. Phone (297) 582-8001.

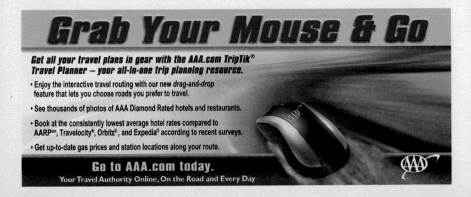

Fontein Cave is s. of Boca Prins in Arikok National Park. Once used by Arawak Indians, this limestone hollow contain pre-Columbian petroglyphs. A ranger is present at the cave entrance to point out important markings. Paths and steps are rocky and uneven; handrails may not be present. Free. Phone (297) 582-8001.

Guadirikiri Cave is s. of Fontein along the coast in Arikok National Park. Sunlight filters into two chambers in this 100-foot tunnel, which features impressive stalagmites and stalactites. Farther south is the Huliba Cave or Tunnel of Love, named for its heart-shaped entrance rather than its romantic atmosphere; paths are cramped and hot, and the smell of guano can be overpowering. Bats in both caves are harmless. Caves free. Flashlight and helmet rental $6. Phone (297) 582-8001.

ORANJESTAD (A-1) pop. 26,355

Oranjestad, which translates to "Orange City," derived its name from the House of Orange, the ruling family of the Netherlands. Dutch architecture in Oranjestad blends nicely with Caribbean colors: Dutch colonial houses are painted green, blue, yellow and brown. This profusion of color is maintained by a local tenet that warns against coveting the color of a neighbor's house. Modern residences, broad boulevards and a park complement the city's charm.

Aruba Tourism Authority: L.G. Smith Blvd. 172, Oranjestad, Aruba; phone (297) 582-3777.

ALTO VISTA CHAPEL is e. of Noord on a dirt road to the coast. Arawak Indians and Spanish missionaries built the first Catholic church on this site in 1750. A priest came to the island several times a year to perform masses, baptisms and marriages. The tiny yellow chapel that stands at the edge of a cliff above the sea was built in 1952. Stations of the cross mark the road leading to the chapel, often called the Pilgrim's Church, a peaceful spot for contemplation. Open daily.

THE ARCHEOLOGICAL MUSEUM OF ARUBA is in the Instituto di Cultura behind the St. Franciscus Church at J.E. Irausquin Blvd. 2-A. Artifacts representing Aruba's cultural heritage include the remains of stone tools dating from 2000 B.C., known as the pre-ceramic period. Items dating from 1000 A.D., the ceramic period, include pottery, sling stones used for hunting and burial artifacts of the Debajuroid Aruban Indians. Also displayed are skeletal remains excavated from an Indian burial site. Mon.-Fri. 8-noon and 1-4. Free. Phone (297) 588-9961.

ARUBA ALOE MUSEUM & FACTORY is .6 mi. (1 km) e. on Rte. 4A from the Eagle Beach traffic circle, then .2 mi. (.5 km) s. to Pitastraat 115. Since 1890, the aloe vera plant has influenced everything on Aruba from art and architecture to health and healing—at one point it covered almost two-thirds of the island's surface. Guided tours of the factory demonstrate how aloe vera leaves are transformed into finished lotions. Museum exhibits reflect aloe's importance to Aruba's history and economy.

Allow 30 minutes minimum. Tours are given Mon.-Fri. 8:30-4, Sat. 9-1. Admission $8; $4 (children). Phone (297) 588-3222.

ARUBA BUTTERFLY FARM is on J.E. Irausquin Blvd. More than 35 species from around the world are housed in a tropical garden. Tours trace the four stages of the butterfly life cycle. Allow 30 minutes minimum. Daily 9-4:30. Last admission 30 minutes before closing. Admission (good for 7 days) $13; $6 (ages 4-16). AX, DS, MC, VI. Phone (297) 586-3656.

ARUBA NUMISMATIC MUSEUM is on Weststraat across from the cruise ship terminals next to Royal Plaza. Various forms of currency from more than 400 countries date from 221 B.C. to the present. The 40,000-piece display, amassed by collector Mario Odor and maintained by his family, includes Aruban Indian shell artifacts used for barter; wampum beads used as money by North American Indians; currency from World Wars I and II, including inflation and occupation money and money used in concentration camps; and bills made of linen and silk.

Mon.-Thurs. 9-4, Fri. 9-1, Sat. 9-noon. Admission (includes a 30-minute guided tour and a commemorative medal for each family) $5. Phone (297) 582-8831.

GEM **_ATLANTIS_ SUBMARINE EXPEDITION** departs from the Seaport Village Marina at L.G. Smith Blvd. 82. This 65-foot-long (20 m), 48-passenger submarine cruises at a maximum depth of 150 feet (46 m), offering excellent views of Barcadera Reef, marine life and coral formations. Trips depart daily at 11, noon and 1. A 10-minute ferry ride transports passengers between the dock and the submarine for the 1-hour tour. Fare $89; $37 (ages 4-16). Children under 36 inches tall are not permitted. Reservations are required. AX, DS, MC, VI. Phone (297) 588-6881.

BALASHI GOLD MILL RUINS is 3 mi. (5 km) s.e. of the airport. Balashi was the site of Aruba's early gold mining industry. Ruins of gold smelters are visible at Frenchman's Pass. Aruba's drinking water is produced at the nearby desalination plant, one of the largest in the world. The water's purity gives it the nickname "Balashi cocktail," and the island brewery uses the same source.

FORT ZOUTMAN AND THE WILLEM III TOWER is on Zoutmanstraat. Dominating the city's skyline, the tower was built in 1798 to protect the island from pirates. It was named in honor of the reigning Dutch king. Historical displays at the Museo Arubano include weights and measures, coins, furniture and antique tools. The Bon Bini Festival is held every Tuesday evening on the patio of the fort from 6:30-8:30; visitors can sample Aruban cuisine, crafts, music and dancing. Museum open Mon.-Fri. 10-noon and 1:30-4:30. Fort admission (includes guided tour and refreshments) $6. Festival $3. Phone (297) 582-6099.

ST. ANNA CHURCH is on Caya F. D. Figueroa in Noord. The first Catholic church on this site was constructed in 1776; the current building dates to 1914. The neo-Gothic altar was intended for a Dutch chapel in Noord-Brabant but shipped to Aruba by accident; the ceiling had to be cut to accommodate the intricate hand-carved piece. Adjoining the church is a cemetery with tomb "houses" painted in pastel colors and adorned with flowers and various mementos. Sunday mass is given in Papiamentu and Latin, with a special English service at 11. Phone (297) 586-1409.

WILHELMINA PARK is off L.G. Smith Blvd. The park was created in 1955 in honor of the visit of Queen Juliana and Prince Bernhard of the Netherlands. A statue of Queen Mother Wilhelmina of the Netherlands, sculpted of white marble in Italy by Arnoldo Lualdi, dominates the plaza. The park is particularly beautiful when the tropical foliage is blooming in June, September and October. Visitors can rest on benches shaded by palm trees. Daily 24 hours.

GAMBLING ESTABLISHMENTS

- **Alhambra Casino** is at J.E. Irausquin Boulevard 47 at Manchebo Beach. Daily 10 a.m.-4 a.m. Phone (297) 583-5000.
- **Allegro Casino at the Occidental Grand Aruba** is at J.E. Irausquin Blvd. 83 in Palm Beach. Daily noon-4 a.m. Phone (297) 586-9039.
- **Casablanca Casino at Aruba Resort, Spa & Casino** is at J.E. Irausquin Blvd. 77 in Palm Beach. Daily noon-4 a.m. Phone (297) 586-2283.
- **The Casino at the Radisson Aruba Resort** is at J.E. Irausquin Blvd. 81 in Palm Beach. Daily 2 p.m.-3 a.m. Phone (297) 586-4045.
- **Casino Merengue at Aruba Grand Beach Resort** is at J.E. Irausquin Blvd. 79 in Palm Beach. Daily 10 a.m.-3 a.m. Phone (297) 586-3900.
- **Copacabana Casino at the Hyatt Regency Aruba Resort** is at J.E. Irausquin Blvd. 85 in Palm Beach. Daily noon-4 a.m. Phone (297) 586-1234.
- **Crystal Casino at Renaissance Aruba Beach Resort** is at L.G. Smith Blvd. 82 in Seaport Village. Daily 24 hours. Phone (297) 583-6000.
- **Excelsior Casino at Holiday Inn Aruba Resort** is at J.E. Irausquin Blvd. 230. Daily 8 a.m.-3 a.m. Phone (297) 586-7777.
- **Royal Cabana Casino** is at J.E. Irausquin Blvd. 250 in Eagle Beach. Daily 11 a.m.-4 a.m. Phone (297) 587-9000.
- **Seaport Casino at Renaissance Aruba Beach Resort** is at L.G. Smith Blvd. 9 at Seaport Village. Daily 10 a.m.-4 a.m. Phone (297) 583-5027.
- **Stellaris Casino at Aruba Marriott Resort** is at L.G. Smith Boulevard 101 at Palm Beach. Daily 10 a.m.-4 a.m. Phone (297) 586-9000 or (800) 223-6388.

SAN NICOLAS (B-2) pop. 15,848

San Nicolas, 12 miles (19 km) southeast of Oranjestad, is Aruba's second largest city. Known as the island's Sunrise Side, San Nicolas was once a bustling company town when Lago Oil and Transport operated 1924-85. The refining of oil is again playing a part in Aruba's economy: Coastal Corp. reopened the oil refinery in 1991, and Valero took ownership in 2003. A Dutch marine camp is off Commanders Bay near the fishing village of Savaneta.

Charlie's Bar, in operation since 1941, once had a colorful reputation as a hangout for rowdy sailors and oil refinery workers. The establishment is known for its amazing variety of bric-a-brac. Pictures, business cards and license plates grace the walls of the bar while the hundreds of items hanging from the ceiling include hats, Frisbees, an inner tube, a life jacket and even shirts from the Boston Braves and Brooklyn Dodgers.

There is a small natural bridge east of Seroe Colorado at the island's southern tip near Colorado Point. Along the road at Seroe Pretoe is the Lourdes Grotto, a shrine to the Virgin Mary built into the limestone rock by a Catholic priest in the 1950s.

New Providence Island / © Jerry Edmanson / age fotostock

The Bahamas

The subtropical Bahamas, where turquoise waters flow along miles of white sand beaches, include more than 2,000 cays, islets and rocks. Of the approximately 700 islands, 30 of the largest ones are inhabited. Beginning 50 miles (80 km) from the Florida coast, The Bahamas form a 760-mile (1,223-km) arc through the Atlantic, creating a natural barrier across the eastern gateway to the Gulf of Mexico. The island of Bimini is closest to Florida, while the southernmost island, Inagua, is 60 miles (97 km) from Haiti. Spaniards named this archipelago *baja mar*, or "shallow sea."

The two most popular tourist destinations in The Bahamas are the city of Nassau/Paradise Island and Grand Bahama Island. The islands' capital, Nassau, on New Providence Island, is rich in colonial history and charm and offers varied opportunities for sports activities, shopping and sightseeing. Prestigious Paradise Island, linked by entry and exit bridges to Nassau, is a playground of the rich. Freeport, the modern resort-residential complex on Grand Bahama Island, is more cosmopolitan and sports oriented than Nassau. Grand Bahama was developed more recently than Nassau and has become a favored resort, due in part to its nearness to Florida. About 80 percent of the people vacationing in The Bahamas are from the United States.

The Out Islands, known the world over for game fishing, scuba diving, sailing, pristine beaches and emerald-blue seas, extend as far as you can see. There are resorts in areas noted for their lack of commercial development, and where only the silver-top thatch palms and flamingoes claim residence. The principal Out Islands are Abaco, Andros, Bimini, Cat Island, Eleuthera, Exuma and Long Island. Abaco has naturally protected

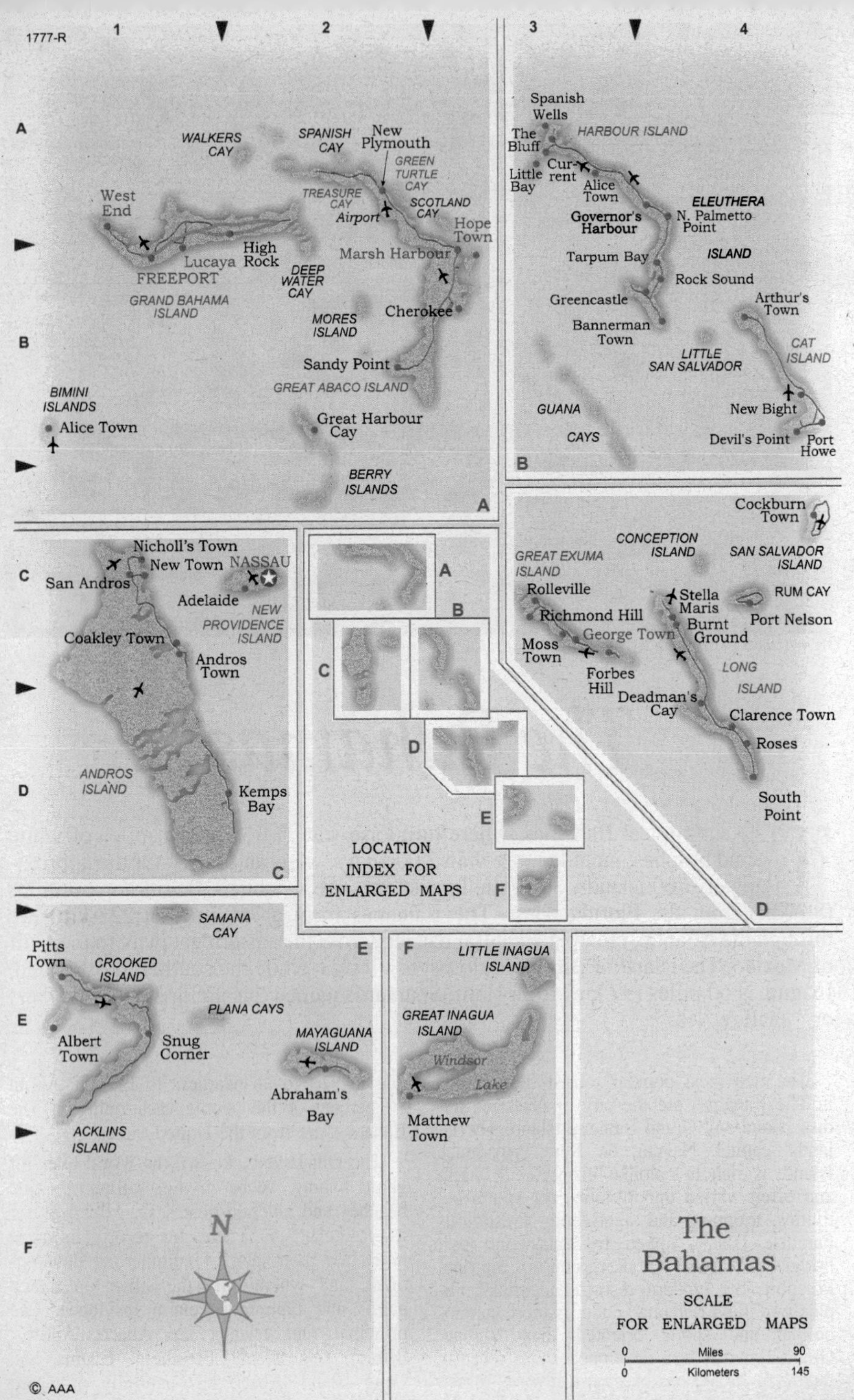
1777-R
1
2
3
4
A
B
C
D
E
F
WALKERS CAY
SPANISH CAY
New Plymouth
GREEN TURTLE CAY
TREASURE CAY
Airport
SCOTLAND CAY
West End
High Rock
Lucaya
FREEPORT
GRAND BAHAMA ISLAND
DEEP WATER CAY
Hope Town
Marsh Harbour
MORES ISLAND
Cherokee
Sandy Point
GREAT ABACO ISLAND
BIMINI ISLANDS
Alice Town
Great Harbour Cay
BERRY ISLANDS
Spanish Wells
The Bluff
HARBOUR ISLAND
Little Bay
Cur-rent
Alice Town
ELEUTHERA
Governor's Harbour
N. Palmetto Point
Tarpum Bay
ISLAND
Rock Sound
Greencastle
Arthur's Town
Bannerman Town
LITTLE SAN SALVADOR
CAT ISLAND
GUANA CAYS
New Bight
Devil's Point
Port Howe
Nicholl's Town
New Town
NASSAU
San Andros
Adelaide
NEW PROVIDENCE ISLAND
Coakley Town
Andros Town
ANDROS ISLAND
Kemps Bay
LOCATION INDEX FOR ENLARGED MAPS
Cockburn Town
CONCEPTION ISLAND
GREAT EXUMA ISLAND
SAN SALVADOR ISLAND
Rolleville
Stella Maris
RUM CAY
Richmond Hill
Burnt Ground
Port Nelson
George Town
Moss Town
Forbes Hill
LONG ISLAND
Deadman's Cay
Clarence Town
Roses
South Point
SAMANA CAY
Pitts Town
CROOKED ISLAND
PLANA CAYS
Albert Town
Snug Corner
MAYAGUANA ISLAND
Abraham's Bay
ACKLINS ISLAND
LITTLE INAGUA ISLAND
GREAT INAGUA ISLAND
Windsor Lake
Matthew Town
N
The Bahamas
SCALE FOR ENLARGED MAPS
0 Miles 90
0 Kilometers 145
© AAA

waters and dozens of offshore cays (pronounced *keys)* that make them a favorite with yachting and fishing enthusiasts. Here there are excellent marinas, guides and boats for hire, and a championship golf course.

Just off the island of Eleuthera, with its picturesque little villages and exclusive resorts, are the charming settlements of Harbour Island, with its pink sandy beaches, and Spanish Wells, which in the old days served as a watering hole for Spanish galleons. The Exumas have many cays, most of which can be reached only by boat.

History

The Bahamas claim the distinction of being Christopher Columbus' first New World discovery. In 1492 he stepped ashore on an island originally called *Guanahani* and renamed it San Salvador. The Lucayan Indians, who then populated the islands, were soon sent by the Spaniards to labor in the mines and sugar mills of Cuba and Hispaniola. However, the Spaniards did not settle here, and in 1629 King Charles I of England granted the islands to Sir Robert Heath, attorney general of England.

A group of English merchants and pioneers from Bermuda, known as the Eleutherian Adventurers, then came seeking religious freedom. They colonized Eleuthera in 1648 and attempted to establish the first republic in the New World. This attempt at colonization and other settlements which followed were, for the most part, unsuccessful. As a result, The Bahamas were soon overrun by pirates such as Blackbeard and Calico Jack, who were finally routed in 1718 by Capt. Woodes Rogers, the first royal governor.

Another wave of immigration occurred after the American Revolution, when Loyalist refugees fled to The Bahamas, taking their slaves with them. England ruled until 1782, when Spain captured the islands; however, the Treaty of Versailles returned them to England once again in 1783.

Throughout The Bahamas' turbulent history their strategically positioned cays and islets played a vital role in international intrigues. Not only were The Bahamas a formidable hideout for pirates, but Confederate blockade runners during the American Civil War and bootleggers during America's Prohibition Era also exploited the islands' proximity to Florida in efforts to smuggle contraband into the United States.

From 1718 to 1969 a governor was appointed by the British Crown; after 1969 the appointment was made in consultation with The Bahamas Government. On July 10, 1973, the islands became an independent sovereign nation headed by a prime minister. Now a member of the British Commonwealth of Nations, the islands retain many legacies from the years of British rule, including the distinctive Bahamian accent and two popular spectator sports—cricket and rugby.

Shopping

Shoppers have a field day exploring the multitude of stores and boutiques lining the streets of Nassau and Grand Bahama Island. Shops also are found just over the bridge on Paradise Island, at Cable Beach and at shopping malls in the outlying areas.

Bay Street is the center of activity in Nassau, where the merchandise consists of imported European goods: perfumes, brass, leather goods, cameras, cashmere, candies, jewelry, china, porcelain, crystal, glass, figurines, linens and designer and sportswear fashions to name just a few. Duty-free prices, made available for the first time in 1992, make these items all the more attractive. Available at discount prices are the island's own liqueur, Nassau Royale, and local banana rums and coconut liqueurs. Festival Place, on Prince George Wharf, features local crafts, food and music in an atmosphere reminiscent of a Bahamian village.

Built in the 1930s, Nassau's Straw Market on Bay Street was famed for its island handicrafts made not only from straw but also from wood and a variety of shells, including coconut and conch (pronounced *konk*). The market was destroyed by fire in 2001, displacing some 500 vendors to smaller booths a block away. Bargaining is expected here, but not in Nassau's shops. Items made from tortoiseshell are banned from importation into the United States. Most shops are open Mon.-Sat. 9-5. Banking hours are Mon.-Thurs. 9:30-3, Fri. 9:30-4:30.

Food and Drink

With the exception of fruit, vegetables and seafood, most food is imported. Many restaurants and hotels feature European, Chinese, Polynesian, Japanese and American cuisines. But Bahamian specialties should not be overlooked: dishes include pigeon peas and rice, rock lobster, baked crab, grouper cutlets, fried jack and fried snapper. Souse is a hearty dish of simmered vegetables and chicken or pig's feet. Conch, a meaty mollusk, is served raw—with fresh lime juice, onions, tomatoes and peppers—and can also be steamed, pounded and deep-fried ("cracked"), or used as an ingredient in soups, chowders and fritters. Rum-raisin ice cream, guava duff (a steamed bread pudding topped with guava sauce) or a coconut tart round off the meal. Tap water is usually safe to drink; bottled water is widely available. Milk is pasteurized.

Graycliff Manor in Nassau, reputedly built by a successful pirate, is currently as renowned for its jet-set clientele as for its cuisine. The resort has its own cigar factory and a wine cellar with more than 250,000 vintage bottles. The Bahamian Club on Paradise Island is one of the most popular restaurants in The Bahamas.

Vendors at the "Fish Fry" on Arawak Cay, just west of Bay Street, provide an array of local specialties, including conch salad and fried fish. The Bamboo Shack and Dirty's on Nassau Street are two of the many take-out restaurants that serve such Bahamian specialties as cracked conch with hot sauce.

Prices for meals in hotels are slightly higher during the winter season, but most lodgings in Nassau offer a modified American plan, which includes breakfast and dinner as an additional option. On the whole, native dishes are usually the least expensive. Most restaurants add a 15-percent service charge to the bill.

Sports and Amusements

Local and international yachting and sailing regattas, golf and tennis tournaments, cricket, rugby and squash are only a few of the activities available in The Bahamas. That golf ranks high in popularity is verified by the number of 18-hole public golf courses on New Providence Island, including the Cable Beach and Ocean Club golf courses. The PGA-rated Ocean Club Golf Course on Paradise Island is exclusively for the guests of Atlantis properties.

Grand Bahama Island offers two championship 18-hole courses at The Westin and Sheraton at Our Lucaya Golf and Beach Resort: the Reef Course, designed by Robert Trent Jones, Jr., and the Lucayan Course by Dick Wilson. Great Abaco Island boasts two more 18-hole courses, the Treasure Cay Golf Club and the Scottish-style Abaco Club on Winding Bay. Exuma's Four Seasons Hotel offers an 18-hole championship golf course designed by Greg Norman, with six signature holes hugging the perimeter of Emerald Bay's scenic peninsula.

Most hotels have tennis courts and information about horseback riding, which is available in Nassau and Freeport.

Though landlubbers enjoy their share of activities, water sports captivate the majority of island travelers. The numerous coves along the beaches of New Providence Island create natural pools ideal for swimming and snorkeling. The 142-mile (228-km) underwater coral reef known for its "blue holes," freshwater springs that well to the surface, offers excellent scuba diving. Paradise Island boasts one of the finest beaches in The Bahamas. Fishing in The Bahamas is good, and light-tackle anglers are amply rewarded.

Peterson Cay National Park, some 15 miles (24 km) east of Freeport, offers excellent opportunities for snorkeling and diving in a pristine setting and is accessible by boat only.

The trade winds ensure fine sailing conditions all year; boats and equipment for sailing, parasailing, fishing, water skiing, windsurfing, snorkeling, scuba diving and spear fishing can be rented from charter firms at the major marinas and from the docks of many waterfront hotels. Hotels that offer parasailing are found in Nassau and Paradise Island; Freeport and Lucaya, Grand Bahama Island; and Cockburn Town, San Salvador Island.

An informative publication for those interested in bareboat charters is the "Yachtsman's Guide to The Bahamas," available at many yachting supply stores, marinas and bookstores in The Bahamas. The 1- or 2-hour scuba diving lessons offered throughout the islands are usually not enough preparation for the sport; you should take a complete course in advance. One of the best places to learn diving is at the Underwater Explorers Society (UNEXSO), in the Grand Bahama's Port Lucaya area, home base of a prominent society of diving experts.

Those who prefer indoor recreation will find nightclubs and casinos on New Providence, Paradise Island and Grand Bahama. Hotel nightclubs and restaurants usually sponsor dancing and after-dinner entertainment. The Chez Willie Restaurant on West Bay Street offers a native show on Saturdays. The Out Island hotels occasionally feature calypso and steel-drum bands. First-run American films are shown in New Providence and Grand Bahama theaters.

Lively festivals and tournaments are offered throughout the year. Junkanoo, the Bahamian national festival, is held on December 26 (Boxing Day) and January 1. Across the islands, competing groups parade through the streets from 1 a.m. to dawn, vying for prizes in costumes and music. The most spectacular parade takes place on Bay Street in Nassau, where the sounds of cowbells, goatskin drums and whistles can be heard for miles. Visitors are free to join in the revelry as part of a "scrap" group.

Smaller versions of Junkanoo are held at various hotels year-round. The Junkanoo Summer Festival is held at Arawak Cay Cultural Park every Saturday in June from 2-10 p.m. Featured are Bahamian food, craft demonstrations, story telling, special children's activities, live entertainment and parades. For additional information, contact the Ministry of Tourism.

Sightseeing

Popular excursions include glass-bottom boat trips, which depart from the Prince George Dock in Nassau and the Port Lucaya Marketplace on Grand Bahama Island, or swimming and snorkeling cruises around Nassau and to Blackbeard's Cay on the catamaran *Coral II*. Several yacht trips depart from the Nassau Yacht Haven for excursions to nearby cays.

Views of the underwater world around Nassau are offered daily aboard the *Seaworld Explorer*, a semi-submarine that operates out of New Mermaid Marina. Glass-bottom boats depart from Prince George Wharf for 90-minute tours of the Sea Gardens, with views of colorful tropical fish and coral formations.

East End Adventures offers all-day tours which include a 54-mile (87-km) drive through pine forests and along deserted beaches with a hike to an inland blue hole and caverns and ending with a 6-mile (9.7-km) speed boat ride to Sweeting's Cay; phone (242) 373-6662.

The tour buses that leave from the major hotels are convenient and economical ways to tour Nassau. A pleasant 2-hour drive might include stops at such sites as the Queen's Staircase, Government House, Ardastra Gardens and forts Fincastle, Montagu and Charlotte.

Transportation

Air service from the East Coast and the Midwest is available aboard many major carriers to Lynden Pindling International Airport and Grand Bahama Island International Airport. American Eagle, Bahamasair, Delta, Continental Connection/Gulfstream International, US Airways and others depart daily from Miami. Jet Blue offers daily non-stop flights between New York and Nassau, and Spirit Airlines flies daily from Ft. Lauderdale. Direct commuter service to some of the Out Islands is available from Fort Lauderdale, Miami, Orlando and Palm Beach.

Some of the large islands have bus service. Bicycles and motor scooters rent by the hour, day or longer. For more luxurious transportation, chauffeur-driven limousines can be hired in Nassau and Freeport. A quaint way to see the sites in Nassau is by horse-drawn carriage. Metered taxis are a convenient way to get around, and the rates are regulated. There are major car rental agencies in Nassau and on Grand Bahama Island; rentals also are available on most of the Out Islands. Driving is on the left side of the road.

More than 145 miles (230 km) of good roads make for pleasant motoring from downtown Nassau to almost all parts of New Providence Island; road conditions on the Out Islands have improved since 1992. Automobiles can be taken duty free to Nassau for up to 6 months. A deposit covering duty charges (between 45 and 60 percent of the car's value plus 4 percent stamp tax), in the form of a customs bond executed by a local bank, is refunded if the vehicle is removed from the Commonwealth before the end of this period. A U.S. driver's license is valid for 3 months.

Island-hopping is possible by both plane and boat. Bahamasair has regularly scheduled interisland flights from Nassau. If there is not a direct flight to the island of your choice, check with the charter companies listed in the telephone directory; information also is available at hotels on the Out Islands.

Many cruise services travel from Miami, Port Everglades and Port Canaveral to Nassau and Grand Bahama Island on a once- or twice-weekly basis. There also is a day cruise from Fort Lauderdale to Freeport on Discovery cruise lines, which sails every day except Wednesday. Traveling by mail boat, though it might be slow and lacking in some comforts, is an inexpensive way to island hop. Since departures are subject to change without notice, advance arrangements with the captain are recommended.

Bahamas Ferries offers a 2-hour ferry ride to Harbour Island, Spanish Wells or mainland Eleuthera. The ferry departs Nassau at 8 a.m. and returns at 6 p.m.; phone (242) 323-2166.

Fast Facts

POPULATION: 304,837.

AREA: 13,934 sq km (5,380 sq mi.).

CAPITAL: Nassau.

HIGHEST POINT: 63 m (206 ft.), Mount Alvernia, Cat Island.

LOWEST POINT: Sea level, Atlantic Ocean.

TIME ZONE(S): Eastern Standard. DST.

LANGUAGE: English (Creole among Haitian immigrants).

GOVERNMENT: Independent. Member of the British Commonwealth of Nations.

UNIT OF CURRENCY: Bahamian dollar. $1 U.S. = 1 Bahamian dollar. U.S. currency is widely accepted.

ELECTRICITY: 110-220 volts, 60 cycles AC; voltage varies with location.

MINIMUM AGE FOR DRIVERS: 21-25, depending on the rental car agency; maximum age 65 without medical certificate. U.S. license valid for 3 months; drive on left.

MINIMUM AGE FOR GAMBLING: 18.

SEAT BELT/CHILD RESTRAINT LAWS: Seat belts are required for all passengers.

HELMETS FOR MOTORCYCLISTS: Required.

HOLIDAYS: Jan. 1; Good Friday; Easter Monday; Whit Monday, May or June (8th Mon. after Easter); Labour Day, June (1st Fri.); Independence Day, July 10; Emancipation Day, Aug. (1st Mon.); Discovery Day, Oct. 12; Christmas, Dec. 25; Boxing Day, Dec. 26.

TAXES: A 10 percent room tax and 10-15 percent service charge are added to most hotel bills. On Grand Bahama Island, a $5 airport security fee is assessed for all ticketed passengers. Departure tax is $15 U.S. from all islands except Grand Bahama, which charges $18 U.S. Departure tax is included in the airline ticket cost.

IMMIGRATION REQUIREMENTS: Passport and a return or onward ticket are required. No visa needed for stays up to 8 months for U.S. citizens. The U.S. Dept. of Homeland Security requires all U.S. citizens returning from the Caribbean to present a valid passport.

PHONING THE ISLANDS: To call The Bahamas from the U.S. or Canada, dial 1 + 242 + the 7-digit local number.

FURTHER INFORMATION FOR VISITORS:

The Bahamas Tourist Office, New York
60 E. 42nd St., Suite 1850
New York, NY 10165
(212) 758-2777
(800) 823-3136

The Bahamas Tourist Office, Florida
1200 South Pine Island Rd., Suite 770
Plantation, Florida 33324
(954) 236-9292

The Bahamas Ministry of Tourism
P.O. Box N-3701
King and George Sts.
Nassau, New Providence Island
The Bahamas
(242) 302-2000
(800) 224-2627
See color ad p. 8.

Points of Interest

See maps on pages 66 and 75.

Andros Island (D-1)

The largest island in The Bahamas but one of the least populous, Andros covers 2,300 square miles (5,957 sq km) replete with stands of virgin pine that often soar to more than 70 feet (21 m). During the early 1840s a group of Seminole Indians and runaway slaves settled at Red Bays, where some of their descendants remain to this day. Legend has it that miniature red-eyed creatures called chickcharnies—a kind of subtropical leprechaun, half man and half bird—nest in the trees and exert both good and bad influence over daily events.

The spectacular reef that borders the island's eastern coast is the world's third-largest barrier reef. Five national parks have been established on Andros and in its surrounding waters to protect 286,080 acres (115,774 hectares) of forest, wetlands and marine ecosystems. Blue holes, many of which have never been explored, abound in the sea floor and offer plentiful opportunities for divers. The Tongue of the Ocean, a canyon in the ocean floor between Andros and Nassau, is the site of oceanographic research. Freshwater lakes harbor waterfowl and provide hunting in season.

Anglers also are drawn to Andros, as the surrounding waters provide many varieties of sea life. The island claims to be the world's premier spot for bonefishing. The 1892 Andros Lighthouse stands at the southern entrance to Fresh Creek Channel. The Androsia Factory at Fresh Creek produces colorful batik with exquisite designs.

Bimini Islands (B-1)

Westernmost of The Bahamas, North and South Bimini and Cat Cay lie on the northwestern edge of the Grand Bahama Bank. With record catches of bonefish, marlin, dolphin, wahoo and tuna, this region is considered one of the world's fishing capitals. Ernest Hemingway's fishing trips in the Biminis in the 1930s inspired him to write his classic story "The Old Man and the Sea." Boats and accommodations are available on both islands; fishing clubs are on Cat Cay. Offshore waters beckon scuba divers with underwater caves, reefs and sunken ships.

Cat Island (B-4)

The pirate Arthur Catt is said to have given his name to this island, one of the least inhabited Out Islands. The main road traverses 50 miles (80 km) of rolling hills and secluded beaches from Arthur's Town in the north to Port Howe in the south. The aptly named Fine Beach is noted for its pristine pink sands. Among many 18th-century plantation ruins that dot the island is Deveaux Mansion, once the home of Col. Andrew Deveaux of the U.S. Navy, who received 1,000 acres (400 hectares) on the island as reward for ousting the Spanish from Nassau in 1783.

At the summit of Mount Alvernia, the highest point in The Bahamas, is the Hermitage of Father Jerome, a stone monastery built by the Jesuit missionary in the 1940s. St. Francis of Assisi Catholic Church in Old Bight is one of several other religious structures built by Father Jerome in the Bahamian islands.

Eleuthera Island (A-4)

Eleuthera has been a refuge for several groups seeking religious freedom since 1648, when the Eleutherian Adventurers established the first settlement here. These settlers gave the island its name, which is derived from the Greek word *eleutheros,* meaning "free."

Settlements at Governor's Harbour and Rock Sound have contributed to Eleuthera's development as a leading family-oriented resort destination. Its miles of secluded beaches and quiet atmosphere are its most appealing features. The main road runs the 110-mile (177-km) length of the island. A marina and a safe harbor are on the ocean side of Rock Sound. Worth seeing is the pineapple plantation in Gregory Town. Ferries connect Eleuthera with Harbour Island and Spanish Wells.

Grand Bahama Island (B-1)

Only 55 miles (89 km) east of Florida, Grand Bahama Island is a major tourist destination. The fourth largest island of the group, it covers more than 530 square miles (1,373 sq km) and is known for excellent bonefishing, reef and deep-sea fishing. Grand Bahama Island's hotels and nightspots have earned it the title of "New World Riviera."

The community of West End gained notoriety during America's Prohibition Era as a jumping-off place for rum runners to the United States. Public beaches include Barbary, Churchill, Fortune, Gold Rock Creek, Paradise Cove and Taíno beaches. The Underwater Explorers Society adjacent to the Port Lucaya Marketplace has a diver-training pool and rental equipment. "The Dolphin Experience," a program offered by UNEXSO, enables visitors to swim and interact with these marine mammals.

FREEPORT (B-1) pop. 26,910

The resort center of the island, Freeport lures outdoor enthusiasts with its many opportunities for fishing, sailing, snorkeling, swimming, golf and tennis.

The Bahamas Ministry of Tourism: Poinciana Drive, Grand Bahama Island, The Bahamas; phone (242) 352-8044. Other tourist information centers are based at Grand Bahama Island International Airport, Lucayan Harbour and Port Lucaya Marketplace.

RAND NATURE CENTRE is 3 mi. (5 km) n.e. of the International Bazaar on E. Settler's Way. A nature trail winds through this 100-acre (40-hectare) sanctuary, which preserves the native flora and fauna of Grand Bahama Island. An ideal spot for birdwatching, the area is home to more than 120 species. Exhibits at the education center reflect the island's ecology, culture and natural history. Mon.-Fri. 9-4. Guided tours Tues. and Thurs. at 10:30. Admission $5; $3 (ages 5-12). Reservations are required for guided tours. Phone (242) 352-5438.

RECREATIONAL ACTIVITIES

Horseback Riding

- **Pinetree Stables** is off East Sunrise Hwy. Guided 2-hour trail rides are offered. Weight limit is 200 pounds and riders limited to ages 8 years and above. Phone (242) 373 3600.
- **Trikk Pony Adventures** provides transportation from local hotels. A variety of beach and nature trail rides are offered. Phone (242) 374-4449.

Kayaking

- **Grand Bahama Nature Tours** offers transportation from local hotels. Kayaking destinations include Lucayan National Park and Peterson Cay National Parks. Snorkeling, bicycling, hiking, and birdwatching tours also are offered. Tours depart daily. Phone (242) 373-2485 or (866) 440-4542.

LUCAYA (B-1) pop. 9,924

Twenty miles east of Freeport along the southern coast of Grand Bahama Island is The Westin and Sheraton at Our Lucayan Golf and Beach Resort. The 6-acre Port Lucaya Marketplace and Marina features shops, restaurants, and live entertainment centered around Count Basie Square, named for the jazz artist who wintered on the island.

LUCAYAN NATIONAL PARK is on Grand Bahama Hwy. The 40-acre (16-hectare) park contains one of the largest explored underwater cave systems in the world. Ecological zones in the park include pineland with hardwood hammocks, rocky coppice, whiteland coppice, mangrove marshes and sand dunes. Hiking trails are available. A trail leading to Ben's Cave and Burial Ground Cave features boardwalk observation decks inside the caves.

Swimming in the caves is prohibited; diving requires special permits. Picnicking is permitted. Daily 9-4. Ben's Cave is closed during the summer to protect the fruit bat nurseries. Park admission $3; free (ages 0-4). Tickets must be purchased in advance at the Rand Nature Center in Freeport (see attraction listing). Phone (242) 393-1317.

GAMBLING ESTABLISHMENTS

- **Isle of Capri Casino at Our Lucaya** is on Sea Horse Lane at the Westin Grand Bahama Island Resort. Daily 10 a.m.-2 a.m. Phone (242) 350-2000.

Great Abaco Island (B-2)

Great Abaco is more than 100 miles (160 km) long with a chain of offshore barrier cays lying east of Grand Bahama Island. Its tourism-based economy is supplemented by agriculture and fishing.

Reports of sunken treasure have brought Great Abaco fame and modern-day explorers. In the 1950s, two Nassau businessmen discovered several 17th-century Spanish coins and a 72-pound silver bar that was identified as the personal property of King Philip IV of Spain and valued at $20,000. Shipwrecks and reefs abound in the waters off Abaco's east coast, making it a popular dive center. A Civil War warship with a huge Dahlgren cannon lies in 30 feet (9 m) of water off Man-O-War Cay.

Many residents, descendants of Loyalists who fled the American Colonies after the Revolution, have carried on the art of shipbuilding, which was introduced here centuries ago. However, local artisans have substituted the use of fine Abaco pine with imported wood and fiberglass to construct the boats. The sailmaker's loft of the Alburys is worth a visit; bags, hats and other canvas items are made here. Marsh Harbour is the commercial center of the island as well as the bareboat charter center of the northern Bahamas.

Abaco's resort potential is enhanced by many secluded, safe harbors along the cays. Such activities as sailing, bonefishing and birdwatching can be arranged. Among the leading vacation spots are Treasure Cay, known for one of the world's top ten beaches and home of endangered wild horses; Elbow Cay, known for its candy-striped lighthouse; the northernmost island of Walker's Cay, a sportfishing resort; Green Turtle Cay, which exudes an early New England atmosphere; Man-O-War Cay, known for the art of boatbuilding; and Guana Cay, site of a Sunday pig roast and live entertainment at Nipper's Beach Bar & Grill.

HOPE TOWN (B-3)

Elbow Cay's famous landmark, the red-and-white-striped Hope Town Lighthouse, was built in 1863. The mechanically-operated beacon is powered by kerosene; its Fresnel lens floats in a bed of mercury. Cars are not permitted in the harbor village.

WYANNIE MALONE HISTORICAL MUSEUM is next to the administration building. Wyannie Malone, the widow of a British Loyalist who fled America during the Revolutionary War, was one of the founders of the settlement of Hope Town in 1783. The museum, in a replica of her century-old white clapboard house, displays historical maps, ships models and items of everyday life. The Balcony House contains historical displays, artifacts and flora and fauna from across the region.

Guided tours of the museum may be arranged by appointment. Allow 30 minutes minimum. Mon.-Sat. 10-3, Oct.-Apr.; Mon.-Sat. 10-12:30, May-July. Admission $3; $5 (family). Phone (242) 366-0293 to schedule a tour.

NEW PLYMOUTH (A-2)

In downtown New Plymouth on Green Turtle Cay, the Loyalist Memorial Sculpture Garden displays 30 bronze busts of famous Bahamian citizens. Green Turtle Kay is a sister city to Key West, Florida, where many Abaco residents moved in the 1800s.

ALBERT LOWE MUSEUM is 1 blk. from the docks on Parliament St. Named for a master builder of model boats, this museum features photographs, antiques and artifacts tracing Abaco's history and development. The restored Loyalist home also houses a display of paintings by Lowe's son Alton, whose work is featured on Bahamian postage stamps; and a fine collection of carved ship models by Vertrum Lowe, who carries on his father's tradition. Mon.-Sat. 9:30-11:45 and 1-4; closed holidays. Admission $5; $2.50 (ages 7-12); free (ages 0-6 with adult). Phone (242) 365-4094.

Great Exuma Island (C-3)

The Exumas consist of 365 islands, ranging from small, uninhabited dots on the map to the two largest islands, Great Exuma and Little Exuma. At the southernmost tip of the Exuma Cays, Great Exuma is 40 miles (64 km) long.

A popular excursion follows the slave route from George Town to Rolleville, a village once owned by Loyalist Lord Rolle, who, upon his death, gave freedom, the land and the name of Rolle to all the tenants. The land may never be sold, but is passed down to each succeeding generation.

Visitors will enjoy touring Elizabeth Harbour and the pristine hidden coves and inlets throughout the 365 cays. Sailing tours often stop to feed swimming pigs at Big Major Cay, iguanas on Allan Cay and nurse sharks at Compass Cay.

Thunderball Grotto is site of colorful underwater reefs, while Dog Rocks is one of the best dive spots in the Bahamas—it starts at 35 feet and slopes off to approximately 50 feet before dropping off into the Exuma Sound. The Exuma Wall, off Highbourne Cay, is a 75-foot sloping wall dive offering views of such tropical creatures as angel fish, grouper, turtles, horse-eye jacks and the occasional shark, billfish and tuna.

Sixty miles of flats on the island's west side offer excellent bonefishing in knee-deep turquoise waters. Sheltered coves and hidden inlets make kayaking in the Exumas ideal for the whole family.

GEORGE TOWN (C-3)

The administrative capital of Exuma, George Town is on Lake Victoria. Several popular festivals entertain visitors. In March, the Bahamian Music and Heritage Festival features popular musicians as well as arts and crafts, Bahamian foods, storytelling, singing, poetry reading and a sloop and Junkanoo exhibition. More than 60 native sloops race at the National Family Island Regatta during the last full week in April. George Town also hosts its own Junkanoo festival on Saturdays in July and August.

EXUMA CAYS LAND AND SEA PARK stretches 22 mi. (35 km) from Wax Cay Cut in the north to Conch Cut in the south and is accessible only by boat. Said to be the first national park of its kind, this marine preserve was established in 1958. The park is made up of 15 major cays and many smaller islands in a pristine area encompassing 176 square miles (456 sq km). The vast underwater park attracts snorkeling and scuba enthusiasts from around the world. The bird and marine life sanctuary is home to sea turtles, rock iguanas and the Bahamas Hutia, a small rodent once thought to be extinct.

The park headquarters at Warderick Wells is open Mon.-Sat. 9-noon and 1-4, Sun. 9-noon. Free. Phone (242) 357-8344.

Harbour Island (A-3)

Harbour Island almost encloses the northeast tip of Eleuthera, forming a harbor 6 miles (10 km) long and 3 miles (5 km) wide. The island boasts 3 miles (5 km) of pink sand beach, the color provided by particles of shell ground against the outer reefs by the force of the sea.

Harbour Island also claims one of the oldest settlements in The Bahamas, Dunmore Town. At the northern end of the island, the town retains an Old World charm through its many restored, brightly colored homes, whose carved shutters and verandas outlined in white create a gingerbread-cottage atmosphere. Many colonial houses were built during the latter part of the 19th century; Loyalist Cottage on Bay Street dates from 1790. A pink municipal building adds the finishing touch to this picturesque town. Snorkeling, scuba diving and bonefishing are popular.

Long Island (C-4)

Long Island is almost wholly within the Tropic of Cancer zone. The island covers 230 square miles (596 sq km), with a width of only a half-mile (.8 km) in some places. It also is one of The Bahamas' chief agricultural islands. According to legend, when Christopher Columbus landed here he found the inhabitants living in tent-shaped buildings and sleeping in nets stretched between posts. The latter idea, adopted by his sailors, evolved into the hammock.

Interesting sites include the ruins of Gray's Plantation in Grays, the Columbus Monument in Seymour's and Dean's Blue Hole in Turtle Cove. Clarence Town has beautiful twin churches on two hilltops: St. Paul's Anglican Church and St. Peter's & St. Paul's Catholic Church. The Stella Maris Inn stands on the island's highest point and affords superb views. The waters off the coast of Long Island are ideal for scuba diving and fishing. Regular flights from Nassau are available.

New Providence Island (C-2)

Home to a majority of the country's population, New Providence Island is the domain of the capital city, Nassau. A prime tourist destination, the island features all the amenities associated with The Bahamas—an array of water sports, golf, tennis, nightlife, casinos, international shopping and a colorful history.

The 21-mile-long (34-km), 7-mile-wide (11-km) island also is home to the popular resort areas of Cable Beach and Paradise Island, linked to Nassau by entry and exit bridges. The tiny island was privately owned for many years until Huntington Hartford, whose fortune came from the A&P supermarket chain, developed it as a resort. In the 1960s, Hartford purchased a ruined 14th-century monastery from William Randolph Hearst, who had imported it piece by piece from France. The stone ruins, known as the Cloisters, overlook Nassau Harbor, surrounded by the Versailles Gardens. A popular wedding site, the gardens are open to the public.

Boasting one of the finest beaches in the Caribbean, Paradise Island offers tennis, golf and parasailing for the sports minded; the "strip" features a casino and other entertainment. Bridge toll is $1.

NASSAU (C-2) pop. 210,832

Capital and principal city of The Bahamas, Nassau is on the northeast coast of New Providence Island. This resort was a battleground for Spanish, British and French colonization efforts and a haven for buccaneers. It was here that the infamous pirate Blackbeard posted a lookout in his tower while he caroused around the islands. In 1718, a century after the first British colony was established, the British sent the first royal governor to The Bahamas. Nassau was named in 1729 for King William III of the House of Orange-Nassau. Residents call themselves "Nassuvians."

There is always plenty to do in downtown Nassau: sightseeing by horse-drawn carriage, photographing the colorful buildings, dining, dancing or duty-free shopping. The focal point of Nassau is Bay Street, which runs along the water from Prince George Wharf. Directly across from the cruise ship docks is Rawson Square, anchored by the Churchill Building. Across the plaza is Parliament Square. Here are the two chambers of Parliament and the Supreme Court. Visitors can watch the proceedings of the House of Assembly when it is in session; arrangements must be made at the House office of the clerk of courts. To find out when the House will be in session, phone (242) 322-2041. Also in the square is the Garden of Remembrance, with its cenotaph honoring Bahamians who died in World Wars I and II; nearby is the octagonal Nassau Public Library and Museum, once a jail.

Nassau's 18th-century forts also are worth visiting. Of the three forts, only Fort Montagu at the eastern entrance to the harbor was confronted by invaders. High above the city, the Government House is host to tea parties held the last Friday of each month from January through November. A colorful changing of the guard ceremony takes place every other Saturday at 10 a.m.

Vibrant, sociable Nassau possesses almost every conceivable sports facility. Tennis courts and golf courses abound, as do local entrepreneurs marketing rentals or lessons for snorkeling, scuba diving, fishing and sailing. Nassau's many fine beaches include

Cabbage, Goodman's Bay, Saunder's, Delaport, Caves, Montagu and Western Esplanade.

The waters, noted for deep-sea and reef fishing, are most famous for giant blue marlin, but white marlin, tuna, wahoo, bonito and sailfish also are abundant. Nassau Yacht Haven on E. Bay Street is the charter and fishing headquarters. Sailing is popular in the bays and around the coral islands; local and international races are held by The Bahamas Sailing Association, Royal Nassau Sailing Club and the Nassau Yacht Club.

Bahamas Tourist Information Center: Festival Place, Prince George Wharf, Nassau, The Bahamas; phone (242) 323-3182.

ARDASTRA GARDENS, ZOO AND CONSERVATION CENTRE is on Chippingham Rd. near Fort Charlotte. More than 4,000 tropical and subtropical plants flourish on 5.5 acres (2 hectares). Against this setting, a flamingo platoon marches to the commands of a friendly drill sergeant. The birds, usually a shy and easily frightened species, will stand while visitors snap pictures at close range. The zoo has more than 300 birds, mammals and reptiles, many of which are endangered Bahamian or Caribbean species.

Food is available. Open daily 9-5; closed Jan. 1 and Dec. 25. Last admission 30 minutes before closing. Flamingos march daily at 10:30, 2 and 4. Lory parrot feedings are offered daily at 11, 1:30 and 3:30. Admission $15; $7.50 (ages 4-12). AX, DS, MC, VI. Phone (242) 323-5806.

DISCOVER ATLANTIS is at the Atlantis Resort on Paradise Island. This 1-hour guided tour includes a 14-acre waterscape and "The Dig," a walk-through aquarium displaying more than 50,000 exotic fish and sea animals among the ruins of the fabled Atlantean civilization.

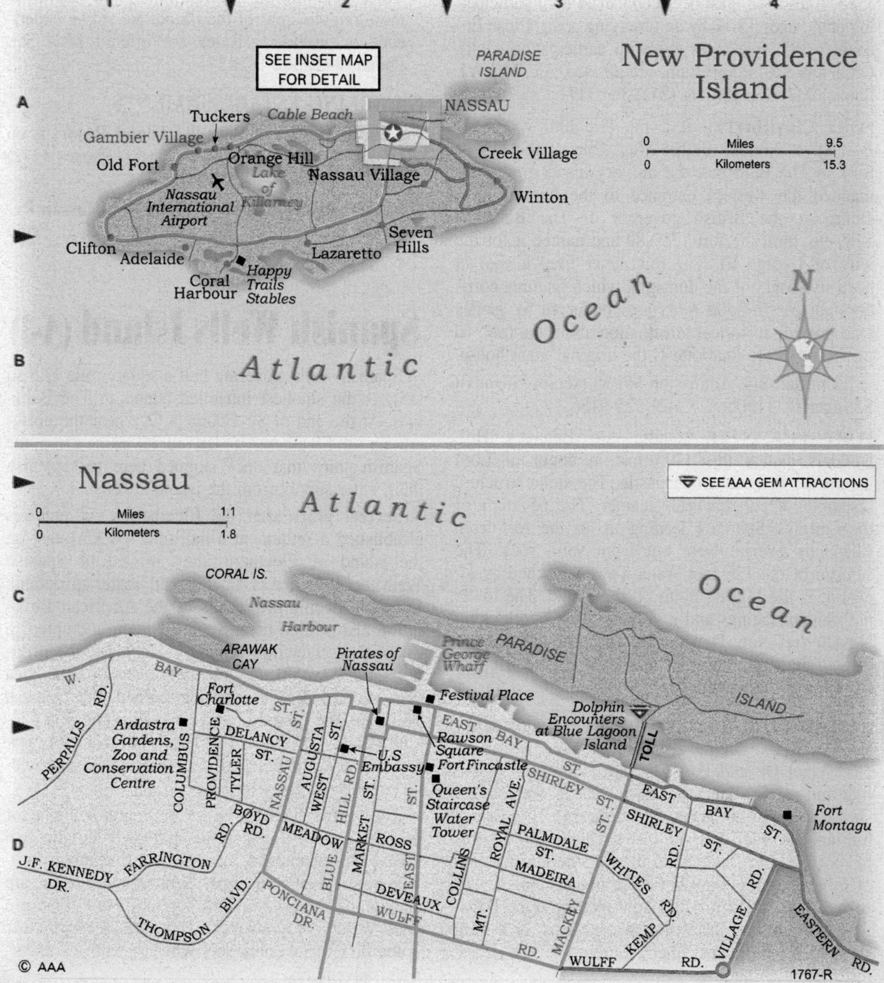

Surrounding water slides and pools are open only to resort guests. Tours depart every 20 minutes daily 9-5. Admission $29; $21 (ages 3-11). AX, DS, MC, VI. Phone (242) 363-3000.

GEM **DOLPHIN ENCOUNTERS AT BLUE LAGOON ISLAND** departs from the Paradise Island Ferry Terminal at 1 Marina Dr. between the bridges. A high-speed catamaran takes visitors to the island, where two interactive programs allow up-close encounters with bottlenose dolphins. A 30-minute Swim includes water acrobatics such as the foot push. The Close Encounter takes place on a waist-deep platform, where participants can touch, kiss and feed the dolphins. Observers can watch from nearby. All programs start with an educational orientation.

Allow 3 hours minimum. Participants should bring a towel and change of clothes. Boats depart daily at 8:30, 10;30, 1:30 and 3:30. Swim with the Dolphins $165. Ages 6-12 must be accompanied by a participating adult, ages 13-17 by an observing adult. Close Encounter $85; free (ages 0-3 with participating adult). Observers $20. Reservations are advised. AX, MC, VI. Phone (242) 363-1003 or (242) 363-7171.

FORT CHARLOTTE is 1 mi. (1.6 km) w. on W. Bay St. at Marcus Bethel Way. One of the largest forts in The Bahamas, the military installation commanded the western entrance to the harbor. Lord Dunmore, the British governor of The Bahamas 1787-96, built the fort 1787-89 and named it for the wife of George III. The fort never fired a shot in hostility. Tours of the dungeon, which features corridors cut out of solid rock, are conducted by guides who provide historical information about the fort. To the east of Fort Charlotte is the original guardhouse.

Mon.-Sat. 8-4. Admission $5; $3 (senior citizens); $2 (ages 0-11). Phone (242) 325-9186.

FORT FINCASTLE stands atop Bennet's Hill. Builders named this 1793 fort in honor of Lord Dunmore, Viscount of Fincastle. The stone structure resembles a paddlewheel steamer. The 65 steps of the Queen's Staircase leading up to the fort from Elizabeth Avenue were cut from solid rock. The summit of the 126-foot Water Tower, reached by elevator, is the highest point on the island. The tower has cannon facings and a viewing deck overlooking Nassau and New Providence. Tours of the fort are offered by local guides. Mon.-Sat. 9-4. Free. Tipping for tours is recommended.

NASSAU BOTANICAL GARDENS is bounded by W. Bay St., N. Dunmore and Infant View rds., Marcus Bethel Dr. and Fort Charlotte. Hundreds of native and exotic plant species, including orchids, are showcased on 20 acres (8 hectares). The British military occupied this site in the 1800s, and according to folklore, slaves who died in the construction of Fort Charlotte were buried in the gardens. Originally designed to introduce new species to the Bahamas from around the world, the gardens have been ravaged by hurricanes many times over the years; restoration is ongoing.

Open Mon.-Fri. 8-4, Sat.-Sun. 9-4. Admission $1; 50c (ages 5-12). Phone (242) 356-6475 or (242) 356-6477.

PIRATES OF NASSAU is near the corner of Marlborough and George sts. The history of local pirate activity 1690-1720 is related through taped commentaries, sound effects and costumed interpreters. Visitors can experience a pirate's life at sea aboard a full-scale replica of Blackbeard's ship *Revenge*. Exhibits about female pirates and the laws that brought an end to area piracy also are offered. Food is available. Allow 1 hour minimum. Mon.-Sat. 9-6, Sun. 9-noon; closed major holidays. Admission $12; $6 (ages 3-18); free (one child age 0-11 per paying adult). AX, DS, MC, VI. Phone (242) 356-3759.

RECREATIONAL ACTIVITIES

Horseback Riding

- **Happy Trails Stables** provides transportation from local hotels. Guided tours take riders to more remote areas of the island. No riding experience is necessary. Rides are offered Mon.-Sat. Phone (242) 362-1820.

GAMBLING ESTABLISHMENTS

- **Atlantis Casino at Paradise Island Resort** is on Casino Drive. Daily 24 hours. Phone (242) 363-3000 or (800) 722-7466.
- **Crystal Palace Casino at Wyndham Nassau Resort** is on West Bay Street at Cable Beach. Daily 24 hours. Phone (242) 327-6200.

Spanish Wells Island (A-3)

Spanish Wells, covering half a square mile (1.3 sq km), is the smallest inhabited island in The Bahamas. At the end of St. George's Cay near the northern tip of Eleuthera, it derived its name from the Spanish ships that once stopped here to replenish their water supply from the island's wells.

Several years after the Eleutherian Adventurers established a settlement a half-mile (.8 km) east on the island of Eleuthera, they moved to Spanish Wells because it was smaller and easier to defend. Loyalists fleeing the results of the American Revolution also settled here. Some of them attempted to establish a plantation economy. However, the original settlers would not tolerate slavery, so the idea was squelched. This attitude earned the Spanish Wellsians the hatred of their slave-trading sister islands. Relics of that era include some colorful New England-style homes and traces of the English dialect spoken by early settlers.

The lobster industry is the most important factor in an economy that depends primarily on the sea. Tomatoes, cucumbers, onions and pineapples provide supplemental income. Sailing and fishing are among the main attractions for tourists. Offshore a wide variety of shipwrecks and coral reefs provide scuba divers and snorkelers with a wealth of underwater adventures.

Bottom Bay / © Geoffrey Clive / age fotostock

Barbados

Easternmost of the Caribbean islands, Barbados is the "Little England of Eternal Summer." Meaning "the bearded ones," its name is said to have been given by a Portuguese discoverer because of the beardlike vines on the fig trees. With nearly 1,600 inhabitants per square mile, Barbados is one of the most densely populated countries in the Caribbean; the friendliness of its people is its foremost charm.

The silver sand beaches on the Caribbean side of the island contrast with the rugged Atlantic coastline. Roads are bordered by fields of cane, royal palms and rolling hills and terraces. Vivid tropical flowers, including fragrant oleander, frangipani, jasmine, cassia, bougainvillea, hibiscus and lady-of-the-night, lie in profusion along neat hedgerows. Scarlet flame trees and coral walls shelter the well-tended lawns of color-washed houses, and windmills of former sugar plantations dot the land, though the Morgan Lewis Sugar Mill is the only one with its arms and wheelhouses still intact.

Bridgetown, the capital, is representative of the island's heritage. Its typically English atmosphere is enhanced by names like Yorkshire and Windsor and by the ritual of afternoon tea, which occurs at "half past four."

History

Once inhabited only by Arawak Indians, Barbados was discovered by the Portuguese in the 16th century. The English claimed it in 1625, and 2 years later the first settlers arrived. The island's population increased significantly during the mid-1600s as English immigrants fled the political unrest in their homeland and slaves were brought from Africa to work the sugar crops. The colony thrived early on as a result of the tobacco and cotton trade and became a prosperous sugar producer in the 17th and 18th centuries. During the struggle for European supremacy in the Caribbean, 35 forts were built along 25 miles (40 km) of coastline. The ruins of many are still visible.

Of all the islands in the West Indies, Barbados is the only one to have remained solely in the hands of its original settlers. This fact helps explain the island's stability and the British flavor that has remained constant over the centuries.

Since 1954 Barbados has had a ministerial system of government with a governor general appointed by the Queen of Great Britain on recommendation of the prime minister, who heads the island's government. Barbados became an independent nation on Nov. 30, 1966. A coat of arms bearing the motto "Pride and Industry" speaks for the high literacy rate and prosperous economy; Barbados is one of the most economically stable Caribbean islands, with tourism, sugar production, financial services and light industry forming the basis of the economy.

Shopping

High-quality English clothing and Scottish and English fabrics are excellent buys in Barbados. Bridgetown tailor shops on Prince Alfred and Tudor streets offer made-to-measure clothing in a variety of materials ranging from Sea Island cotton to imported tweeds. Baskets, seashell trinkets, pottery, English china and silver, silks and Oriental objects and antiques also are popular purchases. Another leading commodity available at a very low price is Barbados rum, said to be the world's oldest. By shopping in the afternoon you can avoid the morning rush.

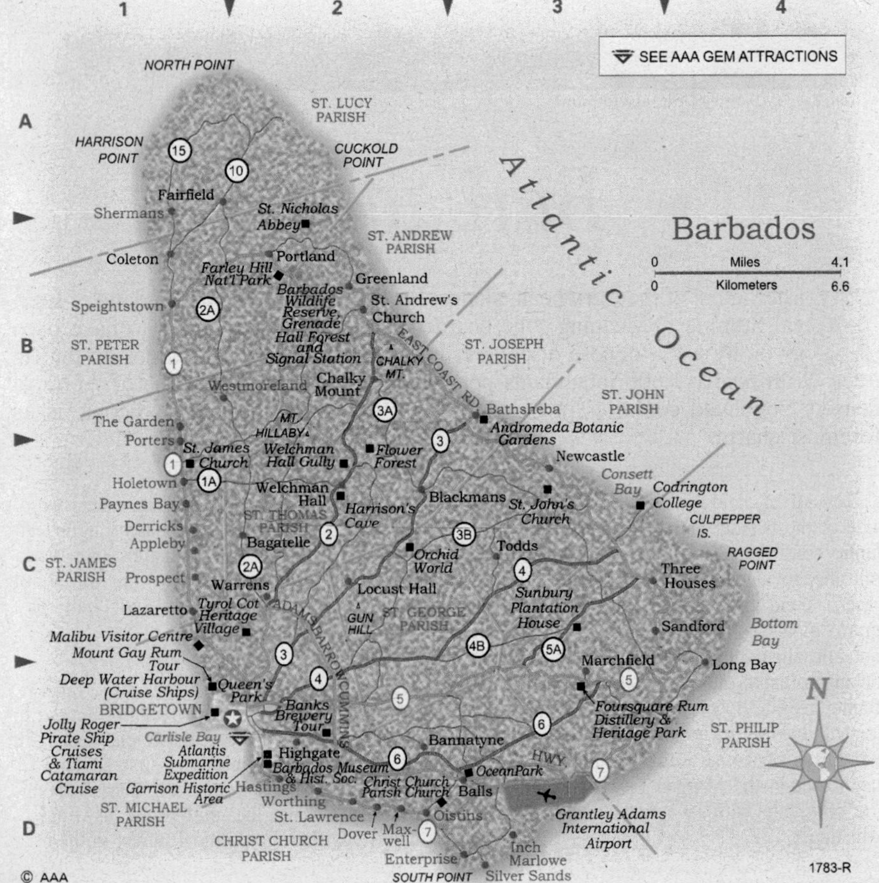

BARBADOS
experience the authentic Caribbean
Estimated wait time
from this point is 2 minutes.
Welcome to Mother Nature's water park. Where the beaches are endless and open to all. Where you won't find the same crowds, the same hotels and the same restaurants. A unique corner of the Caribbean that's a little harder to get to, and a whole lot harder to leave. Welcome, traveler. Welcome to Barbados.
www.visitbarbados.org or call 1.888.BARBADOS

Most of the duty-free shopping in Bridgetown is concentrated on Broad Street. Cave Shepherd, Bridgetown's largest department store, features Waterford, Wedgwood, Royal Doulton and Swarovski china and crystal, an extensive selection of cosmetics and fragrances, leather goods, jewelry, electronics, fashions and a liquor department. Harrison's is a department store containing a vast assortment of luxury items including Lladró figurines, designer sweaters, jewelry and watches by Cartier, Fendi and Gucci.

Da Costa's Mall, also on Broad Street, houses several interesting boutiques. Just opposite is Mall 34, with shops displaying high quality merchandise from India and Europe, and the Royal Shop, with a wide selection of watches.

Malls in the Hastings and Worthing area of Christ Church include Hastings Plaza, Sandy Bank, Skyway Plaza and Quayside Centre. Sheraton Centre, said to be the island's largest shopping establishment, is in Christ Church at Sargeants' Village, less than 20 minutes from the airport.

Chattel House Village, a shopping area in Holetown, St. James, consists of a medley of actual chattel houses, all colorfully painted. The village contains a variety of boutiques, including a Best of Barbados gift shop. Also situated in Holetown is the West Coast Mall, a marketplace popular with locals containing a small Cave Shepherd store, a supermarket and various shops.

Barbados is said to have some of the finest antiques in the West Indies. Reputable dealers include Antiquaria in Holetown, St. James, and Greenwich House Antiques at Greenwich Village, St. James.

Medford Craft World, on White Hall Main Road, specializes in such local handicrafts as pottery, wood carvings, and batik and woven baskets. Shells, metal art, leather, coral and other island-made articles can be found at Pelican Village, on Princess Alice Highway near Deep Water Harbour. Temple Yard, south of Pelican Village in Bridgetown, is where members of the Rastafarian community display crafts. Clothing, jewelry and mahogany pieces are among the items crafted by artisans at Heritage Park in St. Philip.

The Best of Barbados Shops, with several locations throughout the island, sell only products made or designed in Barbados. The shops have a wide assortment of local handicrafts and souvenirs including hand-painted tile, kitchen items, local prints, pottery and T-shirts. Earthworks Pottery atop Shop Hill in St. Thomas offers handmade pottery.

Some stores feature in-bond departments, where certain merchandise has been set aside and marked with two prices. The higher price applies to buy-and-take purchases. The second in-bond price, usually considerably lower, once applied only to merchandise purchased in the store and delivered to the airport or pier. However, most in-bond shops now allow tourists with proper ID (passport and travel ticket) to take their duty-free items from the store. Shopping hours for most stores in Barbados are Mon.-Fri. 8-4, Sat. 8-noon. Banks are open Mon.-Thurs. 9-3, Fri. 9-4.

Food and Drink

In addition to fine Continental and curried dishes, Barbados has many island specialties. These include *bonavist,* small white beans often seasoned with pumpkin and herbs; *jug-jug,* a molded dish of chopped ham and salt beef or pork combined with green peas; *cou-cou,* a savory pudding made with cornmeal and okra; and Barbadian black pudding, similar to a sausage stuffed with seasoned grated sweet potatoes.

Other local foods include pepperpot, a spicy stew made with selected meats; and *conkies,* a steamed concoction of sweet potatoes, cornmeal, pumpkin, coconut, raisins and spices served in a banana leaf. Roast suckling pig and native "flying fish" are favorite specialties. Fresh lobster and seafood are available. The fruits of Barbados are avocados, mangoes, guavas, bananas, breadfruit, golden apples, hog plums, gooseberries, cherries, pears, oranges, limes and grapefruit.

The name "rum" may have originated in Barbados, where a 17th-century observer wrote, "The chief fuddling they make in the Island is Rum Bullion, alias Kill-Devil, and is made of sugarcane distilled, a hot, hellish and terrible liquor." Today, the island rum is known for its smooth, refined taste.

Most hotels and resorts on Barbados include a 10-percent charge on the guest's bill to cover gratuities. However, in nightclubs and restaurants, tipping is at the discretion of the guest.

Sports and Amusements

Most major hotels have a beach or are near one, and all types of aquatic gear can be rented. Motorboats (for water skiing) and sailboats are available for hire at beach club resorts. Conditions are excellent for skiing in the tranquil waters off the west coast, while sailing is favorable on both the west and south coasts. In the path of the trade winds, the east coast beaches are considered dangerous for swimming but ideal for surfing, with the Soup

Bowl at Bathsheba being the best area for this sport.

Popular west coast beaches include Mullins Beach near Speightstown, which features a good snorkeling reef just offshore as well as shaded areas, shower facilities and an open-air restaurant providing a view of the bay. Paynes Bay, recognizable by the neighboring fish market, is a site where numerous water sports are indulged in. Visitors will enjoy the picturesque bay at Sandy Lane, with public access available on either side of the hotel.

Southeast coast beaches are not known for swimming amenities, but rather for their rugged beauty. Bottom Bay is a delightful cove with a white sand beach surrounded by cliffs and a coconut grove. At Crane Beach, pounding waves crash against the rocky shore. The Crane, reputedly the Caribbean's oldest operating hotel, rests atop a dramatic cliff surrounding the beach; parking is available at the beach or hotel. Foul Bay Beach is accessible by a road that travels downward to a paved parking area. This long stretch of beach, nestled between two cliffs, has a wide expanse of seagrape trees.

Popular beaches on the south coast of Barbados include Accra, where water-sports equipment is available for rental and opportunities are good for body surfing. Casuarina Beach is frequented by windsurfers due to large waves and abundant winds. Sandy Beach is preferred by families because of its shallow lagoon and calm seas.

Conditions for windsurfing are excellent on the south coast, due to constant trade winds and year-round water temperatures of about 78 degrees Fahrenheit. The Barbados Windsurfing Classic, held in January, attracts top contenders from throughout the world. Club Mistral at the Windsurf Beach Hotel in Maxwell and the Silver Rock Windsurfing Club at Silver Sands provide equipment rentals and lessons.

At the Folkestone Marine Park off Holetown on the St. James coast, snorkelers and divers can follow an underwater trail along a coral reef where fish, sea anemones and sea fans can be seen.

Scuba diving lessons lasting about 2.5 hours are taught at several dive shops; reputable establishments include Carib Ocean Divers and Underwater Barbados. Scuba gear rentals and dives can be arranged through some hotels.

Numerous shipwrecks in the waters around Barbados provide excellent diving opportunities. A large number of these wrecks are concentrated in Carlisle Bay, including *Sea Trek,* deliberately sunk in about 40 feet (12 m) of water; *The Berwyn,* an old tugboat brimming with sea life less than 10 feet (3 m) from the surface; and *The Fox,* a 120-foot schooner approximately 40 feet (12 m) from the surface that is home to numerous crustaceans. *Friar's Craig* is a small vessel in the area of coast just east of Aquatic Gap. The *Stavronikita,* a Greek freighter, was deliberately sunk by the Park and Beaches Commission in Folkestone Underwater Park.

January through June are the best fishing months; dolphin fish, kingfish, snapper, yellowfin tuna, shark and barracuda are plentiful. Fishing boats and guides can be hired for fishing excursions at most hotels or through the Barbados Game Fishing Association. The association also sponsors an annual fishing contest the last week in April, and visitors may enter the international competition.

Though Barbados calls itself the "Land of the Flying Fish," the national symbol has become scarce in recent years. Schools of the small, leaping fish have migrated south to warmer waters off Trinidad and Tobago, leaving the Bajan fishing fleet without its signature catch.

Check at your hotel's activities desk for information about snorkeling, scuba diving, deep-sea fishing and charter boats. Carlisle Bay is the island's sailing headquarters.

There are tennis courts at many hotels; reservations are recommended. Squash enthusiasts can play at the Almond Beach Village and the Barbados Squash Club.

Golfers also can enjoy their sport at several courses on the island. The 18-hole Barbados Golf Club in Christ Church is open to the public. Renowned golf course architect Tom Fazio has designed two 18-hole courses at the Sandy Lane Golf Club; the "Old Nine" also is available for play. Eighteen holes of a 27-hole championship golf course at Royal Westmoreland in St. James are open to resort guests. Temporary memberships are available for nine-hole courses at Almond Beach Village and Rockley Golf Club.

Horseback riding inland is offered at Caribbean International Riding Centre at the Cleland Plantation in St. Andrew, (246) 422-7433. Beau Geste Farm in St. George, (246) 429-0139, offers riding lessons for new equestrians and trails for experienced riders.

Cricket is the chief spectator sport in Barbados. Visitors can watch matches at the national level at several sports clubs May through December, and at the international level January through March. Queens Park and Kensington Oval, both in Bridgetown, regularly hold matches. Soccer is popular January through April. Polo is played July through February at Holder's in St. James.

The Garrison Savannah has a horse-racing track with races held every other Saturday, except during the month of September. The Sandy Lane Gold Cup, the biggest race in the Caribbean, usually takes place in March; festivities and a parade accompany this exciting event. The Barbados Turf Club's race meetings, held five times a year, are joyous occasions with music, food booths and a general carnival atmosphere.

Many discos, nightclubs and restaurants provide after-dinner entertainment. The limbo and calypso, danced to the haunting rhythm of steel bands, entertain spectators and participants alike. For those who would rather look at the stars than dance beneath them, the Barbados Astronomical Society offers a night of stargazing at the Harry Bayley Observatory in nearby Clapham every Friday from 8:30 to 10:30 (weather permitting); phone (246) 426-1317. Although there are no casinos in Barbados, slot machines are permitted; there are arcades in Bridgetown and at some resorts. The Plantation Restaurant stages a dinner show, "Bajan Roots and Rhythms," on Wednesday and Friday at 6:30 p.m.; phone (246) 428-5048.

Annual events include the Barbados Jazz Festival, a premier 7-day event in mid-January showcasing international, regional and local musicians. The Holetown Festival in February commemorates the arrival of English settlers in 1627. Activities include a parade of vintage cars, a street fair and arts and crafts.

The month of March is Holders Season, a celebration of opera, music and theater. In April, the Oistins Fish Festival pays tribute to Barbados' fishing industry; a Coast Guard exhibition, boat races and a fish-boning contest are among the events. Barbados Gospelfest brings top performers to Bridgetown on Whitsuntide weekend at the end of May.

Barbadians eagerly anticipate the nonstop revelry of the Crop-Over Festival, which occurs from July to early August. The event, an island-wide folk celebration in honor of the completion of the sugar cane harvest, is considered one of the Caribbean's most popular. It features calypso competitions, art shows, food, music, crafts, a costume parade and fireworks on Kadooment Day (a national holiday) and other entertainment. Bajan music, singing, drama, dance and writing are celebrated every year at the National Independence Festival of Creative Arts in November.

The *Barbados Advocate* and *The Nation* are Bridgetown's daily newspapers. *The Nation* also produces *The Weekend Nation, The Sun on Saturday, The Sunday Sun, Better Health Magazine* and *Friends Magazine,* a weekly tourist publication containing entertainment information.

Sightseeing

From January through April the Barbados National Trust offers its Open House Programme, allowing the public to visit some of Barbados' most attractive and interesting private homes and gardens. Tours are offered every Wednesday from 2:30-5:30. Admission is $15; ages 5-12, $7.50. A different house is featured each week, with past highlights including Cluffs Plantation House, Hopefield Manor, Forster Lodge and Sunbury Plantation House; phone the National Trust at (246) 426-2421 for the weekly program. Boyce's Tours provides round-trip transportation from local hotels; tour rates include the house entrance fee; phone (246) 425-1455.

The National Trust also sponsors guided hikes on the Arbib Nature and Heritage Trail, starting at St. Peter's Church in Speightstown. These informative walks of 3 miles (5.5 km) or 5 miles (7.5 km) offer insight into Barbados' history, environment and culture. Tours are offered on Wednesday, Thursday and Saturday, and the fee is $15; ages 5-12, $7.50. Reservations must be made a day in advance.

Barbados has four lighthouses positioned on strategic areas of coastline. Ragged Point Lighthouse, in St. Philip at the island's eastern tip, is constructed of coral limestone and provides an outstanding view of the east coast and Pico Tenerife. South Point Lighthouse, at the island's southernmost point in Christ Church, is a cast-iron structure made in England and shipped to Barbados in 1851. Other lighthouses are at Harrison Point in St. Lucy and Needham's Point in St. Michael.

You can arrange to tour some of the large sugar factories, such as Portvale and Andrews. The Sir Frank Hutson Sugar Museum and Factory, next to the Portvale factory yard near Holetown, is open during the sugar-grinding season from February through June. Visits should be arranged in advance; phone (246) 432-0100.

Tours and tastings also are available at Mount Gay Rum Distillery in Bridgetown on Spring Garden Highway; the Malibu Visitor Centre on Brighton Beach, where Malibu and Cockspur rums are made; and Banks Breweries, producers of the award-winning Banks beer.

Glass-bottom boats afford a fascinating view of sea life among the coral reefs of the west coast; the Folkestone Underwater Park and the old shipwrecks in Carlisle Bay are popular attractions. Lunch cruises aboard the *Jolly Roger* depart from Pirate's Pier in Bridgetown. Music and swimming are featured on four-hour cruises that take passengers along the coast in a replica of a pirate ship. Snorkeling stops are offered on catamaran cruises, which often include a buffet lunch. The MV *Harbour Master* offers a variety of cruises aboard the 4-deck boat complete with a ramp for beach landings and a semi-submersible chamber to view the underwater life.

Cruises to neighboring islands can be arranged through Caribbean Safari Tours, (246) 427-5100; Chantours Caribbean, (246) 432-5591; Grenadine Tours, (784) 458-3795; and St. James Travel and Tours, (246) 432-0774. Helicopter tours are available from Bajan Helicopters in Bridgetown; phone (246) 431-0069.

Tour operators offering a wide variety of land excursions include Boyce's Tours, (246) 425-1455; Island Safari, (246) 429-5337; and Topaz Tours, (246) 435-8451.

One of the most popular sightseeing drives follows the rugged Atlantic coast past such points of interest as Codrington College, St. John's Church and the pottery works at Chalky Mount. Those touring Barbados will notice numerous chattel houses made of wood, historically built up on rocks so they could be dismantled easily and moved to another location. Rum shops also contribute to the local flavor, serving as village meeting places where locals can exchange news.

The East Coast Road, traversing the rolling hills and greenery of the Scotland district and the rocky east coast, provides spectacular sightseeing opportunities. The road travels past Bathsheba, a haven for surfers and identified by the huge boulders protruding from the water; a small park area provides picnic tables and restroom facilities.

Cattlewash, a scenic stretch of coast punctuated by beach houses, took its name from the cattle that occasionally wander through the area. North of Cattlewash, Barclays Park is a popular spot for picnicking and recreation. The park overlooks a scenic stretch of coast lined with seagrape, hog plum and Casuarina trees. Swimming is not recommended due to the strong undercurrent. Visitors have access to a facility with changing rooms, showers and restrooms. A small restaurant in the 50-acre (20-hectare) park serves good Barbadian food on a seasonal basis.

Barbados' famed "Platinum Coast" along the Caribbean is lined with luxury hotels boasting tranquil beaches of powdery sand. A tour through St. Thomas Parish in the center of the island usually includes the botanical garden at Welchman Hall Gully and Harrison's Cave. St. Thomas and neighboring St. George are the only parishes without any coastal area.

Oistins is a picturesque fishing village in Christ Church Parish at the south end of the island. Several restored historic rum shops are in the area and can be visited. Visitors and locals can partake in freshly-cooked fish at the Oistins Fish Fry.

Transportation

Daily nonstop flights from New York and Miami touch down at Barbados' Grantley Adams International Airport. Interisland flights connect Barbados with Trinidad, Grenada, St. Vincent, St. Lucia, Martinique, Jamaica and the islands to the north. Barbados also is a port of call for many cruise ships.

The roads from Bridgetown to the popular districts are good, and the Adams-Barrow-Cummins (ABC) Highway from the airport to

Highway 2A at Warrens enables traffic to bypass Bridgetown, reducing travel time by about 50 percent. You can rent cars, minimokes (resembling small jeeps), scooters, bicycles, chauffeur-driven cars and limousines. You must present a valid U.S. driver's license to obtain a Barbados permit.

Driving is on the left side of the road. Speed limits are 35 mph (60 km/h) in most areas of the island, with the exception being 25 mph (40 km/h) in town and 50 mph (80 km/h) on the Spring Garden and ABC highways. No car may be driven in Barbados without third-party insurance coverage. Slow-moving vehicles should travel on the left side of all double-lane highways.

Frequent bus service connects the parishes with Bridgetown. Transport Board buses, painted blue and trimmed in yellow, depart every half-hour from the three main terminals in Bridgetown: The Lower Green and Princess Alice Highway terminals provide transportation to destinations in the north part of the island and along the west coast, while the Fairchild Street terminal is for southbound travelers. There also is a Transport Board terminal in the north in Speightstown.

Privately owned minibuses, yellow with blue trim, travel shorter distances and therefore have faster turnaround times. The main minibus terminals are in Bridgetown at Probyn Street, River Road and Cheapside. Even when at a designated stop, you must wave at the minibuses to get the driver to come to a halt. Buses run daily 6 a.m.-midnight; fare is $1.50 and exact change is required for the Transport Board buses.

Taxis are readily available in the National Heroes' Square area of Bridgetown; a taxi stand is next to a fountain adorned with dolphins. Check the fixed rates before taking a cab.

Fast Facts

POPULATION: 275,330.

AREA: 430 sq km (166 sq mi.).

CAPITAL: Bridgetown.

HIGHEST POINT: 336 m (1,102 ft.), Mount Hillaby.

LOWEST POINT: Sea level, Atlantic Ocean.

TIME ZONE(S): Atlantic Standard.

LANGUAGE: English.

GOVERNMENT: Independent. Member of the British Commonwealth of Nations.

UNIT OF CURRENCY: Barbados dollar. $1 U.S. = 2 Barbados dollars. U.S. bills and travelers checks are accepted by most hotels.

ELECTRICITY: 110 volts, 50 cycles AC.

MINIMUM AGE FOR DRIVERS: 21-25, depending on the rental car agency. Local license ($5 U.S.) required; drive on left.

SEAT BELT/CHILD RESTRAINT LAWS: Seat belts are required for all passengers.

HOLIDAYS: Jan. 1; Errol Barrow Day, Jan. 21; Good Friday; Easter; Easter Monday; National Heroes Day, Apr. 28, Labour Day, May 1; Whit Monday, May or June (8th Mon. after Easter); Emancipation Day, Aug. 1; Kadooment Day, Aug. (1st Mon.); Independence Day, Nov. 30; Christmas, Dec. 25; Boxing Day, Dec. 26.

TAXES: A 7.5 percent room tax and 10 percent service charge are added to most hotel bills. A 15 percent VAT (value-added tax) is charged for food and beverages. Airport passenger service charge and security fee $30, usually included in airline ticket price.

IMMIGRATION REQUIREMENTS: A valid passport and a return or onward ticket are required. No visa needed for stays up to 28 days. The U.S. Dept. of Homeland Security requires all U.S. citizens returning from the Caribbean to present a valid passport.

PHONING THE ISLANDS: To call Barbados from the U.S. or Canada, dial 1 + 246 + the 7-digit local number.

FURTHER INFORMATION FOR VISITORS:

Barbados Tourism Authority
800 Second Ave., 2nd Floor
New York, NY 10017
(212) 986-6516
(800) 221-9831
See color ad on insert.

Barbados Tourism Authority, Bridgetown
Harbour Road
P.O. Box 242
Bridgetown, Barbados
(246) 427-2623
(246) 426-4080

Points of Interest

See map page 78.

Christ Church Parish (D-2)

One of 11 parishes defining Barbados, Christ Church is at the southern end of the island. Visitors arriving by air see this parish first; it's the home of Grantley Adams International Airport. East of Oistins are Silver Sands and Enterprise beaches, both popular with sunbathers and windsurfers.

St. Lawrence Gap is the parish's hub for dining and entertainment opportunities. The area is punctuated with nightclubs, bistros and upscale restaurants, many with views of the water. A small beach area dotted with fishing boats provides a pedestrian-friendly atmosphere ideal for a daytime or evening stroll. Those interested in bird watching can pay a visit to the nearby Graeme Hall Nature Sanctuary, where a visitor center leads to a boardwalk nature trail that passes through a portion of the reserve area.

BALLS (D-2)

OCEANPARK is at Balls Complex off of the Henry Forde roundabout. The aquarium offers tropical marine displays and represents a variety of marine habitats, including the deep ocean, coral reefs and a ray pool. Additional features include a touch tank, shark and piranha exhibits, a playground and an 18-hole miniature golf course. Visitors also can enjoy the lush landscaped grounds filled with colorful tropical plants. Food is available. Allow 1 hour minimum. Daily 10-6, mid-Jan. through Oct. 31; Tues.-Sun. 10-5, rest of year. Admission $17.50; $12.50 (senior citizens); $10 (ages 4-12). Miniature golf $9; $5 (ages 4-12). MC, VI. Phone (246) 420-7405.

OISTINS (D-2)

The fishing community of Oistins hosts the island's annual fish festival in April and a fish fry every Friday and Saturday night. The local catch is prepared by street vendors for all to enjoy.

CHRIST CHURCH PARISH CHURCH is on Church Hill Road. This Anglican church was the scene of considerable excitement during the 19th-century "Restless Coffins Mystery." Coffins in the sealed Chase Vault were reportedly found in different positions each time the vault was opened. To stem the hysteria provoked by the strange incidents, the governor finally had the coffins buried elsewhere. Open daily. Donations. Phone (246) 428-8087 or (246) 428-2319.

St. Andrew Parish (B-2)

About 850 feet (259 m) above sea level, Cherry Tree Hill offers an excellent view of the hilly Scotland District, where cane fields stretch toward the coast. Mahogany trees on the hill's summit are a playground for monkeys, usually visible in the evening. St. Andrew also is home to Mount Hillaby, the highest point on the island at 1,102 feet (336 m); a narrow, winding road leads from the town of Hillaby to the summit. Nearby Turner's Hall Woods, a 50-acre (20-hectare) ecosystem containing many indigenous plant and animal species, is what remains of a dense tropical forest that once covered the island.

St. Andrew's Parish Church dates from 1846. The previous building withstood the 1780 and 1831 hurricanes. The wooden altar, with stained-glass windows at its center, is surrounded by colorful floor tiles.

CHALKY MOUNT POTTERY is e. of Hwy. 2. Formed by a deposit of clay that looks like a reclining man with hands folded over his chest, Chalky Mount has been nicknamed "Napoleon" by local residents. Only a few pottery businesses continue to operate, several of them located in private homes. Visitors can watch potters form their clay shapes on a kick wheel. A variety of articles are for sale, including plant pots, tableware, pitchers, jugs and cooking utensils. Daily 8:30-5.

MORGAN LEWIS SUGAR MILL is about 1 mi. (1.6 km) s.e. of Cherry Tree Hill. The last working example of some 500 sugar mills that once dotted the island, this massive windmill has been restored by the Barbados National Trust. Stones in the conical tower were cemented together with a mixture of egg whites and coral dust. Visitors can enter the 18th-century mill and observe the machinery used to grind sugar cane until the 1940s; exhibits include historic photographs and plantation artifacts. The window on the top level provides a striking view of the surrounding Scotland District. Mon.-Fri. 9-5. Admission $5; $2.50 (children). Phone (246) 422-7429.

St. George Parish (C-2)

Built in 1784 after a hurricane destroyed the first structure on the site, St. George Parish Church is noted for its altarpiece, "The Resurrection," by American painter Benjamin West.

GUN HILL SIGNAL STATION is off Hwy. 3 on Fusilier Rd. During British occupation of the island, this 700-foot (213-m) rise was one of several points used to relay messages. A monument to Britain's supremacy is the lion carved on the side of a limestone cliff by British soldiers in 1868. The restored 19th-century station contains a collection of military memorabilia. Mon.-Sat. 9-5; closed holidays. Admission $5; $2.50 (ages 0-11). Phone (246) 429-1358.

ORCHID WORLD is off Hwy. 3B between Gun Hill and St. John's Church. This 6-acre (2-hectare) site in the high rainfall sector of Barbados is said to contain more than 35,000 orchids. Paths wind through a lush tropical setting accented by vibrantly colored orchids, most of which are labeled. A number of varieties are displayed in greenhouses, depending on growing conditions. Views of the surrounding countryside are punctuated by sugarcane fields. Food is available. Allow 1 hour minimum. Daily 9-5; closed Good Friday and Dec. 25. Admission $10; $5 (ages 5-13). MC, VI. Phone (246) 433-0306.

St. James Parish (C-1)

The island's first English settlement was established in St. James Parish in 1627, two years after Captain John Powell claimed the island in the name of King James I. Originally named Jamestown, the village came to be called Holetown for the narrow offshore channel where ships were serviced.

North of Holetown, the Folkestone Marine Park is an underwater park and sanctuary where snorkelers and divers can follow an underwater trail along a coral reef. The park includes a beach and the Folkestone Marine Museum, which displays live and mounted fish native to local waters.

HOLETOWN (C-1)

Opening celebrations of the week-long Holetown Festival are held in February at the Holetown Monument, which commemorates the first British landing on Barbados in 1625. Now a major tourist area, this area of upscale resorts, shops and shimmering beaches is called the "Platinum Coast."

Vestiges of the island's sugar industry are preserved at the Sir Frank Hutson Sugar Museum and Factory in the yard of the Portvale sugar factory. Antique and modern machines are displayed February through June during the harvest season.

ST. JAMES' PARISH CHURCH is on Hwy. 1. Most of the present church was built in 1874. Hurricanes destroyed the first wooden structure, erected in 1628, and its stone replacement. The original church bell is inscribed "God Bless King William 1696." Other relics include hand-beaten silver pieces that date from the late 17th century and the original baptismal font with its mahogany cover. A graveyard where many of Barbados' early settlers are interred adjoins the church. Open daily dawn-dusk. Donations. Phone (246) 422-4117.

St. John Parish (B-3)

One of the highest points on the island, Hackleton's Cliff rises 1,000 feet (305 m) above sea level. A steep, winding drive rewards visitors with a panoramic view of the east coast and the Scotland district.

CODRINGTON COLLEGE is on Sargeant St. overlooking Consett Bay. The site of the college originally was a plantation owned by Sir Christopher Codrington, former governor general of the Leeward Islands. Founded in 1745, this is one of the oldest seminaries in the Western Hemisphere. The wooded grounds offer a spectacular view of Consett Bay on the east coast. Daily. Grounds admission $2.50. Phone (246) 423-1140 or (246) 423-1141.

ST. JOHN'S PARISH CHURCH is n.e. on Hwy. 3B. The 1836 Gothic chapel perches on the edge of Hackleton's Cliff, affording a spectacular view of the Atlantic coast. The floor is paved with memorial tablets rescued from earlier churches, all destroyed by hurricane or fire. Ferdinando Paleologus, an alleged descendant of Constantine the Great, was buried in the churchyard in 1646. Daily. Donations. Phone (246) 433-5599.

St. Joseph Parish (B-3)

St. Joseph, on the northeastern shore, is in the heart of the Scotland District, a rugged vista that reminded homesick settlers of their native hills. Near the top of Horse Hill is the Cotton Tower, one of six signal stations built across Barbados by the British as part of the island's defense.

BATHSHEBA (B-3)

A resort 14 miles (23 km) from Bridgetown, Bathsheba has been called a miniature Cornish coast. The Flying Fish Fleet, purveyors of Barbados' national dish, arrives daily at Tent Bay. The outside verandah of the Atlantis Hotel is a popular spot for a typical Barbadian lunch, with Tent Bay and Bathsheba providing a scenic backdrop.

ANDROMEDA BOTANIC GARDENS, .2 mi. (.3 km) off Hwy. 3 following signs, clings to a rocky hillside overlooking the Atlantic coastline. Founded in 1954 by world-renowned horticulturist Iris Bannochie, Andromeda's lush gardens span 6.5 acres and host a collection containing some 650 species from the Caribbean, tropical Americas, Africa, Asia, Australia and the Pacific Islands. Visitors wind their way past flowering trees, palms and orchids, enjoying sea breezes in a tranquil setting. Allow 1 hour minimum. Daily 9-5; closed Good Friday, Easter and Dec. 25. Admission $10; $5 (ages 5-12). MC, VI. Phone (246) 433-9384.

FLOWER FOREST is on Hwy. 2 at Richmond Plantation, following signs. Hillside trails wind among tropical trees and plants, including bamboo, banana, avocado, breadfruit, coconut, coffee, cocoa and Barbados cherry. Relics of the sugar industry can be seen on the 50-acre (20-hectare) Richmond Plantation site. Food is available. Allow 1 hour minimum. Daily 9-5; closed Good Friday and Dec. 25. Admission $10; $5 (ages 5-13). MC, VI. Phone (246) 433-8152.

St. Lucy Parish (A-2)

The Animal Flower Cave in St. Lucy is one of the most scenic coastal areas in Barbados. Steps descend into a coral limestone cave containing three rooms. This sea-sculptured formation obtains its name from the sea anemones that exist in the pools, one of which is deep enough to swim in. Sneakers or reef shoes are recommended since the steps are steep and the rocks can be slippery. A guide leads the way into the cave, which is sometimes closed due to rough seas; phone (246) 439-8797.

From the cliffs surrounding Cove Bay, visitors can watch the tumultuous waves of the Atlantic Ocean crashing against the shore. Towering above the cove is Pico Tenerife, a jagged rock formation rising from the ocean to a height of 269 feet (82 m).

St. Michael Parish (D-1)

With its first English camp in 1628, St. Michael Parish soon gained prominence over earlier settlements in St. James and St. Peter due to its sheltered bay and freshwater access. The area later named Bridgetown would become one of the most important commercial ports in the West Indies.

BRIDGETOWN (D-1) pop. 7,500

Barbados' capital, Bridgetown was founded in 1629 and was the chief residential section during the island's settlement. The exuberance of its people and customs blend with a Victorian austerity typified by the public buildings that house parliament.

A statue of Lord Nelson in National Heroes' Square (formerly Trafalgar Square) was erected by planters in recognition of the British admiral, who saved their sugar profits from the French. St. Michael's Cathedral, on St. Michael's Row, was rebuilt in 1831 of coral rock after the original was destroyed by hurricanes. George Washington is recorded as having attended services in the original cathedral in 1751; it is now one of the town's main attractions.

The parliamentary buildings are on Broad Street facing National Heroes' Square. The House of Assembly meetings, held in the east building's Public Gallery, usually can be observed Tuesday at noon; visitors must be appropriately dressed and cameras are not permitted. The gallery contains stained-glass windows representing the sovereigns of England and a speaker's chair with intricate carvings.

The Careenage, in central Bridgetown alongside Wharf Street, is a picturesque harbor where pleasure craft are docked. Chamberlain Bridge, one of two spans over the Careenage, contains the Independence Arch, originally erected in 1987 and later rebuilt; it commemorates the island's 21st anniversary as a self-governing nation. Next to the arch is an area of shops, craft vendors and restaurants overlooking the water. Fishing and sailing charters as well as scuba diving excursions can be arranged at the waterfront shops.

Off Broad Street, visitors can find duty-free shops offering china, crystal, leather and fine jewelry. The Fairchild Street Market is a bustling center of activity, with merchants selling produce, snacks, clothing, shoes, newspapers and other items. Another colorful market can be found on Cheapside Street.

The Bridgetown Synagogue, on Magazine Lane, dates from 1654. Said to be one of the oldest Jewish synagogues in the Western Hemisphere, the structure was destroyed by a hurricane in 1933 and has been restored. The adjoining cemetery has tombstones dating from the 1630s.

Situated on Bay Street, opposite the Prime Minister's office and next to Bayshore Beach, the Esplanade offers a nice view of Bridgetown's harbor area and Carlisle Bay. The small park, which was once a village of wooden houses, contains benches shaded by trees and a lovely gazebo. St. Patrick's Roman Catholic Cathedral, also on Bay Street, dates from 1839.

East of Bridgetown, in a residential area at the northern end of St. Barnabas Highway, is the Emancipation Statue of Bussa, a national hero. Commemorating the abolition of slavery in 1834, the statue depicts a slave standing with his chains broken and his hands to the sky in triumph. In 1816, Bussa purportedly led a revolt at Bayley's Plantation in St. Philip Parish that was to be the largest revolt on the island.

Barbados Tourism Authority: Harbour Road, Bridgetown, Barbados; phone (246) 427-2623. Information booths at Deep Water Harbour inside the cruise ship terminals and at the airport offer assistance with reservations, sightseeing tours and other services.

GEM **_ATLANTIS_ SUBMARINE EXPEDITION** departs from the Shallow Draft in Deep Water Harbour. The 65-foot-long, 48-passenger submarine cruises at a maximum depth of 150 feet (45 m), offering excellent views of reefs, coral formations, marine life and a sunken ship.

Trips depart daily on the hour 9-4; closed 1 week in Sept. A 15-minute ferry ride transports passengers between the dock and the submarine for the 50-minute tour. Fare $89; $57 (ages 13-17); $44.50 (ages 4-12). Transportation to harbor $7.50; $5 (ages 4-12). Children under 36 inches tall are not permitted on the submarine. Reservations are advised. AX, MC, VI. Phone (246) 436-8929.

BANKS BREWERY TOUR is in the Wildey area. The guided tour begins with a brief orientation video depicting the beer brewing process. Visitors are then led through the plant where they see milling equipment in the Brew House, the fermentation tanks and the Bottling Hall, where bottles are washed, filled, pasteurized and labeled. After the tour, guests are treated to complimentary samples of the various products produced onsite.

Allow 1 hour minimum. Tours Mon.-Fri. at 10, noon and 2; closed major holidays. Under 10 are not permitted. Admission $6; $3 (ages 10-15). DS, MC, VI. Phone (246) 228-6486.

BARBADOS MUSEUM AND HISTORICAL SOCIETY is 2.5 mi. (4 km) s.e. on Bay St. at the Garrison. Exhibits in the 1817 British military prison depict the natural history of the Caribbean, Amerindian prehistory and the history of Barbados. The museum also has collections of ceramics, silver, maps and prints; period rooms from a Barbadian plantation house; a children's gallery; and a prisoner's cell as well as changing exhibits. Mon.-Sat. 9-5, Sun. 2-6; closed holidays. Admission $6; $3 (children). Phone (246) 427-0201 or (246) 436-1956.

GARRISON HISTORIC AREA is 2.5 mi. (4 km) s.e. on Bay St. at the outskirts of Bridgetown. This military site began with construction of Charles Fort by the Barbados Militia in 1650. British troops were garrisoned here 1780-1905. The West India Regiment was the first British unit of black soldiers; their distinctive Zouave uniforms are still worn by the Barbados Defence Force Band.

The community surrounding the Garrison Savannah racetrack features some 70 buildings of historical and architectural interest, including the 1705 St. Ann's Fort and the 1804 Main Guard House with its prominent clock tower. Bush Hill House, where George Washington and his brother lived for three months in 1751, has been restored; tours can be booked by contacting (246) 228-5461. The National Cannon Collection displays several dozen of the more than 400 iron guns that have been excavated on the island, including an Elizabethan cannon forged in 1600. Phone (246) 436-9033.

MALIBU VISITOR CENTRE is off Spring Garden Hwy. on Brighton Beach. A guided tour begins with a 10-minute videotape highlighting the plant's signature products, Malibu and Cockspur rum. Participants view the aging and filling rooms where the rum is blended and bottled. The guide provides a detailed explanation of the fermentation and distillation processes.

Allow 1 hour minimum. Tour fee includes beach chair rental and complimentary drink. Visitor center Mon.-Fri. 9-5. Tours on the half-hour except 11-noon. Last tour 1 hour before closing. Tour $10; free (ages 0-11). DS, MC, VI. Phone (246) 425-9393.

MOUNT GAY RUM TOUR is on Spring Garden Hwy. near Bridgetown's deep water port. The guided 45-minute tour begins with an audiovisual presentation in a theater resembling a rum shop. A knowledgeable guide then offers an in-depth explanation of all aspects of rum production, focusing on the aging process involved in producing a mature rum. The tour also includes a look at the blending and bottling areas of the plant. Afterward, visitors may participate in a tasting.

Traditional tours depart every hour Mon.-Fri. 9:30-3:30. Lunch tour Tues. and Thurs. at noon. Cocktail tour Wed. at 2:30. Closed bank holidays. Traditional tour $7; free (ages 0-11). Lunch tour including transportation $40; $20 (ages 4-11). Cocktail tour including transportation $30 (children not permitted). DC, MC, VI. Phone (246) 425-8757.

QUEEN'S PARK is off Constitution Rd. The British government purchased this area in the 1780s as a residence for the general commanding the British troops. The building, formerly known as "King's House," was later changed to "Queen's House" when Queen Victoria came to power. On the grounds are a playground, a bandstand, a fountain and lush gardens that create an escape from the bustle of Bridgetown. A 1,000-year-old baobab tree stands some 90 feet high and measures more than 81 feet around its trunk.

An art gallery in Queen's Park House features local works, and a theater presents local productions. Park open daily dawn-dusk. Gallery Mon.-Sat. 10-6. Free. Phone (246) 425-1200 or (246) 426-2555.

***TIAMI* CATAMARAN CRUISE** departs from the Shallow Draught harbor of Bridgetown port. Lunch and sunset cruises are offered, both of which include snorkeling stops; sites may vary due to weather conditions. Passengers enjoy views of the island's southwest coast. Food, beverages and hotel transfers are included. Allow a half day. Snorkeling equipment is provided. Bring a swimsuit, towel and sunscreen. Five-hour lunch cruises depart daily at 10. Sunset cruise departs Sun. at 4. Closed Good Friday and Dec. 25. Lunch cruise $80; $40 (ages 4-12). Sunset cruise $47.50; $40 (ages 4-12). AX, MC, VI. Phone (246) 430-0900.

TYROL COT HERITAGE VILLAGE is at Codrington Hill. The home of Sir Grantley Adams, who led the struggle for democracy in Barbados, contains family photographs and articles, as well as antique mahogany pieces. Reproductions of chattel houses in the surrounding village include a replica of an 1820s slave hut, a working blacksmith's shop and a home depicting the domestic life of Barbadians in the 1920s. Allow 1 hour, 30 minutes minimum. Mon.-Fri. 9-5; closed bank holidays. House $6; $3 (ages 0-12). Village free. Phone (246) 424-2074.

St. Peter Parish (B-1)

St. Peter and St. Lucy, which share the northern end of the island, are the only two parishes in Barbados with shorelines on both the Atlantic Ocean and Caribbean Sea. The port of Speightstown was once a vital trading link with England, and British landowners established several large estates here in the 17th century, including Saint Nicholas Abbey and Farley Hill.

Wild green monkeys frolic in their natural habitat at the Barbados Wildlife Reserve, which protects 4 acres (1.6 hectares) of mahogany forest.

SPEIGHTSTOWN (B-1)

This fishing village was once a shipping center known as Little Bristol. In 1663 Sir John Yeamans sailed from Speightstown (pronounced *Spites-town*) on an expedition to colonize South Carolina; he later became the third governor of that colony. His house, St. Nicholas Abbey, is one of the oldest sugar plantation great houses still standing in the Caribbean. Also in the area are the remains of the Old Denmark, Orange and Dover forts. Six Men's Bay north of town is lined with cannons and old buildings once used for drying whale blubber.

FARLEY HILL NATIONAL PARK borders the Barbados Wildlife Reserve. On a cliff 900 feet (275 m) above sea level, the park provides sweeping views of the coast amid gardens and the ruins of a sugar planter's estate. The earliest part of the house, known originally as Grenade Hall, is thought to have been built in 1818. In 1856, original owner Joseph Lyder Briggs gave the property to his son, Thomas Graham Briggs. Thomas spent large sums developing Farley Hill into one of the finest country residences in the West Indies and entertained distinguished guests there. The park also is the site of concerts and festivals. Picnicking is permitted. Daily 8:30-4:30. Entrance fee $3.45 per private vehicle. Phone (246) 422-6700.

GRENADE HALL FOREST AND SIGNAL STATION borders the Barbados Wildlife Reserve and Farley Hill National Park. The station commands a panorama of the island and offers insight into its original role as part of a communications network that was unique in the Caribbean. The site was originally used by the Royal Artillery to communicate between island signal stations and the capital of Bridgetown. Visitors can explore a mile (1.6 km) of coral pathways winding through trees, shrubs, vines and herbs.

Daily 10-5; closed Jan. 1 and Dec. 25. Last admission 1 hour, 30 minutes before closing. Admission (includes the Barbados Wildlife Reserve) $12; $6 (ages 3-12). Phone (246) 422-8826.

ST. NICHOLAS ABBEY is 5.5 mi. (9 km) n.e. via Hwy. 1 following signs. Built about 1660 for a sugar planter, the Jacobean mansion had as its second resident Sir John Yeamans, commissioned by King Charles II as lieutenant general and governor of South Carolina. Visitors tour the ground floor, which is decorated with antique English and Barbadian furniture. An 1890 steam mill grinds sugar cane; sugar and rum products can be sampled. A film depicts the sugar-making process and other island scenes. Mon.-Fri. and Sun. 10-3:30; closed major holidays. Hours may vary; phone ahead. Admission $13. MC, VI. Phone (246) 422-8725.

St. Philip Parish (D-4)

The rugged coastline on the southeast edge of the island is famous for its waves. Crane Beach, with its dramatic limestone cliffs, is considered one of the most beautiful beaches on the island. The area is named for a large winch that was once used to unload ships.

FOURSQUARE RUM DISTILLERY AND HERITAGE PARK is s. of Six Cross Roads on Hwy. 6. The Foursquare Plantation's 19th-century sugar factory has been modified to produce rum. Self-guiding tours of the underground furnace room offer insight about early sugar boiling methods; rum production, from barreling to aging, is explained through displays in the distillery. Rum tastings are offered. The 8-acre (3-hectare) landscaped park contains a folk museum, craft shops, an outdoor sugar museum, an amphitheater and a children's play park.

Food is available. Allow 1 hour minimum. Mon.-Fri. 9-5; closed bank holidays. Free. Phone (246) 420-1977.

SUNBURY PLANTATION HOUSE is .7 mi. (1.1 km) w. of Six Cross Roads on Hwy. 5. Built in 1660, Sunbury is one of the oldest plantation houses on the island. Guides lead 30-minute tours of the house, which is furnished with period pieces and antiques. The yam cellars contain collections of horse-drawn vehicles and an optometrist's artifacts. The surrounding plantation is still being worked. A candlelight dinner is offered Tuesday and Thursday; reservations are required. Tours are offered daily 9:30-4:30; closed Dec. 25. Admission $7.50; $3.75 (ages 5-12). AX, MC, VI. Phone (246) 423-6270.

St. Thomas Parish (C-2)

St. Thomas is one of two land-bound parishes on Barbados; the other is St. George to the south. The 1799 Sharon Moravian Church is one of the few unaltered 18th-century structures on the island.

HARRISON'S CAVE is on Hwy. 2 at the southern end of Welchman Hall Gully. Narrated 30-minute tram rides travel through subterranean stream passages. An introductory slide show at the visitor center depicts the discovery and development of the cave. Food is available. Trams depart every 15 minutes daily 8:30-4; closed Good Friday, Easter and Dec. 25. Admission $16; $7 (ages 3-12). Reservations are recommended. DS, MC, VI. Phone (246) 438-6640.

WELCHMAN HALL GULLY is on Hwy. 2. A ravine created by collapsed limestone caverns contains a 13-acre (5-hectare) tropical garden of fruit and spice trees. The gully is rimmed by cave-pocked cliffs inhabited by monkeys. A massive pillar formed by the joining of stalactites and stalagmites seems to support the rock cliff. With a diameter of more than 4 feet (1.2 m), the limestone pillar is one of the largest of its kind in the world. Daily 9-5; closed Good Friday and Dec. 25. Admission $6; $3 (ages 6-12). Phone (246) 438-6671.

Fort St. Catherine, St. George's / © GlowCam / eStock Photo

Bermuda

Viewed from the air, Bermuda presents a kaleidoscope of pink beaches, blue-green ocean and patchwork isles. The mainland is a graceful chain of eight islands joined by roads and bridges; in all, Bermuda consists of 181 islands and islets. A closer view reveals well-ordered homes with white roofs and a profusion of flowers—Easter lilies, amaryllis, oleander, gladioli, hibiscus and poinsettias. Because Bermuda is the northernmost of the coral islands, limestone, the residual product of coral, is seen everywhere. The island is 650 miles (1,045 km) east of Cape Hatteras, N.C., and about a 2-hour flight from New York, Atlanta and other East Coast gateway cities.

Thanks to a mild climate and beautiful beaches, Bermuda's main business is tourism. However, Bermuda is a subtropical island—the weather during December, January and February can be brisk enough to keep most people out of the water. The peak tourist season runs from spring until fall.

History

Bermuda's discoverer and namesake, Juan de Bermúdez of Spain, is thought to have anchored off the islands as early as 1503. The first settlers, however, were Virginia-bound British colonists who were shipwrecked off St. George's Island in 1609. Some historians credit the event with providing Shakespeare with background for "The Tempest."

Although tourism, banking and international business are today's primary industries, Bermuda relied on shipbuilding as the mainstay of its economy 1684-1775. Vessels constructed of cedar were the basis of the island's flourishing economy until wooden ships were replaced by those made of steel during the late 1800s and tourism began to take on economic importance.

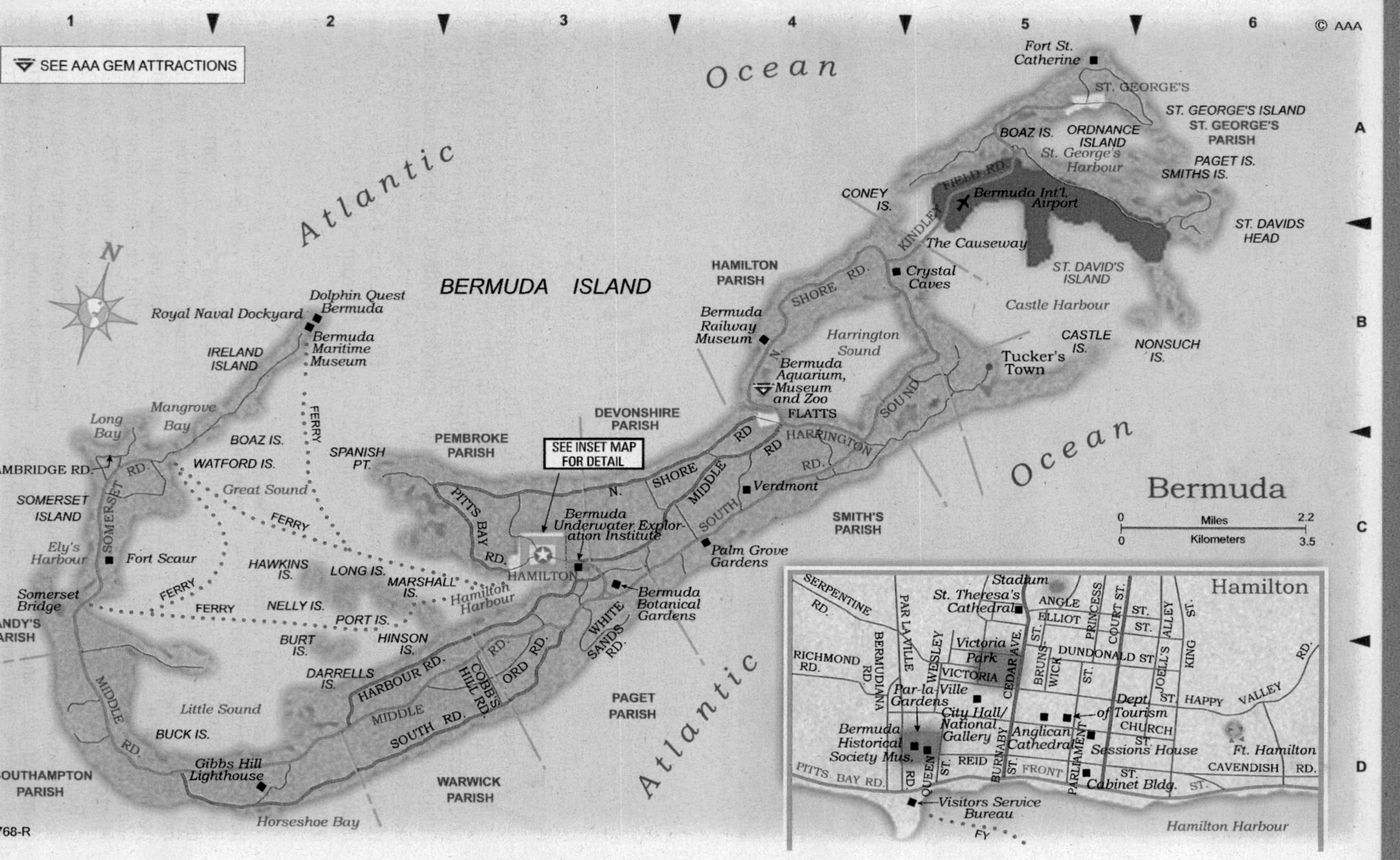
© AAA
SEE AAA GEM ATTRACTIONS
Atlantic Ocean
BERMUDA ISLAND
Fort St. Catherine
ST. GEORGE'S
ST. GEORGE'S ISLAND
ST. GEORGE'S PARISH
BOAZ IS.
ORDNANCE ISLAND
St. George's Harbour
PAGET IS.
SMITHS IS.
CONEY IS.
Bermuda Int'l. Airport
ST. DAVIDS HEAD
The Causeway
HAMILTON PARISH
Crystal Caves
ST. DAVID'S ISLAND
Castle Harbour
Dolphin Quest Bermuda
Royal Naval Dockyard
Bermuda Maritime Museum
IRELAND ISLAND
Bermuda Railway Museum
Harrington Sound
CASTLE IS.
NONSUCH IS.
Tucker's Town
Bermuda Aquarium, Museum and Zoo
FLATTS
Mangrove Bay
Long Bay
DEVONSHIRE PARISH
BOAZ IS.
PEMBROKE PARISH
SPANISH PT.
SEE INSET MAP FOR DETAIL
CAMBRIDGE RD.
WATFORD IS.
Verdmont
Great Sound
SOMERSET ISLAND
Bermuda Underwater Exploration Institute
SMITH'S PARISH
Bermuda
Miles 0 2.2
Kilometers 0 3.5
Ely's Harbour
Fort Scaur
HAWKINS IS.
LONG IS.
Palm Grove Gardens
MARSHALL IS.
HAMILTON
Hamilton Harbour
Bermuda Botanical Gardens
Somerset Bridge
FERRY
NELLY IS.
PORT IS.
SANDY'S PARISH
BURT IS.
HINSON IS.
DARRELLS IS.
PAGET PARISH
Little Sound
BUCK IS.
SOUTHAMPTON PARISH
Gibbs Hill Lighthouse
WARWICK PARISH
Horseshoe Bay
1768-R
Hamilton
Stadium
St. Theresa's Cathedral
Victoria Park
Par-la-Ville Gardens
City Hall/ National Gallery
Bermuda Historical Society Mus.
Anglican Cathedral
Dept. of Tourism
Sessions House
Cabinet Bldg.
Ft. Hamilton
Visitors Service Bureau
Hamilton Harbour

As a British colony Bermuda is administered by a governor appointed by the reigning British monarch; a cabinet appointed by the premier; a senate jointly formed by the governor, the premier and the opposition party; and a house of assembly elected by the citizens. The country's nine parishes are governed by separate advisory councils. The islands hold the distinction of being the oldest self-governing colony in the British Commonwealth. Bermuda's constitution, adopted in June 1967, provides for a large measure of self-government.

Shopping

Browsing for antiques and bric-a-brac is entertaining in itself. Shops in Hamilton have given Bermuda its reputation as the "Showcase of the British Commonwealth." Choice woolens, cashmeres, silver, English china, leather gloves and slacks, French perfumes, German cameras, Swiss watches, Swedish crystal and Italian leather can be purchased at great savings.

A.S. Cooper & Sons Ltd., on Front Street, sells Wedgwood china, and William M. Bluck and Co. deals in fine china and crystal. The Calypso Shop on Front Street and the Irish Linen Shop feature linens from Ireland, Italy and Switzerland. Perfumes can be found at Peniston Brown.

Fine selections of jewelry are displayed at Astwood Dickenson on Front Street and at Crisson's on Queen, Reid and Front streets in Hamilton and York Street in St. George's. The specialty shops composing The Emporium, entered from Front Street, allow visitors with limited time to purchase an array of interesting Bermudian items in one stop.

Bermuda Perfumery preserves the traditional creative processes of this native industry. Branch stores and specialty shops are tucked away in St. George's and Somerset as well as in several of the larger resort hotels throughout the island. Most stores are open Mon.-Sat. 9-5, and some have extended hours during the Christmas holidays and summer months. Banking hours generally are Mon.-Thurs. 9-4, Fri. 9-4:30.

Food and Drink

In Bermuda the lobster season extends from September through March. The delicacy is served steaming with melted butter or one of several rich sauces. Cassava pie filled with chicken and pork is a popular treat during the Christmas season. The secret of its unique flavor is the grated and baked root of the cassava plant. Favorite desserts are sweet potato pudding and *syllabub,* a guava jelly-cream-wine concoction.

Fruits and vegetables are grown locally, but meat is imported from the United States and Canada. Drinking water is distilled from sea water for hotels or collected on rooftops, and milk is pasteurized. All popular American drinks are available; meals in hotels are similar to those served in the United States. Reservations are suggested for lunch and dinner at the best restaurants. A tip of 15 percent, with extra allowance for special service, is customary. However, most hotels, restaurants, cottage colonies and guesthouses add a 15-percent gratuity to the accommodation or food bill. Most hotels and restaurants accept credit cards.

Sports and Amusements

Part of Bermuda's appeal is that it has something for everyone. Golf, tennis, horseback riding, fishing and water sports lure the athletically inclined, while shoppers can enjoy Hamilton's exclusive stores and civic activities. St. George's, the former capital, provides a journey into the past with its 17th-century architecture and narrow lanes. Lazy days are filled by sunning, sightseeing or browsing in out-of-the-way shops.

Bermuda ranks among the most sports-conscious countries of the world: More than 30 sporting clubs are found in an area of 21 square miles (54 sq km). The island's diverse activities include bowling, bridge, cricket, cycling, dog and horse shows, fishing, golfing, parasailing, sailing, swimming, scuba diving, tennis, racquetball, squash, table tennis, horseback riding, water skiing and windsurfing.

Soccer and cricket are the national sports—soccer matches are scheduled September through April, and cricket matches are held May through September. The Annual Cup Match, a national holiday, is a cricket match played between teams representing the island's east and west ends on the Thursday and Friday before the first Monday in August; most shops and eateries close during the event. Rugby also is popular; one major international tournament, the Easter Rugby Classic, is played on Easter and another, the World Rugby Classic, in mid-November.

Other sporting events include golf and tennis tournaments; yacht races on Saturday and Sunday; the Bermuda Game Fishing Tournament, held throughout the year; the Bermuda Triple Crown Billfish Championship in July; and the Escape to Bermuda Triathlon in the fall. Summer is celebrated on Bermuda Day, May 24, with dinghy races in St. George's

Harbour and cycling and inline skating races in Hamilton.

The beaches on the south shore are wild stretches of sand and surf. Horseshoe Bay is one of the most popular. Because Bermuda is not subject to strong ocean currents that stir up sediment, the waters are usually clear and excellent for snorkeling. In addition, more than 600 species of fish live in the surrounding waters. One of the most unusual underwater sports Bermuda offers is helmet diving, or underwater walking. It is an opportunity for nonswimmers and people who wear glasses to see the incredible variety of marine life in Bermuda's waters. Anyone from 5 to 85 can participate in the guided 30-minute tours departing from Flatts Village in Smith's Parish, daily April through November, weather permitting.

You can rent boats and equipment for snorkeling, scuba diving and spear fishing at many places on the island; spear fishing is not permitted within 1 mile (1.6 km) of the shore, and the importation and use of a spear gun in Bermuda is illegal. Since 1- or 2-hour scuba diving lessons are usually insufficient preparation for a novice, you should take a complete course in advance. Several operators offer snorkeling and scuba diving lessons on trips aboard glass-bottom boats.

Information on trips for deep-sea, reef or shore fishing is available from Visitor Service Bureaus on Front Street in Hamilton, King's Square in St. George's and the Royal Naval Dockyard in Sandy's Parish. Boats with tackle and bait can be chartered for both half- and full-day excursions; no license is required. Rentals and lessons for sailing vessels and windsurfing are abundant. Water skiing is best May through September and is permitted in Hamilton Harbour, the Great Sound, Castle Harbour, Mangrove Bay, Spanish Point, Ferry Reach, Ely's Harbour, Riddells Bay and Harrington Sound; the law requires that skiers be towed by a licensed skipper.

If you prefer to play on land, you can choose among golf, tennis, squash, bicycling or horseback riding. Public golf courses include the Belmont Hills Golf Club, Warwick Parish; Fairmont Southampton Golf Club, Southampton Parish; Ocean View Golf Course, Devonshire Parish; Port Royal Golf Course, Southampton Parish; and St. George's Golf Club, St. George's Parish.

Many large hotels have tennis courts. The Bermuda Squash Racquets Club in Devonshire Parish is available to visitors for a fee of $10; reservations are required. Bowlers can pursue their sport at the Warwick Lanes on Middle Road in Warwick Parish.

Bicycling is an engaging pastime, particularly on the Railway Trail, which runs along an old railroad line. The nature trail runs the entire length of Bermuda, St. George to Somerset, except for a 3-mile (4.8-km) section in and around Hamilton. The 21 miles (34 km) of trails are divided into seven sections, each with its own flavor and character. The trail also is a fine walking and equestrian path. A free, 18-page trail guide is published by the Bermuda Department of Tourism *(see Fast Facts box)*. The guide includes a history of the trail, maps, descriptions of various sections of the path and historical photos.

The self-guiding African Diaspora Heritage Trail crisscrosses the island and provides glimpses into Bermuda's role in black history. The trail includes such sights at the slave graveyard at St. Peter's, Crow Lane and the Commissioner's House at Bermuda Maritime Museum.

The Spicelands Riding Centre in Warwick Parish offers a variety of programs, including trail rides, evening rides and lessons; phone (441) 238-8212.

A special enticement for winter visitors is "Fall into Spring," appropriately held from November through March. Some of the events featured during this seasonal observance include a "skirling ceremony" performed by kilted pipers and dancers at Fort Hamilton; an open house of the official residence of the premier; guided tours of St. George's, Hamilton and Somerset; a historical review by the Gombey Dancers; and various golf tournaments.

The Bermuda Festival, which takes place in January and February in Hamilton, is an international gala of music, dance and drama. The Bermuda Regiment Band Beating of the Retreat provides pomp and ceremony as it is performed downtown twice a month on Wednesdays at 9 p.m. from May through October.

Several publications listing weekly events and entertainment are distributed at hotels and other establishments. Dancing and after-dinner entertainment are nightly fare at hotels and large cottage colonies. Calypso bands and local talent fill Hamilton nightclubs, some of which stay open until 3 a.m.

Sightseeing

Excursions can be taken to almost any point on Bermuda by cycle, taxi, boat or bus. A blue flag on a taxi signifies that the driver has been approved as a qualified tour guide by the government. Excellent maps are available at Visitor Service Bureaus on Front Street in Hamilton, King's Square in St. George's and the Royal Naval Dockyard in Sandy's Parish. Some hotels will arrange escorted excursions.

Popular cruises include a 2-hour cruise aboard a glass-bottom boat to the sea gardens and a 3-hour catamaran cruise of Great Sound. Reservations can be made directly through the operator or arranged through a hotel activities desk. Ferries operate daily from Hamilton to the Bermuda Maritime Museum, Royal Naval Dockyard, in Sandy's Parish.

Transportation

Several air carriers provide service to Bermuda International Airport from Atlanta, Washington D.C., Boston, Miami, New York, Philadelphia and Toronto. Flights last from 1 hour, 50 minutes to 2.5 hours.

Because law forbids the use of automobiles by nonresidents, car-rental services are not available. Perhaps the most common and economical means of transportation in Bermuda is cycling. Mopeds can be rented for about $80 a day for a single or $85 a day for a double. For the hardier visitor, bicycles (known as "pedal bikes") can be rented for about $53 for a full day plus $20 for insurance; weekly rates also are available. Cycle rental operations are found throughout the island and at many of the large hotels. Riders should use caution, as roads in Bermuda are narrow, hilly, curving and banked in many spots by coral walls. Carriages with fringed tops also can be hired for sightseeing at $40-$50 per half-hour.

Bus service, priced by zone, is available throughout the island; the central bus terminal is on Washington Street in Hamilton. Exact change, tokens or tickets are required; books of 15 tickets are available at substantial savings at the central terminal or at most sub-post offices throughout the island. Adult fare for up to three zones is $20 cash. The flat fare for ages 5 to 16 is $7.50.

Bermuda Ferry Service runs daily between Hamilton, Paget, Warwick, Somerset, Dockyard and Rockaway. An additional route to St. George's operates mid-April to early November. The Hamilton-Paget-Warwick fare is $2.50 one way; the Hamilton-Somseset fare is $4 one way. The flat fare for ages 5 to 16 is $2. Cash is no longer accepted on the ferries; tickets must be purchased before boarding. Motor-assisted cycles and pedal bikes on the Hamilton-Somserset ferry cost $4 extra one way and are not permitted on other routes. Bus and ferry schedules, which include maps of routes and fare zones and sample fares, can be obtained at the bus and ferry terminals, visitor's service bureaus and most hotels.

Fast Facts

POPULATION: 64,500.

AREA: 54 sq km (21 sq mi.).

CAPITAL: Hamilton.

HIGHEST POINT: 76 m (250 ft.), Town Hill.

LOWEST POINT: Sea level, Atlantic Ocean.

TIME ZONE(S): Atlantic Standard. DST.

LANGUAGE: English.

GOVERNMENT: British Overseas Territory.

UNIT OF CURRENCY: Bermudian dollar, divided into 100 cents. $1 U.S. = 1 Bermudian dollar. Most shops, restaurants and hotels accept U.S. currency.

ELECTRICITY: 110 volt, 60 cycles AC.

MINIMUM AGE FOR DRIVERS: Nonresidents may not drive cars on Bermuda; rental cars are not available. Driving is on the left.

HELMETS FOR MOTORCYCLISTS: Required.

HOLIDAYS: Jan. 1; Good Friday; Bermuda Day, May 24; Queen's Birthday, June (1st or 2nd Mon.); Cup Match and Somers Day, Thurs. and Fri. before 1st Mon. in Aug.; Labour Day, Sept. (1st Mon.); Remembrance Day, Nov. 11; Christmas, Dec. 25; Boxing Day, Dec. 26.

TAXES: A 7.25 percent room tax and 10-15 percent service charge are added to most hotel bills. Most restaurants include a 10-15 percent service charge. There is no sales tax on the island. Departure tax and airport security fee is $35 U.S. by air, $60 by sea.

IMMIGRATION REQUIREMENTS: Passport and a return or onward ticket are required. No visa needed for stays up to 21 days.

PHONING THE ISLANDS: To call Bermuda from the U.S. or Canada, dial 1 + 441 + the 7-digit local number.

FURTHER INFORMATION FOR VISITORS:

Bermuda Department of Tourism
675 Third Ave., 20th Floor
New York, NY 10017
(212) 818-9800
(800) 237-6832
See color ad on insert.

Visitors Service Bureau
Global House
43 Church St.
Hamilton Parish, Bermuda HM12
(441) 292-0023

Points of Interest

See map page 90.

Devonshire Parish (C-3)

One of nine Bermudian parishes, each comprising 1,250 acres (500 hectares), Devonshire is at the geographical center of the island. The area is named for William Cavendish, the first Earl of Devonshire. The Old Devonshire Parish Church on Middle Road dates to 1716, though it has been destroyed and rebuilt at least twice.

PALM GROVE GARDENS is at 38 South Shore Rd. The private estate contains tropical birds and native and exotic trees and flowers. A pond has a relief map of Bermuda. Mon.-Thurs. 8:30-5; closed holidays. Free.

Hamilton Parish (B-4)

Hamilton Parish, north of Harrington Sound, is known for its labyrinth of caves. Though it shares the same name, this parish does not contain the island's capital; the city of Hamilton is in Pembroke Parish.

GEM **BERMUDA AQUARIUM, MUSEUM AND ZOO** is at 40 North Shore Rd. in Flatts Village. Most species of fish found in Bermuda waters are represented, along with tropical birds, lemurs, golden lion tamarins, turtles, seals and binturongs. The 140,000-gallon North Rock Exhibit has two viewing tanks showcasing Bermuda's ocean resources and the underwater environment of the nearby North Rock coral reef. A touch pool and Discovery Cove also are on-site.

The Australasia Exhibit features the wildlife of Australia, New Guinea, Borneo and Malaysia. The museum highlights the unique geological development of Bermuda. A full-sized whale skeleton also is displayed. Self-guiding audio tours are available, and videotapes about Bermuda's marine life run continuously.

Food is available. Allow 1 hour minimum. Daily 9-5; closed Dec. 25. Last admission 1 hour before closing. An interpretive tour is offered daily at 1:10, Apr.-Sept; Sat.-Sun. at 1:10, rest of year. Admission $10; $5 (ages 5-12 and 66+). Phone (441) 293-2727.

BERMUDA RAILWAY MUSEUM is at 37 North Shore Rd. The museum contains memorabilia from the days of the Bermuda Railway, which operated 1931-1948. The 22-mile (35-km) track no longer exists, but most of the roadbed is now part of the Railway Trail. Photographs, documents, equipment, antiques and collectibles are contained in an old station house. Tues.-Fri. 10-4 (weather permitting); closed holidays. Donations. Phone (441) 293-1774 or (441) 334-9297.

THE CRYSTAL & FANTASY CAVES OF BERMUDA is at 8 Crystal Caves Rd. off Wilkinson Ave. on Bailey's Bay. Folklore says that two boys discovered the first cavern in 1905 while searching for a lost cricket ball. The main cave takes its name from the crystal-clear waters of its underground lake, which is 55 feet (17 m) deep. A second passage in the underground network, Fantasy Cave, features rare chandelier clusters of soda straw formations and calcite mineral deposits resembling frozen waterfalls.

The 81 steps in Crystal Cave might be difficult for some; benches are available for resting. Food is available. Allow 30 minutes minimum. Guided tours daily 9:30-4:30; closed Jan. 1, Good Friday, Dec. 24-26. Last admission 30 minute before closing. Admission to one cave $16; $8 (ages 5-12). Combination admission $23; $10 (ages 5-12). Phone (441) 293-0640.

Paget Parish (D-3)

Across the harbor from the capital city of Hamilton, Paget Parish includes the resort area of Elbow Beach.

BERMUDA BOTANICAL GARDENS is at 169 South Rd. via Berry Hill and Point Finger rds. On the property of Camden, the official residence of Bermuda's premier, the 37-acre (15-hectare) gardens display native and introduced flora and feature several display houses and a garden for the blind. A visitor center at the Berry Hill entrance offers educational displays and a videotape presentation.

Food is available. Allow 1 hour, 30 minutes minimum. Gardens open daily dawn-dusk. Display houses open Tues.-Sat. 10-4. Free tours depart from the visitor center Tues.-Wed. and Fri. at 10:30 (weather permitting). The premier's residence is open, except during official functions, Tues. and Fri. noon-2. Free. Phone (441) 236-4201.

Pembroke Parish (C-3)

Once known as Spanish Point, Pembroke Parish is home to the island's capital. Bermuda's most populous parish covers a peninsula between the Atlantic Ocean and Hamilton Harbour.

HAMILTON (C-3) pop. 969

Incorporated in 1793, Hamilton succeeded St. George's as capital in 1815. The city, overlooking

Hamilton Harbour, is a latticework of pastel houses surrounded by tropical flowers. Whitewashed roofs, shuttered windows, arched doorways, Old World carriages and clusters of shops all enhance Hamilton's charm.

The sparkling white tower of City Hall rises 90 feet above Church Street. Its bronze weather vane depicts Sir George Somers' shipwrecked *Sea Venture*. A first floor gallery displays a stamp collection and oil portraits of Queen Victoria and Prince Albert. Upstairs is the Bermuda National Gallery *(see attraction listing)*. Behind the building is Victoria Park with its 19th-century gazebo, built in honor of Queen Victoria's golden jubilee.

Visitors Service Bureau, Hamilton: Front St. near ferry terminal, Hamilton, Bermuda.

BERMUDA HISTORICAL SOCIETY MUSEUM is next to the public library at 13 Queen St. Displayed are china, silver, antique furniture, Bermudian coins, personal belongings of Adm. Sir George Somers and sketches and models of early Bermuda ships. Somers was commander of the fleet carrying settlers to Virginia when it was shipwrecked off St. George's Island in 1609. Also featured is a collection of blue and white Canton porcelain and locally made silver spoons from 1727. Mon.-Fri. 10-3; closed holidays. Free. Phone (441) 295-2487.

BERMUDA NATIONAL GALLERY occupies the second floor of City Hall at 17 Church St. The country's art museum showcases fine and decorative arts from around the world. The permanent collection features Bermudian works, 15th- through 19th-century European art, African sculpture and contemporary pieces. Highlights include paintings by Thomas Gainsborough, Sir Joshua Reynolds and George Romney; photographs by Richard Saunders; and prints by Hale Woodruff.

Allow 1 hour minimum. Mon.-Sat. 10-4; closed holidays. Guided tours of the national gallery are offered Thurs. at 10:30. Free. Phone (441) 295-9428.

BERMUDA UNDERWATER EXPLORATION INSTITUTE (BUEI) is just outside Hamilton on E. Broadway at 40 Crow Lane. Designed to foster an understanding and appreciation of the world's oceans, the BUEI features two floors of interactive exhibits. Through simulator modules, visitors can dive 12,000 feet in a deep-sea submersible or survive an attack in a shark cage. Highlights include the Jack Lightbourne Shell Collection and a display of artifacts discovered by diver and explorer Teddy Tucker. Marine exhibits include diving bells, a bathysphere and the space-like Exosuit, an atmospheric diving suit.

Food is available. Mon.-Fri. 9-5, Sat.-Sun. 10-5; closed Dec. 25. Last admission 1 hour before closing. Admission $12.50; $10 (ages 66+); $6 (ages 7-16). AX, MC, VI. Phone (441) 292-7219.

THE CABINET BUILDING is at 105 Front St. Known as the Secretariat, the 1841 building houses several government offices and the council chamber of the Senate, the upper house of the legislature. Mon.-Fri. 9-5; closed holidays. Free. Phone (441) 292-5501.

CATHEDRAL OF THE MOST HOLY TRINITY is on Church St. Built of native limestone and stones from around the world, the Anglican cathedral was consecrated in 1911. Special features include a marble altar, mosaics and stained-glass windows. The 155 steps to the top of the cathedral's tower lead to a panoramic view of Hamilton. Cathedral open daily and for Sunday services. Tower Mon.-Fri. 10-4 (weather permitting); closed holidays. Tower $3; $2 (senior citizens and students). Phone (441) 292-4033.

CATHEDRAL OF ST. THERESA is on Cedar Ave. Stained-glass windows from Munich, Germany, enhance the Spanish-style architecture of this Roman Catholic church, which was built in 1932. Mon.-Fri. 7 a.m.-8:30 a.m., Sat.-Sun. 8 a.m.-7:30 p.m. Free. Phone (441) 292-0607.

FORT HAMILTON is e. on Happy Valley Rd. This well-preserved coral fortress was built during the American Civil War to prevent blockade running; the underground passageways and large cannons are noteworthy. A semitropical garden occupies the moat. Picnicking is permitted on the lawn, which offers a fine view of Hamilton, Paget and Warwick parishes and the harbor. Daily 9:30-5. Free.

PAR-LA-VILLE GARDENS is on Queen St. just off Front St. Native flowers and plants are presented in a formal arrangement. The Perot Post Office is in the gardens. Gardens open daily 24 hours. Post office open Mon.-Fri. 9-5; closed holidays. Free. Phone (441) 292-9052 for the post office.

SESSIONS HOUSE (PARLIAMENT BUILDING) is at 21 Parliament St. Completed in 1819, this building accommodates the Supreme Court and the House of Assembly, which meets from November to May. Building open Mon.-Fri. 9-12:30 and 2-3; closed holidays. Public gallery free. Phone (441) 292-7408.

St. George's Parish (A-6)

At the eastern end of Bermuda, St. George's Parish comprises several islands, the largest of which is St. George's Island. During World War II, when Bermuda became an important base for Atlantic military operations, four U.S. posts were built here.

ST. DAVID'S ISLAND (A-5)

The 650-acre St. David's Island is connected to the mainland by a bridge on St. George's Harbor. Its U.S. naval air station remained active until 1995. The picturesque St. David's Lighthouse has been in continuous use since 1879.

CARTER HOUSE is off Southside Rd. on the former U.S. Navy base. One of the vicinity's oldest buildings, the former dwelling features original cedar beams and a limestone-flanked open fireplace. Two floors display various items relating to the history of whaling, boat building and farming, while native trees and plants surround the restored 17th-century stone structure. Allow 30 minutes minimum. Tues.-Thurs. and Sat. 10-4, Apr.-Oct.; Sat. 10-4, rest of year. Hours may vary; phone ahead. Admission $2. Phone (441) 293-5960.

ST. GEORGE'S (A-5) pop. 1,752

The town of St. George's is about 12 miles (19 km) northeast of Hamilton and is connected with the mainland by causeway. St. George's was once the seat of Bermuda's government, which was organized in 1612. It would be difficult to find a more delightful storybook town. The quaintness of St. George's is reflected in the names of its narrow, twisting lanes: Old Maids Lane, Shinbone Alley, Featherbed Alley and One Gun Alley.

The Old State House on the town square dates to 1620. In April the governor of Bermuda makes his formal call on the Freemasons to collect the annual rent of one peppercorn for their use of the Old State House.

At the head of Duke of Kent Street stand the stone arches and columns of the Unfinished Church, which was intended as a replacement for St. Peter's Church. Politics, budget problems and storm damage caused the roofless cathedral to be abandoned in the 1870s; the mossy ruins are open to the public.

Visitors Service Bureau, St. George's: King's Square, St. George's, Bermuda.

BERMUDA NATIONAL TRUST MUSEUM is at 32 Duke of York St. on King's Square. Housed in the old Globe Hotel, built 1698-1700 and used as a Confederate headquarters during the American Civil War, the museum chronicles the boom era of blockade running, when small steamships ran goods from St. George's to Confederate ports in the United States. A 12-minute videotape presentation gives an overview of Bermuda's history.

Mon.-Sat. 10-4, Apr.-Oct.; Wed.-Sat. 10-4, rest of year. Closed public holidays. Admission $5; $2 (ages 6-18). Combination ticket with Tucker House and Verdmont $10. MC, VI. Phone (441) 297-1423.

BERMUDIAN HERITAGE MUSEUM is on the corner of Duke of York and Water sts. Artifacts, memorabilia and photographs relating to the cultural history of black Bermudians are displayed in a historic building. The highlight of the two-story museum is a model replica of the slave ship *Enterprise*. Allow 30 minutes minimum. Tues.-Sat. 10-3. Admission $4; $2 (senior citizens); free (ages 0-4).

THE DELIVERANCE is on Ordnance Island at King's Square. The ship is a full-size replica of the vessel built to carry the shipwrecked company of the *Sea Venture* to Jamestown, Va., in 1610. This saga of shipwreck and survival on Bermuda is thought to have been the basis of Shakespeare's play "The Tempest." A bronze sculpture of British admiral Sir George Somers also is here. A taped narration is given. Daily 9-5, Apr.-Nov.; closed Good Friday and Easter. Admission $3; $1 (ages 0-11).

FORT ST. CATHERINE is at 15 Coot Pond Rd. The fortification was completed in 1614 and remodeled in the 19th century. Alterations made in the 19th century remodeled the fort into its present shape. Exhibits in restored rooms and passageways include replicas of the British crown jewels and dioramas depicting key events in Bermuda's history. A videotape about forts in Bermuda runs continuously. Allow 30 minutes minimum. Daily 10-4; closed Jan. 1 and Dec. 25-26. Admission $5; $2 (ages 0-11). Phone (441) 297-1920.

KING'S SQUARE is in the heart of town. In front of the 1782 Town Hall are replicas of stocks, a pillory, a whipping post and a ducking stool, once used to punish gossiping and other 18th-century offenses. Several times a week at noon, St. George's town crier appears in period costume to convene a mock tribunal. Market Night, a local street fair, is held on Tuesday evenings in the summer. Phone (441) 297-1532.

ST. GEORGE'S HISTORICAL SOCIETY MUSEUM is on Featherbed Alley at Duke of Kent St. The 18th-century building of Bermuda limestone contains exhibits of Bermuda furniture, documents and pictures. Behind the museum is the Featherbed Alley Printery, which features a working replica of a Gutenberg-style printing press. Museum open Mon.-Fri. 10-4, Apr.-Oct.; Wed. 11-4, Jan.-Mar. Closed holidays. Admission $5; $2 (ages 0-11). Phone (441) 297-0423.

ST. PETER'S ANGLICAN CHURCH is at 33 York St. Founded in 1612, this is thought to be the oldest Anglican church site in continuous use in the Western Hemisphere. The original cedar-frame structure was erected by Bermuda's first governor, Richard Moore. After a hurricane in 1712, parishioners salvaged the altar, pulpit and beams and rebuilt in stone. Galleries and a tower were added in the 1800s. The silver communion set displayed in the vestry was a gift from King William III in 1697. Open daily 10-4:30. Donations. Phone (441) 297-0216.

SOMERS GARDEN is on Duke of York St. Two memorials are dedicated to Adm. Sir George Somers, who established the first British settlement in 1609. Daily 9-5. Free. Phone (441) 297-1532.

TUCKER HOUSE MUSEUM is at 5 Water St. The 1775 residence of Henry Tucker, president of Bermuda's Governor's Council, contains a collection of family silver, china and antiques. During the American Civil War, Joseph Rainey, a former slave from South Carolina and later the first black member of the U.S. House of Representatives, operated a barbershop at the house.

Heritage Bermuda Passport

The Heritage Bermuda Passport offers visitors an opportunity to visit seven of Bermuda's leading cultural attractions in 7 days for the most value. The attractions are: Bermuda Aquarium, Museum and Zoo; Bermuda National Gallery; Bermuda National Trust Museum; Bermuda Underwater Exploration Institute; Fort St. Catherine; Tucker House; and Verdmont.

Bermuda Aquarium, Museum and Zoo
© Andre Jenny

The cost is $20 for adults and $10 for children. The Bermuda Heritage Passport is available online at www.boxoffice.bm and at the Bermuda National Trust's "Trustworthy" gift shops in Hamilton and St. George's.

Allow 30 minutes minimum. Mon.-Sat. 10-4, Apr.-Oct.; Wed.-Sat. 10-4, rest of year. Closed public holidays. Admission $5; $2 (ages 6-18). Combination ticket with Bermuda National Trust Museum and Verdmont $10. Phone (441) 297-0545.

Sandy's Parish (C-1)

Sandy's Parish is a popular picnicking area in rural Bermuda. Sightseers often arrive by ferry from Hamilton and return by bicycle via the Railway Trail. A visitor's bureau on Somerset Road offers maps and brochures describing the Somerset area; it is open Mon.-Fri. 10-3.

Somerset Bridge on Middle Road is believed to be the world's smallest hand-operated drawbridge. The 13-inch gap allows the masts of sailboats to pass.

THE ROYAL NAVAL DOCKYARD is at the n. end of Ireland Island. The dockyard supported British naval operations from the War of 1812 through World War II. Major construction of this "Gibraltar of the West" began in 1809, involving large land reclamations and the labor of thousands of British convicts. The dockyard's great warehouses and fortifications now house shops and restaurants. The 1823 Commissioner's House, one of the oldest surviving examples of prefabricated cast iron construction, has been restored as a museum. Spectacular views are offered at the 6-acre (2-hectare) citadel keep, which features ramparts, underground magazines and a museum.

Dockyard open daily 24 hours; closing times vary for shops and restaurants. Cruise ships dock Apr.-Nov. Visitors can reach the island via a fast ferry or bus from Hamilton. Buses leave Hamilton and the dockyard every 15 minutes. Free. Phone (441) 234-1709.

Bermuda Maritime Museum is inside the fortress keep of the Royal Naval Dockyard. Among eight historic exhibit halls is the Commissioner's House, which showcases local heritage and military history. Bermuda's maritime history—including shipwrecks, shipbuilding, ocean commerce, transport and the dockyard—is chronicled in converted ammunition storehouses on the lower grounds. Boats, ship models, shipwreck artifacts and artillery also are displayed.

Allow 1 hour minimum. Daily 9:30-5; closed Dec. 25. Last admission 1 hour before closing. Admission $10; $8 (ages 61+); $5 (ages 5-15). Phone (441) 234-1418.

Dolphin Quest Bermuda is located at the Bermuda Maritime Museum at the Royal Naval Dockyard. Visitors of all ages can play and swim with dolphins in a variety of fun and educational encounter programs. Swimsuits and towels are required; water footwear is recommended. Programs are offered daily 9:30-4:30; phone for schedule. Closed Dec.

25. Discover Dolphins $150. Encounter $225. Ultimate Adventure $295. Reservations are required. AX, MC, VI. Phone (441) 234-4464 or (800) 248-3316.

SCAUR HILL FORT PARK is off Somerset Rd. on Somerset Island. Built in the 19th century to protect the Royal Naval Dockyard from possible American invasion after the Civil War, the fort was never tested. Its polygonal shape, based on a Prussian design, makes it nearly invisible from land or sea. The view is exceptional, and picnic facilities are available. Daily 8-5; closed Jan 1. and Dec. 25. Free. Phone (441) 236-5902.

Smith's Parish (C-4)

Bermuda's largest nature and wildlife reserve, Spittal Pond, is in Smith's Parish on South Road. The 59-acre (24-hectare) sanctuary harbors many species of waterfowl and plant life. The best season for bird-watching is September through April. The North Nature Reserve at Mangrove Lake across from Pink Beach also preserves various examples of the island's fauna and flora. Both reserves are open daily.

VERDMONT is at 6 Verdmont Ln. This restored mansion, circa 1710, blends Bermudian and New England design elements and is furnished with period antiques. The three-story house remains virtually unchanged, standing as it did some 300 years ago. The grounds offer ocean views and gardens of herbs, old roses and fruit trees typical of the 18th century. Allow 30 minutes minimum. Tues.-Sat. 10-4, Apr.-Oct.; Wed.-Sat. 10-4, rest of year. Closed holidays. Admission $5; $2 (ages 6-18). Combination ticket with Bermuda National Trust Museum and Tucker House $10. Phone (441) 236-7369.

Southampton Parish (D-1)

On the southwest end of the island, Southampton Parish was originally known as Port Royal, perhaps preceding the town of the same name in Jamaica. The area offers a nature reserve and dramatic coastal views.

GIBBS' HILL LIGHTHOUSE is on Lighthouse Rd. This cast-iron lighthouse was built in 1846 and is believed to be the oldest of its kind in the world. The observation platform, reached by a 185-step climb, affords a magnificent view. Food is available. Daily 9-5, Feb.-Dec.; closed Dec. 25-26. Admission $2.50; free (ages 0-4). AX, MC, VI. Phone (441) 238-8069.

Bonaire

Second largest island in the Netherlands Antilles, Bonaire is the least populated and developed of the "ABC" (Aruba, Bonaire and Curaçao) islands. Pink is the island's official color—flamingos congregate here by the thousands—but a dive into Bonaire's turquoise waters reveals a world of rainbow hues. Not only is Bonaire surrounded by coral reefs, it *is* a reef, harboring an incredible variety of sea life. This, coupled with excellent underwater visibility, makes Bonaire one of the foremost diving and snorkeling spots in the world. Strict laws prohibiting spear fishing and the gathering of shells and coral protect the delicate ecological balance of marine life in Bonaire's waters.

History

When discovered by Amerigo Vespucci, sailing for Spain in 1499, Bonaire was the home of the Arawak Indians. Vespucci named the island after the Arawak word *boynare,* which means "low country." The Spaniards sent some of the natives to Spain and others to Hispaniola to work the copper mines; as a result, within 20 years no Arawak Indians were left on Bonaire. Several caves around the island, particularly those at Boca Onima, bear Indian inscriptions that have never been deciphered.

In 1816 control passed to the Dutch, who realized that the abundant sunshine and scant rainfall created ideal conditions for the manufacture of salt through evaporation. It was the Netherlanders who first brought slaves to work the saltpans at the southern end of the island, an endeavor that thrived until abolition curtailed the labor supply and caused production to cease. The area, already agreeable to flamingos, became even more attractive, and the colorful, exotic birds moved into the deserted saltpans to build thousands of nests.

The Cargill Company has revived the practice using an updated version of the old methods. Thanks to a sanctuary set aside from a portion of the old saltpans, the flamingos continue to exist in harmony with people. Bonaire's other industry—in addition to its main staple of tourism—is an oil storage terminal.

Within the Netherlands Antilles (an autonomous region of the Netherlands), Bonaire is administered by an island council and has its own representative to the Crown. Though Dutch is the official language, the majority of islanders prefer the colloquial tongue of Papiamentu. Spanish and English also are widely spoken.

Shopping

Shopping is not Bonaire's main attraction; even so, the island has many good buys. Most of the shops in Kralendijk are on Kaya Grandi, J.A. Abraham Boulevard and Kaya Simon Bolivar. Such stores as Littmans, Atlantis and Island Fashions offer a wide selection of jewelry, watches, clothing and gifts. Cinnamon Art Gallery, a project of the Bonaire Artists Foundations, displays and sells the work of local artists. Shopping opportunities also are available at Les Galeries, a mall in downtown Kralendijk.

The Divi Flamingo Beach Resort & Casino and Plaza Resort Bonaire have shops that offer fashions, jewelry and perfumes. Sand Dollar Plaza near the hotels on the island's north end features shops and an Internet cafe. The Harbourside Mall in Kralendijk has several shops and restaurants. Store hours are Mon.-Sat. 9-noon and 2-6; some stores remain open during lunch when cruise ships are in port. Banking hours are Mon.-Fri. 8:30-4.

Food and Drink

Most of the best restaurants can be found in Kralendijk or in area hotels. Menus vary from fresh seafood and steaks to Chinese, Tex-Mex, Indonesian and Continental cuisine. Waterfront restaurants specialize in lobster, fresh fish, shrimp and, best of all, wonderful views of the sea, sailboats and sunsets. A number of restaurants serve such local specialties as goat stew, iguana, gumbo and a stuffed cheese known as *keshi yena*. Beer, wine and rum drinks complement meals. There is no lack of fresh drinking water since it is distilled from the sea.

Sports and Amusements

Most visitors come to Bonaire for outdoor recreation: Water sports, including scuba diving, snorkeling, kayaking, kiteboarding and windsurfing, head the list of popular activities, along with birdwatching and mountain biking. The island is home to thousands of tropical birds, including parrots, parakeets, pelicans, pearly-eyed thrashers, mangrove cuckoos and hummingbirds. The flamingo colonies are particularly colorful March through May, when the deep-pink parents raise their gray hatchlings. To photograph or observe these shy birds, approach them slowly and quietly. If you come upon any nest areas, do not disturb them. The best birdwatching places are at Pekelmeer in the southern part of the island and Goto Meer Lake in the northwest (the actual flamingo sanctuary is off-limits to visitors).

Diving is popular in Bonaire; the island and its reef are said to be among the top five dive destinations in the world. Of the more than 80 diving locations around the island, more than half are accessible from the shore. The best spots for diving are off the leeward side of the island. Klein Bonaire, an offshore uninhabited island, is an excellent location for underwater exploring. You can make arrangements for snorkeling, scuba diving, kayaking, sailing or deep-sea fishing for marlin, tuna or bonito at several hotels or at the various commercial establishments on the island. Guided snorkeling programs also are available.

Although diving is what Bonaire is primarily known for, the island also offers opportunities for windsurfing, kiteboarding, sea and mangrove kayaking, hiking, mountain biking, landsailing and horseback riding, all of which provide alternative methods of exploring the island's natural beauty. The Riding

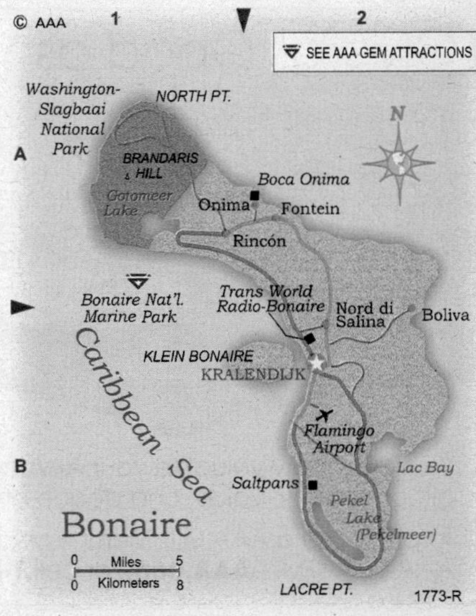

Academy Club at Kunuku Warahama features a beach trail where riders can swim with their horses; phone (599) 560-7949.

Nightlife in Bonaire is mainly centered at the island's hotels, many of which offer theme dinners and live entertainment. Free slide shows are presented weekly at Captain Don's Habitat, Divi Flamingo Beach Resort & Casino and Buddy Dive Resort; more information is available at each establishment. Dancing and live music venues include Karel's and City Café in Kralendijk.

Sightseeing

Guided walking tours of Bonaire's outback, or "kunuku," are available at Rooi Lamoenchi Kunuku, a 56-acre (23-hectare) site highlighting the island's cultural history, flora and fauna. Rooi Lamoenchi, or Lime River, features a restored plantation house, aloe fields, a 1908 dam and marked trails showing such plant varieties as cactus, divi-divi and mesquite. For tour reservations, phone (599) 717-8489.

Bonaire Tours & Vacations features bus tours to destinations across the island, including Washington-Slagbaai National Park, which covers nearly one-fifth of the island; phone (599) 717-8778. Soldachi Tours offers bus and walking tours of Rincon, Bonaire's oldest village, departing on Monday mornings, market days (the first Saturday of the month) and by request; phone (599) 790-5657.

Full- or half-day sailing excursions and cocktail cruises are the perfect way to experience Bonaire's charms and climate; information about charters is available at the Harbour Village, Bonaire Nautico and Plaza marinas.

Transportation

Flights are available every Saturday to Kralendijk's Flamingo Airport via Montego Bay on Air Jamaica from Atlanta, Baltimore (BWI), Boston, Chicago, Fort Lauderdale, Houston, Los Angeles, Miami, Newark, New York (JFK), and Philadelphia. American Eagle flies nonstop from San Juan several times a week with connections to many American Airlines flights. Continental Airlines offers nonstop service from Houston and Newark on weekends. Dutch Antilles Express, the island airline, provides daily service between Aruba, Bonaire, Curaçao and St. Maarten, while Divi Divi provides daily flights between Curacao and Bonaire. There is no regular ferry service between Bonaire and Aruba or Curaçao, but the island is a port of call for cruise ships.

You can tour Bonaire in a day on the island's excellent roads. Several car rental agencies serve the island. Double-cab pickup trucks are ideal for shore diving and tours across Bonaire's desert interior. Taxi rates are fixed, and you should check them before taking a cab.

Fast Facts

POPULATION: 14,203.

AREA: 290 sq km (112 sq mi.).

CAPITAL: Kralendijk.

HIGHEST POINT: 238 m (784 ft.), Mount Brandaris.

LOWEST POINT: Sea level, Caribbean Sea.

TIME ZONE(S): Atlantic Standard.

LANGUAGE: Dutch, Spanish, English and Papiamentu.

GOVERNMENT: Netherlands Antilles, autonomous within the Kingdom of the Netherlands.

UNIT OF CURRENCY: Netherlands Antillean guilder (also called a florin), divided into 100 cents. $1 U.S. = 1.8 guilders. U.S. currency is widely accepted.

ELECTRICITY: 127/220 volts, 50 cycles AC; voltage varies with location.

MINIMUM AGE FOR DRIVERS: 21-25, depending on the rental car agency. U.S. license valid; drive on right.

MINIMUM AGE FOR GAMBLING: 21.

SEAT BELT/CHILD RESTRAINT LAWS: Seat belts and child restraints are required.

HELMETS FOR MOTORCYCLISTS: Required.

HOLIDAYS: Jan. 1; Carnival Rest Day (Jan. or Feb.); Good Friday; Easter; Easter Monday; Queen's Birthday and Rincón Day, Apr. 30; Labor Day, May 1; Ascension Day, May (6th Thurs. after Easter); Bonaire Day, Sept. 6; Christmas, Dec. 25; Boxing Day, Dec. 26.

TAXES: A per-day room tax of $6.50 per person and a 10-15 percent service charge are added to most hotel and restaurant bills. A 5 percent sales tax (NAOB) is assessed on most goods and services. Airport departure tax and security fee $33.40 U.S., interisland tax $5.75 per person over age 2.

IMMIGRATION REQUIREMENTS: Passport or proof of U.S. citizenship and a return or onward ticket are required. No visa needed for stays up to 2 weeks. The U.S. Dept. of Homeland Security requires all U.S. citizens returning from the Caribbean to present a valid passport.

PHONING THE ISLANDS: To call Bonaire from the U.S. or Canada, dial 011 + 599 + 7-digit local number.

FURTHER INFORMATION FOR VISITORS:

Tourism Corporation Bonaire
80 Broad Street, Suite 3202
New York, NY 10004
(212) 956-5912
(800) 266-2473

Tourism Corporation Bonaire, Kralendijk
Kaya Grandi 2
Kralendijk, Bonaire
Netherlands Antilles
(599) 717-8322

Points of Interest

See map page 101.

KRALENDIJK (B-1) pop. 2,000

Kralendijk (crawl-en-dike) is the capital of Bonaire. The tropics and the Netherlands meet in this pink and orange town, whose name means "coral dike." North of town along the coast is Boca Onima, a grotto inscribed with Indian drawings. At the northern end of the island is Bonaire's inland lake, Goto Meer, home to great numbers of flamingos. The best time to view these colorful birds is early morning. The chief breeding ground is south at Pekelmeer *(see attraction listing).*

Bonaire Government Tourist Office: Kaya Grandi 2, Kralendijk, Bonaire, Netherlands Antilles; phone (599) 717-8322.

GEM **BONAIRE NATIONAL MARINE PARK** extends around the coast and coral reefs of Bonaire and Klein Bonaire. This unique environment can be explored by scuba diving, snorkeling and kayaking. The park protects the waters around the island from the high-water mark to a depth of 200 feet (60 m); its restrictions and regulations preserve and allow best use of the island's coastline. Obtain a diving guide at dive operations or in local bookstores for a complete list of park guidelines.

Guide service is available. Nature fee tag (good for the calendar year and includes admission to Washington-Slagbaai National Park) $25 (diving); $10 (swimming and other watersports). Phone (599) 717-8444.

DONKEY SANCTUARY-PARADISE SAFARI PARK is adjacent to Flamingo Airport at Airport and Beloit rds., following signs. These pack animals were brought to Bonaire in the 1800s to work the saltpans, and hundreds of their descendants roamed wild, falling prey to disease and car accidents. The sanctuary cares for sick and orphaned donkeys and provides a home for healthy donkeys.

Visitors are encouraged to bring fruit and bread snacks to hand-feed the residents. The park also contains an iguana forest, watchtower and pond area with pink flamingos. Allow 30 minutes minimum. Daily 10-5 (last admission at 4). Admission $6; $3 (ages 0-12). Phone (599) 560-7607.

PEKELMEER SANCTUARY is on the s.w. end of the island. This vast stretch of salt flats is the chief breeding ground for flamingos. As seawater evaporates, the beds turn various shades of pink, matching these birds that choose to nest near towering stacks of salt crystals. The flamingos skillfully construct nests of mud in which they hatch their young during March and April; the birds must be watched from a distance.

Three 30-foot obelisks used as navigational aids by the salt ships of the 1800s still stand, and primitive stone huts of the slaves who once worked the saltpans have been restored. The majority of salt produced in Bonaire today is used in water softeners.

TRANS WORLD RADIO-BONAIRE is n. of Kralendijk at Kaya Amsterdam 3. Once reputed to be the most powerful privately-owned transmitter in the Western Hemisphere, the Christian station now reaches all of the Caribbean and northern South America. TWR broadcasts on 800 AM with programming in Spanish, Portuguese, English, Creole and Maxuci. The local broadcast on 89.5 FM is carried in English and Papiamentu. Tours are available. Phone (599) 717-8800.

WASHINGTON-SLAGBAAI NATIONAL PARK covers the northwest end of the island. The 13,500-acre (5,463-hectare) wildlife sanctuary—a tropical desert landscape of scrub plains, salt flats, beaches and caves—protects many bird and lizard species unique to Bonaire. Two rugged driving trails lead through the former Washington and Slagbaai plantations, which exported goats, cattle, aloe extract, charcoal, salt and divi-divi pods (used in leather tanning).

A hiking trail leads to the top of Mount Brandaris, and other options include the Kasikunda climbing trail and Lagadishi walking trail. Free maps are available at the park entrance. A visitor center features exhibits about the park's flora and fauna, plantation history, geology and archeology. Mountain biking, kayaking, swimming, snorkeling and scuba diving are popular activities; several companies on the island offer transportation and guided tours.

Allow at least 5 hours for the 22-mile (35-km) driving tour, 3 hours for the 15-mile (24-km) tour. Vehicles should have high ground clearance and a spare tire; motorcycles are not allowed. During rain, the dirt roads may become impassable (four-wheel drive vehicles are recommended). Food is available on weekends. The park is open daily 8-5; closed some national holidays. Last admission at 2:45. Nature fee tag (good for the calendar year and includes non-diving admission to Bonaire National Marine Park) $10; $5 (ages 0-11). Phone (599) 788 9015 or (599) 717-8444.

GAMBLING ESTABLISHMENTS

- **Divi Flamingo Beach Resort & Casino** is at J.A. Abraham Blvd. 40. Mon.-Sat. 8 p.m.-2 a.m. Phone (599) 717-8285.

- **Grand Palace Casino at the Plaza Resort Bonaire** is at J.A. Abraham Blvd. 80. Daily 8 p.m.-4 a.m. Phone (599) 717-2500.

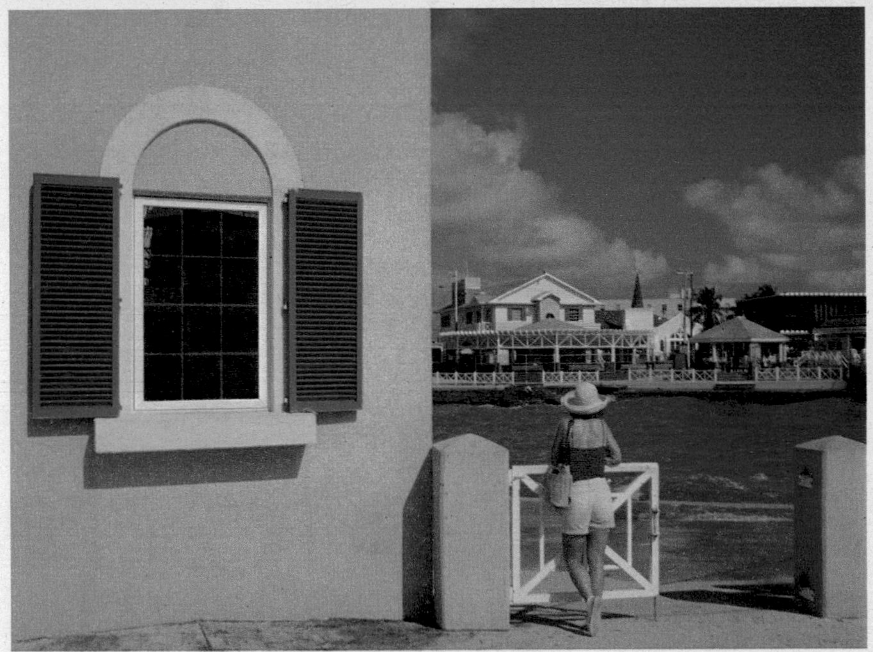

George Town, Grand Cayman / © Richard Cummins / Lonely Planet Images

Cayman Islands

Surrounded by sapphire waters and coral reefs, the Cayman Islands is an outdoor-lover's paradise. Neither a sleepy, secluded destination nor a luxury resort area, the Cayman Islands is the best of both worlds. Its reputation as one of the top diving spots in the Caribbean coupled with its proximity to Florida—the islands are about 480 miles (772 km) due south of Miami—also account for its increasing popularity.

Of the three islands—Grand Cayman, Cayman Brac and Little Cayman—Grand Cayman, 22 miles (35 km) long and 8 miles (13 km) wide, is the largest and the best equipped to handle tourism. Most of the islands' inhabitants live on Grand Cayman near the capital city of George Town.

History

The Cayman Islands were sighted in 1503 by Christopher Columbus while on his fourth and last voyage to the New World. It was Columbus who named them *Las Tortugas* for the large number of turtles in the waters. The present name comes from *caymanas,* a derivation of the Carib Indian name for the crocodile.

Although the islands were ceded to the British by the Treaty of Madrid in 1670, there was no serious attempt to settle them until the early 18th century, when a group from Jamaica moved in; they were recalled 3 years later over problems in protecting them from Spanish pirates. The earliest settlers, however, were believed to be from Oliver Cromwell's army, shipwrecked sailors and refugees fleeing religious persecution in Britain.

With the passing of the days of sail, the Cayman Islands lapsed into isolation until the 1950s, when air travel was introduced. Flights now serve all three islands, making them a readily accessible vacation spot.

1 2 3 4

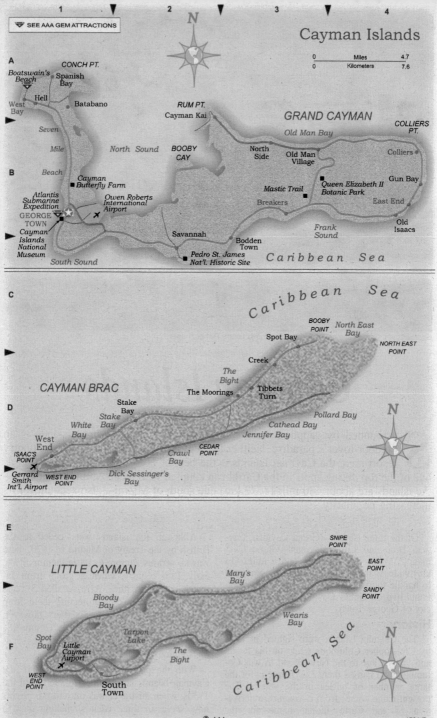

SEE AAA GEM ATTRACTIONS

N

Cayman Islands

0 Miles 4.7
0 Kilometers 7.6

A

CONCH PT.
Boatswain's Beach
Spanish Bay
Hell
West Bay
Batabano
Seven Mile Beach
North Sound
RUM PT.
Cayman Kai
BOOBY CAY

B

Cayman Butterfly Farm
Atlantis Submarine Expedition
Owen Roberts International Airport
GEORGE TOWN
Cayman Islands National Museum
South Sound
Savannah
Pedro St. James Nat'l. Historic Site
Bodden Town

GRAND CAYMAN

Old Man Bay
COLLIERS PT.
North Side
Old Man Village
Colliers
Mastic Trail
Queen Elizabeth II Botanic Park
Gun Bay
Breakers
East End
Old Isaacs
Frank Sound
Caribbean Sea

C

Caribbean Sea
BOOBY POINT
North East Bay
NORTH EAST POINT
Spot Bay
Creek
The Bight
The Moorings
Tibbets Turn

CAYMAN BRAC

D

Stake Bay
Stake Bay
White Bay
West End
ISAAC'S POINT
Gerrard Smith Int'l. Airport
WEST END POINT
Dick Sessinger's Bay
Crawl Bay
CEDAR POINT
Jennifer Bay
Cathead Bay
Pollard Bay
N

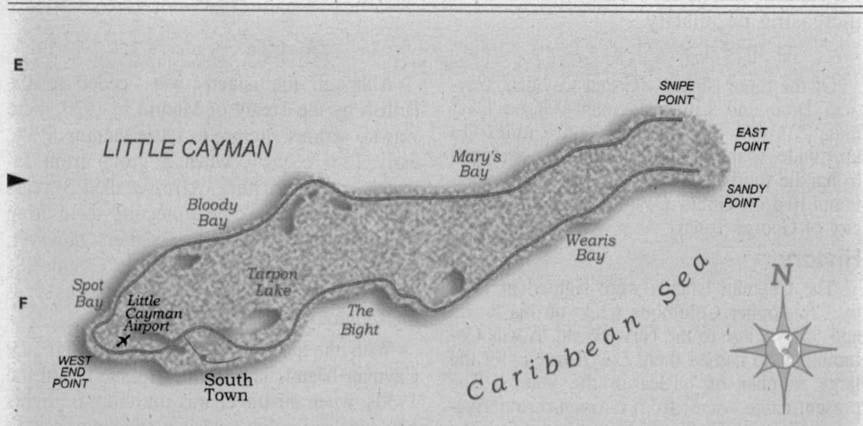

1781-R

Despite independence movements among its neighbors, the Cayman Islands is content with its status as a United Kingdom Overseas Territory. Formerly governed by Jamaica, Cayman is now administered by a governor appointed by the queen.

The governor is president of the Legislative Assembly and chairman of the Cabinet. Electoral districts in the Cayman Islands are George Town, West Bay, Bodden Town, North Side, East End, Cayman Brac and Little Cayman. Every 4 years elections are held to select 15 representatives from these districts, based on each area's population. These representatives form the Legislative Assembly, which is responsible for enacting laws.

The Cabinet consists of five elected ministers, while three members are appointed by the governor—the chief secretary, attorney general and financial secretary. Council ministers are responsible for the administration of the country, advising the governor on policy issues and instituting programs.

Political and economic stability—and tax neutrality—has helped make the Cayman Islands one of the largest financial centers in the world. Laws passed by the Legislative Assembly in the 1960s paved the way for international banking, investments, trusts, insurance, corporate registries and the Cayman Islands Stock Exchange (CSX). The country has no income, corporation, capital gains, estate or gift taxes.

Though the biggest moneymakers are financial services and tourism, some Caymanians still depend upon the sea and soil for their livelihood. Relatively flat with no rivers, the Cayman Islands is covered by the tropical vegetation of mangroves, mangoes and palms. Trade is conducted mainly with Jamaica, the United States and Costa Rica.

Grand Cayman has one of the highest standards of living in the Caribbean. Visitors can explore the island without fear of being approached by street and beach vendors or beggars; the law prohibits such activity.

Shopping

Free-port shopping is plentiful on Cardinal Avenue in George Town. Cameras, perfumes, watches, linens, china and British woolens are sold at reduced prices. Kirk Freeport Plaza contains The Coral Shop, La Parfumerie, Kirk Jewelers and the Waterford/Wedgwood Shop. Treasure Cove, affiliated with Kirk Freeport, is on the opposite side of the street and consists of Fossil, Gucci, Cartier and La Parfumerie II.

Around the corner on Albert Panton Street, Kirk Gallery has such fine china as Royal Doulton and Rosenthal, Hummel figurines and Baccarat crystal. Next to the gallery is Kirk Leather, with products by Cartier, Pierre Balmain, Fendi and Yves Saint Laurent.

Island Plaza, between the shops on Harbour Drive, surrounds an open-air courtyard with a snack area. The mall contains Tropical Traders, with an array of island souvenirs, and jewelry stores Grand Switzerland Diamond Direct, Moissanite Gallery and Island Jewellers.

The English Shoppe, at the intersection of Cardinal Avenue and Harbour Drive, has jewelry and souvenirs among its merchandise. Caymania Freeport, located on Shedden Road, has a vast selection of perfumes and some jewelry. Easily recognized by its flying flags and attractive blue and white buildings, Elizabethan Square is situated on Shedden Road. This complex contains an American Express office and boutiques that offer children's clothing, leather goods, jewelry, sportswear and gift items. Caymania Jewelers is on Edward Street. Bayshore Mall is opposite the cruise ship terminal on South Church Street at Goring Avenue.

The Seven Mile Beach area has several shopping plazas with a wide assortment of goods. These plazas, all on West Bay Road, include Coconut Place, The Falls Shopping Centre, Galleria Plaza, Queen's Court, Seven Mile Shops, West Shore Centre and The Marquee.

Island products make meaningful souvenirs: coral or conch-shell jewelry and sculpture, hammocks, and woven baskets. Antique gold and silver coins and coin jewelry are of high quality and good value in the Cayman Islands. Many shops in Grand Cayman and Cayman Brac offer local arts and crafts. For handicrafts with a unique touch, try Pure Art on South Church Street or the Craft Market on Harbour Drive. The products of the local artistic community can be seen at several galleries, including the National Gallery in Harbour Place, Kennedy/Cayman Fine Art in West Shore and Morgan's Gallery in Galleria Plaza.

Shopping hours are generally Mon.-Sat. 9-5; some hotel shops are open on Sunday. Banking hours are Mon.-Thurs. 9-4, Fri. 9-4:30. Cayman Islands Dollars are available in denominations of $1, $5, $10, $25, $50 and $100.

Food and Drink

Although 90 percent of the islands' food is imported from Florida, noteworthy local dishes include turtle steak, conch, lobster and chowders. Locally grown vegetables and fruit—bananas, plantains, cassava and breadfruit—complement any meal.

Caymanians also enjoy their deep-fried or baked johnny cake, a doughy unseasoned concoction that resembles a heavy dough ball, and patties, pastry stuffed with beef, chicken or vegetables. "Bread Kind" refers to local vegetables such as yams, cassava, breadfruit and potatoes. Pepperpot is a hearty soup that contains *callaloo*, a leafy, spinach-like vegetable, and potatoes seasoned with hot peppers and spices. *Ackee* and saltfish, a dish adopted from Jamaica, is another local favorite. In addition to native fare, there are also restaurants devoted to Chinese, Italian, German, Continental and Thai cuisine. Most dining establishments are in George Town, along Seven Mile Beach or in the hotels.

Desalination provides adequate drinking water, and water is safe in restaurants and hotels. Pasteurized milk is imported from the United States.

Sports and Amusements

Vacationers come to the Cayman Islands to escape the pressures of the outside world; fishing and scuba diving are two means to this end. Rich catches of dolphin, blue marlin, wahoo and yellowfin tuna reward fishing enthusiasts. Little Cayman has bottom fishing outside the reef, bone fishing and fly fishing close to shore and tarpon fishing in a landlocked lake. Half- and full-day deep-sea charters are available. The Cayman Islands International Fishing Tournament takes place in April. For entry information write to the Cayman Islands Angling Club, P.O. Box 30280 SMB, Grand Cayman, Cayman Islands; phone (345) 945-3131.

Due to favorable currents and the proximity of deep open water to the shore, Northwest Point, Rum Point, Southwest Point, South Coast Drop Off and 12-Mile Bank are prime fishing destinations in Grand Cayman. Charter Boat Headquarters, (345) 945-4340, and Bayside Watersports, (345) 949-3200, serve as centralized booking agencies for charter boats in Grand Cayman; trips can be arranged for deep-sea, bottom, reef, bone and tarpon fishing. Marinas that are available to visiting yachtsmen include Cayman Islands Yacht Club and Harbour House Marina, both in the North Sound, and Morgan's Harbour Marina in West Bay.

Grand Cayman's trade winds coupled with water temperatures that average in the 80s provide excellent opportunities for windsurfing. Morritt's Tortuga Club & Resort at East End boasts good winds and calm waters inside the reef area. Winds blow 15-25 knots (17-29 mph) in the winter and 10-20 knots (12-23 mph) in the summer; lessons and rentals are available from Cayman Windsurf at the resort. A windsurfing regatta is held at the Tortuga Club every January. With constant breezes blowing 6-12 knots (7-14 mph), Grand Cayman is a prime place to learn how to windsurf.

Parasailing is available on Grand Cayman; inquire at Red Sail Sports (located within most hotels) for information on equipment rentals. A few operators offer water skiing. Sunfish, Hobie Cat and Jet Ski rentals are available at many hotels. Sailing regattas are scheduled by the local sailing club throughout the year, generally in conjunction with public holidays.

Landlubber activities range from cave exploring to sunbathing. Most of the caves that can be explored are on Cayman Brac. The only caves accessible on Grand Cayman are the Pirate's Caves in Bodden Town.

Birdwatching opportunities abound on all three islands. The Grand Cayman and Cayman Brac parrots are found only in these islands, which also are home to more than 180 other resident and migratory species.

Seven Mile Beach, where 90 percent of the resorts and water sports operations are found, lures swimmers and sun worshipers to the west coast of Grand Cayman. One of the longest unbroken white sand beaches in the Caribbean, Seven Mile Beach is actually about 5.5 miles (9 km) long. The beach received its name from the fact that it is 7 miles (11 km) from the northwest to the southwest point of Grand Cayman.

Colliers Point on the east end of the island also has a lovely beach. Old Man Bay and Cayman Kai, on the north coast of Grand Cayman, are secluded beaches with golden sands that are occasionally punctuated by exquisite beach houses. Smith Cove, on the south coast off South Church Street, is known for swimming and snorkeling rather than for a beach. Picnic tables are available, and shaded areas provide respite from the sun.

Rum Point, on the north central tip of the island, is a park area that overlooks the North Sound. Visitors can relax on the beach, swim or snorkel in the shallow waters and rest in hammocks shaded by casuarina trees, also known as Australian pines. Red Sail Sports operates a full-service water sports and dive facility; activities include diving, jet skiing, snorkeling, sailing, windsurfing and water skiing. A restaurant, snack bar, changing facilities, hammocks, picnic tables and showers also are available.

Hikers are attracted to the eastern tip of the island. Also popular with hikers is Cayman Brac, where a trek along the Bluff is rewarded with a view of the tropical wilderness where 150 species of resident and migratory birds can be spotted. A trail used primarily as a cow path leads to the caves that honeycomb the Bluff.

Many hotels on Grand Cayman and Cayman Brac are equipped with tennis courts. Temporary health club memberships are offered by World Gym, (345) 949-5132, off West Bay Road; The Fitness Connection, (345) 949-8485, just south of George Town on Glen Eden Road; and Kings Sports Centre on Crew Road, (345) 946-5464 or (345) 949-0555, which also features squash courts and a rock-climbing wall.

Two types of golf can be played at the Jack Nicklaus designed Britannia Golf Course—regulation play on a nine-hole course and a Caymanian version on an 18-hole course. The Ritz-Carlton at Seven Mile Beach has a challenging nine-hole course for the exclusive use of its guests; designed by Greg Norman, the course is situated along a scenic saltwater lagoon.

The Truman Bodden Sports Complex and Stadium in George Town features a variety of amateur and professional sporting events.

While water sports dominate the action in the Cayman Islands, most hotels offer some form of evening entertainment. Ports of Call, the bar at The Wharf restaurant at the south end of Seven Mile Beach, is known for its spectacular ocean view. Next Level, Obar and District 6 are popular discos/nightclubs.

The Cayman National Cultural Foundation presents a variety of events from October to June, and the Cayman Drama Society stages productions at the Prospect Playhouse on Shamrock Road year-round. Top-name entertainers perform at the Lion's Centre on Crewe Road in the Red Bay area. Movies are shown regularly at the Marquee Cinema on Lawrence Boulevard just off West Bay Road, and at Hollywood Theatres, in Camana Bay.

Island festivities peak when the Cayman Islands honors its earliest settlers during Pirates Week in November. Celebrations include colorful costumes, parades, treasure hunts and a lively reenactment, when a group of Cayman residents costumed as rogues and wenches board a replica of a pirate ship and approach the harbor. The landing turns into a mock battle with those who ruled the sea lanes more than 200 years ago.

The Cayman Jazz Fest draws international musicians and jazz fans to Grand Cayman in December. Other island events include Batabano, a festival with costume parades and street dances held during the first week of May. An open house and garden party at Government House and a parade are highlights of the Queen's Birthday celebration in mid-June.

Several publications provide information about local events, activities and points of interest. Two island newspapers, *The Caymanian Compass* and *Cayman Net News,* are published Monday through Friday. *Key to Cayman,* a complimentary magazine distributed at hotels, contains a wide assortment of visitor information. *Horizons,* a free magazine published bimonthly by Cayman Airways, can be found at retail establishments and other points throughout Grand Cayman. *What's Hot* is a monthly feature magazine filled with an up-to-date listing of activities; it is available free of charge at many stores.

Scuba Diving

Scuba diving is the Cayman Islands' claim to fame: It is said that these islands are the most popular diving destination in the world. The three islands that make up the Cayman Islands are actually the tips of three undersea mountains surrounded by vertical drop-offs that plunge thousands of fathoms to the bottom of the sea. The Cayman Trench drops to a depth of 25,216 feet.

The Cayman walls encircle the Cayman Islands. The drop-offs begin at 55-60 feet and provide spectacular underwater scenery. A barrier reef encircles Grand Cayman in the shallower depths preceding the walls. Visibility can range from 125 to 200 feet, and conditions for underwater photography are excellent. Surrounded by colorful corals and sponges, the wall at Bloody Bay on Little Cayman begins its drop-off at 18 feet, then plunges to a reported 6,000 feet.

Diving close to the shore often eliminates the need for boats. Sometimes only a mask, snorkel and fins are needed to explore shallow-water reefs. An even more intensive diving experience is available on live-aboard dive boats, which offer divers access to the best sites around the islands. A guided trip with a qualified dive master is recommended. Among the many reputable dive operators are Bob Soto's Reef Divers, (345) 949-2022; Divetech, (345) 946-5658; Don Foster's Dive Cayman, (345) 945-5132; Ocean Frontiers, (345) 947-0000; Red Sail Sports, (345) 945-5965; and Sunset Divers, (345) 949-7111.

All divers must possess a certification card from one of the international diving schools before any island dive shop will rent scuba gear. Most dive operations offer beginning divers a short "resort course" that provides enough familiarity with the equipment to allow them to take supervised, shallow diving trips. Harming or collecting coral or other marine life is illegal, as is spear fishing. A recompression chamber at George Town Hospital is staffed daily 24 hours; for emergencies phone 911.

The Cayman Islands has numerous recorded shipwrecks but divers are only able to see about a dozen. With more than 240 known diving locations it is impossible to list each one, but following are some of the most popular dive sites surrounding Grand Cayman.

The waters off the north side of the island include Eagle Ray Pass, an area of narrow canyons inhabited by eagle rays, barracudas, tarpons and sometimes sharks. For experienced divers only, Grand Canyon consists of giant canyons up to 150 feet wide that were formed by collapsed reefs. Hepp's Pipeline, with depths ranging from 20 to 60 feet, has two mini-walls that provide a home for stingrays and tropical fish. Divers can feed and pet friendly stingrays in 12 feet of water at Stingray City, considered one of the world's best shallow dive sites.

The west side of Grand Cayman also contains several renowned underwater sites. Aquarium, a shallow dive considered ideal for beginners, has tame parrotfish and angelfish that provide excellent photographic opportunities. Experienced divers will want to visit Big Tunnels, where two tunnels lead downward through a reef to open up on the Cayman Wall; one tunnel can be entered at 80 feet, while the other can be entered at 160 feet. At Bonnie's Arch, extraordinary marine life and spectacular arch formations can be viewed. Trinity Caves, a wall dive with dramatic caves and arches, features such sea life as sponges, black coral, sea turtles and eagle rays.

East coast spots favored by divers include Grouper Grotto, situated just before the 6,000 foot drop-off at the Cayman Trench. The Maze is a series of caverns, tunnels and archways that twist through an elaborate coral formation extending 500 feet along the East End Wall. Three Sisters is composed of three massive pinnacles of coral named Agnes, Bertha and Claire; each measures about 70 feet in diameter.

The south side of Grand Cayman also has many underwater wonders. Among them are Japanese Gardens, a series of narrow passages containing beautiful elkhorn coral formations and tropical fish, and Red Bay Gardens, known for striking elkhorn and antler coral, colorful caves and wide areas of sand.

Devil's Grotto has numerous caverns and grottoes as well as a long tunnel that leads to a room. Eden Rock, a good spot for inexperienced divers, consists of a coral cliff inhabited by tropical fish. Parrot's Reef, only 30 yards off the park's dock, contains the wreck of the *Anna Marie* and teems with parrotfish that swim among coral heads and sponges. About 150 yards from the dock, Polly's Perch is a wall dive that starts at 70 feet.

Many shipwrecks lay in the waters off the islands, such as the *Balboa,* a Norwegian freighter that sank off the George Town shore in the 1932 hurricane. The *Cali* is a sunken cargo freighter near George Town harbor that houses such marine life as barracudas, parrotfish and lobsters.

Oro Verde, off the coast of Seven Mile Beach, is the wreckage of an old cargo vessel sunk purposely in 1980 for the enjoyment of underwater explorers. Off Cayman Brac in 1996, the Russian frigate *Capt. Keith Tibbetts* was sunk to form an artificial reef. The MV *Ridgefield,* which ran aground on the coral reef off Gun Bay, attracts divers and snorkelers. Other shipwrecks include the *Doc Polson* wreck, a barge off Grand Cayman's northwest corner, and the wreck of the *David Nicholson,* a vessel in 65 feet of water deliberately sunk offshore from the Sunset House Dive Resort.

Sightseeing

A driving tour of Grand Cayman runs south from George Town along the South Sound coastal road that merges with the Bodden Town Road. Lined with tall casuarina trees, the route travels through the historic outer districts, which were the heart of the island in the 17th and 18th centuries. Once a thriving settlement, Prospect was destroyed by a hurricane in 1846, leaving only a monument erected on the site of an 18th-century fort that was built to protect against Spanish pirates.

About 3 miles (5 km) east of Prospect in Savannah, the Old Savannah Schoolhouse has been restored to reflect a typical 1950s Caymanian school.

Two cannons guard the entrance to Bodden Town, the first capital of the Cayman Islands, where you can explore Gun Square, the Slave Wall and the Pirates' Caves. It is believed that pirates once hid in the caves, an extensive maze of tunnels that eventually connects with underwater caves. Across the street is a cemetery where pirates are supposedly buried. Queen Victoria's Monument, erected by residents to commemorate the queen, is in the center of Bodden Town. Also along the way is caymanite, a multicolored rock found only in these islands.

The road traveling east out of Bodden Town is bordered on the left by a bird sanctuary, where such species as heron, snowy egret and black-necked stilt can be viewed at dawn and dusk. About a mile (1.6 km) before East End are the Blowholes: As the incoming surf surges against the shore, water is forced through crevices in the coral rock, shooting more than 60 feet into the air to create a geyser effect.

Just northeast of the village of East End is Gun Bay, the scene of the "Wreck of the Ten Sails" in 1794. British sailors from the *Cordelia* tried to warn their merchant fleet after running aground; however, the other nine ships misinterpreted their warning and followed onto the reef. Islanders were recognized by King George III for saving all lives aboard. Folk stories claim that the islands were granted freedom from taxation as a reward. The two cannons in Bodden Town are from the wreck, and an anchor that protrudes from the water off East End's shore is believed to be from one of the ships. A monument and scenic overlook commemorating this maritime disaster was unveiled by Queen Elizabeth II in 1994. The coastal road continues through Old Man Bay Village and ends at Rum Point.

You also can drive to Boatswain's Beach on the rugged northwest coast. The forbidding "Hell" coral formations are near West Bay. The coral, which is more than 1.5 million years old, is colored by black algae and caymanite. Even though the coral limestone resembles charred ruins, folklore claims that the spot received its name in the 1930s when a visiting official from England fired at a bird near the formations, missed, and said "Oh, hell." Tourists have made the post office of this tiny town popular by getting their postcards and letters canceled with the stamp of "Hell, Grand Cayman."

Sightseeing tour buses depart from hotels on Seven Mile Beach and head to George Town. The 2-hour tours include stops at Hell and Boatswain's Beach, Tortuga Rum Company bakery and store, and a conch-shell house; the full-day tours also include stops at Cayman Kai and the Pirate's Caves. Cruises along Seven Mile Beach also are available. A walking tour guidebook of the historical districts of West Bay and George Town can be purchased from the National Trust office at Dart Park in South Sound; phone (345) 949-0121.

Several boats offer afternoon and dinner cruises, and glass-bottom boat rides can be arranged at many resorts and water sports outlets. Picnicking, shelling, snorkeling and swimming are other popular activities.

A popular way to spend a day and to experience the Cayman Islands is to participate in a North Sound Beach lunch/snorkeling trip. The all-day boat excursion features a native-style lunch prepared by the captain; diving for a conch (except during off-season, May through October) to be used later as part of the meal; and three snorkeling stops, including Stingray City. These trips, available from more than 20 captains, can be booked through Bayside Watersports at Morgan's Harbour, (345) 949-3200; Charter Boat Headquarters on Birchtree Hill Road in West Bay, (345) 945-4340; and through Captain Marvin's, (345) 945-6975. Half-day excursions without lunch also are offered.

The smaller islands are less developed than Grand Cayman, but they provide a welcome change of pace and an opportunity to see the islands in a more natural state. The dramatic limestone cliffs of Cayman Brac, 89 miles (143 km) east of Grand Cayman, are a popular destination for hikers and birdwatchers. A 2-mile nature trail offers glimpses of frigate birds, boobies and the rare Cayman Brac parrot. The island also offers many opportunities for fishing, scuba diving and exploring, with many hidden caverns reputed to have once been the hideouts of pirates and their treasures.

Snorkeling, scuba diving and deep-sea fishing also are excellent on Little Cayman, 5 miles (8 km) northwest of Cayman Brac. The diving at Bloody Bay Wall has been described as spectacular. A haven for birdwatchers, the island is home to one of the largest breeding colonies of red-footed boobies in the Caribbean. Road signs advise: "Iguanas Have the Right of Way; Drive Slowly."

Transportation

Cayman Airways, the national flag carrier, provides daily direct flights from Miami to Grand Cayman's Owen Roberts International Airport, as well as regular service from Tampa, Houston and New York. American Airlines offers daily flights from Miami, US Airways has flights from Charlotte and Delta Air Lines provides daily service from Atlanta. Saturday flights are available on Continental Airlines from Newark and Northwest Airlines from Detroit.

Air Jamaica and Cayman Airways regularly fly between Grand Cayman and Kingston, Jamaica. Grand Cayman also is a leading port of call for cruise ships, serving an average of 13 vessels per week.

Interisland service to Cayman Brac's Gerrard Smith International Airport is provided by Cayman Airways. Island Air provides charter flights between the Sister Islands. Cayman Airways Express provides day trips to Cayman Brac and Little Cayman leaving from Grand Cayman. Flights from Grand Cayman to Little Cayman take approximately 40 minutes. Service from Grand Cayman to Cayman Brac is 18 minutes by jet, and 45 minutes by propeller plane. There is no jet service to Little Cayman.

It is best to rent a car if your accommodations are not in the Seven Mile Beach area. Major and local car rental agencies serve the island. Hertz, (345) 949-2280, offers discounts to AAA members. Driving permits are issued upon presentation of a valid driver's license and cost $7.50. Speed limits are 40 mph on West Bay Road in the Seven Mile Beach area and 25 mph in George Town; in other parts of the island, speed limits range from 25 to 50 mph. Driving is on the left side of the road. A seat belt law is in effect.

Independent, privately-owned minibuses run between West Bay Road and George Town; buses stop at the side of the road by white circular bus stop signs. At Kirk Gallery on Albert Panton Street in George Town, visitors can catch the bus back to the resort area; a bus depot is next to the library. Roughly, buses run about every half-hour between 7 a.m. and 9 or 10 p.m.

Taxis, motor scooters and bicycles are available on both Grand Cayman and Cayman Brac. Taxis, often driven by islanders versed in local folklore and history, can be chartered for island tours. Jeeps are available on Little Cayman, where bicycling also is very popular. Taxis do not have meters, as rates are fixed by the government. Visitors must be at least 17 to rent a scooter, and a scooter permit is required. The permit, which can be purchased for $10, does not entitle you to drive a car; if you plan to do both, two permits are necessary. Use caution when renting scooters or bicycles; although the island is relatively flat, traffic can be heavy in George Town and on portions of West Bay Road.

Fast Facts

POPULATION: 53,172.

AREA: 259 sq km (100 sq mi.).

CAPITAL: George Town, Grand Cayman.

HIGHEST POINT: 43 m (141 ft.), The Bluff.

LOWEST POINT: Sea level, Caribbean Sea.

TIME ZONE(S): Eastern Standard.

LANGUAGE: English.

GOVERNMENT: British Overseas Territory.

UNIT OF CURRENCY: Caymanian dollar, divided into 100 cents. $1 U.S. = approx. .8 Cayman Islands dollar. U.S. currency is widely accepted.

ELECTRICITY: 110 volts, 60 cycles AC.

MINIMUM AGE FOR DRIVERS: 21-25, depending on the rental car agency. Local license ($7.50 U.S.) required; drive on left.

SEAT BELT/CHILD RESTRAINT LAWS: Seat belts are required for all passengers.

HELMETS FOR MOTORCYCLISTS: Required.

HOLIDAYS: New Year's Day; National Heroes' Day, Jan. 28; Ash Wednesday; Good Friday; Easter Monday; Discovery Day, May (3rd Mon.); Queen's Birthday, June (2nd Mon.); Constitution Day, July (1st Mon.); Remembrance Day, Nov. (closest Mon. to Nov. 11); Christmas, Dec. 25; Boxing Day, Dec. 26. Cayman holidays falling on a weekend are legally observed the following Monday.

TAXES: A 10 percent room tax and 10-15 percent service charge are added to most hotel bills.

IMMIGRATION REQUIREMENTS: Passport and a return or onward ticket are required. No visa needed for stays up to 6 months. The U.S. Dept. of Homeland Security requires all U.S. citizens returning from the Caribbean to present a valid passport.

PHONING THE ISLANDS: To call the Cayman Islands from the U.S. or Canada, dial 1 + 345 + the 7-digit local number.

FURTHER INFORMATION FOR VISITORS:

Cayman Islands Department of Tourism
Doral Centre
8300 N.W. 53rd St., Suite 103
Miami, FL 33166
(305) 599-9033

Cayman Islands Department of Tourism, George Town
Regatta Office Park
Windward 3, West Bay Rd.
P.O. Box 67
George Town, Grand Cayman
Cayman Islands KY1-1102
(345) 949-0623

See color ad p. 395.

Points of Interest

See map page 106.

Cayman Brac

Cayman Brac (brac means "bluff" in Gaelic) is named for the limestone ridge running the length of the island, rising to a height of 140 feet (43 m). The 3,500 residents of this 14-square-mile (36 sq-km) island call themselves "Brackers."

The 180-acre (73-hectare) Brac Parrot Reserve is a protected breeding area of the native Cayman Brac parrot.

CAYMAN BRAC MUSEUM is at Stake Bay on Cotton Tree Bay Road. This small museum in a former customs office displays artifacts pertaining to the island's seafaring history and Brackers' daily lives. Mon.-Fri. 9-noon and 1-4, Sat. 9-noon. Free. Phone (345) 948-2622.

Grand Cayman

Covering about 76 square miles (197 sq km), Grand Cayman is the most developed of the island group. The majority of resorts and diving facilities are found along Seven Mile Beach, where portions of the movie "The Firm" were filmed.

GEORGE TOWN (B-1) pop. 20,626

Named for King George III of England, George Town is the capital of the Cayman Islands. It is a bustling city that serves as a center for shopping, banking, tourism and other businesses.

The post office on Cardinal Avenue is a busy meeting place where locals exchange news; the hundreds of boxes on the outside of the building reflect the fact that there is no home or office mail delivery in Grand Cayman. Just 2 miles (3.2 km) from the airport, George Town is the gateway to Seven Mile Beach, which stretches north to West Bay. The Royal Watler Cruise Terminal opened to passengers in 2006.

Distinctive Caymanian architecture, with its ornate hand-carved trim and zinc roofs, adds a gingerbread character that can be seen in Pantonville, where three original houses have been restored.

George Town's architectural landmarks include the Elmslie Memorial Church, built by Captain Rayal Bodden, a skilled shipbuilder whose signature timber roof framing is a structural highlight; the Peace Memorial, which once served as a town hall; the Clock Tower, built in honor of King George V; and the George Town Public Library, which has elaborate ceilings and houses an assortment of English novels.

A plaque on the corner of Fort Street and North Church Street commemorates the area where Fort George once stood. Just a small portion of the wall remains. The coral-rock fort, which guarded the harbor's entrance, was constructed in the late 1700s to defend the island against the Spanish.

When the legislature is not in session, the sergeant-at-arms is frequently available to provide tours through the Legislative Assembly building on Fort Street. Visitors are permitted to observe the legislature in session from the upstairs gallery; appropriate dress is required.

Cayman Islands Department of Tourism: Regatta Office Park, Windward 3, West Bay Rd., George Town, Grand Cayman, Cayman Islands; phone (345) 949-0623. Tourist information is available at all cruise ship terminals and at Owen Roberts International Airport.

Self-guiding tours: A pamphlet describing a self-guiding historic walking tour of central George Town is available at The National Trust office at Dart Park in South Sound and at the gift shop in the Cayman Islands National Museum.

GEM ***ATLANTIS*** **SUBMARINE EXPEDITION** departs from 131 S. Church St. at the George Town harbor. This 65-foot-long, 48-passenger underwater vessel cruises along the Cayman Wall at a maximum depth of 100 feet (30 m), offering excellent views of coral formations and sea creatures.

Other tours include a shallow water experience aboard the semi-submarine *Seaworld Explorer*. Passengers sit 5 feet below the surface in an air-conditioned glass observatory to view the *Cali* shipwreck, coral reefs and abundant marine life. The 1-hour tour includes a diver fish-feeding show at Cheeseburger Reef. *Atlantis* night trips also are available.

Allow 1 hour, 30 minutes minimum. Morning and afternoon trips depart Mon.-Sat. A 10-minute ferry ride transports passengers between the dock and the submarine for the 45-minute tour. *Atlantis* fare $89; $69 (ages 13-17); $59 (ages 4-12). *Seaworld Explorer* fare $39; $19 (ages 2-12). Children under 36 inches tall are not permitted on *Atlantis*. Reservations are required. AX, MC, VI. Phone (345) 949-7700.

GEM **BOATSWAIN'S BEACH** is 8 mi. (13 km) n. via Seven Mile Beach Rd. to 825 North West Point Rd. in West Bay. Green sea turtles once were a mainstay of the Cayman economy, but their numbers in the wild dwindled toward extinction. This marine park is home to some 16,000 turtles representing five of the seven known species, including the endangered Ridley turtle. The park also includes an interactive turtle area, a snorkel lagoon and an aviary, along with a Caymanian heritage street with craft vendors and local food.

Visitors should be aware that sea turtle products purchased in the Cayman Islands cannot be taken home; U.S. customs officials will confiscate any items brought into the country. Food is available. Allow 2 hours minimum. Park open daily 8:30-4:30; closed Dec. 25. "Wet experience" $55; $25 (ages 2-12). "Dry experience" $18; $9 (ages 2-12). AX, DS, MC, VI. Phone (345) 949-3894.

CAYMAN BUTTERFLY FARM is on Lawrence Blvd. at West Bay Rd. across from Seven Mile Beach. More than 40 species from around the world are housed in a tropical garden, where tour guides provide information about butterfly habits. Exhibits trace the metamorphosis of the butterfly from larva to chrysalis to adult. Food is available. Allow 30 minutes minimum. Daily 9-4. Last tour departs 30 minutes before closing. Admission (good for 7 days) $12; $7 (ages 4-18). Phone (345) 946-3411.

CAYMAN ISLANDS NATIONAL MUSEUM is on Harbour Dr. at the waterfront. Cultural and historic exhibits are displayed in the 19th-century Old Courts Building. Highlights of the 4,000-item collection include natural history specimens, coins, rare documents and a traditional catboat. A children's gallery offers interactive exhibits. **Note:** The museum sustained damage from Hurricane Ivan and is expected to reopen in early 2009. Phone ahead to verify schedule. Allow 30 minutes minimum. Mon.-Fri. 9-5, Sat. 10-2; closed Good Friday, Dec. 25 and first Mon. of the month. Last admission 30 minutes before closing. Admission $5; $2.50 (ages 7-17 and senior citizens). Phone (345) 949-8368.

NORTH SIDE (B-3) pop. 1,079

Once the most remote area of Grand Cayman, the North Side district preserves an ancient forest and a footpath used by islanders for two centuries. On the northern coast is Rum Point, named for the cargo barrels that floated ashore after a shipwreck. Nearby is Stingray City, where divers can swim with hundreds of docile stingrays.

MASTIC TRAIL is s. of Old Man Bay, paralleling Frank Sound Rd. A 200-year-old footpath winds through this 2 million-year-old woodland reserve in the dense interior of the island. The National Trust offers 3-hour hiking tours of the 2-mile (3-km) trail where visitors can view native flora and fauna, including the Grand Cayman parrot and other unique bird species. An ancient yellow mastic tree stands at the midpoint of the trail, which traverses rocks, swamps, high woods and farmland.

Comfortable hiking shoes, drinking water, insect repellent and sunscreen are advised. Hiking tours are not recommended for senior citizens or children under 6. Guided hikes depart Wed. at 9 a.m. and are limited to 15 persons. National Trust fee $15 for members, $20 for non-members. Reservations are required. Phone (345) 947-2084.

QUEEN ELIZABETH II BOTANIC PARK is off Frank Sound Rd. at 367 Botanic Rd. The 65-acre (26-hectare) park is dedicated to preserving the island's native plants and animals. Along the Woodland Trail, visitors can view labeled trees and plants representing 55 percent of the island's native flora. The Color Garden displays flowering plants from around the world. The Heritage Garden features a traditional wooden cottage, sand garden, fruit trees and crops. Aquatic birds including the West Indian whistling duck reside at the lake, and blue iguanas roam the park.

Allow 1 hour, 30 minutes minimum. Daily 9-5:30; closed Good Friday and Dec. 25. Last admission 1 hour before closing. Admission $10; free (ages 0-12). AX, DS, MC, VI. Phone (345) 947-9462.

RECREATIONAL ACTIVITIES

Kayaking

- **Cayman Kayaks** departs from the Kaibo dock in Cayman Kai. Guided 1.5 to 2-hour eco-adventure tours explore the mangroves, bird-nesting areas and coral reefs of the Cayman coastline. Tours are offered daily. Phone (345) 926-4467.

SAVANNAH (C-2)

Savannah was settled in the 18th century by William Eden, who built a stone meeting house and residence named Pedro St. James. The "Pedro Castle" was the only building on the island to survive the hurricane of 1785. The house stood through two centuries of Caribbean storms; it was destroyed by fire in 1967. Pedro St. James has been restored as a national historic site.

PEDRO ST. JAMES NATIONAL HISTORIC SITE is off the South Sound coastal road following signs. The 8-acre (3-hectare) site contains a restoration of one of the island's oldest structures, a 1780 plantation house built by English settler William Eden. Revered as the "Birthplace of Democracy in the Cayman Islands," the house was the 1831 meeting site of residents who established government by representation. The three-story manor features period Caribbean furniture. A multimedia theater offers a 24-minute film about the "Pedro Castle."

Food is available. Allow 1 hour minimum. Daily 9-5; closed Dec. 25. Films are shown on the hour from 10-4. Admission $10; free (ages 0-12). AX, DS, MC, VI ($10). Phone (345) 947-3329.

Little Cayman

Ten miles (16 km) long and two miles (3 km) at its widest point, Little Cayman is the smallest and flattest of the island group. Game fishing, scuba diving and birdwatching attract thousands of visitors, but Little Cayman boasts fewer than 170 permanent residents. Most live near Blossom Village on the island's southernmost tip, where turtle fisherman first settled in the 1600s. The Booby Pond Nature Reserve is home to 20,000 red-footed boobies, considered the largest breeding colony in the Caribbean. More than 200 other species of resident and migratory birds may be sighted on the island.

The National Trust House in Blossom Village offers information about Little Cayman's natural and historic sites.

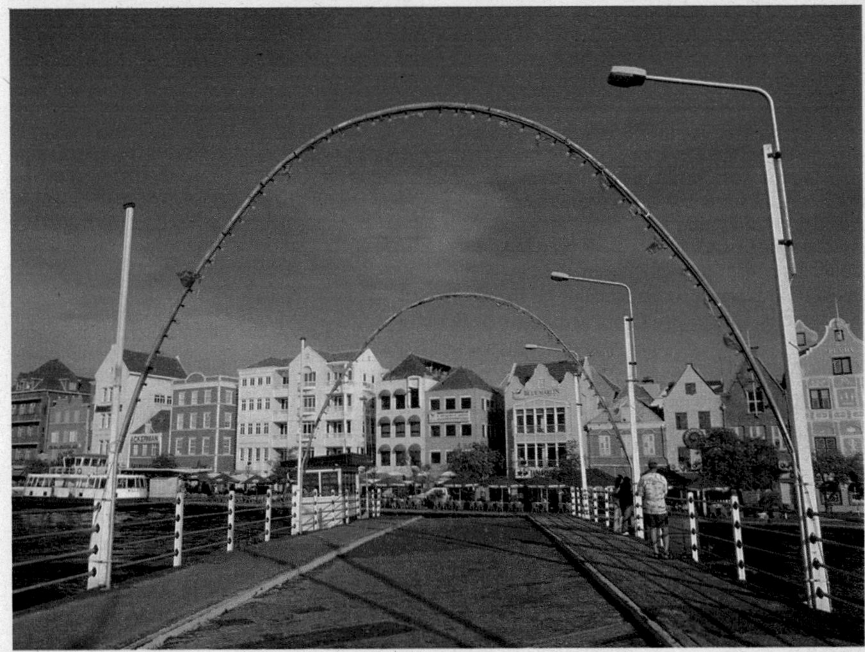

Queen Emma Bridge, Willemstad / Altrendo Travel / Getty Images

Curaçao

Largest of the Netherlands Antilles, Curaçao lies 35 miles (61 km) off the coast of Venezuela. Small hills throughout the island offer a variety of scenery, but vegetation is sparse because of slight rainfall. Willemstad, the capital, is a bright mosaic of narrow streets lined with 18th-century Dutch-Caribbean houses topped with red tile roofs. Each house is painted a pastel shade, which lends a storybook Dutch charm.

History

Curaçao shares much of its history with the other Dutch islands. Discovered in 1499 by Alonso de Ojeda, a lieutenant of Christopher Columbus, the island was named for the tribe of Caiquetios, an Arawak-speaking group which lived here. A more popular legend claims that Curaçao's name was derived from the Spanish word *curación,* meaning "cure," when several malarial sailors miraculously recovered from scurvy after an extended visit to the island. It is pronounced *cure-a-sow.*

The initial Spanish colonizers were displaced early in the 17th century by Dutch settlers, who made the islands flourishing centers of trade. One of the first governors was Peter Stuyvesant, later governor of another island colony: New Amsterdam on Manhattan Island. Sephardic Jews fleeing the Spanish Inquisition sought refuge on the island among the tolerant Dutch and would make up half of the white population by the 18th century. The Netherlands Antilles changed hands several times in the early 19th century, but by 1815 the Dutch were here to stay.

Except for a brisk slave trade that ended in 1863, the 19th century was less than prosperous for Curaçao and its sister islands. Then the discovery in 1914 of oil in Venezuela made their position astride the trade routes important. Curaçao's economic mainstays today are banking, tourism and refinery facilities. It also has several large local industries, including Senior & Co. Curaçao Liqueur; a battery manufacturer; the largest nonmilitary drydock in the hemisphere; and cigarette, soap and paint factories.

Autonomous within the Kingdom of the Netherlands since 1954, the Netherlands Antilles are administered by a governor appointed by the Queen and a legislative and executive council for each island. One of the languages spoken on Curaçao is Papiamentu, a blend of Portuguese, Dutch, Spanish and English with African dialects. In this colorful language, *Dushi Kòrsou* means "Beloved Curaçao."

Shopping

Because of the low import duty on most goods, Curaçao is an excellent shopping center; prices are often lower than in the products' countries of origin. Duty free shops sell perfume, electronics and jewelry. Local handicrafts also make popular souvenirs.

Curaçao's foremost shopping promenades are the Gomezplein and the Heerenstraat in Willemstad. Designed for pedestrians, they are closed to traffic and their roadbeds have been raised to sidewalk level and covered with European bricks.

Smart offerings combined with the excitement of a Middle Eastern bazaar are found on the estraat and Madurostraat in Punda, the oldest section of Willemstad. Mini-malls on the outskirts of Willemstad worth visiting include Salinja Galleries and Bloempot Shopping Center.

Lining the Waaigat Canal is the "Floating Market," a string of schooners from Venezuela, Colombia and other West Indian islands. Alive with color and buzzing with voices haggling over the prices of fresh fish, tropical fruit, vegetables and handicrafts, this seafaring market is a photographer's delight.

Shops in Curaçao are generally open Mon.-Sat. 8:30-noon and 2-6 and when ships are in port. Banking hours are Mon.-Fri. 8-3:30. The bank at the airport is open Mon.-Sat. 8-8 and Sun. 9-4 for currency exchange.

Food and Drink

Like those on the other Dutch islands, restaurants on Curaçao set an international table, often combining Dutch, Spanish, American, Creole, Italian, Indonesian, French and Chinese cuisine on one board. Other specialties include *erwten soep,* a thick pea soup cooked with pork, ham and sausage, and *funchi,* a cornmeal-like dish served steamed or fried.

Local specialties include *keshi yena,* a baked Edam cheese stuffed with chicken or fish; *sopito,* a fish soup flavored with coconut; and *sopi juana,* otherwise known as iguana soup. Another local specialty is *rijsttafel* ("rice table"). This Dutch-Indonesian banquet consists of rice served with up to 20 side dishes. Local tap water distilled from the sea is so pure that minerals must be added for taste. Curaçao produces Curaçao Liqueur made from the *laraha,* a local variety of orange.

Sports and Amusements

With 38 miles (61 km) of shoreline and 12.5 miles (20 km) of protected coral reef,

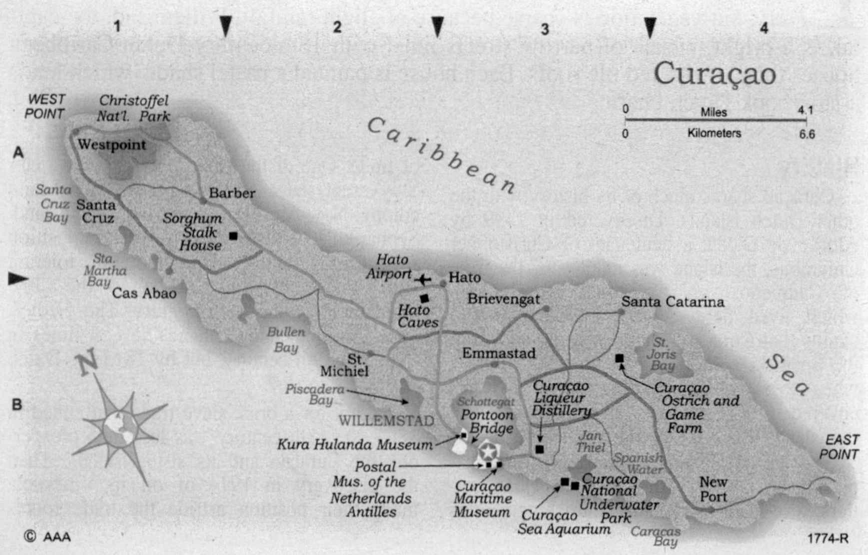

recreation on Curaçao centers on the sea. The clear water draws swimmers, snorkelers, skiers, anglers, sailors, windsurfers and scuba divers, and the secluded coves and beaches at Blauw Bay, Cas Abao, Santa Barbara, Santa Cruz, Westpunt, Jan Thiel, Knip Bay and the Curaçao Sea Aquarium are favorites for lounging. Game fishing for marlin, wahoo, kingfish and dolphin is best July through October. Fishing boats can be chartered for a half-day or a full day, and sailboats and speedboats can be rented by the hour. The Curaçao Yacht Club is in Spanish Water east of Willemstad. Windsurfing and scuba diving lessons also are available; check with your hotel for information.

Caracas Bay Island, on a scenic peninsula south of Willemstad, offers a wide variety of land and water activities, including bicycling, diving, windsurfing, jet skiing and snorkeling. Operators include Windsurfing Curacao, (599) 9-524-4974 and Wannabike, (599) 9-527-3720.

With 68 diverse dive sites, Curaçao is known for its scuba diving opportunities. In 1983, 12.5 miles (20 km) of Curaçao's waters were designated a national marine park. The park features coral beds, steep walls and several shipwrecks. The Curaçao Dive Festival, beginning in late May, is a weeklong event featuring guided dives, seminars, workshops, live entertainment and other activities.

Sports include tennis and basketball, played at the Curaçao Sport Club; golf at the Isla Golf and Squash Club and the Blue Bay Golf Resort, an 18-hole course; and baseball and soccer at S.D.K. Stadium, Antoine Maduro Stadium and smaller fields. Horseback riding and bowling also are available. Schooner races between Curaçao and Bonaire are occasionally held.

Written in the native Papiamentu, Curaçao's *tumba* furnishes a lively and interesting musical comment on island politics and gossip. Spirited visitors can enjoy gambling at island casinos or joining in the songs and dances at discos, beachfront clubs and during the island's many festivals. *Island Tours* or *K-PASA,* available at hotel desks, lists weekly events and entertainment.

Sightseeing

You can tour the island by car in about a day. The western tour along the main road from Piscadera Bay includes most of the island's beaches and plantation houses. Christoffel National Park, at the northwestern end of the island, encompasses a wildlife preserve, gardens, caves, plantation ruins and Mount Christoffel, the highest point on the island.

A shorter trip to Bullen Bay might include stops at the Flamingo Sanctuary and the fishing village of St. Michael. Interesting destinations east of Willemstad are Caracas Bay, site of Fort Beekenburg, and Spanish Water, home of the Curaçao Yacht Club. A popular 45-minute drive northwest from Willemstad heads through Curaçao's *cunucu,* or countryside, punctuated by wind-bent divi-divi trees, cactuses and other drought-resistant plants.

Not far from Willemstad are a botanical garden and zoo, open daily 9-5. Glass-bottom boat tours depart from the Hilton Curaçao Resort daily at 10 and from the Curaçao Sea Aquarium.

North of Santa Barbara is Den Paradera, a historic botanical garden containing herbs and plants that have traditionally been used for the treatment of various ailments. A reconstructed settlement contains small huts with scenes depicting rural life. Tours are offered by appointment; phone (599) 9-767-5608.

Transportation

Two daily nonstop flights to Curaçao are available on American Airlines from Miami, with connections from all major U.S. gateways. Weekly Saturday service direct to Curaçao from Newark is available on Continental Airlines. Dutch Antilles Express and Inselair provide daily service between Aruba, Bonaire, St. Maarten and Curaçao. American Eagle provides connecting flights from San Juan. Hato Airport boasts one of the longest jet landing strips in the West Indies. Many of the major cruise lines visit Curaçao, docking at Willemstad.

There are taxi stands at the airport, major hotels and in Willemstad; check the fixed fares before you ride. Car rentals are available from major U.S. companies and several local firms; a U.S. driver's license is acceptable. Driving is on the right side of the road. Hourly buses connect Willemstad with the airport.

Fast Facts

POPULATION: 130,000.

AREA: 471 sq km (182 sq mi.).

CAPITAL: Willemstad.

HIGHEST POINT: 372 m (1,221 ft.), Mount Christoffel.

LOWEST POINT: Sea level, Caribbean Sea.

TIME ZONE(S): Atlantic Standard.

LANGUAGE: Dutch, Papiamentu, Spanish and English.

GOVERNMENT: Netherlands Antilles, autonomous within the Kingdom of the Netherlands.

UNIT OF CURRENCY: Netherlands Antillean guilder (also called the florin), divided into 100 cents. $1 U.S. = 1.8 guilders. U.S. currency is widely accepted.

ELECTRICITY: 110-130 volts, 50 cycles AC.

MINIMUM AGE FOR DRIVERS: 21-25, depending on the rental car agency. U.S. license valid; drive on right.

MINIMUM AGE FOR GAMBLING: 21.

SEAT BELT/CHILD RESTRAINT LAWS: Seat belts are required for all passengers. Child restraints required for under age 4; children under 12 must ride in the back seat.

HELMETS FOR MOTORCYCLISTS: Required.

HOLIDAYS: Jan. 1; Carnival Monday, Feb. (Mon. before Ash Wednesday); Good Friday; Easter Monday; Queen's Birthday, Apr. 30; Labour Day, May 1; Ascension Day, May (6th Thurs. after Easter); Flag Day, July 2; Antillean Day, Oct. 21; Christmas, Dec. 25; Boxing Day, Dec. 26.

TAXES: A 7 percent room tax and 12 percent service charge are added to most hotel bills. Most restaurants include a 10 percent service charge. Departure tax $22 U.S.; interisland tax $10.

IMMIGRATION REQUIREMENTS: A passport and a return or onward ticket are required. No visa needed for stays of up to 2 weeks. The U.S. Dept. of Homeland Security requires all U.S. citizens returning from the Caribbean to present a valid passport.

PHONING THE ISLANDS: To call Curaçao from the U.S. or Canada, dial 011 + 599 + 9 + the 7-digit local number.

FURTHER INFORMATION FOR VISITORS:

Curaçao Tourism Corp.
One Gateway Center, Suite 2600
Newark, NJ 07102
(973) 353-6200
(800) 328-7222

Curaçao Tourism Board
Pietermaai 19
P.O. Box 3266
Willemstad, Curaçao
Netherlands Antilles
(599) 9-434-8200

Points of Interest

See map page 118.

WILLEMSTAD (B-2) pop. 43,550

Often called "Little Amsterdam," Willemstad is capital of both Curaçao and the islands of the Netherlands Antilles. Its architecture is a tropical adaptation of the traditional Dutch style. The pastel colors characterizing government buildings and private homes alike are a legacy from a governor-general who complained in 1817 that the tropical sun's glare on the white-painted buildings caused his blinding headaches. To ease his discomfort, he decreed that thereafter only other colors would be used.

Curaçao's trademark, Queen Emma Bridge spans Santa Anna Bay. Originally, pedestrians wearing shoes paid a toll of 2c to cross the swinging pontoon bridge; the barefooted walked free. The toll was eventually eliminated after the wealthy routinely discarded their shoes before crossing. Today the bridge links the city's two sections—Punda and Otrobanda—along with the four-lane Queen Juliana Bridge, which arcs nearly 200 feet (60 m) above the bay. Otrabanda means, literally, "the other side." West of the Queen Emma Bridge in Brionplein Square is the Pedro Luis Brion Statue commemorating a local hero who served under Simón Bolívar and pursued the hostile British in 1805.

With its narrow streets and shopping promenade, Punda recalls old Holland. Architectural tours of the city include the classic colonial-style governor's mansion and Department of Finance building on Pietermaai, the Georgian-style Masonic Temple and the stately homes of the merchant princes in Scharloo. A collection of Dutch coins is displayed at the Bank of the Netherlands Antilles Numismatic Museum at 7 Rouvilleweg in Otrabanda; phone (599) 9-462-5913.

Northeast of Punda atop Arrarat Hill is the Franklin D. Roosevelt House, constructed by islanders in 1950 as a symbol of the friendship between the Netherlands and the United States during World War II. It now serves as the residence of the U.S. Consulate General.

Willemstad and Schottegat Harbor, the island's natural harbor, are designated as UNESCO's (United Nations Education, Scientific and Cultural Organization) World Heritage places.

Curaçao Tourism Development Bureau: Pietermaai 19, Willemstad, Curaçao, Netherlands Antilles; phone (599) 9-434-8200.

BETH HAIM JEWISH CEMETERY is n.w. on Schottegatweg West. Consecrated in 1659, the burial ground was one of the first Hebrew cemeteries in the New World. Tombstones marking some 2,500 graves feature ornate sculptures and inscriptions in Portuguese, Spanish, Hebrew, Dutch, English and French. Open Sun.-Fri. dawn-dusk.

CHRISTOFFEL NATIONAL PARK is 17 mi. (27 km) w. of Willemstad at the n.w. end of the island, entered at Landhuis Savonet. This 5,683-acre (2,300-hectare) wildlife preserve encompasses three former plantations. Twenty miles (31 km) of driving trails offer glimpses of rare orchids, bromeliads, cacti, several bird species and Curacao's white-tailed deer. Several bat caves are adorned with Arawak petroglyphs. Well-marked hiking trails traverse the park and ascend Mount Christoffel, the highest point on the island. The Savonet Museum houses a whale exposition with skeletons found on the island's shores.

The 2-hour mountain hike from the visitor center should be planned for the cool morning hours. Safari, deer-spotting and guided walking tours are offered. Park open Mon.-Sat. 7:30-4, Sun. 6-3; closed holidays. Last admission 1 hour before closing. Admission $10; $4.50 (ages 6-12). Deer-spotting tour $30; $20 (ages 6-12). Safari tour $30; $20 (ages 6-12). Reservations are required for all tours. Phone (599) 9-864-0363.

CURAÇAO LIQUEUR DISTILLERY is 3 mi. (5 km) e. at Schottegatweg Oost 129. Housed in the Chobolobo Mansion, the Senior & Co. Distillery produces Curaçao Liqueur from the fruit of the laraha tree. The orange-flavored product is offered for tastings and purchase. Visitors may take self-guiding tours Mon.-Fri. 8-noon and 1-5 and on weekends when cruise ships are in port. Free. Phone (599) 9-461-3526.

CURAÇAO MARITIME MUSEUM is at Van der Brandhofstraat 7 in Scharloo, across from the Floating Market. The island's maritime history is traced with such artifacts as antique ships models and maps. Special exhibits focus on such prominent area residents as American consul Leonard Smith, who brought electricity to the island. Videotape presentations detail the development of the harbor and offer a look at Curaçao's past role as one of the largest slave depots in the Caribbean.

Guided 2-hour tours of the harbor are offered aboard a ferry that also provides transportation to the museum from cruise ships. Food is available. Museum open Tues.-Sat. 10-5. Harbor tours offered Wed. and Sat. at 2. Museum admission $6; $4.50 (ages 8-15). Harbor tour $12; $7 (ages 8-15). Reservations are required. AX, DC, DS, MC, VI. Phone (599) 9-465-2327.

CURAÇAO MUSEUM is .5 mi. (.8 km) w. of the Queen Emma Bridge at Van Leeuwenhoekstraat and Donderstraat in Mundo Nobo. The 1853 military hospital building, a fine example of ornate Dutch architecture, houses historical and geological exhibits, pre-Colombian Indian artifacts, colonial antiques and an art gallery. A special exhibit depicts the lives and occupations of Afro-Curaçaoans after the abolition of slavery. On the grounds is a 47-bell carillon. Mon.-Fri. 8:30-4:30, Sun. 10-4; closed holidays. Admission $4; $2.50 (ages 0-13). Phone (599) 9-462-3873.

CURAÇAO NATIONAL UNDERWATER PARK covers an area from the Curaçao Sea Aquarium to the s.e. tip of the island. Marked underwater trails and sunken ships can be explored by snorkelers and scuba divers. The park features 14 signed dive sites.

CURAÇAO OSTRICH & GAME FARM is 7 mi. (11 km) e. on Groot St. Joris. Visitors to this working farm can hold an egg or a day-old chick while they learn about the life cycle and lifestyle of this large, powerful, flightless bird. Food is available. Allow 2 hours, 30 minutes minimum. Tours are offered on the hour daily 9-4. Fee $10; $6 (ages 2-12). Reservations are required. Phone (599) 9-747-2777.

CURAÇAO SEA AQUARIUM is 4 mi. (6 km) e. on Martin Luther King Blvd. to Bapor Kibra. The facility displays more than 600 species of fish, crabs, lobsters, sea lions, dolphins, sharks, stingrays, sea turtles, anemones, colorful sponges and coral, all natives of the reefs surrounding Curaçao. A variety of diving, snorkeling and educational programs provide hands-on encounters with marine animals. The Seaquarium Beach is nearby.

Food is available. Allow 1 hour minimum. Daily 8:30-5:30. Last admission 1 hour before closing. Animal Encounter dives and snorkeling daily at 9, 11, 1 and 3. Sea Lion Training Experience and Kids Encounters daily at 8:30 and 1. Aquarium admission $15; $7.50 (ages 5-12). Animal Encounter $34 (snorkeling); $54 (scuba dives). Kids Encounter $45 (half-day); $100 (full-day). Sea Lion Encounters $39-$149. Dolphin Encounters $69-$300. Beach admission $3. Reservations are required for marine animal programs. AX, DS, MC, VI. Phone (599) 9-461-6666.

DID YOU KNOW

Curaçao's 185-foot-high Queen Juliana Bridge is said to be the tallest in the Caribbean.

FORT AMSTERDAM is off Breedestraat in Punda, adjoining the waterfront. Built in 1769 to protect the island from invaders, the fort was once the living quarters of the directors of the West Indian Co. It now contains the official residence of the governor-general, the Ministry and government offices.

The Fort Church Museum preserves the island's oldest Protestant church, completed in 1769. Lodged in the southwest wall is a cannonball fired by the British in 1804. A collection of artifacts from the Dutch Protestant congregation includes antique silver chalices, a mahogany and silver baptismal font and historic maps of the island. Museum open Mon.-Fri. 9-noon. Fort free. Church and museum admission $4; $2 (ages 6-14). Phone (599) 9-461-1139.

HATO CAVES is .5 mi. (.8 km) n. of the Hato Airport on F. D. Rooseveltweg. Historical guided tours take visitors into more than 12 limestone chambers that were formed below sea level millions of years ago. A sloping trail leads past unusual formations, pools and a waterfall. Caquetio Indian carvings are visible on the outer walls. A colony of long-nose bats lives inside the cave, and some 100 iguanas roam the surrounding park. Allow 1 hour minimum. Tours depart daily on the hour 10-5. Admission $8; $6 (ages 4-11). Phone (599) 9-868-0379.

MIKVÉ ISRAEL-EMANUEL SYNAGOGUE is at Hanchi di Snoa 29 in Punda. Consecrated in 1732, the synagogue is the oldest active Jewish temple in continuous use in the Western Hemisphere. A thick layer of sand on the floor symbolizes the Israelites' wanderings in the desert before they reached the Promised Land. Open Mon.-Fri. 9-4:30. Services are held Fri. at 6:30 p.m., Sat. and Jewish holidays at 10 a.m. Synagogue admission $3. Phone (599) 9-461-1067.

Jewish Cultural Historical Museum is entered through the synagogue courtyard at Hanchi di Snoa 29. Dating from 1651, the collection includes Torah scrolls, Hanukkah lamps, antique personal and household belongings and a centuries-old ritual bath. Mon.-Fri. 9-4:30; closed Jewish and public holidays. Synagogue and museum admission $6; free (ages 0-12). Phone (599) 9-461-1633.

KAS DI PAL'I MAISHI MUSEUM is 8 mi. (13 km) w. of the airport at Dokterstuin 27 in Weg naar Westpunt. The Sorghum Stalk House, built in the late 19th century, is typical of the rural dwellings in which most of the island's Afro-Curaçaoan population lived until the 1950s. Walls are made of loam and branches, the floor of loam, cow dung and caustic lime; the roof is thatched with sorghum stalks. Period artifacts include furniture and cooking utensils. Food is available. Allow 30 minutes minimum.

Mon.-Fri. 9-3, Sat.-Sun. 9-5. Admission $2; 75c (ages 4-10). Phone (599) 9-864-2742.

KURÁ HULANDA MUSEUM is at Klipstraat 9 in Otrobanda. African culture and history is portrayed in reconstructed 19th-century buildings on the site of a former wharf and slave yard. Exhibits include a collection of original 19th- and 20th-century European prints and artifacts from ancient West African empires. The transatlantic slave trade is depicted through a full-size re-creation of the hold of a slave ship and a plantation worker's cabin. "The Living History," a play about the slave trade, is presented every Wednesday at 7:30. Museum open daily 10-5; closed Dec. 25. Admission $6; $3 (ages 0-11). Phone (599) 9-434-7765.

POSTAL MUSEUM OF THE NETHERLANDS ANTILLES is at Kaya Toni Prince in Punda. The museum features a collection of stamps from the Netherlands Antilles and other countries as well as related artifacts, such as old post boxes and scales. Special exhibits of theme stamps from around the world change quarterly. The museum is housed in Punda's oldest surviving building, which dates from 1693. Allow 30 minutes minimum. Tues.-Fri. 10-4. Admission $2; $1 (ages 6-15). Phone (599) 9-465-8010.

SEAWORLD EXPLORER departs from the Hilton hotel pier on Piscadera Bay. This semi-submarine travels just below the surface of the water, providing dramatic views of Curaçao's shipwrecks and coral reefs through large glass windows. Sightseeing trips depart daily at 10, based upon cruise ship demand. Buses provide transportation to the dive site. Closed holidays. Fare $30; $20 (ages 0-11). Reservations are required. Phone (599) 9-461-0011.

WILLEMSTAD TROLLEY TRAIN TOUR departs from Fort Amsterdam near the Queen Emma Pontoon Bridge. This 1.5-hour narrated tour passes many historic Willemstad sights, including the Floating Market, Scharloo, Bolo di Bruid (the "Wedding Cake House"), Mikve Israel Synagogue, Pietermaai Cathedral, Queen Wilhelmina Park, Waterfort Arches and Fort Amsterdam. Schedule varies, depending upon cruise ship demand. Closed holidays. Fare $20; $15 (children). Reservations are required. Phone (599) 9-461-0011.

GAMBLING ESTABLISHMENTS

- **Breezes Curaçao Resort & Casino** is at 8 Dr. Martin Luther King Blvd. Daily 10 a.m.-4 a.m. Phone (599) 9-736-7888.

- **Curaçao Casino** is on John F. Kennedy Blvd. on Piscadera Bay. Daily 10 a.m.-3 a.m. Phone (599) 9-462-5000.

- **Curaçao Howard Johnson Plaza Hotel & Casino** is at Brionplein z/n in Otrabanda. Phone (599) 9-462-7800.

- **Curaçao Marriott Beach Resort & Emerald Casino** is on Piscadera Bay. Daily 11 a.m.-midnight. Phone (599) 9-736-8800.

- **Holiday Beach Hotel & Casino Royale** is at Pater Euwensweg 31. Daily 11 a.m.-4 a.m. Phone (599) 9-462-5400.

Fort Shirley, Cabrits National Park, Portsmouth / © Bob Krist / eStock Photo

Dominica

Deep tropical rain forests, mountains and isolation have preserved the wild beauty of Dominica (dom-in-EE-ka), reminding visitors of an earlier, less commercial Caribbean. What the island lacks in nightlife, duty-free shops and white sand beaches, it makes up for with the natural splendor of its volcanic mountain ranges swathed in the rich green of towering trees, exotic ferns and flowers. Fed by the ample rainfall in the island's interior, numerous rivers wind through Dominica's primordial forest, which is home to such endangered species as the imperial and red-necked parrots.

History

So named because Christopher Columbus discovered it on a Sunday, Dominica was a stronghold of the Carib Indians, who were the dominant indigenous group found on many of the Caribbean islands. Although the Carib population on many other islands was severely depleted, and in some instances wiped out, the Caribs on Dominica frustrated the efforts of the French and British to successfully colonize the island. In the 18th century the island became the scene of fierce battles between the French and the English for outright possession. The British prevailed in 1783 and remained in control until 1978, when Dominica became independent. Some 3,000 Carib Indians still live on the island.

Since gaining independence from Great Britain, Dominica has carefully nurtured its pristine resources. Rather than depending on high-rise resorts and glittering casinos for its economy, Dominica relies primarily on the export of produce. The island government also is encouraging tourism and light industry.

Shopping

Handcraft centers in the Old Market Plaza in Roseau and in the Carib Territory offer handmade items, including finely woven baskets and Dominica's unique grass mats; also in the marketplace is the Dominican Museum. There are several boutiques in Roseau and at some hotels throughout the island. Other buys include soaps made locally from fresh coconut oil, other toiletries, leather goods, cigars and cigarettes and cassette recordings of the traditional *jing-ping* folk music.

Duty-free shopping is available throughout Roseau. Pirates, on Long Lane, has a wide selection of cheeses and French wines. In the Fort Young Hotel *(See color ad p. 128)* on Victoria Street are Whitchurch Duty Free Shop and Jewellers International. Baroon International is at the Prevo Cinemall on Kennedy Avenue. Duty Free Emporium is on Dame Eugenia Boulevard. Limers Jeans Shop on Cork Street offers brand-name clothing and shoes. Among the duty-free items available at various shops are cosmetics, crystal ware, handicrafts, articles made from pearls, perfume, cigars, liquor, watches and cameras.

Banking hours are Mon.-Thurs. 8-2, Fri. 8-4. Business hours are Mon.-Fri. 8-4, Sat. 8-1.

Food and Drink

Traditional dishes include freshwater crayfish; *tee-tee-ree accras,* fried fish cakes; *callaloo* soup, made from dasheen leaves and coconut cream; and *crab backs,* black and red land crabs stuffed with spicy crab meat. Nectar, syrups, jams and sherbets are available as well as locally made rums and ginger beer. Sea moss is a seaweed shake made with milk, sugar and cinnamon spices.

Crapaud, the local delicacy known as "mountain chicken," has disappeared from restaurant tables. The national dish is not fowl but frog—*leptodactylus fallax,* one of the world's largest frogs. Found only on Dominica and Montserrat, this rare species may be on the brink of extinction.

Sports and Amusements

Dominica's many streams and rivers shaded by giant ferns attract both swimmers and canoeists. A few northern beaches offer swimming; Coconut Beach is the most appealing. About 25 miles (40 km) north of Roseau, it has silver volcanic sand and a mountain backdrop. Other options are Mero Beach, about 12 miles (19 km) north of Roseau, and Purple Turtle Beach Club in Portsmouth, which has restaurant facilities on the beach. Fishing on the island is good; Dive Dominica, (767) 448 2188, provides boats and equipment for deep-sea fishing. Spectators can enjoy cricket, soccer, netball, volleyball, tennis and basketball in season.

Scuba diving also is available and must be arranged through a local dive operator. Establishments include ALDIVE, (767) 440-3483; Anchorage Dive Center, (767) 448-2638; Cabrits Dive Centre, (767) 445-3010; Dive Dominica, (767) 448-2188; East Carib Dive, (767) 449-6575; Fort Young, (767) 448-5000; Irie Safari, (767) 440-5085; Nature Island Dive, (767) 449-8181; and Sunset Bay Club, (767) 446-6522.

The island has several spectacular dive sites, including L'Abyme, or the Abyss. Champagne, outside Pointe Michel, has an incredible reef where divers swim through bubbling waters created by volcanic activity on the sea bed. On the north side of Cabrits National Park, the marine park at Douglas Bay contains a snorkeling trail. There are wrecks at nearby Toucarie and Capuchin.

Sea kayaking and mountain biking are two popular ways to discover Dominica. Nature Island Dive Center, on Soufrière Bay, offers hourly, half-day and full-day trips. In Portsmouth near Coconut Bay kayaking, windsurfing, kneeboarding and snorkeling are just some of the water activities offered by Cabrits Dive Center.

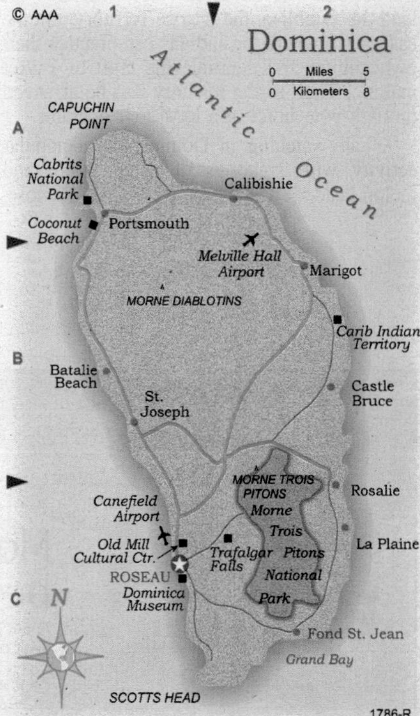

Dominica starts the new year with Mas Domnik (Carnival), in February and March. The arts are celebrated during the Dominica Festival of Arts in May and June. Sports enthusiasts can partake in the Dominica International Sport Fishing Tournament in mid-May and Dive Fest in early July. The World Creole Music Festival is held in late October. National Day and Independence festivities are held during the month of October and continue through early November.

Sightseeing

Dominica is famous for the exotic flora that grows wild around its river pools and rain forests. Morne Trois Pitons National Park, covering 17,000 acres (6,880 hectares) on the southern end of the island, is the first natural heritage site in the Eastern Caribbean and only the second in the insular Caribbean to be listed as a UNESCO World Heritage Site. Its volcanic wonders include mud pots, hot springs, sulphur vents and the Boiling Lake.

Dominica's Carib Indians distinguished themselves from other Caribbean tribes by fighting so fiercely that in 1748 both the English and the French abandoned the island. Consequently, Carib descendants are among the island's inhabitants, and in 1903 the British set aside 3,700 acres (1,497 hectares) of land to establish the Carib Territory on the east coast, where the Indians can practice their own culture and continue the craft of basket making. Trips to the territory can be arranged through your hotel or a local tour operator.

Whale-watching in Dominica is a popular activity with sightings of sperm, pilot and melon-headed whales as well as bottlenose, Risso and spinner dolphins. Excursions can be arranged through Anchorage Dive Center and Dive Dominica.

Roseau, Dominica's capital, occupies a picturesque setting on the banks of the Roseau River. Saturday mornings come alive with the bustle of the colorful market, whose cinnamon scent fills the air. The grass rugs that are in demand throughout the Caribbean are woven at Tropicrafts, opposite the Woodbridge Bay port.

A site pass is required for visiting selected tourist sites. Daily pass $5, weekly pass $10 or $2 per site. Passes can be obtained from tour operators and at attractions.

Transportation

International access into Dominica is facilitated via airports of neighboring Caribbean islands with connections to the island's two small airports: Canefield Airport, 5 minutes from Roseau, and Melville Hall Airport, on the northeastern tip of the island about an hour from Roseau. Airlines servicing Dominica include American Eagle, Carib Aviation and LIAT. Major gateway connections to Dominica are from Antigua, Barbados, Guadeloupe, Martinique, Puerto Rico, St. Lucia and St. Maarten.

Car rentals are available at the airports; taxis meet all flights. City and island sightseeing tours with a driver-guide are available. L'Express des Iles operates high-speed ferries that connect Dominica with Guadeloupe, Martinique and St. Lucia. A departure tax is charged; phone (767) 448-2181 for schedules and fares. Cruise ships call at the docks in Roseau and Woodbridge Bay.

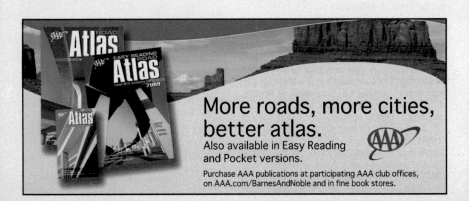

Fast Facts

POPULATION: 69, 625.

AREA: 749 sq km (289 sq mi.).

CAPITAL: Roseau.

HIGHEST POINT: 1,447 m (4,747 ft.), Morne Diablotins.

LOWEST POINT: Sea level, Caribbean Sea.

TIME ZONE(S): Atlantic Standard.

LANGUAGE: English, but a French patois (Creole) is widely spoken.

GOVERNMENT: Independent. Member of the British Commonwealth of Nations.

UNIT OF CURRENCY: Eastern Caribbean (E.C.) dollar. $1 U.S. = 2.7 E.C. dollars.

ELECTRICITY: 220-240 volts, 50 cycles AC.

MINIMUM AGE FOR DRIVERS: 25 to drive a rental car; maximum age 65. Local license ($12 U.S.) required, valid for 30 days; drive on left.

SEAT BELT/CHILD RESTRAINT LAWS: Seat belts are required for all passengers.

HELMETS FOR MOTORCYCLISTS: Required.

HOLIDAYS: Jan. 1; Merchants' Day, Jan. 2; Carnival Monday and Tuesday, Feb. 19-20; Good Friday; Easter Monday; Labour Day, May 5; Whit Monday, May 12; August Monday, Aug. 4; Independence Day, Nov. 3; Community Day of Service, Nov. 4; Christmas, Dec. 25; Boxing Day, Dec. 26.

TAXES: A 10 percent VAT (value-added tax) is charged at all hotels. A 15 percent VAT (value-added tax) and a 10 percent service charge are added to restaurant bills. Departure tax $22 U.S.

IMMIGRATION REQUIREMENTS: A passport and a return or onward ticket are required. The U.S. Dept. of Homeland Security requires all U.S. citizens returning from the Caribbean to present a valid passport.

PHONING THE ISLANDS: To call Dominica from the U.S. or Canada, dial 1 + 767 + the 7-digit local number.

FURTHER INFORMATION FOR VISITORS:

Discover Dominica Authority
Valley Road
P.O. Box 293
Roseau, Dominica
(767) 448-2045
(866) 522-4057

Points of Interest

See map page 125.

PORTSMOUTH (A-1)

Portsmouth sits on the northwest coast at Prince Rupert Bay, where Christopher Columbus moored on his fourth voyage to the New World in 1504. It is said that the swampy terrain around the Indian River prevented Portsmouth from becoming the island's capital.

CABRITS NATIONAL PARK is 1.5 mi. n. of town between Douglas and Prince Rupert's bays. Perched on a forested, twin-peaked peninsula, Cabrits National Park contains the ruins of a military garrison used by British and French forces 1770-1854. Its centerpiece is Fort Shirley, which is surrounded by more than 50 major structures, including gun batteries, powder magazines, storehouses and barracks that housed up to 600 men.

Trails connecting the sites meander through thick tropical growth. Light clothing and comfortable shoes are recommended. Allow 4 hours minimum. Daily 8-4. Admission $2. Phone (767) 448-2401, ext. 3277 or 3429.

ROSEAU (C-1) pop. 16,535

The island's capital, Roseau (Rōzō) was named by the French for the reeds that once grew at the mouth of the river. The busy wharf area north of town caters to large freighters as well as local wooden sloops. High stone walls surround the 19th-century Our Lady of Fair Haven Cathedral and the convent.

Within walking distance are the Government House and the 44-acre (18-hectare) Roseau Botanical Garden. Heavily damaged by Hurricane David in 1979.

Discover Dominica Authority: Valley Road, Roseau, Commonwealth of Dominica, W.I.; phone (767) 448-2045.

DOMINICA MUSEUM is on the bayfront across from the cruise ship port. Housed in the old post office, the museum offers a comprehensive introduction to Dominica and its history. The formation of the island is illustrated with volcanic ash and rocks. Other exhibits depict the first Amerindian settlement, colonial plantation life and Dominica's agricultural and political changes. Mon.-Fri. and major holidays 9-4, Sat. 9-noon. Admission $3. Phone (767) 448-8923.

MORNE TROIS PITONS NATIONAL PARK stretches across the southern half of the island. The visitor center is 14 mi. (23 km) n.e. on Canefield-Castle Bruce Rd. to Pond Casse-Rosalie Rd. Covering 17,000 acres (6,880 hectares), Morne Trois Pitons is the first natural heritage site in the Eastern Caribbean and only the second in the insular Caribbean to be listed as a UNESCO World Heritage Site.

The park centers around the volcanic "mountain of three peaks" with its steaming vents, fumaroles and hot springs. Boiling Lake is said to be the largest of its kind in the world. Bubbling mud pots and sulphur vents mark the barren Valley of Desolation.

The twin torrents at Trafalgar Falls in Roseau Valley offer an ideal setting for a picnic within reach of wild orchids and tropical rain forests. At 300 feet (91 m), Middleham Falls is the highest waterfall in the park. Emerald Pool, a short walk from the visitor center, is a popular destination for cruise ship excursions. A qualified guide must be hired for the 8-mile (13-km) hike to Boiling Lake. Hikers should wear sturdy shoes and raingear and protect cameras from moisture. Park fee $2. Phone (767) 448 2401.

OLD MILL CULTURAL CENTRE is .5 mi. (.8 km) s. of Canefield Airport. The boiling house of what was one of the largest sugar mills on the island is now the venue for training residents in the performing and visual arts, including steel band music, dance and painting. An art gallery presents changing exhibitions. Mon.-Fri. 8-4; closed holidays. Free. Phone (767) 449-1804.

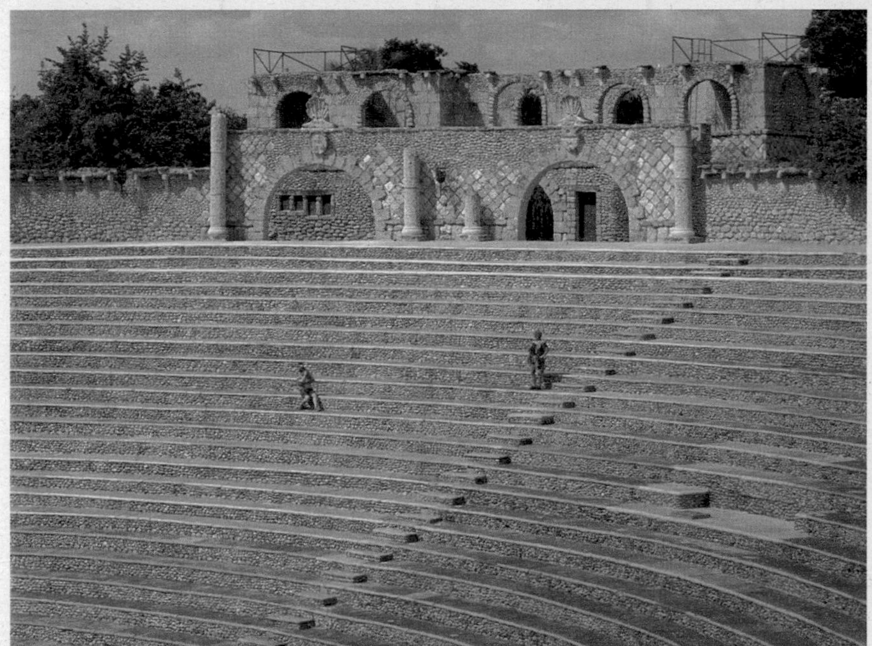

Altos de Chavon, La Romana / © Heeb Photos / eStock Photo

Dominican Republic

When Christopher Columbus came ashore in 1492, he wrote in his diary, "This is the most beautiful land that human eyes have seen." He would leave members of his family behind to colonize the island and would return to it after venturing throughout the Caribbean. In his will, he asked to be buried in Santo Domingo. It's no wonder the Dominican Republic calls itself "the land Columbus loved best."

A relaxed atmosphere is not just a promise here; it is a way of life. Old World charm lingers here in language, food, customs and thought. The emphasis placed on music, dance, history and art as well as the usual island activities of sunbathing and swimming make the Dominican Republic a popular Caribbean vacation destination.

Santo Domingo, capital and cultural center, preserves the Dominican Republic's rich history with its many churches, palaces, museums, forts, monuments and restored homes. Puerto Plata in the north, Punta Cana in the east and La Romana in the southeast are other major resort centers. Pico Duarte, at 10,128 feet (3,087 m), is the highest point in the Caribbean; just 50 miles (80 km) southwest, Lake Enriquillo, at 144 feet (44 m) below sea level, is the lowest point in addition to being the largest salt lake in the Caribbean.

History

The Dominican Republic occupies the eastern two-thirds of the island the Indians called *Quisqueya* and Christopher Columbus named Hispaniola; Haiti occupies the western third. When Columbus ran the *Santa María* aground on the northern coast on Dec. 25, 1492, he used the ship's salvaged lumber to build Fuerte de Navidad, or Fort Christmas. About a year later, Columbus returned to discover the

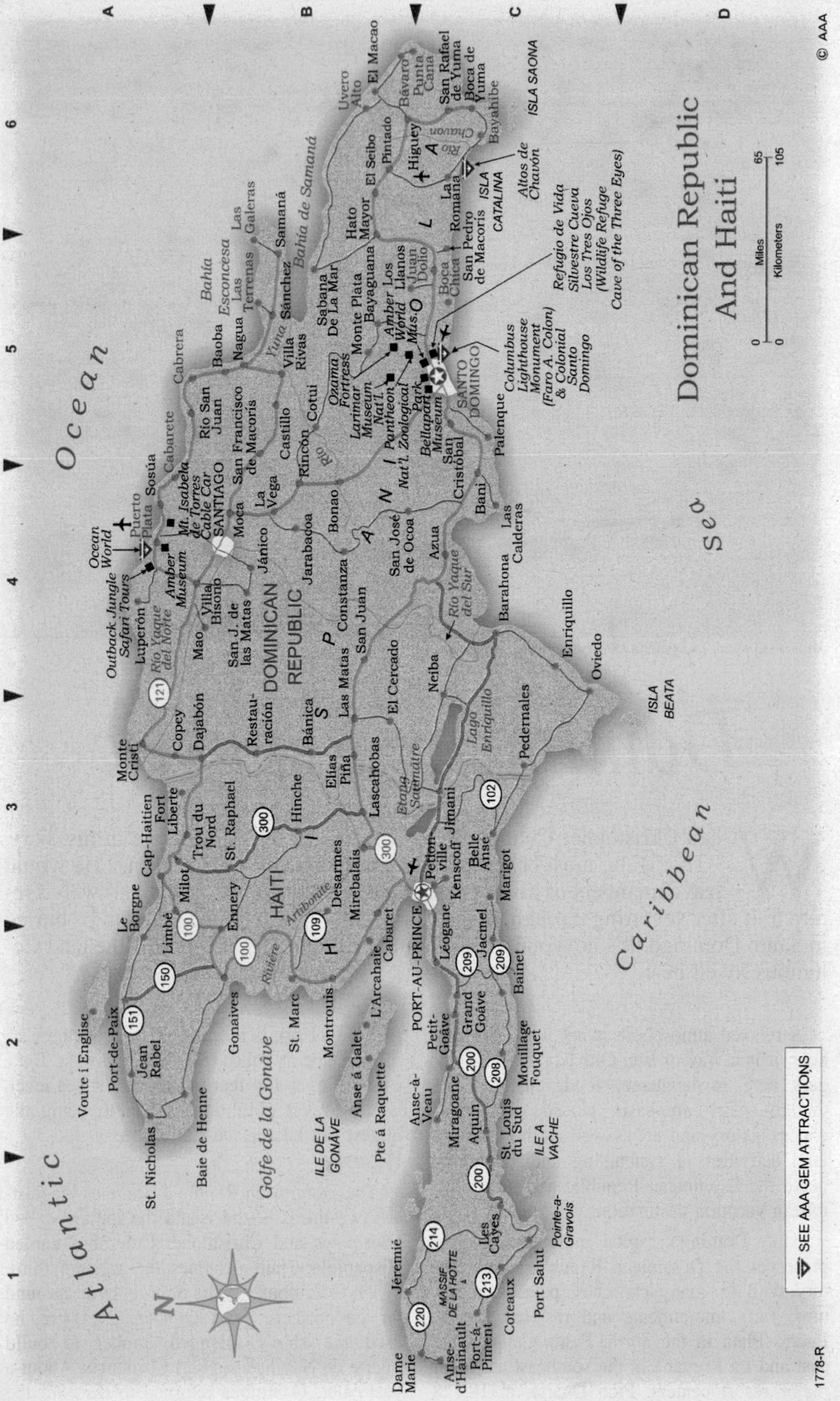

Dominican Republic And Haiti

Miles 0 65
Kilometers 0 105

SEE AAA GEM ATTRACTIONS

Atlantic Ocean
Caribbean Sea
Golfe de la Gonâve
Bahía Escocesa
Bahía de Samaná
HAITI
DOMINICAN REPUBLIC
HISPANIOLA
ILE DE LA GONÂVE
ILE A VACHE
ISLA BEATA
ISLA SAONA
ISLA CATALINA
MASSIF DE LA HOTTE
Lago Enriquillo
Etang Saumâtre
Rio Yaque del Norte
Rio Yaque del Sur
Rivière Artibonite
Rio Yuna
Rio Ozama
Rio Chavón
PORT-AU-PRINCE
SANTO DOMINGO
SANTIAGO
St. Nicholas
Voute i Englise
Port-de-Paix
Jean Rabel
Baie de Henne
Gonaives
Le Borgne
Limbé
Milot
Cap-Haitien
Fort Liberte
Trou du Nord
St. Raphael
Ennery
Hinche
Desarmes
Mirebalais
St. Marc
Montrouis
L'Archahaie
Cabaret
Anse á Galet
Pte á Raquette
Petit-Goâve
Grand Goâve
Léogane
Petion-ville
Kenscoff
Jacmel
Bainet
Marigot
Belle Anse
Anse-à-Veau
Miragoane
Aquin
St. Louis du Sud
Mouillage Fouquet
Les Cayes
Port Salut
Pointe-a-Gravois
Coteaux
Port-á-Piment
Anse-d'Hainault
Dame Marie
Jéremié
Lascahobas
Jimani
Monte Cristi
Copey
Dajabón
Restauración
Bánica
Elías Piña
Las Matas
El Cercado
Neiba
Pedernales
Oviedo
Enriquillo
Barahona
Las Calderas
Baní
San Cristóbal
Palenque
Azua
San José de Ocoa
San Juan
Constanza
Jarabacoa
Bonao
Jánico
Villa Bisonó
Mao
San J. de las Matas
Luperón
Puerto Plata
Sosúa
Cabarete
Moca
La Vega
San Francisco de Macorís
Rio San Juan
Cabrera
Baoba
Nagua
Las Terrenas
Las Galeras
Samaná
Sánchez
Villa Rivas
Castillo
Cotuí
Rincón
Sabana De La Mar
Monte Plata
Bayaguana
Los Llanos
Hato Mayor
El Seibo
Pintado
Uvero Alto
El Macao
Bávaro
Punta Cana
San Rafael de Yuma
Boca de Yuma
Bayahibe
Higuey
La Romana
San Pedro de Macoris
Juan Dolio
Boca Chica
Outback Jungle Safari Tours
Ocean World
Amber Museum
Mt. Isabela de Torres Cable Car
Larimar Museum
Ozama Fortress
Nat'l. Pantheon
Nat'l. Zoological Park
Bellapart Museum
Amber World Mus.
Columbus Lighthouse Monument (Faro A. Colon) & Colonial Santo Domingo
Refugio de Vida Silvestre Cueva Los Tres Ojos (Wildlife Refuge Cave of the Three Eyes)
Altos de Chavón
151 150 100 109 300 209 200 208 214 213 220 102 121

© AAA

1778-R

settlement destroyed and 38 of his men massacred.

Columbus then founded La Isabela farther east in the present-day Dominican Republic. The first European city in the New World, La Isabela was to become Columbus' base of operations for the next 2 years. In 1496 Bartolomeo Columbus, Christopher's brother, founded New Isabela on the southern coast—where the Republic's capital of Santo Domingo thrives today.

The only colony ever governed by its discoverer, Hispaniola was the base for excursions by many famous Spanish explorers, including Francisco Pizarro, Hernando Cortés, Hernando de Soto, Vasco de Balboa, Alonzo de Ojeda, Diego Velásquez and Juan Ponce de León. Considered the oldest university in the Americas, the University of Santo Domingo was founded in 1538.

The French settled in western Hispaniola in 1697, and within 100 years the entire island had come under French rule. Spain regained the eastern two-thirds in 1809. The Dominican Republic declared its independence in 1821 to prevent invasion from Haiti. Shortly thereafter, however, troops from newly independent Haiti overran the Republic and held it for another 22 years.

Led by national hero Juan Pablo Duarte, the Republic gained its independence once again in 1844, but it was to be lost and gained yet one more time: Spain reannexed the territory in 1861 and held it until 1865, when fierce fighting led to the Republic's restoration.

Foreign parties were not the sole source of aggravation; the country has experienced a turbulent internal history as well. Political instability had become the rule by 1904, when Theodore Roosevelt sent U.S. customs agents to oversee the Dominican Republic's finances and enforce payment of its foreign debt. U.S. Marines occupied the country 1916-24 until the installation of a constitutionally elected government. Democracy was restored but short-lived: The dictator Rafael Trujillo came to power in 1930 and held it until his assassination in 1961. U.S. troops intervened again in 1965 following another civil uprising. Democracy was restored the following year, and the nation has enjoyed free elections ever since.

For many years, agriculture was the backbone of the economy. Traditional exports—sugar, cocoa, coffee, bananas and tobacco—flourished in this land of fertile valleys and foliage-clad mountains. Today, tourism is one of the Dominican Republic's primary industries. Resorts have sprung up in the coastal beach towns and around the capital city of Santo Domingo. There also has been an increase of ecotourism in the interior, with hiking, caving, white-water rafting, cascading and biking tours through the mountains and countryside.

Shopping

In Santo Domingo one shopping area extends along Calle El Conde from El Conde Gate eastward to the colonial section; the long thoroughfare is closed to vehicular traffic. There are less expensive shops nearby—along avenidas Duarte and Mella, near Columbus Park and along Mercedes. Plaza Central, at the intersection of avenidas 27th of February and Winston Churchill is a popular shopping center. Mercado Modelo, the public crafts market, is at the corner of avenidas Mella and Santome. Santo Domingo also offers several modern shopping malls.

Shopping opportunities in Puerto Plata can be found around Central Park, the Plaza Turisol and a popular crafts center near Playa Dorada. In Santiago shoppers go to Calle El Sol and the Mercado crafts market. Haggling is expected in the crafts markets but not at the commercial shops.

There are free-port zones at Santo Domingo's Las Americas International Airport and at Puerto Plata International Airport. Duty-free purchases must be made in U.S. dollars and are delivered to your point of departure. Shopping hours are generally Mon.-Sat. 9-7:30. Banking hours are Mon.-Fri. 8:30-5.

One of the best buys is jewel-like amber—the Dominican Republic is one of the few spots in the Western Hemisphere where this fossilized resin is found. Larimar, a blue stone similar to turquoise, also is found in the Dominican Republic. Other good buys include embroidery, woven baskets, dolls, leather goods, art objects and handicrafts of local cedar and mahogany. Imported perfume and jewelry also are available. Local handicrafts made of tortoiseshell, such as combs or jewelry, may not be imported into the United States.

Food and Drink

The national dish, *sancocho,* is a hearty stew of vegetables and meats. The local staple is the plantain, served ripe or green in a variety of ways. *Fritos verdes* are plantain fritters; *mangú* is a puree of boiled plantains and onions. *La bandera*, which means "the flag," is a tri-colored meal of white rice, red beans and meat. Dishes prepared *a la criolla* reflect the country's Creole heritage. Fish in coconut-milk sauce *(pescado con coco)* is a traditional favorite. Stewed goat *(chivo guisado)* is served in most restaurants; goats on the island are said to graze on wild oregano, which lends flavor to the meat. The locals are especially partial to a snack food of fried pork rinds, *chicharones.*

Numerous restaurants provide traditional and contemporary Caribbean specialties along with many Italian, French, Spanish, Indian, Japanese and Chinese dishes. A 10-percent service charge—in addition to a 12-percent sales tax—is added to the bill in all restaurants and hotels; a tip of up to 10 percent more is customary for good service.

Dominican rum is the most popular drink, though imported brands claim a substantial following. Barcelo, Bermudez and Brugal are readily available. Dominican Republic beer rivals German brands for robust flavor. Presidente is the local favorite, but Bohemia also is popular.

If a milder form of refreshment is preferred, try a *batida,* or fruit shake. Dominican coffee is considered excellent, especially by those who like their coffee strong. Tap water is *not* considered safe to drink by visitors, even in the hotels. Water served in restaurants is generally safe, and bottled water is readily available.

Sports and Amusements

With nearly a thousand miles of coastline, the Dominican Republic offers a wide choice of unspoiled beaches for swimming and other water sports. Top destinations include the Amber Coast, near Puerto Plata on the northern shore, Boca Chica and La Romana on the southern shore, Punta Cana on the island's eastern tip and Samaná on the northeast coast.

Marlin, wahoo, kingfish and barracuda are the desired catches of deep-sea anglers. Samaná is noted for excellent bay fishing. Other prime fishing areas are Cumayasa, La Romana and Cabeza de Toro, east of the capital; and Puerto Plata on the north coast.

Charter boats for sailing and yachting can be rented at most resorts by the hour or day. Opportunities for snorkeling and scuba diving are not as widespread as on other Caribbean isles; however, the reefs around Catalina Island, accessible by boat from La Romana, are popular for underwater exploring. Windsurfing, kiteboarding, surfing, water skiing and other water sports can be arranged at the Puerto Plata and Cabarete resorts and at Casa de Campo near La Romana.

Facilities for such land sports as golf, tennis and horseback riding are excellent. With more than 21 golf courses, the island is becoming a popular year-round golf destination. Championship 18-hole courses are available at Playa Grande on the north coast, Punta Cana to the east, Playa Dorada at Puerto Plata, Casa de Campo near La Romana and Coral Costa Caribe near Juan Dolio. Tennis courts are found in the resort areas as well as in the city. Stables are in and around Santo Domingo, Puerto Plata and La Romana, where horseback riding proves to be a practical way to sightsee in the surrounding countryside.

Spectator sports in the Republic include horse racing, basketball, baseball, boxing and polo. Sports facilities built for the 2003 Pan-American games represented the largest public works project in the country's history. A variety of competitions are held at the Juan Pablo Duarte Olympic Center at avenidas Máximo Gómez and 27 de Febrero in the center of Santo Domingo. Nearby are the V Centenario Hipódromo, the horse racing track, and Quisqueya Stadium, where baseball—the national sport—is played.

The country has lent more than its share of baseball talent to U.S. teams. In fact, nearly

10 percent of American Major League baseball players come from the Dominican Republic. Notable names include Bartolo Colón, Vladamir Guerrero, Pedro Martinez, Manny Ramirez, Alex Rodriguez, Alfonso Soriano, Sammy Sosa and Miguel Tejada. Though baseball is played year-round, the more acclaimed winter league plays late October through January.

A country that gave the world dances like the *merengue* is bound to have a lively nightlife. African, Spanish and Indian influences have been sifted, filtered and then combined in a swirl of *Criollo* activity and Latin good times. *Bachata,* a soulful variation on the traditional merengue, has become a Dominican trademark. The nightclubs and casinos in Santo Domingo feature top-name entertainers; dance bands are featured at most restaurants and hotels.

The National Theater in Santo Domingo's Plaza de la Cultura regularly presents dramatic productions and orchestral performances. Plays also are staged at the Palace of Fine Arts (Palacio de Bellas Artes) and the Casa de Teatro in the capital.

Sightseeing

Major hotels and ground tour operators can arrange guided sightseeing tours. Tours away from the city visit coffee, sugar, banana, cocoa and pineapple plantations, rice paddies and tobacco farms. The drive along Duarte Highway, connecting Santo Domingo on the coast to Puerto Plata on the north coast, affords a glimpse of the country's diverse interior. The highway cuts through the mountainous region of the island, an area noted for its coffee plantations. Popular stops along the way are La Vega, a typical island mountain town, and Santiago, where Bermudez Rum is made. Both towns are known for their carnival celebrations, which are held every Sunday in February.

At Puerto Plata are opportunities to relax, swim or ride a cable car to the top of 2,565-foot (782-m) Mount Isabela de Torres, which offers a spectacular view of the countryside. At the top of the mountain is the statue of "Christ the Redeemer." East of town near Río San Juan is Laguna Gri Gri, where boats can be rented to explore the mangrove-lined lagoon and the island's north coast. The mountain town of Jarabacoa, 90 miles (145 km) south of Puerto Plata, is an ecotourism base for river rafting, hiking, horseback riding and mountain biking. About 50 miles (80 km) southeast of Río San Juan is the Samaná Peninsula, noted for its pristine white sand beaches and excellent sailing, diving, whale watching and fishing opportunities.

West of Santo Domingo are San Cristobal, where the dictator Rafael Trujillo built a fabulous palace and college; Barahona, with its miles of unspoiled beaches; and Lake Enriquillo, one of the largest lakes in the Caribbean, complete with flamingos and crocodiles. Another worthwhile excursion is a 2-hour drive east from Santo Domingo to La Romana. Here is Altos de Chavon, a replica of a 16th-century Mediterranean village, with an artists' colony on a cliff overlooking the Chavón River.

More than ten percent of the country's land area is set aside for national parks, natural monuments and scientific reserves. Though few sites offer tourist facilities, many are open to guided tours. In the north, Parque Nacional Monte Cristi covers 212 sq mi. (550 sq km) between the Haitian border and Punta Rucia. The coastal park features beaches, mangrove swamps and the limestone mesa of El Morro. Christopher Columbus's first home in the New World is among the archeological excavations at Parque Nacional La Isabela near Luperón.

At Cabarete, lagoons and underground pools characterize Parqué Nacional El Choco. On Samaná Bay, Parque Nacional Los Haïtises is noted for its bird life, caves and rock formations.

In the central mountain region, Parque Nacional Armando Bermúdez and Parque Nacional José del Carmen Ramírez are home to the highest peaks in the Antilles, including 10,128-foot (3,087-m) Pico Duarte. The ruins of Old Vega, a fort town destroyed by an earthquake in 1562, are preserved at Parque Histórico La Vega Vieja, where Christopher Columbus is said to have erected a wooden cross during a battle with the Taíno Indians.

In the southeast, Parque Nacional del Este covers 166 sq mi. (430 sq km) on the peninsula between Bayahibe and Boca del Yuma, including the island of Saona. Manatees and bottlenose dolphins are among the endangered marine mammals found in the park, which is noted for its caves and coral formations.

Near San Cristóbal, Parque Nacional Cuevas de Bourbón o de El Pomier features a network of 54 caves marked by thousands of Taíno pictographs and petroglyphs.

In the southwest, Parque Nacional Isla Cabritos comprises three islands in Lake Enriquillo. The country's largest protected area, Parque Nacional Jaragua, covers 560 sq mi. (1,450 sq km) on the southern Pedernales Peninsula. The desertlike landscape is home to

130 bird species, including the region's largest flamingo population. Parque Nacional Sierra de Bahoruco, on the Haitian border, is an area of great ecological diversity; some 50 bird species and 166 orchid species are found here.

When visiting any major tourist area, be prepared for the approach of helpful—and sometimes aggressive—freelance tour guides. You may find yourself walking with a friendly stranger who gives directions and then charges for the information. Should you wish to take a guided tour, agree in advance upon a fee, but feel free to decline such services. Tours are optional, even within most attractions.

Transportation

American Airlines, Continental and Delta are among carriers offering regular flights and packages from New York, Newark and Miami to Puerto Plata's Gregorio Luperón International Airport and Santo Domingo's Las Américas International Airport. Connections also are available from San Juan, Puerto Rico. American Airlines and American Eagle also serve La Romana International Airport and Punta Cana International Airport.

Ferry transportation from Puerto Rico to the Dominican Republic is provided by Ferries del Caribe, which operates the *Millennium Express* between Mayagüez and Santo Domingo. The 12-hour overnight crossing operates three times weekly in each direction.

The Dominican Republic has good highways, though the back roads are not as well maintained. The Duarte Highway (Autopista Duarte) bisects the country, connecting Santo Domingo with Santiago and Puerto Plata to the north. The Sanchez Highway stretches westward from Santo Domingo and the Mella Highway eastward. Rental cars are available. Unless otherwise posted, speed limits are 50 mph (80 km/h) on the highway, 35 mph (60 km/h) in suburban areas and 25 mph (40 km/h) in the city. On newer highways, the limit may be raised to 60 mph (100 km/h). A U.S. driver's license is valid in the Dominican Republic for 90 days.

Because Dominican law allows for detaining visitors who have become involved in accidents in which injuries are claimed, extreme caution is advised while driving. For some this possibility rules out driving altogether. Reasonable alternatives are available.

In the city most visitors prefer the convenience of taxis. There are four types. Regular taxis are government-regulated and rates are fixed; they are found at hotels and tourist spots. Radio taxis are dispatched and the rate is set over the phone. Public taxis, or *públicos,* are operated independently; they are available along established routes. Collective taxis, or *conchos,* also operate along major thoroughfares. Rates are fairly inexpensive. Regardless of the type of taxi used, the fare should be agreed upon before entering the vehicle.

Bus service is provided by Caribe Tours and Metro Bus between cities and from Santo Domingo to the airport. Comfortable, inexpensive buses operate several times daily between Santo Domingo and Puerto Plata, a 4-hour ride. Buses depart hourly; reservations are advised.

Note: Rented vehicles cannot cross the border between the Dominican Republic and Haiti.

Fast Facts

POPULATION: 8,950,034.

AREA: 48,443 sq km (18,704 sq mi.).

CAPITAL: Santo Domingo.

HIGHEST POINT: 3,087 m (10,128 ft.), Pico Duarte.

LOWEST POINT: -44 m (-144 ft.), Lago Enriquillo.

TIME ZONE(S): Atlantic Standard.

LANGUAGE: Spanish.

GOVERNMENT: Representative democracy.

UNIT OF CURRENCY: Dominican Republic Peso, divided into 100 centavos, also known as "chele." $1 U.S. = approx. 35 pesos. Keep all exchange receipts to reconvert to U.S. dollars. Only 30 percent of the original amount will be reconverted.

ELECTRICITY: 110 volts, 60 cycles AC.

MINIMUM AGE FOR DRIVERS: 25 to drive a rental car; maximum age 65. U.S. license valid; drive on left.

MINIMUM AGE FOR GAMBLING: 18.

SEAT BELT/CHILD RESTRAINT LAWS: Seat belts are required for all passengers.

HELMETS FOR MOTORCYCLISTS: Required.

HOLIDAYS: Jan. 1; Epiphany Day, closest Mon. to Jan. 6; Lady of Altagracia Day, Jan. 21; Juan Pablo Duarte Day, closest Mon. to Jan. 26; Carnival, Feb. 26; Independence Day, Feb. 27; Good Friday; Labour Day, closest Mon. to May 1; Corpus Christi Day, May or June (9th Thurs. after Easter); Restoration Day, closest Mon. to Aug. 16; Our Lady of Las Mercedes Day, Sept. 24; Constitution Day, Nov. 6; Christmas, Dec. 25.

TAXES: Taxes and service charges totaling 26 percent are added to all hotel and restaurant bills. This includes a 16 percent sales tax and a 10 percent service charge; in restaurants, an additional gratuity of up to 10 percent is customary. Departure tax $20 U.S.

IMMIGRATION REQUIREMENTS: A passport and a return or onward ticket are required. Tourists without a visa must pay $10 U.S. for a 30-day tourist card (available through air or sea carrier or upon arrival); the card must be surrendered upon leaving the country. The U.S. Dept. of Homeland Security requires all U.S. citizens returning from the Caribbean to present a valid passport.

PHONING THE ISLANDS: To call the Dominican Republic from the U.S. or Canada, dial 1 + 809 + the 7-digit local number.

FURTHER INFORMATION FOR VISITORS:

Dominican Republic Tourist Office
848 Brickell Ave., Suite 405
Miami, FL 33131
(305) 358-2899
(888) 358-9594

Ministry of Tourism, Government Offices
Bloque D, Ave. Mexico/30 de Marzo
Santo Domingo, Dominican Republic
(809) 221-4660
(809) 686-4659

Points of Interest

See map page 130.

BÁVARO (B-6)

Part of the Punta Cana destination area, Bávaro Beach stretches for 23 miles along the eastern edge of the island, protected by a coral reef. The first hotel was built here by a group of American investors in the 1970s; some two dozen resorts now line the shore.

MANATÍ PARK is n.w. of the Punta Cana resort district on Carretera Manatí; free bus service is provided from area hotels. This nature park features dolphin, sea lion, horse and parrot shows. Iguanas, exotic birds and reptiles are displayed in a tropical garden setting. An interactive program allows visitors to swim with dolphins. On the grounds is a Taíno village with a museum and demonstrations of native dancing.

Food is available. Allow 3 hours minimum. Daily 9-6. Swimming with Dolphins programs at 9, 2 and 5:15; reservations are required. Park admission $25; $15 (ages 2-12). Swimming with Dolphins (includes admission) $70. MC, VI. Phone (809) 221-9444.

BOCA CHICA (C-5) pop. 46,385

About 20 miles (32 km) east of Santo Domingo, Boca Chica boasts a white sand beach and shallow, crystal-clear waters. The area has been a favorite vacation spot since being discovered by the Republic's elite in the late 1920s. Coral reefs provide a natural barrier, creating excellent conditions for water skiing, windsurfing, scuba diving and snorkeling. Modern accommodations are nearby.

CABARETE (A-5)

A fortuitous combination of wind and geography has created near ideal conditions for windsurfing at Cabarete, and since the 1980s the town has become an internationally renowned destination for the sport's enthusiasts. Surfing and the newer sport of kite-boarding also are popular here.

RECREATIONAL ACTIVITIES

Mountain Biking

- **Iguana Mama** departs from Calle Principal No. 74. The outfitter offers day-long biking trips into the Cordillera Septentrional mountain range. Other activities are offered. Daily 8-5. Phone (809) 571-0908.

LA ROMANA (C-6) pop. 191,303

A sugar town on the southeast coast, La Romana means "the scales"; the cane growers brought their crops here to be weighed and bought. Most of its residents work at the sugar mill, which offers tours by appointment. Recreation includes tennis, polo, horseback riding and golf at three 18-hole courses, all at the nearby 7,000-acre (2,832-hectare) resort of Casa de Campo. An all-day boat excursion to Catalina Island, with its small offshore reef and powdery beaches, can be arranged at the harbor near town. The fishing village of Bayahibe, noted for its pristine beaches and diving sites, is a growing resort area.

Thousands of Dominicans make the yearly pilgrimage to the Basilica of Nuestra Señora de la Altagracia at Higüey (EE-gway), which is 23 mi. (37 km) northeast of La Romana. The large cathedral, built in honor of the country's patron saint, is considered one of the island's finest examples of modern architecture. West of La Romana are the beach resort towns of Juan Dolio, Guyacanes and San Pedro de Macorís, home of some of the country's—and America's—greatest baseball players.

GEM **ALTOS DE CHAVON** is high above the Chavon River, 8 mi. (13 km) e. via Casa de Campo. Built in 1976 to resemble a 16th-century Renaissance village, this artistic community promotes Dominican and international culture. The self-contained campus is host to many Dominican and international writers, painters, musicians and artisans.

The Altos de Chavon Art Gallery displays monthly exhibits by Dominican and international painters, sculptors and photographers. The Regional Museum of Archeology interprets aboriginal evolution from the first pre-ceramic groups to the highly developed Taíno Indians. The museum's fine collection of some 3,000 Taíno art and artifacts was collected along the banks of the Chavon River

Chavon Amphitheater, built in the classic Greek tradition, presents performances all year. The theater was inaugurated by Frank Sinatra in 1982. St. Stanislaus Church was named after Poland's patron saint in honor of Pope John Paul II, who donated the saint's ashes to the community. The church is built entirely of hand-cut stone.

Spanish influences can be seen along the cobblestone streets with their limestone buildings and wrought-iron balconies. Within these buildings are craft workshops, artist studios, ethnic restaurants and fine shops. Art gallery open Tues.-Sun. 10-10. Museum open Tues.-Sun. 8-8. Phone (809) 523-8011.

LA CUEVA DE LAS MARAVILLAS (CAVE OF WONDERS) is w. of La Romana between the Soco and Cumayasa rivers on San Pedro de Macoris Hwy. Guided 1-hour tours take visitors 80 feet (25 m) underground to the Cave of Wonders, which contains dramatic formations and some 500 pre-Columbian pictographs. Knowledgeable guides offer history and anecdotes; tours are available in English.

To protect rock formations, photography is prohibited. The cave is equipped with lighted pathways and an elevator; comfortable walking shoes are advised. Food is available. Allow 1 hour minimum. Tours depart on the hour Tues.-Sun. 9-5. Admission $3; $2.50 (children). Phone (809) 696-1797.

LUPERÓN (A-4)

On the northern coast of Hispaniola, the protected bay at Luperón has long provided shelter for seafaring travelers. Returning on his second voyage to the New World, Christopher Columbus moored near here with 17 ships and 1,500 men to establish the first European town in the Americas. The settlement of La Isabela, named after the queen of Spain, would be abandoned within 5 years.

PARQUE NACIONAL LA ISABELA is 8.5 mi. (14 km) w. of Luperón. In December 1493, Christopher Columbus established the first European settlement in the New World, building a walled city named La Isabela on the east bank of the Bajabonico River. The foundations of a fort, a sentry tower, a chapel and Columbus's limestone house are visible. A small museum features exhibits about Spanish and Taíno culture and artifacts excavated from the site; labels are in Spanish. Mon.-Sat. 9-5:30. Admission $1.

PUERTO PLATA (A-4) pop. 112,036

Puerto Plata, meaning "silver port," was named so by Christopher Columbus in 1493 because of the silver mist that hovers around the nearby mountains at sunset. Soon after its founding by Columbus' brother Bartolomeo in 1496, Puerto Plata began to flourish as a trade center for the Spanish colonies. Increasing competition from newer ports, however, led to its demise, and by 1520 Puerto Plata had become overrun by smugglers. Illegal trade continued well into the 17th century, despite the crown's decree that the town be destroyed and abandoned. Legitimate trade resumed in the mid-1700s, but it is tourism that fuels the local economy today.

Puerto Plata's charm lies in its cobblestone streets, Victorian homes and leisurely pace of life. Horse-drawn carriages are available for city tours. Central Park attracts sightseers; a large gazebo adorns the site. Puerto Plata's Brugal Rum is considered to be among the world's finest; the distillery on Avenida Luis Ginebra offers tours Mon.-Fri. 9-noon and 2-5.

Puerto Plata is the gateway to the 75 miles (120 km) of golden beach known as the Amber Coast. The many beaches along this beautiful strip include Sosúa, Long, Grande, Dorada, Cofresí and Cabarete. This glittering vista is best viewed from the top of Mount Isabela de Torres *(see attraction listing p. 137)*. Most of the major resorts are east of town in Playa Dorada and Costa Dorada.

Other interesting local attractions include Laguna Gri Gri and the town of Sosúa, a refugee colony of European Jews during World War II and the site of the island's largest dairy industry.

AMBER MUSEUM (MUSEO DEL ÁMBAR DOMINICANO) is on the second floor of the Villa Bentz at the corner of Calle Duarte and Padre Castellanos. Housed in an early 20th-century mansion built by wealthy German merchants, the museum features a large collection of amber. One particularly rare specimen contains a small lizard. Exhibits describe how the gem is formed and how and where it is mined in the Dominican Republic. Visitors can also see samples of copal, which is relatively young resin that has not completely hardened into amber.

Allow 30 minutes minimum. Mon.-Sat. 9-6. Admission $1. Phone (809) 586-2848.

MONSTER TRUCK SAFARIS provides shuttle service from area hotels. Narrated day-long tours aboard 8 x 8 all-terrain trucks depart from Puerto Plata and travel the back roads and rivers of the island. Stops include mingling with a local family at a typical Dominican home, visiting with children at a local schoolhouse and going for a river swim. A lunch stop features an island buffet.

English language tours depart from Puerto Plata Mon.-Sat. at 9, with hotel pick-up starting at 8. Guests are returned to their hotels by 5. Fare $89. Phone (809) 244-4060.

MOUNT ISABELA DE TORRES CABLE CAR (PICO ISABELA DE TORRES TELEFÉRICO) is s.w. of downtown near the jct. of Ave. Circunvalación Sur & Ave. Teleférico following signs. The cable car transports visitors to the top of 2,565-foot (782-meter) Mount Isabela de Torres for stunning views of the Cordillera Septentrional mountains, Puerto Plata and the Silver Coast. The statue "Christ the Redeemer" and a botanical garden with tropical plants and winding paths crown the summit. Visitors should arrive in the morning to avoid view-obscuring clouds that often develop. Long waits can be expected on weekends.

Food is available. Allow 3 hours minimum. Thurs.-Tues. 9-6. Hours may vary; phone ahead. Fare $4; $2 (ages 0-12). Phone (809) 970-0501.

GEM **OCEAN WORLD** is 3 mi. (5 km) w. on the Carretera 5 (C-5) to Cofresí Beach following signs. Comprising a series of artificial lagoons and aquariums constructed along the Atlantic shore, Ocean World is home to bottlenose dolphins, sea lions, sharks, stingrays, tropical birds and other exotic animals. Park admission includes snorkeling in a tropical reef aquarium and swimming in Tiger Grotto, a pool where otherwise dangerous cats are separated from guests by a glass wall.

The highlight of the park is its dolphin and sea lion encounter programs, which allow guests to touch and even swim with these intelligent marine mammals. Visitors can also walk through a small aviary and rain forest and relax on a sandy beach. Sea lions perform twice daily at the park's amphitheater.

Allow 4 hours minimum. Guests should wear swimwear and a change of clothes. Daily 10-5:30. Park admission (includes lunch buffet and round-trip bus transfers from larger hotels) $55; $40 (ages 4-12). Admission with an interactive program $25. Dolphin Swim $120; $95 (ages 6-12); under 6 not permitted. Dolphin Encounter $75; $55 (ages 4-12). Sea Lion Encounter $55; under 6 not permitted. Reservations are required. MC, VI. Phone (809) 291-1000.

OUTBACK JUNGLE SAFARI TOURS picks up passengers at area hotels. The tour company provides full-day, narrated excursions into the countryside aboard four-wheel-drive vehicles. Guides acquaint passengers with the lifestyle of average Dominicans through visits to a typical home and a schoolhouse. The excursion features a stop at a petting zoo and a cruise down a tropical river. Activities include swimming in a stream and boogie boarding at a white-sand beach. Food is available. Allow a full day. Daily 8-4:30. Fare $74; $37 (ages 0-12). MC, VI. Phone (809) 244-4886.

SAN FELIPE FORT dominates the Puerto Plata waterfront. It was built in 1520 to protect the country from English pirates and Carib Indians. The fort was used as a prison for political dissidents during the Trujillo regime. Guides conduct narrated tours Mon.-Sat. 9-5, Sun. 9-noon. Tour $1.30; tipping is customary.

PUNTA CANA (B-6)

One of the country's fastest-growing destinations, Punta Cana is known for its quiet beaches and all-inclusive resorts. The silky sand beaches on this eastern tip of the island stretch for some 30 miles (50 km), and watersports offer the chief source of entertainment. A coral reef—the longest in the region—breaks the waves offshore, keeping the surf gentle. Local communities in the Punta Cana area include Arena Gorda, Bávaro *(see place listing p. 136)*, Cabeza de Toro, Cap Cana, El Cortecito, Macao and Uvero Alto.

Punta Cana International Airport, reputedly the world's first privately owned international airport, is located within the 15,000-acre Puntacana Resort and Club. The Punta Cana Ecological Reserve is a natural sanctuary for local flora and fauna.

MANATÍ PARK—*see Bávaro p. 136.*

MONSTER TRUCK SAFARIS provides shuttle service from area resorts. Narrated day-long tours aboard 8 x 8 all-terrain trucks travel the back roads and rivers of the island. Passengers visit a local Dominican family, children at a local schoolhouse, a river where they can swim, a fruit plantation, a tobacco museum and a voodoo doctor. A lunch stop features an island buffet.

English-language tours depart Mon.-Sat. at 9. Guests are returned to their hotels by 5. Fare $99. Phone (809) 244-4060.

SANTIAGO (B-4) pop. 507,418

Santiago is the Dominican Republic's industrial center and second largest city. In addition to being the home of the world-famous *merengue* music, Santiago specializes in fine restaurants, robust Dominican coffee, fine handmade cigars and Bermudez Rum. In February this otherwise conservative city enjoys the merrymaking of Carnival, when revelers don elaborate costumes and colorful horned masks.

Santiago actually had three beginnings. Bartolomeo Columbus founded Santiago de los Caballeros in 1495 after an inland settlement at La Vega was abandoned. The town was moved to present-day Jacagua a few years later, leveled by an earthquake in 1562, then rebuilt at its present site. The ruins at La Vega can still be seen. Just north at Santo Cerro, or Holy Hill, Christopher Columbus reputedly raised the first cross of Christianity in the New World. The hill affords a spectacular view of the valley below.

In Santiago's Duarte Park is the Catedral de Santiago Apostol. The Gothic and neoclassical cathedral was built 1868-95 and features a carved mahogany altar and stained-glass windows by Rincon Mora. Other points of interest are the Tobacco Museum, also in Duarte Park; the Museum of the City of Santiago, in the 19th-century town hall; and the Tomás Morel Museum of Folkloric Art, featuring a display of prizewinning Carnival masks. A good way to take in some of Santiago's historical and architectural sights is by horse-drawn carriage.

MONUMENT TO THE HEROES OF THE RESTORATION OF THE REPUBLIC is in the s.e. section of the city. Constructed in the 1940s during the Trujillo era, the 200-foot column stands on a two-story base faced with native white marble. The monument offers an excellent view of the city. Murals by Spanish painter Vela Zanetti are displayed in an interior museum. Open daily. Free.

SANTO DOMINGO (C-5) pop. 1,887,586

Capital of the Dominican Republic, Santo Domingo was founded in 1496 by Bartolomeo Columbus. During the early 16th century, the city was the prize jewel of the Spanish colonies, enjoying great prosperity as the cultural center of the Caribbean and Spain's stepping stone to further explorations in the New World. It was during this period that many of the city's splendid palaces and churches were built.

However, when Spain turned its interests toward the gold fields of Mexico, Santo Domingo faced a sudden decline in prestige and wealth. The final blow occurred in 1586 when Sir Francis Drake of England pillaged and burned the city, which survived only to be invaded by the French and Haitians.

Many buildings and narrow streets reminiscent of the Old World have escaped the razing of expansive modernization projects. Ruins of city walls, ancient gates and crumbling fortresses in the colonial section (Zona Colonial) are vivid reminders of the city's history. Most notable are the ruins of San Nicolas de Bari Hospital and the Monastery of San Francisco, first of their kind in the New World.

The Atarazana, a restored 16th-century shipyard, covers a city block across from the Alcázar de Colón. Cafes, restaurants and boutiques as well as faithful restoration work make this a most interesting section to visit. A departure from the area's pervasive antiquity is the Mercado Modelo, the modern crafts market at avenidas Mella and Santome. On Calle Padre Billini is the Convent of the Dominicans, which dates from 1510. Inside the church is the Capilla del Rosario, or Chapel of the Rosary, a stone vault embellished with the signs of the Zodiac.

The western section of the city has benefited most from redevelopment. Of particular interest are the National Palace on Calle Moises Garcia and the Palace of Fine Arts (Palacio de Bellas Artes) at avenidas Independencia and Máximo Gómez. University City, site of the University of Santo Domingo, occupies several blocks west of Máximo Gómez. In the northwest section of the city are the Juan Pablo Duarte Olympic Center and Quisqueya Stadium.

BELLAPART MUSEUM (MUSEO BELLAPART) is on the fifth floor of a Honda dealership at Ave. John F. Kennedy & Dr. Luis Lembert Peguero. This small private collection traces the evolution of more than 100 years of Dominican fine art. Divided into four sections corresponding to important artistic trends, the museum features works by native Dominicans as well as expatriates from abroad who were influenced by their years in the Dominican Republic. Artists represented include Yoryi Morel, Jamie Colson, Darío Suro and José Vela Zanetti.

Allow 30 minutes minimum. Mon.-Fri. 10-6, Sat. 9-noon. Free. Phone (809) 541-7721.

GEM **COLONIAL SANTO DOMINGO (ZONA COLONIAL)** extends about 1 mi. (1.6 km) w. from the bank of the Ozama River, bounded on the north by Ave. Mella and on the south by the Caribbean Sea. The New World's first fortress, cathedral, monastery, hospital, palaces and government offices were built here after Christopher Columbus' arrival in 1492.

At the heart of this UNESCO World Heritage Site is Columbus Park. Two blocks east is the Ozama Fortress, within which stands the Tower of Homage (La Torre del Homenaje), built 1503-07. North along Calle de Las Damas is the National Pantheon, where the remains of some of the country's greatest heroes are enshrined.

Visitors to the colonial section are advised to wear comfortable shoes and light clothing, but not shorts; those wearing shorts can be denied admission to some attractions. Caution should be exercised in this area, as tourists are often approached by locals asking for money. Amiable freelance tour guides are eager to offer their services; it is wise to ask to see a government-issued identification card and to agree upon the guide's fee before taking a tour. Visitors should feel free to decline tours despite the insistence of overzealous guides; such tours are optional, even within most of the attractions.

Amber World Museum is on the second floor of a building at the corner of Arzobispo Meriño and Restauración in the Zona Colonial. Formed over the course of millions of years from hardened tree resin, amber is found in abundance in the Dominican Republic. The museum's displays describe the semiprecious gem's origins, the variety of material often contained in amber (leaves, insects, spiders, small frogs, lizards, etc.), how it is mined and what distinguishes Dominican amber from that which is found elsewhere in the world. Allow 30 minutes minimum. Mon.-Sat. 8-6, Sun. 8-2. Admission $1. Phone (809) 682-3309.

Casa del Cordón (Cord House) is at 214 Calle Isabel la Católica in the Zona Colonial. Diego Columbus lived here while the Alcázar was under construction. Built in 1503 and spared by earthquakes, hurricanes and Sir Francis Drake, it is said to be the oldest standing house in the Western Hemisphere. The stone cord carved above the door is the sign of a Franciscan order. The building now houses a bank and offices. Mon.-Fri. 8-4. Free.

Casa del Tostado (Dominican Family Museum) is on Calle Padre Billini and Arzobispo Meriño in the Zona Colonial. The 16th-century Tostado House, once used as the archbishop's palace, contains displays of 19th-century household effects and furnishings. The house's Gothic double window is architecturally unique. Guided tours are available. Mon.-Sat. 9-3. Admission $1. Phone (809) 689-5057.

Casa Duarte (Juan Pablo Duarte Museum) is at 308 Calle Isabel la Católica between calles Restauración and Vicente Celestino Duarte in the Zona Colonial. The 1826 birthplace of Juan Pablo Duarte, father of the Dominican Republic, contains personal possessions and furniture of the patriot and the Duarte-Diez family, as well as portraits of Duarte, paintings with historical themes and artifacts and documents of the independence period. Mon.-Fri. 9-5, Sat. 9-noon. Admission $1. Phone (809) 687-1436 or (809) 687-1475.

Casas Reales (Museum of the Royal Houses) is on Calle de Las Damas at Mercedes in the Zona Colonial. This architecturally interesting and historically important complex includes two palaces built in the early 16th century. Various facets of Spanish colonial life are depicted through artifacts, tapestries, maps and a re-created courtroom. Recovered treasures from sunken Spanish galleons and a large collection of arms and armor from the first through the 18th centuries also are displayed. Guided tours are available. Daily 9-5. Admission $1. Phone (809) 682-4202.

Cathedral Basilica Santa María la Menor is on Arzobispo Meriño next to Columbus Park in the Zona Colonial. Pope Paul III pronounced this the first cathedral in the New World in 1542. Sir Frances Drake reputedly lived in the cathedral for 25 days. With a Gothic vault, Spanish Renaissance facades, Romanesque arches and Baroque ornamentation, the cathedral is an architectural marvel. Exquisite stained-glass windows were crafted by Dominican artist Rincón Mora. Guide service of the cathedral is available. Appropriate attire is required; persons in shorts are not admitted. Daily 9-4:30. Donations. Phone (809) 682-3848.

Fortaleza Ozama is in the southeastern corner of the Zona Colonial at Calle Las Damas and Padre Billini. Begun in 1503 on the banks of the Ozama River, the fortress is said to be the oldest military complex in the New World. Dominating the open space within is the Torre del Homenaje (Tower of Homage), which was used as a prison until the 1960s and offers picturesque views from its battlements. A bronze statue of Gonzalo Fernández de Oviedo, the 16th-century Spanish historian, looms nearby. Allow 30 minutes minimum. Mon.-Sat. 9-5, Sun. 10-3. Admission $1; fee higher during special exhibition in May. Phone (809) 333-8672 or (809) 333-8673.

Larimar Museum is on the second floor of a building at the corner of Isabel La Católica and Padre Billini in the Zona Colonial. While the mineral pectolite can be found all over the world, blue pectolite—also called larimar—has been found only in the Dominican Republic's Barahona province. The small museum features labeled displays describing the semiprecious stone's volcanic formation and how it is mined. Allow 30 minutes minimum. Mon.-Sat. 8-6, Sun. 8-2. Free. Phone (809) 689-6605.

Museo Alcázar de Colón (Columbus Castle Museum) is at the n. end of Calle Las Damas next to the Gate of San Diego on the Plaza de España. This 22-room palace overlooking the Ozama River was built 1510-14 for Columbus' son Diego, first viceroy of the West Indies. The coral-rock castle served as the seat of the Spanish court for 60 years. Colonial furniture and 16th-century works of art add to the elegance of the interior. Guided tours in English are available. Mon.-Sat. 9-5, Sun. 9-4. Admission $2. Phone (809) 682-4750.

Museo de las Atarazanas is at 4 Calle Colon at the corner of Vicente Celestino Duarte Ave. in the Zona Colonial. On the street of taverns and shops that once served Spanish sailors, this museum chronicles 17th-century maritime life. Exhibits include shipwreck artifacts from the galleon *Concepción*, which sank off the coast in 1641. The museum also chronicles the gold, silver and slave trades. Most exhibits are labeled in Spanish. Allow 30 minutes minimum. Tues.-Sat. 9-5. Admission $1. Phone (809) 682-5834.

National Pantheon (Panteón de la Patria) is near the corner of Las Damas and Las Mercedes in the Zona Colonial. Originally a Jesuit church completed in the 1740s, the building endured periods as a warehouse and a theater before it was converted to a mausoleum in 1956 for Dominican dictator Rafael Trujillo. Interred within its walls are the remains of many of the nation's most illustrious political figures. A large bronze chandelier, a gift from Spanish dictator Francisco Franco, hangs beneath the domed ceiling. Allow 30 minutes minimum. Tues.-Sun. 9-6. Free. Phone (809) 689-6010.

San Francisco Monastery Ruins are on a hilltop n. of Ave. Mercedes at Calle Hostos in the Zona Colonial. The Franciscan monastery was thought to be the first in the Americas. Construction began around 1508, but a series of natural disasters, followed by Sir Francis Drake's 1586 rampage, thwarted its completion. Free.

San Nicolás de Bari Hospital Ruins are on Ave. Mercedes in the Zona Colonial. Stone walls remain from the first hospital to be erected in the Americas. A wooden building that had housed the sick and injured since 1503 was replaced in 1530 by the stone structure; records contain accounts of facilities that included a number of wards, a chapel and a cemetery.

GEM **COLUMBUS LIGHTHOUSE MONUMENT (FARO A COLÓN)** is on the east side of the Ozama River at Ave. España in Mirador del Este Park. The massive seven-story, cross-shaped edifice features 145 flood lamps that project a shining cross into the night sky. Displays in mahogany-trimmed rooms illustrate the discoveries of Christopher Columbus and how they changed the world.

Visitors also can see excellent scale models of the *Niña, Pinta* and *Santa María.* An entire hall is devoted to the construction of the monument, which was dedicated in 1992 to commemorate the 500th anniversary of Columbus' landing. Exhibits include photographs and drafts submitted by architects from around the world. An art gallery displays work from Santo Domingo.

The ornate bronze box suspended in a three-story marble monument—and guarded by militia—is said to contain the explorer's remains. DNA tests are under way to determine whether these or a set of bones moved to Spain in 1795 are those of Columbus or his son. Allow 1 hour minimum. Tues.-Sun. 9-5:30. Admission $1.25; 35c (children). Phone (809) 591-1492, ext. 238.

NATIONAL AQUARIUM (ACUARIO NACIONAL) is on Ave. España. A variety of marine and freshwater animals are displayed in tanks reflecting their natural habitats. A short film is presented. Food is available. Allow 30 minutes minimum. Tues.-Sun. 9:30-5:30. Film presented on the hour Tues.-Thurs. and every half-hour Fri.-Sun. Admission $1. Phone (809) 766-1709.

NATIONAL BOTANICAL GARDEN (JARDÍN BOTÁNICO NACIONAL) is n.w. of downtown on Av. Republica de Columbia in Altos de Galá. Highlights of the 400-acre (162-hectare) park include the Japanese Garden, the Great Ravine, the Floral Clock and the Orchid Pavilion. A passenger train transports visitors through the park. Daily 9-5. Admission

$1.50; 25c (children). Train 75c; 35c (children). Phone (809) 385-2611 or (809) 385-0774.

NATIONAL ZOOLOGICAL PARK (PARQUE ZOOLÓGICO NACIONAL) is at Ave. Vega Real and Ave. Los Arroyos Arroyo Hondo. The zoo preserves the natural environment of a wide variety of animals, which are allowed to roam freely. The park includes the African Plain, a children's zoo and one of the largest bird cages in the world. Five miles (8 km) of roads and walks traverse the park. Train tours also are available. Allow 2 hours minimum. Tues.-Sun. 9-5; closed Good Friday. Admission $5; $3 (children). Phone (809) 562-3149.

PARQUE INDEPENDENCIA (INDEPENDENCE PARK) is at the w. end of Calle El Conde at avs. Bolivar and Independencia. The park contains two national icons. At the east end is El Conde Gate, one of the city's original entranceways and the site of the nation's 1844 proclamation of independence. To the west is the Altar of the Nation, a white marble mausoleum containing the remains of founding fathers Juan Pablo Duarte, Francisco del Rosario Sánchez and Ramón Matías Mella. The images of both edifices can be seen on the Dominican 20-peso bill. Daily dawn-dusk.

PLAZA DE LA CULTURA is at avs. Mexico and Máximo Gómez. Representing the modern side of Santo Domingo, this cultural and educational center is distinguished by its progressive architecture. A park inside the plaza contains national cultural buildings and museums, set amid tropical gardens.

Museum of the Dominican Man (Museo del Hombre Dominicano) is on Calle Pedro Henríquez Ureña in the Plaza de la Cultura. The museum presents Dominican history and folklore from pre-Columbian times to the present. Exhibits include Indian artifacts excavated on the island and graphic displays charting migration in the Caribbean. Tues.-Sun. 9-5. Admission $2. Phone (809) 687-3622.

Museum of Modern Art (Museo de Arte Moderno) is on Calle Pedro Henríquez Ureña in the Plaza de la Cultura. The museum displays a collection of contemporary paintings and sculpture by Dominican and foreign artists as well as changing displays by current artists. Tues.-Sun. 10-6. Admission $1; free (children). Phone (809) 685-2153 or (809) 685-2154.

National Library (Biblioteca Nacional) is at Ave. César Nicolás Penson 91 in the Plaza de la Cultura. The library holds half a million books and magazines; its excellent research facilities require a good command of Spanish. Mon.-Fri. 8 a.m.-9 p.m., Sat.-Sun. 8-4. Free. Phone (809) 688-4086.

National Museum of History and Geography is on Ave. César Nicolás Penson in the Plaza de la Cultura. Devoted to Dominican history, the museum highlights the war against Haiti and the dictatorship of Rafael Trujillo. Tues.-Sun. 9-4:30. Admission $1. Phone (809) 686-6668 or (809) 689-9509.

National Museum of Natural History is on Ave. César Nicolás Penson in the Plaza de la Cultura. Exhibits focus on the natural characteristics and ecology of the island, from its creation to future developments. Of note is an extensive collection of mounted birds and fish. Tues.-Sun. 10-5. Admission $1; 50c (children). Phone (809) 689-0106.

National Theater (Teatro Nacional) is on Ave. Máximo Gómez in the Plaza de la Cultura. Architect Teófilo Carbonell's imposing structure is home to ballets, operas, dramas and concerts by local and visiting artists. Changing exhibits and a permanent collection of artwork by Dominican artists are displayed in the third-floor exhibition rooms. Guided tours are offered Mon.-Sat. 9-1. Free. Phone (809) 687-3191.

REFUGIO DE VIDA SILVESTRE CUEVA LOS TRES OJOS (WILDLIFE REFUGE CAVE OF THE THREE EYES) is s.e. via Las Americas Hwy. Three lagoons in 50-foot-deep caverns are accessible by limestone walkways; a fourth can be reached by water taxi. Stalactites, stalagmites and columns have created interesting formations. Several movies were filmed here. Swimming is not permitted. Guided tours are available in English. Open daily 7-5:30. Admission $1.50; 60c (children). Phone (809) 788-7056.

St. George's / © Heeb Photos / eStock Photo

Grenada

Popularly known as "the Spice Island of the Caribbean," Grenada (gre-NAY-da) has a moderate tropical climate that ensures the success of spice production. The island is famous for its cocoa, mace, cloves, vanilla, cinnamon, ginger—and nutmeg. Grenada is the largest nutmeg producer in the Western Hemisphere.

Grenada's balmy climate lures travelers seeking an ideal Caribbean retreat. Its 133 square miles (344 sq km) of tropical landscape, encompassing volcanic mountains, lush valleys and pristine beaches, have distinguished it as one of the most beautiful West Indian islands. Ninety miles (145 km) north of Trinidad, Grenada is the southernmost of the Windward Islands and offers a remoteness that is the essence of its appeal.

History

Though Christopher Columbus discovered Grenada during his third voyage in 1498, the island was relatively neglected until 1650, when it was purchased by the governor of Martinique. The French began their colonization with a series of skirmishes that virtually exterminated the island's native Carib population. The survivors were pushed north to Le Morne des Sauteurs, where rather than surrender they jumped off the cliff to the jagged rocks below. Today the site of the Carib defeat is known as Carib's Leap or Leapers' Hill.

After gaining complete control in 1714, the French introduced the cultivation of cocoa, coffee and cotton. During the wars between France and Great Britain, the island changed hands several times until the Treaty of Versailles finally ceded it to Britain in 1783. Slave labor and large plantation holdings brought prosperity to the island, which served as the headquarters of the British West Indies 1885-1958. After unsuccessful attempts to federate with other West Indian islands, Grenada assumed the status of an Associated State of Britain in 1967. The island became independent from the United Kingdom in 1974 and obtained dominion status within the Commonwealth.

Following a revolution on March 13, 1979, a People's Revolutionary Government replaced the parliamentary system of democracy in Grenada. Revolutionary rumblings and ideological differences erupted into a coup d'etat against the presiding prime minister in October 1983, prompting U.S. and Eastern Caribbean military intervention. Political order in Grenada was reestablished with the election of a representative government on December 3, 1984.

Shopping

A Grenada spice basket—a handwoven pannier of palm leaf or straw filled with cinnamon, nutmeg, ginger, vanilla, cloves and other native spices—is an easy way to bring the aroma of Grenada back home. Spice necklaces also are popular souvenirs. Straw and sisal items are usually bargains, particularly at the Blind Handicraft Center and the Straw Mart on the Carenage in St. George's. Another good buy is woodcarvings.

The Yellow Poui Art Gallery on Young Street in St. George's sells paintings, sculpture, photography, print editions, antique maps and graphics by local artists. Art Fabrik, also on Young Street, offers a large selection of handpainted batik art, clothing and accessories. Other popular shops are Tikal, Ganzee and Amba Kaila Spice Place.

More than 25 shops provide a wide range of quality items in the shopping mall at Melville Street Cruise Ship Terminal. Five shopping centers in the hotel area in Grand Anse contain fine shops, especially ones that sell china, crystal and other luxury items. With 82 booths, the Grand Anse Vendors' Market is an ideal place to purchase handcrafted jewelry, straw goods, clothing and spices. The market is open daily 9-6.

Shops are generally open Mon.-Fri. 8-4, Sat. 8-1. Banking hours are generally Mon.-Fri. 8-2.

Food and Drink

An almost endless list of seafood and homegrown fresh fruit is available at most island hotels and restaurants. *Callaloo* soup, crab backs, *lambi* (conch) dishes and avocado and nutmeg ice cream are local favorites. A liberal dose of Grenadian rum punch, made with lime juice, syrup, Angostura bitters,

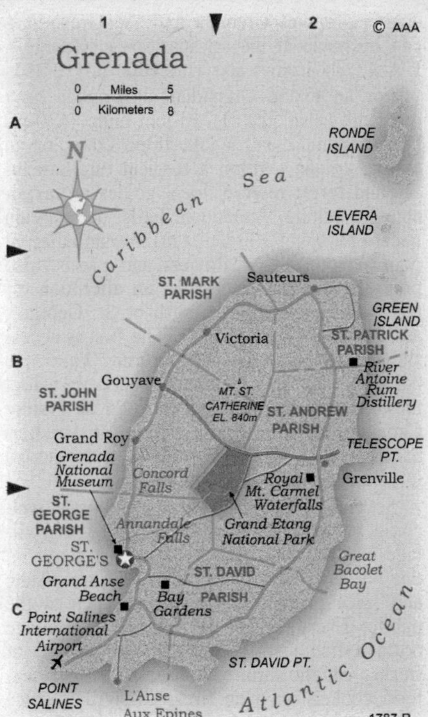

grated nutmeg and local rum, often helps encourage the visitor to experiment with the native cuisine. Gin and coconut water is another popular libation, as is the locally brewed Carib beer.

Sports and Amusements

Since much of the island nation is mountainous, it is easy to understand why hiking is a popular activity. Although guides may be necessary for some excursions, opportunities exist for hikes to waterfalls, historic sites, scenic views and nature study. Sailing the island's clear waters is another available form of outdoor recreation. Grand Anse, a dazzling 2-mile (3-km) stretch of sand on southwestern Grenada, is considered one of the world's finest beaches. Grenada's dependencies of Carriacou and Petite Martinique also have scenic coves with white sand beaches.

Scuba diving has become a major sport and is good off Point Salines and Molinere Point. Viewing the underwater sculptures at Molinere Marine Park also makes for an intriguing dive excursion. Experienced divers can reach the *Bianca C.*, a cruise ship that sank outside St. George's harbor in 1961; it is the largest shipwreck site in the Caribbean. Deep-sea vessels can be chartered for a half- or full-day. Arrangements for day sails and longer charters around Grenada and the Grenadines can be made at the marinas in St. George's, L'Anse aux Epines and True Blue Bay.

For an exotic Grenadian experience back on land, visit the 1,740-foot-high (530-m) Grand Etang Lake, a lake-filled crater of an extinct volcano within a tropical bird sanctuary and forest reserve; local guides are available for hiking. Annandale Falls, a mountain stream plunging 30 feet (9 m) into an adjacent pool surrounded by flowers and plants, also provides an ideal setting for an afternoon off the beaten path. To the north of St. George's are the three Concord Falls. The first is accessible by road; the second and third, known as Au Coin and Fontainbleu, are reached by foot through mountain terrain. La Sagesse Nature Center offers hiking trails, some 86 varieties of tropical birds, a plantation with guided tours and an extensive beach area.

Several spice and cocoa plantations welcome visitors. Gouyave, a small fishing village on the island's west coast, is a center of the nutmeg industry; its Dougaldston Estate and spice processing station are open to the public. Every Friday at 6 p.m., the village hosts a fish festival with a smorgasbord of freshly caught shrimp, lobster and other seafood cooked on open fires. Grenville's spice factory also is open for tours. Saturday in Grenville and St. George's is market day. Pastries, breads, fruits, spices, vegetables and handmade baskets, bags and hats are among the items for sale.

Some hotels have tennis courts, and two tennis clubs are near St. George's. The Grenada Golf Club has a nine-hole course. Cricket and soccer are the most popular spectator sports.

DID YOU KNOW

The first Elvis Presley postage stamp was issued by Grenada in 1978.

Because most visitors come to Grenada to soak up the sun, sail, snorkel or roam, the evenings tend to be much quieter than on some of the larger Caribbean islands. The hotels provide nightly entertainment in season, including dancing to popular music or calypso rhythms. When the sun finally sets, however, the majority of people are content to sit back, sip a rum punch and listen to a steel band.

Sightseeing

Popular tours on Grenada include a 2.5-hour ridge tour past the 18th-century forts on Morne Jaloux Ridge above St. George's; the fishing village of Woburn, where parts of the movie "Island in the Sun" were filmed; a small rum factory at Woodlands; and the beaches at Lance Aux Epines. A city tour of St. George's, which includes the Market Square, the Grenada National Museum, churches and surrounding 18th-century forts, also lasts about 2.5 hours.

A 3-hour mountain tour explores the island's tropical interior and passes spice, cocoa and banana plantations en route to Grand Etang National Park and Annandale Falls. A full-day tour departs St. George's and leads to Dougaldston Estate and the Nutmeg Processing Station at Gouyave before continuing by way of Victoria, Sauteurs, Levera Beach, Tivoli, Grenville and Grand Etang.

Full-day tours usually last 7 hours (including lunch) and visit most of the island's points of interest as well as some beaches. A special photographer's tour, conducted for a minimum of eight people, leads participants past 40 miles (64 km) of landscapes, ruins, villages, wildlife and native vegetation. If you wish to brave Grenada's narrow roads and hairpin turns yourself, road maps are available at the Grenada Board of Tourism on the Carenage in St. George's. Most hotels provide information about guided tours.

Local hotels also can arrange all-day yacht cruises along the island's western and southern coasts. If your time on the island is short, you may want to take a cruise of St. George's harbor and the surrounding area aboard the *Rhum Runner.* Moonlight cruises also are available.

Another popular excursion is a visit to the island of Carriacou (carry-a-KOO), 23 miles (37 km) northeast of Grenada. Noted for some of the best beaches in the Caribbean, the island also is famous for its small boatyards where villagers build wooden schooners using hand tools and centuries-old techniques. Good times to visit are in February during Carnival, in late April for the Carriacou Maroon Music

Festival, early August when the Carriacou Regatta takes place and in December for the Parang Festival on the weekend before Christmas.

Transportation

Flights to Point Salines International Airport are offered by American Eagle from San Juan, Puerto Rico, and by Air Jamaica nonstop from New York, with connections from other cities. There also are air connections to Grenada via Barbados and Trinidad. Many cruise lines also call at Grenada's deep-water port.

Taxis provide transportation between the airport and island hotels. Rental cars equipped for the island's left-hand driving are available in St. George's; a 2-day minimum rental is required. Driving conditions can be treacherous on some shoulderless, one-lane roads. Minibuses provide alternative means of transportation. Buses regularly depart from the St. George's bus terminal and the Esplanade for all parts of the island. Inexpensive water taxis transport passengers across the harbor and to the Grand Anse and Morne Rouge beaches.

Daily 15-minute flights and interisland ferries travel to the island of Carriacou. Local boat service also reaches Grenada's satellite island of Petite Martinique. Several flights depart daily to and from Point Salines International Airport. Boats depart daily from the Carenage.

Fast Facts

POPULATION: 102,632.

AREA: 344 sq km (133 sq mi.).

CAPITAL: St. George's.

HIGHEST POINT: 840 m (2,756 ft.), Mount Saint Catherine.

LOWEST POINT: Sea level, Caribbean Sea.

TIME ZONE(S): Atlantic Standard.

LANGUAGE: English and a French patois.

GOVERNMENT: Independent. Member of the British Commonwealth of Nations.

UNIT OF CURRENCY: Eastern Caribbean (E.C.) dollar. $1 U.S. = 2.7 E.C. dollars.

ELECTRICITY: 220 or 240 volts, 50 cycles AC.

MINIMUM AGE FOR DRIVERS: 21-25, depending on the rental car agency. Local license ($12 U.S.) required; drive on left.

SEAT BELT/CHILD RESTRAINT LAWS: Seat belts are required for front-seat passengers.

HOLIDAYS: Jan. 1; Independence Day, Feb. 7; Good Friday; Easter Monday; Labour Day, May 1; Whit Monday, May or June (8th Mon. after Easter); Feast of Corpus Christi, May or June (9th Thurs. after Easter); Emancipation Day, Aug. (1st Mon.); Carnival, Aug. (2nd Mon. and Tues.); Thanksgiving, Oct. 25; Christmas, Dec. 25; Boxing Day, Dec. 26.

TAXES: An 8 percent GCT (general consumption tax) and a 10 percent service charge are added to most hotel and restaurant bills. Departure tax $20 U.S.; ages 5-12, $10.

IMMIGRATION REQUIREMENTS: Passport and a return or onward ticket are required. No visa is needed for stays up to 3 months. The U.S. Dept. of Homeland Security requires all U.S. citizens returning from the Caribbean to present a valid passport.

PHONING THE ISLANDS: To call Grenada from the U.S. or Canada, dial 1 + 473 + the 7-digit local number.

FURTHER INFORMATION FOR VISITORS:

Grenada Board of Tourism
P.O. Box 1668
Lake Worth, FL 33460
(561) 588-8176
(800) 927-9554

Grenada Board of Tourism, St. George's
Burns Point
P.O. Box 293
St. George's, Grenada
(473) 440-2279

See color ad opposite inside back cover.

Points of Interest

See map page 143.

St. Andrew Parish (B-2)

The largest of Grenada's six parishes, St. Andrew has the longest coastline and is the island's agricultural center. Mangos, pumpkins, yams, lemons and coconuts are just a few of the crops that supplement the region's nutmeg production.

GRAND ETANG NATIONAL PARK (C-2)

Grand Etang National Park is 9.3 mi. (15 km) n.e. of St. George's in St. Andrew Parish, following signs to Snug Corner and St. Margaret. The park preserves 3,816 acres (1,544 hectares) of rain forest in the central mountain range, 1,740 feet (530 m) above sea level. Grand Etang Lake fills the crater of an extinct volcano.

Marked trails include a 15-minute introduction to the rain forest, a 1-hour hike around the lake and a 2-hour climb to the top of Mt. Qua Qua. Trail maps are usually available at the Grand Etang Forest Center, which offers exhibits and videotape presentations about the park's diverse flora and fauna.

Trails are often muddy; waterproof hiking boots are recommended. Allow 1 hour minimum. Mon.-Fri. 8-4, Sat.-Sun. 9-5. Admission $1. Phone (473) 440-6160.

GRENVILLE (B-2)

Grenada's second-largest town is home to one of the island's largest nutmeg factories. The Grenville Nutmeg Processing Station offers guided tours and demonstrations. Saturday morning is market day, when local farmers, anglers and merchants bring their wares to town. Culture, music and exotic foods fill the streets during the Rainbow City Festival on the first weekend in August.

ROYAL MT. CARMEL WATERFALLS is 2 mi. (3.2 km) s. of Grenville following signs. A guided 15-minute hike down a steep, wooded trail leads to the island's highest waterfall, also known as Marquis Falls, set in lush tropical surroundings. While swimming is not permitted at Royal Mt. Carmel, it is permitted at the lower waterfall, which also offers a picnic area. Daily 9-5. Admission $1.

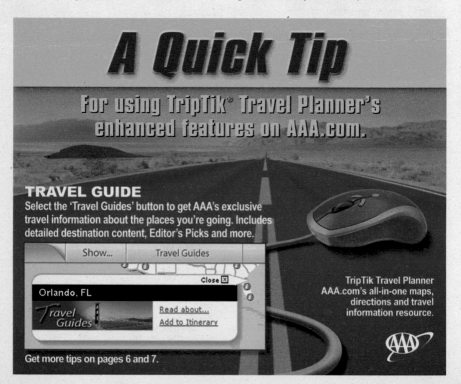

St. George Parish (C-1)

Home to Grenada's capital city, St. George Parish encompasses the southwest corner of the island. A number of historic forts crown the hilltops above St. George's Harbour; the best restored of these is the Fort George, built by the French in 1705.

ST. GEORGE'S (C-1) pop. 37,000

The streets of St. George's wind in a medieval tangle up several steep hillsides. One hill is so steep that it divides St. George's, but a tunnel through the hill connects the two sections. These terraced ways, the red- and white-gabled houses and the lively Saturday morning market lend an Old World charm to the town, considered by many travelers to be among the most picturesque in the Caribbean.

Grenada Board of Tourism: Burns Point, St. George's, Grenada; phone (473) 440-2279.

BAY GARDENS is 4 mi. (6 km) n.e. in the suburb of St. Paul's. On the slope of an old sugar mill, the walkthrough tropical garden is landscaped with fish pools, fruit and spice trees and more than 3,000 species of plants and flowers in tropical bloom. Guides explain the growing and processing of spice plants; tours are available by appointment. Daily 8-5; closed Jan. 1, Easter and Dec. 25. Admission $2. Phone (473) 435-4544 or (473) 414-3240.

GRENADA NATIONAL MUSEUM is on Young St. in the Antilles Bldg. Housed in a former French army barracks and prison built in 1704, the museum traces the island's history with pictorial displays and artifacts from the Indian period, the colonial period, the 1979 revolution and the 1983 intervention. Art galleries and a children's play center also are featured. Mon.-Fri. 9-4:30, Sat. 10-1:30, Sun. by appointment. Admission $4; $1 (ages 3-12). Phone (473) 440-3725.

St. Patrick Parish (B-2)

The northernmost parish on the island, St. Patrick encompasses the 16-acre (6-hectare) Lake Antoine, a shallow crater lake formed by an extinct volcano. Leapers Hill, a cliff near the fishing village of Sauteurs, marks the spot where some 40 Carib Indians jumped to their death in 1651 rather than submit to French colonists who were battling for possession of the island.

The 450-acre (180-hectare) Levera National Park protects mangrove swamps, another volcanic crater lake and a scenic beach. Hiking, swimming and birdwatching are popular activities.

RIVER ANTOINE RUM DISTILLERY is 6 mi. (10 km) n. of Grenville near Lake Antoine. One of the oldest water-driven distilleries still in operation in the Caribbean, the mill was built in 1785. Its signature product is the overproof Rivers Rum, a high-octane drink with an alcohol volume of more than 75 percent, or 151 proof. Guided tours of the distillery's operation include sugar cane crushing, extraction, fermentation and bottling. Allow 30 minutes minimum. Self-guiding tours are offered Mon.-Fri. 8-4, Sat.-Sun. by appointment. Admission $2. Phone (473) 442-7109.

Iles des Saintes / © Wayne Walton / Lonely Planet Images

Guadeloupe

Known as "the Emerald Isle," Guadeloupe (gwa-da-LOOP) lies midway between Puerto Rico and Venezuela. The "island" is really two smaller land masses joined by two bridges over a narrow channel called Rivière-Salée. Grande-Terre to the east typifies the French Antilles with rolling hills and sugarcane fields; Basse-Terre to the west is a rugged, mountainous island dominated by the volcano of La Soufrière. Its hills and ravines are lush with hardwood forests, ferns, bamboo, bananas, hibiscus, bougainvillea and guava. One road follows the coast while another crosses the highlands, providing a spectacular drive.

Pointe-à-Pitre, Guadeloupe's commercial center on Grande-Terre, and Basse-Terre, the capital, contrast busy port life with a French provincial atmosphere. This Gallic ambiance also is evident in Guadeloupe's island dependencies. The closest of these are Marie-Galante; La Désirade; and Les Saintes, where Norman-French speech and customs prevail. Farther north are Guadeloupe's two other island dependencies: St. Barthélémy, once a Swedish colony; and Saint Martin, where French and Dutch influences mingle.

History

Called "the island of beautiful waters" by the Carib Indians, Guadeloupe was discovered by Christopher Columbus in 1493, on his second voyage. He named the island for the Spanish monastery of Santa Maria de Guadalupe de Estremadura, but Spain established no colonies due to fierce opposition from the Caribs. Guadeloupe and her sister island Martinique were settled by French colonists in 1635 and soon became important centers of sugar production.

Both islands were incorporated as departments of France in 1946 and elevated to regions in 1974, with each island holding representation in the French Parliament by two senators, four deputies and two members of the Economic Council. The local government consists of elected General and Regional Councils as well as a prefect, or governor; the island's inhabitants are French citizens.

Shopping

The French islands are excellent shopping centers, where perfumes and other luxury made-in-France products are sold at or below Paris, New York or St. Thomas prices. Le Bonheur des Dames and Passion Beauté on the Rue Frébault are among the most popular places to shop for perfumes. Rues de Nozières and Schoelcher also have shops carrying French imports as well as madras cottons, watches, silver and china. The local outdoor market, Marché d'Epices, and the Place de la Victoire are worth visiting.

Most shops are open Mon.-Fri. 8-noon and 2-6, Sat. 9-1, and are closed holidays. Banking hours are Mon.-Fri. 8-noon and 2-4; summer hours are Mon.-Fri. 8-3. Stores can give up to 20-percent discounts on some luxury goods purchased with travelers checks or certain credit cards.

Food and Drink

Guadeloupe shares its cuisine with France. Delicacies like *escargots* are on the menus of many restaurants and can be savored with excellent French wines. Traditional Creole dishes available in most restaurants lend added zest to dining. *Colombo,* a spicy Indian dish of currylike seeds cooked with either beef, pork, chicken, mutton, conch or goat, is eaten with rice; stuffed crab and crayfish are prepared in a variety of ways; *calalou* soup is made from greens, West Indian herbs and bacon; *court bouillon* combines a thick fish stew with rice; gumbos are eaten with rice and fried codfish; and yams are cooked in their skins and seasoned with butter and cheese. Gourmet menus list roasted wild goat, duckling and a salad of coconut and hearts of palm.

Meals taste best preceded by Punch Guadeloupéen, or "Ti Punch," a delicious and quite potent rum potion. Rum is bottled locally, as is mineral water. Local milk and water are safe. At the airport and around the dock at Terre-de-Haut, one of the Saintes islands, barefoot children sell a delicious coconut

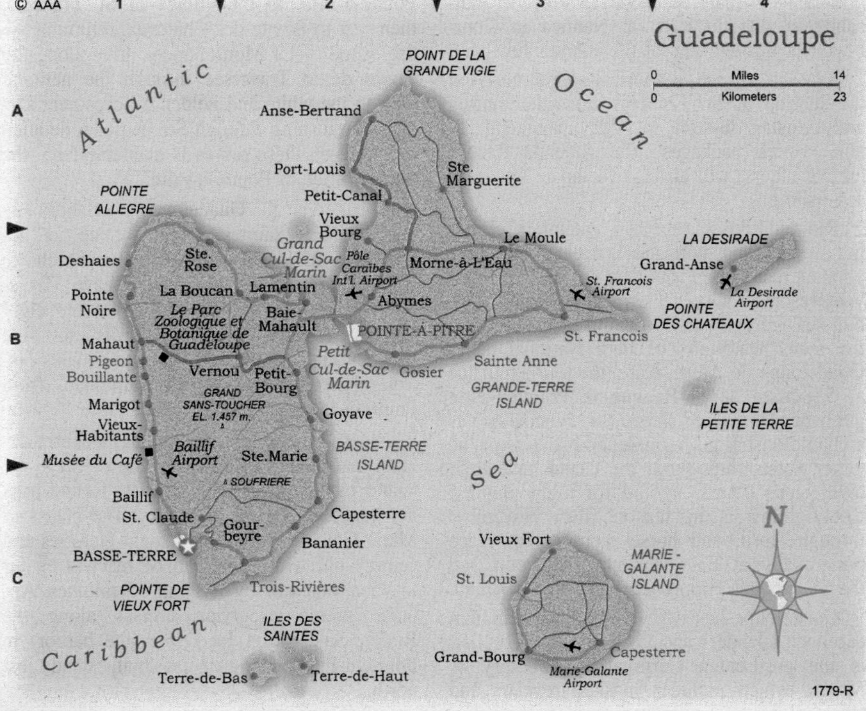

pastry called *tourment d'amour,* or "torment of love."

Guadeloupe boasts more than 200 restaurants, often modest in appearance but superior in cuisine. Served after noon, lunch is a big meal in Guadeloupe, as evidenced by multi-course Creole lunches. Most hotels and restaurants include a 10- to 15-percent service charge in their prices. If not, this charge will be added to the final bill.

Sports and Amusements

Beaches of white, ochre and black volcanic sand offer almost unlimited opportunities for swimming, snorkeling, scuba diving, water skiing, windsurfing and other aquatic sports. Grande-Terre's southern coast boasts several good public beaches, including those at Ste. Anne, St. François and Gosier as well as tiny coves of white powdery sands only a hike away from the main beach road. Favorable trade winds called *les alizés* create conditions ideal for sailing, water skiing and windsurfing between Grande-Terre and the islet of Gosier, just offshore from Gosier.

Beginning scuba divers can enroll in several diving schools based at local hotels. Several water sports concessions are congregated on the beach at Gosier. Yacht chartering has become increasingly popular in recent years; arrangements can be made at Port de Plaisance in Bas du Fort; at Nautica in Gourbeyre; or through any of the island's hotels.

Evasion Marine, a nautical school based at the marina at St. François, provides sailing and cruising lessons in 1-day, weekend, 2- and 3-week packages. The Kalenda Resort, among others, will arrange for boats for deep-sea fishing.

Riding, hiking, camping, mountain climbing, tennis and golf are some of the most popular recreational pursuits on land. The adventuresome, wise to arm themselves with bug spray, might wish to camp or hike around the many waterfalls of Parc National de la Guadeloupe on Basse-Terre; the tourism office at 5 Square de la Banque in Pointe-à-Pitre publishes *Walks and Hikes.* St. François boasts a championship golf course, and several of the larger hotels throughout the island have their own tennis courts, lighted for night playing. Cockfighting is in season from November through April, and horse racing takes place periodically at Baie-Mahault, Bellecourt and the St. Jacques Hippodrome at Anse Bertrand.

Guadeloupe has two seasonal festivals that captivate islanders and visitors alike. The first is the pre-Lenten Carnival in February or March, which includes masked revelers and costumed dancers winding through the streets, parades with elaborate floats and street parties. The second, on the Saturday closest to August 10, is called the *Fête des Cuisinières,* or the Women Cooks' Festival. The celebration begins with a religious service in the cathedral in Pointe-à-Pitre. Then there is a procession of women in Creole dress carrying exotic island specialties through the capital, followed by a 5-hour feast with much singing and dancing.

Sightseeing

Guadeloupe's major road system encompasses about 1,200 miles (1,930 km). A day tour of Grande-Terre might include a drive from Pointe-à-Pitre to Port-Louis and Anse Bertrand. After the spectacular cliffs at Pointe de la Vigie, the return trip leads through Le Moule, Pointe des Châteaux, Ste. Anne and Gosier. Another all-day excursion can be made by crossing the channel to Basse-Terre, following Route de la Traversèe as it winds through the 73,240-acre (29,640-hectare) Parc National, then turning south along the coast to Basse-Terre and on to the archeological park at Trois-Rivières, and returning to Pointe-à-Pitre via the coast road.

Other excursions include a drive from Pointe-à-Pitre to the village of St. François, then east to Pointe des Châteaux, returning via Ste. Anne or Le Moule; and a drive along the Route de la Traversèe through the national park to the white and golden beaches near Deshaies, returning through Ste. Rose. A detailed brochure on these drives is available from the tourist office in Pointe-à-Pitre.

Excursions to Guadeloupe's offshore islands of Les Saintes, Marie-Galante and La Désirade offer an alternative approach to sightseeing. Boat excursions leave Trois-Rivières for Terre-de-Haut, one of the eight Saintes islands, affording visits to fine beaches and a small village with quaint bistros. Ferries also travel round-trip from Pointe-à-Pitre.

Ninety-minute minibus tours of Terre-de-Haut (narrated in French) include a visit to the island bastion Le Fort Napoléon. Round trips are available via Air Caraïbes. The island of Marie-Galante, dotted with sugar factories and century-old windmills, can be reached by air in 15 minutes or by ferry in 35 minutes. Another scenic excursion cruises along the Rivière-Salée from La Darse (the harbor) in Pointe-à-Pitre to one of the small islands just north.

Transportation

Pôle Caraïbes International Airport, just north of Pointe-à-Pitre, services flights from New York, Newark, Miami, San Juan and other U.S. cities and Caribbean islands. Air Caraïbes makes frequent flights to Guadeloupe's island dependencies and to the other islands of the French West Indies. Charter flights can be arranged at the small airports at St. François on Grande-Terre and Baillif on Basse-Terre. Pointe-à-Pitre is a port of call for many cruise ships.

Taxi fare from the airport to Pointe-à-Pitre is approximately $11.50-$14; from 9 p.m. to 7 a.m. and all day Sunday the fare increases by 40 percent. Crowded buses used largely by islanders also are available. Car rental plans should be made in advance; a valid U.S. driver's license is required. Rates are approximately $50 a day plus a kilometer charge; gas is not included. Camper-car rentals are available at Abymes.

Daily ferry transportation to the islands of Marie-Galante and Les Saintes is offered by Brudey Frères and TMC Archipel. These island routes are also serviced by Caribbean Express and L'Express des Iles, high-speed passenger ferries that connect Guadeloupe with Dominica, Martinique and St. Lucia.

Fast Facts

POPULATION: 431,170.

AREA: 1,373 sq km (530 sq mi.).

CAPITAL: Basse-Terre.

HIGHEST POINT: 1,484 m (4,869 ft.), La Soufrière.

LOWEST POINT: Sea level, Caribbean Sea.

TIME ZONE(S): Atlantic Standard.

LANGUAGE: French and Creole.

GOVERNMENT: Overseas Department of France.

UNIT OF CURRENCY: Euro Dollar. $1 U.S. = approx. .6 Euro.

ELECTRICITY: 220 volts, 50 cycles AC.

MINIMUM AGE FOR DRIVERS: 21-25, depending on the rental car agency. U.S. license valid; drive on right.

MINIMUM AGE FOR GAMBLING: 18.

SEAT BELT/CHILD RESTRAINT LAWS: Seat belts are required for all passengers. Children under 12 must ride in the back seat.

HOLIDAYS: Jan. 1; Easter Monday; Labour Day, May 1; Victory Day, May 8; Ascension Day, May (6th Thurs. after Easter); Whit Monday, May or June (8th Mon. after Easter); Abolition Day, May 27; Bastille Day, July 14; Schoelcher Day, July 21; Feast of the Assumption, Aug. 15; All Saints' Day, Nov. 1; Remembrance Day, Nov. 11; Christmas, Dec. 25.

TAXES: A 10-15 percent service charge is added to most hotel and restaurant bills. Departure tax $20 U.S. (included in plane fare).

IMMIGRATION REQUIREMENTS: A valid passport and return or onward ticket are required for U.S. citizens entering the French West Indies. No visa needed for stays up to 3 months. The U.S. Dept. of Homeland Security requires all U.S. citizens returning from the Caribbean to present a valid passport.

PHONING THE ISLANDS: To call Guadeloupe from the U.S. or Canada, dial 011 + 590 + 590 + the 6-digit local number.

FURTHER INFORMATION FOR VISITORS:

French Government Tourist Office
825 3rd Ave.
New York, NY 10022
(212) 838-7800

Guadeloupe Tourist Office
5 Square de la Banque
B.P. 555, F-97166 edex
Pointe-à-Pitre, Guadeloupe
(590) 82-09-30

Points of Interest

See map page 149.

Basse-Terre Island (C-2)

The mountainous island of Basse-Terre (boss-TARE) is dominated by 4,869-foot (1,484 m) La Soufrière. The village of St. Claude, noted for its coffee and banana plantations and stately homes, is the starting point for many trips up the volcano. After driving through the East Indian village of Matouba, where such ancient rites as animal sacrifice are still practiced, another road runs through the Bains Jaunes Rain Forest to within a 20-minute climb of the summit.

Southeast of the capital city of Basse-Terre are the engraved rocks at Trois-Rivières, a string of fishing hamlets and Ste. Marie, where Christopher Columbus landed in 1493. Inland from Trois-Rivières are the well-known thermal baths at Ravine Chaude.

BASSE-TERRE (C-1) pop. 12,410

Basse-Terre is the administrative capital of Guadeloupe. Known for its 17th-century Cathedral of Our Lady of Guadeloupe, French provincial atmosphere and colorful port life, this charming city offers fine shops and open-air markets.

FORT LOUIS DELGRÈS is near the village of Gourbeyre. The fortification was built about 1650 by Charles Houel, the island governor appointed Marquis de Guadeloupe by Louis XIV. Guarding the approach to Basse-Terre, the fort served in several battles against the British. Daily 7-5. Free. Phone (590) 81-37-48.

PARC ARCHÉOLOGIQUE DES ROCHES GRAVÉES is in Trois-Rivières. Deep in a forest grotto, the Archeological Park of Engraved Rocks protects carvings left by Arawak Indians. A botanical garden is on the grounds. Tours are available. Daily 9-5. Admission $2.50. Phone (590) 92-91-88.

BOUILLANTE (B-1) pop. 7,336

The steep Mamelles mountain range plunges into the sea at the picturesque bay of Bouillante on the western coast. Offshore is Pigeon Island and the Cousteau Marine Reserve, considered one of the best dive sites in the world. Snorkeling, scuba diving and glass-bottom boat tours depart from Malendure Beach.

LE PARC ZOOLOGIQUE ET BOTANIQUE DE GUADELOUPE is 5.6 mi. (9 km) n.e. The zoo and botanical garden is home to monkeys, raccoons, agoutis, mongooses, turtles and tropical birds. A boardwalk canopy tour takes visitors high above the dense forest, and a self-guiding nature walk follows a series of suspension bridges. Food is available. Allow 1 hour minimum. Daily 9-5. Admission $13.80; $9 (children). Phone (590) 98-83-52.

PETIT-BOURG (B-2) pop. 20,528

DOMAINE DE VALOMBREUSE is on Cabout St. A 9-acre (3.6-hectare) tropical garden contains more than 450 varieties of plants and flowers. Also within the 20-acre (8-hectare) park is a bird sanctuary featuring some 300 species. Food is available. Allow 1 hour minimum. Daily 8-6. Last admission 1 hour before closing. Admission $9.50; $4.50 (ages 0-11). AX, MC, VI. Phone (590) 95-50-50.

POINTE NOIRE (B-1) pop. 7,689

Named "Black Point," this small coastal village gets its name from the black volcanic sand on its beaches. Sand paintings are offered at local craft markets.

LA MAISON DU BOIS (HOUSE OF WOOD) is on Les Plaines Road. Traditional woodworking and the island's tree varieties are showcased at this house, which is made of local woods and contains permanent exhibits of furniture, boats and musical instruments. Tues.-Sun. 9:30-5, Oct.-July. Admission $12. Phone (590) 98-16-90.

LA MAISON DU CACAO (HOUSE OF COCOA) is .8 mi. (1 km) s. at the jct. of Route de la Traversée. The history of cocoa and chocolate are represented at this working cocoa plantation, where cocoa is harvested by traditional methods. Tastings are offered. Food is available. Allow 30 minutes minimum. Mon.-Sat. 9:30-5, Sun. 9:30-1; reduced hours Sept. 1-15. Admission $6.25; $5 (children and senior citizens). AX, MC, VI. Phone (590) 98-25-23.

STE. ROSE (B-1) pop. 17,574

LE DOMAINE DE SÉVERIN is just w. of La Boucan traffic circle on road RN2, following signs. Originally called the Bellevue Plantation, this 18th-century sugar estate was purchased by the Marsolle family in 1928. The working rum distillery is operated by a paddlewheel. Tropical gardens and crawfish pools are among the sights on a narrated train tour. Rum tastings are offered, and food is available. Allow 1 hour minimum. Open Mon.-Sat. 8:30-5:30. Train tours depart at 9:30, 10:45 and 11:30. Admission $7.75; $6 (ages 5-12). MC, VI. Phone (590) 28-91-86 or (590) 28-28-11.

MUSÉE DU RHUM is at Belle Vue. The Rum Museum chronicles three centuries of sugar cane history, leading to the distilling of rum. Exhibits include early production equipment, models of trade ships and information about Caribbean customs and daily life. An extensive butterfly and arthropod collection also is displayed. Tastings at the Reimonenq Distillery are offered. Allow 2 hours minimum. Mon.-Sat. 9-5. Admission $6.50; $4.35 (ages 10-18); $3.25 (ages 0-9). VI. Phone (590) 28-70-04.

VIEUX-HABITANTS (B-1) pop. 7,611

Coffee, vanilla and cocoa flourish on Basse Terre's west-central coast. Vieux-Habitants, the first village on the island, was settled here in 1636. Its name means "old inhabitants." The 18th-century Saint-Joseph Church is noted for its collection of gold and silver relics.

MUSÉE DU CAFÉ is .6 km (.4 mi) n. The museum traces the cultivation of coffee in Guadeloupe from 1721 to the present. Historic exhibits at this working plantation include antique coffee mills and roasters. Visitors may observe the processing of bonifière coffee and taste the finished product. Allow 30 minutes minimum. Daily 9-5. Admission $6; $5 (ages 0-12). Phone (590) 98-54-96.

Grande-Terre Island (B-3)

Unlike its mountainous sister, Grande-Terre (gron-tare) is characterized by rolling hills, sandy beaches and sugarcane fields. The limestone islet of Gosier, off the coast of the town of the same name, has a white coral beach. Farther east, swimming is delightful at Ste. Anne, Le Moule, Port-Louis and St. François, a fishing village noted for its square and buildings. The coastline is particularly scenic between Le Moule beach and Pointe des Châteaux. A small airport at the Hamak and Kalenda hotels offers charter flights to local islands.

LE MOULE (B-3) pop. 20,827

The former capital of Guadeloupe, Le Moule has a beach that was once the battleground for Carib warriors and French and English soldiers. In the 19th century, nearly all of the sugar and rum produced on Grande-Terre was shipped from Le Moule's harbor.

EDGAR CLERC ARCHEOLOGICAL MUSEUM is 1.2 mi. (2 km) n. at 440 Route de la Rosette in Parc de la Rosette. Two rooms house the permanent collection of archeological artifacts of the Carib and Arawak Indians. The building is surrounded by a tropical garden that overlooks the ocean. Mon.-Wed. 9-5; closed holidays. Free. Phone (590) 23-57-57 or (590) 23-57-43.

DID YOU KNOW

England once considered trading Canada in exchange for the French island of Guadeloupe.

POINTE-À-PITRE (B-2) pop. 20,948

Pointe-à-Pitre is the commercial capital of Guadeloupe and seat of the sub-prefecture of Grande-Terre. About 40 miles (64 km) northeast of Basse-Terre, Pointe-à-Pitre is reached by either of two bridges from Basse-Terre Island. Colonial and modern buildings complement each other; white bungalows with red roofs are separated by tree-lined parks and a large market square. Place de la Victoire, punctuated by royal palms, shade trees and poincianas, is bordered by attractive wooden houses with balconies.

Guadeloupe Tourist Office: 5 Square de la Banque, Pointe-à-Pitre, Guadeloupe 97163; phone (590) 82-09-30.

AQUARIUM DE LA GUADELOUPE is .6 mi. (1 km) w. of the marina in Bas du Fort. The facility displays marine life found in the waters around Guadeloupe, including sharks and piranhas. Food is available. Allow 30 minutes minimum. Daily 9-7. Admission $12; $6 (ages 5-12). AX, MC, VI. Phone (590) 90-92-38.

FORT FLEUR D'EPÉE overlooks the bay. The point offers a fine view of the islands of Le Saints and Dominica and the mountains of Basse-Terre. Because of its strategic location, this 18th-century fort was the scene of fierce struggles between the French and English. Today preserved battlements, dungeons with underground passageways, some walls and a small chapel remain. Daily 9-6. Free. Phone (590) 90-94-61.

SCHOELCHER MUSEUM is at 24 rue Peynier behind the market. The museum is dedicated to abolitionist Victor Schoelcher, who is credited with ending slavery in the French West Indies in 1848. Housed in a 19th-century setting, the museum contains some of Schoelcher's personal belongings and traces the island's recent history. Mon.-Fri. 9-5; closed holidays. Admission $1.60; 80c (ages 0-12). Phone (590) 82-08-04.

Iles des Saintes (C-2)

The Saints Islands are a cluster of eight islands considered among the most beautiful in the Caribbean. Their isolation from the plantation system distinguishes them from sister islands and enabled them to maintain a way of life in which fishing is still the main occupation and source of income.

Only two of the islands are inhabited; the fishing village of Bourg is found on Terre-de-Haut. Standing over the bay is Pain de Sucre (Sugar Loaf), a mountain named for its resemblance to a mound of sugar. Terre-de-Haut can be reached by boat from Trois-Rivières or by daily ferry or flights from Pointe-à-Pitre. *Taxis de l'Ile,* or minibuses, provide transportation to the island's points of interest, including Le Fort Napoléon with its modern art gallery and cactus garden. There is a good view of Terre-de-Haut from the old stone watchtower on 1,014-foot Le Chameau, the island's highest point.

Marie-Galante Island (C-3)

On his second voyage to the New World, Columbus named this island after his flagship, the *Maria Galanda*. Fifteen miles (24 km) southeast of Pointe-à-Pitre, Marie-Galante is Guadeloupe's largest dependency. The round, flat island is often called *la grande galette*, or "the big pancake." More than 100 windmills once dotted the countryside, and many ruins are still visible.

About half of the rural island's 12,500 inhabitants live on the southwest coast at Grand-Bourg, the administrative capital. To the north is the fishing village of Saint-Louis, and to the east is Capesterre, home of the Bielle and Bellevue rum distilleries. Transportation to Marie-Galante is available by ferry from Pointe-à-Pitre and St. François or by air.

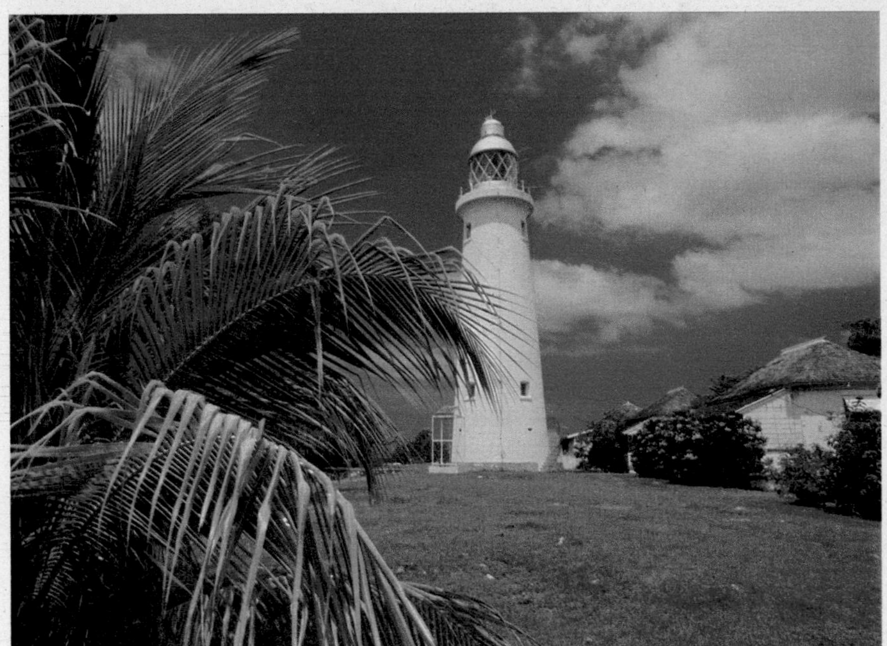

Negril Point Lighthouse, Negril / © Greg Johnston / Lonely Planet Images

Jamaica

A multiracial population and varied scenery are primary components of Jamaica's charm. Most Jamaicans are descendants of African slaves brought to the island between the 17th and 19th centuries, but Chinese, East Indians, Lebanese, Europeans and North Americans as well as nationals from neighboring republics, also have made the island their home. This multiplicity, most evident in the port city of Kingston, reflects a special unity in the country's motto, "Out of many, one people."

Third largest of the Greater Antilles, Jamaica is 550 miles (885 km) south of Florida. About 146 miles (235 km) long and 51 miles (82 km) wide, the landscape is primarily one of contrasts, ranging from misty forest-clad mountains to bare scrubland and fields. The island's diverse terrain also is reflected in its beaches, which vary from fine coral sand in sheltered bays and inlets to black sand along the rugged coastline, where the mountains plunge straight into the sea. Montego Bay, Negril, Ocho Rios and Port Antonio are some of the most popular resort centers. Small towns and mountain villages might lack the comforts of the developed port cities but are rich in island lore and natural beauty. Blanketed with peach trees and strawberry fields, the summit of 7,402-foot Blue Mountain Peak provides a 90-mile (145-km) panorama on clear days.

History

The Indians in Cuba had told Christopher Columbus of *Xaymaca,* the "land of wood and water." He attempted to land at St. Ann's Bay in May 1494, but was met by hostile Taínos and had to remain offshore. After overcoming lighter resistance, he came ashore at Discovery Bay the next day, then landed at Montego Bay before moving on. Columbus made an inauspicious return in 1503; the last

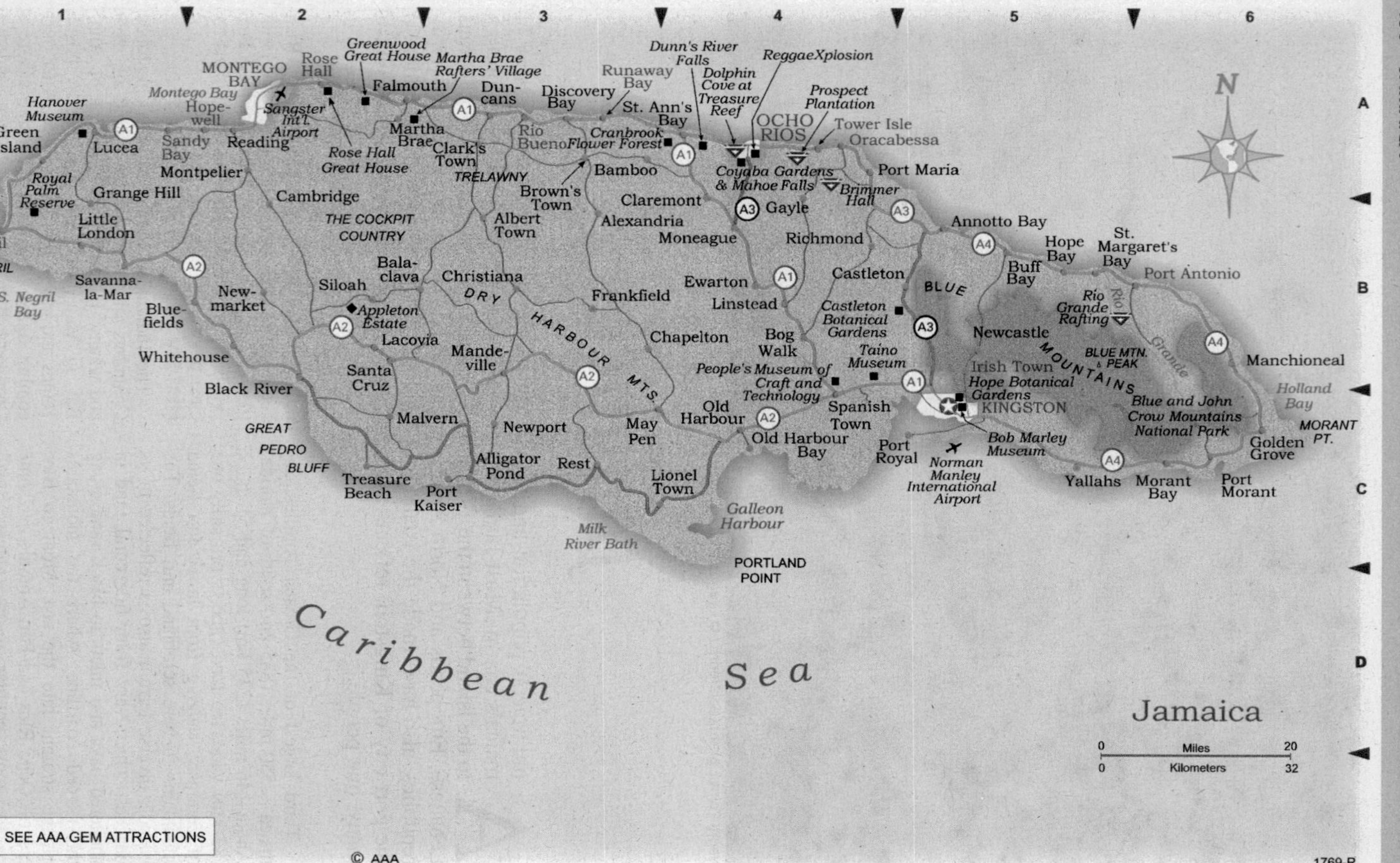
1
2
3
4
5
6
A
B
C
D
N
Hanover Museum
Green Island
Lucea
Royal Palm Reserve
Long Bay
Negril
S. NEGRIL POINT
S. Negril Bay
Little London
Grange Hill
Savanna-la-Mar
MONTEGO BAY
Montego Bay
Hopewell
Sandy Bay
Montpelier
Reading
Sangster Int'l. Airport
Rose Hall
Rose Hall Great House
Greenwood Great House
Falmouth
Martha Brae Rafters' Village
Martha Brae
Clark's Town
TRELAWNY
Duncans
Rio Bueno
Discovery Bay
Runaway Bay
St. Ann's Bay
Cranbrook Flower Forest
Brown's Town
Dunn's River Falls
Dolphin Cove at Treasure Reef
ReggaeXplosion
OCHO RIOS
Prospect Plantation
Tower Isle
Oracabessa
Coyaba Gardens & Mahoe Falls
Brimmer Hall
Port Maria
Bamboo
Claremont
Alexandria
Moneague
Gayle
Richmond
Cambridge
THE COCKPIT COUNTRY
Albert Town
Blue-fields
New-market
Whitehouse
Black River
Siloah
Bala-clava
Appleton Estate
Lacovia
Santa Cruz
Malvern
GREAT PEDRO BLUFF
Treasure Beach
Port Kaiser
Christiana
DRY HARBOUR MTS.
Mande-ville
Newport
Alligator Pond
Rest
Milk River Bath
Frankfield
May Pen
Lionel Town
Ewarton
Linstead
Chapelton
Bog Walk
People's Museum of Craft and Technology
Old Harbour
Old Harbour Bay
Galleon Harbour
PORTLAND POINT
Castleton
Castleton Botanical Gardens
Taino Museum
Spanish Town
Port Royal
Norman Manley International Airport
Annotto Bay
Buff Bay
Hope Bay
St. Margaret's Bay
Port Antonio
Rio Grande Rafting
Rio Grande
BLUE MOUNTAINS
BLUE MTN. PEAK
Newcastle
Irish Town
Hope Botanical Gardens
KINGSTON
Bob Marley Museum
Blue and John Crow Mountains National Park
Manchioneal
Holland Bay
MORANT PT.
Golden Grove
Port Morant
Morant Bay
Yallahs
A1
A2
A3
A4
Caribbean Sea
Jamaica
0 Miles 20
0 Kilometers 32
SEE AAA GEM ATTRACTIONS
© AAA
1769-R

two ships of his fourth voyage were forced to run aground at St. Ann's Bay, and he and his crew were marooned there for more than a year. It wasn't until a small charter could be sent from Hispaniola that Columbus was able to return home, where he died 2 years later.

Diego Columbus, son of the explorer, returned to St. Ann's Bay in 1509 and founded Sevilla Nueva. The marshy site was soon abandoned, however, in favor of Santiago de la Vega (St. James of the Plain) at present-day Spanish Town. Having depleted the Taíno population through overwork and disease, the Spaniards turned to Africa for slaves and in 1517 imported the first of Jamaica's current majority race. The island was never fully developed as a Spanish colony, however, and in 1655 a British expedition literally walked into Spanish Town and took it over. The island was officially ceded to England in 1670 by the Treaty of Madrid.

Also during this time, West Indian buccaneers had made Port Royal their headquarters, giving the city a reputation as a bawdy mecca for the adventurous and the wicked. These were the days when Sir Henry Morgan rose to a commanding position among the privateers who dominated the Caribbean. His widespread successful adventures, however, overlapped the signing of peace with Spain, and he was recalled to England under arrest in 1672. When the Spanish again became a threat, he was knighted by Charles II and returned to Jamaica in 1674 as the deputy governor and the island's only honored pirate.

Kingston, the present capital, was built after an earthquake destroyed Port Royal on June 7, 1692. The flourishing slave trade and sugar and cotton plantations made Jamaica rich during the 18th century.

The cause of the slaves was supported by a group known as the Maroons, slaves freed by the Spanish to harass the English before the Spanish fled the island in 1660. Taking refuge in the hills of the Cockpit Country, these former slaves were joined by other fugitives. Together they successfully waged a guerrilla war against the English, and in 1738 the Maroons were granted self-rule and given title to their lands free of taxes. Descendants of the Maroons still live in this area; they are free of taxation and all government laws, except in the case of murder.

Although the slave trade was finally abolished in 1808, the oppression of this group did not improve. An uprising against the treatment of slaves took place in 1831; Baptist preacher Sam Sharpe led an islandwide revolt that forced the governor to declare martial law. So incensed were members of Britain's Parliament at the government's bloody crackdown, during which Sharpe and thousands more were executed, that abolition came shortly thereafter. Today Sam Sharpe is a national hero.

As a result of these frequent rebellions, slavery was abolished in 1834. Jamaica's newly freed population underwent years of economic and social hard times. As plantation life came to a gradual end, most workers took to the hills and practiced subsistence farming, a way of life that was to continue for generations. The 20th century, however, brought about sweeping reforms and a national identity. Marcus Garvey engendered racial pride, Alexander Bustamante organized a labor union and Norman Manley a political party. Increasingly, Jamaicans were making a place in the world.

The first civil governor of Jamaica was appointed in 1661, and the island was governed by a representative council until 1866, when a crown-colony government was established by act of Parliament. The island became independent within the British Commonwealth on August 6, 1962. A prime minister heads the government, which has its executive power vested in a cabinet; a governor general represents the British monarch. Legislative functions are assigned to a bicameral house. Sugar, bananas and coffee continue to fluctuate in prominence but are still the chief export crops. Since the 1960s bauxite and alumina exports and tourism have become the main earners of foreign exchange for the island.

Shopping

Jamaica was rich with the plunder of a continent in the days when Capt. Henry Morgan swaggered down the streets of Port Royal. Today the island is rich with merchandise from the four corners of the Earth. Free-port shops in Kingston, Montego Bay, Negril and Ocho Rios have good buys on Swiss watches, cameras, French perfumes, British woolens and cashmeres, imported liquor, silverware, crystal, jewelry and bone china. Boutiques feature Jamaican resort clothes.

Island handicrafts include woodcarvings, inlaid boxes and trays, Jamaican dolls, straw hats, colorful baskets, pottery, shell articles and yard goods with vivid tropical prints. They are sold in specialty shops at the Kingston Crafts Market, north of the cruise ship pier in Kingston, and the Crafts Market at Harbour and Church streets in Montego Bay. Port Antonio has a straw market downtown, and the Ocho Rios Craft Park and the Olde Market are along Main Street in Ocho Rios.

At Wassi Art Pottery Works near Fern Gully, visitors can watch potters create ethnic designs from clay.

East of Falmouth, the Caribatik factory produces regionally famous batik paintings and garments. Islanders often set up stalls along the roadside; you should be prepared to barter for good prices. The skill of Jamaican needlewomen has made the island's embroidered Irish linen dresses valued throughout the world. Paintings and sculptures by local artists make lasting souvenirs. A pound or so of Jamaica's excellent Blue Mountain Coffee also is a favorite take-home item.

Several shopping centers cover the southern end of Constrant Spring Road leading to the Half Way Tree area, Kingston's main shopping district. A shopping complex is on the grounds of Devon House, a 19th-century great house on Hope Road. There also are several shopping malls in the Kingston area. Mall shopping in Montego Bay is available at the Hip Strip (Gloucester Avenue), Fairview Shopping Centre and the town center. In Ocho Rios there are the Island Plaza, Island Village, Little Pub Shopping Complex, Ocean Village Shopping Centre, Soni's Plaza and the Taj Mahal—all on Main Street. Kingston shops are open Mon.-Sat. 9-5, but shops close at noon on Wed. in downtown Kingston and on Thurs. in New Kingston and Montego Bay. In Ocho Rios retail stores also are open Mon.-Sat. 9-5. Banking hours are Mon.-Thurs. 9-2, Fri. 9-4.

Food and Drink

The Jamaican national dish is *ackee* and saltfish, a dish made from imported salted cod and the fleshy lobes of the seeds of the ackee tree, cooked with onions, tomatoes and pepper in oil. Another staple is boiled rice and peas (red beans). On more exotic menus, gourmets will find goat cooked with Indian curry and served hot with boiled green bananas and rice, baked crab and pepperpot soup, a thick green "hot-pot" made of *callaloo* (a spinach-like vegetable), Indian kale, salted pork, vegetables and pepper. West Indian lobster and red snapper dishes are abundant.

Another peppery-hot island specialty is jerk pork. This was a favorite dish of the Maroons, who roasted wild hogs over a wood fire. The special flavoring is achieved through spices from a rich, peppery marinade and the type of wood used—the pimento (allspice) wood. Jerk pork and jerk chicken are available at roadside stands throughout the island.

Jamaica has a mouthwatering assortment of locally grown fruits and vegetables: mangoes, pawpaws, naseberries, sweetsops, soursops, ortaniques, otaheites, star apples, melons, rose apples, guinep, avocado pears, ugli fruit, tangerines, limes, pineapples, yams, green bananas, plantains, breadfruit, yampie, cocoa, cho-cho, turnips, pumpkins and beetroot. A delicious ice cream is made from coconut, pawpaw, pineapple and soursop. Another favorite dessert is matrimony, a refreshing dish of oranges and the pulp of the star apple.

Rum is Jamaica's national drink. Consumed in an endless variety of concoctions, it can be mixed with ginger ale or coconut water, brewed with pimento berries to produce Pimento Dram Liqueur, aged with citrus peel, heated to a toddy or blended with coffee to produce Tia Maria Liqueur. Rumona is another rum liqueur. The island's most popular rum-based beverage is Planters Punch. Popular rum brands are Appleton, Myers's and Wray and Nephew's White Overproof.

Jamaica also brews a strong light beer called Red Stripe. Cooling nonalcoholic drinks include homemade ginger beer; sorrel, a Christmas favorite; and fruit punches made with pineapple, banana, orange, melon and tamarind juices and coconut water. Also popular is Ting, a grapefruit-flavored soft drink. Tap water is chlorinated and filtered.

Among eateries offering local cuisine, Montego Bay and Ocho Rios also have their share of Chinese, Italian, French and Continental restaurants. Tips average 15 to 20 percent.

Sports and Amusements

Swimming heads the list of sports and amusements in Jamaica. The most noted beaches with miles of white sand and crystal waters are on the north shore; Doctor's Cave Beach and Cornwall Beach at Montego Bay share an excellent strand. Negril Beach is on the western shore. Good beaches on the south shore include Alligator Pond and Bluefields near Savanna-La-Mar, and the black sand beaches in Kingston and Black River. Outside Kingston Harbour are the white sand beaches of Lime Cay and Maiden Cay. Mineral spas reputed to cure certain rheumatic ailments are Milk River in Clarendon, Rockfort Spa in Kingston and the Bath Fountain in St. Thomas.

Countless water sports opportunities await guests not content to merely lie on the beaches. The offshore islands and cays near Kingston, the coves around Ocho Rios, the offshore reefs at Montego Bay and the waters surrounding Port Antonio and Negril are good diving areas. Diving operators offer both guide services and courses for beginners.

Snorkel and scuba equipment, water skis, jet skis and small sailing craft can be rented from the larger resort hotels and at Turtle Beach in Ocho Rios. Arrangements for sailing can be made through the Morgan's Harbor Hotel in Kingston and the Montego Bay Yacht Club, where colorful regattas are held each winter. The Jamaica Tourist Board maintains a current list of charter companies.

Rafting is popular on the Río Grande, Martha Brae and Great rivers. Less adventuresome visitors can discover the mysteries of the undersea world in a glass-bottom boat.

Mountain streams offer good fishing for mullet; the sea yields marlin, dolphin, tarpon, barracuda, bonefish, snook, wahoo and small tuna. Boats can be chartered for deep-sea fishing for half- or full-day trips at Kingston, Port Antonio, Ocho Rios, Montego Bay, Negril and Whitehouse. A fishing license is not required. Annual fishing tournaments include the Port Antonio International Spring Fishing Tournament in mid-March and the Montego Bay, Ocho Rios and Port Antonio marlin tournaments in early autumn.

You can attend horse racing Wednesday, Saturday and holidays at Caymanas Park, 6 miles (10 km) west of Kingston; pari-mutuel and quinella betting are permitted. Kingston has cricket matches on Saturday afternoons, January through April. Polo matches are held at Caymanas in Kingston, at Chukka Cove near Ocho Rios and at Drax Hall, also near Ocho Rios. Horseback riding is offered at Chukka Cove, the Double A Ranch near Montego Bay and at resort centers.

The island has 11 golf courses as well as tennis and squash courts that are open to hotel and villa guests. Among the major golf tournaments held are the World Cup of Golf tournament qualifier in September, the Jamaica Open Pepsi Pro-Am in October and the Caribbean Golf Association Classic of Golf in December.

Most hotels in Jamaica offer after-dinner entertainment, with many doubling as nightclubs and restaurants. Nightclubs and cabarets are available to suit almost every taste. Many clubs offer conventional orchestras; others echo with the distinctive rhythms of calypso and reggae bands. Floor shows are presented regularly in many of the larger clubs.

Jamaica's reggae sound, made world famous by Bob Marley, Peter Tosh and associates, is a prominent fixture in the lives of young Jamaicans. Shows featuring the nation's top performers take place regularly throughout the island. The most popular is Reggae Sumfest, held in August in Montego Bay.

Winter visitors to Kingston can enjoy a series of local plays, as well as the "Pantomime"—colorful social commentary—at the Ward Theatre and The Little Theatre. The National Dance Theatre Company also performs in Kingston. Films are shown in Kingston, Montego Bay, Ocho Rios, Port Antonio and Mandeville. For more information contact the Jamaica Tourist Board, which publishes two calendars of events during the year.

Aqua Sol Theme Park at Montego Bay is the scene of colorful beach parties on selected Fridays at 7 p.m. The Jamaica Tourist Board regularly schedules entertainment programs that include river rafting trips, dances, parties and barbecues, usually set in a secluded area near the major hotels. Inquire at your hotel for more information.

Sightseeing

With more than 7,800 miles (12,550 km) of primary roads and 2,800 miles (4,500 km) of secondary roads linking every village and hamlet, Jamaica is popular for motor tours. Possible itineraries are numerous, the only limitation being the time you can spend.

Beginning and ending at Kingston, a driving tour around the island takes about 2 days. A condensed circle tour of the island out of Kingston might follow Rte. A3 to Ocho Rios and St. Ann's Bay on the north coast and return via A1 by way of Spanish Town, and include such sites as Castleton Botanical Gardens, restored plantations, Dunn's River Falls, Fern Gully, the Ewarton aluminum plant and the Cathedral of St. James.

South and west of Claremont via unimproved roads is the village of Rhoden Hall. Musician Bob Marley was born in Rhoden Hall in 1945 and interred there in 1981. The mausoleum grounds are open to the public; admission is charged.

Rte. A2 heading east from Negril skirts the pristine South Coast and passes through quaint seaside villages, their shores lined with colorful fishing boats. Near Black River roadside vendors tempt visitors with such local delicacies as fresh escoveitch fish, bammy and shrimp. A coastal road south leads to the peaceful town of Treasure Beach.

Tour buses offering 3-hour tours of Kingston drive past the historic residences of the prime minister and governor general and through the campus of the University of the West Indies. They also include stops at the National Gallery of Jamaica, Hope Botanical Gardens and the Kingston Crafts Market.

The 3-hour Ocho Rios Tour takes in such area highlights as Prospect Estate, Dunn's River Falls, Shaw Park Gardens and Fern Gully. A 3-hour trip from Ocho Rios to Port Maria and Brimmer Hall Plantation also is available. Departing from Montego Bay, the 3- to 4-hour Great Houses Tour includes a complimentary drink at either Rose Hall or Greenwood; reservations can be made through your hotel. Bus tours that include stops at YS Falls, the Black River and Appleton Estate provide lunch, drinks and hotel pickup; inquire at your hotel for information and reservations.

Scheduled morning and sunset cruises are available for tours of Montego Bay; snorkeling cruises also are available. Arrangements can be made through the tour desks at most hotels.

Transportation

Jamaica is easily accessible by air from several North American cities to Kingston's Norman Manley International Airport and Montego Bay's Sangster International Airport. Air service linking Kingston, Port Antonio, Ocho Rios, Negril and Montego Bay is available on Jamaica Air Link or by charter. Ocho Rios and Montego Bay are ports of call for many cruise ships; a few smaller ships also call on Port Antonio.

There are nearly 11,000 miles (17,700 km) of roadway in Jamaica. Since long-distance cab and limousine rides can be expensive, it is recommended that you secure an accommodations package that includes transportation between your hotel and the airport.

Two types of taxis operate on the island: those affiliated with the Jamaica Union of Travellers Association (JUTA) or Jamaica Co-operative Automobile & Limousine (JCAL)—and those that are not. Non-affiliated taxis can be distinguished from private vehicles by their red license plate. Taxis are unmetered; maximum rates are merely suggested by the government, so it is always wise to determine the fare in advance.

Cars can be rented by the day or week; a U.S. driver's license is valid for 1 year. Driving in Jamaica is complicated, and, at times, dangerous. Driving on the left side of the road (with the steering wheel on the right side of the vehicle) complicates navigation of narrow, ill-maintained, two-lane roads often found in the interior of the island. Be prepared to relinquish your right-of-way. Though traffic is relatively light in smaller towns, sidewalks are nearly nonexistent, and thus roadways are shared with animals, pedestrians and those on mopeds and bicycles. Maps are often not helpful, as streets may or may not be marked. When driving across the island, allow 40 miles (64 km) to the hour. In larger cities, expect congestion; busy, unmarked intersections; poor road conditions and streets crowded with pedestrians.

If you're not up for a challenge, it is recommended you rent a car with a driver or hire a tour operator. Half- and full-day excursions are available from all the resort areas. Minibuses, inexpensive but usually very crowded, serve all areas of the island.

Fast Facts

POPULATION: 2,500,000.

AREA: 10,991 sq km (4,244 sq mi.).

CAPITAL: Kingston.

HIGHEST POINT: 2,256 m (7,402 ft.), Blue Mountain Peak.

LOWEST POINT: Sea level, Caribbean Sea.

TIME ZONE(S): Eastern Standard.

LANGUAGE: English and a local patois.

GOVERNMENT: Independent. Member of the British Commonwealth of Nations.

UNIT OF CURRENCY: Jamaican dollar. $1 U.S. = approx. 74 Jamaica dollars. While Jamaican law requires that Jamaican currency be used when paying for all goods and services, this is not enforced. Most hotels, restaurants and attractions accept U.S. dollars, and credit cards may be used. Jamaican currency is available at airport and hotel exchange bureaus and commercial banks. Keep all exchange receipts; you must present them upon departure when you reconvert unspent Jamaican currency.

ELECTRICITY: 110-220 volts, 50 cycles AC, single and three phases; voltage varies with location.

MINIMUM AGE FOR DRIVERS: 21-25, depending on the rental car agency; an underage surcharge may apply. U.S. license valid; drive on left.

SEAT BELT/CHILD RESTRAINT LAWS: Seat belts are required for driver and front-seat passengers.

HELMETS FOR MOTORCYCLISTS: Required.

HOLIDAYS: Jan. 1; Ash Wednesday; Good Friday; Easter Monday; National Labour Day, May 23; Emancipation Day, Aug. 1; Independence Day, Aug. 6; National Heroes Day, Oct. (3rd Mon.); Christmas, Dec. 25; Boxing Day, Dec. 26.

TAXES: A 10-15 percent room tax and a 10 percent service charge are added to most hotel bills. A 16.25 percent government tax is charged on food, beverages, merchandise and rental cars. Departure tax $28 over age 11.

IMMIGRATION REQUIREMENTS: Passport or proof of U.S. citizenship and a return or onward ticket are required. No visa needed for stays up to 6 months. The U.S. Dept. of Homeland Security requires all U.S. citizens returning from the Caribbean to present a valid passport.

PHONING THE ISLANDS: To call Jamaica from the U.S. or Canada, dial 1 + 876 + the 7-digit local number.

FURTHER INFORMATION FOR VISITORS:

Jamaica Tourist Board
5201 Blue Lagoon Drive, Suite 670
Miami, FL 33126
(305) 665-0557
(800) 233-4582

Jamaica Tourist Board, Kingston
64 Knutsford Blvd.
P.O. Box 360
Kingston, Jamaica
(876) 929-9200
(888) 995-9999

Points of Interest

See map page 156.

DISCOVERY BAY (A-3)

Christopher Columbus landed at Discovery Bay in 1494. Dedicated to this historic event is 2.75-acre (1-hectare) Columbus Park, 1.5 miles (2.4 km) west of Discovery Bay on Rte. A1. The park is open during daylight hours and provides a fine view of Discovery Bay. Interesting artifacts of early Jamaican life are present on the nicely landscaped grounds. Puerto Seco Beach also is worth visiting.

FALMOUTH (A-2) pop. 7,245

Falmouth is surrounded by sugar estates and cattle land. Once a leading port, the town has excellent examples of 19th-century Georgian architecture along with a faithful restoration of the early 19th-century courthouse destroyed by fire in 1926. Of special interest is the 1796 Falmouth Anglican Church on Rte. A1. Fresh fruit and vegetables are sold along Market Street.

MARTHA BRAE RAFTERS' VILLAGE is 3.5 mi. (5.6 km) s. on Market St., following signs. A relaxing trip down the Martha Brae River is offered aboard a 30-foot bamboo raft. Food is available. Allow 1 hour, 30 minutes minimum. Raft trips are offered daily 9-4. Fare $45 per raft (accommodates two adults and one child under 12). Return transportation to Montego Bay can be included in the fare upon request. Phone (876) 952-0889.

KINGSTON (C-5) pop. 587,798

Kingston was founded in 1692 when survivors of the Port Royal earthquake resettled around a piggery across the harbor. It became Jamaica's capital in 1872 and is today considered the island's cultural center. An earthquake and fire in 1907 destroyed most of the city, but it was immediately rebuilt. On a broad plain beneath the Blue Mountains, Kingston is built around one of the largest natural harbors in the world.

The new Kingston is even busier than the old; suburbs have grown up around residences of officials and wealthy merchants. The town and surrounding districts are well supplied with good hotels, and the Kingston Crafts Market on Port Royal Street is a shopper's mecca. North of downtown is 74-acre (30-hectare) National Heroes Park, where Jamaican leaders Alexander Bustamante, Norman Manley and Marcus Garvey are buried.

King's House on Hope Road was built around 1770 as the official residence for the governor-general. Fire gutted the stately building in 1925; only the facade survives. Surrounding the ruins are 175 acres (71 hectares) of landscaped grounds, which are open by appointment; phone (876) 927-6424.

Hellshire Beach, 14 miles (23 km) southwest of Kingston on the coast, has 200,000-year-old Two Sisters Cave with rare Taíno petroglyphs. Nearby is Fort Clarence Beach, a seaside recreational complex. Both beaches are popular with the locals on weekends.

Jamaica Tourist Board, Kingston: 64 Knutsford Blvd., P.O. Box 360, Kingston 5, Jamaica; phone (876) 929-9200.

BLUE AND JOHN CROW MOUNTAINS NATIONAL PARK has three main recreation areas in eastern Jamaica: Portland Gap, which is on the Blue Mountain Peak Trail; Holywell, on the road to Buff Bay; and Millbank, in the Rio Grande Valley.

This pristine preserve, covering nearly 200,000 acres (81,000 hectares), offers mountain vistas, waterfalls, streams, lush rain forests and exotic flora and fauna. The park is the natural habitat for the Giant Swallowtail, the largest butterfly in the Americas. Numerous roads approach the park; however some roads can only be accessed by four-wheel-drive vehicles. Footpaths branch off of the main roads, making hiking a popular way to explore the park.

Mule rides and hiking treks to the top of Blue Mountain offer thrilling views; Cuba is visible on a clear day. At 7,402 feet (2,256 m), this is the highest peak on the island. Guided tours of the park are offered. Cabins are available for rent. Park open Tues.-Sun. Admission $5; $2 (ages 4-12). Phone (876) 920-8278.

BOB MARLEY MUSEUM is .5 mi. (.8 km) e. of jct. Waterloo and Hope rds. at 56 Hope Rd. The museum is contained in the former home of Jamaican reggae singer Bob Marley. His life and career are recounted through his personal belongings, tour memorabilia and extensive information about his religion, politics and music. The guided tour also includes an herb garden and meditation area. Photography and tape recording are restricted to certain areas. One-hour tours are offered Mon.-Sat. 9:30-4. Admission $10; $9 (ages 13-18 and students with ID); $5 (ages 4-12). Phone (876) 927-9152.

CASTLETON BOTANICAL GARDENS is 19 mi. (31 km) n. at Junction Rd. in St. Mary. Many species of tropical plants, including spice and fruit trees and a palm grove, flourish on 15 acres (6 hectares). Swimming is permitted in Wag Water River, which runs through the gardens. Daily 6-6. Free. Phone (876) 927-1257.

DEVON HOUSE HERITAGE SITE is at 26 Hope Rd. Following the lines of classical Georgian architecture, Devon House is one of the few buildings left from 19th-century Jamaica where the opulence of the time is preserved in the architecture and the finely crafted antiques and decorations within its walls. The current Devon House property formed part of 600 acres owned by the St. Andrew Parish Church in the 17th and 18th centuries.

George Stiebel, Jamaica's first millionaire of African descent, purchased the rectory and lands from the parish church in 1879 and built Devon House on its foundations in 1881 after amassing wealth from investments in gold mines in Venezuela. Guided 30-minute tours are available. Food is available. Allow 30 minutes minimum. Mon.-Sat. 9:30-4:30. Admission $5; $2 (ages 0-12). Phone (876) 926-0829.

HOPE BOTANICAL GARDENS is 6 mi. (10 km) n. on Hope Rd. The park has more than 150 acres (61 hectares) of flower beds, lawns and borders as well as a sunken garden. On the grounds are an orchid house, a zoo and a cactus garden. A 1758 stone aqueduct built on the old Hope sugar estate is still in use. Gardens daily 6-6. Zoo daily 10-5. Gardens free. Zoo $2; $1 (ages 3-11). Phone (876) 927-1257 for the gardens or (876) 927-1085 for the zoo.

INSTITUTE OF JAMAICA is at 10-16 East St. The facility houses an outstanding West Indies reference library, a reading room, an art gallery and a natural history museum that highlights Jamaica's native plants and animals. An herbarium features more than 30,000 specimens. There also are maps and folklore exhibits, including the "shark papers," incriminating journals thrown overboard by a guilty sea captain and found years later in the belly of a shark. Mon.-Thurs. 8:30-4:30, Fri. 8:30-3:30; closed holidays. Admission $3; $1 (children). Phone (876) 922-0620.

KINGSTON PARISH CHURCH is at King St. and South Parade. Founded in 1695, the Church of St. Thomas the Apostle was reconstructed after the 1907 earthquake and contains monuments to prominent Jamaicans. The clock tower honors those killed in World War I. Tombstones in the church graveyard date to the 17th century. Daily. Phone (876) 922-6888 or (876) 948-0065.

NATIONAL GALLERY OF JAMAICA is at 12 Ocean Blvd. in the Kingston Mall on the harborfront. The gallery houses the definitive collection of Jamaican art, tracing its development through different periods and movements. Works represent realism, symbolism, expressionism and surrealism as well as abstract and intuitive styles. The works of Edna Manley are featured prominently. Other artists represented include Carl Abrahams, Henry Daley, John Dunkley, Colin Garland, Albert Huie, Kapo and Namba Roy. Tues.-Thurs. 10-4:30, Fri. 10-4, Sat. 10-3. Admission $1; 50c (children). MC, VI. Phone (876) 922-1561.

UNIVERSITY OF THE WEST INDIES is about 3 mi. (5 km) n. at Mona. The campus features modern architecture and a collection of 18th-century artifacts. The 1799 chapel was moved from its original location on a sugar plantation and meticulously rebuilt. Original stone aqueducts are scattered throughout the campus. The university, established in 1948, is attended by students from all areas of the Caribbean. Visitors may drive through the grounds. Phone (876) 977-5941.

LACOVIA (B-2)

This crossing place on the Black River was the site of a clash between Spanish and English forces in 1655. The town's name is derived from a Spanish word for mahogany, once one of the area's chief exports. Cashew nuts remain a staple of the local economy.

LUCEA (A-1) pop. 6,002

West of Montego Bay, Lucea (pronounced *Lucy*) was the site of Fort Charlotte, one of five 18th-century English forts built to protect the Hanover coast. The 1817 clock atop the courthouse was intended for St. Lucia, but when the timepiece arrived by mistake in Lucea, town fathers raised enough money to keep it.

HANOVER MUSEUM is w. on Rte. A1 to Watson Taylor Dr., just past the library. Centered around a 1776 prison, the museum chronicles the history of Hanover Parish. Displays include official weights and measures; colonial-era artifacts and tools; and exhibits dedicated to Sir Alexander Bustamante, the first Jamaican prime minister, and Capt. William Bligh, owner of the ship *The Bounty*. A small village re-creates the life of Taíno Indians who greeted Columbus in 1494. Allow 30 minutes minimum. Mon.-Thurs. 8:30-5, Fri. 8:30-4; closed public holidays. Admission $2; $1 (ages 0-12). Phone (876) 956-2584.

MANDEVILLE (B-3) pop. 39,430

A quiet elegance pervades the resort of Mandeville, 64 miles (103 km) west of Kingston in the 2,000-foot Manchester Mountains. Resembling a town in the English Midlands, Mandeville exudes backcountry charm with its prim cottages and private gardens, town square and clock tower. The town's avid gardeners compete each May in the Manchester Flower Show, which draws visitors from all over the island.

Founded in 1814, Mandeville was named after the Earl of Mandeville, son of the Duke of Manchester—a governor of Jamaica. The town quickly became a retreat for wealthy Jamaican growers drawn by the peaceful setting and cool mountain breezes. Bauxite and alumina mining sustained the area economy beyond the 1940s. Mandeville is now at the heart of the island's citrus industry; the town market overflows with colorful fruits and flowers in season. Dominating Mandeville Square is the 1820 Georgian-style Mandeville Courthouse. Just south is the Parish Church, also built in 1820.

Golf, tennis and sightseeing are enjoyable in the bracing mountain air. Golf and tennis can be played at the Manchester Club on Brumalia Road, the Caribbean's first golf course. Golf Week, Jamaica's oldest tournament, is played on the club's nine-hole course in July. Tennis Week, purportedly the oldest tournament in the Caribbean, is played in August.

A noteworthy attraction is nearby Marshall's Pen, an 18th-century great house on a 300-acre (12-hectare) cattle farm; extensive gardens, a bird sanctuary and hiking trails are on the property. House tours and village tours are offered by appointment; phone (876) 904-5454.

About 20 miles (32 km) west of Mandeville, Rte. A2 enters Bamboo Avenue, a grove of giant bamboo that creates a tropical canopy for about 3 miles (5 km). Paralleling the route southward is Black River. Once the center for crocodile hunting before the sport was prohibited, Black River is the largest navigable river in Jamaica and offers excellent freshwater fishing. Regular boat tours are available.

Only the most courageous sightseers will venture near the edge of Lover's Leap. On the coast about 40 miles (64 km) southwest of Mandeville, the sheer cliff stands about 1,700 feet (518 m) over the sea. The cliff is said to be the spot where two slaves once jumped to avoid separation; this romantic story is re-told daily by interpretive guides. A museum houses area artifacts; phone (876) 965-6634.

About 30 miles (48 km) southeast of town is Milk River Bath. The spring water is a constant 92 degrees Fahrenheit and is purportedly the most radioactive in the world. Bathers are limited to three 15-minute treatments per day; phone (876) 965-6577.

MONTEGO BAY (A-2) pop. 83,446

On the northwest coast 119 miles (191 km) from Kingston, Montego Bay is an exciting, cosmopolitan resort with beautiful beaches and excellent accommodations. The shoreline is dotted with sparkling coves and luxury hotels offering the gamut of water sports. The main resort area is east of the airport in Rose Hall *(see place listing p. 168)*, where such great houses as Greenwood and Rose Hall are open to the public. The ruins of the old British Fort Montego bears further witness to a rich history.

MoBay, as the resort is known locally, was one of Jamaica's original settlements. Christopher Columbus called it *El Golfo de Buen Tiempo,* or "Fair Weather Gulf," back in 1494, but his successors were apparently not as impressed; the current name comes from the Spanish *manteca,* or lard, an early major export. Montego Bay later prospered as a sugar and banana port. Tourism was born in the late 19th century when Dr. Alexander McCatty began attracting wealthy North Americans to the "curative" waters off Doctor's Cave Beach.

At the center of town is busy Sam Sharpe Square, where the slave rebellion leader and hundreds more were hanged in 1832. The colonial government's harsh response to the uprising led England to abolish slavery 2 years later. A monument to Sharpe stands on the site. Northeast on Union Street is the Slave Ring, where slaves were bought, sold and traded.

The strand of MoBay's famous beaches begins just north of town at Aqua Sol Theme Park. Farther north are Doctor's Cave, Cornwall and Chatham beaches. All but Chatham Beach have changing facilities, food and a slight admission charge. More resorts and beaches extend eastward from the airport to Rose Hall. South of town on a man-made peninsula is Freeport, home to the Montego Bay Yacht Club and the Catherine Hall Entertainment Centre. The municipal bus company serves the airport and the hotel strip.

The wild and forbidding Cockpit Country southeast of Montego Bay once harbored the Maroons, slaves who established their own villages after being freed by the Spanish. They were fierce warriors whose relentless guerrilla tactics were successful in frightening the British colonists into riding back-to-back on a single horse whenever they traveled through Maroon territory. Today their descendants welcome travelers to the historic "Land of Look Behind," though some may still warn, "Me no call you, you no come."

About 6 miles (8 km) southwest of Montego Bay on Rte. B8 near Anchovy is the Rocklands Feeding Station, where a wide variety of birds can be observed. Bird feedings take place daily at 3:30; admission is charged. For additional information phone (876) 952-2009. Rafting on the Great River west of the city is offered daily 9-5, with a two-person maximum per raft; consult any tour operator or ask your hotel for information.

Jamaica Tourist Board, Montego Bay: Cornwall Beach, Montego Bay, Jamaica; phone (876) 952-4425.

DOCTOR'S CAVE BEACH is off Gloucester Ave. in the hotel area. One of the best beaches in the West Indies was once the property of Jamaican tourism pioneer Dr. Alexander McCatty. The beach now has changing rooms and water sports rentals and is Blue-Flag certified for environmental standards. Food is available. Daily 8:30-dusk. Admission $5; $2.50 (children). Snorkeling $5 per set. Phone (876) 952-2566.

ST. JAMES PARISH CHURCH is at Church and King sts. The gray stone cruciform building was dedicated in 1775. Almost destroyed by an earthquake in 1957, the church has been restored. It is considered to be one of the finest churches in Jamaica. Daily dawn-dusk. Phone (876) 952-5500.

RECREATIONAL ACTIVITIES

Summer Activities

- **Chukka Caribbean Adventures** includes transportation from local hotels. Rain forest canopy tours feature high-wire traverses across mountain ravines. Other tours include river tube rides, horseback riding trips, bike excursions and jeep safari rides. Trips depart daily; reservations are required. Phone (876) 684-9934 or (876) 953-6699.

NEGRIL (B-1) pop. 1,500

On Jamaica's western tip, Negril (neh-GRILL) is a 90-minute drive down the coast from Montego Bay. Two bays sheltered by coral reefs lie along a 7-mile (11 km) stretch of unbroken shoreline, creating excellent conditions for swimming, snorkeling, scuba diving, sailing, windsurfing, parasailing, water skiing and horseback riding. The longer and more popular beach is at Long Bay. To the north is the more private Bloody Bay—its name dates back to the whaling era. Swimsuits are optional at Bloody Bay.

Pirates knew Negril well during their time. The coastal setting was a favored hideaway of Jamaica's notorious "Calico Jack" Rackham. He was finally apprehended in 1720 while lounging at Bloody Bay with two female mates. Negril remained largely undiscovered, however, until the late 1960s when it became a haven for young escapists seeking freedom from the modern world. It remains an uncluttered destination; in order to preserve the beauty of the area, an ordinance prohibits the building of any structure taller than the average palm tree.

Given its location at the island's westernmost point, Negril is famous for its spectacular sunsets. Popular vantage points are the numerous cafes at the rock cliffs along West End (also called Lighthouse) Road; Rick's Cafe is one of the most popular. At some cafes locals and visitors can be seen diving off the tall cliffs into the calm sea below. At the end of West End Road is the 100-foot Negril Point Lighthouse. Contact the caretaker for permission to climb to the top.

ROYAL PALM RESERVE is 6 mi. (10 km) e. on Sheffield Rd. (Rte. A1), then n.w. on Springfield Rd., following signs. The reserve protects 300 acres (121 hectares) within the Negril Great Morass. A small museum details native flora and fauna of this wetlands area. A 2-mile (3-km) boardwalk leads to an observation tower. Visitors may glimpse the endangered West Indian whistling duck and 50 other bird species. Guided nature walks, horseback rides and birdwatching tours are offered by appointment.

Food is available. Picnicking is permitted. Allow 30 minutes minimum. Daily 9-6. Admission $10; $5 (ages 0-12). Phone (876) 957-3736.

OCHO RIOS (A-4) pop. 7,800

Ocho Rios, or Ochi as the locals call it, is on the north shore about 54 miles (87 km) from Kingston. A ballooning tourist industry has reinforced the town's bauxite harvesting, manufacturing and mining industries. The town's antique charm is complemented by its fine hotels, beautiful scenery, good shopping, active nightlife and stable climate. All manner of water sports are available both within the bay and along the coast. Ocho Rios is a popular port of call for private yachts as well as cruise ships.

Some of the island's oldest communities are within a few miles of Ocho Rios. St. Ann's Bay, 7 miles (11 km) west via Rte. A3, is said to be the final resting place of Christopher Columbus' last ships. The ruins of Sevilla Nueva, Jamaica's first settlement, are 9 miles (14 km) west. Laid out by the Spanish in 1509, the site is currently the subject of archeological research.

Popular local tours include an excursion to Dunn's River Falls, a raft trip on the White River and a visit to Shaw Park Botanical Gardens, which has 34 acres (14 hectares) of tropical flora and a waterfall. The gardens are .75 miles (1.2 km) south on Rte. A3 then 1 mile (1.6 km) west, following signs; admission is charged. Visitors can view the pottery-making process at Wassi Art Pottery Works, 1 mile (1.6 km) south on Rte. A1, where glazed earthenware is produced by local artisans. Ocho Rios' central location makes day trips to Kingston, Montego Bay and the interior manageable.

COYABA GARDENS AND MAHOE FALLS is 1.5 mi (2.4 km) s. on Rte. A3, then w. on Millford Rd. at St. John's Anglican Church to Shaw Park Rd., following signs. Named for the Arawak word meaning "heaven," Coyaba features gardens, ponds, fountains, waterfalls and a raised boardwalk above the Milford mineral springs. A small museum chronicles the island's history. Food is available. Allow 1 hour minimum. Daily 8-5. Admission $10; $5 (ages 0-12). MC, VI. Phone (876) 974-6235.

GEM **DOLPHIN COVE AT TREASURE REEF** is 2 mi. (3.5 km) w. on Belmont Rd. (Rte. A1). Visitors can touch, kiss and swim with these friendly marine mammals at a seaside park. For swimming participants over age 8, two programs offer deep-water encounters in a natural cove: the Swim with two bottlenose dolphins includes play time, a kiss, a foot push and a dorsal pull; and the Encounter offers splashing and dancing with a single dolphin. A program is offered where visitors can swim with and feed the sharks.

Children and non-swimmers can enjoy the Touch, which takes place in knee-deep water. Visitors also can interact with stingrays, snorkel, and take mini-boat and glass-bottom kayak rides. The park also offers a beach and a jungle trail, where guides encourage interaction with parrots, snakes and iguanas.

Food is available. Allow 2 hours minimum. Park open daily 8:30-5:30. All-inclusive general admission ($45) includes mini-boat and kayak rides, petting and snorkeling with stingrays, shark show and nature trail adventures. Dolphin Swim $195, Encounter $129, Touch $67, shark program $119. Dolphin and shark interaction program fees include general admission. Reservations are required. AX, MC, VI. Phone (876) 974-5335.

DUNN'S RIVER FALLS is 3 mi. (5 km) w. on Rte. A3. The waterfall cascades 600 feet (183 m) through tropical foliage, rushing over layered tiers of smooth rock to the beach. A paved walkway parallels the falls; visitors may also climb to the top with the assistance of guides. Official guides are available only inside the falls' gates.

Aqua shoes or water socks and swim wear are recommended; footholds have been carved in the most difficult places. Cameras should remain secured when not in use and in waterproof protection if you climb the falls (guides are not permitted to secure cameras for guests). Swimming is permitted, and food and changing rooms are available. Allow 1 hour, 30 minutes minimum. Daily 8:30-4 (open at 7 a.m. during DST). Admission $15; $12 (ages 2-12). Tipping is optional for the guided climb to the top. Water shoe rental $5. Phone (876) 974-4767 or (954) 974-5944.

FERN GULLY is along Rte. A3, 1.5 mi. (2.4 km) s. of Rte. A1. The tree-covered canyon features lush growths of ferns and tropical plants. The gorge descends for about 3 miles (5 km), following the course of a dry riverbed. Visitors should exercise caution, as the road is narrow and normally damp. Heavy rains can cause floods as well as mudslides and rockslides. There are a limited number of areas wide enough for vehicles to pull off the road.

HARMONY HALL is 4 mi. (6.4 km) e. on main road to Oracabessa. Works by renowned Jamaican artists and artisans are featured at this gallery, housed in a restored 19th-century Methodist manse. Monthly exhibitions are held from Thanksgiving through Easter. Allow 30 minutes minimum. Tues.-Sun. 10-6; closed Good Friday and Dec. 25. Free. Phone (876) 975-4222.

GEM **PROSPECT PLANTATION** is 2 mi. (5 km) e. on Rte. A3, following signs. A comprehensive jitney tour takes visitors through a working 1,180-acre (478-hectare) plantation, including stops at the White River Gorge and Sir Harold's Viewpoint. Narrators provide the history and background of the various fruits grown on the plantation as well as information about native flora. Highlights of the tour include the Prospect College Chapel with its handmade furnishings and such demonstrations as coconut picking. A butterfly farm also can be toured.

Guided horseback and camel rides are offered; reservations are required. Food is available. Allow 1 hour, 30 minutes minimum. Tours depart Mon.-Sat. at 10:30, 2 and 3:30, Sun. at 11, 1:30 and 3. Plantation $32; free (ages 0-7). Horseback and camel riding $58. Phone (876) 994-1058.

REGGAEXPLOSION is in the Island Village complex on Turtle River Rd. This interactive museum explores the history of reggae music from the 1940s to the present through art, photographs, videos and listening stations. Exhibitions detail the music styles of mento, ska, rock steady, roots rock reggae, 1970s club music and present-day dance hall music. A gallery is dedicated to Bob Marley. Allow 1 hour minimum. Mon.-Fri. 9-5, Sat. 10-6. Admission $15; $7.50 (ages 0-12). MC, VI. Phone (876) 675-8895.

RECREATIONAL ACTIVITIES

Summer Activities

- **Chukka Caribbean Adventures** offers transportation from local hotels. Activities include a river tubing safari, a jungle canopy tour, horseback riding, a mountain-to-sea biking tour, jeep safaris, ATV safari tours and bus tours to Bob Marley's mausoleum. Tours depart daily; reservations are required. Phone (876) 972-2506 or (876) 972-2727.

PORT ANTONIO (B-6) pop. 13,246

About 60 miles (97 km) northeast of Kingston on the windward coast, Port Antonio was one of Jamaica's first tourist destinations. Its beautiful twin harbors at the foothills of the lush Blue Mountains lured North America's elite in the early 20th century. Among the likes of William Randolph Hearst, Bette Davis, Ginger Rogers and J.P. Morgan was the irrepressible Errol Flynn, who made Port Antonio his home.

The two harbors, sheltered by Navy Island and Titchfield Peninsula, were largely responsible for the town's early success as a banana port. Since 1729 imposing Fort George has overlooked the harbors, once busy with lines of steamers waiting for their shipments of bananas. Today the docks no longer hum with the rhythm of banana loaders and the colorful refrain "come mister tallyman, tally me banana," but the charm of this port town has survived.

Of interest to sightseers and photographers are the port's ruins of Folly. Built in 1905 by a wealthy American engineer, this extravagant 60-room mansion lay vacant within 30 years, a victim of poor construction and neglect. Its crumbling walls and pillars are all that remain. The Folly Point Lighthouse stands at the end of the peninsula. Dominating the skyline on Bridge Street is the Romanesque Christ Church, built in 1840. Produce and crafts can be had at Musgrave Market on West Harbour east of the ferry dock.

Among the nearby scenic spots is Somerset Falls, about 10 miles (16 km) west, where the Daniels River plunges through a gorge in a series of cascades and pools; admission is charged. Most of the area's beaches extend east of town. Two of the most popular are San San and Boston. Frenchman's Cove and Blue Lagoon also are frequented; admission is $5 for both beaches.

GEM **RÍO GRANDE RAFTING** departs 5.5 mi. (9 km) w. on Rte. A4. A memorable 2.5-hour trip down the Río Grande River is offered on a 33-foot bamboo raft. Maximum capacity is two adults and one child under 12 per raft. Return transportation is available, or licensed drivers are available on request to transport cars to the journey's end, where they can be picked up by their owners. Food is available. Allow 2 hours, 30 minutes minimum. Daily 9-4; closed Good Friday and Dec. 25. Last trip begins 1 hour before closing. Fare $45 per raft. Car transport $15. MC, VI. Phone (876) 913-5434.

PORT MARIA (A-4) pop. 7,651

Port Maria was an important commercial center during the Spanish era, made possible in large part by its deep natural harbor. Of interest in town is St. Mary Parish Church, built in 1861. Northwest toward Oracabessa are several small, fine beaches, among them Pagee and Murdock's. At Galina is the Galina Point Lighthouse.

On a mountain north of Port Maria is Firefly, the small retreat of Noel Coward, noted English playwright, actor and director. The house, 2.2 miles (3.6 km) north on Rte. A3, then 1 mile (1.6 km) west on Stuart Place track, contains the playwright's possessions; his grave is in the garden. Firefly is open Mon.-Sat. 9-4. Firefly was inspired by Coward's visit to nearby Goldeneye, the home of Ian Fleming, author of the James Bond novels. Goldeneye is not open to the public.

BRIMMER HALL is 5 mi. (8 km) s., following signs. Jitney tours explore a 2,000-acre (809-hectare) working plantation that produces bananas, cocoa, sugarcane and pineapple. Guides identify and describe the crops and tropical flora encountered along the route. The 18th-century great house is furnished with period antiques. Swimming is permitted. Tours daily at 9, 11, 1:30 and 3:30. Admission-$18. Additional fee for house tours. Phone (876) 994-2309.

PORT ROYAL (C-5)

At the tip of a 10-mile (16 km) strip of land called the Palisadoes, Port Royal became the focus of British fortification efforts soon after their takeover in 1655. Construction of Fort Charles began in 1656, and within a few years there were five more forts manned by more than 2,500 soldiers. Port Royal also became headquarters for buccaneers and privateers who preyed on Spanish ships throughout the Caribbean. This era brought Port Royal great wealth and a reputation as one of the wickedest cities in the world.

Shortly before noon on June 7, 1692, as if by divine judgment, an earthquake and tidal wave destroyed 90 percent of the city and claimed more than 2,000 lives; most of the city sank beneath the sea. Attempts were made to rebuild Port Royal, but a 1703 fire and numerous hurricanes thwarted all efforts and the site was eventually abandoned for Kingston across the harbor. Somewhere offshore are the remains of Sir Henry Morgan, who was buried in Port Royal in 1688.

Port Royal is reached by water taxi or bus from Kingston or by a 10-minute drive from Norman Manley International Airport. Boat trips can be arranged to visit the cays offshore from the Palisadoes. Lime Cay is the most popular.

FORT CHARLES is next to the Jamaican Coast Guard headquarters. Built in 1656, the fort was one of few Port Royal structures to survive the 1692 disaster. The installation retains many of its old battlements. Horatio Nelson served as a naval lieutenant at Fort Charles in 1779. Food is available. Fort open daily 9-5. A maritime museum is open daily 10-4. Admission $5; $2 (children). Phone (876) 967-8438.

Bob Marley

Jamaica's distinctive reggae sound found its way onto the world's popular music scene in the early 1970s. Desmond Dekker announced its arrival with his 1969 hit "The Israelites," and in 1972 Johnny Nash popularized the sound with "I Can See Clearly Now," as did Paul Simon with "Mother and Child Reunion." But it was Bob Marley and his group the Wailers, featuring Peter Tosh and Bunny Livingston, and later the back-up vocals of the I-Threes (Rita Marley, Marcia Griffiths and Judy Mowatt), who brought reggae to worldwide prominence.

As his European and American contemporaries did to rock 'n' roll, Bob Marley brought to reggae lyrics of pride and protest. He sang of black unity, in the tradition of national hero Marcus Garvey, and of the tenets of Rastafari, the uniquely Jamaican religion of which he was a devout follower. Bob Marley and the Wailers released nine albums, as well as several compilations, outside of Jamaica. Among his more popular songs are "Get Up Stand Up," "Jamming" and "Is This Love." Eric Clapton recorded Marley's song "I Shot the Sheriff" in 1974, bringing international acclaim to both Marley and the reggae sound.

Bob Marley passed away from cancer in 1981; he was just 36 years old. During his lifetime, many Jamaicans granted Marley the veneration usually accorded to their political and religious leaders. Shortly before his passing, Marley was awarded the Order of Merit—Jamaica's third highest honor—and he is still spoken of in legendary terms. His birthday, February 6th, is recognized as Bob Marley Day.

ST. PETER'S CHURCH is next to the Morgan's Harbour Hotel on Church St. Built in 1725 to replace Christ's Church, which slid into the sea in 1692, this Anglican church houses an 18th-century candelabrum, altar railings, an elaborate organ loft and monuments to a number of distinguished citizens. It also boasts a silver communion plate that was a gift from Sir Henry Morgan. In the churchyard is the tomb of Lewis Galdy, a famous survivor of the Great Earthquake. Mon.-Sat. 9-5. Services on Sun. Donations.

ROSE HALL (A-2)

Montego Bay's resort area, Rose Hall was established in 1750 by George Ash, a wealthy Englishman who named his 6,600-acre (2,670-hectare) sugar plantation after his wife. The estate fell into ruin after the 1831 slave rebellion and was restored in the 1960s. Of the 700 great houses built on Jamaica in the 18th century, Rose Hall and neighboring Greenwood are two of the finest to survive.

GREENWOOD GREAT HOUSE is 4 mi. (6 km) e. on Rte. A1, then 2 mi. (3 km) on a steep, rutted road. The house was built in 1790 by Richard Barrett, a relative of poet Elizabeth Barrett Browning. Having amassed considerable wealth from their sugar plantations, the Barretts presided over an estate that extended about 12 miles (19 km) along the coast from Little River to Falmouth. Antiques include period furniture, family portraits, rare musical instruments and Wedgwood china made exclusively for the Barrett family.

Visitors can see the curvature of the Earth from a 70-foot-long veranda overlooking the Caribbean Sea. Allow 1 hour minimum. Guided 45-minute tours are offered daily 9-5:15. Admission $14; $7 (ages 5-12). Phone (876) 953-1077.

ROSE HALL GREAT HOUSE is on Rte. A1 following signs. The original owner named the house after his wife, Rose, who survived him to remarry three times. Rose's fourth husband, John Palmer, completed the Georgian mansion in 1780. Fifty years later, a Palmer descendant married Annie Mae Patterson, the plantation's last mistress. Known as the "White Witch of Rose Hall," she is rumored to have killed three husbands and countless lovers, many of them slaves. Legend says that Annie Palmer, murdered during the 1831 uprising, haunts the house.

Guided tours are available. Food is available. Allow 30 minutes minimum. Daily 9-6. Admission $15; $10 (ages 6-12). MC, VI. Phone (876) 953-2323.

DID YOU KNOW

Ian Fleming wrote all of his James Bond novels in Jamaica.

ST. ANN'S BAY (A-3) pop. 10,518

On the coast west of Ocho Rios, St. Ann's Bay and the surrounding parish were named for Lady Anne Hyde, wife of King James II of England.

CRANBROOK FLOWER FOREST is 1 mi. (1.6 km) w. of Chukka Cove on Rte. A1, then 1 mi. s. on Llandovery Rd. The River Head Adventure Tour follows a hiking trail through a 130-acre (53-hectare) botanical garden along the Little River. Flowering plants and ornamentals include royal palms, ginger lilies, orchids, hibiscus, begonias and bromeliads. Other activities include picnicking, horseback riding, swimming, mountain biking, pond fishing or visiting a petting zoo.

Food is available. Comfortable hiking boots and insect repellent are advised. Allow 2 hours minimum. Daily 9-5; closed Good Friday and Dec. 25. Admission $10; $5 (ages 4-12). Phone (876) 770-8071 or (876) 995-3097.

SILOAH (B-2)

At the western end of the Siloah Valley is the rural town of Maggotty, where hydroelectricity is generated by nearly thirty waterfalls on the Black River. Views of the river gorge are offered along Route A2.

APPLETON ESTATE RUM TOUR is 7 mi. (11 km) n. on Rte. A2 to Maggotty, then 3 mi. (5 km) e. The Appleton plantation has been producing sugar, molasses and rum since 1749. The distillery is set in a valley along the Black River. A 90-minute guided tour provides a demonstration of various stages of the production process and a tasting of "wet" sugar. A rum tasting venue is on the premises. Mon.-Sat. 9-4. Admission $15; $10 (ages 0-9). AX, MC, VI. Phone (876) 963-9215 or (876) 963-9217.

SPANISH TOWN (C-4) pop. 92,383

First known as Santiago de la Vega (St. James of the Plain), Spanish Town was founded by the Spaniards about 1534 after they abandoned their first city at Sevilla Nueva on the north coast. The British destroyed much of the original town in 1655, but remained to build new structures, many of them fine examples of Georgian architecture. Spanish Town served as capital of Jamaica until 1872, when the capital was moved to Kingston.

The heart of Spanish Town is Emancipation Square with its stately Georgian buildings. Here are the Assembly House, the King's House and the Rodney Memorial. The old courthouse was gutted by fire and has not been restored.

The ruins of 17th-century Colbeck Castle, reached by a slight detour off the road to Old Harbour, are worth visiting. The main facade is more than 100 feet (30 m) high, and the four fortresslike towers are each 40 feet (12 m) high with walls 3 feet (.9 m) thick. The monumental construction hints that this castle was not only a residence but also a bastion against the fierce Maroons.

CATHEDRAL OF ST. JAMES (ST. JAGO DE LA VEGA) is at Barrett and White Church sts. Built by the British in 1662, this is considered the oldest church in the former British colonies. It has served the Church of England for more than 300 years. Many English nobles and islanders are buried in the crypts beneath its floors. Daily 9-4:30. Free. Phone (876) 984-2535.

JAMAICAN ARCHIVES is at the corner of King and Manchester sts. on Emancipation Square. Records begin with the British occupation of Jamaica in 1655; Spanish records prior to that period did not survive. Mon.-Thurs. 9-4:30, Fri. 9-3:30. Free. Phone (876) 984-2581.

PEOPLE'S MUSEUM OF CRAFT AND TECHNOLOGY is on the w. side of Emancipation Square. Rebuilt in 1802 following its destruction in 1761, only the Georgian facade remains of the house; the rest burned in 1925. The house was once the official residence of colonial British governors. Early Jamaican relics are displayed in the coach house and stables. Mon.-Thurs. 9-4:30, Fri. 9-3:30; closed public holidays. Admission $3; $1 (children). Phone (876) 907-0322 or (876) 922-0620.

RODNEY MEMORIAL is on the n. side of Emancipation Square. This domed building with colonnades honors British admiral George Rodney and his 1782 victory over French forces off the shores of Dominica. His victory assured the safety of Jamaica and other British possessions in the Caribbean. Rodney is portrayed as a Roman emperor in a toga. His 200-ton statue was moved to Kingston in 1872, but outraged Spanish Town citizens reclaimed it in 1889. One stone hand was lost in the process.

TAÍNO MUSEUM is 3 mi. (5 km) e. at White Marl. At the 7-acre (2.8-hectare) Taíno Indian settlement, the museum features a small collection of relics and exhibits covering early migrations into the Western Hemisphere and the early history of Jamaica. Mon.-Thurs. 9-4:30, Fri. 9-3:30; closed public holidays. Admission $3; $1 (ages 0-11). Phone (876) 922-0620.

Diamant Beach / © Wysocki Pawel / age fotostock

Martinique

One of the largest islands in the Lesser Antilles, Martinique is 50 miles (80 km) long and 22 miles (35 km) wide. The volcanic Mont Pelée in the north and Les Pitons du Carbet in the central section are the main peaks on this mountainous island.

It is easy to see why the Carib Indians once designated Martinique as the Isle of Flowers—bougainvillea, hibiscus, anthuriums, bamboo and wild orchids deck the woodlands; forests with many varieties of flowering trees rim the hills. Plantation fields with crops containing bananas, pineapples, sugarcane and coffee can be found throughout this fertile island. Martinique's tropical visage is scarred only by the ruins of St. Pierre, the result of an eruption of Mont Pelée in 1902.

History

Christopher Columbus sighted Martinique in 1493 but did not land until his fourth voyage in 1502. Arawak and Carib Indians called the island *Madinina,* the "island of flowers." Because of opposition from the Indians, no settlement took place until 1635, when the French made the island a center for sugar production. France and Britain battled for the island throughout the 17th and 18th centuries until France gained permanent control in 1814.

Like Guadeloupe, Martinique is a department and region of France, represented in the French Parliament by two senators and four deputies. The island is administered by elected general and regional councils as well as by a prefect. The seat of government is Fort-de-France.

Shopping

Martinique offers enough goods and bargains to suit the needs of most shoppers. French perfumes, china, linens, jewelry, crystal and other luxury imports are sold at or below prices in Paris, New York or St. Thomas.

The main shopping district is in Fort-de-France along rues Antoine Siger, Victor Hugo and Schoelcher, where shops sell madras cottons, watches, silver and crystal at low prices. Just south of town is La Galleria, billed as the largest shopping center in the West Indies.

Roger Albert's duty-free department store on rue Victor Hugo specializes in French perfume; leather goods, sportswear and crystal, Cadet-Daniel on rue Antoine Siger is known for its jewelry, china, silver and crystal. Most jewelry stores in the district feature handcrafted gold and Creole pieces, including a traditional beaded necklace known as a *collier chou*. Fort-de-France is not truly a "free port," but instead offers a 20 percent discount on purchases paid for with travelers checks or charged to a credit card.

At the Caribbean Arts Center on the seafront, artisans sell their tapestries, Creole dolls, straw baskets, ceramics, handmade jewelry and souvenirs. As on many other Caribbean islands, rum is a popular purchase; Martinique offers 17 varieties. Most distilleries offer free tours and rum tastings.

Shops are open Mon.-Fri. 8:30-6, Sat. 9-noon, and are closed on holidays. Banking hours are Mon.-Fri. 7:30-noon and 2:30-4:30. Stores can give up to 20-percent discounts on some luxury goods purchased with travelers checks or certain credit cards.

Food and Drink

Martinique's cuisine is a mix of classic French and Creole. Local specialties include *colombo,* an Indian curry dish cooked with either beef, pork, chicken, mutton, conch or goat and eaten with rice; *boudin,* a spicy local blood sausage; and *callaloo,* a soup made from greens and West Indian herbs. Typical Creole seafood dishes might include such exotic ingredients as *oursins,* sea urchins; *lambi,* conch; and *langouste,* local rock lobster or crayfish. For dessert, try coconut sorbet or *amour caché,* a traditional pastry made with coconut jam. Local beverages include a potent mix known as "ti punch," bottled rums from a dozen distilleries, and *bière de Lorraine*, the local ale. Didier Water, bottled on the island, is a naturally carbonated mineral water. Tap water and milk are safe to drink.

More than 350 restaurants in Martinique have elevated Creole and French cooking to its highest level of artistic perfection. Most hotels and restaurants include a 10- to 15-percent service charge in their prices or add it to the final bill.

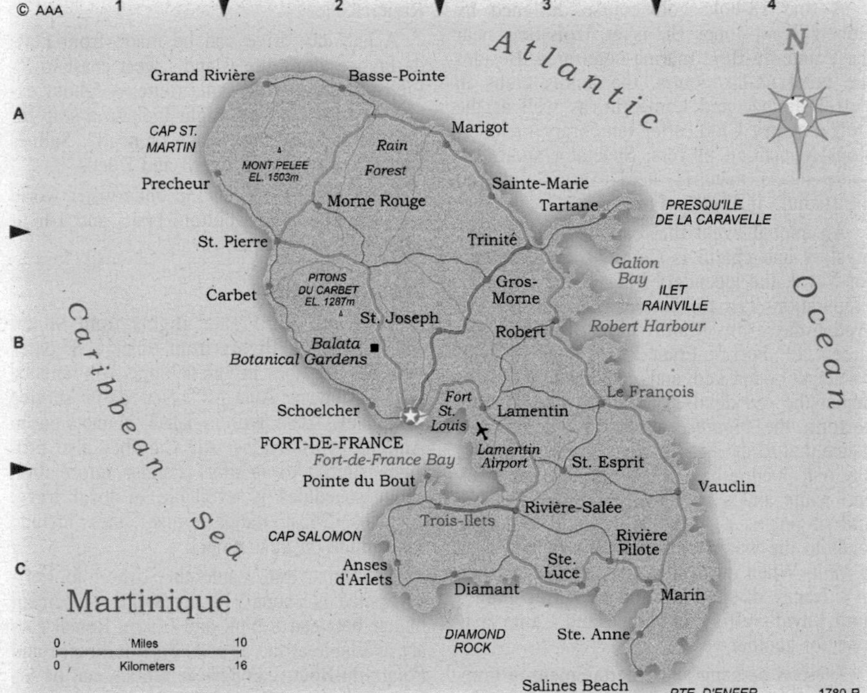

Sports and Amusements

Beaches of white, ochre and silver-gray volcanic sand offer unlimited opportunities for swimming, skin diving, scuba diving, water skiing and other aquatic sports. Among the island's most popular beaches are Diamant Beach, about 21 miles (34 km) from Fort-de-France on the southwest coast, and the sandy strand at Salines near Ste. Anne. Scuba diving services, including courses for beginners, are available to guests at hotels in the Pointe-du-Bout and Diamant resort areas and elsewhere.

The Pointe-du-Bout area also is a popular spot for sailing. Large boats can be chartered at Pointe-du-Bout and through Moorings, Stardust and several other charter companies at the island's largest marina in Marin. Memberships of most U.S. yacht clubs are honored at the two yacht clubs in Fort-de-France. Most of the larger hotels and the marina at Fort-de-France charter boats for deep-sea fishing.

Other recreational pursuits include horseback riding, hiking, mountain climbing, tennis and golf. An alternative to the resort environment is camping. Campgrounds with showers are found in Ste. Anne, Trois-Ilets and Le Vauclin. Horseback rides through the country and cane fields are conducted through several private clubs and ranches.

A fine 18-hole golf course designed by Robert Trent Jones Sr. is at Trois-Ilets near the Pointe-du-Bout marina-hotel area. Besides the hotel tennis courts, the tennis clubs in Fort-de-France and Lamentin, as well as the Golf Country Club, offer temporary memberships to visiting players. Spectator sports include soccer matches, held every Sunday at the stadium in Fort-de-France.

An annual event that captures the island's mystery and charm is Carnival, a celebration for Vaval, the legendary king of the Carnival. Preparations last for 5 weeks, ending on Ash Wednesday. On Mardi Gras Tuesday, the streets of Fort-de-France are jammed with participants masked and costumed in red to depict the red devils, or *diables rouge*. They perform the *biguine*, a twisting, uninhibited dance that to the Martiniquais is a way of life. On Ash Wednesday, the costumes are black and white and a parade of rhythmic dancing and singing is a wake for Vaval. The parade leads to the waterfront where his funeral pyre is built. When dusk falls, the spectators dance in a frenzy of shadows and flickering flames until Vaval's effigy is burned and Carnival is over for another year.

There is dancing and entertainment in Fort-de-France at L'Alibi, Le Cheyenne, Le Négresco and Xenakis Club as well as at several major hotels, such as Le Kalenda Resort Hotel, which features a discotheque.

L'Atrium, Fort-de-France's cultural center, features concerts as well as dance and opera performances by internationally known artists. Theater life in Fort-de-France revolves around the Théâtre Municipal. Dance exhibitions performed by the Grands Ballets de la Martinique and other groups are frequently held at the major hotels. Several theaters show French and American films with French soundtracks.

Sightseeing

Good roads, including many four-lane highways, afford pleasant excursions. These include a 5-hour drive to the old capital of St. Pierre, where the historical museum can be visited, and on to Grand Rivière, returning through quaint fishing villages on the eastern coast. A 4-hour trip from Fort-de-France to the southern half of the island includes stops at Trois-Ilets, birthplace of Empress Josephine; Pointe-du-Bout, which offers a fine view of the capital across the bay; and Anses d'Arlets, a small fishing village. Diamant Beach affords a view of Diamond Rock, a giant offshore monolith. Return is through Rivière-Salée.

A half-day drive can be made from Fort-de-France along the island's west coast to St. Pierre, returning the same route. A 5-hour excursion to Ste. Anne might include a stop for a swim at Ste. Anne Beach or nearby Salines Beach; return via St. Esprit and Ducos.

Fascinating views of the underwater world are offered on glass-bottom boats and 1-hour aquascope excursions.

Transportation

There are Air France flights from Miami and connecting flights from other U.S. cities with Air Caraïbes in Guadeloupe. Air Jamaica and Caribbean Airways offer daily service from New York with a LIAT connection in Antigua or Barbados. Air Caraïbes also provides flights to nearby islands; information about schedules is available at local travel agencies. Most major cruise lines include Martinique on their itinerary.

Taxi fare from Lamentin Airport to Fort-de-France is about $12; fares are 40 percent higher between 8 p.m. and 6 a.m. Rental cars are available at the airport, Fort-de-France and Pointe-du-Bout; camper-car rentals can be arranged at Anse Mitan.

Collective taxis, private cars or minibuses that serve as jitney buses, will take up to eight passengers to many standard destinations. The name of the final destination is marked on the car. These "group" taxis stop running at 6 p.m. A one-way taxi fare from Fort-de-France to Ste. Anne is approximately $4. Crowded buses, used primarily by islanders, also serve sections of Fort-de-France.

Ferries link Fort-de-France with the main resort areas of Trois-Ilets and Ste. Anne. High-speed passenger ferries operated by Brudey Frères and L'Express des Iles connect Martinique with Dominica, Guadeloupe and St. Lucia.

Fast Facts

POPULATION: 429,510.

AREA: 1,101 sq km (425 sq mi.).

CAPITAL: Fort-de-France.

HIGHEST POINT: 1,397 m (4,584 ft.), Mont Pelée.

LOWEST POINT: Sea level, Caribbean Sea.

TIME ZONE(S): Atlantic Standard.

LANGUAGE: French and Creole.

GOVERNMENT: Overseas Department of France.

UNIT OF CURRENCY: Euro Dollar. $1 U.S. = approx. .6 Euro. U.S. currency is widely accepted.

ELECTRICITY: 220 volts, 50 cycles AC.

MINIMUM AGE FOR DRIVERS: 21-25, depending on the rental car agency. An international driver's license is required; drive on right.

MINIMUM AGE FOR GAMBLING: 18.

SEAT BELT/CHILD RESTRAINT LAWS: Seat belts are required for all passengers. Children under 12 must ride in the back seat.

HOLIDAYS: Jan. 1; Carnival (Mardi Gras and Ash Wednesday); Good Friday; Easter Monday; Labour Day, May 1; Victory Day, May 8; Slavery Abolition Day, May 22; Ascension Day, May (6th Thurs. after Easter); Whit Monday, May or June (8th Mon. after Easter); Bastille Day, July 14; Assumption Day, Aug. 15; All Saints Day, Nov. 1; Armistice Day, Nov. 11; Christmas, Dec. 25.

TAXES: A 5 percent room tax and 10 percent service charge are added to most hotel bills. Restaurants include a 15 percent service charge.

IMMIGRATION REQUIREMENTS: A valid passport and return or onward ticket are required for U.S. citizens entering the French West Indies. No visa needed for stays up to 3 months. The U.S. Dept. of Homeland Security requires all U.S. citizens returning from the Caribbean to present a valid passport.

PHONING THE ISLANDS: To call Martinique from the U.S. or Canada, dial 011 + 596 + 596 + the 6-digit local number.

FURTHER INFORMATION FOR VISITORS:

French Government Tourist Office/Martinique Promotion Bureau
825 3rd Ave.
New York, NY 10022
(212) 838-7800

Martinique Tourist Office (Comité Martiniquais du Tourisme)
Immeuble Le Beaupré
Pointe de Jaham
Schoelcher, Martinique 97233
(596) 61-61-77

Points of Interest

See map page 171.

CARBET (B-1) pop. 3,316

Christopher Columbus landed near Carbet (car-BAY) in 1502. Paul Gauguin lived in this village on the scenic coastal route between Fort-de-France and St. Pierre for 5 months in 1887.

CENTRE D'ART MUSÉE PAUL GAUGUIN is at Turin Cove between Carbet and St. Pierre. The museum documents Paul Gauguin's stay on Martinique with copies of manuscripts, letters and a dozen paintings of the island. Art exhibits by local artists also are featured. Daily 9-5:30. Admission $5; $1 (children). Phone (596) 78-22-66.

FORT-DE-FRANCE (B-2) pop. 134,727

Capital of the "island of flowers," Fort-de-France is stepped like an amphitheater around the celebrated Place de la Savane. This lovely park contains the statue of Pierre Belain D'esnambuc, founder of the French colony here in 1635, the island's first European settlement. Nearby is the marble statue of the Empress Josephine, who was born across the bay near Trois-Ilets. Fort St. Louis dominates the harbor promontory.

The Schoelcher Library, across from La Savane, was designed by French architect Henri Picq for the Paris exposition of 1889, then later disassembled and shipped to the island. The building is named for Victor Schoelcher, a French abolitionist who helped end slavery in Martinique in the mid-1800s. A statue of Schoelcher stands at the entrance to the Court of Justice Building at the corner of rues Schoelcher and Moreau de Jones.

DID YOU KNOW

Josephine, Empress of France, was born in Martinique.

On Rue Schoelcher is the 1895 Saint-Louis Cathedral, a neo-classical church featuring Byzantine decor, stained-glass windows and a massive pipe organ. Built upon the site of six previous churches, the iron structure was designed to withstand fire, earthquake and hurricane. The Sacré-Coeur de Balata basilica is in the suburbs north of Fort-de-France.

BALATA BOTANICAL GARDENS (JARDIN DE BALATA) is 6 mi. (10 km) n. on Route de Balata, following signs. Entered through a restored Creole house furnished in period, the gardens showcase labeled plant varieties including anthuriums, heliconias, begonias, orchids and many others. Ornamental lakes feature water lilies and lotus blossoms. Free-flying hummingbirds are often sighted. Allow 1 hour minimum. Daily 9-6. Last admission 1 hour before closing. Admission $9; $3 (ages 7-12). MC. Phone (596) 64-48-73.

PRE-COLUMBIAN MUSEUM is at 9 rue de la Liberté. The Musée Départemental d'Archéologie Précolombienne features relics from prehistoric Arawak Indian excavations and exhibits about contemporary everyday life. Mon.-Fri. 8-5, Sat. 9-noon. Admission $6. Phone (596) 71-57-05.

GAMBLING ESTABLISHMENTS

- **Casino Batelière Plazza** is north of Fort-de-France on Rue des Alizés in Schoelcher. Daily 8:30 p.m.-3 a.m. Phone (596) 61-73-23.

LE FRANÇOIS (B-3) pop. 18,559

This east coast village was the site of a March 1991 summit meeting between presidents George Bush and François Mitterand to discuss the Middle East peace process. The Atlantic coast at Le François is noted for its breakers and sand bars.

HABITATION CLÉMENT is at the L'Acajou Estate 1.2 mi. (2 km) w. toward Le St-Esprit. The Clement House is home to one of the finest rum distilleries on the island. Visitors can tour the distillery and estate, and free tastings are offered. The 18th-century house of the company's founder evokes plantation life, and an old distillery has been restored as a museum. Tropical gardens are on the grounds. Allow 1 hour minimum. Daily 9-5:30, Oct.-Aug. Admission $9. Phone (596) 54-62-07.

ST. PIERRE (B-1) pop. 4,453

Sometimes called the Pompeii of the New World, St. Pierre is 20 miles (32 km) northwest of Fort-de-France. Amid this active tropical town are the ruins of the old St. Pierre, which was destroyed by the eruption of Mont Pelée. Now dormant, the volcano roared into life on May 8, 1902, annihilating all but one of St. Pierre's 30,000 inhabitants—a local drunk imprisoned in the basement of the jail. The village was never buried under lava, which bypassed the town on its run to the sea some miles north; it was destroyed within 3 minutes by the exploding volcano's intense heat and gas.

Walls and foundations are all that remain of the magnificent theater that was once the heart of the "Paris of the West Indies." Cars can be driven to within an hour's walk of the summit, and rental vehicles, drivers and guides are available at Morne Rouge, a popular vacation spot for Martiniquais.

MUSÉE VOLCANOLOGIQUE DE FRANCK A. PERRET is on rue Victor Hugo in the center of town. Founded by an American volcanologist, the museum displays items salvaged after the eruption of Mont Pelée along with photographs of the ruins. Photography is not permitted. Allow 30 minutes minimum. Daily 9-5. Admission $3; free (ages 0-6). Phone (596) 78-15-16.

TROIS-ILETS (C-2) pop. 5,162

Across the bay from Fort-de-France is Trois-Ilets, named for the three islets floating offshore. Nearby is the birthplace of Marie Josèphe Rose Tascher de la Pagerie, the Creole beauty who later reigned as Napoleon's Empress Josephine. La Pagerie, her partially restored home and the church where she was christened can be visited. The town also contains La Maison de la Canne, a museum featuring exhibits about the sugar industry; phone (596) 68-32-04.

MUSÉE DE LA PAGERIE is near Pointe-du-Bout. Empress Josephine was born here in 1763, the daughter of Joseph Tascher de la Pagerie, a French planter. A museum in the old kitchen quarters of the family home contains mementos of the Empress and of the Napoleonic period. A few of Napoleon's love letters are displayed. A tropical garden is on the grounds of the sugar plantation. Tues.-Fri. 9-5:30, Sat.-Sun. 9:30-1 and 3-5. Admission $7; $5 (ages 0-11). Phone (596) 68-38-34 or (596) 68-33-06.

GAMBLING ESTABLISHMENTS

- **Trois Ilets Casino at Kalenda Resort** is at Pointe du Bout. Daily 9 p.m.-3 a.m. Phone (596) 66-00-00.

Rendezvous Bay / David Mac Gillivary / Montserrat Tourist Board

Montserrat

During his second voyage to the New World, Christopher Columbus paid homage to a hill-encircled abbey near Barcelona, Spain, naming a tiny, mountainous island Montserrat after the Spanish landmark. Although the Caribbean land mass 27 miles (43 km) southwest of Antigua outwardly resembles Spain's venerated peak, geologically, it greatly differs from its namesake. The ruggedly beautiful slopes of the "saw-toothed mountain" actually are those of a 3,000-foot (914-meter) volcano, which drew worldwide attention in the 1990s as torrents of hot volcanic debris destroyed its southern portion.

Although the disaster claimed Montserrat's capital and sole airport, the tropical oasis endures today, affording dramatic rock formations, lush vegetation, and secluded, sandy retreats. The government of the overseas British territory now operates out of Brades, with a new $18.5-million airport receiving travelers. In the aftermath of nature's fury, the eruption yielded more fertile soil; healthier and more diverse underwater environments; and an unusual natural attraction—the active Soufrière Hills Volcano.

History

The Arawaks and Caribs resided on *Alliouagana,* "the land of the prickly bush," before Columbus sailed Montserrat's waters in 1493. Irish-Catholic settlers from St. Kitts arrived in 1632 and were later joined by Irish exiles fleeing Lord Cromwell's troops in Britain. France twice attempted to claim the island, having purchased it from Spain, but Britain maintained control.

Tobacco, sugar and cotton plantations once flourished; the rich, fertile soil produced an abundance of crops. When world markets declined, lime orchards were planted and the juice bottled and exported. In the 1960s, real estate development replaced agricultural pursuits, as Americans, Canadians and Britons flocked to the island to build homes and businesses. Such musicians as Elton John, Stevie Wonder and Eric Clapton also began arriving to record at AIR Studios Montserrat, built by Beatles producer George Martin in 1979.

As the economy became more diversified and with tourism thriving, disaster struck. Hurricane Hugo damaged more than 90 percent of the island's structures, even forcing AIR Studios Montserrat to close. The vital tourist industry was eventually re-established

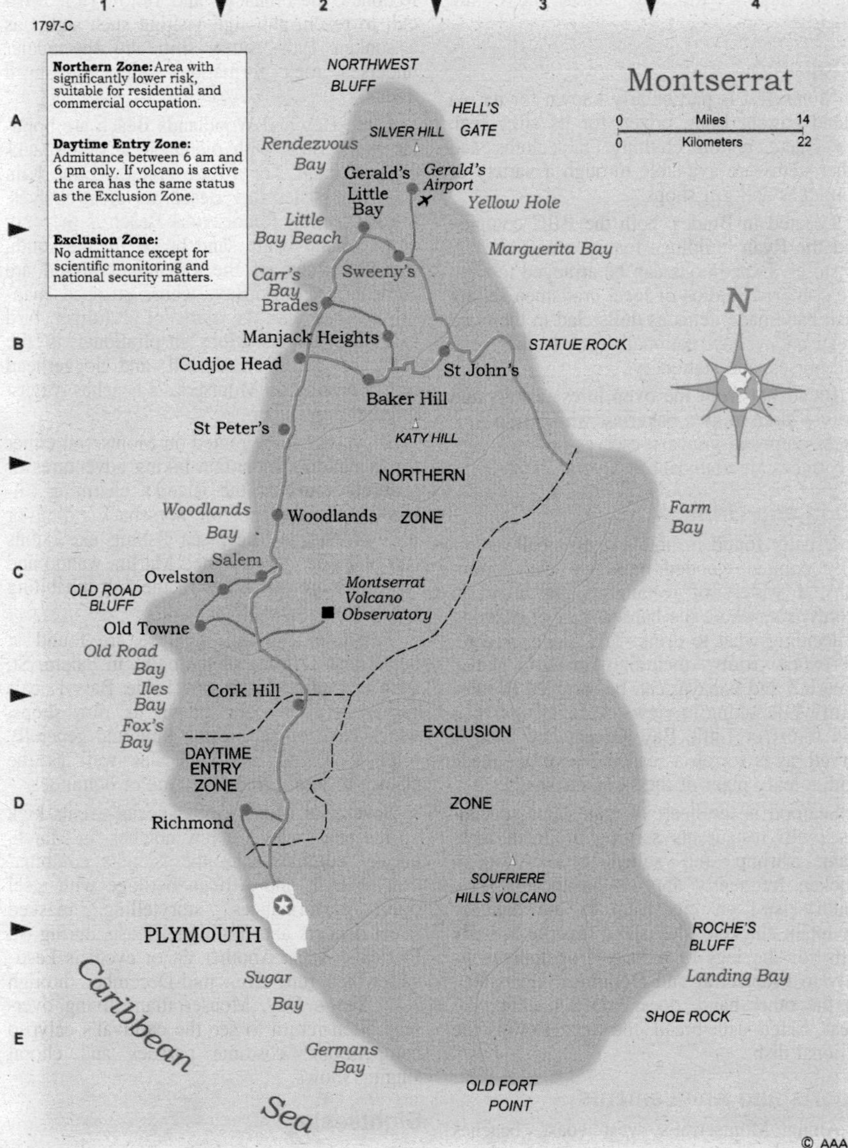

but again crumbled in 1995 when the long-dormant Soufrière Hills Volcano began spewing hot gas and rock. Ash darkened the skies over Plymouth, forcing evacuation to the north as volcanic mudflows buried the capital.

Today, the Exclusion Zone prohibits most entry into the island's southern half. Resilient Monserratians continue to add modern facilities in the north, which also boasts such ecological lures as Runaway Ghaut and Centre Hills.

Shopping

Montserrat is particularly known for its sea island cotton. Long prized for its silky feel, sea island cotton clothing, tablecloths and other items are available through a variety of boutiques and gift shops.

Located in Brades, both the BBC complex and the Ryan buildings feature small clusters of stores. Expeditions can be arranged to shop the scattered studios of local craftsmen selling such handmade items as dolls clad in the plaid green and yellow national dress, leather belts and purses, and stationery.

Bread hot from the oven lures visitors and natives alike to area bakeries, while fresh produce, domestic guava preserves and hot pepper sauces are abundant at several markets.

Food and Drink

Usually found in hotels or in small, colorfully painted wooden buildings with verandahs, a variety of restaurants are found in Montserrat, where the hardest part of ordering is deciding what to drink. The island's wealth of exotic fruits, including mango, guava, tamarind and papaya, can be sampled in juice form while taking in views of the Centre Hills rain forest or Little Bay. Ginger beer also is served, as is sorrel, a seasonal beverage made from a leafy plant of the same name.

Seafood is the heart of many area specialties, with restaurants serving up fresh mahi mahi, shrimp and salted cod. Although chicken frequently appears on local menus, poultry isn't an ingredient in the delicacy mountain chicken. The island favorite actually calls for the legs of a large frog indigenous only to Montserrat and Dominica. Goatwater, on the other hand, does indeed feature goat meat. Eaten with bread, the thick stew is the national dish.

Sports and Amusements

Along Montserrat's west coast, beaches with pearl-grey volcanic sand provide plenty of swimming and water sports opportunities; equipment can be obtained through most local hotels. Snorkeling and scuba diving are popular sports, and the island offers numerous coral reefs for exploration.

Beginners can dive at Lime Kiln Bay, with a maximum depth of 45 feet (14 m). Schools of reef fish dart past swimmers at Northwest Bluff, while Rendezvous Bay cave divers encounter thousands of fruit bats dangling from the chasm's ceiling. High waves make Little Redonda, the Pinnacles and Yellow Hole difficult to reach, although visiting such sights as a sunken 19th-century ship and spectacular undersea rock formations tempt advanced divers.

Little Bay and Woodlands Beach are popular shore sites, with picnic areas and snacks close at hand. For a little privacy, Lime Kiln Beach and Isles Bay Beach are great choices. Furthest north, Rendezvous Beach is the only non-volcanic white sand beach. In the south, the aftereffects of the volcanic eruption are evident at Foxes Bay, where stripped mangrove trees and the ruins of a former bird sanctuary linger. More inspirational is the sight of green, hawksbill and loggerhead turtles nesting on Montserrat's beaches August through September.

Bicycles can be rented on Montserrat either for demanding mountain biking adventures or leisurely tours of the island's charming villages. Arrangements for horseback riding or full- or half-day deep-sea fishing excursions can be made at your hotel. Marlin, wahoo and swordfish are just a few of the fish inhabiting the surrounding waters.

Entertainment and nightlife are found at hotels and at some of the clubs in Salem, St. John's, Cudjoe Head and Little Bay. Locals gather at cozy bars known as rum shops, which have no set closing time and generally offer food and live music as well as the chance to join a friendly game of dominoes.

Several of Montserrat's special events kick up the energy level a few notches. In March, natives commemorate the island's combination of Irish and African heritage with steel drum performances, storytelling, masked street dancers and traditional feasts during St. Patrick's Week. Another major event is Festival, which runs from mid-December through New Year's Day. Monserratians living overseas often return to see the carnival's calypso competitions, costume parades and choral singing shows.

Sightseeing

Built almost exclusively of volcanic rocks, Montserrat is only 12 miles (19 km) long and 7 miles (11 km) wide. Galway's Soufrière, a volcanic crater on the southern half of the island, lies within the Exclusion Zone that covers nearly half the island.

Visitors can view the Soufrière Hills from a safe distance; several companies offer guided tours of accessible areas. Patrons of Caribbean Helicopters fly over the active volcano; phone (268) 460-5900. Across the Belham Valley, the Daytime Entry Zone affords panoramas of devastating volcanic mudflows. The abandoned capital of Plymouth can be seen from St. George's, Garibaldi and Richmond hills. A viewing facility at Jack Boy Hill includes a platform, picnic areas, a walking trail and a telescope imparting close-ups of Montserrat's destroyed WH Bramble Airport and eastern villages.

The Montserrat Volcano Observatory provides the best vantage point along with insight into the island's famous, unruly tenant. Scientific staff explain the volcano monitoring program during short tours.

Although the southern portion of the island is uninhabitable, Montserrat remains worthy of the designation "Emerald Isle." The pure, open terrain demands extensive exploration by foot; most trails take hikers through Centre Hills, where the national bird, the Montserrat oriole, and the mountain chicken dwell.

A trail through The Cot, the historic site of an old banana plantation, provides glimpses of varied flora and fauna in their lush environs as well as views of Salem and the surrounding areas. Oriole Walkway and Silver Hills Trail are home to some of Montserrat's 34 species of birds, including the mangrove cuckoo. The latter route lies within one of the island's oldest inactive volcanic centers.

The Montserrat National Trust and Natural History Centre, displays many relics of the island's past, including pre-Columbian, agricultural and volcanic exhibits. Montserrat's senior citizens recount local history through a video display. A small historical library, botanical gardens and the Montserrat Philatelic Bureau, filled with valuable and unusual stamps, also are on site; phone (664) 491-3086 for the history center or (664) 491-2042 for the philatelic bureau.

Transportation

Daily flights aboard Winair connect Montserrat with Antigua and St. Maarten, where air travel to neighboring islands, North America and Europe is available. Charter flights to Montserrat's modern Gerald's Airport are available as well. Several Antigua tour operators offer day trips to Montserrat that include sightseeing and transportation; check with the tourist board for more information.

Transportation on the island is by car, taxi or minibus. There are no scheduled times or official stops for minibuses, but most can be hailed off main thoroughfares. Both buses and taxis have green license plates beginning with "H"; agree on the appropriate fare to be paid in advance.

When exploring by rental car, a valid U.S. driver's license must be presented to obtain a temporary driving permit. The permit costs $19 and is available at your port of entry or from Montserrat's police headquarters. Be sure to fill up at one of the two gas stations before maneuvering the island's lengthy roads peppered with twists and steep hills. In addition, driving is on the left and there are no traffic lights; however, names are posted on most streets. If driving seems too challenging, your hotel or the tourist board can provide a road map or a list of local guides.

Fast Facts

POPULATION: 9,341.

AREA: 102 sq km (39 sq mi.).

CAPITAL: Plymouth (abandoned in 1997 due to volcanic activity; interim government buildings have been built in Brades).

HIGHEST POINT: 914 m (3,000 ft.), Chances Peak (in the Soufrière Hills volcanic complex).

LOWEST POINT: Sea level, Caribbean Sea.

TIME ZONE(S): Atlantic Standard.

LANGUAGE: English.

GOVERNMENT: British Overseas Territory.

UNIT OF CURRENCY: Eastern Caribbean (E.C.) dollar. $1 U.S. = 2.7 E.C. dollars.

ELECTRICITY: 110-220 volts, 60 cycles AC.

MINIMUM AGE FOR DRIVERS: 21-25, depending on the rental car agency. A valid U.S. driver's license must be presented to obtain a temporary driving permit. The $19 permit is available at port of entry or from Montserrat's police headquarters at Brades or in Salem.

HOLIDAYS: Jan. 1; St. Patrick's Day, March 17; Good Friday; Easter; Easter Monday; Labour Day, May (1st Mon.); Whit Monday, May or June (8th Mon. after Easter); Queen's Birthday, June (2nd Sat.); August Monday, Aug. (1st Mon.); Dec. 25; Boxing Day, Dec. 26; Festival Day, Dec. 31.

TAXES: A 7-10 percent room tax (depending on the size of the resort) and a 10 percent service charge are added to most hotel and restaurant bills. Departure tax $21 U.S.

IMMIGRATION REQUIREMENTS: Passport and a return or through ticket are required. No visa needed for stays up to 3 months. The U.S. Dept. of Homeland Security requires all U.S. citizens returning from the Caribbean to present a valid passport.

PHONING THE ISLANDS: To call Montserrat from the U.S. or Canada, dial 1 + 664 + the 7-digit local number.

FURTHER INFORMATION FOR VISITORS:

Montserrat Tourist Board
#7 Farara Plaza, Buildings B&C
P.O. Box 7
Brades, Montserrat
(664) 491-2230
(664) 491-8730

Points of Interest

See map page 177.

SALEM (C-2)

Just north of the exclusion zone, Salem is a few miles inland on the west coast of the island. Residents were temporarily evacuated in 1997 but returned a year later. On Old Road Beach, souvenir hunters may find bits of pumice and charred wood washed down from the volcano during heavy rains.

MONTSERRAT VOLCANO OBSERVATORY (MVO) is up a steep hill from Salem in Flemmings, following signs. Established soon after the first eruption of the Soufrière Hills volcano on July 18, 1995, the observatory monitors daily seismic activity. An observation deck offers one of the best views of the volcano and the surrounding countryside, including the abandoned capital of Plymouth.

Twice-weekly tours include a video presentation of recent eruptions and a description of monitoring techniques and equipment. Allow 1 hour minimum. Mon.-Fri. 8:30-4:30. Guided tours are offered Tues. and Thurs. at 2. Observatory free. Tours $4. Phone (664) 491-5647.

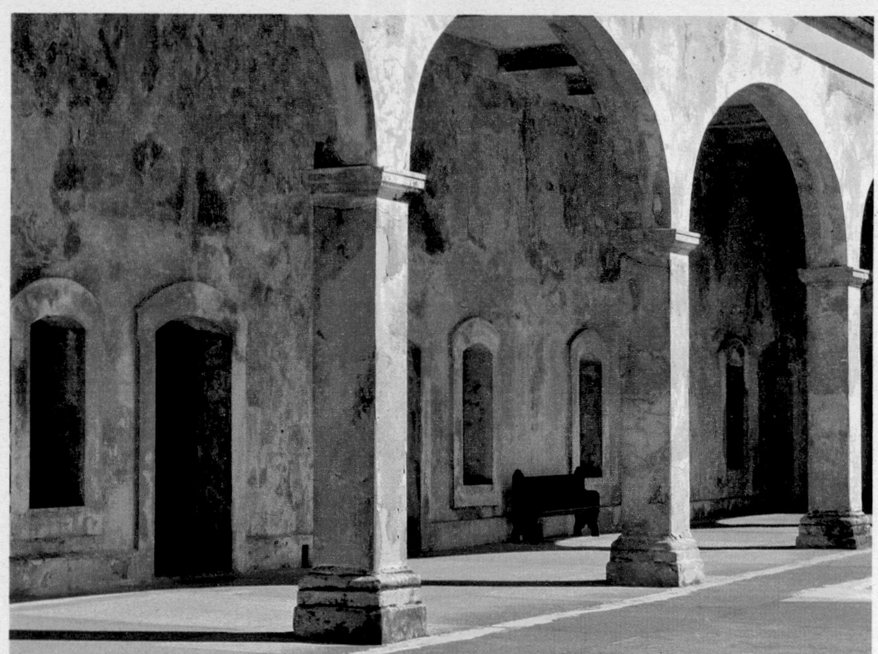

Fort San Cristóbal, Old San Juan / © Kim Karpeles / age fotostock

Puerto Rico

A diverse tropical landscape awaits the visitor to the U.S. Commonwealth of Puerto Rico, which boasts more than 300 miles (500 km) of palm-fringed coastline and a lush interior of montage thicket, palm, dwarf and rain forests. The island is a progressive blend of old and new. Nowhere is this more evident than in the capital city of San Juan, with its centuries-old Spanish fortresses and glamorous resort hotels. "Out on the island," as the Puerto Ricans refer to the remainder of the island, the changes are less dramatic but no less important.

Puerto Rico has made great strides economically and today enjoys one of the highest standards of living in the Caribbean. The island is a major banking and business center, and San Juan is the Caribbean's primary air and cruise hub. Complementing this progress, the Commonwealth, with the Institute of Puerto Rican Culture, has fostered an atmosphere in which writers, painters, sculptors, musicians and actors flourish, and has taken steps to preserve the island's crafts, folklore, dances, music and architecture.

History

Originally named *Borikén* (Island of the Brave Lord) by the Taíno Indians, Puerto Rico was discovered by Christopher Columbus in 1493 during his second voyage to the New World. He landed on the northwestern part of the island and named the island San Juan Bautista. The island derived its present name, however, from the exclamation "*¡Qué puerto rico!*" (What a rich port!), said to have been made by *conquistador* Juan Ponce de León upon entering the bay. He established the first settlement at Caparra in 1508 and in 1510 he was appointed the island's first governor by Spain's King Ferdinand. The capital was transferred to its present site and named San Juan Bautista de Puerto Rico in 1521, the year of de León's death.

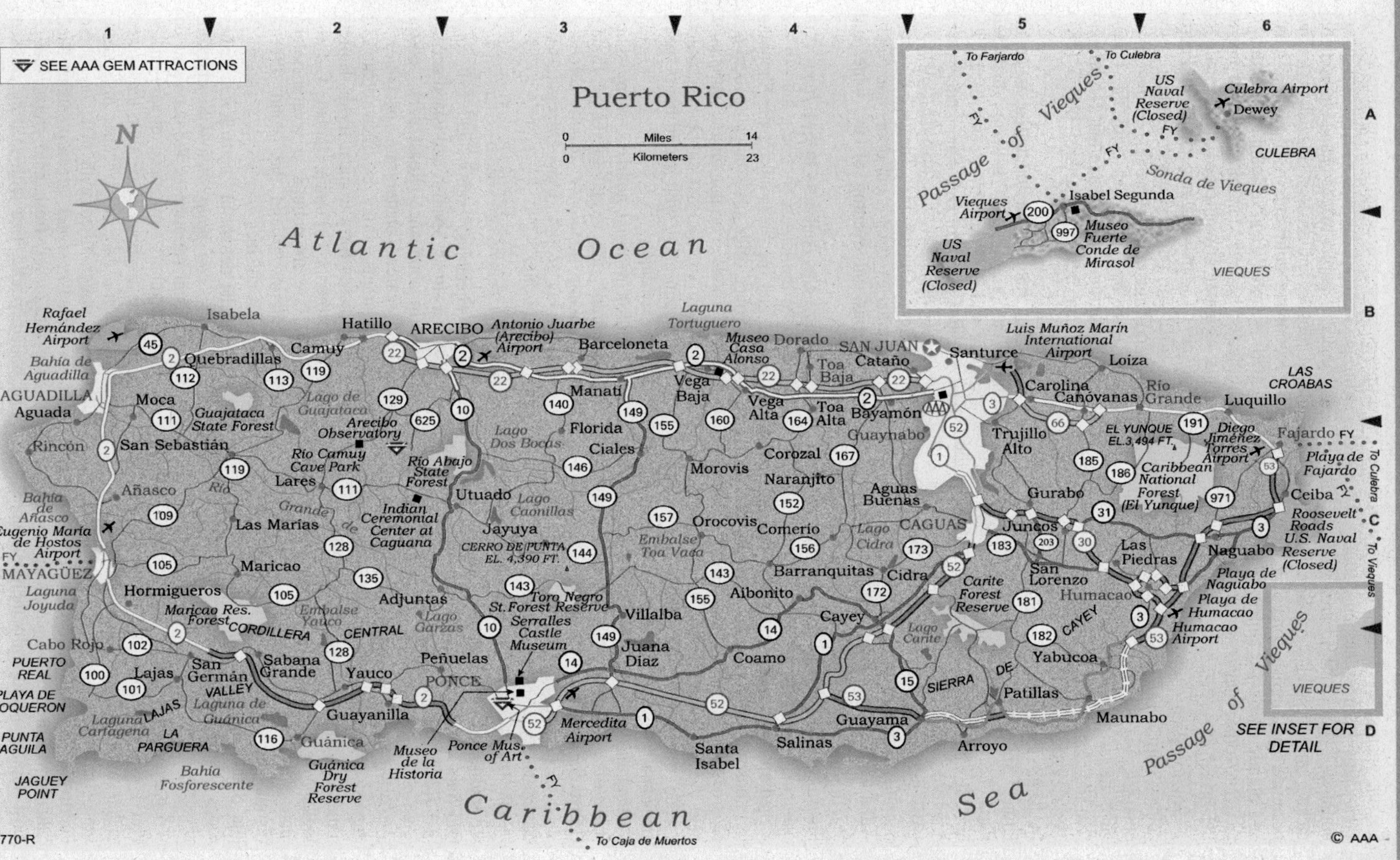
SEE AAA GEM ATTRACTIONS
Puerto Rico
Miles
Kilometers
Atlantic Ocean
Caribbean Sea
Passage of Vieques
Sonda de Vieques
To Farjardo
To Culebra
US Naval Reserve (Closed)
Culebra Airport
Dewey
CULEBRA
Isabel Segunda
Vieques Airport
Museo Fuerte Conde de Mirasol
VIEQUES
SAN JUAN
Santurce
Luis Muñoz Marín International Airport
ARECIBO
Antonio Juarbe (Arecibo) Airport
Rafael Hernández Airport
AGUADILLA
MAYAGÜEZ
Eugenio María de Hostos Airport
PONCE
Mercedita Airport
Ponce Mus. of Art
Museo de la Historia
CAGUAS
Humacao Airport
Diego Jiménez Torres Airport
EL YUNQUE EL.3,494 FT.
Caribbean National Forest (El Yunque)
CERRO DE PUNTA EL. 4,390 FT.
CORDILLERA CENTRAL
SIERRA DE CAYEY
Río Camuy Cave Park
Arecibo Observatory
Indian Ceremonial Center at Caguana
Serralles Castle Museum
Toro Negro St. Forest Reserve
Carite Forest Reserve
Guajataca State Forest
Río Abajo State Forest
Maricao Res. Forest
Guánica Dry Forest Reserve
Roosevelt Roads U.S. Naval Reserve (Closed)
To Dominican Republic
To Caja de Muertos
To Culebra
To Vieques
SEE INSET FOR DETAIL
1770-R
© AAA

The Spanish used San Juan Bay to protect their ships from pirates and attacks by other countries. This strategic area of land was attacked unsuccessfully by Sir Francis Drake, occupied by English forces in 1598, burned and plundered by the Dutch in 1625 and subjected to other sieges until a last attempt by the British in 1797.

Puerto Rico remained a loyal Spanish colony until 1897, when Luis Muñoz Rivera obtained the Charter of Autonomy, which gave the island dominion status. However, before the charter could go into effect, Spain became engaged in the Spanish-American War. In 1898 Puerto Rico became part of the United States by the terms of the Treaty of Paris. The Foraker Act of 1900 enabled the island to establish a civil government under the direction of a U.S.-appointed governor; in 1917 the Jones Act made the Puerto Rican people citizens of the United States and provided for the creation of a local senate.

The first native-born governor was Jesús T. Piñero, appointed by President Harry S. Truman in 1946. The following year Truman signed an act giving Puerto Rico the authority to choose its chief executive by popular vote. Luis Muñoz Marín, the first elected governor, held the office until 1965, when he was succeeded by Roberto Sánchez Vilella. A Congressional resolution signed by President Truman in 1952 elevated Puerto Rico to the status of a commonwealth associated with the United States.

Shopping

The best buys to look for in Puerto Rico are traditional island crafts. Calle Fortaleza in Old San Juan, a 20-minute bus or 10-minute taxi ride from the Condado section of resort hotels, is the center of a large and varied collection of shops selling both local crafts and imports—Thai silks, Spanish furniture and antiques, jewelry and items from the Philippines, India, Mexico and Europe. The tourist information center at La Casita at Pier 1 and the Institute of Puerto Rican Culture in the Ballajá Sector have lists of the numerous craft shops where artisans ply their trade in front of visitors.

Local artisans can be seen at La Casita at Pier 1 every Saturday and Sunday from noon to late evening. On Calle Marina in Old San Juan, opposite Pier 3, is the Plazoleta del Puerto—a delightful collection of shops specializing in traditional crafts. Some of the most notable island crafts include mundillo or bobbin lace; *santos,* or hand-carved, wooden religious figurines; *cuatros,* handmade 10-string guitars; festival masks made from coconut husks or papier-mâché; hand-embroidered linens, blouses and dresses; Spanish-style jewelry of copper, gold and silver filigree; hand-painted scarves and clothing; handbags; hammocks; baskets; ceramics; musical instruments; original artwork; and items made of mahogany. Cigars and rum made in Puerto Rico also are popular buys. Though some plants and fruits may be brought to the United States, it is best to check with the USDA Plant Protection and Quarantine Department in San Juan before departure; phone (787) 253-4551.

Old San Juan has a reputation as an art center, harboring many galleries that sell paintings and sculpture by Puerto Rican artists. Calle Cristo in Old San Juan houses many well-known art galleries such as the Botello Gallery. On the first Tuesday of every month, galleries open their doors for Noche de Gallerias, an evening of art, wine and socializing.

The Plaza Las Américas in San Juan, considered to be the largest shopping mall in the Caribbean, and the Plaza del Caribe Shopping Center in Ponce offer a full range of local and continental goods. For last-minute purchases, San Juan's airport also has shopping counters which are open daily, with varied hours based on airline schedules.

In addition to usual holidays, many shops and restaurants are closed on Good Friday. While banking hours are usually Monday through Friday 8:30-4, some banks also are open on Saturday.

Food and Drink

Fruits, vegetables, poultry and fish, prepared with a strong Spanish and island accent, are found in abundance. Roast pork, lobster dishes and seafood platters are specialties in many restaurants. Fruit is often combined with main dishes for a tropical flavor. Buffets featuring American, French, Italian, Chinese and native fare are popular at several hotels. Upscale eateries around the island offer a wide range of cuisines.

Some of the delightful Puerto Rican dishes include *arroz con pollo,* rice with chicken; *pasteles,* a local variation of the tamale made of ground plantain with meat, olives, raisins and chickpeas wrapped in plantain leaves and boiled; *lechón asado,* or barbecued pig; *pastelillos,* thin dough filled with meat or cheese and deep fried; *tostones,* green plantains fried in deep fat; *jueyes,* fresh land crabs, shelled and boiled; *paella,* rice with saffron, chicken and seafood; and *asopao,* a traditional Puerto

Rican soup made with rice and chicken or shrimp, cooked with wine sauce and often garnished with peas, pimientos, asparagus and hard-boiled eggs. Tap water is safe to drink and milk is pasteurized. A tip of 15 percent, with more for special service, is customary.

Sports and Amusements

The Caribbean, with its clear, warm water, is ideal for both scuba diving and snorkeling. Coral reefs and cays in many areas provide natural harbors for an array of beautiful and exotic sea life—coral, sea horses, starfish and tropical fish.

One of the best diving spots is off the northeastern coast of Puerto Rico around a small chain of islands. Visibility is exceptionally good in these waters, which range in depth from about 15 to 60 feet (5 to 18 m). The southwestern coast near La Parguera and the waters surrounding the eastern islands of Vieques and Culebra, dotted with many reefs, also are excellent spots for diving. Along the northwestern coast, the towns of Rincón and Aguadilla offer diving excursions to Mona and Desecheo islands.

Diving or snorkeling excursions from either the beach or a charter boat can be arranged for an hour, a day or longer; beginners might want to stay along the beach where there is a sheltered cove. There are courses for both beginning and advanced snorkelers and divers. The longer and more expensive advanced courses usually feature night dives or search and recovery expeditions. Major hotels and resorts have information about lessons and packages.

With 272 miles (438 km) of coastline, the island is ringed with good beaches with public facilities, called *balnearios,* which offer lockers, showers and parking for a nominal fee. They are open Tues.-Sun. 8-6 and are closed election days, Good Friday and the Tuesday following Monday holidays. Balneario de Luquillo, east of San Juan near El Yunque, is one of the most beautiful and popular beaches; the scenic bay at Balneario Boquerón near Cabo Rojo is a favorite among islanders.

Like Costa Rica, Panama and many other Central American countries, Puerto Rico is also widely known as a mecca for surfing. Thousands of pro and amateur surfers come here to ride some of the best beach and reef breaks in the Caribbean. The surfing season begins in September and runs through May. Surfing conditions are excellent along the north and west coast. Rincón, on the west coast of the island facing the Mona Passage, is popular with winter surfers, with typical swells delivering 15-foot waves. Surf shops abound in Rincón, as well as throughout the rest of the island.

Steady trade winds provide excellent opportunities for boating and sailing, particularly in San Juan Bay and the waters off Fajardo and La Parguera, which are well protected by coral reefs. Boats and equipment for sailing or deep-sea fishing can be rented from charter operators and marinas in San Juan, Mayagüez, Fajardo, Humacao and other towns. Game fish abound in Puerto Rico's waters, where more than 30 world records have been set, and include marlin, sailfish, mackerel, dolphin fish and wahoo. Snook, grouper, snapper, tarpon and amberjack teem along the southern coast. The International Billfish Tournament is held in late August; other fishing tournaments take place through September.

Puerto Rico offers golfers more than 20 courses to play. Most of these are of championship caliber, designed by some of the best-known architects in the golf world and host to local and international tournaments. Landscaped championship golf courses are at the Westin Río Mar in Río Grande, the Hyatt Dorado Beach in Dorado, El Conquistador Resort in Fajardo, Palmas del Mar Golf Club in Humacao, Punta Borinquen Golf Club in Aguadilla and Coco Beach in Río Grande. Other golf courses on the island include Aguirre Golf Club in Salinas; Bahía Beach Plantation (temporarily closed for renovation), Berwind Country Club in Río Grande; Club Deportivo del Oeste in Mayagüez; Coamo Springs and Costa Caribe in Ponce; the Dorado del Mar and Plantation Club in Dorado; El Legado in Guayama; and Bambuas Golf Course in Gurabo.

Tennis courts are available at San Juan Central Park and at many of the hotels in the Condado and Isla Verde areas of San Juan. Hotels out on the island with more than 10 tennis courts are Hyatt Dorado Beach, El Conquistador Resort & Country Club in Fajardo and the Palmas del Mar Resort in Humacao. Horseback riding is available at Doral Resort at Palmas del Mar Resort in Humacao, Hacienda Carabalí and Tropical Trail Rides in Isabela.

Spectator sports in Puerto Rico cover a wide range of interests reflecting both Spanish and American cultures. One of the local favorites is basketball; Puerto Ricans eagerly await the beginning of the basketball season in May. Second only to basketball in popularity is baseball, whose season runs from October through February; the game is played at the Hiram Bithorn Stadium in San Juan. Another popular and exciting sport is horse racing;

races with pari-mutuel and daily double betting take place at Hipódromo El Comandante. Paso Fino horse shows, featuring Puerto Rico's own smooth-gaited breed, take place regularly around the island.

Activities in Puerto Rico do not end at sundown. Supper clubs feature elaborate floor shows, dining and dancing. The Luis A. Ferré Performing Arts Center (also known as the Centro de Bellas Artes) in San Juan regularly presents internationally acclaimed musicians, opera and ballet stars in its three theaters. One of the oldest municipal theaters in the Western Hemisphere, Old San Juan's restored El Tapía Theater offers performances every weekend. Another historic cultural center in Old San Juan is the Ateneo , which produces all kinds of cultural events throughout the year. The Puerto Rico Symphony Orchestra, a top-ranked ensemble, kicks off its concert season every year at Bellas Artes in September and wraps up in May.

Elegant government-regulated casinos are found in most of the large hotels. Various hotels offer a weekly rendition of the Le Lo Lai Festival, sponsored by the Puerto Rico Tourism Co. This colorful extravaganza of Puerto Rican folk songs and dances showcases the European and Afro-Antillean heritage of the island.

In January is the Pablo Casals Festival, which pays tribute to the life and musical career of the famous Spanish cellist. In mid-January, internationally acclaimed opera singers, ballet dancers and chamber music artists from around the globe perform at the Luis A. Ferré Performing Arts Center in the Santurce sector of San Juan. San Juan Bautista Day is celebrated on June 24, with public parties, bonfires on the beaches, street dances and concerts. Constitution Day on July 25 marks the anniversary of the island's commonwealth status; parades, fireworks and regattas are held throughout the island.

A copy of *Qué Pasa!* (What's Happening!) is available at hotel desks and at the Puerto Rico Tourism Co.'s information centers. This quarterly magazine lists events, scenic tours, points of interest, restaurants, nightclubs, shops and visitor information for San Juan and places out on the island.

Sightseeing

With about 3,000 miles (4,800 km) of good roads, Puerto Rico is popular for motor excursions. Though San Juan receives the majority of attention, it is a good idea to venture out on the island to get a true picture of Puerto Rico. Currently, there are 20 forest reserve areas in the island. For detailed information about guided driving tours, consult the Puerto Rico Tourism Co.'s information centers at the International Airport in Isla Verde, La Casita near Pier 1 in Old San Juan and the PRTC Headquarters at the La Princesa Building, also in Old San Juan. Self-guiding driving and walking tours are detailed in *Qué Pasa!,* the official guide to Puerto Rico.

Many interesting sites are only a short distance from San Juan—famous resorts, craft villages, forests, beaches and scenic areas. For example, a half-day tour from San Juan to the Palo Colorado Recreation Site in the El Yunque National Forest might include a drive through the towns of Río Grande, Luquillo and Loíza, where intricate masks are carved out of coconut shells by descendants of the town's original black plantation slaves.

Another half-day trip from San Juan is a visit to Las Cabezas de San Juan Nature Preserve, a beautiful, ecologically diverse area operated by the Conservation Trust of Puerto Rico. Known locally as El Faro (the lighthouse), the reserve is home to indigenous and endangered species and features each of Puerto Rico's unique ecosystems.

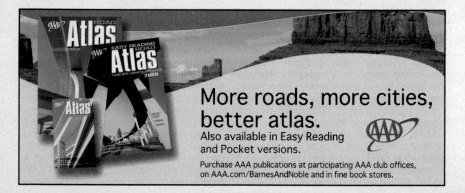

A full day should be allotted for a round-trip drive from San Juan to Arecibo, including stops at Vega Baja, Manatí, the grounds of the Arecibo Observatory and, near Lares, the Río Camuy Cave Park, featuring the world's third largest underground river. Part of the drive follows a scenic coastal road, Rte. 681.

A drive through coffee country from Manatí to Ponce on rtes. 140 and 10, then to San Juan via Rte. 1, might include stops at rock formations and at Central Mercedita near Ponce, where sugar is refined.

Longer excursions out on the island are usually worth the extra effort. A 3-day tour from San Juan to Ponce might include over-night stops in Mayagüez and La Parguera, then passing through San Germán and Ponce. Evening boat trips to La Parguera's bioluminescent bay offer an "illuminating" experience. Miniscule marine life known as dinoflagellates produce a glowing chemical light in the water when disturbed on moonless nights.

An interesting attraction in the southwestern area is the Guánica Dry Forest, a scrub and cactus landscape that was the site of the American landing in 1898. For the hardy traveler, a 4-day tour beginning and ending in San Juan and reaching Ponce via Barranquitas can include extensive sightseeing along the highway winding through the Cordillera Central, Puerto Rico's mountain range.

Guided tours provide insight into some of the island's more popular attractions. A 3-hour guided tour of Old San Juan includes visits to the Capitol Building, Fort San Felipe del Morro (El Morro), Fort San Cristóbal, La Iglesia de San José, San Juan Gate, Capilla del Cristo (Christ) and La Princesa and its paseo. The 4-hour El Yunque Rain Forest Tour explores the rain forest's waterfalls, observation tower and tropical plants; a full-day tour that includes swimming at the beach of Balneario de Luquillo also is available.

Boat and airplane charters to Mona Island, about 50 miles (80 km) west of Puerto Rico and inhabited by a variety of wildlife, are available on the west coast; for information phone the Department of Natural Resources at (787) 999-2200. The islands of Vieques and Culebra off the east coast are reached by plane from San Juan or ferry service from Fajardo.

Transportation

Puerto Rico is accessible by air from most mainland cities including Atlanta, Boston, Chicago, Dallas, Houston, Miami, Newark, New York City, Orlando and Philadelphia. There also is air service between San Juan and Mayagüez, Aguadilla, Ponce or Fajardo. American Airlines provides daily nonstop service from Miami to Ponce. Several U.S. carriers operate out of San Juan's Luis Muñoz Marín International Airport and reach most major U.S. cities. Many of the flights continue to other Caribbean islands. Caribbean Sun Airlines connects San Juan with Antigua, St. Croix, St. Kitts, Tortola and St. Thomas. Rafael Hernandez Airport in Aguadilla and Eugenio María de Hostos Airport in Mayagüez serve the west coast of the island.

Having long been a popular port of call, Puerto Rico is one of the largest home-based cruise ship ports in the world. The terminal is in Old San Juan.

Transportation in San Juan includes metered taxicabs at the airport, hotels and other locations throughout the city; taxis can be rented by the hour. Taxis are the fastest way to get to San Juan from the airport. Flat fares from the airport to Isla Verde, to Condado and to Old San Juan are $8, $12 and $16, respectively, aboard Taxis Turísticos. The fare from the piers to Old San Juan or Puerto de Tierra is $6, to Condado $10, to Isla Verde $16. All fares include two pieces of luggage.

The bus system also operates throughout the metropolitan area. Stops are designated by a magenta, orange and white sign bearing the word *Parada;* fare 50c. *Públicos,* public cars that follow established routes between most towns on the island, run during daylight hours. Marked by the letters P or PD following the numbers on their license plate, *públicos* can usually be hailed from the main plaza of a town. *Públicos* are the least expensive

DID YOU KNOW

Puerto Ricans are U.S. citizens but pay no federal income tax.

transportation available, but prospective riders must wait until the car is full.

Free trolley rides are available within the Old San Juan historic district and along the beachfront in Isla Verde.

Rental cars also are available, as are chauffeur-driven cars. A valid U.S. driver's license is good in Puerto Rico for up to 120 days. Speed limits are posted in miles per hour and are strictly enforced; metric measurements generally are used on distance signs.

In the future, Tren Urbano will provide fast and reliable mass transit to the municipalities of San Juan, Bayamón and Guyanabo. This $2.25-billion project, which includes 16 stations along 11 miles of track, hit many snags and cost overruns between its initial proposal in 1989 and its inauguration in 2005. The "urban train" is scheduled to run daily from 5:30 a.m. to 11:30 p.m.; one-way fare is $1.50. For information, phone (787) 765-0927.

Ferry service provides interesting and inexpensive interisland links. Crossing the bay every 30 minutes, La Lancha de Cataño connects Old San Juan with the municipality of Cataño; fares are very inexpensive. The Fajardo Ferry carries passengers and cars on a triangular route linking Fajardo on the east end of the island with the islands of Vieques and Culebra. Transportation to other Caribbean islands includes Ferries del Caribe, which operates the Millennium Express between Puerto Rico and the Dominican Republic. The 12-hour overnight crossing between Mayagüez and Santo Domingo is offered three times weekly in each direction.

Fast Facts

POPULATION: 3,806,610.

AREA: 8,897 sq km (3,435 sq mi.).

CAPITAL: San Juan.

HIGHEST POINT: 1,338 m (4,390 ft.), Cerro de Punta.

LOWEST POINT: Sea level, Caribbean Sea.

TIME ZONE(S): Atlantic Standard.

LANGUAGE: Spanish and English.

GOVERNMENT: Commonwealth associated with the United States.

UNIT OF CURRENCY: U.S. dollar.

ELECTRICITY: 110 volts, 60 cycles AC.

MINIMUM AGE FOR DRIVERS: 21-25, depending on the rental car agency; daily surcharge for ages 21-24, $10-$25. U.S. license valid for 3 months; drive on right.

MINIMUM AGE FOR GAMBLING: 18.

SEAT BELT/CHILD RESTRAINT LAWS: Seat belts are required for driver and front-seat passengers. Child restraints required for under age 2; seat belts required for ages 2-12.

HELMETS FOR MOTORCYCLISTS: Required.

HOLIDAYS: Jan. 1; Three Kings Day (Epiphany), Jan. 6; Eugenio María de Hostos' Birthday, Jan. (2nd Mon.); Martin Luther King Jr. Day, Jan. (3rd Mon.); Presidents Day, Feb. (3rd Mon.); Emancipation Day, Mar. 22; Good Friday; Easter; José de Diego's Birthday, Apr. (3rd Mon.); Memorial Day, May (last Mon.); July 4; Luis Muñoz Rivera's Birthday, July (3rd Mon.); Constitution Day, July 25; José Celso Barbosa's Birthday, July 27; Labor Day, Sept. (1st Mon.); Columbus Day, Oct. (2nd Mon.); Veterans Day, Nov. 11; Discovery of Puerto Rico Day, Nov. 19; Thanksgiving, Nov. (4th Thurs.); Christmas, Dec. 25.

TAXES: A 7-11 percent room tax (depending on the size of the resort) and 10 percent service charge are added to most hotel bills.

IMMIGRATION REQUIREMENTS: There are no immigration requirements for U.S. citizens, but a passport is required when travel may involve stops on other Caribbean islands.

PHONING THE ISLANDS: To call Puerto Rico from the U.S. or Canada, dial 1 + area code + the 7-digit local number.

FURTHER INFORMATION FOR VISITORS:

Puerto Rico Tourism Company
666 Fifth Ave., 15th Floor
New York, NY 10103
(212) 586-6262
(800) 223-6530
See color ad on insert.

Puerto Rico Tourism Company, Old San Juan
La Princesa Bldg. #2, Paseo La Princesa
P.O. Box 902-3960
San Juan, Puerto Rico 00902-3960
(787) 721-2400
(800) 866-7827

Points of Interest

See maps on pages 183 and 196.

AGUADA (B-1) pop. 42,042

On the western coast, Aguada (ah-GWAH-da) is traditionally considered the first landing place of Christopher Columbus when he arrived on the island of Puerto Rico in 1493. There is no historical evidence, however, and the nearby town of Aguadilla makes a similar claim. Nevertheless, a 15th-century settlement was established at Aguada, and its port became a stopping point for ships traveling from Spain to South America. The ruins of Ermita Espinar, a chapel built in 1525, are evidence of early attempts to convert Taíno Indians to Christianity.

The Museo de Aguada, housed in a former railroad station, displays Taíno and African art, railroad exhibits and artifacts relating to Puerto Rican history; phone (787) 868-6300.

LA IGLESIA DE SAN FRANCISCO DE ASÍS is on the central plaza at calles Colón and Paz. Completed in 1936, the Church of Saint Francis of Assisi features two towers standing more than 100 feet high. A series of stained glass windows adorns the interior. Franciscan friars built the first monastery on this site in 1516, but it was destroyed by Carib Indians. A later church was leveled by the earthquake of 1918. Mon.-Fri. 6:30-11 a.m. Mass held daily. Donations. Phone (787) 868-2630.

AGUADILLA (B-1) pop. 64,685

On the northwest edge of the island, Aguadilla (ah-gwah-DEE-ya) calls itself "the garden of the Atlantic." With its red-tiled roofs and mountain backdrop, the city is often described as having a Mediterranean feel. Aguadilla was founded in 1775.

Once a fishing village and now a manufacturing center, the city is perhaps best known for its world-class surfing beaches, with colorful names such as Gas Chambers, Survivor and Wilderness. The most popular is Crashboat Beach, prized for its crystal-clear water. Parque de Colón, or Christopher Columbus Park, is on the southernmost beach and features monuments, a boardwalk, a playground and a banyan tree house. A statue of composer Rafael Hernández, who was born in Aguadilla, stands on the town square.

Six miles north at Punta Borinquen, Ramey Air Force Base operated 1939-1971. It boasted one of the longest runways in the Caribbean—more than 2 miles long. Planes flying into the western part of the island now land on this runway at Rafael Hernandez Airport. The Punta Borinquen Lighthouse was destroyed by the tidal wave of 1918; ruins are still visible. The Coast Guard light station that replaced it is not open to the public.

LAS CASCADAS WATER PARK is on Hwy. 2. Aquatic features include giant waterslides, a wave pool and the long, winding Crazy River. Daily 10-5, late May to early Sept.; Sat.-Sun. 10-5, Mar. 1 to late May. Admission $15.95; $13.95 (children); $7.95 (senior citizens). MC, VI. Phone (787) 819-0950 or (787) 819-1030.

ARECIBO (B-2) pop. 100,131

Arecibo, on the north coast, is the island's largest city in geographical size. It has been called *El Diamante Del Norte,* or "the diamond of the north." The city was settled in 1556. Capt. Antonio Correa and a handful of soldiers repelled a British sea invasion here in 1702 and were later honored for their bravery by King Philip V of Spain.

Cambalache State Forest (Bosque Estatal), midway between Arecibo and Barceloneta on Highway 22, is noted for its plantations of eucalyptus, teak, and mahoe trees. The forest is a popular destination for hiking and mountain biking; a permit is required for camping.

ARECIBO LIGHTHOUSE AND HISTORICAL PARK is off Hwy. 22 exit 71 (Domingo Ruiz), following Rd. 2 to Rds. 681 and 655. The park offers five cultural representations of Puerto Rico's history, from the 1493 Spanish Conquest to the building of the lighthouse in 1898 during the Spanish-American War. Historic replicas include a Taíno Indian village, slave quarters, Blackbeard's pirate ship and the three sailing vessels of Christopher Columbus. Marine artifacts are displayed in the restored lighthouse. The surrounding park on rocky Punta Morillo includes a playground; a small petting zoo; and a pirate's cave containing a saltwater aquarium with sharks, rays and eels.

Mon.-Fri. 9-6, Sat.-Sun. 10-7. Admission $9; $7 (ages 2-12 and 66+). Parking $2. Phone (787) 880-7540.

GEM **ARECIBO OBSERVATORY** is at the end of Hwy. 625. The world's largest and most sensitive radio telescope consists of a 1,000-ton, suspended platform that hovers above a 20-acre (8-hectare) dish set in a sinkhole 565 feet (172 m) deep. Built under the direction of Cornell University in 1963, the observatory is the home base for SETI, the Search for Extraterrestrial Life.

The telescope is used by scientists from around the world to study deep-space objects, natural radio emissions, the planets and Earth's atmosphere. Moviegoers have seen the giant reflector dish in such films as "Goldeneye" and "Contact."

The observatory's Ángel Ramos Foundation Visitor Center provides a platform for viewing the telescope and houses a variety of interactive exhibits, audiovisual displays and informative panels. Allow 2 hours minimum. Wed.-Fri. noon-4, Sat.-Sun. and major holidays 9-4. Admission $5; $3 (ages 3-10 and senior citizens). Phone (787) 878-2612.

RÍO CAMUY CAVE PARK is 12 mi. (19 km) s. off Hwy. 129. The 250-acre (102-hectare) park's massive cave network encompasses one of the largest underground river systems in the world. Trams transport visitors to the mouth of one of the caves, where guided walking tours begin.

Tours require a moderate level of physical activity that includes climbing stairs; non-slip shoes are recommended. Food is available. Allow 3 hours minimum. Two-hour tours depart Wed.-Sun. 8-3:30 (weather permitting). Visitors should arrive early, as the park reaches maximum capacity quickly. Tram waits may exceed 15 minutes. Admission $12; $7 (ages 4-12); $6 (ages 76+). Parking $3-$5. Phone (787) 898-3100.

ARROYO (D-5) pop. 19,117

The telegraph was introduced to Puerto Rico and Latin America in 1858 when Samuel F. B. Morse installed the first line at Arroyo. His daughter and son-in-law owned a sugarcane plantation here known as Hacienda La Enriqueta.

On the southeast coast, Arroyo is popular for its beaches, especially Punta Guilarte on the west side of Puerto Patillas bay. The yellow lighthouse at Faro de Punta Figuras has been restored; it offers a striking view of the Caribbean.

MUSEO ANTIGUA ADUANA is on Morse St. next to City Hall. Historical exhibits in this ornate pink building, the former customs house, include memorabilia related to the installation of Puerto Rico's first telegraph line by Samuel F.B. Morse. Taíno artifacts and local artworks also are displayed. **Note:** The museum is currently closed for remodeling; phone ahead to verify schedule. Wed.-Fri. 9-noon and 1-4, Sat.-Sun. 9-4. Free. Phone (787) 839-8096.

BARRANQUITAS (C-4) pop. 28,909

Near the center of the island, the mountain town of Barranquitas (bahr-rahn-KEE-tahs) has been called the "cradle of the greats" for the many distinguished Puerto Ricans it has produced. Among them was Luis Muñoz Rivera, who negotiated the island's Charter of Autonomy with the Spanish government in 1897. The small house where he was born, Casa Natal de Luis Muñoz Rivera, has been restored by the Institute of Puerto Rican Culture as a library and museum. The bodies of Rivera and his son, Luis Muñoz Marín—who became Puerto Rico's first elected governor—are entombed at the nearby Mausoleo Luis Muñoz Marín.

Islanders flock to Barranquitas in July for the Feria Nacional de Artesanías, considered the longest-running artisan fair in Puerto Rico and one of its most significant. The fair features food, music and exhibits by some 200 local artists and craftspeople.

South of Barranquitas is the only volcanic rift in Puerto Rico, San Cristóbal Canyon. This rugged and nearly inaccessible gorge is more than 650 feet (198 m) deep, with rushing streams and plunging waterfalls along the Río Usabón. Best viewed with a guide, the canyon is an emerging destination for rock climbing and adventure tours.

CABO ROJO (D-1) pop. 46,911

On the southwestern coast, the limestone cliffs of Cabo Rojo rise several hundred feet above the Atlantic. The Spanish-style Cabo Robo Lighthouse, or Faro de Los Morillos, was built in 1881 and is now automated. The bay at Boquerón, part of the municipality, extends several miles inland; salt has been mined in the surrounding flats since the time of the Taíno Indians. The public beach at Balneario Boquerón is a long-time favorite of Puerto Ricans for its scenic setting on the bay.

Mona Island, 50 miles (80 km) off the coast, is a unique island preserve in the straits between Puerto Rico and the Dominican Republic. It has often been compared to the Galápagos Islands for its rare species of wildlife, including giant iguanas, sea turtles and red-footed boobies. The iron Isla Mona Lighthouse was designed by Gustave Eiffel. Boat and airplane charters are available; for information phone the Department of Natural Resources at (787) 724-8774.

CABO ROJO NATIONAL WILDLIFE REFUGE is 3 mi. s. on Hwy. 301 from Hwy. 101 in Boquerón. This bird-watcher's haven in the subtropical dry forest region is home to the endangered yellow-shouldered blackbird.

The Cabo Rojo Salt Flats have been called the single most important point of convergence for migratory shorebirds in Puerto Rico and the U.S. Virgin Islands. The flats are a vital nesting ground for the snowy plover, least tern, peregrine falcon and brown pelican. The refuge features a visitor center, a 2-mile interpretive trail and 12 miles of hiking trails. Mon.-Fri. 7:30-4. Free. Phone (787) 851 7258.

CANÓVANAS (B-5) pop. 43,335

East of San Juan in the metropolitan area, *La Cuna de los Indios* (the Indian Cradle) was once home to a large Taíno population and took its name from a local chief. To this day, Canóvanas sports teams are nicknamed the Indios.

In modern times, Canóvanas is known as *La Ciudad de las Carreras* (the Racetrack City) for its famous horse-racing complex, El Comandante. Races are held Monday, Wednesday and Friday through Sunday; phone (787) 876-2450. The annual Clásico del Caribe, or Caribbean Classic, is considered the richest horse race in Latin America.

Note: Policies concerning admittance of children to pari-mutuel betting facilities vary. Phone for information.

Casa Jesús T. Piñero, the home of Puerto Rico's first native governor, contains a small museum commemorating Piñero's life. He was appointed to the governor's post in 1946 by President Harry S. Truman; the island's first democratic election was held 2 years later.

COAMO (D-4) pop. 37,597

One of the oldest settlements on the island, Coamo (ko-AH-mo) is known for its thermal springs, long believed to have therapeutic properties. Local legend says that Juan Ponce de León, who traveled to the New World with Christopher Columbus and colonized Puerto Rico in 1508, mistakenly went off to Florida in search of the Fountain of Youth after hearing natives speak about the Baños de Coamo.

The lovely white Iglesia Católica San Blás de Illesca on the main plaza was established in 1563. Just off the square, the Museo Histórico de Coamo displays archeological artifacts, local exhibits and colonial-style furnishings.

CULEBRA (A-6) pop. 1,868

About 17 miles off the eastern coast, Culebra is the smallest of the inhabited Spanish Virgin Islands. The larger Vieques is 8 miles south. Though a few beach resorts have opened on Culebra in recent years, the island remains largely undeveloped, a laid-back destination for sunning and scuba diving. The pristine Flamenco Beach is considered one of the most stunning beaches in the Caribbean.

Culebra and nearly two dozen islets are part of a national wildlife refuge that protects nesting sea turtles and colonies of endangered sea birds, including nearly 60,000 sooty terns. The abandoned Culebrita Lighthouse was built in 1882 to establish Spanish dominion over the main island. Culebra can be reached by ferry from Fajardo.

DORADO (B-4) pop. 34,017

West of San Juan on the northern coast, Dorado is home to several beachside golf resorts. The recreation area of El Ojo del Buey is named for a large rock formation resembling the eye of an ox. The public beaches at Sardinera and Cerro Gordo are particularly scenic.

MUSEO Y CENTRO CULTURAL CASA DEL REY is at Calle Mendez Vigo 292 next to city hall. Once a garrison for Spanish military personnel and later the home of writer Manuel Alonso y Pacheco, this 1823 inn has been restored by the Institute of Puerto Rican Culture. Exhibits chronicle the island's Taíno culture and its Spanish colonization. Mon.-Fri. 8-4:30. Free. Phone (787) 796-5740.

EL YUNQUE NATIONAL FOREST (C-6)

Elevations in the forest range from 1,000 ft. to 3,533 ft. (305 m to 1,077 m) at El Yunque. Refer to AAA maps for additional elevation information.

The El Yunque National Forest is 25 miles (40 km) east of San Juan near the town of Palmer on Hwy. 191. Three other forest roads, rtes. 186, 966 and 988, skirt the western, northern and eastern boundaries. The scenic beach of Balneario Luquillo is off Rte. 3.

The forest, which takes its name from El Yunque (JUNE-kay), a 3,533-foot (1,077-m) peak in the Luquillo Mountains, covers 28,000 acres (11,287 hectares). Proclaimed a forest reserve by Theodore Roosevelt in 1903, El Yunque is the only tropical U.S. National Forest; it is administered by the U.S. Department of Agriculture Forest Service.

The annual rainfall is extremely heavy, and at the high elevations it exceeds 200 inches. Moisture drips from massive trees, dense plants, ferns and moss. Hundreds of streams course down the mountainsides, creating countless falls and pools. The rain forest receives more than 100 billion gallons of rain a year.

Moist, misty and generally cool, the forest supports a dense system of vegetation. Largest are the towering hardwoods, their crowns hung with vines; many trunks or limbs support a fringe of air plants, a large number containing blossoms. Beneath these giants are smaller trees and shrubs that shade flowers, herbs, mosses and tree ferns growing as high as 30 feet (9 m).

The montane thicket covering valleys and slopes above 2,000 feet (610 m) is generally composed of trees and a ground cover of ferns, vines and bromeliads. Extensive stands of sierra palms grow on steep slopes at higher elevations and along streams. The cloud forest, its trees about 12 feet (4 m) high, is found on the highest peaks. In all, the forest harbors more than 240 species of trees, four forest types and dozens of waterfalls. More than 50 of these species of trees are found only in Puerto Rico.

Such resplendent birds as tanagers, woodpeckers, cuckoos, euphonia and the Puerto Rican inhabit the forest. The birds usually remain hidden, but their calls and whistles are heard frequently. The Puerto Rican Parrot, an extremely rare and endangered species, also inhabits the rain forest and is found only in this part of the island. *Coquíes,* tiny inch-long tree frogs, fill the forest with their high-pitched notes, which resemble the singing of their own name.

The forest's main visitor center, El Portal, is just inside the entrance on Hwy. 191 at Km 4.3. Near Km 8 is La Coca Falls, named for 14th-century settler Juan Diego de La Coca. The Yokahú Observation Tower at Km 8.9 offers a magnificent view of the forest and the northeast coast of Puerto Rico. Food and picnic facilities are available at the Sierra Palm Information Center at Km 11.6.

The Palo Colorado Recreation Site, the most visited section of the forest, includes an information center and picnic shelters. In this area around Km 12 are trailheads leading to La Mina Falls, Mt. Britton Lookout Tower and El Toro Peak, the summit of El Yunque. Guided 1-hour interpretive hikes of the recreation area are offered by the Forest Service. In all, the forest contains 24 miles (39 km) of soft and paved hiking trails.

Rain gear and hiking boots are recommended, as trails are often wet and slippery. Information centers are open daily 9:30-5. Hiking tours depart daily 10:30-3:30, Feb.-Aug.; based upon guide availability rest of year. Tour tickets are sold at the Palo Colorado Information Center on a first-come, first-served basis. Park admission is free. Hiking tours $5, ages 4-12, $3. Phone (787) 888-1880.

EL PORTAL RAIN FOREST CENTER is on Hwy. 191 at Km 4.3, just inside the El Yunque National Forest entrance. An elevated walkway through the forest canopy takes visitors into the environmental education center, which offers information about the natural features and importance of the El Yunque National Forest and tropical forests worldwide. Noted for its award-winning tropical architecture, the center features four multimedia exhibit pavilions, an orientation film and an interpretive trail through landscaped grounds. Food is available. Daily 9-5. Admission $3; $1.50 (ages 61+); free (ages 0-15). Phone (787) 888-1880.

FAJARDO (C-6) pop. 40,712

On the eastern coast, Fajardo is a major boating center and the departure point for ferry and plane trips to the islands of Vieques and Culebra. With more than 1,000 boat slips, Puerto del Rey Marina is one of the largest marinas in the Caribbean.

The Ceiba Forest stretches from Fajardo to Ceiba along the coast and west to the El Yunque National Forest. It is a subtropical dry woodland, predominantly mangrove.

LAS CABEZAS DE SAN JUAN NATURE PRESERVE is on Hwy. 987. Surrounded on three sides by the Atlantic Ocean, this reserve protects a variety of ecological systems, including coral reefs, offshore cays, lagoons, mangroves, a dry forest and a bioluminescent lagoon. The park is accessible only by a 2.5-hour guided tour that combines riding aboard an open-air trolley and walking along boardwalks and nature trails. The last stop is the castle-like lighthouse, Faro de las Cabezas de San Juan, one of the oldest on the island.

English-language tours depart Fri.-Sun. at 2; three other tours are offered in the morning. The number of visitors is strictly limited to protect the park's fragile ecosystem; reservations are required. Admission $7; $4 (children and ages 64+). Phone (787) 722-5882 or (787) 860-2560.

GAMBLING ESTABLISHMENTS

- **El Conquistador Casino** is at 1000 Avenida Conquistador. Daily noon-2 a.m. Phone (787) 863-1000.

GUÁNICA (D-2) pop. 21,888

After landing on the northwest tip of the island during his second voyage to the New World, Christopher Columbus founded a settlement at Guánica on the southern coast. During the Spanish-American War, U.S. troops landed here on July 25, 1898, surprising Spain's forces. Fuerte Caprón, which stands on a hill 450 feet above the bay, was built by American soldiers after the invasion.

Although best known for its mangrove and cactus forest, Guánica is a popular excursion for diving, snorkeling and sunbathing. A small cay off the coast is named Gilligan's Island for its resemblance to the TV show setting. Manatees and endangered hawksbill and leatherback turtles may be found in the crystal blue lagoon at Ballenas Beach.

GUÁNICA DRY FOREST RESERVE (BOSQUE ESTATAL) is off Hwy. 2 on rds. 116, 333 and 334 to the visitor center. One of the largest tropical dry coastal forests in the world, Guánica covers nearly 10,000 acres along the southern coast. This UNESCO Biosphere Reserve, known as *El Bosque Seco,* is home to more than 600 types of rare plants and animals, including 48 endangered species. A population of the supposedly extinct Puerto Rican whippoorwills was discovered here in 1961. One lignum vitae tree is said to be more than 1,000 years old. The ruins of a Spanish lighthouse, El Faro Guánica, are visible.

More than 36 miles of trails lead through the forest, but hiking is recommended only during cool morning hours. Visitors should wear protective clothing and carry drinking water. Daily 8:30-4. Forest free. Trail guide $1. Phone (787) 821-5706.

HUMACAO (C-5) pop. 59,035

Named for a Taíno chieftain, Humacao (oo-mah-KOU) was once home to a large sugar plantation. This quiet town on the eastern coast is drawing an increasing number of tourists to its resorts, golf courses and beaches.

The Observatorio Astronómico on the campus of the University of Puerto Rico at Humacao is open to the public every Thursday evening at 7:30 for viewings of the planets and stars; phone (787) 850-9344.

Just offshore is the island of Cayo Santiago, a field station of the Caribbean Primate Research Center. More than 400 Rhesus monkeys were released here in 1938, and their descendants roam the island today. Access is restricted, but diving and fishing charters provide an offshore glimpse of the colony.

CASA ROIG MUSEUM is at 66 Calle Antonio López. The 1920 home of sugar baron Antonio Roig was designed by architect Antonín Nechodoma, who took his inspiration from Frank Lloyd Wright. Restored by the University of Puerto Rico, the house museum displays regional history exhibits and works of contemporary art. Mon.-Fri. 8:30-4:30. Free. Phone (787) 852-8380.

ISABELA (B-1) pop. 44,444

On the northwest coast, Isabela was founded by European settlers in 1725. Ruins of the original church and village are visible along the Guajataca River at San Antonio de la Tuna.

GUAJATACA STATE FOREST (BOSQUE ESTATAL) is e. on Rte. 2, then s. on Rte. 446. In the "karst country" of northwest Puerto Rico, where underground limestone dissolves into sinkholes, tunnels and caves, Guajataca (wa-ha-TA-ka) encompasses more than 25 miles of hiking trails through this unusual topography. A walking map is available at the ranger station, and an observation tower provides a scenic view of man-made Guajataca Lake. Cueva de Viento (Wind Cave) features dramatic formations of stalactites and stalagmites. Daily dawn-dusk. Free. Phone (787) 724-3724.

LA PARGUERA (D-1) pop. 1,141

Settled in 1883, the fishing village of La Parguera has become a modest tourist area centered around the southwest coast's eerie neon waters. Along the coast, dozens of mangrove cays and islets form ornate channels that are popular among kayakers. The Lajas valley is known for its major crop, a large and delicious pineapple called the *Piña Cabezona.*

LA PARGUERA BIOLUMINESCENT BAY is 5 mi. (8 km) s. on the harbor. La Parguera is one of three bioluminescent bays in Puerto Rico; the others are found at Las Cabezas de San Juan Nature Preserve in Fajardo and at Mosquito Bay off the island of Vieques *(see attraction listings).* The eerie blue-green light is produced by microorganisms that cause the water to shimmer and glow when disturbed. Viewing is best on cloudy or moonless nights. Boats leave from the La Parguera dock.

LOÍZA (B-5) pop. 32,537

East of San Juan on the northern coast, Loíza (loo-EE-zah) has been nicknamed "the capital of traditions." The village was settled by Yoruban slaves in the 1500s and retains one of the highest percentages of African descendants on the island. The week-long Fiesta de Santiago Apóstol in late July is a colorful celebration of Taíno and African culture. Religious processions lead from the 17th-century Iglésia de San Patricio (St. Patrick's Church), considered the island's oldest church in continuous use. The festivities continue with music, food, fireworks and dancing the *bomba.* Loíza's festival masks, made from coconut husks and intricately painted, are highly prized.

MARICAO (C-2) pop. 6,449

High in the central mountain range east of Mayagüez, Maricao (mah-ree-KOU) is one of the island's premier coffee-growing villages. The 3-day Maricao Coffee Festival in February celebrates the annual harvest.

MARICAO FOREST RESERVE (BOSQUE ESTATAL) is on Rte. 20. A prime bird-watching site, the forest has a stone observation tower that provides fine views of the west and south coasts. The elfin woods warbler, the Puerto Rican woodpecker and many other endangered species can be spotted here. Some 25,000 fish, including largemouth bass, channel catfish and Congo perch, are raised yearly at the Maricao Fish Hatchery for release into Puerto Rican rivers and reservoirs. Tues.-Sun. 8-4. Free. Phone (787) 838-1040.

MAYAGÜEZ (C-1) pop. 98,434

On the west coast, Mayagüez (mah-yah-GWES) is the island's fifth-largest city and an important commercial port for sugar, coffee and fruit as well as one of the world's largest tuna-packing centers. It also is the home of the College of Agriculture and Engineering of the University of Puerto Rico. An elegant plaza dominates the center of the city, which was almost destroyed by an earthquake in 1918. Mayagüez is about 95 miles (153 km) from San Juan; half-hour flights depart frequently.

JUAN A. RIVERO ZOO is 1 mi. (1.6 km) n. off Rte. 108, following signs. The Mayagüez zoo displays tropical plants and animals in their natural settings. More than 340 animal species, including Bengal tigers and Andean condors, have been collected from tropical climates around the world. Walk-through aviaries highlight birds from Central and South America and the Caribbean. All birds, mammals and reptiles are identified in English and Spanish. Wed.-Sun. 8:30-4. Admission $6; $4 (ages 11-17); $3 (ages 60-74); $2 (ages 5-10); free (ages 0-4 and 75+). Parking $3. MC, VI. Phone (787) 832-6330.

TROPICAL AGRICULTURE RESEARCH STATION is on Rte. 65 between rtes. 2 and 108. Since its establishment on an old plantation in 1901, the tropical research center of the U.S. Department of Agriculture has fostered the development of more than 2,000 tropical plant species from around the world. A well-marked self-guiding tour covers most of the important areas. Because of frequent afternoon rains, morning visits are best. Mon.-Fri. 7-4; closed holidays. Free. Phone (787) 831-3435.

GAMBLING ESTABLISHMENTS

- **Holiday Inn Mayagüez & El Tropical Casino** is at 2701 Ave. Hostos. Daily 24 hours. Phone (787) 833-1100.
- **The Mayagüez Resort and Casino** is at jct. Hwy. 2 and 104, just n. of Rt. 104 km .3. Daily 24 hours. Phone (787) 832-3030.

MOCA (B-1) pop. 39,697

The lace center of the island, Moca is famous for its mundillo lace. Woven by hand on a pillow loom with dozens or hundreds of bobbins, the intricate lace can be found in wedding gowns, tapestries, linens and accessories. A bronze statue on the town square, *La tejedora de mundillo,* honors the women who carry on this time-honored tradition. The Festival del Mundillo in June features weaving demonstrations, traditional music and food.

PALACETE LOS MOREAU is off Hwy. 2 on Rte. 464 near Isabela. This beautiful two-story manor, once part of a French coffee and sugar plantation, was completed in 1905. One of the first houses on the island built with concrete, it was originally called Castillo Labadie. Novelist Enrique Arturo Laguerre immortalized the estate in his best-known work, "La Llamarada." Newly restored, the yellow mansion features stained-glass windows and period furnishings. Daily 8-4. Free. Phone (787) 830-2540.

PONCE (D-3) pop. 186,475

An important commercial port on the south coast, Ponce (PONE-say) is the center of the island's sugar, rum and coffee industries and has some of the largest textile mills in the Caribbean. In its center are two tree-shaded plazas bordering the graceful Cathedral of Our Lady of Guadalupe. The Carnaval de Ponce, which coincides with Mardi Gras celebrations around the world, is famous for its papier-maché masks and brightly colored costumes.

The Alhambra residential section has more than 125 Spanish-style estates. And throughout the city more than 600 of its 1,000 historic buildings have been restored, particularly on Isabel and Reina streets. A visitor information center is located in the Fox Delicias Mall, facing the plaza. A steep hill called *El Vigía* (The Watchman) was once a lookout post. At the top, a 100-foot observation tower in the shape of a cross, La Cruceta del Vigía, offers dramatic views of the city.

On the corner of avs. Marina and Esquina Aurora, a yellow house known as Casa de la Masacre de Ponce marks a bloody chapter in Puerto Rico's political history. On Easter Sunday 1937, police fired upon Nationalist demonstrators, killing 20 people and injuring hundreds.

HACIENDA BUENA VISTA is 10 mi. (16 km) n. on SR 10 in Barrio Magüeyes. Considered one of the best surviving examples of a Puerto Rican coffee plantation, this 19th-century estate includes nearly a dozen restored buildings, including a working mill and a two-story hacienda furnished with period antiques. The farm was one of the first to establish a nutrition program for slaves. A scenic waterfall provides power to the coffee mill. Guided 2-hour tours describe the history of the plantation and the cultivation of coffee.

Tours are offered Sat.-Sun. at 8:30, 10:30, 1:30 and 3:30; reservations are required. Admission $7; $4 (ages 5-8). Phone (787) 722-5882 or (787) 284-7020.

PARQUE DE BOMBAS (OLD PONCE FIRE STATION) is on Plaza de las Delicias behind the cathedral. Built as the main pavilion for the 1882 Exhibition Trade Fair, this Moorish building with bold red and black stripes is one of the most photographed features on the island. Now a museum, the building houses an antique fire engine and historical exhibits dedicated to Ponce's volunteer fire brigade. Wed.-Mon. 8-6. Free. Phone (787) 284-4141.

PONCE HISTORY MUSEUM (MUSEO DE LA HISTORIA) is on the town square at Isabel and Mayor sts. Ten exhibition halls in two neoclassical buildings contain displays depicting the city's ecology, economy, architecture, government and elements of daily life. A videotape documentary is available in English. Guided tours are available. Tues. and Sun. 9-4. Free. Phone (787) 844-7071.

GEM **PONCE MUSEUM OF ART (MUSEO DE ARTE DE PONCE)** is at 2325 Avenue Las Américas opposite Catholic University. Important paintings and sculpture from Europe and the Americas span the 13th through 20th centuries. Highlights from the permanent collection include works by such artists as Eugène Delacroix, Lord Frederick Leighton, Bartolomé Esteban Murillo, José Ribera, Auguste Rodin, Peter Paul Rubens, Anthony Van Dyck and Diego Velázquez.

The Puerto Rican and Latin American galleries includes pieces by Myrna Báez, José Campeche, Rafael Coronel, López Dirube, Luis Hernández, Carlos Mérida, Francisco Oller and Francisco Rodón. Traveling exhibits also are presented.

The building was designed by Edward Durell Stone, architect of the Kennedy Center in Washington, D.C. The Granada Garden is a replica of the gardens in Spain. Food is available. Allow 1 hour, 30 minutes minimum. Daily 10-5; closed Jan. 1, Jan. 6, Good Friday, Thanksgiving and Dec. 25. Admission $5; $2.50 (ages 0-11). AX, MC, VI. Phone (787) 848-0505.

SERRALLÉS CASTLE (MUSEO CASTILLO SERRALLÉS) is at 17 El Vigía. Guided tours of this Spanish Revival home, built in the 1930s, provide insights into the lifestyle of its owner, a wealthy sugar and rum merchant. Scenic city and coastal views are offered from an upstairs terrace. Tues.-Sun. 9:30-5:30. Admission to museum and castle gardens $9.63; $4.82 (60+); $4.24 (children and students). AX, MC, VI. Phone (787) 259-1774.

TIBES INDIGENOUS CEREMONIAL PARK (CENTRO CEREMONIAL INDÍGENA) is on Rte. 503 at km 2.2. The site features seven pre-Taíno ball courts as well as the oldest burial ground yet uncovered in the Antilles. Excavations conducted 1975-1982 revealed 124 human remains believed to belong to an aboriginal Indian population called the Igneris. The center includes a re-created Indian village and a museum with permanent and temporary exhibits.

Food is available. Tues.-Sun. 9-4; park opens on Mon. holidays and closes the following day. Closed Jan. 1, Good Friday, Mothers' and Father's Days, Thanksgiving and Dec. 25. Admission $3; $2.25 (ages 60-64); $2 (ages 5-12); $1.80 (ages 65-74); free (ages 75+). Phone (787) 840-2255 or (787) 840-5685.

TORO NEGRO STATE FOREST (BOSQUE ESTATAL) is 17 mi. (27 km) n.e. via rtes. 10 and 143. This scenic reserve contains the island's tallest peak, Cerro de Punta, and its highest reservoir, the bamboo-fringed Lake Güineo. Coffee plantations once dotted the mountain's lower elevations. The forest offers hiking trails, an observation tower and picnic, swimming and camping facilities at the Doña Juana Recreational Area. Daily dawn-dusk. Free. Phone (787) 817-0984.

GAMBLING ESTABLISHMENTS

- **Hilton Ponce Golf & Casino Resort** is at 1150 Caribe Ave. Daily 8 a.m.-4 a.m. Phone (787) 259-7676.

- **Holiday Inn Ponce & El Tropical Casino**, 3315 Ponce Bypass. Daily 24 hrs. Phone (787) 844-1200.

RINCÓN (C-1) pop. 14,767

The Atlantic Ocean meets the Caribbean Sea at Rincón (rin-KONE), where 8 miles of reef-lined beaches produce some spectacular waves. This sleepy village on Puerto Rico's west coast—the Porta del Sol, or "Door to the Sun"—has become a winter mecca for experienced surfers. Rincón first gained international attention during the 1968 World Surfing Championship, and many surfers now live here year-round.

Waves during the main season from November to March are generally too rough for swimming, but the surf quiets down the rest of the year for snorkeling, scuba diving and watersports. The largest breaks are at Domes Beach, Playa Marias and Tres Palmas. Most restaurants, hotels and surf shops are clustered around Sandy Beach. More secluded spots include Pools Beach, Antonio's Beach and River Mouth. Tres Palmas Marine Reserve protects an offshore reef of elkhorn coral and other shallow-water varieties. The reserve also is home to hawksbill and leatherback turtles.

Whale watching is popular from January through March, when humpbacks winter in the warm waters of Rincón Bay. The best view is from the park surrounding the Rincón Lighthouse, El Faro Punta Higüero, which was built by the Spanish in 1892 and reconstructed in 1922 after a tsunami.

RÍO GRANDE (B-6) pop. 52,362

East of San Juan, Río Grande is the closest town to El Yunque National Forest. Several beach and golf resorts have opened here in recent years, drawing new visitors to the northeast coast.

GAMBLING ESTABLISHMENTS

- **Paradisus Puerto Rico Casino** is at 1000 Cocoa Beach Blvd. Phone (787) 809-1770.
- **Westin Rio Mar Beach Resort & Casino** is at 6000 Rio Mar Blvd. Daily noon-2 a.m. Phone (787) 888-6000.

SAN GERMÁN (D-1) pop. 37,105

Midway between Mayagüez and Ponce and surrounded by mountains, San Germán (her-MON) has been nicknamed *Ciudad de Las Lomas,* or City of the Hills. This is Puerto Rico's second oldest Spanish village, settled in 1511. It features two plazas with buildings representing a variety of architectural styles. The centerpiece of Parque de Santo Domingo is the famous Porta Coéli Church. Crowning the Plaza Francisco Mariano Quiñones is the Church of San Germán Auxerre, which was founded in 1688 and has undergone countless reconstructions over the centuries. The church features a crystal chandelier and a trompe l'oeil ceiling.

IGLESIA PORTA COÉLI is at Ramas and Dr. Veve sts., overlooking one of San Germán's two plazas, the Parque de Santo Domingo. Built in 1606, Porta Coéli is one of the oldest churches under the American flag. Its name means "gate of heaven."

Restored as a museum, the church has wooden statues, paintings, ornaments and liturgical objects from Puerto Rico's historic churches; images carved by 16th-century *santeros* (saint makers); Spanish mosaics of Biblical scenes; and paintings by the 18th-century artist José Campeche. Wed.-Sun. 9-noon and 1-4; closed holidays. Admission $1; free (ages 0-11 and 56+). Phone (787) 892-5845.

MUSEO DE ARTE ALFREDO ARELLANO & ROSELL is at 7 Calle Esperanza. This museum contains collections of religious art and objects, including antique altar pieces and vestments worn by Puerto Rico's first cardinal. Taíno artifacts and changing exhibits by local artists also are displayed. Wed.-Sun. 10-noon and 1-3; closed major holidays. Free. Phone (787) 892-8870.

SAN JUAN (B-4) pop. 434,374

One of the oldest capital cities in the Western Hemisphere, San Juan is the principal city of the Commonwealth of Puerto Rico. Enveloped within the metropolitan core are the inner districts of Hato Rey, Río Piedras and Santurce, all bonded to San Juan by the public transportation system. The sprawling urban area also encompasses the municipalities of Bayamón, Carolina, Cataño, Guaynabo and San Juan. The Aqua Express, a daily ferry service, connects Old San Juan at Pier 2 with Cataño and Hato Rey.

Luxury hotels lining Avenida Ashford distinguish the Condado Beach section, known as the Gold Coast. Attractive shops, dining spots, supper clubs, casinos and beachfronts dotted with umbrellas, palm trees and Spanish residences grace this popular resort area.

On Avenida Ponce de León is Puerto Rico's Archives and General Library, one of the last buildings to be erected by the Spanish. Built in 1877, it has functioned as a prison, a cigar factory and a rum plant. Red-tiled floors, stained-glass windows, chandeliers and a chapel make this building interesting.

The 580,000-square-foot Puerto Rico Convention Center, which opened in 2005, is considered the largest and most technologically advanced meeting facility of its kind in the Caribbean. The architectural style is "techno-tropic," and a 113-acre business and entertainment complex is planned for the surrounding peninsula of Isla Grande. The convention center can accommodate up to 10,000 delegates.

Tourism Information Center: Luis Muñoz Marín International Airport, Isla Verde, San Juan, Puerto Rico; phone (787) 791-1014.

CAPARRA RUINS HISTORICAL MUSEUM AND PARK is 10 mi. (16 km) s. at Km. 6.4 on Hwy. 2 in Guaynabo. The site includes ruins of the ancient fort and settlement founded by explorer Juan Ponce de León in 1508. The small Museum of the Conquest and Colonization of Puerto Rico contains items found during excavations in the area and exhibits

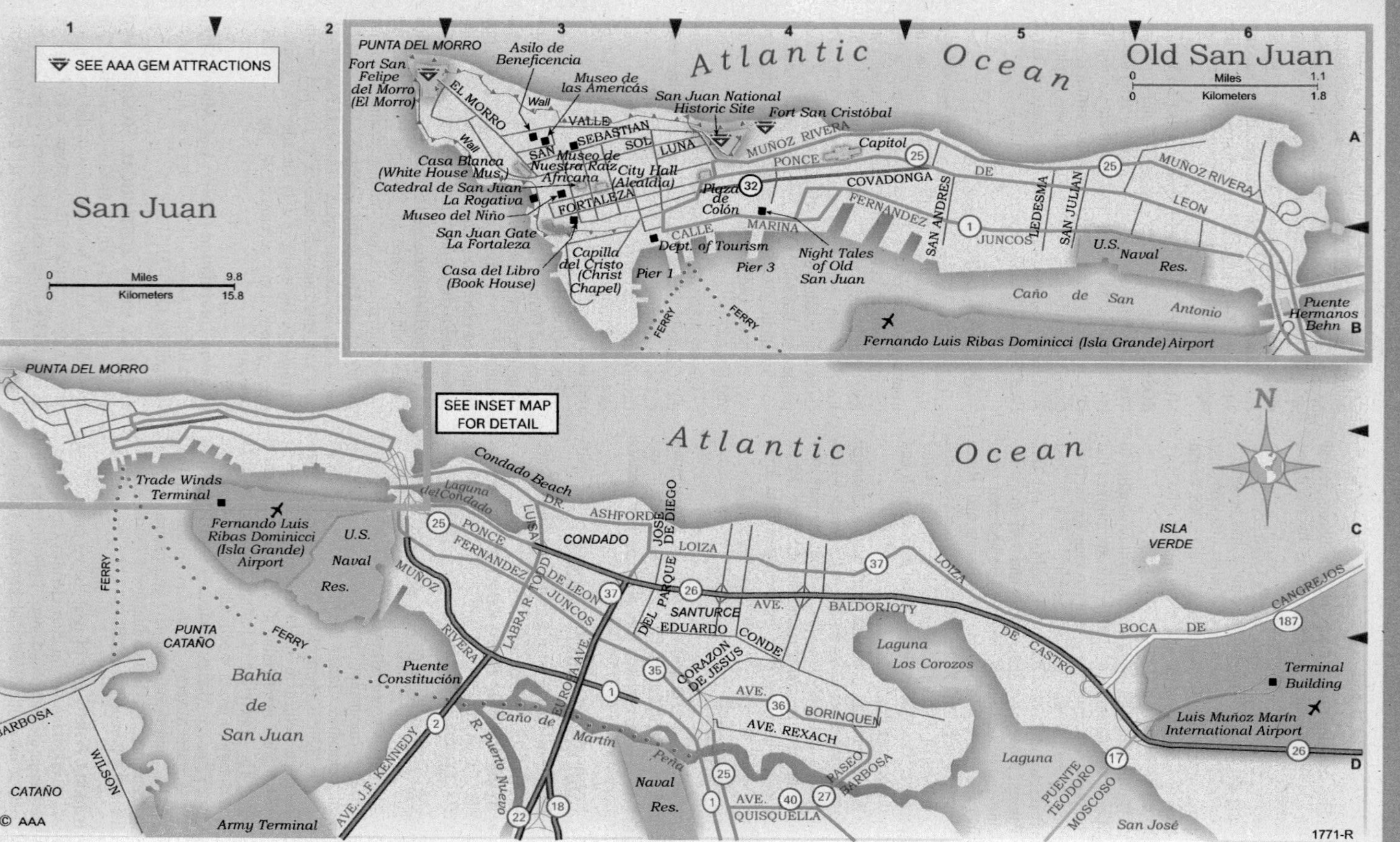
SEE AAA GEM ATTRACTIONS
San Juan
Miles 0 9.8
Kilometers 0 15.8
Old San Juan
Miles 0 1.1
Kilometers 0 1.8
Atlantic Ocean
PUNTA DEL MORRO
Fort San Felipe del Morro (El Morro)
EL MORRO
Wall
Asilo de Beneficencia
Museo de las Américas
San Juan National Historic Site
Fort San Cristóbal
Capitol
VALLE
SAN SEBASTIAN
SOL
LUNA
Casa Blanca (White House Mus.)
Museo de Nuestra Raíz Africana
City Hall (Alcaldía)
Catedral de San Juan
La Rogativa
FORTALEZA
Museo del Niño
San Juan Gate La Fortaleza
Capilla del Cristo (Christ Chapel)
Casa del Libro (Book House)
Plaza de Colón
CALLE MARINA
Dept. of Tourism
Night Tales of Old San Juan
Pier 1
Pier 3
FERRY
MUÑOZ RIVERA
PONCE DE LEON
COVADONGA
FERNANDEZ JUNCOS
SAN ANDRES
LEDESMA
SAN JULIAN
U.S. Naval Res.
Caño de San Antonio
Puente Hermanos Behn
Fernando Luis Ribas Dominicci (Isla Grande) Airport
PUNTA DEL MORRO
SEE INSET MAP FOR DETAIL
Atlantic Ocean
N
Condado Beach
Laguna del Condado
ASHFORD DR.
CONDADO
JOSE DE DIEGO
LOIZA
ISLA VERDE
Trade Winds Terminal
Fernando Luis Ribas Dominicci (Isla Grande) Airport
U.S. Naval Res.
PONCE
FERNANDEZ
DE LEON
JUNCOS
LUISA
R. TODD
LABRA
MUÑOZ RIVERA
DEL PARQUE
SANTURCE
EDUARDO CONDE
CORAZON DE JESUS
AVE. BALDORIOTY DE CASTRO
BOCA DE CANGREJOS
Laguna Los Corozos
Terminal Building
Luis Muñoz Marín International Airport
Laguna San José
PUENTE TEODORO MOSCOSO
AVE. BORINQUEN
AVE. REXACH
PASEO BARBOSA
AVE. QUISQUELLA
EUROPA AVE
Caño de Martín Peña
R. Puerto Nuevo
Naval Res.
Puente Constitución
AVE. J.F. KENNEDY
FERRY
PUNTA CATAÑO
Bahía de San Juan
BARBOSA
WILSON
CATAÑO
Army Terminal
© AAA
1771-R

about the early colonial period. Mon.-Sat. 8:30-4:20. Free. Phone (787) 781-4795.

EL CAPITOLIO (THE CAPITOL) is on Ave. Ponce de León. Built of Georgia marble in the Renaissance style, the building is flanked by the commonwealth's legislative offices. The rotunda features an illuminated coat of arms; a pamphlet available on the second floor explains the symbolism of the rotunda's mosaics. Mon.-Fri. 8:30-5. Free. Phone (787) 721-6040, ext. 2458.

CASA BACARDÍ VISITOR CENTER is 2.5 mi. (4 km) w. on SR 888 at km 2.6 in Cataño. A public ferry connects Old San Juan port and the dock at Cataño, where visitors can take a taxi to the "Cathedral of Rum," said to be the world's largest rum distillery. Displays and samples are offered. One-hour tours of the visitor center are offered Mon.-Sat. 8:30-4:30; closed holidays. Tours free. Round-trip transportation from the ferry $12-$24. Phone (787) 788-1500.

FUNDACIÓN LUIS MUÑOZ MARÍN is 1.3 mi. s. on Rd. 877, Km 0.4 off Trujillo Alto Expressway in Río Piedras. Luis Muñoz Marín, the island's first democratically elected governor, is known as the "Father of Modern Puerto Rico." After taking office in 1949, he engineered the island's unique commonwealth status with the United States. His 4-acre estate and gardens feature displays of photographs and memorabilia, a library and changing art exhibitions. Guided tours are offered by reservation. Open Mon.-Fri. 8-5, Sat.-Sun. 10-3. Guided tours depart Mon.-Fri. at 10 and 2, Sat.-Sun. at 10:30 and 1. Admission $2; $1 (children). AX, MC, VI. Phone (787) 755-7979, ext. 22.

MUSEO DE ARTE CONTEMPORÁNEO DE PUERTO RICO is at the corner of Ave. Ponce de León and Ave. Roberto H. Todd in Santurce. The museum features contemporary art works from Latin America, the Caribbean and Puerto Rico. Tues.-Sat. 10-4, Sun. noon-4. Free. Phone (787) 977-4030.

MUSEO DE ARTE DE PUERTO RICO is at 299 Ave. de Diego in Santurce. Paintings, sculpture, photography, folk art and other media are housed within an expansive neoclassical building. The collection focuses on Puerto Rico's artistic tradition, with pieces ranging from colonial times to the present. Peppered with sculptures and waterfalls, a nature trail weaves through a verdant setting of native island flora, encircling the center.

Guided tours are available by reservation. Picnicking is permitted. Food is available. Allow 1 hour minimum. Tues.-Sat. 10-5 (also Wed. 5-8), Sun. 11-6. Admission $6.39; $3.20 (ages 5-12 and 60-74); free (ages 75+ and on Wed. 2-8). Additional fee for guided group tours. AX, DS, MC, VI. Phone (787) 977-6277.

PARQUE NACIONAL LUIS MUÑOZ RIVERA is on Avenida Luis Muñoz Rivera in Puerta de Tierra. The 27-acre oceanside park honors the statesman and poet who helped Puerto Rico gain its autonomy from Spain in 1897. This land was once a key part of San Juan's military defense; the 1769 powder house that supplied Fort San Jerónimo still stands on the grounds. Cultural events are held at the open-air Pabellón de la Paz. Daily 24 hours. Free. Parking $1. Phone (787) 721-6133.

UNIVERSITY OF PUERTO RICO is on Ave. Ponce de León in Río Piedras. The university has an enrollment of more than 42,000 students. A museum exhibits paintings by José Campeche and Francisco Oller as well as archeological displays. Museum open Mon.-Fri. 9-4:30 (also Wed.-Thurs. 4:30-8:30). Free. Phone (787) 764-0000, ext. 2452.

Botanical Garden of the University of Puerto Rico (El Jardín Botánico) is at jct. SR 847 and Hwy. 1 at the entrance to Barrio Venezuela in Río Piedras. The 289-acre (117-hectare) garden of the University of Puerto Rico features native and tropical flora, including aquatic and herb gardens and areas devoted to heliconia, bamboo, orchids and palms. Guided tours are available. Open daily 9-4:30. Free. Phone (787) 767-1710.

GAMBLING ESTABLISHMENTS

- **Condado Plaza Hotel & Casino** is at 999 Ashford Ave. in Condado. Daily 24 hrs. Phone (787) 721-1000.
- **Diamond Palace Hotel & Casino** is at 55 Condado Ave. Daily 10 a.m.-4 a.m. Phone (787) 721-0810.
- **El San Juan Hotel & Casino** is at 6063 Isla Verde Ave. in Carolina. Daily noon-4 a.m. Phone (787) 791-1000.
- **Embassy Suites Hotel & Casino San Juan** is at 8000 Tartak St. in Isla Verda. Daily noon-4 a.m. Phone (787) 791-0505.
- **Intercontinental San Juan Resort & Casino** is at 5961 Isla Verde Ave. in Carolina. Daily 10 a.m.-4 a.m. Phone (787) 791-6100.
- **Radisson Ambassador Plaza Hotel & Casino** is at 1369 Ashford Ave. in Condado. Daily 24 hrs. Phone (787) 721-7300.
- **The Ritz-Carlton San Juan Hotel, Spa & Casino** is at 6961 Avenue of the Governors at Isla Verde in Carolina. Daily 24 hrs. Phone (787) 253-1700.
- **San Juan Marriott Resort & Stellaris Casino** is at 1309 Ashford Ave. in Condado. Daily 24 hours. Phone (787) 724-8545 or (800) 737-9559.
- **Sheraton Old San Juan Hotel & Casino** is at 100 Brumbaugh St. Daily 10:30 a.m.-2 a.m. Phone (787) 721-5100.

Old San Juan

Settled in 1521, the seven-square-block area of *Viejo* San Juan remains partially enclosed by walls which once were believed necessary to protect San Juan Harbor. Spain continued this construction for

244 years. By the 19th century the military stronghold, protected by the fortresses of San Felipe del Morro and San Cristóbal, had developed into a quaint residential and commercial community. Restored to its former grandeur, Old San Juan exudes the atmosphere of colonial Spain with its pastel-colored houses, filigreed balconies, hidden plazas and narrow streets.

Paved with *adoquines,* bluish glazed bricks used for ballast in Spanish galleons, some streets in the old quarter are so narrow that the walls on both sides can be touched with outstretched arms. Other charming remnants of early times are the street staircases that scaled this hilly section. Halfway between the cathedral and San Juan Gate on Callejón de las Monjas and one block above it are two of these survivors. A prime example of colonial opulence is *La Fortaleza,* reputedly the oldest executive mansion still in use in the Western Hemisphere.

A series of bridges link the islet with the resort areas of Condado and Isla Verde as well as the residential communities of Santurce and the suburbs of Hato Rey and Río Piedras. The Plaza de Colón, where Old San Juan begins, is dominated by a statue of Christopher Columbus erected in 1893 to commemorate the 400th anniversary of his discovery of Puerto Rico. Today the plaza adjoins the main shopping district on Calle Fortaleza; city buses and free trolleys make frequent stops here. Plaza de San José is bounded by calles San Sebastián, Cristo and San José. Several historic structures and museums border the plaza, where a statue of Juan Ponce de León was fashioned from bronze cannons captured from the British in 1797. Narrow streets and slow-moving traffic make walking the most practical way to explore the old city.

La Casita, the little yellow building near Pier 1 in the Plaza Dársena, serves as a visitor information center. Maps, brochures and free daiquiri samples are offered.

Puerto Rico Tourism Company: 259 Recinto Sur St., La Princesa Bldg. #2, Paseo La Princesa, Old San Juan, Puerto Rico 00902; phone (787) 721-2400.

ANTIGUO ASILO DE BENEFICENCIA (OLD HOME FOR THE POOR) is off El Morro at 9 Calle Norzagaray. The Home for the Poor, built in the 1840s, now houses the Institute of Puerto Rican Culture. Exhibits include archeological items, rocks, tools, masks and copper geometric figures. The grounds are accented with gardens and courtyards. The Museo del Indio de Puerto Rico displays artifacts belonging to several Indian cultures that inhabited Puerto Rico and neighboring islands in the pre-Columbian era.

Allow 1 hour minimum. Building Mon.-Fri. 8-5. Museum Tues.-Sat. 9-4. Closed major holidays. Free. Phone (787) 724-0700.

CAPILLA DEL CRISTO (CHRIST CHAPEL) is on Calle Cristo. The tiny chapel, which has room for only some 30 worshipers, was built on the spot where a horse and rider plunged over the 70-foot bluff during a festival race in 1753. One version of the legend says the rider was saved by prayer; another recounts that only his mount survived. The chapel contains an elaborate altar made of silver and gold with antique ornaments and paintings. Tues. 10-4. Free. Phone (787) 723-1895.

CASA ALCALDÍA (CITY HALL) fronts the Plaza de Armas on Calle San Francisco. Construction began on this building in 1602 and wasn't completed until 1789. The facade is said to have been inspired by the city hall in Madrid, Spain. A small museum chronicles San Juan's history. An information center is near the Calle San Francisco entrance. Mon.-Fri. 8-4; closed holidays. Free. Phone (787) 724-7171, ext. 2000.

CASA BLANCA (WHITE HOUSE MUSEUM) is at 1 Calle San Sebastián above the seawall. A wooden fort on the site burned in 1521, and this fortified mansion was built in its place 2 years later for Juan Ponce de León by his son-in-law. The conquistador died before its completion. His family lived here for 250 years, until the Spanish government acquired it for a military headquarters. Gardens surround the mansion, which is furnished with 16th- and 17th-century antiques.

Allow 30 minutes minimum. Tues.-Sat. 9-noon and 1-4; closed Jan. 1 and Good Friday. Guided tours are offered by appointment. Admission $3; $2 (children and senior citizens). Phone (787) 725-1454.

CASA DEL LIBRO (BOOK HOUSE) is at 255 Calle Cristo. A restored and furnished 18th-century residence holds a specialized library of 4,000 books including many pre-16th-century and rare editions. The emphasis of the museum is upon book arts and the book as an art form. Tues.-Sat. 11-4:30; closed holidays. Donations. Phone (787) 723-0354.

CASA RAMÓN POWER Y GIRALT is at 155 Calle Tetuán. The former home of a Spanish military commander, the building is now headquarters for the Conservation Trust of Puerto Rico. Interactive media exhibits explore the island's environmental issues. Tues.-Sat. 9-4. Free. Phone (787) 722-5834.

CATEDRAL DE SAN JUAN is at 151 Calle Cristo. Built in 1521 and damaged repeatedly by the elements, the present structure is the result of several restorations. The cathedral is a rare example of New World medieval architecture, featuring a circular staircase, vaulted ceilings, 16th-century chalices, the relic of San Pio and a Renaissance madonna. The marble tomb of Juan Ponce de León rests near the transept. Open daily 8-5; mass is held Mon.-Fri. at 12:15, Sat. at 7 p.m., Sun. at 9 and 11 a.m. Donations. Phone (787) 723-1895.

CONVENTO DE LOS DOMINICOS is at 98 Calle Norzagaray. The 16th-century convent now houses the Institute of Puerto Rican Culture and a chapel museum. Cultural activities are regularly presented in the interior patio, which is surrounded by arcaded galleries. One room is devoted to the display of wooden *santos*. Tues.-Sat. 8:30-4:20. Free. Phone (787) 977-2700 or (787) 977-2701.

LA FORTALEZA is at the foot of Calle Fortaleza. The oldest executive mansion in the Western Hemisphere still in use, the Palacio de Santa Catalina has been the residence of more than 150 governors and the seat of Puerto Rico's government for more than 4 centuries. Tours through the gardens are offered; proper attire is required. Guided 30-minute garden tours in English depart Mon.-Fri. 9-3:30 from Fortaleza Street (lobby of Real Audiencia building). Closed holidays. Admission $3. Phone (787) 721-7000, ext. 2211, 2323 and 2358.

LA IGLESIA DE SAN JOSÉ is on Calle San Sebastián on Plaza de San José. The Spanish Gothic church is considered the second oldest house of worship in the Western Hemisphere. Dominican friars began construction on this original chapel for a monastery in 1532. Its interior features vaulted Gothic ceilings, a collection of religious paintings and frescoes, Ponce de León's family coat of arms and a figure of Christ on the cross that may date to the mid-16th century.

Note: the church is currently closed for restoration. Mon.-Sat. 7-2; mass is held Sun. at noon. Donations. Phone (787) 725-7501.

LA PRINCESA is on Paseo de la Princesa at 259 Recinto Sur St. The former San Juan Penitentiary, built in 1837, now serves as an art gallery and home to the Puerto Rico Tourism Company. The gallery features contemporary works by island artists, as well as examples of traditional crafts. Elegantly restored and landscaped, the building faces San Juan Bay, overlooking the *Raíces* fountain sculpture. Mon.-Fri. 9-noon and 1-4. Free. Phone (787) 721-2400, ext. 2175.

LA ROGATIVA is just n. of the San Juan Gate on Calle Recinto del Oeste. This striking statue, commissioned for San Juan's 450th anniversary, pays homage to a celebrated legend. During the British siege by Sir Ralph Abercromby's troops in 1797, it is said that the local bishop led his parishioners in a prayer procession through the streets. The enemy, seeing the line of torches, thought Spanish reinforcements had arrived—and fled. The little plaza atop the city wall offers a bird's-eye view of the western harbor and the Paseo del Morro.

MUSEO DE LAS AMÉRICAS is on the second floor of the Cuartel de Ballajá on Calle Norzagaray. Housed in a massive three-story building designed to house Spanish soldiers and their families, the museum presents permanent and temporary exhibits with a concentration on the artwork of the Americas. Displays include archeological artifacts, sculpture, Amazon Indian photographs and objects, folk art, a peasant's house and a replica of a country chapel. A permanent exhibit highlights African heritage. Guided tours are available by reservation. Allow 30 minutes minimum. Thurs.-Fri. 9-4, Tues.-Wed. and Sat.-Sun. 10-4; closed major holidays. Free. Indian exhibit $2. Phone (787) 724-5052.

MUSEO DEL NIÑO DE PUERTO RICO (CHILDREN'S MUSEUM) is at 150 Calle Cristo next to El Hotel Convento. The museum features three floors of hands-on exhibits highlighting health, nature, science and society. A re-creation of a town features a grocery store, a shoeshine shop and a plaza for playing hopscotch and dominoes. Allow 1 hour minimum. Tues.-Fri. 11-6, Sat.-Sun. noon-6, June-July and 1st week in Aug.; Tues.-Thurs. 9-3:30, Fri. 9-5, Sat.-Sun. 12:30-5, rest of year. Closed holidays. Last admission 1 hour before closing. Children's admission $7; $5 (adults). AX, MC, VI. Phone (787) 722-3791.

MUSEO DE NUESTRA RAÍZ AFRICANA is at 101 Calle San Sebastián on Plaza de San José. The Museum of Our African Roots is housed in the heavily buttressed building known as Casa de los Contrafuertes, one of the oldest private residences in Viejo San Juan. Exhibits chronicle the history of slavery and the influence of African music, language and culture in Puerto Rico. Photographs, maps, artifacts and musical instruments are labeled in Spanish. Allow 30 minutes minimum. Tues.-Sat. 8:30-4:20. Admission $2; $1 (children). Phone (787) 724-4294.

MUSEO DE SAN JUAN is at 150 Calle Norzagaray. Puerto Rican art is displayed in the east and west galleries. Concerts and other cultural events take place in the museum's interior patio. Audiovisual shows trace the history of San Juan. Tues.-Fri. 9-4, Sat.-Sun. 10-4. Free. Phone (787) 724-1875.

MUSEO PABLO CASALS is at 101 Calle San Sebastián on Plaza de San José. Museum exhibits include memorabilia, manuscripts and photographs of the famous Spanish cellist who lived in Puerto Rico for nearly 20 years. Videotapes of Festival Casals concerts can be viewed upon request. Tues.-Sat. 9:30-4:30. Admission $1.07; 58c (ages 0-11 and 60+). Phone (787) 723-9185.

NIGHT TALES OF OLD SAN JUAN departs from the flagpole outside the Sheraton Old San Juan Hotel at Pier 3. This guided 2-hour walking tour explores the famous sites of Viejo San Juan, covering approximately 2 miles of the historic district with several rest stops. The tour company, Legends of Puerto Rico, also offers other city and island excursions. Walking tours take place rain or shine. Streets can be slippery; wear comfortable walking shoes. Tours depart Mon. at 7 p.m., Tues.-Wed. and Fri.-Sat. at 6 p.m. Fee $30; free (ages 0-5). Reservations are required. MC, VI. Phone (787) 605-9060.

GEM **SAN JUAN NATIONAL HISTORIC SITE** is on the north shore of Old San Juan overlooking the bay. The extensive site contains the fortifications built by the Spanish to protect San Juan and the treasure-laden fleets that sailed past the city en route to Spain. Puerta de San Juan at the foot of Caleta de San Juan is the most impressive and last remaining of six gates of the old city wall. The 1639 structure stands more than 16 feet (5 m) tall.

The site encompasses two large forts and a small inlet fortification, Castillo de San Juan de la Cruz. El Cañuelo, as the smallest fort is known, was built on Isla de Cabras at the entrance to San Juan Harbor, about 1610 as a wooden structure. Destroyed by the Dutch in 1625, it was rebuilt in stone in the 1660s. The tiny fort is closed to the public.

Guided tours of the national historic site are available by reservation. Comfortable walking shoes are recommended. Site open daily 9-5; closed Dec. 25. Last admission 1 hour before closing. Admission per fort (valid for 24 hours) $3; free (ages 0-15). Both forts (valid for 7 days) $5; free (ages 0-15). Parking $2. Phone (787) 729-6960.

GEM **Fort San Cristóbal** stands on a hill at the e. edge of Old San Juan n. of Ave. Muñoz Rivera. at San Juan National Historic Site. The 27-acre (11-hectare) fortification was the largest ever built by the Spanish in the New World. Constructed 1635-1783, the castle fort is connected to outworks by a series of tunnels and dry moats. Gunrooms, barracks and officers quarters surround the main courtyard. The fort's powerful artillery repelled British forces attacking from the east in 1797. The first shot of the Spanish-American War in Puerto Rico was fired from the fort in 1898.

Daily 9-5; closed Dec. 25. Last admission 1 hour before closing. Admission per fort (good for 24 hours) $3; free (ages 0-15). Both forts (good for 7 days) $5; free (ages 0-15). Phone (787) 729-6960.

GEM **Fort San Felipe del Morro (El Morro)** was built on a promontory at the n.w. tip of Old San Juan, now part of San Juan National Historic Site. The grounds are closed to motor vehicles; visitors walk one-quarter mile (.4 km) to the fort from underground parking at Plaza del Quinto Centenario on Calle Norzagaray.

The most strategic of San Juan's defense systems, El Morro repelled attacks by the British, Dutch and French over the course of 300 years. Six levels of impressive batteries rising 140 feet (43 m) out of the sea afford a beautiful harbor view. A network of ramps and stairways connects the ramparts.

Construction began in 1539 with a simple tower designed to guard the channel to the harbor. Most of the massive earthworks and fortifications were built between 1589 and the 1650s, and the fort was completed by 1787. The fort contains a museum with examples of 16th- and 17th-century armor and weapons, a chapel and audiovisual exhibits. Daily 9-5; closed Dec. 25. Last admission 1 hour before closing. Admission per fort (good for 24 hours) $3; free (ages 0-15). Both forts (good for 7 days) $5; free (ages 0-15). Phone (787) 729-6960.

AAA Walking Tour

This walking tour of Old San Juan will take 2-4 hours, depending on your pace as well as the number of listed sites you visit. *Those attractions appearing in bold type have detailed listings in the Old San Juan section.* The historic district is small—a seven-square-block area of pastel-colored colonial buildings—but the cobbled streets are often steep and uneven; wear comfortable shoes and walk with care. Don't forget sunscreen, bottled water and a hat in the hottest months.

Begin your walking tour at La Casita, the visitor center of the Puerto Rico Tourism Company. The little yellow building is on the waterfront at Plaza de la Dársena, just west of the first cruise ship pier. Here you can pick up maps, brochures and a free daiquiri sample before venturing into the heart of Old San Juan.

From the visitor center, follow the paved brick walkway west along the port toward El Paseo de La Princesa. The U.S. Customs House with its pink stucco exterior and Moorish details will be on your left; the towering Art Deco edifice of Banco Popular will be on your right across the street. Two orange columns mark the entrance to the Paseo, the tree-lined promenade winding along the ancient city wall and the rocky shore of San Juan Bay. Pocket parks and benches provide resting places along the way. The massive wall, known as "La Muralla," stands 42 feet high and was constructed with parallel sections of sandstone blocks. Sand poured between the sections helped absorb the impact of cannon balls. Completed in 1782, the towering fortification stretches for 3.4 miles and once enclosed the entire colonial capital. *Garitas,* or sentry boxes, crown the wall at prominent points along the bay.

Toward the end of the main promenade is **La Princesa**, the old penitentiary. Now restored, the gray-and-white building houses a visitor center for the Puerto Rico Tourism Company and a gallery for local artists. At the point where the Paseo meets San Juan Bay, the *Raíces* fountain by sculptor Luís Sanguino honors the three cultures—Taíno, Spanish and African—comprising modern Puerto Rico.

Following the walkway into the deep shade of banyan trees, you'll pass the jagged metal spikes of *Crecimiento,* a sculpture by Carmen Inés Blondet. Above the wall are the gardens of La Fortaleza, the governor's mansion.

Rounding a bend in the stone wall, you'll approach the Puerta de San Juan, or San Juan Gate, as seafaring guests approached the city for centuries. The red gate was one of six in the original fortification, and its massive wooden doors were locked at sundown to guard against attack. Disembarking from their ships, visiting dignitaries were greeted here and escorted to the cathedral for an official blessing. The Latin inscription reads, "Blessed is he who comes in the name of the Lord."

From here, the Paseo continues along the wall to the foot of El Morro. Future plans call for the trail to access the fort, but for now, it ends below the water battery. Should you decide to walk out to the point and back, you'll see many of Old San Juan's furry residents lazing in the sun; a colony of feral cats is protected by the national park service and fed by a local organization called "Save a Gato."

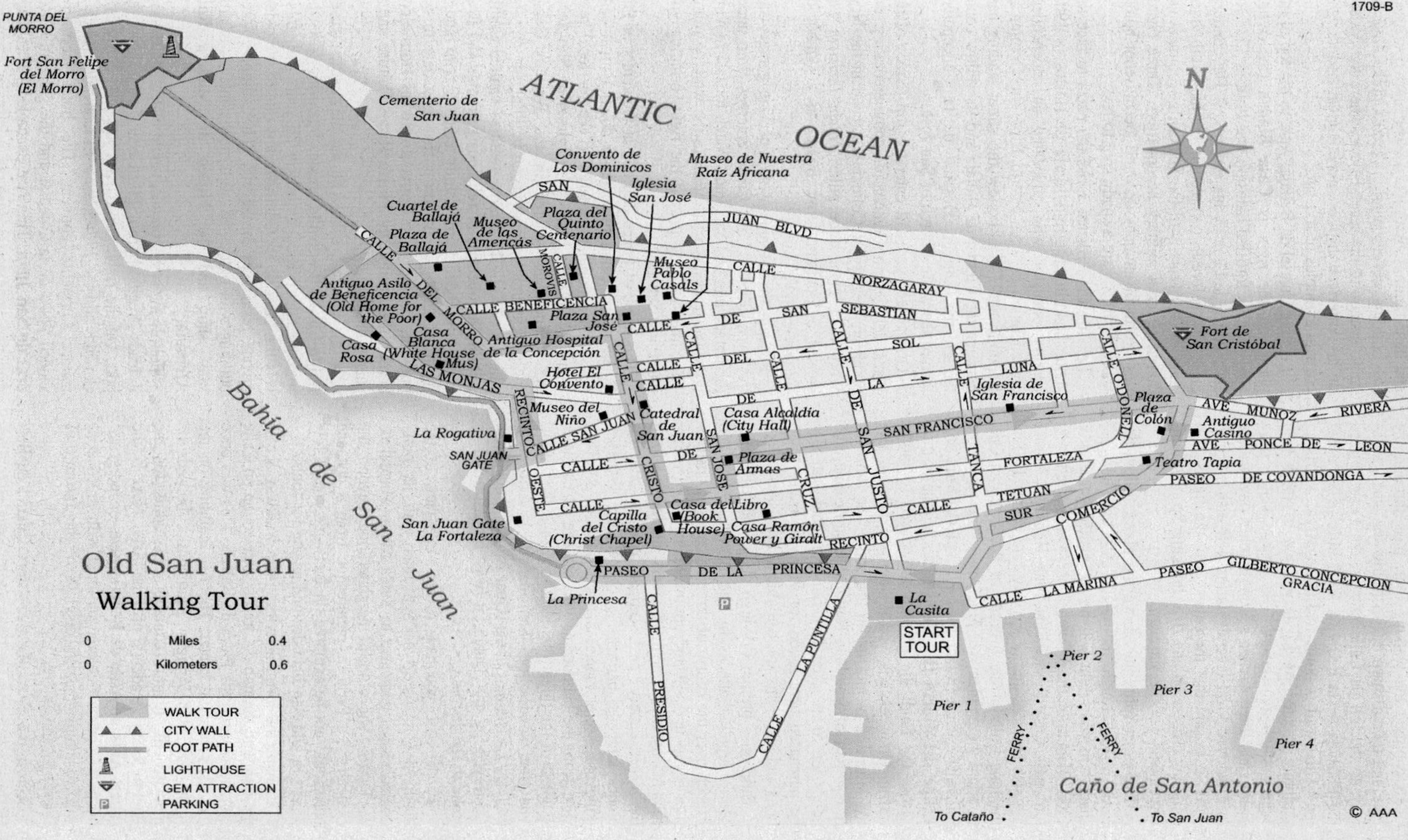
1709-B
PUNTA DEL MORRO
Fort San Felipe del Morro (El Morro)
Cementerio de San Juan
ATLANTIC
OCEAN
N
Convento de Los Dominicos
Museo de Nuestra Raíz Africana
Iglesia San José
Cuartel de Ballajá
Museo de las Américas
Plaza del Quinto Centenario
Plaza de Ballajá
Museo Pablo Casals
Antiguo Asilo de Beneficencia (Old Home for the Poor)
Plaza San José
Casa Blanca (White House Mus)
Antiguo Hospital de la Concepción
Casa Rosa
Hotel El Convento
Museo del Niño
Catedral de San Juan
Casa Alcaldía (City Hall)
Iglesia de San Francisco
Plaza de Colón
Antiguo Casino
Teatro Tapia
La Rogativa
SAN JUAN GATE
Plaza de Armas
Casa del Libro (Book House)
Capilla del Cristo (Christ Chapel)
Casa Ramón Power y Giralt
San Juan Gate
La Fortaleza
Fort de San Cristóbal
Bahía de San Juan
La Princesa
La Casita
START TOUR
Pier 1
Pier 2
Pier 3
Pier 4
FERRY
FERRY
Caño de San Antonio
To Cataño
To San Juan
© AAA
SAN JUAN BLVD
CALLE NORZAGARAY
CALLE SAN SEBASTIAN
CALLE DEL SOL
CALLE DE LA LUNA
CALLE SAN FRANCISCO
CALLE FORTALEZA
CALLE TETUAN
CALLE SUR
COMERCIO
CALLE LA MARINA
CALLE TANCA
CALLE DE SAN JUSTO
CALLE DE LA CRUZ
CALLE DE SAN JOSE
CALLE CRISTO
CALLE SAN JUAN
CALLE BENEFICENCIA
CALLE DEL MORRO
CALLE MOROVIS
CALLE O'DONELL
RECINTO OESTE
RECINTO
LAS MONJAS
PASEO DE LA PRINCESA
CALLE PRESIDIO
CALLE LA PUNTILLA
PASEO GILBERTO CONCEPCION GRACIA
PASEO DE COVANDONGA
AVE PONCE DE LEON
AVE MUÑOZ RIVERA
Old San Juan
Walking Tour
0 Miles 0.4
0 Kilometers 0.6
WALK TOUR
CITY WALL
FOOT PATH
LIGHTHOUSE
GEM ATTRACTION
PARKING

To continue the walking tour, pass through the gate and take a sharp left to follow the steep walkway up the hill on Calle Recinto del Oeste toward the Plazuela de la Rogativa. This little plaza at the top of the wall is home to **La Rogativa**, a striking sculpture created by Lindsay Daen to mark San Juan's 450th anniversary. The bronze statue of a bishop and three women bearing torches pays tribute to a beloved local legend: during a British siege in 1797, it is said that the enemy saw the lights of a religious procession and fled, thinking Spanish reinforcements were on the way.

The street splits just above the plaza; follow the lower road through the white gate and into the shade. On your right will be the walled gardens of Casa Blanca, or the White House. On the left, you will pass Casa Rosada, the Pink House, a former Spanish barracks and now a day-care center. Follow the long walls of the Institute of Puerto Rican Culture and the Academy of Fine Arts to the top of the hill, where you will face the low citadel of **Fort San Felipe del Morro (El Morro)**. It's a quarter-mile across the field; the grounds are closed to motor traffic. On weekends, you'll often see families flying kites and picnicking on the grass. The fortification is part of San Juan National Historic Site, and admission to its sister fort, San Cristóbal, can also be purchased here (good for 7 days). Water fountains and restrooms are available at both sites.

Built on a promontory high above the harbor, El Morro repelled attacks by the British, Dutch and French over the course of three centuries. Construction began in 1539 and continued until 1787. Surrounded by a dry moat, it covers six levels—from the water battery to the upper bastions—and includes kitchens, barracks, a chapel, gun batteries, dungeons, secret tunnels and a lighthouse. Looking west from the battlements you can see El Cañuelo, smallest of the three forts built to defend the harbor. The first wooden fort, San Juan de la Cruz, was built on La Isla de Cabras (Goat Island) about 1610. Destroyed by the Dutch, it was reconstructed in stone in the 1670s.

To the east, you have a bird's-eye view of the beautiful Cementerío de San Juan with its pink-domed chapel dedicated to Santa Maria Magdalena de Pazzis. The colorful neighborhood beyond the cemetery, La Perla, is picturesque from a distance but should not be explored on foot—it's one of few places in Old San Juan deemed unsafe for tourists.

Leaving the fort, follow the main walkway across the field and through the traffic intersection on Calle Norzagaray into the Plaza de Ballajá. This was once the city's hospital center. The first building on the right, the 1858 Antiguo Manicomio, housed the mentally ill. It now contains classrooms for the Puerto Rican Academy of Fine Arts. Next is the stately **Antiguo Asilo de Beneficencia**, or indigents' hospital. The buff-colored building with green ironwork contains museum displays of the Institute of Puerto Rican Culture.

Across the plaza, the three-story Cuartel de Ballajá was a barracks for 19th-century Spanish soldiers and their families. With its massive inner courtyard, the building covers nearly 3 acres. Take time to walk upstairs to the second floor, where the **Museo de las Américas** displays archeological artifacts and colorful examples of folk art.

Leaving Cuartel de Ballajá, walk to the top of the plaza; on the right is **Casa Blanca** (the White House). This fortified mansion was built in 1523 for Juan Ponce de León by his son-in-law. The conquistador died before its completion, but his family lived here for 250 years until the Spanish government acquired it for a military headquarters. Three centuries' worth of antiques decorate the museum home, and the gardens are a shady spot to rest.

Leaving Casa Blanca, cross the plaza to face the statue honoring Eugenio Maria de Hostos, a 19th-century educator who advocated an independent confederation between Puerto Rico, the Dominican Republic and Cuba. Follow the street leading east between the Cuartel de Ballajá and its yellow counterpart, the Antiguo Hospital de la Concepción, toward the white Church of San José.

On the left, you will enter the top terrace of the Plaza del Quinto Centenario, commemorating the 500th anniversary of Columbus' arrival in the New World. The giant stone pillar, *Tótem Telúrico*, was created by sculptor Jaime Suárez as a symbol of Caribbean Indian cultures.

Beneath the monument is a parking garage, and the busy street of Calle Cristo emerges from under the terrace into Old San Juan. Watch for fast-moving taxis and trucks as you return to the walking route. The street will jog toward the right, bringing you into Plaza San José.

The statue of Ponce de León at the center of this square was created by melting down British cannons. It's a popular gathering place for local residents. The plaza's heart is **La Iglesia de San José**, the second-oldest church in the Western Hemisphere. Dominican friars began building the original chapel in 1532. The interior features vaulted Gothic ceilings, a collection of religious paintings and frescoes, Ponce de León's family coat of arms and a figure of Christ on the cross that may date to the mid-16th century. The **Convento de los Dominicos** houses the Institute of Puerto Rican Culture and a chapel museum.

In the northern corner of the plaza, the **Museo Pablo Casals** honors the famous Spanish cellist who lived in Puerto Rico for nearly 20 years. Adjoining it is the Casa de los Contrafuertes, one of the oldest private residences in the city. The salmon-colored building with buttressed walls now contains an artisans' shop and the **Museo de Nuestra Raíz Africana**.

Follow the steep, cobbled street of Calle Cristo as it leads downhill from Plaza San José toward the port. On the right, you'll pass the 1842 Seminario Concilar and the 17th-century El Convento Hotel, a former Carmelite convent. The hotel faces the shaded Plaza de la Catedral and the graceful **Catedral de San Juan**. This rare example of Caribbean medieval architecture features a circular staircase, vaulted ceilings and venerated relics. The marble tomb of Juan Ponce de León stands near the transept. On the western edge of the plaza is the **Museo del Niño de Puerto Rico**, a children's museum with three floors of hands-on exhibits.

Continue south on Calle Cristo past the designer shops and T-shirt stores to Calle Fortaleza. One block to your right is the oldest executive mansion still in use in the Western Hemisphere, **La Fortaleza**. Also known as El Palacio de Santa Catalina, the blue-and-white building has been the residence of Puerto Rico's governors and the seat of government for more than 4 centuries. Guided tours of the gardens are offered in English; proper attire is required.

Calle Cristo ends at the gated **Capilla del Cristo**, a small stone chapel built in honor of a fabled miracle. Legend says that a horse and rider plunged off this cliff during a festival race in 1753, but prayers saved the rider's life. (Some versions of the story say he died but his mount survived.) Nevertheless, this tiny chapel was erected in thanksgiving. The building is only open to the public on Tuesdays, when the glass doors are unlocked to reveal a golden altar and painted icons. The Parque de las Palomas atop the city wall offers a good view of the port. Keep your camera handy—when a visitor buys a bag of dried corn to feed the pigeons, it can look like a scene from Hitchcock's "The Birds."

Also within the cul-de-sac at the end of Calle Cristo are the **Casa del Libro**, a restored and furnished 18th-century residence holding a specialized library of 4,000 antique books; and the Centro Nacional de Artes Populares y Artesanías, a popular place to shop for handcrafted souvenirs.

To end the tour early and take a shortcut back to the waterfront, walk behind the chapel and follow Calle Tetuán east, passing **Casa Ramón Power y Giralt**—the former home of a Spanish military hero and now headquarters of the Conservation Trust of Puerto Rico—and the pink Iglesia de Santa Ana. Turn right on Calle San Justo to finish your tour at the cruise ship piers.

To continue the full walking tour, return north on Calle Cristo to Calle Fortaleza and turn right. Take a left at the next corner onto Calle de San José to reach Old San Juan's main square, Plaza de Armas. The statues on the fountain represent the four seasons. The former Spanish treasury on the left, La Intendencia, is headquarters of the Puerto Rico Department of State. **Casa Alcaldía** (City Hall) fronts the plaza on Calle San Francisco. The building's façade was said to have been inspired by the city hall in Madrid.

There are two drug stores on the northeast corner if you need to pick up any supplies. Continue past them on Calle San Francisco. On the left, you'll come to La Bombanera, a local cafe famous for its fresh-baked pastries. A little farther on is the Plaza de Salvador Brau with its seated statue of the 19th-century Puerto Rican writer. Adjoining the plaza is the 1756 Franciscan Chapel.

The street will open onto Plaza de Colón (Columbus Square), where a statue of the explorer stands on the stone column above a fountain. A two-sided sign with maps of the island and Old San Juan will help you get your bearings. At the bottom of the plaza is El Teatro Tapía, one of Puerto Rico's most cherished cultural monuments. Built in 1832, the restored theater is one of the oldest still in use in the Western Hemisphere. To the east, the gray-and-white Antiguo Casino is an opulent example of French Second Empire architecture, now used for state functions.

The walls of **Fort San Cristóbal** dominate the northeast corner. From Plaza de Colón, follow the street up the hill to the gate of the city's main defense against land attacks. The 27-acre (11-hectare) fortification was the largest ever built by the Spanish in the New World. Visitors can climb the ramparts and wander a maze of tunnels inside this UNESCO World Heritage Site, which remains a monument to military engineering. Take time to explore the museum exhibits of armor and weaponry.

From Fort San Cristóbal it's a short walk back down to the waterfront. If you're ready for a break, hop aboard the free trolley (although it may be crowded if cruise ships are in port).

On foot, walk back through Plaza de Colón and follow Recinto Sur; El Teatro Tapía will be on your left. At the intersection of Recinto Sur and Calle Tetuán, you'll pass a triangular plaza and a statue of Arturo Somohano, composer and director of the San Juan Symphony Orchestra. International restaurants along Recinto Sur offer everything from sushi to Italian to Transylvanian cuisine. Passing the six-story Galeria, you'll see the U.S. Post Office and Courthouse with its Moorish roof. Turn left on Calle Tanca to come full circle on your walking tour of Old San Juan.

UTUADO (C-3) pop. 35,336

In the Cordillera Central Mountain Range, Utuado (oo-too-AH-do) is a departure point for trips to Río Abajo State Forest. Nearby off Rte. 10 is man-made Lago Dos Bocas, a long, winding hydroelectric reservoir. One- or 2-hour launch trips on the lake, including stops at several mountain villages, depart from the wharf several times daily.

The Indian Ceremonial Center at Caguana, 7.5 miles (12 km) west of Utuado on Rte. 111, was constructed by Taíno Indians more than 700 years ago. A soccer-like game was played here on dozens of ritual courts, or *bateyes*; many are lined with inscribed monoliths. The park is open daily; phone (787) 894-7325.

RÍO ABAJO STATE FOREST (BOSQUE ESTATAL) is reached via Rte. 10 to Rte. 621. Teak and mahogany trees cover the oddly shaped karst hills of the 5,730-acre (2,319-hectare) forest, which contains a recreation area and offers exploring possibilities in dozens of mountain caves and ruined sugar mills. Daily dawn-dusk. Free. Reservations are required. Phone (787) 880-6557 or (787) 999-2200, ext. 5158.

VEGA BAJA (B-3) pop. 61,929

MUSEO CASA ALONSO is at Calle Betances #4. A guided tour of the 1776 Neoclassic-Criolla structure includes the music room, library, kitchens and bedrooms. Visitors encounter artifacts of Caribbean history and culture, including tiles, ceramics, coins and pottery unearthed in area archeological excavations. Guides discuss the various families that owned the house and their influence on Puerto Rico's history. Allow 1 hour minimum. Mon.-Sat. 9-noon and 1-4; closed public holidays. Admission $2; $1 (senior citizens and 0-12). Phone (787) 855-1364.

VIEQUES (B-6, D-6) pop. 9,106

Long a missile range for the U.S. Navy, Vieques (vee-AY-kays) finally saw an end to the bombing in May 2003. The military had purchased part of the island in the 1940s to use for weapons testing. After many years of protest, the base was finally turned over to the government of Puerto Rico, which is working to reclaim the land. Only the eastern tip of the island remains restricted. The Vieques National Wildlife Refuge has been established on nearly 18,000 acres on both ends of the island to protect such endangered animals as the brown pelican, the Antillean manatee and four species of sea turtles.

With its quiet beaches, coral reefs and bioluminescent bay, Vieques has become a popular destination for eco-tourism. The Punta Mulas Lighthouse, known as Morropó, has been protecting the port town of Isabel Segunda since 1893. Vieques lies about 8 miles off the eastern shore of Puerto Rico; daily ferries run from Fajardo and San Juan, and air flights are available from San Juan International Airport.

BAHÍA MOSQUITO BIOLUMINESCENT BAY TOURS depart from the Biobay Eco-Center on Rte. 996 at Km 4.5, just west of Esperanza. The waters literally glow in the dark at Mosquito Bay, one of the brightest bioluminescent bays in the world. Tiny microorganisms called dinoflagellates create the mysterious blue-green light, which is best viewed on cloudy or moonless nights. Narrated 2.5-hour trips to the bay include a star and planet lecture and a chance to swim in the glowing waters. Electric pontoon boats prevent pollution of the fragile ecosystem.

Passengers who wish to swim should wear bathing suits under their clothes and refrain from using insect repellent or skin lotion. Trips depart nightly when the moon is not in full phase. Fare $30; $15 (ages 3-12). MC, VI. Phone (787) 741 0720.

MUSEO FUERTE CONDE DE MIRASOL is in the Barriada Fuerte sector of Isabel Segunda. Built 1845-1855 by order of the governor of Puerto Rico, the fort was one of the last Spanish military structures to be erected in the New World. The restored fort displays local artwork and exhibits about the island's archeology, slavery, sugar production, colonial influences and military presence. Wed.-Sun. 8:30-4:30. Donations. Phone (787) 741-1717.

Gustavia / © Sylvain Grandadam / age fotostock

St. Barthélemy

Affectionately called St. Barths, St. Barthélemy (bar-TELL-a-mee) lies 125 miles (200 km) northwest of Guadeloupe at the northern end of the Leeward Islands. St. Barths' residents are probably the least "Caribbean" of the islands' people. Because the island's rocky, arid soil supported few slave plantations—and due to an unlikely 100-year ownership by Sweden—most residents are fair-skinned. Remnants of the Swedish ownership remain, most notably in the name of the capital, Gustavia. A trip around the tiny island, however, reveals scenes reminiscent of 17th-century France, a legacy of the island's original settlers maintained by today's reserved and self-sufficient residents. A quiet island with more than a dozen white sand beaches, St. Barths also has rocky hillsides and lush green valleys.

History

Discovered by Christopher Columbus in 1493 and named for his brother Bartolomeo, St. Barths was first settled by French colonists from nearby St. Kitts in 1648. The settlement failed, however, and in 1651 the French sold the island to the Knights of Malta. Five years later it was raided by the fierce Caribs, then abandoned until 1673 when it was again settled by the French, but from Normandy and Brittany.

This colony succeeded, in large part because French buccaneers brought to the island vast quantities of plunder from Spanish galleons. One such pirate, Monbars the Exterminator, reputedly maintained his headquarters on St. Barths, and his treasure is said to be hidden among the coves and buried in the island sands.

Except for a brief British takeover in 1758, St. Barths remained in French hands until

1784 when it was ceded to Sweden in exchange for trading rights in Gothenburg, Sweden. The Swedes declared St. Barths a neutral and free port, and made fortunes in trade for many years. Following a protracted economic decline, the Swedish people voted to sell the island back to France. France agreed to repurchase the island and maintained its free-port status. St. Barths is a dependency of Guadeloupe, which is a department and region of France.

The people of St. Barths are industrious, spiritual and soft-mannered. Some work in the expanding tourist trade, but these private people return quietly to their homes at the end of the day. Lacking significant agricultural and industrial opportunities, the men have taken to the sea and are considered superb sailors and fishermen. Many women have become skilled at weaving straw hats, baskets and similar items to sell to tourists. Sailboats and yachts fill the harbor, but St. Barths doesn't promote itself as a cruise destination. Government officials hope to control growth on the island, thus preserving its reputation as a chic hideaway for the rich and famous.

Shopping

St. Barths is a duty-free port; therefore, perfumes, cosmetics, china, crystal, watches, imported jewelry, resort wear, liquor and tobacco sell at bargain prices. Some selections are limited, but there are enough bargains to warrant setting aside time for shopping, particularly for "name" merchandise. Besides duty-free items, there is delicately woven reed work unique to St. Barths as well as bonnets, seashells, pottery and island artwork. The village of Corossol is known for its straw goods.

Downtown Gustavia is a center for boutiques and duty-free shops. Shopping centers include La Villa Créole and Pelican Plage in St. Jean and La Savane Commercial Center opposite the airport. An array of lotions and cosmetics is produced in Lorient.

Most shops are open daily 9-noon and 2-6, although some close for the day at noon on Saturday. Banking hours are Mon.-Fri. 8-noon and 2-3:30; a bank at Les Galeries du Commerce in St. Jean is open Tues.-Sat. until 5. The currency exchange office in downtown Gustavia is open Mon.-Fri. 8:30-noon and 2:30-5, Sat. 8:30-noon. Banks are closed on holidays and some afternoons preceding holidays. U.S. dollars are accepted everywhere, and prices are often quoted in dollars. Major credit cards are usually accepted.

Food and Drink

Dining on St. Barths can be a memorable experience. Young chefs who have trained in some of France's greatest restaurants enjoy plying their trade on the island. Combining local fruits and spices with classical French traditions, they have created a Caribbean showcase of French cuisine.

Most restaurants are small, but each is different either in food, setting or atmosphere. Some are beach cafes featuring fresh lobster and charcoal-grilled steaks; some specialize in seafood; and some, particularly in the finer

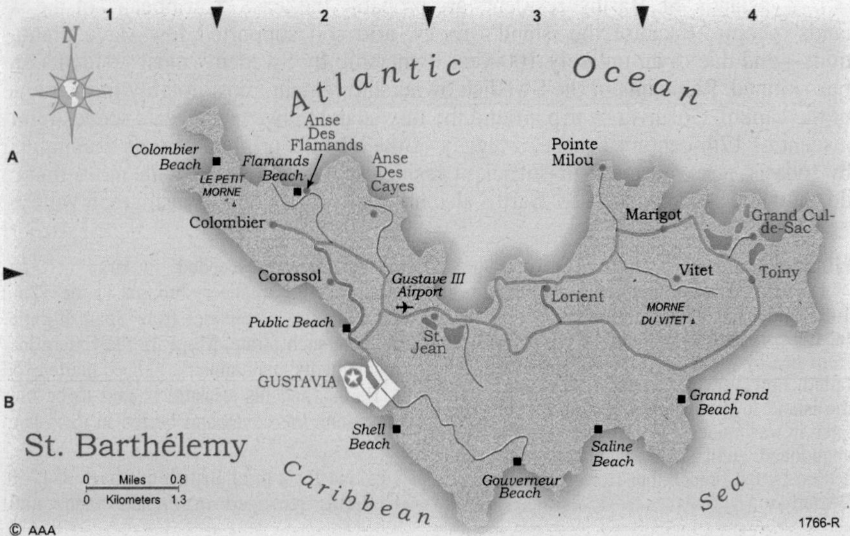

hotels, present traditional French cuisine and international menus.

In Gustavia some of the restaurants are housed in quaint little buildings dating back to the Swedes and early French settlers. La Rotisserie is a deluxe French deli offering picnic fare and afternoon gourmet treats. Another popular daytime eatery is Cheeseburger in Paradise, next to Le Select. Restaurants are required by law to add a 10-15 percent service charge *(service compris)* to their prices. Reservations are always a good idea. Some hotels and restaurants might be closed in the fall for refurbishing or due to their owners' vacations.

St. Barths offers the usual Caribbean fare in the way of beer and potent rum punch. The wine connoisseur, however, will appreciate the island's wine cellars, where more than a million bottles of France's best vintages are kept under strictly controlled conditions.

Sports and Amusements

For many the attraction to St. Barths is its quiet, leisurely pace. There are no casinos, large resorts or organized activities and few nightclubs. You won't find a single golf course on the island, though there is a driving range, and only a few tennis courts. Instead the emphasis is on sand and surf. Opportunities abound for swimming, yachting and sailing, windsurfing, deep-sea fishing, scuba diving and snorkeling.

The gleaming white sand beaches are all public and free; most are never crowded, and complete privacy is often readily available. Swimming and sunbathing *au naturel* are prohibited, and the law is enforced by local police. The beaches of Grand Cul de Sac, on the northeast shore, and St. Jean are both in the vicinity of hotels, restaurants and water sports outlets. Flamands, to the northwest of St. Jean, is a classic stretch of white sand fringed with palm trees. Favored by island families on Sundays, the secluded beaches at Marigot and Lorient on the north shore are otherwise quiet.

In the south, Gouverneur offers complete privacy; Saline, just to the east, is more popular. Shell Beach, so named because it is partially covered with seashells, can be reached on foot from Gustavia. Public Beach is near the commercial pier on the other side of town. The least accessible is Colombier in the northwest. It can be reached by boat from Gustavia or by car to the villages of Colombier or Flamands, then a 20-minute hike down a scenic path.

Lying about midway between the major yachting centers of Antigua and Virgin Gorda Island, St. Barths is naturally a popular yachting destination. Gustavia's harbor has docking facilities for about 40 yachts, and there also are anchorages at nearby Public, Corossol and Colombier; mooring instructions are available from the Marine Reserve at Colombier. Shipchandler du Port Franc in Gustavia carries yachting supplies and accessories; phone (590) 27-86-29. Sailing information is available from the Office du Tourisme on the harborfront in Gustavia. A full-day round-trip sail from Gustavia to Ile Fourchue, an uninhabited island, and Colombier is available. Other charter trips also can be arranged.

Windsurfing is perhaps the most popular sport on the island; the colorful, billowing sails are a common offshore sight. Rentals and lessons are available at outlets in St. Jean and Grand Cul de Sac. Sailing enthusiasts can rent Hobie Cats in St. Jean. Carib Waterplay in St. Jean offers specialized instruction.

The waters around St. Barths abound in tazard, wahoo, dolphin, bonito, barracuda and marlin. Fishing is prohibited in several offshore zones protected by the St. Barthélemy Marine Reserve; information about deep-sea fishing expeditions is available through Ocean Must Marine Service, Masterski Pilou and Yannis Marine.

Licensed, accredited divemasters at West Indies Dive-Marine Service in Gustavia conduct dive schools and have all the necessary gear available; phone (590) 27-70-34. Other scuba clubs in Gustavia include La Bulle-Ocean Must, (590) 27-62-25; Plongée Caraïbes, (690) 54-66-14; St. Barth Plongée, (590) 27-54-44; Big Blue, (590) 27-83-74; and Splash, (590) 29-64-23. Diving equipment and lessons also are available at Ouanalao Dive in Grand Cul de Sac, (690) 63-74-34. Snorkeling is good in many areas off the beaches and islets; the waters off Gouverneur, St. Jean and Grand Cul de Sac are usually the calmest. Gear is sold in Gustavia and St. Jean.

The landlubber might enjoy horseback riding on the island. Ranch des Flamands offers 2-hour rides and instruction for beginning riders; phone (690) 39-87-01 or (590) 27-13-87.

Although limited, nightlife on St. Barths is not totally lacking. Sailors and young locals gather at Le Select, across the street at the Bar de l'Oubli or at the BAZ Bar (Bêtes A Z'Ailes) in Gustavia. The lounges at the upscale Hotel Carl Gustaf and the Mandala Restaurant, both overlooking the harbor, are popular with visiting yachtsmen. During the winter season, live jazz is on the menu at some spots. *St. Barth Magazine, Le Journal de St. Barth, Le News* and *St Barth Weekly* contain information about current entertainment. Published regularly during the winter season, they are distributed free all over the island.

With its Carnival festivities kicking off in early January and continuing through Ash Wednesday, St. Barthélemy is one of few countries in the world not to end its celebration on the traditional "Fat Tuesday" of Mardi Gras. The St. Barthélemy Music Festival in mid-January features world-renowned classical and jazz musicians. The St. Barths Bucket Regatta is a 3-day mega-yacht race held in late March. At the St. Barthélémy Caribbean Film Festival during the last week in April, all films are presented in French. The St. Barthélémy Theater Festival follows in the first week of May.

The year's most important event is the annual Festival of St. Barthélemy, celebrated on the weekends before and after August 24—feast day of the island's patron saint. Colorful booths line the streets of Gustavia, giving it the look and feel of a French country fair. July and August events featuring regattas, live music and fireworks also are held in the villages of Corossol at the St. Louis Festival and Lorient at the Fête du Vent.

Sightseeing

Just four or five roads meander around St. Barths, so it's nearly impossible to get off the beaten path; you can drive all around the island in about an hour. An island map can be obtained in Gustavia at the Office du Tourisme on the harborfront. Gustavia also is a good place to get an introduction to island life; this quaint little harbor town can be explored on foot. At about 11 a.m., sleek catamarans start arriving with day trippers from St. Maarten, filling the streets and shops with visitors. From Monday afternoon through Thursday morning, visitors can mingle with the locals at a small public market on rue du Roi Oscar II.

Northwest of Gustavia is the village of Corossol, where colorful fishing boats bob at anchor in the harbor and women at roadside stands weave palm fronds into baskets. Even while displaying their wares, villagers are camera shy and do not like to be photographed. Similar scenes can be found in the nearby village of Colombier.

From Colombier you can continue north to the secluded beach where an easy hike takes you to viewpoint at Grande Roche. Here you can see the uninhabited offshore islands to the north and Pointe Milou to the east.

Another possible trip is through the busy resort town of St. Jean, east through Lorient, along the north shore to Pointe Milou and Marigot, then south to the rocky coast of Grand Fond. The hilly vicinity of Vitet is just a short drive from Marigot. The volcanic Morne du Vitet, at 938 feet (286 m), is the highest peak on the island. From Grand Fond the road turns inland and back to Lorient, St. Jean and Gustavia.

Island tours are available for up to eight people by minibus or taxi, and there are a number of tour operators.

Transportation

St. Jean's Gustave III Airport has a short landing strip able to handle nothing larger than 20-seat STOL (Short Take-Off and Landing) aircraft, and it is not equipped for night landings. The steep landing approach tests the nerves of even veteran air travelers. From the United States, the principal gateway to St. Barths is St. Maarten, where Air Caraïbes and Windward Island Airways fly in from Princess Juliana International Airport. St. Barth Commuter also flies from Esperance Airport on the French side in St. Martin. These flights take about 15 minutes.

Other flights are available from San Juan, Guadeloupe and Antigua. Most carriers offer several flights daily. St. Barths also is a port of call for some cruise ships.

Taxis are available at the airport; the minimum fare is around $11, and the fare to most hotels is about $25. Fares increase by 50 percent Mon.-Sat. from 8 p.m. to 6 a.m. and all day Sun. and holidays. Rates are not fixed, so it is always a good idea to agree upon the fare in advance. There are just two taxi stands on St. Barths: at the airport, (590) 27-75-81, and on the Rue de la République harborfront in Gustavia, (590) 27-66-31.

Several major and local car rental agencies operate from the airport. Rates are about $70 per day and include unlimited mileage, collision damage insurance and free delivery and pickup; rates are discounted in the summer. A U.S. driver's license is valid. Small sport utility vehicles are replacing the familiar gurgels, minimokes and other jeeplike conveyances for traveling the island's narrow, hilly roads.

Car rental plans can sometimes be made in advance through your hotel. Reservations are required during peak season. Motorbikes also are available for rent at about $50 per day with a $100 deposit; a valid driver's license is required. Helmets are required on the island when operating two-wheeled vehicles.

Edge Catamaran departs for Simpson Bay, St. Maarten, Tuesday through Saturday. This is a 1-day round-trip excursion, but the skippers will take one-way passengers on a space-available basis for about $50. The ferry *Voyager* travels between Gustavia and Marigot or Oyster Pond, St. Martin, four times daily; phone (590) 87-10-68.

Fast Facts

POPULATION: 8,732.

AREA: 21 sq km (8 sq mi.).

CAPITAL: Gustavia.

HIGHEST POINT: 286 m (938 ft.), Morne du Vitet.

LOWEST POINT: Sea level, Caribbean Sea.

TIME ZONE(S): Atlantic Standard.

LANGUAGE: French and English.

GOVERNMENT: Dependency of the French Overseas Department of Guadeloupe.

UNIT OF CURRENCY: Euro Dollar. $1 U.S. = approx. .6 Euro. U.S. currency is widely accepted.

ELECTRICITY: 220 volts, 60 cycles AC.

MINIMUM AGE FOR DRIVERS: 18-25, depending on the rental car agency. An international driving permit is advised; drive on right.

HOLIDAYS: Jan. 1; Epiphany, Jan. 6; Mardi Gras (day before Ash Wednesday); Easter Monday; Labour Day, May 1; Victory Day, May 8; Ascension Day, May (6th Thurs. after Easter); Bastille Day, July 14; Festival of St. Barthélemy, Aug. 24; All Saints Day, Nov. 1; All Souls Day, Nov. 2; Armistice Day, Nov. 11; Assumption Day and St. Barths' Pitea Day, Nov. 16; Christmas, Dec. 25.

TAXES: A 10-15 percent service charge is added to all restaurant prices and most hotel bills. Departure tax $6 U.S.

IMMIGRATION REQUIREMENTS: A valid passport and return or onward ticket are required for U.S. citizens entering the French West Indies. No visa needed for stays up to 3 months. The U.S. Dept. of Homeland Security requires all U.S. citizens returning from the Caribbean to present a valid passport.

PHONING THE ISLANDS: To call St. Barthélemy from the U.S. or Canada, dial 011 + 590 + 590 + the 6-digit local number.

FURTHER INFORMATION FOR VISITORS:

French Government Tourist Office
825 3rd Ave.
New York, NY 10022
(212) 838-7800

Office du Tourisme
Quai du Général de Gaulle
BP 113
Gustavia, St. Barthélemy
(590) 27-87-27

Points of Interest

See map page 206.

COROSSOL (B-2)

In the "straw village" of Corossol, women carry on the tradition of weaving palm fronds into baskets, hats and handbags. Past generations in this tiny fishing hamlet wore modest, long-sleeved dresses and shoulder-length bonnets called *quichenottes* or "kiss-me-nots," vestiges of their French provincial origins. The bonnets offered protection from the sun but also thwarted the unwanted advances of suitors. Visitors may still see these traditional costumes during celebrations, most notably the St. Louis Festival on Aug. 25.

INTER OCEANS MUSEUM is on the waterfront. A private collector amassed this eclectic display of some 9,000 seashells from around the world, including more than a thousand pieces from Caribbean waters and examples of sand from far-flung beaches. Tues.-Sun. 9-12:30 and 2-5. Admission $4. Phone (590) 27-62-97.

GUSTAVIA (B-2) pop. 6,825

St. Barths' harbor town and capital, Gustavia was called Carénage by the French for the shelter it provided to damaged ships. The present name dates back to 1784, which marked the beginning of the island's Swedish era. The Anglican Episcopal Church on the harborfront was completed in 1855.

Three forts built in the mid- to late 17th century protected the harbor. The sites of Fort Karl, overlooking Shell Beach south of town, and Fort Gustave, at the base of the Gustavia Lighthouse to the north, reward hikers with idyllic panoramas. Fort Oscar, at the tip of Gustavia Peninsula, houses the National Police.

Office du Tourisme: Quai du Général de Gaulle, BP 113, Gustavia, St. Barthélemy F.W.I.; phone (590) 27-87-27.

WALL HOUSE MUSEUM is on rue de Pitea. Dating from the Swedish period 1785-1878, this restored building houses a variety of exhibits pertaining to the island's history and culture. Traditional costumes, farming tools and old documents are of special interest. Allow 30 minutes minimum. Mon.-Tues. and Thurs.-Fri. 8:30-12:30 and 2:30-6, Wed. 8:30-12:30; Sat. 9-12:30, closed holidays. Admission $3. Phone (590) 29-71-55.

Lower Town, Oranjestad, St. Eustatius / © Helene Rogers / Alamy

St. Eustatius and Saba

Quiet and tiny, with an area of merely 11.8 square miles (31 sq km), St. Eustatius (also called Statia) consists of two dormant volcanoes linked by a central plain. While the northern volcano has been eroded to a cluster of hills, the southern one, known as the Quill, is perfectly formed and rises precipitously to nearly 2,000 feet (610 m). Home to some 58 species of birds and 18 species of orchids, the Quill derived its name from English settlers because they could not pronounce the Dutch word *Kuil*.

Climatic conditions vary strikingly for such a small island: The Atlantic side has strong winds and low vegetation; the Caribbean side is calm with tall coconut, almond, cotton and mango trees.

Even smaller is Saba (SAY-ba), only 5 square miles (13 sq km) and located just north of Statia. Saba is unusual among Caribbean islands—its steep volcanic cliffs rise straight out of the water, leaving no room for beaches. What it lacks in sand, the island makes up for in breathtaking views of the sea.

Along with St. Maarten, Statia and Saba form the Windward Islands of the Dutch Caribbean.

History

Christopher Columbus first sighted St. Eustatius on his second voyage in 1493. Never settled by Spain, the island was first colonized by France in 1629, then by Holland in 1636. St. Eustatius changed hands 22 times between the French and Dutch—and the English in 1665—before Dutch possession finally became permanent in 1816.

During its early years St. Eustatius developed into a prosperous center for the slave trade and mercantile exchange of the eastern Caribbean, earning the nickname "The Golden Rock." It also was a vital depot for supplies shipped from Europe to the American

Revolutionaries. In 1776 St. Eustatius became the first foreign government to officially recognize the United States by firing a salute from Fort Oranje to the American brig *Andrew Doria.* But the Dutch settlers' pro-American sympathies ultimately led to the sacking of St. Eustatius by George Bridges Rodney, a British admiral based in St. Lucia. Rodney arrived in St. Eustatius with a fleet of 15 ships and a crew of 3,000 men on Feb. 3, 1781, an event that marked the end of the tiny island's prosperity.

Shopping

Saba's local specialties are Saba lace, including handcrafted blouses, handkerchiefs and linens, and Saba Spice, an aromatic blend of 150 proof cask rum, brown sugar, fennel seed, cinnamon, nutmeg and cloves. The Windwardside is an ideal place to purchase these and one-of-a-kind handmade glass beads, jewelry, folk art and original paintings by local artisans and artists.

Food and Drink

Spiny lobster in garlic sauce, whelk stew, bread baked in stone ovens and various shrimp and goat dishes are popular on St. Eustatius. Local restaurants serve such specialties as tripe, bullfoot soup, conch soup and curried vegetables.

Fare on Saba includes gourmet seafood and duck dishes as well as Caribbean and Creole meals.

Sports and Amusements

Reef and wreck diving is popular in St. Eustatius. Several vendors offer PADI certification, dive packages and equipment rental, including Dive Statia, (599) 318-2435; Golden Rock Dive Center, (599) 318-2964; and Scubaqua, (599) 318-5450. In Saba, various dive

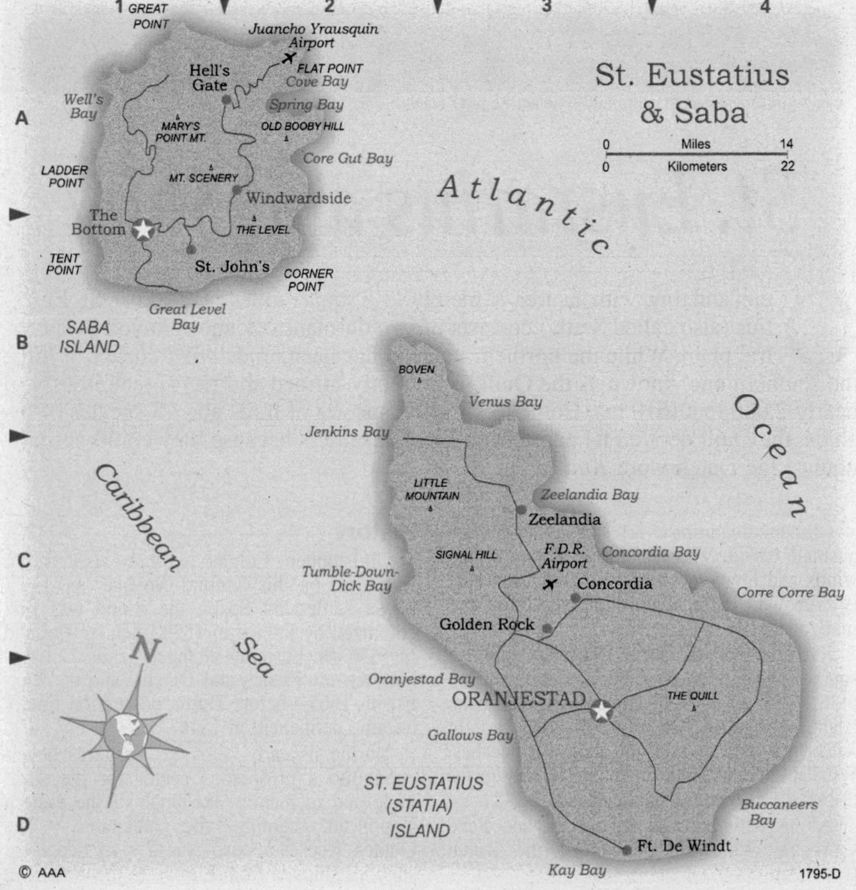

packages are offered by Saba Deep Dive Center, (599) 416-3347; Saba Divers, (599) 416-2740; and Sea Saba Dive Center, (599) 416-2246.

The St. Eustatius Marine Park offers more than 30 sites where divers can view pristine coral reefs, drop-offs, walls, pinnacles, canyons and historical wrecks with an abundance of fish, lobster and sea turtles. The park covers more than 10 square miles (27.5 sq km), encompassing the entire coast. Sites range from Gallows Bay to the White Wall area and from Jenkins Bay to North Point and Oranjebaai. No boat anchoring is permitted in the park. Fee $4 per dive, annual pass $20.

The Saba Marine Park, which encircles the entire island, has marked dive sites and snorkeling trails. Surrounded by waters with a visibility up to 200 feet (60 m), Saba is ideal for divers.

Sightseeing

Sightseeing is concentrated near Fort Oranje in Oranjestad, the capital of St. Eustatius. The fort was built in 1629 by the French and enlarged in 1636 by the Dutch to include bigger cannons from Amsterdam. Maps for walking tours past many 17th-, 18th- and 19th-century buildings are available at the St. Eustatius Historical Foundation Museum in Upper Town. Three Widows' Corner near the fort features an 18th-century townhouse and a 19th-century Victorian home in a charming tropical courtyard.

In addition to a few shops and inns, the town also contains the historic Government's Guest House, where government is headquartered; the Dutch Reformed Church, a 1755 structure with a 75-foot tower; the ruins of the 1739 Honen Dalim Synagogue, one of the oldest Jewish synagogues in the Western Hemisphere; and a library. The St. Eustatius Historical Foundation Museum contains exhibits about the pre-Columbian and Colonial periods.

Fort de Windt, built in the mid-18th century presumably under the command of Jan de Windt, lies at the southern tip of the island, offering breathtaking views of St. Kitts. Fort de Windt and Fort Oranje are the only two forts that are restored out of 19 surrounding the island. On the island's northeastern side is Lynch Plantation Museum, which features an impressive collection of domestic artifacts and antiques.

The tourist office has information about tours, history, cruises, swimming, kayaking, snorkeling and scuba diving. Guides lead hikes to the top of The Quill, an extinct volcano whose cone rises 2,000 feet (610 m); the crater contains a lush tropical rain forest. Near the Quill is the Miriam C. Schmidt Botanical Garden, which includes floral collections, walking paths and a variety of uncommon plants and tea bush along with a breathtaking view of St. Kitts, St. Barths and St. Maarten.

Day trips from St. Eustatius to Saba are possible. The smallest of the Netherlands Antilles and possibly the only island in the Caribbean without a beach, Saba is a tiny volcanic island draped with lush vegetation. The rocky shoreline of the island contains tidepools home to numerous sealife.

A rain forest exists some 3,000 feet (915 m) above sea level; a constant cloud of moisture surrounds the area. Various trails lead hikers into the rain forest where 15 species of wild orchids live along with such other tropical foliage as ferns, giant elephant ears and banana and mango trees. Here 1,064 steps chiseled from vertical rock connect the village of Windwardside with The Bottom, the island's capital. These steps were the island's only thoroughfare until a twisting road was built by hand in the 1940s. At 1,900 feet (580 m), Windwardside offers a superb view of the Caribbean. Trail maps and information can be obtained from The Trail Shop, Windwardside, Saba.

The Saba Museum is housed in an 1840s sea captain's cottage; contact the tourist bureau for more information. Descend by jeep to The Bottom, 1,000 feet (305 m) below, and head for the Saba Artisans' Foundation for locally designed fashions.

Transportation

St. Eustatius' Franklin Delano Roosevelt Airport has daily flights to St. Maarten via Windward Islands Airways (WinAir) as well as flights to Saba's Juancho E. Yrausquin Airport and St. Kitts. Windjammer cruises call here twice monthly. Car rental information can be obtained at the airport information desk.

Fast Facts

POPULATION: St. Eustatius: 3,183. Saba: 1,500.

AREA: St. Eustatius: 31 sq km (11.8 sq mi.). **Saba:** 13 sq km (5 sq mi.).

CAPITAL: St. Eustatius: Oranjestad. **Saba:** The Bottom.

HIGHEST POINT: 862 m (2,828 ft.), Mount Scenery, Saba.

LOWEST POINT: Sea level, Caribbean Sea.

TIME ZONE(S): Atlantic Standard.

LANGUAGE: Dutch, English, Spanish and Papiamentu.

GOVERNMENT: Netherlands Antilles, autonomous within the Kingdom of the Netherlands.

UNIT OF CURRENCY: Netherlands Antillean guilder, divided into 100 cents. $1 U.S. = 1.8 guilders.

ELECTRICITY: 110 volts, 60 cycles AC.

MINIMUM AGE FOR DRIVERS: 18; a valid license is required; drive on right.

SEAT BELT/CHILD RESTRAINT LAWS: Seat belts are required for all passengers. Child restraints required for under age 4; children under 12 must ride in the back seat.

HELMETS FOR MOTORCYCLISTS: Required.

HOLIDAYS: Jan. 1; Good Friday; Easter Monday; Queen's Birthday, Apr. 30; Labour Day, May 1; Ascension Day, May (6th Thurs. after Easter); Carnival Monday, July; Antillean Day, Oct. 21; Statia/America Day, Nov. 16; Christmas, Dec. 25; Boxing Day, Dec. 26.

TAXES: A 7 percent room tax and 10-15 percent service charge are added to most hotel bills. In lieu of a gratuity, restaurants may add a 15 service charge on food and beverage items. Departure tax $12 U.S.; Dutch interisland tax $5.65.

IMMIGRATION REQUIREMENTS: Passport or proof of U.S. citizenship and a return or onward ticket are required. No visa needed for stays up to 2 weeks. The U.S. Dept. of Homeland Security requires all U.S. citizens returning from the Caribbean to present a valid passport.

PHONING THE ISLANDS: To call St. Eustatius and Saba from the U.S. or Canada, dial 011 + 599 + the 7-digit local number.

FURTHER INFORMATION FOR VISITORS:

St. Eustatius Tourist Office
Fort Oranje
Oranjestad, St. Eustatius
Netherlands Antilles
(599) 318-2433

Saba Tourist Bureau
P.O. Box 527
Windwardside, Saba
Netherlands Antilles
(599) 416-2231
(599) 416-2322

Points of Interest

See map page 212.

St. Eustatius

Discovered in 1493, the diminutive island known as Statia changed hands at least 22 times before the Dutch took possession in 1636. St. Eustatius was a major arms supplier to the American colonies during the Revolutionary War.

ORANJESTAD (D-3)

The capital city of Oranjestad was considered the first foreign port to acknowledge the sovereignty of the United States. On Nov. 16, 1776, an American ship flying the stars and stripes entered Statia's harbor and fired a salute; the guns at Fort Oranje returned the greeting. A plaque presented by Pres. Franklin D. Roosevelt in 1939 commemorates the event.

Oranjestad is divided by coastal cliffs into two sections. Traditionally, Lower Town was the base for mercantile operations, while residents built their homes in Upper Town.

St. Eustatius Tourist Office: Fort Oranje, Oranjestad, St. Eustatius, Netherlands Antilles; phone (599) 318-2433.

ST. EUSTATIUS HISTORICAL FOUNDATION MUSEUM is across from Fort Oranje at Wilhelminaweg #3 in Upper Town. The museum chronicles the island's pre-Columbian and colonial history. Special exhibits depict sugar production, shipping and commerce. Built by prominent merchant Simon Doncker, the house served as headquarters for Admiral George Rodney after he invaded the island in 1781. Allow 30 minutes minimum. Mon.-Thurs. 9-5, Fri. 9-3:30, Sat.-Sun. 9-noon. Admission $3; $1 (ages 3-18). Phone (599) 318-2288.

Botanical Garden of Nevis, Charlestown / © Donatella Marmaggi / age fotostock

St. Kitts and Nevis

Separated by a mere 2 miles (3.2 km), St. Kitts and Nevis (NEE-vis) constitute one of the world's tiniest nations. Their beauty and charm, however, are not proportional to their size. Dominated by 3,792-foot (1,156-m) Mount Liamuiga, mountainous St. Kitts contains some of the islands' finest beaches. Nevis embraces a single peak rising from the sea to a cloud-shrouded height of 3,232 feet (985 m). Beaches of coral sand are found along its shores. Missing from St. Kitts and Nevis is the profusion of towering resorts found on many of the bigger, more developed islands, as by law no building can be taller than the palm trees. Its visitors can still enjoy the rustic atmosphere and slow-paced "island time" that some say makes for real relaxation.

History

When Christopher Columbus discovered the two sister islands in 1493, the cloud-encircled volcanic peak of the smaller island inspired him to call it *Las Nieves,* meaning "the snows." Over the years the island's name has evolved into simply Nevis. The larger island is said to be named St. Christopher after the explorer, but the British adopted the diminution St. Kitts after Sir Thomas Warner established a settlement, the first English colony in the West Indies, at Old Road Town in 1623. The next year the French also established a colony, and the Anglo-French rivalry for control of the islands was to last for the next 160 years.

After changing hands several times, the islands fell under British rule in 1783 through the Treaty of Versailles. Evidence of their turbulent history remains in the battlegrounds and ruined forts on St. Kitts. Today inhabitants pursue the more peaceful activities of accommodating tourists and growing the island's agriculture and other industries.

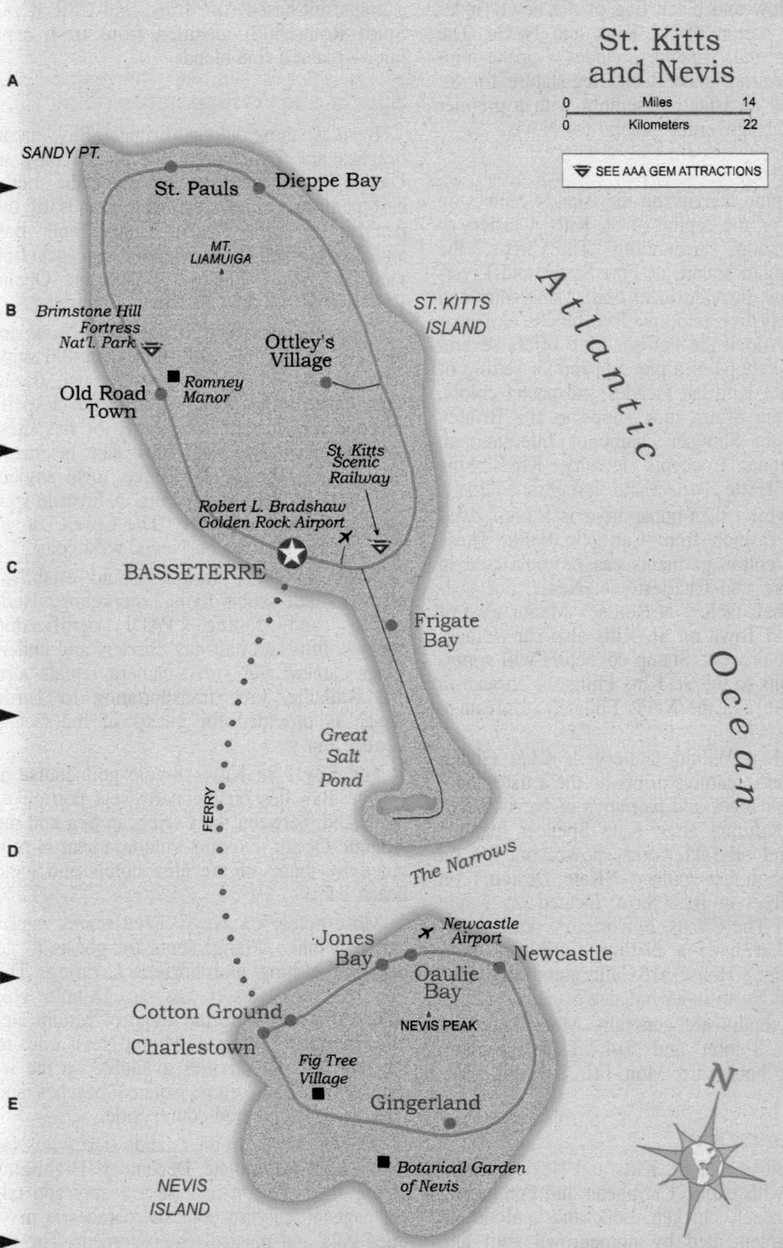

St. Kitts and Nevis
0 Miles 14
0 Kilometers 22
SEE AAA GEM ATTRACTIONS
1
2
3
4
A
B
C
D
E
F
SANDY PT.
St. Pauls
Dieppe Bay
MT. LIAMUIGA
Brimstone Hill Fortress Nat'l. Park
ST. KITTS ISLAND
Atlantic
Ottley's Village
Romney Manor
Old Road Town
St. Kitts Scenic Railway
Robert L. Bradshaw Golden Rock Airport
BASSETERRE
Frigate Bay
Ocean
Great Salt Pond
FERRY
The Narrows
Newcastle Airport
Jones Bay
Newcastle
Oaulie Bay
Cotton Ground
NEVIS PEAK
Charlestown
Fig Tree Village
Gingerland
N
Botanical Garden of Nevis
NEVIS ISLAND
© AAA
1792-D

The two islands became an Associated British State in 1967. On Sept. 19, 1983, the British Union Jack was replaced by the green, red, yellow and black flag of the newly independent nation of St. Kitts and Nevis. The governmental structure includes a prime minister, governor-general and legislature for St. Kitts and an Island Assembly with a premier and deputy governor-general for Nevis.

Shopping

Shopping activity on the islands centers on Basseterre, the capital of St. Kitts. Clusters of modern shops surrounding "The Circus," the town's main square at Fort Street and Liverpool Row, provide local crafts, souvenirs and some duty-free imports. Two blocks east near the ferry dock the Pelican Mall offers several duty-free shops in a pleasant indoor setting of traditional Kittitian facades and pastel colors. Port Zante offers such shops as the Brinley Gold Rum Shoppe, Diamonds International, International Concepts Jewelry, Kay's Fine Jewelry, Little Switzerland and Piranha Joe's.

A favorite take-home item is a hand-dyed tropical fashion from Caribelle Batik. These colorful cotton garments can be purchased in Basseterre and Charlestown, Nevis, but visitors to their factory at Romney Manor west of Old Road Town on St. Kitts also can witness the batik process. Stamp collectors will appreciate visits to the St. Kitts Philatelic Bureau in Basseterre and the Nevis Philatelic Bureau in Charlestown.

The Eva Wilkin Gallery at Clay Ghaut, Gingerland, features prints by the artist known for her sketches and paintings of Nevis. Well-known Kittitian artist Kate Spencer features prints and original works showcasing life on St. Kitts in her gallery, "Kate Design," on Bank Street in Basseterre, located on a side street off The Circus. For original pottery creations that have a distinct Caribbean flair, visit Potter's House Art Gallery and Studio on St. Kitts' North Independence Square.

Store hours are generally Mon.-Wed. and Fri.-Sat. 8-noon and 1-4, Thurs. 8-noon. Banking hours are Mon.-Fri. 8-3 (also Fri. 3-5).

Food and Drink

The cuisine of St. Kitts and Nevis is highlighted with exotic Caribbean and continental flavors. Beef, chicken, pork and seafood all are complemented by homegrown fruit and vegetables. Such favorite native dishes as Creole red bean soup, conch chowder, goat water (a soup) and boiled saltfish stew are served in several local restaurants. Conch fritters and saltfish balls make good appetizers.

St. Kitts' own Carib Beer or Brinley Gold Rum are good complements to a hearty West Indian meal. Two other local products—Ting, a grapefruit-based soft drink, and CSR (Cane Spirit Rothschild), distilled from fresh cane juice—make a fine blend.

Sports and Amusements

Besides those along Frigate Bay, good beaches are found along the south coast, at Dieppe Bay in the north and along the southeast peninsula. From the white sands of the peninsula's Turtle Beach, Sandy Bank Bay and Cockleshell Bay, visitors can get fine views of Nevis. Pinney's Beach and Oualie Beach on Nevis offer excellent swimming.

The waters between St. Kitts and Nevis are the final resting place for more than 400 ships sunk 1492-1825, yet only some one dozen sites have been identified thus far. Experienced divers can explore many of the sites. Arrangements for dive trips can be made through most hotels. For a fee, local anglers will take you deep-sea fishing. A favorite spot for experienced divers is "The Caves," a series of coral grottoes on Nevis' west coast.

Water sports at various island establishments include scuba diving, snorkeling, windsurfing and sailing. PADI certification courses, full- and half-day charters and underwater camera and video camera rentals also are available. Free transportation to Turtle Beach is provided for guests of the Ocean Terrace Inn.

The Royal St. Kitts 18-hole golf course at Frigate Bay lies on the narrowest portion of the island, between the Caribbean Sea and the Atlantic Ocean. Evening entertainment is provided by many of the area hotels and local beach bars.

Most hotels on Nevis have tennis courts and will make arrangements for guests to go deep-sea fishing and horseback riding. The Four Seasons Resort has an 18-hole golf course that winds up the slope of Mount Nevis. Hiking to the top of Mount Nevis adds to the recreational activities available on the island. Nevis also offers isolated beaches and unspoiled, uncluttered countryside.

Special events on the islands start with National Carnival in late December. Highlights of the 10-day event include a beauty and talent pageant, calypso contests, parades, a masqued gala and musical entertainment. The St. Kitts and Nevis Triathlon, in mid-May, starts with a 2.5-mile (4-km) ocean swim from Nevis to St. Kitts and is followed by a 45-mile (72 km) mountain bicycle race and a 14-mile (23-km) run. The St. Kitts Music Festival is held in June and features an eclectic mix of local and international artists.

Sightseeing

Excursions on St. Kitts can be breathtaking—both aesthetically and physically. Climbing Mount Liamuiga (lee-a-MWEE-ga) is an all-day affair; the crater, 1,192 feet (363 m) below the peak, is the usual stopping point. Hikers can explore the tropical rain forest, which abounds with monkeys, birds, butterflies, fruits and flowers, while enjoying a coastal view of the sea. The monkeys, left behind by the French who kept them as pets, now outnumber the human population by a ratio of approximately 2.5-to-1.

Other sites worth investigating are Brimstone Hill Fortress, a UNESCO World Heritage site, positioned approximately 800 feet (244 m) atop a rock cliff; the Carib Indian petroglyphs at Old Road; Bloody Point near Challengers village, the site of a Carib Indian massacre in 1626; and Caribelle Batik, housed at Romney Manor, a 17th-century great house set above Old Road Town. In a churchyard at Middle Island is the tomb of Sir Thomas Warner, the British founder of St. Kitts.

Eco-Tours Nevis offers various walking tours, including a stroll through Historic Charlestown, a walk through the uninhabited east coast to the 18th-century New River and Coconut Walk Estates and a visit to Montravers House, a former sugar plantation; phone (869) 469-2091 for information and reservations.

Fun-loving seafarers will enjoy an all-day cruise aboard the catamaran *Spirit of St. Kitts.* The day includes a beach barbecue and snorkeling. For information and reservations phone (869) 465-7474.

St. Kitts' scenic southeast peninsula is accessible via the Dr. Kennedy A. Simmonds Highway, a modern roadway completed in 1990. The 6-mile (10-km) highway leads from Frigate Bay east of Basseterre to Major's Bay, just 2 miles (3.2 km) from Nevis. The peninsula's mountainous terrain affords spectacular views of the sea and offshore islands.

Transportation

Non-stop service to St. Kitts' Robert L. Bradshaw International Airport is available from Charlotte aboard U.S. Airways. American Airlines offers direct flights from Miami and New York's JFK International Airport. Delta Airlines offers direct flights from Atlanta. American Eagle, Windward Island Airways (WinAir) and LIAT provide flights and connections from Antigua, San Juan and St. Maarten. Port Zante in St. Kitts is a leading port of call for cruise ships.

Taxis are readily available. An approximate fare from Robert L. Bradshaw International Airport to Basseterre is $8. A taxi tour around St. Kitts takes about 4 hours. Minimokes are also a fun way to get around. Car rentals also are available. A local driver's license is required to drive on the islands and can be obtained for about $20 at the Police Traffic Department in Basseterre.

Nevis is accessible from St. Kitts via a brief flight to Vance W. Amory International Airport or regular ferry trips aboard the *Caribe Queen* and MV *Sea Hustler.*

Fast Facts

POPULATION: 38,756.

AREA: St. Kitts: 176 sq km (68 sq mi.). **Nevis:** 93 sq km (36 sq mi.).

CAPITAL: St. Kitts: Basseterre. **Nevis:** Charlestown.

HIGHEST POINT: 1,156 m (3,792 ft.), Mount Liamuiga, St. Kitts.

LOWEST POINT: Sea level, Caribbean Sea.

TIME ZONE(S): Atlantic Standard.

LANGUAGE: English.

GOVERNMENT: Independent. Member of the British Commonwealth of Nations.

UNIT OF CURRENCY: Eastern Caribbean (E.C.) dollar. $1 U.S. = 2.7 E.C. dollars.

ELECTRICITY: 230 volts, 60 cycles AC.

MINIMUM AGE FOR DRIVERS: 21-25, depending on the rental car agency. Local license ($25) required; drive on left.

MINIMUM AGE FOR GAMBLING: 21.

HOLIDAYS: Jan. 1; Carnival, Jan. 2; Good Friday; Easter Monday; Labour Day, May (1st Mon.); Whit Monday, May or June (8th Mon. after Easter); Queen's Birthday, June (2nd Sat.); August Monday, Aug. (1st Mon.); Culturama Last Lap, Aug. (1st Tues.); National Heroes Day, Sept. 16; Independence Day, Sept. 19; Christmas, Dec. 25; Boxing Day, Dec. 26.

TAXES: A 7 percent room tax and 10-15 percent service charge are added to most hotel bills. Departure tax $19 U.S.; a tourism enhancement tax of $1.50 also is charged.

IMMIGRATION REQUIREMENTS: Passport or proof of U.S. citizenship and a return or onward ticket are required. No visa needed for stays up to 1 month. The U.S. Dept. of Homeland Security requires all U.S. citizens returning from the Caribbean to present a valid passport.

PHONING THE ISLANDS: To call St. Kitts and Nevis from the U.S. or Canada, dial 1 + 869 + the 7-digit local number.

FURTHER INFORMATION FOR VISITORS:

St. Kitts Tourism Authority New York
414 E. 75th St., Suite 5
New York, NY 10021
(212) 535-1234
(800) 582-6208

St. Kitts Tourism Office, Basseterre
Pelican Mall, Bay Road
P.O. Box 132
Basseterre, St. Kitts
St. Kitts and Nevis
(869) 465-4040

Nevis Tourism Authority
Main Street
Charlestown, Nevis
St. Kitts and Nevis
(869) 469-7550

Points of Interest

See map page 217.

Nevis

Nevis is a volcanic island surrounded by coral reefs. Forested slopes rise from palm-lined beaches to the island's cloud-shrouded summit. Relatively untouched by tourism, Nevis attracts those in search of a quiet escape. Except for the Four Seasons Resort, lodging consists mostly of small family-run businesses—guest cottages, hotels and a few sugar plantations converted to inns, many of which are nestled among the foothills of Nevis Peak.

As on many of the Caribbean isles, the use of slave labor at sugar plantations on Nevis created a wealthy upper class. During the 19th century the islands, including Nevis, quickly became the haunt of the elite of British society, who frequented the island's mineral baths and hot springs at the Bath Hotel, considered one of the most ambitious structures built in the West Indies in 1778.

Jamestown, the former capital that fell prey to an earthquake and tidal wave in 1680, is accessible by the main road that circles Nevis. Snorkelers and scuba divers frequent the area.

Among the historic figures associated with Nevis is Alexander Hamilton, the American author and statesman, who was born here in 1757. When he was a captain, Horatio Nelson courted and married Fanny Nisbet in Nevis. Montpelier Plantation was the site of their 1787 marriage, in which the future King William IV of England acted as best man. Their vows were recorded at St. John's Church in Fig Tree Village.

CHARLESTOWN (E-1) pop. 1,820

During the Spanish Inquisition many Jews fled South America to the Caribbean to escape persecution. The Jewish community on Nevis can be traced to the early 17th century with a tombstone in the Nevis Jewish Cemetery dated 1658. Visitors to Charlestown can view the Nevis Synagogue archeological dig taking place at an old stone building in partial ruin. The site, adjacent to the government administration building, is believed to be one of the Caribbean's oldest synagogues.

BOTANICAL GARDEN OF NEVIS is 3 mi. (5 km) s. at the Montpelier Estate in Gingerland. Orchids, bromeliads, rare palms, flowering vines and fruit trees are among the hundreds of species at this 7-acre (3-hectare) tropical hillside haven, which features fountains, waterfalls, lily pools and a rain forest conservatory. The estate offers striking views of Nevis. Food is available seasonally. Allow 2 hours minimum. Mon.-Sat. 9-4, Jan.-Mar.; Mon.-Fri. 9-4, Apr.-mid-Oct. Closed holidays. Admission $9. AX, MC, VI. Phone (869) 469-3509 or (869) 469-3399.

THE HORATIO NELSON MUSEUM is .5 mi. (.8 km) s. behind the Bath Hotel. A large collection of memorabilia associated with Adm. Horatio Nelson, a frequent visitor to Nevis, includes glassware, ceramics, paintings, prints and ship models. Permanent and changing exhibits chronicle the history of Nevis and its people. Allow 30 minutes minimum. Mon.-Fri. 9-4, Sat. 9-noon; closed holidays. Admission $5; $2 (ages 0-11). MC, VI. Phone (869) 469-0408.

MUSEUM OF NEVIS HISTORY AT THE BIRTHPLACE OF ALEXANDER HAMILTON is .2 mi. (.3 km) n. on Low St. Housed in a reconstruction of Alexander Hamilton's birthplace, the museum features a series of small exhibits related to both Hamilton and the history of Nevis. Of interest is a bronze plaque commemorating the visit made by a group of 144 Englishmen in 1607 who landed on the island, spent 6 days and went on to found Jamestown, Virginia, the first permanent English settlement. Mon.-Fri. 9-4, Sat. 9-noon; closed holidays. Admission $5; $2 (ages 0-11). MC, VI. Phone (869) 469-5786.

St. Kitts

While it retains its charm as an off-the-beaten-track destination, St. Kitts is welcoming an ever-increasing number of tourists. Accommodations on the island range from grand beach-front resorts to intimate plantation inns, and activities range from sightseeing and shopping to deep-sea fishing and water sports. Beaches are quiet and secluded, with sands of volcanic black, gold or powder white.

BASSETERRE (C-1) pop. 13,220

Bordering a harbor on the island's southern end, Basseterre (boss-tare) is the principal city and capital of St. Kitts. The town has preserved many early examples of West Indian and Georgian architecture; a good example of the former is the Treasury building on the waterfront. But the architectural legacy of British colonialism can best be seen in Independence Square, originally the slave market. This park of manicured lawns and shade trees includes the Catholic church and several 18th-century homes. Another landmark is the ornate Victorian clock in "The "Circus," a roundabout in the town's main square that was modeled after Piccadilly Circus in London.

St. Kitts Tourism Authority Office: Pelican Mall, Bay Road, Basseterre, St. Kitts, W.I.; phone (869) 465-4040.

GREG'S SAFARIS offers Land Rover tours with pickup service from local hotels, the airport and cruise-ship dock. The half-day Plantation Tour takes in some of the island's sugar plantations. The half-day Rainforest Tour features a nature walk through a lush rain forest. The physically challenging full-day Volcano Tour involves a 1,600-foot (488-m) hike to the rim of Mount Liamuiga; lunch is included. Tours are available daily. Half-day tours $60. Full-day tours $90. Phone (869) 465-4121 or (869) 663-6008.

ST. KITTS SCENIC RAILWAY departs from Needsmust Station on Bay Rd., just e. of the airport. The narrow gauge railway, once used to transport sugar cane, has been converted for double-deck sightseeing cars. Given seats on both levels, passengers are free to move between the lower air-conditioned compartment and the open-air upper deck. Each trip includes colorful narration, live musical entertainment and complimentary refreshments.

The 3-hour, 30-minute scenic rail tour makes a complete circuit around the island, providing views of old sugar estates, villages and farms, cane fields, rain forests and the volcanic cone of Mt. Liamuiga. Historic sites include St. Paul, home of the prime minister; Old Road Town, where Thomas Jefferson's great grandfather is buried; and Brimstone Hill Fortress *(see place listing)*.

Trains depart Mon. at 1 and Wed. at 9:30, June-Sept.; based upon cruise ship arrivals rest of year. Scenic tour $89; $44.50 (ages 3-11). AX, DS, MC, VI. Phone (869) 465-7263.

GAMBLING ESTABLISHMENTS

- **Royal Beach Casino at St. Kitts Marriott Resort** is at 858 Frigate Bay Rd. Phone (869) 466-1200.

BRIMSTONE HILL FORTRESS NATIONAL PARK (B-1)

Nine miles (14 km) west of Basseterre, this massive British fortress on a hill 800 feet (244 m) above the sea was built by slaves over a 100-year period beginning in the late 1600s. Once known as "The Gibraltar of the West Indies," Brimstone Hill was so intimidating that ship captains often changed course rather than come within range of its powerful guns. The British believed the fort to be impregnable, but the French proved them quite wrong in 1782. Despite the French victory, the British regained the fort a year later through the Treaty of Versailles.

Today visitors can explore the fortress, look out over the now dormant cannons and enjoy the panoramic view that inspired Her Majesty, Queen Elizabeth II, to declare Brimstone Hill a national monument. The UNESCO World Heritage Site covers 38 acres (15 hectares). A visitor center in the Commissariat features a 10-minute film orientation and audio tours for rental; all presentations are available in four languages. At the citadel museum, artifacts, paintings and exhibits chronicle the history of the fortress and the struggle between the British and French for control of the islands during the 1700s.

Food is available. Allow 1 hour minimum. Daily 9:30-5:30; closed Good Friday and Dec. 25. Last admission 30 minutes before closing. Admission $8, children $4. Audio tour rental $5. Phone (869) 465-2609 or (869) 465-6771.

OLD ROAD TOWN (B-1)

Founded in 1623 by Sir Thomas Warner, Old Road Town was the first permanent English colony in the West Indies. English and French troops banded together in 1626 to attack the native Carib Indians at a spot known as Bloody Point. Here, some 2,000 Caribs were massacred. Near Romney Manor is a cluster of large boulders carved with petroglyphs, bearing mute witness to the island's original inhabitants.

ROMNEY MANOR is on Old Road. On the grounds of this 17th-century plantation are gardens, sugar mill ruins and a 350-year-old saman tree. The original estate, Wingfield, is said to have belonged to an ancestor of Thomas Jefferson. The Earls of Romney owned the property 1713-1819. Wild tobacco grows in the ruins, though the plant hasn't been cultivated in 400 years. At Caribelle Batik, visitors can watch the production of wax-dyed cotton fabric. Allow 30 minutes minimum. Mon.-Fri. 8:30-4; closed holidays. Free. Phone (869) 465-6253.

Marigot Bay, south of Castries / © SIME s.a.s. / eStock Photo

St. Lucia

Lush greenery, endless banana plantations, wooded mountains and fertile valleys are just some of the elements that harmonize to make St. Lucia (LOO-sha) "the Helen of the West Indies." This tropical paradise, which is 27 miles (43 km) long and 14 miles (23 km) wide, contains 19,000 acres (7,689 hectares) of rain forest. Quaint fishing villages and enticing beaches provide a backdrop that complements the diverse landscape of the interior. Gros and Petit Pitons, regal twin peaks separated by a picturesque bay, are prominent landmarks.

History

The first settlers were the peace-loving Arawak Indians, who probably came to St. Lucia to escape the warlike Caribs. However, the Arawaks did not endure—the Caribs eventually followed and succeeded in driving them off the island by A.D. 800.

Although it has not been established whether Christopher Columbus or Juan de la Cosa discovered St. Lucia, the first European to settle on the island was pirate François de Clerc. In 1550, de Clerc attacked passing Spanish ships from his base on Pigeon Island.

The English attempted to settle the island in 1605 and 1639, but the fierce Caribs thwarted their efforts on both occasions. In 1650 the French finally established the first permanent settlement; a treaty with the Caribs was signed in 1660. About this time, a bitter dispute originated in which each country claimed ownership of the territory.

A 150-year-long struggle for control ensued, as St. Lucia changed hands between the feuding French and British 14 times. The island was ultimately ceded to the British in 1814 and became one of the Windward Islands in 1838.

Sugar plantations flourished from the mid-1700s to the mid-1800s. With African slaves providing free labor, the industry thrived.

Once slavery was abolished in 1834, a labor shortage ensued that contributed to the industry's decline. Such epidemics as smallpox and cholera also impeded prosperity during the remainder of the 19th century. The economy improved in the early 20th century, as a greater emphasis was placed on the cultivation of bananas and cocoa. Although the sugar industry briefly resurged, production eventually ceased in the 1960s.

As a provision of the West Indies Act of 1967, St. Lucia became entirely self-governing in internal affairs. The United Kingdom retained authority in regard to defense and external matters. On Feb. 22, 1979, the island obtained full independence. That same year, St. Lucia became a member of the British Commonwealth of Nations.

The country remains a stable parliamentary democracy, with a governor-general designated by Queen Elizabeth II. Agriculture and tourism are economic mainstays, accounting for about 80 percent of total economic revenue.

Shopping

Local goods available on St. Lucia include batik fabrics, perfumes, straw works, unglazed pottery, and handicrafts produced from wood and shell. The island is particularly known for its cane furniture and batik designs. These items can be found in duty-free shopping complexes at La Place Carenage in Castries and at Pointe Seraphine on the north side of the bay on Vigie Peninsula; both places are expanding to meet cruise ship demand.

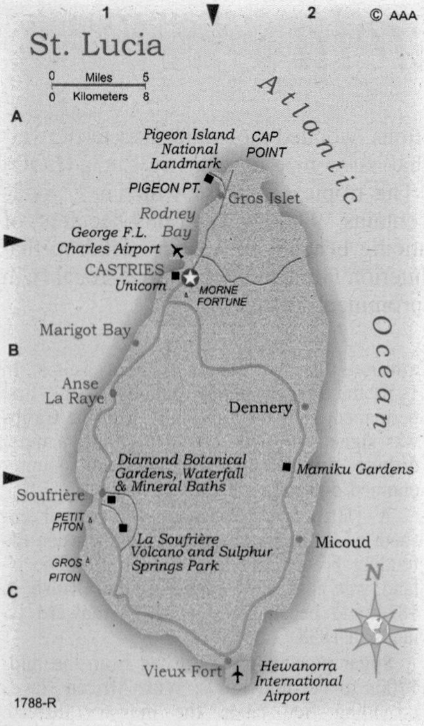

Gemstone jewelry; fine china, crystal, figurines, perfume, international apparel and colorful silk-screened clothing are among choice buys. Local straw work is sold at two large open-air markets, the Vendor's Arcade and the Castries Market. For a dollar fare, water taxis provide transportation across the bay.

Several shops and restaurants can be found at the Rodney Bay Marina, near Gros Islet at the north end of the island. While browsing in boutiques offering beachwear, local crafts, electronics and island souvenirs, visitors can enjoy splendid views of the bay and of gleaming yachts docked in the marina.

Downtown Castries also provides shopping opportunities such as those at the Castries Market Arcade. William Peter Boulevard, lined with department stores, souvenir shops and banks, is the city's center of shopping activity. A multitude of street vendors make their home on the boulevard as well as on many other streets in the downtown area. Gablewoods is a small shopping complex just north of Castries off the Castries-Gros Islet Highway.

Eudovic Art Studio is about 15 minutes south of Castries off the road that snakes up the slopes of Morne Fortune. Woodcarvings fashioned from mahogany, teak and cedar are exhibited in a small gallery; works available for purchase at the adjacent shop include whisk-broom dolls in traditional madras costumes.

Also on Morne Fortune is Caribelle Batik, situated in Hewelton House on Old Victoria Road. Clothing enhanced by unique colors and patterns is available for purchase, and the dye-resistant method incorporated by the batik process is demonstrated by workers as they create freehand designs. On the terrace at the rear of the facility, shoppers can sip a refreshing drink and relish the view of Castries.

Another Morne Fortune landmark is Bagshaw Studios, which features clothing, place mats, tablecloths, wall hangings and other fabrics hand painted with cheery island motifs. Workers create brightly colored designs from a stenciled pattern during the silk-screening process, which can be observed in the print shop. Caribbean Perfumes, also on the Morne, creates exotic fragrances from herbs and tropical flowers found throughout St. Lucia.

Choiseul, a small coastal village in the southwest portion of the island, is the site of the Choiseul Art and Craft Center. Artists produce traditional Carib Indian crafts, including clay pottery and handwoven baskets constructed from straw and wicker.

In addition, St. Lucia's major resorts usually have shops on the premises. Shopping hours throughout the island are generally Mon.-Fri. 8:30-12:30 and 1:30-4:30, Sat. 8:30-12:30. Shopping malls are usually open until 6.

Food and Drink

Restaurants on St. Lucia are concentrated in Castries and Gros Islet. Many specialize in Creole cuisine, while others offer Italian, Chinese and Continental food. The national dish is "green fig," boiled green bananas usually served with saltfish. Other local specialties include lobster, snapper, dolphin, kingfish, swordfish, *callaloo* soup, breadfruit, plantain and pumpkin soufflé. Hearty pepperpot stew and spicy curries also are popular.

Fresh juices—including tamarind, guava, passion fruit, mango and grapefruit—accompany most meals. Bounty Rum is distilled near Roseau in the Cul-de-Sac Valley. The local Piton beer is often mixed with fruit juice for a lighter taste. Restaurants providing native fare include The Still, an establishment in Soufrière that was once a rum distillery, and the Green Parrot, which presents Creole delights in a scenic setting at the top of Morne Fortune.

Sports and Amusements

Aquatic pastimes—water skiing, snorkeling and boating among them—are popular recreational pursuits on St. Lucia. Conditions for windsurfing are good at Reduit Beach on the northwest coast and at Vieux Fort at the island's southern tip; The Rex St. Lucian and The Royal St. Lucian hotels on Reduit Beach rent equipment to the public. The Rex St. Lucian also offers parasailing.

Day or sunset cruises operate out of Castries Harbour; longer excursions to Martinique or south to St. Vincent and the Grenadines also are available. Sailing enthusiasts can charter boats with or without a crew at Marigot Bay, Rodney Bay Marina and Vigie Marina. Deep-sea fishing charters are provided by Mako Watersports, (758) 452-0412, and Captain Mike's, (758) 452-7044. The main catches are barracuda, blue marlin, kingfish, tuna, swordfish and wahoo.

Because of St. Lucia's volcanic origins, black sand is found on many beaches. All of St. Lucia's beaches, even those fronted by resorts, are open to the public. The most popular are on the north and west coasts; waves are very powerful on the Atlantic side, where only the strongest swimmers should venture. Anse Chastanet, just north of Soufrière, is named for the hotel that graces its shores. The beach area, accented by a hilly panorama, is flanked by a restaurant and dive shop. Water taxis provide transportation to Anse Chastanet and the hideaway beach of Anse Mamim; be sure to reserve a ride for the return trip.

Farther north, the quaint fishing village of Anse la Raye boasts a picturesque beach with a wealth of graceful palms. South of Castries, Marigot Bay is a charming tropical cove peppered with colorful yachts. Visitors can just relax and sip a refreshing drink in the shade, or take a swim in the cove's tranquil waters where the original "Dr. Doolittle" was filmed. Yachts anchor offshore at the little beach at Soufrière, which is perfect for sunning and a leisurely lunch.

Although the beige-sand beach at La Toc Bay, south of Castries, is a great place to soak up the sun and enjoy the view, swimming is not advised due to occasional strong currents. Choc Bay, north of Castries in the vicinity of several major resorts, has calm waters ideal for swimming. Windsurfing is popular at Vieux Fort in the south and Cas-en-Bas in the north; beginners prefer the calmer waters of the resort area of Reduit Beach, where a variety of watersports rental equipment is available.

Sun worshipers will revel in the fine selection of secluded white-sand beaches at Pigeon Point; the area is connected to the island by a man-made causeway. Conditions are excellent for swimming, and a nearby restaurant provides refreshment. At the extreme southern tip of the island, Vieux Fort consists of miles of white-sand beaches against a backdrop of coconut palms. From this expanse of land, the contrast between the deep blue Caribbean waters and the murky hues of the Atlantic is apparent. The island also possesses several isolated stretches of beach accessible only by boat.

Scuba St. Lucia offers diving courses geared toward certification as well as daytime and evening diving expeditions; locations include the Anse Chastanet Hotel in Soufrière, (758) 459-7755, and the St. Lucian Hotel in Rodney Bay, (758) 452-8009. Also at Rodney Bay is Buddies Scuba, (758) 450-8406. Dive Fair Helen, (758) 451-7716, operates in Marigot at the Wyndham Morgan Bay Resort. Marigot Beach Club & Dive Resort, (758) 451-4974 offers PADI training facilities with dives at several sites around St Lucia.

Divers can experience a spectacular sampling of steep underwater drop-offs and unspoiled marine life. The waters off the west coast provide the best opportunities for diving, with most of the sites concentrated between Marigot Bay and Choiseul. *Lesleen M.*, a 165-foot vessel south of Marigot Bay that was deliberately sunk in the 1980s, has several compartments that can be explored. For the less adventurous, *Volga* is an easy 20-foot wreck dive near Castries.

Anse Chastanet Reef contains a colorful display of coral and a 150-foot-deep wall; this reef also is home to a large school of squid. Keyhole Pinnacles is another popular dive site just south of Anse Chastanet. Piton Wall, a site that features a vibrant assortment of coral and sponges, begins at about 30 feet and plunges to a depth of 1,300 feet.

Horseback riding, an excellent way to tour St. Lucia, can be arranged through Trim's National Riding Stables, (758) 450-8273, at Cas-en-Bas in Gros Islet; Country Saddles, (758) 450-5467, east of Castries in Babonneau; Trekkers, (758) 459-7340, at the Morne Coubaril Estate in Soufrière; and the Fox Grove Inn, (758) 454-0281, on the east coast.

St. Lucia Golf and Country Club's 18-hole course, the island's only public golf course, is scenically situated on the northern end of the island at Cap Estate. Reservations are advised; phone (758) 450-8523. Sandals La Toc Resort, (758) 452-3081, ext. 6054, has nine holes for guests. Tennis courts are open to non-guests at the Rex St. Lucian and Windjammer Landing, as well as at the St. Lucia Racquet Club. The St. Lucia Golf and Country Club and the St. Lucia Yacht Club offer squash courts. Legacies of the island's English heritage are the popular spectator sports of soccer and cricket. Cricket matches can be observed on Sunday near the Choc Bay War Memorial in the northwestern portion of the island.

Two villages host Friday night street parties, known locally as "jump-ups." The most popular of these is held in Gros Islet, a small fishing town in northern St. Lucia. Locals and tourists alike enjoy the carnival atmosphere, where the pulsating beat of reggae and soca music permeates the air. Food vendors stationed on the sidewalk grill spicy Caribbean delights as merrymakers dance to the latest soca tunes. Many hotels arrange round-trip bus transportation to the Gros Islet "jump-up."

Seafood Friday, the second "jump-up," is held weekly in the fishing village of Anse la Raye on the west coast. Vendors sell a variety of prepared seafood, much like they do in Gros Islet. The popular event draws locals from all over the island for its fried mackerel, dorado and tuna, as well as lambi (conch), lobster, octopus and the national dish, green fig and saltfish.

Island nightlife centers on the hotels, where steel bands perform folk music, calypso and reggae. The island also plays host to a number of cultural events.

The St. Lucia Jazz Festival, now one of the world's top jazz events, draws international acts—and their fans—for two weeks in early May. Free lunchtime and evening concerts are held at Derek Walcott Square in Castries. Many hotels also host shows in conjunction with official jazz events. A day-long concert known as Jazz in the South, held at the Balembouche Estate south of Choiseul, is popular with locals.

Masquerade bands take to the streets during the annual Carnival celebration held the third Monday and Tuesday in July; a multitude of activities takes place in the days preceding these holidays, among the island's biggest events. The festivals of La Rose and La Marguerite occur on Aug. 30 and Oct. 17, and St. Lucia's Day on Dec. 13. October is Creole Heritage Month, featuring a series of cultural activities leading up to International Creole Day, or *Jounen Kweyol*, celebrated by Creole-speaking people around the world.

Sightseeing

Those exploring St. Lucia's interior will be rewarded with views of the island's lush greenery. Drivers will often encounter roosters and other farm animals during their travels and may have to stop and wait patiently while a stray cow or goat wanders slowly across the road.

It is not unusual to see natives diligently walking with a huge display of bananas perched precariously on their heads. Sightseers will be overwhelmed by the seemingly endless maze of banana plants, sometimes wrapped in peculiar plastic bags which serve as protection against insects. Colorful rum shops, often ramshackle in appearance, serve as neighborhood meeting spots where locals exchange the latest news.

Pigeon Island off the northwestern coast is named for Admiral Rodney's carrier pigeons, which were once housed at the ruined fort. Joined to the main island by a causeway, the area is now a national park which contains Arawak remnants, lookouts, gun batteries and barracks set amid tropical plant life. Union Agricultural Station, also in the northern portion of the island, is the headquarters of the Forestry Division. The station has a small zoo with animals native to St. Lucia, a medicinal herb garden and a nature trail; phone (758) 450-2078.

Just north of Castries, Rodney Bay Village is being developed as a yachting center and resort area. Marigot Bay, a popular yacht harbor with an inviting beach, is a half-hour coastal drive south of Castries. Nearby, at the colorful fishing village of Anse la Raye, fishermen continue to craft their vessels out of logs. Also south of Castries is Soufrière, which can be reached by a long but scenic drive or by boat, which also provides an oceangoing view of *Les Pitons*. Soufrière's volcano acts as a safety valve; it releases small amounts of pressure, forestalling a major volcanic eruption.

From Soufrière the road toward Fond St. Jacques penetrates the island's rain forest, which can be seen by organized tour. Hikers may spot the endangered St. Lucia parrot and are rewarded with views such as orchids and anthuriums growing wild, and agoutis and manicous playing. The rain forest also can be toured by arranging a guide through the Forestry and Lands Division; phone (758) 451-1691. Visitors are cautioned to dress appropriately, as the forest can be extremely muddy in areas.

Flora-loving travelers may tour the Diamond Botanical Gardens in Soufrière, Mamiku Gardens off the East Coast Highway, Tropica Gardens on the northern end of the island and La Sikwi Sugar Mill and Gardens at Anse La Raye.

Excursions also can be made to two of the island's working banana plantations: Marquis Estate in the northern part of the island and Errard Plantation in the Dennery area. The Marquis tour provides a trip down the unspoiled Marquis River. Practical footwear and clothing are advised, as grounds are often muddy. The rise and fall of St. Lucia's once-thriving sugar industry is the subject of an organized tour at Invergoil Estate; a restored sugar mill is on the grounds. Excursions to the Cap Moule à Chique Lighthouse also are available.

Most boat excursions sail from Castries to Soufrière and include bus tours of Sulphur Springs and Diamond Falls. Tours usually include lunch and time for snorkeling.

Dramatic views of St. Lucia's rugged terrain and lush rain forest are possible by helicopter. Flights glide past such sites as the inspiring twin Pitons and the 18th-century fortifications on Morne Fortune. Narrated tours are offered by St. Lucia Helicopters, (758) 453-6950, and Eastern Caribbean Helicopters, (758) 453-6952.

DID YOU KNOW

Great Britain went to war with France 14 times to gain control of St. Lucia.

Transportation

Non-stop flights arrive at Hewanorra International Airport from Miami aboard American Airlines, Philadelphia via US Airways and Atlanta aboard Delta Airlines. Caribbean Airways offers service from both Miami and New York. George F.L. Charles Airport, just outside of Castries, services on-island charters and interisland flights to and from Barbados, Trinidad, Antigua, San Juan and several other islands; flights also arrive from Puerto Rico aboard American Eagle. Most resorts in the northern end of the island furnish complimentary transportation to guests flying into Hewanorra; the trip usually takes about an hour.

While there is no organized public bus system in St. Lucia, minibuses do run frequently between Castries and such points as Vigie, Gros Islet and Vieux Fort. There is no set schedule, and buses are often crowded, but they stop at designated sites about every half hour, and the longest trip costs no more than $3. Service between Castries and some outlying villages may be limited to once a day. Taxis are available but relatively expensive; establish the fare before your ride. The cab rate for sightseeing tours is usually around $20 per hour. Cars can be rented; a temporary license, which costs $20 and is valid for 3 months, is required. Hertz, with outlets at both airports and Rodney Bay Marina, offers discounts to AAA members; phone (758) 452-0679.

Water taxis provide one of the quickest routes between Castries and Soufrière. Expect to pay around $20 per person, depending on the boat or yacht. Service also is available north to Anse Chastanet and points along the coast. High-speed passenger ferries operated by Caribbean Express and L'Express des Iles connect St. Lucia with Dominica, Guadeloupe and Martinique. Channel Shuttles also travels between St. Lucia and Martinique.

Fast Facts

POPULATION: 158,178.

AREA: 616 sq km (238 sq mi.).

CAPITAL: Castries.

HIGHEST POINT: 950 m (3,117 ft.), Mount Gimie.

LOWEST POINT: Sea level, Caribbean Sea.

TIME ZONE(S): Atlantic Standard.

LANGUAGE: English and Kweyol.

GOVERNMENT: Independent. Member of the British Commonwealth of Nations.

UNIT OF CURRENCY: Eastern Caribbean (E.C.) dollar. $1 U.S. = 2.7 E.C. dollars.

ELECTRICITY: 220 volts, 50 cycles AC.

MINIMUM AGE FOR DRIVERS: 21-25, depending on the rental car agency. Local license ($20) required, valid for 3 months; drive on left.

SEAT BELT/CHILD RESTRAINT LAWS: Seat belts are required for all passengers.

HELMETS FOR MOTORCYCLISTS: Required.

HOLIDAYS: Jan. 1; Carnival, Jan. 2; Independence Day, Feb. 22; Good Friday; Easter; Easter Monday; Labour Day, first Mon. in May; Whit Monday, May or June (8th Mon. after Easter); Feast of Corpus Christi, May or June (9th Thurs. after Easter); Carnival, July; Emancipation Day, Aug. 1; Thanksgiving, Oct.; St. Lucia Day, Dec. 13; Christmas, Dec. 25; Boxing Day, Dec. 26.

TAXES: An 8 percent room tax and 10-15 percent service charge are added to most hotel bills. Departure tax $26 U.S. over age 12.

IMMIGRATION REQUIREMENTS: Passport and a return or onward ticket are required. No visa needed for stays up to 6 months. The U.S. Dept. of Homeland Security requires all U.S. citizens returning from the Caribbean to present a valid passport.

PHONING THE ISLANDS: To call St. Lucia from the U.S. or Canada, dial 1 + 758 + the 7-digit local number.

FURTHER INFORMATION FOR VISITORS:

St. Lucia Tourist Board
800 Second Ave., Suite 910
New York, NY 10017
(212) 867-2950
(800) 456-3984

St. Lucia Tourist Board, Castries
Pointe Seraphine
P.O. Box 221
Castries, St. Lucia
(758) 452-4094

Points of Interest

See map page 224.

CASTRIES (B-1) pop. 64,344

St. Lucia's capital, Castries (CASS-trees) is a bustling harbor town surrounded by rolling hills. Only a few historic landmarks stand; since its founding by the French in the 18th century, Castries has been destroyed by fire four times.

The town's colorful downtown market on Jeremie Street has been in existence since 1895; it is open Monday through Saturday 6-6. Saturday is the best time to visit the market, which is renowned for its lush tropical fruits, fresh vegetables, exotic spices, wicker furniture, wood carvings and handicrafts. Boutiques in town sell European perfumes, jewelry, clothes and fabric. Some shops sell handmade cane furniture and batik clothing, for which the island is noted.

Bordered by Peynier, Laborie and Micoud streets, the 1890s Cathedral of the Immaculate Conception reveals impressive murals by St. Lucian artist Dunstan St. Omer. Derek Walcott Square, next to the cathedral, is named for the island's Nobel prizewinning poet. The square contains a 400-year-old samaan tree and a monument to the St. Lucians who died in World Wars I and II. An antique map collection focusing on St. Lucia and the Caribbean Sea can be found at the National Library on Bourbon Street.

Morne Fortune, or "hill of good fortune," is on the southern side of Castries. The 845-foot-high hill offers a striking view of Castries Harbour, Vigie Peninsula and the northern portion of the island. The road winds past Government House, a Victorian-style residence occupied by the governor-general. At the top of the Morne are the remains of Fort Charlotte, which changed hands between British and French forces during the 18th and 19th centuries. A monument marks the site of a battle fought in 1796. Many of the structures have been restored to house the University of the West Indies.

St. Lucia Tourist Board: Pointe Seraphine, Castries, St. Lucia, W.I.; phone (758) 452-4094.

THE BRIG *UNICORN* docks at Rodney Bay Marina. The working sailing ship is a 140-foot replica of a 19th-century brig. The impressive vessel, with its billowing white sails, appeared in the television series "Roots" and the film "Pirates of the Caribbean." Passengers depart for a land-based tour of Soufrière's volcano and waterfall at Rodney Bay. On the return boat trip, visitors can take a swim at Anse Cochon. Farther north, *Unicorn* sails through picturesque Marigot Bay. Sunset cruises also are offered.

Seven-hour trips depart Tues.-Fri. at 8:30. Fare $90; $45 (ages 0-10). Fare includes lunch, beverages and transfers. MC, VI. Phone (758) 452-8644.

PIGEON ISLAND NATIONAL LANDMARK is 7 mi. (11 km) n. via a man-made causeway. The 44-acre (18-hectare) park preserves the crumbling barracks, magazines and ramparts of Fort Rodney, built in the late 1700s and named for British Adm. George Rodney. From the fort's excellent vantage points, Rodney monitored the French fleet in Martinique. A hike to the top of the fort will reward visitors with a contrasting view of the lush landscape of the Caribbean side of St. Lucia and the rugged terrain of the east coast.

The Pigeon Island Interpretive Centre is devoted to the historical significance of the park's stone-and-brick military ruins. Visitors can interact with the exhibits by listening to narratives through headphones and participating in other hands-on exercises. Food is available. Daily 9-5. Admission $5; $1 (ages 6-12). Phone (758) 453-7656 or (758) 450-0603.

MICOUD (C-2) pop. 16,041

Baron de Micoud, former governor of St. Lucia, acquired this estate on the island's east coast in 1766. The Creole plantation came to be known as "Mamiku" after the baron's wife, Madame de Micoud. Later a British military post under Gen. John Moore, the estate house was destroyed in 1796 and stood abandoned for 200 years. Mamiku is now a working plantation again.

MAMIKU GARDENS is off the East Coast Hwy. A haven of tropical flowers, fruits and birds, the 15-acre (6-hectare) botanical garden includes a banana plantation, forest trails, a medicinal herb garden and an archeological dig. The Mystic Garden features wild and cultivated orchids. On the grounds is the site of a battle between British and French forces in 1796. At the gate house, visitors may borrow plant guidebooks, maps and walking sticks. Food is available. Allow 1 hour minimum. Daily 9-5; closed Good Friday and Dec. 25. Guided tours are offered at 10 and 1. Admission $6; $3 (ages 5-16). Guided tours $8. Phone (758) 455-3729.

SOUFRIÈRE (C-1) pop. 7,656

Established by the French in 1746, the quaint west coast village of Soufrière (soo-free-AIR) is actually a low-lying volcanic crater. The town derived its name from the bubbling pits of sulphur at the nearby volcano and sulphur springs. Once the flourishing French capital, Soufrière is now a sleepy fishing village characterized by traces of French Colonial architecture and black sand beaches.

Soufrière is perhaps most renowned as the home of the towering twin Pitons, volcanic peaks that spring forth majestically from the ocean to a height of more than a half-mile (.8 km). Gros Piton (2,619 ft./798 m) can be climbed by experienced hikers;

Petit Piton (2,438 ft./743 m) is not considered safe to climb. Anse des Pitons, a picturesque bay, separates the Pitons.

The town's marketplace, especially active on Saturday, can be recognized by its charming gingerbread trim. Situated near the waterfront on Bay Street, the market offers fresh fruits and vegetables, spices and island crafts. Le Toc Battery, built in 1888, overlooks Castries Harbor. The military installation includes cartridge and shell stores, underground tunnels and an original 18-ton cannon.

DIAMOND BOTANICAL GARDENS, WATERFALL AND MINERAL BATHS is about 1.5 mi. (2.4 km) s.e. on Diamond Rd. King Louis XVI of France had bathhouses built for his troops at this site just prior to the French Revolution. Visitors can bathe in the mineral-rich pools. The exotic tropical garden is filled with colorful flora and fauna. A path that winds through landscaped grounds leads to a magnificent waterfall; the unique coloration of the rocks is due to mineral deposits left by the streaming water. A nature trail takes visitors past a restored sugar mill and water wheel.

Food is available. Mon.-Sat. 10-5, Sun. and holidays 10-3. Admission $6; $3.50 (ages 0-11). Public bathing charge $4; private bathing charge $6. Phone (758) 459-7565 or (758) 452-4759.

LA SOUFRIÈRE VOLCANO AND SULPHUR SPRINGS PARK is 2 mi. (3.2 km) s.e. The 25-acre (10-hectare) park contains a high-temperature geothermal system that last erupted in 1766. A road winds alongside hot pools that bubble and steam with sulphurous gases, and cars were once allowed to enter the crater—hence the park's nickname, "the world's only drive-in volcano." An interpretive center features information about the volcano that erupted and collapsed here some 40,000 years ago, forming a crater 8 miles (13 km) wide. Guided 30-minute tours are offered. Open daily 9-5. Admission (including guided tour) $2.50. Phone (758) 459-7686 or (758) 459-5726.

MORNE COUBARIL ESTATE is 1 mi. (6 km) s. on West Coast Road. Costumed guides conduct 90-minute tours of this working cocoa plantation, the first major estate on the island. The 250-acre site includes the ruins of an 18th-century sugar mill, a renovated great house and a re-created Carib workers' village. Food is available. Reservations are suggested. Open daily 9-5:30. Admission $6. Phone (758) 459-7340.

Cupecoy, St. Maarten / © SIME s.a.s. / eStock Photo

St. Martin/St. Maarten

Shared between France and the Netherlands, St. Martin/St. Maarten is the smallest territory in the world governed by two sovereign states. Until a few years ago the island was a largely undiscovered hideaway; today modern tourist accommodations are plentiful. Philipsburg, the capital of St. Maarten, is on a sandbar between Great Bay and the Great Salt Pond. Marigot, the quintessentially French capital of St. Martin, is known for its fine shopping and as a haven for yachts, as are Oyster Pond and Great Bay in St. Maarten.

History

The Arawaks were the first to inhabit the island in pre-Columbian times. The Caribs, who eventually replaced their peace-loving predecessors, called the island *Soualiga,* meaning "land of salt," due to its numerous salt ponds. When Christopher Columbus discovered the island during his second voyage in 1493, he named it after St. Martin of Tours.

Spanish colonization didn't come until about 1640; until then they battled with the Dutch and French for the island's coveted anchorages and valuable salt ponds. In 1634 a Spanish battery went up at Pointe Blanche, southeast of present-day Philipsburg, and on the peninsula where the ruins of Fort Amsterdam can now be found, and the island was defended successfully until the Spanish finally abandoned it in 1648. The island was then settled by French and Dutch prisoners and their countrymen from nearby St. Kitts and St. Eustatius.

The two remaining contestants decided to divide the island, and local legend holds that they defined the border through a walking contest. A Frenchman and a Dutchman started in the same spot, walked around the island in opposite directions and drew the boundary line where they met. In reality, though, the 1648 Treaty of Concordia granted France the greater portion of the island because its navy could offer greater protection. Though claims to the territory remained in some dispute for another 170 years, the settlers' idea of harmonious coexistence has lasted. In 1948 the islanders, who by this time considered themselves one people, erected a monument commemorating their 300 years as neighbors.

The salt ponds remained important economically through the 19th century. Sugar cane and tobacco, however, brought only brief prosperity; slaves were imported to work the plantations in the late 1700s, but following abolition in 1848 most of the plantations fell to ruin. A devastating hurricane followed by an earthquake in 1819 foreshadowed the island's economic decline. It was not until 1939 when the island declared itself a free port that the economy began to turn around. An airport was built in the late 1950s, and the tourism industry was born.

Dutch St. Maarten became part of the Netherlands Antilles in 1845. French St. Martin has been a dependency of the French overseas department of Guadeloupe since 1946.

Shopping

The two capitals of Philipsburg and Marigot are a treasureland for shoppers. Duty-free luxury imports include Dutch and French silver, crystal, Delftware, cameras, French perfume, china, fashions, jewelry, Italian leather and electronics. Inexpensive souvenirs are available among such plentiful island wares as hand-drawn and embroidered linens, ceramics, woodcarvings, straw goods, original paintings, St. Martin music and books, cane furniture and *pareu,* a length of fabric that is twisted and turned depending on how it is worn.

The island's shopping mecca is Philipsburg's Frontstreet, where more than 100 shops line the mile-long (1.6 km-long) thoroughfare. Hidden behind Frontstreet are numerous shops along Backstreet and Cannegieter Street—all connected by *steegjes,* or alleyways. Island handicrafts are for sale along the pier and in nearby Wathey Square. Other shopping opportunities are available west of town in the Simpson Bay and Maho Bay areas.

In Marigot the shops center on Port la Royale on the marina and across the street along rue Général de Gaulle and rue de la Liberté. Rue de la République, the road leading to the ferry pier, also has several fine shops. Boutiques in Marigot specialize in European designer fashions and tropical clothing. Wednesday and Saturday mornings Market

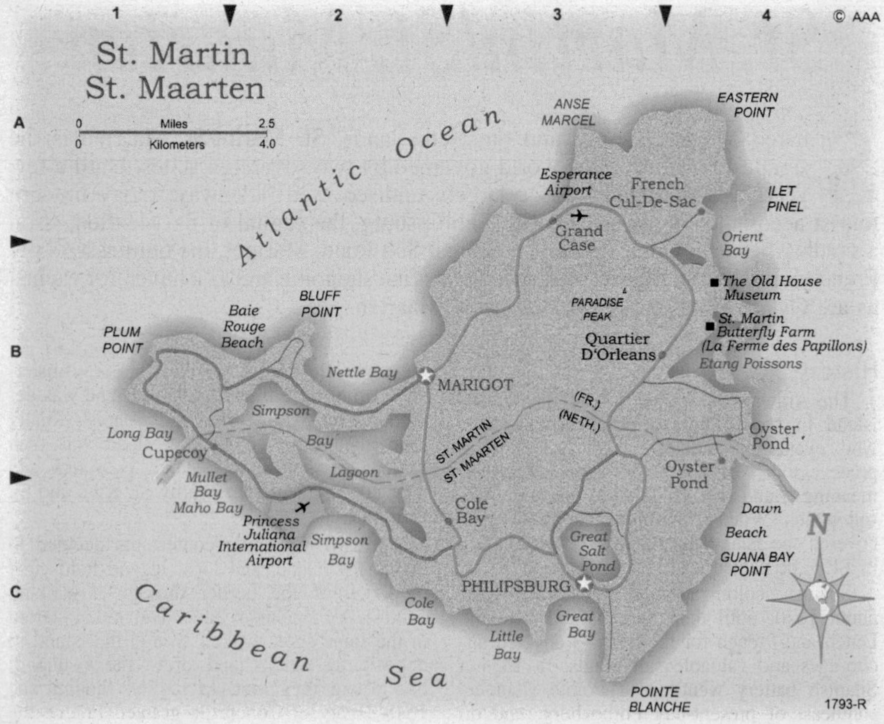

Square on the harbor bustles with the activity of locals selling fresh food and handicrafts.

Shopping hours on the Dutch side are generally Mon.-Sat. 8-noon and 2-6, and on the French side Mon.-Sat. 9-12:30 and 3-7. Banking hours in Philipsburg are Mon.-Fri. 8:30-3. In Marigot banking hours are Mon.-Fri. 8:30-4.

Food and Drink

Few experienced travelers would disagree that St. Martin/St. Maarten offers some of the best dining in the Caribbean. The dual nationality of the island adds a dimension of culinary variety, and there are more than 375 restaurants to choose from. French and West Indian menus predominate, though Italian and American also are popular.

As expected of a former French colony, St. Martin is especially renowned for its cuisine, both in its classic version and its Creole cousin. Northeast of Marigot is the tiny village of Grand Case, considered the island's gourmet capital; some of the island's best French and West Indian restaurants can be found here. In Marigot there are several Gallic restaurants as well as those offering other cuisines. Marigot also features several French-style sidewalk cafes.

The restaurants in Philipsburg and elsewhere in St. Maarten offer greater variety. In addition to French, the finest in West Indian, Italian, American, Mexican, Thai, sushi, Argentinean, Indonesian and even Chinese cuisines can be found. Restaurants add a 10- to 15-percent service charge to the bill.

St. Maarten's own Guavaberry Island Folk Liqueur makes a good take-home item. Six bittersweet flavors are available and can be sampled at a tasting house at the east end of Frontstreet in Philipsburg. The island's tap water is purified; bottled water also is widely available.

Sports and Amusements

Most daytime activities on the island are water oriented and take place on white sand beaches and in secluded coves. The island is fringed with some three dozen beaches. Great Bay and Little Bay beaches are the most accessible from Philipsburg. To the west are Simpson Bay Beach, replete with water sports outlets; Mullet Bay Beach, with convenient facilities; and secluded Cupecoy Beach. Scenic Dawn Beach on the east coast also is good for snorkeling. Tiny but popular Maho Beach offers an unusually close view of jets landing at Princess Juliana International Airport.

On the French side west of Simpson Bay Lagoon are the unspoiled beaches of Baie Longue and intimate Baie Rouge. Mile-long (1.6 km) Grand Case Beach on the northwest shore has calm, clear waters. Orient Beach on the northeast shore is the island's most popular. Topless bathing is common on the French side; bathing *au naturel* is possible at Orient.

Such water sports concessions as scuba diving, snorkeling, windsurfing, parasailing, water skiing and jet skiing are concentrated around Grand Case Beach, Anse Marcel and Orient Beach in St. Martin and Great Bay, Little Bay and Simpson Bay in St. Maarten. Ocean Explorers at Simpson Bay offers the Sea Walk, in which participants don specially made bell helmets for a walk on the sea floor; swimming is not required.

The island's coral reefs teem with marine life, and its waters allow for visibility of up to 200 feet. Experienced divers have many interesting diving spots to choose from, including the Alleys, bound by cliffs and ledges; Green Key; Flat Island; and Hen and Chick, small islands with beautiful elkhorn coral reefs. Outside Great Bay is the 1801 wreck of the British warship HMS *Proselyte.*

Several firms offer scuba diving lessons lasting about 3 hours. Picnic sails and snorkeling trips to such nearby deserted islands as Tintamarre (Flat Island) and Pinel or Prickly Pear islands also are available. Arrangements for diving and snorkeling trips and lessons can be made through all the island's marinas and major hotels. Deep-sea fishing charters can be arranged at Bobby's Marina and Great Bay Marina in Philipsburg, Port la Royale in Marigot and Port Lonvilliers in Anse Marcel. Dolphin, kingfish, sailfish, blue marlin and wahoo are the main catches.

But those seeking land-based activities need not feel so out of the swim of things. Horseback riding is available at Crazy Acres Riding Center in Cole Bay, St. Maarten, and Caid and Isa in Anse Marcel, St. Martin; guided excursions are available. Tennis courts can be found at most hotels and resorts, and many are lighted. Le Privilège, a sports and spa complex in Anse Marcel, has six lighted courts as well as exercise equipment, squash courts and a pool. An 18-hole golf course is available on the Dutch side at Mullet Bay Resort.

The island is definitely not lacking in nighttime diversions. Evening entertainment takes place primarily at 13 hotel casinos, all on the Dutch side, and the resorts, where carnival shows and Caribbean music are on tap. St. Maarten's club scene centers on the Maho area, where Cheri's Cafe and The Q Club attract youthful revelers. Another popular night spot is Salsa at the Atlantis Casino. In St. Martin, Atmos 2000 is at the Marigo Marina.

The first weekend in March, the St. Maarten Regatta includes yacht races and soirees. A popular event is Carnival, held around Shrove Tuesday and Ash Wednesday in St. Martin and for two weeks beginning in late April in St. Maarten.

Sightseeing

The island is easily toured by car, but caution should be exercised—many side roads are rough and narrow, and wandering livestock are common, especially on the French side. Steep roads should not be attempted following rains. The border between the Dutch and French sides can be traversed freely. Road maps are available at the airport, car rental agencies located at the airport and the tourist offices in Philipsburg and Marigot.

On a peninsula between Great Bay and Little Bay is Fort Amsterdam, built by the Dutch in 1631 but occupied by the Spanish 1633-48. Peter Stuyvesant, eventual governor of America's New Netherlands colony, lost his right leg here while battling the Spanish in 1644. The unimproved site is accessible via the Divi Little Bay Beach Resort. Due north atop Fort Hill are the ruins of Fort William, which dates to 1801. A steep hike to the top rewards the adventurous with a spectacular panorama; driving is not recommended.

Another excellent vantage point is the roadside lookout a few miles west on Cole Bay Hill. Several neighboring islands can be seen, including on a clear day St. Kitts and Nevis—about 45 miles (72 km) southeast. Union Road, the route north from Cole Bay Hill, is the quickest way to Marigot; at the halfway point stands the Border Monument, erected in 1948 to commemorate the islanders' 300 years as neighbors. A longer but worthwhile route proceeds west past the airport and through the island's lowlands, circling Simpson Bay Lagoon. En route are some of the island's finest resorts.

From Philipsburg the especially scenic east coast of St. Maarten is accessible via Sucker Garden Road. The first turnoff leads to Guana Bay Point and the second to Dawn Beach and Oyster Pond. Both paved routes are steep and meandering, but the vistas to be enjoyed are worth the effort. Most noticeable among the numerous offshore landmarks is the French island of St. Barthélemy, about 14 miles (23 km) offshore. Picturesque Oyster Pond, reminiscent of the French Riviera, is a favorite anchorage of Caribbean boaters.

North of Oyster Pond is the rural area of Orléans, seemingly untouched by time and tourism, and the large Etang aux Poissons, or Fish Lake. Farther north along the coast are popular Orient Beach and several smaller, more secluded spots. Off the eastern shore of rural French Cul de Sac is uninhabited Pinel Island, a favorite day-sail destination where water sports and facilities are available.

From French Cul de Sac the road turns westward through Grand Case. This charming former fishing village has earned its reputation as the island's gourmet capital. The Creole-style structures along the main road house some of the island's best restaurants. And at numerous roadside food stands, or *lolos,* barbecued lobster, chicken and ribs and such Caribbean specialties as plantains and johnnycakes are sold.

The road south passes Paradise Peak; at 1,391 feet (424 m) it is the highest point on the island. On clear days the view encompasses both capitals and the island's patchwork of blue and green. The road to the inland village of Colombier, south of Paradise Peak, is lined on the north by lush tropical flora and on the south by rolling green hills decorated with long, meandering stone walls.

Glass-bottom boat trips, picnic sails and luncheon, sunset and moonlight yacht cruises are available out of the marinas at Philipsburg, Simpson Bay, Cole Bay, Marigot, Anse Marcel and Oyster Pond. Day trips to nearby Anguilla, St. Barthélemy, Saba, St. Eustatius and St. Kitts and Nevis also can be arranged.

Transportation

Princess Juliana International Airport has direct flights from San Juan, Miami, Dallas/Fort Worth and New York. Dutch Caribbean Airlines offers daily service from Curaçao; LIAT from Antigua, Montserrat, St. Croix, St. Kitts, St. Thomas and Tortola; and Windward Islands Airways from Anguilla, St. Eustatius and Saba. Dutch Antilles Express provides daily service between Aruba, Bonaire, Curaçao and St. Maarten. Air Caraïbes has daily flights from Guadeloupe, St. Barthélemy and Martinique. In addition to Juliana Airport, Air Caraïbes flies into Esperance Airport, a small domestic airstrip in Grand Case. Philipsburg is a port of call for many cruise ships. Smaller ships dock at Marigot.

Automobiles rented from companies with outlets at Princess Juliana Airport cannot be picked up at the airport; courtesy shuttles transport visitors to the rental car lots. Automobiles rented from outlets not near the airport are delivered free to hotels, and many hotels have car rental offices on the premises. Most cars have automatic transmissions and air conditioning. Motor scooters also are available; caution is advised due to rough roads and steep hills. Major credit cards are accepted.

Taxis are abundant on both the Dutch and French sides. Taxi rates are regulated, but it is always wise to agree on the fare in advance. Rates increase by 25 percent from 10 p.m. to midnight and by 50 percent from midnight to 6 a.m. Each additional passenger over two is an extra $2. The rates from Princess Juliana Airport are posted at the taxi stand outside. Tipping is customary. The two capitals of Philipsburg and Marigot are connected by inexpensive public buses that operate from 6 a.m. to 10 p.m.

The islands of Anguilla, St. Barthélemy, Saba and St. Eustatius are accessible by any one of several boats operating out of Philipsburg in St. Maarten. High-speed ferries can make the trip in 40 minutes. Several ferries to St. Barthélemy and Anguilla operate out of Marigot in St. Martin.

Fast Facts

POPULATION: St. Martin: 29,888. St. Maarten: 38,876.

AREA: 96 sq km (37 sq mi.)

CAPITAL: **St. Martin**: Marigot. **St. Maarten:** Philipsburg.

HIGHEST POINT: 424 m (1,391 ft.), Pic du Paradis (Paradise Peak), St. Martin.

LOWEST POINT: Sea level, Caribbean Sea.

TIME ZONE(S): Atlantic Standard.

LANGUAGE: St. Martin: French and English. **St. Maarten:** Dutch, English and a local patois.

GOVERNMENT: St. Martin: Dependency of the French Overseas Department of Guadeloupe. **St. Maarten:** Netherlands Antilles, autonomous within the Kingdom of the Netherlands.

UNIT OF CURRENCY: St. Martin: Euro Dollar. $1 U.S. = approx. .6 Euro. **St. Maarten:** Netherlands Antillean guilder (also called the florin), divided into 100 cents. $1 U.S. = 1.8 guilders. U.S. currency is widely accepted on both sides of the island.

ELECTRICITY: St. Martin: 220 volts, 60 cycles AC. **St. Maarten:** 110 volts, 60 cycles AC.

MINIMUM AGE FOR DRIVERS: 25; maximum age 65-70. U.S. license valid; drive on right.

MINIMUM AGE FOR GAMBLING: 18.

SEAT BELT/CHILD RESTRAINT LAWS: Seat belts are required for all passengers. Child restraints required for under age 4; children under 12 must ride in the back seat.

HELMETS FOR MOTORCYCLISTS: Required.

HOLIDAYS: St. Martin: Jan. 1; Epiphany, Jan. 6; Mardi Gras; Good Friday; Easter; Easter Monday; Queen's Birthday, Apr. 30; Labour Day, May 1; Ascension Day, May (6th Thurs. after Easter); Whit Monday, May or June (8th Mon. after Easter); Bastille Day, July 14; Schoelcher Day, July 21; Feast of the Assumption, Aug. 15; All Saints Day, Nov. 1; Concordia Day/Armistice Day, Nov. 11; Christmas, Dec. 25; Boxing Day, Dec. 26. **St. Maarten:** Jan. 1; Good Friday; Easter and Easter Monday; Queen's Birthday, Apr. 30; Labour Day, May 1; Day after Carnival (early May); Antillean Day (Oct. 21); St. Maarten's Day, Nov. 11; Christmas, Dec. 25; Boxing Day, Dec. 26.

TAXES: St. Martin: A 5 percent room tax and 10-15 percent service charge are added to most hotel bills. Departure tax $20 U.S.; interisland tax $5 U.S. **St. Maarten:** A 5-8 percent room tax and 10-15 percent service charge are added to most hotel bills. Departure tax $30 U.S., ages 2 and up; interisland tax $10 U.S.

IMMIGRATION REQUIREMENTS: St. Martin: A valid passport and return or onward ticket are required for U.S. citizens entering the French West Indies. No visa needed for stays up to 3 months. **St. Maarten:** Passport and return or onward ticket are required. No visa needed for stays up to 2 weeks. The U.S. Dept. of Homeland Security requires all U.S. citizens returning from the Caribbean to present a valid passport.

PHONING THE ISLANDS: St. Martin: From the U.S. or Canada, dial 011 + 590 + 590 + the 6-digit local number. **St. Maarten:** Dial 011 + 599 + the 7-digit local number.

FURTHER INFORMATION FOR VISITORS:

St. Martin/St. Maarten Tourist Office
675 Third Ave., Suites 1807
New York, NY 10017
(212) 475-8970 (St. Martin)
(877) 956-1234 (St. Martin)
(212) 953-2084 (St. Maarten)
(800) 786-2278 (St. Maarten)

St. Martin Tourist Office
Route de Sandy Ground
Marigot, St. Martin
Guadeloupe
(590) 87-57-21

St. Maarten Tourist Bureau
Vineyard Office Park
W.G. Buncamper Rd. #33
Philipsburg, St. Maarten
Netherlands Antilles
(599) 542-2337
See color ad p. 5.

Points of Interest

See map page 232.

St. Maarten

Covering 16 square miles (41 sq km) on the southern half of the island, the Dutch dependency of St. Maarten is characterized by rolling hills and white sand beaches. Arawak Indians harvested salt from the many lagoons and salt lakes in the area.

CUPECOY (B-1)

The last Dutch beach on the western end of the island, picturesque Cupecoy Beach was once a series of coves running along the sandstone cliffs and caves. Time and the sea have washed away most of the sand, and a single cove remains. The beach is clothing-optional and was once fairly secluded; condo development has changed the landscape in recent years.

GAMBLING ESTABLISHMENTS

- **Atlantis Casino** is at 106 Rhine Rd. Daily 24 hours. Phone (599) 545-4601.

MAHO BAY (C-1)

The island's largest resort area, Mayo Bay is famous for a tiny stretch of sand at the end of the airport runway. Jumbo jets roar overhead at Maho Beach, and signs warn about the danger of engine blasts. Even so, many thrillseekers come here for the chance to be blown off their feet by incoming aircraft.

GAMBLING ESTABLISHMENTS

- **Casino Royale at Sonesta Maho Beach Resort** is at 1 Rhine Rd. Daily 1 p.m.-4 a.m. Phone (599) 545-2115.

PHILIPSBURG (C-3)

Philipsburg is the busy Dutch capital. Its three main thoroughfares are usually crammed with shoppers browsing through stores stocked with duty-free luxuries. Among the jumble of shops, restaurants and modern buildings are remnants of an earlier Philipsburg. One of the most notable of the town's historic buildings is the 18th-century Philipsburg Courthouse. The courthouse borders Wathey Square, the town center of activity. Fort Amsterdam, built in 1631 on a peninsula between Great Bay and Little Bay, was the first Dutch military outpost in the Caribbean.

St. Maarten Tourist Bureau: W.G. Buncamper Rd. #33, Philipsburg, St. Maarten; phone (599) 542-2337.

ST. MAARTEN NATIONAL HERITAGE FOUNDATION & MUSEUM is at 7 Frontstreet. Revolving exhibits depict the island's history and culture. Among the items displayed are pre-Columbian artifacts; old maps and photos; and articles from the island's forts and plantations, including an 18th-century Chinese porcelain dinner service. Exhibits related to nature, environment and geology also are featured. Mon.-Fri. 10-4. Donations. Phone (599) 542-4917.

ST. MAARTEN PARK is on the n. side of Great Salt Pond on Arch Rd. More than 80 species at this tropical garden zoo include Caribbean parrots, squirrel monkeys, ocelots, golden lion tamarins and capybaras. On the grounds are a walk-through aviary, a reptile house, a nocturnal exhibit and a petting zoo. Guided night safari tours are offered by reservation. Food is available. Allow 1 hour minimum. Daily 9-5, June-Sept.; 9-6, rest of year. Admission $10; $5 (children). MC, VI. Phone (599) 543-2030.

ST. MAARTEN'S 12 METRE CHALLENGE departs from Bobby's Marina downtown at Front St. and Yrausquin Blvd. Participants experience the thrill of riding aboard multi-million-dollar America's Cup race boats. Crew members can grind, winch, trim sails or sit back and relax aboard Dennis Conner's *Stars & Stripes, Canada II* or *True North*. Prior sailing experience is not necessary. Allow 3 hours minimum. Departures daily at 8:30, 10, 11:45 and 1:30; closed Dec. 25. Schedule may vary; phone ahead. Fare $75. Children under 12 are not permitted. MC, VI. Phone (599) 542-0045 or (599) 542-0046.

***SEAWORLD EXPLORER* CORAL REEF TOUR** departs from the Atlantis dock on Grand Case Blvd. This 51-foot-long semi-submarine cruises to Creole Rock for excellent views above deck of French Grand Case and British Anguilla, and below deck of marine life and coral formations. Morning and afternoon trips depart daily, based upon cruise ship demand. Closed holidays. Fare $39; $25 (ages 2-12). Reservations are required. Phone (599) 542-4078.

GAMBLING ESTABLISHMENTS

- **Casino Rouge et Noir** is at 66 Front St. Daily 9 a.m.-4 a.m. Phone (599) 545-4601.
- **Coliseum Casino** is at 71 Front St. Daily 10 a.m.-2 a.m. Phone (599) 543-2101.
- **Diamond Casino** is in the StreetKaanal Bldg. at 1 Front St. Daily 11 a.m.-3 a.m. Phone (599) 543-2583.
- **Jump Up Casino** is at the end of Frontstreet at 1 Emmaplein. Daily 10 a.m.-4 a.m. Phone (599) 542-0862.
- **Princess Casino at Port de Plaisance Resort** is at 155 Union Rd. Daily 2 p.m.-4 a.m. Phone (599) 544-4311.
- **Tropicana Casino** is at Cole Bay at 34 Welfare Rd. Daily 2 p.m.-4 a.m. Phone (599) 544-5654.

SIMPSON BAY (C-2)

One of the largest landlocked bodies of water in the Caribbean, Simpson Bay Lagoon sprawls across the western end of the island. The saltwater bay is popular for yachting and watersports, including jet-skiing, waterskiing and parasailing. Rental equipment is available at several outlets along Simpson Bay Beach.

GAMBLING ESTABLISHMENTS

- **Hollywood Casino** is at the Pelican Resort at 37 Billy Folly Rd. Phone (599) 544-4463.

St. Martin

Occupying 21 square miles (54 sq km) on the northern half of the island, the French dependency of St. Martin is known for its secluded beaches and resort areas.

ANSE MARCEL (A-3)

On the northern tip of the island, the pleasant family beach at Anse Marcel is prized for its white sands, shallow waters and shady coves. The resort Le Meridien L'Habitation was the site of a summit meeting between United States President George Bush and French President François Mitterand in 1989.

PLANTATION MONT VERNON is just e. of jct. Anse Marcel Rd. and Main Rd., following signs. Visitors take a walking tour of this 1786 plantation while listening to a personal audio narration of the history of St. Martin and the cultivation of coffee, cotton, indigo and sugar cane. Free samples are available at coffee and rum distillery exhibits. Allow 1 hour minimum. Daily 9-5. Admission $16; $7 (ages 3-12). MC, VI. Phone (590) 29-50-62.

GRAND CASE (A-3)

Considered the island's gourmet capital, Grand Case is home to some of the island's best French and West Indian restaurants. The tiny village is also known for the elaborate gingerbread trim on its pastel-colored houses.

LOTERIE FARM is on the road to Pic Paradis, following signs. On the site of a former sugar plantation, the nature park features interesting rock formations and caves, thriving vegetation and a historic mill. Such species as the yellow-, black- and white-colored sugarbird can be spotted in the island's sole tropical humid forest. Marked trails that vary in degree of difficulty are available for hikers and nature enthusiasts.

Guided tours are available. Picnicking is permitted. Food is available. Comfortable walking shoes are recommended. Allow 1 hour minimum. Daily 9-5. Admission $5. Phone (590) 87-86-16 or (599) 57-28-55.

MARIGOT (B-3) pop. 29,078

The quaint harbor town of Marigot (MAR-ee-go) is thoroughly French. The traditional architecture of wrought-iron balconies and fretwork trim is visible along its busy streets and residential roads, and a stroll among the shops and sidewalk cafes of Port la Royale transports visitors to the French Riviera. The restored ruins of 18th-century Fort St. Louis overlook Marigot's harbor, providing an excellent view; the fort can be reached on foot via the steps behind the Sous-Préfecture off rue de L'Hôpital.

Adding to the quaintness, a tree-lined promenade borders the water's edge and a series of pleasure boat slips. At the far end of the boulevard is the town marketplace.

St. Martin Tourist Office: Rue the Sandy Ground, Marigot, St. Martin; phone (590) 87-57-21.

ST. MARTIN MUSEUM is at Sandy Ground just outside the city center on the waterfront. "On the Trail of the Arawaks" is a permanent collection of pre-Columbian pottery and artifacts depicting the cultures of the island's first inhabitants. Early island photographs also are displayed. Mon.-Sat. 9-1 and 3-7. Admission $5; $3 (ages 0-11). Phone (590) 29-22-84.

QUARTIER D'ORLEANS (B-3)

Some of the original 17th-century structures of the island's first French settlement are preserved at Quartier d'Orleans, or the French Quarter. This quaint village is a mile south of clothing-optional Orient Beach, one of the island's most popular stretches of sand.

THE OLD HOUSE MUSEUM is on the main road between Orient Beach and Quartier d'Orleans. Preserved as a historic site, this Creole house contains artifacts from the 1800s to the present. Farm implements from the sugar plantation's history also are displayed. Guided tours are available. Allow 30 minutes minimum. Tues.-Fri. and Sun. 10-4. Admission $5; free (ages 0-10). Phone (590) 87-32-67.

ST. MARTIN BUTTERFLY FARM (LA FERME DES PAPILLONS) is off Philipsburg/Marigot Rd. at Galion Beach Rd. More than 40 butterfly species from around the world are housed in a tropical garden, where tour guides provide information about butterfly names, characteristics and life cycles. Brightly-colored clothing and perfume will attract these colorful insects. Allow 30 minutes minimum. Daily 9-3:30. Admission (good for 7 days) $12; $6 (ages 0-12). AX, DS, MC, VI. Phone (590) 87-31-21.

Bequia / © Steve Vidler / SuperStock

St. Vincent and The Grenadines

The barefoot life of a traditional West Indian island is readily available on St. Vincent, 18 miles (29 km) long and 11 miles (18 km) wide. Relatively unknown to tourists until recently, St. Vincent is one of the most picturesque of the Windwards, with quaint fishing villages, coconut and arrowroot plantations and palm-fringed coves of black volcanic sand. St. Vincent and its string of Grenadine islands, which reach south to Grenada, offer some of the best sailing, swimming, diving and snorkeling in the Caribbean. Complementing these pleasures are the small comfortable inns that provide much of the guest accommodations on St. Vincent and its sun-swept satellite islands, which include Bequia (beck-way), Mayreau (my-row), Mustique (mus-teek), Canouan (can-no-wan), Petit St. Vincent, Palm, Union and Young islands.

History

Generations before Christopher Columbus arrived in the area in 1498, fierce Carib Indians from the South American mainland had annihilated St. Vincent's original population of gentle Arawaks. St. Vincent was left relatively undisturbed until the 18th century when, despite the hostility of the Caribs, the French, Dutch and British began to vie for settlement. Near the close of the 18th century the Caribs were deported to the Bay of Honduras. By the Treaty of Paris in 1763, France ceded the island to Britain but recaptured it in 1779. Britain gained final possession in 1783 by the Treaty of Versailles. Independence from Britain was finally granted in 1979.

That same year La Soufrière, the 4,048-foot volcano in the north, erupted, spewing ash that filtered all the way to Barbados, 100 miles (160 km) east. While necessitating the evacuation of Carib descendants living on the volcano's slopes, the eruption posed no threat to the capital of Kingstown, 30 miles (48 km) south.

Sharing the characteristics of the other Windward Islands, St. Vincent relies on tourism and agriculture as its main sources of income. Cut flowers have become St. Vincent's newest export. Green mountains and productive valleys cover the island. The rural Mesopotamia Valley, also called Marriaqua Valley, is the focus of much agricultural activity. Besides breadfruit, introduced from Tahiti by Captain Bligh of "Mutiny on the Bounty" fame, bananas, coconuts and arrowroot constitute the principal crops.

Shopping

Kingstown's main street has several interesting shops, a few selling clothing with island motifs. Sea island cotton with screened designs is available at the cruise ship terminal. Local artisans offer a large variety of macramé items, jewelry and straw handicrafts, some made on the spot. A cluster of shops is tucked in the courtyard of the Cobblestone Inn, inland from the main waterfront road. The dockside Market Square comes alive on Friday and Saturday mornings when vendors and anglers gather to sell their goods; the weekly loading of the banana boats enhances this vibrant scene.

Shopping hours are generally Mon.-Fri. 8-noon and 1-4, Sat. 8-noon, though some stores are open Mon.-Fri. 8-4. Banking hours are Mon.-Thurs. 8-2, Fri. 8-5.

Food and Drink

Traditional West Indian cuisine—local fish, island produce and thick soups—as well as international flavors are available at hotels. Wilkie's, in the Grand View Beach Hotel at Villa Point, 10 minutes southeast of Kingstown, offers a typical island meal. Other hotel restaurants worth investigating are in the Cobblestone Inn, Mariners Hotel and Grenadine House. Hotel kitchens often use the bountiful produce from the native market at the far end of the main street.

Sports and Amusements

The beaches at Villa Bay, Indian Bay and in the Grenadines are excellent for swimming, sunning, snorkeling and scuba diving. Sailing, boating, fishing and diving equipment can be rented for either half- or full-days. Cumberland Bay on the leeward coast is a secluded beach, ideal for snorkeling and diving. Just minutes from Port Elizabeth in Bequia, Princess Margaret is a tree-lined stretch of soft sand, named after the princess who enjoyed a dip there in 1958. Casuarina is a white-sand beach that runs the entire length of Palm Island. Boating enthusiasts consider Saltwhistle Bay in Mayreau to be one of the Grenadines' most stunning; sailors favor this bay due to its calm waters. Macaroni Bay, on Mustique's east coast, is one of the island's most popular beaches and includes a covered picnic area. The main dive centers are on St. Vincent, Bequia, Mustique, Canouan and Union Island.

Tennis courts are available; the Kingstown Tennis Club offers its facilities to nonmembers. Spectator sports include cricket, netball and soccer.

The Emerald Valley Resort Casino, 30 miles (48 km) outside of Kingstown in Penniston Valley, is a popular nightspot for gambling, dancing and socializing. Hotels also offer evening entertainment—local steel or string bands play live music. Grand View Hotel and Young Island Resort are two that host performances, usually on Friday and Saturday.

Sightseeing

A hike to La Soufrière involves a full day and requires good physical conditioning. The trip to the still-active volcano begins by car along the coast and crosses the Yurumein/Taiwan bridge, then proceeds on foot through the Bamboo Forest and straight up the 4,048-foot summit for an unparalleled view. The Vermont Nature Trail and Trinity Falls also provide scenic outlooks. Another all-day excursion for the adventurous leaves Chateaubelair by boat for the spectacular Falls of Baleine. Dark View Falls, two majestic falls set in the forest-clad Richmond Valley on the island's northwest side, can be reached via a natural bamboo bridge spanning across a tumbling river. Elevations rise up to 229 feet.

Day trips also can be made on island schooners and motorized mailboats to Bequia and other islands of the Grenadines. Bequia, Union Island and Canouan are accessible by plane. Port Elizabeth's harbor area has colorful shops along the waterfront as well as lodgings, restaurants and water sports facilities. The production of hand-carved wooden sailboats is a prosperous industry on Bequia.

If you have less time you can take a half-day drive through the Mesopotamia Valley, which includes hillsides covered with banana

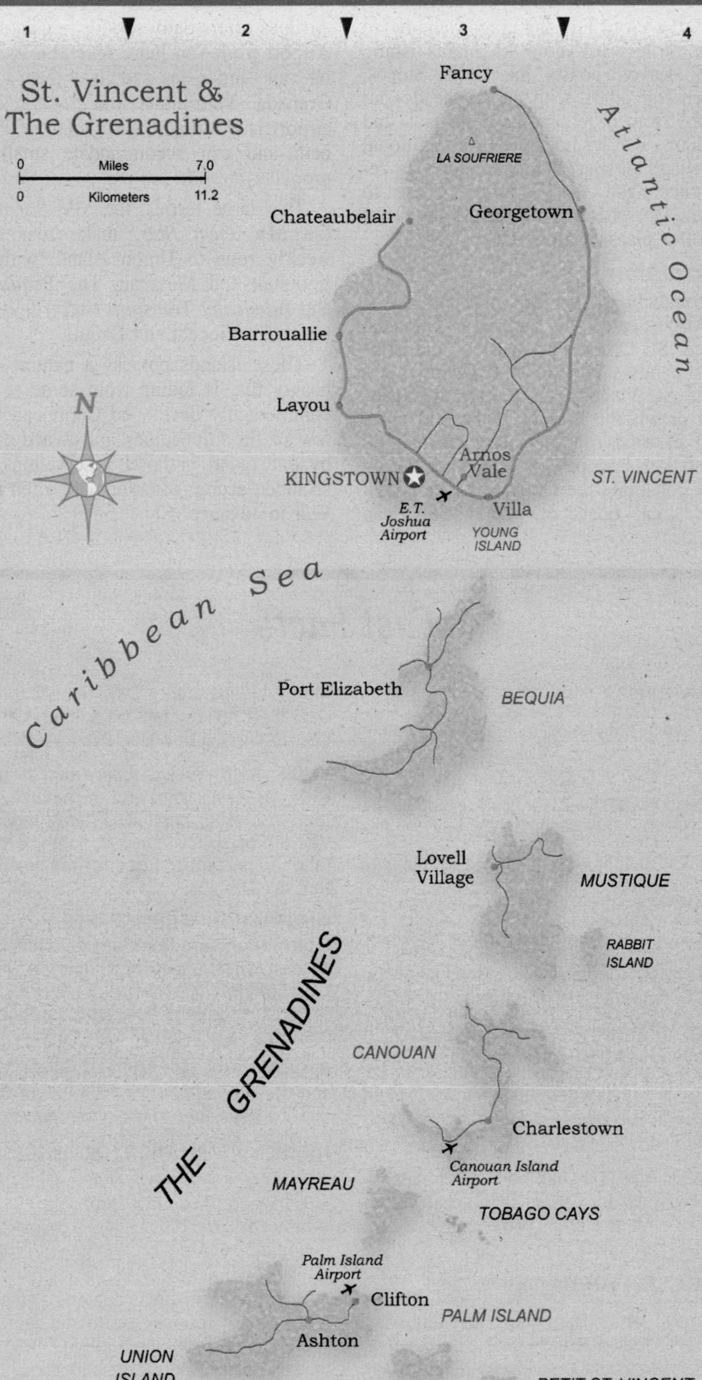

St. Vincent &
The Grenadines
0 Miles 7.0
0 Kilometers 11.2
N
Fancy
LA SOUFRIERE
Atlantic Ocean
Chateaubelair
Georgetown
Barrouallie
Layou
Arnos Vale
KINGSTOWN
ST. VINCENT
E.T. Joshua Airport
Villa
YOUNG ISLAND
Caribbean Sea
Port Elizabeth
BEQUIA
Lovell Village
MUSTIQUE
RABBIT ISLAND
THE GRENADINES
CANOUAN
Charlestown
Canouan Island Airport
MAYREAU
TOBAGO CAYS
Palm Island Airport
Clifton
PALM ISLAND
Ashton
UNION ISLAND
PETIT ST. VINCENT
1789-R
© AAA

and arrowroot crops and the craggy windward shore. On the leeward shore the quaint fishing village of Layou boasts the Carib Stones, huge sacrificial altars with carved heads and petroglyphs from pre-Columbian, Arawak and Carib Indians. Farther north lies the traditional fishing village of Barrouallie, which has remained unchanged for centuries. Close to Kingstown, Dorsetshire Hill and Mount Saint Andrew offer pleasant climbs.

Transportation

Air connections to St. Vincent's E.T. Joshua Airport are via Barbados, Grenada, Martinique, St. Lucia, Puerto Rico, and Trinidad. Public buses operate in Kingstown and throughout St. Vincent; rental cars are available with or without driver. Of the 600 miles (960 km) of roads on the island, about 360 miles (580 km) are paved. The other 31 islands that constitute the Grenadines are accessible via small boats or planes. American Airlines offers daily service to Canouan Island Airport from San Juan; several resorts also offer air limousine service from Barbados, Grenada, Martinique and St. Lucia. Bequia airport is 4 miles (6 km) south of Port Elizabeth and can accommodate small capacity propeller aircraft.

Two large ferries, the MV *Barracuda* and the MV *Gem Star*, make two and three weekly runs to Union Island, with stops in Canouan and Mayreau. The *Bequia Express* and *Admiralty Transport* make daily trips between St. Vincent and Bequia.

These islands possess a natural, unspoiled beauty that is fading from some of the more commercially developed Caribbean islands. A few of the Grenadines are owned exclusively by one resort or hotel; reservations for these secluded accommodations are often required a year in advance.

Fast Facts

POPULATION: 110,000.

AREA: 344 sq km (133 sq mi.).

CAPITAL: Kingstown.

HIGHEST POINT: 1,234 m (4,048 ft.), La Soufrière.

LOWEST POINT: Sea level, Caribbean Sea.

TIME ZONE(S): Atlantic Standard.

LANGUAGE: English and French patois.

GOVERNMENT: Independent. Member of the British Commonwealth of Nations.

UNIT OF CURRENCY: Eastern Caribbean (E.C.) dollar. $1 U.S. = 2.7 E.C. dollars.

ELECTRICITY: 220 volts, 50 cycles AC (except for Petit St. Vincent and Palm Island, which have 110 volts, 60 cycles).

MINIMUM AGE FOR DRIVERS: 21-25, depending on the rental car agency. Local license ($28) or international driver's license required. Drive on left.

MINIMUM AGE FOR GAMBLING: 18.

HOLIDAYS: Jan. 1; National Heroes Day, Mar. 14; Good Friday; Easter Monday; Labour Day, May (1st Mon.); Whit Monday, May or June (8th Mon. after Easter); Carnival, July (2nd Mon. and Tues.); August Monday, Aug. (1st Mon.); Independence Day, Oct. 27 (or Mon., Oct. 28, if holiday falls on a Sun.); Christmas, Dec. 25; Boxing Day, Dec. 26.

TAXES: A 10 percent service tax, 10 percent VAT on hotel room, and 15 percent tax on food and other purchased items; service and VAT are often combined at hotels, with a total of 10 percent charged for the two. Departure tax $15 U.S.

IMMIGRATION REQUIREMENTS: Passport and return or onward ticket are required. No visa needed for stays up to 6 months. The U.S. Dept. of Homeland Security requires all U.S. citizens returning from the Caribbean to present a valid passport.

PHONING THE ISLANDS: To call St. Vincent and the Grenadines from the U.S. or Canada, dial 1 + 784 + the 7-digit local number.

FURTHER INFORMATION FOR VISITORS:

St. Vincent and The Grenadines
801 Second Ave., 21st Floor
New York, NY 10017
(212) 687-4981
(800) 729-1726

St. Vincent and The Grenadines, Kingstown
Ministry of Tourism, Youth and Sports
Cruise Ship Terminal, Harbour Quay
Kingstown, St. Vincent
St. Vincent and The Grenadines
(784) 457-1502

Points of Interest

See map page 241.

CANOUAN (E-3)

Named "turtle island" by the Carib Indians, this once deserted sugar plantation and whaling outpost is now home to the 300-acre Raffles Resort and luxury villas and estate properties developed by Donald Trump. The 18-hole course at the Trump International Golf Club was designed by Jim Fazio. An extensive coral reef offers excellent snorkeling and scuba diving.

GAMBLING ESTABLISHMENTS

- **Casino at Trump Club Privée** is at the Raffles Resort. Phone (784) 458 8000.

KINGSTOWN (B-2) pop. 13,212

The capital city of Kingstown is an enjoyable place to explore, with its mixture of English and French architectural styles, exemplified by 19th-century houses and such historic buildings as Wesleyan Hall and St. George's Anglican Cathedral.

St. Mary's Catholic Cathedral is an architectural wonder incorporating a variety of styles; it has Roman arches, Gothic spires and a myriad of balconies, turrets, battlements and courtyards.

FORT CHARLOTTE is on Berkshire Hill west of town. Completed by the British in 1806, the fortification perches 600 feet (183 m) above the city. The fort ruins afford a commanding view of the harbor and the Grenadines. Mounted guns face inland, not out to sea, evidence of the struggle for possession among the British, French and Carib Indians. Paintings that trace the island's history are in the old officers' quarters, now a museum. Daily dawn-dusk. Free. Phone (784) 456-1165.

ST. VINCENT BOTANICAL GARDENS is just s. of Fort Charlotte. Founded in 1762, the 20-acre (8-hectare) gardens are considered the oldest in the Western Hemisphere. Lush with tropical palms, lilies, hibiscus and bougainvillea, the gardens are home to Captain Bligh's breadfruit tree, grown from the original plant, along with such unusual trees as the flowering cannonball and the sealing wax palm. Also at the gardens is an aviary housing the rare St. Vincent parrot, and an archeology museum.

Allow 30 minutes minimum. Daily 8-4. The gardens are free, and plants are labeled in English for self-guiding tours. Local guides offer their services for $3-$5 per hour; be sure to negotiate a rate in advance. Phone (784) 457-1003.

GAMBLING ESTABLISHMENTS

- **Emerald Valley Resort & Casino** is 7 mi. (11 km) outside of Kingstown in Penniston Valley. Wed.-Mon. 9 a.m.-3 a.m. Phone (784) 430-9296.

Maracas Bay, northern Trinidad / © Henry Beeker / age fotostock

Trinidad and Tobago

Trinidad is the southernmost island of the West Indies. It was once an extension of the northern coast of Venezuela, but the lowlands were washed away by the Orinoco River centuries ago; at the closest point only 7 miles (11 km) of sea separate Trinidad and Venezuela. Port of Spain, the capital, is one of the Caribbean's most cosmopolitan cities. People from Africa, China, Britain, India, France, Holland, Portugal, Spain and many other countries make their home here along with descendants of the Arawak and Carib Indians. The architecture is as varied, with ornate mansions, Spanish patios and tiled roofs, French grillwork, cathedrals, mosques and temples.

Christopher Columbus is said to have encountered the island of Trinidad on July 31, 1498, naming it after the Holy Trinity. Many Trinidadians leave the hustle and bustle of their island to vacation on subdued Tobago, some 20 miles (32 km) away. Columbus reported seeing Tobago, which he named Bella Forma, but did not land on the island. Tobago's present name may be derived from the Spanish word for tobacco, but exactly when and how the island was named is unknown. It is believed that Tobago was the inspiration for the shipwreck tales of the Swiss Family Robinson and Robinson Crusoe. Today's visitors will find wide, white beaches and small contemporary hotels.

History

Trinidad was originally inhabited by several Amerindian tribes, including the Caribs, who called the island *Iere,* meaning "land of the hummingbird." However, Christopher Columbus' was inspired by three mountain peaks when he sighted land in 1498, and he called the island La Trinidad, a confirmation of his vow to name his next discovery after the Holy

Trinity. He claimed it for Spain, but a permanent settlement, San Jose de Oruña, was not established until 1577 by Don José de Oruña. Now known as St. Joseph, the town was named as the capital in 1592 upon the arrival of the Spanish governor to Trinidad and Guyana, Don Antonio de Berrio y Oruña,

The 1600s saw raids by the Dutch and French, but the Spanish retained control. Crop failures kept the island poor until 1783, when a Spanish proclamation offered land grants to immigrants willing to develop agriculture and commerce. In 1797, attracted by the resulting prosperity, the British sent an expedition that gained control of the island. Trinidad was formally ceded to Great Britain by the Treaty of Amiens in 1802.

Inhabited by Caribs when first sighted by Columbus, Tobago was subsequently coveted as a strategic position by every major power

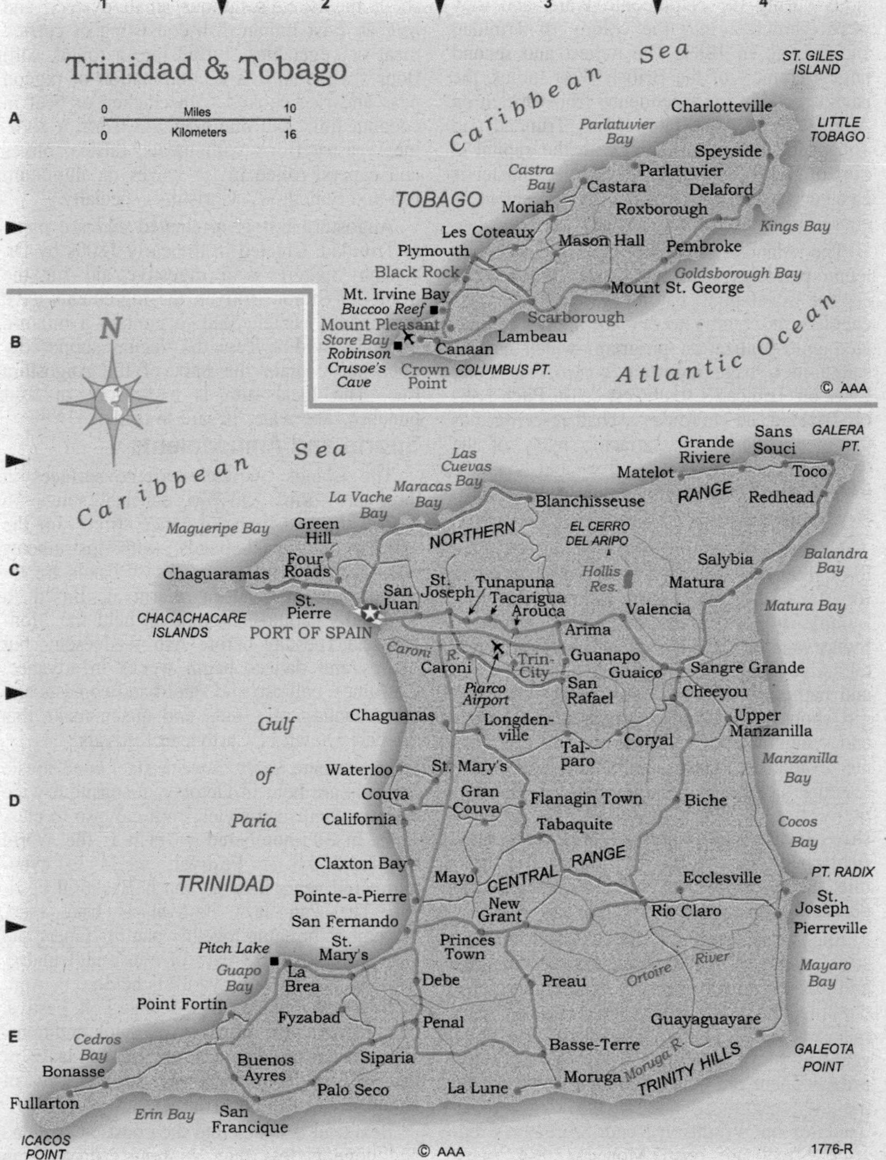

operating in the Caribbean. As a result the island changed hands more than any other in the West Indies; during the 17th and 18th centuries it was taken and retaken by France, Britain, Holland and Spain. In accordance with an agreement in 1749, the island was left unmolested for 13 years, but the struggle began anew when the reprieve ran out. Tobago finally became a crown colony of the Windward Island group in 1814.

Britain consolidated its hold on both islands during the Napoleonic Wars, and they were combined into the colony of Trinidad and Tobago in 1889. The richest and second largest country of the British West Indies, the islands acquired independence from Britain on Aug. 31, 1962. In March 1976, Trinidad and Tobago became a republic, with the capital at Port of Spain, Trinidad. The prime minister is elected by the people, and the president is chosen by the electoral college.

The islands' principal exports are petroleum, petrochemicals and sugar. The discovery of substantial natural gas reserves has enabled the country to embark upon a revitalized industrialization program, which has resulted in a large industrial complex at Point Lisas off Trinidad's southwest coast. Pitch Lake on Trinidad, an enormous asphalt reservoir, has provided material for surfacing many of the world's roads. Cocoa, coffee and—increasingly—tourism also are important economically.

Shopping

Frederick Street in Port of Spain is known throughout the Caribbean and South America for its fascinating shops and merchandise. Luxury imports include French perfumes, Swiss watches, jewelry, china, porcelain, crystal, silver, cameras, leather handbags, beads and petitpoint. Modern department stores and gift shops offer English tweeds and worsteds and synthetic fibers. Irish linens and fine silks are available; dresses, suits and sports and evening jackets are custom tailored on short notice from imported materials. The Oriental shops feature ivory carvings, brassware, saris, richly patterned silks, carved curios and furniture, native filigree jewelry, embroidered slippers and silk apparel.

Such local crafts as hand-carved articles, straw and sisal goods, imaginative ceramics and tiles, vivid paintings, hand-embroidered clothing and gold, silver and copper jewelry make good souvenirs. Trinidad's fine rums and Angostura bitters are available at bargain prices. There are several malls in and around the city, including one at the Cruise Ship Complex on Wrightson Road. Stores on Frederick Street are open Mon.-Fri. 8-4; some stores are open until 5, on Fri. until 6 and on Sat. until noon. Malls are open daily 10-6. Banking hours are Mon.-Thurs. 9-2 and Fri. 9-1 and 3-5 at banks and daily 10-6 at malls.

Food and Drink

The food on Trinidad is as cosmopolitan as the island; British, American, Continental, Creole, Chinese and Indian dishes are available. Popular dishes include *sancoche* and *callaloo,* excellent thick soups; stuffed cascadura, a freshwater fish; crabmeat served in the shell; the island's famous small oysters; and *roti,* an East Indian dish consisting of curried meat or vegetables stuffed into a rolled, soft, flour shell. *Pelau* is a combination of pigeon peas and rice cooked with chicken or beef in coconut milk and pumpkin. *Pastelles,* a cornmeal pastry filled with meats, raisins, olives and capers, rolled in fig leaves or aluminum foil and boiled, is a Christmas specialty.

Angostura bitters originated and are made in Trinidad. Created in the early 1800s by Dr. Johann Siegert as a digestive aid for the troops of Simon Bolivar, the ingredients have remained a secret. Said to contain a mixture of herbs and spices, the recipe supposedly does not contain the bark of the Angostura tree. The local rum is a favorite in fruit punches. The water is safe to drink.

Sports and Amusements

The islands' African heritage surfaces in three art forms: calypso, satirical songs on topical themes; limbo, a dance strictly for the athletic; and steel bands, with instruments fashioned from oil drums. These bands are especially popular during Carnival. Based in Trinidad's capital, Carnival is held the Monday and Tuesday before Ash Wednesday, but parties and dances begin weeks in advance. Costumes, calypso and steel-band contests and the crowning of a king and queen make this the best known of Caribbean festivals.

In alternate years, 3-week steel band music festivals are held in October, featuring a wide variety of musical styles from calypso to classical: In odd-numbered years it is the World Steelband Music Festival, while in even-numbered years it is the Pan is Beautiful Festival. The Pan Jazz Festival is held every November, bringing together pan drummers and jazz musicians for 3 days of music in Trinidad, while Pan Jazz "in de yard" is held every April in Tobago. Yearly, the Best Village Folk Festival in late November offers displays of traditional skills, dance and drama combined with tastes of local cuisine. The islands also are the scene of Hindu and Muslim festivals.

Beautiful beaches line the coast of Trinidad and none is less than an hour's drive from

Port of Spain. Maracas Beach, with its white sand, limpid water and coconut palms, is considered one of the world's most beautiful beaches. Trinidad's efforts to develop the natural beauty of the coastland are focused on Maracas and Las Cuevas bays northwest of Port of Spain and Manzanilla and Mayaro beaches on the east coast.

Good fishing in the Gulf of Paria and adjacent waters is available all year, but the best fishing is from June through September. Boats, guides and equipment are available for hire. Yachting is best during hurricane season, usually falling between July and November; the Trinidad Yacht Club will arrange sailing parties.

Inland activities on Trinidad include golf, hunting and some lively spectator sports. Eighteen-hole golf is played at St. Andrew's (Moka) Golf Club and Pointe-a-Pierre Golf Course. Large hotels usually have facilities catering to tennis buffs. Hunting season in Trinidad runs October through February.

Horse racing takes place at the Santa Rosa Racing Track in Arima during late May, July and August. For spectators and players alike Trinidad offers such popular sports as cricket, January through April; field hockey, January through June; and soccer, which generally runs July through December.

The calypso singers, steel bands and Port of Spain's long history as a sailor's town have earned the island a reputation for its own raucous, gaudy, exciting brand of nightlife. Clubs throughout town vibrate with the beat of Trinidadian dance and music, and stay open until the wee hours of the morning. Hotels also have entertainment, but it is geared toward those with more conservative tastes.

Recreation on Tobago centers on the sea. The island's many inlets, bays, shoals and reefs are excellent for fishing with line or spear; boats, guides and equipment are available for hire. Scuba diving and snorkeling are excellent at Buccoo Reef, and there is bathing at the Nylon Pool, 2 miles (3.2 km) out in the Caribbean. For landlubbers, Trinidad has three 18-hole golf courses: Millennium Lakes Golf and Country Club, Pointe-a-Pierre and St. Andrews. On the sister island of Tobago, golfers can choose from Mt. Irvine Golf Club or the Tobago Plantations Golf and Country Club.

Sightseeing

Lovely drives around Port of Spain enable visitors to relish the island's tropical beauty. Lady Chancellor Road affords a panorama of the city, the Gulf of Paria and San Fernando Hill. Lady Young Road also offers fine views of the city and the hills. Excellent views of the countryside, Venezuela and the sea are available from the Shrine of Our Lady of Fatima in Laventille and from Fort George, both a short distance from Port of Spain.

The North Coast Road to Las Cuevas Bay is spectacular; most of it is between 500 and 1,500 feet (150-450 m) above sea level and overlooks La Vache and Balata bays. This 34-mile (55-km) round trip from Port of Spain is the most popular shore excursion with Caribbean cruise passengers, as it highlights Trinidad's great scenic variety. Also high in Trinidad's northern mountain range at 1,200 feet (365 m) is the very secluded Asa Wright Nature Center. Tours can be arranged out of Port of Spain to the center, which has a former estate house and day- and week-long nature programs.

The northwest coast road to Carenage and Chaguaramas also is particularly scenic. This area includes the islands of Monos and Gaspar Grande (described by the locals as "down the islands"), the latter containing an interesting group of caves on its southern end. The Gasparee Caves are entered by a long winding staircase to the bottom, where stalactites and stalagmites can be seen. A nature trail on Gaspar Grande leads to mounted guns left from World War II and offers a panoramic view of the sea and surrounding islands.

The driving tour from Port of Spain to the Maraval Valley passes through the San Juan cocoa plantations and the Santa Cruz Valley, where planters' houses of French and Spanish colonial days and the great samaan trees still stand. Maracas Bay and Maracas Beach climax the drive from Port of Spain along the Saddle Road.

From Port of Spain the trip to Pitch Lake travels along the Uriah Butler Highway through Chaguanas, noted for its East Indian jewelry; Pointe-à-Pierre, the site of a large oil refinery and the Wildfowl Trust; and San Fernando. Circle tours of Trinidad, lasting 7 hours, travel past the Gulf of Paria, across the central plains, through Pointe-à-Pierre and San Fernando, continue past sugarcane and coconut plantations to Mayaro Beach and return via Manzanilla Beach. Lunch and swimming are included.

An excursion on Tobago might include a tour of Old Fort King George, the Botanical Gardens and the shopping district in Scarborough, combined with a drive past coconut plantations and beaches to Store Bay and Plymouth. A cruise to the Coral Gardens and the Natural Aquarium at Buccoo Reef provides an opportunity for snorkeling and swimming.

Both of these excursions take about a half day.

A pleasant full-day drive on Tobago follows Windward Road along the Atlantic coast from Scarborough to Charlotteville. Visitors can take a pleasant detour off Windward Road, traveling northwest from Roxborough to Parlatuvier. The well-maintained, two-lane Roxborough-Parlatuvier Road climbs across the spine of the island, passing through forest and cultivated land. As the road descends to Parlatuvier, it provides a fine view of the Caribbean side of the island.

Boats depart from Speyside to Little Tobago, where guides conduct walks through a 450-acre (182-hectare) bird sanctuary.

Transportation

Daily direct flights to Trinidad's Piarco International Airport leave New York, Atlanta, Houston, Newark and Miami; other flights from New York and Miami stop at San Juan, Barbados and other intermediate islands. There is regular and frequent air service between Trinidad and the other Caribbean islands and nearby Venezuela. Trinidad also is a port of call for some cruise lines. Cars can be rented by the day or week; driving is on the left. Trinidad's 4,600 miles (7,400 km) of asphalt highways are among the best in the Caribbean. City and island sightseeing tours with a driver-guide are available in Port of Spain. Taxis are abundant.

Twenty-minute flights between Piarco Airport and Tobago's Crown Point Airport are available several times a day. There are two ways visitors can travel on ferry between Trinidad and Tobago—fast ferry or conventional. Fast ferry sailing time is under 2 hours. The conventional ferry takes 5 1/2 hours; these car/passenger ferries have dining rooms and bars. For additional information, phone (868) 625-3055. Cars can be rented on Tobago, which has about 220 miles (354 km) of good roads. Public buses traverse the island several times daily and charge very reasonable rates.

Fast Facts

POPULATION: 1,305,000.

AREA: Trinidad: 4,828 sq km (1,864 sq mi.). **Tobago:** 300 sq km (116 sq mi.).

CAPITAL: Port of Spain, Trinidad.

HIGHEST POINT: 940 m (3,084 ft.), El Cerro del Aripo, Trinidad.

LOWEST POINT: Sea level, Caribbean Sea.

TIME ZONE(S): Atlantic Standard.

LANGUAGE: English.

GOVERNMENT: Independent. Member of the British Commonwealth of Nations.

UNIT OF CURRENCY: Trinidad and Tobago dollar. $1 U.S. = approx. 6 Trinidad/Tobago dollars.

ELECTRICITY: 110-230 volts, 60 cycles AC; voltage varies with location.

MINIMUM AGE FOR DRIVERS: 21-25, depending on the rental car agency. U.S. license valid for 3 months; drive on left.

SEAT BELT/CHILD RESTRAINT LAWS: Seat belts are required for driver and front-seat passengers.

HOLIDAYS: Jan. 1; Spiritual Baptist Shouter Liberation Day, Mar. 30; Good Friday; Easter Monday; Indian Arrival Day, May 30; Feast of Corpus Christi, May or June (9th Thurs. after Easter); Labour Day, June 19; Emancipation Day, Aug. 1; Independence Day, Aug. 31; Republic Day, Sept. 24; Divali Day, Nov. 12; Eid-ul-Fitr (Muslim Holy Day), Nov. or Dec; Christmas, Dec. 25; Boxing Day, Dec. 26.

TAXES: A 10 percent room tax and 10-15 percent service charge are added to most hotel bills. Many restaurants include a 10-15 percent service charge. A 15 percent VAT (value-added tax) is added to most consumer goods. Departure tax $16 U.S.

IMMIGRATION REQUIREMENTS: A valid passport and return or onward ticket are required. No visa needed for stays up to 90 days. The U.S. Dept. of Homeland Security requires all U.S. citizens returning from the Caribbean to present a valid passport.

PHONING THE ISLANDS: To call Trinidad and Tobago from the U.S. or Canada, dial 1 + 868 + the 7-digit local number.

FURTHER INFORMATION FOR VISITORS:

Trinidad and Tobago Tourism Development Co.
P.O. Box 222
Maritime Centre, 29 Tenth Ave.
Barataria, Trinidad
Trinidad and Tabago
(868) 675-7034

Tobago Department of Tourism
Doretta's Court
197 Mount Marie
Scarborough, Tobago
Trinidad and Tobago
(868) 639-2125
(868) 639-4636
See color ad inside back cover.

Points of Interest

See map page 245.

Tobago

The island of Tobago, 21 miles (34 km) northeast of Trinidad, covers 116 square miles (300 sq km). A low mountain ridge divides the island, which is a sanctuary for hummingbirds, green parrots, jacamars, motmots and nightjars.

Robinson's Crusoe's Cave, 10 miles (16 km) west of Scarborough, is named for Daniel Defoe's fictional castaway. The subterranean cave traverses Crown Point and Store Bay. The ruins of Fort James are nearby at Plymouth; a powder magazine on the grounds has been restored.

SCARBOROUGH (B-3) pop. 15,830

Scarborough, the main town and administrative center of Tobago, is on Rockley Bay on the island's southern shore. Its native market is most active Friday and Saturday. The Coral Gardens on Buccoo Reef is a popular spot for both snorkelers and divers.

The ruins of Fort King George overlook the city at its highest point. Built 1784-87, the fort originally was named Fort Castries by the French. When the British took over, they renamed the fort after their king. Within the fort is the Tobago Museum, where exhibits include prehistoric Amerindian artifacts, historical maps and documents and local history displays. The Rockery Vale sugar estate, parceled out in the late 1800s, now is home to a 17-acre (7-hectare) botanic garden and the Welbeck House.

Trinidad

Just 7 miles (11 km) off the coast of Venezuela, Trinidad is the southernmost island in the Caribbean archipelago. Trinidad covers 1,864 square miles (4,828 sq km), roughly the size of Rhode Island. Three mountain ranges cross the island; at 3,085 feet (940 m), El Cerro del Aripo is the highest point. Half of the island is forest, and mangrove swamps provide wildlife habitats on both the east and west coasts.

The Pitch Lake at San Fernando prompted interest in Trinidad's petrochemical resources; the first oil well was drilled here in 1857. By the early 20th century, oil had replaced sugar as the island's chief export. A surplus of Navy oil drums led to the invention of Trinidad's famed steel drums.

The church of Notre Dame de Montserrat in Tortuga contains the statue of the Black Virgin. The wooden figure is said to have been brought from Spain by Capuchin monks. In nearby Carapichaima stands the 85-foot-tall Hanuman Murti, reputed to be the tallest Hindu statue of its kind outside India. The brightly-colored effigy of a monkey-faced god is east of the Waterloo Temple, also known as the Temple-in-the-Sea. A laborer built this shrine in the Gulf of Paria after he was forbidden from using sugar land.

PORT OF SPAIN (C-2) pop. 49,031

Busy markets, exotic houses of worship and modern buildings give Port of Spain a cosmopolitan atmosphere. The city has been the capital of Trinidad since 1757 and the capital of both Trinidad and Tobago since they were united in 1899. From the hills north of the city, the coast of Venezuela can be seen across the Gulf of Paria.

Just outside of Port of Spain on the Eastern Main Road in Laventille is the House of Angostura, maker of several varieties of rum and its signature, Angostura aromatic bitters. The distillery features a museum, art gallery and butterfly collection; factory tours are available by reservation. Phone (868) 623-1841.

CARONI LAGOON NATIONAL PARK AND BIRD SANCTUARY is 7 mi. (11 km) s. on the Uriah Butler Hwy. This 15,000-acre (6,000-hectare) mangrove swamp is nesting ground to the scarlet ibis, now threatened by pollution and poachers. At sunset, thousands of the brilliantly colored birds return to roost in the mangrove trees, offering a spectacular sight. Guided 2.5-hour boat trips are offered by Nanan's Bird Sanctuary Tours.

Insect repellent and binoculars are advised; boats do not disturb the birds by approaching closely. Tours depart daily at 4; passengers should arrive at the sanctuary 15 minutes before departure. Closed Dec. 25. Fare $10; $5 (children); free (ages 0-4). Reservations are required. Phone (868) 645-1305.

CATHEDRAL OF THE HOLY TRINITY faces the southern side of Woodford Square on Abercromby St. and is entered from Queen St. This Anglican church was built 1816-18; a 1908 fire destroyed the original building and the church was subsequently rebuilt. The Georgian and Gothic structure has a mahogany ceiling patterned after the one in London's Westminster Hall. The altar and choir stalls also are noteworthy. Open daily 6-6. Free. Phone (868) 623-7271.

CATHEDRAL OF THE IMMACULATE CONCEPTION is at Independence Square. Begun in 1816, this Catholic cathedral with dual towers was consecrated in 1851. Daily 9-5. Free. Phone (868) 623-5232.

NATIONAL MUSEUM AND ART GALLERY is on the s.w. corner of Queen's Park Savannah at 117 Frederick St. Guarded by Spanish cannons that date from 1797, the museum houses an anchor that Columbus lost in Trinidad. Displays relate to natural history, industry, geology and archeology. Of special note are elaborate costumes worn during Carnival Week celebrations as well as a display of folk art and crafts. Allow 1 hour minimum. Tues.-Sat. 10-6, Sun. 2-6. Free. Phone (868) 623-5941.

QUEEN'S PARK SAVANNAH is in the center of the fashionable residential district. The park covers nearly 200 grassland acres (81 hectares). The Stollmeyer House in the eastern section was built in 1904 as a copy of a wing of Balmoral Castle in Scotland; other excellent examples of Grand Colonial Architecture surround the park. Cricket, football and rugby events are held here. The Emperor Valley Zoo and the Royal Botanic Gardens, laid out in 1820, face the northern side of the park; Memorial Square and the National Museum are on the park's east side.

Park open daily 24 hours. Zoo Wed.-Mon. 9:30-6; closed Dec. 25 and Carnival Monday and Tuesday. Park and botanic gardens free. Zoo $2; $1 (ages 3-12). Phone (868) 622-3530 for the zoo.

RED HOUSE is on Abercromby Street opposite Woodford Square. The handsome building once housed the legislative council and other government agencies and now serves as the seat of the nation's parliament. The main chamber is noted for its ornate gesso ceiling, which was created in England, shipped in panels and installed by an Italian craftsman in 1906. An eternal flame symbolizing "the need to be ever vigilant in the protection of democracy" burns on the eastern lawn atop a marble cenotaph. Guided tours are offered by appointment. Daily 8-4. Free. Phone (868) 624-7275.

ROYAL BOTANIC GARDENS adjoins the president's house at Queen's Park Savannah. Tropical plants and trees, including lotus lilies, monkey pods and Ceylon willows, grow on about 70 acres (28 hectares). Evening band concerts occasionally take place. Guided tours are available by appointment. Open daily 6-6. Free. Phone (868) 622-4221.

SAN FERNANDO (D-2) pop. 55,419

San Fernando, Trinidad's second largest city, is built on a hill on the Gulf of Paria. Sugar estates and factories are nearby; oil fields lie to the southeast.

PITCH LAKE is s.w. at La Brea. One of three natural asphalt lakes in the world, the tar pit covers 100 barren acres (40 hectares). Its hard surface will bear foot traffic—with caution. About 165,000 tons of asphalt are excavated yearly. Local legend attributes the origin of this lake to the Great Spirit, anguished by the Chayma Indians' sacrifice of the sacred hummingbird. In retribution, the Great Spirit caused the earth to swallow up the guilty, leaving the lake as a reminder.

Cockburn Town, Grand Turk / © Walter Bibikow / Danita Delimont Stock Photography

Turks and Caicos Islands

The tiny islands of Turks and Caicos (KAY-kos) lie southeast of The Bahamas and north of the Dominican Republic and Haiti. The Turks and Caicos are comprised of eight major islands and some 40 smaller cays, most of which remain uninhabited. Grand Turk and Salt Cay are in the Turks, and North, Middle (also known as Grand), South, East and West Caicos and Providenciales (also known as Provo) are in the Caicos. The two groups are separated by the Turks Island Passage. Of the Atlantic group, these beautiful islands resemble those found farther south, with dazzling white or gold sand and sparkling waters. Most of the resorts are on Provo and Grand Turk; more intimate accommodations are available on the other islands. The islands' business, banking and government center is Cockburn Town on Grand Turk.

History

The Turks and Caicos might have been among the islands mentioned in Christopher Columbus' 1492 diary, but there is no official record of discovery until Juan Ponce de León arrived in 1512. The native inhabitants were the Arawak Indians, whose population was almost destroyed by the French and Spanish. The British finally took control of the islands under the Treaty of Madrid, and during the American Revolution they were the territory of Loyalists and pirates. At the end of the war the Loyalists and settlers from Bermuda began producing salt and set up cotton and sisal plantations, ventures that eventually supported the islands for many years. Tourism is now the mainstay of the economy. The Turks are named for the Turk's Head Cactus, while Caicos is a derivation of *cayos,* the Spanish word for "small island."

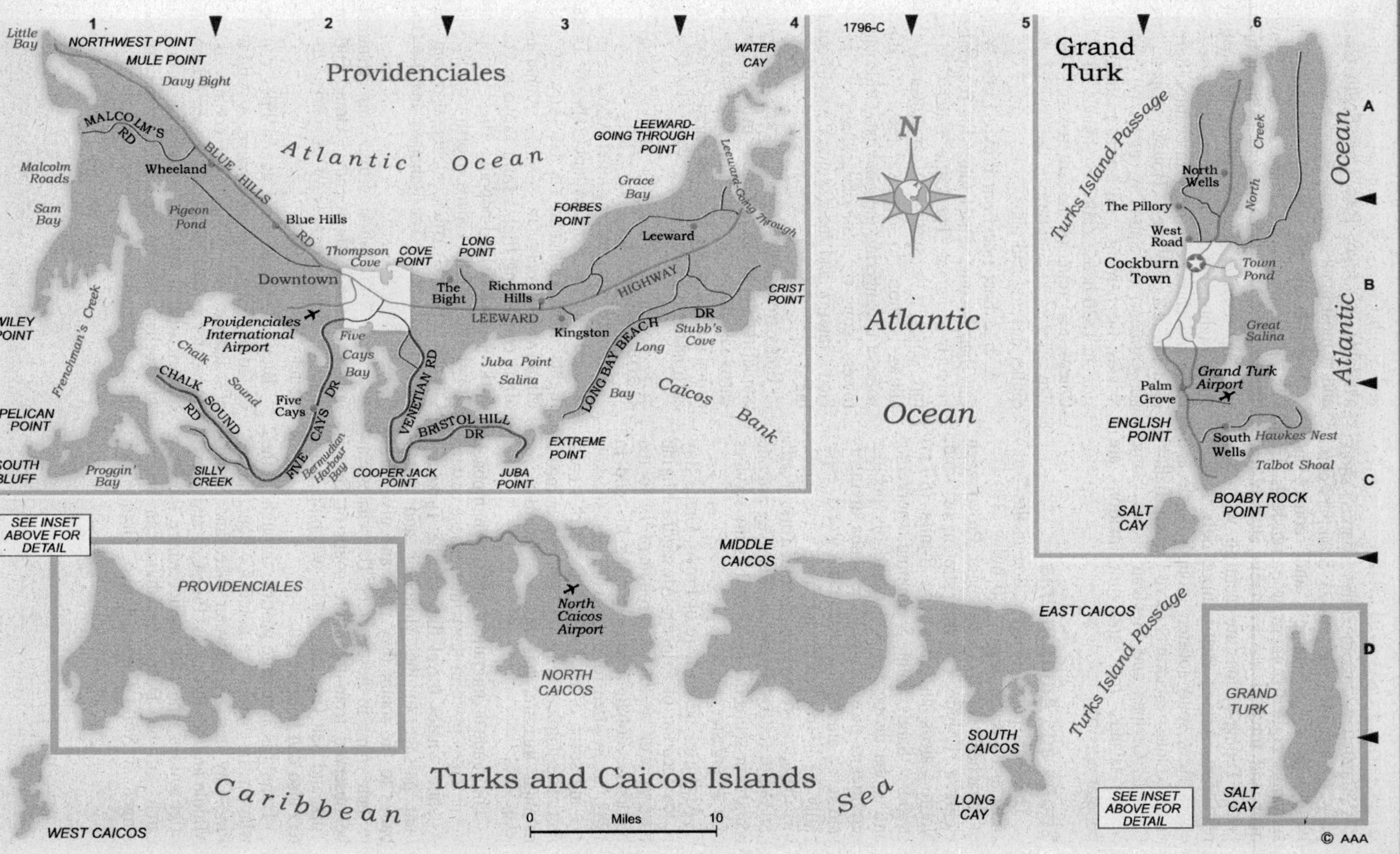
1796-C
Providenciales
Atlantic Ocean
Little Bay
NORTHWEST POINT
MULE POINT
Davy Bight
MALCOLM'S RD
Malcolm Roads
Sam Bay
Wheeland
BLUE HILLS RD
Blue Hills
Pigeon Pond
Downtown
Thompson Cove
COVE POINT
LONG POINT
The Bight
Richmond Hills
LEEWARD HIGHWAY
Kingston
FORBES POINT
Grace Bay
LEEWARD-GOING THROUGH POINT
Leeward
Leeward-Going Through
WATER CAY
CRIST POINT
Stubb's Cove
LONG BAY BEACH DR
Long Bay
Caicos Bank
EXTREME POINT
Juba Point Salina
BRISTOL HILL DR
JUBA POINT
VENETIAN RD
COOPER JACK POINT
Five Cays Bay
FIVE CAYS DR
Bermudian Harbour Bay
Five Cays
Providenciales International Airport
Chalk Sound
CHALK SOUND RD
SILLY CREEK
Proggin' Bay
Frenchman's Creek
WILEY POINT
PELICAN POINT
SOUTH BLUFF
N
Atlantic Ocean
Grand Turk
Turks Island Passage
North Wells
The Pillory
West Road
Cockburn Town
North Creek
Town Pond
Great Salina
Grand Turk Airport
Palm Grove
ENGLISH POINT
South Wells
Hawkes Nest
Talbot Shoal
BOABY ROCK POINT
SALT CAY
Ocean
Atlantic
SEE INSET ABOVE FOR DETAIL
PROVIDENCIALES
North Caicos Airport
NORTH CAICOS
MIDDLE CAICOS
EAST CAICOS
Turks Island Passage
SOUTH CAICOS
LONG CAY
GRAND TURK
SALT CAY
SEE INSET ABOVE FOR DETAIL
Turks and Caicos Islands
Caribbean Sea
0 Miles 10
WEST CAICOS
© AAA

Shopping, Food and Drink

Compared with some other islands, shopping opportunities are limited. Shoppers commonly purchase stamps and coins and souvenirs crafted from straw or seashells. Liquor and tobacco are available at duty-free prices. Dining options are plentiful, with local restaurants serving such seafood delicacies as conch stew, spiny lobster, grouper, turtle and wahoo. Other restaurants serve French, Italian, Chinese, German and Mexican dishes. Some of the islands' fruit and rum libations are popular aperitifs.

Sports and Amusements

The focal point for recreation in the Turks and Caicos is the nearly 230 miles (370 km) of beaches. North Caicos and Provo each claim a 12-mile (19-km) stretch of sand; North Caicos also boasts a 5-mile (8-km) strand at Sandy Point. Swimming, snorkeling and scuba diving are understandably popular activities at most resorts. The scuba diving is said to be among the best in the world, especially off Provo and Grand Turk. Dive operators based at resorts on Grand Turk, North and South Caicos, Provo and Salt Cay provide rentals for scuba diving as well as the services of a divemaster.

Along the north shore of Provo, Grace Bay is the location of Princess Alexandra Marine Park as well as the playground of Jo Jo the bottlenose dolphin. Since leaving his pod in 1983, Jo Jo often follows swimmers, snorkelers and scuba divers through the park's coral reef. The dolphin, who has been proclaimed a national treasure, has his own warden for protection.

The annual migration of the humpback whale takes place in the winter. These eastern Atlantic whales travel through the Turks Island passage to the Mouchoir and Silver banks to the south; they mate and give birth to their young in these waters. The whales can be observed from the shore south of Grand Turk and Salt Cay, and whale-watching charters also can be arranged.

Fishing is a favorite pastime throughout the islands; the Caicos are noted for bonefishing. Pine Cay has a freshwater lake, and South, Middle and North Caicos, Pine Cay and Provo offer guides who can predict where the best catch will be. Deep-sea fishing can be arranged at North Caicos, Provo, Grand Turk and South Caicos. Boat rentals for sailing are available at Provo, Pine Cay, South Caicos and at most hotels.

Tennis courts are available to guests of hotels on North Caicos, Pine Cay and Provo. The Provo Golf Club offers an 18-hole championship course. Hotels offer information about sightseeing. Some interesting sites include old churches, the 19th-century Bermudian Great White House (open by appointment) on Salt Cay, caves on Middle Caicos, the herd of wild horses roaming outside an 1820 house called Highlands on South Caicos, and ruins of the salt industry. Hotels also offer some nightlife in the way of after-dinner dancing and pubs.

A short boat ride from Provo, Little Water Cay has become a sanctuary for the endangered rock iguana. The Little Water Cay Nature Trail is a system of boardwalks that allows visitors to observe these creatures without endangering their habitat. Observation towers along the trail offer views of the island's interior and the azure waters surrounding it.

Boats from many towns participate in the annual regatta at South Caicos in May. Carnival is celebrated in September with the coronation of the queen and the parade in which each island is represented.

Transportation

Providenciales International Airport can be reached by air from Atlanta aboard Delta flights, from Charlotte via US Airways and Miami with American Airlines. Bahamasair offers connecting flights from Provo to Grand Turk Airport. Island-hopping flights stop at Grand Turk, South Caicos, North Caicos, Salt Cay and Provo. Arrangements also can be made for flights to The Bahamas and the Dominican Republic.

A new $45-million cruise ship terminal opened on the southern end of Grand Turk in 2005, bringing a new wave of tourists to the island.

Bicycles, mopeds and automobiles can be rented on Grand Turk and Provo. A valid driver's license from your home country is required for rentals, and vehicles are driven on the left side of the road. Chartering a boat is an excellent way to see a wide variety of islands while you enjoy the sun and sea.

Fast Facts

POPULATION: 18,122.

AREA: 430 sq km (166 sq mi.).

CAPITAL: Grand Turk.

HIGHEST POINT: 49 m (161 ft.), Blue Hills, Providenciales.

LOWEST POINT: Sea level, Atlantic Ocean.

TIME ZONE(S): Eastern Standard. DST.

LANGUAGE: English.

GOVERNMENT: British Overseas Territory.

UNIT OF CURRENCY: U.S. dollar.

ELECTRICITY: 110-120 volts, 60 cycles AC.

MINIMUM AGE FOR DRIVERS: 21-25, depending on the rental car agency. U.S. license valid; drive on left.

MINIMUM AGE FOR GAMBLING: 18.

SEAT BELT/CHILD RESTRAINT LAWS: Seat belts are required for all passengers.

HOLIDAYS: Jan. 1; Commonwealth Day, Mar. (2nd Mon.); Good Friday; Easter Monday; National Heroes Day, May 26; Queen's Birthday, June (3rd weekend); Emancipation Day, Aug. (1st Mon.); Constitution Day, Aug. 30; National Youth Day, Sept. 30; Columbus Day, Oct. 13; International Human Rights Day, Oct. 24; Christmas, Dec. 25; Boxing Day, Dec. 26.

TAXES: A 7 percent room tax and 10-15 percent service charge are added to most hotel bills. Departure tax $45 U.S.

IMMIGRATION REQUIREMENTS: Passport and a return or onward ticket are required. No visa needed for stays up to 30 days. The U.S. Dept. of Homeland Security requires all U.S. citizens returning from the Caribbean to present a valid passport.

PHONING THE ISLANDS: To call the Turks and Caicos Islands from the U.S. or Canada, dial 1 + 649 + the 7-digit local number.

FURTHER INFORMATION FOR VISITORS:

Turks and Caicos Tourist Board
The Lincoln Building
60 E. 42nd St., Suite 2817
New York, NY 10165
(646) 375-8830
(800) 241-0824

Turks and Caicos Tourist Board, Grand Turk
Front Street
P.O. Box 128
Grand Turk, Turks and Caicos Islands
(649) 946-2321

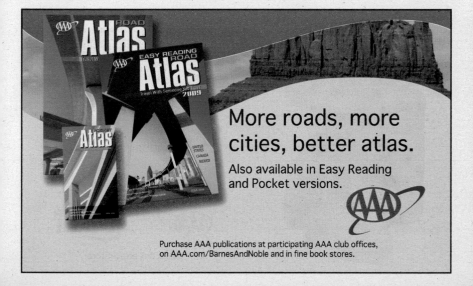

Points of Interest

See map page 253.

Grand Turk (B-6)

Grand Turk island, 6 miles (9.7 km) long, is noted for its beaches and scuba-diving. Flat and dry, the island was used as a salt-making station in the 1600s. Cockburn Town, the nation's administrative capital, features Bermuda-style architecture in many of its 18th- and 19th-century buildings.

The Grand Turk Lighthouse at the north end was constructed in 1852, though its whale-oil lamps failed to prevent shipwrecks until the addition of a Fresnel lens and kerosene lights in 1943. Now electrified, the lighthouse remains in service.

TURKS AND CAICOS NATIONAL MUSEUM is in Guinep House on Front Street. The building, constructed in the mid-1800s of native stone, houses artifacts from the Molasses Reef shipwreck, said to be the oldest European wreck discovered in the Western Hemisphere. Several exhibits portray the culture and natural history of the islands. A 7-minute film is presented. Artifacts from what is thought to be the oldest Lucayan Indian site in the Bahamian archipelago, dating to 750 A.D., also are displayed.

Guided tours are available. Allow 1 hour minimum. Mon.-Fri. 9-4, Sat. 9-1; closed major holidays. Admission $5. Phone (649) 946-2160.

Providenciales (B-2)

Larger in size than Bermuda, Providenciales (known as Provo) has become the Turks and Caicos Islands' tourism center. Not a single wheeled vehicle was in use on the island until 1965; it now has miles of good roads and a variety of fine accommodations and restaurants. On a hilltop overlooking Sapodilla Bay, stones bear the inscriptions of 18th-century sailors.

CAICOS CONCH FARM is on the n.e. tip of the island at Leeward. Guided 20-minute tours educate visitors about the queen conch (pronounced *konk*), which is raised here for food and pearl production. The 5-acre (2-hectare) working farm includes a hatchery, nursery ponds, sea pens and a processing facility. Two "trained" conches are introduced during the tour. Mon.-Fri. 9-4, Sat. 9-2; closed holidays. Last tour departs 20 minutes before closing. Admission $6; $3 (ages 0-11). Phone (649) 946-5643.

The Baths, Virgin Gorda Island / British Virgin Island Tourist Board

Virgin Islands, British

Islands tinged with the warm colors of a Paul Gauguin painting and white sand beaches cooled by refreshing breezes characterize the Virgin Islands. About 60 miles (97 km) east of Puerto Rico, the archipelago lies directly in the path of the trade winds and enjoys a pleasant climate with moderate rainfall and maximum sunlight. The principal British islands are Tortola, Virgin Gorda, Anegada (ah-nee-GAH-da) and Jost Van Dyke; except for the flat coral island of Anegada, both the U.S. and British Virgins are volcanic in origin.

Though not as developed as their U.S. sisters, the British Virgin Islands have a distinctive appeal. Tortola has the capital, Road Town, with its serene harbor and rugged 1,709-foot (521-m) Mount Sage. Virgin Gorda Island has an untamed natural beauty, and uninhabited Norman Island is reputed to be the "Treasure Island" of Robert Louis Stevenson fame. Some of the smaller, secluded islands are privately owned and offer the ultimate in escapist vacations.

History

The British Virgin Islands saw their first Europeans when Christopher Columbus arrived in 1493. Except for some copper on Virgin Gorda, the Spanish found little of interest on the islands and eventually lost them to the British in 1628. However, it was the Dutch who settled Tortola and initiated the lucrative sugar trade, which sparked the envy of other countries. Yet, despite battles between the

French, Spanish, Dutch, Danes and various pirates, Britain regained the islands in 1666 and has held them ever since. Today the islands constitute a territory, administered by a queen-appointed governor and a locally elected government headed by a Chief Minister. While livestock raising is still important, offshore banking and tourism and its related industries dominate the islands' economy.

Shopping

Most of the retail shops in the islands are found along Main Street in Road Town or along the harbor in Virgin Gorda. Because there is no duty on British imports, bargains can be found on some English china, fabrics and foods. Among other bargains are rum, whiskey and gin as well as intricate straw goods, island crafts, jewelry and fabric designs. One popular shopping area in Road Town is Main Street, which has shops offering souvenirs, spices, jewelry and china. Such native spices as Tortola's rum, pepper sauce and BVI Caribbean seasoning are found at the retail outlets of Tortola's two spice factories. Locations include Main Street, Crafts Alive Market, Soper's Hole Marina and the Beef Island Airport.

Local stamps are unique in that they are the only stamps in the British Commonwealth sold in a denomination of U.S. currency, official tender in the British Virgins. Stamps are available in Road Town or at the small post office at West End on Tortola. Major credit cards and travelers checks are accepted at most hotels and restaurants.

Food and Drink

Except for seafood, mutton, beef or home-grown vegetables and fruit, all food is imported. Tortola and Virgin Gorda have the largest selection of restaurants. On other inhabited islands a small hotel or inn is often the only establishment. Hotels usually serve three meals a day and have wine lists as well as a wide assortment of liquors and fruit drinks. Island cuisine is characterized by fish or seafood dishes, the most popular being *fungee*. This type of Caribbean polenta is made from corn meal, mixed with onions, sweet peppers and okra, boiled into cakes and served with boiled fish and green vegetables.

Sports and Amusements

The islands' most popular activity and biggest drawing card is sailing. Their reputation as a mecca for yachting enthusiasts, though long known by advocates of the sport, has been discovered by amateur sailors and tourists. As a result hundreds of yachts are available for charter. The more than 40 islands and cays are ripe for exploring.

Many half- or full-day cruises include a picnic lunch, snorkeling, swimming or tours of such sites as Virgin Gorda's Baths—gigantic boulders forming a labyrinth of grottoes

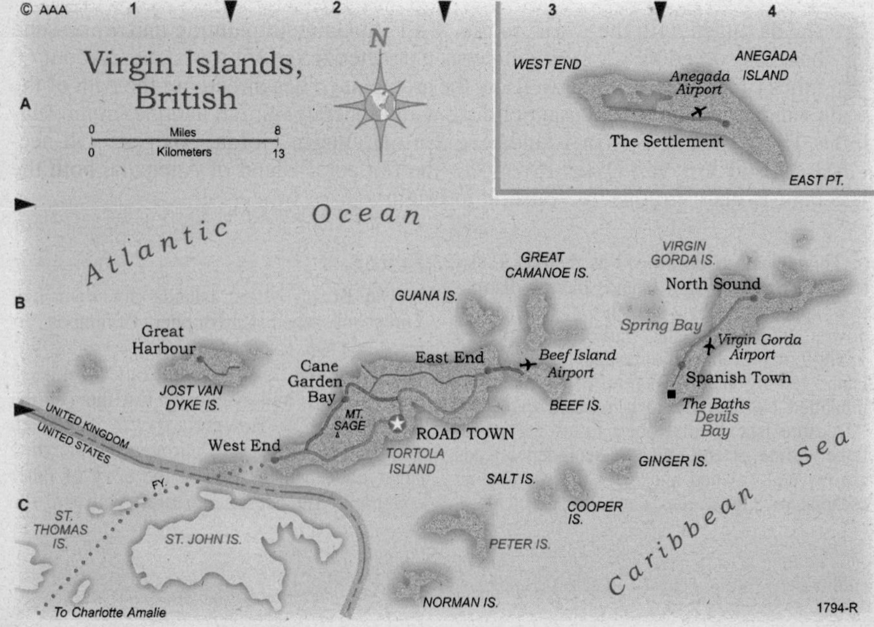

and beaches. The best equipped marinas are on Tortola, Virgin Gorda and Peter Island. You should make reservations for longer sailing excursions during the peak season, December through February.

Deep-sea fishing is another popular activity in the British Virgin Islands, where record catches of blue marlin, tuna and wahoo have been made. Special competitions take place June through November.

The clarity of the waters off these islands creates superb scuba and snorkeling conditions. Especially notable is the wreck of the RMS *Rhone* located off Salt Island; this wreck is ranked as one of the top-rated sites by several diving publications. Expert guides are available, and arrangements can be made through any of the islands' many dive shops or hotels. Caribbean Images and Rainbow Visions in Tortola rent cameras and offer courses on underwater photography.

The variety of birds, including pink flamingos, inhabiting the flat island of Anegada also make a visit worthwhile. Some 154 species of birds are found throughout the British Virgin Islands. Tennis courts can be found at hotels on Virgin Gorda, Tortola and Peter Island.

The appeal of the British Virgin Islands is tranquility, which means few dance clubs and no high-rises, jets or mammoth cruise ships. Evening diversions, therefore, are minimal. Moonlight cruises, listening to a steel band or dancing to after-dinner music at one of the hotels constitute most of the organized activities. Tortola's Festival, held the last week in July through the first weekend in August, incorporates the Emancipation Day Parade; Virgin Gorda's Festival celebrations take place Easter weekend. The festivities, popular with visitors and residents alike, include parades, dances, food fairs, beauty contests and band competitions.

The Welcome, the bimonthly tourist news magazine available free throughout the islands, provides up-to-date information. *The Limin' Times Entertainment Guide* is a good source for news about entertainment and activities. The British Virgin Islands Tourist Board maintains an office in Road Town and at the yacht harbor on Virgin Gorda Island.

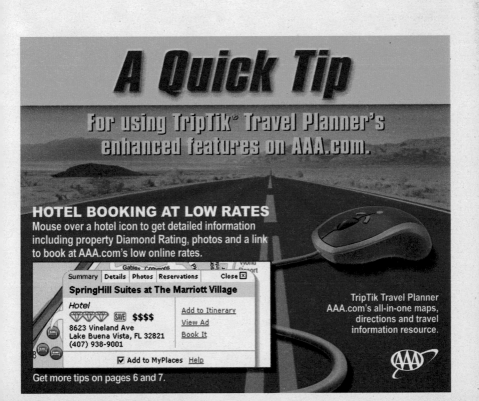

Transportation

Tortola's Beef Island Airport can be reached by plane from St. Thomas, St. Maarten, St. Croix, Antigua, St. Kitts or San Juan via Air Sunshine, American Eagle, Cape Air or LIAT. Virgin Gorda has frequent connections with St. Thomas and San Juan. Frequent interisland flights link Tortola with Anegada. Charter flights are available through Fly BVI and Clair Aero.

While inland transportation is fairly limited, taxis are available on Tortola, Virgin Gorda, Anegada and Jost Van Dyke; all offer island tours. Rental cars can be hired on Tortola, Virgin Gorda and Anegada, and with limited availability on Jost Van Dyke; a local driver's license good for 90 days is required and can be obtained at car rental agencies or the traffic licensing office.

Virgin Islands Ferries operate daily between both Charlotte Amalie and Red Hook, St. Thomas in the U.S. Virgin Islands, and West End, Tortola. Trips take 30-45 minutes. A 90-minute ferry runs to Road Town, Tortola. Phone (284) 495-4617 or (284) 995-4495 for fares and schedules. Within the British Virgin Islands, ferry service operates daily from Road Town, Tortola, to Virgin Gorda and Peter Island. A ferry also connects West End, Tortola, with Jost Van Dyke. Phone Jost Van Dyke Ferry, (284) 494-2997; New Horizon Ferry, (284) 495-9477; Peter Island Ferry, (284) 495-2000; Smith's Ferry, (284) 495-4495; or Speedy's Ferry (284) 495-5240. North Sound Express operates a ferry between Beef Island and North Sound, Virgin Gorda, with stops in the valley; phone (284) 495-2138. Some of the more remote islands can only be reached by sailboat or motorboat out of Tortola and Virgin Gorda.

Fast Facts

POPULATION: 19,100.

AREA: 153 sq km (59 sq mi.).

CAPITAL: Road Town, Tortola.

HIGHEST POINT: 521 m (1,709 ft.), Mount Sage, Tortola.

LOWEST POINT: Sea level, Caribbean Sea.

TIME ZONE(S): Atlantic Standard.

LANGUAGE: English.

GOVERNMENT: British Overseas Territory.

UNIT OF CURRENCY: U.S. dollar.

ELECTRICITY: 110-120 volts, 60 cycles AC; voltage varies with location.

MINIMUM AGE FOR DRIVERS: 25. Local license ($10) required, valid for 3 months; drive on left.

SEAT BELT/CHILD RESTRAINT LAWS: Seat belts are required for all passengers.

HOLIDAYS: Jan. 1; H.L. Stoutt's Birthday, Mar. (1st Mon.); Commonwealth Day, Mar. (2nd Mon.); Good Friday; Easter; Easter Monday; Whit Monday, May or June (8th Mon. after Easter); Sovereign's Birthday, June (2nd Sat.); Territory Day, July 1; Festival Monday, Tuesday and Wednesday, Aug. (1st Mon., Tues. and Wed.); St. Ursula's Day, Oct. 20; Prince of Wales' Birthday, Nov. 14; Christmas, Dec. 25; Boxing Day, Dec. 26.

TAXES: A 7 percent room tax and 10-15 percent service charge are added to most hotel bills. Departure tax is $20 U.S. by air, $7 by cruise ship, $5 by ferry,

IMMIGRATION REQUIREMENTS: Passport and return or onward ticket are required. No visa needed for stays up to 30 days. The U.S. Dept. of Homeland Security requires all U.S. citizens returning from the Caribbean to present a valid passport.

PHONING THE ISLANDS: To call the British Virgin Islands from the U.S. or Canada, dial 1 + 284 + the 7-digit local number.

FURTHER INFORMATION FOR VISITORS:

British Virgin Islands Tourist Board
1 West 34th Street, Suite 302
New York, NY 10001
(212) 696-0400
(800) 835-8530

British Virgin Islands Tourist Board, Road Town
DeCastro Street
2nd Floor, AKARA Building
Road Town, Tortola
Virgin Islands, British
(284) 494-3134

Points of Interest

See map page 258.

Tortola Island (B-2)

Its name meaning "turtledove" in Spanish, 24-square-mile (62-sq-km) Tortola is the largest of the British Virgin Islands. It rests in the shadow of 1,709-foot Mount Sage, where traces of a primeval rain forest can still be found. Settled first by the Dutch and then the English in 1666, Tortola was granted its charter in 1773.

Road Town is the business center and seat of government. Fishing, scuba diving, snorkeling, sailing, swimming, windsurfing, kayaking, hiking, bicycling and horseback riding are popular diversions that can be enjoyed island-wide. Cane Garden Bay is one of the island's most popular beaches; others include Brewer's Bay Beach, Smuggler's Cove and Lambert Bay.

OLD GOVERNMENT HOUSE is on Waterfront Dr. in Road Town. This elegant house for the Commissioner of the British Virgin Islands was built in 1926 after the original was destroyed by a hurricane. The first floor and gardens are open to the public; historical exhibits include period furniture, cannonballs and glass bottles recovered during excavation of the grounds. Murals in the dining room depicting 19th-century island life were painted by the governor's wife. Mon.-Fri. 9-2. Free. Guided tours are offered for a fee. Phone (284) 494-4091.

Virgin Gorda Island (B-4)

Expanses of unspoiled beaches characterize Virgin Gorda (The Fat Virgin). Ten miles (16 km) long and almost 2 miles (3.2 km) wide in some places, the 8-square-mile (21-sq-km) island is the third largest of the British group and commands the Anegada Passage. Settled by the English in the late 1600s, Virgin Gorda was developed into agricultural estates. With the abolition of slavery in 1834, the population—once more than 8,000—dwindled to about 3,000.

Excursions on Virgin Gorda include trips to serene Spring Bay, Valley Trunk Bay, North Sound, Gorda Peak National Park, Devil's Bay, the boulder-strewn labyrinth of grottoes and beaches known as The Baths, and the ruins of a 19th-century Cornish mine at Copper Mine National Park.

Paradise Point, Charlotte Amalie, St. Thomas Island / US Virgin Islands Department of Tourism

Virgin Islands, U.S.

Taken together, all three U.S. Virgin Islands—St. Thomas, St. Croix and St. John—create the ideal West Indies vacation package. Charlotte Amalie (a-MAL-ya), capital of the islands, typifies the Caribbean town with its delightful shops and patios, winding streets and Old World, Continental flavor. Its picturesque harbor is among the busiest cruise ports in the Caribbean. Varied nightlife and a resort atmosphere make St. Thomas the liveliest of the U.S. Virgins. The largest of the islands, St. Croix is dotted with the ruins of plantation great houses and secluded beaches. St. Croix also offers shopping and amusement opportunities, but at a slower, less hectic pace. For those seeking peace, quiet and natural beauty, St. John is the archetype of the remote and undeveloped Caribbean isle. The beautiful Virgin Islands National Park covers two-thirds of the island.

History

Christopher Columbus discovered the Virgin Islands during his second voyage in 1493. His fleet of 17 ships first anchored off the north coast of Santa Cruz, or St. Croix as the French would later call it, then sailed off to the chain of smaller islands on their northern horizon. Columbus named the chain in honor of the 11,000 virgins who in legend were martyred with St. Ursula in a battle with a pagan ruler in the third century.

The English and French attempted to colonize St. Croix as early as 1625; the Dutch and Spanish made later appearances. After changing hands several times, St. Croix was ceded to the Knights of Malta in 1653, then sold to the French. The Danish West India & Guinea

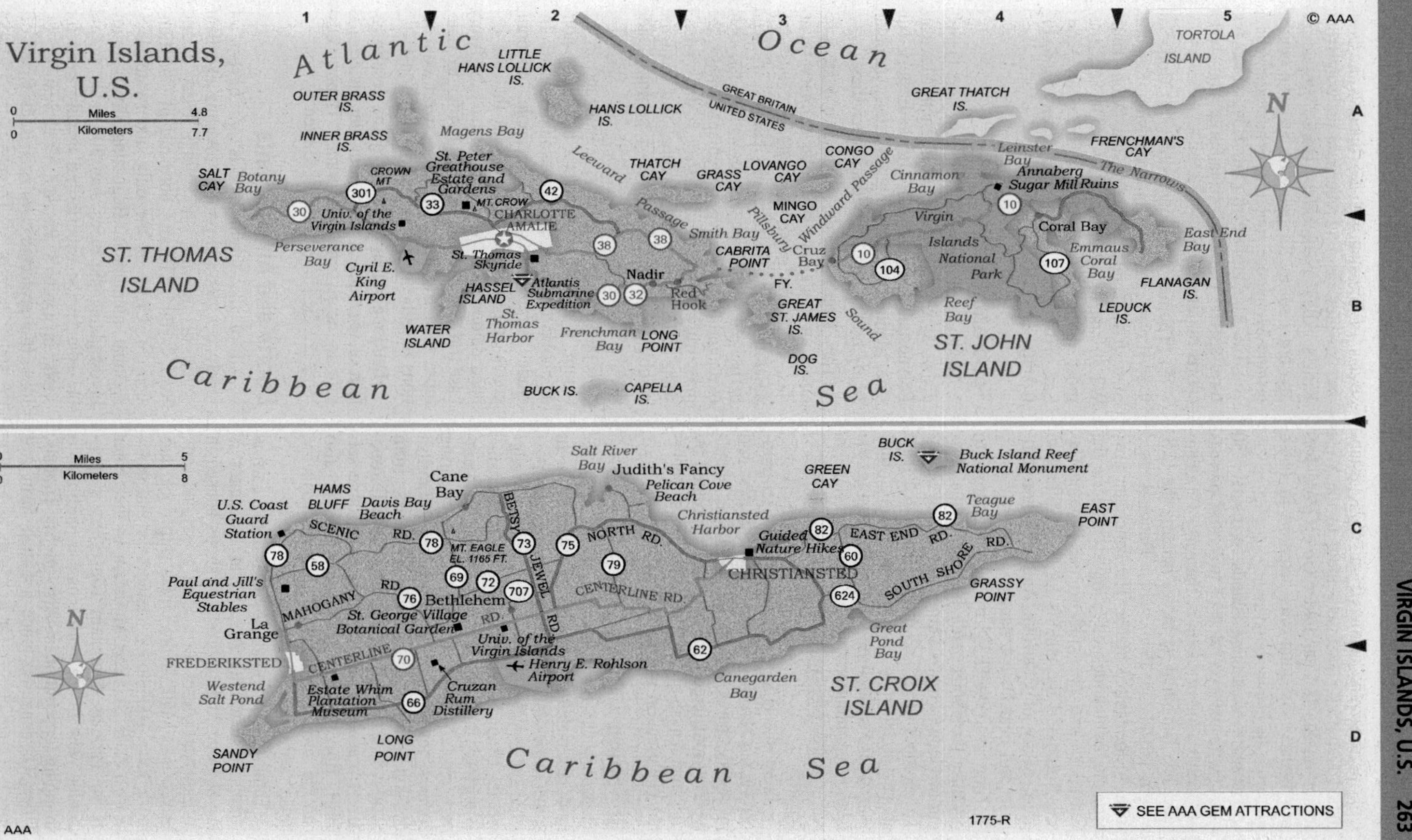
Virgin Islands, U.S.
Miles 0 4.8
Kilometers 0 7.7
Atlantic Ocean
Caribbean Sea
LITTLE HANS LOLLICK IS.
HANS LOLLICK IS.
OUTER BRASS IS.
INNER BRASS IS.
GREAT BRITAIN
UNITED STATES
GREAT THATCH IS.
TORTOLA ISLAND
FRENCHMAN'S CAY
Magens Bay
SALT CAY
Botany Bay
CROWN MT
St. Peter Greathouse Estate and Gardens
MT. CROW
CHARLOTTE AMALIE
Leeward Passage
THATCH CAY
GRASS CAY
LOVANGO CAY
CONGO CAY
MINGO CAY
Windward Passage
Pillsbury Sound
Cinnamon Bay
Leinster Bay
Annaberg Sugar Mill Ruins
The Narrows
Univ. of the Virgin Islands
Perseverance Bay
Cyril E. King Airport
St. Thomas Skyride
HASSEL ISLAND
Atlantis Submarine Expedition
Smith Bay
CABRITA POINT
Nadir
Red Hook
Cruz Bay
FY.
Virgin Islands National Park
Coral Bay
Emmaus Coral Bay
East End Bay
FLANAGAN IS.
LEDUCK IS.
ST. THOMAS ISLAND
WATER ISLAND
St. Thomas Harbor
Frenchman Bay
LONG POINT
GREAT ST. JAMES IS.
DOG IS.
Reef Bay
ST. JOHN ISLAND
BUCK IS.
CAPELLA IS.
Miles 0 5
Kilometers 0 8
Salt River Bay
Judith's Fancy
Pelican Cove Beach
BUCK IS.
Buck Island Reef National Monument
GREEN CAY
Christiansted Harbor
Teague Bay
EAST POINT
U.S. Coast Guard Station
HAMS BLUFF
Davis Bay Beach
Cane Bay
SCENIC RD.
MT. EAGLE EL. 1165 FT.
BETSY JEWEL RD
NORTH RD.
Guided Nature Hikes
EAST END RD.
SOUTH SHORE RD.
GRASSY POINT
Paul and Jill's Equestrian Stables
MAHOGANY RD
Bethlehem
CENTERLINE RD.
CHRISTIANSTED
St. George Village Botanical Garden
La Grange
Univ. of the Virgin Islands
Henry E. Rohlson Airport
FREDERIKSTED
CENTERLINE
Westend Salt Pond
Estate Whim Plantation Museum
Cruzan Rum Distillery
Canegarden Bay
Great Pond Bay
ST. CROIX ISLAND
SANDY POINT
LONG POINT
SEE AAA GEM ATTRACTIONS
1775-R
© AAA

Co., permanently chartered in 1671, established Denmark's first settlement in the West Indies on St. Thomas under Gov. Georg Jorgen Iversen. St. John was acquired in 1684, St. Croix in 1733.

Denmark ruled these islands for nearly 250 years, with the exception of two brief periods of British administration in the early 19th century. The Danish West Indies became the U.S. Virgin Islands in 1917, when Denmark sold them to the United States. The American government, which desired a naval base in the Caribbean and proximity to the Panama Canal, purchased the islands for $25 million in gold. Many of Charlotte Amalie's thoroughfares still bear Danish names.

Tourism to the U.S. Virgin Islands began to boom in the 1960s partly because of the closing of Cuba to tourists from the United States. The number of visitors quickly escalated from about 100,000 per year to more than 2 million. At the same time tourism was rising, the islands' population tripled. Other islanders were attracted by the relative economic security.

Today the U.S. Virgin Islands are an unincorporated territory of the United States, and its people are American citizens. The islands were administered by a governor appointed by the president until 1970, when the first gubernatorial election was held.

Shopping

Among the bargains in the U.S. Virgin Islands are imported liqueurs and local rums. In some instances, considerable savings are possible on Royal Copenhagen, Limoges, Wedgwood, Bing and Grondahl china; Baccarat, Waterford, Lalique, Daum and Val St. Lambert crystal; Swiss watches; island wearing apparel; jewelry and precious gems; English doeskin products; cashmere sweaters from Scotland; and designer fashions from Europe. Silver bracelets, earrings, cuff links, table settings, fine perfumes and Danish silver also can be found. Handicrafts include basketry, hats, handbags, dolls and embroideries.

Hundreds of tiny shops crowd the narrow streets of Charlotte Amalie; at its center is Royal Dane Mall, a group of shops housed in former warehouses for trading goods and rum. Havensight Mall, at the cruise ship dock, has more than 100 stores, restaurants and businesses. Atop St. Peter Mountain in the center of St. Thomas, Mountain Top offers a spectacular view of the north coast in addition to shopping opportunities. Also in St. Thomas, Tillett Gardens was once a Dutch farm and now is a marketplace for local arts and crafts. In St. Croix, King, Strand and Company streets in Christiansted are lined with shops and arcades, as is Frederiksted's waterfront; King's Alley Walk offers stores, restaurants and hotel suites. Shopping on St. John centers around Mongoose Junction, Wharfside Village and The Marketplace in Cruz Bay, which feature specialty shops, restaurants and water sports outlets.

St. Thomas shopping hours are Mon.-Sat. 9-5; Havensight Mall is open Mon.-Sat. 8-6, Sun. 9-1. Banking hours are Mon.-Thurs. 9-2:30 and Fri. 9-2 and 3:30-5. On St. Croix, most shops in Christiansted are open Mon.-Sat. 10-6, and banks are open Mon.-Fri. 9-3:30.

Food and Drink

Restaurants serve West Indian and Danish dishes as well as American, French, Mexican, Polynesian, Oriental and Middle Eastern cuisine, with seafood being especially popular. Many hotels have individual specialties.

The Virgin Islands' tropical climate produces an abundance of exotic culinary favorites, including papayas, mangoes, avocados, passion fruit and bananas. Leaves of wild herbs and plants, combined with meat, fish, okra and other native ingredients, make the most truly native of all dishes, a thick island soup called *kallaloo*. Cornmeal and okra are combined to make *fungee*, a common side dish.

Ripe soursop is used as a fruit and in ice cream; it also is made into a refreshing nonalcoholic drink, as is tamarind. Desserts include tarts made with pineapple, coconut, guava and guavaberry. It is said that the banana daiquiri was perfected at the U.S. Army base on Signal Hill in the 1940s; to date, more than 6 million of these sweet concoctions have been served at Mountain Top.

Drinking water, obtained by the desalinization of seawater or from rainwater cisterns, is safe in hotels and restaurants. Tipping customs are the same as in the United States.

Sports and Amusements

All of the Virgin Islands are havens of lovely beaches and pools, providing excellent scuba diving and snorkeling. Buck Island Reef, 6 miles (10 km) northeast of Christiansted, St. Croix, is the only underwater U.S. national monument. Beginning divers enjoy investigating the more than 300 reefs around the islands; the experienced usually head for spots in Drake's Passage northwest of St. John. In a protected cove near Buck Island off the south shore of St. Thomas is the 190-foot World War I cargo vessel *Cartenser Sr.* On St.

Thomas and St. John, dive shops operating through major hotels offer equipment rental, diving excursions and lessons; there are independent shops as well. The National Park Service offers similar services at Cinnamon Bay in St. John. Independent and resort dive shops in St. Croix are located near dive sites in Cane Bay, Christiansted, Frederiksted and Salt River.

For swimming and sunbathing, Magens Bay on the north coast of St. Thomas is considered one of the top 10 beaches in the world, as is Trunk Bay on St. John. On St. Croix, some of the out-of-the-way inns and hotels have superb beaches and plenty of privacy. Popular beaches include Half Penny, Cramer's Park and Jack's and Isaac's Bays. For sailors, and landlubbers with binoculars, there is the Rolex Regatta in late March or early April.

Deep-sea fishing is popular. The most important gamefish are blue marlin, sailfish, dolphin, kingfish, tuna and wahoo. The USVI Open/Atlantic Blue Marlin Tournament is held in mid-August. Fishing boats are available for charter on all three islands. Sailboats and yachts also can be chartered on all three islands; private cruises are available around the Virgin Islands to Puerto Rico.

For those who prefer land-based pastimes, St. Croix has an 18-hole championship golf course at the Carambola Beach Resort, an 18-hole course at The Buccaneer and a 9-hole course at The Reef Condominiums at Teague Bay. St. Thomas also sports an 18-hole championship course at the Mahogany Run Golf Course. You can play tennis at hotels and on public courts. St. Croix has many magnificent trails for horseback riding. Horse races are held on holidays at Clinton Phipps Race Track on St. Thomas and Randall "Doc" James Racetrack on St. Croix. Softball and baseball are played during the season on both St. Thomas and St. Croix, and some locals gather for cricket matches on Sunday.

Though sea, sun and sand are the islands' main attractions, there are enough evening pastimes to keep the spirit alive well after sunset. Dinner dancing, jazz, calypso music, limbo dancing and native acts are featured in many hotels and nightclubs. There are dance clubs on all three islands and movie theaters on St. Croix and St. Thomas.

Island Center, a cultural complex on Peppertree Hill on St. Croix, presents plays, musicals and other performances by well-known artists from the United States and neighboring islands. Similar fare is offered at the Reichhold Center for the Arts, an amphitheater on St. Thomas. The St. John School of the Arts and the Cinnamon Bay Amphitheater periodically host vocal, instrumental and theatrical performances. Check with *St. Thomas This Week* and *St. Croix This Week* magazines to find out what's happening and where.

Sightseeing

Island tours are most easily arranged through your hotel activities desk. A 2-hour tour of St. Thomas stops at Drake's Seat and Mountain Top. Trips to the island's eastern end visit beach clubs and fishing centers. Sunset and harbor cruises are available from Charlotte Amalie.

A scenic trip to Magens Bay for swimming also departs from Charlotte Amalie; sailboats and beach equipment can be rented. A 2-hour tour to the island's western end passes a World War II submarine base, the University of the Virgin Islands and Brewer's Bay on the way to Crown Mountain. The return trip includes a stop at the old sugar mill at Estate Contant; admission is included. Safari bus tours of the island are often less expensive than taxi tours.

Perhaps the best of the many excellent scenic vantage points in Charlotte Amalie is Paradise Point atop Flag Hill. Southeast of Havensight Mall via a steep roadway, the site is especially popular at sunset. St. Thomas Skyride transports visitors to the hilltop. West of the harbor is the fishing village of Frenchtown, where the descendants of settlers from St. Barths continue to live off the sea.

Popular excursions on St. Croix include 3-hour glass-bottom boat or catamaran trips to Buck Island Reef National Monument for snorkeling. Beach barbecues are available with some all-day sails. Arrangements can be made at local dive shops in Christiansted Harbor. Full- and half-day tours of local highlights are available, including the rain forest and Salt River, where Columbus landed. In February and March the St. Croix Landmarks Society conducts house tours that include restored sugar mills, great houses and elegant mansions.

You can hire one of several safari guides for exploring St. John. A popular day excursion tours the Virgin Islands National Park, visits the Annaberg Sugar Mill ruins and includes lunch and swimming at Trunk Bay. For those more interested in aquatic sports, boat trips to St. John are available that include 2 hours in Francis Bay for swimming and snorkeling.

Transportation

Direct jet service is available from the U.S. mainland via several airlines. Commuter airlines fly between Puerto Rico, St. Thomas'

Cyril E. King Airport and St. Croix's Henry E. Rohlson Airport. Many cruise ships call at Charlotte Amalie and Frederiksted.

The Vitran bus service on St. Croix, St. John and St. Thomas is mainly for local traffic. Taxi service on St. Thomas and on St. Croix is good, and you also can rent cars on all three islands. Taxi rates are set in advance and apply per passenger. It is always wise to agree on the fare in advance. Parking is usually very scarce in Charlotte Amalie; a public lot east of Fort Christian costs 50c per hour. Taxi service is available on St. John as well, and jeeps can be rented by the day or week. A U.S. driver's license is valid.

Daily ferry service to Cruz Bay, St. John, is offered from two St. Thomas ports: Red Hook, a 20-minute trip, and Charlotte Amalie, a 45-minute trip. Daily ferry service connects both Charlotte Amalie and St. John with the British Virgin Islands of Jost Van Dyke, Tortola and Virgin Gorda; proof of citizenship is required.

Fast Facts

POPULATION: 108,612.

AREA: 344 sq km (133 sq mi.).

CAPITAL: Charlotte Amalie, St. Thomas.

HIGHEST POINT: 474 m (1,555 ft.), Crown Mountain, St. Thomas.

LOWEST POINT: Sea level, Caribbean Sea.

TIME ZONE(S): Atlantic Standard.

LANGUAGE: English; Spanish or Spanish creole; French or French creole.

GOVERNMENT: Unincorporated U.S. territory.

UNIT OF CURRENCY: U.S. dollar.

ELECTRICITY: 110-120 volts, 60 cycles AC.

MINIMUM AGE FOR DRIVERS: 21-25, depending on the rental car agency. U.S. license valid; drive on left.

SEAT BELT/CHILD RESTRAINT LAWS: Seat belts are required for driver and front-seat passengers. Child restraints required for under age 3; seat belts required for ages 3-5.

HELMETS FOR MOTORCYCLISTS: Required.

HOLIDAYS: Jan. 1; Three Kings Day, Jan. 6; Martin Luther King Jr. Day, Jan. (3rd Mon.); Presidents Day, Feb. (3rd Mon.); Holy Thursday; Good Friday; Easter Monday; Transfer Day, Mar. 31; Memorial Day, May (last Mon.); Danish West Indies Emancipation Day, July 3; U.S. Independence Day, July 4; Supplication Day, July (4th Mon.); Labor Day, Sept. (1st Mon.); Columbus/Puerto Rico Friendship Day, Oct. (2nd Mon.); Local Thanksgiving, Oct. (3rd Mon.); D. Hamilton Jackson Day, Nov. 1; Veterans Day, Nov. 11; U.S. Thanksgiving, Nov. (4th Thurs.); Christmas, Dec. 25.

TAXES: An 8 percent room tax and 10-15 percent service charge are added to most hotel bills. Departure fee is $3 U.S. by air.

IMMIGRATION REQUIREMENTS: Proof of U.S. citizenship is not needed to enter the U.S. Virgin Islands, but it is required to reenter the United States. A valid passport or birth certificate accompanied by a photo ID are accepted. A passport is required when travel involves stops on other Caribbean islands.

PHONING THE ISLANDS: To call the U.S. Virgin Islands from the U.S. or Canada, dial 1 + 340 + the 7-digit local number.

FURTHER INFORMATION FOR VISITORS:

U.S. Virgin Islands Department of Tourism, St. Thomas
P.O. Box 6400
Charlotte Amalie, St. Thomas
Virgin Islands, U.S. 00804
(340) 774-8784
(800) 372-8784
See color ad opposite inside front cover.

U.S. Virgin Islands Department of Tourism, St. Croix
P.O. Box 4538
Christiansted, St. Croix
Virgin Islands, U.S. 00822
(340) 772-0357

Points of Interest

See map page 263.

St. Croix Island

Old Danish towns rising above the Caribbean characterize the lovely island of St. Croix. Santa Cruz, as it was known by Christopher Columbus, rivaled Barbados as the leading sugar producer in the West Indies; great plantation houses recall these days of wealth on the 82-square-mile (212-sq-km) island. Modern St. Croix, the easternmost point in the United States territories, is the agricultural and industrial center of the U.S. Virgin Islands as well as a major tourist destination.

Self-guiding tours: The U.S. Virgin Islands Department of Tourism provides a walking/driving tour brochure covering Christiansted and Frederiksted.

GEM BUCK ISLAND REEF NATIONAL MONUMENT (C-4)

Abour 6 miles (10 km) off the northeast coast of St. Croix, Buck Island Reef offers snorkeling, swimming, picnicking, birdwatching and exploring. The foremost attraction of the national monument—one of only a few underwater parks in the U.S. national park system—is the fine barrier reef. Buck Island, which covers 176 acres (71 hectares), is the only dry land in the park. The remaining 18,800 acres (7,600 hectares) comprise "one of the finest marine gardens in the Caribbean sea." Underwater trails offer excellent opportunities for snorkeling; markers identify the reef's fauna and flora.

Full- and half-day trips to Buck Island from St. Croix can be arranged with licensed concession boats at Christiansted Wharf or Green Cay Marina; snorkeling equipment and instruction are available. Park open daily dawn-dusk. Park admission free. Full-day boat trips (including meals) $70-$80; ages 6-12, $50-$60; under 6, $20. Half-day trip $45-$50; ages 6-12, $35-$40; under 6, $15. Phone (340) 773-1460 for the park office.

CHRISTIANSTED (C-3) pop. 2,637

Christiansted has preserved the 18th-century buildings of its Danish settlers. Solid stone buildings in pastel colors with bright red tile roofs line the cobblestone sidewalks, adding a touch of European charm. The town's symmetry, with streets running at right angles to the waterfront, makes it popular for walking tours. The shopping area centers on King, Strand and Company streets, next to Christiansted National Historic Site.

CHRISTIANSTED NATIONAL HISTORIC SITE covers three city blocks along the waterfront and town square. The 7-acre (3-hectare) site includes such landmarks of the Danish colonial period as 1749 Fort Christiansvaern, the best preserved of the five remaining Danish forts in the Virgin Islands; the Old Scalehouse; the Old Danish Customs House; the Danish West India & Guinea Co. Warehouse; and the Government House, once capitol of the Danish West Indies.

The Steeple Building, St. Croix's first Lutheran church, houses a museum with Arawak and Carib Indian relics. A self-guiding tour brochure is available from the National Park Service headquarters; caution is advised on the area's uneven sidewalks and stairs. Site open daily 8-5. Museum open Mon.-Fri. 8-5, Sat.-Sun. 9-5. Admission $3; free (ages 0-15 with adult). Phone (340) 773-1460.

FREDERIKSTED (D-1) pop. 732

The emancipation of slaves was proclaimed on July 3, 1848, at Fort Frederik on the waterfront at the northern edge of Frederiksted. Destroyed by a fire in 1878, Frederiksted was restored during the Victorian era, as reflected in the town's architecture.

Modern Frederiksted operates at a slower pace than Christiansted, except when cruise ships dock in Frederiksted's deepwater port. Visitor information is available at the entry to the pier. Fort Frederik houses art and cultural exhibits, including a police museum which details the history of the town.

Of historical interest are the palatial ruins of Judith's Fancy, the former residence of the governor of the Knights of Malta. Set on an estate of several hundred acres, it has a view of the site where Christopher Columbus anchored at Salt River in 1493. Due to the greeting he received from the Carib Indians, Columbus named it the Cape of the Arrows.

CRUZAN RUM DISTILLERY, on West Airport Rd. at 3A Estate Diamond, is the world's only facility where this rum is produced. Tours and rum tastings are offered at the Estate Diamond visitor's pavilion. Mon.-Fri. 9-11:30 and 1-4:15. Admission $4; $1 (ages 6-18). DS, MC, VI. Phone (340) 692-2280.

ESTATE WHIM PLANTATION MUSEUM is 1.5 mi. (2.4 km) e. on Queen Mary Hwy. The restored three-room plantation house is furnished with antiques, china, paintings and silver. A museum in the cookhouse contains sugar- and rum-making equipment, household and military articles and reproductions of old engravings. A restored stone sugar mill with large grinding mechanisms typical of those used in the late 18th century also is on the grounds.

Guided tours depart every 30 minutes Mon.-Sat. 10-4, Nov.-Apr.; Mon.-Sat. 10-3, rest of year. Admission $10; $5 (senior citizens); $4 (ages 6-12). MC, VI. Phone (340) 772-0598.

LAWAETZ MUSEUM is n. on Rte. 63, then 1.5 mi. e. on Mahogany Rd. (Rte. 76). The 19th-century

house of a prominent Danish-Crucian family has been restored at Little La Grange, a working plantation since the 1750s. The West Indian great house contains handcrafted furniture, antiques, photographs and memorabilia. Guided tours reflect rural life during the first half of the twentieth century.

Mon., Wed. and Fri.-Sat. 10-3, May-Oct.; Tues., Thurs. and Sat. 10-2, rest of year. Admission $10; $5 (senior citizens); $4 (ages 6-12). Phone (340) 772-1539.

ST. GEORGE VILLAGE BOTANICAL GARDEN is 4 mi. (6 km) e. at 127 Estate St., just n. of Centerline Rd. This 16-acre (6-hectare) tropical garden surrounds the ruins of a 19th-century workers' village. Royal Poinciana trees burst into flamboyant bloom in summer; hibiscus unfold all year. Daily 9-5; closed Dec. 25. Admission $8; $6 (senior citizens); $1 (ages 0-11). MC, VI. Phone (340) 692-2874.

RECREATIONAL ACTIVITIES

Horseback Riding

- **Paul and Jill's Equestrian Stables** is off Rte. 58. Guided horseback rides are offered; riding lessons are provided. Weight limit is 220 pounds for men, 200 pounds for women. Tours depart Mon.-Sat. Phone (340) 772-2880 or (340) 772-2627.

St. John Island

St. John owes its reputation as a quiet, largely undeveloped haven to the generosity of Laurance Rockefeller. His love of the island's beauty moved Rockefeller in the 1950s to purchase as much of St. John as he could acquire, then to donate most of it to the United States for the creation of a national park, ensuring that "this thing of beauty will be a joy forever." Rockefeller saw his wish fulfilled in 1956 with the dedication of Virgin Islands National Park.

Smaller than Manhattan Island, 19-square-mile (49-sq-km) St. John is scalloped by lovely bays rimmed with white sand beaches of pristine beauty. The most famous is Trunk Bay, where the National Park Service maintains an underwater snorkel trail. Bordeaux Mountain, at 1,277 feet (390 m), dominates the island's rugged topography, and the lush forests conceal ruins of forts and plantation houses and traces of the Arawak and Carib Indians, the island's pre-Columbian inhabitants. Small museums at Cruz Bay exhibit relics of these peoples; their cryptic petroglyphs can be seen on rocks at Reef Bay, along Reef Bay Trail and other places.

The subdued atmosphere of Cruz Bay, the island's main town, conceals a history as a bustling center for the cotton, sugar and rum trade in the days when plantations thrived on St. John. A slave revolt occurred in 1733; the rebels held St. John for 6 months against the Danes and the British before the French finally overran them. Prosperous plantation farming continued through the mid-1830s and limited production continued until 1916, lasting through the emancipation of slaves in 1848.

Accommodations on St. John range from rustic to rich. Platform campsites front the beach at Cinnamon and Maho bays, while Caneel Bay, the world-renowned luxury resort developed by Laurance Rockefeller, occupies the site of an 18th-century sugar estate.

VIRGIN ISLANDS NATIONAL PARK (B-4)

Virgin Islands National Park covers about two-thirds of St. John and most of Hassel Island in St. Thomas Harbor off Charlotte Amalie. Encompassing nearly 15,000 acres (6,000 hectares), including 5,600 acres (2,300 hectares) of offshore waters, the park protects tropical forests, white-sand beaches and coral reefs. Pre-Columbian petroglyphs and the ruins of Danish sugar plantations also are found within its borders. The Cruz Bay Visitor Center, north of the ferry dock, offers park information and exhibits.

Swimming, snorkeling and boating are popular at the park; equipment can be rented. To protect the coral reefs and seagrass beds, moorings have been installed in many areas. Boaters are encouraged to contact the park for information related to safe boating.

Hiking trails lead to scenic overlooks and into deep valleys such as Reef Bay. Park programs range from guided hiking and snorkeling trips to illustrated evening programs at the campground amphitheater.

Annaberg Sugar Mill, built in 1718, is one of the island's best preserved examples of colonial sugar production. A self-guiding walking trail leads through the factory ruins, including a windmill and slave quarters; guided tours are offered by park rangers.

Camping is permitted at Cinnamon Bay, 4 miles (6 km) northeast of Cruz Bay, where accommodations include cottages, tents and tent sites. Maho Bay Campground, on privately-owned land within park boundaries 6 miles (10 km) northeast of Cruz Bay, features canvas cottages connected by wooden walkways that meander through the thickly wooded hillside. Supplies and water sports equipment are available at both sites. Reservations must be made well in advance, often up to a year before the desired date.

The park is open daily 24 hours. Cruz Bay Visitor Center open daily 8-4:30; closed Dec. 25. Ferry service from Red Hook, St. Thomas, to St. John departs hourly 7 a.m.-midnight. Park admission is free. A $4 user fee is charged at Annaberg Ruins and Trunk Bay; under 17 free. For park information, phone (340) 776-6201, ext. 238. For camping reservations, phone Cinnamon Bay at (340) 776-6330 or (800) 539-9998; or Maho Bay at (340) 776-6240 or (800) 392-9004.

St. Thomas Island

Settled by Danes in 1672, St. Thomas covers 32 square miles (83 sq km) of hilly terrain about 40 miles (64 km) east of Puerto Rico. Crown Mountain, at 1,555 feet (472 m), and Signal Hill, at 1,505 feet (460 m), are the highest points. From the road that cuts through the mountain range, both sides of the island can be seen. Near the top of the range is Drake's Seat, from which Sir Francis Drake is supposed to have charted the course of the channel now bearing his name. From this point there is a fine view of Magens Bay, many islands and the Atlantic Ocean.

In the days of piracy, St. Thomas was a favorite hideout for Captain Kidd, Bluebeard and Blackbeard. The towers from which buccaneers are said to have searched the sea for potential victims are now hotels.

St. Thomas' checkered past has left the landscape dotted with contrasting architectural styles. Pastel houses line narrow cobblestone streets and alleys, where the doors reflect the Dutch heritage and the red tile roofs, the Danish. The elaborate iron grillwork was left by the French, and the patios lend a Spanish accent.

Tourism is the chief means of livelihood on St. Thomas. Tennis, golf, boating, swimming and fishing are available; spear fishing and snorkeling are excellent near the coral reefs around the island. Magens Bay on the north coast has a beautiful heart-shaped sand beach.

CHARLOTTE AMALIE (B-2) pop. 19,000

The only town on St. Thomas, Charlotte Amalie is the territorial capital of the U.S. Virgin Islands. This town, climbing up the steep sides of Mafolie Mountain, Frenchman's Hill and Solberg, once served as the home port for such unsavory characters as Captain Kidd, Bluebeard and Blackbeard. Sir Francis Drake employed the port's favorable location to descend upon the gold-laden galleons that sailed through the Anegada Passage en route to Spain.

Under the Danish colonial government the port accommodated one of the world's biggest slave trade operations, routing slaves from Africa to other areas in the Caribbean and on the mainland. From Emancipation Garden, the city's central square, slaves heard the proclamation giving them freedom in 1848.

Valdemar Hill Drive offers a panoramic view of Charlotte Amalie and its deepwater harbor, usually busy with several major cruise ships, container ships, island sloops and yachts. The 17th-century warehouses now house shops and restaurants that accommodate the tourist trade. Distinctive among the city's old buildings is the governor's office, the Government House, furnished with antiques and paintings by native impressionist Camille Pissarro.

At the base of the nearby "Ninety-Nine Steps," one of the few remaining stair-streets that once helped residents traverse the hilly town, is Government Hill, a wealthy residential community of the 18th century. Crown House, a national historic landmark, is a fine example of how wealthy Danish planters lived during the sugar heyday.

Historically significant churches include the Dutch Reformed Church, one of the first outside New York's Dutch colony; and the Frederick Lutheran Church, where silver equipment more than 2 centuries old is still in use. The Jewish Synagogue is one of the oldest in the Western Hemisphere and still has sand on its floor to symbolize the Jews' flight from Egypt through the desert. The New Hernhut Moravian Church, about 2.5 miles (4 km) east of town, was built by missionaries in 1738.

U.S. Virgin Islands Department of Tourism, St. Thomas: P.O. Box 6400, St. Thomas, Virgin Islands 00804; phone (340) 774-8784.

GEM *ATLANTIS* **SUBMARINE EXPEDITION** departs from the West Indian Co. dock in Building VI of Havensight Mall. After a 20-minute boat ride through St. Thomas harbor, guests board the submarine and descend 90 feet while observing colorful undersea gardens of sea fans, dramatic coral formations and rich sea life. Throughout the 2-hour tour, the copilot provides informative and entertaining narration.

Trips depart daily. Fare $99; $49 (ages 0-12). Children under 36 inches tall are not permitted. Reservations are required. AX, DS, MC, VI. Phone (340) 776-5650.

CORAL WORLD OCEAN PARK is 7.5 mi. (12 km) n.e. at 6450 Coki Point. This 5-acre (2-hectare) marine park features exotic aquariums, outdoor pools, nature trails and the Undersea Observatory. Visitors can pet sharks, stingrays and turtles during feeding shows. Additional activities include the Sea Trek helmet dive, sea lion swim, turtle and shark encounter programs, parasailing and a semi-submarine ride.

Food, lockers and fresh-water showers are available. Allow 1 hour minimum. Open daily 9-5. Last admission 1 hour before closing. Summer hours may vary; phone ahead. Admission $19 (not including special activities or water sports); $10 (ages 3-12). Sea Trek helmet dive $74; under age 8 or under 80 pounds not permitted. Sea lion swim $100; under age 5 or under 50 pounds not permitted, under age 12 must be accompanied by adult swimmer. Shark and turtle encounters $49; under 57 inches not permitted. Semi-submarine $38. Parasailing $75; under age 5 or under 50 pounds not permitted. Reservations are recommended for all activities. AX, DC, DS, MC. Phone (340) 775-1555, ext. 233, or (888) 695-2073.

FORT CHRISTIAN MUSEUM stands on the waterfront near Emancipation Garden Park. The red masonry structure once housed the entire St. Thomas colony. Built by the Danes in 1672, it has been reconstructed several times. Several cells display a collection of Arawak and Carib artifacts and items relating to the early Danish settlers. **Note:** The museum is closed for renovations with no opening date established. Please phone ahead to verify schedule. Mon.-Fri. 9-4; closed holidays. Admission $3; free (children). Public parking $1 per hour, $5 per day. Phone (340) 776-4566.

ST. PETER GREATHOUSE ESTATE AND GARDENS is at 2A St. Peter Mountain Rd. Part of a French plantation built in the 1800s, the restored manor is surrounded by 11 acres (4.5 hectares) of landscaped botanical gardens with an elevated nature trail. An observation deck 1,000 feet (305 m) above sea level provides a panoramic view of more than 20 islands. Caribbean artwork is displayed throughout the house.

Mountain Top, the highest point on the island, offers duty-free shopping and banana daiquiris, the signature drink said to have been invented here in the 1940s. Estate open daily 9-4:30. Admission $10; $5 (ages 0-11). MC, VI. Phone (340) 774-4999.

ST. THOMAS SKYRIDE is across from Havensight Mall and the cruise ship dock. Aerial gondolas transport passengers 700 feet (213 m) up a mountainside to Paradise Point. The 15-minute round trip offers views of the harbor and Charlotte Amalie. At the top, tropical bird shows are presented daily, and local musicians provide entertainment most afternoons. Food is available. Daily 9-5 (also Tues.-Wed. 5-9) when cruise ships are in port. Bird shows are offered at 10:30, 1:30 and 3:30. Fare $19; $9.50 (ages 6-12). AX, MC, VI. Phone (340) 774-9809.

America on the Move is made possible by generous support from General Motors Corporation, AAA, State Farm Companies Foundation, The History Channel, United States Congress, U.S. Department of Transportation, Exxon Mobil, American Public Transportation Association, American Road & Transportation Builders Association, Association of American Railroads, National Asphalt Pavement Association, The UPS Foundation

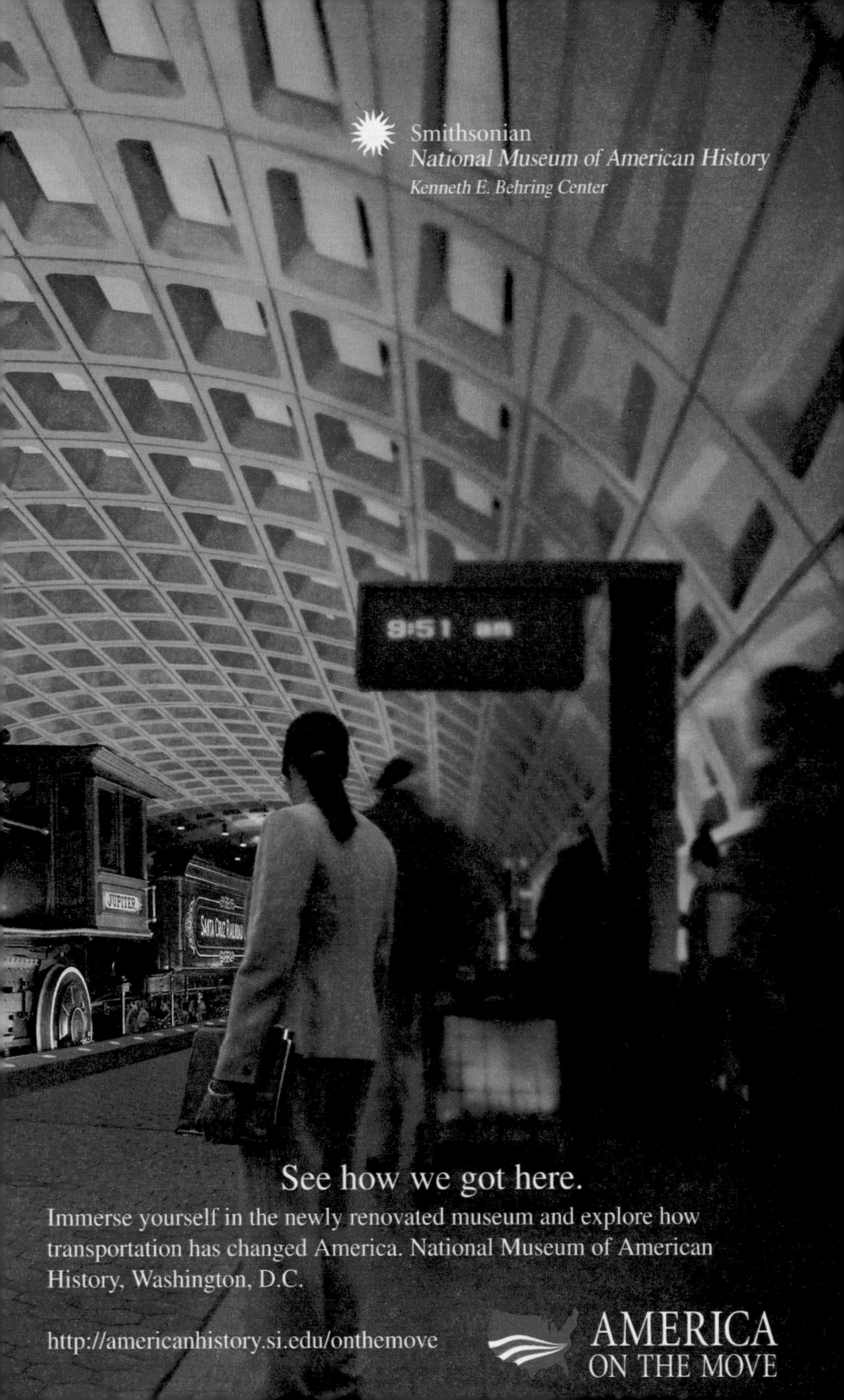
Smithsonian
National Museum of American History
Kenneth E. Behring Center
9:51
JUPITER
See how we got here.
Immerse yourself in the newly renovated museum and explore how transportation has changed America. National Museum of American History, Washington, D.C.
http://americanhistory.si.edu/onthemove
AMERICA
ON THE MOVE

Caribbean

Annaberg Sugar Mill, St John Island, U.S. Virgin Islands

ANGUILLA

This index helps you "spot" where approved lodgings and restaurants are located on the corresponding detailed maps. Lodging daily rate range is for comparison only and show the property's high season. Restaurant rate range is a combination of lunch and/or dinner. Turn to the listing page for more detailed rate information and consult display ads for special promotions.

MEADS BAY

Map Page	OA	Lodging	Diamond Rated	High Season	Page
1 / p. 279		Malliouhana Hotel & Spa	◆◆◆◆	$345-$1180	281

Map Page	OA	Restaurants	Diamond Rated	Cuisine	Meal Range	Page
1 / p. 279		The Michel Rostang at Malliouhana Restaurant	◆◆◆	International	$20-$60	281
3 / p. 279		Blanchard's	◆◆◆	International	$42-$55	281

RENDEZVOUS BAY

Map Page	OA	Lodgings	Diamond Rated	High Season	Page
4 / p. 279		Anguilla Great House Beach Resort - see color ad p 281	◆◆	$210-$340	281
5 / p. 279	AAA	**CuisinArt Resort & Spa**	◆◆◆◆	$400-$3500 SAVE	282

Map Page	OA	Restaurant	Diamond Rated	Cuisine	Meal Range	Page
4 / p. 279	AAA	**Santorini**	◆◆◆◆	International	$28-$54	282

MAUNDAYS BAY

Map Page	OA	Lodgings	Diamond Rated	High Season	Page
6 / p. 279	AAA	**Sheriva**	◆◆◆◆	$1100-$6400 SAVE	280
8 / p. 279		Cap Juluca	◆◆◆◆	$400-$2875	280

SHOAL BAY EAST

Map Page	OA	Lodging	Diamond Rated	High Season	Page
10 / p. 279		Ku'	◆◆◆	$180-$420	282

ISLAND HARBOUR

Map Page	OA	Restaurants	Diamond Rated	Cuisine	Meal Range	Page
5 / p. 279		Smitty's World Famous Seaside Bar & Restaurant	◆	Barbecue	$13-$25	280
6 / p. 279		Cote Mer Seaside Restaurant	◆◆	French	$19-$32	279

GEORGE HILL

Map Page	OA	Restaurant	Diamond Rated	Cuisine	Meal Range	Page
8 / p. 279		Old House Restaurant & Bar	◆◆	Caribbean	$12-$28	279

SANDY GROUND

Map Page	OA	Restaurant	Diamond Rated	Cuisine	Meal Range	Page
10 / p. 279		Johnno's	◆	Caribbean	$11-$25	282

SOUTH HILL

Map Page	OA	Restaurant	Diamond Rated	Cuisine	Meal Range	Page
12 / p. 279		Bistro Phil	◆◆◆	French	$24-$40	283

THE VALLEY

Map Page	OA	Restaurant	Diamond Rated	Cuisine	Meal Range	Page
14 / p. 279	AAA	**KoalKeel**	◆◆◆	International	$28-$45	283

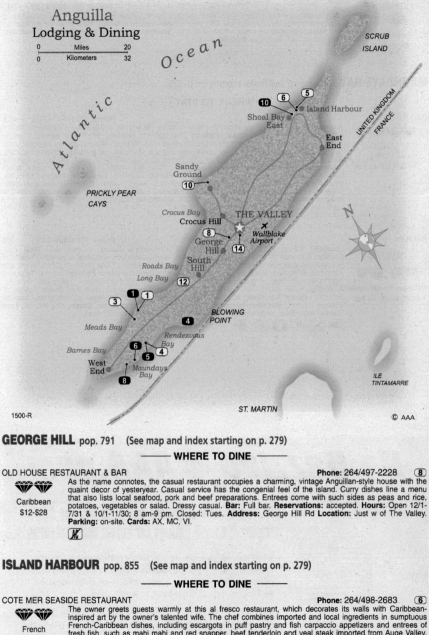

Anguilla
Lodging & Dining

0 Miles 20
0 Kilometers 32

Atlantic Ocean
SCRUB ISLAND
Island Harbour
Shoal Bay East
East End
UNITED KINGDOM
FRANCE
Sandy Ground
PRICKLY PEAR CAYS
Crocus Bay
Crocus Hill
THE VALLEY
Wallblake Airport
George Hill
South Hill
Roads Bay
Long Bay
BLOWING POINT
Meads Bay
Rendezvous Bay
Barnes Bay
West End
Maundays Bay
ILE TINTAMARRE
ST. MARTIN
1500-R
© AAA

GEORGE HILL pop. 791 (See map and index starting on p. 279)

WHERE TO DINE

OLD HOUSE RESTAURANT & BAR **Phone:** 264/497-2228 (8)

Caribbean
$12-$28

As the name connotes, the casual restaurant occupies a charming, vintage Anguillan-style house with the quaint decor of yesteryear. Casual service has the congenial feel of the island. Curry dishes line a menu that also lists local seafood, pork and beef preparations. Entrees come with such sides as peas and rice, potatoes, vegetables or salad. Dressy casual. **Bar:** Full bar. **Reservations:** accepted. **Hours:** Open 12/1-7/31 & 10/1-11/30; 8 am-9 pm. Closed: Tues. **Address:** George Hill Rd **Location:** Just w of The Valley. **Parking:** on-site. **Cards:** AX, MC, VI.

ISLAND HARBOUR pop. 855 (See map and index starting on p. 279)

WHERE TO DINE

COTE MER SEASIDE RESTAURANT **Phone:** 264/498-2683 (6)

French
$19-$32

The owner greets guests warmly at this al fresco restaurant, which decorates its walls with Caribbean-inspired art by the owner's talented wife. The chef combines imported and local ingredients in sumptuous French-Caribbean dishes, including escargots in puff pastry and fish carpaccio appetizers and entrees of fresh fish, such as mahi mahi and red snapper, beef tenderloin and veal steak imported from Auge Valley. Among homemade desserts are creme brulee, chocolate mousse and tarte Tatin. Casual dress. **Bar:** Full bar. **Reservations:** suggested. **Hours:** noon-2:30 & 6:30-9 pm. Closed: Sun. **Address:** Island Harbour Rd **Location:** Just w of center. **Parking:** on-site. **Cards:** MC, VI.

(See map and index starting on p. 279)

SMITTY'S WORLD FAMOUS SEASIDE BAR & RESTAURANT

Barbecue
$13-$25

Phone: 264/497-4300 (5)

Owner Smitty prepares ribs, chicken, fish, steak, shrimp, conch, lobster and crawfish on the barbecue out back. Accompaniments include peas and rice, fries, coleslaw and other fixings. Save room for the luscious coconut cream pie. Casual dress. **Bar:** Full bar. **Hours:** 11 am-9:30 pm. **Address:** East End **Location:** Across from Scilly Cay. **Parking:** on-site.

MAUNDAYS BAY (See map and index starting on p. 279)

WHERE TO STAY

CAP JULUCA

Resort Hotel
$400-$2875 All Year

Phone: (264)497-6666 (8)

Address: Maundays Bay **Location:** Oceanfront. 10 mi (16 km) sw of Wallblake International Airport; situated on the southwest coast. **Facility:** The high-end property, which has earned a stellar reputation, offers all ocean-view units in Moorish-style villas. 98 units. 74 one-bedroom standard units. 13 one- and 11 two-bedroom suites, some with kitchens. 2 stories (no elevator), exterior corridors. *Bath:* combo or shower only. **Parking:** on-site. **Terms:** age restrictions may apply, 30 day cancellation notice-fee imposed. **Amenities:** high-speed Internet (fee), dual phone lines, voice mail, safes, honor bars, irons, hair dryers. *Some:* CD players. **Pool(s):** outdoor. **Leisure Activities:** sailboats, windsurfing, waterskiing, snorkeling, putting green, 3 tennis courts (2 lighted), exercise room, volleyball. *Fee:* bicycles, massage. **Guest Services:** TV in common area, valet laundry, wireless Internet. **Business Services:** meeting rooms, PC. **Cards:** AX, MC, VI.

  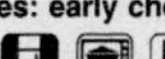 / SOME UNITS

SHERIVA

Vacation Rental House
$1100-$6400 All Year

Phone: (264)498-9898 (6)

Location: 9.7 mi (15.7 km) sw of Wallblake International Airport; situated near West End. **Facility:** Spacious villas are well-appointed with upscale comforts, including a personal chef and housekeeper assigned to each villa. 8 units. 3 one-, 2 two- and 1 three-bedroom suites, some with whirlpools. 2 houses. 2 stories (no elevator), interior/exterior corridors. **Parking:** on-site. **Terms:** 3 night minimum stay - seasonal and/or weekends, 30 day cancellation notice-fee imposed. **Amenities:** video library, DVD players, CD players, voice mail, safes, irons, hair dryers. **Pool(s):** 7 outdoor. **Leisure Activities:** whirlpools, exercise room. **Guest Services:** complimentary laundry, wireless Internet. **Business Services:** meeting rooms, business center. **Cards:** AX, MC, VI. **Free Special Amenities: early check-in/late check-out and high-speed Internet.**

MEADS BAY (See map and index starting on p. 279)

WHERE TO STAY

MALLIOUHANA HOTEL & SPA — **Phone:** (264)497-6111 **1**

Resort Hotel

$345-$1180 12/1-8/31 & 11/1-11/30

Address: Leeward Island **Location:** Oceanfront. 7 mi (11.2 km) w of Wallblake International Airport. **Facility:** Mediterranean-style, spacious, luxurious units and villas are set on a terraced hillside overlooking a white-sand beach; find a well-trained staff. 55 units. 38 one-bedroom standard units. 15 one- and 2 two-bedroom suites, some with whirlpools. 3 stories (no elevator), exterior corridors. **Parking:** on-site. **Terms:** open 12/1-8/31 & 11/1-11/30, 7 night minimum stay - seasonal, 30 day cancellation notice-fee imposed. **Amenities:** high-speed Internet (fee), dual phone lines, voice mail, safes, honor bars, hair dryers. **Pool(s):** 4 outdoor. **Leisure Activities:** saunas, whirlpool, steamrooms, waterslide, sailboats, windsurfing, waterskiing, snorkeling, 4 lighted tennis courts, playground, spa, basketball, volleyball. *Fee:* boats, bicycles. **Guest Services:** TV in common area, valet laundry. **Business Services:** meeting rooms, PC. **Cards:** AX, MC, VI.

/ SOME UNITS

WHERE TO DINE

BLANCHARD'S — **Phone:** 264/497-6100 **3**

International

$42-$55

The candlelit, open-air dining room overlooks a garden pathway to the sea. Innovative preparations of fresh local seafood draw on inspirations from the Caribbean, Asia and America and are nicely complemented by offerings from the extensive wine cellar. Among delicious choices are crispy crusted snapper with Thai citrus glaze and Jamaican jerk chicken with grilled cinnamon bananas. Whole-roasted lobster is the specialty. Service is unpretentious. Casual dress. **Bar:** Full bar. **Reservations:** suggested. **Hours:** Open 12/1-9/1 & 10/26-11/30; 6:30 pm-9:30 pm. Closed: Sun, also Mon 6/1-8/30. **Address:** Main Rd **Location:** 7 mi (11.2 km) w of Wallblake International Airport. **Parking:** on-site. **Cards:** AX, MC, VI.

THE MICHEL ROSTANG AT MALLIOUHANA RESTAURANT — **Phone:** 264/497-6111 **1**

International

$20-$60

At the Malliouhana Resort Anguilla, this romantic open-air restaurant features candlelit tables facing the sea. The sophisticated setting is perfect for a leisurely dining experience. The menu features a fine mix of international dishes prepared with a Caribbean influence. Semi-formal attire. **Bar:** Full bar. **Reservations:** suggested. **Hours:** Open 12/1-8/31 & 11/1-11/30; 7-11 am, 12:30-3 & 7:30-10:30 pm. **Address:** Leeward Island **Location:** 7 mi (11.2 km) w of Wallblake International Airport; in Malliouhana Hotel & Spa. **Parking:** on-site. **Cards:** AX, MC, VI.

RENDEZVOUS BAY (See map and index starting on p. 279)

WHERE TO STAY

ANGUILLA GREAT HOUSE BEACH RESORT — **Phone:** (264)497-6062 **4**

Hotel

$210-$340 All Year

Address: Rendezvous Bay Rd **Location:** Oceanfront. 5 mi (6 km) sw of Wallblake International Airport. **Facility:** 31 one-bedroom standard units. 1-2 stories (no elevator), exterior corridors. *Bath:* shower only. **Parking:** on-site. **Terms:** office hours 6:30 am-11 pm, 30 day cancellation notice-fee imposed. **Amenities:** irons. **Pool(s):** outdoor. **Leisure Activities:** rental sailboats, snorkeling equipment rental, volleyball. *Fee:* massage. **Guest Services:** valet laundry, wireless Internet. **Business Services:** meeting rooms, PC. **Cards:** AX, MC, VI. ***(See color ad below)***

/ SOME UNITS FEE

▼ *See AAA listing above* ▼

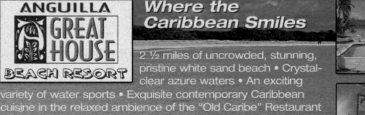

(See map and index starting on p. 279)

THE BACCARAT HOTEL AND RESIDENCES AT TEMENOS

Phone: 264/222-8000

fyi

Resort Hotel

Under construction, scheduled to open March 2009. **Address:** Cove Bay **Location:** West end. **Amenities:** 114 units, refrigerators, pool, tennis.

CUISINART RESORT & SPA Book great rates at AAA.com **Phone:** (264)498-2000 5

AAA SAVE

Resort Hotel

$400-$3500 All Year

Address: Rendezvous Bay **Location:** Oceanfront. 8 mi (12.8 km) sw of Wallblake International Airport. **Facility:** This distinctive resort with architecture reminiscent of the Greek Isle of Mykonos is on a white-sand beach; posh guest rooms are extremely spacious. Meets AAA guest room security requirements. 93 units. 71 one-bedroom standard units. 10 one-, 10 two- and 2 three-bedroom suites, some with whirlpools. 3 stories (no elevator), interior/exterior corridors. **Parking:** on-site and valet. **Terms:** 30 day cancellation notice-fee imposed. **Amenities:** video library, DVD players, CD players, high-speed Internet (fee), dual phone lines, voice mail, safes, honor bars, irons, hair dryers. **Dining:** 3 restaurants, also, Santorini, see separate listing, entertainment. **Pool(s):** outdoor. **Leisure Activities:** saunas, whirlpool, steamrooms, boating, sailboats, windsurfing, snorkeling, hobie cat, kayak, 3 lighted tennis courts, recreation programs, billiards, bocci, croquet, one mile par course with exercise stations, playground, exercise room, spa, volleyball. *Fee:* charter fishing, catamaran sailing trip, tennis instruction, bicycles. **Guest Services:** valet laundry, wireless Internet. **Business Services:** meeting rooms, PC. **Cards:** AX, MC, VI.

S D / SOME UNITS

WHERE TO DINE

SANTORINI **Phone:** 264/498-2000 4

AAA

International

$28-$54

Choose from air-conditioned interior dining or al fresco with a pool view. The attentive service leaves nothing to chance. Much of the menu centers around the on-site, hydroponically grown fruits, vegetables and herbs. Dressy casual. Entertainment. **Bar:** Full bar. **Reservations:** suggested. **Hours:** Open 12/1-9/5 & 10/30-11/30; 7 pm-10 pm. **Address:** Rendezvous Bay **Location:** 8 mi (12.8 km) sw of Wallblake International Airport; in CuisinArt Resort & Spa. **Parking:** on-site and valet. **Cards:** AX, MC, VI.

SANDY GROUND pop. 274 (See map and index starting on p. 279)

WHERE TO DINE

JOHNNO'S **Phone:** 264/497-2728 10

Caribbean

$11-$25

The popular local favorite is a hit with tourists as well for its casual mood and filling food. Casual dress. **Bar:** Full bar. **Reservations:** accepted. **Hours:** 10 am-10 pm. Closed: 12/25; also Mon & Good Friday. **Address:** Johnno's Beach **Location:** 3 mi (4.8 km) w of Wallblake International Airport. **Parking:** on-site. **Cards:** AX, MC, VI.

AC

SHOAL BAY EAST (See map and index starting on p. 279)

WHERE TO STAY

KU' Book at AAA.com **Phone:** (264)497-2011 10

Hotel

$180-$420 1/4-11/30

$180-$220 12/1-12/19

Address: Shoal Bay E **Location:** Oceanfront. Northwest coast; just s of Island Harbour. **Facility:** Designated smoking area. 27 units. 22 one- and 5 two-bedroom suites with kitchens. 1-3 stories (no elevator), exterior corridors. *Bath:* shower only. **Parking:** on-site. **Terms:** open 12/1-12/19 & 1/4-11/30, office hours 7 am-11 pm, age restrictions may apply, 30 day cancellation notice. **Amenities:** video library, DVD players, high-speed Internet (fee), voice mail, safes, irons, hair dryers. **Pool(s):** outdoor. **Leisure Activities:** exercise room. *Fee:* sailboats, windsurfing, waterskiing, scuba diving, snorkeling, massage. **Guest Services:** valet laundry. **Business Services:** PC. **Cards:** AX, MC, VI.

ASK FEE D VCR

SOUTH HILL pop. 1,495 (See map and index starting on p. 279)

WHERE TO DINE

BISTRO PHIL

Phone: 264/497-6810 (12)

French
$24-$40

Situated on a bluff over the Caribbean is the Parisian style bistro serving French food with a Caribbean twist. The gracious owner greets every guest. The seafood kabobs with shrimp, sea scallops, tuna, snapper, and mahi mahi are a favorite as is the lamb shank confit. Desserts are mouthwatering and the large bar area adjacent to the restaurant is perfect for enjoying a before or after dinner drink. Casual dress. **Bar:** Full bar. **Reservations:** required, 12/1-4/30. **Hours:** Open 12/1-9/1 & 10/1-11/30; 6:30 pm-9:30 pm. Closed: Sun. **Address:** Isaac Rd **Location:** Just se of Sandy Ground Village. **Parking:** on-site. **Cards:** MC, VI.

THE VALLEY pop. 1,169 (See map and index starting on p. 279)

WHERE TO DINE

KOALKEEL

Phone: 264/497-2930 (14)

International
$28-$45

On the site of an old sugar and cotton mill plantation, the pleasant dining room reflects on the history of days gone by. The menu features a wonderful mix of international fare and tandoori specialties. Candlelit tables lend to the romantic feel. Main courses arrive under silver dome covers to add a sense of drama to the meal. All of the not-to-be-missed desserts are prepared fresh to order. Complimentary shuttle service is offered from many island hotels. Semi-formal attire. **Bar:** Full bar. **Reservations:** suggested. **Hours:** 7 pm-9:30 pm. Closed: Sun. **Address:** Coronation Ave **Location:** Centre. **Parking:** on-site. **Cards:** MC, VI.

WEST END pop. 736

WHERE TO STAY

VICEROY ANGUILLA RESORT & RESIDENCES

fyi

Hotel
Rates not provided

Too new to rate, opening scheduled for November 2008. **Address:** Meads Bay **Location:** Main Road to West End. **Amenities:** 172 units, restaurant, coffeemakers, refrigerators, pool, tennis.

ANTIGUA AND BARBUDA

This index helps you "spot" where approved lodgings and restaurants are located on the corresponding detailed maps. Lodging daily rate range is for comparison only and show the property's high season. Restaurant rate range is a combination of lunch and/or dinner. Turn to the listing page for more detailed rate information and consult display ads for special promotions.

CEDAR GROVE

Map Page	OA	Lodging	Diamond Rated	High Season	Page
1 / p. 286		Blue Waters Antigua	♦♦♦	$300-$1775	287

Map Page	OA	Restaurant	Diamond Rated	Cuisine	Meal Range	Page
1 / p. 286		Le Bistro	♦♦♦	French	$35-$56	287

DICKENSON BAY

Map Page	OA	Lodging	Diamond Rated	High Season	Page
4 / p. 286		Siboney Beach Club	♦♦	$150-$325	288

Map Page	OA	Restaurants	Diamond Rated	Cuisine	Meal Range	Page
2 / p. 286		Bay House Restaurant	♦♦	International	$14-$38	288
3 / p. 286		Coconut Grove	♦♦	International	$8-$31	288
4 / p. 286		The Beach	♦♦	International	$17-$42	288
5 / p. 286		Pari's Pizza & Steak House	♦	International	$17-$34	288
6 / p. 286		Warri Pier	♦♦	International	$29-$40	288

JUMBY BAY (LONG ISLAND)

Map Page	OA	Lodging	Diamond Rated	High Season	Page
5 / p. 286		Jumby Bay Resort	♦♦♦♦	$775-$3350	289

FIVE ISLANDS

Map Page	OA	Lodging	Diamond Rated	High Season	Page
9 / p. 286	AAA	**Galley Bay Resort & Spa** - see color ad p 289	♦♦♦	$665-$1300 SAVE	289

WILLIKIES

Map Page	OA	Lodgings	Diamond Rated	High Season	Page
13 / p. 286	AAA	**The Verandah Resort & Spa** - see color ad p 293	♦♦♦	$345-$395 SAVE	293
14 / p. 286		Long Bay Hotel	♦♦	$300-$645	292
15 / p. 286	AAA	**Grand Pineapple Beach** - see color ad p 292	♦♦	$460-$630 SAVE	292

BOLANS

Map Page	OA	Lodging	Diamond Rated	High Season	Page
16 / p. 286	AAA	**Jolly Beach Resort Antigua** - see color ad p 287	♦	$380-$508 SAVE	287

MAMORA BAY

Map Page	OA	Lodging	Diamond Rated	High Season	Page
17 / p. 286	AAA	**St. James's Club & Villas** - see color ad p 290	♦♦♦	$395-$890 SAVE	290

Map Page	OA	Restaurant	Diamond Rated	Cuisine	Meal Range	Page
13 / p. 286		The Hideout Restaurant & Art Gallery	♦♦	International	$22-$33	290

ST. MARY'S

Map Page	OA	Lodging	Diamond Rated	High Season	Page
19 / p. 286		Carlisle Bay	♦♦♦♦	$775-$3700	292

Map Page	OA	Restaurant	Diamond Rated	Cuisine	Meal Range	Page
16 / p. 286		East	♦♦♦	Asian	$19-$32	292

CODRINGTON

Map Page	OA	Lodging	Diamond Rated	High Season	Page
23 / p. 286		The Beach House	◆◆◆	$750	287

ENGLISH HARBOUR

Map Page	OA	Restaurants	Diamond Rated	Cuisine	Meal Range	Page
14 / p. 286		The Admiral's Inn Restaurant	◆	International	$18-$35	288
15 / p. 286		The Terrace Restaurant	◆◆◆	International	$22-$32	288

ST. JOHN'S

Map Page	OA	Restaurants	Diamond Rated	Cuisine	Meal Range	Page
18 / p. 286		Hemingways Caribbean Cafe	◆◆	Caribbean	$10-$28	291
19 / p. 286		Home	◆◆◆	Caribbean	$28-$39	291
20 / p. 286		George Restaurant & Bar	◆◆	Caribbean	$13-$43	291
21 / p. 286		Cafe Napoleon	◆	International	$8-$22	291

NEW WINTHORPES

Map Page	OA	Restaurants	Diamond Rated	Cuisine	Meal Range	Page
26 / p. 286		The Pavilion Antigua	◆◆◆◆◆	Creole	$44-$63	290
27 / p. 286	AAA	**The Sticky Wicket Restaurant and Bar**	◆◆	International	$11-$23	290

Antigua and Barbuda

Lodging & Dining

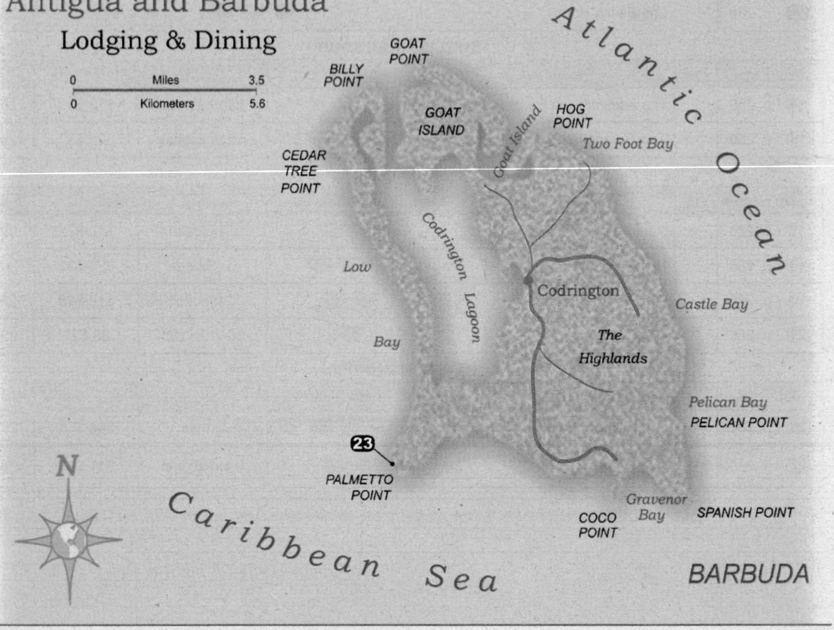

0 Miles 3.5
0 Kilometers 5.6

Atlantic Ocean
GOAT POINT
BILLY POINT
GOAT ISLAND
Goat Island
HOG POINT
Two Foot Bay
CEDAR TREE POINT
Codrington Lagoon
Low Bay
Codrington
Castle Bay
The Highlands
Pelican Bay
PELICAN POINT
23
PALMETTO POINT
N
Caribbean Sea
Gravenor Bay
COCO POINT
SPANISH POINT
BARBUDA

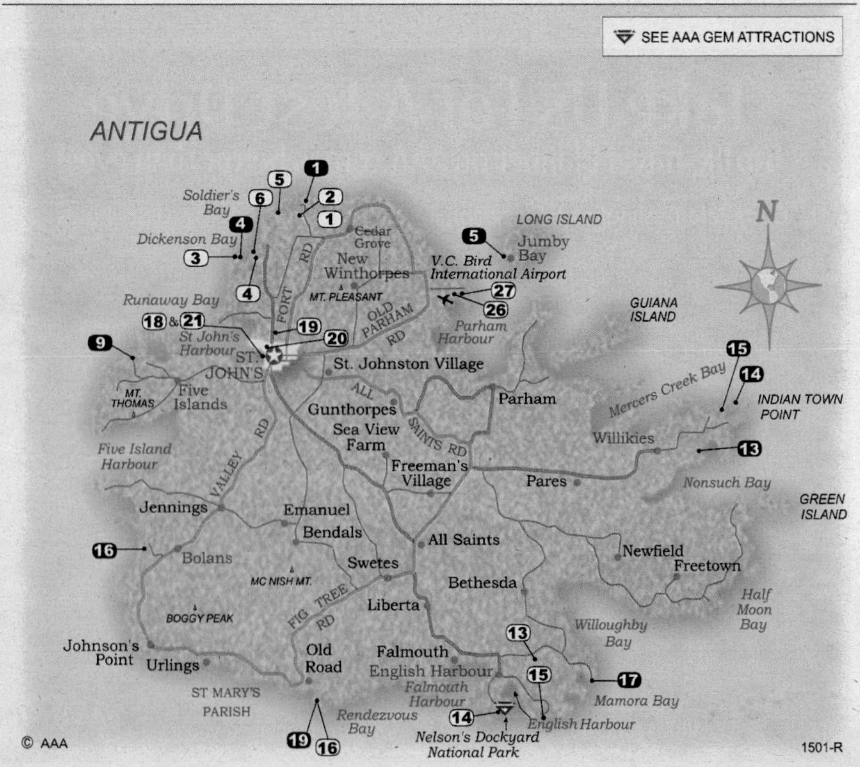

SEE AAA GEM ATTRACTIONS

ANTIGUA

1
5
Soldier's Bay
6
2
1
4
Dickenson Bay
3
Cedar Grove
New Winthorpes
5
LONG ISLAND
Jumby Bay
V.C. Bird International Airport
N
4
FORT RD
MT. PLEASANT
27
26
Runaway Bay
18 & 21
OLD PARHAM RD
GUIANA ISLAND
19
St John's Harbour
20
Parham Harbour
9
ST. JOHN'S
St. Johnston Village
15
14
MT. THOMAS
Five Islands
ALL SAINTS RD
Gunthorpes
Parham
Mercers Creek Bay
INDIAN TOWN POINT
Sea View Farm
Willikies
Five Island Harbour
VALLEY RD
Freeman's Village
13
Pares
Nonsuch Bay
GREEN ISLAND
Jennings
Emanuel
Bendals
All Saints
16
Bolans
Newfield
Freetown
Swetes
MC NISH MT.
Bethesda
Half Moon Bay
FIG TREE RD
Liberta
BOGGY PEAK
Willoughby Bay
13
Johnson's Point
Urlings
Old Road
Falmouth
English Harbour
15
17
ST MARY'S PARISH
Falmouth Harbour
Mamora Bay
Rendezvous Bay
14
English Harbour
Nelson's Dockyard National Park
19
16

1501-R

BOLANS pop. 1,447 (See map and index starting on p. 286)

WHERE TO STAY

JOLLY BEACH RESORT ANTIGUA Book great rates at AAA.com **Phone:** (268)462-0061 16

Resort Hotel

$380-$508 12/1-4/15
$346-$442 4/16-11/30

Address: Jolly Beach, St. Mary's Parish **Location:** Oceanfront. 6 mi (9.6 km) s of downtown St. John's; 12.3 mi (19.7 km) se of airport. **Facility:** The expansive, oceanfront resort offers many water sports activities and five room categories ranging from compact super-savers to junior suites. 462 one-bedroom standard units. 4 stories (no elevator), exterior corridors. *Bath:* combo or shower only. **Parking:** on-site. **Terms:** 7 day cancellation notice-fee imposed. **Amenities:** voice mail, safes (fee), hair dryers. *Some:* irons. **Dining:** 5 restaurants, entertainment. **Pool(s):** 2 outdoor. **Leisure Activities:** whirlpool, canoeing, paddleboats, sailboats, windsurfing, snorkeling, kayaks, table tennis, recreation programs, playground, exercise room, spa, basketball, shuffleboard, volleyball, game room. *Fee:* scuba diving, 4 lighted tennis courts. **Guest Services:** valet laundry, wireless Internet. **Business Services:** conference facilities, PC (fee). **Cards:** AX, DC, MC, VI. *(See color ad below)*

/ SOME UNITS

CEDAR GROVE (See map and index starting on p. 286)

WHERE TO STAY

BLUE WATERS ANTIGUA **Phone:** (268)462-0290 1

Resort Hotel

$300-$1775 All Year

Address: Soldiers Bay **Location:** Oceanfront. On north coast; 4.4 mi (7 km) nw of airport; at Soldiers Point. **Facility:** The oceanfront resort has a large, open-air lobby and offers several room categories with extra amenities; water sports activities also are offered. 105 units. 100 one-bedroom standard units, some with whirlpools. 4 two-bedroom suites. 1 house. 2-3 stories, exterior corridors. **Parking:** on-site. **Terms:** 28 day cancellation notice-fee imposed. **Amenities:** CD players, high-speed Internet, dual phone lines, voice mail, safes, honor bars, irons, hair dryers. **Pool(s):** 3 outdoor. **Leisure Activities:** whirlpool, beach access, paddleboats, sailboats, windsurfing, snorkeling, lighted tennis court, recreation programs in winter, exercise room, game room. *Fee:* massage. **Guest Services:** valet laundry, beauty salon, wireless Internet. **Business Services:** PC (fee). **Cards:** AX, DC, DS, MC, VI.

D

WHERE TO DINE

LE BISTRO **Phone:** 268/462-3881 1

French

$35-$56

Diners enjoy a spacious, candlelit dining room and a menu of traditional French cuisine prepared with an island flair. Fresh fish and Caribbean lobster are favorites. Dressy casual. **Bar:** Full bar. **Reservations:** suggested. **Hours:** Open 12/1-9/1 & 10/1-11/30; 6:30 pm-10:30 pm. Closed: 12/25; also Mon. **Address:** Hodges Bay **Location:** In Hodges Bay; 5 mi (8 km) e of downtown; 2 mi (3.2 km) n of airport. **Parking:** on-site. **Cards:** AX, MC, VI.

CODRINGTON pop. 814 (See map and index starting on p. 286)

WHERE TO STAY

THE BEACH HOUSE **Phone:** 268/764-4042 23

Hotel

$750 12/1-9/1 & 11/16-11/30

Address: Palmetto Point **Location:** Oceanfront. At Palmetto Point. **Facility:** 22 units. 21 one-bedroom standard units. 1 two-bedroom suite. 1 story, exterior corridors. **Parking:** on-site. **Terms:** open 12/1-9/1 & 11/16-11/30, age restrictions may apply. **Amenities:** video library, DVD players, irons, hair dryers. **Pool(s):** outdoor. **Leisure Activities:** beach access, snorkeling, fishing. *Fee:* massage. **Guest Services:** TV in common area, valet laundry, wireless Internet. **Business Services:** PC. **Cards:** AX, CB, DC, DS, JC, MC, VI.

24

DICKENSON BAY (See map and index starting on p. 286)

WHERE TO STAY

SIBONEY BEACH CLUB **Phone:** (268)462-0806 4

Hotel
$150-$325 All Year

Address: Dickenson Bay **Location:** Oceanfront. 7.5 mi (12 km) w of airport. **Facility:** 13 units. 1 one-bedroom standard unit. 12 one-bedroom suites with efficiencies. 3 stories (no elevator), exterior corridors. *Bath:* shower only. **Parking:** on-site. **Terms:** office hours 7 am-11 pm, 7 night minimum stay - seasonal, 21 day cancellation notice-fee imposed. **Amenities:** safes. **Dining:** Coconut Grove, see separate listing. **Pool(s):** outdoor. **Guest Services:** valet laundry, wireless Internet. **Business Services:** PC (fee). **Cards:** AX, MC, VI.

ASK / SOME UNITS

WHERE TO DINE

BAY HOUSE RESTAURANT **Phone:** 268/462-1223 2

International
$14-$38

Perched on a hill with panoramic views, the restaurant offers touches of island elegance in an al fresco setting. Tasty coconut shrimp are a great beginning. Lamb, numerous fresh fish dishes and a variety of pasta creations are among hearty entrees. Creme brulee and panna cotta are tempting finales. Dressy casual. **Bar:** Full bar. **Reservations:** suggested. **Hours:** 7 am-11 pm. **Address:** Dickenson Bay **Location:** 6.7 mi (10.7 km) w of airport; 4 mi (6.5 km) n of downtown St. John's; in Tradewinds Hotel. **Parking:** on-site. **Cards:** AX, MC, VI.

THE BEACH **Phone:** 268/480-6940 4

International
$17-$42

The beachside al fresco restaurant presents a broad menu of pizza, burgers, lamb, pasta and fresh seafood. Preparation styles span the culinary world. Service is languid and easygoing at the popular spot. Top off the meal with tiramisu or a lemon-lime tart. Casual dress. **Bar:** Full bar. **Reservations:** suggested, for dinner. **Hours:** 8:30 am-11 pm. **Address:** Dickenson Bay **Location:** 7.3 mi (11.7 km) w of airport; in Antigua Village. **Parking:** on-site. **Cards:** AX, DC, MC, VI.

COCONUT GROVE **Phone:** 268/462-1538 3

International
$8-$31

The covered, open-air beach shack—with cloth-covered tables and a fine menu selection—adds sophistication to beachfront dining. Diners find good food, primarily seafood and island fare, friendly service and stunning views of Dickenson Bay. Dressy casual. **Bar:** Full bar. **Reservations:** suggested, for dinner. **Hours:** 7:30 am-10:30 pm. **Address:** Dickenson Bay Rd **Location:** 7.5 mi (12 km) w of airport; in Siboney Beach Club. **Parking:** on-site. **Cards:** AX, MC, VI.

PARI'S PIZZA & STEAK HOUSE **Phone:** 268/462-1501 5

International
$17-$34

The long-established eatery on the northwest coast of Antigua is well known as a pizza and take-out joint, but dining in is also a popular option. In addition to pizza, the menu lists steak, ribs, grilled or steamed fish. The relaxed rustic decor attracts locals and tourists alike. Casual dress. **Bar:** Full bar. **Reservations:** suggested. **Hours:** 6 pm-11 pm. Closed: 12/25; also Mon. **Address:** Tradewinds Hill **Location:** 6.8 mi (10.9 km) w of airport; just n of town. **Parking:** on-site. **Cards:** AX, MC, VI.

WARRI PIER **Phone:** 268/462-0256 6

International
$29-$40

At the end of a wooden pier overlooking the sea, this open-air restaurant is a romantic choice for dinner. Peaceful sea breezes wash over the dining room, which is appointed in pleasant island decor. The menu centers on international fare, including fresh fish, steak and lamb, as well as a nice selection of tasty desserts. Casual dress. **Bar:** Beer only. **Reservations:** required. **Hours:** 6:30 pm-10 pm. Closed: Sun. **Address:** Dickenson Bay **Location:** 7 mi (11.2 km) w of airport; in Halcyon Cove by Rex Resorts. **Parking:** on-site. **Cards:** MC, VI.

ENGLISH HARBOUR pop. 614 (See map and index starting on p. 286)

WHERE TO DINE

THE ADMIRAL'S INN RESTAURANT **Phone:** 268/460-1027 14

International
$18-$35

The restaurant is an ideal stop for lunch or dinner while touring the historic Nelson Dockyard. The blackboard menu changes frequently but always features fresh seafood and meats often prepared West Indies style. The staff is laid-back. Casual dress. **Bar:** Full bar. **Reservations:** accepted. **Hours:** Open 12/1-8/20 & 10/15-11/30; 7 am-10, noon-2:30 & 7-9 pm. **Address:** Nelson's Dockyard **Location:** 15 mi (24 km) s of St. John's; on south coast; in Nelson's Dockyard National Park overlooking Falmouth Harbour. **Parking:** on-site. **Cards:** AX, MC, VI. **Historic**

THE TERRACE RESTAURANT **Phone:** 268/460-1014 15

International
$22-$32

High on a hill overlooking English Harbour, the restaurant offers open-air and terrace dining and a romantic ambience. Tables are candlelit, and diners enjoy gazing at the stars and the twinkling lights of the harbor below as they feast on fine Continental cuisine. The menu is ever-changing, with a focus on fresh local and regional ingredients. Sophisticated, attentive servers exude warm island hospitality. Dressy casual. **Bar:** Full bar. **Reservations:** required. **Hours:** Open 12/1-9/8 & 10/21-11/30; 7 pm-10 pm. **Address:** Shirley Heights Rd **Location:** In Dockyard National Park on road to Shirley Heights; 16 mi (25.6 km) s of airport; in The Inn at English Harbour. **Parking:** on-site. **Cards:** AX, MC, VI.

FIVE ISLANDS (See map and index starting on p. 286)

WHERE TO STAY

GALLEY BAY RESORT & SPA — **Phone:** (268)462-0302 **9**

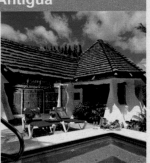

AAA SAVE

Resort Hotel

$665-$1300 All Year

Address: Galley Bay **Location:** Oceanfront. 4 mi (6.4 km) w of St. John's Harbor via New Rd to Five Island, follow signs. **Facility:** The luxurious romantic hideaway has rooms that vary from Polynesian-style cottages to junior suites; some guest units feature private plunge pools. 100 units. 87 one-bedroom standard units. 13 cottages. 1-2 stories (no elevator), exterior corridors. *Bath:* combo or shower only. **Parking:** on-site. **Terms:** 5 night minimum stay, age restrictions may apply, 30 day cancellation notice-fee imposed. **Amenities:** safes, honor bars, hair dryers. *Some:* irons. **Dining:** 3 restaurants, entertainment. **Pool(s):** 2 outdoor. **Leisure Activities:** sailboats, windsurfing, snorkeling, kayaks, tennis court, table tennis, bicycles, jogging, exercise room, spa. *Fee:* charter fishing. **Guest Services:** valet laundry, beauty salon, wireless Internet. **Business Services:** meeting rooms, PC. **Cards:** AX, MC, VI. **Free Special Amenities: early check-in/late check-out.**

(See color ad below)

Long Island

JUMBY BAY (See map and index starting on p. 286)

WHERE TO STAY

JUMBY BAY RESORT — *Book at AAA.com* — **Phone:** (268)462-6000 **5**

Resort Hotel

$775-$3350 All Year

Address: Long Island **Location:** Oceanfront. Private island 2 mi (3.2 km) ne of airport; accessed by boat launch on the hour between 7 am and midnight; behind Beach Comber Hotel. **Facility:** Set on 300 acres, this idyllic private island resort boasts three beaches; renovated guest rooms have British Colonial-style furnishings. 58 units. 32 one-bedroom standard units. 8 one- and 11 three-bedroom suites. 7 houses. 1-2 stories, exterior corridors. *Bath:* combo or shower only. **Parking:** no self-parking. **Terms:** 45 day cancellation notice. **Amenities:** video library, CD players, voice mail, safes, honor bars, irons, hair dryers. *Some:* DVD players. **Pool(s):** outdoor. **Leisure Activities:** paddleboats, sailboats, windsurfing, boat dock, waterskiing, snorkeling, putting green, 3 tennis courts (2 lighted), recreation programs, bicycles, playground, exercise room. *Fee:* scuba diving, massage. **Guest Services:** valet laundry, wireless Internet. **Business Services:** meeting rooms, PC. **Cards:** AX, DC, DS, MC, VI.

D / SOME UNITS

This ends listings for Long Island.
The following resumes the alphabetical listings
of cities in Antigua and Barbuda.

MAMORA BAY (See map and index starting on p. 286)

WHERE TO STAY

ST. JAMES'S CLUB & VILLAS **Phone:** (268)460-5000 17

AAA SAVE

Resort Hotel

$395-$890 12/1-3/31
$315-$835 4/1-11/30

Address: Mamora Bay **Location:** Oceanfront. 16 mi (25.6 km) se of airport. Located in a remote secluded area. **Facility:** Tropical grounds and two beaches give this property set on a secluded peninsula a distinctive island ambience; guest units vary. Meets AAA guest room security requirements. 257 units. 171 one-bedroom standard units. 13 one-, 69 two- and 4 three-bedroom suites, some with kitchens. 1-3 stories (no elevator), interior/exterior corridors. *Bath:* combo or shower only. **Parking:** on-site. **Terms:** 3 night minimum stay, 14 day cancellation notice-fee imposed. **Amenities:** safes, hair dryers. *Some:* irons. **Dining:** 4 restaurants, entertainment. **Pool(s):** 4 outdoor. **Leisure Activities:** whirlpool, sailboats, windsurfing, snorkeling, 6 tennis courts (4 lighted), recreation programs, exercise room, spa, volleyball. *Fee:* boats, paddleboats, boat dock, waterskiing, fishing, charter fishing, kayaks, tennis instruction. **Guest Services:** valet laundry, wireless Internet. **Business Services:** PC (fee). **Cards:** AX, MC, VI. **Free Special Amenities: early check-in/late check-out.** *(See color ad below)*

WHERE TO DINE

THE HIDEOUT RESTAURANT & ART GALLERY **Phone:** 268/460-3666 13

International
$22-$33

The gracious husband and wife who own and manage the restaurant are delightfully welcoming. Preparations of lamb, beef, duck and local fish blend Continental, French and West Indies ingredients and preparation styles. An ever-changing art gallery decorates the covered, open-air dining room. Dressy casual. **Bar:** Full bar. **Reservations:** required. **Hours:** 7 pm-9:30 pm. Closed: Sun. **Address:** Willoughby Bay **Location:** 16 mi (25.6 km) s of airport; on south coast; between English Harbour and Mamora Bay. **Parking:** on-site. **Cards:** MC, VI.

NEW WINTHORPES (See map and index starting on p. 286)

WHERE TO DINE

THE PAVILION ANTIGUA **Phone:** 268/480-6800 26

Creole
$44-$63

Exquisite cuisine served in one of the most refined dining rooms in the Caribbean. Entrees include Colorado lamb, Maine lobster and Berkshire pork chop. Formal service with precise attention to details. Formal attire. **Bar:** Full bar. **Reservations:** required. **Hours:** 7 pm-10 pm. Closed: 4/12; also Sun, Mon & Good Friday. **Address:** 7 Pavilion Dr **Location:** At V.C. Bird International Airport Complex. **Parking:** valet. **Cards:** AX, MC, VI.

THE STICKY WICKET RESTAURANT AND BAR Menu on AAA.com **Phone:** 268/481-7000 27

AAA

International
$11-$23

The novel, newly built restaurant is "where carnival meets cricket." Part sports bar with televised events, this place also boasts its own cricket field. The location near the airport is a hub of activity nightly and on weekend afternoons. On the menu are many options, including prime cuts of beef, barbecue and fresh fish dishes. Casual dress. **Bar:** Full bar. **Reservations:** accepted. **Hours:** 11 am-11 pm. Closed major holidays. **Address:** 20 Pavilion Dr **Location:** Just e of town; at V.C. Bird International Airport. **Parking:** on-site. **Cards:** AX, DS, MC, VI.

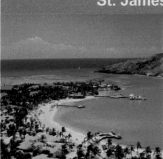

ST. JOHN'S pop. 22,342 (See map and index starting on p. 286)

WHERE TO DINE

CAFE NAPOLEON — **Phone:** 268/562-1820 (21)

International
$8-$22

Patrons can enjoy al fresco breakfast and lunch dining at the bustling downtown shopping and cruise ship docking area. Gourmet sandwiches, entree-size salads and such international entrees as lamb moussaka line the menu. Casual dress. **Bar:** Full bar. **Reservations:** suggested. **Hours:** 8 am-5 pm. Closed: 12/25; also Sun. **Address:** Redcliffe Quay **Location:** Downtown waterfront. **Parking:** street. **Cards:** MC, VI.

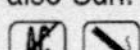

GEORGE RESTAURANT & BAR — **Phone:** 268/562-4866 (20)

Caribbean
$13-$43

Centrally located in the upstairs of a downtown historic building is the popular restaurant, which serves hearty fare with island-friendly service. Start with pumpkin soup topped with a swirl of creme fraiche. Local fish, such as kingfish, is popular, as are the barbecue ribs and steak entrees. Middle Eastern spices and ingredients influence a few dishes. All entrees include a choice of starch and vegetable. Saturday is Antiguan night, featuring local specialties. Casual dress. **Bar:** Full bar. **Reservations:** accepted. **Hours:** 9 am-10 pm. Closed: 12/25; also Sun & Mon. **Address:** Corner Market & Redcliffe Sts **Location:** Center. **Parking:** street. **Cards:** MC, VI. **Historic**

HEMINGWAYS CARIBBEAN CAFE — **Phone:** 268/462-2763 (18)

Caribbean
$10-$28

Upstairs in a historical building overlooking downtown, the restaurant offers fresh fish, lobster, steaks, lamb and some pasta dishes, all made fresh with the use of local herbs and spices. Dressy casual. **Bar:** Full bar. **Reservations:** suggested. **Hours:** Open 12/1-9/1 & 10/1-11/30; 8:30 am-10 pm. Closed major holidays; also Sun. **Address:** St. Mary's St **Location:** Downtown; at Heritage Quay. **Parking:** street. **Cards:** MC, VI. **Historic**

HOME — **Phone:** 268/461-7651 (19)

Caribbean
$28-$39

Warm hospitality exudes from the childhood home of acclaimed chef Carl Thomas. The owner/chef serves Caribbean haute cuisine inspired by the freshest seafood and local produce. The media hold this place in high esteem. Casual dress. **Bar:** Full bar. **Reservations:** suggested. **Hours:** Open 12/1-5/31 & 8/15-11/30; 6:30 pm-11 pm. Closed major holidays; also Sun & local holidays. **Address:** Gambles Terrace **Location:** Just n of downtown, then just e of Fort Rd, follow signs. **Parking:** street. **Cards:** AX, MC, VI.

ST. MARY'S pop. 10,000 (See map and index starting on p. 286)

WHERE TO STAY

CARLISLE BAY *Book at AAA.com* **Phone:** (268)484-0000 19

Resort Hotel

$775-$3700 All Year

Address: Old Rd **Location:** Oceanfront. Carlisle Bay; on the south coast. **Facility:** The newest luxury property in Antigua boasts a spa, gym and Asian-inspired restaurant as well as a 50-seat, indoor, air-conditioned movie theater. 82 units. 50 one-bedroom standard units. 28 one- and 4 three-bedroom suites. 2-3 stories (no elevator), exterior corridors. **Parking:** on-site and valet. **Terms:** 28 day cancellation notice-fee imposed. **Amenities:** video library, DVD players, CD players, high-speed Internet, dual phone lines, safes, honor bars, hair dryers. **Dining:** East, see separate listing. **Pool(s):** outdoor. **Leisure Activities:** saunas, sailboats, windsurfing, boat dock, snorkeling & rental equipment, 9 tennis courts (4 lighted), recreation programs, playground, exercise room, spa, yoga, basketball. *Fee:* scuba diving. **Guest Services:** valet laundry, wireless Internet. **Business Services:** meeting rooms, PC. **Cards:** AX, DC, MC, VI.

FEE / SOME UNITS

WHERE TO DINE

EAST **Phone:** 268/484-0000 16

Asian

$19-$32

In Antigua's newest Four Diamond hotel, the sleekly refined restaurant displays Asian minimalist decor and presents a menu that mixes Chinese, Thai and Japanese cuisine. Many dishes are seafood based, with ingredients such as shrimp, sea bass and crab, but the duck is also especially succulent. Sauces are delicately prepared, and portions are not overbearing so as to encourage the sampling of several dishes. Service is polished and attentive. Casual dress. **Bar:** Full bar. **Reservations:** suggested. **Hours:** Open 12/1-8/31 & 10/16-11/30; 7 pm-10 pm. **Address:** Old Rd **Location:** Carlisle Bay; on the south coast; in Carlisle Bay. **Parking:** on-site. **Cards:** AX, CB, DC, JC, MC, VI.

WILLIKIES pop. 1,042 (See map and index starting on p. 286)

WHERE TO STAY

GRAND PINEAPPLE BEACH *Book great rates at AAA.com* **Phone:** (268)463-2006 15

AAA SAVE

Resort Hotel

$460-$630 All Year

Address: Long Bay #2000 Rd **Location:** Oceanfront. 11.8 mi (18.9 km) e of St. John's; 1.3 mi (2.1 km) e of town; on northeast coast, follow signs. **Facility:** This sprawling, family-friendly, all-inclusive resort is on 25 acres and offers sporting activities, nightly entertainment and four room categories. 180 one-bedroom standard units. 1-3 stories (no elevator), exterior corridors. *Bath:* combo or shower only. **Parking:** on-site. **Terms:** 3 night minimum stay, 14 day cancellation notice-fee imposed. **Amenities:** voice mail, safes, hair dryers. **Dining:** 3 restaurants, nightclub, entertainment. **Pool(s):** 2 outdoor. **Leisure Activities:** sailboats, windsurfing, snorkeling, kayaks, 4 tennis courts, recreation programs, slot machines, exercise room, basketball, shuffleboard, volleyball. *Fee:* scuba diving, massage. **Guest Services:** valet laundry, wireless Internet. **Business Services:** PC (fee). **Cards:** AX, MC, VI. *(See color ad below)*

LONG BAY HOTEL **Phone:** 268/463-2005 14

Hotel

$300-$645 12/1-5/15 & 11/1-11/30

Address: Long Bay #442 Dr **Location:** Oceanfront. On northeast coast, 2.9 mi (1.8 km) e of town. **Facility:** 25 units. 20 one-bedroom standard units. 5 cottages. 1-2 stories, exterior corridors. *Bath:* shower only. **Parking:** on-site. **Terms:** open 12/1-5/15 & 11/1-11/30, office hours 7 am-10 pm, 21 day cancellation notice-fee imposed. **Leisure Activities:** sailboats, windsurfing, boat dock, snorkeling, tennis court, game room. *Fee:* waterskiing. **Guest Services:** valet laundry, wireless Internet. **Business Services:** PC (fee). **Cards:** AX, MC, VI.

/ SOME UNITS

(See map and index starting on p. 286)

THE VERANDAH RESORT & SPA Phone: 268/562-6840 13

Resort Hotel

$345-$395 All Year

Address: Dian Bay **Location:** Oceanfront. At Dian Bay; 12.8 mi (20.5 km) e of St. John's; follow signs; 2.3 mi (3.7 km) e of town; on east coast. **Facility:** Nestled on a bluff, the newly build resort offers cottage-like units with varied amenities, rattan-style furniture, a wet bar and a LCD television. 145 one-bedroom standard units. 1 story, exterior corridors. **Parking:** on-site. **Terms:** 3 day cancellation notice-fee imposed. **Amenities:** safes, irons, hair dryers. **Dining:** 3 restaurants, entertainment. **Pool(s):** 2 outdoor. **Leisure Activities:** canoeing, paddleboats, sailboats, windsurfing, snorkeling, kayaks, personal watercraft, 2 lighted tennis courts, recreation programs, kids club, playground, exercise room, spa, horseshoes, shuffleboard, volleyball. *Fee:* sauna. **Guest Services:** valet laundry, wireless Internet. **Business Services:** meeting rooms, PC. **Cards:** AX, DS, MC, VI. *(See color ad below)*

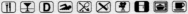

ARUBA

Airport Accommodations

Map Page	OA	QUEEN BEATRIX AIRPORT	Diamond Rated	High Season	Page
30 / p. 296	AAA	**Renaissance Aruba Resort & Casino, 2.7 mi (4.3 km) of terminal**	4 diamonds	$230-$475 SAVE	301

Aruba

This index helps you "spot" where approved lodgings and restaurants are located on the corresponding detailed maps. Lodging daily rate range is for comparison only and show the property's high season. Restaurant rate range is a combination of lunch and/or dinner. Turn to the listing page for more detailed rate information and consult display ads for special promotions.

PALM BEACH

Map Page	OA	Lodgings	Diamond Rated	High Season	Page
3 / p. 296	AAA	**Aruba Marriott Resort & Stellaris Casino** - see color ad p 309, on insert	fyi	$338-$761 SAVE	308
4 / p. 296	AAA	**Hyatt Regency Aruba Resort & Casino** - see color ad p 310	4 diamonds	$255-$695 SAVE	311
8 / p. 296		Holiday Inn SunSpree Resort Aruba - see color ad p 310	3 diamonds	$180-$445	310
9 / p. 296	AAA	**Radisson Aruba Resort, Casino & Spa** - see color ad p 312	4 diamonds	$250-$775 SAVE	311
10 / p. 296	AAA	**The Westin Aruba Resort** - see color ad p 313, on insert	4 diamonds	$269-$659 SAVE	314
12 / p. 296	AAA	**Divi Aruba Phoenix Beach Resort**	3 diamonds	$290-$824 SAVE	308

Map Page	OA	Restaurants	Diamond Rated	Cuisine	Meal Range	Page
3 / p. 296		Tango Argentine Grill - see color ad p 315	2 diamonds	Argentine	$23-$36	315
4 / p. 296		Hostaria da' Vittorio	2 diamonds	Italian	$23-$39	314
5 / p. 296		Amazonia Churrascaria	2 diamonds	Steak	$27-$43	314
6 / p. 296	AAA	**Blossom's**	3 diamonds	Asian	$22-$40	314
10 / p. 296		Pago Pago	3 diamonds	Steak & Seafood	$29-$45	315
11 / p. 296		Cafe Japengo	3 diamonds	Asian	$21-$36	314
12 / p. 296		Las Ruinas del Mar	3 diamonds	Continental	$24-$38	314
13 / p. 296	AAA	**Sunset Grille** - see color ad p 312	4 diamonds	Steak & Seafood	$27-$40	315
14 / p. 296		Aqua Grill	3 diamonds	Seafood	$26-$39	314

BUBALI

Map Page	OA	Lodgings	Diamond Rated	High Season	Page
15 / p. 296	AAA	**Costa Linda Beach Resort** - see color ad p 302	3 diamonds	$259-$1467 SAVE	297
16 / p. 296		Bucuti Beach Resort	3 diamonds	$250-$535	297
17 / p. 296	AAA	**Manchebo Beach Resort & Spa** - see color ad p 304	3 diamonds	$169-$305 SAVE	300
18 / p. 296	AAA	**Divi Aruba All Inclusive** - see color ad p 303	3 diamonds	$388-$600 SAVE	297
19 / p. 296		Aruba Beach Club	2 diamonds	$175-$368	297
21 / p. 296	AAA	**Tamarijn Aruba All Inclusive**	2 diamonds	$338-$488 SAVE	300
24 / p. 296	AAA	**Amsterdam Manor Beach Resort** - see color ad p 303	3 diamonds	$169-$440 SAVE	296
26 / p. 296		Paradise Beach Villas	2 diamonds	$118-$780	300
28 / p. 296	AAA	**Divi Village Golf & Beach Resort/Divi Dutch Village Resort** - see color ad p 304	3 diamonds	$150-$845 SAVE	297

Map Page	OA	Restaurants	Diamond Rated	Cuisine	Meal Range	Page
17 / p. 296		Le Dome Restaurant	◆◆◆	Belgian	$18-$40	301
18 / p. 296		Chalet Suisse Restaurant	◆◆◆	International	$24-$38	300
20 / p. 296	AAA	**French Steakhouse Restaurant** - see color ad p 304	◆◆	Steak & Seafood	$23-$36	301

ORANJESTAD

Map Page	OA	Lodging	Diamond Rated	High Season	Page
30 / p. 296	AAA	**Renaissance Aruba Resort & Casino** - see color ad p 305, on insert	◆◆◆◆	$230-$475 SAVE	301

Map Page	OA	Restaurants	Diamond Rated	Cuisine	Meal Range	Page
22 / p. 296		Jamaica Me Krazy	◆	Jamaican	$9-$14	306
23 / p. 296		L.G. Smith's Steak & Chop House	◆◆◆	Steak	$23-$36	307
24 / p. 296	AAA	**Iguana Joe's Caribbean Bar & Grill**	◆	International	$9-$20	306
26 / p. 296		Rumba Bar & Grill	◆◆	International	$7-$28	307
28 / p. 296	AAA	**Matilde Restaurant & Downtown Monument** - see color ad p 307	◆◆◆◆	International	$22-$46	307
29 / p. 296		Don Carlo's Ristorante Italiano	◆◆	Italian	$17-$34	306
30 / p. 296		Driftwood Restaurant	◆◆	Seafood	$18-$36	306
31 / p. 296		El Gaucho	◆◆	Argentine	$20-$37	306
32 / p. 296		Cuba's Cookin	◆◆	Cuban	$17-$28	306
35 / p. 296		La Fondue d' Aruba	◆◆	Fondue	$19-$42	307

NOORD

Map Page	OA	Restaurants	Diamond Rated	Cuisine	Meal Range	Page
16 / p. 296		Madame Janette	◆◆	International	$20-$32	301
19 / p. 296	AAA	**Gasparito Restaurant & Gallery**	◆◆	Caribbean	$18-$28	301
21 / p. 296	AAA	**Buccaneer Restaurant**	◆◆	Seafood	$17-$30	301

ARASHI

Map Page	OA	Restaurant	Diamond Rated	Cuisine	Meal Range	Page
38 / p. 296		La Trattoria El Faro Blanco	◆◆	Italian	$15-$33	296

© AAA

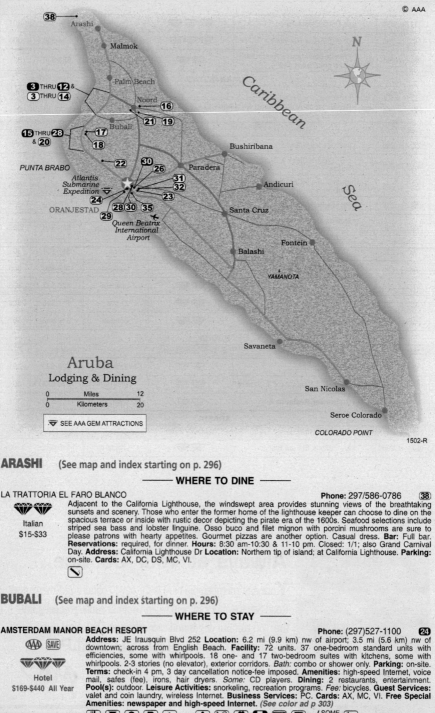

Aruba
Lodging & Dining

38 Arashi
Malmok
Palm Beach
3 THRU 12 & 3 THRU 14
Noord 16 21 19
Bubali
15 THRU 28 & 20
17
18
22
PUNTA BRABO
30 26
Atlantis Submarine Expedition
24
31 32 23
ORANJESTAD
28 30 35
29
Queen Beatrix International Airport
Caribbean Sea
N
Bushiribana
Paradera
Andicuri
Santa Cruz
Fontein
Balashi
YAMANOTA
Savaneta
San Nicolas
Seroe Colorado
COLORADO POINT
0 Miles 12
0 Kilometers 20
SEE AAA GEM ATTRACTIONS
1502-R

ARASHI (See map and index starting on p. 296)

WHERE TO DINE

LA TRATTORIA EL FARO BLANCO — **Phone:** 297/586-0786 (38)

Italian
$15-$33

Adjacent to the California Lighthouse, the windswept area provides stunning views of the breathtaking sunsets and scenery. Those who enter the former home of the lighthouse keeper can choose to dine on the spacious terrace or inside with rustic decor depicting the pirate era of the 1600s. Seafood selections include striped sea bass and lobster linguine. Osso buco and filet mignon with porcini mushrooms are sure to please patrons with hearty appetites. Gourmet pizzas are another option. Casual dress. **Bar:** Full bar. **Reservations:** required, for dinner. **Hours:** 8:30 am-10:30 & 11-10 pm. Closed: 1/1; also Grand Carnival Day. **Address:** California Lighthouse Dr **Location:** Northern tip of island; at California Lighthouse. **Parking:** on-site. **Cards:** AX, DC, DS, MC, VI.

BUBALI (See map and index starting on p. 296)

WHERE TO STAY

AMSTERDAM MANOR BEACH RESORT — **Phone:** (297)527-1100 (24)

Hotel
$169-$440 All Year

Address: JE Irausquin Blvd 252 **Location:** 6.2 mi (9.9 km) nw of airport; 3.5 mi (5.6 km) nw of downtown; across from English Beach. **Facility:** 72 units. 37 one-bedroom standard units with efficiencies, some with whirlpools. 18 one- and 17 two-bedroom suites with kitchens, some with whirlpools. 2-3 stories (no elevator), exterior corridors. *Bath:* combo or shower only. **Parking:** on-site. **Terms:** check-in 4 pm, 3 day cancellation notice-fee imposed. **Amenities:** high-speed Internet, voice mail, safes (fee), irons, hair dryers. *Some:* CD players. **Dining:** 2 restaurants, entertainment. **Pool(s):** outdoor. **Leisure Activities:** snorkeling, recreation programs. *Fee:* bicycles. **Guest Services:** valet and coin laundry, wireless Internet. **Business Services:** PC. **Cards:** AX, MC, VI. **Free Special Amenities: newspaper and high-speed Internet.** *(See color ad p 303)*

(See map and index starting on p. 296)

ARUBA BEACH CLUB — **Phone:** 297/582-3000 19

Condominium

$175-$368 All Year

Address: JE Irausquin Blvd 53 **Location:** Oceanfront. Punto Bravo; 4.9 mi (7.8 km) nw of airport; 2.2 mi (3.5 km) nw of downtown. **Facility:** Meets AAA guest room security requirements. 131 units. 89 one-bedroom standard units with efficiencies. 42 one-bedroom suites with kitchens. 2-4 stories, interior corridors. *Bath:* shower only. **Parking:** on-site. **Terms:** check-in 4 pm, cancellation fee imposed. **Amenities:** high-speed Internet (fee), voice mail, safes, irons. *Some:* DVD players (fee), hair dryers. **Pool(s):** outdoor. **Leisure Activities:** 4 lighted tennis courts, recreation programs, playground. **Guest Services:** valet and coin laundry, wireless Internet. **Business Services:** PC (fee). **Cards:** AX, DS, MC, VI.

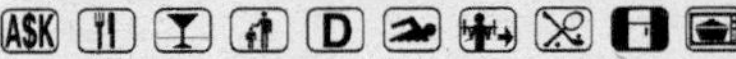

BUCUTI BEACH RESORT — Book at AAA.com — **Phone:** (297)583-1100 16

Hotel

$250-$535 All Year

Address: L.G. Smith Blvd 55B **Location:** Oceanfront. 5.1 mi (8.1 km) nw of airport; 2.4 mi (3.8 km) nw of downtown; at Eagle Beach. Located behind Alhambra Casino Complex. **Facility:** Meets AAA guest room security requirements. Designated smoking area. 104 units. 63 one-bedroom standard units, some with efficiencies. 41 one-bedroom suites, some with efficiencies. 1-4 stories, interior/exterior corridors. *Bath:* combo or shower only. **Parking:** on-site. **Terms:** 5-7 night minimum stay - seasonal, age restrictions may apply, 14 day cancellation notice-fee imposed. **Amenities:** high-speed Internet, voice mail, safes, honor bars, irons, hair dryers. **Pool(s):** outdoor. **Leisure Activities:** whirlpool, exercise room, spa, activity desk. **Guest Services:** valet and coin laundry, wireless Internet. **Business Services:** business center. **Cards:** AX, DS, MC, VI.

ASK S D

COSTA LINDA BEACH RESORT — Book great rates at AAA.com — **Phone:** (297)583-8000 15

AAA SAVE

Resort Hotel

$259-$1467 All Year

Address: JE Irausquin Blvd 59 **Location:** Oceanfront. 5.1 mi (8.1 km) nw of airport; 2.4 mi (3.8 km) nw of downtown; at Eagle Beach. **Facility:** The new condominium-style property located directly on the beach has many room categories to choose from, all with numerous amenities. Designated smoking area. 159 units. 3 one-, 140 two- and 16 three-bedroom suites with kitchens. 5 stories, exterior corridors. **Parking:** on-site. **Terms:** check-in 4 pm, 30 day cancellation notice-fee imposed. **Amenities:** voice mail, safes, irons, hair dryers. *Some:* DVD players (fee). **Dining:** 5 restaurants, entertainment. **Pool(s):** 2 outdoor. **Leisure Activities:** whirlpools, 2 tennis courts (Fee: 2 lighted), recreation programs, bocci, playground, exercise room, spa, basketball, shuffleboard, volleyball, game room. **Guest Services:** valet and coin laundry, beauty salon, wireless Internet. **Cards:** AX, MC, VI. *(See color ad p 302)*

S D / SOME UNITS FEE VCR

DIVI ARUBA ALL INCLUSIVE — Book great rates at AAA.com — **Phone:** (297)525-5200 18

AAA SAVE

Resort Hotel

$388-$600 All Year

Address: JE Irausquin Blvd 45 **Location:** Oceanfront. 4.7 mi (7.5 km) nw of airport; 2 mi (3.2 km) nw of downtown. Located across from the Alhambra Casino Complex. **Facility:** This recently renovated resort shares facilities with Tamarijn Aruba All Inclusive; all units have a balcony or patio and Caribbean-style decor. 203 one-bedroom standard units, some with whirlpools. 1-3 stories (no elevator), interior/exterior corridors. *Bath:* combo or shower only. **Parking:** on-site. **Terms:** 3-5 night minimum stay - seasonal, 30 day cancellation notice. **Amenities:** voice mail, safes (fee), irons, hair dryers. **Dining:** 3 restaurants, entertainment. **Pool(s):** 2 outdoor. **Leisure Activities:** recreation programs, bocci, recreational facilities privileges at sister property, spa, volleyball. **Guest Services:** valet laundry, beauty salon, wireless Internet. **Business Services:** meeting rooms. **Cards:** AX, DS, MC, VI. **Free Special Amenities: preferred room (subject to availability with advance reservations).** *(See color ad p 303)*

D

DIVI VILLAGE GOLF & BEACH RESORT/DIVI DUTCH VILLAGE RESORT — Book great rates at AAA.com — **Phone:** (297)583-5000 28

AAA SAVE

Resort Condominium

$150-$845 All Year

Address: JE Irausquin Blvd 93 **Location:** Oceanfront. 4.5 mi (7.2 km) nw of airport; 1.8 mi (2.9 km) nw of downtown. **Facility:** The modern condo-style operation across from Druif Beach features well-equipped units, all with balcony, ideal for long term stays. Meets AAA guest room security requirements. 385 units. 191 one-bedroom standard units, some with kitchens and/or whirlpools. 126 one-, 66 two- and 2 three-bedroom suites with kitchens, some with whirlpools. 3-5 stories, exterior corridors. **Parking:** on-site. **Terms:** check-in 4 pm, 3-7 night minimum stay - seasonal, 7 day cancellation notice-fee imposed. **Amenities:** safes, irons, hair dryers. *Some:* DVD players. **Dining:** 3 restaurants. **Pool(s):** 3 outdoor. **Leisure Activities:** whirlpools, kayak, putting green, golf learning center, 3 lighted tennis courts, recreation programs, rock climbing wall & use of recreational facilities at Divi properties, exercise room, volleyball. *Fee:* golf-9 holes. **Guest Services:** valet and coin laundry, wireless Internet. **Business Services:** business center. **Cards:** AX, DS, MC, VI. *(See color ad p 304)*

S D / SOME UNITS VCR

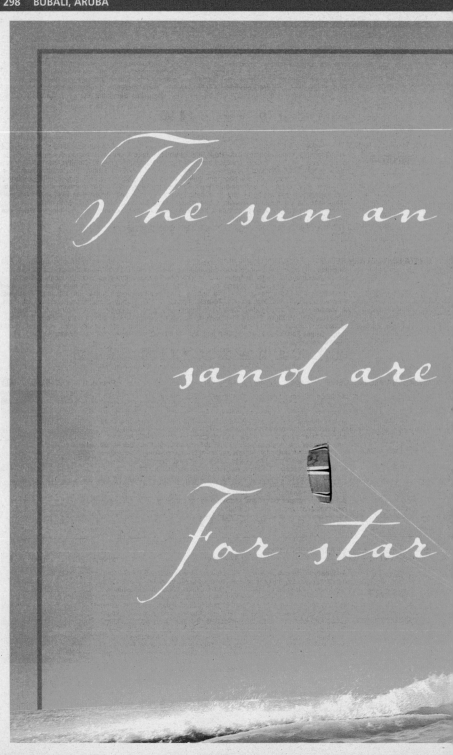

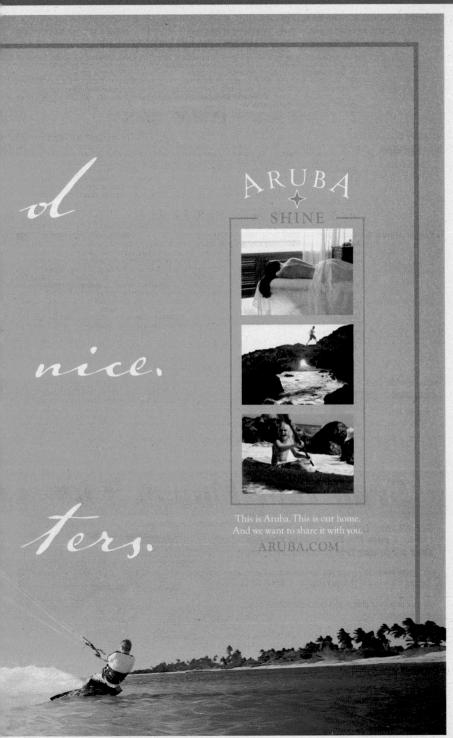

(See map and index starting on p. 296)

MANCHEBO BEACH RESORT & SPA Book great rates at AAA.com **Phone:** (297)582-3444 17

AAA SAVE

Hotel
$169-$305 All Year

Address: JE Irausquin Blvd 55 **Location:** Oceanfront. 5 mi (8 km) nw of airport; 2.3 mi (3.7 km) nw of downtown at Punto Bravo. Located behind the Alhambra Casino Complex. **Facility:** Meets AAA guest room security requirements. 71 one-bedroom standard units. 2 stories (no elevator), exterior corridors. **Parking:** on-site. **Terms:** 3 night minimum stay - seasonal and/or weekends, 7 day cancellation notice, 14 day in winter-fee imposed. **Amenities:** voice mail, safes, irons, hair dryers. **Dining:** 2 restaurants, also, French Steakhouse Restaurant, see separate listing, entertainment. **Pool(s):** outdoor. **Leisure Activities:** exercise room, spa, volleyball. *Fee:* whirlpool, steamroom. **Guest Services:** valet and coin laundry, wireless Internet. **Business Services:** meeting rooms, PC. **Cards:** AX, DC, MC, VI. **Free Special Amenities: newspaper and high-speed Internet.** *(See color ad p 304)*

D / SOME UNITS

PARADISE BEACH VILLAS **Phone:** (297)587-4000 26

Condominium
$118-$780 All Year

Address: JE Irausquin Blvd 64 **Location:** Oceanfront. 5.8 mi (9.3 km) nw of airport; 3.1 mi (4.9 km) nw of downtown. **Facility:** Meets AAA guest room security requirements. 80 units. 4 one-bedroom standard units with efficiencies and whirlpools. 45 one-, 30 two- and 1 three-bedroom suites with kitchens and whirlpools. 3-4 stories, interior/exterior corridors. **Parking:** on-site. **Terms:** office hours 6:30 am-10 pm, check-in 4 pm, cancellation fee imposed. **Amenities:** high-speed Internet (fee), voice mail, safes, irons, hair dryers. **Pool(s):** 2 outdoor. **Leisure Activities:** whirlpools, exercise room. *Fee:* massage. **Guest Services:** coin laundry, beauty salon, wireless Internet. **Business Services:** PC (fee). **Cards:** AX, DS, MC, VI.

S D

TAMARIJN ARUBA ALL INCLUSIVE Book great rates at AAA.com **Phone:** (297)525-5200 21

AAA SAVE

Resort Hotel
$338-$488 All Year

Address: JE Irausquin Blvd 41 **Location:** Oceanfront. 4.5 mi (7.2 km) nw of airport; 1.8 mi (2.9 km) nw of downtown. **Facility:** An active, all-inclusive resort with a new lobby, new gym and new restaurant as well as a rock climbing wall and rooms with tropical decor. 236 one-bedroom standard units. 2 stories (no elevator), exterior corridors. *Bath:* combo or shower only. **Parking:** on-site. **Terms:** 3 night minimum stay, 30 day cancellation notice. **Amenities:** voice mail, irons, hair dryers. *Fee:* high-speed Internet, safes. **Dining:** 4 restaurants, entertainment. **Pool(s):** outdoor. **Leisure Activities:** beach access, canoeing, sailboats, windsurfing, snorkeling, beginner's windsurfing equipment, beach games, snorkeling instruction, 2 lighted tennis courts, recreation programs, rock climbing wall, kids club, lawn chess, use of recreational facilities, bicycles, exercise room, shuffleboard, volleyball, game room. **Guest Services:** valet laundry, wireless Internet. **Business Services:** PC (fee). **Cards:** AX, DS, MC, VI. **Free Special Amenities: preferred room (subject to availability with advance reservations).**

D

WHERE TO DINE

CHALET SUISSE RESTAURANT **Phone:** 297/587-5054 18

International
$24-$38

The restaurant has earned a solid reputation since it opened in 1988. International and Continental flavors influence the French-trained chef's preparations, which include dishes made from prime cuts of meat and fresh seafood. Portions are ample. Swiss-style architecture and decor characterizes the bustling dining room, where diners often linger over the decadent chocolate fondue. Repeat guests often favor the early-bird specials. Dressy casual. **Bar:** Full bar. **Reservations:** suggested. **Hours:** 5:30 pm-10 pm. Closed: 1/1; also 12/31 & Sun. **Address:** JE Irausquin Blvd 246 **Location:** 3.1 mi (4.9 km) nw of downtown; across from Eagle Beach. **Parking:** on-site. **Cards:** AX, DS, MC, VI.

(See map and index starting on p. 296)

FRENCH STEAKHOUSE RESTAURANT *Menu on AAA.com* **Phone:** 297/582-3444 (20)

Steak & Seafood
$23-$36

The restaurant specializes in beef and seafood. The French decor touches accent a dining room comfortable for casual dining or a special occasion. Both indoor and outdoor dining available. Extensive wine list. Casual dress. **Bar:** Full bar. **Reservations:** required. **Hours:** 5:30 pm-10:30 pm. **Address:** JE Irausquin Blvd 55 **Location:** 5 mi (8 km) nw of airport; 2.3 mi (3.7 km) nw of downtown at Punto Bravo; in Manchebo Beach Resort & Spa. **Parking:** on-site. **Cards:** AX, DC, DS, MC, VI. *(See color ad p 304)*

LE DOME RESTAURANT **Phone:** 297/587-1517 (17)

Belgian
$18-$40

Patrons are seated in one of four distinct themed dining rooms—Old World, Dali, L'Orangerie or Terrace Galleria—for exquisite cuisine served by a European staff. Warm and cold appetizers include duck liver mousse, escargot and frog legs. The Belgian owners' large selection of entrees is influenced by French cuisine. Among fish entrees are Dover sole and steamed salmon in puff pastry. Meat selections include Chateaubriand and grilled rosemary veal chop. Dressy casual. **Bar:** Full bar. **Reservations:** suggested. **Hours:** noon-3 & 6-10:30 pm, Sat & Sun from 6 pm; Sunday brunch 11 am-3 pm. Closed: Mon. **Location:** 6 mi (9.6 km) nw of airport; 3.3 mi (5.3 km) nw of downtown. **Parking:** on-site. **Cards:** AX, DS, MC, VI.

NOORD (See map and index starting on p. 296)

WHERE TO DINE

BUCCANEER RESTAURANT **Phone:** 297/586-6172 (21)

Seafood
$17-$30

The popular, casual spot might make diners feel as though they are eating in a ship's cabin; windows display saltwater aquariums, and two bars are made from old ships. Patrons should stop in early for a good table, as reservations are not accepted. Seafood, beef and European specialties, all served in large portions, line the menu. Casual dress. **Bar:** Full bar. **Hours:** 5:30 pm-10 pm. Closed: 12/25; also Sun. **Address:** Gasparito 11-C **Location:** 0.3 mi (0.5 km) e from Palm Beach, then 0.3 mi (0.5 km) s, follow signs. **Parking:** on-site. **Cards:** AX, DS, MC, VI.

GASPARITO RESTAURANT & GALLERY **Phone:** 297/586-7044 (19)

Caribbean
$18-$28

The romantic restaurant is in an Aruban-style house with a candlelit courtyard. Original gallery-quality artwork lines the walls of the air-conditioned interior dining area. Representative of Antillean cuisine are keshi yena and stoba. Casual dress. **Bar:** Full bar. **Reservations:** required. **Hours:** 5:30 pm-10 pm. Closed major holidays; also Aruba public holidays. **Address:** Gasparito #3 **Location:** 0.5 mi (0.8 km) e of Palm Beach, 0.6 mi (0.9 km) s; follow signs; in Gasparito. **Parking:** on-site. **Cards:** MC, VI. **Historic**

MADAME JANETTE **Phone:** 297/587-0184 (16)

International
$20-$32

The restaurant is a perennial favorite with repeat tourists and locals alike. Guests can savor the international flavors of Caribbean-influenced cuisine in the al fresco garden courtyard. Rich rock lobster a la creme in a puff pastry and crab cakes with spicy island remoulade are great beginnings. Among offerings in a sea of fresh fish are snapper, grouper, mahi mahi and sea bass. Carnivores might try the veal chop with marinara sauce or beef stroganoff. Casual dress. **Bar:** Full bar. **Reservations:** required. **Hours:** Open 12/1-6/1 & 6/22-11/30; 6 pm-10 pm. Closed: 1/1; also 12/31 & Tues. **Address:** Cunucu Abao 37 **Location:** 3.5 mi (5.6 km) n of downtown; just e of LG Smith Blvd. **Parking:** on-site. **Cards:** AX, MC, VI.

ORANJESTAD pop. 26,355 (See map and index starting on p. 296)

WHERE TO STAY

RENAISSANCE ARUBA RESORT & CASINO *Book great rates at AAA.com* **Phone:** (297)583-6000 (30)

SAVE

Resort Hotel
$230-$475 All Year

Address: LG Smith Blvd 82 **Location:** Oceanfront. 2.7 mi (4.3 km) nw of airport; downtown. Part of Seaport Village Complex. **Facility:** Accommodations are offered in the resort's beach and marina towers downtown; transportation to a private island beach is available. Smoke free premises. 556 units. 298 one-bedroom standard units. 258 one-bedroom suites. 5-6 stories, interior corridors. **Parking:** on-site and valet. **Terms:** check-in 4 pm, 7 day cancellation notice-fee imposed. **Amenities:** high-speed Internet (fee), dual phone lines, voice mail, safes, irons, hair dryers. **Dining:** 15 restaurants, also, L.G. Smith's Steak & Chop House, see separate listing, entertainment. **Pool(s):** 3 outdoor. **Leisure Activities:** saunas, marina, 2 lighted tennis courts, recreation programs, spa, basketball, volleyball, game room. *Fee:* boats, canoes, paddleboats, sailboats, windsurfing, scuba diving, snorkeling, charter fishing, kayaks, water bicycles. **Guest Services:** valet and coin laundry, wireless Internet. **Business Services:** conference facilities, business center. **Cards:** AX, DS, MC, VI. *(See color ad p 305 & on insert)*

RENAISSANCE. HOTELS & RESORTS

AAA Benefit:
Members save a minimum 5% off the best available rate.

▼ See AAA listing p 297 ▼

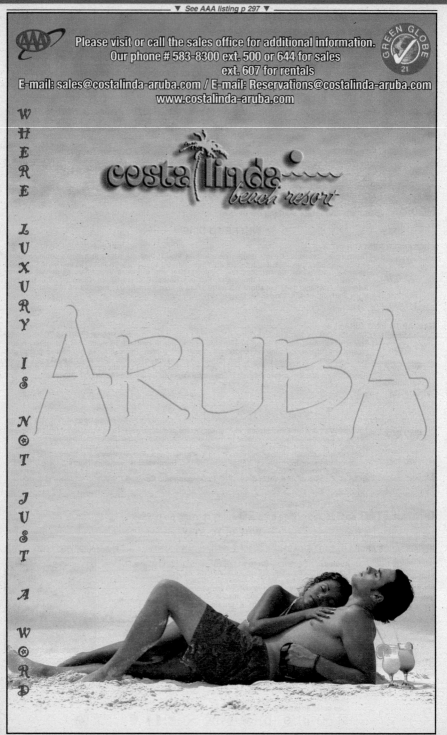

▼ See AAA listing p 297 ▼

▼ See AAA listing p 296 ▼

▼ See AAA listing p 297 ▼
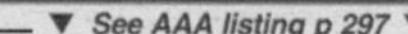

▼ See AAA listing p 300 ▼

▼ See AAA listing p 301 ▼

(See map and index starting on p. 296)

WHERE TO DINE

CARLOS 'N CHARLIE'S **Phone:** 297/582-0355

Mexican
$11-$23

The fun, festive and sometimes raucous chain restaurant and cantina welcomes occasional live entertainment, including a magician. On the familiar menu are tacos, burritos, chimichangas and enchiladas, as well as ceviche and nachos. The younger crowd gravitates here in the evening for the creative libations that have made this place well known. Casual dress. **Bar:** Full bar. **Hours:** noon-midnight. **Address:** Westraat #3A **Location:** Center; downtown near waterfront. **Parking:** street. **Cards:** MC, VI.

CUBA'S COOKIN **Phone:** 297/588-0626 (32)

Cuban
$17-$28

With captivating original Cuban art on the walls, the rustic, intimate interior reflects the ambience of old Havana. Hearty portions of Cuban-inspired cuisine—such as lechon (roast pork), ropa vieja (skirt steak), churrasco Cubano and lobster enchiladas—are satisfying. Among side dishes are yucca and plantains. Effervescent servers are traditionally attired. Live music is featured most late evenings. Casual dress. Entertainment. **Bar:** Full bar. **Reservations:** suggested. **Hours:** noon-2:30 & 5:30-11 pm. Closed: Sun. **Address:** Wilhelminastraat #27 **Location:** Downtown; just se of Seaport Village; across from police station. **Parking:** on-site. **Cards:** AX, DS, MC, VI.

DON CARLO'S RISTORANTE ITALIANO **Phone:** 297/583-6246 (29)

Italian
$17-$34

Situated on the downtown waterfront of Oranjestad, this family favorite for hearty portions and fair value. Besides an array of gourmet style pizzas there are pastas and risottos as well as dishes like Ossobuco alla Milanese made with braised veal. The service is casual yet crisp. Casual dress. **Bar:** Full bar. **Reservations:** suggested. **Hours:** 11 am-11:30 pm. **Address:** L.G. Smith Blvd 82 **Location:** Center at Renaissance Seaport Marina; in front of Crystal Palace Casino Oceanside. **Parking:** street. **Cards:** AX, DS, MC, VI.

DRIFTWOOD RESTAURANT **Phone:** 297/583-2515 (30)

Seafood
$18-$36

For almost 20 years the owner of this restaurant has been catching the fish for this downtown restaurant daily. Meals are served in the rustic ambience of a natural driftwood dining room. The chefs prepare a wide variety of fish and seafood dishes Arubian style. All meals come with pan bati, a type of cornbread. Casual dress. **Bar:** Full bar. **Reservations:** suggested. **Hours:** 5:30 pm-10:30 pm. Closed: Tues & Carnival. **Address:** Klipstraat 12 **Location:** Downtown; just s of corner of Rifstraat and Klipstraat sts. **Parking:** street. **Cards:** AX, DS, MC, VI.

EL GAUCHO **Phone:** 297/582-3677 (31)

Argentine
$20-$37

Excellent charcoal-grilled churrasco steak, quality meats and fresh seafood are served in a cozy dining room that reflects a touch of the Pampas. The well-established eatery is popular among locals and visitors alike. Casual dress. Entertainment. **Bar:** Full bar. **Reservations:** suggested. **Hours:** 11:30 am-11 pm. Closed: 1/1, 12/24, 12/25; also 12/31, Sun & Good Friday. **Address:** Wilhelminastraat 80 **Location:** 0.3 mi (0.5 km) s of Seaport Village; downtown. **Parking:** street. **Cards:** DC, DS, MC, VI.

IGUANA JOE'S CARIBBEAN BAR & GRILL **Phone:** 297/583-9373 (24)

International
$9-$20

The fun, festive grill has an open-air upstairs terrace overlooking the gallery of downtown shops. The easy-to-spot restaurant is not far from the cruise ship docks. Burgers, barbecue, quesadillas and fajitas are favorites. Sangria is refreshing on a hot day. Casual dress. **Bar:** Full bar. **Hours:** 11 am-11 pm, Sun from 5 pm. Closed: 1/1, 12/25; also Carnival Day. **Address:** Royal Plaza Mall, Suite 302 **Location:** Downtown; across from cruise ship docks; upstairs in Royal Plaza Mall. **Parking:** street. **Cards:** AX, DS, MC, VI.

JAMAICA ME KRAZY **Phone:** 297/583-4692 (22)

Jamaican
$9-$14

Tucked in the corner of a shopping center is a slice of Jamaica come alive. The eatery is marked by rasta and reggae decor. Jerk pork, chicken and fish share menu space with curried goat and mackerel rundown. Adventurous diners might try cow foot with tripe and beans. Made in house, the ginger beer satisfyingly complements the flavorful cuisine, which is served in large portions. Take-out orders are popular. Casual dress. **Bar:** Full bar. **Hours:** 11 am-10 pm. Closed major holidays. **Address:** Italiestraat #13 **Location:** 2 mi (3.2 km) nw of downtown; behind Certified Mega Mall. **Parking:** on-site. **Cards:** AX, DS, MC, VI.

(See map and index starting on p. 296)

LA FONDUE D' ARUBA — **Phone:** 297/582-4073 (35)

Fondue
$19-$42

Fondue is hard to come by in Aruba, but guests of this place can choose and help prepare flavorful cheese pots and other dip-worthy bowls. A refined atmosphere and skilled wait staff make for a memorable experience. It's hard to beat a grand finale of chocolate fondue for dessert. Dressy casual. **Bar:** Full bar. **Reservations:** suggested. **Hours:** 5:30 pm-10 pm. Closed: Sun. **Address:** Wilhelminastraat #64 **Location:** Just se of Seaport village; next to Masy-Fral; downtown. **Parking:** street. **Cards:** DS, MC, VI.

L.G. SMITH'S STEAK & CHOP HOUSE — **Phone:** 297/523-6195 (23)

Steak
$23-$36

A relatively new addition to the Aruba dining scene, the contemporary steakhouse serves aged Certified Angus beef in a hip, stylish atmosphere. Steak choices range from the 8-ounce petit filet mignon to a whopping 22-ounce porterhouse. Dressy casual. Entertainment. **Bar:** Full bar. **Reservations:** required. **Hours:** 5:30 pm-11 pm. **Address:** L.G. Smith Blvd #82 **Location:** 2.7 (4.3 km) nw of airport; downtown; in Renaissance Aruba Resort & Casino. **Parking:** on-site and valet. **Cards:** AX, CB, DC, DS, JC, MC, VI.

MATILDE RESTAURANT & DOWNTOWN MONUMENT *Menu on AAA.com* — **Phone:** 297/583-9200 (28)

International
$22-$46

With a chic and contemporary edge this popular restaurant offers innovative French cuisine with touches of Asian and Caribbean mixed in. The service is fresh and crisp. The decor is stunning. Dressy casual. **Bar:** Full bar. **Reservations:** required. **Hours:** 11:30 am-11 pm. Closed: Carnival Day. **Address:** Havenstraat 23 **Location:** Downtown; one street inland from Seaport shopping area. **Parking:** on-site. **Cards:** AX, DS, MC, VI. **Historic** *(See color ad below)*

RUMBA BAR & GRILL — **Phone:** 297/588-7900 (26)

International
$7-$28

The restaurant is a great place to check out for lunch while shopping downtown. The laid-back setting offers indoor or streetside al fresco seating. The menu reflects European influences and a German flair. Casual dress. **Bar:** Full bar. **Reservations:** suggested. **Hours:** 8 am-11 pm. Closed: for lunch 1/1. **Address:** Havenstraat 4 **Location:** Downtown; behind Renaissance Aruba Resort & Casino. **Parking:** street. **Cards:** AX, DS, MC, VI.

▼ See AAA listing above ▼

PALM BEACH (See map and index starting on p. 296)

WHERE TO STAY

ARUBA MARRIOTT RESORT & STELLARIS CASINO — Phone: (297)586-9000 — 3

AAA SAVE fyi

Resort Hotel

$338-$761 All Year

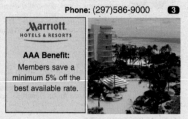

Under major renovation, scheduled to be completed October 2008. Last rated: ◆◆◆◆ **Address:** L.G. Smith Blvd 101 **Location:** Oceanfront. 8.6 mi (13.7 km) nw of airport; 6.9 mi (11 km) nw of downtown; north end of Palm Beach. **Facility:** Handsome guest rooms and a fine beach are offered at this service-oriented property, which also features expansive, tropical public areas. Meets AAA guest room security requirements. Smoke free premises. 411 units. 376 one-bedroom standard units. 35 one-bedroom suites. 8 stories, interior corridors. **Parking:** on-site. **Terms:** check-in 4 pm, 7 day cancellation notice-fee imposed. **Amenities:** high-speed Internet (fee), dual phone lines, voice mail, safes, irons, hair dryers. **Dining:** 7 restaurants, entertainment. **Pool(s):** outdoor. **Leisure Activities:** saunas, whirlpool, rental canoes, rental paddleboats, rental sailboats, rental sailboards, 2 lighted tennis courts, recreation programs, kids club, playground, spa, basketball, volleyball. *Fee:* waterskiing, scuba diving, snorkeling, charter fishing, kayaks, game room. **Guest Services:** valet laundry, wireless Internet. **Business Services:** conference facilities, PC (fee). **Cards:** AX, VI.
(See color ad p 309 & on insert)

Marriott HOTELS & RESORTS

AAA Benefit:
Members save a minimum 5% off the best available rate.

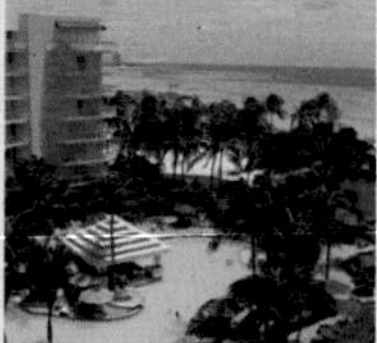

DIVI ARUBA PHOENIX BEACH RESORT — Book great rates at AAA.com — Phone: (297)586-6066 — 12

AAA SAVE ◆◆◆

Condominium

$290-$824 All Year

Address: JE Irausquin Blvd 75 **Location:** Oceanfront. 6.9 mi (11 km) nw of airport; 4.2 mi (6.7 km) nw of downtown. **Facility:** A variety of room types are available to choose from, all with contemporary decor, as well as well-appointed public areas. Meets AAA guest room security requirements. Designated smoking area. 101 units. 66 one-bedroom standard units with efficiencies and whirlpools. 26 one- and 9 two-bedroom suites with efficiencies, some with whirlpools. 4-14 stories, interior/exterior corridors. **Parking:** on-site. **Terms:** check-in 4 pm, 3 night minimum stay, 7 day cancellation notice. **Amenities:** voice mail, safes, irons, hair dryers. **Dining:** 2 restaurants, entertainment. **Pool(s):** outdoor. **Leisure Activities:** sauna, whirlpool, racquetball court, recreation programs, use of recreational facilities at Divi properties, volleyball. *Fee:* massage. **Guest Services:** valet and coin laundry, wireless Internet. **Business Services:** meeting rooms, PC (fee). **Cards:** AX, DC, DS, MC, VI.

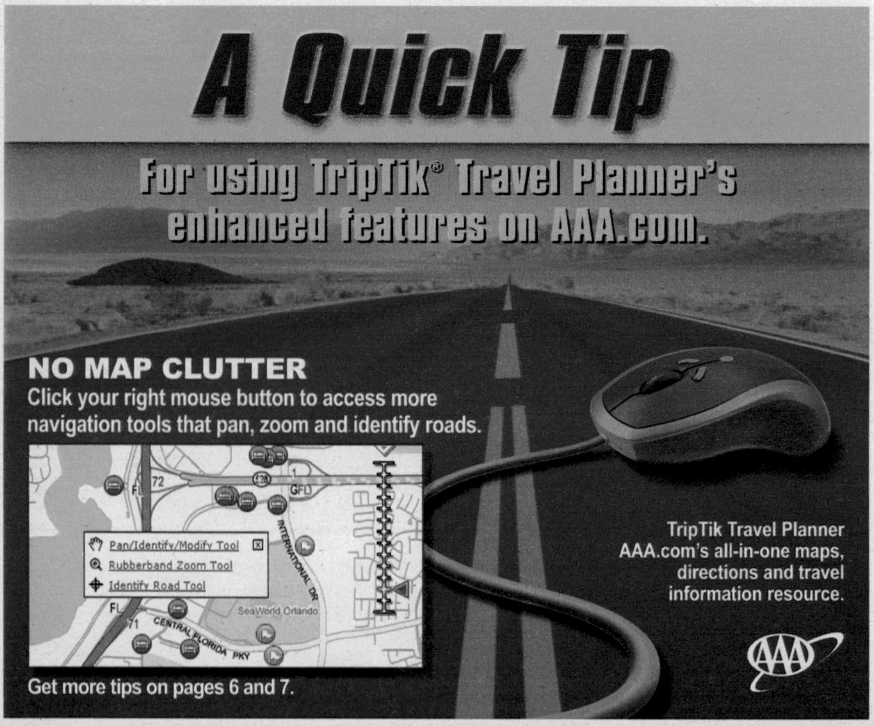

▼ See AAA listing p 308 ▼

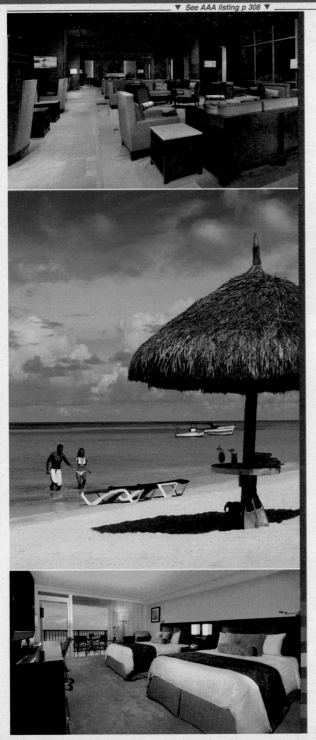

(See map and index starting on p. 296)

HOLIDAY INN SUNSPREE RESORT ARUBA *Book great rates at AAA.com* **Phone:** (297)586-3600 **8**

Resort Hotel

$180-$445 All Year

Address: JE Irausquin Blvd 230 **Location:** Oceanfront. 8 mi (12.8 km) nw of airport; 6.3 mi (11.3 km) nw of downtown. **Facility:** A family-style resort on the ever-popular Palm Beach, the property offers large guest rooms with an updated, contemporary appeal. Meets AAA guest room security requirements. 600 units. 591 one-bedroom standard units. 7 one- and 2 two-bedroom suites. 6-7 stories, interior corridors. *Bath:* combo or shower only. **Parking:** on-site. **Terms:** check-in 4 pm, 2-3 night minimum stay - weekends, 7 day cancellation notice-fee imposed. **Amenities:** voice mail, safes, irons, hair dryers. **Pool(s):** 2 outdoor. **Leisure Activities:** whirlpools, beach access, rental paddleboats, rental sailboats, boat dock, snorkeling equipment rental, 5 tennis courts (4 lighted), recreation programs, playground, exercise room, spa, basketball, volleyball. *Fee:* saunas, waterskiing, scuba diving, game room. **Guest Services:** valet and coin laundry, beauty salon, wireless Internet. **Business Services:** conference facilities, PC (fee). **Cards:** AX, CB, DC, DS, MC, VI. *(See color ad below)*

▼ *See AAA listing p 311* ▼

▼ *See AAA listing above* ▼

(See map and index starting on p. 296)

HYATT REGENCY ARUBA RESORT & CASINO *Book great rates at AAA.com* **Phone:** (297)586-1234 **4**

Resort Hotel

$255-$695 All Year

Address: JE Irausquin Blvd 85 **Location:** Oceanfront. 7.4 mi (11.8 km) nw of airport; 5.7 mi (9.1 km) nw of downtown. **Facility:** Well-appointed rooms and extensive tropically landscaped grounds enhance this beachfront high-rise resort with popular nightlife. Refined service. Meets AAA guest room security requirements. 358 units. 334 one-bedroom standard units. 24 one-bedroom suites. 9 stories, interior corridors. *Bath:* combo or shower only. **Parking:** on-site. **Terms:** check-in 4 pm, cancellation fee imposed. **Amenities:** high-speed Internet (fee), voice mail, safes, honor bars, irons, hair dryers. **Dining:** 3 restaurants, also, Cafe Japengo, Las Ruinas del Mar, see separate listings, entertainment. **Pool(s):** 2 outdoor. **Leisure Activities:** sauna, whirlpools, steamroom, waterslide, rental paddleboats, rental sailboats, rental sailboards, snorkeling, fishing, 2 lighted tennis courts, recreation programs, playground, exercise room, spa, basketball, shuffleboard, volleyball, game room. *Fee:* boats, waterskiing, scuba diving, charter fishing, banana boats, catamaran rides. **Guest Services:** valet laundry, wireless Internet. **Business Services:** conference facilities, business center. **Cards:** AX, CB, DC, DS, JC, MC, VI. *(See color ad p 310)*

HYATT HOTELS & RESORTS

AAA Benefit:

Ask for the AAA rate and save 10%.

/ SOME UNITS

RADISSON ARUBA RESORT, CASINO & SPA *Book great rates at AAA.com* **Phone:** (297)586-6555 **9**

Resort Hotel

$250-$775 All Year

Address: JE Irausquin Blvd 81 **Location:** Oceanfront. 7.6 mi (12.1 km) nw of airport; 4.9 mi (7.8 km) nw of downtown. **Facility:** This property features spectacular landscaping, a superlative beachfront location along with rich, tropical decor and furnishings in the guest rooms. 353 units. 326 one-bedroom standard units. 27 one-bedroom suites, some with whirlpools. 4-8 stories, interior corridors. *Bath:* combo or shower only. **Parking:** on-site and valet. **Terms:** check-in 4 pm, 14 day cancellation notice-fee imposed. **Amenities:** video library, high-speed Internet, dual phone lines, voice mail, safes, honor bars, irons, hair dryers. *Some:* DVD players, CD players. **Dining:** 3 restaurants, also, Sunset Grille, see separate listing, entertainment. **Pool(s):** 2 outdoor. **Leisure Activities:** whirlpools, rental boats, rental canoes, rental paddleboats, rental sailboats, rental sailboards, recreation programs, playground, spa, shuffleboard, volleyball, game room. *Fee:* saunas, steamrooms, waterskiing, scuba diving, snorkeling, charter fishing, kayaks, parasailing. **Guest Services:** valet laundry, wireless Internet. **Business Services:** conference facilities, business center. **Cards:** AX, DC, DS, MC, VI. **Free Special Amenities: high-speed Internet.** *(See color ad p 312)*

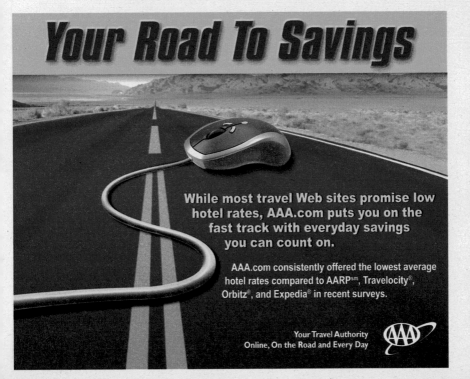

▼ See AAA listing p 311 ▼

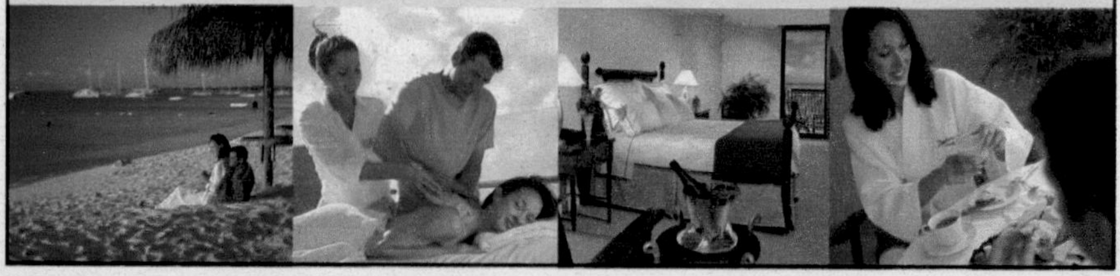

▼ See AAA listing p 314 ▼

(See map and index starting on p. 296)

THE WESTIN ARUBA RESORT Book great rates at AAA.com **Phone:** (297)586-4466 10

Resort Hotel

$269-$659 All Year

Address: JE Irausquin Blvd 77 **Location:** Oceanfront. 7.2 mi (11.5 km) nw of airport; 4.5 mi (7.2 km) nw of downtown. **Facility:** Comprehensive resort facilities with a variety of restaurants featured and new spa facilities. The spacious guest rooms provide numerous amenities. Meets AAA guest room security requirements. Smoke free premises. 481 units. 442 one-bedroom standard units. 39 one-bedroom suites, some with whirlpools. 18 stories, interior corridors. **Parking:** on-site and valet. **Terms:** check-in 4 pm. **Amenities:** high-speed Internet (fee), voice mail, safes, honor bars, irons, hair dryers. *Some:* CD players. *Fee:* DVD players. **Dining:** 7 restaurants, also, Blossom's, Pago Pago, see separate listings, entertainment. **Pool(s):** outdoor. **Leisure Activities:** steamrooms, rental paddleboats, recreation programs, kids club, playground, spa, volleyball. *Fee:* waterskiing, scuba diving, snorkeling, banana boat, kayaks, parasailing, personal watercraft. **Guest Services:** valet laundry, wireless Internet. **Business Services:** conference facilities, business center. **Cards:** AX, CB, DC, DS, JC, MC, VI. **Free Special Amenities: newspaper.** *(See color ad p 313 & on insert)*

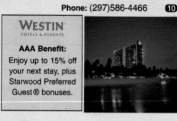

WESTIN HOTELS & RESORTS

AAA Benefit:

Enjoy up to 15% off your next stay, plus Starwood Preferred Guest® bonuses.

/ SOME UNITS FEE VCR FEE FEE

WHERE TO DINE

AMAZONIA CHURRASCARIA **Phone:** 297/586-4444 5

Steak

$27-$43

The memorable dining experience is nirvana for the indisputable carnivore. Besides the extensive selection of Brazilian hot dishes and salad bar fixings, there are specialized carvers who, on command, bring cuts of rodizio charcoal-grilled beef, lamb, pork and chicken to the table. Try a refreshing Brazilian Caipirinha to wash everything down. Casual dress. **Bar:** Full bar. **Reservations:** suggested. **Hours:** 6 pm-10 pm, Sun from 4 pm. **Address:** JE Irausquin Blvd 374 **Location:** 7.8 mi (12.5 km) nw at Palm Beach; across from Hyatt Regency Aruba Resort & Casino. **Parking:** on-site. **Cards:** AX, DC, DS, MC, VI.

CALL

AQUA GRILL **Phone:** 297/586-5900 14

Seafood

$26-$39

One of the newest seafood restaurants has hit the Aruba dining scene with a splash. It serves not only freshly caught local seafood but also other seafood that is flown in daily. August is lobster month. The attentive and engaging staff serves meals in stylish dining rooms. Dressy casual. **Bar:** Full bar. **Reservations:** required. **Hours:** 6 pm-9:30 pm, Sun 5 pm-10 pm. **Address:** JE Irausquin Blvd 374 **Location:** 7.8 mi (12.5 km) nw of town at Palm Beach; across from Hyatt Regency Aruba Resort & Casino. **Parking:** on-site. **Cards:** AX, DS, MC, VI.

BLOSSOM'S **Phone:** 297/586-4466 6

Asian

$22-$40

Lending to the upscale Oriental motif are teak furnishings and statues. The menu lists great Japanese and Chinese dishes. Teppanyaki tables add theatrics to the dining experience. Dressy casual. **Bar:** Full bar. **Reservations:** required. **Hours:** 11:30 am-3 & 6-11 pm, Sun from 5 pm. **Address:** JE Irausquin Blvd 77 **Location:** 7.2 mi (11.5 km) nw of airport; 4.5 mi (7.2 km) nw of downtown; in The Westin Aruba Resort. **Parking:** on-site. **Cards:** AX, DS, MC, VI.

CAFE JAPENGO **Phone:** 297/586-1234 11

Asian

$21-$36

Crisp, attentive service awaits diners at the distinctly Asian restaurant. Among at least six catches of the day are ahi tuna, Chilean sea bass and grouper. Fish can be broiled, blackened or pan-fried, and three signature sauces accompany each. Other specialties include char-su duck, seared ginger beef and cashew chicken. Patrons also can order from a full sushi menu. A 15 percent service charge is added to the bill. Dressy casual. **Bar:** Full bar. **Reservations:** required. **Hours:** 6 pm-10:30 pm. Closed: Tues. **Address:** JE Irausquin Blvd 85 **Location:** 7.4 mi (11.8 km) nw of airport; 5.7 mi (9.1 km) nw of downtown; in Hyatt Regency Aruba Resort & Casino. **Parking:** on-site. **Cards:** AX, DC, DS, MC, VI.

HOSTARIA DA' VITTORIO **Phone:** 297/586-3838 4

Italian

$23-$39

Vittorio Muscariello, recipient of many culinary awards including "maestro di cucina," prepares guaranteed authentic Italian cuisine. Guests can begin a culinary tour of Italy with a carpaccio appetizer or a zuppa di minestrone. Varied pastas are prepared using an array of ingredients. Veal, lamb, pork and a fresh selection of fish are skillfully prepared. The European staff provides superb service and conveys exceptional food preparation and menu knowledge. Dressy casual. **Bar:** Full bar. **Reservations:** required. **Hours:** 11 am-3 & 6-11 pm. **Address:** L.G. Smith Blvd #380 **Location:** 6.1 mi (9.7 km) nw of downtown; just e of Hyatt Regency Aruba Resort & Casino. **Parking:** on-site. **Cards:** AX, DS, MC, VI.

LAS RUINAS DEL MAR **Phone:** 297/586-1234 12

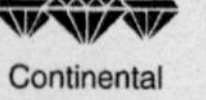

Continental

$24-$38

Continental cuisine incorporates Mediterranean influences in this establishment, which replicates the 19th-century ruins of Bushiribana Gold Mill. Guests can request indoor or patio seating in a romantic setting overlooking a pond of water with black swans. Dressy casual. **Bar:** Full bar. **Reservations:** required. **Hours:** 7 am-noon & 5:30-10:30 pm; Sunday brunch 9 am-2 pm. Closed: for dinner Sun. **Address:** JE Irausquin Blvd 85 **Location:** 7.4 mi (11.8 km) nw of airport; 5.7 mi (9.1 km) nw of downtown; in Hyatt Regency Aruba Resort & Casino. **Parking:** on-site. **Cards:** AX, CB, DC, DS, JC, MC, VI.

(See map and index starting on p. 296)

PAGO PAGO — Phone: 297/586-4466 (10)

Steak & Seafood
$29-$45

Enjoy prime cuts of American aged beef and chops as well as fresh seafood in a sophisticated, romantic setting. The finely tuned service is pleasantly accommodating. Dressy casual. **Bar:** Full bar. **Reservations:** suggested. **Hours:** 6 pm-11 pm. Closed: Wed. **Address:** JE Irausquin Blvd 77 **Location:** 7.2 mi (11.5 km) nw of airport; 4.5 mi (7.2 km) nw of downtown; in The Westin Aruba Resort. **Parking:** on-site. **Cards:** AX, DC, DS, MC, VI.

SUNSET GRILLE — **Phone:** 297/526-6612 (13)

AAA

Steak & Seafood
$27-$40

The upscale restaurant offers indoor and outdoor seating in an atmosphere that remains casually elegant. The menu lists Angus steaks, lamb, pork, chicken and assorted seafood from around the world prepared in the open grill area. Although the emphasis is on hearty meat portions, the spectacular desserts are no letdown. Oysters Rockefeller, escargots, the monster seafood appetizer for two and assorted bread offerings make it hard to push back from the table. Dressy casual. Entertainment. **Bar:** Full bar. **Reservations:** required. **Hours:** 6 pm-11 pm. **Address:** JE Irausquin Blvd 81 **Location:** 7.6 mi (12.1 km) nw of airport; 4.9 mi (7.8 km) nw of downtown; in Radisson Aruba Resort, Casino & Spa. **Parking:** on-site. **Cards:** AX, DC, DS, MC, VI. *(See color ad p 312)*

TANGO ARGENTINE GRILL — **Phone:** 297/586-8600 (3)

Argentine
$23-$36

Patrons can enjoy live music while feasting on the best of Argentine beef. South American memorabilia enhances the spacious dining room. Those with a hearty appetite might try the mixed grill. Casual dress. **Bar:** Full bar. **Reservations:** suggested. **Hours:** 5 pm-11 pm. **Address:** JE Irausquin Blvd #370 **Location:** 5.1 mi (8.1 km) nw of downtown; across from Palm Beach; in Arawak Garden Shopping Plaza. **Parking:** on-site. **Cards:** AX, DS, MC, VI. ***(See color ad below)***

TEXAS DE BRAZIL — **Phone:** 297/586-4686

Brazilian
$30-$45

"Gauchos" bring skewered meat selections directly to the table at the Brazilian-style steakhouse, and diners use a small colored coaster to let the server know when they are ready for another selection of beef, chicken, pork or lamb. The extensive salad bar gets meals off to the right start. Desserts are worthy of serious consideration. Casual dress. **Bar:** Full bar. **Reservations:** required. **Hours:** 6 pm-10:30 pm, Fri from 11 am. Closed: 12/25. **Address:** JE Irausquin Blvd 382 **Location:** 5.1 mi (8.1 km) nw of downtown in Palm Beach area; at Hacienda Mall. **Parking:** on-site. **Cards:** AX, DS, MC, VI.

▼ *See AAA listing above* ▼

THE BAHAMAS

This index helps you "spot" where approved lodgings and restaurants are located on the corresponding detailed maps. Lodging daily rate range is for comparison only and show the property's high season. Restaurant rate range is a combination of lunch and/or dinner. Turn to the listing page for more detailed rate information and consult display ads for special promotions.

WEST END (GRAND BAHAMA ISLAND)

Map Page	OA	Lodging	Diamond Rated	High Season	Page
1 / p. 319	AAA	**Old Bahama Bay by Ginn Sur Mer** - see color ad p 326	◆◆◆◆	$190-$1280 SAVE	326

Map Page	OA	Restaurant	Diamond Rated	Cuisine	Meal Range	Page
27 / p. 319		The Aqua Restaurant	◆◆◆	International	$26-$50	326

LUCAYA (GRAND BAHAMA ISLAND)

Map Page	OA	Lodgings	Diamond Rated	High Season	Page
3 / p. 319		Taino Beach Resorts & Club	◆◆	$125-$375	324
4 / p. 319	AAA	**Pelican Bay at Lucaya**	◆◆	$139-$379 SAVE	323
5 / p. 319	AAA	**Sheraton Grand Bahama Island Our Lucaya Resort** - see color ad p 323	◆◆◆	$135-$600 SAVE	323
7 / p. 319	AAA	**The Westin Grand Bahama Island Our Lucaya Resort** - see color ad p 323	◆◆◆◆	$189-$289 SAVE	324

Map Page	OA	Restaurants	Diamond Rated	Cuisine	Meal Range	Page
1 / p. 319	AAA	**Pisces Seafood**	◆◆	Seafood	$14-$32	325
2 / p. 319		Cappuccino's Italian Restaurant	◆◆◆	Italian	$20-$30	324
3 / p. 319		China Beach	◆◆	Chinese	$18-$35	324
4 / p. 319	AAA	**Giovanni's Cafe**	◆◆	Italian	$14-$33	324
5 / p. 319	AAA	**The Harbour Room**	◆◆◆	International	$18-$42	325
6 / p. 319		Zorba's Greek Cuisine	◆	Greek	$9-$22	326
7 / p. 319	AAA	**The Pub at Port Lucaya**	◆	American	$7-$27	326
8 / p. 319		La Dolce Vita	◆◆	Regional Italian	$20-$36	325
9 / p. 319	AAA	**The Ferry House Restaurant**	◆◆◆	International	$20-$48	324
11 / p. 319	AAA	**Shenanigan's Irish Pub & Eatery**	◆◆	Irish	$10-$25	326
12 / p. 319		Iries	◆◆	Caribbean	$18-$30	325
14 / p. 319		Churchill's Chophouse	◆◆◆	Steak & Seafood	$28-$42	324
15 / p. 319	AAA	**Luciano's**	◆◆◆	Continental	$26-$36	325

FREEPORT (GRAND BAHAMA ISLAND)

Map Page	OA	Lodging	Diamond Rated	High Season	Page
8 / p. 319	AAA	**Best Western Castaways Resort & Suites**	◆◆	$135-$155 SAVE	322

Map Page	OA	Restaurants	Diamond Rated	Cuisine	Meal Range	Page
33 / p. 319	AAA	**Ruby Swiss European Restaurant**	◆◆	Continental	$10-$28	322
34 / p. 319		Hong Kong Cuisine	◆	Chinese	$8-$22	322
35 / p. 319		Silvano's Italian Restaurant	◆◆	Italian	$14-$29	322

TREASURE CAY (GREAT ABACO ISLAND)

Map Page	OA	Lodging	Diamond Rated	High Season	Page
10 / p. 319		Treasure Cay Hotel Resort & Marina	◆◆	Rates not provided	329

GREEN TURTLE CAY (GREAT ABACO ISLAND)

Map Page	OA	Lodgings	Diamond Rated	High Season	Page
13 / p. 319	AAA	**Green Turtle Club and Marina**	◆◆◆	$180-$675 SAVE	327
14 / p. 319		Coco Bay Cottages	◆◆	$275-$550	327

Map Page	OA	Restaurant	Diamond Rated	Cuisine	Meal Range	Page
38 / p. 319		Laura's Kitchen	◆	American	$10-$21	327

MARSH HARBOUR (GREAT ABACO ISLAND)

Map Page	OA	Lodgings	Diamond Rated	High Season	Page
18 / p. 319		Conch Inn Hotel & Marina	◆◆	$120-$160	328
19 / p. 319		Abaco Beach Resort & Boat Harbour	◆◆◆	$255-$748	328

Map Page	OA	Restaurants	Diamond Rated	Cuisine	Meal Range	Page
16 / p. 319		Curly Tails Restaurant and Bar	◆◆◆	International	$18-$29	329
17 / p. 319		Snappas Grill and Chill	◆	American	$8-$22	329
18 / p. 319		Sapodilly's	◆◆	Caribbean	$10-$32	329
19 / p. 319		Wally's	◆◆	Caribbean	$10-$27	329
20 / p. 319	AAA	**Angler's Restaurant**	◆◆◆	Steak & Seafood	$11-$32	328
21 / p. 319	AAA	**The Hummingbird Restaurant & Lounge**	◆◆	Caribbean	$9-$20	329
22 / p. 319		Mangoes Restaurant	◆◆◆	Seafood	$11-$27	329

HOPE TOWN (GREAT ABACO ISLAND)

Map Page	OA	Lodgings	Diamond Rated	High Season	Page
23 / p. 319		Hope Town Hideaways	◆◆◆	Rates not provided	327
26 / p. 319		Sea Spray Resort & Marina	◆◆	$950-$2450	328

Map Page	OA	Restaurants	Diamond Rated	Cuisine	Meal Range	Page
23 / p. 319		Harbour's Edge Restaurant	◆	Caribbean	$10-$26	328
24 / p. 319		Cap'N Jacks	◆	American	$8-$19	328
25 / p. 319		Abaco Inn Dining Room	◆◆	International	$12-$33	328
26 / p. 319		Boat House Restaurant	◆	International	$11-$29	328

HARBOUR ISLAND

Map Page	OA	Lodging	Diamond Rated	High Season	Page
31 / p. 319		Pink Sands	◆◆◆◆	$750-$2350	331

Map Page	OA	Restaurant	Diamond Rated	Cuisine	Meal Range	Page
29 / p. 319		The Landing Restaurant	◆◆◆	International	$36-$42	331

CAT ISLAND

Map Page	OA	Lodgings	Diamond Rated	High Season	Page
35 / p. 319		Sammy T's Beach Resort	◆◆	$135-$255	321
36 / p. 319		The Bridge Inn	◆	$88-$200	321
37 / p. 319		Greenwood Beach Resort	◆	$110-$130	321

LONG ISLAND

Map Page	OA	Lodging	Diamond Rated	High Season	Page
41 / p. 319		Cape Santa Maria Beach Resort	◆◆◆	$235-$795	331

GEORGE TOWN (GREAT EXUMA ISLAND)

Map Page	OA	Lodgings	Diamond Rated	High Season	Page
42 / p. 319		The Exuma Palms at Three Sisters Resort Ltd	◆	$120-$160	330
43 / p. 319		Grand Isle Resort and Spa	◆◆◆	$380-$6000	330

GEORGE TOWN (GREAT EXUMA ISLAND) (cont'd)

Map Page	OA	Lodgings (cont'd)	Diamond Rated	High Season	Page
44 / p. 319		Four Seasons Resort Great Exuma at Emerald Bay	◆◆◆◆	$350-$6800	330
45 / p. 319		Palm Bay Beach Resort	◆◆◆	$265-$775	330
46 / p. 319		Peace & Plenty Bonefish Lodge	◆◆	$225	330

Map Page	OA	Restaurants	Diamond Rated	Cuisine	Meal Range	Page
30 / p. 319		Il Cielo	◆◆◆◆	Italian	$22-$45	330
31 / p. 319		Coconut Cove	◆◆	American	$15-$54	330
32 / p. 319		Wahoo's	◆◆	Caribbean	$18-$32	331

ANDROS ISLAND

Map Page	OA	Lodgings	Diamond Rated	High Season	Page
50 / p. 319		Lighthouse Yacht Club and Marina	◆◆	$115-$170	320
51 / p. 319		Small Hope Bay Lodge	◆	$220-$310	320
52 / p. 319		Andros Island Bonefish Club	◆	$823	320
54 / p. 319		Emerald Palms	◆◆◆	$105-$695	320

Map Page	OA	Restaurants	Diamond Rated	Cuisine	Meal Range	Page
40 / p. 319		Beacon Bar and Dining Room	◆◆	Seafood	$11-$40	321
41 / p. 319		Airport Deli	◆	American	$4-$10	321
43 / p. 319		Dining Room at Emerald Palms	◆◆◆	Caribbean	$7-$25	321

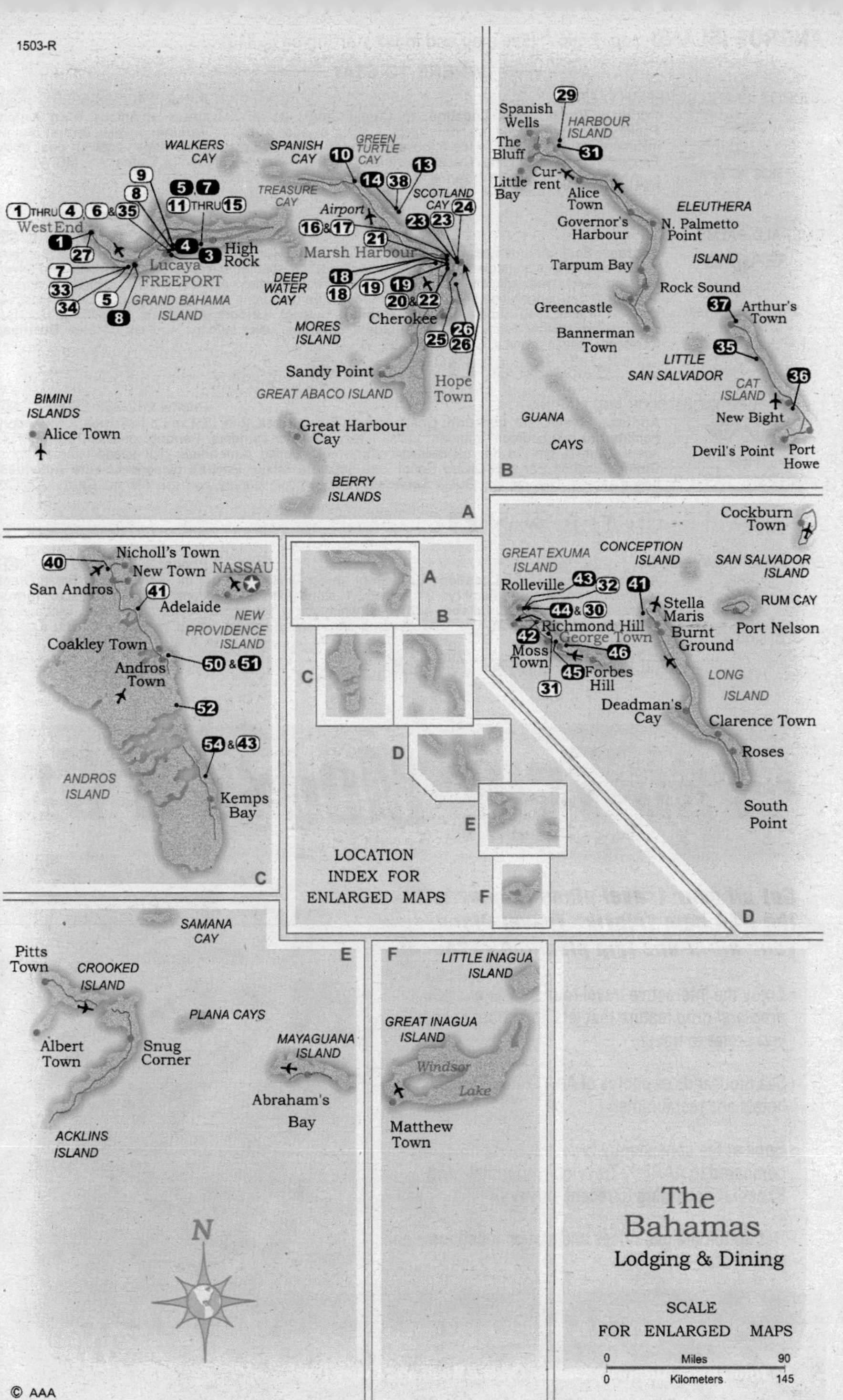
1503-R
WALKERS CAY
SPANISH CAY
GREEN TURTLE CAY
TREASURE CAY
SCOTLAND CAY
Airport
West End
Lucaya
FREEPORT
High Rock
GRAND BAHAMA ISLAND
Marsh Harbour
DEEP WATER CAY
MORES ISLAND
Cherokee
Sandy Point
GREAT ABACO ISLAND
Hope Town
BIMINI ISLANDS
Alice Town
Great Harbour Cay
BERRY ISLANDS
A
Spanish Wells
HARBOUR ISLAND
The Bluff
Little Bay
Current
Alice Town
ELEUTHERA
Governor's Harbour
N. Palmetto Point
ISLAND
Tarpum Bay
Rock Sound
Greencastle
Arthur's Town
Bannerman Town
LITTLE SAN SALVADOR
CAT ISLAND
New Bight
GUANA CAYS
Devil's Point
Port Howe
B
Nicholl's Town
New Town
NASSAU
San Andros
Adelaide
NEW PROVIDENCE ISLAND
Coakley Town
Andros Town
ANDROS ISLAND
Kemps Bay
C
LOCATION INDEX FOR ENLARGED MAPS
Cockburn Town
GREAT EXUMA ISLAND
CONCEPTION ISLAND
SAN SALVADOR ISLAND
Rolleville
Stella Maris
RUM CAY
Richmond Hill
George Town
Burnt Ground
Port Nelson
Moss Town
Forbes Hill
LONG ISLAND
Deadman's Cay
Clarence Town
Roses
South Point
D
SAMANA CAY
Pitts Town
CROOKED ISLAND
PLANA CAYS
Albert Town
Snug Corner
MAYAGUANA ISLAND
Abraham's Bay
ACKLINS ISLAND
E
F
LITTLE INAGUA ISLAND
GREAT INAGUA ISLAND
Windsor Lake
Matthew Town
N
The Bahamas
Lodging & Dining
SCALE FOR ENLARGED MAPS
0 Miles 90
0 Kilometers 145
© AAA

ANDROS ISLAND pop. 7,686 (See map and index starting on p. 319)

WHERE TO STAY

ANDROS ISLAND BONEFISH CLUB — Phone: 242/368-5395 (52)

Hotel
$823 All Year

Address: Cargill Creek **Location:** In Cargill Creek; 21 mi (33 km) s of Andros Town Airport. **Facility:** 12 one-bedroom standard units. 1 story, exterior corridors. **Parking:** on-site. **Terms:** 3 night minimum stay, cancellation fee imposed. **Pool(s):** outdoor. **Leisure Activities:** boating, boat dock. *Fee:* fishing, charter fishing. **Guest Services:** coin laundry, wireless Internet. **Cards:** AX, MC, VI.

EMERALD PALMS — Phone: 242/369-2713 (54)

Hotel
$105-$695 All Year

Address: South Andros **Location:** Oceanfront. In Driggs Hill; 3 mi (4.8 km) n of airport, also s of ferry dock. **Facility:** Designated smoking area. 34 units. 16 one-bedroom standard units. 13 one- and 5 two-bedroom suites with efficiencies, some with whirlpools. 1 story, exterior corridors. **Parking:** on-site. **Terms:** 30 day cancellation notice-fee imposed. **Amenities:** irons, hair dryers. **Dining:** Dining Room at Emerald Palms, see separate listing. **Pool(s):** outdoor. **Leisure Activities:** snorkeling, bicycles. *Fee:* fishing, charter fishing, massage. **Guest Services:** valet laundry, wireless Internet. **Business Services:** meeting rooms. **Cards:** AX, MC, VI.

/ SOME UNITS

LIGHTHOUSE YACHT CLUB AND MARINA — Phone: 242/368-2305 (50)

Hotel
$115-$170 All Year

Address: Fresh Creek **Location:** Oceanfront. In Fresh Creek; 2 mi (3.2 km) n of Andros Town Airport. **Facility:** 20 one-bedroom standard units. 1 story, exterior corridors. **Parking:** on-site. **Terms:** office hours 7 am-11 pm, 14 day cancellation notice-fee imposed. **Amenities:** high-speed Internet, irons. **Dining:** Beacon Bar and Dining Room, see separate listing. **Pool(s):** outdoor. **Leisure Activities:** beach access. *Fee:* marina. **Guest Services:** valet and coin laundry, wireless Internet. **Cards:** AX, CB, DC, DS, JC, MC, VI.

D

SMALL HOPE BAY LODGE — Phone: 242/368-2014 (51)

Cabin
$220-$310 All Year

Address: Queens Hwy **Location:** Oceanfront. In Small Hope Bay; 3 mi (4.8 km) n of Fresh Creek (Andros Town) Airport. **Facility:** 21 cabins. 1 story, exterior corridors. **Parking:** on-site. **Terms:** cancellation fee imposed. **Leisure Activities:** whirlpool, beach access, boating, sailboats, windsurfing, boat dock, snorkeling, bicycles. *Fee:* scuba diving, fishing, charter fishing, massage. **Cards:** AX, CB, DC, DS, JC, MC, VI.

/ SOME UNITS

(See map and index starting on p. 319)

WHERE TO DINE

AIRPORT DELI — Phone: 242/329-4445 (41)

American
$4-$10

The delicatessen, which whips up a wide choice of sandwiches and salads, offers great convenience for those wishing to grab a quick meal upon arrival or departure. Casual dress. **Bar:** Beer & wine. **Hours:** 6 am-7 pm; to 5 pm 9/4-10/31. **Address:** Mastic Point **Location:** At airport terminal. **Parking:** on-site.

BEACON BAR AND DINING ROOM — Phone: 242/368-2305 (40)

Seafood
$11-$40

This indoor/outdoor dining spot is a fantastic place to enjoy drinks and local favorites, like lobster or cracked conch, while soaking in the picturesque views of the harbor. Staff are friendly and accommodating. Casual dress. **Bar:** Full bar. **Reservations:** accepted. **Hours:** 7 am-2 & 6-9 pm. **Address:** Fresh Creek **Location:** In Fresh Creek; 2 mi (3.2 km) n of Andros Town Airport; in Lighthouse Yacht Club and Marina. **Parking:** on-site. **Cards:** AX, DS, MC, VI.

DINING ROOM AT EMERALD PALMS — Phone: 242/369-2713 (43)

Caribbean
$7-$25

Friendly staff serve such scrumptious local treats as lobster, conched crab and fresh, home-grown veggies. Not only are they delicious, the desert plates are a beautiful work of art. Casual dress. **Bar:** Full bar. **Reservations:** accepted. **Hours:** 7 am-11, noon-2 & 7-10 pm. **Address:** The Bluff, Driggs Hill **Location:** In Driggs Hill; 3 mi (4.8 km) n of airport, also s of ferry dock; in Emerald Palms. **Parking:** on-site. **Cards:** AX, MC, VI.

CAT ISLAND pop. 1,647 (See map and index starting on p. 319)

WHERE TO STAY

THE BRIDGE INN — Phone: 242/342-3013 (36)

Hotel
$88-$200 All Year

Address: New Bight Gen'l Delivery **Location:** Fly into New Bight Airport, just s of downtown. **Facility:** 17 units. 10 one-bedroom standard units. 6 two- and 1 three-bedroom suites. 1-2 stories (no elevator), exterior corridors. *Bath:* combo or shower only. **Parking:** on-site. **Leisure Activities:** fishing. *Fee:* scuba diving, snorkeling. **Cards:** AX, MC, VI.

/ SOME UNITS

GREENWOOD BEACH RESORT — Phone: 242/342-3053 (37)

Hotel
$110-$130 All Year

Address: Port Howe **Location:** 1.7 mi (2.8 km) ne of Port Howe. **Facility:** 15 one-bedroom standard units. 1 story, exterior corridors. *Bath:* shower only. **Parking:** on-site. **Terms:** office hours 7:30 am-9:30 pm, 14 day cancellation notice-fee imposed. **Amenities:** hair dryers. **Pool(s):** outdoor. **Leisure Activities:** limited beach access. *Fee:* scuba diving, snorkeling. **Guest Services:** TV in common area, valet laundry, wireless Internet. **Business Services:** PC. **Cards:** MC, VI.

ASK D / SOME UNITS

SAMMY T'S BEACH RESORT — Phone: 242/354-6009 (35)

Cottage
$135-$255 12/1-8/30 & 10/1-11/30

Address: Bennetts Harbour **Location:** Oceanfront. 5 mi (8 km) s of Arthur's Town Airport. **Facility:** Designated smoking area. 7 cottages. 1 story, exterior corridors. **Parking:** on-site. **Terms:** open 12/1-8/30 & 10/1-11/30, office hours 8 am-10 pm, 30 day cancellation notice. **Amenities:** video library, DVD players, CD players, irons, hair dryers. **Pool(s):** outdoor. **Leisure Activities:** limited beach access, paddleboats, windsurfing, snorkeling, bicycles, volleyball. *Fee:* fishing. **Guest Services:** wireless Internet. **Cards:** MC, VI.

D

Grand Bahama Island

FREEPORT pop. 26,910 (See map and index starting on p. 319)

WHERE TO STAY

BEST WESTERN CASTAWAYS RESORT & SUITES *Book great rates at AAA.com* **Phone:** (242)352-6682 8

Hotel
$135-$155 12/1-4/18
$125-$145 4/19-11/30

Address: E Mall Dr **Location:** Center. **Facility:** 118 units. 97 one-bedroom standard units. 21 one-bedroom suites. 4 stories, interior/exterior corridors. **Parking:** on-site. **Terms:** 3 day cancellation notice. **Amenities:** high-speed Internet, safes (fee), irons, hair dryers. *Some:* DVD players, dual phone lines. **Pool(s):** outdoor. **Leisure Activities:** playground, exercise room. **Guest Services:** valet and coin laundry, wireless Internet. **Business Services:** meeting rooms, business center. **Cards:** AX, DS, MC, VI.

  / SOME UNITS 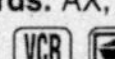

Best Western

AAA Benefit:
Members save up to 20%, plus 10% bonus points with rewards program.

WHERE TO DINE

HONG KONG CUISINE **Phone:** 242/352-7662 34

Chinese
$8-$22

Upstairs at the International Bazaar shopping complex, this simple Chinese eatery offers seating in multiple dining rooms or the separate bar area. Daily meal specials with soup, egg roll, entree and dessert are attractively priced. The menu features standard Chinese fare of rice, noodle, curry and stir-fry dishes. Casual dress. **Bar:** Full bar. **Reservations:** accepted. **Hours:** 10:30 am-10:30 pm. **Address:** International Bazaar **Location:** At International Bazaar. **Parking:** on-site. **Cards:** MC, VI.

RUBY SWISS EUROPEAN RESTAURANT **Phone:** 242/352-8507 33

Continental
$10-$28

The extensive menu caters to all tastes and appetites. Selections range from lighter fare to full tableside presentations by skilled servers. The atmosphere is relaxed, yet sophisticated. Entertainers perform Tuesday through Sunday from 7 pm. Casual dress. Entertainment. **Bar:** Full bar. **Reservations:** accepted. **Hours:** 11 am-4 & 6-4 am, Sat & Sun from 6 pm. Closed: for lunch on public holidays. **Address:** W Sunrise Hwy **Location:** Next to International Bazaar. **Parking:** on-site. **Cards:** AX, DS, MC, VI.

SILVANO'S ITALIAN RESTAURANT **Phone:** 242/352-5111 35

Italian
$14-$29

Informal is the mode in the small, elegant dining room, across from the popular International Bazaar. Formally attired servers bring an array of seafood, meats and house-prepared pastas. Casual dress. **Bar:** Full bar. **Reservations:** suggested. **Hours:** Open 12/1-9/1 & 11/1-11/30; noon-3 & 5:30-11 pm. Closed: 12/25; also Sun 4/15-11/30 & for lunch major holidays. **Address:** E Mall at Sunrise Hwy **Location:** Facing International Bazaar. **Parking:** on-site. **Cards:** AX, DS, MC, VI.

LUCAYA pop. 9,924 (See map and index starting on p. 319)

WHERE TO STAY

PELICAN BAY AT LUCAYA

Book great rates at AAA.com — **Phone:** (242)373-9550 — 4

SAVE

Hotel

$139-$379 All Year

Address: Seahorse Rd at Port Lucaya **Location:** 6 mi (9.6 km) se of Freeport. Located adjacent to UNEXSO. **Facility:** 182 units. 90 one-bedroom standard units. 92 one-bedroom suites. 3-4 stories, exterior corridors. **Parking:** on-site. **Terms:** 3 day cancellation notice-fee imposed. **Amenities:** voice mail, safes, irons, hair dryers. *Some:* DVD players (fee), dual phone lines, honor bars. **Dining:** 2 restaurants, also, The Ferry House Restaurant, see separate listing. **Pool(s):** 3 outdoor. **Leisure Activities:** whirlpool, marina, guest privileges at The Ritz Taino Beach Resort. *Fee:* charter fishing. **Guest Services:** valet and coin laundry, wireless Internet. **Business Services:** business center. **Cards:** AX, MC, VI.

D / SOME UNITS

SHERATON GRAND BAHAMA ISLAND OUR LUCAYA RESORT

Book great rates at AAA.com — **Phone:** (242)373-1444 — 5

SAVE

Resort Hotel

$135-$600 All Year

Address: Royal Palm Way **Location:** Oceanfront. 6 mi (9.6 km) se of Freeport on Lucaya Beach; opposite Port Lucaya Marketplace. **Facility:** The largest beachfront resort on Grand Bahama Island, this family-oriented property offers three themed pool areas, one with a water slide. Meets AAA guest room security requirements. 477 units. 465 one-bedroom standard units. 11 one- and 1 two-bedroom suites. 5 stories, interior corridors. *Bath:* combo or shower only. **Parking:** on-site. **Terms:** 3 day cancellation notice-fee imposed. **Amenities:** high-speed Internet, dual phone lines, voice mail, safes, irons, hair dryers. *Some:* CD players. **Dining:** 13 restaurants, also, Iries, see separate listing, nightclub, entertainment. **Pool(s):** 6 outdoor. **Leisure Activities:** whirlpools, waterslide, lifeguard on duty, recreation programs, shared facilities with The Westin Grand Bahama Island Our Lucaya Resort, playground, spa, basketball, shuffleboard, volleyball. *Fee:* saunas, steamrooms, boats, paddleboats, sailboats, windsurfing, scuba diving, snorkeling, charter fishing, kayaks, personal watercraft, parasailing, golf-36 holes, 4 lighted tennis courts, game room. **Guest Services:** valet and coin laundry, wireless Internet. **Business Services:** conference facilities, business center. **Cards:** AX, CB, DC, DS, JC, MC, VI. *(See color ad below)*

Sheraton HOTELS & RESORTS

AAA Benefit:

Members get up to 15% off, plus Starwood Preferred Guest® bonuses.

24 S D / SOME UNITS VCR

(See map and index starting on p. 319)

TAINO BEACH RESORTS & CLUB — Phone: 242/373-4682 — 3

Condominium
$125-$375 All Year

Address: Jolly Rodger Rd **Location:** Oceanfront. Just e of Port Lucaya. **Facility:** 157 condominiums. 4 stories, exterior corridors. *Bath:* combo or shower only. **Parking:** on-site. **Terms:** office hours 7 am-11 pm, check-in 4 pm. **Amenities:** DVD players, safes, irons, hair dryers. **Pool(s):** outdoor. **Leisure Activities:** whirlpool, waterslide, marina, lighted tennis court, playground, shuffleboard, volleyball. *Fee:* boats, sailboats, snorkeling, charter fishing, bicycles, massage. **Guest Services:** coin laundry, area transportation (fee). **Business Services:** business center. **Cards:** AX, DS, MC, VI.

/ SOME UNITS

THE WESTIN GRAND BAHAMA ISLAND OUR LUCAYA RESORT — *Book great rates at AAA.com* — **Phone:** (242)373-1333 — 7

SAVE

Resort Hotel
$189-$289 All Year

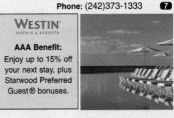

Address: Sea Horse Ln **Location:** 6 mi (9.6 km) se of Freeport on Lucaya Beach; opposite Port Lucaya Marketplace. **Facility:** The full-scale resort facilities offer an array of leisure activities; choose from several room categories, all tastefully furnished and well-equipped. Smoke free premises. 735 units. 683 one-bedroom standard units. 51 one- and 1 three-bedroom suites. 2-10 stories, interior/exterior corridors. *Bath:* combo or shower only. **Parking:** on-site and valet. **Terms:** 3 day cancellation notice-fee imposed. **Amenities:** video games (fee), high-speed Internet, dual phone lines, voice mail, safes, honor bars, irons, hair dryers. *Some:* CD players. **Dining:** 12 restaurants, also, China Beach, Churchill's Chophouse, see separate listings, nightclub, entertainment. **Pool(s):** 6 outdoor. **Leisure Activities:** whirlpools, waterslide, lifeguard on duty, limited beach access, recreation programs, shared facilities with Sheraton at Our Lucaya Resort Beach & Golf Resort, playground, spa, basketball, shuffleboard, volleyball. *Fee:* saunas, steamrooms, boats, paddleboats, sailboats, windsurfing, scuba diving, snorkeling, charter fishing, kayaks, personal watercraft, parasailing, golf-36 holes, 4 lighted tennis courts, game room. **Guest Services:** valet and coin laundry, wireless Internet. **Business Services:** conference facilities, business center. **Cards:** AX, CB, DC, DS, JC, MC, VI.
(See color ad p 323)

/ SOME UNITS

WHERE TO DINE

CAPPUCCINO'S ITALIAN RESTAURANT — **Phone:** 242/373-1584 — 2

Italian
$20-$30

This quaint eatery serves a wide selection of homemade Italian fare and seafood in an intimate setting. Diners can kick back on the pleasant patio or in the cozy air-conditioned dining room. In addition to tasty pasta, the chef also prepares grilled meats and seafood, including excellent broiled island lobster. Early-bird specials appeal to tourists. Casual dress. **Bar:** Full bar. **Reservations:** suggested. **Hours:** Open 12/1-9/1 & 10/1-11/30; 5 pm-10 pm. Closed: Wed. **Address:** Port Lucaya Marketplace **Location:** 6 mi (9.6 km) se of Freeport; at Port Lucaya Marketplace. **Parking:** on-site. **Cards:** AX, MC, VI.

CHINA BEACH — **Phone:** 242/373-1333 — 3

Chinese
$18-$35

Diners can sit indoors or on the patio to explore the menu of tasty Chinese food. The oceanfront setting offers a visual distraction outside, while the kitchen view of chefs at work entertains inside. Among offerings of Asian fare are traditional spring rolls, won ton soup and stir-fries. The chef also incorporates many seafood items into his dishes. Casual dress. **Bar:** Full bar. **Reservations:** suggested. **Hours:** 6 pm-11 pm; hours vary off season. **Address:** Sea Horse Ln **Location:** 6 mi (9.6 km) se of Freeport on Lucaya Beach; in The Westin Grand Bahama Island Our Lucaya Resort. **Parking:** on-site and valet. **Cards:** AX, CB, DC, DS, JC, MC, VI.

CHURCHILL'S CHOPHOUSE — **Phone:** 242/373-1333 — 14

Steak & Seafood
$28-$42

Rich, dark woods and crystal chandeliers adorn the elegant dining room. Food is presented with an artistic flair. Traditional cuts of beef are available. Before or after dinner, patrons can settle into overstuffed chairs in the well-appointed lounge. Semi-formal attire. **Bar:** Full bar. **Reservations:** required. **Hours:** 6 pm-11 pm. Closed: Sun & Mon. **Address:** Sea Horse Ln **Location:** 6 mi (9.6 km) se of Freeport on Lucaya Beach; opposite Port Lucaya Marketplace; in The Westin Grand Bahama Island Our Lucaya Resort. **Parking:** on-site and valet. **Cards:** AX, MC, VI.

THE FERRY HOUSE RESTAURANT — **Phone:** 242/373-1595 — 9

International
$20-$48

Enjoy a dining experience that blends global cuisine with the distinctive flavors of the Caribbean. Tantalizing appetizers include roasted fennel soup and steamed mussels. Sumptuous main courses range from cumin-scented buffalo tenderloin to caribou with sauteed oyster mushrooms. Incredible desserts, including baked-to-order hot chocolate cake and tiramisu, are too tempting to pass up. The ever-changing five-course chef's exotic menu is worthy of a splurge. Dressy casual. **Bar:** Full bar. **Reservations:** required. **Hours:** noon-2:30 & 6-9 pm, Mon-2:30 pm. **Address:** Port Lucaya **Location:** 6 mi (9.6 km) se of Freeport; across from UNEXSO; adjacent to Pelican Bay Hotel. **Parking:** on-site. **Cards:** AX, MC, VI.

GIOVANNI'S CAFE — **Phone:** 242/373-9107 — 4

Italian
$14-$33

This bustling eatery is very popular with the family market due to its good value and hearty portions of freshly prepared Italian fare. Guests can choose from the cozy indoor dining area with a distinct European decor or the popular outdoor patio. In addition to the extensive selections of pastas, also featured are steak, seafood and grilled meats. Casual dress. **Bar:** Full bar. **Reservations:** accepted. **Hours:** Open 12/1-9/30 & 10/15-11/30; 4 pm-11 pm. **Address:** Port Lucaya Marketplace **Location:** 6 mi (9.6 km) se of Freeport; at Port Lucaya Marketplace. **Parking:** street. **Cards:** AX, MC, VI.

(See map and index starting on p. 319)

THE HARBOUR ROOM — **Phone:** 242/374-4466 (5)

International
$18-$42

Elegance marks the indoor dining room, which incorporates fine wood accents, while candlelit tables on the romantic patio afford views of the harbor. On the menu are pasta, fresh fish and other seafood dishes, as well as grilled meat selections. Casual dress. **Bar:** Full bar. **Reservations:** suggested. **Hours:** 5 pm-11 pm; Sunday brunch 11 am-4:30 pm. Closed: Mon & Tues. **Address:** Port Lucaya Marina **Location:** At Port Lucaya Marina; 6 mi (9.6 km) se of Freeport. **Parking:** street. **Cards:** AX, MC, VI.

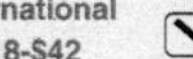

IRIES — **Phone:** 242/373-1333 (12)

Caribbean
$18-$30

Distinctive Jamaican cuisine is served in surroundings that replicate a Caribbean great house. Congenial servers wear traditional island dress. Cracked conch, jerked meat, seafood bouillabaisse and curries are some of the favorites. Dressy casual. **Bar:** Full bar. **Reservations:** required. **Hours:** 6 pm-11 pm. Closed: Wed. **Address:** Royal Palm Way **Location:** 6 mi (9.6 km) se of Freeport on Lucaya Beach; opposite Port Lucaya Marketplace; in Sheraton Grand Bahama Island Our Lucaya Resort. **Parking:** on-site. **Cards:** AX, DS, MC, VI.

LA DOLCE VITA — **Phone:** 242/373-8652 (8)

Regional Italian
$20-$36

Offering a sophisticated atmosphere, the upscale restaurant has an indoor dining room and an outdoor terrace overlooking the marina. The creative menu lists excellent house-prepared pasta dishes, gourmet pizzas and a full complement of seafood, veal, beef and poultry selections. Casual dress. **Bar:** Full bar. **Reservations:** suggested. **Hours:** 5 pm-10:30 pm. Closed: 12/25. **Address:** Port Lucaya Marketplace **Location:** In Port Lucaya Marketplace; facing marina. **Parking:** on-site. **Cards:** AX, MC, VI.

LUCIANO'S — **Phone:** 242/373-9100 (15)

Continental
$26-$36

Located on the waterfront, this second floor location offers marina and bandstand views from the outdoor patio. Blending French and Continental cuisine to serve a truly satisfying meal, the restaurant also features the most extensive wine list on the island. Casual dress. **Bar:** Full bar. **Reservations:** required. **Hours:** 5:30 pm-9:45 pm. Closed: 1/1; also 7/10 & Sun 9/1-9/30. **Address:** Seahorse Rd at Port Lucaya **Location:** In Port Lucaya Marketplace. **Parking:** on-site. **Cards:** AX, MC, VI.

PISCES SEAFOOD — **Phone:** 242/373-5192 (1)

Seafood
$14-$32

A nautical motif punctuates the Port Lucaya Marketplace restaurant, which offers cozy seating indoors or on the sidewalk. Patrons are often swayed to ordering from the huge selection of gourmet pizzas, many with seafood toppings, but seafood pasta dishes, veal and chicken parmigiana, entree-size salads and curry dishes also merit a look. Casual dress. **Bar:** Full bar. **Reservations:** suggested. **Hours:** 5 pm-1:30 am. Closed: Sun. **Address:** Port Lucaya Marketplace **Location:** At Port Lucaya Marketplace. **Parking:** on-site. **Cards:** AX, MC, VI.

(See map and index starting on p. 319)

THE PUB AT PORT LUCAYA **Phone:** 242/373-8450 (7)

American
$7-$27

Adjacent to a popular marketplace, the bustling pub invites diners to unwind indoors or outdoors. Lining the menu is a good selection of American, Bahamian and English specialties, all dished in hearty portions. Casual dress. **Bar:** Full bar. **Reservations:** accepted. **Hours:** 11 am-11 pm. Closed: 12/25. **Address:** Port Lucaya Marketplace **Location:** In Port Lucaya Marketplace; facing the marina. **Parking:** on-site. **Cards:** AX, DS, MC, VI.

SHENANIGAN'S IRISH PUB & EATERY **Phone:** 242/373-4734 (11)

Irish
$10-$25

This friendly pub has touches of Dublin and an authentic Irish menu. Casual dress. **Bar:** Full bar. **Reservations:** accepted. **Hours:** 5 pm-10 pm. Closed: 1/1, 12/25; also Sun, Mon holidays. **Address:** Seahorse Rd at Port Lucaya **Location:** In Port Lucaya Marketplace. **Parking:** on-site. **Cards:** DS, MC, VI.

ZORBA'S GREEK CUISINE **Phone:** 242/373-6137 (6)

Greek
$9-$22

Popular for take-away, the eatery is also nice for a quick bite on the wraparound porch. For the hearty appetite try the Greek platter which includes moussaka, lamb, Greek lasagna, dolmades and taziaka. Casual dress. **Bar:** Full bar. **Hours:** 7 am-10:30 pm. Closed: 12/25. **Address:** Sea Horse Rd **Location:** 6 mi (9.6 km) se of Freeport; in Port Lucaya Marketplace. **Parking:** on-site. **Cards:** AX, CB, DC, DS, JC, MC, VI.

WEST END pop. 4,827 (See map and index starting on p. 319)

WHERE TO STAY

OLD BAHAMA BAY BY GINN SUR MER **Phone:** 242/350-6500 (1)

SAVE

Condominium
$190-$1280 All Year

Address: West End **Location:** Oceanfront. West end of island; 25 mi (40 km) w of airport; follow signs. **Facility:** Located oceanfront, near a marina, the property offers well-appointed guest rooms with residential appointments and luxurious comforts. Designated smoking area. 79 condominiums. 2 stories (no elevator), exterior corridors. **Parking:** on-site. **Terms:** 21 day cancellation notice. **Amenities:** video library, DVD players, CD players, dual phone lines, voice mail, safes, irons, hair dryers. **Dining:** 2 restaurants, also, The Aqua Restaurant, see separate listing, entertainment. **Pool(s):** outdoor. **Leisure Activities:** fishing, recreation programs, bicycles, playground, exercise room, volleyball. *Fee:* charter fishing, massage. **Guest Services:** valet and coin laundry, wireless Internet. **Business Services:** PC. **Cards:** AX, DS, MC, VI. *(See color ad below)*

WHERE TO DINE

THE AQUA RESTAURANT **Phone:** 242/350-6500 (27)

International
$26-$50

In a AAA Four Diamond hotel, this refined restaurant serves a mix of French, Continental and Bahamian cuisine, including the chef's skillful preparations of lamb, beef, fish and other seafood. The well-attired staff provides personalized attention. Dressy casual. Entertainment. **Bar:** Full bar. **Reservations:** required. **Hours:** 6 pm-10 pm. **Address:** West End **Location:** West end of island; 25 mi (40 km) w of airport; in Old Bahama Bay by Ginn Sur Mer. **Parking:** on-site. **Cards:** AX, DS, MC, VI.

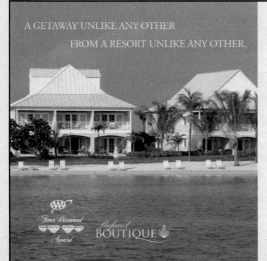

Great Abaco Island

GREEN TURTLE CAY

(See map and index starting on p. 319)

WHERE TO STAY

COCO BAY COTTAGES — Phone: 561/202-8149 — 14

Cottage
$275-$550 All Year

Address: North End of Green Turtle Cay **Location:** Fly into Treasure Cay Airport, taxi to Green Turtle Cay Ferry. Green Turtle Cay Ferry Dock is 25 mi (40 km) n of Marsh Harbour. **Facility:** 5 cottages. 1 story, exterior corridors. *Bath:* combo or shower only. **Parking:** on-site. **Terms:** cancellation fee imposed. **Amenities:** hair dryers. **Guest Services:** TV in common area, valet laundry, wireless Internet. **Cards:** MC, VI.

GREEN TURTLE CLUB AND MARINA — Phone: 242/365-4271 — 13

AAA SAVE

Hotel
$180-$675 12/1-9/5 & 9/29-11/30

Address: White Sound Harbour **Location:** Oceanfront. Treasure Cay Airport, taxi to Green Turtle Cay ferry; request Green Turtle Club dock. Green Turtle Cay ferry dock is 25 mi n of Marsh Harbour. **Facility:** Designated smoking area. 33 units. 14 one- and 9 two-bedroom standard units. 2 one- and 1 two-bedroom suites. 7 cottages. 1 story, exterior corridors. *Bath:* combo or shower only. **Parking:** on-site. **Terms:** open 12/1-9/5 & 9/29-11/30, office hours 7:45 am-8 pm, 2 night minimum stay, 14 day cancellation notice-fee imposed. **Amenities:** video library, irons, hair dryers. **Pool(s):** outdoor. **Leisure Activities:** beach access, marina, fishing. *Fee:* scuba diving, snorkeling, charter fishing, kayaks, golf carts, bicycles, massage. **Guest Services:** coin laundry, wireless Internet. **Business Services:** PC (fee). **Cards:** AX, DS, MC, VI. **Free Special Amenities: room upgrade (subject to availability with advance reservations) and high-speed Internet.**

/ SOME UNITS VCR

WHERE TO DINE

LAURA'S KITCHEN — Phone: 242/365-4287 — 38

American
$10-$21

Simple decor and informal service are apparent at the laid-back eatery. Ample portions of island and American dishes are served. Casual dress. **Bar:** Beer & wine. **Reservations:** accepted. **Hours:** Open 12/1-9/15 & 11/1-11/30; 11 am-3 & 6-9 pm. Closed: 12/25; also Sun. **Address:** King St **Location:** Just above Town Dock; in New Plymouth. **Parking:** on-site. **Cards:** MC, VI.

HOPE TOWN

(See map and index starting on p. 319)

WHERE TO STAY

HOPE TOWN HIDEAWAYS — Phone: 242/366-0224 — 23

Cottage
Rates not provided

Address: 1 Purple Porpoise Pl **Location:** Oceanfront. On Elbow Cay; accessed from Marsh Harbour by ferry boat. **Facility:** Set across from Hope Town and reached only by boat, the property boasts privacy in a lush, tropical garden setting; cottages are equipped with boats. 4 cottages. 1 story, exterior corridors. **Parking:** on-site. **Terms:** office hours 9 am-5 pm, check-out 9 am. **Amenities:** video library, DVD players, CD players. **Pool(s):** outdoor. **Leisure Activities:** beach access, boating. *Fee:* marina. **Guest Services:** coin laundry, area transportation, wireless Internet.

VCR

(See map and index starting on p. 319)

SEA SPRAY RESORT & MARINA **Phone:** 242/366-0065 26

Cottage
$950-$2450 All Year

Address: White Sound, Elbow Cay **Location:** 3.5 mi (5.6 km) s of village; on White Sound. Located in a secluded area. **Facility:** 6 cottages. 1 story, exterior corridors. *Bath:* combo or shower only. **Parking:** on-site. **Terms:** office hours 8 am-5 pm, 3 night minimum stay - seasonal, 30 day cancellation notice-fee imposed. **Amenities:** irons, hair dryers. **Dining:** Boat House Restaurant, see separate listing. **Pool(s):** outdoor. **Leisure Activities:** *Fee:* marina. **Guest Services:** coin laundry. **Business Services:** PC (fee). **Cards:** AX, MC, VI.

WHERE TO DINE

ABACO INN DINING ROOM **Phone:** 242/366-0133 25

International
$12-$33

Patio and inside tables afford spectacular daylight views of the Atlantic Ocean. Included in dishes of delicious, well-prepared island and American cuisine are some vegetarian preparations. A comfortable and relaxed atmosphere prevails. Casual dress. **Bar:** Full bar. **Reservations:** required, for dinner. **Hours:** Open 12/1-9/3 & 10/25-11/30; 8 am-10:30, noon-3 & 6:30-9 pm. **Location:** 2.5 mi (4 km) s of village; on White Sound; in Abaco Inn. **Parking:** on-site. **Cards:** AX, DS, MC, VI.

BOAT HOUSE RESTAURANT **Phone:** 242/366-0359 26

International
$11-$29

On the dock in White Sound, the simple, relaxed eatery is known for serving ample-size portions of island cuisine. Indoor and patio seating overlooks the marina. Complimentary transportation is available from anywhere on the island. Casual dress. **Bar:** Full bar. **Reservations:** required, for dinner. **Hours:** 8 am-9 pm. **Address:** White Sound, Elbow Cay **Location:** 3.5 mi (5.6 km) s of village; on White Sound; in Sea Spray Resort & Marina. **Parking:** on-site. **Cards:** AX, MC, VI.

CAP'N JACKS **Phone:** 242/366-0247 24

American
$8-$19

The waterfront restaurant is wholly informal, from the atmosphere to the service. Diners who sit indoors or on the patio can tackle hearty portions of burgers, pasta, sandwiches, seafood and nightly changing specials. Casual dress. **Bar:** Full bar. **Hours:** Open 12/1-8/10 & 10/1-11/30; 8:30 am-10 & 11-9 pm. Closed: 12/25; also Sun. **Address:** Queens Hwy **Location:** Harbourfront. **Parking:** street. **Cards:** MC, VI.

AC

HARBOUR'S EDGE RESTAURANT **Phone:** 242/366-0292 23

Caribbean
$10-$26

The open-air deck overlooks Hope Town Harbor and sets the tone for a casual mood. Local specialties of island and American cuisine line an often-changing menu. Casual dress. **Bar:** Full bar. **Hours:** Open 12/1-8/15 & 11/15-11/30; 11:30 am-9 pm. Closed: 12/25; also Tues. **Address:** Main Rd **Location:** In center of village; adjacent to town dock. **Parking:** on-site. **Cards:** MC, VI.

AC

MARSH HARBOUR pop. 4,700 (See map and index starting on p. 319)

WHERE TO STAY

ABACO BEACH RESORT & BOAT HARBOUR **Phone:** (242)367-2158 19

Hotel
$255-$748 All Year

Location: 3.5 mi (5.6 km) n from airport. **Facility:** Meets AAA guest room security requirements. 82 units. 73 one-bedroom standard units. 4 one-bedroom suites with efficiencies. 5 cottages. 3-4 stories (no elevator), exterior corridors. **Parking:** on-site. **Terms:** 14 day cancellation notice-fee imposed. **Amenities:** high-speed Internet, voice mail, safes, irons, hair dryers. **Dining:** Angler's Restaurant, see separate listing. **Pool(s):** outdoor, heated outdoor. **Leisure Activities:** limited beach access, rental boats, canoeing, sailboats, windsurfing, 2 lighted tennis courts, playground, exercise room, horseshoes, volleyball. *Fee:* marina, scuba diving, snorkeling, charter fishing. **Guest Services:** valet and coin laundry, wireless Internet. **Business Services:** meeting rooms, PC (fee). **Cards:** AX, DS, MC, VI.

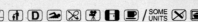

D / SOME UNITS

CONCH INN HOTEL & MARINA **Phone:** (242)367-4000 18

Motel
$120-$160 All Year

Address: E Bay St **Location:** 3 mi (4.8 km) n from airport. Located at marina. **Facility:** 9 one-bedroom standard units. 1 story, exterior corridors. *Bath:* shower only. **Parking:** on-site. **Terms:** office hours 7:30 am-6 pm, cancellation fee imposed. **Amenities:** irons. **Pool(s):** outdoor. **Leisure Activities:** *Fee:* boats, sailboats, marina, scuba diving, snorkeling. **Cards:** AX, MC, VI.

ASK D

WHERE TO DINE

ANGLER'S RESTAURANT **Phone:** 242/367-2158 20

AAA

Steak & Seafood
$11-$32

The dining room affords a lovely view of the ocean, beach and marina. The full menu specializes in fresh local seafood but also offers a selection of meat entrees. Servers are pleasant and attentive. Casual dress. **Bar:** Full bar. **Reservations:** suggested. **Hours:** 7 am-2:30 & 6-9:30 pm. **Address:** Queen Elizabeth Dr **Location:** 3.5 mi (5.6 km) n from airport; in Abaco Beach Resort & Boat Harbour. **Parking:** on-site. **Cards:** AX, DS, MC, VI.

(See map and index starting on p. 319)

CURLY TAILS RESTAURANT AND BAR — Phone: 242/367-4444 (16)

International
$18-$29

This popular waterfront eatery offers a choice of an outdoor open-air patio or indoor air conditioned dining; the menu features an innovative mix of island and international fare in an upbeat yet relaxed setting. Casual dress. Entertainment. **Bar:** Full bar. **Reservations:** accepted. **Hours:** 7 am-10 pm. **Address:** E Bay St **Location:** 3 mi (4.8 km) n from airport; located at marina. **Parking:** on-site. **Cards:** MC, VI.

THE HUMMINGBIRD RESTAURANT & LOUNGE — Phone: 242/367-2922 (21)

Caribbean
$9-$20

In a small shopping complex, the popular restaurant specializes in fresh local seafood but also serves a selection of steaks and comfort foods. A separate cigar lounge bar is on site. Casual dress. **Bar:** Full bar. **Reservations:** accepted, for dinner. **Hours:** 8 am-3 & 6-9 pm, Fri & Sat-10 pm, Mon & Tues-3 pm, Wed 5:30 pm-10 pm. Closed: 4/12, 12/25; also Bahamian Labor Day. **Address:** Bay St **Location:** 3 mi (4.8 km) s of airport; in Memorial Plaza. **Parking:** on-site. **Cards:** AX, MC, VI.

MANGOES RESTAURANT — Phone: 242/367-2366 (22)

Seafood
$11-$27

The attractive waterfront dining room borders an active marina and offers guests complimentary use of the dock. The menu lists well-prepared local seafood and meat entrees. An all-day lighter menu is presented at the bar. Casual dress. **Bar:** Full bar. **Reservations:** accepted. **Hours:** Open 12/1-9/7 & 11/5-11/30; 11:30 am-2:30 & 6-9:30 pm. Closed: 4/12, 12/25; also Good Friday & Bahamas Independence Day. **Address:** Bay St **Location:** Center. **Parking:** on-site. **Cards:** AX, MC, VI.

SAPODILLY'S — Phone: 242/367-3498 (18)

Caribbean
$10-$32

The casual eatery offers outdoor dining in a busy tourist area and is within walking distance of several marinas. Casual dress. Entertainment. **Bar:** Full bar. **Reservations:** accepted. **Hours:** Open 12/1-8/15 & 9/8-11/30; 11:30 am-9 pm. Closed: 1/1, 12/25; also Sun & Emancipation Day. **Address:** Bay St **Location:** Center. **Parking:** on-site. **Cards:** AX, MC, VI.

SNAPPAS GRILL AND CHILL — Phone: 242/367-2278 (17)

American
$8-$22

A popular local hangout and a great place to grab some casual fare in a relaxed setting. This eatery offers waterfront semi-open dining. The daily Happy Hour is popular with tourists and locals alike. Casual dress. **Bar:** Full bar. **Reservations:** accepted. **Hours:** 11 am-11 pm. **Address:** E Bay St **Location:** 3 mi (4.8 km) n from airport. **Parking:** on-site. **Cards:** MC, VI.

WALLY'S — Phone: 242/367-2074 (19)

Caribbean
$10-$27

Close to the harbor, the restaurant lures diners with its open-air setting and pleasant service. Local specialties are highlighted on a daily changing menu of Caribbean and American cuisine. Freshly prepared food is dished in hearty portions. Live music adds to the atmosphere on many nights. Casual dress. **Bar:** Full bar. **Reservations:** suggested. **Hours:** Open 12/1-9/30 & 11/1-11/30; 11:30 am-3 pm, Fri & Sat also 6 pm-9 pm. Closed major holidays; also Sun. **Address:** Bay St **Location:** On waterfront; center. **Parking:** on-site. **Cards:** AX, DS, MC, VI.

TREASURE CAY

(See map and index starting on p. 319)

WHERE TO STAY

TREASURE CAY HOTEL RESORT & MARINA — Book at AAA.com — Phone: 242/365-8810 (10)

Resort Hotel
Rates not provided

Address: Treasure Cay Rd **Location:** 7 mi (11.2 km) s from Treasure Cay Airport. **Facility:** An ideal spot for an escape, the resort offers a marina, a non-intimidating golf course and one-bedroom, apartment-style units. 96 units. 62 one-bedroom standard units. 33 one- and 1 two-bedroom suites with kitchens. 2 stories (no elevator), exterior corridors. **Parking:** on-site. **Terms:** office hours 7 am-10 pm. **Amenities:** high-speed Internet, irons, hair dryers. **Pool(s):** outdoor. **Leisure Activities:** beach access, volleyball. *Fee:* boats, marina, scuba diving, snorkeling, fishing, charter fishing, golf-18 holes, 6 tennis courts (4 lighted), bicycles. **Guest Services:** valet and coin laundry. **Business Services:** meeting rooms, PC (fee).

Great Exuma Island

GEORGE TOWN (See map and index starting on p. 319)

WHERE TO STAY

THE EXUMA PALMS AT THREE SISTERS RESORT LTD Book at AAA.com — Phone: (242)358-4040 42

Motel
$120-$160 All Year

Address: Queens Hwy **Location:** Oceanfront. Center. **Facility:** Designated smoking area. 12 one-bedroom standard units. 2 stories (no elevator), exterior corridors. *Bath:* shower only. **Parking:** on-site. **Terms:** office hours 8 am-9 pm. **Guest Services:** wireless Internet. **Business Services:** PC. **Cards:** MC, VI.

FOUR SEASONS RESORT GREAT EXUMA AT EMERALD BAY Book at AAA.com — Phone: (242)336-6800 44

Resort Hotel
$350-$6800 All Year

Address: Queens Hwy **Location:** 6.5 mi (10.4 km) nw of Exuma International Airport; 15.6 mi (24.9 km) nw of town. **Facility:** Luxury resort located on a remote island. Colonial-style buildings with spacious guest units and secluded terraces. Meets AAA guest room security requirements. Designated smoking area. 219 units. 140 one-bedroom standard units. 43 one- and 36 three-bedroom suites, some with kitchens. 3 stories, interior corridors. *Bath:* combo or shower only. **Parking:** on-site and valet. **Terms:** 30 day cancellation notice-fee imposed. **Amenities:** video library, DVD players, CD players, high-speed Internet (fee), dual phone lines, voice mail, safes, irons, hair dryers. **Dining:** Il Cielo, see separate listing. **Pool(s):** 2 heated outdoor. **Leisure Activities:** whirlpools, steamrooms, lifeguard on duty, paddleboats, sailboats, windsurfing, snorkeling, recreation programs, playground, spa, basketball, volleyball, game room. *Fee:* charter fishing, golf-18 holes, 6 lighted tennis courts. **Guest Services:** valet laundry, area transportation (fee), wireless Internet. **Business Services:** conference facilities, business center. **Cards:** AX, DC, DS, MC, VI.

FEE

/ SOME UNITS

GRAND ISLE RESORT AND SPA Book at AAA.com — Phone: (242)358-5000 43

Condominium
$380-$6000 All Year

Address: Emerald Bay **Location:** Oceanfront. 6.5 mi (10.4 km) nw of Exuma International Airport; 15.6 mi (24.9 km) nw of town. **Facility:** A new upscale condo-resort community located near the marina with very spacious units and upgraded appliances, well-appointed decor and a 50 inch flat screen TV. Smoke free premises. 57 condominiums. 2-3 stories, exterior corridors. *Bath:* combo or shower only. **Parking:** on-site. **Terms:** office hours 7 am-11 pm, check-in 4 pm, 30 day cancellation notice. **Amenities:** video library, DVD players, CD players, high-speed Internet, voice mail, fax, safes, irons, hair dryers. **Pool(s):** heated outdoor. **Leisure Activities:** whirlpool, snorkeling, fishing, recreation programs in winter, exercise room. *Fee:* charter fishing, bicycles, massage. **Guest Services:** complimentary laundry, wireless Internet. **Business Services:** meeting rooms, PC. **Cards:** AX, MC, VI.

PALM BAY BEACH RESORT Book at AAA.com — Phone: (242)336-2787 45

Hotel
$265-$775 All Year

Address: Queens Hwy **Location:** 7.5 mi (12 km) se of Exuma International Airport; 1.6 mi (2.6 km) nw of town. **Facility:** Designated smoking area. 65 units. 20 one-bedroom standard units. 45 cottages. 1 story, exterior corridors. *Bath:* combo or shower only. **Parking:** on-site. **Terms:** office hours 7 am-11 pm, 14 day cancellation notice-fee imposed. **Amenities:** irons, hair dryers. *Some:* safes. **Pool(s):** outdoor. **Leisure Activities:** whirlpool, paddleboats, sailboats, windsurfing, volleyball. **Guest Services:** area transportation, wireless Internet. **Business Services:** meeting rooms, PC. **Cards:** AX, MC, VI.

/ SOME UNITS FEE

PEACE & PLENTY BONEFISH LODGE — Phone: (242)345-5555 46

Motel
$225 All Year

Address: Queens Hwy **Location:** Oceanfront. 18.8 mi (30.8 km) se of Exuma International Airport; 9.7 mi (15.5 km) se of town. Located in a quiet area. **Facility:** 8 one-bedroom standard units. 2 stories (no elevator), exterior corridors. **Parking:** on-site. **Terms:** office hours 8 am-5 pm, age restrictions may apply. **Pool(s):** outdoor. **Leisure Activities:** snorkeling, fishing, bicycles. *Fee:* charter fishing. **Guest Services:** TV in common area, wireless Internet. **Business Services:** PC. **Cards:** MC, VI.

WHERE TO DINE

COCONUT COVE — Phone: 242/336-2659 31

American
$15-$54

The unassuming, low-key eatery prepares lamb, lobster, seafood and curry dishes. Laid-back service and healthy portions are the norm. Casual dress. **Bar:** Full bar. **Reservations:** suggested. **Hours:** Open 12/1-9/1 & 11/1-11/30; 6 pm-9 pm. Closed: 12/25; also Mon & Tues. **Address:** Queens Hwy **Location:** 7.5 mi (12 km) se of Exuma International Airport; 1.6 mi (2.6 km) nw of town. **Parking:** on-site. **Cards:** AX, MC, VI.

IL CIELO — Phone: 242/336-6800 30

Italian
$22-$45

The elegant, two-tiered dining room overlooks the manicured lawns of this luxury resort and distant ocean. Refined service delivers expertly prepared Italian dishes like osso bucco, risotto and insalata caprese. Dressy casual. **Bar:** Full bar. **Reservations:** required. **Hours:** 5:30 pm-10 pm. **Address:** Queens Hwy **Location:** 6.5 mi (10.4 km) nw of airport; 15.6 mi (24.9 km) nw of town; in Four Seasons Resort Great Exuma at Emerald Bay. **Parking:** on-site. **Cards:** AX, CB, DC, DS, JC, MC, VI.

(See map and index starting on p. 319)

WAHOO'S **Phone:** 242/358-5000 32

Caribbean
$18-$32

The simple marina eatery offers al fresco seating and a subtle nautical theme. For starters, patrons enjoy appetizers such as lobster-crab fritters, mushroom bisque or one of several salads. Entrees include preparations of pasta, lamb and seafood, including conch and lobster. Casual dress. **Bar:** Full bar. **Reservations:** accepted. **Hours:** 6:30 pm-10 pm. **Address:** Emerald Bay **Location:** 6.5 mi (10.4 km) nw of Exuma International Airport; 15.6 mi (24.9 km) nw of town; in Grand Isle Resort and Spa. **Parking:** on-site. **Cards:** AX, MC, VI.

This ends listings for Great Exuma Island.
The following resumes the alphabetical listings
of cities in The Bahamas.

HARBOUR ISLAND pop. 1,639 (See map and index starting on p. 319)

WHERE TO STAY

PINK SANDS **Phone:** (242)333-2030 31

Cottage
$750-$2350 12/1-4/30
$600-$1600 5/1-11/30

Address: Chapel St **Location:** Oceanfront. Reached from N Eleuthera Airport via taxi and ferry; also by Fast Ferry from Nassau 2 hours one way. **Facility:** Owned by record magnate Chris Blackwell, handsome individual and duplex cottages with distinctive decor are set above three miles of pink-sand beach. 25 cottages. 1 story, exterior corridors. *Bath:* combo or shower only. **Parking:** on-site. **Terms:** 3 night minimum stay, 30 day cancellation notice. **Amenities:** video library, DVD players, CD players, dual phone lines, voice mail, safes, honor bars, irons, hair dryers. **Pool(s):** heated outdoor. **Leisure Activities:** limited beach access, snorkeling, fishing, 3 tennis courts (1 lighted), exercise room. *Fee:* charter fishing, bicycles, massage. **Guest Services:** valet laundry, wireless Internet. **Business Services:** meeting rooms, PC. **Cards:** AX, MC, VI.

D

WHERE TO DINE

THE LANDING RESTAURANT **Phone:** 242/333-2707 29

International
$36-$42

The diverse menu combines Mediterranean, Bahamian and American cuisine. The charming, attractive waterfront setting features indoor and patio seating. Friendly, attentive servers help nurture the relaxed atmosphere. Casual dress. **Bar:** Full bar. **Reservations:** suggested. **Hours:** Open 12/1-8/28 & 11/2-11/30; 8 am-10 & 6:30-10 pm, Sun 8-11 am; 7 pm-10 pm in summer. Closed: 12/25; also Tues & Wed. **Address:** Bay St **Location:** Just above Town Dock; overlooking harbor. **Parking:** street. **Cards:** AX, MC, VI. **Historic**

LONG ISLAND pop. 2,992 (See map and index starting on p. 319)

WHERE TO STAY

CAPE SANTA MARIA BEACH RESORT **Phone:** (242)338-5273 41

Cottage
$235-$795 12/1-8/29 & 11/3-11/30

Address: Northwest Coast **Location:** 6 mi (9.6 km) n from Stella Maris Airport at Cape Santa Maria. **Facility:** A superb beach and attractive cottages dot the shoreline of this isolated popular getaway for anglers and romantics alike. 30 units. 10 houses and 20 cottages. 1-2 stories (no elevator), exterior corridors. *Bath:* combo or shower only. **Parking:** on-site. **Terms:** open 12/1-8/29 & 11/3-11/30, office hours 7 am-10:30 pm, 30 day cancellation notice. **Amenities:** video library, safes, hair dryers. **Leisure Activities:** bicycles, exercise room. *Fee:* scuba diving, snorkeling, fishing, charter fishing, massage. **Guest Services:** complimentary laundry, wireless Internet. **Business Services:** PC (fee). **Cards:** AX, MC, VI.

D / SOME UNITS VCR

New Providence Island

This index helps you "spot" where approved lodgings and restaurants are located on the corresponding detailed maps. Lodging daily rate range is for comparison only and show the property's high season. Restaurant rate range is a combination of lunch and/or dinner. Turn to the listing page for more detailed rate information and consult display ads for special promotions.

CABLE BEACH (NEW PROVIDENCE ISLAND)

Map Page	OA	Lodgings	Diamond Rated	High Season	Page
1 / p. 334		Wyndham Nassau Resort & Crystal Palace Casino	♦♦♦	$129-$299	335
2 / p. 334	AAA	**Sheraton Cable Beach Resort** - see color ad on insert	♦♦♦	$269-$449 SAVE	335

Map Page	OA	Restaurants	Diamond Rated	Cuisine	Meal Range	Page
2 / p. 334		The Poop Deck Sandyport	♦♦♦	Seafood	$16-$43	335
4 / p. 334		Capriccio Ristorante	♦♦♦	Italian	$12-$28	335

GAMBIER VILLAGE (NEW PROVIDENCE ISLAND)

Map Page	OA	Lodging	Diamond Rated	High Season	Page
6 / p. 334		Compass Point Beach Resort	♦♦♦	$215-$460	335

Map Page	OA	Restaurant	Diamond Rated	Cuisine	Meal Range	Page
8 / p. 334		Compass Point Restaurant	♦♦	Caribbean	$11-$34	335

NASSAU (NEW PROVIDENCE ISLAND)

Map Page	OA	Lodgings	Diamond Rated	High Season	Page
12 / p. 334	AAA	**British Colonial Hilton Nassau** - see color ad p 336, opposite title page	♦♦♦	$129-$409 SAVE	336
14 / p. 334	AAA	**Graycliff Hotel & Restaurant** - see color ad p 337	♦♦♦	$225-$700 SAVE	336

Map Page	OA	Restaurants	Diamond Rated	Cuisine	Meal Range	Page
12 / p. 334		Twin Brothers Seafood & Steakhouse	♦♦	Caribbean	$10-$28	339
13 / p. 334		Cricket Club Restaurant and Lounge	♦	British	$10-$20	338
15 / p. 334		Chez Willie Restaurant	♦♦♦	French	$15-$35	338
16 / p. 334		Clay Oven	♦♦	Indian	$12-$27	338
17 / p. 334		Hard Rock Cafe	♦♦	American	$12-$24 SAVE	338
18 / p. 334		Cafe Matisse	♦♦♦	Italian	$15-$32	338
20 / p. 334		Graycliff - see color ad p 337	♦♦♦♦	International	$24-$60	338
21 / p. 334		Humidor Churrascaria Restaurant	♦♦♦	Brazilian	$40	338
24 / p. 334		The Poop Deck Yacht Haven Marina	♦♦	Seafood	$13-$36	338
25 / p. 334		East Villa Restaurant	♦♦	Chinese	$12-$34	338
28 / p. 334	AAA	**'Sun and —' Restaurant**	♦♦♦	International	$34-$44	339

PARADISE ISLAND (NEW PROVIDENCE ISLAND)

Map Page	OA	Lodgings	Diamond Rated	High Season	Page
20 / p. 334		Atlantis Paradise Island	♦♦♦♦	$250-$1705	339
21 / p. 334		Riu Paradise Island	♦♦♦	$266-$460	343
22 / p. 334		One & Only Ocean Club	♦♦♦♦	$560-$870	343
24 / p. 334	AAA	**Club Land'Or Resort** - see color ad p 340	♦♦	$255-$375 SAVE	340
25 / p. 334	AAA	**Comfort Suites Paradise Island** - see color ad p 341	♦♦♦	$239-$373 SAVE	342
26 / p. 334		Paradise Island Harbour Resort	♦♦♦	$310-$500	343

PARADISE ISLAND (NEW PROVIDENCE ISLAND) (cont'd)

Map Page	OA	Lodgings (cont'd)	Diamond Rated	High Season	Page
28 / p. 334	AAA	**Best Western Bay View Suites** - see color ad p 339	♦♦♦	$259-$325 SAVE	340

Map Page	OA	Restaurants	Diamond Rated	Cuisine	Meal Range	Page
30 / p. 334	AAA	**Bahamian Club**	♦♦♦	Steak	$30-$42	343
31 / p. 334		Seafire Steakhouse	♦♦♦	Steak	$32-$54	344
33 / p. 334	AAA	**Casa D'Angelo**	♦♦♦	Italian	$32-$60	344
34 / p. 334	AAA	**Nobu**	♦♦♦	Asian	$18-$70	344
35 / p. 334		Cafe Martinique	♦♦♦♦	International	$38-$65	344
38 / p. 334		Dune	♦♦♦♦	International	$22-$58	344
40 / p. 334		The Green Parrot	♦	American	$9-$24	344
42 / p. 334		Anthony's Caribbean Grill	♦♦	Caribbean	$10-$23	343

New Providence Island
Lodging & Dining
0 Miles 9.5
0 Kilometers 15.3
SEE INSET MAP FOR DETAIL
PARADISE ISLAND
NASSAU
Cable Beach
Tuckers
Gambier Village
Orange Hill
Old Fort
Lake of Killarney
Nassau International Airport
Nassau Village
Creek Village
Winton
Clifton
Adelaide
Seven Hills
Lazaretto
Coral Harbour
Atlantic Ocean
N
1
2
2
4
6
8

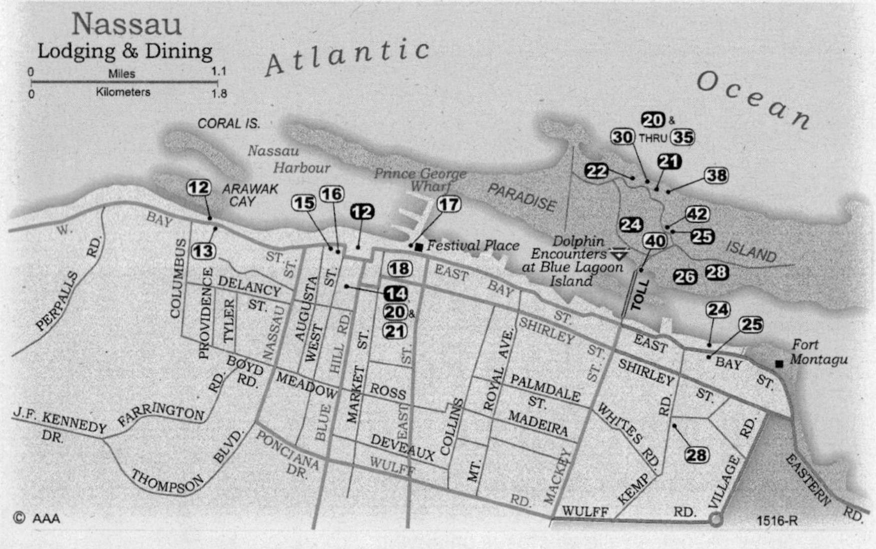
Nassau
Lodging & Dining
0 Miles 1.1
0 Kilometers 1.8
Atlantic Ocean
CORAL IS.
Nassau Harbour
Prince George Wharf
PARADISE ISLAND
ARAWAK CAY
Festival Place
Dolphin Encounters at Blue Lagoon Island
TOLL
Fort Montagu
W. BAY ST.
EAST BAY ST.
PERPALLS RD.
COLUMBUS
PROVIDENCE
TYLER
NASSAU ST.
AUGUSTA ST.
WEST ST.
HILL RD.
BLUE
MARKET ST.
EAST ST.
DELANCY ST.
BOYD RD.
MEADOW
ROSS
DEVEAUX
WULFF
COLLINS
ROYAL AVE.
MT.
MACKEY ST.
SHIRLEY ST.
PALMDALE ST.
MADEIRA
WHITES RD.
KEMP RD.
VILLAGE RD.
EASTERN RD.
WULFF RD.
FARRINGTON RD.
J.F. KENNEDY DR.
THOMPSON BLVD.
PONCIANA DR.
12
13
15
16
12
17
18
14
20 & 21
20 & 30 THRU 35
21
22
38
24
42
40
25
26
28
24
25
28
© AAA
1516-R

CABLE BEACH (See map and index starting on p. 334)

WHERE TO STAY

SHERATON CABLE BEACH RESORT — **Phone:** 242/327-6000 **2**

AAA SAVE

Resort Hotel

$269-$449 All Year

Address: West Bay St **Location:** 5 mi (8 km) w of Rawson Square; 3.5 mi (5.6 km) e of airport. **Facility:** On Cable Beach, the hotel boasts 25,000 square feet of lagoon-style swimming pools, hot tubs and cascading waterfalls surrounded by lush landscaping. 694 units. 678 one-bedroom standard units. 16 one-bedroom suites. 9 stories, interior corridors. *Bath:* combo or shower only. **Parking:** on-site and valet. **Terms:** 2 night minimum stay, 7 day cancellation notice. **Amenities:** dual phone lines, voice mail, irons, hair dryers. *Fee:* video games, high-speed Internet, safes. *Some:* CD players. **Dining:** 4 restaurants, entertainment. **Pool(s):** 3 outdoor. **Leisure Activities:** whirlpools, lifeguard on duty, canoeing, paddleboats, sailboats, windsurfing, snorkeling, kayaks, 5 tennis courts, recreation programs, playground, basketball, volleyball. *Fee:* golf-18 holes, massage. **Guest Services:** valet laundry, wireless Internet. **Business Services:** conference facilities, business center. **Cards:** AX, DC, MC, VI. ***(See color ad on insert)***

D / SOME UNITS

WYNDHAM NASSAU RESORT & CRYSTAL PALACE CASINO — **Phone:** (242)327-6200 **1**

Resort Hotel

$129-$299 All Year

Address: West Bay St **Location:** Oceanfront. On Cable Beach; 5 mi (8 km) w of Rawson Square; 4.2 mi (6.7 km) e of airport. Located in a developed commercial and residential area. **Facility:** This large resort designed to resemble a cruise ship offers many activities and a variety of views. 850 units. 762 one-bedroom standard units. 88 one-bedroom suites with whirlpools. 11-15 stories, interior corridors. **Parking:** on-site and valet. **Terms:** check-in 4 pm, 3 day cancellation notice. **Amenities:** high-speed Internet, voice mail, safes, irons, hair dryers. **Pool(s):** outdoor. **Leisure Activities:** saunas, whirlpools, waterslide, lifeguard on duty, rental paddleboats, recreation programs, playground, spa, volleyball. *Fee:* sailboats, windsurfing, game room. **Guest Services:** valet laundry, wireless Internet. **Business Services:** conference facilities, business center. **Cards:** AX, CB, DC, DS, JC, MC, VI.

ASK S D / SOME UNITS

WHERE TO DINE

CAPRICCIO RISTORANTE — **Phone:** 242/327-8547 **4**

Italian

$12-$28

A local favorite, the restaurant lets patrons choose to dine inside or outdoors on the terrace. Italian dishes are prepared to order with the diner's preferred pasta and sauces. Casual dress. **Bar:** Full bar. **Reservations:** required. **Hours:** 11 am-10 pm, Sun from 5 pm. Closed: 4/12, 12/25; also for lunch on public holidays. **Address:** West Bay St **Location:** At west end of Cable Beach. **Parking:** on-site. **Cards:** MC, VI.

THE POOP DECK SANDYPORT — **Phone:** 242/327-3325 **2**

Seafood

$16-$43

A warm reception always can be found at the popular restaurant. The popular raw bar serves conch ceviche, raw oysters, sushi and sashimi. Mouthwatering appetizer standouts are blue mussels, soft-shell crab and escargots. Expertly prepared entrees range from the fisherman's platter to hog snapper, Angus beef and seafood bouillabaisse. Guests can sit in the air-conditioned dining room or enjoy balmy breezes on the al fresco deck. Dressy casual. **Bar:** Full bar. **Reservations:** suggested. **Hours:** Open 12/1-9/1 & 9/15-11/30; noon-10:30 pm, Sun-10 pm. Closed: 12/25, 12/26; also Mon. **Address:** West Bay St **Location:** W of Cable Beach; at Sandyport. **Parking:** on-site. **Cards:** AX, DC, MC, VI.

GAMBIER VILLAGE (See map and index starting on p. 334)

WHERE TO STAY

COMPASS POINT BEACH RESORT — **Phone:** (242)327-4500 **6**

Cottage

$215-$460 All Year

Address: West Bay St, Gambier **Location:** Oceanfront. Adjacent to Love Beach; 10 mi (16 km) w of Rawson Square; 1.5 mi (2.4 km) w of airport on John F Kennedy. **Facility:** Brightly colored cottages and cabanas face the sea, each with a private deck; an upbeat, chic atmosphere prevails here. Short walk to the beach. 18 cottages. 1-2 stories (no elevator), exterior corridors. *Bath:* shower only. **Parking:** on-site. **Amenities:** video library (fee), DVD players, CD players, safes, irons, hair dryers. **Dining:** Compass Point Restaurant, see separate listing. **Pool(s):** outdoor. **Leisure Activities:** whirlpool. **Guest Services:** valet laundry, wireless Internet. **Business Services:** PC. **Cards:** AX, CB, DC, DS, JC, MC, VI.

D

WHERE TO DINE

COMPASS POINT RESTAURANT — **Phone:** 242/327-4500 **8**

Caribbean

$11-$34

The creative menu lists offerings of American and Caribbean cuisine. A tropical feeling—thanks to bright, island decor and pretty ocean views—prevails. Light luncheon selections also are available. Casual dress. Entertainment. **Bar:** Full bar. **Reservations:** suggested, for dinner. **Hours:** 7 am-10 pm. **Address:** West Bay St **Location:** Adjacent to Love Beach; 10 mi (16 km) w of Rawson Square; 1.5 mi (2.4 km) w of airport on John F Kennedy; in Compass Point Beach Resort. **Parking:** on-site. **Cards:** AX, MC, VI.

NASSAU pop. 210,832 (See map and index starting on p. 334)

WHERE TO STAY

BRITISH COLONIAL HILTON NASSAU

Phone: (242)322-3301 **12**

Historic Hotel

$129-$409 All Year

Address: No 1 Bay St **Location:** Just w of Rawson Square. Located in the downtown commercial and financial district. **Facility:** In the heart of the downtown Nassau shopping area, the Spanish Colonial-style hotel has modern amenities and a cabana bar spilling out to the beach. Meets AAA guest room security requirements. 288 units. 271 one-bedroom standard units. 17 one-bedroom suites, some with whirlpools. 7 stories, interior corridors. *Bath:* combo or shower only. **Parking:** on-site and valet. **Terms:** 1-30 night minimum stay, cancellation fee imposed. **Amenities:** high-speed Internet (fee), voice mail, safes, honor bars, irons, hair dryers. *Some:* CD players, dual phone lines. **Dining:** 3 restaurants, entertainment. **Pool(s):** heated outdoor. **Leisure Activities:** lifeguard on duty, limited beach access, paddleboats, boat dock, snorkeling, kayaks, exercise room, basketball, volleyball. **Guest Services:** valet laundry, wireless Internet. **Business Services:** meeting rooms, business center. **Cards:** AX, DC, DS, JC, MC, VI. ***(See color ad below & opposite title page)***

AAA Benefit:
Members save 5% or more everyday!

S D / SOME UNITS

GRAYCLIFF HOTEL & RESTAURANT

Phone: (242)302-9150 **14**

Classic Historic Country Inn

$225-$700 12/1-4/23
$195-$550 4/24-11/30

Address: 8-12 West Hill St **Location:** Downtown; opposite the Government House. **Facility:** The 250-year-old mansion in a private, downtown setting has meticulous grounds; find elegantly furnished rooms and suites and a cigar factory on site. 20 units. 12 one-bedroom standard units, some with whirlpools. 8 one-bedroom suites, some with whirlpools. 2 stories (no elevator), interior/exterior corridors. *Bath:* combo or shower only. **Parking:** on-site. **Terms:** office hours 7:30 am-11:30 pm, 14 day cancellation notice. **Amenities:** high-speed Internet, dual phone lines, voice mail, safes, honor bars, irons, hair dryers. **Dining:** Graycliff, Humidor Churrascaria Restaurant, see separate listings. **Pool(s):** 2 outdoor. **Leisure Activities:** sauna, whirlpool, steamroom, spa. **Guest Services:** valet laundry, wireless Internet. **Business Services:** PC (fee). **Cards:** AX, DS, MC, VI. ***(See color ad p 337)***

D / SOME UNITS 

▼ *See AAA listing above* ▼

See AAA listing p 336

(See map and index starting on p. 334)

WHERE TO DINE

CAFE MATISSE — **Phone:** 242/356-7012 (18)

Italian
$15-$32

Quaint European decor and a bustling atmosphere characterize the popular restaurant. The menu blends a good selection of homemade pasta, seafood and Bahamian dishes, all of which can be enjoyed indoors or on the terrace. Dressy casual. **Bar:** Full bar. **Reservations:** required. **Hours:** Open 12/1-8/1 & 9/5-11/30; noon-3 & 6-11 pm. Closed major holidays; also Sun & Mon. **Address:** Bank Ln **Location:** Across from the courthouse; behind Parliament Square; just off Bay St; downtown. **Parking:** valet and street. **Cards:** AX, DS, MC, VI. **Historic**

CHEZ WILLIE RESTAURANT — **Phone:** 242/322-5364 (15)

French
$15-$35

The restaurant is a good choice for finer dining. Several pleasant sections include a landscaped courtyard. The staff projects a professional flair that is further enhanced in the evening. Semi-formal attire. **Bar:** Full bar. **Reservations:** suggested. **Hours:** noon-3 & 6:30-10 pm, Sat from 6:30 pm, Sun 11:30 am-4:30 & 6:30-10 pm. Closed: for lunch 4/15-11/30. **Address:** West Bay St **Location:** Corner of Dorchester and West Bay sts. **Parking:** on-site and valet. **Cards:** AX, DS, MC, VI.

CLAY OVEN — **Phone:** 242/325-2525 (16)

Indian
$12-$27

The distinctive marrying of specific herbs and spices in the cuisine creates a sensuous tasting experience. Begin with an order of samosas: either seasoned diced vegetables or diced seasoned lamb and vegetables stuffed in a pastry shell, then deep-fried and served with tamarind chutney. Entree choices include curry specialties made with tender lamb, grouper fillets, jumbo shrimp or boneless chicken. Obvious favor is given to tandoori meals, which are cooked to perfection in a clay oven. Casual dress. **Bar:** Full bar. **Reservations:** accepted. **Hours:** noon-3 & 6-10 pm, Sun from 6 pm. Closed: for lunch on Bahamian public holidays. **Address:** 100 W Bay St **Location:** Center of downtown. **Parking:** street. **Cards:** AX, MC, VI.

CRICKET CLUB RESTAURANT AND LOUNGE — **Phone:** 242/326-4720 (13)

British
$10-$20

A favorite gathering spot, the friendly, casual club's open-air dining balcony overlooks the cricket grounds. British pub fare is prepared with a Bahamian twist. Casual dress. **Bar:** Full bar. **Hours:** 8 am-11:30 pm. Closed: 12/25. **Address:** West Bay St **Location:** At Haynes Oval; just w of downtown. **Parking:** on-site. **Cards:** MC, VI.

EAST VILLA RESTAURANT — **Phone:** 242/393-3377 (25)

Chinese
$12-$34

Popular with locals and tourists alike, the restaurant prepares mainly Chinese cuisine but also offers some Continental specialties. With more than 50 items, the menu lists something for every palate. House favorites include pineapple duck, Szechuan lobster and mu shu pork, as well as classic preparations of shrimp scampi, chicken parmigiana and broiled rack of lamb. Top off the meal with an after-dinner coffee concoctions laced with rum or liqueur. Dressy casual. Entertainment. **Bar:** Full bar. **Reservations:** suggested. **Hours:** noon-3 & 6-11 pm, Sat from 6 pm, Sun 12:30 pm-3 & 6-10 pm. Closed: 12/25; also for lunch on public holidays. **Address:** East Bay St **Location:** 1 mi (1.6 km) e of downtown. **Parking:** valet. **Cards:** AX, MC, VI.

GRAYCLIFF — **Phone:** 242/322-2796 (20)

International
$24-$60

In a 260-year-old Bahamian mansion, the upscale dining room boasts an impressive wine cellar of 175,000 rare and vintage wines, as well as an excellent choice of ports and Armagnacs. At a cigar factory on the premises, a team of Cuban-born workers roll the highly reputed house-blend cigars. Imported Cuban cigars also are available. The menu blends Bahamian and Continental fine cuisine. Service reflects elements of Old World formality. Semi-formal attire. Entertainment. **Bar:** Full bar. **Reservations:** required. **Hours:** noon-3 & 6:30-9:30 pm, Sat & Sun from 6:30 pm. Closed: 12/25. **Address:** 8-12 W Hill St **Location:** Downtown; opposite Government House; in Graycliff Hotel & Restaurant. **Parking:** on-site and valet. **Cards:** AX, MC, VI. **Historic** ***(See color ad p 337)***

HARD ROCK CAFE — **Phone:** 242/325-7625 (17)

American
$12-$24

Rock 'n' roll memorabilia decorates the walls of the popular theme restaurant. Live music on the weekends contributes to the bustling atmosphere. On the menu is a wide variety of American cuisine—from burgers and sandwiches to seafood, steaks and pasta. Casual dress. **Bar:** Full bar. **Hours:** 11 am-11 pm. **Address:** Charlotte St N **Location:** Corner of Bay and Charlotte sts; downtown. **Parking:** street. **Cards:** AX, DS, JC, MC, VI.

HUMIDOR CHURRASCARIA RESTAURANT — **Phone:** 242/322-2796 (21)

Brazilian
$40

Adjacent to a cigar factory, the upscale Brazilian steakhouse lets guests watch rollers making cigars. Dinners begin with a buffet of well-prepared appetizers before moving on to the main course: more than 20 cuts of meat, including beef, ribs, pork, chicken and lamb, carved at the table by the roving, well-attired staff. Casual dress. **Bar:** Full bar. **Reservations:** required. **Hours:** 7 pm-9:30 pm. Closed: 12/25; also Sun. **Address:** 8-12 W Hill St **Location:** Downtown; opposite Government House; in Graycliff Hotel & Restaurant. **Parking:** street. **Cards:** AX, MC, VI. **Historic**

THE POOP DECK YACHT HAVEN MARINA — **Phone:** 242/393-8175 (24)

Seafood
$13-$36

The popular casual eatery and pub offers guests a full view of the active marina. On the menu are fresh local seafood, including some traditional dishes, and various comfort foods, such as sandwiches, burgers and fish and chips. Casual dress. **Bar:** Full bar. **Reservations:** suggested. **Hours:** Open 12/1-9/10 & 9/21-11/30; noon-4:30 & 5-10:30 pm. Closed: 1/1, 12/25, 12/26; also 12/31. **Address:** East Bay St **Location:** At Nassau Yacht Haven Marina; just e of Paradise Island Bridge. **Parking:** on-site. **Cards:** AX, DC, MC, VI.

(See map and index starting on p. 334)

SENOR FROG'S — **Phone:** 242/323-1777

Tex-Mex
$9-$21

Part of the chain of Mexican restaurants that also includes Carlos 'n Charlie's, the fun and festive eatery is a great place to eat with the family or rendezvous with friends. The menu is lined with Tex-Mex, American and Mexican favorites, such as Buffalo wings, quesadillas, fajitas and burritos. After hours, a bar atmosphere prevails. Casual dress. Entertainment. **Bar:** Full bar. **Reservations:** accepted. **Hours:** 11 am-10 pm. **Address:** Woodes Rogers Walk **Location:** At the British Colonial Centre of Commerce; waterfront downtown. **Parking:** street. **Cards:** AX, DS, MC, VI.

'SUN AND —' RESTAURANT — **Phone:** 242/393-1205 (28)

International
$34-$44

Guests can sample imaginative dishes that incorporate local and international influences in the charming garden courtyard. Dessert souffles are worth saving room for. Dressy casual. **Bar:** Full bar. **Reservations:** suggested. **Hours:** Open 12/1-7/30 & 10/1-11/30; 11:30 am-3 & 6:30-9:30 pm, Sat from 6:30 pm. Closed: 1/1; also Sun & Mon. **Address:** Lakeview Dr **Location:** 1.5 mi (2.4 km) e of Rawson Square off Shirley St, just nw. **Parking:** on-site. **Cards:** AX, DS, MC, VI.

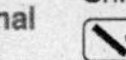

TWIN BROTHERS SEAFOOD & STEAKHOUSE — **Phone:** 242/328-5033 (12)

Caribbean
$10-$28

Located in always busy Arawak Cay, be prepared to wait for a table as this place draws a crowd with its authentic spin on Bahamian food served hot; the focus is beef and fresh seafood. Casual dress. **Bar:** Full bar. **Hours:** noon-11 pm, Fri-Sun to midnight. Closed: 12/25; also Mon. **Address:** Arawak Cay **Location:** W of downtown. **Parking:** on-site. **Cards:** MC, VI.

PARADISE ISLAND (See map and index starting on p. 334)

WHERE TO STAY

ATLANTIS PARADISE ISLAND Book at AAA.com — **Phone:** (242)363-3000 (20)

Resort Hotel
$250-$1705 All Year

Address: Casino Dr **Location:** Reached by toll bridge from Nassau. **Facility:** Marine life-stocked lagoons, underwater viewing tunnels, a water theme park, a lazy river, entertainment and extensive shops complete this property. 2318 units. 2147 one-bedroom standard units. 6 one- and 165 two-bedroom suites with whirlpools. 4-24 stories, interior/exterior corridors. *Bath:* combo or shower only. **Parking:** valet. **Terms:** 14 day cancellation notice-fee imposed. **Amenities:** high-speed Internet (fee), dual phone lines, voice mail, safes, honor bars, irons, hair dryers. **Dining:** Bahamian Club, Cafe Martinique, Casa D'Angelo, Nobu, Seafire Steakhouse, see separate listings. **Pool(s):** 11 heated outdoor. **Leisure Activities:** sauna, whirlpools, waterslide, lifeguard on duty, beach access, rental paddleboats, recreation programs, playground, spa, basketball, shuffleboard, volleyball. *Fee:* canoes, sailboats, marina, scuba diving, snorkeling, fishing, charter fishing, golf-18 holes, 6 lighted tennis courts, game room. **Guest Services:** valet laundry, area transportation, wireless Internet. **Business Services:** conference facilities, business center. **Cards:** AX, DC, DS, MC, VI. Affiliated with A Preferred Hotel.

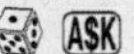   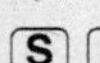     FEE / SOME UNITS

▼ See AAA listing p 340 ▼

(See map and index starting on p. 334)

BEST WESTERN BAY VIEW SUITES Book great rates at AAA.com **Phone:** (242)363-2555 28

Condominium
$259-$325 12/1-4/18
$205-$280 4/19-11/30

Address: Bay View Dr **Location:** Reached by toll bridge from Nassau. **Facility:** Attractive one- and two-bedroom suites, townhouses and villas are set in a peaceful tropical setting, with a public beach just a short walk away. 25 units. 23 one- and 2 two-bedroom suites with kitchens. 1-2 stories (no elevator), exterior corridors. **Parking:** on-site. **Terms:** office hours 8:30 am-10 pm, 1-5 night minimum stay - seasonal, 7 day cancellation notice-fee imposed. **Amenities:** high-speed Internet, voice mail, safes (fee), irons, hair dryers. **Pool(s):** 3 outdoor. **Leisure Activities:** lighted tennis court, playground. **Guest Services:** coin laundry, wireless Internet. **Business Services:** PC (fee). **Cards:** AX, DC, DS, MC, VI. *(See color ad p 339)*

Best Western

AAA Benefit: Members save up to 20%, plus 10% bonus points with rewards program.

D / SOME UNITS

CLUB LAND'OR RESORT **Phone:** (242)363-2400 24

Hotel
$255-$375 All Year

Address: Marina Dr **Location:** Reached by toll bridge from Nassau. **Facility:** Meets AAA guest room security requirements. 72 condominiums. 3 stories (no elevator), interior/exterior corridors. *Bath:* combo or shower only. **Parking:** on-site. **Terms:** check-in 4 pm, 3 day cancellation notice-fee imposed. **Amenities:** safes, irons. **Dining:** entertainment. **Pool(s):** outdoor. **Leisure Activities:** whirlpool, exercise room, use of Atlantis Paradise Island beach only. **Guest Services:** wireless Internet. **Cards:** AX, DS, MC, VI. *(See color ad below)*

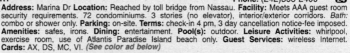

D

▼ See AAA listing p 342 ▼

(See map and index starting on p. 334)

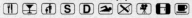

COMFORT SUITES PARADISE ISLAND Book great rates at AAA.com **Phone:** (242)363-3680 

Hotel

$239-$373 All Year

Address: 1 Paradise Island Dr **Location:** Reached by toll bridge from Nassau. **Facility:** Meets AAA guest room security requirements. Smoke free premises. 228 one-bedroom standard units. 2-4 stories, interior corridors. **Parking:** on-site. **Terms:** 5 day cancellation notice-fee imposed. **Amenities:** voice mail, irons, hair dryers. *Fee:* high-speed Internet, safes. *Some:* dual phone lines. **Pool(s):** outdoor. **Leisure Activities:** facility privileges at Atlantis Paradise Island. **Guest Services:** valet and coin laundry, wireless Internet. **Business Services:** meeting rooms, PC (fee). **Cards:** AX, DC, DS, MC, VI. **Free Special Amenities: continental breakfast and newspaper.** *(See color ad p 341)*

(See map and index starting on p. 334)

ONE & ONLY OCEAN CLUB Book at AAA.com Phone: (242)363-2501 22

Resort Hotel
$560-$870 All Year

Address: Paradise Island **Location:** Oceanfront. Reached by toll bridge from Nassau. **Facility:** Find luxurious accommodations at this world-class resort, including 24-hour butler service, a spa and the use of recreational facilities at Atlantis Paradise Island. 105 units. 83 one-bedroom standard units. 14 one-, 2 two- and 1 three-bedroom suites, some with whirlpools. 3 houses and 2 cottages. 1-2 stories, exterior corridors. **Parking:** valet. **Terms:** 3 night minimum stay. **Amenities:** video library, DVD players, CD players, high-speed Internet, dual phone lines, voice mail, safes, honor bars, irons, hair dryers. **Dining:** Dune, see separate listing. **Pool(s):** 2 outdoor. **Leisure Activities:** steamrooms, lifeguard on duty, beach access, snorkeling, 6 lighted tennis courts, bicycles, jogging, spa, shared facilities with Atlantis Paradise Island. *Fee:* golf-18 holes, kids club. **Guest Services:** valet laundry, area transportation (fee), wireless Internet. **Business Services:** meeting rooms, PC. **Cards:** AX, MC, VI.

24 S D

PARADISE ISLAND HARBOUR RESORT Phone: 242/363-2561 26

Hotel
$310-$500 All Year

Address: Harbour Dr **Location:** Oceanfront. Reached by toll bridge from Nassau. **Facility:** Meets AAA guest room security requirements. 246 units. 242 one-bedroom standard units. 4 one-bedroom suites. 12 stories, interior corridors. *Bath:* combo or shower only. **Parking:** on-site. **Terms:** check-in 4 pm, 7 day cancellation notice-fee imposed. **Amenities:** dual phone lines, voice mail, safes, irons, hair dryers. *Fee:* video games, high-speed Internet. **Pool(s):** outdoor. **Leisure Activities:** whirlpool, 2 lighted tennis courts, recreation programs, exercise room, basketball, horseshoes, volleyball. *Fee:* massage, game room. **Guest Services:** valet and coin laundry, wireless Internet. **Business Services:** PC (fee). **Cards:** AX, DC, DS, MC, VI.

ASK CALL S D / SOME UNITS

RIU PARADISE ISLAND Book great rates at AAA.com Phone: (242)363-3500 21

Resort Hotel
$266-$460 All Year

Address: Casino Dr **Location:** Oceanfront. Reached by toll bridge from Nassau. **Facility:** Well-suited for families, the expansive property boasts multiple recreation opportunities; units in the Reef building have been recently renovated. Meets AAA guest room security requirements. 379 one-bedroom standard units. 15 stories, interior corridors. *Bath:* combo or shower only. **Parking:** on-site. **Terms:** 3 night minimum stay, 3 day cancellation notice-fee imposed. **Amenities:** safes, honor bars, irons, hair dryers. **Pool(s):** outdoor. **Leisure Activities:** saunas, whirlpools, lifeguard on duty, beach access, lighted tennis court, recreation programs, exercise room, spa, volleyball. *Fee:* scuba diving, snorkeling. **Guest Services:** valet laundry, wireless Internet. **Business Services:** conference facilities, PC (fee). **Cards:** AX, MC, VI.

ASK S D / SOME UNITS

WHERE TO DINE

ANTHONY'S CARIBBEAN GRILL Phone: 242/363-3152 42

Caribbean
$10-$23

Enjoy bright tropical decor, Casablanca fans and lively music playing in the background at the decidedly Caribbean grill. An array of island-inspired dishes line the menu including steaks, local fish, seafood platters, conch, baby back ribs and gourmet burgers. There's Key lime pie for dessert, and try one of the limbering potent libations. Casual dress. Entertainment. **Bar:** Full bar. **Hours:** 7:30 am-11 pm. Closed: 12/25. **Address:** Casino Dr **Location:** Across from Atlantis Paradise Island; in Paradise Village Shopping Center. **Parking:** on-site. **Cards:** AX, DS, MC, VI.

BAHAMIAN CLUB Phone: 242/363-3000 30

AAA

Steak
$30-$42

The mood is elegant and sophisticated, yet relaxed, at the upscale restaurant. Specialties include chateaubriand for two, steak and grilled seafood. Some dishes are prepared tableside. Semi-formal attire. **Bar:** Full bar. **Reservations:** required. **Hours:** 6 pm-10 pm. Closed: Tues. **Address:** Casino Dr **Location:** On Paradise Island; reached by toll bridge from Nassau; in Atlantis Paradise Island. **Parking:** valet. **Cards:** AX, DC, DS, MC, VI.

(See map and index starting on p. 334)

CAFE MARTINIQUE **Phone:** 242/363-3000 (35)

International
$38-$65

The sophisticated servers, expertly provide tableside preparation and the diners are entertained with live music throughout the night. Expect to be pampered and enjoy a wonderful selection of grilled meats and fresh local and regional seafood as well as fine International fare. Dressy casual. **Bar:** Full bar. **Reservations:** required. **Hours:** 6 pm-10 pm. Closed: Thurs. **Address:** Casino Dr **Location:** On Paradise Island; reached by toll bridge; in Atlantis Paradise Island. **Parking:** on-site and valet. **Cards:** AX, DC, DS, MC, VI.

CASA D'ANGELO **Phone:** 242/363-3000 (33)

Italian
$32-$60

A trendy, comfortably upscale atmosphere is what diners have come to expect at this pleasant spot. Creative menu selections include many freshly made pasta dishes with homemade sauces, as well as preparations of veal, lamb and fresh fish. One popular item is veal ravioli in a creamy tomato sauce. Freshly baked bread is served with a sun-dried tomato spread and roasted garlic. Semi-formal attire. **Bar:** Full bar. **Reservations:** required. **Hours:** 6 pm-11 pm. Closed: Wed & Thurs. **Address:** Casino Dr **Location:** From Nassau; reached by toll bridge from Nassau; in Atlantis Paradise Island. **Parking:** on-site (fee) and street. **Cards:** AX, DC, DS, MC, VI.

DUNE **Phone:** 242/363-2501 (38)

International
$22-$58

Developed by famed celebrity chef and restaurateur Jean Georges Vongerichten, the oceanfront restaurant takes Paradise Island dining to new heights. Herbs from an on-site garden punch up the flavor in dishes that draw on Asian and French inspiration. Well-rehearsed and attentive team service and a congenial atmosphere enhance the dining experience. Dressy casual. **Bar:** Full bar. **Reservations:** required, for dinner. **Hours:** 7 am-11, noon-3 & 6-10:30 pm. **Address:** Paradise Island **Location:** On Paradise Island; in One & Only Ocean Club. **Parking:** on-site. **Cards:** AX, DC, DS, MC, VI.

THE GREEN PARROT **Phone:** 242/363-3633 (40)

American
$9-$24

This is a casual marina bar where locals and tourists interact. Stop at the bar as you enter to pick up a menu and place your order then select a table and wait for the comfort food to arrive while you gaze upon the passing boats or watch marina life unfold. Casual dress. **Bar:** Full bar. **Hours:** 11 am-10 pm. **Address:** Hurricane Hole Marina **Location:** On Paradise Island; reached by toll bridge from Nassau; at Hurricane Hole Marina. **Parking:** on-site. **Cards:** MC, VI.

NOBU **Phone:** 242/363-3000 (34)

Asian
$18-$70

Well-known Chef Nobu Matsuhisa and actor Robert De Niro join forces to create a sleek, modern and hip dining venue. Combining the flavors and techniques of Japanese cuisine with South American Peruvian ingredients, the menu features such favorites as baby abalone, arctic char and halibut cheeks with wasabi pepper sauce. Semi-formal attire. **Bar:** Full bar. **Reservations:** required. **Hours:** 6 pm-10 pm. **Address:** Casino Dr **Location:** On Paradise Island; reached by toll bridge from Nassau; in Atlantis Paradise Island. **Parking:** valet. **Cards:** AX, DC, DS, MC, VI.

SEAFIRE STEAKHOUSE **Phone:** 242/363-3000 (31)

Steak
$32-$54

A popular dining spot for boaters moored at the Atlantis Marina. This bustling hotspot is trendy and hip. Diners enjoy the menu of fine wines and huge cuts of fresh prime beef as well as fresh seafood specialties. Dressy casual. **Bar:** Full bar. **Reservations:** required. **Hours:** 6 pm-10 pm. **Address:** Casino Dr **Location:** On Paradise Island; reached by toll bridge; at Marina Village; in Atlantis Paradise Island. **Parking:** valet. **Cards:** AX, DC, DS, MC, VI.

BARBADOS

This index helps you "spot" where approved lodgings and restaurants are located on the corresponding detailed maps. Lodging daily rate range is for comparison only and show the property's high season. Restaurant rate range is a combination of lunch and/or dinner. Turn to the listing page for more detailed rate information and consult display ads for special promotions.

SHERMANS (ST. LUCY PARISH)

Map Page	OA	Lodging	Diamond Rated	High Season	Page
1 / p. 349	AAA	**Little Good Harbour**	◆◆◆	$237-$895 SAVE	366

SPEIGHTSTOWN (ST. PETER PARISH)

Map Page	OA	Lodgings	Diamond Rated	High Season	Page
3 / p. 349	AAA	**Almond Beach Village**	◆◆◆	$429-$1150 SAVE	367
4 / p. 349	AAA	**Cobblers Cove**	◆◆◆	$440-$2500 SAVE	367

Map Page	OA	Restaurant	Diamond Rated	Cuisine	Meal Range	Page
1 / p. 349		Mango's by the Sea	◆◆◆	International	$25-$50	368

THE GARDEN (ST. JAMES PARISH)

Map Page	OA	Lodging	Diamond Rated	High Season	Page
10 / p. 349	AAA	**Cove Spring**	◆◆◆	$542-$1122 SAVE	364

PORTERS (ST. JAMES PARISH)

Map Page	OA	Lodgings	Diamond Rated	High Season	Page
12 / p. 349	AAA	**Lone Star Restaurant & Hotel**	◆◆◆	$400-$850 SAVE	363
13 / p. 349	AAA	**The Fairmont Royal Pavilion**	◆◆◆◆	$740-$1336 SAVE	363
15 / p. 349	AAA	**Colony Club Hotel** - see color ad p 350	◆◆◆	$400-$1512 SAVE	362
16 / p. 349	AAA	**Coral Reef Club**	◆◆◆◆	$245-$1400 SAVE	363

Map Page	OA	Restaurant	Diamond Rated	Cuisine	Meal Range	Page
2 / p. 349	AAA	**Lone Star Restaurant**	◆◆◆	International	$24-$40	363

HOLETOWN (ST. JAMES PARISH)

Map Page	OA	Lodgings	Diamond Rated	High Season	Page
18 / p. 349	AAA	**The Sandpiper**	◆◆◆	$385-$1080 SAVE	359
20 / p. 349	AAA	**Settlers Beach Villa Hotel**	◆◆◆	$134-$1230 SAVE	360
21 / p. 349	AAA	**MangoBay**	◆◆◆	$385-$690 SAVE	359
23 / p. 349	AAA	**Almond Beach Club & Spa**	◆◆	$730-$1325 SAVE	359
24 / p. 349	AAA	**Sandy Lane Hotel** - see color ad p 361	◆◆◆◆◆	$950-$4900 SAVE	360

Map Page	OA	Restaurants	Diamond Rated	Cuisine	Meal Range	Page
3 / p. 349		The Mews Restaurant	◆◆	International	$21-$38	360
4 / p. 349		Olives Bar & Bistro	◆◆	Mediterranean	$13-$33	360
5 / p. 349		The Tides Restaurant	◆◆◆	International	$13-$35	360
6 / p. 349		The Sandpiper Dining Room	◆◆◆	International	$35-$45	360
7 / p. 349		Spago Restaurant & Bar	◆◆	Italian	$14-$28	360

WESTMORELAND (ST. JAMES PARISH)

Map Page	OA	Lodging	Diamond Rated	High Season	Page
26 / p. 349	AAA	**Royal Westmoreland**	◆◆◆	$300-$2500 SAVE	364

PAYNES BAY (ST. JAMES PARISH)

Map Page	OA	Lodgings	Diamond Rated	High Season	Page
30 / p. 349	AAA	**Treasure Beach**	◆◆◆	$325-$1860 SAVE	362

PAYNES BAY (ST. JAMES PARISH) (cont'd)

Map Page	OA	Lodgings (cont'd)	Diamond Rated	High Season	Page
31 / p. 349	AAA	**Tamarind Cove Hotel** - see color ad p 350	♦♦♦	$380-$1027 SAVE	362
32 / p. 349	AAA	**The St. James Luxury Apartment Hotel**	♦♦	$180-$865 SAVE	362
34 / p. 349	AAA	**Tropical Escape**	♦♦	$218-$290 SAVE	362

Map Page	OA	Restaurants	Diamond Rated	Cuisine	Meal Range	Page
9 / p. 349		Daphne's	♦♦♦	New Italian	$27-$60	362
10 / p. 349	AAA	**'Al Fresco' At Treasure Beach**	♦♦♦	International	$15-$50	362

APPLEBY (ST. JAMES PARISH)

Map Page	OA	Lodging	Diamond Rated	High Season	Page
38 / p. 349	AAA	**Crystal Cove Hotel** - see color ad p 350	♦♦♦	$386-$1197 SAVE	359

PROSPECT (ST. JAMES PARISH)

Map Page	OA	Lodging	Diamond Rated	High Season	Page
40 / p. 349	AAA	**Escape Hotel & Spa by Virgin Holidays**	♦♦♦	$377-$507 SAVE	363

Map Page	OA	Restaurants	Diamond Rated	Cuisine	Meal Range	Page
12 / p. 349		Calabaza Restaurant	♦♦♦	International	$65-$78	363
13 / p. 349	AAA	**Il Tempio Restaurant & Bar**	♦♦	Italian	$16-$48	364

BRIDGETOWN (ST. MICHAEL PARISH)

Map Page	OA	Lodging	Diamond Rated	High Season	Page
44 / p. 349	AAA	**Hilton Barbados** - see color ad opposite title page	♦♦♦♦	$379-$859 SAVE	366

Map Page	OA	Restaurants	Diamond Rated	Cuisine	Meal Range	Page
19 / p. 349	AAA	**Brown Sugar Restaurant**	♦♦	Caribbean	$5-$35	366
15 / p. 349		Careenage Grille	♦♦♦	Steak & Seafood	$27-$42	366

BATHSHEBA (ST. JOSEPH PARISH)

Map Page	OA	Lodging	Diamond Rated	High Season	Page
48 / p. 349	AAA	**The New Edgewater Hotel**	♦♦	$116-$212 SAVE	365

ST. PHILIP PARISH

Map Page	OA	Lodging	Diamond Rated	High Season	Page
52 / p. 349	AAA	**The Crane Resort & Residences**	♦♦♦	$150-$850 SAVE	368

Map Page	OA	Restaurant	Diamond Rated	Cuisine	Meal Range	Page
42 / p. 349		Zen	♦♦♦	Japanese	$26-$45	368

HASTINGS (CHRIST CHURCH PARISH)

Map Page	OA	Lodgings	Diamond Rated	High Season	Page
55 / p. 349	AAA	**The Savannah Barbados**	♦♦♦	$265-$660 SAVE	351
56 / p. 349	AAA	**Amaryllis Beach Resort**	♦♦	$178-$663 SAVE	351
57 / p. 349	AAA	**Hotel PomMarine**	♦♦	$97-$170 SAVE	351
58 / p. 349	AAA	**Pirate's Inn**	♦	$90-$120 SAVE	351
60 / p. 349	AAA	**Allamanda Beach Hotel**	♦♦	$145-$265 SAVE	351

Map Page	OA	Restaurants	Diamond Rated	Cuisine	Meal Range	Page
16 / p. 349		Aqua Restaurant & Lounge	♦♦♦	International	$28-$40	351
17 / p. 349		Bistro Monet	♦♦	International	$21-$44	352
18 / p. 349		Opa! Greek Restaurant & Bar	♦♦	Greek	$14-$32	352

WORTHING (CHRIST CHURCH PARISH)

Map Page	OA	Lodgings	Diamond Rated	High Season	Page
64 / p. 349	AAA	**Accra Beach Hotel & Resort** - see color ad p 357	◆◆◆	$185-$404 SAVE	356
66 / p. 349	AAA	**Blue Orchids Beach Hotel**	◆◆	$187-$246 SAVE	356
67 / p. 349	AAA	**Coral Mist Beach Hotel**	◆◆	$112-$290 SAVE	356
70 / p. 349	AAA	**Melrose Beach Apartments**	◆	$80-$120 SAVE	357
71 / p. 349	AAA	**Sandy Bay Beach Club**	◆◆	$170-$406 SAVE	357
72 / p. 349	AAA	**Rockley Plumtree Club**	◆◆	$100-$240 SAVE	357
73 / p. 349	AAA	**South Beach Resort and Vacation Club**	◆◆◆	$170-$304 SAVE	358

Map Page	OA	Restaurants	Diamond Rated	Cuisine	Meal Range	Page
20 / p. 349		Champers	◆◆◆	International	$16-$43	358
21 / p. 349		Lucky Horseshoe	◆	International	$9-$24	358
22 / p. 349		Bert's	◆◆	International	$10-$28	358
24 / p. 349	AAA	**Apsara & Tamnak Thai Restaurant**	◆◆◆	Indian	$15-$35	358
25 / p. 349	AAA	**Bubba's Sports Bar & Restaurant**	◆	American	$9-$33	358

ST. LAWRENCE (CHRIST CHURCH PARISH)

Map Page	OA	Lodgings	Diamond Rated	High Season	Page
75 / p. 349	AAA	**Yellow Bird Hotel**	◆	$100-$200 SAVE	354
76 / p. 349	AAA	**South Gap Hotel**	◆◆	$90-$160 SAVE	354
78 / p. 349	AAA	**Divi Southwinds Resort**	◆◆	$229-$469 SAVE	354
79 / p. 349	AAA	**Rostrevor Hotel**	◆	$57-$192 SAVE	354
80 / p. 349	AAA	**Southern Palms Beach Club**	◆◆	$145-$430 SAVE	354
81 / p. 349	AAA	**Escape at the Gap**	◆◆	$376-$400 SAVE	354
82 / p. 349	AAA	**Dover Beach Apartment Hotel**	◆◆	$145-$200 SAVE	354

Map Page	OA	Restaurants	Diamond Rated	Cuisine	Meal Range	Page
26 / p. 349		Bellini's Trattoria	◆◆◆	Italian	$13-$35	355
27 / p. 349		Flying Fish Restaurant and Bar	◆◆	Seafood	$13-$30	355
28 / p. 349	AAA	**The Restaurant at Southsea** - see color ad p 355	◆◆◆◆	International	$30-$44	356
29 / p. 349		Cafe Sol	◆	Mexican	$9-$20	355
30 / p. 349		David's Place by the Sea	◆◆	International	$23-$43	355
31 / p. 349		Harlequin Restaurant	◆◆	International	$20-$35	355
32 / p. 349		Sweet Potatoes	◆	Caribbean	$14-$40	356
33 / p. 349		Josef's	◆◆◆	International	$31-$48	356
34 / p. 349		Aqua Pisces Restaurant	◆	Seafood	$17-$29	355

MAXWELL (CHRIST CHURCH PARISH)

Map Page	OA	Lodgings	Diamond Rated	High Season	Page
86 / p. 349	AAA	**Bougainvillea Beach Resort** - see color ad p 352	◆◆◆	$167-$644 SAVE	353
88 / p. 349	AAA	**Sea Breeze Beach Hotel**	◆◆	Rates not provided SAVE	353
89 / p. 349	AAA	**Barbados Beach Club**	◆◆	$320-$450 SAVE	352

Map Page	OA	Restaurant	Diamond Rated	Cuisine	Meal Range	Page
36 / p. 349		Water's Edge Restaurant	◆◆◆	International	$32-$70	353

ENTERPRISE (CHRIST CHURCH PARISH)

Map Page	OA	Lodging	Diamond Rated	High Season	Page
92 / p. 349	AAA	**Little Arches Hotel**	3 diamonds	$200-$552 SAVE	351

SILVER SANDS (CHRIST CHURCH PARISH)

Map Page	OA	Lodging	Diamond Rated	High Season	Page
95 / p. 349	AAA	**Silver Point Hotel**	3 diamonds	$210-$420 SAVE	356

INCH MARLOWE (CHRIST CHURCH PARISH)

Map Page	OA	Lodging	Diamond Rated	High Season	Page
98 / p. 349	AAA	**Peach and Quiet Inn**	2 diamonds	$89-$109 SAVE	352

OISTINS (CHRIST CHURCH PARISH)

Map Page	OA	Lodging	Diamond Rated	High Season	Page
99 / p. 349	AAA	**Cumber's Tropical Apartment Complex**	1 diamond	$90-$130 SAVE	353

DERRICKS (ST. JAMES PARISH)

Map Page	OA	Restaurant	Diamond Rated	Cuisine	Meal Range	Page
14 / p. 349		The Cliff	4 diamonds	International	$94-$104	359

DOVER (CHRIST CHURCH PARISH)

Map Page	OA	Lodging	Diamond Rated	High Season	Page
84 / p. 349	AAA	**Turtle Beach Resort** - see color ad p 350	3 diamonds	$440-$965 SAVE	350

Map Page	OA	Restaurant	Diamond Rated	Cuisine	Meal Range	Page
38 / p. 349		Luigi's "The" Italian Restaurant	2 diamonds	Italian	$18-$35	350

SEE AAA GEM ATTRACTIONS

Barbados
Lodging & Dining

0 Miles 4.1
0 Kilometers 6.6

NORTH POINT
ST. LUCY PARISH
HARRISON POINT
CUCKOLD POINT
Atlantic Ocean
Fairfield
Shermans
Coleton
Portland
ST. ANDREW PARISH
Greenland
St. Andrew's Church
Speightstown
Barbados Wildlife Reserve, Grenade Hall Forest and Signal Station
ST. PETER PARISH
Chalky Mount
CHALKY MT.
EAST COAST RD
ST. JOSEPH PARISH
Westmoreland
Bathsheba
ST. JOHN PARISH
MT. HILLABY
The Garden
Porters
Welchman Hall
Holetown
Newcastle
Consett Bay
Blackmans
Paynes Bay
Derricks
ST. THOMAS PARISH
Appleby
CULPEPPER IS.
ST. JAMES PARISH
Prospect
Todds
RAGGED POINT
Three Houses
Warrens
Locust Hall
Lazaretto
ADAMS BARROW CUMMINS
GUN HILL
ST. GEORGE PARISH
Sandford
Bottom Bay
Marchfield
Long Bay
ST. MICHAEL PARISH
BRIDGETOWN
Atlantis Submarine Expedition
Carlisle Bay
Highgate
Bannatyne
ST. PHILIP PARISH
HWY.
Balls
Hastings
Dover
Worthing
Maxwell
Oistins
Chancery Lane
Grantley Adams International Airport
CHRIST CHURCH PARISH
Inch Marlowe
St. Lawrence
Enterprise
Silver Sands

1504-R

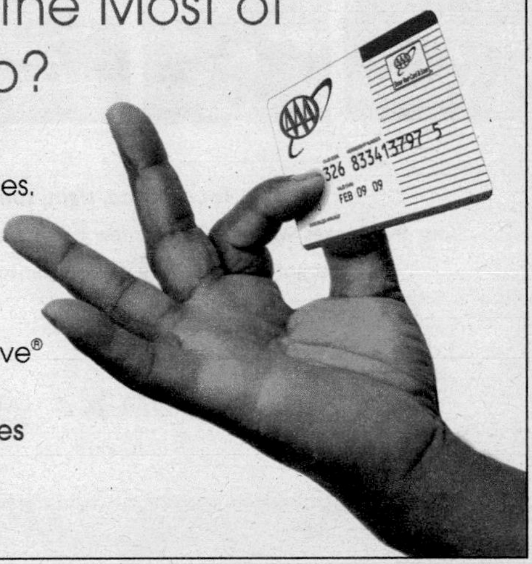

Christ Church Parish

DOVER (See map and index starting on p. 349)

— WHERE TO STAY —

TURTLE BEACH RESORT *Book great rates at AAA.com* **Phone:** (246)428-7131 84

AAA SAVE

Resort Hotel

$440-$965 All Year

Address: Dover, Christ Church **Location:** Oceanfront. South end of St. Lawrence Gap. **Facility:** Premier resort with a multi-tiered lobby area surrounded by restaurants and gift shops; varying room types cater to everyone's needs. Meets AAA guest room security requirements. 164 units. 146 one-bedroom standard units. 18 one-bedroom suites. 4 stories, exterior corridors. **Parking:** on-site. **Terms:** 5 night minimum stay - seasonal, 21 day cancellation notice-fee imposed. **Amenities:** high-speed Internet (fee), voice mail, safes, irons, hair dryers. **Dining:** 3 restaurants, entertainment. **Pool(s):** 2 outdoor. **Leisure Activities:** whirlpool, sailboats, windsurfing, 2 lighted tennis courts, recreation programs, playground, exercise room, kids club, volleyball. *Fee:* massage. **Guest Services:** valet laundry, wireless Internet. **Business Services:** meeting rooms, PC (fee). **Cards:** AX, MC, VI. *(See color ad below)*

D / SOME UNITS

— WHERE TO DINE —

LUIGI'S "THE" ITALIAN RESTAURANT **Phone:** 246/428-9218 38

Italian

$18-$35

In business at the same location for more than 25 years, this family-owned-and-operated restaurant serves authentic Italy-inspired cuisine in a large house setting with a wrap-around porch. The husband and wife team circulates the dining room to chat with guests. The extensive menu includes seven soups, six salads, personal-size pizzas and more than two dozen pasta dishes. Silky panna cotta is a tempting way to conclude the meal. Casual dress. **Bar:** Full bar. **Reservations:** suggested. **Hours:** 6:30 pm-9:45 pm. Closed: Sun. **Address:** Dover Woods **Location:** South end of St. Lawrence Gap, follow signs. **Parking:** on-site. **Cards:** MC, VI.

ENTERPRISE (See map and index starting on p. 349)

WHERE TO STAY

LITTLE ARCHES HOTEL *Book great rates at AAA.com* **Phone:** (246)420-4689 92

AAA SAVE

Country Inn
$200-$552 All Year

Address: Enterprise Beach Rd **Location:** Oceanfront. Just s of Oistins; follow signs; opposite Enterprise Beach. **Facility:** Originally a mansion-villa, this stylish Mediterranean property with Caribbean influences boasts a range of individually decorated room categories and floor plans. 10 units. 7 one-bedroom standard units, some with whirlpools. 3 one-bedroom suites, some with efficiencies or kitchens. 3 stories (no elevator), exterior corridors. *Bath:* shower only. **Parking:** on-site. **Terms:** office hours 7 am-10 pm, 3-7 night minimum stay - seasonal, age restrictions may apply, 30 day cancellation notice-fee imposed. **Amenities:** voice mail, safes, irons, hair dryers. *Some:* DVD players, CD players. **Pool(s):** outdoor. **Leisure Activities:** golf privileges, tamden bicycles, bicycles. **Guest Services:** valet laundry, wireless Internet. **Business Services:** PC. **Cards:** MC, VI.

D / SOME UNITS

HASTINGS (See map and index starting on p. 349)

WHERE TO STAY

ALLAMANDA BEACH HOTEL **Phone:** (246)438-1000 60

AAA SAVE

Hotel
$145-$265 All Year

Address: Main Rd **Location:** Oceanfront. Center. **Facility:** 50 units. 49 one-bedroom standard units with efficiencies. 1 one-bedroom suite with kitchen. 4 stories (no elevator), exterior corridors. *Bath:* shower only. **Parking:** on-site. **Terms:** office hours 7 am-11 pm, check-in 4 pm, 14 day cancellation notice, 7 day in summer-fee imposed. **Amenities:** voice mail, irons, hair dryers. *Fee:* high-speed Internet, safes. **Pool(s):** outdoor. **Leisure Activities:** guest privileges at sister property Ameryllis. **Guest Services:** coin laundry, area transportation-Amaryllis. **Business Services:** PC (fee). **Cards:** AX, MC, VI.

D

AMARYLLIS BEACH RESORT **Phone:** 246/438-8000 56

AAA SAVE

Hotel
$178-$663 All Year

Address: Garrison Historic Area **Location:** Oceanfront. 9.5 mi (15.2 km) w of international airport; 1.9 mi (3 km) s of downtown Bridgetown. **Facility:** Designated smoking area. 145 units. 107 one-bedroom standard units. 36 one- and 2 two-bedroom suites with efficiencies. 3-4 stories, interior/exterior corridors. *Bath:* combo or shower only. **Parking:** on-site. **Terms:** check-in 4 pm, 3 day cancellation notice. **Amenities:** voice mail, irons, hair dryers. *Fee:* high-speed Internet, safes. *Some:* DVD players. **Dining:** 3 restaurants, entertainment. **Pool(s):** 2 outdoor. **Leisure Activities:** whirlpool, snorkeling, kayaks, recreation programs in winter, billiards, exercise room, volleyball, game room. *Fee:* massage. **Guest Services:** valet and coin laundry, beauty salon. **Business Services:** conference facilities, business center. **Cards:** AX, MC, VI.

D / SOME UNITS VCR

HOTEL POMMARINE **Phone:** 246/228-0900 57

AAA SAVE

Hotel
$97-$170 All Year

Address: Marine Gardens **Location:** At Hospitality Institute; just e of Hastings Main Rd. **Facility:** Designated smoking area. 21 units. 20 one-bedroom standard units. 1 one-bedroom suite with kitchen. 3 stories, exterior corridors. **Parking:** on-site. **Amenities:** high-speed Internet, safes, irons. **Dining:** 2 restaurants. **Pool(s):** outdoor. **Leisure Activities:** *Fee:* lighted tennis court. **Guest Services:** valet laundry, wireless Internet. **Business Services:** meeting rooms, business center. **Cards:** AX, MC, VI.

D

PIRATE'S INN *Book great rates at AAA.com* **Phone:** (246)426-6273 58

AAA SAVE

Motel
$90-$120 All Year

Address: Browne's Gap **Location:** Just w of Hastings Main Rd; at Browne's Gap, just e of Hastings Plaza. **Facility:** 22 units. 21 one-bedroom standard units with efficiencies. 1 one-bedroom suite with kitchen. 2 stories (no elevator), exterior corridors. *Bath:* shower only. **Parking:** on-site. **Terms:** office hours 8 am-4:30 pm, cancellation fee imposed. **Amenities:** safes. **Pool(s):** outdoor. **Guest Services:** valet laundry, wireless Internet. **Business Services:** PC (fee). **Cards:** MC, VI.

D / SOME UNITS

THE SAVANNAH BARBADOS *Book great rates at AAA.com* **Phone:** (246)228-3800 55

AAA SAVE

Hotel
$265-$660 All Year

Address: Hastings Main Rd **Location:** Oceanfront. 11.3 mi (18.1 km) w of international airport; 1.8 mi (2.9 km) s of downtown Bridgetown. **Facility:** Meets AAA guest room security requirements. Designated smoking area. 98 units. 89 one-bedroom standard units. 9 one-bedroom suites. 4 stories, exterior corridors. **Parking:** on-site. **Terms:** 7 day cancellation notice-fee imposed. **Amenities:** video library, high-speed Internet (fee), voice mail, safes, irons, hair dryers. *Some:* DVD players, CD players, honor bars. **Dining:** 2 restaurants, entertainment. **Pool(s):** 2 outdoor. **Leisure Activities:** putting green, tennis privileges, spa. **Guest Services:** valet laundry, area transportation-Rockley Beach, wireless Internet. **Business Services:** conference facilities, business center. **Cards:** AX, MC, VI.

D / SOME UNITS VCR

WHERE TO DINE

AQUA RESTAURANT & LOUNGE **Phone:** 246/420-2995 16

International
$28-$40

Oceanfront. One of the newest restaurants on the Barbados dining scene. French and Asian influenced cuisines with additional inspiration from around the world help elevate and push the cuisine into a category all its own. Attentive servers and a lounge area add to the experience. Dressy casual. **Bar:** Full bar. **Reservations:** suggested. **Hours:** noon-2:30 & 6:30-10:30 pm. Closed: 1/1, 12/25; also Easter Monday & for lunch on public holidays. **Address:** Hastings Main Rd **Location:** Center; oceanfront; in Keswick Centre. **Parking:** on-site. **Cards:** AX, MC, VI.

(See map and index starting on p. 349)

BISTRO MONET — Phone: 246/435-9389 (17)

International
$21-$44

In a cottage-style building with French cafe decor, the bistro gives diners the choice of indoor or outdoor seating. The menu offers a lot of variety, with French, Continental, West Indies and American fare. Menu items include local fish cakes, Greek salad, escargot, seafood gumbo and create-your-own pasta dishes. A favorite option is shrimp and lobster coquille. Casual dress. **Bar:** Full bar. **Reservations:** suggested. **Hours:** 11 am-10 pm, Sat from 6 pm. Closed: 1/1, 12/24, 12/25; also Sun & Barbados public holidays. **Address:** Hastings Main Rd **Location:** 2.6 mi (4.1 km) s of Bridgetown; on South Coast. **Parking:** on-site. **Cards:** MC, VI.

OPA! GREEK RESTAURANT & BAR — Phone: 246/435-1234 (18)

Greek
$14-$32

This place is the only Greek restaurant in Barbados owned and operated by an American-Greek family. The spacious dining room is comfortable and airy. The menu lists all the expected Greek dishes, including moussaka, as well as some non-Greek seafood and a few local Bajan dishes. Baklava made with honey, phyllo dough and nuts is an ultrasweet convection. Casual dress. **Bar:** Full bar. **Reservations:** suggested. **Hours:** 11:30 am-10 pm, Sat & Sun from 6 pm. Closed: 1/1, 12/24, 12/25; also Kadooment Day & for lunch on Bajan public holidays. **Address:** Shak Shak Complex, Hastings Rd **Location:** 2.3 mi (3.7 km) s of downtown Bridgetown; 10.4 mi (16.7 km) w of international airport. **Parking:** on-site. **Cards:** AX, DS, MC, VI.

INCH MARLOWE (See map and index starting on p. 349)

WHERE TO STAY

PEACH AND QUIET INN — **Phone:** 246/428-5682 (98)

AAA SAVE

Country Inn
$89-$109 All Year

Address: Inch Marlowe **Location:** Oceanfront. 4 mi (6.4 km) sw of airport; next to Surfer's Point. **Facility:** Designated smoking area. 22 one-bedroom standard units. 2 stories (no elevator), exterior corridors. *Bath:* shower only. **Parking:** on-site. **Terms:** age restrictions may apply, 30 day cancellation notice. **Amenities:** safes, hair dryers. **Pool(s):** outdoor. **Leisure Activities:** snorkeling. *Fee:* massage. **Guest Services:** valet laundry. **Cards:** DS, MC, VI.

MAXWELL (See map and index starting on p. 349)

WHERE TO STAY

BARBADOS BEACH CLUB *Book great rates at AAA.com* — **Phone:** (246)428-9900 (89)

AAA SAVE

Hotel
$320-$450 All Year

Address: Maxwell Coast Rd **Location:** Oceanfront. 8.5 mi (13.6 km) w of international airport; 1.4 mi (2.2 km) nw of Oistins. **Facility:** Designated smoking area. 112 units. 110 one-bedroom standard units. 2 one-bedroom suites. 3-6 stories, interior corridors. **Parking:** on-site. **Terms:** 14 day cancellation notice-fee imposed. **Amenities:** voice mail, safes (fee), hair dryers. **Dining:** 3 restaurants, entertainment. **Pool(s):** outdoor. **Leisure Activities:** sailboats, snorkeling, kayaks, miniature golf, tennis court, billiards, exercise room, volleyball. *Fee:* windsurfing. **Guest Services:** valet laundry, wireless Internet. **Business Services:** meeting rooms, PC (fee). **Cards:** AX, MC, VI.

▼ See AAA listing p 353 ▼

(See map and index starting on p. 349)

BOUGAINVILLEA BEACH RESORT Book great rates at AAA.com **Phone:** (246)418-0990 86

Resort Hotel

$167-$644 All Year

Address: Maxwell Coast Rd, Christ Church **Location:** Oceanfront. 8.6 mi (13.7 km) w of international airport; 1.5 mi (2.4 km) nw of Oistins. **Facility:** The small scale-resort has a free-form cascading pool and bright, colorful guest room decor that matches the tropical ambience. 138 units. 64 one-bedroom standard units with efficiencies. 68 one- and 6 two-bedroom suites with kitchens. 4 stories (no elevator), exterior corridors. *Bath:* combo or shower only. **Parking:** on-site. **Terms:** check-in 4 pm, 4-7 night minimum stay - seasonal, 28 day cancellation notice-fee imposed. **Amenities:** video library (fee), voice mail, safes, irons, hair dryers. **Dining:** 2 restaurants, entertainment. **Pool(s):** 3 outdoor. **Leisure Activities:** canoeing, snorkeling, kayaks, lighted tennis court, recreation programs, shuffleboard, volleyball, game room. *Fee:* sailboats, windsurfing, waterskiing, kite surfing, banana boat, kids club, massage. **Guest Services:** valet laundry, beauty salon, wireless Internet. **Business Services:** meeting rooms, PC (fee). **Cards:** MC, VI. *(See color ad p 352)*

SEA BREEZE BEACH HOTEL Book great rates at AAA.com **Phone:** 246/428-2825 88

Resort Hotel

Rates not provided

Address: Maxwell Coast Rd **Location:** Oceanfront. Center. **Facility:** Some units recently received marked upgrades while the remaining units are still comfortable with tasteful decor. 78 units. 76 one-bedroom standard units, some with efficiencies. 2 two-bedroom suites with kitchens. 3 stories (no elevator), exterior corridors. **Parking:** on-site. **Amenities:** voice mail, safes (fee), hair dryers. **Dining:** 2 restaurants, entertainment. **Pool(s):** 2 outdoor. **Leisure Activities:** whirlpools, paddleboats, sailboats, windsurfing, snorkeling, kayaks, recreation programs, exercise room, sports court, basketball, volleyball. *Fee:* waterskiing, personal watercraft, massage. **Guest Services:** coin laundry. **Business Services:** PC (fee).

WHERE TO DINE

WATER'S EDGE RESTAURANT **Phone:** 246/428-2592 36

International

$32-$70

Diners enjoy the romantic open-air setting and the peaceful sounds of the sea. The menu features a fine mix of international fare prepared with an island flair. Menu highlights include grilled mahi mahi, sauteed Caribbean shrimp and red snapper fillets, as well as a good mix of beef, lamb, poultry and pasta offerings. Desserts are a treat, and all are homemade and decadent. Hot bread pudding served with rum custard is an island favorite. Casual dress. **Bar:** Full bar. **Reservations:** suggested. **Hours:** 6:30 pm-9:30 pm. Closed: Fri. **Address:** Maxwell Coast Rd **Location:** 8.6 mi (13.7 km) w of international airport; 1.5 mi (2.4 km) nw of Oistins. **Parking:** on-site. **Cards:** MC, VI.

OISTINS (See map and index starting on p. 349)

WHERE TO STAY

CUMBER'S TROPICAL APARTMENT COMPLEX **Phone:** 246/418-9957 99

Motel

$90-$130 All Year

Address: Oistins Main Rd **Location:** Just s of town center; in Pegwell Gardens. **Facility:** 8 units. 4 one- and 4 two-bedroom suites with kitchens. 3 stories (no elevator), exterior corridors. *Bath:* shower only. **Parking:** on-site. **Terms:** office hours 9 am-5 pm. **Amenities:** irons, hair dryers. **Guest Services:** complimentary laundry. **Cards:** MC, VI.

ST. LAWRENCE (See map and index starting on p. 349)

WHERE TO STAY

DIVI SOUTHWINDS RESORT Book great rates at AAA.com **Phone:** (246)428-7181 78

AAA SAVE

Resort Hotel

$229-$469 All Year

Address: St. Lawrence Main Rd **Location:** Center. **Facility:** Extensive landscaped grounds. Spacious one- and two-bedroom units with garden, pool or ocean view. Short walk to beach from main building, 34 units on the beach. Meets AAA guest room security requirements. 133 units. 121 one- and 12 two-bedroom suites with kitchens, some with whirlpools. 3-5 stories, exterior corridors. *Bath:* combo or shower only. **Parking:** on-site. **Terms:** check-in 4 pm, 3 night minimum stay, cancellation fee imposed. **Amenities:** DVD players, voice mail, safes, irons, hair dryers. **Dining:** 2 restaurants, entertainment. **Pool(s):** 4 outdoor. **Leisure Activities:** snorkeling, 2 lighted tennis courts, recreation programs, playground, exercise room, basketball, shuffleboard, volleyball, game room. *Fee:* miniature golf, massage. **Guest Services:** coin laundry, wireless Internet. **Business Services:** meeting rooms, PC (fee). **Cards:** AX, MC, VI.

DOVER BEACH APARTMENT HOTEL Book great rates at AAA.com **Phone:** (246)428-8076 82

AAA SAVE

Motel

$145-$200 12/1-4/15
$120-$175 4/16-11/30

Address: St. Lawrence Gap Rd **Location:** Oceanfront. South end of St. Lawrence Gap. **Facility:** 59 units. 49 one-bedroom standard units, some with efficiencies. 10 one-bedroom suites with efficiencies. 3 stories (no elevator), interior/exterior corridors. **Parking:** on-site. **Terms:** office hours 7 am-10 pm, check-in 4 pm, 21 day cancellation notice-fee imposed. **Amenities:** safes (fee). **Pool(s):** outdoor. **Guest Services:** valet laundry, wireless Internet. **Business Services:** PC (fee). **Cards:** AX, MC, VI.

/ SOME UNITS

ESCAPE AT THE GAP Book great rates at AAA.com **Phone:** (246)428-6131 81

AAA SAVE

Resort Hotel

$376-$400 All Year

Address: St. Lawrence Gap Rd **Location:** Oceanfront. Center. **Facility:** Guest units have a simple decor with up-to-date amenities. Bathrooms are modest in size with basic enhancements. 66 units. 49 one-bedroom standard units, some with efficiencies. 13 one- and 4 two-bedroom suites, some with efficiencies and/or whirlpools. 3 stories (no elevator), interior/exterior corridors. *Bath:* combo or shower only. **Parking:** on-site. **Terms:** 3 night minimum stay. **Amenities:** voice mail, safes, hair dryers. *Some:* irons. **Dining:** 2 restaurants, entertainment. **Pool(s):** 2 outdoor. **Leisure Activities:** sailboats, windsurfing, snorkeling, kayaks, recreation programs, playground, exercise room, volleyball. *Fee:* kids club. **Guest Services:** valet and coin laundry. **Business Services:** PC (fee). **Cards:** MC, VI.

/ SOME UNITS

ROSTREVOR HOTEL Book great rates at AAA.com **Phone:** (246)428-9298 79

AAA SAVE

Hotel

$57-$192 All Year

Address: St. Lawrence Gap Rd **Location:** Oceanfront. Center. **Facility:** 61 units. 45 one-bedroom standard units with efficiencies. 8 one- and 8 two-bedroom suites with efficiencies. 3-4 stories (no elevator), exterior corridors. *Bath:* shower only. **Parking:** on-site. **Terms:** 14 day cancellation notice, 21 day in winter-fee imposed. **Amenities:** voice mail, safes (fee), irons. *Some:* hair dryers. **Pool(s):** outdoor. **Leisure Activities:** shuffleboard. **Guest Services:** valet laundry, wireless Internet. **Business Services:** PC. **Cards:** MC, VI.

/ SOME UNITS

SOUTHERN PALMS BEACH CLUB Book great rates at AAA.com **Phone:** (246)428-7171 80

AAA SAVE

Hotel

$145-$430 All Year

Address: St. Lawrence Gap Rd **Location:** Oceanfront. Center. **Facility:** 92 units. 72 one-bedroom standard units, some with efficiencies. 20 one-bedroom suites with efficiencies. 1-3 stories (no elevator), exterior corridors. *Bath:* combo or shower only. **Parking:** on-site. **Amenities:** high-speed Internet, voice mail, safes (fee), hair dryers. *Some:* irons. **Dining:** entertainment. **Pool(s):** 2 outdoor. **Leisure Activities:** beach access, windsurfing, snorkeling, miniature golf, limited exercise equipment, shuffleboard, volleyball. *Fee:* 2 lighted tennis courts, massage. **Guest Services:** valet and coin laundry, beauty salon, wireless Internet. **Business Services:** meeting rooms, PC. **Cards:** MC, VI.

SOUTH GAP HOTEL **Phone:** 246/420-7597 76

AAA SAVE

Hotel

$90-$160 All Year

Address: St. Lawrence Gap Rd **Location:** Oceanfront. At St. Lawrence Gap; center. **Facility:** 34 units. 28 one-bedroom standard units with efficiencies. 6 one-bedroom suites with kitchens. 3 stories (no elevator), interior/exterior corridors. **Parking:** on-site. **Terms:** 14 day cancellation notice. **Amenities:** voice mail, irons, hair dryers. *Some:* safes (fee). **Pool(s):** outdoor. **Guest Services:** valet laundry, wireless Internet. **Cards:** AX, MC, VI.

YELLOW BIRD HOTEL Book great rates at AAA.com **Phone:** (246)418-8444 75

AAA SAVE

Motel

$100-$200 All Year

Address: St. Lawrence Gap Rd **Location:** At entrance of St. Lawrence Gap; center. **Facility:** 13 units. 12 one-bedroom standard units with efficiencies. 1 two-bedroom suite with kitchen and whirlpool. 4 stories (no elevator), exterior corridors. **Parking:** on-site. **Amenities:** high-speed Internet, voice mail, irons, hair dryers. **Pool(s):** outdoor. **Guest Services:** valet laundry, wireless Internet. **Cards:** AX, MC, VI.

(See map and index starting on p. 349)

WHERE TO DINE

AQUA PISCES RESTAURANT Phone: 246/420-8353 (34)

Seafood
$17-$29

The owner-operated seafood restaurant is on the terrace of a Bajan-style chattel house and plays background reggae music. Catches of local fish, including barracuda and flying fish, are prepared in varied ways and served with assorted accompaniments. Tempting meal toppers include Bajan rum cake and bread pudding. Casual dress. **Bar:** Full bar. **Reservations:** accepted. **Hours:** Open 12/1-8/30 & 10/1-11/30; 6 pm-9:30 pm. Closed: 1/1, 12/25; also Good Friday & Easter Monday. **Address:** St. Lawrence Gap Rd **Location:** In St. Lawrence Gap; 7.6 mi (12.1 km) w of international airport; 4.1 mi (6.5 km) s of downtown Bridgetown. **Parking:** street. **Cards:** DC, DS, MC, VI.

BELLINI'S TRATTORIA Phone: 246/420-7587 (26)

Italian
$13-$35

This distinctly Caribbean open-air restaurant offers a wonderful setting overlooking the sea. The varied menu brings together freshly prepared pasta dishes, seafood and grilled items. Warm hospitality emanates from the personable staff. Casual dress. **Bar:** Full bar. **Reservations:** suggested. **Hours:** 6 pm-10 pm. Closed: 12/25. **Address:** St. Lawrence Gap **Location:** St. Lawrence Gap; at Little Bay Hotel. **Parking:** street. **Cards:** AX, DS, MC, VI.

CAFE SOL Phone: 246/435-9531 (29)

Mexican
$9-$20

Ole! Ole! This place is a slice of Mexico transplanted smack dab in the middle of lively St. Lawrence Gap. In the festively decorated open-air Bajan house, the familiar fare includes fajitas, burritos, tacos and enchiladas. Pitchers of sangria and designer margaritas are just a few offerings from the exciting and creative drink menu. Casual dress. **Bar:** Full bar. **Hours:** noon-11 pm, Mon from 6 pm. Closed: 12/25. **Address:** St. Lawrence Gap, Christ Church **Location:** In St. Lawrence Gap; 7.3 mi (11.7 km) w of international airport; 2.6 mi (4.1 km) s of downtown Bridgetown. **Parking:** street. **Cards:** MC, VI.

DAVID'S PLACE BY THE SEA Phone: 246/435-9755 (30)

International
$23-$43

A very popular oceanfront dining spot owned by cheerful David; well-rounded menu with everything from steak to local seafood, curry dishes, lamb, rabbit and goat is served by an attentive staff. Dressy casual. **Bar:** Full bar. **Reservations:** suggested. **Hours:** Open 12/1-7/1 & 8/1-11/30; 6 pm-10 pm. Closed: 1/1, 12/25; also Mon. **Address:** St. Lawrence Main Rd **Location:** Entrance to St. Lawrence Gap. **Parking:** on-site. **Cards:** AX, DS, MC, VI.

FLYING FISH RESTAURANT AND BAR Phone: 246/418-9772 (27)

Seafood
$13-$30

Island decor brightens the casual, open-air dining room, where patrons enjoy fresh local fish and other seafood cooked up with a Caribbean flair. The menu also lists comfort foods, such as hearty burgers and sandwiches, steaks and good old-fashioned fish and chips. Casual dress. **Bar:** Full bar. **Reservations:** suggested. **Hours:** 7:30 am-9:30 pm. **Address:** St. Lawrence Gap **Location:** At Yellow Bird Apartment Hotel. **Parking:** street. **Cards:** MC, VI.

HARLEQUIN RESTAURANT Phone: 246/420-7677 (31)

International
$20-$35

In the heart of the trendy entertainment and dining district of St. Lawrence Gap, the Baja-style chattel house presents an international menu that represents offerings from the Caribbean, Asia and the Mediterranean. Among entree choices are tuna with tropical fruit salsa, duck breast with raspberry au jus and nut-crusted salmon. Tempting desserts include pina colada cheesecake, bread and butter pudding and hot apple pie. Casual dress. **Bar:** Full bar. **Reservations:** suggested. **Hours:** 6 pm-10 pm. **Address:** St. Lawrence Gap Rd **Location:** Center St. Lawrence Gap; adjacent to Rostrevor Hotel; across from Ship's Inn. **Parking:** street. **Cards:** AX, MC, VI.

▼ *See AAA listing p 356* ▼

(See map and index starting on p. 349)

JOSEF'S — **Phone:** 246/435-8245 (33)

International
$31-$48

Enjoy a unique brand of international haute cuisine blended with elements of Asian and Caribbean influences at this romantic seaside restaurant. Dressy casual. **Bar:** Full bar. **Reservations:** suggested. **Hours:** 6:30 pm-9:30 pm. Closed: 12/25. **Address:** Waverly House **Location:** In St. Lawrence Gap; 7.5 mi (12 km) w of international airport; 4 mi (6.4 km) s of downtown Bridgetown. **Parking:** street. **Cards:** AX, MC, VI.

THE RESTAURANT AT SOUTHSEA *Menu on AAA.com* — **Phone:** 246/420-7423 (28)

International
$30-$44

Relish in the views while dining beside the sea or request a romantic setting at an outdoor table complete with linen tablecloth and candles. The owner/chef is renowned for his imaginative and tasteful creations of the finest local and worldly cuisine. Plan for an evening that will long be remembered. Dressy casual. Entertainment. **Bar:** Full bar. **Reservations:** suggested. **Hours:** Open 12/1-9/1 & 9/22-11/30; 6 pm-10 pm. Closed major holidays; also Sun 4/1-12/14. **Address:** St. Lawrence Gap **Location:** In St. Lawrence Gap; 7.3 mi (11.7 km) w of international airport; 2.6 mi (4.1 km) s of downtown Bridgetown. **Parking:** on-site and valet. **Cards:** AX, MC, VI. *(See color ad p 355)*

SWEET POTATOES — **Phone:** 246/435-9638 (32)

Caribbean
$14-$40

This down-home Bajan eatery is located in hip St. Lawrence Gap, in a converted home with veranda-style dining. There are many items to choose from, but some favorites include the vegetable stuffed flying fish and jerked pork. The large drink menu offers some very creative concoctions. Save room for the moist bread pudding with rum sauce. Dressy casual. Entertainment. **Bar:** Full bar. **Reservations:** accepted. **Hours:** 11 am-3 & 6-10:30 pm. **Address:** St. Lawrence Gap, Christ Church **Location:** In St. Lawrence Gap; 7.3 mi (11.7 km) w of international airport; 3.8 mi (4.8 km) s of downtown Bridgetown. **Parking:** on-site (fee). **Cards:** AX, DS, MC, VI.

SILVER SANDS (See map and index starting on p. 349)

WHERE TO STAY

SILVER POINT HOTEL *Book great rates at AAA.com* — **Phone:** (246)420-4416 (95)

SAVE
Hotel
$210-$420 All Year

Address: Silver Sands Rd **Location:** On south coast. **Facility:** Meets AAA guest room security requirements. 37 units. 12 one-bedroom standard units with efficiencies. 22 one- and 3 two-bedroom suites with efficiencies. 3 stories (no elevator), exterior corridors. *Bath:* shower only. **Parking:** on-site. **Terms:** office hours 8 am-11 pm, check-in 4 pm, 21 day cancellation notice. **Amenities:** video library (fee), DVD players, voice mail, safes, irons, hair dryers. **Pool(s):** 2 outdoor. **Guest Services:** valet laundry, wireless Internet. **Business Services:** PC. **Cards:** AX, MC, VI.

WORTHING (See map and index starting on p. 349)

WHERE TO STAY

ACCRA BEACH HOTEL & RESORT — **Phone:** (246)435-8920 (64)

SAVE
Hotel
$185-$404 All Year

Address: Rockley, Christ Church **Location:** Oceanfront. 7.7 mi (12.3 km) w of international airport; 2 mi (3.2 km) s of downtown. **Facility:** Designated smoking area. 224 units. 212 one-bedroom standard units. 9 one- and 3 two-bedroom suites. 4 stories, interior corridors. *Bath:* shower only. **Parking:** on-site. **Terms:** 14 day cancellation notice-fee imposed. **Amenities:** high-speed Internet, voice mail, safes, irons, hair dryers. **Dining:** entertainment. **Pool(s):** 2 outdoor. **Leisure Activities:** beach access, snorkeling, exercise room, volleyball. **Guest Services:** valet laundry, wireless Internet. **Business Services:** meeting rooms, business center. **Cards:** AX, DS, MC, VI. *(See color ad p 357)*

D / SOME UNITS

BLUE ORCHIDS BEACH HOTEL — **Phone:** (246)435-8057 (66)

SAVE
Hotel
$187-$246 12/1-4/15
$123-$188 4/16-11/30

Address: 18 Worthing **Location:** Oceanfront. Center. **Facility:** 31 units. 16 one-bedroom standard units with efficiencies. 11 one- and 4 two-bedroom suites with kitchens. 2-4 stories, exterior corridors. *Bath:* combo or shower only. **Parking:** on-site. **Terms:** 3 night minimum stay, 21 day cancellation notice-fee imposed. **Amenities:** high-speed Internet (fee), voice mail, irons, hair dryers. **Pool(s):** outdoor. **Leisure Activities:** windsurfing, snorkeling, kayaks, recreation programs, bocci, croquet, exercise room, volleyball, game room. **Guest Services:** valet laundry, wireless Internet. **Cards:** AX, MC, VI.

CORAL MIST BEACH HOTEL — **Phone:** (246)435-7712 (67)

SAVE
Hotel
$112-$290 All Year

Address: Worthing, Christ Church **Location:** Oceanfront. Center. **Facility:** 32 units. 21 one-bedroom standard units. 8 one- and 3 two-bedroom suites with kitchens, some with whirlpools. 4 stories, exterior corridors. *Bath:* combo or shower only. **Parking:** on-site. **Terms:** 3 night minimum stay, 21 day cancellation notice-fee imposed. **Amenities:** voice mail, irons, hair dryers. **Pool(s):** outdoor. **Leisure Activities:** windsurfing, snorkeling, kayaks, recreation programs, croquet, bocci, exercise room, volleyball, game room. **Guest Services:** valet laundry, wireless Internet. **Cards:** AX, MC, VI.

(See map and index starting on p. 349)

MELROSE BEACH APARTMENTS Phone: (246)435-7984 70

AAA SAVE

Motel
$80-$120 All Year

Address: Worthing Main Rd **Location:** Center. **Facility:** 15 one-bedroom suites with efficiencies. 3 stories (no elevator), exterior corridors. *Bath:* combo or shower only. **Parking:** on-site. **Terms:** 14 day cancellation notice. **Guest Services:** valet laundry, wireless Internet. **Cards:** DC, MC, VI.

ROCKLEY PLUMTREE CLUB Phone: (246)435-7606 72

AAA SAVE

Condominium
$100-$240 All Year

Address: Plumtree Cluster Golf Club Rd **Location:** 10.2 mi (16.3 km) n of international airport; 2.8 mi (4.5 km) s of downtown Bridgetown; in Club Rockley. **Facility:** 40 units. 34 one- and 6 two-bedroom suites with kitchens. 2 stories (no elevator), exterior corridors. *Bath:* combo or shower only. **Parking:** on-site. **Terms:** office hours 8:30 am-7 pm, 3 night minimum stay, 21 day cancellation notice. **Amenities:** safes, irons. **Pool(s):** outdoor. **Leisure Activities:** *Fee:* golf-9 holes, 4 lighted tennis courts. **Guest Services:** valet and coin laundry, area transportation-Accra Beach, wireless Internet. **Business Services:** PC (fee). **Cards:** MC, VI.

SANDY BAY BEACH CLUB Phone: (246)435-8000 71

AAA SAVE

Hotel
$170-$406 All Year

Address: Worthing Main Rd **Location:** Oceanfront. Center. **Facility:** Designated smoking area. 129 units. 48 one-bedroom standard units. 72 one- and 9 two-bedroom suites with kitchens (no utensils). 3-4 stories (no elevator), exterior corridors. *Bath:* combo or shower only. **Parking:** on-site. **Terms:** 14 day cancellation notice, 7 day in summer-fee imposed. **Amenities:** voice mail, safes (fee), irons, hair dryers. **Dining:** 2 restaurants, entertainment. **Pool(s):** 2 outdoor. **Leisure Activities:** whirlpool, paddleboats, sailboats, snorkeling, kayak, recreation programs, billiards, kids club, volleyball. *Fee:* waterskiing, massage. **Guest Services:** valet laundry, wireless Internet. **Business Services:** PC (fee). **Cards:** AX, MC, VI.

▼ *See AAA listing p 356* ▼

(See map and index starting on p. 349)

SOUTH BEACH RESORT AND VACATION CLUB **Phone:** 246/435-8561 73

Condominium
$170-$304 All Year

Address: Rockley Beach, Christ Church **Location:** In Rockley Beach; 7.7 mi (9.3 km) w of international airport; 2.1 mi (3.3 km) s of downtown Bridgetown. **Facility:** This time-share property operates like a hotel and offers residential-style units with numerous amenities; all units face the ocean across the street. Designated smoking area. 47 units. 21 one-bedroom standard units with efficiencies and whirlpools. 26 one-bedroom suites with kitchens and whirlpools. 5 stories, interior corridors. **Parking:** street. **Terms:** cancellation fee imposed. **Amenities:** high-speed Internet, voice mail, safes, irons, hair dryers. **Pool(s):** outdoor. **Leisure Activities:** limited beach access. **Guest Services:** valet and coin laundry, wireless Internet. **Business Services:** PC (fee). **Cards:** AX, MC, VI.

WHERE TO DINE

APSARA & TAMNAK THAI RESTAURANT **Phone:** 246/435-5454 24

Indian
$15-$35

Outstanding Indian cuisine is served in an upscale and refined dining area with an Indian motif. The restaurant boasts a solidly attentive and congenial wait staff attired in traditional dress. On the menu are varied curry dishes, lamb cutlets, lobster tail and flying fish, in addition to popular and healthy meats prepared in the tandoori oven. The dining experience here rises way above the ordinary. Dressy casual. **Bar:** Full bar. **Reservations:** suggested. **Hours:** 11:30 am-3 & 6:30-10 pm, Sat & Sun from 6:30 pm. Closed: for lunch on public holidays. **Address:** Worthing Main Rd **Location:** In Morecambe House; center of town. **Parking:** on-site. **Cards:** AX, MC, VI. **Historic**

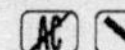

BERT'S **Phone:** 246/435-7924 22

International
$10-$28

Dine al fresco while being surrounded by pools of fish. Large bar area is great for sports fans to unwind with a beer and some pizza. The dinner menu offers something for everyone including local specialties like flying fish, pizzas, burgers and entree size salads. Casual dress. **Bar:** Full bar. **Reservations:** accepted. **Hours:** 11:30 am-10:30 pm. Closed: 12/25. **Address:** Rockley Main Rd **Location:** 2.7 mi (4.3 km) s of Bridgetown on Hwy 7; 10 mi (16 km) w of international airport. **Parking:** on-site. **Cards:** MC, VI.

BUBBA'S SPORTS BAR & RESTAURANT **Phone:** 246/435-8731 25

American
$9-$33

Diners can escape the heat inside the air-conditioned restaurant and enjoy live satellite sporting events while imbibing and noshing on a freshly prepared meal. For a warm-up, try fish fingers, chicken wings or coconut shrimp. Main-event entrees range from shrimp Provencal to flying fish, kebabs, fajitas and porterhouse steak. Also popular are satisfying burgers and a good selection of sandwiches all served with a jacket potato. Casual dress. **Bar:** Full bar. **Reservations:** accepted. **Hours:** 11:30 am-11 pm, Fri-1 am, Sat 10 am-1 am, Sun 8 am-11 pm. Closed: 12/25; also Kadooment Day & for lunch on Bajan public holidays. **Address:** Rockley Main Rd **Location:** 2.4 mi (3.9 km) s of Bridgetown on Hwy 7; 10.3 mi (16.6 km) w of international airport. **Parking:** on-site. **Cards:** AX, MC, VI.

CALL

CHAMPERS **Phone:** 246/434-3463 20

International
$16-$43

The dining room excels in comfort and service; the menu has been refined with many gourmet selections including the variety of fish that are among the most popular choices; also available is lamb, chicken, duck dishes, all cooked to perfection. Dressy casual. **Bar:** Full bar. **Reservations:** required. **Hours:** 11:30 am-3 & 6-9:45 pm. Closed: 1/1, 12/25; also Sun, Kadooment Day & Easter Monday. **Address:** Skeetes Hill, Torrington House **Location:** 2.3 mi (3.7 km) s of downtown Bridgetown; at Rockley Beach. **Parking:** on-site. **Cards:** AX, MC, VI.

LUCKY HORSESHOE **Phone:** 246/435-5825 21

International
$9-$24

With an International and American menu, there is something for everyone at this 24-hour eatery including a wide selection of sandwiches, hamburgers, beef and fish. Casual dress. **Bar:** Full bar. **Hours:** 24 hours. **Address:** Worthing Main Rd **Location:** Center; across from beach. **Parking:** on-site. **Cards:** AX, DS, MC, VI.

OISTINS —*See Christ Church Parish p. 353.*

St. James Parish

APPLEBY (See map and index starting on p. 349)

WHERE TO STAY

CRYSTAL COVE HOTEL — **Phone:** (246)432-2683 **33**

Resort Hotel
$386-$1197 All Year

Address: Main Rd **Location:** Oceanfront. 15.5 mi (24.8 km) nw of international airport; 5.3 mi (8.5 km) n of downtown Bridgetown. **Facility:** Multi-level, meandering pools with a grotto-like cave bar are distinct features of this all-inclusive resort. Room categories are based on location. 88 units. 62 one-bedroom standard units. 26 one-bedroom suites. 2-3 stories (no elevator), exterior corridors. **Parking:** on-site. **Terms:** 7 night minimum stay - seasonal, 21 day cancellation notice, 7 day in summer-fee imposed. **Amenities:** safes, irons, hair dryers. **Dining:** 2 restaurants, entertainment. **Pool(s):** 3 outdoor. **Leisure Activities:** sailboats, windsurfing, waterskiing, snorkeling, kayaks, exercise room. **Guest Services:** valet laundry, area transportation-water taxi, wireless Internet. **Business Services:** business center. **Cards:** AX, DC, DS, MC, VI. *(See color ad p 350)*

DERRICKS (See map and index starting on p. 349)

WHERE TO DINE

THE CLIFF — **Phone:** 246/432-1922 **14**

International
$94-$104

Located on top of a coral cliff; open-air, tiered dining room. Varied international, Thai and Caribbean menu offering creative, and innovative entrees. Flavorful food and delectable desserts capably served in a setting of candlelight and art. Dressy casual. **Bar:** Full bar. **Reservations:** required. **Hours:** 6:30 pm-9:30 pm; to 10 pm 12/15-4/30. Closed: 1/1, 12/24, 12/25; also Sun 4/30-11/30 & Kadooment Day. **Address:** Hwy 1, Derricks **Location:** 5 mi (8 km) n of Bridgetown on Hwy 1. **Parking:** valet. **Cards:** AX, MC, VI.

HOLETOWN (See map and index starting on p. 349)

WHERE TO STAY

ALMOND BEACH CLUB & SPA *Book great rates at AAA.com* — **Phone:** (246)432-7840 **23**

Resort Hotel
$730-$1325 All Year

Address: Vauxhall, St. James **Location:** Oceanfront. In Vauxhall; 17.4 mi (27.8 km) nw of international airport; 7.1 mi (11.3 km) n of downtown Bridgetown. **Facility:** The property's grounds are well-landscaped and most units have balconies or patios, some beachfront; a hospitality suite is available. 161 units. 98 one-bedroom standard units, some with whirlpools. 63 one-bedroom suites. 3-4 stories (no elevator), exterior corridors. **Parking:** on-site. **Terms:** 3 night minimum stay, age restrictions may apply, 21 day cancellation notice-fee imposed. **Amenities:** voice mail, safes, irons, hair dryers. **Dining:** 3 restaurants, entertainment. **Pool(s):** 3 outdoor. **Leisure Activities:** saunas, whirlpool, steamrooms, boating, sailboats, windsurfing, waterskiing, snorkeling, fishing, aqua cycles, kayaks; guest use privileges at sister properties, lighted tennis court, recreation programs, spa, volleyball, game room. **Guest Services:** valet laundry, area transportation-Almond Beach Village & Bridgetown, wireless Internet. **Cards:** AX, MC, VI. **Free Special Amenities: full breakfast.**

/ SOME UNITS

MANGOBAY *Book great rates at AAA.com* — **Phone:** (246)432-1384 **21**

Hotel
$385-$690 All Year

Address: 2nd St **Location:** Oceanfront. 17.2 mi (27.5 km) nw of international airport; 7.7 mi (12.3 km) n of downtown Bridgetown. **Facility:** Designated smoking area. 67 units. 65 one-bedroom standard units. 2 one-bedroom suites. 2-4 stories, exterior corridors. **Parking:** on-site. **Terms:** 3 day cancellation notice-fee imposed. **Amenities:** CD players, voice mail, safes, irons, hair dryers. **Dining:** entertainment. **Pool(s):** outdoor. **Leisure Activities:** paddleboats, sailboats, waterskiing, snorkeling, kayaks, sailing trips, complimentary introduction to scuba, recreation programs, library, volleyball. *Fee:* scuba diving, massage. **Guest Services:** valet laundry, wireless Internet. **Business Services:** meeting rooms, business center. **Cards:** AX, MC, VI.

/ SOME UNITS

THE SANDPIPER — **Phone:** (246)422-2251 **18**

Hotel
$385-$1080 All Year

Address: Hwy 1, St James **Location:** Oceanfront. 17.7 mi (28.3 km) nw of international airport; 8 mi (12.8 km) n of downtown Bridgetown. **Facility:** 47 units. 22 one-bedroom standard units. 25 one-bedroom suites, some with efficiencies. 2-3 stories (no elevator), exterior corridors. **Parking:** on-site. **Terms:** age restrictions may apply, 28 day cancellation notice, 14 day in summer-fee imposed. **Amenities:** CD players, voice mail, safes, hair dryers. **Dining:** The Sandpiper Dining Room, see separate listing, entertainment. **Pool(s):** outdoor. **Leisure Activities:** sailboats, windsurfing, waterskiing, snorkeling, kayaks, 2 lighted tennis courts, shared facilities with sister property, exercise room. **Guest Services:** TV in common area, valet laundry, area transportation-Bridgetown, wireless Internet. **Business Services:** PC. **Cards:** AX, MC, VI.

/ SOME UNITS

(See map and index starting on p. 349)

SANDY LANE HOTEL **Phone:** (246)444-2000 24

Resort Hotel
$950-$4900 All Year

Address: St. James **Location:** Oceanfront. 17.2 mi (27.5 km) nw of international airport; 6.9 mi (11 km) n of downtown Bridgetown. **Facility:** Boutiques, Bentleys and the beach await at this luxurious destination offering state-of-the-art amenities, gourmet dining and a fully appointed spa. Meets AAA guest room security requirements. 113 units. 95 one-bedroom standard units, some with whirlpools. 4 one-, 11 two- and 2 three-bedroom suites, some with whirlpools. 1 house. 4 stories, interior corridors. **Parking:** valet. **Terms:** check-in 4 pm, 28 day cancellation notice-fee imposed. **Amenities:** DVD players, video games, CD players, high-speed Internet, dual phone lines, voice mail, fax, safes, honor bars, hair dryers. **Dining:** 4 restaurants, entertainment. **Pool(s):** outdoor. **Leisure Activities:** sauna, whirlpools, steamroom, beach access, boating, canoeing, paddleboats, sailboats, windsurfing, snorkeling, plunge pool, ice room, 9 lighted tennis courts, recreation programs, hiking trails, jogging, playground, spa, volleyball, game room. *Fee:* waterskiing, scuba diving, charter fishing, golf-45 holes. **Guest Services:** valet laundry, airport transportation-Grantley Adams International Airport, area transportation-country club/golf course, wireless Internet. **Business Services:** meeting rooms, business center. **Cards:** AX, DC, DS, MC, VI. Affiliated with A Preferred Hotel. *(See color ad p 361)*

/ SOME UNITS

SETTLERS BEACH VILLA HOTEL **Phone:** (246)422-3052 20

Cottage
$134-$1230 12/1-8/31 & 10/27-11/30

Address: Trents **Location:** Oceanfront. 17.8 mi (28.5 km) nw of international airport; 8.1 mi (13 km) n of downtown Bridgetown. **Facility:** Stylish and spacious cottages located on the Platinum coast of Barbados. 23 units. 1 one-bedroom suite with kitchen. 22 cottages. 1-2 stories (no elevator), exterior corridors. **Parking:** on-site. **Terms:** open 12/1-8/31 & 10/27-11/30, office hours 8 am-10 pm, 60 day cancellation notice, 30 day off season-fee imposed. **Amenities:** voice mail, safes, irons, hair dryers. **Pool(s):** outdoor. **Leisure Activities:** croquet, badminton. **Guest Services:** TV in common area, valet laundry, wireless Internet. **Business Services:** PC. **Cards:** AX, MC, VI.

WHERE TO DINE

THE MEWS RESTAURANT **Phone:** 246/432-1122 3

International
$21-$38

The cuisine, a blend of International and Caribbean dishes with an occasional mix of Asian, will please any appetite. The more popular upstairs dining area offers a comfortable decorative ambiance with tables tightly tucked together. Dressy casual. Entertainment. **Bar:** Full bar. **Reservations:** suggested. **Hours:** 6:30 pm-10 pm. Closed: 12/25; also Sun & Kadooment Day. **Address:** 2nd St **Location:** In the 2nd St Restaurant Row. **Parking:** street. **Cards:** AX, MC, VI.

OLIVES BAR & BISTRO **Phone:** 246/432-2112 4

Mediterranean
$13-$33

The welcoming bistro offers a choice of interior or al fresco seating. The creative cuisine has a blend of earthy Mediterranean and Caribbean ingredients and culinary influences. The upstairs lounge is a comfortable place to snack on appetizers or one of the thin crusted gourmet pizzas. The main event entrees include dishes like duckling cooked two ways, jerked pork tenderloin and local black belly lamb as well as a catch of the day. Dressy casual. **Bar:** Full bar. **Reservations:** suggested. **Hours:** Open 12/1-8/30 & 9/26-11/30; 6:30 pm-10 pm. Closed: 1/1, 12/25. **Address:** 2nd St **Location:** 17.2 mi (27.5 km) nw of international airport; 7.7 mi (12.3 km) n of downtown Bridgetown; just past Holetown Police Station. **Parking:** street. **Cards:** AX, MC, VI.

THE SANDPIPER DINING ROOM **Phone:** 246/422-2251 6

International
$35-$45

At this popular, elegant spot, twice a week patrons can take advantage of a specialty buffet dinner in lieu of the a la carte menu. Dim lighting and candlelit tables lend to the romantic feel of the covered open-air dining room, where high ceiling fans create a refreshing breeze. The chef changes the menu daily to feature the freshest local and international ingredients, which combine with global cooking influences and island flair. Semi-formal attire. **Bar:** Full bar. **Reservations:** suggested. **Hours:** 7-9:30 am, 12:30-2:30 & 7-9:30 pm. **Address:** Hwy 1, St. James **Location:** 17.7 mi (28.3 km) nw of international airport; 8 mi (12.9 km) n of downtown Bridgetown; in The Sandpiper. **Parking:** on-site. **Cards:** AX, MC, VI.

SPAGO RESTAURANT & BAR **Phone:** 246/432-7394 7

Italian
$14-$28

In the city's restaurant row area, this cute Bajan chattel-style cottage restaurant lets patrons relax indoors or on the porch over plates of Italy-influenced fare, including varied pasta dishes, gourmet pizzas, entree salads and the catch of the day. Casual dress. **Bar:** Full bar. **Reservations:** required. **Hours:** 11:30 am-4 & 6:30-10 pm. **Address:** 2nd St **Location:** 17.2 mi (27.5 km) nw of international airport; 7.7 mi (12.3 km) n of downtown Bridgetown; just n of Holetown Center. **Parking:** street. **Cards:** MC, VI.

THE TIDES RESTAURANT **Phone:** 246/432-8356 5

International
$13-$35

Set directly on the edge of the mesmerizing azure sea. The proprietor creates memorable meals incorporating culinary techniques, ingredients and flavors that span the globe in order to suit any palate. Savory starters like the crab cakes with Thai sauce, entree-size salads, pasta, gourmet pizzas and sandwiches are served up for lunch. Dinner really showcases the chef's talent and may include his special preparations of lamb, shrimp, scallops, beef, pork and duck. Dressy casual. **Bar:** Full bar. **Reservations:** required. **Hours:** noon-2:30 & 6:30-9:30 pm, Sat & Sun from 6:30 pm. Closed: 1/1, 12/25; also Good Friday. **Address:** Queens Hwy **Location:** 16.8 mi (26.9 km) nw of international airport; 7.5 mi (12 km) n of downtown Bridgetown; in St. James. **Parking:** on-site and valet. **Cards:** MC, VI.

▼ See AAA listing p 360 ▼

PAYNES BAY (See map and index starting on p. 349)

WHERE TO STAY

THE ST. JAMES LUXURY APARTMENT HOTEL — **Phone:** 246/432-0489 — 32

Hotel
$180-$865 All Year

Address: Paynes Bay **Location:** Oceanfront. Center. **Facility:** Designated smoking area. 14 units. 3 one-bedroom standard units with efficiencies. 2 one-, 8 two- and 1 three-bedroom suites with kitchens. 2-4 stories (no elevator), interior/exterior corridors. *Bath:* combo or shower only. **Parking:** on-site. **Terms:** office hours 9:30 am-5:30 pm. **Amenities:** CD players, high-speed Internet, voice mail, safes, irons, hair dryers. *Some:* DVD players. **Leisure Activities:** golf privileges. **Guest Services:** valet laundry. **Business Services:** PC. **Cards:** MC, VI.

TAMARIND COVE HOTEL — **Phone:** 246/432-1332 — 31

Resort Hotel
$380-$1027 All Year

Address: Paynes Bay **Location:** Oceanfront. Center; on Gold Coast. **Facility:** Rooms at the expansive hotel offer views of the pool, garden or ocean; planned recreational programs offer plenty of fun activities. Smoke free premises. 110 units. 96 one-bedroom standard units. 14 one-bedroom suites. 3 stories (no elevator), exterior corridors. **Parking:** on-site. **Terms:** 5-6 night minimum stay - seasonal, 14 day cancellation notice, 7 day in summer-fee imposed. **Amenities:** voice mail, safes, irons, hair dryers. *Some:* DVD players, CD players. **Dining:** 2 restaurants, entertainment. **Pool(s):** 3 outdoor. **Leisure Activities:** paddleboats, sailboats, windsurfing, waterskiing, snorkeling, banana boat, kayaks, recreation programs, exercise room. *Fee:* scuba diving, massage. **Guest Services:** valet laundry, area transportation-water taxi to sister hotels, beauty salon, wireless Internet. **Business Services:** meeting rooms, business center. **Cards:** AX, MC, VI. *(See color ad p 350)*

TREASURE BEACH — *Book great rates at AAA.com* — **Phone:** (246)432-1346 — 30

Hotel
$325-$1860 All Year

Address: Paynes Bay **Location:** Oceanfront. Center. **Facility:** 35 one-bedroom suites. 3 stories (no elevator), exterior corridors. **Parking:** on-site. **Terms:** age restrictions may apply, 28 day cancellation notice, 14 summer-fee imposed. **Amenities:** high-speed Internet, voice mail, safes, honor bars, irons, hair dryers. *Some:* DVD players, CD players, dual phone lines. **Dining:** entertainment. **Pool(s):** outdoor. **Leisure Activities:** snorkeling, exercise room. *Fee:* massage. **Guest Services:** valet laundry, wireless Internet. **Business Services:** business center. **Cards:** AX, MC, VI.

/ SOME UNITS

TROPICAL ESCAPE — **Phone:** (246)432-5153 — 34

Hotel
$218-$290 All Year

Address: Main Rd **Location:** Center; on Gold Coast. **Facility:** 58 one-bedroom standard units. 3 stories (no elevator), interior/exterior corridors. **Parking:** on-site. **Terms:** 3 night minimum stay. **Amenities:** voice mail, safes, hair dryers. **Dining:** entertainment. **Pool(s):** outdoor. **Leisure Activities:** sailboats, kayaks, limited exercise equipment. **Guest Services:** valet laundry. **Business Services:** PC (fee). **Cards:** MC, VI.

/ SOME UNITS FEE

WHERE TO DINE

'AL FRESCO' AT TREASURE BEACH — **Phone:** 246/432-1346 — 10

International
$15-$50

This elegant dining room offers a sophisticated yet relaxed dining experience in a covered open-air setting. The well-trained staff provides fine service, while the chef prepares fine international fare. During the day, diners enjoy nice views of the surrounding gardens, while at night, the atmosphere is more romantic. Casual dress. **Bar:** Full bar. **Reservations:** suggested. **Hours:** 7:30 am-9 pm. **Address:** Paynes Bay, St. James **Location:** At Treasure Beach Hotel. **Parking:** on-site. **Cards:** AX, MC, VI.

DAPHNE'S — **Phone:** 246/432-2731 — 9

New Italian
$27-$60

A chic oasis on the Platinum Coast, the elegantly rustic al fresco dining area sustains a romantic air and has muslin sheets draped from the ceiling. The sophisticated menu lines up such selections as carpaccio marlin, sashimi-grade tuna and lamb cutlets, as well as a range of Italian-inspired pasta dishes, including tagliatelle, rigatoni and linguine; potato dumpling gnocchi; and risotto. Dressy casual. **Bar:** Full bar. **Reservations:** suggested. **Hours:** 12:30 pm-3 & 6:30-9:30 pm. Closed: Mon 6/1-12/4. **Address:** Payne's Bay Rd **Location:** 20.3 mi (32.5 km) nw of international airport; 7.5 mi (12 km) n of Bridgetown; in The House at Tamarind Cove. **Parking:** on-site and valet. **Cards:** AX, MC, VI.

PORTERS (See map and index starting on p. 349)

WHERE TO STAY

COLONY CLUB HOTEL — *Book great rates at AAA.com* — **Phone:** (246)422-2335 — 15

Hotel
$400-$1512 All Year

Address: Porters **Location:** Oceanfront. 18 mi (28.8 km) nw of international airport; 8.3 mi (13.3 km) n of downtown Bridgetown. **Facility:** 96 units. 92 one-bedroom standard units. 4 one-bedroom suites with whirlpools. 1-3 stories (no elevator), exterior corridors. **Parking:** on-site. **Terms:** 7 night minimum stay - seasonal, age restrictions may apply, 21 day cancellation notice, 7 day off season-fee imposed. **Amenities:** CD players, voice mail, safes, irons, hair dryers. *Some:* DVD players, high-speed Internet, honor bars. **Dining:** 2 restaurants, entertainment. **Pool(s):** 4 outdoor. **Leisure Activities:** sailboats, windsurfing, waterskiing, snorkeling, kayaks, 2 lighted tennis courts, table tennis, seasonal kids club, limited exercise equipment. *Fee:* golf privileges, massage. **Guest Services:** valet laundry, area transportation-water taxi, beauty salon, wireless Internet. **Business Services:** meeting rooms, PC. **Cards:** AX, MC, VI. *(See color ad p 350)*

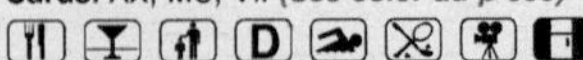

(See map and index starting on p. 349)

CORAL REEF CLUB — **Phone:** (246)422-2372 16

Hotel
$245-$1400 All Year

Address: Hwy 1 **Location:** Oceanfront. 17.9 mi (28.6 km) n of international airport; 8.2 mi (13.1 km) n of downtown Bridgetown. **Facility:** Varied guest-room categories are offered at this family-operated beachfront property, which was recently renovated. Designated smoking area. 88 units. 60 one-bedroom standard units. 18 one-bedroom suites, some with efficiencies. 10 cottages. 1-3 stories (no elevator), exterior corridors. **Parking:** on-site. **Terms:** 7-14 night minimum stay - seasonal, age restrictions may apply, 28 day cancellation notice-fee imposed. **Amenities:** video library (fee), CD players, voice mail, safes, hair dryers. *Some:* DVD players. **Dining:** entertainment. **Pool(s):** 2 outdoor. **Leisure Activities:** paddleboats, sailboats, windsurfing, waterskiing, snorkeling, kayaks, 3 lighted tennis courts, billiards, TV lounge, playground, exercise room, shuffleboard. *Fee:* scuba diving, sailing cruises, massage. **Guest Services:** valet laundry, area transportation-Bridgetown, beauty salon, wireless Internet. **Business Services:** meeting rooms, business center. **Cards:** AX, MC, VI.

D / SOME UNITS

THE FAIRMONT ROYAL PAVILION — Book great rates at AAA.com — **Phone:** (246)422-5555 13

Hotel
$740-$1336 12/1-4/30
$442-$569 5/1-11/30

Address: Porters **Location:** Oceanfront. 18.5 mi (29.6 km) nw of international airport; 8.8 mi (14.1 km) n of downtown Bridgetown. **Facility:** This picturesque beachfront resort, renovated in 2003, features pink buildings set against colorful, lush landscaping. Meets AAA guest room security requirements. 75 units. 74 one-bedroom standard units. 1 house. 3 stories, exterior corridors. **Parking:** on-site. **Terms:** check-in 4 pm, age restrictions may apply, 30 day cancellation notice-fee imposed. **Amenities:** video library, DVD players, CD players, high-speed Internet, voice mail, safes, honor bars, irons, hair dryers. **Dining:** 2 restaurants, entertainment. **Pool(s):** outdoor. **Leisure Activities:** whirlpool, sailboats, windsurfing, waterskiing, snorkeling, kayaks, 2 lighted tennis courts, exercise room. *Fee:* scuba diving, massage. **Guest Services:** valet laundry, beauty salon, wireless Internet. **Business Services:** meeting rooms, PC. **Cards:** AX, DS, MC, VI.

24 D

LONE STAR RESTAURANT & HOTEL — **Phone:** (246)419-0599 12

Bed & Breakfast
$400-$850 12/1-5/31 & 7/2-11/30

Address: Mount Standfast **Location:** Oceanfront. 22.2 mi (35.5 km) nw of international airport; 9.4 mi (15 km) n of Bridgetown. **Facility:** All units are spacious with large balconies facing the ocean, giving the property a retreat-like ambiance; property is closed 6/1-7/31 and 9/1-9/30. 5 units. 4 one-bedroom standard units. 1 house. 2 stories (no elevator), exterior corridors. *Bath:* combo or shower only. **Parking:** on-site. **Terms:** open 12/1-5/31 & 7/2-11/30, office hours 8 am-11 pm, 90 day cancellation notice-fee imposed. **Amenities:** video library, DVD players, CD players, high-speed Internet, voice mail, safes, honor bars, hair dryers. **Dining:** Lone Star Restaurant, see separate listing. **Leisure Activities:** snorkeling. **Guest Services:** valet laundry, wireless Internet. **Business Services:** PC. **Cards:** AX, MC, VI.

VCR

WHERE TO DINE

LONE STAR RESTAURANT — **Phone:** 246/419-0599 2

International
$24-$40

Attached to a hotel by the same name, the oceanfront al fresco dining room reflects a romantic ambience. Well-presented cuisine incorporates Asian and Mediterranean influences. The meze plate appetizer—which includes baba ghanoush, hummus, goat cheese truffles and kalamata olives—is ideal for sharing. Savory main plates range from lamb cutlets and duck to mahi mahi and lobster. A real favorite is tuna nicoise. Dressy casual. **Bar:** Full bar. **Reservations:** required, in winter. **Hours:** 11:30 am-3:30 & 6:30-10:30 pm. **Address:** Mount Standfast **Location:** 22.2 mi (35.5 km) nw of international airport; 9.4 mi (15 km) n of Bridgetown; in Lone Star Restaurant & Hotel. **Parking:** on-site. **Cards:** MC, VI.

AC

PROSPECT

(See map and index starting on p. 349)

WHERE TO STAY

ESCAPE HOTEL & SPA BY VIRGIN HOLIDAYS — **Phone:** 246/424-7571 40

Hotel
$377-$507 All Year

Address: Main Rd **Location:** Oceanfront. Center. **Facility:** 83 one-bedroom standard units. 2-3 stories, exterior corridors. **Parking:** on-site. **Amenities:** video library, voice mail, safes, hair dryers. *Some:* DVD players, CD players, irons. **Dining:** 2 restaurants, entertainment. **Pool(s):** 2 outdoor. **Leisure Activities:** sauna, whirlpool, waterslide, sailboats, windsurfing, snorkeling, kayaks, table tennis, recreation programs, exercise room, spa, billiards, volleyball, game room. **Guest Services:** valet laundry, wireless Internet. **Business Services:** PC (fee). **Cards:** MC, VI.

D / SOME UNITS

WHERE TO DINE

CALABAZA RESTAURANT — **Phone:** 246/424-4557 12

International
$65-$78

This al fresco Moroccan motif restaurant is an ideal place to cool off from the midday sun—not only because of the proximity to ocean breezes, but with the portable air conditioning units at each table as well. The cuisine is artistically composed to accentuate the color and texture of each dish. The flavors' and ingredients' main influences are from Asia and the Mediterranean. The staff of local servers are congenial and efficient. Top your meal off with the French pressed coffee. Dressy casual. **Bar:** Full bar. **Reservations:** required. **Hours:** 6:30 pm-9:30 pm. Closed: 1/1, 12/25, 12/26; also Kadooment Day. **Address:** Prospect, St. James **Location:** 14 mi (22.4 km) nw of international airport; 4.3 mi (6.9 km) n of downtown Bridgetown. **Parking:** on-site and valet. **Cards:** AX, DS, MC, VI.

(See map and index starting on p. 349)

IL TEMPIO RESTAURANT & BAR Menu on AAA.com Phone: 246/417-0057 (13)

Italian
$16-$48

A young Italian operates the casual oceanfront restaurant. A favorite on the menu of savory pasta, meat and seafood dishes is tortellini stuffed with lamb. A broad selection of appetizers, such as beef carpaccio, and salads, such as caprese, whets the appetite. Tutto bene! Dressy casual. **Bar:** Full bar. **Reservations:** required, for dinner. **Hours:** Open 12/1-7/31 & 10/1-11/30; noon-2:30 & 6-10 pm. Closed: Mon. **Address:** Fitts Village, St. James **Location:** At Fitts Village; 5 mi (8 km) n of downtown Bridgetown; 14.7 mi (23.5 km) nw of international airport. **Parking:** on-site. **Cards:** MC, VI.

THE GARDEN

(See map and index starting on p. 349)

WHERE TO STAY

COVE SPRING Phone: 246/422-3166 (10)

SAVE
Hotel
$542-$1122 All Year

Address: The Garden **Location:** Oceanfront. Center; on main road. **Facility:** Designated smoking area. 10 one-bedroom standard units, some with whirlpools. 2 stories (no elevator), interior corridors. *Bath:* combo or shower only. **Parking:** on-site. **Amenities:** video library, DVD players, CD players, high-speed Internet, voice mail, hair dryers. *Some:* safes. **Pool(s):** outdoor. **Leisure Activities:** whirlpool, snorkeling, kayak, exercise room, movie theatre. *Fee:* massage. **Guest Services:** complimentary laundry, wireless Internet. **Business Services:** PC. **Cards:** MC, VI.

WESTMORELAND

(See map and index starting on p. 349)

WHERE TO STAY

ROYAL WESTMORELAND Phone: 246/422-4653 (26)

SAVE
Vacation Rental House
$300-$2500 All Year

Location: Just e of Reads Bay and Porters, follow signs. **Facility:** Located inland, this residential-style resort community is ideal for large families or groups traveling together. 27 houses. 2 stories (no elevator), exterior corridors. **Parking:** on-site. **Terms:** office hours 8 am-5 pm. **Amenities:** DVD players, CD players, voice mail, safes, irons, hair dryers. **Leisure Activities:** whirlpool, driving range, 2 lighted tennis courts, recreation programs, exercise room, basketball. *Fee:* golf-18 holes, massage. **Guest Services:** complimentary laundry, area transportation-Mullins Beach, wireless Internet. **Business Services:** PC. **Cards:** AX, MC, VI.

FEE

St. Joseph Parish

BATHSHEBA (See map and index starting on p. 349)

WHERE TO STAY

THE NEW EDGEWATER HOTEL **Phone:** (246)433-9900 48

AAA SAVE

Hotel

$116-$212 12/1-4/14
$82-$163 4/15-11/30

Address: Bathsheba Rd **Location:** Oceanfront. Just n. **Facility:** Designated smoking area. 24 units. 20 one-bedroom standard units, some with whirlpools. 4 one-bedroom suites. 2 stories (no elevator), interior/exterior corridors. *Bath:* combo or shower only. **Parking:** on-site. **Terms:** office hours 8 am-8 pm, 3-7 night minimum stay - seasonal and/or weekends, 30 day cancellation notice. **Amenities:** high-speed Internet, safes, irons, hair dryers. *Some:* DVD players (fee). **Pool(s):** outdoor. **Leisure Activities:** billiards, limited exercise equipment. **Guest Services:** valet laundry. **Business Services:** business center. **Cards:** MC, VI.

FEE D / SOME UNITS

St. Lucy Parish

SHERMANS (See map and index starting on p. 349)

WHERE TO STAY

LITTLE GOOD HARBOUR Phone: 246/439-3000 1

AAA SAVE

Hotel

$237-$895 12/1-8/31
$237-$544 10/10-11/30

Address: Fort Rupert **Location:** 23.4 mi (37.5 km) nw of airport; 13.2 mi (21.2 km) n of downtown Bridgetown. **Facility:** Meets AAA guest room security requirements. 21 units. 10 one-, 4 two- and 7 three-bedroom suites with kitchens. 1-2 stories, exterior corridors. *Bath:* combo or shower only. **Parking:** on-site. **Terms:** open 12/1-8/31 & 10/10-11/30, office hours 8:30 am-5:30 pm, 28 day cancellation notice. **Amenities:** video library, CD players, voice mail, safes, irons, hair dryers. *Some:* DVD players. **Pool(s):** 2 outdoor. **Leisure Activities:** limited beach access, snorkeling, kayaks, limited exercise equipment. **Guest Services:** valet and coin laundry, wireless Internet. **Business Services:** PC. **Cards:** MC, VI.

St. Michael Parish

BRIDGETOWN pop. 7,500 (See map and index starting on p. 349)

WHERE TO STAY

HILTON BARBADOS Phone: (246)426-0200 44

AAA SAVE

Resort Hotel

$379-$859 All Year

Address: Needham Point **Location:** Oceanfront. 1.5 mi (2.4 km) s of downtown, 0.4 mi (0.6 km) w at Aquatic Gap turn off. **Facility:** On the site of Old Fort Charles, between the Caribbean Sea and Carlisle Bay. Extensive landscaped grounds. Meets AAA guest room security requirements. 350 units. 317 one-bedroom standard units. 33 one-bedroom suites. 8-10 stories, interior corridors. **Parking:** on-site. **Terms:** 1-30 night minimum stay, cancellation fee imposed. **Amenities:** high-speed Internet (fee), dual phone lines, voice mail, safes, honor bars, irons, hair dryers. *Some:* CD players. **Dining:** 4 restaurants, also, Careenage Grille, see separate listing, entertainment. **Pool(s):** 2 outdoor. **Leisure Activities:** whirlpool, sailboats, snorkeling, kayaks, 4 lighted tennis courts, recreation programs, exercise room, volleyball. *Fee:* scuba diving, massage. **Guest Services:** valet laundry, area transportation, wireless Internet. **Business Services:** conference facilities, business center. **Cards:** AX, MC, VI. *(See color ad opposite title page)*

CALL / SOME UNITS

WHERE TO DINE

BROWN SUGAR RESTAURANT *Menu on AAA.com* Phone: 246/426-7684 19

AAA

Caribbean

$5-$35

Veranda and garden terrace seating are options in the converted home. The Creole cooking style is applied in such dishes as flying fish, jerk pork and fish chowder, as well as many other Bajan favorites. Lamp-lit tropical tables lend to the relaxed ambience. The three-course buffet luncheon is popular. Casual dress. Entertainment. **Bar:** Full bar. **Reservations:** suggested. **Hours:** noon-2:30 & 6-9:30 pm, Sat from 6 pm. Closed: 12/25; also for lunch on public holidays. **Address:** Aquatic Gap, Bay St **Location:** At Aquatic Gap turnoff; 1.2 mi (1.9 km) s of downtown. **Parking:** on-site. **Cards:** AX, DS, MC, VI.

CAREENAGE GRILLE Phone: 246/426-0200 15

Steak & Seafood

$27-$42

In a AAA Four Diamond hotel, the fine-dining establishment envelops patrons in plush, comfortable surroundings characterized by rich decor. Seafood and steaks pair with choices from an excellent wine list prepared to impress the true connoisseur. The adjacent lounge offers live music most nights. Dressy casual. Entertainment. **Bar:** Full bar. **Reservations:** required. **Hours:** 6:30 pm-10 pm. **Address:** Needham's Point **Location:** 1.5 mi (2.4 km) s of downtown, 0.4 mi (0.6 km) w at Aquatic Gap turnoff; in Hilton Barbados. **Parking:** on-site. **Cards:** AX, MC, VI.

St. Peter Parish

SPEIGHTSTOWN

(See map and index starting on p. 349)

—— WHERE TO STAY ——

ALMOND BEACH VILLAGE Book great rates at AAA.com Phone: (246)422-4900 3

AAA SAVE

Resort Hotel

$429-$1150 All Year

Address: Hwy 1 Heywoods-St. Peter **Location:** Oceanfront. 12.5 mi (20 km) n of Bridgetown on Hwy 1; 1.2 mi (1.9 km) n of town. **Facility:** This former sugar plantation is on 30 acres of landscaped grounds; all units have a patio or balcony, some with garden, pool or ocean views. 400 units. 379 one-bedroom standard units. 21 one-bedroom suites. 2-5 stories, exterior corridors. **Parking:** on-site. **Terms:** 3 night minimum stay, 21 day cancellation notice-fee imposed. **Amenities:** voice mail, safes, irons, hair dryers. **Dining:** 4 restaurants, nightclub, entertainment. **Pool(s):** 11 outdoor. **Leisure Activities:** whirlpools, paddleboats, sailboats, windsurfing, waterskiing, snorkeling, fishing, kayaks, banana boats, water trykes, golf-9 holes, 4 lighted tennis courts, 2 squash courts, recreation programs, billiards, table tennis, kids club, playground, exercise room, shuffleboard, volleyball, game room. *Fee:* turtle feeding, massage. **Guest Services:** valet laundry, area transportation-sister property Almond Beach Club & Spa, beauty salon, wireless Internet. **Business Services:** meeting rooms, business center. **Cards:** AX, MC, VI. **Free Special Amenities: full breakfast.**

D / SOME UNITS

COBBLERS COVE Book great rates at AAA.com Phone: (246)422-2291 4

AAA SAVE

Hotel

$440-$2500 All Year

Address: Road View, St. Peter **Location:** Oceanfront. 22.2 mi (35.5 km) nw of international airport; 11.9 mi (19 km) n of downtown Bridgetown; 1 mi (1.6 km) s of town. **Facility:** Designated smoking area. 40 units. 38 one- and 2 two-bedroom suites. 2 stories (no elevator), exterior corridors. **Parking:** on-site. **Terms:** age restrictions may apply, 14 day cancellation notice-fee imposed. **Amenities:** high-speed Internet, voice mail, safes, honor bars, irons, hair dryers. **Dining:** entertainment. **Pool(s):** outdoor. **Leisure Activities:** sailboats, windsurfing, waterskiing, snorkeling, lighted tennis court, kids club, bocci, exercise room, spa. *Fee:* banana boat. **Guest Services:** TV in common area, valet laundry, wireless Internet. **Business Services:** PC. **Cards:** AX, DC, MC, VI.

     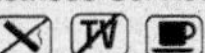

(See map and index starting on p. 349)

WHERE TO DINE

MANGO'S BY THE SEA **Phone:** 246/422-0704 (1)

International
$25-$50

In an outstanding location overlooking the sea, this second-level island eatery entices patrons with its covered open-air setting and fine views. The small dining room has a distinct island feel in both its decor and its menu offerings, which include homemade chicken pate, grilled meats and fresh fish and other seafood prepared with island spices. Tempting passion fruit cheesecake exemplifies the lush desserts that also reflect the island. Semi-formal attire. **Bar:** Full bar. **Reservations:** suggested. **Hours:** 6 pm-9:45 pm. Closed: 12/25. **Address:** West End #2 Queen St **Location:** Centre; waterfront. **Parking:** street. **Cards:** AX, MC, VI.

St. Philip Parish

ST. PHILIP PARISH (See map and index starting on p. 349)

WHERE TO STAY

THE CRANE RESORT & RESIDENCES *Book great rates at AAA.com* **Phone:** (246)423-6220 (52)

AAA SAVE

Resort Hotel
$150-$850 All Year

Address: Crane Beach, St. Philip **Location:** Oceanfront. In Crane; 4.8 mi (7.7 km) se of international airport; 17.6 mi (28.1 km) se of downtown Bridgetown. **Facility:** Reputed to be the oldest continuous operating resort in the Caribbean, this property is in a stunning location built around a former plantation. Meets AAA guest room security requirements. 202 units. 86 one-bedroom standard units, some with efficiencies and/or whirlpools. 106 one- and 10 two-bedroom suites, some with kitchens and/or whirlpools. 2-5 stories, exterior corridors. **Parking:** on-site. **Terms:** check-in 4 pm, 3-7 night minimum stay - seasonal. **Amenities:** video library, DVD players, CD players, high-speed Internet (fee), dual phone lines, voice mail, safes, irons, hair dryers. **Dining:** 3 restaurants, also, Zen, see separate listing, entertainment. **Pool(s):** 5 outdoor. **Leisure Activities:** whirlpool, boogie boards, exercise room. *Fee:* massage. **Guest Services:** valet and coin laundry, area transportation-supermarket & Bridgetown, wireless Internet. **Business Services:** meeting rooms, PC. **Cards:** AX, MC, VI.

WHERE TO DINE

ZEN **Phone:** 246/423-6220 (42)

Japanese
$26-$45

Diners here can select preparations from a fine menu of freshly prepared Thai and Japanese cuisine, which can be ordered a la carte or via full tasting menus. Japanese elements, including a large sushi bar and tatami room, enhance the dining room. **Bar:** Full bar. **Hours:** 6 pm-9:15 pm. Closed: Tues. **Address:** Crane Beach, St. Philip **Location:** In Crane; 4.8 mi (7.7 km) se of international airport; 17.6 mi (28.1 km) se of downtown Bridgetown; in The Crane Resort and Residences. **Parking:** on-site. **Cards:** AX, MC, VI.

BERMUDA

This index helps you "spot" where approved lodgings and restaurants are located on the corresponding detailed maps. Lodging daily rate range is for comparison only and show the property's high season. Restaurant rate range is a combination of lunch and/or dinner. Turn to the listing page for more detailed rate information and consult display ads for special promotions.

HAMILTON (PEMBROKE PARISH)

Map Page	OA	Lodgings	Diamond Rated	High Season	Page
1 / p. 372	AAA	**Royal Palms Hotel**	◆◆◆	$266-$354 SAVE	379
3 / p. 372	AAA	**The Oxford House**	◆◆	$183-$220 SAVE	377
4 / p. 372	AAA	**Rosemont Guest Apartments**	◆◆	$214-$256 SAVE	379
5 / p. 372	AAA	**Edgehill Manor Guest House**	◆◆	$208-$220 SAVE	377
6 / p. 372	AAA	**Rosedon Hotel**	◆◆	$260-$402 SAVE	379
7 / p. 372	AAA	**The Fairmont Hamilton Princess** - see color ad p 378	◆◆◆	$199-$689 SAVE	377
9 / p. 372	AAA	**Mazarine by the Sea**	◆	$120-$180 SAVE	377
10 / p. 372	AAA	**Robin's Nest**	◆◆	$150-$240 SAVE	377
11 / p. 372	AAA	**Bay City Guest House**	◆◆◆	$220-$310 SAVE	377

Map Page	OA	Restaurants	Diamond Rated	Cuisine	Meal Range	Page
1 / p. 372	AAA	**House of India**	◆◆	Indian	$10-$18	380
2 / p. 372		Harley's Bistro	◆◆◆	Continental	$27-$39	379
3 / p. 372		La Trattoria	◆◆	Italian	$10-$29	380
4 / p. 372		Ascots Restaurant	◆◆◆	Mediterranean	$15-$38	379
5 / p. 372		The Lobster Pot Restaurant & Boathouse Bar	◆◆	Seafood	$11-$32	380
6 / p. 372		The Red Carpet	◆◆	Continental	$17-$36	381
7 / p. 372		L'Oriental	◆◆◆	Asian	$16-$48	380
8 / p. 372		The Little Venice	◆◆◆	Italian	$22-$40	380
9 / p. 372		Ristorante Primavera	◆◆◆	Italian	$17-$38	381
10 / p. 372		Portofino	◆◆	Italian	$12-$29	381
11 / p. 372		The Harbourfront Restaurant & Sushi Bar	◆◆◆	International	$15-$37	379
12 / p. 372		Port O' Call Restaurant	◆◆◆	Steak & Seafood	$10-$45	381
13 / p. 372		Hog Penny Restaurant & Pub	◆◆	English	$16-$34	380
14 / p. 372		Barracuda Grill	◆◆◆	Steak & Seafood	$14-$40	379
15 / p. 372		Silk	◆◆	Thai	$12-$23	381
16 / p. 372		The Robin Hood Pub & Restaurant	◆	English	$12-$28	381
17 / p. 372		Cafe Cairo Restaurant & Bar	◆◆◆	Middle Eastern	$12-$28	379
18 / p. 372		The Spot Restaurant	◆◆	American	$7-$18	381
19 / p. 372	AAA	**Chopsticks**	◆◆	Asian	$9-$23	379
21 / p. 372	AAA	**Rosa's Cantina**	◆	Tex-Mex	$13-$25	381

SMITH'S PARISH

Map Page	OA	Lodging	Diamond Rated	High Season	Page
13 / p. 372	AAA	**Pink Beach Club & Cottages**	◆◆◆	$440-$925 SAVE	384

Map Page	OA	Restaurants	Diamond Rated	Cuisine	Meal Range	Page
56 / p. 372		Speciality Inn	◆	International	$9-$20	384
57 / p. 372		North Rock Brewing Company	◆◆	English	$15-$39	384

ST. GEORGE'S (ST. GEORGE'S PARISH)

Map Page	OA	Lodgings	Diamond Rated	High Season	Page
16 / p. 372	AAA	**The St. George's Club**	◆◆◆	$360-$460 SAVE	382
17 / p. 372	AAA	**Aunt Nea's Inn at Hillcrest**	◆◆	$125-$240 SAVE	382

Map Page	OA	Restaurants	Diamond Rated	Cuisine	Meal Range	Page
24 / p. 372		The Carriage House	◆◆	International	$10-$32	382
26 / p. 372		Cafe' Gio	◆◆	International	$10-$29	382

SANDY'S PARISH

Map Page	OA	Lodgings	Diamond Rated	High Season	Page
20 / p. 372	AAA	**Cambridge Beaches - see color ad p 383**	◆◆◆◆	$275-$1690 SAVE	382
21 / p. 372	AAA	**9 Beaches**	◆◆◆	$270-$470 SAVE	382
22 / p. 372	AAA	**The Willowbank**	◆◆	$331-$419 SAVE	384

Map Page	OA	Restaurants	Diamond Rated	Cuisine	Meal Range	Page
28 / p. 372		Beethoven's Restaurant & Bar	◆◆	International	$9-$26	384
29 / p. 372		The Frog & Onion Pub	◆	English	$12-$25	384

SOUTHAMPTON PARISH

Map Page	OA	Lodgings	Diamond Rated	High Season	Page
25 / p. 372	AAA	**Pompano Beach Club**	◆◆◆	$260-$590 SAVE	385
28 / p. 372	AAA	**The Reefs**	◆◆◆	$314-$574 SAVE	385
30 / p. 372	AAA	**The Fairmont Southampton - see color ad p 386**	◆◆◆◆	$199-$4789 SAVE	385

Map Page	OA	Restaurants	Diamond Rated	Cuisine	Meal Range	Page
32 / p. 372	AAA	**The Waterlot Inn Steakhouse**	◆◆◆◆	Steak & Seafood	$30-$57	387
33 / p. 372		Lighthouse Tea Room	◆◆	International	$12-$52	387
34 / p. 372	AAA	**The Newport Room**	◆◆◆◆◆	French	$95-$115	387
35 / p. 372	AAA	**Bacci's**	◆◆◆	Italian	$14-$38	387
36 / p. 372	AAA	**Henry VIII Restaurant and Pub**	◆◆◆	English	$16-$40	387
37 / p. 372		Tio Pepe	◆◆	Italian	$14-$29	387

PAGET PARISH

Map Page	OA	Lodgings	Diamond Rated	High Season	Page
34 / p. 372	AAA	**Valley Cottages & Apartments**	◆	Rates not provided SAVE	376
35 / p. 372	AAA	**Greenbank & Cottages**	◆◆	$155-$215 SAVE	374
36 / p. 372	AAA	**Salt Kettle House**	◆	$150-$170 SAVE	376
37 / p. 372	AAA	**Erith Guest House**	◆◆	$170-$245 SAVE	374
38 / p. 372	AAA	**The Wharf Executive Suites**	◆◆◆	$245-$440 SAVE	376
39 / p. 372	AAA	**Fourways Inn Cottage Colony**	◆◆◆	$235-$305 SAVE	374
40 / p. 372	AAA	**Grape Bay Beach Hotel**	◆◆	$175-$195 SAVE	374
41 / p. 372	AAA	**Little Pomander Guest House**	◆	$110-$150 SAVE	376
42 / p. 372	AAA	**Elbow Beach Bermuda, A Mandarin Oriental Hotel**	◆◆◆	$295-$795 SAVE	374
44 / p. 372	AAA	**Coco Reef Resort**	◆◆◆	$343-$830 SAVE	374

Map Page	OA	Restaurants	Diamond Rated	Cuisine	Meal Range	Page
44 / p. 372		**Fourways Inn**		International	$30-$42	376
48 / p. 372		**Seahorse Grill**		International	$24-$45	376

WARWICK PARISH

Map Page	OA	Lodgings	Diamond Rated	High Season	Page
43 / p. 372		**Granaway Guest House & Cottage**		$170-$200 SAVE	388
45 / p. 372		**Blue Horizons**		$125-$175 SAVE	388
46 / p. 372		**Sandpiper Guest Apartments**		$155-$245 SAVE	388
47 / p. 372		**Surf Side Beach Club**		$160-$1260 SAVE	388
48 / p. 372		**Clairfont Apartments**		$150-$175 SAVE	388

HAMILTON PARISH

Map Page	OA	Lodging	Diamond Rated	High Season	Page
49 / p. 372		**Grotto Bay Beach Resort** - see color ad p 373		$185-$360 SAVE	373

Map Page	OA	Restaurants	Diamond Rated	Cuisine	Meal Range	Page
52 / p. 372		Hibiscus Room		Continental	$20-$29	373
53 / p. 372		Swizzle Inn		English	$11-$28	373
54 / p. 372		**Tom Moore's Tavern**		International	$28-$45	373

ST. DAVID'S ISLAND (ST. DAVID'S PARISH)

Map Page	OA	Restaurant	Diamond Rated	Cuisine	Meal Range	Page
55 / p. 372		The Black Horse Tavern		Seafood	$17-$37	381

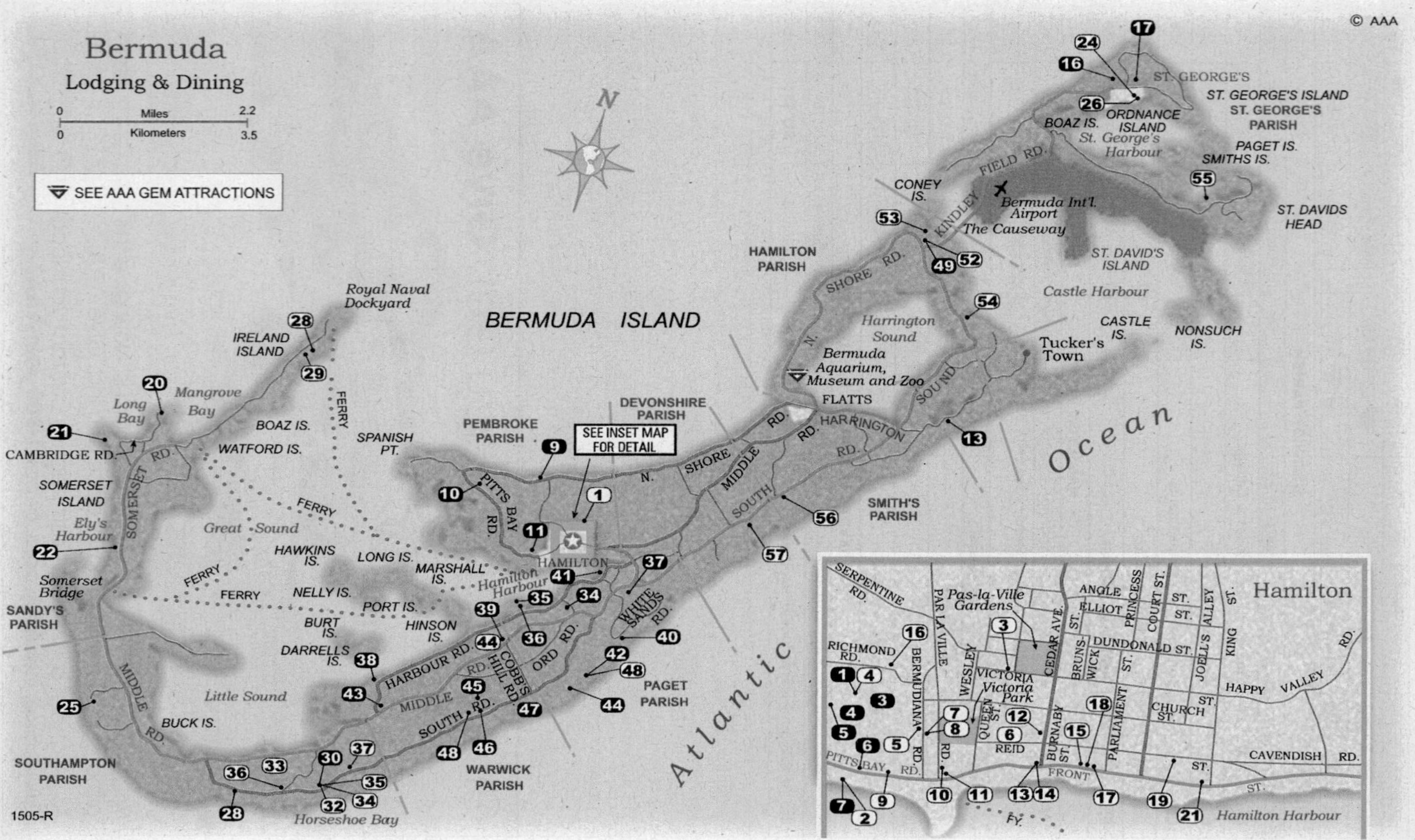

Bermuda
Lodging & Dining
Miles
Kilometers
SEE AAA GEM ATTRACTIONS
© AAA
N
BERMUDA ISLAND
SEE INSET MAP FOR DETAIL
Atlantic
Ocean
ST. GEORGE'S
ST. GEORGE'S ISLAND
ST. GEORGE'S PARISH
ORDNANCE ISLAND
BOAZ IS.
St. George's Harbour
PAGET IS.
SMITHS IS.
ST. DAVIDS HEAD
FIELD RD.
KINDLEY
Bermuda Int'l. Airport
The Causeway
CONEY IS.
ST. DAVID'S ISLAND
Castle Harbour
CASTLE IS.
NONSUCH IS.
Tucker's Town
HAMILTON PARISH
Harrington Sound
Bermuda Aquarium, Museum and Zoo
FLATTS
HARRINGTON SOUND RD.
SMITH'S PARISH
DEVONSHIRE PARISH
PEMBROKE PARISH
Royal Naval Dockyard
IRELAND ISLAND
BOAZ IS.
WATFORD IS.
SPANISH PT.
Mangrove Bay
Long Bay
CAMBRIDGE RD.
SOMERSET ISLAND
SOMERSET RD.
Ely's Harbour
Great Sound
FERRY
HAWKINS IS.
LONG IS.
MARSHALL IS.
Hamilton Harbour
HAMILTON
PITTS BAY RD.
N. SHORE RD.
MIDDLE RD.
SOUTH RD.
WHITE SANDS RD.
ORD RD.
COBB'S HILL RD.
HARBOUR RD.
NELLY IS.
PORT IS.
HINSON IS.
BURT IS.
DARRELLS IS.
Somerset Bridge
SANDY'S PARISH
Little Sound
BUCK IS.
SOUTHAMPTON PARISH
Horseshoe Bay
WARWICK PARISH
PAGET PARISH
1505-R
Hamilton
SERPENTINE RD.
RICHMOND RD.
PAR LA VILLE RD.
BERMUDIANA RD.
Pas-la-Ville Gardens
WESLEY ST.
VICTORIA ST.
Victoria Park
QUEEN ST.
CEDAR AVE.
BRUNSWICK ST.
BURNABY ST.
ANGLE ST.
ELLIOT ST.
PRINCESS ST.
COURT ST.
DUNDONALD ST.
PARLIAMENT ST.
JOELL'S ALLEY
KING ST.
CHURCH ST.
REID ST.
FRONT ST.
HAPPY VALLEY RD.
CAVENDISH RD.
PITTS BAY RD.
FY.
Hamilton Harbour

Hamilton Parish

HAMILTON PARISH pop. 5,270 (See map and index starting on p. 372)

WHERE TO STAY

GROTTO BAY BEACH RESORT *Book great rates at AAA.com* **Phone:** (441)293-8333 (49)

AAA SAVE

Resort Hotel

$185-$360 All Year

Address: 11 Blue Hole Hill **Location:** Oceanfront. On Baileys Bay; just w of the causeway bridge. **Facility:** Situated on a lovely hillside overlooking Bailey's Bay and 21 acres of landscaped grounds, all guest rooms have bay views from private balconies. 201 one-bedroom standard units. 3 stories (no elevator), exterior corridors. **Parking:** on-site. **Terms:** 14 day cancellation notice-fee imposed. **Amenities:** voice mail, safes, irons, hair dryers. **Dining:** 3 restaurants, also, Hibiscus Room, see separate listing. **Pool(s):** heated outdoor. **Leisure Activities:** whirlpool, cave swimming, recreation programs, playground, exercise room, shuffleboard. *Fee:* boats, paddleboats, sailboats, windsurfing, scuba diving, snorkeling, charter fishing, 4 tennis courts (2 lighted), motor bikes; croquet, bicycles, massage. **Guest Services:** valet and coin laundry, wireless Internet. **Business Services:** meeting rooms, PC (fee). **Cards:** AX, MC, VI. *(See color ad below)*

D / SOME UNITS FEE VCR

WHERE TO DINE

HIBISCUS ROOM **Phone:** 441/293-8333 (52)

Continental

$20-$29

The contemporary dining room with a tropical theme presents a daily changing menu with a mix of European and Bermudian influences. Guests might start the day with the all-inclusive breakfast buffet or wrap it up with a la carte service at dinner. Outdoor terrace seating is an option. A 15 percent service charge applies to all meals. Dressy casual. **Bar:** Full bar. **Reservations:** suggested. **Hours:** 7:30 am-10:30 & 6:30-9 pm. **Address:** 11 Blue Hole Hill **Location:** On Baileys Bay; just w of causeway bridge; in Grotto Bay Beach Resort. **Parking:** on-site. **Cards:** AX, MC, VI.

SWIZZLE INN **Phone:** 441/293-1854 (53)

English

$11-$28

Legend has it that the historic pub is the birthplace of the rum swizzle. Patrons' business cards cover the walls and ceiling. Alfresco seating is available. The menu centers on English pub fare: sandwiches to full meals. Portions are hearty. Live entertainment is lined up in the summer. Casual dress. Entertainment. **Bar:** Full bar. **Hours:** 11 am-10 pm. Closed: 12/25; also 1st day of Cup Match (July). **Address:** 3 Blue Hole Hill **Location:** On Blue Hole Hill; in Baileys Bay. **Parking:** on-site. **Cards:** MC, VI. **Historic**

TOM MOORE'S TAVERN **Phone:** 441/293-8020 (54)

AAA

International

$28-$45

Considered to be Bermuda's oldest restaurant, the carefully restored mid-17th-century home occupies a lovely, peaceful setting. Contributing to the graceful atmosphere are handsome table settings, original woodwork and antiques. The cadre of servers is pampering and attentive. Continental cuisine with Bermudian influences is skillfully prepared, delicious and visually appealing. Semi-formal attire. **Bar:** Full bar. **Reservations:** required. **Hours:** Open 12/1-1/1 & 2/14-11/30; 6:30 pm-10 pm. Closed: 12/25; also 1st day of Cricket Match (August). **Address:** 7 Walsingham Ln **Location:** Walsingham Bay; off Harrington Sound Rd. **Parking:** on-site. **Cards:** AX, MC, VI. **Historic**

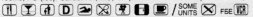

▼ *See AAA listing above* ▼

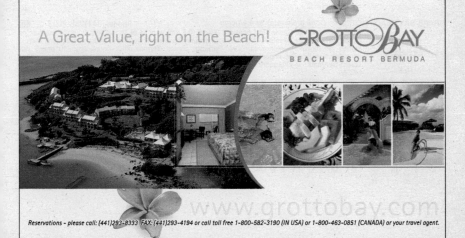

Paget Parish

PAGET PARISH pop. 5,088 (See map and index starting on p. 372)

WHERE TO STAY

COCO REEF RESORT Phone: (441)236-5416 44

Hotel
$343-$830 All Year

Address: 3 Stonington Cir **Location:** Oceanfront. Off South Shore Rd; on Elbow Beach. **Facility:** Designated smoking area. 64 units. 60 one-bedroom standard units. 2 one-bedroom suites. 2 cottages. 2 stories (no elevator), exterior corridors. **Parking:** on-site. **Terms:** 14 day cancellation notice, 7 day in winter-fee imposed. **Amenities:** voice mail, safes, irons, hair dryers. **Dining:** 2 restaurants. **Pool(s):** heated outdoor. **Leisure Activities:** 2 tennis courts. *Fee:* motor bikes. **Guest Services:** valet laundry, wireless Internet. **Business Services:** meeting rooms, PC. **Cards:** AX, MC, VI.

ELBOW BEACH BERMUDA, A MANDARIN ORIENTAL HOTEL Phone: (441)236-3535 42

Resort Hotel
$295-$795 All Year

Address: 60 S South Shore Rd **Location:** Oceanfront. At Elbow Beach; on the south coast. **Facility:** Recently renovated, the refined property offers a variety of guest unit categories set on 50 landscaped acres that slope down to a pink-sand beach. 235 units. 151 one-bedroom standard units. 79 one-, 3 two- and 2 three-bedroom suites, some with whirlpools. 1-4 stories, interior/exterior corridors. **Parking:** on-site. **Terms:** 14 day cancellation notice-fee imposed. **Amenities:** video library, CD players, high-speed Internet (fee), dual phone lines, voice mail, safes, honor bars, irons, hair dryers. *Some:* DVD players, fax. **Dining:** 5 restaurants, also, Seahorse Grill, see separate listing, entertainment. **Pool(s):** heated outdoor. **Leisure Activities:** whirlpool, rental paddleboats, snorkeling equipment rental, putting green, recreation programs in season, kids club, exercise room, spa, volleyball. *Fee:* scuba diving, kayaks, 5 tennis courts (3 lighted), motor bikes, bicycles. **Guest Services:** valet laundry, beauty salon, wireless Internet. **Business Services:** conference facilities, business center. **Cards:** AX, DC, MC, VI.

24 S D / SOME UNITS

ERITH GUEST HOUSE Phone: 441/232-1827 37

Bed & Breakfast
$170-$245 4/1-11/30
$140-$200 12/1-3/31

Address: 15 Pomander Rd **Location:** Jct The Lane, just w. **Facility:** Smoke free premises. 8 units. 7 one-bedroom standard units, some with kitchens. 1 one-bedroom suite with kitchen. 1-2 stories (no elevator), interior/exterior corridors. *Bath:* combo or shower only. **Parking:** on-site. **Terms:** office hours 8 am-6 pm, 21 day cancellation notice. **Amenities:** high-speed Internet (fee), voice mail, safes, irons, hair dryers. **Pool(s):** outdoor. **Leisure Activities:** whirlpool, gas grill. **Guest Services:** valet laundry, wireless Internet. **Cards:** AX, MC, VI.

D / SOME UNITS VCR

FOURWAYS INN COTTAGE COLONY Phone: (441)236-6517 39

Cottage
$235-$305 4/1-11/30
$190-$220 12/1-3/31

Address: 1 Middle Rd **Location:** Jct Cobbs Hill and Middle rds. Located in a quiet, secluded area. **Facility:** Luxurious units in refined cottage setting. Smoke free premises. 11 cottages. 2 stories (no elevator), exterior corridors. **Parking:** on-site. **Terms:** office hours 7 am-midnight, 21 day cancellation notice-fee imposed. **Amenities:** voice mail, safes, irons, hair dryers. **Dining:** Fourways Inn, see separate listing. **Pool(s):** outdoor. **Leisure Activities:** shared facilities at Coco Reef Resort. **Guest Services:** valet laundry, wireless Internet. **Business Services:** meeting rooms. **Cards:** AX, MC, VI.

D

GRAPE BAY BEACH HOTEL Phone: (441)236-2023 40

Hotel
$175-$195 All Year

Address: 55 White Sands Rd **Location:** 0.3 mi (0.5 km) w of jct of Middle and South Shore rds; on Grape Bay. **Facility:** Meets AAA guest room security requirements. 24 one-bedroom standard units. 3 stories (no elevator), interior corridors. **Parking:** on-site. **Terms:** office hours 7 am-10 pm, 7 day cancellation notice-fee imposed. **Amenities:** voice mail, safes, irons, hair dryers. **Pool(s):** outdoor. **Guest Services:** valet laundry, wireless Internet. **Business Services:** meeting rooms, PC. **Cards:** AX, MC, VI.

D

GREENBANK & COTTAGES Phone: (441)236-3615 35

Cottage
$155-$215 4/1-11/30
$130-$180 12/1-3/31

Address: 17 Salt Kettle Rd **Location:** Oceanfront. On Salt Kettle Peninsula; off Harbour Rd. Located in a secluded area. **Facility:** Smoke free premises. 11 cottages. 1 story, exterior corridors. *Bath:* combo or shower only. **Parking:** on-site. **Terms:** office hours 9 am-5 pm, 3 night minimum stay, 21 day cancellation notice-fee imposed. **Amenities:** irons, hair dryers. **Leisure Activities:** boat dock. **Guest Services:** TV in common area, wireless Internet. **Cards:** AX, MC, VI.

D / SOME UNITS

(See map and index starting on p. 372)

LITTLE POMANDER GUEST HOUSE Phone: 441/236-7635 41

AAA SAVE

Bed & Breakfast
$110-$150 All Year

Address: 16 Pomander Rd **Location:** Jct The Lane, just w. **Facility:** Smoke free premises. 5 one-bedroom standard units. 2 stories (no elevator), interior/exterior corridors. **Parking:** on-site. **Terms:** office hours 9 am-midnight, 3 night minimum stay, 21 day cancellation notice-fee imposed. **Amenities:** irons, hair dryers. **Guest Services:** wireless Internet. **Cards:** AX, MC, VI.

D

SALT KETTLE HOUSE Phone: (441)236-0407 36

AAA SAVE

Bed & Breakfast
$150-$170 3/1-11/30
$120-$140 12/1-2/28

Address: 10 Salt Kettle Rd **Location:** Oceanfront. On Salt Kettle Peninsula; off Harbour Rd. Located in a secluded area. **Facility:** Smoke free premises. 9 units. 5 one-bedroom standard units. 4 cottages. 1 story, exterior corridors. *Bath:* combo or shower only. **Parking:** on-site. **Terms:** office hours 8 am-8 pm, 21 day cancellation notice-fee imposed. **Amenities:** hair dryers. **Leisure Activities:** gas grill. **Guest Services:** TV in common area, complimentary laundry.

D / SOME UNITS

VALLEY COTTAGES & APARTMENTS Phone: 441/236-0628 34

AAA SAVE

Cottage
Rates not provided

Address: 2 Simons Ln **Location:** Jct Middle, just n on Valley Rd, then just w. Across from Oleander Scooter Rentals. **Facility:** 9 units. 3 one-bedroom standard units with efficiencies. 6 two-bedroom suites with kitchens. 1-2 stories (no elevator), exterior corridors. *Bath:* combo or shower only. **Parking:** on-site. **Amenities:** irons. *Some:* high-speed Internet. **Guest Services:** coin laundry.

D

THE WHARF EXECUTIVE SUITES *Book great rates at AAA.com* Phone: (441)232-5700 38

AAA SAVE

Motel
$245-$440 All Year

Address: 1 Harbour Rd **Location:** Oceanfront. At Darrell's Wharf. **Facility:** Meets AAA guest room security requirements. 15 units. 10 one-bedroom standard units. 5 one-bedroom suites with kitchens. 2 stories (no elevator), interior corridors. **Parking:** on-site. **Terms:** 3 day cancellation notice-fee imposed. **Amenities:** high-speed Internet, dual phone lines, voice mail, fax, safes, irons, hair dryers. **Leisure Activities:** use of facilities at sister properties. **Guest Services:** valet laundry. **Business Services:** meeting rooms, PC. **Cards:** AX, MC, VI.

S D

WHERE TO DINE

FOURWAYS INN Phone: 441/236-6517 44

AAA

International
$30-$42

The 1727 Georgian-style Bermuda manor house, now handsomely restored, is a picture of charming elegance. Service is outstanding, and even the most sophisticated palate will be pleased by the exceptional menu of haute cuisine. Try the signature dish: foie gras prepared with caramelized pineapple in a cranberry and black grape reduction. The entrees range from Chateaubriand to Arctic Char. Indulge in a souffle du jour for dessert. Dressy casual. Entertainment. **Bar:** Full bar. **Reservations:** required. **Hours:** 6:30 pm-9:30 pm; Sunday brunch 11:30 am-2:30 pm. **Address:** 1 Middle Rd **Location:** Jct Cobbs Hill and Middle rds; in Fourways Inn Cottage Colony. **Parking:** on-site. **Cards:** AX, MC, VI. **Historic**

SEAHORSE GRILL Phone: 441/236-3535 48

AAA

International
$24-$45

Patrons can relax in refined surroundings and enjoy attentive service while savoring choice dishes from the ever-changing menu. Some starter offerings might include lobster bisque, seared foie gras or baked Caesar salad with anchovy tempura. Creative entrees range from soft-shell crab with soy risotto and loquat chutney to braised beef short rib with taro gnocchi to pancetta-wrapped monkfish. The desserts are simply too tempting to pass up. Dressy casual. **Bar:** Full bar. **Reservations:** required. **Hours:** 7 am-11 & 6:30-10:30 pm, Sun 7 am-10:30 & noon-3 pm. **Address:** 60 South Shore Rd **Location:** At Elbow Beach; on the south coast; in Elbow Beach Bermuda, A Mandarin Oriental Hotel. **Parking:** on-site. **Cards:** AX, MC, VI.

Pembroke Parish

HAMILTON pop. 969 (See map and index starting on p. 372)

WHERE TO STAY

BAY CITY GUEST HOUSE Phone: 441/295-1275 **11**

AAA SAVE

Bed & Breakfast
$220-$310 All Year

Address: 53 Pitts Bay Rd **Location:** 0.6 mi w of Hamilton Ferry terminal. **Facility:** Just west of town, this recently renovated establishment is geared toward the business traveler in need of modern conveniences and technology. Smoke free premises. 12 one-bedroom standard units, some with whirlpools. 2 stories (no elevator), interior/exterior corridors. *Bath:* combo or shower only. **Parking:** on-site. **Terms:** office hours 9 am-6 pm, age restrictions may apply, cancellation fee imposed. **Amenities:** high-speed Internet, voice mail, irons, hair dryers. *Some:* CD players. **Guest Services:** valet laundry. **Cards:** AX, MC, VI.

D / SOME UNITS

EDGEHILL MANOR GUEST HOUSE Phone: 441/295-7124 **5**

AAA SAVE

Bed & Breakfast
$208-$220 4/2-11/30
$182-$192 12/1-4/1

Address: 36 Rosemont Ave **Location:** Just w on Pitts Bay Rd, 0.5 mi (0.8 km) n. **Facility:** Smoke free premises. 14 one-bedroom standard units, some with kitchens. 2 stories (no elevator), interior/exterior corridors. *Bath:* combo or shower only. **Parking:** on-site. **Terms:** 14 day cancellation notice-fee imposed. **Amenities:** safes, irons, hair dryers. *Some:* high-speed Internet. **Pool(s):** outdoor. **Guest Services:** valet laundry, wireless Internet. **Cards:** AX, MC, VI.

D / SOME UNITS VCR

THE FAIRMONT HAMILTON PRINCESS *Book great rates at AAA.com* Phone: (441)295-3000 **7**

AAA SAVE

Hotel
$199-$689 All Year

Address: 76 Pitts Bay Rd **Location:** Oceanfront. Downtown. **Facility:** Meets AAA guest room security requirements. Smoke free premises. 410 units. 367 one-bedroom standard units. 43 one-bedroom suites. 3-7 stories, interior/exterior corridors. *Bath:* combo or shower only. **Parking:** on-site. **Terms:** check-in 4 pm, 3 day cancellation notice. **Amenities:** video library, high-speed Internet (fee), voice mail, safes, honor bars, irons, hair dryers. *Some:* DVD players, CD players, dual phone lines. **Dining:** Harley's Bistro, see separate listing, entertainment. **Pool(s):** outdoor, heated outdoor. **Leisure Activities:** fishing, putting green, exercise room, spa. *Fee:* sailboats, boat dock, scuba diving, snorkeling, charter fishing, personal watercraft, water tours, golf privileges, motorbikes. **Guest Services:** valet laundry, area transportation-ferry to beach club at Fairmont Southampton, wireless Internet. **Business Services:** conference facilities, business center. **Cards:** AX, DC, MC, VI. *(See color ad p 378)*

S D / SOME UNITS FEE

MAZARINE BY THE SEA Phone: (441)292-1690 **9**

AAA SAVE

Motel
$120-$180 All Year

Address: 91 North Shore Rd **Location:** Oceanfront. Jct Blackwatch Pass, just w. **Facility:** Smoke free premises. 7 one-bedroom standard units with efficiencies. 1 story, exterior corridors. *Bath:* combo or shower only. **Parking:** on-site. **Terms:** office hours 8:30 am-11 pm, off-site registration, 2 night minimum stay - seasonal, 14 day cancellation notice-fee imposed. **Amenities:** voice mail, irons. **Pool(s):** outdoor. **Leisure Activities:** charcoal grill. **Cards:** MC, VI.

D

THE OXFORD HOUSE Phone: 441/295-0503 **3**

AAA SAVE

Bed & Breakfast
$183-$220 All Year

Address: 20 Woodbourne Ave **Location:** Between Pitts Bay and Richmond rds. **Facility:** Designated smoking area. 12 one-bedroom standard units. 2 stories (no elevator), interior/exterior corridors. *Bath:* combo or shower only. **Parking:** street. **Terms:** office hours 7 am-6 pm, 14 day cancellation notice-fee imposed. **Amenities:** irons, hair dryers. **Guest Services:** valet laundry. **Cards:** AX, MC, VI.

D

ROBIN'S NEST Phone: 441/292-4347 **10**

AAA SAVE

Motel
$150-$240 All Year

Address: 37 Mount View Rd **Location:** Jct St. John's Rd, just n. **Facility:** Smoke free premises. 11 units. 9 one-bedroom standard units with efficiencies. 2 one-bedroom suites with efficiencies. 2 stories (no elevator), exterior corridors. **Parking:** on-site. **Terms:** 3 night minimum stay, age restrictions may apply, 14 day cancellation notice. **Amenities:** voice mail, safes, irons, hair dryers. *Some:* CD players. **Pool(s):** outdoor. **Cards:** MC, VI.

▼ See AAA listing p 377 ▼

(See map and index starting on p. 372)

ROSEDON HOTEL Book great rates at AAA.com **Phone:** (441)295-1640 6

Hotel

$260-$402 4/1-11/30
$204-$336 12/1-3/31

Address: 57 Pitts Bay Rd **Location:** Downtown; across from waterfront. **Facility:** 44 one-bedroom standard units. 2 stories (no elevator), interior/exterior corridors. *Bath:* combo or shower only. **Parking:** on-site. **Terms:** office hours 7 am-8 pm, 14 day cancellation notice-fee imposed. **Amenities:** video library, high-speed Internet, voice mail, safes, irons, hair dryers. *Some:* CD players, dual phone lines. **Pool(s):** heated outdoor. **Guest Services:** valet laundry, area transportation-Elbow Beach, wireless Internet. **Business Services:** PC. **Cards:** AX, MC, VI.

/ SOME UNITS

ROSEMONT GUEST APARTMENTS Book great rates at AAA.com **Phone:** (441)292-1055 4

Motel

$214-$256 All Year

Address: 41 Rosemont Ave **Location:** 0.5 mi (0.8 km) w of downtown; just w on Pitts Bay Rd, just n. **Facility:** Smoke free premises. 47 units. 37 one-bedroom standard units with efficiencies, some with whirlpools. 10 one-bedroom suites with efficiencies. 3 stories, exterior corridors. *Bath:* combo or shower only. **Parking:** on-site. **Terms:** office hours 8 am-8 pm, 14 day cancellation notice-fee imposed. **Amenities:** voice mail, irons, hair dryers. **Pool(s):** outdoor. **Guest Services:** valet and coin laundry, wireless Internet. **Business Services:** PC. **Cards:** AX, MC, VI.

ROYAL PALMS HOTEL Book great rates at AAA.com **Phone:** (441)292-1854 1

Country Inn

$266-$354 4/1-11/30
$239-$319 12/1-3/31

Address: 24 Rosemont Ave **Location:** Just w on Pitts Bay Rd, 0.8 mi (1.3 km) n. Located in a quiet residential area. **Facility:** This small, charming inn has an ambience recalling Bermuda in an earlier time; restored residences house richly furnished lodgings. Smoke free premises. 32 units. 28 one-bedroom standard units. 4 one-bedroom suites. 2 stories (no elevator), interior/exterior corridors. *Bath:* some combo or shower only. **Parking:** on-site. **Terms:** office hours 7 am-9 pm, 7 day cancellation notice-fee imposed. **Amenities:** high-speed Internet (fee), dual phone lines, voice mail, safes, irons, hair dryers. **Dining:** Ascots Restaurant, see separate listing. **Pool(s):** outdoor. **Guest Services:** valet laundry, wireless Internet. **Cards:** AX, MC, VI.

/ SOME UNITS

WHERE TO DINE

ASCOTS RESTAURANT **Phone:** 441/295-9644 4

Mediterranean
$15-$38

The former Bermuda home boasts a gracious Victorian-style dining room and a charming veranda. The cedar-lined bar's pleasant atmosphere is fitting for relaxing before or after dinner. The chef/owner prepares creative cuisine with an international flair, and the four-course chef's surprise menu changes daily. Dressy casual. **Bar:** Full bar. **Reservations:** required. **Hours:** noon-2:30 & 6:30-10 pm, Sat from 6:30 pm. Closed: Sun, 1st day of Cup Match (July) & for lunch on public holidays. **Address:** 24 Rosemont Ave **Location:** Just w on Pitts Bay Rd, 0.8 mi (1.3 km) n ; in Royal Palms Hotel. **Parking:** on-site. **Cards:** AX, MC, VI.

BARRACUDA GRILL **Phone:** 441/292-1609 14

Steak & Seafood
$14-$40

A very cool and contemporary-style restaurant with dark mahogany furnishings. Fresh, creatively prepared seafood and chops are served in a friendly, crisp manner. Over fifteen wines by the glass are featured. Dressy casual. **Bar:** Full bar. **Reservations:** required. **Hours:** noon-2:30 & 5:30-10 pm, Fri-11 pm, Sat 5:30 pm-11 pm, Sun 5:30 pm-10 pm. Closed: 12/25, 12/26; also for lunch on Bermuda public holidays. **Address:** 5 Burnaby Hill **Location:** Just off Front St; downtown; above Hog Penny Restaurant & Pub. **Parking:** street. **Cards:** AX, MC, VI.

CAFE CAIRO RESTAURANT & BAR **Phone:** 441/295-5155 17

Middle Eastern
$12-$28

One of the latest and most unique restaurants on the Bermuda dining scene, the authentic Middle Eastern restaurant combines the best elements of Egyptian, Lebanese and Moroccan cuisine with a decorative motif in three distinct dining areas. Some of the favorite dishes include the stuffed grape leaves and the moussaka. Also offered are a mixed cold appetizer platter as well as a hot appetizer platter—both are great for sharing. Belly dancing is featured on some nights. Dressy casual. Entertainment. **Bar:** Full bar. **Reservations:** suggested. **Hours:** noon-2:30 am, Sat & Sun from 6 pm. Closed: for lunch on public holidays. **Address:** 93 Front St **Location:** Downtown; on waterfront. **Parking:** street. **Cards:** AX, MC, VI.

CHOPSTICKS **Phone:** 441/292-0791 19

Asian
$9-$23

The popular establishment serves well-prepared Chinese and Thai food. Made-to-order meals allow guests' dietary restrictions to be taken into account. Dressy casual. **Bar:** Full bar. **Reservations:** suggested. **Hours:** 11:30 am-2:30 & 5-11 pm, Sat, Sun & major holidays from 5 pm. Closed: 12/25. **Address:** 88 Reid St **Location:** Between King and Court sts. **Parking:** street. **Cards:** AX, MC, VI.

THE HARBOURFRONT RESTAURANT & SUSHI BAR **Phone:** 441/295-4207 11

International
$15-$37

The menu sports well-prepared Mediterranean and Asian cuisines like duck breast with orange anise sauce, veal Oscar with shiitake mushroom sauce and the "bento box" with an array of sushi, sashimi, black cod and tempura shrimp. Escargot or salmon and tuna carpaccio are excellent starters while the chocolate truffle with coconut ice cream ends the dining experience on a fine note. Dressy casual. **Bar:** Full bar. **Reservations:** suggested. **Hours:** 11:45 am-3:30 & 6-10 pm. Closed: 1/1, 12/25, 12/26; also Sun & for lunch on Bermuda public holidays. **Address:** 40 Crow Ln **Location:** Just e of downtown Hamilton; on E Broadway; in Bermuda Underwater Exploration Institute. **Parking:** on-site. **Cards:** AX, MC, VI.

HARLEY'S BISTRO **Phone:** 441/295-3000 2

Continental
$27-$39

Overlooking Hamilton Harbor, the tastefully-appointed dining room offers a relaxed dining experience. A varied menu features such international favorites as sword fish, rack of lamb and seafood cioppino. The fish chowder or Bermuda onion bisque is a great way to start the meal. Dressy casual. **Bar:** Full bar. **Reservations:** required. **Hours:** 7 am-11 & noon-9:30 pm. **Address:** 76 Pitts Bay Rd **Location:** Downtown; in The Fairmont Hamilton Princess. **Parking:** on-site. **Cards:** AX, DC, MC, VI.

(See map and index starting on p. 372)

HOG PENNY RESTAURANT & PUB — Phone: 441/292-2534 (13)

English
$16-$34

One of the oldest pubs in Bermuda, the cozy, informal spot prepares traditional pub fare—such as fish and chips, steak and kidney pie and bangers and mash—as well as Indian curry selections, sandwiches and burgers. The staff is cheerful and unpretentious. Casual dress. **Bar:** Full bar. **Reservations:** suggested. **Hours:** 11:30 am-3 & 5:30-10 pm. Closed: 1/1, 12/25. **Address:** 5 Burnaby Hill **Location:** Just off Front St; downtown. **Parking:** street. **Cards:** AX, MC, VI. **Historic**

HOUSE OF INDIA — **Phone:** 441/295-6450 (1)

Indian
$10-$18

The little hole-in-the-wall operation across from the Salvation Army barracks in an area of Hamilton known locally as "Back of Town" offers Indian and Pakistani dishes that come highly recommended by locals. You'll find an excellent selection of breads, meats, seafood and vegetarian delights. A buffet-only lunch makes way for a much wider, a la carte selection for dinner. Dressy casual. **Bar:** Beer & wine. **Reservations:** suggested. **Hours:** 11 am-2:30 & 5-9:45 pm, Sat & Sun 5 pm-10 pm. Closed major holidays. **Address:** 57 North St **Location:** Just e of north end of Court St; in Park View Plaza. **Parking:** street. **Cards:** AX, MC, VI.

LA TRATTORIA — **Phone:** 441/295-1877 (3)

Italian
$10-$29

Guests can follow their nose to the aroma of garlic. Checkered tablecloths and a bustling, upbeat atmosphere make for a cozy, informal experience. The all-Italian staff serves authentic food. Dressy casual. **Bar:** Full bar. **Reservations:** suggested, for dinner. **Hours:** 11:30 am-3:30 & 5:30-10:30 pm, Sun 5:30 pm-10 pm; 5:30 pm-10 pm 11/15-4/15. Closed: 1/1, 12/25; also 1st day of Cup Match (July) & for lunch on public holidays. **Address:** 22 Washington Ln **Location:** Between Reid and Church sts; downtown; adjacent to Washington Mall. **Parking:** on-site. **Cards:** AX, MC, VI.

THE LITTLE VENICE — **Phone:** 441/295-3503 (8)

Italian
$22-$40

The restaurant is very popular with locals and out-of towners alike. The antipasto, carpaccio or the calamari are great beginnings to a fine meal. For pasta lovers there are savory preparations of gnocchi, risotto, penne, ravioli, lasagna and pappardelle to choose from. Salmon, clams, sea bass and scallops top the seafood portion of the menu while meats include rack of lamb, veal tenderloin, free range chicken and Barberry duck breast. Fabulous desserts round off the menu. Dressy casual. **Bar:** Full bar. **Reservations:** required. **Hours:** noon-2 & 6:30-10 pm, Sat & Sun from 6 pm. Closed: 12/24, 12/25; also 1st day of Cup Match (July); for lunch on public holidays. **Address:** 32 Bermudiana Rd **Location:** Between Church and Front sts; downtown. **Parking:** street. **Cards:** AX, MC, VI.

THE LOBSTER POT RESTAURANT & BOATHOUSE BAR — **Phone:** 441/292-6898 (5)

Seafood
$11-$32

A popular spot with locals and tourists alike, the casual eatery sports nautical decor and sustains a bustling atmosphere. Traditional and island seafood dishes are prepared in a number of ways. Tempting meat and poultry selections appeal to landlubbers. Casual dress. **Bar:** Full bar. **Reservations:** suggested. **Hours:** 11 am-3 & 5:30-9:45 pm, Sat from 5:30 pm, Sun from 6 pm. Closed major holidays. **Address:** 6 Bermudiana Rd **Location:** Just off Front St; center of downtown. **Parking:** street. **Cards:** AX, MC, VI.

L'ORIENTAL — **Phone:** 441/296-4477 (7)

Asian
$16-$48

The bustling dining room features Teppanyaki tables and two sushi bars. Fusion cuisine is served here blending the finest elements of Asian and Mediterranean cooking. An array of sushi, sashimi and tempura dishes are offered. Main course offerings may include grilled pork chop with oriental five spice, Thai beef curry or giant scallops with mushroom pasta and smoked tomato concasse. Don't neglect dessert with such temptations as orange infused creme caramel or Asian peach tart. Dressy casual. **Bar:** Full bar. **Reservations:** required. **Hours:** noon-2:15 & 6-10 pm, Sat & Sun from 6 pm. Closed: 12/24, 12/25; also 1st day of Cup Match (July); lunch on Bermuda public holidays. **Address:** 32 Bermudiana Rd **Location:** Between Church and Front sts; downtown. **Parking:** street. **Cards:** AX, DC, DS, MC, VI.

(See map and index starting on p. 372)

PORT O' CALL RESTAURANT **Phone:** 441/295-5373 (12)

Steak & Seafood
$10-$45

Located across from the waterfront, this popular dining spot offers fresh seafood and well-prepared steaks in a casual upscale setting. Enjoy dining al fresco at sidewalk tables in the warmer weather. An award-winning, lengthy wine list is featured. Dressy casual. **Bar:** Full bar. **Reservations:** suggested. **Hours:** noon-2:30 & 6-10 pm, Sat & Sun from 6 pm. Closed: for lunch on public holidays. **Address:** 87 Front St **Location:** Downtown, on waterfront. **Parking:** street. **Cards:** AX, MC, VI.

PORTOFINO **Phone:** 441/292-2375 (10)

Italian
$12-$29

Pasta, pizza and creative daily specials tempt diners at the lively eatery, which is in the hub of activity. Dressy casual. **Bar:** Full bar. **Reservations:** accepted. **Hours:** 11:30 am-2:30 & 6-10:30 pm, Sat 6 pm-11:45 pm, Sun 6 pm-11 pm. Closed: 1/1, 12/24, 12/25; also Bermuda Day, 1st day of Cup Match (July) & for lunch on Bermuda public holidays. **Address:** 48 Bermudiana Rd **Location:** Corner of Front St; west side of downtown. **Parking:** on-site. **Cards:** AX, MC, VI.

THE RED CARPET **Phone:** 441/292-6195 (6)

Continental
$17-$36

Popular with local businesspeople, the comfortable dining room incorporates copious amounts of red into the decor. Well-prepared cuisine blends Continental, Italian and German elements. Dressy casual. **Bar:** Full bar. **Reservations:** suggested. **Hours:** 11:30 am-2:45 & 6:30-10 pm. Closed major holidays; also Sun. **Address:** 37 Reid St **Location:** In Armory Building. **Parking:** street. **Cards:** AX, MC, VI.

RISTORANTE PRIMAVERA **Phone:** 441/295-2167 (9)

Italian
$17-$38

The restaurant's comfortable dining room offers subtle elegance in a traditional Italian setting. The mostly Italian staff provides attentive service. The chef prepares fresh seafood selections, as well as dishes ranging from ravioli to saltimbocca alla romana. Dressy casual. **Bar:** Full bar. **Reservations:** suggested. **Hours:** 11:45 am-2 & 6-10 pm, Sat & Sun from 6 pm. Closed: 1/1, 12/25; also for lunch on Bermuda public holidays. **Address:** 69 Pitts Bay Rd **Location:** Just e of The Fairmont Hamilton Princess and across from Barcardi Headquarters. **Parking:** on-site. **Cards:** AX, DC, MC, VI.

THE ROBIN HOOD PUB & RESTAURANT **Phone:** 441/295-3314 (16)

English
$12-$28

The boisterous tavern draws a mixed crowd of locals, tourists and sports enthusiasts who watch the big-screen TVs. Those who like to imbibe a favorite brew will find pleasure here, as well. Straightforward service matches well with the large portions of comfort food. Besides the familiar pub fare, menu items include bangers and mash, fish and chips and hearty chowders. Casual dress. **Bar:** Full bar. **Reservations:** accepted. **Hours:** noon-2:30 & 4:30-10 pm, Sat & Sun 11 am-10 pm. Closed: 1/1, 12/25; also for lunch on public holidays. **Address:** 25 Richmond Rd **Location:** Between Pitts Bay Rd and Woodbourne Ave; downtown. **Parking:** on-site. **Cards:** AX, MC, VI.

ROSA'S CANTINA **Phone:** 441/295-1912 (21)

AAA

Tex-Mex
$13-$25

Representative of Tex-Mex food are fajitas, burritos and tacos. The menu also lists steak and seafood. Locals enjoy unwinding here. Try fried ice cream for dessert. Casual dress. **Bar:** Full bar. **Reservations:** suggested. **Hours:** 11:30 am-11 pm. Closed: 12/25. **Address:** 121 Front St **Location:** Between King and Court sts. **Parking:** street. **Cards:** AX, MC, VI.

SILK **Phone:** 441/295-0449 (15)

Thai
$12-$23

The island's only Thai restaurant, the award-winning spot has earned international accolades. Well-planned decor transports guests to far-off Thailand. Among dishes are red, green and yellow curries combined with seafood, chicken, pork or beef, in addition to four delicately prepared soups. After a savory meal, such desserts as chocolate and banana custard cake are a great finale. Dressy casual. **Bar:** Full bar. **Reservations:** suggested. **Hours:** noon-2:30 & 6:30-10 pm, Sat 6:30 pm-10 pm. Closed: Sun & for lunch on public holidays. **Address:** 55 Front St **Location:** Downtown; across from waterfront; in Masters Building. **Parking:** street. **Cards:** AX, MC, VI.

THE SPOT RESTAURANT **Phone:** 441/292-6293 (18)

American
$7-$18

Popular with the locals and tourists for more than 60 years for their down-home favorites with a Bermudian twist. Roast turkey, fried chicken, and a daily vegetable selection are just a few samples from the lengthy menu that also offers sandwiches, wraps and seafood. Casual dress. **Hours:** 6:30 am-8 pm. Closed major holidays; also Sun. **Address:** 6 Burnaby Hill **Location:** Jct Front St, 2 blks n. **Parking:** street.

St. David's Parish

ST. DAVID'S ISLAND (See map and index starting on p. 372)

WHERE TO DINE

THE BLACK HORSE TAVERN **Phone:** 441/297-1991 (55)

Seafood
$17-$37

The simple restaurant is known for fresh seafood. Visitors to St. David's Lighthouse often stop in for lunch. Hearty fish chowder and English-style fish and chips are favorites. Casual dress. **Bar:** Full bar. **Reservations:** accepted. **Hours:** Open 12/1-12/9 & 1/21-11/30; noon-9:30 pm. Closed major holidays; also Mon. **Address:** 34 Great Bay Rd **Location:** Beside St. David's Post Office; overlooking Great Bay. **Parking:** on-site. **Cards:** AX, MC, VI.

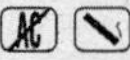

St. George's Parish

ST. GEORGE'S pop. 1,752 (See map and index starting on p. 372)

WHERE TO STAY

AUNT NEA'S INN AT HILLCREST *Book great rates at AAA.com* **Phone:** (441)297-1630 17

AAA SAVE

Historic Bed & Breakfast
$125-$240 All Year

Address: 1 Nea's Alley **Location:** 0.3 mi (0.5 km) w from Kings Square, off Duke of York St. **Facility:** Family-owned for many generations, this home converted into an inn features some unique, collector furnishings. A new addition is across the street. Designated smoking area. 13 units. 11 one-bedroom standard units, some with efficiencies and/or whirlpools. 2 one-bedroom suites. 2 stories, interior/exterior corridors. *Bath:* combo or shower only. **Parking:** on-site. **Terms:** office hours 9 am-noon, 2 night minimum stay, 14 day cancellation notice-fee imposed. **Amenities:** dual phone lines, voice mail. *Some:* DVD players. **Leisure Activities:** recreational privileges at St. George's Club. **Guest Services:** valet laundry, wireless Internet. **Cards:** AX, MC, VI.

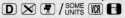

D / SOME UNITS VCR

THE ST. GEORGE'S CLUB **Phone:** (441)297-1200 16

AAA SAVE

Condominium
$360-$460 3/2-11/30
$179-$260 12/1-3/1

Address: 6 Rose Hill St **Location:** Just n of York St. **Facility:** These modern, well-equipped and attractively furnished cottage-style units are in a time-share colony with a choice of harbor or golf course views. Designated smoking area. 71 condominiums. 1-2 stories, exterior corridors. **Parking:** on-site. **Terms:** check-in 4 pm, 2 night minimum stay, 21 day cancellation notice. **Amenities:** CD players, voice mail, safes, irons, hair dryers. *Some:* DVD players (fee). **Dining:** 2 restaurants. **Pool(s):** 2 outdoor, heated outdoor. **Leisure Activities:** snorkeling equipment rental, golf privileges, 3 lighted tennis courts, exercise room. *Fee:* kayaks, motor scooters. **Guest Services:** coin laundry, wireless Internet. **Business Services:** PC (fee). **Cards:** AX, MC, VI.

D

WHERE TO DINE

CAFE' GIO **Phone:** 441/297-1307 26

International
$10-$29

The cafe's varied menu has something to suit most palates, from daily creative specials, Thai noodles and Monte Cristo sandwiches to gourmet burgers, fish and chips and an array of pasta dishes. Diners with hearty appetites might opt for distinctly prepared full-size entrees of beef, seafood and chicken. Savor one of the scrumptious in-house-prepared desserts. Patrons can choose waterfront terrace seating or a cozy indoor table. Dressy casual. **Bar:** Full bar. **Reservations:** suggested. **Hours:** 11:30 am-10:30 pm. Closed: 1/1, 12/25; also 1st day of Cup Match (July). **Address:** 36 Water St **Location:** Center; between Somer's Wharf and Ordinance Island. **Parking:** street. **Cards:** AX, MC, VI.

THE CARRIAGE HOUSE **Phone:** 441/297-1730 24

International
$10-$32

The restored 18th-century warehouse maintains an Old World atmosphere. The cozy terrace overlooks the harbor. Among offerings are Continental preparations of fresh local fish and lobster and prime rib carved to order from the trolley. Dressy casual. **Bar:** Full bar. **Reservations:** suggested. **Hours:** 11:30 am-3 & 5:30-9:30 pm; Sunday brunch. **Address:** 22 Water St **Location:** At Somers Wharf; just below police station. **Parking:** street. **Cards:** AX, MC, VI. **Historic**

Sandy's Parish

SANDY'S PARISH pop. 7,275 (See map and index starting on p. 372)

WHERE TO STAY

9 BEACHES **Phone:** 441/232-6655 21

AAA SAVE

Cottage
$270-$470 4/1-11/30
$195-$370 12/1-1/3

Address: 4 Daniel's Head Ln **Location:** Oceanfront. On Daniel's Head Beach. **Facility:** A large resort on the water, its over-the-sea cabanas have canvas interior walls and a section of glass floor so guests can look into the ocean. 84 cottages. 1 story, exterior corridors. *Bath:* shower only. **Parking:** on-site. **Terms:** open 12/1-1/3 & 4/1-11/30, 21 day cancellation notice-fee imposed. **Amenities:** DVD players, voice mail, safes, irons, hair dryers. **Dining:** 2 restaurants. **Pool(s):** outdoor. **Leisure Activities:** tennis court, bocci, croquet, playground, exercise room, volleyball. *Fee:* paddleboats, sailboats, windsurfing, kayak, kite surfing, personal watercraft, bicycles. **Guest Services:** TV in common area, wireless Internet. **Business Services:** PC. **Cards:** AX, MC, VI.

TV

CAMBRIDGE BEACHES *Book great rates at AAA.com* **Phone:** (441)234-0331 20

AAA SAVE

Hotel
$275-$1690 All Year

Address: 30 Kings Point Rd **Location:** Kings Point west side of island. **Facility:** This multi-award winning, luxurious cottage colony is located on a 25-acre peninsula surrounded by five beaches. Designated smoking area. 94 units. 65 one-bedroom standard units, some with whirlpools. 26 one- and 3 two-bedroom suites, some with whirlpools. 1-2 stories (no elevator), exterior corridors. **Parking:** on-site. **Terms:** office hours 7 am-11 pm, 4 night minimum stay - seasonal, age restrictions may apply, 28 day cancellation notice-fee imposed. **Amenities:** video library, CD players, high-speed Internet, dual phone lines, voice mail, safes, irons, hair dryers. *Some:* DVD players. **Dining:** 3 restaurants, entertainment. **Pool(s):** outdoor, heated indoor. **Leisure Activities:** whirlpool, rental boats, rental sailboats, rental sailboards, resistance pool, putting green, 3 tennis courts, recreation programs, badminton, croquet, labyrinth, exercise room, spa, horseshoes, volleyball. *Fee:* sauna, steamroom, marina, kayak, personal watercraft, motor scooters, bicycles. **Guest Services:** valet laundry. **Business Services:** meeting rooms, PC. **Cards:** AX, DS, MC, VI. *(See color ad p 383)*

▼ See AAA listing p 382 ▼

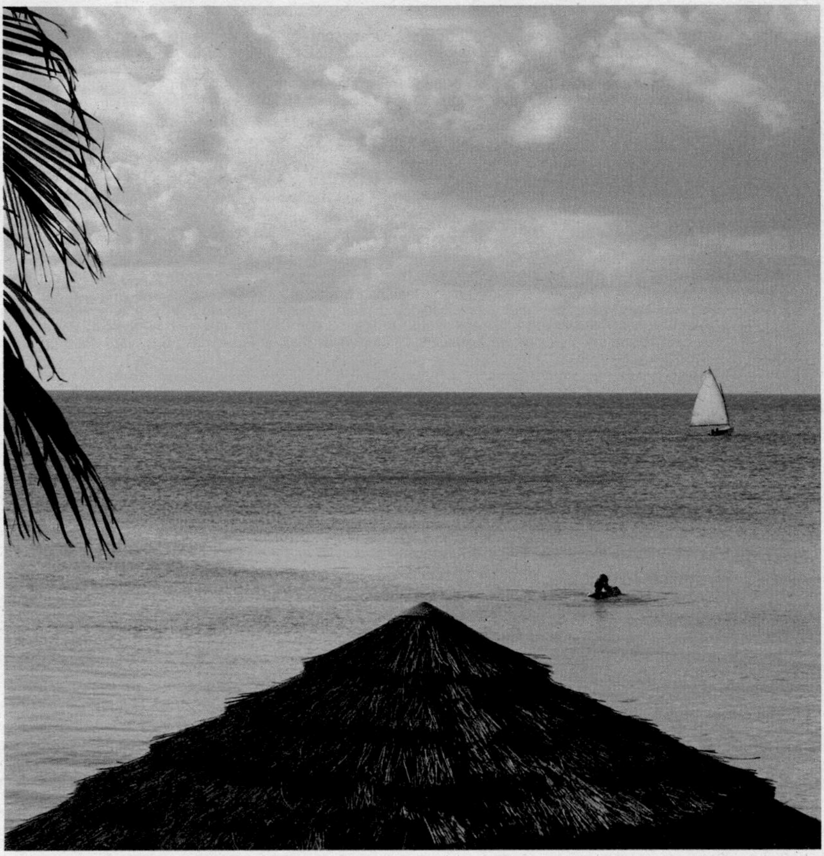

(See map and index starting on p. 372)

THE WILLOWBANK **Phone:** 441/234-1616 22

Hotel
$331-$419 4/1-11/30
$281-$349 12/1-3/31

Address: 126 Somerset Rd **Location:** Oceanfront. At Ely's Harbour. **Facility:** 69 units. 67 one-bedroom standard units. 2 one-bedroom suites. 1 story, exterior corridors. **Parking:** on-site. **Terms:** office hours 9 am-6 pm, 2 night minimum stay, 21 day cancellation notice-fee imposed. **Amenities:** irons, hair dryers. **Dining:** 2 restaurants. **Pool(s):** heated outdoor. **Leisure Activities:** 2 tennis courts, library, playground. **Guest Services:** TV in common area, coin laundry. **Business Services:** conference facilities. **Cards:** MC, VI.

WHERE TO DINE

BEETHOVEN'S RESTAURANT & BAR **Phone:** 441/234-5009 28

International
$9-$26

A family-friendly pub with a lengthy menu featuring a wide array of sandwiches and wraps, all served with crispy fries and a small salad; pasta, salad and seafood selections round out the offerings. Casual dress. **Bar:** Full bar. **Reservations:** accepted. **Hours:** 9 am-6 pm; to 5 pm 11/1-4/30. Closed: 12/25; also Good Friday. **Address:** 5 Freeport Rd **Location:** In Clocktower Mall, at Royal Navy Dockyard. **Parking:** on-site. **Cards:** AX, MC, VI.

THE FROG & ONION PUB **Phone:** 441/234-2900 29

English
$12-$25

The English-style pub exhibits a fine display of nautical artifacts. Representative of traditional pub fare are sausage and mash, shepherd's pie and fish and chips. Seasonal entertainment and a large game room keep guests amused. Dressy casual. **Bar:** Full bar. **Reservations:** accepted. **Hours:** 11:30 am-9:30 pm, Sun noon-9 pm; noon-9:30 pm 11/1-2/28. Closed: 12/25; also 12/31 & Mon 12/1-3/31. **Address:** Royal Naval Dockyard **Location:** Within the walls of Royal Naval Dockyard. **Parking:** on-site. **Cards:** MC, VI. **Historic**

Smith's Parish

SMITH'S PARISH pop. 5,658 (See map and index starting on p. 372)

WHERE TO STAY

PINK BEACH CLUB & COTTAGES **Phone:** (441)293-1666 13

Hotel
$440-$925 3/13-11/30
$415-$595 12/1-12/10

Address: 116 South Rd **Location:** Oceanfront. Jct South Rd and Devil's Hole Hill, just e. **Facility:** 94 one-bedroom standard units. 1-2 stories (no elevator), exterior corridors. **Parking:** on-site. **Terms:** open 12/1-12/10 & 3/13-11/30, 21 day cancellation notice-fee imposed. **Amenities:** CD players, voice mail, safes, irons, hair dryers. *Some:* DVD players (fee). **Dining:** 2 restaurants. **Pool(s):** heated outdoor. **Leisure Activities:** snorkeling, 2 tennis courts, exercise room. *Fee:* scooters, massage. **Guest Services:** TV in common area, valet laundry, wireless Internet. **Business Services:** PC. **Cards:** AX, MC, VI.

/ SOME UNITS FEE VCR

WHERE TO DINE

NORTH ROCK BREWING COMPANY **Phone:** 441/236-6633 57

English
$15-$39

Bermuda's only microbrewery features such hand-crafted brews as Blackwatch stout, India Pale Ale and Porter. The broad menu lists traditional English fare, including fish and chips, cottage pie and steak and ale pie. Tempting desserts range from prune Armagnac mousse to raspberry creme brulee to chocolate truffle cake. Casual dress. **Bar:** Full bar. **Reservations:** suggested. **Hours:** 11:30 am-3 & 6-9:30 pm, Sat & Sun 11:30 am-4:30 & 6-9:30 pm. Closed: 9/7; also 12/24-1/2, Good Friday, Bermuda Day & 1st day of Cup Match (July). **Address:** 10 South Shore Rd **Location:** Jct South Shore and Collectors Hill rds. **Parking:** on-site. **Cards:** AX, MC, VI.

SPECIALITY INN **Phone:** 441/236-3133 56

International
$9-$20

Shhhh - you're not supposed to know about this popular hangout for locals. It offers the island's idea of comfort food which includes burgers, sandwiches, pasta, pizza and, of all things, a sushi bar. Don't forget to check out the daily specials on the menu board before ordering. Seafood is most popular with Bermudians, but don't be afraid to experiment. Casual dress. **Hours:** 6 am-10 pm. Closed major holidays; also Sun. **Address:** 4 South Shore Rd **Location:** Jct Collectors Hill Rd. **Parking:** on-site. **Cards:** MC, VI.

Southampton Parish

SOUTHAMPTON PARISH pop. 6,117 (See map and index starting on p. 372)

WHERE TO STAY

THE FAIRMONT SOUTHAMPTON Book great rates at AAA.com **Phone:** (441)238-8000 30

Resort Hotel
$199-$4789 All Year

Address: 101 South Shore Rd **Location:** Oceanfront. Between Middle and South Shore rds. **Facility:** In an impressive hilltop setting buffered by manicured grounds, the recently renovated property offers a spa and luxurious guest rooms. Meets AAA guest room security requirements. Smoke free premises. 593 units. 557 one-bedroom standard units. 27 one- and 9 two-bedroom suites, some with whirlpools. 6 stories, interior corridors. **Parking:** on-site. **Terms:** check-in 4 pm, 3 day cancellation notice-fee imposed. **Amenities:** high-speed Internet (fee), dual phone lines, voice mail, safes, honor bars, irons, hair dryers. *Some:* DVD players, CD players. **Dining:** 8 restaurants, also, Bacci's, The Newport Room, The Waterlot Inn Steakhouse, see separate listings, entertainment. **Pool(s):** heated outdoor, heated indoor. **Leisure Activities:** whirlpools, rental boats, rental paddleboats, putting green, recreation programs, croquet, jogging, spa, volleyball. *Fee:* saunas, steamrooms, scuba diving, snorkeling, charter fishing, kayaks, personal watercraft, golf-18 holes, 6 tennis courts (3 lighted), motor scooters, game room. **Guest Services:** valet laundry, area transportation-beach/property restaurant, golf course, ferry dock, Hamilton, wireless Internet. **Business Services:** conference facilities, business center. **Cards:** AX, DC, MC, VI.
(See color ad p 386)

FEE

POMPANO BEACH CLUB Book great rates at AAA.com **Phone:** (441)234-0222 25

Hotel
$260-$590 All Year

Address: 36 Pompano Beach Rd **Location:** Oceanfront. Off Middle Rd, 0.5 mi (0.8 km) w via Pompano Beach Rd; adjacent to Port Royal Golf Club. **Facility:** Smoke free premises. 74 units. 58 one-bedroom standard units. 16 one-bedroom suites. 1-2 stories, exterior corridors. **Parking:** on-site. **Terms:** office hours 6:30 am-midnight, 21 day cancellation notice-fee imposed. **Amenities:** voice mail, safes, irons, hair dryers. **Dining:** 2 restaurants, entertainment. **Pool(s):** heated outdoor. **Leisure Activities:** whirlpools, rental paddleboats, rental sailboats, rental sailboards, boat dock, fishing, 5 tennis courts (2 lighted), exercise room, game room. *Fee:* snorkeling, massage. **Guest Services:** valet and coin laundry, area transportation-golf course & ferry, wireless Internet. **Business Services:** meeting rooms, PC. **Cards:** AX, MC, VI.

THE REEFS Book great rates at AAA.com **Phone:** (441)238-0222 28

Hotel
$314-$574 All Year

Address: 56 South Shore Rd **Location:** Oceanfront. At Christian Bay. **Facility:** 65 units. 56 one-bedroom standard units, some with whirlpools. 1 one-bedroom suite with whirlpool. 8 cottages. 2 stories, interior/exterior corridors. **Parking:** on-site. **Terms:** 5 night minimum stay - seasonal, 28 day cancellation notice-fee imposed. **Amenities:** video library, DVD players, voice mail, safes, irons, hair dryers. *Some:* CD players, dual phone lines. **Dining:** 3 restaurants. **Pool(s):** heated outdoor. **Leisure Activities:** whirlpool, snorkeling, kayak, 2 tennis courts, hiking trails, exercise room, shuffleboard. *Fee:* massage. **Guest Services:** valet laundry, wireless Internet. **Business Services:** PC. **Cards:** AX, DC, MC, VI.

/ SOME UNITS

▼ See AAA listing p 385 ▼

(See map and index starting on p. 372)

WHERE TO DINE

BACCI'S **Phone:** 441/238-8000 (35)

Italian
$14-$38

Refined surroundings and a sumptuous antipasti bar are hallmarks of the popular resort restaurant. Lining the menu are many pasta, ravioli, gnocchi and risotto dishes, in addition to such heartier entrees as osso buco alla milanese, grilled veal chop and striped sea bass. Popular as well are create-your-own individual gourmet pizzas. Irresistible desserts range from chocolate fudge cake to classic tiramisu. Diners can count on precision service. Dressy casual. **Bar:** Full bar. **Reservations:** required. **Hours:** 6 pm-10 pm. **Address:** 101 South Shore Rd **Location:** Between Middle and South Shore rds; in The Fairmont Southampton. **Parking:** on-site. **Cards:** AX, CB, DC, DS, JC, MC, VI.

HENRY VIII RESTAURANT AND PUB *Menu on AAA.com* **Phone:** 441/238-1977 (36)

English
$16-$40

Tudor decor is befitting of the English-style fare, including well-thought-out daily specials. Service is friendly and efficient. Guests can enjoy entertainment seasonally in the pub lounge. Dressy casual. **Bar:** Full bar. **Reservations:** suggested. **Hours:** noon-2:30 & 6-10 pm, Sun noon-3 & 6:30-10 pm. Closed: 1st day of Cup Match (July). **Address:** 69 South Shore Rd **Location:** Across from Wyndham Bermuda Resort & Spa. **Parking:** on-site. **Cards:** AX, MC, VI.

LIGHTHOUSE TEA ROOM **Phone:** 441/238-8679 (33)

International
$12-$52

The fortuitous location affords vistas of the island and surrounding ocean. Light English fare and traditional tea are served anytime. Entrees range from vegetable lasagna and red snapper with juniper berry sauce to roasted rack of lamb with pommery mustard sauce. Dressy casual. **Bar:** Full bar. **Reservations:** required, for dinner. **Hours:** Open 12/1-1/1 & 2/1-11/30; 9 am-4:45 & 6:30-8:30 pm, Tues 9 am-4:45 pm. Closed: 12/25. **Address:** 68 St. Anne's Rd **Location:** Jct South Shore Rd, just n on Lighthouse Rd, then just w; at Gibbs Hill Lighthouse. **Parking:** on-site. **Cards:** AX, MC, VI.

THE NEWPORT ROOM **Phone:** 441/238-8000 (34)

French
$95-$115

Modern and classical cuisine is served in a luxurious dining room designed after the grand salon of an ocean yacht. Waiters are attired in a formal nautical uniform befitting of the atmosphere. The staff sees to each diner's every need. Jackets are required. Semi-formal attire. **Bar:** Full bar. **Reservations:** required. **Hours:** 6:30 pm-9:30 pm. Closed: Sun, Mon, 12/1-12/18 & 1/1-3/19. **Address:** 101 South Shore Rd **Location:** Between Middle and South Shore rds; in The Fairmont Southampton. **Parking:** on-site. **Cards:** AX, DC, JC, MC, VI.

CALL

TIO PEPE **Phone:** 441/238-1897 (37)

Italian
$14-$29

The menu includes basic, home-style Italian food and some Spanish dishes. Seafood linguine is a local favorite. Nine-inch thin-crust pizzas are cooked in a brick oven. Guests can order from the lunch menu until 5 pm When the weather is nice, the terrace is a nice spot for seating. Dressy casual. **Bar:** Full bar. **Reservations:** suggested. **Hours:** 11:30 am-10 pm; from noon 10/1-4/30. Closed: 12/25. **Address:** 117 South Rd **Location:** 0.5 mi (0.8 km) e of Southampton Princess Hotel. **Parking:** on-site. **Cards:** AX, MC, VI.

THE WATERLOT INN STEAKHOUSE *Menu on AAA.com* **Phone:** 441/238-8000 (32)

Steak & Seafood
$30-$57

By popular demand, the restaurant has changed its theme to an American steakhouse offering aged steaks and chops as well as an assortment of seafood selections; while a massive 90-ounce porterhouse is billed as a two-person entree, some have certainly tried to earn their wings tackling it solo. Dressy casual. **Bar:** Full bar. **Reservations:** required. **Hours:** 6 pm-10 pm. **Address:** 101 South Shore Rd **Location:** Between Middle and South Shore rds; in The Fairmont Southampton. **Parking:** on-site. **Cards:** AX, DC, MC, VI. **Historic**

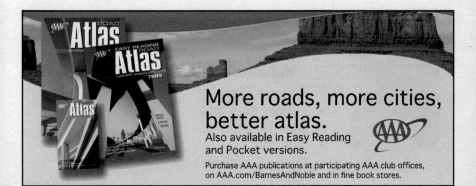

Warwick Parish

WARWICK PARISH pop. 8,587 (See map and index starting on p. 372)

WHERE TO STAY

BLUE HORIZONS **Phone:** 441/236-6350 45

Motel

$125-$175 All Year

Address: 93 South Rd **Location:** Jct Cobbs Hill Rd, 0.8 mi (1.3 km) w. **Facility:** 6 one-bedroom standard units, some with efficiencies. 2 stories (no elevator), exterior corridors. **Parking:** on-site. **Terms:** office hours 9 am-5 pm, 2 night minimum stay, 14 day cancellation notice-fee imposed. **Amenities:** DVD players, irons, hair dryers. *Some:* safes. **Guest Services:** coin laundry, beauty salon, wireless Internet. **Cards:** AX, MC, VI.

CLAIRFONT APARTMENTS **Phone:** 441/238-3577 48

Bed & Breakfast

$150-$175 All Year

Address: 6 Warwickshire Rd **Location:** Jct South Shore Rd, just n. **Facility:** Smoke free premises. 8 units. 2 one-bedroom standard units with kitchens. 6 one-bedroom suites with kitchens. 2 stories (no elevator), exterior corridors. **Parking:** on-site. **Terms:** office hours 10 am-4 pm, 14 day cancellation notice. **Amenities:** video library, DVD players, high-speed Internet, voice mail, safes, irons, hair dryers. **Pool(s):** outdoor. **Guest Services:** valet laundry. **Cards:** AX, MC, VI.

GRANAWAY GUEST HOUSE & COTTAGE **Phone:** 441/236-3747 43

Bed & Breakfast

$170-$200 4/1-11/30
$120-$170 12/1-3/31

Address: 1 Longford Rd **Location:** Belmont Ferry dock, just w on Harbour Rd. **Facility:** Smoke free premises. 5 units. 4 one-bedroom standard units. 1 cottage. 2 stories (no elevator), interior/exterior corridors. *Bath:* combo or shower only. **Parking:** on-site. **Terms:** office hours 9 am-6 pm, 3 night minimum stay, 30 day cancellation notice-fee imposed. **Amenities:** video library, DVD players, CD players, irons, hair dryers. **Pool(s):** heated outdoor. **Leisure Activities:** croquet, grill. **Guest Services:** valet laundry, wireless Internet. **Business Services:** PC. **Cards:** AX, MC, VI.

SANDPIPER GUEST APARTMENTS **Phone:** 441/236-7093 46

Motel

$155-$245 4/1-11/30
$110-$185 12/1-3/31

Address: 1 Sandy Mount Ln **Location:** Jct Cobbs Hill Rd, 0.8 mi (1.3 km) w. **Facility:** 14 units. 9 one-bedroom standard units with kitchens. 5 one-bedroom suites with kitchens. 2 stories (no elevator), exterior corridors. **Parking:** on-site. **Terms:** office hours 9 am-8 pm, 2 night minimum stay, 14 day cancellation notice-fee imposed. **Amenities:** voice mail, safes, irons, hair dryers. **Pool(s):** outdoor. **Leisure Activities:** barbecue grills. **Guest Services:** coin laundry, wireless Internet. **Cards:** AX, MC, VI.

SURF SIDE BEACH CLUB *Book great rates at AAA.com* **Phone:** (441)236-7100 47

Hotel

$160-$1260 All Year

Address: 90 South Shore Rd **Location:** Oceanfront. Corner of Cobbs Hill and South Shore rds. **Facility:** 38 units. 25 one-bedroom standard units, some with kitchens. 10 one-, 2 two- and 1 three-bedroom suites with kitchens. 1-2 stories (no elevator), exterior corridors. *Bath:* combo or shower only. **Parking:** on-site. **Terms:** office hours 8 am-10 pm, 14 day cancellation notice-fee imposed. **Amenities:** voice mail, safes, irons, hair dryers. **Pool(s):** outdoor. **Leisure Activities:** sauna, whirlpool. *Fee:* snorkeling, massage. **Guest Services:** valet and coin laundry, beauty salon, wireless Internet. **Business Services:** meeting rooms, PC. **Cards:** AX, CB, DC, DS, JC, MC, VI.

SOME UNITS

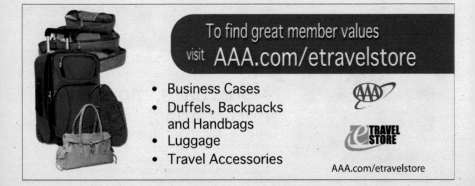

BONAIRE

Airport Accommodations

Map Page	OA	BONAIRE, NETHERLAND ANTILLES - FLAMINGO FIELD	Diamond Rated	High Season	Page
5 / p. 390		Bellafonte Chateau de la Mer, just s of airport	◆◆	$125-$495	390
1 / p. 390	AAA	**Divi Flamingo Beach Resort & Casino, 0.8 mi (1.3 km) n of terminal**	◆◆	$163-$367 SAVE	391
4 / p. 390		Happy Holiday Homes, 2.5 mi (4 km)	◆	$65-$75	391

Kralendijk

This index helps you "spot" where approved lodgings and restaurants are located on the corresponding detailed maps. Lodging daily rate range is for comparison only and show the property's high season. Restaurant rate range is a combination of lunch and/or dinner. Turn to the listing page for more detailed rate information and consult display ads for special promotions.

KRALENDIJK

Map Page	OA	Lodgings	Diamond Rated	High Season	Page
1 / p. 390	AAA	**Divi Flamingo Beach Resort & Casino**	◆◆	$163-$367 SAVE	391
2 / p. 390		Den Laman Condominiums	◆◆	$110-$275	390
4 / p. 390		Happy Holiday Homes	◆	$65-$75	391
5 / p. 390		Bellafonte Chateau de la Mer	◆◆	$125-$495	390

Map Page	OA	Restaurants	Diamond Rated	Cuisine	Meal Range	Page
1 / p. 390		Papaya Moon Cantina	◆◆	Tex-Mex	$15-$23	391
3 / p. 390		It Rains Fishes	◆◆	International	$15-$22	391
4 / p. 390		Richard's	◆	Steak & Seafood	$19-$30	391
6 / p. 390		Casablanca Argentinian Grill	◆◆	Argentine	$15-$26	391
7 / p. 390		Le Flamboyant Bar, Restaurant & Shop	◆◆	International	$10-$30	391
8 / p. 390	AAA	**Chibi Chibi**	◆◆	International	$9-$23	391

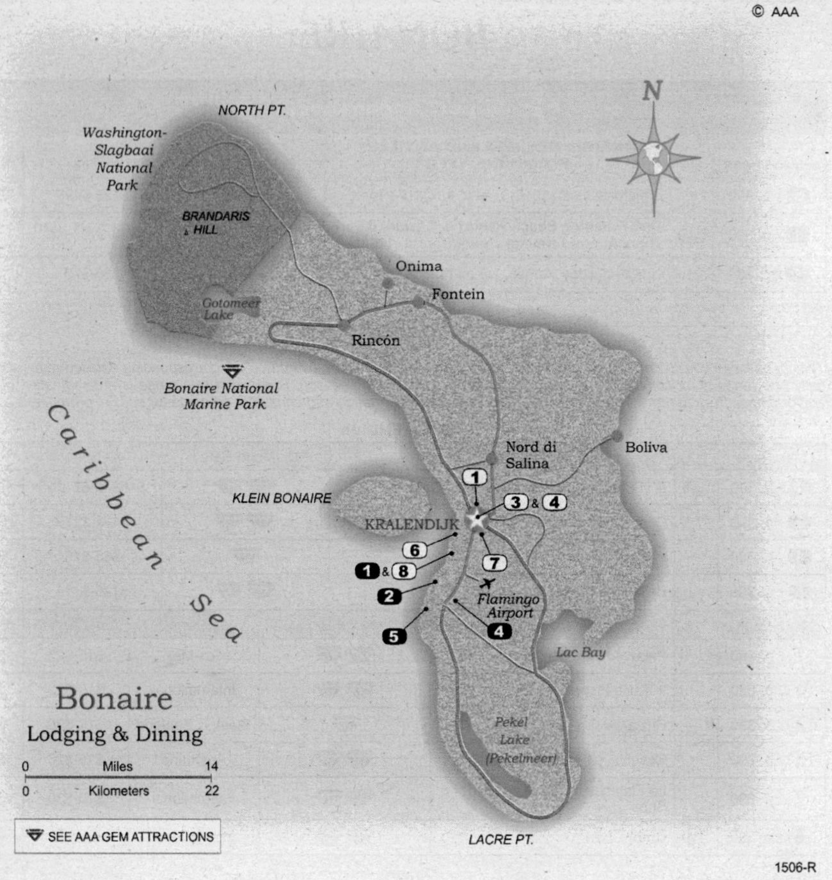

N
NORTH PT.
Washington-Slagbaai National Park
BRANDARIS HILL
Onima
Fontein
Gotomeer Lake
Rincón
Bonaire National Marine Park
Caribbean Sea
Nord di Salina
Boliva
KLEIN BONAIRE
1
3 & 4
KRALENDIJK
6
1 & 8
7
2
Flamingo Airport
4
5
Lac Bay
Pekel Lake (Pekelmeer)
LACRE PT.

Bonaire
Lodging & Dining

0 Miles 14
0 Kilometers 22

SEE AAA GEM ATTRACTIONS

1506-R

KRALENDIJK pop. 2,000 (See map and index starting on p. 390)

WHERE TO STAY

BELLAFONTE CHATEAU DE LA MER — **Phone:** 599/717-3333 — 5

Condominium
$125-$495 All Year

Address: EEG Boulevard 10 **Location:** Oceanfront. Just s of airport. **Facility:** 22 units. 6 one-bedroom standard units. 8 one- and 8 two-bedroom suites, some with whirlpools. 4 stories, exterior corridors. *Bath:* shower only. **Parking:** on-site. **Terms:** office hours 8 am-5 pm. **Amenities:** CD players, safes. *Some:* irons. **Leisure Activities:** whirlpool, boat dock, snorkeling. *Fee:* massage. **Guest Services:** wireless Internet. **Business Services:** PC. **Cards:** AX, MC, VI.

DEN LAMAN CONDOMINIUMS — **Phone:** (599)717-1700 — 2

Condominium
$110-$275 All Year

Address: Kaya Gobernador N. Debrot 77 **Location:** 0.8 mi (1.3 km) n of downtown. **Facility:** 14 units. 5 one-bedroom standard units with efficiencies. 5 one- and 4 two-bedroom suites with kitchens. 3 stories (no elevator), interior corridors. *Bath:* shower only. **Parking:** on-site. **Terms:** office hours 8 am-5 pm, off-site registration, 45 day cancellation notice-fee imposed. **Amenities:** DVD players, CD players, safes, hair dryers. **Leisure Activities:** boat dock. *Fee:* scuba diving, snorkeling. **Guest Services:** valet laundry, wireless Internet. **Cards:** AX, DC, MC, VI.

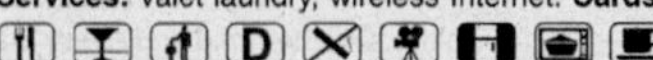

(See map and index starting on p. 390)

DIVI FLAMINGO BEACH RESORT & CASINO Book great rates at AAA.com **Phone:** (599)717-8285 **1**

AAA SAVE

Hotel

$163-$367 All Year

Address: JA Abraham Blvd #40 **Location:** Oceanfront. 0.8 mi (1.3 km) s of town; 1.4 mi (2.2 km) n of airport. **Facility:** Ideal haven for divers. Enjoy the new beach bar with award wining cocktails. Rooms remodeled this year with spanish woven wood, shower tower, new bath amenitites, seaside boardwalk. 129 one-bedroom standard units, some with efficiencies. 2 stories (no elevator), exterior corridors. *Bath:* combo or shower only. **Parking:** on-site. **Amenities:** voice mail, safes (fee), irons, hair dryers. **Dining:** 2 restaurants, also, Chibi Chibi, see separate listing, entertainment. **Pool(s):** 2 outdoor. **Leisure Activities:** boat dock, kayaks, recreation programs, bocci, lawn chess, exercise room, shuffleboard. *Fee:* scuba diving, snorkeling, charter fishing, boat trips, massage. **Guest Services:** valet laundry, airport transportation (fee)-Flamingo Airport, wireless Internet. **Business Services:** meeting rooms, business center. **Cards:** AX, CB, DC, DS, JC, MC, VI.

FEE D / SOME UNITS

HAPPY HOLIDAY HOMES **Phone:** (599)717-8405 **4**

Cottage

$65-$75 All Year

Address: Punt Vierkant #9 **Location:** 2.5 mi (4 km) s of airport. Located in a quiet residential area. **Facility:** Designated smoking area. 14 cottages. 1 story, exterior corridors. *Bath:* shower only. **Parking:** on-site. **Terms:** 2 night minimum stay, 45 day cancellation notice-fee imposed. **Amenities:** CD players, irons. *Fee:* high-speed Internet, safes. *Some:* DVD players (fee). **Guest Services:** coin laundry, wireless Internet.

ASK / SOME UNITS FEE FEE VCR

WHERE TO DINE

CASABLANCA ARGENTINIAN GRILL **Phone:** 599/717-4433 **6**

Argentine

$15-$26

Within walking distance of downtown, this restaurant lets guests enjoy al fresco meals on the verandah or in the rear courtyard. Menu selections include various cuts of Argentinean beef, various sausages, pork ribs and chicken. One night a week is all-you-can-eat night. The congenial hands-on owner enjoys circulating the dining room and chatting with patrons. Casual dress. **Bar:** Full bar. **Reservations:** suggested. **Hours:** noon-2 & 6-10 pm, Sun & Mon from 6 pm. **Address:** Abraham Blvd #6 **Location:** Just s of downtown center. **Parking:** on-site. **Cards:** MC, VI.

AC

CHIBI CHIBI **Phone:** 599/717-8285 **8**

International

$9-$23

Named after a local sweet bird, the over-the-water restaurant offers captivating views and also features a beach entrance. The bright and colorful restaurant offers a complete and varied international menu. The menu consists of fresh local fish, pastas, steak and a variety of entrée size salads. International award winning bartender with cocktail menu of over 30 fresh fruit concoctions. Casual dress. **Bar:** Full bar. **Reservations:** suggested. **Hours:** noon-3 & 5-10 pm. **Address:** JA Abraham Blvd #40 **Location:** 0.8 mi (1.3 km) s of town; 1.4 mi (2.2 km) n of airport; in Divi Flamingo Beach Resort & Casino. **Parking:** on-site. **Cards:** AX, CB, DC, DS, MC, VI.

AC

IT RAINS FISHES **Phone:** 599/717-8780 **3**

International

$15-$22

Great waterfront location for people watching in a casual and frolicking atmosphere. Mostly a seafood centered menu focusing on local fish and fresh lobster but the barbecue ribs are a favorite here as well. Casual dress. **Bar:** Full bar. **Reservations:** required. **Hours:** 5:30 pm-10 pm. Closed: 12/26; also Sun. **Address:** Kaya Jan NE Crane #24 **Location:** Waterfront; downtown. **Parking:** street. **Cards:** AX, CB, DC, DS, JC, MC, VI.

AC

LE FLAMBOYANT BAR, RESTAURANT & SHOP **Phone:** 599/717-3919 **7**

International

$10-$30

In the heart of town, this courtyard restaurant seats diners in a garden setting. Well-prepared and nicely presented cuisine includes four soups, escargot, the catch of the day, seafood pasta and a few different cuts of beef. Good choices to top off the meal are the imported cheese plate and local ice cream. Casual dress. **Bar:** Full bar. **Reservations:** suggested. **Hours:** noon-3 & 6-10 pm. Closed: Sun. **Address:** Kaya Grandi 12 **Location:** Center of town. **Parking:** street. **Cards:** AX, DC, MC, VI. **Historic**

AC

PAPAYA MOON CANTINA **Phone:** 599/717-5025 **1**

Tex-Mex

$15-$23

A Mexican motif unites the colorful and charming Antillean-style house, where patrons dine on the front verandah, in interior saloon-style rooms or in the rear courtyard. Tex-Mex cuisine is decidedly more uptown than most, with a selection ranging from fish tacos and shrimp and lobster enchiladas to fajitas, seviche and gazpacho. One of the tempting designer martinis makes a good accompaniment. Grandma's sizzlin' pie served in an iron skillet is a must. Casual dress. **Bar:** Full bar. **Reservations:** suggested. **Hours:** 6 pm-11 pm. Closed: Mon & Tues. **Address:** Kaya Grandi 48 **Location:** Just n of downtown. **Parking:** street. **Cards:** MC, VI.

RICHARD'S **Phone:** 599/717-5263 **4**

Steak & Seafood

$19-$30

The tropical dining room is open to the harbor and offers great views. A pleasant, informal atmosphere prevails. Regional specialties and American cuisine line a menu that includes many fresh seafood selections. Portions are hearty. Casual dress. **Bar:** Full bar. **Reservations:** accepted. **Hours:** Open 12/1-9/1 & 9/21-11/30; 6 pm-10 pm. Closed: 1/1, 12/25; also Mon. **Address:** JA Abraham Blvd #60 **Location:** 0.9 mi (1.5 km) s of center (Post Office); on waterfront. **Parking:** on-site. **Cards:** MC, VI.

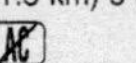

Cayman Brac

This index helps you "spot" where approved lodgings and restaurants are located on the corresponding detailed maps. Lodging daily rate range is for comparison only and show the property's high season. Restaurant rate range is a combination of lunch and/or dinner. Turn to the listing page for more detailed rate information and consult display ads for special promotions.

WEST BAY (GRAND CAYMAN)

Map Page	OA	Lodging	Diamond Rated	High Season	Page
1 / p. 394	AAA	**Cobalt Coast Resort & Suites** - see color ad p 398		$240-$495 SAVE	404

Map Page	OA	Restaurants	Diamond Rated	Cuisine	Meal Range	Page
2 / p. 394		Ristorante Pappagallo		Northern Italian	$25-$46	404
3 / p. 394		Cracked Conch by the Sea		Caribbean	$12-$37	404

SEVEN MILE BEACH (GRAND CAYMAN)

Map Page	OA	Lodgings	Diamond Rated	High Season	Page
3 / p. 394		Aqua Bay Club Condos		$275-$625	398
4 / p. 394		The Christopher Columbus Condos		$210-$495	399
5 / p. 394	AAA	**Westin Casuarina Resort & Spa-Grand Cayman** - see color ad on insert, p 401		$288-$659 SAVE	402
8 / p. 394		Tamarind Bay		$285-$510	400
10 / p. 394		Plantana Condominiums		$240-$680	400
11 / p. 394	AAA	**The Meridian**		$420-$950 SAVE	400
12 / p. 394		Caribbean Club		$800-$2500	399
13 / p. 394	AAA	**The Ritz-Carlton, Grand Cayman**		$399-$3800 SAVE	400
14 / p. 394		7 Mile Beach Resort & Club		$300-$675	398
15 / p. 394		Regal Beach Club		$325-$975	400
16 / p. 394	AAA	**Comfort Suites and Resort** - see color ad p 399		$185-$360 SAVE	399
17 / p. 394	AAA	**Treasure Island Condos**		$205-$630 SAVE	402
18 / p. 394	AAA	**Grand Cayman Marriott Beach Resort** - see color ad on insert		$259-$403 SAVE	400
20 / p. 394		Plantation Village Beach Resort		$185-$595	400

Map Page	OA	Restaurants	Diamond Rated	Cuisine	Meal Range	Page
4 / p. 394	AAA	**Casa Havana** - see color ad p 401		International	$33-$49	402
5 / p. 394		Prime Brazilian Steak House		Steak Brazilian	$24-$55	403
6 / p. 394		Deckers Bistro & Grill		International	$24-$48	403
7 / p. 394		Gateway of India		Indian	$19-$33	403
8 / p. 394	AAA	**7 Prime Cuts and Sunsets**		Steak	$20-$60	402
9 / p. 394		Copper Falls Steakhouse		Steak	$23-$46	403
10 / p. 394		Ristorante Ragazzi		Italian	$14-$44	404
13 / p. 394		Chicken! Chicken!		Caribbean	$8-$16	403
14 / p. 394		Cimboco, A Caribbean Cafe		International	$13-$21	403
15 / p. 394		Cafe Med		Italian	$14-$40	402

Map Page	OA	Restaurants (cont'd)	Diamond Rated	Cuisine	Meal Range	Page
16 / p. 394		Bamboo Lounge	◆◆◆	Japanese	$27-$58	402
17 / p. 394		Hemingway's Beach Club Restaurant	◆◆◆	Continental	$17-$45	403
18 / p. 394	AAA	**Blue**	◆◆◆◆◆	Seafood	$81-$120	402
19 / p. 394		Little Tokyo Mongolian Grill & Lounge	◆	Asian	$13-$19	403
20 / p. 394		Thai Orchid	◆◆	Thai	$18-$30	404
21 / p. 394		The Reef Grill at the Royal Palms	◆◆◆	International	$10-$40	403
23 / p. 394		Fidel Murphy's	◆◆	Irish	$14-$28	403

COLLIERS (GRAND CAYMAN)

Map Page	OA	Lodging	Diamond Rated	High Season	Page
25 / p. 394	AAA	**The Reef Resort** - see color ad p 397	◆◆◆	$175-$595 SAVE	397

LITTLE CAYMAN

Map Page	OA	Lodgings	Diamond Rated	High Season	Page
34 / p. 394		Paradise Villas	◆◆	$175-$200	405
35 / p. 394		The Club at Little Cayman	◆◆◆	$285-$525	405
36 / p. 394		Conch Club Condominiums	◆◆	$250-$450	405
37 / p. 394		Southern Cross Club	◆◆◆	$335-$400	405

Map Page	OA	Restaurant	Diamond Rated	Cuisine	Meal Range	Page
38 / p. 394		Hungry Iguana	◆	American	$14-$28	405

CAYMAN BRAC

Map Page	OA	Lodging	Diamond Rated	High Season	Page
40 / p. 394	AAA	**Brac Reef Beach Resort**	◆◆	$140-$195 SAVE	396

Map Page	OA	Restaurants	Diamond Rated	Cuisine	Meal Range	Page
41 / p. 394		Biggie's Restaurant	◆◆	International	$8-$36	396
42 / p. 394		Captain's Table	◆	Continental	$7-$31	396

GEORGE TOWN (GRAND CAYMAN)

Map Page	OA	Restaurants	Diamond Rated	Cuisine	Meal Range	Page
22 / p. 394		The Wharf Restaurant	◆◆	International	$30-$46	398
29 / p. 394		Hard Rock Cafe	◆◆	American	$12-$24 SAVE	398
30 / p. 394	AAA	**Bacchus Restaurant and Wine Bar**	◆◆◆	International	$18-$40	397
33 / p. 394	AAA	**The Brasserie**	◆◆◆	International	$17-$40	398
35 / p. 394		Grand Old House	◆◆◆	International	$28-$43	398

BREAKERS (GRAND CAYMAN)

Map Page	OA	Restaurant	Diamond Rated	Cuisine	Meal Range	Page
45 / p. 394		The Lighthouse Restaurant at the Breakers	◆◆	International	$11-$50	397

EAST END (GRAND CAYMAN)

Map Page	OA	Restaurant	Diamond Rated	Cuisine	Meal Range	Page
47 / p. 394		Portofino	◆◆	International	$13-$38	397

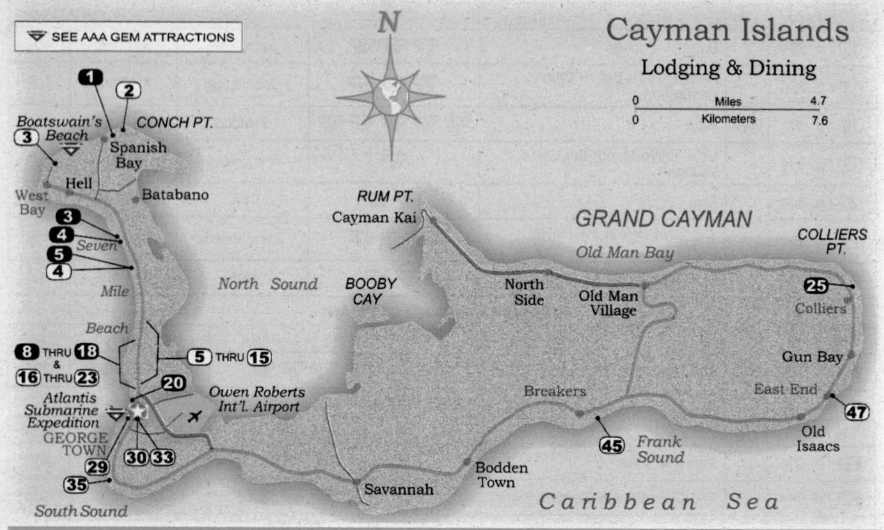
SEE AAA GEM ATTRACTIONS
Cayman Islands
Lodging & Dining
0 Miles 4.7
0 Kilometers 7.6
N
Boatswain's Beach
CONCH PT.
Spanish Bay
Hell
West Bay
Batabano
Seven Mile Beach
North Sound
BOOBY CAY
RUM PT.
Cayman Kai
GRAND CAYMAN
Old Man Bay
COLLIERS PT.
North Side
Old Man Village
Colliers
Gun Bay
East End
Breakers
Owen Roberts Int'l. Airport
Atlantis Submarine Expedition
GEORGE TOWN
8 THRU 18 & 16 THRU 23
5 THRU 15
Frank Sound
Old Isaacs
Bodden Town
Savannah
South Sound
Caribbean Sea

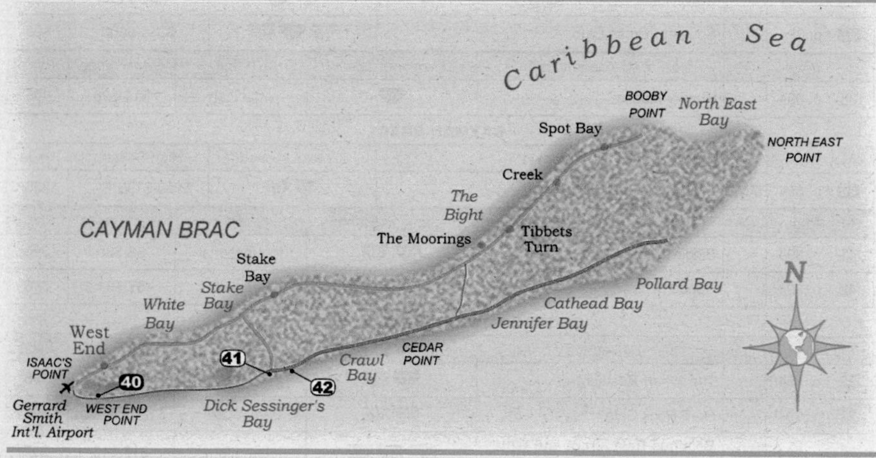
Caribbean Sea
BOOBY POINT
North East Bay
NORTH EAST POINT
Spot Bay
Creek
The Bight
CAYMAN BRAC
The Moorings
Tibbets Turn
Stake Bay
Stake Bay
White Bay
Pollard Bay
Cathead Bay
Jennifer Bay
West End
ISAAC'S POINT
CEDAR POINT
Crawl Bay
Gerrard Smith Int'l. Airport
WEST END POINT
Dick Sessinger's Bay
N

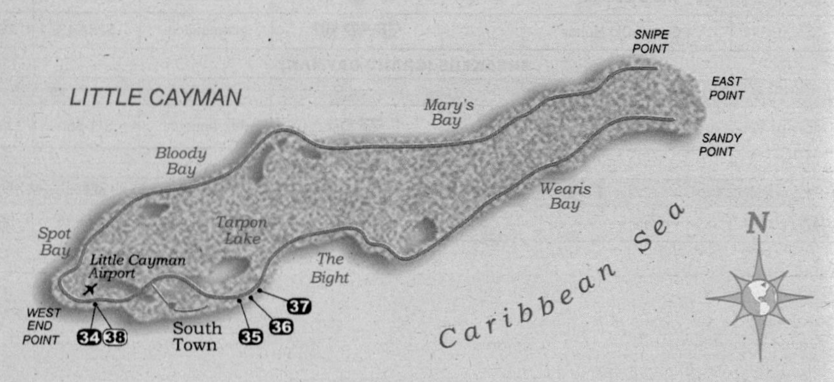
SNIPE POINT
EAST POINT
SANDY POINT
LITTLE CAYMAN
Mary's Bay
Bloody Bay
Wearis Bay
Tarpon Lake
Spot Bay
Little Cayman Airport
The Bight
WEST END POINT
South Town
Caribbean Sea
N

CAYMAN BRAC pop. 1,822 (See map and index starting on p. 394)

WHERE TO STAY

BRAC REEF BEACH RESORT Phone: 345/948-1323 (40)

AAA SAVE

Hotel

$140-$195 All Year

Address: 383 South Side Rd **Location:** Oceanfront. 2.6 mi (4.1 km) se of airport. **Facility:** Designated smoking area. 41 one-bedroom standard units. 2 stories (no elevator), exterior corridors. **Parking:** on-site. **Terms:** office hours 7 am-9 pm, 30 day cancellation notice-fee imposed. **Amenities:** high-speed Internet, irons, hair dryers. **Dining:** 2 restaurants. **Pool(s):** outdoor. **Leisure Activities:** whirlpool, beach access, paddleboats, boat dock, kayaks, lighted tennis court, hammocks, bicycles, exercise room, basketball, volleyball. *Fee:* scuba diving, snorkeling, massage. **Guest Services:** valet and coin laundry, wireless Internet. **Business Services:** meeting rooms, PC (fee). **Cards:** AX, MC, VI. **Free Special Amenities: full breakfast and high-speed Internet.**

WHERE TO DINE

BIGGIE'S RESTAURANT Phone: 345/948-2449 (41)

International

$8-$36

Cayman influenced international cuisine, the menu boasts homemade Atlantis conch chowder, quesadillas, Szechwan chicken and Biggie's special fish tea, a locally caught red snapper served with cassava, yam and pumpkin. Casual dress. **Bar:** Full bar. **Hours:** 7:30 am-2:30 & 5-9 pm. Closed: 4/12, 12/25. **Address:** Main Rd **Location:** 1.2 mi (2 km) nw of airport. **Parking:** on-site. **Cards:** CB, DC, DS, MC, VI.

CAPTAIN'S TABLE Phone: 345/948-1418 (42)

Continental

$7-$31

Local fish and traditional preparations of beef, lamb and veal are served in an island-casual atmosphere. All desserts are made in house. Diners can sit in the air-conditioned interior or on the deck, which is cooled by refreshing breezes. Casual dress. **Bar:** Full bar. **Reservations:** suggested. **Hours:** 11:30 am-3 & 6-9:30 pm. Closed: 12/25; also 9/15-9/30. **Address:** Stake Bay **Location:** 2.4 mi (3.8 km) se of airport; in Carib Sands and Brac Caribbean Beach Village. **Parking:** on-site. **Cards:** AX, MC, VI.

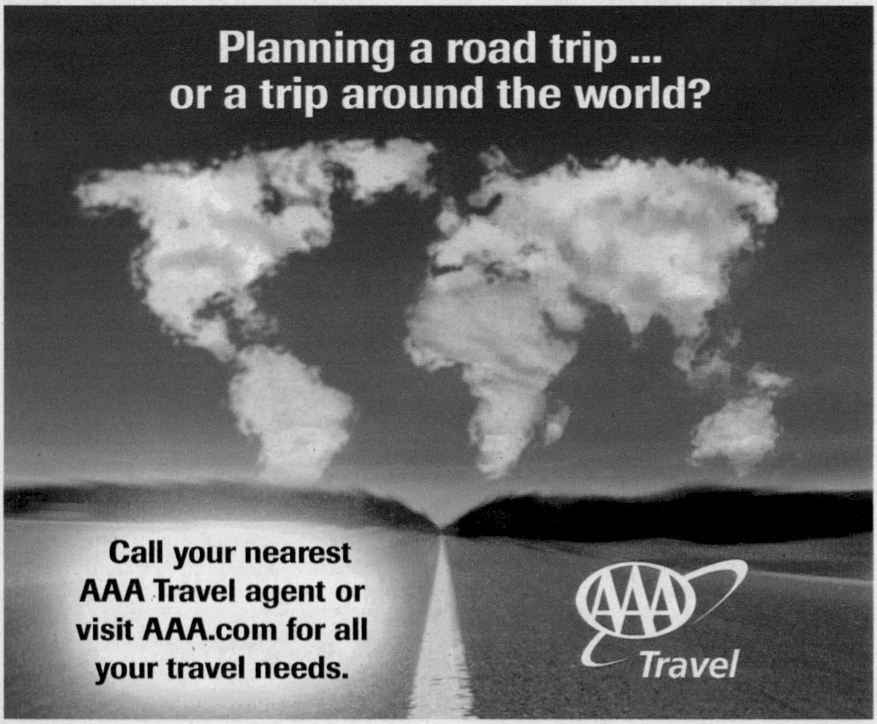

Grand Cayman

BREAKERS (See map and index starting on p. 394)

WHERE TO DINE

THE LIGHTHOUSE RESTAURANT AT THE BREAKERS

International
$11-$50

Phone: 345/947-2047 (45)

The varied menu lists an extensive selection of seafood and Italian dishes. Both indoor and patio seating overlook the ocean. The setting is upscale yet relaxed. Luncheon choices center on lighter fare, such as burgers, sandwiches and salads. Casual dress. **Bar:** Full bar. **Reservations:** suggested. **Hours:** noon-3 & 6-10 pm. **Address:** Queens Hwy **Location:** Just s of Bodden. **Parking:** on-site. **Cards:** MC, VI.

COLLIERS (See map and index starting on p. 394)

WHERE TO STAY

THE REEF RESORT

AAA SAVE

Hotel
$175-$595 All Year

Phone: 345/947-0100 (25)

Address: 1 Queens Hwy **Location:** Oceanfront. At Colliers Bay; 24 mi (38.4 km) e of George Town; 23 mi (36.8 km) e of Owen Roberts International Airport. **Facility:** Smoke free premises. 108 units. 46 one-bedroom standard units, some with whirlpools. 48 one- and 14 two-bedroom suites with kitchens. 2-3 stories, exterior corridors. **Parking:** on-site. **Terms:** office hours 7 am-11 pm, check-in 4 pm, 14 day cancellation notice-fee imposed. **Amenities:** video library, DVD players, CD players, high-speed Internet, voice mail, safes, irons, hair dryers. **Dining:** entertainment. **Pool(s):** 3 outdoor. **Leisure Activities:** whirlpools, lighted tennis court, basketball, volleyball. *Fee:* scuba diving, snorkeling, bicycles. **Guest Services:** coin laundry, wireless Internet. **Business Services:** meeting rooms, PC. **Cards:** AX, MC, VI. *(See color ad below)*

D / SOME UNITS VCR

EAST END pop. 1,371 (See map and index starting on p. 394)

WHERE TO DINE

PORTOFINO

International
$13-$38

Phone: 345/947-2700 (47)

Quaint Old World Italian and Mediterranean decor typifies the oceanfront restaurant, which boasts views of the "Wreck of the Ten Sails." Lasagna is among the familiar pasta dishes offered. Hearty portions are the norm, so bring an appetite. Casual dress. **Bar:** Full bar. **Reservations:** suggested. **Hours:** 11:30 am-4:30 & 5-10 pm; Sunday brunch. **Address:** East End Grand Bay **Location:** Center of town; 25.8 mi (41.4 km) e of George Town. **Parking:** on-site. **Cards:** AX, MC, VI.

GEORGE TOWN pop. 20,626 (See map and index starting on p. 394)

WHERE TO DINE

BACCHUS RESTAURANT AND WINE BAR

AAA

International
$18-$40

Phone: 345/949-5747 (30)

In the heart of downtown, the lively fine-dining restaurant bakes a variety of breads and desserts in-house. The prix fixe menu, which incorporates a wide variety of tastes, is a good value. Save room for warm banana-chocolate bread pudding with mango ice cream. Dressy casual. **Bar:** Full bar. **Reservations:** suggested. **Hours:** 10 am-10 pm. Closed: 12/25; also Sun. **Address:** Fort St **Location:** Center of downtown; in Jack & Jill Building. **Parking:** street. **Cards:** AX, MC, VI.

(See map and index starting on p. 394)

THE BRASSERIE **Phone:** 345/945-1815 (33)

International
$17-$40

A slightly hidden downtown gem, the cool, swanky restaurant is well worth searching out. An on-site bakery creates a wonderful array of breads and desserts. For starters, try the refreshing chunky gazpacho with crabmeat. Roasted sea bass, duck and lamb are just a few of the notable entree offerings. For dessert, banana bread pudding with bourbon caramel sauce receives rave reviews. Those with light appetites might order from the tapas menu. There is a large selection of wines by the glass. Dressy casual. **Bar:** Full bar. **Reservations:** suggested. **Hours:** Open 12/1-8/1 & 9/1-11/30; 11:30 am-2:30 & 6-10 pm, Sat & Sun from 6 pm. Closed: for lunch on public holidays. **Address:** Elgin Ave **Location:** Just s of downtown; in Cricket Square. **Parking:** on-site. **Cards:** AX, MC, VI.

GRAND OLD HOUSE **Phone:** 345/949-9333 (35)

International
$28-$43

On the sea's edge, the circa 1900 residence now is home to a restaurant where guests unwind on the seaside veranda or inside dining rooms. The fine menu selection includes a wide variety of seafood, island cuisine and international specialties. The wine list is outstanding. Dressy casual. Entertainment. **Bar:** Full bar. **Reservations:** suggested. **Hours:** Open 12/1-9/5 & 10/5-11/30; 11:45 am-2 & 6-10 pm, Sat & Sun from 6 pm. **Address:** 648 S Church St **Location:** 1.5 mi (2.4 km) s of town. **Parking:** on-site. **Cards:** AX, DS, MC, VI. **Historic**

HARD ROCK CAFE **Phone:** 345/945-2020 (29)

SAVE

American
$12-$24

Rock 'n' roll memorabilia decorates the walls of the popular theme restaurant. Live music on the weekends contributes to the bustling atmosphere. On the menu is a wide variety of American cuisine—from burgers and sandwiches to seafood, steaks and pasta. Casual dress. **Bar:** Full bar. **Hours:** 11 am-11 pm. **Address:** 43 S Church St **Location:** Center; on the waterfront just s of cruiseship docks. **Parking:** on-site. **Cards:** AX, DS, JC, MC, VI.

THE WHARF RESTAURANT **Phone:** 345/949-2231 (22)

International
$30-$46

Sophisticated yet relaxed, the waterfront location boasts a large outdoor terrace with cozy, candlelit tables. A highlight here is the tarpon feeding off the dock every evening at 9 pm. On the menu is island and Continental cuisine. Dressy casual. **Bar:** Full bar. **Reservations:** suggested. **Hours:** 6 pm-10 pm; 11:30 am-2:30 pm 12/1-4/1. **Address:** West Bay Rd #43 **Location:** 1 mi (1.6 km) n of town. **Parking:** on-site. **Cards:** AX, MC, VI.

SEVEN MILE BEACH (See map and index starting on p. 394)

WHERE TO STAY

7 MILE BEACH RESORT & CLUB **Phone:** (345)949-0332 (14)

Condominium
$300-$675 All Year

Address: 19 D Piper Ln **Location:** 1.4 mi (2.2 km) n of town; 2.6 mi (4.1 km) n of Owen Roberts International Airport. **Facility:** 36 two-bedroom suites with kitchens and whirlpools. 3 stories (no elevator), exterior corridors. **Parking:** on-site. **Terms:** office hours 9 am-6 pm, check-in 4 pm, 30 day cancellation notice. **Amenities:** video library, DVD players, high-speed Internet, voice mail, safes, irons, hair dryers. **Pool(s):** outdoor. **Leisure Activities:** whirlpool, recreation programs, volleyball. *Fee:* scuba diving, snorkeling. **Guest Services:** coin laundry, wireless Internet. **Business Services:** PC. **Cards:** AX, DS, MC, VI.

 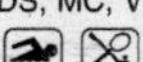   

AQUA BAY CLUB CONDOS **Phone:** 345/945-4728 (3)

Condominium
$275-$625 All Year

Address: 2093 West Bay Rd **Location:** Oceanfront. West end of Seven Mile Beach. **Facility:** Smoke free premises. 19 condominiums. 3 stories (no elevator), exterior corridors. *Bath:* combo or shower only. **Parking:** on-site. **Terms:** office hours 9 am-5 pm. **Amenities:** video library, DVD players, high-speed Internet, voice mail, safes, irons, hair dryers. **Pool(s):** outdoor. **Leisure Activities:** whirlpool. **Guest Services:** coin laundry. **Cards:** AX, MC, VI.

(See map and index starting on p. 394)

CARIBBEAN CLUB Phone: 345/623-4500 12

Condominium
$800-$2500 All Year

Address: 871 West Bay Rd **Location:** Oceanfront. Center. **Facility:** Situated oceanfront, the property offers luxurious residential-style units with features like granite countertops, LCD televisions and plush bedding. Meets AAA guest room security requirements. Smoke free premises. 23 condominiums. 7 stories, interior/exterior corridors. **Parking:** on-site. **Terms:** check-in 4 pm. **Amenities:** video library, DVD players, high-speed Internet, safes, irons, hair dryers. **Pool(s):** outdoor. **Leisure Activities:** limited exercise equipment. **Guest Services:** complimentary laundry. **Business Services:** PC. **Cards:** AX, DC, DS, MC, VI.

S D

THE CHRISTOPHER COLUMBUS CONDOS Phone: 345/945-4354 4

Condominium
$210-$495 All Year

Address: 2013 West Bay Rd **Location:** Oceanfront. West end of Seven Mile Beach. **Facility:** Smoke free premises. 30 condominiums. 3 stories (no elevator), exterior corridors. **Parking:** on-site. **Terms:** office hours 9 am-5 pm. **Amenities:** DVD players, irons. **Pool(s):** outdoor. **Leisure Activities:** 2 lighted tennis courts. **Guest Services:** coin laundry, wireless Internet. **Cards:** AX, DS, MC, VI.

D VCR

COMFORT SUITES AND RESORT Phone: (345)945-7300 16

AAA SAVE

Hotel
$185-$360 All Year

Address: 22 Piper Way **Location:** 1.5 mi (2.4 km) n of town; 2.5 mi (4 km) n of Owen Roberts International Airport; at Seven Mile Beach. **Facility:** Meets AAA guest room security requirements. Smoke free premises. 108 units. 62 one-bedroom standard units. 28 one- and 18 two-bedroom suites with efficiencies. 5 stories, interior corridors. *Bath:* combo or shower only. **Parking:** on-site. **Terms:** cancellation fee imposed. **Amenities:** high-speed Internet, dual phone lines, voice mail, safes (fee), irons, hair dryers. *Some:* DVD players (fee). **Pool(s):** outdoor. **Leisure Activities:** whirlpool, limited beach access, limited exercise equipment. *Fee:* scuba diving, snorkeling, massage. **Guest Services:** valet and coin laundry, wireless Internet. **Business Services:** meeting rooms, PC. **Cards:** AX, MC, VI. **Free Special Amenities: expanded continental breakfast and high-speed Internet.** *(See color ad below)*

CALL S D / SOME UNITS FEE VCR

▼ See AAA listing above ▼

(See map and index starting on p. 394)

GRAND CAYMAN MARRIOTT BEACH RESORT *Book great rates at AAA.com* **Phone:** (345)949-0088 **18**

AAA SAVE

Hotel
$259-$403 All Year

Address: 389 West Bay Rd **Location:** Oceanfront. 1.8 mi (2.9 km) n of town; 2.8 mi (4.5 km) n of Owen Roberts International Airport. **Facility:** Smoke free premises. 295 one-bedroom standard units. 5 stories, interior corridors. *Bath:* combo or shower only. **Parking:** on-site. **Terms:** check-in 4 pm, 3 day cancellation notice-fee imposed. **Amenities:** voice mail, safes, irons, hair dryers. **Dining:** 3 restaurants. **Pool(s):** outdoor. **Leisure Activities:** whirlpool, rental paddleboats, rental sailboats, rental sailboards, scuba equipment rental, snorkeling equipment rental, exercise room, spa. *Fee:* waterskiing, kayak, personal watercraft. **Guest Services:** valet laundry, beauty salon, wireless Internet. **Business Services:** meeting rooms, PC (fee). **Cards:** AX, CB, DC, DS, JC, MC, VI.
(See color ad on insert)

THE MERIDIAN **Phone:** (345)945-4002 **11**

AAA SAVE

Condominium
$420-$950 All Year

Address: 917 West Bay Rd **Location:** Center. **Facility:** Quiet beachfront setting; rooms with balcony or patio. Barbecue. Smoke free premises. 22 condominiums. 6 stories, exterior corridors. **Parking:** on-site. **Terms:** office hours 9 am-5 pm, check-in 4 pm, 3 night minimum stay, 60 day cancellation notice-fee imposed. **Amenities:** DVD players, high-speed Internet, safes, irons, hair dryers. **Pool(s):** outdoor. **Leisure Activities:** whirlpool, exercise room. **Guest Services:** complimentary laundry. **Cards:** AX, DC, DS, MC, VI. **Free Special Amenities: local telephone calls and high-speed Internet.**

PLANTANA CONDOMINIUMS **Phone:** 345/945-4430 **10**

Condominium
$240-$680 All Year

Address: 1293 West Bay Rd **Location:** Center. **Facility:** Smoke free premises. 36 condominiums. 3 stories (no elevator), exterior corridors. **Parking:** on-site. **Terms:** office hours 8:30 am-4:30 pm, 3 night minimum stay, 60 day cancellation notice. **Amenities:** DVD players, CD players, high-speed Internet, safes, irons, hair dryers. **Pool(s):** outdoor. **Guest Services:** complimentary laundry. **Cards:** AX, MC, VI.

PLANTATION VILLAGE BEACH RESORT **Phone:** 345/949-4199 **20**

Condominium
$185-$595 All Year

Address: 323 West Bay Rd **Location:** Oceanfront. Center; east end of Seven Mile Beach. **Facility:** Meets AAA guest room security requirements. Designated smoking area. 20 condominiums. 3 stories (no elevator), exterior corridors. **Parking:** on-site. **Terms:** office hours 8:30 am-5 pm, 30 day cancellation notice-fee imposed. **Amenities:** DVD players, CD players, high-speed Internet, voice mail, safes, irons. **Pool(s):** 2 outdoor. **Leisure Activities:** lighted tennis court, bicycles. **Guest Services:** complimentary laundry. **Business Services:** PC. **Cards:** AX, DS, MC, VI.

REGAL BEACH CLUB **Phone:** (345)945-6189 **15**

Condominium
$325-$975 All Year

Address: 431 West Bay Rd **Location:** 1.9 mi (3.4 km) n of town; 2.7 mi (4.3 km) n of Owen Roberts International Airport; on Seven Mile Beach. **Facility:** Meets AAA guest room security requirements. Designated smoking area. 21 units. 20 two- and 1 three-bedroom suites with kitchens. 3 stories (no elevator), exterior corridors. **Parking:** on-site. **Terms:** office hours 9 am-5 pm, 3 night minimum stay - seasonal, 30 day cancellation notice-fee imposed. **Amenities:** DVD players, CD players, safes, irons, hair dryers. *Some:* high-speed Internet, voice mail. **Pool(s):** outdoor. **Leisure Activities:** whirlpool, lighted tennis court, limited exercise equipment. **Guest Services:** complimentary laundry. **Business Services:** PC. **Cards:** AX, DS, MC, VI.

ASK / SOME UNITS VCR

THE RITZ-CARLTON, GRAND CAYMAN **Phone:** 345/943-9000 **13**

AAA SAVE

Resort Hotel
$399-$3800 All Year

Address: West Bay Rd **Location:** Oceanfront. 4 mi (6.4 km) n of town; 5 mi (8 km) n of Owen Roberts International Airport. **Facility:** The epitome of a tropical island location, this crown jewel offers spacious guest units with either an island or ocean view. Meets AAA guest room security requirements. Smoke free premises. 365 units. 329 one-bedroom standard units. 12 one- and 24 two-bedroom suites. 5-7 stories, interior corridors. *Bath:* combo or shower only. **Parking:** valet. **Amenities:** DVD players, CD players, high-speed Internet (fee), dual phone lines, voice mail, safes, honor bars, irons, hair dryers. **Dining:** 3 restaurants, also, 7 Prime Cuts and Sunsets, Blue, see separate listings, entertainment. **Pool(s):** 2 outdoor. **Leisure Activities:** saunas, whirlpools, steamrooms, beach access, rental sailboards, scuba equipment rental, snorkeling equipment rental, recreation programs, spa, volleyball. *Fee:* paddleboats, sailboats, personal watercraft, kayaks, golf-9 holes, 4 lighted tennis courts. **Guest Services:** valet laundry, car rental, beauty salon, wireless Internet. **Business Services:** conference facilities, business center. **Cards:** AX, CB, DC, DS, JC, MC, VI.

FEE 24

TAMARIND BAY **Phone:** 345/949-4593 **8**

Condominium
$285-$510 All Year

Address: 37 Piper Way **Location:** Oceanfront. Center. **Facility:** Meets AAA guest room security requirements. 6 condominiums. 3 stories, exterior corridors. **Parking:** on-site. **Terms:** office hours 9 am-5 pm, 21 day cancellation notice-fee imposed. **Amenities:** high-speed Internet, irons. *Some:* DVD players, CD players, voice mail. **Pool(s):** outdoor. **Guest Services:** complimentary laundry. **Cards:** AX, DS, MC, VI.

/ SOME UNITS VCR

▼ See AAA listing p 402 ▼

(See map and index starting on p. 394)

TREASURE ISLAND CONDOS **Phone:** (345)949-8533 17

Condominium

$205-$630 All Year

Address: 299 West Bay Rd **Location:** Oceanfront. 1.5 mi (2.4 km) n of town; 2.5 mi (4 km) n of Owen Roberts International Airport; on Seven Mile Beach. **Facility:** Built in the 1980s steps from the beach and a reef, each spacious condo features rattan furniture, a fully-equipped kitchen and two full bathrooms. Designated smoking area. 26 condominiums. 3 stories (no elevator), exterior corridors. *Bath:* combo or shower only. **Parking:** on-site. **Terms:** office hours 10 am-5 pm, 3-7 night minimum stay - seasonal, 30 day cancellation notice-fee imposed. **Amenities:** DVD players, CD players, voice mail, safes, irons, hair dryers. *Some:* high-speed Internet. **Pool(s):** 3 outdoor. **Leisure Activities:** whirlpool, exercise room. *Fee:* scuba diving, snorkeling. **Guest Services:** complimentary laundry, wireless Internet. **Cards:** AX, DC, DS, MC, VI.

WESTIN CASUARINA RESORT & SPA-GRAND CAYMAN **Phone:** (345)945-3800 5

AAA SAVE

Resort Hotel

$288-$659 All Year

Address: West Bay Rd **Location:** Oceanfront. 3.2 mi (5.1 km) n of town; 4.2 mi (6.7 km) n of Owen Roberts International Airport; on Seven Mile Beach. **Facility:** Named for the stately casuarina tree, the resort is on Seven Mile Beach; find a large pool area, a spa and well-appointed guest rooms. Meets AAA guest room security requirements. Smoke free premises. 343 units. 339 one-bedroom standard units. 4 one-bedroom suites. 5 stories, interior corridors. **Parking:** on-site. **Terms:** 15 day cancellation notice-fee imposed. **Amenities:** high-speed Internet (fee), voice mail, safes, honor bars, irons, hair dryers. *Some:* DVD players (fee), CD players. **Dining:** 2 restaurants, also, Casa Havana, see separate listing, entertainment. **Pool(s):** outdoor. **Leisure Activities:** whirlpools, rental sailboards, recreation programs, kids camp, exercise room, spa, volleyball. *Fee:* sailboats, waterskiing, scuba diving, snorkeling, fishing, charter fishing, aqua trykes, banana boats, kayak, dinner & sunset cruise, personal watercraft, parasailing. **Guest Services:** valet laundry, wireless Internet. **Business Services:** conference facilities, business center. **Cards:** AX, MC, VI. *(See color ad on insert & p 401)*

24 S D / SOME UNITS FEE VCR

WHERE TO DINE

7 PRIME CUTS AND SUNSETS **Phone:** 345/943-9000 8

Steak

$20-$60

Diners enjoy upscale, refined dining either outdoors with direct views of the beach and ocean, or in the cool indoors amid elegant surroundings. Experienced servers are very knowledgeable and assist in exploring the menu. Numerous beef cuts include U.S. prime beef, Angus and Kobe. Besides beef, there are some fish and seafood dishes, and the desserts are heavenly. Dressy casual. **Bar:** Full bar. **Reservations:** required. **Hours:** 5:30 pm-10 pm. **Address:** West Bay Rd **Location:** ocean side, 4 mi n of town; 5 mi (8 km) n of Owen Roberts International Airport, in The Ritz-Carlton, Grand Cayman. **Parking:** on-site. **Cards:** AX, CB, DC, DS, JC, MC, VI.

BAMBOO LOUNGE **Phone:** 345/947-8744 16

Japanese

$27-$58

Sleek, chic surroundings epitomize the sushi bar, which is on the ocean side of the Hyatt Regency complex. The considerable menu lists an assortment of sushi rolls, sashimi and tempura, as well as some designer martinis. Unobtrusive service allows for a relaxing evening most weekday nights, but expect large crowds on the weekends as the locals arrive to imbibe and dine. Dressy casual. **Bar:** Full bar. **Hours:** 5:30 pm-11 pm. Closed: Sun. **Address:** West Bay Rd **Location:** 2.5 mi (4 km) n of town; 3.5 mi (5.6 km) n of Owen Roberts International Airport at Seven Mile Beach; in Hyatt Regency Grand Cayman Resort. **Parking:** on-site. **Cards:** AX, MC, VI.

BLUE **Phone:** 345/943-9000 18

Seafood

$81-$120

Celebrity chef Eric Ripert originated this restaurant concept, which centers on artistically presented offerings of creative and bold fish and other seafood. Those interested in exploring flavors in depth should consider the chef's tasting menu. Blue hues and blue roses lend to the water-inspired theme, and the experienced, international wait staff carries out world-class service with grace and charm. Dressy casual. **Bar:** Full bar. **Reservations:** suggested. **Hours:** 6 pm-10 pm. Closed: Sun & Mon. **Address:** West Bay Rd **Location:** 4 mi (6.4 km) n of town; in The Ritz-Carlton, Grand Cayman. **Parking:** valet. **Cards:** AX, CB, DC, DS, JC, MC, VI.

CAFE MED **Phone:** 345/949-8669 15

Italian

$14-$40

The casual bistro holds popular theme entertainment nights, such as salsa dancing and cabarets. The menu—which includes pizza, pasta and veal dishes—blends elements of Mediterranean and Italian cuisine. Listed are at least seven salads, including the Monte Carlo salad with Parma ham, feta cheese, artichoke hearts and asparagus. A favorite dish is capellini D'Angelo Veneziana: angel hair pasta with shrimp, cherry tomatoes and broccoli in garlic olive oil sauce and finished off with pesto. Dressy casual. **Bar:** Full bar. **Reservations:** suggested. **Hours:** 11 am-11 pm. **Address:** West Bay Rd **Location:** 2.4 mi (3.8 km) n of town; 3.4 mi (5.4 km) n of Owen Roberts International Airport; in Galleria Plaza at Seven Mile Beach. **Parking:** on-site. **Cards:** AX, DC, MC, VI.

CASA HAVANA **Phone:** 345/945-3800 4

International

$33-$49

Creative menu selections center on Cuban and Caribbean specialties. Indoor and outdoor tables in the oceanfront restaurant lend an air of upscale elegance. Good food choices include certified Angus beef, rack of lamb and some innovative seafood dishes. Dressy casual. **Bar:** Full bar. **Reservations:** suggested. **Hours:** 6 pm-10:30 pm. **Address:** West Bay Rd **Location:** 3.2 mi (5.1 km) n of town; 4.2 mi (6.7 km) n of Owen Roberts International Airport; on Seven Mile Beach; in Westin Casuarina Resort & Spa-Grand Cayman. **Parking:** on-site. **Cards:** AX, MC, VI. *(See color ad p 401)*

(See map and index starting on p. 394)

CHICKEN! CHICKEN! **Phone:** 345/945-2290 (13)

Caribbean
$8-$16

For a quick, value-priced and nutritious meal, this is the place for dining in or take-out. Wood-roasted chicken comes Caribbean-style or in citrus- or herb-marinated versions. Guests can choose from a whole, half or quarter bird. Among the many side options are mashed potatoes, rice and beans, jicama coleslaw or garlic- and herb-roasted potatoes. Casual dress. **Bar:** Beer & wine. **Hours:** 11 am-10 pm. Closed: 12/25. **Address:** West Shore Center SMB **Location:** 3.2 mi (5.1 km) n of town; in West Shore Shopping Center. **Parking:** on-site. **Cards:** AX, MC, VI.

CIMBOCO, A CARIBBEAN CAFE **Phone:** 345/947-2782 (14)

International
$13-$21

Dine in festively decorated surroundings or choose to take-away a meal. Individual wood-fired gourmet pizzas and some creative pasta dishes are the specialties here. Casual dress. **Bar:** Full bar. **Hours:** 7 am-10 pm, Fri-11 pm. Closed: 12/25. **Address:** Harquail Bypass **Location:** 2 mi (3.2 km) n of town at The Marquee; Seven Mile Beach. **Parking:** on-site. **Cards:** AX, MC, VI.

COPPER FALLS STEAKHOUSE **Phone:** 345/945-4755 (9)

Steak
$23-$46

Diners are treated to pleasant dining in attractive surroundings, both indoors and on the patio. The creative menu blends pasta, seafood and meat entrees, as well as some Caribbean specialties. Dressy casual. **Bar:** Full bar. **Reservations:** suggested. **Hours:** 5:30 pm-10:30 pm. **Address:** 43 Canal Point Rd **Location:** Across from Strand Shopping Plaza. **Parking:** on-site. **Cards:** AX, MC, VI.

DECKERS BISTRO & GRILL **Phone:** 345/945-6600 (6)

International
$24-$48

A distinctive bar built in an original London double-decker bus sets the comfortable restaurant apart. Among creative menu selections are Caribbean, pasta and seafood specialties. Guests can sit indoors or on the patio. Casual dress. **Bar:** Full bar. **Reservations:** suggested. **Hours:** 5:30 pm-10:30 pm. Closed: 12/25. **Address:** West Bay Rd **Location:** 2.5 mi (4 km) n of town; across from Seven Mile Beach; in front of Hyatt Regency Grand Cayman Resort. **Parking:** on-site. **Cards:** AX, MC, VI.

FIDEL MURPHY'S **Phone:** 345/949-5189 (23)

Irish
$14-$28

Dark woods, stained and frosted glass and an Irish pride and sports motif set the tone at the pub, which is a popular place to meet and watch sporting events. Those who don't go for the create-your-own-sandwich menu might try a pasta or seafood dish or maybe a traditional Irish choice, such as fish and chips, shepherd's pie and Irish stew. Casual dress. **Bar:** Full bar. **Reservations:** accepted. **Hours:** 10 am-11 pm. **Address:** West Bay Rd **Location:** 1.2 mi (1.9 km) n of town; in Queen's Court Shopping Plaza. **Parking:** on-site. **Cards:** AX, DS, MC, VI.

GATEWAY OF INDIA **Phone:** 345/946-2815 (7)

Indian
$19-$33

Close-fitting tables nurture a cozy feel in a dining room neatly adorned with East Indian art and curios. The descriptive menu details varied curries made with a choice of lamb, beef, chicken or seafood, in addition to tandoori specialties, which are slow-cooked in a clay oven. A bountiful lunch buffet is the highlight of weekday afternoons. Casual dress. **Bar:** Full bar. **Reservations:** suggested, for dinner. **Hours:** 11:30 am-2 & 5:30-9:30 pm, Sat & Sun from 5:30 pm. Closed: for lunch on Caymanian public holidays. **Address:** Canal Point Rd **Location:** 3 mi (4.8 km) n of town; across from Strand Shopping Center. **Parking:** on-site. **Cards:** AX, MC, VI.

HEMINGWAY'S BEACH CLUB RESTAURANT **Phone:** 345/945-5700 (17)

Continental
$17-$45

Handsome tropical decor characterizes the charming and sophisticated dining room and outdoor patio, which overlook the beach. The attentive staff serves well-prepared regional and Continental cuisine, which is ably complemented by the good wine list. Candlelit tables make the setting romantic. Although parking is limited, additional spaces can be found across the street. Dressy casual. **Bar:** Full bar. **Reservations:** required. **Hours:** 7-10:30 am, 11:30-2:30 & 6-10 pm; Sunday champagne brunch. **Address:** West Bay Rd **Location:** 2.5 mi (4 km) n of town; in Hyatt Regency Grand Cayman Resort. **Parking:** on-site. **Cards:** AX, CB, DC, DS, JC, MC, VI.

LITTLE TOKYO MONGOLIAN GRILL & LOUNGE **Phone:** 345/949-4944 (19)

Asian
$13-$19

Red walls, plasma TVs and a semi-open kitchen define the setting of this relatively new eatery in Seven Mile Beach. A distinctive concept of the Japanese, Chinese and Mongolian menu is the assemble-it-yourself option that lines up a long list of ingredients such as bok choy, baby corn, pork, beef and scallops and sauces along the lines of hoison, teriyaki and oyster. Starters include pot stickers, Buffalo wings and egg rolls. Casual dress. **Bar:** Full bar. **Hours:** 11:30 am-2:30 & 5:30-10 pm. **Address:** 215 West Bay Rd **Location:** Center; in Seven Mile Shops Shopping Complex. **Parking:** on-site. **Cards:** AX, MC, VI.

PRIME BRAZILIAN STEAK HOUSE **Phone:** 345/623-7272 (5)

Steak Brazilian
$24-$55

Polished wood, elegant window treatments and decorative light fixtures lend to a rich and upscale backdrop for the Brazilian rodizio experience, believed to be the first of its kind in the Cayman Islands. For starters, the restaurant offers a fabulous buffet to whet the appetite. Afterward, the real fun begins as carvers circulate the dining room with skewers of grilled and roasted meat such as suckling pig, jerk pork, leg of lamb and steak. Dressy casual. **Bar:** Full bar. **Reservations:** suggested. **Hours:** 11:30 am-3 & 5:30-11 pm. **Address:** Governor's Square **Location:** In Governor's Square. **Parking:** on-site. **Cards:** AX, MC, VI.

THE REEF GRILL AT THE ROYAL PALMS **Phone:** 345/945-6358 (21)

International
$10-$40

Examples of American and island cuisine—such as lobster ravioli, seared tuna with Asian slaw or beef tenderloin—line the restaurant's innovative menu. The modern dining room offers indoor or patio dining in a tropical garden setting. Dressy casual. **Bar:** Full bar. **Reservations:** suggested. **Hours:** 11 am-3 & 6-10 pm. Closed: Sun 5/1-11/15; Mon-Wed 9/1-9/30. **Address:** 537 West Bay Rd **Location:** 2.1 mi (3.3 km) n of town; on Seven Mile Beach; in Royal Palms Beach Club. **Parking:** on-site. **Cards:** AX, MC, VI.

(See map and index starting on p. 394)

RISTORANTE RAGAZZI **Phone:** 345/945-3484 (10)

Italian
$14-$44

The voguish trattoria employs Italian and international servers. The extensive menu includes skillfully prepared pasta dishes—ranging from tortellini to lasagna to gnocchi—as well as tempting grilled meat plates, such as marinated pork tenderloin and grilled rosemary chicken. Also popular are traditional thin-crusted pizzas with a plethora of topping combinations. Casual dress. **Bar:** Full bar. **Reservations:** suggested. **Hours:** 11:30 am-11 pm. Closed: for lunch on public holidays. **Address:** West Bay Rd **Location:** 2.4 mi (3.8 km) n of town; across from Seven Mile Beach; in Buckingham Square. **Parking:** on-site. **Cards:** AX, MC, VI.

THAI ORCHID **Phone:** 345/949-7955 (20)

Thai
$18-$30

Bangkok chefs prepare an extensive selection of savory cuisine. Meals are made a la minute so the diner's taste and preferences are taken into account. The staff is cordial and attentive. The owner is an accomplished artist, and the decor is distinguished by her intriguing work on the walls. Dressy casual. **Bar:** Full bar. **Reservations:** accepted. **Hours:** 11:30 am-2:30 & 5-10 pm, Sat 11:30 am-10 pm. Closed: for lunch on public holidays. **Address:** West Bay Rd **Location:** 1.1 mi (1.7 km) n of town; in Queens Court Plaza. **Parking:** on-site. **Cards:** AX, MC, VI.

WEST BAY pop. 8,243 (See map and index starting on p. 394)

WHERE TO STAY

COBALT COAST RESORT & SUITES *Book great rates at AAA.com* **Phone:** (345)946-5656 (1)

Country Inn
$240-$495 All Year

Address: 18A Sea Fan Dr **Location:** Oceanfront. 7 mi (11.2 km) n of George Town to West Bay four-way stop, 2.5 mi (4 km) n, follow signs. **Facility:** A diver's paradise, this plantation-style country inn is far enough from Seven Mile Beach to ensure tranquility but near enough for a quick visit. Meets AAA guest room security requirements. Designated smoking area. 18 units. 5 one-bedroom standard units. 7 one- and 4 two-bedroom suites. 2 cottages. 2 stories (no elevator), exterior corridors. *Bath:* combo or shower only. **Parking:** on-site. **Terms:** 14 day cancellation notice-fee imposed. **Amenities:** CD players, high-speed Internet, voice mail, safes, irons, hair dryers. *Some:* DVD players. **Pool(s):** outdoor. **Leisure Activities:** whirlpool, snorkeling equipment rental. *Fee:* scuba diving, massage. **Guest Services:** valet laundry, wireless Internet. **Cards:** AX, DS, MC, VI. **Free Special Amenities: full breakfast and high-speed Internet.** *(See color ad p 398)*

  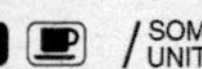 / SOME UNITS VCR

WHERE TO DINE

CRACKED CONCH BY THE SEA **Phone:** 345/945-5217 (3)

Caribbean
$12-$37

Select from seafood, pasta, burgers and lighter fare; the extensive Caribbean Sunday brunch is popular. Seating is on the oceanfront patio or at the indoor dining room. Casual dress. **Bar:** Full bar. **Reservations:** suggested. **Hours:** 11 am-3 & 5:30-10 pm. Closed: 12/25. **Address:** NW Point Rd **Location:** 8 mi (12.8 km) n of George Town; 9 mi (14.4 km) n of Owen Roberts International Airport; adjacent to Turtle Farm. **Parking:** on-site. **Cards:** AX, MC, VI.

RISTORANTE PAPPAGALLO **Phone:** 345/949-3479 (2)

Northern Italian
$25-$46

Diners are treated to a secluded tropical setting on the edge of a lagoon. Thatched-roof dining rooms with live parrots add to the tropical mood. Pasta, beef and seafood selections make up the creative cuisine. Dressy casual. **Bar:** Full bar. **Reservations:** suggested. **Hours:** 6 pm-10:30 pm. Closed: Super Bowl Sun. **Address:** 444B Conch Point Rd **Location:** 7 mi (11.2 km) n to West Bay, 2.5 mi (4 km) n, follow signs to Conch Point/Barkers. **Parking:** on-site. **Cards:** AX, MC, VI.

Little Cayman

LITTLE CAYMAN pop. 115 (See map and index starting on p. 394)

WHERE TO STAY

THE CLUB AT LITTLE CAYMAN — Phone: (345)948-1033 — 35

Condominium
$285-$525 12/1-4/30
$225-$525 5/1-11/30

Address: Guy Banks Rd **Location:** Oceanfront. 0.4 mi (0.7 km) e of airstrip. **Facility:** Recently built, spacious condos feature upscale, residential-quality appointments. Meets AAA guest room security requirements. Designated smoking area. 8 three-bedroom suites with kitchens. 2 stories (no elevator), exterior corridors. **Parking:** on-site. **Terms:** office hours 7 am-8 pm, off-site registration, 21 day cancellation notice-fee imposed. **Amenities:** DVD players, CD players, voice mail, irons, hair dryers. **Pool(s):** outdoor. **Leisure Activities:** whirlpools, limited beach access, bicycles. **Guest Services:** complimentary laundry, wireless Internet. **Business Services:** meeting rooms, PC (fee). **Cards:** AX, MC, VI.

S D

CONCH CLUB CONDOMINIUMS — Phone: (345)948-1033 — 36

Condominium
$250-$450 12/1-4/30
$250-$350 5/1-11/30

Address: Guy Banks Rd **Location:** Oceanfront. 0.6 mi (0.9 km) e of airstrip. **Facility:** Designated smoking area. 12 units. 10 two- and 2 three-bedroom suites with kitchens. 2 stories (no elevator), exterior corridors. **Parking:** on-site. **Terms:** office hours 7 am-8 pm, off-site registration, 21 day cancellation notice-fee imposed. **Amenities:** DVD players, CD players, voice mail, irons, hair dryers. **Pool(s):** 2 outdoor. **Leisure Activities:** whirlpool, bicycles. **Guest Services:** complimentary laundry, wireless Internet. **Business Services:** meeting rooms, PC (fee). **Cards:** AX, MC, VI.

S D

PARADISE VILLAS — Phone: (345)948-0001 — 34

Cottage
$175-$200 All Year

Address: Guy Banks Rd **Location:** Oceanfront. Just e of airstrip. **Facility:** Designated smoking area. 12 cottages. 1 story, exterior corridors. **Parking:** on-site. **Terms:** office hours 9 am-5 pm, 2 night minimum stay, 45 day cancellation notice-fee imposed. **Amenities:** *Some:* DVD players (fee). **Dining:** Hungry Iguana, see separate listing. **Pool(s):** outdoor. **Leisure Activities:** *Fee:* scuba diving, snorkeling, bicycles. **Guest Services:** valet laundry, wireless Internet. **Cards:** AX, MC, VI.

ASK D / SOME UNITS FEE VCR

SOUTHERN CROSS CLUB — Phone: (345)948-1099 — 37

Bed & Breakfast
$335-$400 All Year

Address: Guy Banks Rd **Location:** Oceanfront. 0.7 mi (1.1 km) e of airstrip. **Facility:** Popular with divers, these well-equipped, charming cottages are spaced along an enchanting stretch of beach; diving and fishing options are offered. Designated smoking area. 12 one-bedroom standard units. 1 story, exterior corridors. *Bath:* shower only. **Parking:** on-site. **Terms:** office hours 7 am-8:30 pm, 5 night minimum stay - seasonal, age restrictions may apply, 45 day cancellation notice-fee imposed. **Pool(s):** outdoor. **Leisure Activities:** boat dock, snorkeling, bicycles, horseshoes, volleyball. *Fee:* scuba diving, fishing, charter fishing, massage. **Guest Services:** TV in common area, valet laundry, area transportation, wireless Internet. **Business Services:** PC. **Cards:** MC, VI.

D / SOME UNITS FEE

WHERE TO DINE

HUNGRY IGUANA — Phone: 345/948-0007 — 38

American
$14-$28

Near the airport, the inviting restaurant has a resident retinue of iguanas. The familiar menu features American and island-inspired dishes. Daily lunch specials range from stewed conch and meatloaf to barbecue chicken and spaghetti with meatballs. Monday is pizza night. Casual dress. **Bar:** Full bar. **Reservations:** accepted. **Hours:** Open 12/1-9/15 & 10/15-11/30; noon-2:30 & 6-9 pm. **Address:** Guy Banks Rd **Location:** Just e of airstrip; in Paradise Villas. **Parking:** on-site. **Cards:** AX, MC, VI.

CURACAO

Airport Accommodations

Map Page	OA	**CURACAO AEROPUERTO HATO**	Diamond Rated	High Season	Page
1 / p. 407	AAA	**Best Western Blue Bay Village, 1.9 mi (5 km)**	◆◆◆	$320-$550 SAVE	410

Curacao

This index helps you "spot" where approved lodgings and restaurants are located on the corresponding detailed maps. Lodging daily rate range is for comparison only and show the property's high season. Restaurant rate range is a combination of lunch and/or dinner. Turn to the listing page for more detailed rate information and consult display ads for special promotions.

WILLEMSTAD

Map Page	OA	Lodgings	Diamond Rated	High Season	Page
1 / p. 407	AAA	**Best Western Blue Bay Village**	◆◆◆	$320-$550 SAVE	410
2 / p. 407		Floris Suite Hotel	◆◆◆	$170-$350	412
3 / p. 407		Hilton Curacao - see color ad opposite title page, p 412	◆◆◆	$119-$330	414
4 / p. 407	AAA	**Curacao Marriott Beach Resort & Emerald Casino - see color ad p 411, on insert**	◆◆◆	$195-$432 SAVE	412
7 / p. 407		Clarion Hotel & Suites Curacao - see color ad p 410	◆◆◆	$135-$145	412
11 / p. 407	AAA	**Avila Hotel - see color ad p 409**	◆◆◆	$230-$575 SAVE	409
12 / p. 407		Breezes Curacao Resort Spa & Casino	fyi	$129-$249	410

Map Page	OA	Restaurants	Diamond Rated	Cuisine	Meal Range	Page
1 / p. 407		Fort Nassau Restaurant	◆◆	International	$10-$32	414
2 / p. 407		Hook's Hut Beach Bar & Restaurant	◆◆	International	$10-$26	415
3 / p. 407		Zanta Restaurant	◆◆	International	$15-$28	415
4 / p. 407		Rysttafel Restaurant	◆◆	Indonesian	$15-$27	415
7 / p. 407		Gouverneur de Rouville Restaurant	◆	International	$11-$29	415
10 / p. 407	AAA	**Craving Sushi**	◆	Sushi	$12-$26	414
12 / p. 407	AAA	**Bistro Le Clochard**	◆◆◆	French	$17-$42	414
13 / p. 407		La Pergola	◆◆	Italian	$18-$28	415
16 / p. 407		Larousse Restaurant	◆◆◆	Continental	$22-$33	415
17 / p. 407		Blue's Restaurant	◆◆	International	$17-$26	414
18 / p. 407		Belle Terrace	◆◆◆	International	$17-$34	414

JAN THIEL

Map Page	OA	Lodging	Diamond Rated	High Season	Page
14 / p. 407		Papagayo Beach & Lounge Resort - see color ad p 408	◆◆◆	$224-$410	408

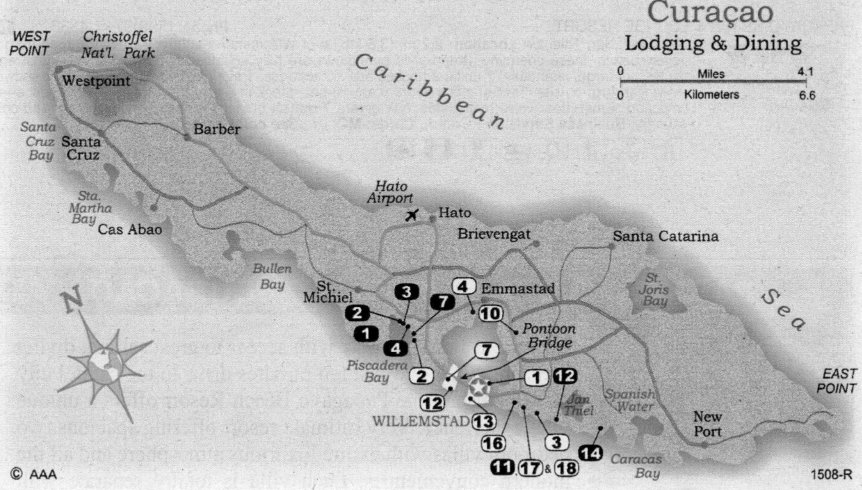
Curaçao
Lodging & Dining
0 Miles 4.1
0 Kilometers 6.6
WEST POINT
Christoffel Nat'l. Park
Westpoint
Caribbean
Barber
Santa Cruz Bay
Santa Cruz
Sta. Martha Bay
Cas Abao
Hato Airport
Hato
Brievengat
Santa Catarina
Bullen Bay
St. Michiel
Emmastad
Pontoon Bridge
St. Joris Bay
Sea
Piscadera Bay
WILLEMSTAD
Jan Thiel
Spanish Water
EAST POINT
New Port
Caracas Bay
© AAA
1508-R

JAN THIEL

(See map and index starting on p. 407)

WHERE TO STAY

PAPAGAYO BEACH & LOUNGE RESORT — Phone: (599)9747-4333 — 14

Cottage
$224-$410 All Year

Address: Jan Thiel z/n **Location:** 2.2 mi (3.5 km) e of Willemstad. **Facility:** Across the road from a lovely beach, these charming, island-style bungalows are fully equipped for extended vacations, and all feature large verandas. 77 units. 2 houses and 75 cottages. 1 story, exterior corridors. *Bath:* shower only. **Parking:** on-site. **Terms:** office hours 8 am-10 pm, check-in 4 pm, 30 day cancellation notice-fee imposed. **Amenities:** voice mail, safes, hair dryers. **Pool(s):** outdoor. **Guest Services:** valet and coin laundry. **Business Services:** PC (fee). **Cards:** MC, VI. ***(See color ad below)***

▼ *See AAA listing above* ▼

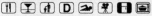

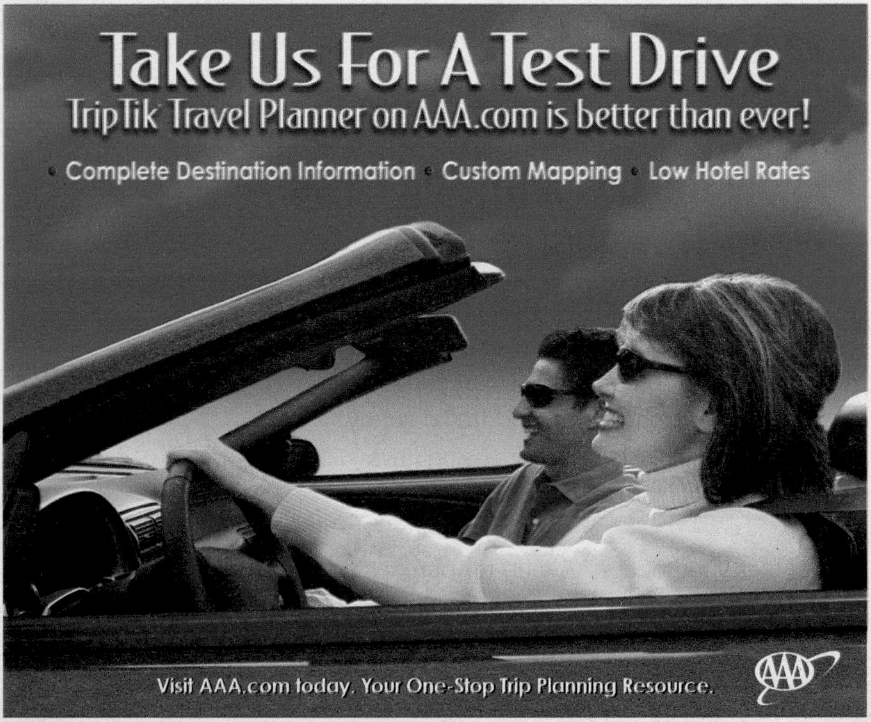

WILLEMSTAD pop. 43,550 (See map and index starting on p. 407)

WHERE TO STAY

AVILA HOTEL *Book great rates at AAA.com* **Phone:** (599)9461-4377 **11**

AAA SAVE

Hotel

$230-$575 All Year

Address: Penstraat 130 **Location:** Oceanfront. 0.9 mi (1.4 km) e from Punda side of downtown. **Facility:** 152 units. 142 one-bedroom standard units, some with efficiencies and/or whirlpools. 10 one-bedroom suites with kitchens. 2-4 stories, interior/exterior corridors. *Bath:* combo or shower only. **Parking:** on-site. **Terms:** 7 day cancellation notice-fee imposed. **Amenities:** voice mail, safes, honor bars, irons, hair dryers. *Some:* high-speed Internet. **Dining:** 2 restaurants, also, Belle Terrace, Blue's Restaurant, see separate listings, entertainment. **Pool(s):** outdoor. **Leisure Activities:** lighted tennis court, spa. **Guest Services:** valet laundry, area transportation-Punda side & Willemstad, wireless Internet. **Business Services:** meeting rooms, business center. **Cards:** AX, MC, VI. *(See color ad below)*

D / SOME UNITS

(See map and index starting on p. 407)

BEST WESTERN BLUE BAY VILLAGE Phone: 599/9888-8800 1

Vacation Rental House
$320-$550 All Year

Location: 1.9 mi (3 km) s of airport, 3.1 mi (5 km) w of downtown, follow signs. **Facility:** Located in a gated community and a short stroll of a premium beach, the villas feature a wrap-around veranda, large living room and complete kitchen. 52 houses. 1-2 stories (no elevator), exterior corridors. *Bath:* shower only. **Parking:** on-site. **Amenities:** voice mail, safes, irons, hair dryers. **Leisure Activities:** limited beach access, 2 tennis courts (Fee: 2 lighted), recreation programs, playground, exercise room. *Fee:* scuba diving, snorkeling, golf-18 holes. **Guest Services:** complimentary laundry, wireless Internet. **Business Services:** business center. **Cards:** AX, CB, DC, DS, JC, MC, VI.

AAA Benefit:
Members save up to 20%, plus 10% bonus points with rewards program.

BREEZES CURACAO RESORT SPA & CASINO Phone: 599/9736-7888 12

fyi

Resort Hotel
$129-$249 All Year

Under major renovation, scheduled to be completed March 2008. **Last rated:** **Address:** Dr Martin Luther King Blvd #78 **Location:** Oceanfront. 2.5 mi (4 km) e from Punda side of downtown. **Facility:** The newly renovated all-inclusive resort is ideal for family vacationers, with plenty of organized games and activities throughout the day. 333 units. 328 one-bedroom standard units, some with kitchens. 3 one- and 2 two-bedroom suites, some with kitchens and/or whirlpools. 2-5 stories, interior/exterior corridors. *Bath:* combo or shower only. **Parking:** on-site. **Terms:** 3 night minimum stay, 21 day cancellation notice. **Amenities:** CD players, dual phone lines, voice mail, safes, irons, hair dryers. **Pool(s):** 4 outdoor. **Leisure Activities:** sauna, whirlpools, steamroom, paddleboats, sailboats, windsurfing, scuba diving, snorkeling, 2 lighted tennis courts, recreation programs, bicycles, playground, spa, basketball, horseshoes, shuffleboard, volleyball, game room. **Guest Services:** valet laundry, area transportation, wireless Internet. **Business Services:** conference facilities, PC (fee). **Cards:** AX, DS, MC, VI.

/ SOME UNITS

▼ See AAA listing p 412 ▼

▼ See AAA listing p 412 ▼

(See map and index starting on p. 407)

CLARION HOTEL & SUITES CURACAO

Phone: (599)9433-6666 **7**

Hotel
$135-$145 All Year

Address: John F Kennedy Blvd **Location:** Piscadera Bay; 3.1 mi (5 km) w of Otrobanda side of town; 5.5 mi (8.9 km) s of airport. **Facility:** 97 units. 81 one-bedroom standard units. 16 one-bedroom suites with efficiencies (no utensils). 4 stories, interior corridors. *Bath:* combo or shower only. **Parking:** on-site. **Amenities:** high-speed Internet, voice mail, safes, hair dryers. *Some:* honor bars, irons. **Pool(s):** outdoor. **Leisure Activities:** playground. **Guest Services:** valet and coin laundry, wireless Internet. **Business Services:** conference facilities, business center. **Cards:** AX, CB, DC, DS, JC, MC, VI. ***(See color ad p 410)***

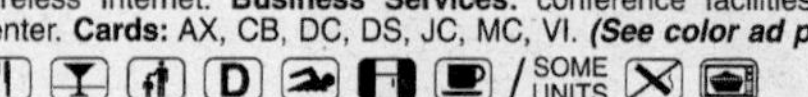

CURACAO MARRIOTT BEACH RESORT & EMERALD CASINO

Phone: 599/9736-8800 **4**

AAA SAVE

Resort Hotel
$195-$432 All Year

Address: John F Kennedy Blvd **Location:** Oceanfront. On Piscadera Bay; 3.1 mi (5 km) w of Otrobanda side of town; 5.5 mi (8.9 km) s of airport. **Facility:** Large, well-appointed resort facilities on Piscadera Bay with spacious rooms, many with ocean views, and an onsite upscale casino. Meets AAA guest room security requirements. Smoke free premises. 247 one-bedroom standard units. 3 stories, exterior corridors. *Bath:* combo or shower only. **Parking:** on-site and valet. **Terms:** cancellation fee imposed. **Amenities:** high-speed Internet (fee), voice mail, safes, irons, hair dryers. **Dining:** 4 restaurants, entertainment. **Pool(s):** outdoor. **Leisure Activities:** saunas, whirlpools, steamrooms, beach access, recreation programs, playground, exercise room, volleyball. *Fee:* sailboats, windsurfing, scuba diving, snorkeling, massage. **Guest Services:** valet laundry, wireless Internet. **Business Services:** conference facilities, PC (fee). **Cards:** AX, CB, DC, DS, MC, VI. ***(See color ad p 411 & on insert)***

Marriott HOTELS & RESORTS
AAA Benefit:
Members save a minimum 5% off the best available rate.

FLORIS SUITE HOTEL

Phone: (599)9462-6111 **2**

Hotel
$170-$350 All Year

Address: John F Kennedy Blvd **Location:** Oceanfront. Across from beach at Piscadera Bay; 3.1 mi (5 km) w of Otrobanda side of town. **Facility:** 72 units. 41 one-bedroom standard units with efficiencies. 29 one- and 2 two-bedroom suites with kitchens. 2 stories (no elevator), exterior corridors. *Bath:* combo or shower only. **Parking:** on-site. **Terms:** cancellation fee imposed. **Amenities:** high-speed Internet (fee), voice mail, safes, hair dryers. *Some:* DVD players (fee). **Pool(s):** outdoor. **Leisure Activities:** lighted tennis court, exercise room. *Fee:* scuba diving, snorkeling. **Guest Services:** valet laundry, area transportation, wireless Internet. **Business Services:** meeting rooms, PC (fee). **Cards:** AX, DC, MC, VI.

/ SOME UNITS FEE VCR

▼ ***See AAA listing p 414*** ▼

▼ See AAA listing p 414 ▼

(See map and index starting on p. 407)

HILTON CURACAO *Book great rates at AAA.com* **Phone:** (599)9462-5000 3

Resort Hotel

$119-$330 All Year

Address: John F Kennedy Blvd **Location:** Oceanfront. Piscadera Bay; 3.1 mi (5 km) w of Otrobanda side of town; 5.5 mi (8.9 km) s of airport. **Facility:** Mid-rise hotel with resort facilities including a free-form lagoon style pool. Guest rooms are well-appointed including marble bathrooms. 196 one-bedroom standard units. 5 stories, interior corridors. *Bath:* combo or shower only. **Parking:** on-site. **Terms:** 1-30 night minimum stay, cancellation fee imposed. **Amenities:** high-speed Internet (fee), voice mail, safes, irons, hair dryers. *Some:* honor bars. **Pool(s):** 2 outdoor. **Leisure Activities:** sauna, steamroom, boat dock, miniature golf, 2 lighted tennis courts, recreation programs, playground, spa, volleyball. *Fee:* paddleboats, sailboats, waterskiing, scuba diving, snorkeling, fishing, charter fishing. **Guest Services:** valet laundry, area transportation. **Business Services:** conference facilities, business center. **Cards:** AX, DC, DS, MC, VI. ***(See color ad opposite title page & p 412)***

Hilton

AAA Benefit:

Members save 5% or more everyday!

/ SOME UNITS FEE

RENAISSANCE CURACAO RESORT & CASINO **Phone:** 599/9435-5000

fyi

Resort Hotel

$197-$262 All Year

Too new to rate, opening scheduled for October 2008. **Address:** Baclen Puzellweg #2. **Amenities:** 237 units, coffeemakers, refrigerators, pool. **Terms:** cancellation fee imposed. **Cards:** AX, DS, MC, VI. ***(See color ad on insert & p 413)***

AAA Benefit:

Members save a minimum 5% off the best available rate.

WHERE TO DINE

BELLE TERRACE **Phone:** 599/9461-4377 18

International

$17-$34

Flamboyant trees in the open-air dining room intertwine to create a large, canopy-like roof. Such items as baked butterfish coated with macadamia nuts and rack of lamb with rosemary sauce are representative of the fare. Some of the more exotic selections center on ostrich, pigeon and rabbit. On Wednesday nights, the chef creates an Antillean-themed menu, while Saturday is Caribbean grill night with live music. Dressy casual. **Bar:** Full bar. **Reservations:** required. **Hours:** 12:30 pm-2:30 & 7-10 pm. **Address:** Penstraat 130 **Location:** 0.9 mi (1.4 km) e from Punda side of downtown; in Avila Hotel. **Parking:** on-site. **Cards:** AX, DC, MC, VI.

BISTRO LE CLOCHARD **Phone:** 599/9462-5666 12

AAA

French

$17-$42

In a picturesque setting at the mouth of a ship channel, the restaurant is known for its savory French/Swiss cuisine and attentive service. Well-prepared and attractively presented dishes employ fresh seafood, lamb, duck and veal. Diners are offered a choice of seating in the cozy interior or on the refreshing terrace. Dressy casual. **Bar:** Full bar. **Reservations:** required, for dinner. **Hours:** noon-2 & 6:30-10:45 pm. **Address:** Riffort Village **Location:** Downtown in the Riffort Village; Otrobanda side of town; at entrance to ship channel near Queen Emma Pontoon Bridge. **Parking:** street. **Cards:** AX, CB, DC, DS, JC, MC, VI. **Historic**

BLUE'S RESTAURANT **Phone:** 599/9461-4377 17

International

$17-$26

Waves lap beneath the pier as rhythm-and-blues recordings play in the background. Tempting, skillfully prepared dishes include grilled wahoo with goat cheese ravioli, marinated veal on tarragon risotto and baked grouper a la Parmesan with gnocchi. A vegetarian plate du jour also is available. Guests should stay for the encore of exotic desserts. The menu changes periodically. The youthful staff is pleasantly accommodating. Happy hour lures locals and tourists alike. Casual dress. **Bar:** Full bar. **Reservations:** suggested. **Hours:** 7 pm-11 pm. **Address:** Penstraat 130 **Location:** 0.9 mi (1.4 km) e from Punda side of downtown; in Avila Hotel. **Parking:** on-site. **Cards:** AX, DC, MC, VI.

CRAVING SUSHI **Phone:** 599/9736-6711 10

AAA

Sushi

$12-$26

Located in a shopping mall area, this cozy eatery is considered to be the island's only sushi bar. All of the familiar choices are here including an array of sushi rolls, sashimi, tempura, soups and salads. Casual dress. **Bar:** Full bar. **Reservations:** suggested. **Hours:** 11:30 am-2:30 & 5-10 pm. Closed: Sun. **Address:** Promenade Shopping Center **Location:** 3 mi (4.8 km) e. **Parking:** on-site. **Cards:** AX, MC, VI.

FORT NASSAU RESTAURANT **Phone:** 599/9461-3450 1

International

$10-$32

Within the walls of a historic fort on a hill above Willemstad, the restaurant affords stunning views. In addition to Continental standards, the menu lists Dutch and Caribbean dishes. Dressy casual. **Bar:** Full bar. **Reservations:** accepted. **Hours:** noon-2 & 6:30-10:30 pm, Sat & Sun from 6:30 pm. **Address:** Seru Fort Nassau **Location:** At historical Fort Nassau; just n of downtown on Sablica Hill. **Parking:** on-site. **Cards:** AX, DC, MC, VI. **Historic**

(See map and index starting on p. 407)

GOUVERNEUR DE ROUVILLE RESTAURANT **Phone:** 599/9462-5999 (7)

International
$11-$29

The restaurant is a great place to watch the activity along the Otrobanda Waterfront or cool off in the shaded courtyard. The longtime local favorite has a varied menu of Mexican burgers, banana soup, Bombay chicken, pasta, satays and tuna sashimi, just to name a few. The house specialty is keshi yena, a sweet chicken dish with raisins and Gouda cheese. A quaint pub atmosphere prevails later in the evening. Casual dress. **Bar:** Full bar. **Reservations:** accepted. **Hours:** noon-10:30 pm. **Address:** De Rouvilleweg 9 **Location:** On Otrobanda side of Queen Emma Pontoon Bridge; center of downtown. **Parking:** street. **Cards:** AX, MC, VI. **Historic**

HOOK'S HUT BEACH BAR & RESTAURANT **Phone:** 599/9462-6575 (2)

International
$10-$26

A beach side eatery with a large bar and tables set on the sand or al fresco under the various gazebos; known for its local and imported seafood and fresh fish; also offered are a few Dutch dishes; food preparation is simple to maintain freshness and flavor. Casual dress. Entertainment. **Bar:** Full bar. **Reservations:** accepted. **Hours:** 8 am-11 pm. **Address:** Pisadera Bay **Location:** Oceanfront; on Piscadera Bay; 3.2 mi (5.1 km) w of Otrobanda side of town. **Parking:** on-site. **Cards:** CB, MC, VI.

LA PERGOLA **Phone:** 599/9461-3482 (13)

Italian
$18-$28

Within the walls of an old fort, the restaurant is in a historic waterfront location affording fine ocean views. Well-prepared Italian dishes include many made from fresh seafood. Diners have a choice of indoor or terrace seating. Dressy casual. **Bar:** Full bar. **Reservations:** required. **Hours:** noon-10:30 pm, Sun from 6 pm. Closed: 12/31. **Address:** Waterfront Arches #12 **Location:** On Punda side of downtown; east side of the Queen Emma Pontoon Bridge. **Parking:** street. **Cards:** AX, MC, VI. **Historic**

LAROUSSE RESTAURANT **Phone:** 599/9465-5418 (16)

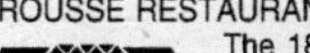

Continental
$22-$33

The 18th-century home is a charming site for intimate, elegant dining in a candlelit, European-style dining room. The chef visits every table to explain the menu. Hot and cold appetizers, rich entrees and outstanding desserts blend French and Dutch cooking traditions. Dressy casual. **Bar:** Full bar. **Reservations:** suggested. **Hours:** Open 12/1-9/1 & 9/22-11/30; 6 pm-midnight. Closed: 12/24; also 12/31 & Mon. **Address:** Penstraat 5 **Location:** 0.7 mi (1.1 km) e of Queen Emma Pontoon Bridge; on Punda side. **Parking:** on-site. **Cards:** AX, DS, MC, VI. **Historic**

RYSTTAFEL RESTAURANT **Phone:** 599/9461-2606 (4)

Indonesian
$15-$27

The restaurant is known specifically for Indonesian rysttafel (rice table) dishes served buffet-style on warming trays at cozy tables. Stunning varieties of 16, 20 or 25 small plates are brought to the table. Contributing to the decor are wall-displayed copper pots and pans, batiks and a wonderful Wayang doll collection in the lounge. Casual dress. **Bar:** Full bar. **Reservations:** suggested. **Hours:** noon-2 & 6-10 pm. Closed: 1/1; also 12/31 & Mon. **Address:** Mercuriusstraat 13-15 **Location:** 2.5 mi (4 km) n from intersection with Schottegat weg (oost) just e. **Parking:** on-site. **Cards:** AX, CB, DC, DS, JC, MC, VI.

ZANTA RESTAURANT **Phone:** 599/9465-0663 (3)

International
$15-$28

Known as a hip party place after hours, this chic restaurant displays Ibiza-style decor in its stylish interior and has bed-style seating outside by the beach. The menu spans the globe with choices such as green lip mussels, yellowfin tuna tartare, tenderloin carpaccio and escargot. Extensive tapas choices lend themselves to sharing and sampling. Dressy casual. **Bar:** Full bar. **Reservations:** suggested. **Hours:** 6 pm-11 pm. Closed: Sun & Mon. **Address:** Seaquarium Beach **Location:** 1.7 mi (2.8 km) e from Punda side of downtown. **Parking:** on-site. **Cards:** MC, VI.

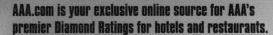

DOMINICA

This index helps you "spot" where approved lodgings and restaurants are located on the corresponding detailed maps. Lodging daily rate range is for comparison only and show the property's high season. Restaurant rate range is a combination of lunch and/or dinner. Turn to the listing page for more detailed rate information and consult display ads for special promotions.

ROSEAU

Map Page	OA	Lodgings	Diamond Rated	High Season	Page
5 / p. 417		The Garraway Hotel	◆◆	$100-$200	418
6 / p. 417	AAA	**Fort Young Hotel** - see color ad p 128	◆◆	$105-$230 SAVE	418
7 / p. 417		Papillote Wilderness Retreat and Nature Sanctuary	◆◆	$115-$130	418

Map Page	OA	Restaurants	Diamond Rated	Cuisine	Meal Range	Page
1 / p. 417		Fort Young Waterfront Restaurant	◆◆◆	Caribbean	$12-$36	418
2 / p. 417		La Robe Creole Tavern Restaurant and Bar	◆◆	Creole	$10-$24	418

FOND ST. JEAN

Map Page	OA	Lodging	Diamond Rated	High Season	Page
10 / p. 417		Zandoli Inn, Roche Cassee-Stowe	◆◆	$145	418

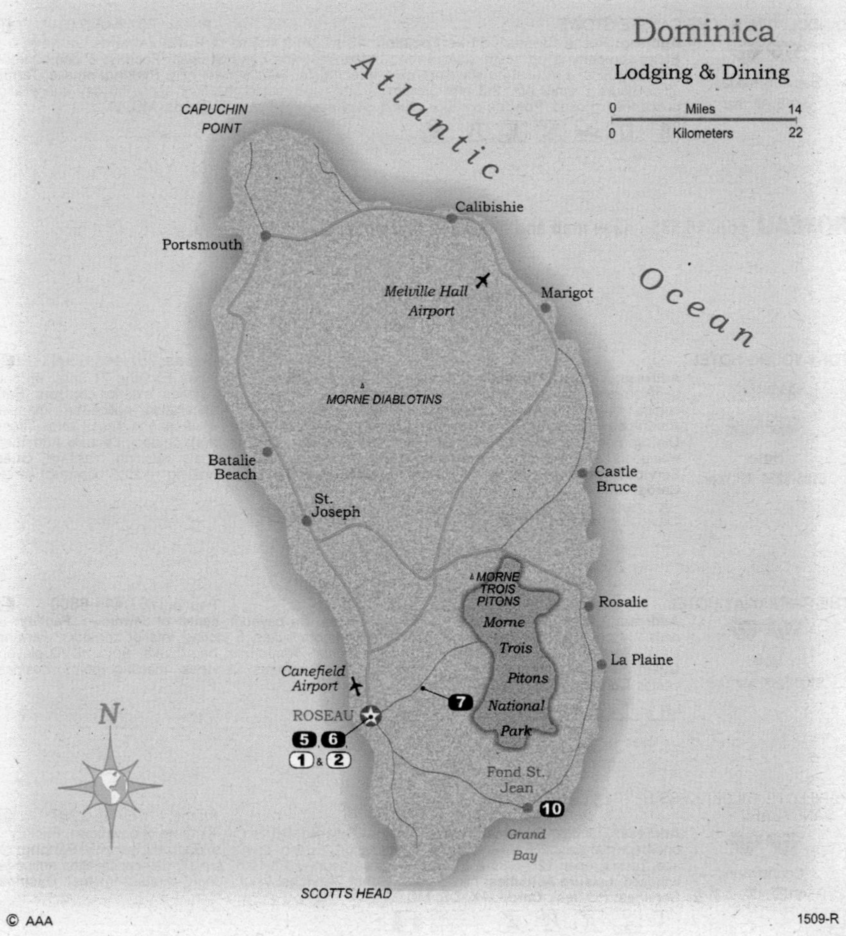

Dominica
Lodging & Dining

0 Miles 14
0 Kilometers 22

Atlantic Ocean

CAPUCHIN POINT
Calibishie
Portsmouth
Melville Hall Airport
Marigot
MORNE DIABLOTINS
Batalie Beach
Castle Bruce
St. Joseph
MORNE TROIS PITONS
Morne Trois Pitons National Park
Rosalie
La Plaine
Canefield Airport
ROSEAU
7
5 6
1 & 2
Fond St. Jean
10
Grand Bay
SCOTTS HEAD
N

1509-R

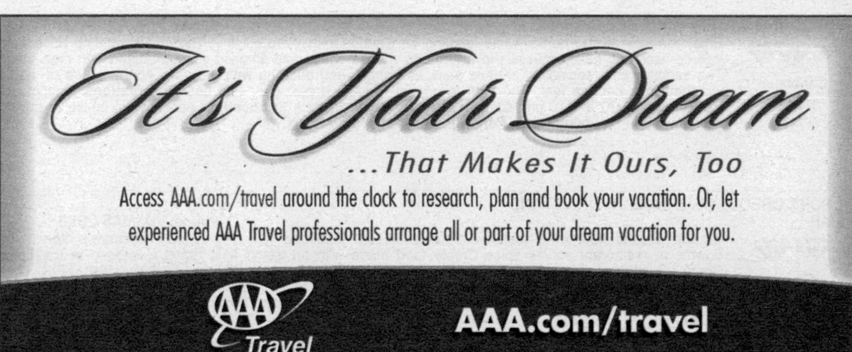

FOND ST. JEAN (See map and index starting on p. 417)

WHERE TO STAY

ZANDOLI INN, ROCHE CASSEE-STOWE **Phone:** 767/446-3161 10

Bed & Breakfast
$145 All Year

Address: Roche Cassee - Stowe **Location:** 13 mi (20.8 km) se of Roseau towards Loubiere, e to Stowe, property is on south side of road before reaching Fond St Jean. **Facility:** 5 one-bedroom standard units. 3 stories (no elevator), exterior corridors. *Bath:* shower only. **Parking:** on-site. **Terms:** office hours 7 am-9 pm, 2-3 night minimum stay, age restrictions may apply, 60 day cancellation notice-fee imposed. **Pool(s):** outdoor. **Guest Services:** valet laundry. **Cards:** MC, VI.

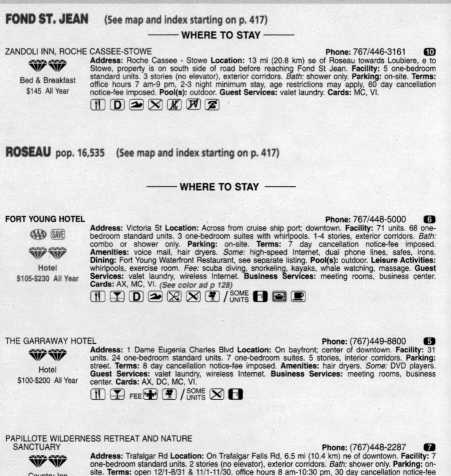

ROSEAU pop. 16,535 (See map and index starting on p. 417)

WHERE TO STAY

FORT YOUNG HOTEL **Phone:** 767/448-5000 6

AAA SAVE
Hotel
$105-$230 All Year

Address: Victoria St **Location:** Across from cruise ship port; downtown. **Facility:** 71 units. 68 one-bedroom standard units. 3 one-bedroom suites with whirlpools. 1-4 stories, exterior corridors. *Bath:* combo or shower only. **Parking:** on-site. **Terms:** 7 day cancellation notice-fee imposed. **Amenities:** voice mail, hair dryers. *Some:* high-speed Internet, dual phone lines, safes, irons. **Dining:** Fort Young Waterfront Restaurant, see separate listing. **Pool(s):** outdoor. **Leisure Activities:** whirlpools, exercise room. *Fee:* scuba diving, snorkeling, kayaks, whale watching, massage. **Guest Services:** valet laundry, wireless Internet. **Business Services:** meeting rooms, business center. **Cards:** AX, MC, VI. *(See color ad p 128)*

/ SOME UNITS

THE GARRAWAY HOTEL **Phone:** (767)449-8800 5

Hotel
$100-$200 All Year

Address: 1 Dame Eugenia Charles Blvd **Location:** On bayfront; center of downtown. **Facility:** 31 units. 24 one-bedroom standard units. 7 one-bedroom suites. 5 stories, interior corridors. **Parking:** street. **Terms:** 8 day cancellation notice-fee imposed. **Amenities:** hair dryers. *Some:* DVD players. **Guest Services:** valet laundry, wireless Internet. **Business Services:** meeting rooms, business center. **Cards:** AX, DC, MC, VI.

FEE / SOME UNITS

PAPILLOTE WILDERNESS RETREAT AND NATURE SANCTUARY **Phone:** (767)448-2287 7

Country Inn
$115-$130 12/1-8/31 & 11/1-11/30

Address: Trafalgar Rd **Location:** On Trafalgar Falls Rd, 6.5 mi (10.4 km) ne of downtown. **Facility:** 7 one-bedroom standard units. 2 stories (no elevator), exterior corridors. *Bath:* shower only. **Parking:** on-site. **Terms:** open 12/1-8/31 & 11/1-11/30, office hours 8 am-10:30 pm, 30 day cancellation notice-fee imposed. **Leisure Activities:** hiking trails. **Guest Services:** valet laundry, wireless Internet. **Business Services:** PC (fee). **Cards:** AX, DS, MC, VI.

/ SOME UNITS

WHERE TO DINE

FORT YOUNG WATERFRONT RESTAURANT **Phone:** 767/448-5000 1

Caribbean
$12-$36

Enjoy the vista of the harbor while feasting on Caribbean-inspired cuisine. The mouthwatering appetizers include escargot, baked mussels in a turmeric cheese sauce and smoked salmon stuffed with crab meat. The versatile chef serves up entrees such as Long Island duckling with balsamic honey sauce or marlin wrapped in a banana leaf. The staff is cordial. Casual dress. **Bar:** Full bar. **Reservations:** suggested. **Hours:** noon-2:30 & 7-10 pm. Closed: Mon. **Address:** Victoria St **Location:** Across from cruise ship port; downtown; in Fort Young Hotel. **Parking:** on-site. **Cards:** AX, MC, VI.

LA ROBE CREOLE TAVERN RESTAURANT AND BAR **Phone:** 767/448-2896 2

Creole
$10-$24

On the second floor of a restored Colonial house appointed with 19th-century decorative items, the downtown restaurant serves spicy Creole food made with an island flair. Servers dressed in traditional Creole costumes match the bright, colorful table linens. Dressy casual. **Bar:** Full bar. **Reservations:** suggested. **Hours:** noon-3 & 6:30-10 pm. Closed major holidays; also Sun. **Address:** 3 Victoria St **Location:** Center of downtown; directly across from Fort Young Hotel. **Parking:** street. **Cards:** MC, VI. **Historic**

DOMINICAN REPUBLIC

Airport Accommodations

Map Page	OA	SANTO DOMINGO - LAS AMERICAS INTERNATIONAL AIRPORT	Diamond Rated	High Season	Page
42 / p. 421	AAA	**Quality Hotel Real Aeropuerto Santo Domingo, 1.2 mi (1.9 km)**	◆◆◆	$110-$140 SAVE	433

This index helps you "spot" where approved lodgings and restaurants are located on the corresponding detailed maps. Lodging daily rate range is for comparison only and show the property's high season. Restaurant rate range is a combination of lunch and/or dinner. Turn to the listing page for more detailed rate information and consult display ads for special promotions.

PUERTO PLATA

Map Page	OA	Lodgings	Diamond Rated	High Season	Page
2 / p. 421		Club Hotel Riu Bachata	◆◆◆	Rates not provided	429
4 / p. 421		Club Hotel Riu Mambo	◆◆◆	$81-$168	430
5 / p. 421		Club Hotel Riu Merengue	◆◆◆	Rates not provided	430
6 / p. 421	AAA	**Casa Colonial Beach & Spa Hotel** - see color ad p 429	◆◆◆◆	$260-$750 SAVE	428
7 / p. 421		Grand Oasis Marien Beach Resort & Spa - see color ad p 430	◆◆◆	$296-$400	430

Map Page	OA	Restaurants	Diamond Rated	Cuisine	Meal Range	Page
1 / p. 421	AAA	**Lucia**	◆◆◆◆	International	$13-$38	431
2 / p. 421		Cariatides Restaurant & Bar	◆◆	International	$6-$27	431

BAVARO

Map Page	OA	Lodgings	Diamond Rated	High Season	Page
10 / p. 421	AAA	**Melia Caribe Tropical** - see color ad p 423	◆◆◆	$190-$500 SAVE	422
11 / p. 421	AAA	**Paradisus Punta Cana** - see color ad p 425	◆◆◆◆	$440-$700 SAVE	426
18 / p. 421	AAA	**Paradisus Palma Real** - see color ad p 424	◆◆◆◆	$360-$600 SAVE	422

Map Page	OA	Restaurants	Diamond Rated	Cuisine	Meal Range	Page
6 / p. 421		Le Flamboyan	◆◆	Spanish	$8-$20	426
7 / p. 421		Blu II Restaurante	◆◆	International	$16-$26	426

SANTO DOMINGO

Map Page	OA	Lodgings	Diamond Rated	High Season	Page
32 / p. 421	AAA	**Hilton Santo Domingo** - see color ad opposite title page, p 432	◆◆◆◆	$149-$279 SAVE	432
34 / p. 421		Courtyard by Marriott Santo Domingo	◆◆◆	$112-$121	432
42 / p. 421	AAA	**Quality Hotel Real Aeropuerto Santo Domingo** - see color ad p 433	◆◆◆	$110-$140 SAVE	433
46 / p. 421		Hotel Santo Domingo	◆◆	$140-$260	433
47 / p. 421	AAA	**Renaissance Jaragua Hotel & Casino**	◆◆◆	$133-$138 SAVE	434
48 / p. 421	AAA	**InterContinental V Centenario & Casino**	◆◆◆	$175-$225 SAVE	433

Map Page	OA	Restaurants	Diamond Rated	Cuisine	Meal Range	Page
8 / p. 421		Cafe Bellini	◆◆◆	Mediterranean	$11-$26	434
9 / p. 421		Los Tres Mosqueteros Cafe & Restaurant	◆◆	International	$9-$20	435
12 / p. 421		El Conuco	◆◆	Caribbean	$10-$19	434
13 / p. 421		La Residence	◆◆◆	International	$14-$50	435
16 / p. 421		Pat'e Palo European Brasserie	◆◆	International	$11-$38	435

Map Page	OA	Restaurants (cont'd)	Diamond Rated	Cuisine	Meal Range	Page
17 / p. 421		El Patio	◆◆◆	International	$10-$25	435
18 / p. 421		Museo del Jamon	◆◆	Spanish	$8-$17	435
19 / p. 421		Restaurante Samurai	◆◆	Japanese	$9-$21	436
21 / p. 421		La Briciola Ristorante	◆◆	Italian	$12-$35	435
22 / p. 421		Restaurante La Llave del Mar	◆◆	Seafood	$12-$28	436
23 / p. 421		Restaurante Cantabrico	◆◆◆	Spanish	$15-$32	436
24 / p. 421		Restaurant Don Pepe	◆◆◆	Spanish	$16-$31	436
25 / p. 421		Reina de Espana	◆◆◆	Spanish	$16-$31	435
27 / p. 421		Meson de la Cava	◆◆◆	Spanish	$16-$34	435
29 / p. 421		Vesuvio del Malecon	◆◆◆	Italian	$17-$30	436
30 / p. 421		La Parilla Steak House	◆	Steak	$10-$24	435

BOCA CHICA

Map Page	OA	Lodging	Diamond Rated	High Season	Page
59 / p. 421		Oasis Hamaca - see color ad p 430	◆◆◆	$311-$400	427

Map Page	OA	Restaurant	Diamond Rated	Cuisine	Meal Range	Page
38 / p. 421		Neptuno's Club	◆◆	Seafood	$9-$21	427

BAYAHIBE

Map Page	OA	Lodgings	Diamond Rated	High Season	Page
60 / p. 421		Viva Wyndham Dominicus Palace	◆◆◆	$132-$340	426
61 / p. 421		Oasis Canoa - see color ad p 430	◆◆◆	$311-$444	426

PUNTA CANA

Map Page	OA	Lodging	Diamond Rated	High Season	Page
63 / p. 421		Grand Oasis Punta Cana - see color ad p 430	◆◆◆	$311-$459	431

CABARETE

Map Page	OA	Lodging	Diamond Rated	High Season	Page
64 / p. 421		Viva Wyndham Tangerine	◆◆◆	$198-$336	427

CABRERA

Map Page	OA	Lodging	Diamond Rated	High Season	Page
65 / p. 421		La Catalina	◆◆	Rates not provided	427

LAS GALERAS

Map Page	OA	Lodging	Diamond Rated	High Season	Page
69 / p. 421		Villa Serena Hotel	◆◆	$130-$150	428

LAS TERRENAS

Map Page	OA	Lodging	Diamond Rated	High Season	Page
71 / p. 421		Las Palmas Residence	◆◆	$62-$87	428

UVERO ALTO

Map Page	OA	Lodging	Diamond Rated	High Season	Page
75 / p. 421	AAA	**Sivory Punta Cana** - see color ad p 431	◆◆◆◆	$290-$2400 SAVE	436

JUAN DOLIO

Map Page	OA	Restaurants	Diamond Rated	Cuisine	Meal Range	Page
31 / p. 421		El Sueno Ristorante	◆	Italian	$8-$19	428
32 / p. 421		El Concon Restaurante	◆◆	International	$8-$18	427
33 / p. 421		El Meson	◆◆	Spanish	$8-$16	427

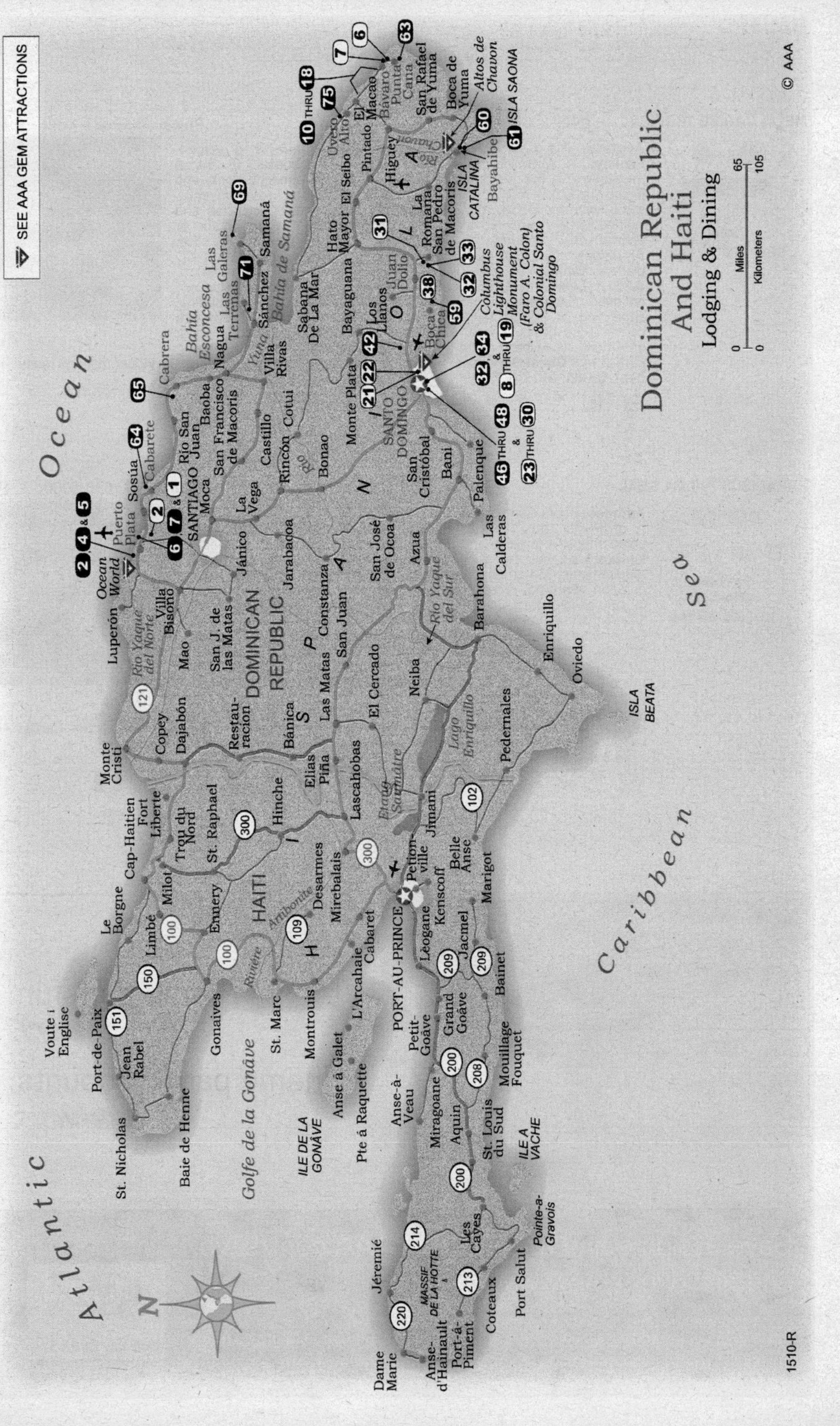

Dominican Republic And Haiti

Lodging & Dining

SEE AAA GEM ATTRACTIONS

Miles 0 65
Kilometers 0 105

© AAA

1510-R

BAVARO (See map and index starting on p. 421)

WHERE TO STAY

MELIA CARIBE TROPICAL Book great rates at AAA.com Phone: (809)221-1290 10

Resort Hotel

$190-$500 All Year

Address: Playa de Bavaro **Location:** Oceanfront. Ne of airport. **Facility:** A sprawling, all-inclusive mega-resort boasts 13 theme restaurants, a live performance theater, multiple swimming pools and junior suite-style rooms. 1110 units. 990 one-bedroom standard units, some with whirlpools. 120 one-bedroom suites with efficiencies and whirlpools. 2 stories (no elevator), exterior corridors. *Bath:* combo or shower only. **Parking:** on-site. **Terms:** 3 day cancellation notice. **Amenities:** voice mail, safes, irons, hair dryers. *Some:* video games, CD players. **Dining:** 14 restaurants, nightclub, entertainment. **Pool(s):** 6 outdoor. **Leisure Activities:** saunas, whirlpools, steamrooms, lifeguard on duty, beach access, canoeing, paddleboats, sailboats, windsurfing, snorkeling, 8 lighted tennis courts, recreation programs, adventure center, rock climbing wall, kids club, playground, spa, sports court, basketball, volleyball, game room. *Fee:* scuba diving, golf-27 holes, parasailing. **Guest Services:** valet laundry, wireless Internet. **Business Services:** meeting rooms, PC (fee). **Cards:** AX, CB, DC, DS, JC, MC, VI. *(See color ad p 423)*

/ SOME UNITS

PARADISUS PALMA REAL Phone: 809/688-5000 18

Resort Hotel

$360-$600 All Year

Address: Punta Cana Higuey Rd **Location:** Oceanfront. 11 mi (17.6 km) n of Punta Cana Airport. **Facility:** An all-inclusive resort offering comprehensive facilities and recreational opportunities that are ideal for families, couples or singles. Meets AAA guest room security requirements. 554 one-bedroom suites with whirlpools. 3 stories, exterior corridors. **Parking:** on-site and valet. **Terms:** 7 day cancellation notice, in season-fee imposed. **Amenities:** video library, DVD players, high-speed Internet, voice mail, safes, honor bars, irons, hair dryers. *Some:* CD players. **Dining:** 6 restaurants, nightclub, entertainment. **Pool(s):** 3 outdoor. **Leisure Activities:** whirlpools, beach access, paddleboats, sailboats, windsurfing, snorkeling, 3 lighted tennis courts, recreation programs, table tennis, bicycles, horseback riding, playground, spa, kids club, horseshoes, volleyball, game room. *Fee:* saunas, steamrooms, scuba diving, charter fishing, golf-18 holes. **Guest Services:** valet laundry, wireless Internet. **Business Services:** conference facilities, business center. **Cards:** AX, MC, VI. **Free Special Amenities: expanded continental breakfast and newspaper.** *(See color ad p 424)*

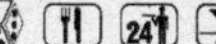

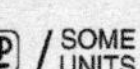

/ SOME UNITS

▼ See AAA listing p 422 ▼

▼ See AAA listing p 422 ▼

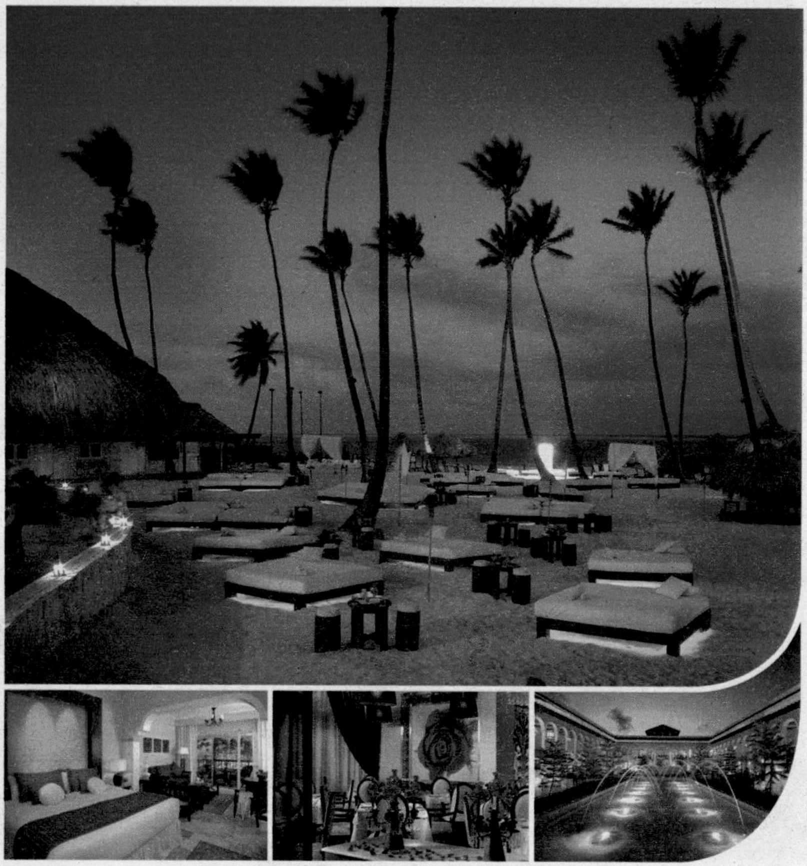

▼ See AAA listing p 426 ▼

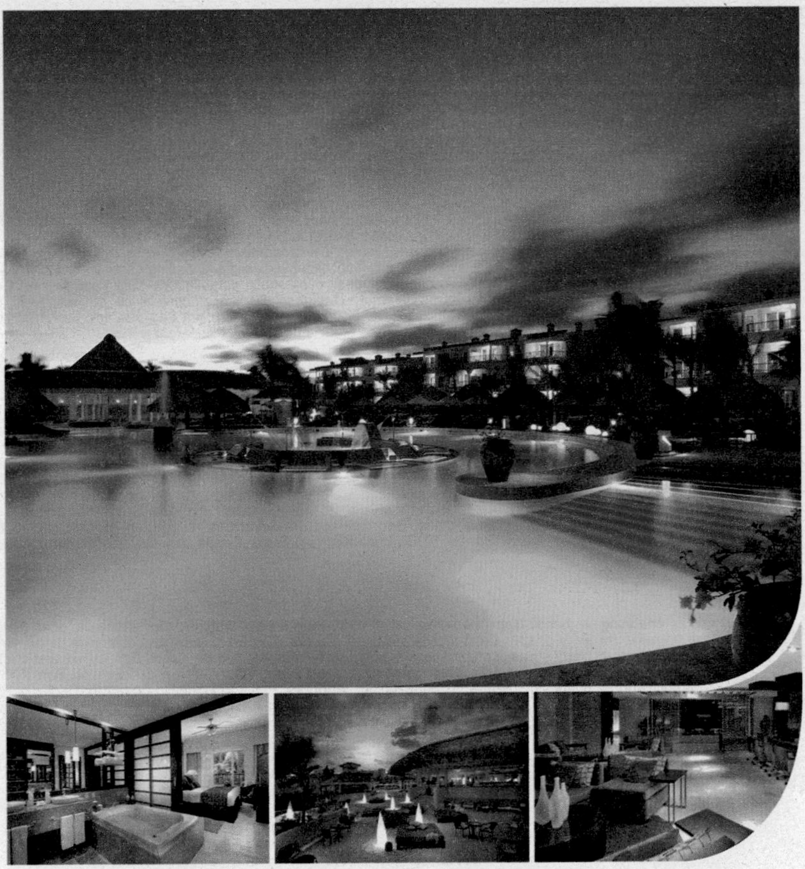

(See map and index starting on p. 421)

PARADISUS PUNTA CANA **Phone:** (809)687-9923 11

AAA SAVE

Resort Hotel
$440-$700 All Year

Address: Playa de Bavaro **Location:** Oceanfront. 13.5 mi (21.6 km) n from Punta Cana Airport; just off Punta Cana Higuey Rd. **Facility:** This is truly a complete resort, with a plethora of leisure and recreational activities; find spacious, junior suite-size units and a pleasant staff. Meets AAA guest room security requirements. 695 units. 503 one-bedroom standard units, some with whirlpools. 96 one- and 96 two-bedroom suites with whirlpools. 2-3 stories (no elevator), exterior corridors. *Bath:* combo or shower only. **Parking:** on-site. **Terms:** cancellation fee imposed. **Amenities:** video library, voice mail, safes, honor bars, irons, hair dryers. *Some:* DVD players, CD players. **Dining:** 11 restaurants, nightclub, entertainment. **Pool(s):** 8 outdoor. **Leisure Activities:** saunas, whirlpools, steamrooms, canoeing, paddleboats, sailboats, windsurfing, scuba diving, snorkeling, kayaks, golf-27 holes, 4 lighted tennis courts, recreation programs, bicycles, jogging, horseback riding, playground, exercise room, spa, archery, batting cage, kids club, 3 paddle courts, rock climbing wall, soccer, basketball, volleyball, game room. *Fee:* parasailing. **Guest Services:** valet laundry, wireless Internet. **Business Services:** conference facilities, PC (fee). **Cards:** AX, CB, DC, DS, JC, MC, VI. **Free Special Amenities: room upgrade and preferred room (each subject to availability with advance reservations).** *(See color ad p 425)*

WHERE TO DINE

BLU II RESTAURANTE **Phone:** 809/552-1793 7

International
$16-$26

The dapper staff provides impeccable service and is attentive to guest needs. On the varied menu are many choices, including an array of seafood and steaks, as well as Italian and local Dominican dishes. Some nights feature live music. Casual dress. **Bar:** Full bar. **Reservations:** suggested. **Hours:** noon-3 & 6-midnight. **Address:** Plaza Brisas 103D **Location:** In Plaza Brisas de Bavaro. **Parking:** on-site. **Cards:** MC, VI.

LE FLAMBOYAN **Phone:** 809/552-0639 6

Spanish
$8-$20

The charming, authentic Dominican-style dining room, with a palm-thatched roof and walls, often features live music. An array of soups and salads are great starters. The extensive menu combines Italian, Criolla and Spanish culinary styles in preparations of pork, pasta, mussels, lobster, conch, fish, steaks and chicken. Meat dishes grilled paridilla style over a wood fire boast exceptional flavor. Entertainment. **Bar:** Full bar. **Reservations:** suggested. **Hours:** 11 am-midnight. **Address:** Playa El Cortecito **Location:** Center of Playa El Cortecito; adjacent to Cortecito Inn. **Parking:** on-site. **Cards:** AX, CB, DC, DS, MC, VI.

BAYAHIBE

(See map and index starting on p. 421)

WHERE TO STAY

OASIS CANOA **Phone:** 809/682-2662 61

Resort Hotel
$311-$444 12/1-4/30
$222-$237 5/1-11/30

Address: Playa Dominicus **Location:** Oceanfront. At Playa Dominicus; 1 mi (1.6 km) e of town; 11.5 mi (18.4 km) e of La Romana International Airport, follow signs. **Facility:** Just outside a national park, this ultra-all-inclusive property offers at least four room categories, all of which are well-equipped. 532 units. 516 one-bedroom standard units, some with whirlpools. 16 one-bedroom suites, some with whirlpools. 3 stories (no elevator), exterior corridors. **Parking:** on-site. **Terms:** 7 day cancellation notice-fee imposed. **Amenities:** voice mail, safes, honor bars, irons, hair dryers. **Pool(s):** outdoor. **Leisure Activities:** saunas, whirlpools, steamrooms, lifeguard on duty, beach access, canoeing, paddleboats, sailboats, windsurfing, snorkeling, miniature golf, 3 lighted tennis courts, recreation programs, bicycles, playground, exercise room, spa, basketball, volleyball, game room. *Fee:* waterskiing, scuba diving, charter fishing. **Guest Services:** valet laundry, beauty salon, wireless Internet. **Business Services:** meeting rooms, PC (fee). **Cards:** AX, CB, DC, DS, JC, MC, VI. ***(See color ad p 430)***

/ SOME UNITS

VIVA WYNDHAM DOMINICUS PALACE **Phone:** (809)686-5658 60

Resort Hotel
$132-$340 All Year

Address: Bayahibe Rd **Location:** Oceanfront. Center; at Playa Dominicus; 10.5 mi (16.8 km) e of La Romana International Airport. **Facility:** The all-inclusive resort has everything for a complete vacation, including a multitude of international restaurants and a plethora of activities. 330 one-bedroom standard units. 3 stories, exterior corridors. **Parking:** on-site. **Terms:** 7 day cancellation notice. **Amenities:** safes, irons, hair dryers. **Pool(s):** outdoor. **Leisure Activities:** whirlpools, steamroom, lifeguard on duty, beach access, canoeing, sailboats, windsurfing, snorkeling & rental equipment, 4 lighted tennis courts, recreation programs, rental bicycles, spa. *Fee:* sauna, scuba diving. **Guest Services:** valet laundry. **Business Services:** meeting rooms, business center. **Cards:** AX, DC, MC, VI.

BOCA CHICA pop. 46,385 (See map and index starting on p. 421)

WHERE TO STAY

OASIS HAMACA — Phone: (809)523-4611 59

Resort Hotel

$311-$400 12/1-4/30
$237-$252 5/1-11/30

Address: Ave Duarte **Location:** Oceanfront. 5 mi (8 km) e of Las Americas Airport; 20 mi (32 km) e of Santo Domingo. **Facility:** The guest units at this sprawling, fully comprehensive resort feature Spanish style decor and come in two different categories. 565 units. 560 one-bedroom standard units. 5 one-bedroom suites. 3-6 stories, interior/exterior corridors. **Parking:** on-site. **Terms:** 7 day cancellation notice-fee imposed. **Amenities:** voice mail, safes (fee), honor bars, irons, hair dryers. **Pool(s):** 2 outdoor. **Leisure Activities:** saunas, whirlpool, canoeing, paddleboats, sailboats, windsurfing, snorkeling, fishing, miniature golf, 3 lighted tennis courts, recreation programs, bicycles, playground, exercise room, spa, basketball, volleyball, game room. *Fee:* waterskiing, scuba diving, charter fishing. **Guest Services:** valet laundry, beauty salon. **Business Services:** conference facilities, business center. **Cards:** AX, MC, VI. ***(See color ad p 430)***

WHERE TO DINE

NEPTUNO'S CLUB — Phone: 809/523-4703 38

Seafood
$9-$21

Ahoy there, mate! Servers dressed in pirate garb are here to feed guests, not to make them walk the plank. The dining room is a series of covered floating docks surrounded by ocean holding tanks for sharks, turtles, lobsters and stingrays. The extensive menu lists paellas, Thermidor-style lobster or shrimp, seviche, mussels, calamari and croquettes stuffed with crab or fish, just to name a few. Stop by the pirate ship bar moored at the end of the dock for some grog. Aarrgghh! Casual dress. **Bar:** Full bar. **Reservations:** suggested. **Hours:** noon-midnight. Closed: 12/24, 12/25. **Address:** Duarte No. 12 **Location:** Waterfront of Boca Chica; center, follow signs; adjacent to Hamaca Coral by Hilton. **Parking:** on-site. **Cards:** AX, CB, DC, DS, JC, MC, VI.

CABARETE (See map and index starting on p. 421)

WHERE TO STAY

VIVA WYNDHAM TANGERINE *Book at AAA.com* — Phone: (809)571-0402 64

Resort Hotel

$198-$336 All Year

Address: Carretera Sosua-Cabarete **Location:** Oceanfront. Just w of center. **Facility:** The all-inclusive resort features a performance theater for nightly entertainment; guest units vary in size, but all are fully equipped for comfort. Meets AAA guest room security requirements. 223 units. 219 one-bedroom standard units. 4 one-bedroom suites with whirlpools. 3 stories, interior/exterior corridors. *Bath:* combo or shower only. **Parking:** on-site. **Terms:** cancellation fee imposed. **Amenities:** voice mail, safes, irons, hair dryers. **Pool(s):** outdoor. **Leisure Activities:** sauna, whirlpool, steamroom, beach access, sailboats, windsurfing, lighted tennis court, recreation programs, playground, exercise room, spa, basketball, volleyball, game room. *Fee:* snorkeling. **Guest Services:** valet laundry. **Business Services:** business center. **Cards:** AX, DC, DS, MC, VI.

ASK / SOME UNITS

CABRERA (See map and index starting on p. 421)

WHERE TO STAY

LA CATALINA — Phone: 809/589-7700 65

Hotel
Rates not provided

Address: Las Farollones Nagua MTS Rd **Location:** 1.1 mi (1.7 km) n of town, then just e, follow signs. **Facility:** 32 units. 12 one-bedroom standard units. 13 one- and 7 two-bedroom suites with kitchens. 2 stories (no elevator), exterior corridors. *Bath:* combo or shower only. **Parking:** on-site. **Terms:** office hours 7 am-11 pm. **Amenities:** video library. *Some:* safes. **Pool(s):** 2 outdoor. **Leisure Activities:** whirlpool, lighted tennis court. *Fee:* charter fishing, massage. **Guest Services:** valet laundry, area transportation (fee), wireless Internet. **Business Services:** PC.

FEE / SOME UNITS

JUAN DOLIO (See map and index starting on p. 421)

WHERE TO DINE

EL CONCON RESTAURANTE — Phone: 809/526-2652 32

International
$8-$18

Owned and operated by two Italians, the covered outdoor restaurant offers a wide variety of options. There is a brick oven for baking pizzas and a paradilla (wood-fired grill) for grilling meats and some Italian and Continental specialties. Escalloped pork, rellenos shrimp, Creole-style goat and chicken cordon bleu are just a few of the dishes found here. Casual dress. **Bar:** Full bar. **Reservations:** accepted. **Hours:** 11 am-11 pm. Closed: 7/1 & Wed. **Address:** Avenida Blvd **Location:** Center; at Villas del Mar. **Parking:** on-site (fee). **Cards:** AX, CB, DC, DS, MC, VI.

EL MESON — Phone: 809/526-2666 33

Spanish
$8-$16

Across from the beach is this al fresco restaurant with well-groomed servers. Gazpacho is a refreshing favorite. Entrees include Dominican-Spanish preparations of chicken, veal, beef, pork and seafood. There is a huge variety of soups, appetizers and desserts. Casual dress. **Bar:** Full bar. **Reservations:** accepted. **Hours:** 11 am-11 pm. Closed: 12/25; also 12/31. **Address:** Calle Blvd **Location:** Center; follow signs; across from Hotel Metro. **Parking:** on-site. **Cards:** AX, CB, DC, MC, VI.

(See map and index starting on p. 421)

EL SUENO RISTORANTE

Phone: 809/526-3903 31

Italian
$8-$19

Across from the ocean on the mini-malecon is the Italian-owned-and-operated eatery. Fresh seafood dishes ranging from calamari and shrimp to fish and octopus are popular. Lackadaisical service prevails, so relax with a cold beer or glass of wine and savor the moment while the meal is prepared. Casual dress. Entertainment. **Bar:** Full bar. **Reservations:** accepted. **Hours:** noon-3:30 & 7-11 pm. Closed: Mon. **Address:** Calle Principal **Location:** Center; on Malecon. **Parking:** street. **Cards:** AX, MC, VI.

LAS GALERAS (See map and index starting on p. 421)

WHERE TO STAY

VILLA SERENA HOTEL

Phone: (809)538-0000 69

Country Inn
$130-$150 All Year

Address: Las Galeras Beach **Location:** Oceanfront. On Samana Peninsula; near downtown. **Facility:** 21 one-bedroom standard units. 2 stories (no elevator), interior corridors. **Parking:** on-site. **Terms:** office hours 7 am-9 pm, 14 day cancellation notice-fee imposed. **Amenities:** safes (fee), hair dryers. **Pool(s):** outdoor. **Leisure Activities:** snorkeling, bicycles. *Fee:* massage. **Guest Services:** valet laundry. **Cards:** AX, MC, VI.

/ SOME UNITS

LAS TERRENAS (See map and index starting on p. 421)

WHERE TO STAY

LAS PALMAS RESIDENCE

Phone: (809)240-6436 71

Cottage
$62-$87 All Year

Address: Calle Esq Benelux #1 **Location:** Just e of commercial center; across from Playa Las Terrenas. **Facility:** 17 cottages. 2 stories (no elevator), exterior corridors. *Bath:* shower only. **Parking:** on-site. **Terms:** office hours 8 am-7 pm, 2-7 night minimum stay - seasonal and/or weekends, 14 day cancellation notice. **Amenities:** safes. **Cards:** MC, VI.

PUERTO PLATA pop. 112,036 (See map and index starting on p. 421)

WHERE TO STAY

CASA COLONIAL BEACH & SPA HOTEL Book great rates at AAA.com

Phone: (809)320-3232 6

Hotel
$260-$750 All Year

Address: Playa Dorada Complex **Location:** Oceanfront. 8.1 mi (13 km) w of Puerto Plata Airport; in Playa Dorada Beach Complex. **Facility:** Guest rooms at the boutique-style, oceanfront resort are spacious and well appointed with fine furnishings and plenty of amenities. Meets AAA guest room security requirements. Smoke free premises. 50 units. 42 one-bedroom standard units. 8 one-bedroom suites. 4 stories, interior/exterior corridors. **Parking:** on-site. **Amenities:** CD players, high-speed Internet, voice mail, safes, honor bars, irons, hair dryers. *Some:* DVD players. **Dining:** 3 restaurants, also, Lucia, see separate listing. **Pool(s):** outdoor. **Leisure Activities:** saunas, whirlpools, steamrooms, paddleboats, sailboats, windsurfing, 2 tennis courts, recreation facilities at sister resorts, spa. **Guest Services:** valet laundry, wireless Internet. **Business Services:** meeting rooms, PC. **Cards:** AX, MC, VI. *(See color ad p 429)*

(See map and index starting on p. 421)

CLUB HOTEL RIU BACHATA Book at AAA.com **Phone:** 809/320-1010 **2**

Resort Hotel

Rates not provided

Address: Bahia de Maimon **Location:** Oceanfront. 4.4 mi (7 km) w of town; 17.5 mi (28 km) w of Puerto Plata Airport. **Facility:** More upscale than the sister hotels, the mega all-inclusive resort features spacious units with island-style decor; each room has a balcony. 592 units. 580 one-bedroom standard units. 12 one-bedroom suites. 2-3 stories (no elevator), interior corridors. **Parking:** on-site. **Amenities:** safes, honor bars, hair dryers. **Pool(s):** 2 outdoor. **Leisure Activities:** whirlpool, paddleboats, sailboats, windsurfing, snorkeling, 2 lighted tennis courts, recreation programs, playground, exercise room, spa, sports court, volleyball, game room. *Fee:* sauna, scuba diving. **Guest Services:** valet laundry, beauty salon. **Business Services:** business center.

▼ *See AAA listing p 428* ▼

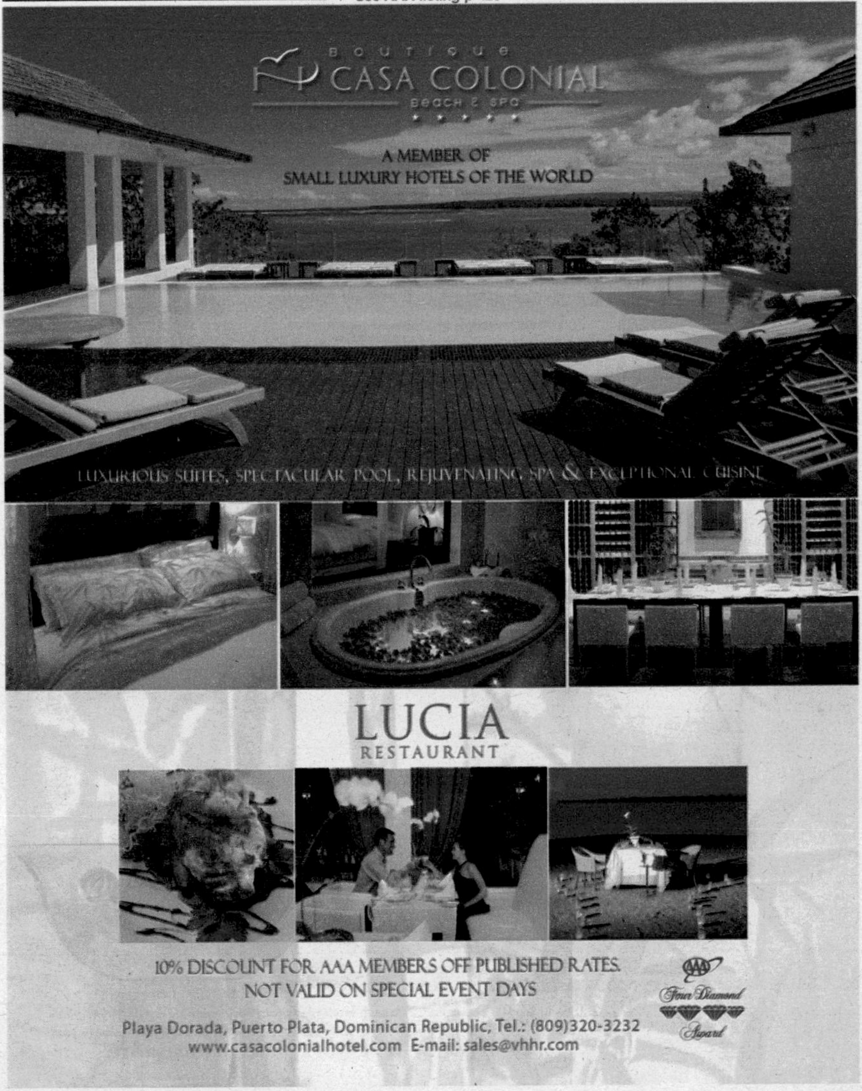

(See map and index starting on p. 421)

CLUB HOTEL RIU MAMBO

Phone: 809/320-1212 **4**

Resort Hotel

$81-$168 All Year

Address: Bahia de Maimon **Location:** Oceanfront. 4.4 mi (7 km) w of town; 17.5 mi (28 km) w of Puerto Plata Airport. **Facility:** The mega all-inclusive resort provides all the facilities for a complete vacation; the plentiful staff ensures the enjoyment of the guests. 454 units. 442 one-bedroom standard units. 12 one-bedroom suites. 2-3 stories (no elevator), interior corridors. **Parking:** on-site. **Terms:** 3 night minimum stay - seasonal, 3 day cancellation notice-fee imposed. **Amenities:** safes, honor bars. *Some:* hair dryers. **Pool(s):** 2 outdoor. **Leisure Activities:** paddleboats, sailboats, windsurfing, snorkeling, lighted tennis court, recreation programs, playground, exercise room, spa, basketball, volleyball, game room. *Fee:* waterskiing, scuba diving. **Guest Services:** valet laundry, beauty salon. **Business Services:** business center. **Cards:** AX, MC, VI.

ASK

CLUB HOTEL RIU MERENGUE *Book at AAA.com*

Phone: 809/320-4000 **5**

Resort Hotel

Rates not provided

Address: Bahia de Maimon **Location:** Oceanfront. 4.4 mi (7 km) w of town; 17.5 mi (28 km) w of Puerto Plata Airport. **Facility:** The hotel, part of a mega complex, is well suited for families; there are two room categories to choose from, all with Spanish-style decor. Meets AAA guest room security requirements. 544 units. 532 one-bedroom standard units. 12 one-bedroom suites. 2 stories (no elevator), interior corridors. **Parking:** on-site. **Amenities:** safes, honor bars, hair dryers. **Pool(s):** outdoor. **Leisure Activities:** paddleboats, sailboats, windsurfing, snorkeling, 2 lighted tennis courts, recreation programs, playground, spa, volleyball, game room. *Fee:* waterskiing, scuba diving, charter fishing. **Guest Services:** valet laundry, beauty salon. **Business Services:** business center.

GRAND OASIS MARIEN BEACH RESORT & SPA

Phone: (809)320-1515 **7**

Resort Hotel

$296-$400 12/1-4/30
$222-$237 5/1-11/30

Address: Carretera Luperon **Location:** Oceanfront. Costa Dorada; 8.5 mi (13.6 km) w of Puerto Plata Airport; in Costa Dorada Beach Complex. **Facility:** The complete all-inclusive resort well suited for families offers two room categories, all featuring Spanish-style decor. Service orientated staff. 332 units. 310 one-bedroom standard units. 22 one-bedroom suites with whirlpools. 3 stories (no elevator), interior corridors. **Parking:** on-site. **Terms:** 7 day cancellation notice-fee imposed. **Amenities:** voice mail, safes (fee), irons, hair dryers. *Some:* CD players. **Pool(s):** outdoor. **Leisure Activities:** saunas, whirlpools, beach access, canoeing, sailboats, windsurfing, snorkeling, miniature golf, 2 lighted tennis courts, recreation programs, playground, exercise room, spa, basketball, volleyball, game room. *Fee:* scuba diving, horseback riding. **Guest Services:** valet laundry. **Business Services:** meeting rooms, PC (fee). **Cards:** AX, MC, VI. ***(See color ad below)***

ASK D / SOME UNITS

(See map and index starting on p. 421)

WHERE TO DINE

CARIATIDES RESTAURANT & BAR — **Phone:** 809/320-1410 (2)

International
$6-$27

Patrons enjoy a "semi-al fresco" experience at the inviting eatery, which has a background waterfall in its garden setting. The international menu lists at least six soups, varied pasta dishes, pork chops, lamb and paella, in addition to eight tempting desserts. Casual dress. **Bar:** Full bar. **Reservations:** suggested. **Hours:** 11 am-11 pm. **Address:** Plaza el Doral **Location:** Just e of downtown; in Plaza el Doral. **Parking:** on-site. **Cards:** AX, CB, DC, DS, JC, MC, VI.

LUCIA — **Phone:** 809/320-3232 (1)

AAA

International
$13-$38

Combining the best elements of Dominican, Italian and Asian cuisine, the chef creates such delicacies as Caribbean lobster, duo of duck, curried goat and Chilean sea bass. Expect to find a refined atmosphere and attentive service. The desserts are tempting and wrap up the dining experience nicely. Dressy casual. **Bar:** Full bar. **Reservations:** required. **Hours:** 6:30 pm-10:30 pm. **Address:** Playa Dorada Comlex **Location:** 8.1 mi (13 km) w of Puerto Plata Airport; in Play Dorada Beach Complex; in Casa Colonial Beach & Spa Hotel. **Parking:** valet. **Cards:** AX, MC, VI.

PUNTA CANA (See map and index starting on p. 421)

WHERE TO STAY

GRAND OASIS PUNTA CANA Book at AAA.com — **Phone:** (809)686-9898 (63)

Resort
Hotel

$311-$459 12/1-4/30
$252-$267 5/1-11/30

Address: Cabeza de Toro **Location:** Oceanfront. 14 mi (22 km) e of Punta Cana International Airport. **Facility:** Spacious public areas with an array of activities are available at this new chain exclusive to Dominican Republic. 467 one-bedroom standard units, some with whirlpools. 3 stories (no elevator), interior/exterior corridors. **Parking:** on-site. **Amenities:** voice mail, safes, irons, hair dryers. **Pool(s):** 3 outdoor. **Leisure Activities:** saunas, whirlpools, steamrooms, paddleboats, sailboats, windsurfing, snorkeling, 2 lighted tennis courts, recreation programs, bicycles, horseback riding, playground, exercise room, spa, volleyball, game room. *Fee:* waterskiing, scuba diving. **Guest Services:** valet laundry, wireless Internet. **Business Services:** business center. **Cards:** AX, MC, VI.
(See color ad p 430)

24 D  / SOME UNITS

SANTO DOMINGO pop. 1,887,586 (See map and index starting on p. 421)

WHERE TO STAY

COURTYARD BY MARRIOTT SANTO DOMINGO

Book great rates at AAA.com

Phone: (809)685-1010 34

Hotel
$113-$121 All Year

Address: 50 A Maximo Gomez Ave **Location:** Center of downtown; 12.5 mi (20 km) w of Las Americas International Airport. **Facility:** Meets AAA guest room security requirements. Smoke free premises. 145 units. 141 one-bedroom standard units, some with whirlpools. 4 one-bedroom suites with efficiencies and whirlpools. 5 stories, interior corridors. *Bath:* combo or shower only. **Parking:** on-site. **Terms:** cancellation fee imposed. **Amenities:** high-speed Internet, dual phone lines, voice mail, safes, irons, hair dryers. *Some:* DVD players (fee). **Pool(s):** outdoor. **Leisure Activities:** exercise room. **Guest Services:** valet and coin laundry, wireless Internet. **Business Services:** meeting rooms, business center. **Cards:** AX, CB, DC, MC, VI.

/ SOME UNITS

AAA Benefit:
Members save a minimum 5% off the best available rate.

HILTON SANTO DOMINGO

Phone: 809/685-0000 32

Hotel
$149-$279 All Year

Address: 500 Ave George Washington **Location:** Center; on Malecon; at Malecon Center. **Facility:** Located adjacent to the Malecon Shopping Center; expect to find contemporary, stylish guest rooms and a rooftop pool offering nice views. Meets AAA guest room security requirements. 228 units. 196 one-bedroom standard units, some with whirlpools. 32 one-bedroom suites with whirlpools. 21 stories, interior corridors. *Bath:* combo or shower only. **Parking:** on-site and valet. **Terms:** cancellation fee imposed. **Amenities:** high-speed Internet (fee), dual phone lines, voice mail, safes, honor bars, irons, hair dryers. *Some:* DVD players, CD players. **Dining:** 3 restaurants, entertainment. **Pool(s):** outdoor. **Leisure Activities:** exercise room. *Fee:* massage. **Guest Services:** valet laundry, wireless Internet. **Business Services:** conference facilities, business center. **Cards:** AX, DC, MC, VI. *(See color ad opposite title page & below)*

 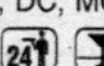       / SOME UNITS  

AAA Benefit:
Members save 5% or more everyday!

▼ See AAA listing above ▼

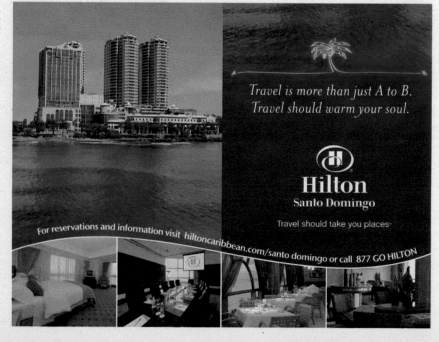

(See map and index starting on p. 421)

HOTEL SANTO DOMINGO — Phone: (809)221-1511 46

Hotel
$140-$260 All Year

Address: Ave Independencia Abraham Lincoln **Location:** Corner of Independencia and Abraham Lincoln aves. **Facility:** 215 units. 210 one-bedroom standard units. 5 one-bedroom suites. 4 stories, interior corridors. **Parking:** on-site and valet. **Terms:** cancellation fee imposed. **Amenities:** video games, high-speed Internet, voice mail, safes, honor bars, hair dryers. *Some:* fax. **Pool(s):** outdoor. **Leisure Activities:** saunas, 3 lighted tennis courts, exercise room. *Fee:* massage. **Guest Services:** valet laundry, wireless Internet. **Business Services:** conference facilities, business center. **Cards:** AX, MC, VI.

ASK 24 D / SOME UNITS

INTERCONTINENTAL V CENTENARIO & CASINO *Book great rates at AAA.com* — Phone: (809)221-0000 48

AAA SAVE

Hotel
$175-$225 All Year

Address: 218 Ave George Washington **Location:** Downtown; on Malecon. **Facility:** Some guest rooms have balconies at this hotel promising sweeping views and comprehensive public areas; recent renovations have upgraded the property. 196 units. 162 one-bedroom standard units. 34 one-bedroom suites. 15 stories, interior corridors. **Parking:** on-site and valet. **Terms:** cancellation fee imposed. **Amenities:** video games, high-speed Internet, dual phone lines, voice mail, safes, honor bars, irons, hair dryers. **Dining:** entertainment. **Pool(s):** outdoor. **Leisure Activities:** saunas, whirlpool, steamrooms, lighted tennis court, exercise room, spa. **Guest Services:** valet laundry, wireless Internet. **Business Services:** conference facilities, business center. **Cards:** AX, DC, DS, MC, VI. **Free Special Amenities: room upgrade (subject to availability with advance reservations) and high-speed Internet.**

24 S D / SOME UNITS

QUALITY HOTEL REAL AEROPUERTO SANTO DOMINGO *Book great rates at AAA.com* — Phone: (809)549-2525 42

AAA SAVE

Hotel
$110-$140 All Year

Address: KM 22 Autopista Las Americas **Location:** 11.2 mi (18 km) e of downtown; 1.2 mi (1.9 km) w of Las Americas International Airport. 1.2 mi (1.9 km) w of airport. **Facility:** Meets AAA guest room security requirements. 124 one-bedroom standard units. 4 stories, interior corridors. *Bath:* combo or shower only. **Parking:** on-site. **Terms:** cancellation fee imposed. **Amenities:** high-speed Internet, dual phone lines, voice mail, irons, hair dryers. *Some:* CD players. **Dining:** entertainment. **Pool(s):** outdoor. **Leisure Activities:** exercise room, spa. **Guest Services:** valet and coin laundry, wireless Internet. **Business Services:** meeting rooms, business center. **Cards:** AX, MC, VI. **Free Special Amenities: full breakfast and high-speed Internet.** *(See color ad below)*

24 CALL &M S D / SOME UNITS

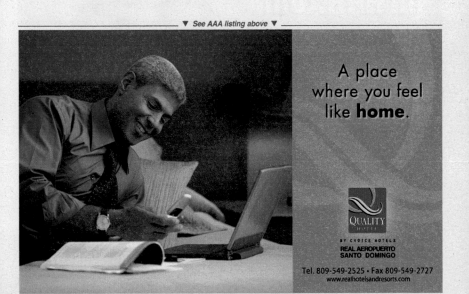

▼ See AAA listing above ▼

(See map and index starting on p. 421)

RENAISSANCE JARAGUA HOTEL & CASINO **Phone:** (809)221-2222 

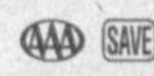

Hotel
$133-$138 All Year

Address: 367 Ave George Washington **Location:** Downtown; on Malecon. **Facility:** Handsome accommodations and luxurious public areas are featured in the tower, while the garden building offers more-modest guest rooms. Smoke free premises. 300 units. 285 one-bedroom standard units. 15 one-bedroom suites, some with whirlpools. 2-10 stories, interior/exterior corridors. **Parking:** on-site and valet. **Terms:** cancellation fee imposed. **Amenities:** video games (fee), high-speed Internet, dual phone lines, voice mail, safes, honor bars, irons, hair dryers. **Dining:** 3 restaurants, nightclub, entertainment. **Pool(s):** outdoor. **Leisure Activities:** saunas, steamrooms, 4 lighted tennis courts, spa, volleyball. **Guest Services:** valet laundry, beauty salon, wireless Internet. **Business Services:** conference facilities, business center. **Cards:** AX, CB, DC, DS, MC, VI. **Free Special Amenities: newspaper and early check-in/late check-out.**

AAA Benefit:
Members save a minimum 5% off the best available rate.

WHERE TO DINE

CAFE BELLINI **Phone:** 809/686-3387 (8)

Mediterranean
$11-$26

In the soul of the Zona Colonial is the romantic Italian-Mediterranean restaurant, which is characterized by refined service and delicately prepared cuisine. Skillful chefs prepare a bountiful array of seafood—such as lobster, shrimp, calamari, mussels and various fish dishes—as well as entrees utilizing veal, beef and pork. The pasta is homemade, as are the tempting and decadent desserts. The list of wines and other beverages is extensive. Dressy casual. **Bar:** Full bar. **Reservations:** suggested. **Hours:** noon-3 & 7-midnight, Mon from 7 pm. **Address:** Plazoleta Padre Billini #155 **Location:** Corner of Arzobispo and Padre Billini; in Zona Colonial. **Parking:** street. **Cards:** AX, DS, MC, VI. **Historic**

EL CONUCO **Phone:** 809/686-0129 (12)

Caribbean
$10-$19

Under several festively decorated bohios, the semi-al fresco and decidedly Dominican eatery provides not only island cuisine but also nightly Dominican entertainment. Diners are in for a treat with signature dishes such as tostones, platanos, yuca and chicharrones (fried chicken and pork), besides the sancocho, an obligatory national dish. Casual dress. Entertainment. **Bar:** Full bar. **Reservations:** suggested. **Hours:** noon-midnight. Closed: 12/25. **Address:** Casimiro de Moya 152 **Location:** In Sector Gazcue; next to Iglesia San Antonio. **Parking:** street. **Cards:** AX, MC, VI.

(See map and index starting on p. 421)

EL PATIO **Phone:** 809/685-9331 (17)

International
$10-$25

In a recently renovated 16th-century mansion, the restaurant offers indoor air-conditioned seating as well as spots in the romantic garden courtyard; well-prepared cuisine shows off the skills of an experienced chef, especially the foie gras or escargot appetizer. Dressy casual. **Bar:** Full bar. **Reservations:** suggested. **Hours:** 7 am-midnight. **Address:** Calle Las Mercedes **Location:** Center of Colonial City District; corner of Las Mercedes and Arzobispo Merino sts; in Sofitel Frances Santo Domingo. **Parking:** on-site. **Cards:** AX, DC, MC, VI. **Historic**

LA BRICIOLA RISTORANTE **Phone:** 809/688-5055 (21)

Italian
$12-$35

The restaurant offers dining in a refined setting but is challenged by the mediocre service and cuisine descriptions that sound better than what is actually delivered. Various beef, chicken and pasta dishes are featured. Dressy casual. **Bar:** Full bar. **Reservations:** suggested. **Hours:** noon-3 & 7-midnight. Closed: Sun. **Address:** 152 A Arzobispo Merino **Location:** Corner of Calle Padre Bellini and Arzobispo Merino; across from Plaza Colon in Zona Colonial. **Parking:** street. **Cards:** MC, VI. **Historic**

LA PARILLA STEAK HOUSE **Phone:** 809/688-1511 (30)

Steak
$10-$24

The ultra-casual eatery on the Malecon is popular with locals. Almost all entrees, which include various cuts of steak, ribs, chicken, pork, chicken and salmon, are grilled, and meals are brought to the table in a sizzling cast-iron skillet. Casual dress. **Bar:** Full bar. **Reservations:** accepted. **Hours:** noon-midnight. **Address:** 553 Ave George Washington **Location:** Downtown; on Malecon. **Parking:** street. **Cards:** AX, DS, MC, VI.

LA RESIDENCE **Phone:** 809/685-9955 (13)

International
$14-$50

In a restored 14th-century mansion is the exquisite restaurant, which presents a menu of gourmet meals enhanced by plate presentations. Dapper servers exude congenial hospitality. The broad menu lists expertly prepared roasted duck breast, veal cutlet, steamed sea bream in a banana leaf and hand-made ravioli stuffed with prawns and wild mushrooms. One house-favorite dessert is the warm chocolate cake with mint-cinnamon ice cream. Dressy casual. Entertainment. **Bar:** Full bar. **Reservations:** required. **Hours:** 6:30 am-10:30, noon-3 & 6-11 pm. **Address:** Calle Las Damas **Location:** Entrance to Colonial City District; in Sofitel Nicolas de Ovando Santo Domingo. **Parking:** on-site. **Cards:** AX, DC, DS, MC, VI. **Historic**

LOS TRES MOSQUETEROS CAFE & RESTAURANT **Phone:** 809/689-1114 (9)

International
$9-$20

In the historic Zona Colonial, very close to major shopping streets, is this Spanish/Mediterranean influenced bodega. The extensive menu includes a variety of pasta dishes, imported meats and cheeses as well as conch, lobster and mussels; an ideal place for enjoying a full meal or nibbling on appetizers and enjoying an affordable bottle of wine. The smartly attired servers are very congenial. Casual dress. **Bar:** Full bar. **Reservations:** accepted. **Hours:** 11 am-11 pm. **Address:** 56 Calle El Conde **Location:** Corner of El Conde and Las Dama sts; in Zona Colonial. **Parking:** street. **Cards:** AX, MC, VI. **Historic**

MESON DE LA CAVA **Phone:** 809/533-2818 (27)

Spanish
$16-$34

The spectacular restaurant is built in a natural cavern 50 feet underground. Service is formal. Flavorful cuisine is well-presented and served in sizable portions. Dressy casual. Entertainment. **Bar:** Full bar. **Reservations:** required. **Hours:** noon-1 am. **Address:** Ave Mirador Sur, #1 **Location:** Near southeast end of Paseo de los Indios; 0.6 mi (1 km) w from jct Jimenez Nova and Mirador Sur aves. **Parking:** on-site and valet. **Cards:** AX, CB, DC, DS, JC, MC, VI.

MUSEO DEL JAMON **Phone:** 809/688-9644 (18)

Spanish
$8-$17

In the restaurant row area of Zona Colonial the restaurant features seating al fresco or indoors with hams suspended from the ceiling. Besides the famed Serrano ham, the Spanish menu features items such as rabbit, mussels, pork loin and chicken dishes. Dressy casual. **Bar:** Full bar. **Reservations:** accepted. **Hours:** 11 am-midnight. **Address:** Calle Atarazana 17 **Location:** In Zona Colonial; at Atarazana across from Alcazar de Colon; between General Cabral and Vincent C Duarte sts. **Parking:** on-site (fee) and street. **Cards:** AX, MC, VI. **Historic**

PAT'E PALO EUROPEAN BRASSERIE **Phone:** 809/687-8089 (16)

International
$11-$38

Pat'e Palo translates to "peg leg," hence the charming pirate-clad waiters. The broad menu features such starters as tuna carpaccio, ceviche, frog legs and a range of pates. Among entree choices are seafood preparations—including dorado, sea bass and red snapper—and the double-cut pork chop. Most dishes go well with a pitcher of sangria. Indoor seating reflects the Spanish decor of the street-side courtyard and offers views of the oldest city in the New World. Dressy casual. **Bar:** Full bar. **Reservations:** suggested. **Hours:** 4:30 pm-midnight, Fri & Sat 1 pm-1 am, Sun 1 pm-midnight. **Address:** La Atarazana #25 **Location:** Zona Colonial; across from Plaza Colon; at Atarazana. **Parking:** street. **Cards:** AX, MC, VI. **Historic**

REINA DE ESPANA **Phone:** 809/685-2588 (25)

Spanish
$16-$31

Cuisine reflecting Spanish, Dominican, Italian and French influences is served in a Medieval-style villa referred to locally as "the castle." The major emphasis is on seafood, but imported beef, veal, lamb and goat receive a good share of the billing. Service is attentive. Dressy casual. **Bar:** Full bar. **Reservations:** suggested. **Hours:** noon-midnight. **Address:** Calle Cervantes #103 **Location:** Corner of Cervantes and Santiago; just n from Malecon. **Parking:** on-site and valet. **Cards:** AX, CB, DC, DS, JC, MC, VI.

(See map and index starting on p. 421)

RESTAURANT DON PEPE **Phone:** 809/686-8481 (24)

Spanish
$16-$31

Elegant decor lends an air of sophistication to the dining room, which is well attended by a formal cadre of servers. The menu emphasizes beef, pork, chicken and seafood dishes, all prepared with Spanish culinary influences. The dessert cart showcases some mouthwatering temptations. Dressy casual. **Bar:** Full bar. **Reservations:** suggested. **Hours:** noon-3 & 7-midnight, Fri & Sat noon-midnight. **Address:** Santiago Ave Pasteur #41 Ave **Location:** Corner Pasteur Ave and Santiago Esq St, just n from Malecon and close to Hotel V Centenario Intercontinental Santo Domingo; in Gazcue neighborhood. **Parking:** valet. **Cards:** AX, MC, VI.

RESTAURANTE CANTABRICO **Phone:** 809/687-5101 (23)

Spanish
$15-$32

Attractively presented and flavorful seafood and Dominican specialties are served in a European atmosphere. Impressive works by local artists decorate the Spanish-style restaurant. The courteous staff provides attentive service. Dressy casual. **Bar:** Full bar. **Reservations:** suggested. **Hours:** noon-midnight. **Address:** Ave Independencia 54 **Location:** On Ave Independencia; adjacent to Cemetery and just w of Independence Park. **Parking:** on-site. **Cards:** AX, MC, VI.

RESTAURANTE LA LLAVE DEL MAR **Phone:** 809/682-5961 (22)

Seafood
$12-$28

The nautical-themed restaurant is just on the fringe of Zona Colonial. A variety of simply prepared fish dishes line the menu including snapper, mahi mahi and sea bass. Besides fish there is conch, scallops, beef and chicken. Dressy casual. **Bar:** Full bar. **Reservations:** accepted. **Hours:** 11 am-midnight, Sun 6 pm-11 pm. **Address:** Calle Santome 43 **Location:** Corner of Ave George Washington and Calle Santome; entrance to Zona Colonial. **Parking:** on-site. **Cards:** MC, VI.

RESTAURANTE SAMURAI **Phone:** 809/565-1621 (19)

Japanese
$9-$21

Essentially the only Japanese restaurant in Santo Domingo, the restaurant features a sushi bar and tatami table seating. Besides a large sushi and sashimi menu, it also offers tempura combinations and teriyaki plates. Dressy casual. **Bar:** Full bar. **Reservations:** accepted. **Hours:** noon-3 & 7-midnight, Sun noon-4 & 7-11 pm. **Address:** Ave Abraham Lincoln 902 **Location:** 0.9 mi (1.5 km) n of jct George Washington (Malecon) and Abraham Lincoln aves. **Parking:** on-site. **Cards:** MC, VI.

VESUVIO DEL MALECON **Phone:** 809/221-1954 (29)

Italian
$17-$30

Since 1954, the landmark restaurant's dapper staff has been serving Spain- and Italy-inspired meals in well-appointed surroundings. Entrees include deft preparations of lamb, chicken, octopus, rabbit and conch. The finale is when the dessert cart is rolled around, and the temptation for one more indulgence is too great. Dressy casual. **Bar:** Full bar. **Reservations:** suggested. **Hours:** noon-midnight. Closed: 1/1, 12/24, 12/25; also 12/31. **Address:** 521 Ave George Washington **Location:** On Malecon; facing Caribbean Sea. **Parking:** valet. **Cards:** AX, DC, DS, JC, MC, VI.

UVERO ALTO (See map and index starting on p. 421)

WHERE TO STAY

SIVORY PUNTA CANA **Phone:** 809/333-0500 (75)

AAA SAVE

Hotel
$290-$2400 All Year

Address: Uvero Alto, Main Rd **Location:** Oceanfront. 25 mi (40 km) n of Punta Cana International Airport. **Facility:** These bungalow-style units are spaced apart in natural garden areas, some with ocean views; an attentive staff caters to the details for a memorable experience. Meets AAA guest room security requirements. 55 units. 48 one-bedroom standard units. 6 one- and 1 two-bedroom suites with whirlpools. 2 stories (no elevator), exterior corridors. **Parking:** on-site and valet. **Terms:** 31 day cancellation notice-fee imposed. **Amenities:** video library, DVD players, CD players, high-speed Internet, voice mail, safes, hair dryers. **Dining:** 3 restaurants. **Pool(s):** outdoor. **Leisure Activities:** sauna, whirlpool, steamroom, sailboats, snorkeling, kayaks, putting green, tennis court, exercise room, spa, volleyball. *Fee:* horseback riding. **Guest Services:** valet laundry, airport transportation (fee)-Punta Cana International Airport, wireless Internet. **Business Services:** meeting rooms, PC. **Cards:** AX, MC, VI. **Free Special Amenities: continental breakfast and early check-in/late check-out.** *(See color ad p 431)*

FEE   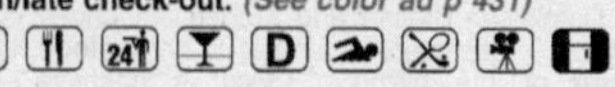

GRENADA

Airport Accommodations

Map Page	OA	POINT SALINE INTL	Diamond Rated	High Season	Page
8 / p. 438		Grenadian by Rex Resorts, 0.3 mi (0.5 km)	◆◆	$263-$548	441

This index helps you "spot" where approved lodgings and restaurants are located on the corresponding detailed maps. Lodging daily rate range is for comparison only and show the property's high season. Restaurant rate range is a combination of lunch and/or dinner. Turn to the listing page for more detailed rate information and consult display ads for special promotions.

ST. GEORGE'S (ST. GEORGE PARISH)

Map Page	OA	Lodgings	Diamond Rated	High Season	Page
2 / p. 438	AAA	**Spice Island Beach Resort**	◆◆◆◆	$635-$1815 SAVE	441
3 / p. 438		South City Plaza Hotel	◆◆	$125-$206	441
4 / p. 438		Coyaba Beach Resort	◆◆◆	$205-$326	441
5 / p. 438		Blue Horizons Garden Resort	◆◆	$150-$225	439
6 / p. 438	AAA	**Flamboyant Hotel & Villas**	◆◆	$175-$215 SAVE	441
7 / p. 438		Allamanda Beach Resort	◆	$125-$270	439
8 / p. 438		Grenadian by Rex Resorts	◆◆	$263-$548	441

Map Page	OA	Restaurants	Diamond Rated	Cuisine	Meal Range	Page
7 / p. 438		Coconut Beach	◆	Caribbean	$18-$27	441
8 / p. 438		Laluna	◆◆◆	International	$24-$36	441

L'ANSE AUX EPINES (ST. GEORGE PARISH)

Map Page	OA	Lodgings	Diamond Rated	High Season	Page
9 / p. 438		The Calabash Hotel	◆◆◆◆	$295-$750	439
10 / p. 438		Lance Aux Epines Cottages	◆◆	$154-$335	439
11 / p. 438		Coral Cove	◆◆	$85-$190	439

Map Page	OA	Restaurants	Diamond Rated	Cuisine	Meal Range	Page
1 / p. 438		Rhodes Restaurant	◆◆◆	International	$31-$39	439
5 / p. 438		The Red Crab	◆◆	Steak & Seafood	$11-$35	439

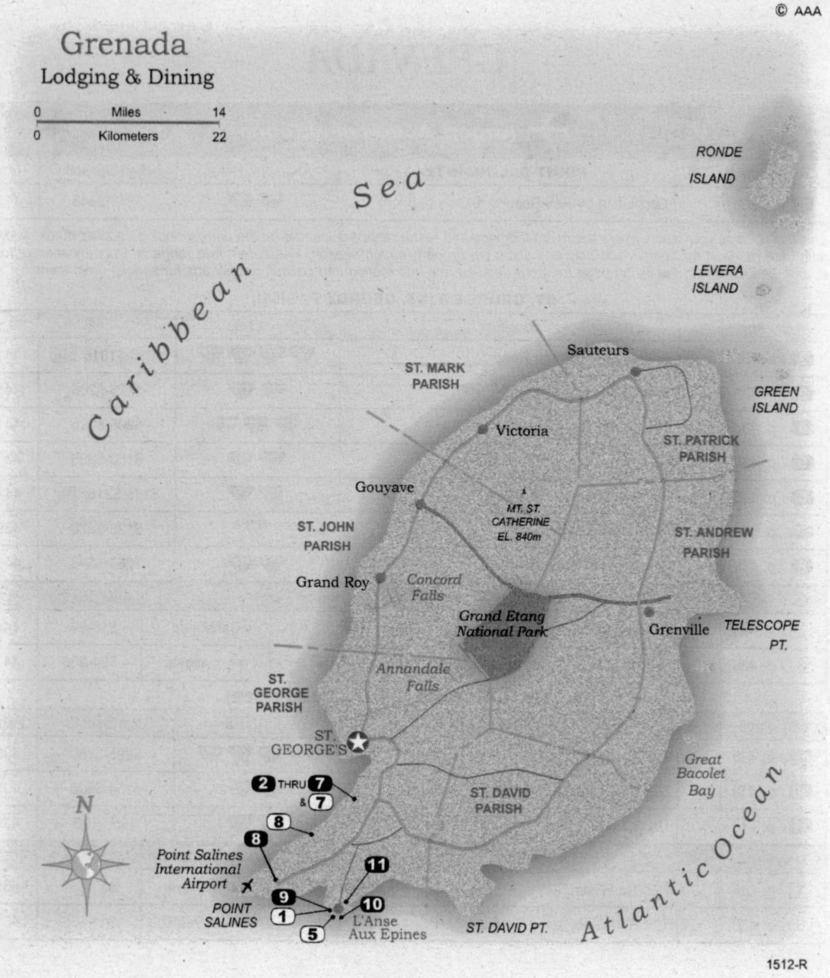

© AAA

Grenada
Lodging & Dining

0 Miles 14
0 Kilometers 22

Caribbean Sea

RONDE ISLAND
LEVERA ISLAND
Sauteurs
ST. MARK PARISH
GREEN ISLAND
Victoria
ST. PATRICK PARISH
Gouyave
MT. ST. CATHERINE EL. 840m
ST. JOHN PARISH
ST. ANDREW PARISH
Grand Roy
Concord Falls
Grand Etang National Park
Grenville
TELESCOPE PT.
Annandale Falls
ST. GEORGE PARISH
ST. GEORGE'S
Great Bacolet Bay
2 THRU 7 & 7
ST. DAVID PARISH
8
8
N
Point Salines International Airport
11
9
10
POINT SALINES
1
L'Anse Aux Epines
5
ST. DAVID PT.
Atlantic Ocean

1512-R

St. George Parish

L'ANSE AUX EPINES (See map and index starting on p. 438)

WHERE TO STAY

THE CALABASH HOTEL — **Phone:** (473)444-4334 — 9

Hotel
$295-$750 All Year

Address: L'Anse aux Epines **Location:** Oceanfront. 5 mi (8 km) s of town; 3.3 mi (5.3 km) ne of airport. **Facility:** These duplex cottages and two-story apartments on tropical grounds face a secluded cove of Prickley Bay; the decor is fresh and inviting. Televisions on request. 30 units. 6 one-bedroom standard units with whirlpools. 24 one-bedroom suites with whirlpools. 2 stories (no elevator), exterior corridors. **Parking:** on-site. **Terms:** office hours 7 am-11 pm, 7-14 night minimum stay - seasonal, age restrictions may apply, 14 day cancellation notice, in summer, 30 day in winter-fee imposed. **Amenities:** DVD players, CD players, voice mail, safes, honor bars, irons, hair dryers. **Dining:** Rhodes Restaurant, see separate listing. **Pool(s):** outdoor. **Leisure Activities:** beach access, sailboats, snorkeling, lighted tennis court, exercise room, shuffleboard. *Fee:* scuba diving, massage. **Guest Services:** valet laundry, wireless Internet. **Business Services:** PC. **Cards:** AX, MC, VI.

CORAL COVE — **Phone:** 473/444-4422 — 11

Cottage
$85-$190 All Year

Address: L'Anse aux Epines **Location:** Oceanfront. 5.2 mi (8.3 km) s of town; 4 mi (6.4 km) nw of airport. **Facility:** 11 cottages. 1 story, exterior corridors. *Bath:* shower only. **Parking:** on-site. **Terms:** 3 night minimum stay - seasonal and/or weekends, 21 day cancellation notice-fee imposed. **Pool(s):** outdoor. **Leisure Activities:** beach access, snorkeling, tennis court. **Guest Services:** coin laundry. **Cards:** AX, MC, VI.

LANCE AUX EPINES COTTAGES Book at AAA.com — **Phone:** (473)444-4565 — 10

Cottage
$154-$335 12/1-4/30
$112-$233 5/1-11/30

Address: L'Anse aux Epines **Location:** Oceanfront. 5.2 mi (8.3 km) s of town; 3.5 mi (13.3 km) ne of airport; on south coast. **Facility:** 11 units. 4 one-bedroom suites with kitchens. 7 cottages. 1-2 stories (no elevator), exterior corridors. *Bath:* shower only. **Parking:** on-site. **Terms:** office hours 8 am-4 pm, 1-3 night minimum stay - seasonal, 60 day cancellation notice, 30 day in summer-fee imposed. **Amenities:** CD players, high-speed Internet (fee), safes, hair dryers. **Leisure Activities:** paddleboats, sailboats, game room. **Guest Services:** TV in common area, complimentary laundry, wireless Internet. **Business Services:** PC (fee). **Cards:** MC, VI.

WHERE TO DINE

THE RED CRAB — **Phone:** 473/444-4424 — 5

Steak & Seafood
$11-$35

Both indoors and outdoors, the restaurant sustains a relaxed English pub atmosphere. Guests can choose from a selection of local seafood dishes and house specialties as well as lighter meals and sandwiches. Casual dress. **Bar:** Full bar. **Reservations:** suggested, in season. **Hours:** 11 am-2 & 6-10:30 pm. Closed major holidays; also 12/26, Sun & Grenada public holidays. **Address:** L'Anse aux Epines **Location:** 8 mi (12.8 km) s of town; 4 mi (6.4 km) ne of airport. **Parking:** on-site. **Cards:** AX, MC, VI.

RHODES RESTAURANT — **Phone:** 473/444-4334 — 1

International
$31-$39

This elegant restaurant nurtures an upscale feel in its covered open-air setting, where diners enjoy pleasant Caribbean-style entertainment as they sample the chef's highly innovative fare. The freshest regional ingredients mingle with island spices and exotic fruits in preparations such as chilled gazpacho with melon balls to start and Caribbean spiced steak with green peppercorn sauce or many fresh fish and other seafood selections as entrees. Exotic flavors burst from the homemade desserts. Semi-formal attire. **Bar:** Full bar. **Reservations:** suggested. **Hours:** 7 pm-9:30 pm. **Address:** L'Anse aux Epines **Location:** 5 mi (8 km) s of town; 3.3 mi (5.3 km) ne of airport; in The Calabash Hotel. **Parking:** on-site. **Cards:** AX, MC, VI.

ST. GEORGE'S pop. 37,000 (See map and index starting on p. 438)

WHERE TO STAY

ALLAMANDA BEACH RESORT Book at AAA.com — **Phone:** (473)444-0095 — 7

Hotel
$125-$270 All Year

Address: Grand Anse **Location:** Oceanfront. 5.7 mi (9.1 km) s of town; 4.2 mi (6.7 km) nw. **Facility:** 50 units. 48 one-bedroom standard units, some with whirlpools. 2 two-bedroom suites. 3 stories (no elevator), exterior corridors. *Bath:* combo or shower only. **Parking:** on-site. **Terms:** 21 day cancellation notice-fee imposed. **Amenities:** safes, irons, hair dryers. **Pool(s):** outdoor. **Leisure Activities:** exercise room, volleyball. *Fee:* lighted tennis court. **Guest Services:** valet laundry, wireless Internet. **Business Services:** PC (fee). **Cards:** MC, VI.

/ SOME UNITS

BLUE HORIZONS GARDEN RESORT — **Phone:** (473)444-4316 — 5

Hotel
$150-$225 All Year

Address: Morne Rouge **Location:** 5.5 mi (8.8 km) s of town; 3.8 mi (6 km) nw of airport. **Facility:** 32 units. 6 one-bedroom standard units with efficiencies. 26 one-bedroom suites with efficiencies. 1 story, exterior corridors. **Parking:** on-site. **Terms:** office hours 7 am-10:30 pm, 7 night minimum stay - seasonal, 30 day cancellation notice. **Amenities:** safes, irons, hair dryers. **Pool(s):** outdoor. **Leisure Activities:** playground. **Guest Services:** valet laundry, wireless Internet. **Business Services:** meeting rooms, PC (fee). **Cards:** AX, DC, DS, MC, VI.

(See map and index starting on p. 438)

COYABA BEACH RESORT Book great rates at AAA.com Phone: (473)444-4129 4

Hotel

$205-$326 All Year

Address: Grand Anse **Location:** Oceanfront. 5.4 mi (8.6 km) s of town; 3.9 mi (6.2 km) nw of airport. **Facility:** Designated smoking area. 80 one-bedroom standard units. 2 stories (no elevator), exterior corridors. *Bath:* combo or shower only. **Parking:** on-site. **Terms:** 2-3 night minimum stay - seasonal, 14 day cancellation notice, 21 day in winter-fee imposed. **Amenities:** high-speed Internet, voice mail, safes, irons, hair dryers. **Pool(s):** outdoor. **Leisure Activities:** canoeing, sailboats, snorkeling, lighted tennis court, recreation programs, exercise room, croquet, shuffleboard. *Fee:* scuba diving, massage. **Guest Services:** valet laundry, wireless Internet. **Business Services:** meeting rooms, PC. **Cards:** AX, MC, VI.

FLAMBOYANT HOTEL & VILLAS Book great rates at AAA.com Phone: (473)444-4247 6

Hotel

$175-$215 12/1-4/30

$125-$150 5/1-11/30

Address: Morne Rouge **Location:** 6.1 mi (9.7 km) s of town; 4.5 mi (7.2 km) nw of airport. Located on Grand Anse Beach. **Facility:** Designated smoking area. 68 units. 60 one-bedroom standard units. 8 one-bedroom suites with efficiencies. 1-3 stories (no elevator), exterior corridors. **Parking:** on-site. **Terms:** 7 day cancellation notice, 14 day 12/16-4/15-fee imposed. **Amenities:** safes, honor bars, irons, hair dryers. **Dining:** 2 restaurants, entertainment. **Pool(s):** outdoor. **Leisure Activities:** whirlpool, paddleboats, snorkeling, kayaks, golf privileges, billiards, exercise room. *Fee:* scuba diving. **Guest Services:** valet laundry, wireless Internet. **Business Services:** conference facilities, PC (fee). **Cards:** AX, DC, DS, MC, VI. **Free Special Amenities: early check-in/late check-out and room upgrade (subject to availability with advance reservations).**

/ SOME UNITS

GRENADIAN BY REX RESORTS Phone: 473/444-3333 8

Resort Hotel

$263-$548 All Year

Address: Point Salines **Location:** Oceanfront. 9.5 mi (15.2 km) s of town; 0.3 mi (0.5 km) n of airport. **Facility:** On 32 acres of well manicured grounds. Public areas reflect flirtations with upscale decor. Room categories vary from Spartan to well-appointed. Designated smoking area. 212 one-bedroom standard units. 3 stories (no elevator), exterior corridors. *Bath:* combo or shower only. **Parking:** on-site. **Terms:** cancellation fee imposed. **Amenities:** *Some:* irons, hair dryers. **Pool(s):** outdoor. **Leisure Activities:** beach access, 2 tennis courts, recreation programs, jogging, playground, exercise room, volleyball. *Fee:* sailboats, windsurfing, scuba diving, snorkeling, massage. **Guest Services:** valet laundry, wireless Internet. **Business Services:** meeting rooms, business center. **Cards:** AX, DC, DS, MC, VI.

SOUTH CITY PLAZA HOTEL Phone: 473/439-3949 3

Hotel

$125-$206 All Year

Address: Grand Anse **Location:** Just s of town; at South City Plaza Shopping Complex. **Facility:** Designated smoking area. 25 one-bedroom standard units, some with whirlpools. 3 stories, interior corridors. **Parking:** on-site. **Amenities:** irons, hair dryers. **Guest Services:** valet laundry, wireless Internet. **Business Services:** meeting rooms, PC (fee). **Cards:** MC, VI.

SPICE ISLAND BEACH RESORT Phone: (473)444-4258 2

Hotel

$635-$1815 All Year

Address: Grand Anse Beach **Location:** Oceanfront. 5.5 mi (8.8 km) s of town; 4 mi (6.4 km) nw of airport. Located on Grand Anse Beach. **Facility:** On 1,600 feet of beachfront grounds, the resort offers attractively decorated accommodations with furnished balconies or terraces. Meets AAA guest room security requirements. Designated smoking area. 64 units. 58 one-bedroom standard units with whirlpools. 6 one-bedroom suites with whirlpools. 1-2 stories (no elevator), exterior corridors. **Parking:** on-site. **Terms:** 7-10 night minimum stay - seasonal, 3 day cancellation notice-fee imposed. **Amenities:** video library, DVD players, CD players, high-speed Internet, voice mail, safes, honor bars, irons, hair dryers. *Some:* dual phone lines. **Dining:** 2 restaurants, entertainment. **Pool(s):** outdoor. **Leisure Activities:** sailboats, snorkeling, kayaks, lighted tennis court, kids club, library, bicycles, exercise room, spa. *Fee:* sauna, whirlpool, scuba diving. **Guest Services:** valet laundry, wireless Internet. **Business Services:** meeting rooms, business center. **Cards:** AX, MC, VI. **Free Special Amenities: early check-in/late check-out and high-speed Internet.**

WHERE TO DINE

COCONUT BEACH Phone: 473/444-4644 7

Caribbean

$18-$27

Located in a historic house right on Grande Anse Beach, the classic beachside al fresco restaurant offers the option of dining al fresco or indoors. The cuisine is cooked with Grenadian herbs and spices in a French Creole fashion; some of the popular dishes include lobster thermidor, calypso conch and pepper steak. Casual dress. **Bar:** Full bar. **Reservations:** suggested. **Hours:** 12:30 pm-10:30 pm. Closed major holidays; also Tues. **Address:** Grand Anse Beach **Location:** 3.1 mi (5 km) s of downtown; 1.6 mi (2.5 km) n of Grand Anse Beach roundabout. **Parking:** on-site. **Cards:** AX, CB, DC, DS, JC, MC, VI.

LALUNA Phone: 473/439-0001 8

International

$24-$36

In a remote and romantic location high on a hill, this covered open-air dining room incorporates contemporary flair into its Caribbean atmosphere, which includes candlelit tables and upbeat background music. The menu features an innovative mix of island-influenced Italian and international cuisine, including the grilled catch of the day in pineapple citrus salsa, Sicilian-style shrimp, grilled meats and freshly prepared pasta dishes. Bread pudding is a popular choice among the decadent desserts. Casual dress. **Bar:** Full bar. **Reservations:** suggested. **Hours:** 7 pm-9 pm. **Address:** Morne Rouge **Location:** 7 mi (11.2 km) s of town; 5.4 mi (8.6 km) nw of airport. **Parking:** on-site. **Cards:** MC, VI.

GUADELOUPE

Basse-Terre Island

This index helps you "spot" where approved lodgings and restaurants are located on the corresponding detailed maps. Lodging daily rate range is for comparison only and show the property's high season. Restaurant rate range is a combination of lunch and/or dinner. Turn to the listing page for more detailed rate information and consult display ads for special promotions.

GOSIER (GRANDE-TERRE ISLAND)

Map Page	OA	Lodgings	Diamond Rated	High Season	Page
3 / p. 444		Auberge de la Vieille Tour	◆◆◆	$437-$777	445
4 / p. 444		La Creole Beach Hotel & Spa	◆◆	$177-$500	445

Map Page	OA	Restaurants	Diamond Rated	Cuisine	Meal Range	Page
1 / p. 444		L'Agouba Grill	◆	Barbecue	$11-$21	445
2 / p. 444		Les Langoustes Grill-Restaurant	◆◆	Creole	$18-$33	446
4 / p. 444		Restaurant Rosini	◆◆	Northern Italian	$16-$34	446
6 / p. 444		Auberge de la Vieille Tour	◆◆◆	Continental	$50-$71	445
7 / p. 444		Villa Fleur d'Epee	◆◆◆	French	$105	446
8 / p. 444		Le Bananier	◆◆◆	Creole	$16-$28	446
14 / p. 444		Le Tam Tam	◆	Creole	$12-$30	446
15 / p. 444		L'Agouba Restaurant Dampierre Grill	◆	Barbecue	$11-$21	446
34 / p. 444		Le Pirate Caribeen	◆◆	Creole	$15-$30	446
36 / p. 444		Banana's Cafe	◆◆	Creole	$13-$31	445
37 / p. 444		La Mandala	◆◆	International	$17-$31	446
38 / p. 444		Le Cafe des Arts	◆◆◆	Seafood	$24-$40	446

SAINTE ANNE (GRANDE-TERRE ISLAND)

Map Page	OA	Lodging	Diamond Rated	High Season	Page
8 / p. 444		Hotel La Toubana	◆◆◆	$260-$345	447

Map Page	OA	Restaurants	Diamond Rated	Cuisine	Meal Range	Page
18 / p. 444		Kote Sud Le Restaurant	◆◆	Creole	$17-$30	448
19 / p. 444		Le Bananeraie	◆◆	Creole	$20-$35	448
21 / p. 444		Chez DouDou	◆	Creole	$13-$23	447

TROIS-RIVIERES (BASSE-TERRE ISLAND)

Map Page	OA	Lodging	Diamond Rated	High Season	Page
15 / p. 444		Le Jardin Malanga	◆◆◆	$396-$437	444

ST. LOUIS (MARIE-GALANTE ISLAND)

Map Page	OA	Lodging	Diamond Rated	High Season	Page
19 / p. 444		La Cohoba Hotel	◆◆	$174-$249	449

CAPESTERRE (MARIE-GALANTE ISLAND)

Map Page	OA	Lodging	Diamond Rated	High Season	Page
25 / p. 444		Cap Re'va Residence Hoteliere	◆◆	$83-$177	449

Map Page	OA	Restaurant	Diamond Rated	Cuisine	Meal Range	Page
31 / p. 444		La Braise Marine	◆	Caribbean	$9-$22	449

ST. FRANCOIS (GRANDE-TERRE ISLAND)

Map Page	OA	Restaurants	Diamond Rated	Cuisine	Meal Range	Page
25 / p. 444		La Dinette Gourmande	◆◆	International	$13-$25	448
26 / p. 444		Chez Man Michel	◆	Creole	$12-$25	448
27 / p. 444		Resto des Artistes	◆◆	Creole	$15-$30	448

POINTE-A-PITRE (GRANDE-TERRE ISLAND)

Map Page	OA	Restaurants	Diamond Rated	Cuisine	Meal Range	Page
40 / p. 444		Cote du Boeuf	◆◆	Steak & Seafood	$18-$38	447
41 / p. 444		Cote Jardin	◆◆◆	French	$16-$38	447
42 / p. 444		La Route du Rhum	◆◆	Creole	$17-$39	447

BOUILLANTE (BASSE-TERRE ISLAND)

Map Page	OA	Restaurant	Diamond Rated	Cuisine	Meal Range	Page
46 / p. 444		Restaurant La Touna	◆◆	Creole	$17-$35	444

PIGEON (BASSE-TERRE ISLAND)

Map Page	OA	Restaurant	Diamond Rated	Cuisine	Meal Range	Page
48 / p. 444		Le Meltipot	◆◆	French	$17-$28	444

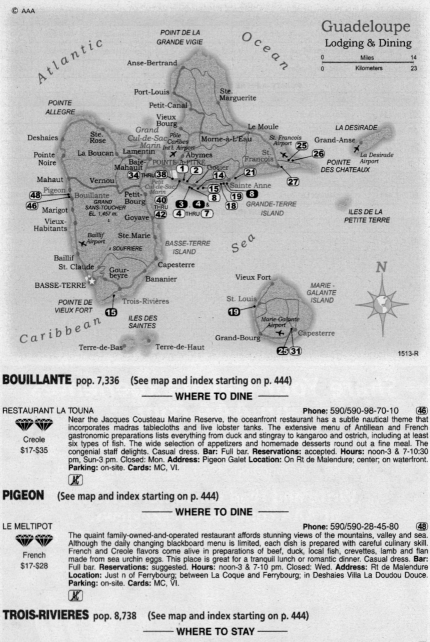

Guadeloupe
Lodging & Dining

1513-R

BOUILLANTE pop. 7,336 (See map and index starting on p. 444)

WHERE TO DINE

RESTAURANT LA TOUNA — Phone: 590/590-98-70-10 (46)

Creole
$17-$35

Near the Jacques Cousteau Marine Reserve, the oceanfront restaurant has a subtle nautical theme that incorporates madras tablecloths and live lobster tanks. The extensive menu of Antillean and French gastronomic preparations lists everything from duck and stingray to kangaroo and ostrich, including at least six types of fish. The wide selection of appetizers and homemade desserts round out a fine meal. The congenial staff delights. Casual dress. **Bar:** Full bar. **Reservations:** accepted. **Hours:** noon-3 & 7-10:30 pm, Sun-3 pm. Closed: Mon. **Address:** Pigeon Galet **Location:** On Rt de Malendure; center; on waterfront. **Parking:** on-site. **Cards:** MC, VI.

PIGEON (See map and index starting on p. 444)

WHERE TO DINE

LE MELTIPOT — Phone: 590/590-28-45-80 (48)

French
$17-$28

The quaint family-owned-and-operated restaurant affords stunning views of the mountains, valley and sea. Although the daily changing blackboard menu is limited, each dish is prepared with careful culinary skill. French and Creole flavors come alive in preparations of beef, duck, local fish, crevettes, lamb and flan made from sea urchin eggs. This place is great for a tranquil lunch or romantic dinner. Casual dress. **Bar:** Full bar. **Reservations:** suggested. **Hours:** noon-3 & 7-10 pm. Closed: Wed. **Address:** Rt de Malendure **Location:** Just n of Ferrybourg; between La Coque and Ferrybourg; in Deshaies Villa La Doudou Douce. **Parking:** on-site. **Cards:** MC, VI.

TROIS-RIVIERES pop. 8,738 (See map and index starting on p. 444)

WHERE TO STAY

LE JARDIN MALANGA — Phone: 590/590-92-67-57 (15)

Country Inn
$396-$437 All Year

Address: La Rue Hermitage **Location:** Basse Terre side of Guadeloupe south coast; from southern highway, just s at Hermitage turn off, follow sign. **Facility:** Situated on six acres of a former banana plantation circa 1927 is this charming inn with mahogany furnishings and stunning views of Les Saintes. Hotel closed 6/1-7/11 and 9/1-10/19. 9 one-bedroom standard units. 1-2 stories (no elevator), interior/exterior corridors. *Bath:* combo or shower only. **Parking:** on-site. **Terms:** office hours 6:30 am-9 pm, 3 day cancellation notice. **Amenities:** hair dryers. **Pool(s):** outdoor. **Leisure Activities:** garden walks. **Cards:** AX, CB, MC, VI.

Grande-Terre Island

GOSIER pop. 25,360 (See map and index starting on p. 444)

WHERE TO STAY

AUBERGE DE LA VIEILLE TOUR Book at AAA.com Phone: (590)590-84-23-23 3

Hotel
$437-$777 All Year

Address: Montauban **Location:** Oceanfront. Center; in Mantauban area. **Facility:** 176 one-bedroom standard units. 1-3 stories (no elevator), interior/exterior corridors. **Parking:** on-site. **Terms:** 30 day cancellation notice. **Amenities:** safes, honor bars, hair dryers. **Dining:** restaurant, see separate listing. **Pool(s):** outdoor. **Leisure Activities:** 2 lighted tennis courts. *Fee:* massage. **Guest Services:** valet laundry, beauty salon, wireless Internet. **Business Services:** meeting rooms, PC. **Cards:** AX, CB, DC, DS, JC, MC, VI.

/ SOME UNITS

LA CREOLE BEACH HOTEL & SPA Book at AAA.com Phone: (590)590-90-46-46 4

Resort Hotel
$177-$500 All Year

Address: Pointe de la Verdure **Location:** Oceanfront. On Pointe de la Verdure; 6.4 mi (10.2 km) se of Pointe-a-Pitre Airport. **Facility:** This beachfront vacation complex offers a wide range of units from modest to upscale, with views of the ocean or gardens. 331 units. 313 one-bedroom standard units. 12 one- and 6 two-bedroom suites with efficiencies, some with whirlpools. 3-5 stories, interior/exterior corridors. *Bath:* combo or shower only. **Parking:** on-site. **Terms:** check-in 4 pm, 30 day cancellation notice-fee imposed. **Amenities:** safes, hair dryers. *Some:* honor bars. **Pool(s):** outdoor. **Leisure Activities:** snorkeling, recreation programs, exercise room, volleyball. *Fee:* canoes, sailboats, windsurfing, waterskiing, scuba diving. **Guest Services:** valet laundry, wireless Internet. **Business Services:** PC. **Cards:** AX, DC, MC, VI.

/ SOME UNITS

WHERE TO DINE

AUBERGE DE LA VIEILLE TOUR Phone: 590/590-84-23-23 6

Continental
$50-$71

In a restored sugar mill, the restaurant nurtures a refined atmosphere with an island flair. Diners often arrive early to enjoy a tropical cocktail or glass of wine before the meal. Fine Continental and French cuisine is listed on a la carte and prix fixe menus. Dressy casual. **Bar:** Full bar. **Reservations:** required. **Hours:** 7 pm-10 pm. Closed: Thurs. **Address:** Montauban **Location:** 3.7 mi (5.9 km) se of Point-a-Pitre Airport; in Hotel Auberge de la Vieille Tour. **Parking:** on-site. **Cards:** AX, MC, VI.

BANANA'S CAFE Phone: 590/590-90-97-34 36

Creole
$13-$31

Patrons can dine al fresco on the waterfront along the marina's restaurant row. The chef specializes in French Antillean Creole cuisine with featured items such as crab farci, lambi boudin, gratin de christophenes, accras and fish prepared in a court bouillon. Among sweet desserts are flan au coco and creme brulee. Casual dress. **Bar:** Full bar. **Reservations:** accepted. **Hours:** noon-midnight. **Address:** Le Mole Portuaire La Marina **Location:** At Marina de Pointe-A-Pitre and Marina Bas du Fort. **Parking:** on-site. **Cards:** CB, MC, VI.

L'AGOUBA GRILL Phone: 590/590-84-64-97 1

Barbecue
$11-$21

A perennial favorite, the roadside grill barbecues tasty chicken, ribs, lobster and fish. Affordably priced dishes are great for take-out or dine in. All plates come with french fries or salad. Casual dress. **Bar:** Full bar. **Hours:** noon-4 & 7-11 pm. Closed: Sun. **Address:** Montauban **Location:** In Montauban. **Parking:** on-site. **Cards:** AX, DC, MC, VI.

(See map and index starting on p. 444)

L'AGOUBA RESTAURANT DAMPIERRE GRILL **Phone:** 590/590-68-14-50 (15)

Barbecue
$11-$21

A perennial favorite for the locals, this roadside grillade barbecues some tasty chicken, ribs, lobster and fish at affordable prices. Great for take-away or dine-in, all plates have the option of french fry or salad accompaniments. Casual dress. **Bar:** Full bar. **Hours:** noon-4 & 7-11 pm. Closed: Sun. **Address:** Rt de Dampierre **Location:** Just e of town. **Parking:** on-site. **Cards:** AX, DC, MC, VI.

LA MANDALA **Phone:** 590/590-20-39-87 (37)

International
$17-$31

On the ever-popular marina restaurant row, the waterfront restaurant offers interior or al fresco seating. The menu centers on Asian and French cuisine, including a full sushi-sashimi menu, beef tartare, fresh fish and duck. Each dish has an artistically detailed presentation. For dessert, it's worth savoring the warm chocolate fondant. Dressy casual. **Bar:** Full bar. **Reservations:** suggested. **Hours:** noon-3 & 7-11 pm, Sat & Sun from 7 pm. **Address:** La Marina Gosier 9 Quai **Location:** At Marina de Pointe-a-Pitre/Gosier. **Parking:** street. **Cards:** CB, MC, VI.

LE BANANIER **Phone:** 590/590-84-34-85 (8)

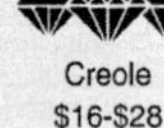

Creole
$16-$28

In a cozy Creole-style house, the restaurant creates delicious French-Creole cuisine. Formal-style service is enhanced with the theatrics of tableside flambe. The vast menu lists preparations of beef, lamb, pork, beef and fresh seafood, including lobster. The ubiquitous foie gras seen on most Guadeloupe menus is here as well and should not be missed. Dressy casual. **Bar:** Full bar. **Reservations:** suggested. **Hours:** Open 12/1-8/31 & 10/7-11/30; noon-2 & 7-10 pm. Closed: Sun & Mon. **Address:** Montauban **Location:** On Pointe de la Verdure; 6.2 mi (10 km) se from Pointe-a-Pitre Airport. **Parking:** on-site. **Cards:** AX, DC, MC, VI.

LE CAFE DES ARTS **Phone:** 590/590-20-17-80 (38)

Seafood
$24-$40

Recently renovated in decor that follows feng shui, the popular restaurant has a following among European screen stars. The fisherman's platter of select exotic seafood is renowned as among the best on the island. Also on the menu are foie gras, roasted onglet and artistically prepared duck and lamb dishes. A trip here is not complete without one of the exquisite desserts. Service, including that provided by the personable and colorful maitre d', is attentively refined. Dressy casual. **Bar:** Full bar. **Reservations:** suggested. **Hours:** 7 pm-11 pm. Closed: Mon. **Address:** 11 La Marina **Location:** At Marina de Pointe-A-Pitre. **Parking:** on-site. **Cards:** CB, MC, VI.

LE PIRATE CARIBEEN **Phone:** 590/590-90-73-00 (34)

Creole
$15-$30

Seafood and Creole dishes are served on a garden terrace along the marina's restaurant row. A good choice is assiette pirate: a bountiful sampler plate of crudites, fish accras, Tahitian-style fish, pulled barbecue chicken, crab farci, boudin Antilles and various salads. At noon, a planteur cocktail or ti punch is on the house. Tanks full of enormous live lobsters lend to the decor. **Bar:** Full bar. **Reservations:** suggested. **Hours:** 8 am-1 am. **Address:** La Marina Pointe-A-Pitre #1 **Location:** At Marina de Pointe-A-Pitre/Gosier. **Parking:** on-site. **Cards:** CB, MC, VI.

LES LANGOUSTES GRILL-RESTAURANT **Phone:** 590/590-90-85-43 (2)

Creole
$18-$33

Lobster tanks fill the room of this rustic, nautical-themed eatery. Enjoy flavorful Creole dishes with a broad selection from the extensive menu including over five types of fish prepared various ways, conch, lobster, accras, crab farci and boudin. Casual, prompt and efficient service. Casual dress. **Bar:** Full bar. **Reservations:** accepted. **Hours:** noon-3 & 7-11 pm. **Address:** Bas du Fort **Location:** At Bas du Fort; next to Hotel Novotel. **Parking:** on-site. **Cards:** AX, MC, VI.

LE TAM TAM **Phone:** 590/590-84-07-08 (14)

Creole
$12-$30

Natives beat the tam-tam (drum), and locals and tourists alike beat a path to the popular eatery for hearty and satisfying meals. The young, no-nonsense wait staff serves French Creole cuisine—including such signature dishes as boudin, farci, fish blaff, chevil, goat and colombo—in an al fresco garden atmosphere. Casual dress. **Bar:** Full bar. **Hours:** 11 am-1 am. **Address:** Rue Montauban **Location:** Montauban section; center. **Parking:** on-site. **Cards:** CB, MC, VI.

RESTAURANT ROSINI **Phone:** 590/590-90-87-81 (4)

Northern Italian
$16-$34

Near tourist hotels in the Bas du Fort area, the restaurant tempts diners with freshly prepared Italian cuisine, including a wide selection of homemade pasta, pizzas and meats. The service is warm and personable. The relaxed family feel appeals to locals and tourists alike. Dressy casual. **Bar:** Full bar. **Reservations:** suggested. **Hours:** noon-2:30 & 6:30-10:30 pm. Closed: 12/25. **Address:** La Porte des Carabies **Location:** In Bas du Fort. **Parking:** on-site. **Cards:** AX, MC, VI.

VILLA FLEUR D'EPEE **Phone:** 590/590-90-86-59 (7)

French
$105

Up a winding hill in a tranquil area, the restaurant's setting is peaceful and relaxing. The menu features an exotic blend of French and island cuisine. Favorites include shredded coconut salad, simmered shrimp in spicy Creole sauce with grilled plantains and house-prepared dessert. Bright, tropical artwork adds to the charm of the cozy dining room, while the small outdoor veranda is ideal for sipping a drink. Dressy casual. **Bar:** Full bar. **Reservations:** required. **Hours:** 7:30 pm-10 pm. Closed: 1/1, 12/24, 12/25; also 12/31, 1/2, Sun & Mon. **Address:** Rue du Fort Fleur d'Epee **Location:** In Bas-du-Fort; 3.3 mi (5.3 km) se of Pointe-a-Pitre, follow signs. **Parking:** street. **Cards:** AX, MC, VI.

POINTE-A-PITRE pop. 20,948 (See map and index starting on p. 444)

WHERE TO DINE

COTE DU BOEUF — Phone: 590/590-21-23-59 (40)

Steak & Seafood
$18-$38

Outdoor seats afford the best views of the marina, but if a controlled climate is a higher priority, the air-conditioned indoor seats meet that need. The menu focuses mainly on various beef preparations but also lists pork, chicken and local and imported seafood. Casual dress. **Bar:** Full bar. **Reservations:** suggested, weekends. **Hours:** noon-2:30 & 7-11 pm, Fri & Sat-11:30 pm. Closed: 12/25. **Address:** La Marina Pointe-a-Pitre **Location:** At Marina de Pointe-a-Pitre. **Parking:** on-site. **Cards:** MC, VI.

COTE JARDIN — Phone: 590/590-90-91-28 (41)

French
$16-$38

Tucked in a quiet corner of the busy Pointe-a-Pitre Marina, the restaurant treats guests to an exceptional menu of fine French cuisine. Sophistication—in the form of rich sauces and specialty ingredients—marks each made-to-order course. Charming French country appointments lend character to the quaint dining room, where diners can hear chefs assembling their creations from the open-concept kitchen. Dressy casual. **Bar:** Full bar. **Reservations:** suggested. **Hours:** noon-2 & 7:30-10 pm, Sat from 7:30 pm. Closed: Sun. **Address:** La Marina, Pointe-a-Pitre **Location:** At Marina de Pointe-a-Pitre. **Parking:** street. **Cards:** AX, CB, MC, VI.

LA ROUTE DU RHUM — Phone: 590/590-90-90-00 (42)

Creole
$17-$39

Extra attention is given to plate presentation at this waterfront marina eatery. The easygoing wait staff serves French West Indies Creole cuisine, including crevettes, lambi, boudin, christophene, Colombo and accras. Two local fish worth trying are dorado and red snapper. Flan du coco, mousse and creme brulee provide a sweet finishing touch. Casual dress. **Bar:** Full bar. **Reservations:** accepted. **Hours:** noon-3 & 7-11 pm. Closed: Sun. **Address:** Bas du Fort Marina **Location:** At Marina de Pointe-A-Pitre; Bas du Fort. **Parking:** street. **Cards:** AX, CB, DC, MC, VI.

AC

SAINTE ANNE pop. 20,410 (See map and index starting on p. 444)

WHERE TO STAY

HOTEL LA TOUBANA — Phone: (590)590-88-25-78 (8)

Cottage
$260-$345 All Year

Address: 97180 Fonds Thezan **Location:** Oceanfront. 1 mi (1.6 km) w of town village, then just s; follow signs. **Facility:** Perched on a hillside with an infinity pool and overlooking the beach. All individually decorated garden or ocean view cottages come with a terrace. 32 cottages. 1 story, exterior corridors. **Parking:** on-site. **Terms:** 7 day cancellation notice-fee imposed. **Amenities:** safes, hair dryers. **Pool(s):** outdoor. **Leisure Activities:** whirlpool, snorkeling. **Guest Services:** valet laundry, wireless Internet. **Cards:** AX, MC, VI.

WHERE TO DINE

CHEZ DOUDOU — Phone: 590/590-23-08-65 (21)

Creole
$13-$23

Oceanfront at Sainte Anne's well-known beach, the covered, open-air eatery features farcis made with conch, crab and christophene. Popular entrees include ribs, chicken, poached fish blaff and Colombo carbi, a spicy curry goat dish. DouDou is French Creole for "attractive lady.". Casual dress. **Bar:** Full bar. **Hours:** noon-10 pm. **Address:** Rue Plage de Sainte Anne **Location:** Center; on Plage Sainte Anne, follow signs. **Parking:** on-site.

AC

(See map and index starting on p. 444)

KOTE SUD LE RESTAURANT — Phone: 590/590-88-17-31 (18)

Creole
$17-$30

The popular restaurant earns rave reviews from locals and tourists alike. The Creole-style home's covered porch creates a casual ambience for al fresco dining. Food is the highlight here. Choices from the ever-changing menu might include ostrich, Tahitian-style fish, brochette of conch and grilled red snapper with fennel emulsion. Dressy casual. **Bar:** Full bar. **Reservations:** suggested. **Hours:** Open 12/1-9/8 & 10/1-11/30; 7 pm-10:30 pm, Fri & Sat-11 pm. **Address:** 16 Lot Dore Durivage **Location:** 0.8 mi (1.2 km) w of town; just s, follow signs; on Route de Rotabas. **Parking:** street. **Cards:** AX, CB, DC, MC, VI.

LE BANANERAIE — Phone: 590/590-85-35-41 (19)

Creole
$20-$35

Tasteful decor complements the charming West Indies Creole-style cottage, where guests sit down to well-prepared French and Creole dishes listed on the blackboard menu. Beef, lamb, conch and local fish are deftly prepared and served by a pleasant hostess. Casual dress. **Bar:** Full bar. **Reservations:** suggested. **Hours:** 7 pm-10 pm. Closed: Sun & Mon 5/1-12/5. **Address:** 180 Dupier **Location:** Just w of town. **Parking:** on-site. **Cards:** MC, VI.

ST. FRANCOIS pop. 10,659 (See map and index starting on p. 444)

WHERE TO DINE

CHEZ MAN MICHEL — Phone: 590/590-88-72-79 (26)

Creole
$12-$25

Just a short walk from the beach is the rustic al fresco eatery, which serves home-style Creole cuisine. Fish blaff, court-bouillon fish and conch, as well as goat and chicken Colombo, are house specialties. A selection of salads, accras and crab farci accompanies the entrees. The broad choice of ice creams cools the after-dinner palate. Casual dress. **Bar:** Full bar. **Hours:** noon-10 pm. **Address:** Plage de Tarare **Location:** At Pointe des Chateaux; Plage de Tarare; east coast of island. **Parking:** on-site.

LA DINETTE GOURMANDE — Phone: 590/590-90-14-79 (25)

International
$13-$25

A bit off the beaten path, the restaurant is worth the drive to the outskirts of town. The groovy little place has an ever-changing menu of creative tapas. Service is pleasant in the relaxed atmosphere. Casual dress. **Bar:** Full bar. **Reservations:** accepted. **Hours:** 7 pm-10 pm, Sun noon-9 pm. Closed: Mon. **Address:** La Coulee **Location:** Just n of St. Francois; on route de la Pointe des Chateaux. **Parking:** on-site. **Cards:** MC, VI.

RESTO DES ARTISTES — Phone: 590/590-88-75-44 (27)

Creole
$15-$30

Laid-back servers circulate through the cozy and familiar marina-front al fresco restaurant. Large entree-size salads are dressed with duck, seafood, chicken or beef, and seafood entrees can be steamed, grilled or sauteed. A local dish especially worth trying is Colombo de porc, a Creole curry dish. Casual dress. **Bar:** Full bar. **Reservations:** accepted. **Hours:** noon-3 & 7-11 pm. **Address:** Marina Golf **Location:** 0.6 mi (1 km) from town; at Marina Golf. **Parking:** street. **Cards:** MC, VI.

Marie-Galante Island

CAPESTERRE pop. 3,559 (See map and index starting on p. 444)

WHERE TO STAY

CAP RE'VA RESIDENCE HOTELIERE Phone: 590/590-97-50-00 25

Hotel
$83-$177 All Year

Address: Plage de la Feuillere **Location:** Just s; on southeast coast. **Facility:** 32 units. 20 one-bedroom standard units with kitchens. 12 one-bedroom suites with kitchens. 2 stories (no elevator), exterior corridors. **Parking:** on-site. **Amenities:** hair dryers. **Pool(s):** outdoor. **Leisure Activities:** volleyball. *Fee:* scuba diving, snorkeling, bicycles, massage. **Guest Services:** valet laundry. **Business Services:** meeting rooms, PC (fee). **Cards:** AX, CB, MC, VI.

/ SOME UNITS

WHERE TO DINE

LA BRAISE MARINE Phone: 590/590-97-42-57 31

Caribbean
$9-$22

Savor the quaint surroundings of this husband-and-wife-operated seaside eatery on the south coast. Order from the blackboard menu that changes often. Chicken Colombo is the house specialty but goat, beef and fresh fish are also offered. Casual dress. **Bar:** Full bar. **Reservations:** accepted. **Hours:** noon-3 & 6-10 pm. **Address:** rue Marine **Location:** Just s of Capesterre; across from Plaige Ferriere. **Parking:** on-site.

ST. LOUIS pop. 2,995 (See map and index starting on p. 444)

WHERE TO STAY

LA COHOBA HOTEL Book at AAA.com Phone: (590)590-97-50-50 19

Hotel
$174-$249 All Year

Address: Cocoyer **Location:** Oceanfront. Just s of St. Louis; at Folle Anse. **Facility:** 100 units. 60 one-bedroom standard units. 40 one-bedroom suites with efficiencies. 1-2 stories (no elevator), exterior corridors. *Bath:* shower only. **Parking:** on-site. **Terms:** 21 day cancellation notice-fee imposed. **Amenities:** safes, hair dryers. **Pool(s):** outdoor. **Leisure Activities:** beach access, volleyball, game room. *Fee:* snorkeling, 2 lighted tennis courts, bicycles. **Guest Services:** wireless Internet. **Business Services:** meeting rooms. **Cards:** AX, MC, VI.

ASK / SOME UNITS

JAMAICA

This index helps you "spot" where approved lodgings and restaurants are located on the corresponding detailed maps. Lodging daily rate range is for comparison only and show the property's high season. Restaurant rate range is a combination of lunch and/or dinner. Turn to the listing page for more detailed rate information and consult display ads for special promotions.

KINGSTON

Map Page	OA	Lodgings	Diamond Rated	High Season	Page
1 / p. 453		Hilton Kingston Jamaica - see color ad opposite title page	◆◆◆	$229-$269	454
2 / p. 453		The Jamaica Pegasus Hotel	◆◆	$180-$300	455
7 / p. 453		The Courtleigh Hotel & Suites	◆◆◆	$145-$400	454

Map Page	OA	Restaurants	Diamond Rated	Cuisine	Meal Range	Page
1 / p. 453		Norma's on the Terrace	◆◆◆	Jamaican	$11-$32	455
2 / p. 453		Redbones-The Blues Cafe	◆◆◆	New Jamaican	$11-$30	455
4 / p. 453		Heather's Garden Restaurant and Bar	◆◆	International	$7-$21	455
6 / p. 453		Jade Garden Restaurant	◆◆◆	Chinese	$12-$40	455

HOPEWELL

Map Page	OA	Lodging	Diamond Rated	High Season	Page
8 / p. 453		Round Hill Hotel and Villas	◆◆◆◆	$410-$2820	454

MONTEGO BAY

Map Page	OA	Lodgings	Diamond Rated	High Season	Page
10 / p. 453	AAA	**Sunset Beach Resort & Spa**	◆◆◆	$260-$560 SAVE	457
11 / p. 453	AAA	**Half Moon - see color ad p 463**	◆◆◆◆	$250-$1680 SAVE	456
12 / p. 453		Holiday Inn SunSpree Resort Montego Bay - see color ad p 456	◆◆◆	$315-$415	456
16 / p. 453		Coyaba Beach Resort & Club	◆◆◆	$230-$440	456

Map Page	OA	Restaurants	Diamond Rated	Cuisine	Meal Range	Page
8 / p. 453		The Houseboat Grill	◆◆	International	$15-$29	457
11 / p. 453		Marguerite's	◆◆◆	Caribbean	$25-$53	457
13 / p. 453		Pelican Grill	◆	Jamaican	$10-$30	457
15 / p. 453		The Native Restaurant & Bar	◆◆	Jamaican	$9-$30	457
16 / p. 453		The Royal Stocks English Pub & Steakhouse	◆◆	English	$10-$30	457
17 / p. 453		The Akbar Restaurant	◆◆	Indian	$11-$30	457

ROSE HALL

Map Page	OA	Lodgings	Diamond Rated	High Season	Page
18 / p. 453	AAA	**Rose Hall Resort & Spa, a Hilton Resort**	◆◆◆	$123-$557 SAVE	464
19 / p. 453	AAA	**The Ritz-Carlton Golf & Spa Resort, Rose Hall, Jamaica**	◆◆◆◆◆	$279-$1100 SAVE	463

Map Page	OA	Restaurants	Diamond Rated	Cuisine	Meal Range	Page
18 / p. 453		Sugar Mill Restaurant	◆◆◆	Jamaican	$19-$35	464
19 / p. 453		Jasmine	◆◆◆◆	Caribbean	$35-$50	464
23 / p. 453		Luna di Mare	◆◆◆	Italian	$20-$34	464
24 / p. 453		Three Palms	◆◆◆	Jamaican	$24-$38	465

OCHO RIOS

Map Page	OA	Lodgings	Diamond Rated	High Season	Page
21 / p. 453		Club Hotel Riu Ocho Rios	◆◆◆	Rates not provided	460
24 / p. 453		Couples Sans Souci	◆◆◆◆	$614-$1000	460
25 / p. 453	AAA	**Hibiscus Lodge Hotel**	◆	$140-$229 SAVE	460
26 / p. 453	AAA	**Jamaica Inn**	◆◆◆◆	$290-$1760 SAVE	460

Map Page	OA	Restaurants	Diamond Rated	Cuisine	Meal Range	Page
29 / p. 453	AAA	**Evita's**	◆◆	Italian	$11-$29	461
31 / p. 453	AAA	**The Almond Tree Restaurant**	◆◆	International	$12-$33	461
32 / p. 453		Jamaica Inn Dining Room	◆◆◆	Continental	$14-$46	461
36 / p. 453		Passage to India	◆◆	Indian	$10-$26	462
37 / p. 453		Blue Runnings	◆◆	Jamaican	$10-$17	461
38 / p. 453		Toscanini Italian Restaurant	◆◆◆	Italian	$15-$29	462

NEGRIL

Map Page	OA	Lodgings	Diamond Rated	High Season	Page
38 / p. 453		Club Hotel Riu Negril	◆◆◆	$260-$338	458
39 / p. 453		Riu Tropical Bay	◆◆◆	Rates not provided	458
42 / p. 453	AAA	**Grand Lido Negril Resort & Spa**	◆◆◆◆	$558-$1430 SAVE	458
43 / p. 453		Rondel Village	◆◆	$75-$260	459
45 / p. 453		Couples Swept Away	◆◆◆	$269-$703	458
46 / p. 453		Couples Negril	◆◆◆	Rates not provided	458
48 / p. 453	AAA	**Sea Splash**	◆◆	$83-$227 SAVE	459
51 / p. 453		The Caves	◆◆◆	$495-$875	458

Map Page	OA	Restaurants	Diamond Rated	Cuisine	Meal Range	Page
39 / p. 453		Cosmo's Seafood Restaurant	◆	Jamaican	$6-$22	459
40 / p. 453	AAA	**Norma's Restaurant at Sea Splash Resort**	◆◆◆	Jamaican	$10-$32	459
45 / p. 453		Sweet Spice Restaurant	◆	Jamaican	$10-$20	460
49 / p. 453		Rock House Restaurant	◆◆	Jamaican	$11-$22	460
51 / p. 453		Rick's Cafe	◆◆	American	$8-$24	459

Map Page	OA	Restaurants (cont'd)	Diamond Rated	Cuisine	Meal Range	Page
52 / p. 453		Xtabi On The Cliff	◆◆	Jamaican	$10-$26	460

PORT ANTONIO

Map Page	OA	Lodging	Diamond Rated	High Season	Page
55 / p. 453		Jamaica Palace Hotel	◆◆	$170-$400	462

Map Page	OA	Restaurant	Diamond Rated	Cuisine	Meal Range	Page
54 / p. 453		Panorama Restaurant and Lounge	◆◆	Jamaican	$12-$27	462

SANDY BAY

Map Page	OA	Lodging	Diamond Rated	High Season	Page
57 / p. 453	AAA	**Tryall Club**	◆◆◆	$345-$2600 SAVE	465

IRISH TOWN

Map Page	OA	Lodging	Diamond Rated	High Season	Page
59 / p. 453		Strawberry Hill	◆◆◆	$275-$775	454

RIO BUENO

Map Page	OA	Lodging	Diamond Rated	High Season	Page
61 / p. 453	AAA	**Grand Lido Braco Resort & Spa**	◆◆◆◆	$400-$1400 SAVE	462

RUNAWAY BAY

Map Page	OA	Lodging	Diamond Rated	High Season	Page
63 / p. 453		Superclubs Breezes Runaway Bay Resort & Golf Club	◆◆◆	$193-$384	465

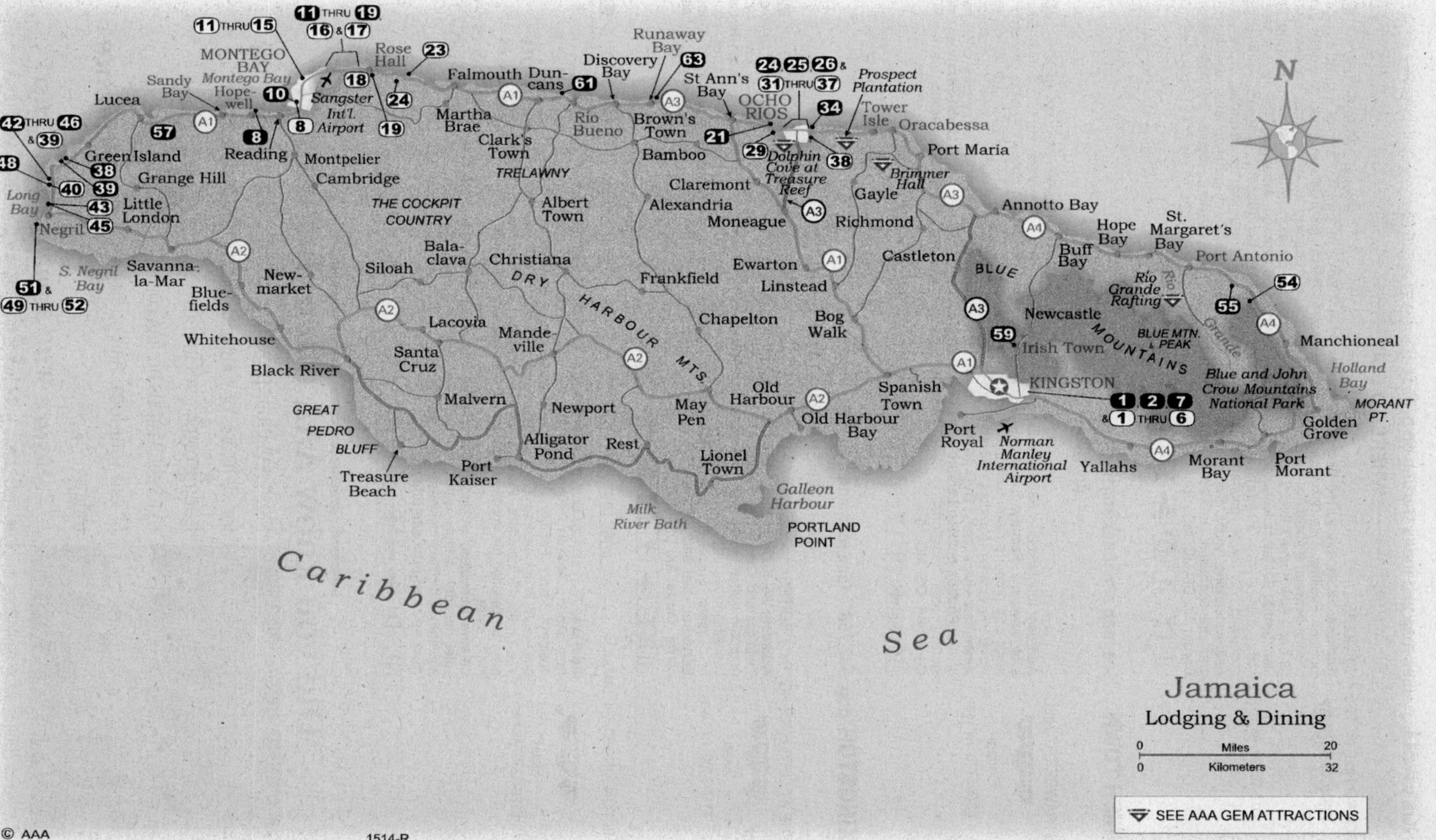

Jamaica
Lodging & Dining
Miles
Kilometers
0
20
32
SEE AAA GEM ATTRACTIONS
N
Caribbean
Sea
MONTEGO BAY
Montego Bay
Sangster Int'l. Airport
Rose Hall
Falmouth
Martha Brae
Duncans
Rio Bueno
Discovery Bay
Runaway Bay
St Ann's Bay
Brown's Town
OCHO RIOS
Dolphin Cove at Treasure Reef
Tower Isle
Prospect Plantation
Oracabessa
Port Maria
Brimmer Hall
Annotto Bay
Buff Bay
Hope Bay
St. Margaret's Bay
Port Antonio
Rio Grande
Rio Grande Rafting
BLUE MOUNTAINS
BLUE MTN. PEAK
Blue and John Crow Mountains National Park
Manchioneal
Holland Bay
MORANT PT.
Golden Grove
Port Morant
Morant Bay
Yallahs
KINGSTON
Irish Town
Newcastle
Norman Manley International Airport
Port Royal
Spanish Town
Old Harbour Bay
Old Harbour
Bog Walk
Linstead
Ewarton
Moneague
Richmond
Gayle
Castleton
PORTLAND POINT
Galleon Harbour
Lionel Town
May Pen
Rest
Milk River Bath
Chapelton
Frankfield
Claremont
Alexandria
Bamboo
Albert Town
TRELAWNY
Clark's Town
Christiana
DRY HARBOUR MTS.
Mandeville
Newport
Alligator Pond
Port Kaiser
Malvern
Lacovia
Santa Cruz
Balaclava
Siloah
THE COCKPIT COUNTRY
Cambridge
Montpelier
Reading
Hopewell
Sandy Bay
Lucea
Green Island
Grange Hill
Little London
Negril
Long Bay
S. Negril Bay
Savanna-la-Mar
Bluefields
Newmarket
Whitehouse
Black River
GREAT PEDRO BLUFF
Treasure Beach
A1
A2
A3
A4
© AAA
1514-R

HOPEWELL (See map and index starting on p. 453)

WHERE TO STAY

ROUND HILL HOTEL AND VILLAS Phone: 876/956-7050 8

Resort Hotel
$410-$2820 All Year

Address: Rt A1, Round Hill Bluff **Location:** 1.1 mi (1.7 km) e of town. Located in a quiet secluded location. **Facility:** This beachfront setting offers scenic hillside grounds and gardens. Guests may choose between a traditional hotel unit or an upscale villa. 110 units. 36 one-bedroom standard units. 59 one-, 8 two- and 7 three-bedroom suites. 1-2 stories (no elevator), exterior corridors. **Parking:** on-site. **Terms:** 30 day cancellation notice, 14 day in winter-fee imposed. **Amenities:** CD players, safes, irons, hair dryers. **Pool(s):** outdoor. **Leisure Activities:** paddleboats, sailboats, windsurfing, snorkeling, 5 tennis courts (2 lighted), recreation programs, jogging, exercise room, spa. *Fee:* waterskiing, scuba diving, charter fishing. **Guest Services:** TV in common area, valet laundry, area transportation, wireless Internet. **Business Services:** meeting rooms, business center. **Cards:** AX, DC, JC, MC, VI.

IRISH TOWN (See map and index starting on p. 453)

WHERE TO STAY

STRAWBERRY HILL Phone: (876)944-8400 59

Cottage
$275-$775 All Year

Address: Kingston Bluff Bay Rd **Location:** N of Kingston on Kingston Bluff Bay Rd (B1), 6 mi (9.6 km) s of Newcastle. **Facility:** Set in the scenic Blue Mountains, 3,100 feet above Kingston, this stylish, rustic-chic property offers well-appointed cottages and common areas. 13 cottages. 1-2 stories (no elevator), exterior corridors. **Parking:** on-site. **Terms:** 14 day cancellation notice-fee imposed. **Amenities:** video library, DVD players, CD players, high-speed Internet, safes, honor bars, irons, hair dryers. **Pool(s):** outdoor. **Leisure Activities:** sauna, exercise room, spa, yoga. **Guest Services:** valet laundry, area transportation (fee), wireless Internet. **Business Services:** meeting rooms, PC. **Cards:** AX, DS, MC, VI.

ASK FEE / SOME UNITS

KINGSTON pop. 587,798 (See map and index starting on p. 453)

WHERE TO STAY

THE COURTLEIGH HOTEL & SUITES Book at AAA.com Phone: (876)929-9000 7

Hotel
$145-$400 All Year

Address: 85 Knutsford Blvd **Location:** In New Kingston; 14 mi (22.4 km) from airport; between Trafalgar and Oxford rds. **Facility:** 127 units. 89 one-bedroom standard units. 37 one- and 1 two-bedroom suites, some with efficiencies. 1-10 stories, interior corridors. **Parking:** on-site. **Terms:** cancellation fee imposed. **Amenities:** high-speed Internet, dual phone lines, voice mail, safes, irons, hair dryers. *Some:* CD players, fax. **Pool(s):** outdoor. **Leisure Activities:** exercise room. **Guest Services:** valet and coin laundry, wireless Internet. **Business Services:** meeting rooms, business center. **Cards:** AX, DS, MC, VI.

/ SOME UNITS

HILTON KINGSTON JAMAICA Book great rates at AAA.com Phone: (876)926-5430 1

Hotel
$229-$269 All Year

Address: 77 Knutsford Blvd **Location:** In New Kingston; 14 mi (22.4 km) from airport; between Trafalgar and Oxford rds. Located in the downtown business district. **Facility:** 303 units. 290 one-bedroom standard units. 11 one- and 2 two-bedroom suites, some with whirlpools. 2-17 stories, interior/exterior corridors. **Parking:** on-site. **Terms:** 1-30 night minimum stay, cancellation fee imposed. **Amenities:** high-speed Internet (fee), voice mail, safes, irons, hair dryers. *Some:* CD players. **Pool(s):** outdoor. **Leisure Activities:** whirlpool. *Fee:* saunas, massage. **Guest Services:** valet laundry, beauty salon, wireless Internet. **Business Services:** conference facilities, business center. **Cards:** AX, DC, DS, JC, MC, VI.
(See color ad opposite title page)

FEE / SOME UNITS

(See map and index starting on p. 453)

THE JAMAICA PEGASUS HOTEL *Book at AAA.com* **Phone:** (876)926-3690 2

Hotel

$180-$300 All Year

Address: 81 Knutsford Blvd **Location:** In New Kingston; 14 mi (22.4 km) from airport; between Trafalgar and Oxford rds. Located in the downtown business district. **Facility:** 300 units. 280 one-bedroom standard units. 17 one- and 3 two-bedroom suites, some with whirlpools. 17 stories, interior corridors. **Parking:** on-site. **Amenities:** voice mail, safes, irons, hair dryers. *Some:* DVD players, CD players, high-speed Internet (fee), dual phone lines, honor bars. **Pool(s):** outdoor. **Leisure Activities:** jogging, exercise room, massage. *Fee:* 2 lighted tennis courts. **Guest Services:** valet laundry, wireless Internet. **Business Services:** conference facilities, business center. **Cards:** AX, DC, DS, MC, VI.

SOME UNITS VCR

WHERE TO DINE

HEATHER'S GARDEN RESTAURANT AND BAR **Phone:** 876/926-2826 4

International

$7-$21

English and Middle Eastern specialties, along with some Jamaican dishes, are offered. Many American and other expatriates in Kingston frequent the pleasant, informal restaurant bar. The covered garden-view terrace, kept cool by ceiling fans, is a popular dining spot. Casual dress. **Bar:** Full bar. **Reservations:** accepted. **Hours:** 10 am-11:30 pm. Closed major holidays; also Sun. **Address:** 9 Haining Rd **Location:** In New Kingston; on Haining Rd off Oxford Rd. **Parking:** on-site. **Cards:** AX, MC, VI.

JADE GARDEN RESTAURANT **Phone:** 876/978-3476 6

Chinese

$12-$40

On the second floor of an upscale shopping center near a movie theater, the pleasant, cool and comfortable restaurant presents an extensive menu of Chinese fare. The well-attired wait staff provides formalized, attentive service. Dressy casual. **Bar:** Full bar. **Reservations:** accepted. **Hours:** noon-10 pm, Sun 11 am-9 pm. Closed major holidays. **Address:** 106 Hope Rd **Location:** Corner of Hope and Barbican rds; in Sovereign Shopping Center. **Parking:** on-site. **Cards:** AX, MC, VI.

NORMA'S ON THE TERRACE **Phone:** 876/968-5488 1

Jamaican

$11-$32

Located on the verandah of the mansion of the first native Jamaican millionaire is the restaurant of celebrity chef Norma Shirley. The menu utilizes many fresh local ingredients. Try the smoked marlin as an appetizer, or the flavorful island salad. Jerked pork, escoveitch fish, oxtail stew and curried goat are some of the favorites that line the menu. Tempting desserts like bread pudding and orange infused trifle are hard to pass up. Dressy casual. **Bar:** Full bar. **Reservations:** suggested. **Hours:** 10 am-10 pm. Closed major holidays; also Sun & Good Friday. **Address:** 26 Hope Rd **Location:** Just n of New Kingston; corner of Hope and Waterloo rds; in Devon House. **Parking:** on-site. **Cards:** AX, DS, MC, VI. **Historic**

REDBONES-THE BLUES CAFE **Phone:** 876/978-8262 2

New Jamaican

$11-$30

The vibrantly decorated restaurant with a jazz-inspired theme was once a Spanish-colonial house. The husband and wife owners designed the restaurant to create an ambience to complement the nouvelle Jamaican cuisine. The menu changes frequently but the uptown comfort food may include dishes such as the grilled baby lamb chops with glazed guava or grilled fish in a caper-lime sauce. Save room for the sweet potato pudding. Dressy casual. **Bar:** Full bar. **Reservations:** suggested. **Hours:** noon-11 pm. Closed: 1/1, 12/25, 12/26; also Sun & Good Friday. **Address:** 21 Braemar Ave **Location:** Center New Kingston; off Oxford Rd. **Parking:** on-site. **Cards:** AX, DS, MC, VI.

MONTEGO BAY pop. 83,446 (See map and index starting on p. 453)

WHERE TO STAY

COYABA BEACH RESORT & CLUB *Book at AAA.com* **Phone:** (876)953-9150 **16**

Hotel
$230-$440 All Year

Address: Mahoe Bay, Rosehall **Location:** 6.3 mi (10 km) e on Rt A1; 4.2 mi (6.7 km) e of airport. **Facility:** Meets AAA guest room security requirements. 50 one-bedroom standard units. 3 stories (no elevator), interior/exterior corridors. **Parking:** on-site. **Terms:** age restrictions may apply, 14 day cancellation notice. **Amenities:** video library (fee), CD players, voice mail, safes, irons, hair dryers. *Some:* DVD players. **Pool(s):** outdoor. **Leisure Activities:** whirlpool, lifeguard on duty, limited beach access, boating, paddleboats, sailboats, windsurfing, boat dock, snorkeling, lighted tennis court, playground, exercise room, spa, game room. **Guest Services:** valet laundry, wireless Internet. **Business Services:** meeting rooms, PC (fee). **Cards:** AX, DS, MC, VI.

A$K D VCR / SOME UNITS FEE

HALF MOON **Phone:** (876)953-2211 **11**

AAA SAVE

Resort Hotel
$250-$1680 All Year

Address: Rt A1 **Location:** Oceanfront. 7.6 mi (12.1 km) e on Rt A1; 5.1 mi (8.1 km) e of airport. Located in a gated area. **Facility:** This renovated oceanfront resort offers mostly spacious guest rooms and suites as well as staffed villas and extensive recreational facilities. 398 units. 259 one-bedroom standard units. 98 one-, 9 two- and 32 three-bedroom suites, some with efficiencies or kitchens. 1-2 stories (no elevator), interior/exterior corridors. **Parking:** on-site. **Terms:** 3 day cancellation notice-fee imposed. **Amenities:** high-speed Internet, dual phone lines, voice mail, safes, honor bars, irons, hair dryers. *Some:* DVD players, CD players, fax. **Dining:** 6 restaurants, also, Sugar Mill Restaurant, see separate listing, entertainment. **Pool(s):** 3 outdoor. **Leisure Activities:** whirlpools, lifeguard on duty, limited beach access, rental sailboats, miniature golf, 13 lighted tennis courts, squash-4 courts, recreation programs, aerobic instruction, badminton, bocci, internationally certified croquet court, rental bicycles, hiking trails, jogging, playground, spa, basketball, shuffleboard, volleyball, game room. *Fee:* saunas, steamrooms, paddleboats, windsurfing, waterskiing, scuba diving, snorkeling, fishing, golf-18 holes, golf instruction, tennis instruction, dolphin encounters, horseback riding. **Guest Services:** valet laundry, area transportation (fee)-Montego Bay, beauty salon, wireless Internet. **Business Services:** conference facilities, business center. **Cards:** AX, CB, DC, DS, JC, MC, VI. **Free Special Amenities: preferred room (subject to availability with advance reservations).** *(See color ad p 463)*

FEE D / SOME UNITS VCR

HOLIDAY INN SUNSPREE RESORT MONTEGO BAY **Phone:** (876)953-2485 **12**

Resort Hotel
$315-$415 All Year

Address: Queens Hwy (Rt A1) **Location:** 6.8 mi (10.8 km) e; 4.7 mi (7.5 km) e of airport. **Facility:** Built in the 1960s, this renovated family-oriented beachfront resort offers large rooms and spacious suites, all with balconies or patios. Meets AAA guest room security requirements. 524 units. 498 one-bedroom standard units. 26 one-bedroom suites with whirlpools. 4 stories, interior/exterior corridors. *Bath:* combo or shower only. **Parking:** on-site. **Terms:** 3 day cancellation notice-fee imposed. **Amenities:** voice mail, safes, irons, hair dryers. *Some:* DVD players (fee). **Pool(s):** 3 outdoor. **Leisure Activities:** whirlpools, lifeguard on duty, limited beach access, paddleboats, sailboats, windsurfing, snorkeling, miniature golf, 4 lighted tennis courts, recreation programs, playground, exercise room, basketball, shuffleboard, volleyball. *Fee:* scuba diving, massage, game room. **Guest Services:** valet and coin laundry, wireless Internet. **Business Services:** meeting rooms. *Fee:* administrative services, PC. **Cards:** AX, CB, DC, DS, MC, VI. *(See color ad below)*

A$K D / SOME UNITS FEE VCR

(See map and index starting on p. 453)

SUNSET BEACH RESORT & SPA *Book great rates at AAA.com* **Phone:** (876)979-8800 **10**

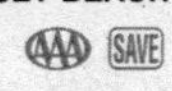

Resort Hotel

$260-$560 All Year

Address: Sunset Dr **Location:** 2.2 mi (3.6 km) sw of Montego Bay "Hip Strip"; 4.4 mi (7 km) sw of the airport. Near the "Freeport" cruise ship docks. **Facility:** Most of the property's rooms have been recently renovated in a tropical decor at this comprehensive, oceanfront resort with theme restaurants. 430 units. 423 one-bedroom standard units. 7 one-bedroom suites, some with whirlpools. 2-10 stories, exterior corridors. **Parking:** on-site. **Terms:** 3 night minimum stay - seasonal, 30 day cancellation notice-fee imposed. **Amenities:** voice mail, safes, irons, hair dryers. **Dining:** 5 restaurants, nightclub, entertainment. **Pool(s):** 4 outdoor. **Leisure Activities:** saunas, whirlpools, steamrooms, lifeguard on duty, limited beach access, paddleboats, sailboats, windsurfing, snorkeling, kayaks; waterpark, miniature golf, 4 lighted tennis courts, recreation programs, playground, spa, basketball, horseshoes, shuffleboard, volleyball, game room. *Fee:* slot machines. **Guest Services:** valet and coin laundry, beauty salon, wireless Internet. **Business Services:** meeting rooms, business center. **Cards:** AX, DS, MC, VI. **Free Special Amenities: early check-in/late check-out and room upgrade (subject to availability with advance reservations).**

/ SOME UNITS FEE

WHERE TO DINE

THE AKBAR RESTAURANT **Phone:** 876/953-8240 **17**

Indian

$11-$30

The menu lists both Indian and Thai dishes, which are prepared exquisitely with spiciness adjusted for the more timid and served on copper-plated dinnerware. Efficient servers circulate in the exotic Asian-decorated dining room. Complimentary transportation is provided to and from local hotels. Casual dress. **Bar:** Full bar. **Reservations:** accepted. **Hours:** noon-3:30 & 6-10:30 pm. **Address:** Half Moon Shopping Village **Location:** 7.6 mi (12 km) e on Rt A1; 5.1 mi w of airport; in Half Moon Shopping Village. **Parking:** on-site. **Cards:** AX, MC, VI.

CALL

THE HOUSEBOAT GRILL **Phone:** 876/979-8845 **8**

International

$15-$29

True to its name, the restaurant is truly a houseboat in the water. Guests are ferried across on a small barge to enjoy well-prepared cuisine. Examples of the types of dishes on the menu, which changes every three weeks, include smoked marlin dip and New Zealand mussels starters, fresh fish entrees, blue cheese-encrusted beef fillet and potato gnocchi in apple-hazelnut creme sauce. Warm banana cake with sabayon sauce is not to be missed. Dressy casual. **Bar:** Full bar. **Reservations:** required. **Hours:** 6 pm-10 pm. Closed: 1/1, 12/25. **Address:** Southern Cross Blvd **Location:** 2 mi (3.2 km) w of Montego Bay; in Montego Freeport District. **Parking:** on-site. **Cards:** MC, VI.

JIMMY BUFFET'S MARGARITAVILLE **Phone:** 876/952-4777

Caribbean

$12-$28

Amenities at the lively bayfront bar and grill include a water slide, floating trampolines and a terrace with a hot tub. Among Caribbean-style specialties are jerk chicken, mango snapper, conch, Jamaican pizza and lobster tail, all complemented by an impressive array of 52 varieties of margaritas. Musicians perform most nights. Casual dress. **Bar:** Full bar. **Hours:** 11 am-9:30 pm. **Address:** Glouster Ave **Location:** 2 mi (3.2 km) se of airport; just s of Doctor's Cave Beach; center of "Hip Strip". **Parking:** valet. **Cards:** AX, DS, MC, VI.

MARGUERITE'S **Phone:** 876/952-4777 **11**

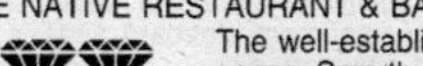

Caribbean

$25-$53

Overlooking the bay, the pleasant dining room affords beautiful sunset views. Menu offerings include preparations of regional fresh fish and seafood, such as lobster, shrimp, kingfish, tuna and red snapper, as well as pasta, chicken piccata and filet mignon. Cigar smoking is popular here. Dressy casual. **Bar:** Full bar. **Reservations:** suggested. **Hours:** 6 pm-10:30 pm. **Address:** Gloucester Ave **Location:** 2 mi (3.2 km) se of airport; just s of Doctor's Cave Beach; center of "Hip Strip". **Parking:** valet. **Cards:** MC, VI.

THE NATIVE RESTAURANT & BAR **Phone:** 876/979-2769 **15**

Jamaican

$9-$30

The well-established restaurant is perched on a terrace above the streets of the Hip Strip with views of the ocean. Smartly attired servers provide island-friendly service in the al fresco eatery adorned with Jamaican art. The extensive menu offers many Jamaican specialties including ackee, codfish fritters, stuffed crabback, oxtail stew and of course escoveitch fish. Casual dress. **Bar:** Full bar. **Reservations:** accepted. **Hours:** 7:30 am-10 pm. Closed: 12/25; also Good Friday. **Address:** 29 Gloucester Ave **Location:** Center of "Hip Strip". **Parking:** on-site. **Cards:** AX, DC, DS, MC, VI.

PELICAN GRILL **Phone:** 876/952-3171 **13**

Jamaican

$10-$30

Hearty, home-style meals are served in a Jamaican-style diner. Favorite selections include curried chicken and goat, escoveitch fish and callaloo soup. Be sure to try the lofty and luscious banana-rum cream pie. Casual dress. **Bar:** Full bar. **Hours:** 7 am-11 pm. **Address:** Gloucester Ave **Location:** In the "Hip Strip"; downtown. **Parking:** on-site. **Cards:** AX, MC, VI.

THE ROYAL STOCKS ENGLISH PUB & STEAKHOUSE **Phone:** 876/953-9770 **16**

English

$10-$30

Patrons can enjoy a taste of merry old England at the pub-style eatery. In addition to tender steaks, the menu lists local lobster and seafood dishes. Some of the more typical British preparations include bangers and mash, steak and kidney pie and shepherd's pie. Meals can be washed down with one of the many traditional ales. For entertainment, guests can watch cricket on the telly or play any of several games. Dressy casual. **Bar:** Full bar. **Reservations:** suggested. **Hours:** 10 am-10 pm. **Address:** #11 Half Moon Shopping Village **Location:** 7.6 mi (12.1 km) e on Rt A1; 5.1 mi (8.1 km) e of airport. **Parking:** on-site. **Cards:** AX, DS, MC, VI.

NEGRIL pop. 1,500 (See map and index starting on p. 453)

WHERE TO STAY

THE CAVES — Phone: (876)957-0270 — 51

Cottage
$495-$875 All Year

Address: Light House Rd **Location:** Oceanfront. 5 mi (8 km) s of Negril Airport via West End Rd; 2.1 mi (3.4 km) w of downtown. **Facility:** Stylish cliffside wooden cottages perched above grotto caves and honeycombed cliffs give this ocean-view property the ambience of a tropical oasis. 12 cottages. 1-2 stories, exterior corridors. *Bath:* combo or shower only. **Parking:** on-site. **Terms:** office hours 8:30 am-8:30 pm, age restrictions may apply, 30 day cancellation notice-fee imposed. **Amenities:** CD players, safes, honor bars, hair dryers. **Leisure Activities:** sauna, whirlpools, snorkeling, bicycles. *Fee:* massage. **Guest Services:** TV in common area, wireless Internet. **Business Services:** PC. **Cards:** AX, DC, DS, MC, VI.

ASK / SOME UNITS

CLUB HOTEL RIU NEGRIL — Book at AAA.com — Phone: (876)957-5700 — 38

Resort Hotel
$260-$338 All Year

Address: Norman Manley Blvd **Location:** Oceanfront. 1.2 mi (1.8 km) n of Negril Airport; 5.9 mi (9.4 km) n of downtown. **Facility:** This newly built, all-inclusive mega-resort is ideal for families, couples or singles and features lavish, elegantly appointed public areas. 420 one-bedroom standard units. 3 stories (no elevator), interior/exterior corridors. *Bath:* combo or shower only. **Parking:** on-site. **Terms:** 3 night minimum stay, 3 day cancellation notice-fee imposed. **Amenities:** safes, honor bars, hair dryers. **Pool(s):** 2 outdoor. **Leisure Activities:** saunas, whirlpool, steamroom, limited beach access, paddleboats, sailboats, windsurfing, 2 lighted tennis courts, recreation programs, playground, exercise room, spa, basketball, volleyball. *Fee:* scuba diving, snorkeling. **Guest Services:** valet laundry. **Business Services:** meeting rooms, PC (fee). **Cards:** AX, MC, VI.

ASK

COUPLES NEGRIL — Book great rates at AAA.com — Phone: 876/957-5960 — 46

Resort Hotel
Rates not provided

Address: Norman Manley Blvd **Location:** Oceanfront. Just n of Negril Airport; 4.8 mi (7.7 km) n of downtown. **Facility:** Built for romance, this couples-only resort is an idyllic escape. The spacious guest rooms are stylishly chic with a bright color scheme. 234 one-bedroom standard units, some with whirlpools. 3 stories (no elevator), exterior corridors. **Parking:** on-site. **Terms:** check-in 4 pm, age restrictions may apply. **Amenities:** CD players, voice mail, safes, irons, hair dryers. *Some:* honor bars. **Pool(s):** 2 outdoor. **Leisure Activities:** whirlpools, lifeguard on duty, boating, paddleboats, sailboats, windsurfing, waterskiing, scuba diving, snorkeling, 4 tennis courts (2 lighted), recreation programs, exercise room, spa, basketball, horseshoes, shuffleboard, volleyball, game room. **Guest Services:** valet laundry, wireless Internet. **Business Services:** PC.

COUPLES SWEPT AWAY — Phone: (876)957-4062 — 45

Resort Hotel
$269-$703 All Year

Address: Norman Manley Blvd **Location:** Oceanfront. 2.3 mi (3.6 km) s of Negril Airport; 2.4 mi (3.9 km) n of downtown. **Facility:** On the beach, this all-inclusive resort has an elaborate sports complex; the villa-style accommodations have large balconies or patio. 312 one-bedroom standard units. 2-3 stories (no elevator), exterior corridors. *Bath:* combo or shower only. **Parking:** on-site. **Terms:** 3 night minimum stay, age restrictions may apply, 30 day cancellation notice-fee imposed. **Amenities:** CD players, voice mail, safes, irons, hair dryers. *Some:* honor bars. **Pool(s):** 2 outdoor. **Leisure Activities:** saunas, whirlpools, steamrooms, paddleboats, sailboats, windsurfing, waterskiing, scuba diving, snorkeling, 10 lighted tennis courts, racquetball courts, recreation programs, jogging, spa, sports court, basketball, volleyball. *Fee:* charter fishing. **Guest Services:** valet laundry, beauty salon, wireless Internet. **Business Services:** conference facilities, business center. **Cards:** AX, MC, VI.

/ SOME UNITS

GRAND LIDO NEGRIL RESORT & SPA — Book great rates at AAA.com — Phone: (876)957-5010 — 42

AAA SAVE

Resort Hotel
$558-$1430 All Year

Address: Norman Manley Blvd **Location:** Oceanfront. Just s of Negril Airport; 4.4 mi (7.1 km) n of downtown. **Facility:** The popular, all-inclusive resort sits on a magnificent stretch of beach along Bloody Bay with extensive recreational facilities. 210 units. 182 one-bedroom standard units, some with whirlpools. 28 one-bedroom suites with whirlpools. 2 stories (no elevator), exterior corridors. *Bath:* combo or shower only. **Parking:** on-site and valet. **Terms:** 2 night minimum stay, age restrictions may apply, cancellation fee imposed. **Amenities:** CD players, high-speed Internet (fee), dual phone lines, voice mail, safes, honor bars, irons, hair dryers. **Dining:** 6 restaurants, nightclub, entertainment. **Pool(s):** 2 outdoor. **Leisure Activities:** sauna, whirlpools, steamroom, lifeguard on duty, paddleboats, sailboats, windsurfing, waterskiing, kayaks, glass-bottom boat, golf-18 holes, 4 tennis courts (2 lighted), recreation programs, slot machines, bicycles, exercise room, spa, volleyball, game room. *Fee:* scuba diving, snorkeling, charter fishing, catamaran sunset cruise. **Guest Services:** valet laundry, airport transportation-Montego Bay & Negril airports, beauty salon, wireless Internet. **Business Services:** conference facilities, PC (fee). **Cards:** AX, DS, MC, VI. **Free Special Amenities: full breakfast and early check-in/late check-out.**

/ SOME UNITS VCR

RIU TROPICAL BAY — Book at AAA.com — Phone: 876/957-5900 — 39

Resort Hotel
Rates not provided

Address: Norman Manley Blvd **Location:** Oceanfront. Just n of Negril Airport; 5.1 mi (8.1 km) n of downtown. **Facility:** This newly built all-inclusive mega resort is ideal for families, couples or singles, and features lavish, elegantly appointed public areas. 416 one-bedroom standard units, some with whirlpools. 3 stories (no elevator), exterior corridors. *Bath:* combo or shower only. **Parking:** on-site. **Amenities:** safes, honor bars, irons, hair dryers. **Pool(s):** 2 outdoor. **Leisure Activities:** sauna, whirlpool, steamroom, limited beach access, paddleboats, sailboats, windsurfing, 2 lighted tennis courts, recreation programs, playground, exercise room, spa, volleyball. *Fee:* scuba diving, snorkeling. **Guest Services:** valet laundry. **Business Services:** PC (fee).

(See map and index starting on p. 453)

RONDEL VILLAGE Book at AAA.com Phone: (876)957-4413 43

Hotel

$75-$260 All Year

Address: Norman Manley Blvd **Location:** 3.2 mi (5.1 km) s of Negril Airport; 1.4 mi (2.2 km) n of downtown. **Facility:** 40 units. 32 one-bedroom standard units. 4 one- and 4 two-bedroom suites with kitchens and whirlpools. 1-3 stories (no elevator), exterior corridors. **Parking:** on-site. **Terms:** office hours 7 am-9:30 pm, 4-7 night minimum stay - seasonal, 22 day cancellation notice-fee imposed. **Amenities:** safes (fee). *Some:* irons. **Pool(s):** 2 outdoor. **Leisure Activities:** whirlpools. **Guest Services:** valet laundry. **Business Services:** PC (fee). **Cards:** AX, DS, JC, MC, VI.

ASK D / SOME UNITS

SEA SPLASH Book great rates at AAA.com Phone: (876)957-4041 48

SAVE

Hotel

$83-$227 All Year

Address: Norman Manley Blvd **Location:** Oceanfront. 2.5 mi (4 km) s of Negril Airport; 2.1 mi (3.3 km) n of downtown. **Facility:** 20 units. 10 one-bedroom standard units. 10 one-bedroom suites with efficiencies. 2 stories (no elevator), exterior corridors. **Parking:** on-site. **Terms:** office hours 7 am-11 pm, 21 day cancellation notice-fee imposed. **Amenities:** safes, irons, hair dryers. **Dining:** Norma's Restaurant at Sea Splash Resort, see separate listing. **Pool(s):** outdoor. **Leisure Activities:** whirlpool, bicycles. **Guest Services:** valet laundry, wireless Internet. **Business Services:** PC (fee). **Cards:** AX, DS, MC, VI. **Free Special Amenities: local telephone calls and high-speed Internet.**

D / SOME UNITS

WHERE TO DINE

COSMO'S SEAFOOD RESTAURANT **Phone:** 876/957-4784 39

Jamaican

$6-$22

Native Jamaican cuisine is served at covered and open tables in a casual beachside setting. Try bammy—a fried cassava cake—or red pea soup with dumplings. The more daring might order escoveitched fish prepared with vinegar, onions and hot peppers. Casual dress. **Bar:** Full bar. **Hours:** noon-10 pm. Closed: 4/12, 12/25; also Good Friday. **Address:** Norman Manley Blvd **Location:** 1 mi (1.6 km) s of Negril Airport; 1.7 mi (2.7 km) n of downtown. **Parking:** on-site. **Cards:** CB, DC, DS, MC, VI.

AC

JIMMY BUFFET'S MARGARITAVILLE **Phone:** 876/957-4467

Caribbean

$12-$28

This is a "no prude zone" type of place to kick back, relax, listen to music and enjoy some great island-inspired fare. Begin with one of the refreshing libations while perusing a menu of choices as colorful and whimsical as the festive decor. Favorites are peel-and-eat shrimp, conch chowder and whole fish served escoveitched style. The menu also abounds with fajitas, jerks, pizzas, pastas and cheeseburgers—in paradise, of course. Casual dress. **Bar:** Full bar. **Reservations:** accepted, for dinner. **Hours:** 9 am-11 pm. **Address:** Norman Manley Blvd **Location:** 1.6 mi (2.5 km) s of Negril Airport; 1.1 mi (1.7 km) n of downtown. **Parking:** on-site. **Cards:** AX, DS, MC, VI.

AC

NORMA'S RESTAURANT AT SEA SPLASH RESORT **Phone:** 876/957-4041 40

Jamaican

$10-$32

Famed celebrity chef Norma Shirley's most recent restaurant features oceanfront seating, where you can enjoy lobster tail, coconut chicken or Rasta pasta for lunch. All dinner entrees are available after 2:00 and include such dishes as pork loin chop marinated in ginger and beer, filet au poivre and filet of red snapper. An array of desserts are also available. Casual dress. **Bar:** Full bar. **Reservations:** suggested. **Hours:** 7:30 am-10 pm. **Address:** Norman Manley Blvd **Location:** 2.5 mi (4 km) s of Negril Airport; 2.1 mi (3.3 km) n of downtown; in Sea Splash. **Parking:** on-site. **Cards:** AX, MC, VI.

AC

RICK'S CAFE **Phone:** 876/957-0380 51

American

$8-$24

Visitors to the popular informal restaurant, on a rocky oceanfront cliff, can watch daring divers plunge into clear grotto waters below. The menu features fresh fish, lobster, pasta and chicken. Casual dress. Entertainment. **Bar:** Full bar. **Reservations:** accepted. **Hours:** noon-11 pm. **Address:** Lighthouse Rd **Location:** 3 mi (4.8 km) w on West End Rd (Lighthouse Rd). **Parking:** on-site. **Cards:** AX, DS, MC, VI.

AC

(See map and index starting on p. 453)

ROCK HOUSE RESTAURANT **Phone:** 876/957-4373 (49)

Jamaican
$11-$22

Tucked away along the lush cliffs of this chic boutique-style hotel is this relaxing restaurant. Enjoy some traditional Jamaican cuisine with an updated twist. Favorites are the pepperpot soup and the escoveitch fish that is tantalizingly spicy. The coconut cream pie is luscious. Casual dress. **Bar:** Full bar. **Reservations:** accepted. **Hours:** 7:30 am-10 pm. **Address:** West End Rd **Location:** 4.2 mi (6.7 km) s of Negril Airport; 1.1 mi (1.7 km) w of downtown via West End Rd; in Rock House Hotel. **Parking:** on-site. **Cards:** AX, MC, VI.

SWEET SPICE RESTAURANT **Phone:** 876/957-4621 (45)

Jamaican
$10-$20

A local favorite, the simple diner uses fresh fruit in all-natural drinks and milkshakes. Depending on the season, lobster, shrimp and curried conch are offered along with Jamaican preparations of chicken, goat and oxtail. Filet of snapper is a favorite. Casual dress. **Hours:** 8:30 am-10:30 pm. **Address:** 1 White Hall Rd **Location:** 0.5 mi (0.8 km) e on Rt A2, jct Whitehall Rd. **Parking:** street. **Cards:** AX, DS, MC, VI.

XTABI ON THE CLIFF **Phone:** 876/957-0121 (52)

Jamaican
$10-$26

A fun place to relax and hang out or enjoy an evening cocktail as the sun sets over the ocean, this eatery is perfectly situated over the cliffs for breathtaking views as you listen to gentle music and enjoy simple island dishes. Casual dress. **Bar:** Full bar. **Reservations:** accepted. **Hours:** 8 am-10:30 pm. **Address:** West End Rd **Location:** 1.7 mi (2.8 km) w on West End Rd (Lighthouse Rd). **Parking:** on-site. **Cards:** AX, MC, VI.

OCHO RIOS pop. 7,800 (See map and index starting on p. 453)

— WHERE TO STAY —

CLUB HOTEL RIU OCHO RIOS **Phone:** 876/972-2200 (21)

Resort Hotel
Rates not provided

Address: Mammee Bay **Location:** Oceanfront. 4.6 mi (7.3 km) w of town. **Facility:** Located on an enviable stretch of beach, this brand new all-inclusive resort is ideal for singles, couples and families, and features grand public areas, comfortable guest units and an array of activities. 856 one-bedroom standard units, some with whirlpools. 4-5 stories, interior corridors. *Bath:* some shower only. **Parking:** on-site. **Amenities:** safes, honor bars, hair dryers. *Some:* irons. **Pool(s):** 2 outdoor. **Leisure Activities:** saunas, whirlpools, lifeguard on duty, beach access, paddleboats, sailboats, windsurfing, snorkeling, 2 lighted tennis courts, recreation programs, playground, exercise room, spa, volleyball, game room. *Fee:* scuba diving. **Guest Services:** valet laundry. **Business Services:** conference facilities, business center.

COUPLES SANS SOUCI **Phone:** 876/994-1206 (24)

Resort Hotel
$614-$1000 All Year

Address: White River, St Mary **Location:** Oceanfront. 3 mi (4.8 km) e of downtown. **Facility:** An all-inclusive beachfront resort offering extensive recreational facilities catering to adults only, the property hosts a weekly beach party. 150 units. 149 one- and 1 two-bedroom suites, some with whirlpools. 2-3 stories (no elevator), exterior corridors. *Bath:* combo or shower only. **Parking:** on-site. **Terms:** 3 night minimum stay, age restrictions may apply, 7 day cancellation notice-fee imposed. **Amenities:** CD players, high-speed Internet, voice mail, safes, honor bars, irons, hair dryers. **Pool(s):** 4 outdoor. **Leisure Activities:** sauna, whirlpools, lifeguard on duty, boating, paddleboats, sailboats, windsurfing, waterskiing, scuba diving, snorkeling, fishing, 2 lighted tennis courts, recreation programs, bicycles, jogging, exercise room, spa, sports court, basketball, volleyball, game room. *Fee:* charter fishing. **Guest Services:** valet laundry, wireless Internet. **Business Services:** conference facilities, PC. **Cards:** AX, MC, VI.

/ SOME UNITS

HIBISCUS LODGE HOTEL **Phone:** 876/974-2676 (25)

AAA SAVE

Hotel
$140-$229 12/1-4/30
$128-$205 5/1-11/30

Address: 83 Main St **Location:** Oceanfront. 0.5 mi (0.8 km) e of downtown. **Facility:** 26 one-bedroom standard units. 2 stories (no elevator), exterior corridors. *Bath:* combo or shower only. **Parking:** on-site. **Terms:** office hours 7 am-11 pm, 14 day cancellation notice-fee imposed. **Amenities:** *Some:* hair dryers. **Dining:** The Almond Tree Restaurant, see separate listing. **Pool(s):** outdoor. **Leisure Activities:** whirlpool, lighted tennis court. *Fee:* snorkeling. **Guest Services:** valet laundry, wireless Internet. **Business Services:** meeting rooms. **Cards:** AX, DS, MC, VI.

/ SOME UNITS

JAMAICA INN *Book great rates at AAA.com* **Phone:** (876)974-2514 (26)

AAA SAVE

Hotel
$290-$1760 All Year

Address: 1 Old Rd **Location:** Oceanfront. 1.7 mi (2.7 km) e on Rt A3, just n of road to Shaw Park. **Facility:** Reflecting a bygone era of Jamaica, the understated guest rooms and tranquil ambience set this property apart from the frenzied mega-resorts. 51 units. 44 one-bedroom standard units. 3 one-bedroom suites. 4 cottages. 2 stories (no elevator), exterior corridors. **Parking:** on-site. **Terms:** age restrictions may apply, 14 day cancellation notice, 30 day in winter-fee imposed. **Amenities:** safes, hair dryers. *Some:* CD players. **Dining:** restaurant, see separate listing, entertainment. **Pool(s):** outdoor. **Leisure Activities:** sailboats, snorkeling, kayaks, tennis privileges, croquet, library, exercise room, spa. **Guest Services:** TV in common area, valet laundry, airport transportation (fee)-Montego Bay & Kingston airports, wireless Internet. **Business Services:** PC. **Cards:** AX, DS, MC, VI.

FEE / SOME UNITS

(See map and index starting on p. 453)

WHERE TO DINE

THE ALMOND TREE RESTAURANT *Menu on AAA.com* **Phone:** 876/974-2813 (31)

International
$12-$33

The beautiful terrace overlooks the Caribbean Sea. Examples of European and island specialties include veal piccata, beef tenderloin, seafood platter, filet mignon and chateaubriand for two. An attractive bar with swinging chairs complements the decor. Dressy casual. **Bar:** Full bar. **Reservations:** required. **Hours:** 7:30 am-10:30, noon-2:30 & 6-9:30 pm. **Address:** 83 Main St **Location:** 0.5 mi (0.8 km) e of downtown; in Hibiscus Lodge Hotel. **Parking:** on-site. **Cards:** AX, DS, MC, VI.

BLUE RUNNINGS **Phone:** 876/675-8794 (37)

Jamaican
$10-$17

The eatery, found in a tranquil setting in the Island Village, is great for a quick bite or take-out coffee as well as a casual sit-down meal as you relax on the porch and watch the fish and ducks swim lazily around the pond below. The menu features items such as jerk fish, cheese festivals and rice and peas. Casual dress. **Bar:** Beer & wine. **Hours:** 8 am-6 pm. Closed: 1/1, 12/25. **Address:** Shop #72/13 Island Village **Location:** Just w of town center; in Island Village Complex. **Parking:** on-site. **Cards:** AX, MC, VI.

EVITA'S *Menu on AAA.com* **Phone:** 876/974-2333 (29)

Italian
$11-$29

The charming converted 1860 gingerbread house sits high on a hillside overlooking the town and bay. Well-prepared Italian food, made with fresh pasta, and some Jamaican specialties make up the diverse menu. Guests should reserve early for one of the popular veranda tables. Some nights feature live music. Dressy casual. **Bar:** Full bar. **Reservations:** required. **Hours:** 11 am-10:30 pm. **Address:** Eden Bower Rd **Location:** Jct Rt A1, just s. **Parking:** on-site. **Cards:** AX, DS, MC, VI. **Historic**

JAMAICA INN DINING ROOM **Phone:** 876/974-2514 (32)

Continental
$14-$46

Well-trained servers move around the romantic terrace dining room, which affords views of the beach and sea. An international wine list complements preparations of excellent Continental, French and island cuisine. Most nights feature live music. Dressy casual. Entertainment. **Bar:** Full bar. **Reservations:** required. **Hours:** Open 12/1-9/1 & 10/1-11/30; 8-10 am, 1-2:30 & 7:30-9:30 pm. **Address:** Shaw Park Rd **Location:** 1.7 mi (2.7 km) e on Rt A3, just n of road to Shaw Park; in Jamaica Inn. **Parking:** on-site. **Cards:** AX, MC, VI.

JIMMY BUFFET'S MARGARITAVILLE **Phone:** 876/675-8800

Caribbean
$12-$28

Adjacent to the cruise ship docks is the newest restaurant opened by famed singer and songwriter Jimmy Buffett. More than a restaurant, the facility also includes a rooftop hot tub, 100-foot-long waterslide and three bars, including a swim-up pool bar. Caribbean decor complements island-inspired fare, such as jerk pork and chicken, conch chowder and, of course, the cheeseburger in paradise. Copious margaritas, beer and a variety of "boat drinks" leave patrons saying, "Irie, mon!". Casual dress. **Bar:** Full bar. **Reservations:** accepted, for dinner. **Hours:** 9 am-10 pm. **Address:** Island Village Shopping Mall **Location:** Just w of town center; in Island Village Complex. **Parking:** on-site. **Cards:** AX, DS, MC, VI.

(See map and index starting on p. 453)

PASSAGE TO INDIA **Phone:** 876/795-3182 (36)

Indian
$10-$26

Patrons can sample tandoori and North Indian dishes at the rooftop restaurant in Soni's Plaza. Palate-teasers include kebabs and tikka, fish or meat marinated in spices then baked in a tandoor oven. Main-event entrees include mutton, fish and chicken simmered in various sauces, including vindaloo, masala and begum bahar sauce: a tomato-and-cashew-nut gravy. Dressy casual. **Bar:** Full bar. **Reservations:** suggested. **Hours:** 11:30 am-10:30 pm. Closed: Mon. **Address:** 50 Main St **Location:** Center; at Soni's Plaza; across from Sunset Jamaica Grande. **Parking:** on-site. **Cards:** AX, CB, DC, DS, MC, VI.

TOSCANINI ITALIAN RESTAURANT **Phone:** 876/975-4785 (38)

Italian
$15-$29

Patrons are treated to al fresco dining on the veranda of a gingerbread mansion. Italian dishes, served in large portions, incorporate a hint of island influences and are nicely matched with the selection of imported wines. Take time to tour the art collection. Dressy casual. **Bar:** Full bar. **Reservations:** required. **Hours:** noon-2:30 & 7-10:30 pm. Closed: Mon. **Address:** Oracabessa Main Rd **Location:** 4.5 mi (7.2 km) e on Rt A3; at Harmony Hall. **Parking:** on-site. **Cards:** AX, MC, VI. **Historic**

PORT ANTONIO pop. 13,246 (See map and index starting on p. 453)

WHERE TO STAY

JAMAICA PALACE HOTEL *Book at AAA.com* **Phone:** (876)993-7720 (55)

Hotel
$170-$400 12/1-4/14
$150-$370 4/15-11/30

Address: Williamsfield **Location:** 5 mi (8 km) e of Port Antonio. **Facility:** 60 units. 57 one-bedroom standard units. 3 one-bedroom suites. 2 stories (no elevator), exterior corridors. **Parking:** on-site. **Terms:** 30 day cancellation notice. **Amenities:** safes (fee). **Pool(s):** outdoor. **Guest Services:** valet laundry, wireless Internet. **Business Services:** PC (fee). **Cards:** AX, MC, VI.

/ SOME UNITS

WHERE TO DINE

PANORAMA RESTAURANT AND LOUNGE **Phone:** 876/993-7374 (54)

Jamaican
$12-$27

On the outskirts of town, the restaurant is nestled high in the hills overlooking the ocean. The covered al fresco dining room provides spectacular views. Choices on the Jamaican-West Indies-influenced menu range from rich red pea soup and jerked meats to oxtail stew and curried chicken. Casual dress. **Bar:** Full bar. **Reservations:** accepted. **Hours:** 7:30 am-10 pm. **Address:** Fern Hill **Location:** 5.5 mi (8.8 km) e on Rt A4; in Fern Hill Hotel and Villa Resort. **Parking:** on-site. **Cards:** AX, DS, MC, VI.

RIO BUENO (See map and index starting on p. 453)

WHERE TO STAY

GRAND LIDO BRACO RESORT & SPA **Phone:** 876/954-0000 (61)

SAVE

Resort Hotel
$400-$1400 All Year

Address: Jamaica S North Coast **Location:** Oceanfront. On Rt A1, between Montego Bay and Ocho Rios; 1 mi (1.6 km) w of Rio Bueno Village. **Facility:** This luxurious, seaside, all-inclusive resort has a quaint courtyard with a re-created Jamaican village; a good beach and upscale rooms are featured. 226 units. 188 one-bedroom standard units. 38 one-bedroom suites. 3 stories (no elevator), exterior corridors. **Parking:** on-site. **Terms:** 2 night minimum stay - weekends, age restrictions may apply, cancellation fee imposed. **Amenities:** CD players, voice mail, safes, honor bars, irons, hair dryers. **Dining:** 7 restaurants, nightclub, entertainment. **Pool(s):** 2 outdoor. **Leisure Activities:** sauna, whirlpools, steamroom, lifeguard on duty, paddleboats, sailboats, windsurfing, waterskiing, snorkeling, fishing, kayaks, glass bottom boat, golf-27 holes, 3 tennis courts (2 lighted), recreation programs, jogging, exercise room, spa, basketball, volleyball, game room. *Fee:* scuba diving, charter fishing. **Guest Services:** valet laundry, airport transportation-Sangster International Airport, area transportation-golf courses, beauty salon, wireless Internet. **Business Services:** conference facilities, business center. **Cards:** AX, DS, MC, VI. **Free Special Amenities: full breakfast and early check-in/late check-out.**

ROSE HALL (See map and index starting on p. 453)

WHERE TO STAY

THE RITZ-CARLTON GOLF & SPA RESORT, ROSE HALL, JAMAICA

AAA SAVE

Resort Hotel

$279-$1100 All Year

Phone: (876)953-2800 19

Address: 1 Ritz-Carlton Dr **Location:** 8.6 mi (13.7 km) e on Rt A1; 6.1 mi (9.7 km) e of airport. **Facility:** A modern spa, golf courses and other recreational facilities combine with luxury lodgings to give the upscale resort a refined, world-class ambiance. Smoke free premises. 427 units. 375 one-bedroom standard units. 52 one-bedroom suites. 5 stories, interior corridors. *Bath:* combo or shower only. **Parking:** valet. **Terms:** 3-7 night minimum stay - seasonal, cancellation fee imposed. **Amenities:** CD players, high-speed Internet, dual phone lines, voice mail, safes, honor bars, irons, hair dryers. *Some:* DVD players (fee). **Dining:** 4 restaurants, also, Jasmine's, see separate listing, entertainment. **Pool(s):** outdoor. **Leisure Activities:** saunas, whirlpool, steamrooms, lifeguard on duty, limited beach access, sailboats, windsurfing, kayaks, water aerobics, 2 lighted tennis courts, recreation programs, bocci, croquet, pool table, table tennis, jogging, playground, spa, horseshoes, volleyball. *Fee:* scuba diving, snorkeling, fishing, charter fishing, golf-18 holes. **Guest Services:** valet laundry, airport transportation (fee)-Sangster International Airport, area transportation-within 1 mi, wireless Internet. **Business Services:** conference facilities, business center. **Cards:** AX, DC, DS, JC, MC, VI. **Free Special Amenities: newspaper and high-speed Internet.**

FEE 24 CALL S D / SOME UNITS

▼ See AAA listing p 456 ▼

(See map and index starting on p. 453)

ROSE HALL RESORT & SPA, A HILTON RESORT Phone: (876)953-2650 18

Resort Hotel

$123-$557 All Year

Address: Rose Hall Rd, Montego Bay **Location:** 9.7 mi (15.5 km) e on Rt A1; 7.7 mi (12.3 km) e of airport. **Facility:** The property offers a mini water park as well as manicured grounds, a golf course and a fine beach; the guest rooms are simple and compact. 483 units. 470 one-bedroom standard units. 13 one-bedroom suites. 7 stories, interior corridors. *Bath:* combo or shower only. **Parking:** on-site. **Terms:** 1-30 night minimum stay, cancellation fee imposed. **Amenities:** *Some:* CD players. **Dining:** 3 restaurants, also, Luna di Mare, Three Palms, see separate listings, nightclub, entertainment. **Pool(s):** 2 outdoor. **Leisure Activities:** whirlpools, waterslide, lifeguard on duty, limited beach access, canoeing, sailboats, windsurfing, snorkeling, hobie cats, kayaks, water park, recreation programs, jogging, playground, exercise room, spa, basketball, horseshoes, volleyball, game room. *Fee:* waterskiing, scuba diving, golf-18 holes, 6 lighted tennis courts, tennis instruction. **Guest Services:** valet laundry, beauty salon, wireless Internet. **Business Services:** conference facilities, PC (fee). **Cards:** AX, CB, DC, DS, MC, VI. **Free Special Amenities: newspaper and preferred room (subject to availability with advance reservations).**

AAA Benefit:

Members save 5% or more everyday!

S D / SOME UNITS

WHERE TO DINE

JASMINE Phone: 876/953-2800 19

Caribbean

$35-$50

Caribbean ingredients combine with Asian-cuisine influences to produce delectable dishes at this luxurious resort restaurant, which offers both indoor and terrace seating. The menu specializes in excellent quality fish and other seafood, including blue crab, lobster, shrimp and Jamaican-style fresh fish preparations. Meat lovers may chose from lamb loin, filet mignon, pork loin and Mongolian beef. Service is refined and friendly. Dressy casual. **Bar:** Full bar. **Reservations:** suggested. **Hours:** 6 pm-11 pm. **Address:** 1 Ritz-Carlton Dr **Location:** 8.6 mi (13.7 km) e on Rt A1; 6.1 mi (9.7 km) e of airport; in The Ritz-Carlton Golf & Spa Resort, Rose Hall, Jamaica. **Parking:** valet. **Cards:** AX, CB, DC, DS, JC, MC, VI.

CALL

LUNA DI MARE Phone: 876/953-2656 23

Italian

$20-$34

The adroit staff serves well-prepared cuisine in a refined and elegant setting. Antipasti del giorno is a cornucopia of Italian morsels to whet the appetite. Pastas are traditionally prepared with such ingredients as pancetta, baby cockle clams, Italian sausage, tomato sauces and lots of garlic. Additional specialties include roasted rosemary chicken, saltimbocca and balsamic glazed salmon. Dressy casual. **Bar:** Full bar. **Reservations:** required. **Hours:** 6 pm-10 pm. Closed: Sun. **Address:** Rt A1 **Location:** 9.7 mi (15.5 km) e on Rt A1; 7.7 mi (12.3 km) e of airport; in Rose Hall Resort & Spa, a Hilton Resort. **Parking:** on-site. **Cards:** AX, DS, MC, VI.

SUGAR MILL RESTAURANT Phone: 876/953-2314 18

Jamaican

$19-$35

The innovative menu intertwines European and Caribbean dishes. Shaded by an almond tree, the patio overlooks the golf course and the sea. Dressy casual. Entertainment. **Bar:** Full bar. **Reservations:** required. **Hours:** 7 pm-10 pm. **Address:** Rt A1 **Location:** 7.6 mi (12.1 km) e on Rt A1; 5.1 mi (8.1 km) e of airport; in Half Moon. **Parking:** on-site. **Cards:** AX, MC, VI. **Historic**

AC

(See map and index starting on p. 453)

THREE PALMS

Jamaican
$24-$38

Phone: 876/953-2650 (24)

Terrace dining at the golf course of this major resort. The chef utilizes select ingredients in preparing the dishes. The international cuisine is inspired by a Caribbean culinary approach and sometimes with a Mediterranean flair like the plantain encrusted snapper with basil orzo. Charming servers cater to the needs of the diners. Dressy casual. **Bar:** Full bar. **Reservations:** required. **Hours:** 6 pm-10:30 pm. Closed: Mon. **Address:** The Queens Dr **Location:** 9.7 mi (15.5 km) e on Rt A1; 7.7 mi (12.3 km) e of airport; in Rose Hall Resort & Spa, a Hilton Resort. **Parking:** on-site. **Cards:** AX, MC, VI.

RUNAWAY BAY (See map and index starting on p. 453)

WHERE TO STAY

SUPERCLUBS BREEZES RUNAWAY BAY RESORT & GOLF CLUB

Resort Hotel

$193-$384 12/1-4/16
$210-$340 4/17-11/30

Phone: 876/973-4820 (63)

Address: Rt A1 **Location:** On Rt A1; between Montego Bay and Ocho Rios. **Facility:** The all-inclusive resort caters to guests 14 years and older with a variety of activities and restaurants—not to mention a good beach. 264 units. 250 one-bedroom standard units. 14 one-bedroom suites. 2 stories (no elevator), interior corridors. **Parking:** on-site. **Terms:** 3 night minimum stay, age restrictions may apply. **Amenities:** CD players, voice mail, safes, irons, hair dryers. **Pool(s):** 3 outdoor. **Leisure Activities:** whirlpools, lifeguard on duty, limited beach access, paddleboats, sailboats, windsurfing, waterskiing, snorkeling, golf-18 holes, 4 lighted tennis courts, recreation programs, bicycles, jogging, exercise room, basketball, shuffleboard, volleyball, game room. *Fee:* scuba diving, massage. **Guest Services:** valet laundry, wireless Internet. **Business Services:** meeting rooms. *Fee:* PC, fax. **Cards:** AX, DC, DS, MC, VI.

D

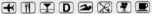

SANDY BAY (See map and index starting on p. 453)

WHERE TO STAY

TRYALL CLUB

AAA SAVE

Vacation Rental House

$345-$2600 All Year

Phone: 876/956-5660 (57)

Location: Between Hopewell and Lucea; 12 mi (19.2 km) w of Montego Bay Airport. **Facility:** A 2200-acre property, this resort evokes the gentile atmosphere of yesteryear. Each elegantly appointed villa comes with a cook and a maid. 77 units. 64 houses and 13 cottages. 2 stories (no elevator), exterior corridors. *Bath:* combo or shower only. **Parking:** on-site. **Terms:** 7 night minimum stay - seasonal, 60 day cancellation notice, 30 day in summer-fee imposed. **Amenities:** irons. *Some:* DVD players, CD players, safes, hair dryers. **Dining:** 2 restaurants. **Pool(s):** outdoor. **Leisure Activities:** lifeguard on duty, limited beach access, sailboats, snorkeling, hobie cat, golf cart, 9 tennis courts (2 lighted), recreation programs, bocci, croquet, kids club, limited exercise equipment, basketball, volleyball. *Fee:* golf-18 holes. **Guest Services:** complimentary laundry, beauty salon, wireless Internet. **Business Services:** meeting rooms, PC. **Cards:** AX, DC, DS, MC, VI.

/ SOME UNITS VCR

MARTINIQUE

This index helps you "spot" where approved lodgings and restaurants are located on the corresponding detailed maps. Lodging daily rate range is for comparison only and show the property's high season. Restaurant rate range is a combination of lunch and/or dinner. Turn to the listing page for more detailed rate information and consult display ads for special promotions.

LE FRANCOIS

Map Page	OA	Lodgings	Diamond Rated	High Season	Page
4 / below		Fregate Bleue Inn	2 Diamonds	$157-$455	467
6 / below	AAA	**Cap Est Lagoon Resort & Spa**	4 Diamonds	$706-$1884 SAVE	467

TROIS-ILETS

Map Page	OA	Restaurant	Diamond Rated	Cuisine	Meal Range	Page
4 / below		Restaurant La Marine	2 Diamonds	Creole	$11-$41	467

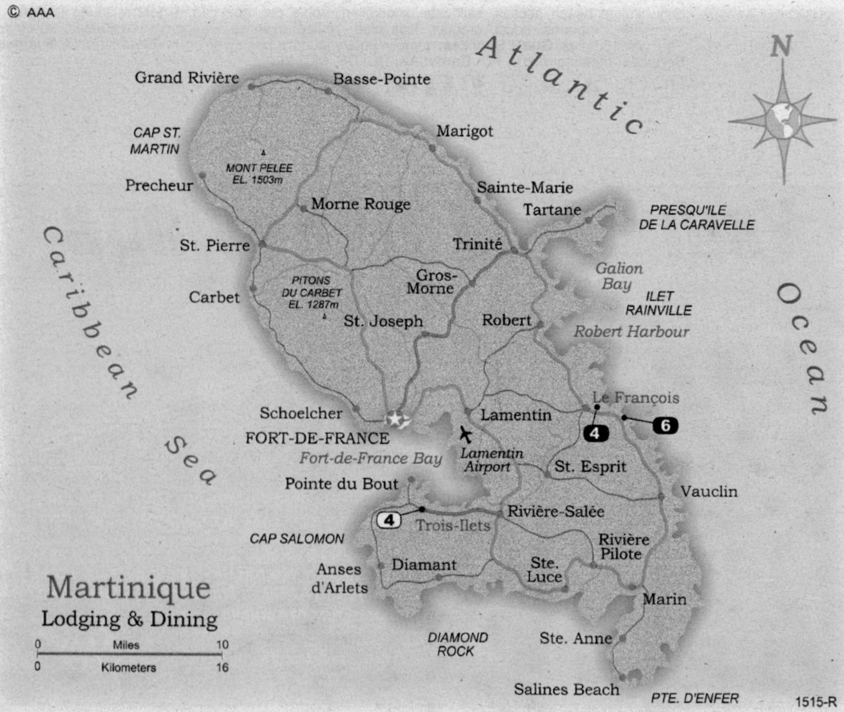

LE FRANCOIS pop. 18,559 (See map and index starting on p. 466)

WHERE TO STAY

CAP EST LAGOON RESORT & SPA — **Phone:** 596/54-80-80 (6)

AAA SAVE — Hotel — $706-$1884 All Year

Address: Quartier La Prairie **Location:** Oceanfront. 15 mi (25 km) e of airport; just s of Le Francois; on east coast of island. **Facility:** The guest units are tastefully decorated with every conceivable amenity. A well-trained European staff attends to every detail. 50 one-bedroom suites. 2 stories (no elevator), exterior corridors. **Parking:** on-site. **Terms:** 22 day cancellation notice. **Amenities:** video library, DVD players, CD players, high-speed Internet, voice mail, safes, honor bars, hair dryers. **Dining:** 2 restaurants. **Pool(s):** outdoor. **Leisure Activities:** beach access, sailboats, windsurfing, boat dock, snorkeling, kayaks, kite surfing, boat tours, lighted tennis court, exercise room, spa. **Guest Services:** valet laundry, wireless Internet. **Business Services:** meeting rooms, PC. **Cards:** AX, DS, MC, VI.

D / SOME UNITS

FREGATE BLEUE INN — **Phone:** (596)54-54-66 (4)

Bed & Breakfast — $157-$455 All Year

Address: Pass Francois **Location:** 2.5 mi (4 km) se of Le Francois towards Vauclin; on Hwy N6, just s of Ravine Fregate, follow signs on Fregate East 4; in Dostaly. **Facility:** 8 units. 7 one-bedroom standard units. 1 house. 1-2 stories (no elevator), interior/exterior corridors. *Bath:* combo or shower only. **Parking:** on-site. **Amenities:** hair dryers. **Pool(s):** outdoor. **Guest Services:** coin laundry, wireless Internet. **Business Services:** PC (fee). **Cards:** AX, CB, MC, VI.

A$K

TROIS-ILETS pop. 5,162 (See map and index starting on p. 466)

WHERE TO DINE

RESTAURANT LA MARINE — **Phone:** 596/66-02-32 (4)

Creole — $11-$41

The open air terrace restaurant offers a pleasant atmosphere featuring views of the marina. Seafood dishes are very popular here as are the satisfying pizzas and salads for the more thrifty traveler. Casual dress. **Bar:** Full bar. **Reservations:** accepted. **Hours:** noon-11 pm. **Address:** La Marina Pointe du Bout **Location:** At the Marina Pointe du Bout. **Parking:** street. **Cards:** MC, VI.

AC

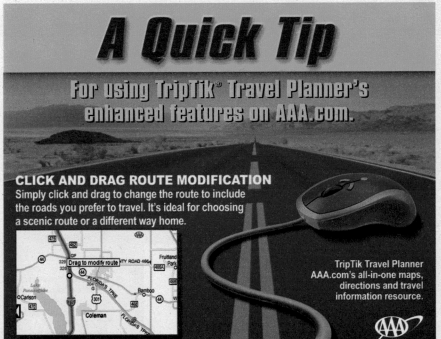

MONTSERRAT

This index helps you "spot" where approved lodgings and restaurants are located on the corresponding detailed maps. Lodging daily rate range is for comparison only and show the property's high season. Restaurant rate range is a combination of lunch and/or dinner. Turn to the listing page for more detailed rate information and consult display ads for special promotions.

SWEENEY'S

Map Page	OA	Lodging	Diamond Rated	High Season	Page
1 / p. 469		Tropical Mansion Suites	2 Diamonds	$119-$150	470

SALEM

Map Page	OA	Restaurant	Diamond Rated	Cuisine	Meal Range	Page
2 / p. 469		Gourmet Gardens	1 Diamond	Caribbean	$6-$20	470

BRADES

Map Page	OA	Restaurant	Diamond Rated	Cuisine	Meal Range	Page
3 / p. 469		Tina's Restaurant	1 Diamond	Caribbean	$8-$18	470

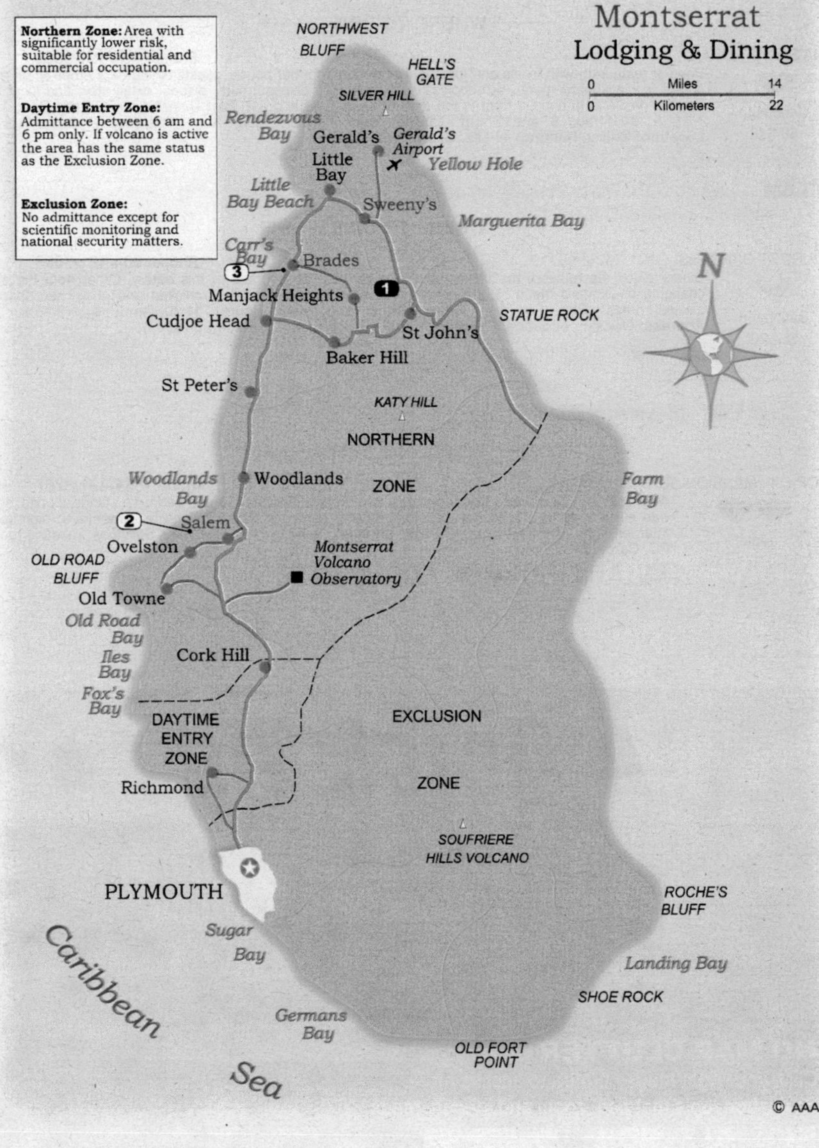
1528-C
Montserrat
Lodging & Dining
0 Miles 14
0 Kilometers 22
Northern Zone: Area with significantly lower risk, suitable for residential and commercial occupation.
Daytime Entry Zone: Admittance between 6 am and 6 pm only. If volcano is active the area has the same status as the Exclusion Zone.
Exclusion Zone: No admittance except for scientific monitoring and national security matters.
NORTHWEST BLUFF
HELL'S GATE
SILVER HILL
Rendezvous Bay
Gerald's
Gerald's Airport
Yellow Hole
Little Bay
Little Bay Beach
Sweeny's
Marguerita Bay
Carr's Bay
Brades
3
1
Manjack Heights
Cudjoe Head
St John's
STATUE ROCK
N
Baker Hill
St Peter's
KATY HILL
NORTHERN
ZONE
Woodlands Bay
Woodlands
Farm Bay
2
Salem
Ovelston
OLD ROAD BLUFF
Montserrat Volcano Observatory
Old Towne
Old Road Bay
Iles Bay
Cork Hill
Fox's Bay
DAYTIME ENTRY ZONE
EXCLUSION
ZONE
Richmond
SOUFRIERE HILLS VOLCANO
PLYMOUTH
ROCHE'S BLUFF
Sugar Bay
Landing Bay
SHOE ROCK
Caribbean Sea
Germans Bay
OLD FORT POINT
© AAA

BRADES (See map and index starting on p. 469)

WHERE TO DINE

TINA'S RESTAURANT — Phone: 664/491-3538 (3)

Caribbean
$8-$18

Popular restaurant with locals and tourists. Located in a former house, guests dining here order off an ever-changing blackboard menu with choices such as baked chicken, curry dishes, oxtail stew and local fish. Several desserts to choose from in the dessert case. Casual dress. **Bar:** Beer & wine. **Hours:** Open 12/1-7/31 & 9/1-11/30; 8 am-10 pm. Closed major holidays; also Sun. **Address:** Brades Main Rd **Location:** Center. **Parking:** on-site. **Cards:** MC, VI.

SALEM (See map and index starting on p. 469)

WHERE TO DINE

GOURMET GARDENS — Phone: 664/491-7859 (2)

Caribbean
$6-$20

Diners enjoy the relaxed, rustic ambience and no rush atmosphere of this eatery. Order from the ever-changing chalkboard menu with offerings such as curried beef, baked chicken and grilled red snapper. Casual dress. **Bar:** Full bar. **Reservations:** suggested. **Hours:** 11:30 am-2 & 6:30-8:30 pm. **Address:** Olveston **Location:** Center; below the Police Station. **Parking:** on-site.

SWEENEY'S (See map and index starting on p. 469)

WHERE TO STAY

TROPICAL MANSION SUITES — Book at AAA.com — Phone: (664)491-8767 (1)

Motel
$119-$150 All Year

Address: 404 Sweeney's **Location:** Just w of airport. **Facility:** 18 one-bedroom standard units, some with efficiencies. 3 stories (no elevator), exterior corridors. **Parking:** on-site. **Amenities:** high-speed Internet, irons. **Pool(s):** outdoor. **Guest Services:** valet laundry. **Business Services:** meeting rooms, PC. **Cards:** MC, VI.

ASK / SOME UNITS 

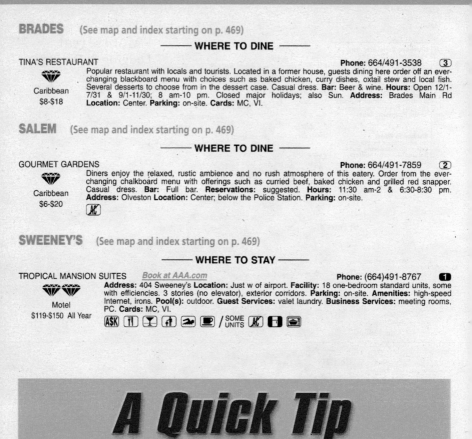

PUERTO RICO

This index helps you "spot" where approved lodgings and restaurants are located on the corresponding detailed maps. Lodging daily rate range is for comparison only and show the property's high season. Restaurant rate range is a combination of lunch and/or dinner. Turn to the listing page for more detailed rate information and consult display ads for special promotions.

DORADO

Map Page	OA	Lodging	Diamond Rated	High Season	Page
1 / p. 473		Embassy Suites Dorado del Mar Beach & Golf Resort	♦♦♦	$149-$299	479

RIO GRANDE

Map Page	OA	Lodgings	Diamond Rated	High Season	Page
2 / p. 473	AAA	**Gran Melia Puerto Rico Resort & Villas** - see color ad p 488	♦♦♦♦	$194-$354 SAVE	487
3 / p. 473	AAA	**Rio Mar Beach Resort & Spa - A Wyndham Grand Resort** - see color ad p 489	♦♦♦♦	$289-$979 SAVE	487

RINCON

Map Page	OA	Lodgings	Diamond Rated	High Season	Page
7 / p. 473		The Lazy Parrot Inn & Restaurant	♦♦	$110-$155	486
8 / p. 473		Rincon of the Seas Grand Caribbean Hotel	♦♦♦	$190-$495	487

ANASCO

Map Page	OA	Lodging	Diamond Rated	High Season	Page
10 / p. 473	AAA	**Rincon Beach Resort** - see color ad p 486	♦♦♦	$190-$630 SAVE	478

FAJARDO

Map Page	OA	Lodgings	Diamond Rated	High Season	Page
12 / p. 473	AAA	**El Conquistador Golf Resort & Casino** - see color ad p 496	♦♦♦	$179-$479 SAVE	479
13 / p. 473	AAA	**Las Casitas Village & Golden Door (R) Spa**	♦♦♦♦	$239-$2470 SAVE	479
14 / p. 473		The Fajardo Inn	♦♦	$110-$354	479

Map Page	OA	Restaurant	Diamond Rated	Cuisine	Meal Range	Page
1 / p. 473		Strip House	♦♦♦	Steak & Seafood	$26-$48	480

HUMACAO

Map Page	OA	Lodgings	Diamond Rated	High Season	Page
16 / p. 473	AAA	**Four Points by Sheraton at Palmas del Mar** - see color ad on insert, p 500	♦♦♦	$165-$225 SAVE	480
17 / p. 473		The Villas at Palmas	♦♦♦	$340-$1005	481

Map Page	OA	Restaurant	Diamond Rated	Cuisine	Meal Range	Page
8 / p. 473		Chez Daniel	♦♦♦	French	$27-$35	481

PONCE

Map Page	OA	Lodgings	Diamond Rated	High Season	Page
19 / p. 473	AAA	**Holiday Inn Ponce & El Tropical Casino** - see color ad p 484	♦♦	$157-$197 SAVE	484
20 / p. 473		Hilton Ponce Golf & Casino Resort - see color ad opposite title page	♦♦♦	$139-$269	483
21 / p. 473	AAA	**Howard Johnson Hotel Ponce** - see color ad p 484	♦♦	$119-$160 SAVE	484
22 / p. 473		Quality Inn El Tuque - see color ad p 485	♦♦	$90-$193	485

Map Page	OA	Restaurants	Diamond Rated	Cuisine	Meal Range	Page
(10) / p. 473		Marks at the Melia	◆◆◆	International	$17-$33	486
(11) / p. 473		La Cava Restaurant	◆◆◆	International	$29-$34	486
(12) / p. 473		Pito's Seafood Restaurant	◆◆	Seafood	$18-$35	486

GUANICA

Map Page	OA	Lodging	Diamond Rated	High Season	Page
(24) / p. 473	AAA	**Copamarina Beach Resort & Spa** - see color ad p 480	◆◆◆	$175-$275 SAVE	480

VIEQUES

Map Page	OA	Lodgings	Diamond Rated	High Season	Page
(29) / p. 473		Inn on the Blue Horizon	◆◆◆	$130-$400	518
(30) / p. 473		Hacienda Tamarindo	◆◆◆	$135-$325	518

CAGUAS

Map Page	OA	Lodging	Diamond Rated	High Season	Page
(32) / p. 473	AAA	**Four Points by Sheraton Caguas Real** - see color ad p 500	◆◆◆	Rates not provided SAVE	478

Map Page	OA	Restaurant	Diamond Rated	Cuisine	Meal Range	Page
(14) / p. 473		Faccio Pizza	◆	Italian	$6-$18	478

MAYAGUEZ

Map Page	OA	Lodgings	Diamond Rated	High Season	Page
(35) / p. 473	AAA	**Holiday Inn of Mayaguez & Tropical Casino** - see color ad p 482	◆◆	$130-$250 SAVE	481
(36) / p. 473		Mayaguez Resort and Casino - see color ad p 482	◆◆	$185-$325	481

Map Page	OA	Restaurant	Diamond Rated	Cuisine	Meal Range	Page
(17) / p. 473		El Castillo	◆◆	International	$16-$34	483

AGUADILLA

Map Page	OA	Restaurant	Diamond Rated	Cuisine	Meal Range	Page
(3) / p. 473		Molina's Restaurant	◆	International	$16-$38	478

ISABELA

Map Page	OA	Restaurant	Diamond Rated	Cuisine	Meal Range	Page
(20) / p. 473		Eclipse Restaurant	◆◆	International	$10-$26	481

CABO ROJO

Map Page	OA	Restaurant	Diamond Rated	Cuisine	Meal Range	Page
(24) / p. 473		Tino's Restaurant	◆	Regional Seafood	$12-$27	478

GUAYNABO

Map Page	OA	Restaurant	Diamond Rated	Cuisine	Meal Range	Page
(26) / p. 473		Faccio Pizza	◆	Italian	$6-$18	480

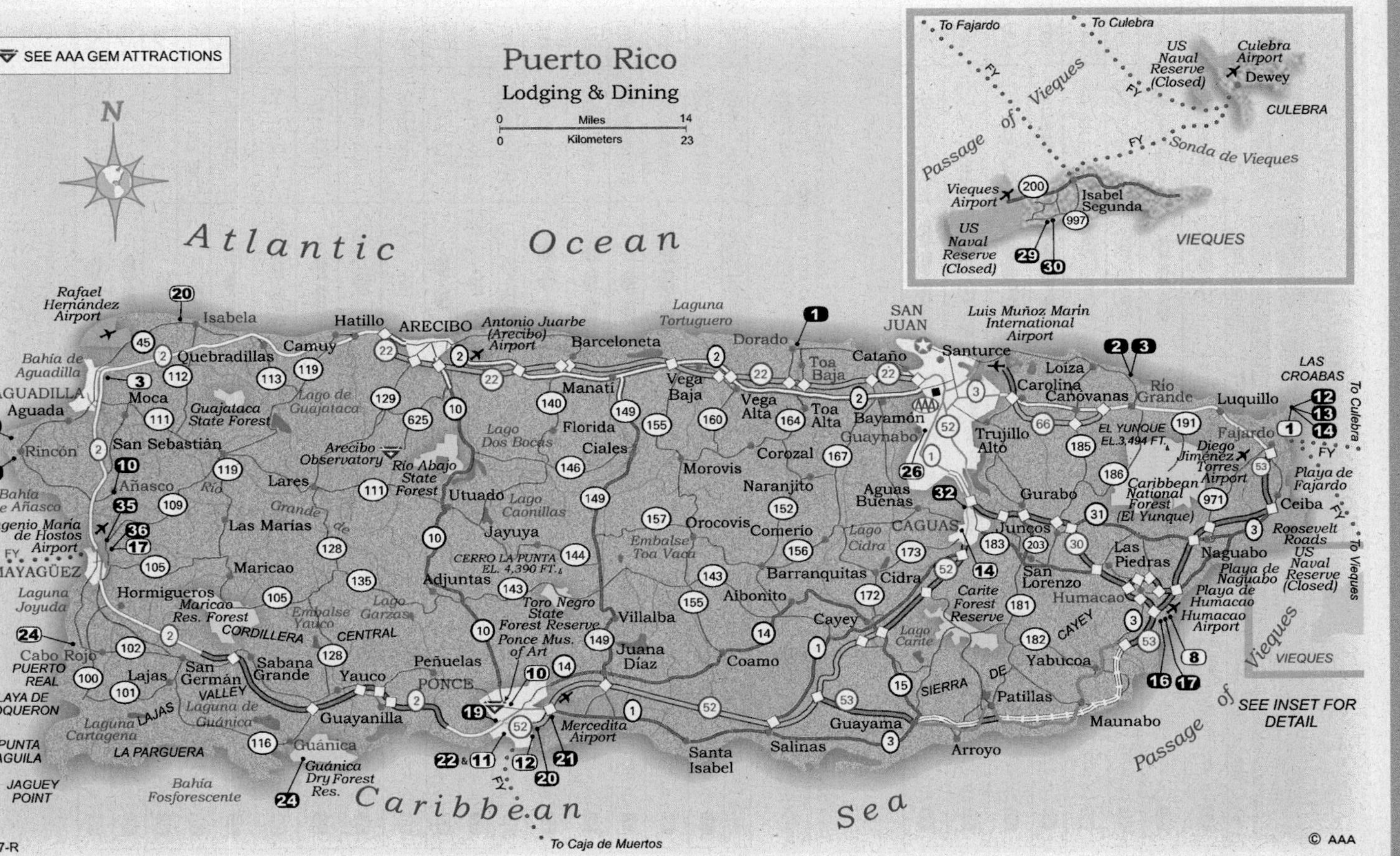
SEE AAA GEM ATTRACTIONS
Puerto Rico
Lodging & Dining
0 Miles 14
0 Kilometers 23
N
Atlantic Ocean
Caribbean Sea
Passage of Vieques
SEE INSET FOR DETAIL
To Fajardo
To Culebra
US Naval Reserve (Closed)
Culebra Airport
Dewey
CULEBRA
Sonda de Vieques
Vieques Airport
Isabel Segunda
VIEQUES
To Vieques
To Dominican Republic
To Caja de Muertos
Rafael Hernández Airport
Isabela
Hatillo
ARECIBO
Antonio Juarbe (Arecibo) Airport
Barceloneta
Laguna Tortuguero
Dorado
SAN JUAN
Luis Muñoz Marín International Airport
Santurce
Cataño
Toa Baja
Loíza
Carolina
Canóvanas
Río Grande
LAS CROABAS
Luquillo
Bahía de Aguadilla
AGUADILLA
Aguada
Quebradillas
Camuy
Moca
Guajataca State Forest
Lago de Guajataca
Manatí
Vega Baja
Vega Alta
Toa Alta
Bayamón
Guaynabo
Trujillo Alto
EL YUNQUE EL.3,494 FT.
Fajardo
Diego Jiménez Torres Airport
Playa de Fajardo
Rincón
San Sebastián
Arecibo Observatory
Río Abajo State Forest
Lago Dos Bocas
Florida
Ciales
Morovis
Corozal
Naranjito
Aguas Buenas
Gurabo
Caribbean National Forest (El Yunque)
Ceiba
Bahía de Añasco
Añasco
Río Grande de
Lares
Utuado
Lago Caonillas
Eugenio María de Hostos Airport
Las Marías
Jayuya
Orocovis
Comerío
Lago Cidra
CAGUAS
Juncos
Roosevelt Roads
MAYAGÜEZ
Maricao
CERRO LA PUNTA EL. 4,390 FT.
Embalse Toa Vaca
Barranquitas
Cidra
Las Piedras
Naguabo
Playa de Naguabo
Adjuntas
Toro Negro State Forest Reserve
Aibonito
Cayey
Carite Forest Reserve
San Lorenzo
Humacao
Playa de Humacao
Humacao Airport
Laguna Joyuda
Hormigueros
Maricao Res. Forest
Embalse Yauco
Lago Garzas
CORDILLERA CENTRAL
Villalba
Ponce Mus. of Art
Lago Carite
CAYEY
Cabo Rojo
PUERTO REAL
Lajas
San Germán
Sabana Grande
Yauco
Peñuelas
Juana Díaz
Coamo
Yabucoa
PLAYA DE BOQUERON
LAJAS VALLEY
Laguna de Guánica
PONCE
Mercedita Airport
SIERRA DE
Patillas
Laguna Cartagena
Guayanilla
Guayama
Maunabo
PUNTA AGUILA
LA PARGUERA
Guánica
Guánica Dry Forest Res.
Santa Isabel
Salinas
Arroyo
JAGUEY POINT
Bahía Fosforescente
1517-R
© AAA

San Juan

Airport Accommodations

Map Page	OA	SAN JUAN INTERNATIONAL AIRPORT	Diamond Rated	High Season	Page
50 / p. 477	AAA	**Best Western San Juan Airport Hotel, in airport**	◆◆	$160-$250 SAVE	490
52 / p. 477	AAA	**Courtyard by Marriott-Isla Verde Beach Resort, 0.3 mi (0.5 km) n of airport**	◆◆◆	$216-$319 SAVE	494
41 / p. 477	AAA	**El San Juan Hotel & Casino, 2 mi (3.2 km)**	◆◆◆	$189-$505 SAVE	497
46 / p. 477	AAA	**Embassy Suites Hotel & Casino San Juan, 1.5 mi (2.4 km)**	◆◆◆	$180-$360 SAVE	497
43 / p. 477		Hampton Inn & Suites-San Juan, 2 mi (3.2 km)	◆◆◆	$144-$279	497
48 / p. 477	AAA	**Holiday Inn San Juan, 1.6 mi (2.5 km) w of airport**	◆◆◆	$195-$320 SAVE	501
40 / p. 477	AAA	**InterContinental San Juan Resort & Casino, 2.1 mi (3.3 km)**	◆◆◆◆	$199-$659 SAVE	504
44 / p. 477		The Ritz-Carlton San Juan Hotel, Spa & Casino, 1 mi (1.6 km)	◆◆◆◆	$249-$579	508

San Juan

This index helps you "spot" where approved lodgings and restaurants are located on the corresponding detailed maps. Lodging daily rate range is for comparison only and show the property's high season. Restaurant rate range is a combination of lunch and/or dinner. Turn to the listing page for more detailed rate information and consult display ads for special promotions.

SAN JUAN

Map Page	OA	Lodgings	Diamond Rated	High Season	Page
1 / p. 477	AAA	**Hotel El Convento** - see color ad p 501	fyi	$235-$425 SAVE	502
4 / p. 477	AAA	**Sheraton Old San Juan Hotel** - see color ad p 510	◆◆◆	$149-$449 SAVE	510
7 / p. 477	AAA	**Normandie Hotel** - see color ad p 506	◆◆◆	$190-$300 SAVE	504
10 / p. 477		Caribe Hilton - see color ad opposite title page, p 491	◆◆◆	$139-$429	491
14 / p. 477	AAA	**Condado Plaza Hotel & Casino** - see color ad p 493	◆◆◆	$199-$329 SAVE	492
16 / p. 477	AAA	**Holiday Inn Express** - see color ad p 501	◆◆	$140-$199 SAVE	499
17 / p. 477		Comfort Inn San Juan - see color ad p 492	◆	$109-$139	492
18 / p. 477		Coral Princess Inn	◆◆	$99-$160	492
19 / p. 477		La Concha - A Renaissance Resort - see color ad p 505	fyi	$239-$369	504
20 / p. 477	AAA	**El Canario by the Lagoon** - see color ad p 495	◆	$120-$165 SAVE	495
22 / p. 477		Courtyard by Marriott San Juan Miramar - see color ad p 495.	◆◆	$153-$227	494
24 / p. 477	AAA	**San Juan Marriott Resort & Stellaris Casino** - see color ad p 509	◆◆◆◆	$211-$345 SAVE	508
25 / p. 477		Radisson Ambassador Plaza Hotel & Casino - see color ad p 506	◆◆◆	$239-$279	507
28 / p. 477	AAA	**Acacia Boutique Hotel**	◆◆	$85-$225 SAVE	490
30 / p. 477		Quality Inn El Portal - see color ad p 507	◆	$116-$129	504
32 / p. 477		At Wind Chimes Inn	◆◆	$65-$145	490
33 / p. 477		Le Consulat - A Clarion Collection Hotel	◆◆	$120-$165	504

SAN JUAN (cont'd)

Map Page	OA	Lodgings (cont'd)	Diamond Rated	High Season	Page
36 / p. 477	AAA	**Best Western Hotel Pierre** - see color ad p 490	fyi	$155-$279 SAVE	490
40 / p. 477	AAA	**InterContinental San Juan Resort & Casino** - see color ad p 503	♦♦♦♦	$199-$659 SAVE	504
41 / p. 477	AAA	**El San Juan Hotel & Casino** - see color ad p 498	♦♦♦	$189-$505 SAVE	497
42 / p. 477		San Juan Water & Beach Club Hotel	♦♦♦	$149-$695	510
43 / p. 477		Hampton Inn & Suites-San Juan	♦♦♦	$144-$279	497
44 / p. 477		The Ritz-Carlton San Juan Hotel, Spa & Casino	♦♦♦♦	$249-$579	508
46 / p. 477	AAA	**Embassy Suites Hotel & Casino San Juan** - see color ad p 499	♦♦♦	$180-$360 SAVE	497
48 / p. 477	AAA	**Holiday Inn San Juan** - see color ad p 502	♦♦♦	$195-$320 SAVE	501
50 / p. 477	AAA	**Best Western San Juan Airport Hotel**	♦♦	$160-$250 SAVE	490
52 / p. 477	AAA	**Courtyard by Marriott-Isla Verde Beach Resort** - see color ad p 494	♦♦♦	$216-$319 SAVE	494

Map Page	OA	Restaurants	Diamond Rated	Cuisine	Meal Range	Page
2 / p. 477		Ristorante Il Perugino	♦♦♦	Northern Italian	$28-$40	515
3 / p. 477		Cafe' Bohemio	♦♦	Caribbean	$8-$15	511
6 / p. 477		Old Harbor Brewery Steak & Lobster House	♦♦	International	$12-$38	514
8 / p. 477		Sofia Italian Kitchen & Wine Bar	♦♦♦	Italian	$12-$36	515
9 / p. 477		The Parrot Club	♦♦	New Latin American	$12-$36	514
10 / p. 477		Trois Cent Onze	♦♦♦	French	$16-$38	516
12 / p. 477		Sonne' Ambience Bar & Restaurant	♦♦	International	$15-$28	515
14 / p. 477	AAA	**Tantra**	♦♦♦	Indian	$16-$30	515
15 / p. 477		Dragonfly	♦♦	New Latin American	$12-$25	512
16 / p. 477		Aguaviva Seaside Latino Cuisine	♦♦♦	Seafood	$16-$35	511
17 / p. 477		Fratelli Ristorante	♦♦	Italian	$17-$29	512
20 / p. 477		El Alcazar Marisqueria y Tasca Espanola	♦♦♦	Spanish	$15-$33	512
21 / p. 477		Makarios Arabian Cuisine & Bar	♦♦	Arabic	$10-$24	513
24 / p. 477		Al Dente Ristorante and Wine Bar	♦♦	Italian	$15-$35	511
25 / p. 477		Mofongo Criollo Cuisine & Bar	♦♦	Puerto Rican	$15-$25	513
28 / p. 477		Panza Restaurant at Chateau Cervantes	♦♦♦	International	$25-$49	514
30 / p. 477		Morton's of Chicago, The Steakhouse	♦♦♦	Steak	$29-$50	513
31 / p. 477		Madrid-San Juan	♦♦	Spanish	$14-$34	513
32 / p. 477		Restaurante Escambron Beach Club	♦♦	Caribbean	$10-$21	514
34 / p. 477		Lemon Grass	♦♦♦	New Asian	$18-$36	513
38 / p. 477		Jose Jose Restaurant	♦♦♦	International	$30-$46	512

Map Page	OA	Restaurants (cont'd)	Diamond Rated	Cuisine	Meal Range	Page
39 / p. 477	AAA	**Restaurant Ajili-Mojili**	2 Diamonds	Caribbean	$16-$28	514
42 / p. 477		Chayote Restaurant	3 Diamonds	International	$12-$35	511
44 / p. 477		Augusto's Cuisine	4 Diamonds	Continental	$24-$45	511
46 / p. 477		Ropa Vieja Grill	2 Diamonds	Cuban	$16-$32	515
47 / p. 477		Zabo Creative Cuisine	2 Diamonds	International	$16-$28	516
50 / p. 477		Che's Restaurant Argentino	2 Diamonds	Argentine	$12-$25	512
52 / p. 477		Buenos Ayres Bar & Grill	1 Diamond	Argentine	$17-$33	511
54 / p. 477		Restaurant Antonio	3 Diamonds	International	$12-$36	514
55 / p. 477		Tijuana's Bar & Grill	1 Diamond	Mexican	$10-$24	516
56 / p. 477		Latin Star Restaurant	1 Diamond	Caribbean	$9-$32	513
57 / p. 477		El Mariachi Restaurante	2 Diamonds	Mexican	$10-$26	512
58 / p. 477		Migas Innovative Cuisine	2 Diamonds	International	$18-$30	513
60 / p. 477		Pikayo	4 Diamonds	International	$21-$60	514
62 / p. 477		Restaurant Compostela	3 Diamonds	Spanish	$14-$38	514
63 / p. 477		BLT Steak	4 Diamonds	Steak	$28-$48	511
64 / p. 477		La Casona Restaurante	3 Diamonds	Spanish	$19-$37	512
66 / p. 477		Restaurante Los Chavales	3 Diamonds	Spanish	$14-$37	514
67 / p. 477		Tierra Santa Restaurant	2 Diamonds	Arabic	$11-$23	516
68 / p. 477		Tierra del Fuego	2 Diamonds	Argentine	$12-$26	515
70 / p. 477		Al Salem Restaurant	1 Diamond	Arabic	$12-$24	511
71 / p. 477		Yum Yum Tree	2 Diamonds	Asian	$12-$25	516
72 / p. 477		El Zipperle Restaurante	2 Diamonds	International	$17-$32	512
74 / p. 477		Shogun Japanese Restaurant	2 Diamonds	Japanese	$19-$37	515
76 / p. 477		Faccio Pizza	1 Diamond	Italian	$6-$18	512
80 / p. 477		Faccio Pizza	1 Diamond	Italian	$6-$18	512
81 / p. 477		Momoyama	2 Diamonds	Japanese	$13-$36	513
82 / p. 477		Ruth's Chris Steak House	3 Diamonds	Steak	$27-$43	515
83 / p. 477		Tangerine	3 Diamonds	International	$24-$36	515
84 / p. 477		La Piccola Fontana	3 Diamonds	Italian	$22-$35	513
85 / p. 477		Platos Restaurant	2 Diamonds	Caribbean	$18-$45	514
86 / p. 477		Metropol Restaurant	1 Diamond	Cuban	$11-$27	513
87 / p. 477		Il Mulino	3 Diamonds	Italian	$24-$65	512

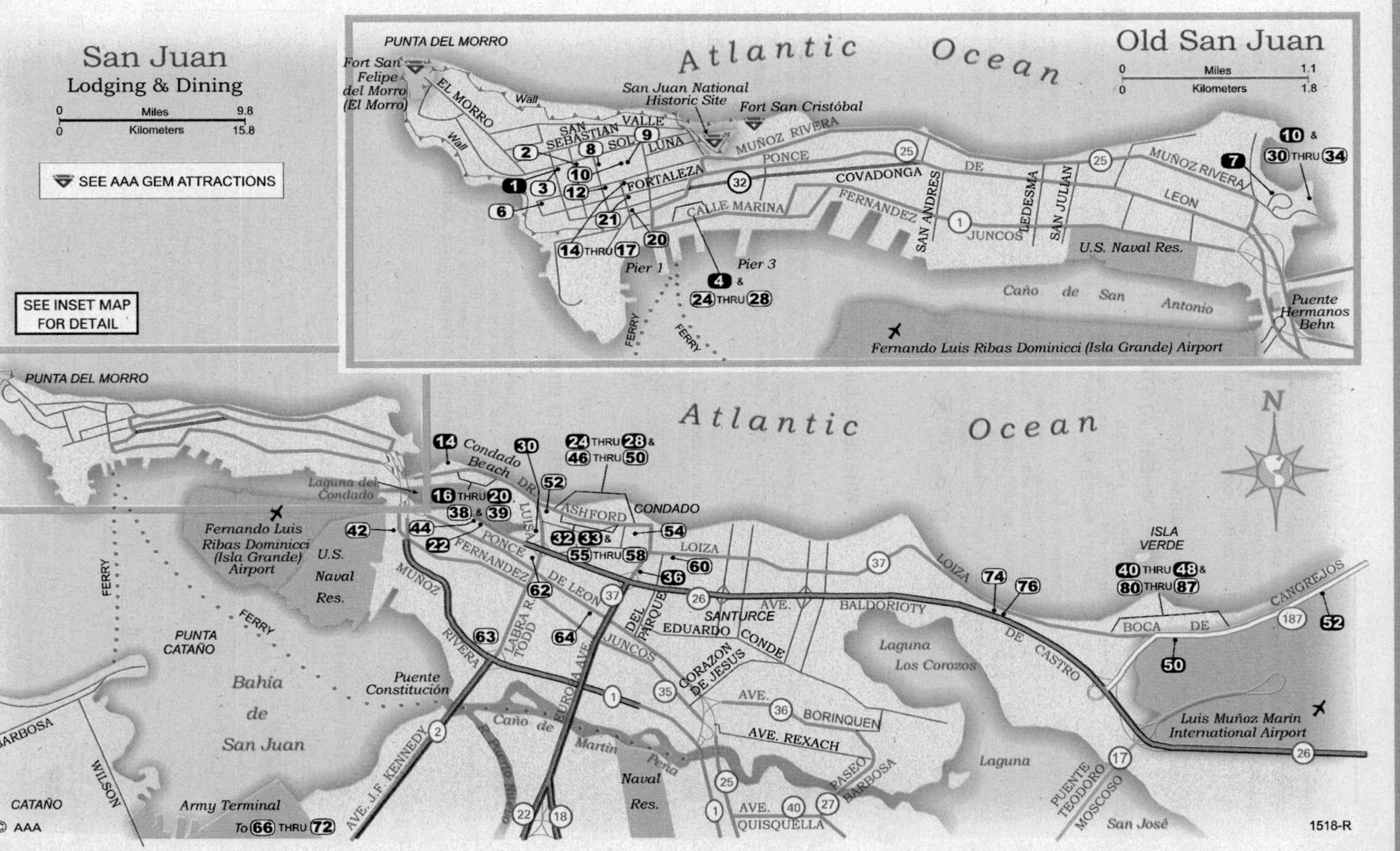
San Juan
Lodging & Dining
0 Miles 9.8
0 Kilometers 15.8
SEE AAA GEM ATTRACTIONS
SEE INSET MAP FOR DETAIL
Old San Juan
0 Miles 1.1
0 Kilometers 1.8
Atlantic Ocean
PUNTA DEL MORRO
Fort San Felipe del Morro (El Morro)
San Juan National Historic Site
Fort San Cristóbal
EL MORRO
Wall
SAN SEBASTIAN
VALLE
SOL
LUNA
FORTALEZA
MUÑOZ RIVERA
PONCE
COVADONGA
CALLE MARINA
FERNANDEZ
SAN ANDRES
JUNCOS
LEDESMA
SAN JULIAN
DE
LEON
U.S. Naval Res.
Pier 1
Pier 3
FERRY
Caño de San Antonio
Puente Hermanos Behn
Fernando Luis Ribas Dominicci (Isla Grande) Airport
Condado Beach
CONDADO
ASHFORD
LUISA
DR.
Laguna del Condado
Fernando Luis Ribas Dominicci (Isla Grande) Airport
U.S. Naval Res.
PONCE
FERNANDEZ
DE LEON
MUÑOZ RIVERA
LABRA R.
TODD
EUROPA AVE.
JUNCOS
DEL PARQUE
SANTURCE
EDUARDO CONDE
CORAZON DE JESUS
LOIZA
AVE. BALDORIOTY DE CASTRO
BOCA DE CANGREJOS
ISLA VERDE
Laguna Los Corozos
Laguna
AVE. BORINQUEN
AVE. REXACH
PASEO BARBOSA
AVE. QUISQUELLA
Caño de Martín Peña
R. Puerto Nuevo
Naval Res.
Puente Constitución
PUNTA CATAÑO
Bahía de San Juan
AVE. J.F. KENNEDY
BARBOSA
WILSON
CATAÑO
Army Terminal
To 66 THRU 72
Luis Muñoz Marín International Airport
PUENTE TEODORO MOSCOSO
San José
N
© AAA
1518-R

AGUADILLA pop. 64,685 (See map and index starting on p. 473)

WHERE TO DINE

MOLINA'S RESTAURANT **Phone:** 787/882-1487 (3)

International
$16-$38

The popular restaurant prepares halibut, mahi mahi, salmon and other fish, as well as various cuts of steak and pork and a good selection of soups made on site. Presentation of the meal is straightforward with little embellishment. The decor shows attractive enhancements. Dressy casual. **Bar:** Full bar. **Reservations:** suggested. **Hours:** 11 am-10 pm, Fri & Sat-midnight. Closed: 11/26. **Address:** Carr #2 KM 117.6 **Location:** Bo Ceiba Baja section of town. **Parking:** on-site. **Cards:** AX, MC, VI.

ANASCO pop. 28,348 (See map and index starting on p. 473)

WHERE TO STAY

RINCON BEACH RESORT *Book great rates at AAA.com* **Phone:** (787)589-9000 (10)

AAA SAVE

Hotel
$190-$630 All Year

Address: Carr 115, KM 5.8, Bo Caguabo **Location:** Oceanfront. 5.4 mi (8.6 km) s of Rincon; just n of jct Hwy 429 and 115. **Facility:** Meets AAA guest room security requirements. Designated smoking area. 112 units. 88 one-bedroom standard units, some with whirlpools. 12 one- and 12 two-bedroom suites with kitchens. 4-6 stories, exterior corridors. *Bath:* combo or shower only. **Parking:** on-site. **Terms:** 2-3 night minimum stay - weekends, 3 day cancellation notice. **Amenities:** video games (fee), dual phone lines, voice mail, safes, irons, hair dryers. **Dining:** 2 restaurants. **Pool(s):** outdoor. **Leisure Activities:** whirlpool, putting green, lighted tennis court, playground, exercise room, volleyball. *Fee:* paddleboats, kayaks, massage. **Guest Services:** valet laundry, wireless Internet. **Business Services:** meeting rooms, business center. **Cards:** AX, MC, VI. **Free Special Amenities: early check-in/late check-out.** Affiliated with A Preferred Hotel. *(See color ad p 486)*

/ SOME UNITS

BAYAMON pop. 224,044

WHERE TO DINE

FACCIO PIZZA **Phone:** 787/799-5777

Italian
$6-$18

Family owned and operated for many decades, this popular eatery serves outstanding thin crust pizza and a variety of pastas and other Italian dishes. All moderately priced, it is difficult to choose from the varied menu selections including lasagna, ravioli, manicotti and seafood. Casual dress. **Bar:** Full bar. **Hours:** 11 am-11 pm, Fri & Sat-midnight. Closed: 11/26, 12/25. **Address:** Carr 167 **Location:** In Rexville Paradise Mall. **Parking:** on-site. **Cards:** AX, DC, DS, MC, VI.

FACCIO PIZZA **Phone:** 787/778-2222

Italian
$6-$18

Family owned and operated for many decades, this popular eatery serves outstanding thin crust pizza and a variety of pastas and other Italian dishes. All moderately priced, it is difficult to choose from the varied menu selections including lasagna, ravioli, manicotti and seafood. Casual dress. **Bar:** Full bar. **Hours:** 10:30 am-11 pm, Fri-Sun to midnight. Closed: 11/26, 12/25. **Address:** Carr 167 Esq C/24 Sierra Bayamon **Location:** In Plaza di Luna; across from Plaza del Sol. **Parking:** on-site. **Cards:** AX, DC, DS, MC, VI.

CABO ROJO pop. 46,911 (See map and index starting on p. 473)

WHERE TO DINE

TINO'S RESTAURANT **Phone:** 787/851-2976 (24)

Regional Seafood
$12-$27

The casual restaurant nurtures a family atmosphere. Puerto Rican seafood specialties—such as mofongo relleno con mariscos, which is loaded with fish, octopus and shrimp inside a mashed fried plantain shell—line the menu. Casual dress. **Bar:** Full bar. **Hours:** 11 am-10 pm, Fri & Sat-11 pm, Sun-9:30 pm. Closed: Tues. **Address:** Rd 102, KM 13.6 **Location:** In Joyuda's Beach; Hwy 2 or 52 to Cabo Rojo, 4 mi (6.4 km) s on Hwy 100, 3.4 mi (5.4 km) w on Hwy 102 at KM 13.6. **Parking:** on-site. **Cards:** AX, MC, VI.

CAGUAS pop. 140,502 (See map and index starting on p. 473)

WHERE TO STAY

FOUR POINTS BY SHERATON CAGUAS REAL **Phone:** 787/653-1111 (32)

AAA SAVE

Hotel
Rates not provided

Address: 500 Alambra & Granada Blvd **Location:** 22 mi (35.2 km) s of airport; Hwy 52, exit 22, follow signs. **Facility:** The newly built hotel is perfect for corporate travelers; it features spacious, tasteful guest units and a brand-new, state-of-the-art casino. Meets AAA guest room security requirements. Designated smoking area. 126 units. 92 one-bedroom standard units. 34 one-bedroom suites. 4 stories, interior corridors. *Bath:* combo or shower only. **Parking:** on-site (fee) and valet. **Amenities:** video games (fee), high-speed Internet, voice mail, irons, hair dryers. *Some:* DVD players, safes. **Dining:** 2 restaurants. **Pool(s):** outdoor. **Leisure Activities:** whirlpool, exercise room. **Guest Services:** valet and coin laundry, wireless Internet. **Business Services:** meeting rooms. *(See color ad p 500)*

CALL / SOME UNITS

WHERE TO DINE

FACCIO PIZZA **Phone:** 787/746-4185 (14)

Italian
$6-$18

Family owned and operated for many decades, this popular eatery serves outstanding thin crust pizza and a variety of pastas and other Italian dishes. All moderately priced, it is difficult to choose from the varied menu selections including lasagna, ravioli, manicotti and seafood. Casual dress. **Bar:** Full bar. **Hours:** noon-midnight. Closed: 11/26, 12/25. **Address:** Ave Luis Munoz Marin #AB-10 **Location:** In Urb Caguas Norte. **Parking:** on-site. **Cards:** AX, DC, DS, MC, VI.

DORADO pop. 34,017 (See map and index starting on p. 473)

— WHERE TO STAY —

EMBASSY SUITES DORADO DEL MAR BEACH & GOLF RESORT *Book great rates at AAA.com* **Phone:** (787)796-6125 1

Resort Hotel

$149-$299 All Year

Address: 201 Dorado del Mar Blvd **Location:** Oceanfront. From San Juan, 25 mi (40 km) w on Hwy 22 to exit 22 (Dorado), 2 mi (3.2 km) n on Hwy 165; 3.5 mi (5.6 km) w on Hwy 693/6165. **Facility:** Spacious, well-equipped units at this contemporary resort-hotel are on the beach and adjacent to the golf course. Meets AAA guest room security requirements. 174 one-bedroom suites. 7 stories, interior corridors. *Bath:* combo or shower only. **Parking:** on-site (fee) and valet. **Terms:** check-in 4 pm, 1-30 night minimum stay, cancellation fee imposed. **Amenities:** high-speed Internet, dual phone lines, voice mail, safes, irons, hair dryers. **Pool(s):** outdoor. **Leisure Activities:** whirlpool, snorkeling equipment rental, 2 lighted tennis courts, recreation programs, playground, exercise room, volleyball. *Fee:* golf-18 holes, massage, game room. **Guest Services:** valet and coin laundry, wireless Internet. **Business Services:** conference facilities, business center. **Cards:** AX, CB, DC, DS, MC, VI.

/ SOME UNITS

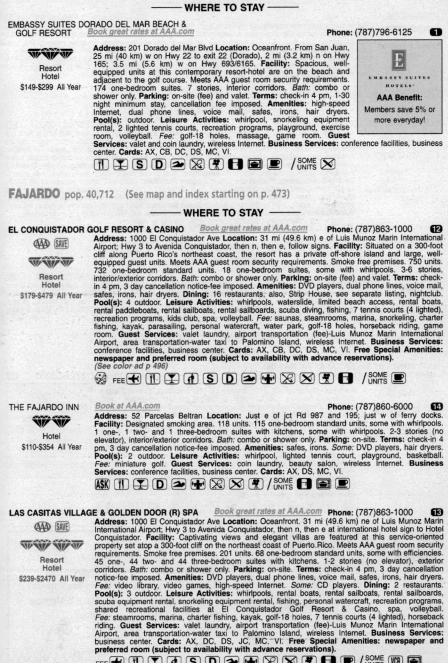

FAJARDO pop. 40,712 (See map and index starting on p. 473)

— WHERE TO STAY —

EL CONQUISTADOR GOLF RESORT & CASINO *Book great rates at AAA.com* **Phone:** (787)863-1000 12

AAA SAVE

Resort Hotel

$179-$479 All Year

Address: 1000 El Conquistador Ave **Location:** 31 mi (49.6 km) e of Luis Munoz Marin International Airport; Hwy 3 to Avenida Conquistador, then n, then e, follow signs. **Facility:** Situated on a 300-foot cliff along Puerto Rico's northeast coast, the resort has a private off-shore island and large, well-equipped guest units. Meets AAA guest room security requirements. Smoke free premises. 750 units. 732 one-bedroom standard units. 18 one-bedroom suites, some with whirlpools. 3-6 stories, interior/exterior corridors. *Bath:* combo or shower only. **Parking:** on-site (fee) and valet. **Terms:** check-in 4 pm, 3 day cancellation notice-fee imposed. **Amenities:** DVD players, dual phone lines, voice mail, safes, irons, hair dryers. **Dining:** 16 restaurants, also, Strip House, see separate listing, nightclub. **Pool(s):** 4 outdoor. **Leisure Activities:** whirlpools, waterslide, limited beach access, rental boats, rental paddleboats, rental sailboats, rental sailboards, scuba diving, fishing, 7 tennis courts (4 lighted), recreation programs, kids club, spa, volleyball. *Fee:* saunas, steamrooms, marina, snorkeling, charter fishing, kayak, parasailing, personal watercraft, water park, golf-18 holes, horseback riding, game room. **Guest Services:** valet laundry, airport transportation (fee)-Luis Munoz Marin International Airport, area transportation-water taxi to Palomino Island, wireless Internet. **Business Services:** conference facilities, business center. **Cards:** AX, CB, DC, DS, MC, VI. **Free Special Amenities: newspaper and preferred room (subject to availability with advance reservations).** *(See color ad p 496)*

FEE / SOME UNITS

THE FAJARDO INN *Book at AAA.com* **Phone:** (787)860-6000 14

Hotel

$110-$354 All Year

Address: 52 Parcelas Beltran **Location:** Just e of jct Rd 987 and 195; just w of ferry docks. **Facility:** Designated smoking area. 118 units. 115 one-bedroom standard units, some with whirlpools. 1 one-, 1 two- and 1 three-bedroom suites with kitchens, some with whirlpools. 2-3 stories (no elevator), interior/exterior corridors. *Bath:* combo or shower only. **Parking:** on-site. **Terms:** check-in 4 pm, 3 day cancellation notice-fee imposed. **Amenities:** safes, irons. *Some:* DVD players, hair dryers. **Pool(s):** 2 outdoor. **Leisure Activities:** whirlpool, lighted tennis court, playground, basketball. *Fee:* miniature golf. **Guest Services:** coin laundry, beauty salon, wireless Internet. **Business Services:** conference facilities, business center. **Cards:** AX, DS, MC, VI.

ASK / SOME UNITS

LAS CASITAS VILLAGE & GOLDEN DOOR (R) SPA *Book great rates at AAA.com* **Phone:** (787)863-1000 13

AAA SAVE

Resort Hotel

$239-$2470 All Year

Address: 1000 El Conquistador Ave **Location:** Oceanfront. 31 mi (49.6 km) ne of Luis Munoz Marin International Airport; Hwy 3 to Avenida Conquistador, then n, then e at international hotel sign to Hotel Conquistador. **Facility:** Captivating views and elegant villas are featured at this service-oriented property set atop a 300-foot cliff on the northeast coast of Puerto Rico. Meets AAA guest room security requirements. Smoke free premises. 201 units. 68 one-bedroom standard units, some with efficiencies. 45 one-, 44 two- and 44 three-bedroom suites with kitchens. 1-2 stories (no elevator), exterior corridors. *Bath:* combo or shower only. **Parking:** on-site. **Terms:** check-in 4 pm, 3 day cancellation notice-fee imposed. **Amenities:** DVD players, dual phone lines, voice mail, safes, irons, hair dryers. *Fee:* video library, video games, high-speed Internet. *Some:* CD players. **Dining:** 2 restaurants. **Pool(s):** 3 outdoor. **Leisure Activities:** whirlpools, rental boats, rental sailboats, rental sailboards, scuba equipment rental, snorkeling equipment rental, fishing, personal watercraft, recreation programs, shared recreational facilities at El Conquistador Golf Resort & Casino, spa, volleyball. *Fee:* steamrooms, marina, charter fishing, kayak, golf-18 holes, 7 tennis courts (4 lighted), horseback riding. **Guest Services:** valet laundry, airport transportation (fee)-Luis Munoz Marin International Airport, area transportation-water taxi to Palomino Island, wireless Internet. **Business Services:** business center. **Cards:** AX, DC, DS, JC, MC, VI. **Free Special Amenities: newspaper and preferred room (subject to availability with advance reservations).**

FEE / SOME UNITS VCR

(See map and index starting on p. 473)

WHERE TO DINE

STRIP HOUSE — Phone: 787/863-6789 (1)

Steak & Seafood
$26-$48

One of the hottest new steakhouse concepts from New York City has reached the shores of Puerto Rico. Tastefully done burlesque decor sets a sexy mood for dining on thick Choice steaks, veal, lamb and fish, such as salmon and tuna. Large portions make the side dishes and appetizers great for sharing. The well-trained staff is attentive to many details. Dressy casual. **Bar:** Full bar. **Reservations:** required. **Hours:** 6 pm-midnight, Fri & Sat-1 am, Sun 5 pm-11 pm. **Address:** 1000 El Conquistador Ave **Location:** 31 mi (49.6 km) e of Luis Munoz Marin International Airport; in El Conquistador Golf Resort & Casino. **Parking:** on-site (fee) and valet. **Cards:** AX, CB, DC, DS, JC, MC, VI.

GUANICA pop. 21,888 (See map and index starting on p. 473)

WHERE TO STAY

COPAMARINA BEACH RESORT & SPA — **Phone:** (787)821-0505 (24)

AAA SAVE

Resort Hotel
$175-$275 All Year

Address: Rt 333, KM 6.5 **Location:** Oceanfront. Hwy 2, exit 194 (SR 16), 2.4 mi (3.8 km) s, then 3.8 mi (6.1 km) e on SR 333, follow signs to Cana Gorda. **Facility:** This beachfront resort on 20 landscaped acres provides a laid-back alternative to the frenetic pace of the cities. Designated smoking area. 106 units. 102 one-bedroom standard units. 2 one- and 2 three-bedroom suites, some with kitchens. 1-2 stories, exterior corridors. *Bath:* combo or shower only. **Parking:** on-site. **Terms:** 7 day cancellation notice-fee imposed. **Amenities:** dual phone lines, voice mail, safes, hair dryers. **Dining:** 2 restaurants. **Pool(s):** 2 outdoor. **Leisure Activities:** whirlpools, beach access, rental boats, rental paddleboats, rental sailboats, boat dock, 2 lighted tennis courts, recreation programs, hiking trails, playground, exercise room, spa, volleyball, game room. *Fee:* steamrooms, scuba diving, snorkeling, kayaks, trips to Gilligan's Island. **Guest Services:** valet and coin laundry, wireless Internet. **Business Services:** meeting rooms, business center. **Cards:** AX, MC, VI. *(See color ad below)*

FEE

GUAYNABO pop. 100,053 (See map and index starting on p. 473)

WHERE TO DINE

FACCIO PIZZA — **Phone:** 787/731-6566 (26)

Italian
$6-$18

Family owned and operated for many decades, this popular eatery serves outstanding thin crust pizza and a variety of pastas and other Italian dishes. All moderately priced, it is difficult to choose from the varied menu selections including lasagna, ravioli, manicotti and seafood. Casual dress. **Bar:** Full bar. **Hours:** 11 am-midnight. Closed: 11/26, 12/25. **Address:** Ave Esmeralda **Location:** Urb Munoz Rivera. **Parking:** on-site. **Cards:** AX, DC, DS, MC, VI.

HUMACAO pop. 59,035 (See map and index starting on p. 473)

WHERE TO STAY

FOUR POINTS BY SHERATON AT PALMAS DEL MAR Book great rates at AAA.com — **Phone:** (787)850-6000 (16)

AAA SAVE

Hotel
$165-$225 All Year

Address: Candelero Dr, #170 Palmas del Mar **Location:** 2 mi (3.2 km) s off Hwy 53 on Hwy 906, exit 35B; in Palmas del Mar residential resort. **Facility:** Choose from several spacious room categories at this recently renovated hotel in a sprawling, residential resort community. Smoke free premises. 107 units. 96 one-bedroom standard units. 11 one-bedroom suites. 3 stories (no elevator), exterior corridors. *Bath:* combo or shower only. **Parking:** on-site. **Terms:** 3 day cancellation notice. **Amenities:** video games (fee), high-speed Internet, dual phone lines, voice mail, safes, irons, hair dryers. *Some:* CD players. **Dining:** 3 restaurants. **Pool(s):** outdoor. **Leisure Activities:** whirlpool, shared facilities at Palmas del Mar, exercise room, game room. *Fee:* massage. **Guest Services:** valet laundry, wireless Internet. **Business Services:** conference facilities, PC. **Cards:** AX, CB, DC, DS, JC, MC, VI. **Free Special Amenities: high-speed Internet.** *(See color ad on insert & p 500)*

S D / SOME UNITS

FOUR POINTS BY SHERATON
AAA Benefit:
Members get up to 15% off, plus Starwood Preferred Guest® bonuses.

▼ See AAA listing above ▼

(See map and index starting on p. 473)

THE VILLAS AT PALMAS Book at AAA.com Phone: (939)645-0916 17

Condominium
$340-$1005 All Year

Address: 295 Palmas Inn Way, Suite 6 **Location:** 2 mi (3.2 km) s off Hwy 53 on Hwy 906, exit 35B (Palmanova Plaza). **Facility:** Well-appointed rental condominiums, some of which have been recently remodeled, are set in a residential resort area. Smoke free premises. 50 condominiums. 2 stories (no elevator), exterior corridors. **Parking:** on-site. **Terms:** office hours 7 am-1:30 am. **Amenities:** CD players, voice mail, irons, hair dryers. *Some:* DVD players. **Pool(s):** outdoor. **Leisure Activities:** whirlpool. *Fee:* horseback riding. **Guest Services:** complimentary laundry, wireless Internet. **Business Services:** PC. **Cards:** MC, VI.

D FEE / SOME UNITS VCR

WHERE TO DINE

CHEZ DANIEL Phone: 787/850-3838 8

French
$27-$35

Owner-chef Daniel Vasse has treated local and tourist clientele for numerous years at the marina restaurant. Offerings of French cuisine include preparations of duck, lamb venison, halibut and seafood bouillabaisse. Starters of frog's legs and escargots are worth consideration. This place gets busy for Sunday brunch. Dressy casual. **Bar:** Full bar. **Reservations:** suggested. **Hours:** Open 12/1-6/1 & 7/1-11/30; 6:30 pm-10 pm, Fri-Sun also noon-4 pm. Closed: Tues. **Address:** 110 Harbour Dr, Suite 5 **Location:** 2 mi (3.2 km) s off Hwy 53 on Hwy 906, exit 35B to Palmas del Mar; at Palmas del Mar Marina. **Parking:** on-site. **Cards:** AX, MC, VI.

ISABELA pop. 44,444 (See map and index starting on p. 473)

WHERE TO DINE

ECLIPSE RESTAURANT Phone: 787/872-9554 20

International
$10-$26

One of Puerto Rico's hot new chefs is carving a nice niche at the chic, oceanside restaurant. Among inspiring dishes are five-spice-crusted calamari, curry-marinated duck breast, pan-roasted tilapia and chimichurri-marinated lamb chops with goat cheese and tamarind sauce. Tempting desserts, such as the baked Bosc pear tart and bourbon pecan pie, are difficult to pass up. Casual dress. **Bar:** Full bar. **Reservations:** suggested. **Hours:** 7 am-6 & 6:30-9:30 pm. **Address:** Carr 1.9 KM 4466 **Location:** SR 2, exit Hwy 110, 3 mi (4.8 km) n to Rt 4466 toward Playa Jobo S; follow signs to Villa Montana Beach Resort. **Parking:** on-site. **Cards:** AX, CB, DC, DS, JC, MC, VI.

AC

MAYAGUEZ pop. 98,434 (See map and index starting on p. 473)

WHERE TO STAY

HOLIDAY INN OF MAYAGUEZ & TROPICAL CASINO Phone: (787)833-1100 35

Hotel
$130-$250 All Year

Address: 2701 Hwy 2 **Location:** Hwy 2, n of downtown; 1.2 mi (2 km) from Mayaguez Airport; at KM 149.9. **Facility:** The hotel's no-nonsense decor appeals to corporate travelers and some leisure travelers; a casino and large pool area provide outlets to relax. Meets AAA guest room security requirements. 141 units. 137 one-bedroom standard units. 4 one-bedroom suites. 6 stories, interior corridors. *Bath:* combo or shower only. **Parking:** on-site. **Terms:** cancellation fee imposed. **Amenities:** high-speed Internet, safes, irons, hair dryers. **Pool(s):** outdoor. **Leisure Activities:** exercise room. *Fee:* game room. **Guest Services:** valet and coin laundry, wireless Internet. **Business Services:** meeting rooms, business center. **Cards:** AX, DC, DS, MC, VI. **Free Special Amenities: newspaper and high-speed Internet.**
(See color ad p 482)

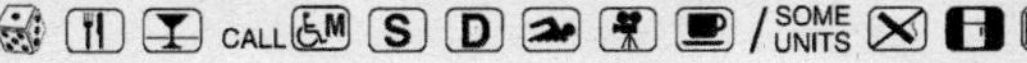

MAYAGUEZ RESORT AND CASINO Book great rates at AAA.com Phone: (787)832-3030 36

Hotel
$185-$325 All Year

Address: Rt 104 KM 0.3, Bo Algarrobo **Location:** Jct Hwy 2 and 104, just n. **Facility:** A garden setting, hilltop views and an Olympic-size pool give this hotel appeal; guest rooms are modestly sized, and some have private balconies. Meets AAA guest room security requirements. Smoke free premises. 140 units. 137 one-bedroom standard units. 3 one-bedroom suites. 5 stories, interior corridors. *Bath:* combo or shower only. **Parking:** on-site (fee) and valet. **Terms:** cancellation fee imposed. **Amenities:** high-speed Internet, voice mail, irons, hair dryers. **Dining:** El Castillo, see separate listing. **Pool(s):** 6 outdoor. **Leisure Activities:** whirlpool, 3 tennis courts (Fee: 3 lighted), playground, limited exercise equipment, volleyball. *Fee:* massage, game room. **Guest Services:** valet laundry, wireless Internet. **Business Services:** conference facilities, business center. **Cards:** AX, DC, DS, MC, VI.
(See color ad p 482)

▼ See AAA listing p 481 ▼

▼ See AAA listing p 481 ▼

(See map and index starting on p. 473)

WHERE TO DINE

EL CASTILLO — **Phone:** 787/832-3030 (17)

International
$16-$34

Diners can sample well-prepared Continental and Caribbean cuisine in an attractive dining room. Popular draws include the daily lunch buffet, Friday night seafood buffet and Saturday night international buffet. Dressy casual. **Bar:** Full bar. **Reservations:** accepted. **Hours:** 6:30 am-11:30 pm, Sat & Sun from 7 am. **Address:** Rt 104, KM 0.3, Bo Algarrobo **Location:** Jct Hwy 2 and 104, just n; in Mayaguez Resort and Casino. **Parking:** on-site (fee). **Cards:** AX, DC, DS, MC, VI.

PONCE pop. 186,475 (See map and index starting on p. 473)

WHERE TO STAY

HILTON PONCE GOLF & CASINO RESORT — Book great rates at AAA.com — **Phone:** (787)259-7676 (20)

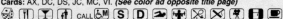

Resort Hotel
$139-$269 All Year

Address: 1150 Caribe Ave, Suite 201 **Location:** Oceanfront. Hwy 52, exit 104B; 1 mi (1.6 km) s on Hwy 12, then 0.5 mi (0.8 km) e, follow signs. **Facility:** Surrounded by lush tropical landscaping, the property's tasteful rooms all have private balconies; new golf course and clubhouse opened in 2003. Designated smoking area. 253 units. 243 one-bedroom standard units. 5 one- and 5 two-bedroom suites, some with whirlpools. 4-5 stories, exterior corridors. *Bath:* combo or shower only. **Parking:** on-site (fee) and valet. **Terms:** 1-30 night minimum stay, cancellation fee imposed. **Amenities:** high-speed Internet, dual phone lines, voice mail, safes, irons, hair dryers. **Dining:** La Cava Restaurant, see separate listing. **Pool(s):** 2 outdoor. **Leisure Activities:** whirlpools, miniature golf, 4 lighted tennis courts, recreation programs, bicycles, playground, spa, basketball, volleyball, game room. *Fee:* saunas, steamrooms, sailboats, golf-27 holes. **Guest Services:** valet laundry, beauty salon, wireless Internet. **Business Services:** conference facilities, business center. **Cards:** AX, DC, DS, JC, MC, VI. ***(See color ad opposite title page)***

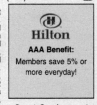

CALL S D

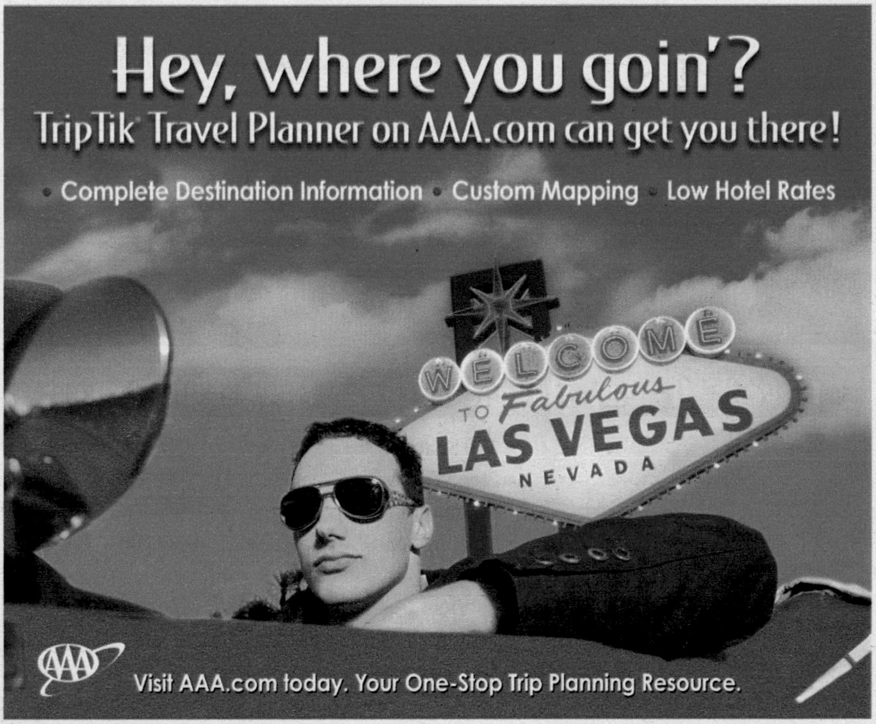

(See map and index starting on p. 473)

HOLIDAY INN PONCE & EL TROPICAL CASINO Book great rates at AAA.com **Phone:** (787)844-1200 19

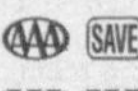
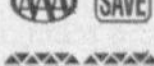

Hotel
$157-$197 All Year

Address: 3315 Ponce Bypass **Location:** Just off Hwy 2, 1.9 mi (3 km) e at end of Hwy 52 (autopista); in sector El Tuque. **Facility:** On the outskirts of Ponce on a hill overlooking the Caribbean, the hotel boasts a popular 24-hour casino; refurbishments give the hotel a fresh feel. Meets AAA guest room security requirements. 116 one-bedroom standard units. 5 stories, interior corridors. *Bath:* combo or shower only. **Parking:** on-site. **Amenities:** high-speed Internet, voice mail, irons, hair dryers. **Pool(s):** outdoor. **Leisure Activities:** limited exercise equipment. *Fee:* game room. **Guest Services:** valet and coin laundry, wireless Internet. **Business Services:** meeting rooms, business center. **Cards:** AX, DC, DS, MC, VI. **Free Special Amenities: newspaper and high-speed Internet.** *(See color ad below)*

CALL S D / SOME UNITS

HOWARD JOHNSON HOTEL PONCE Book great rates at AAA.com **Phone:** (787)841-1000 21

Hotel
$119-$160 All Year

Address: Turpo Industrial Park, #103 **Location:** Hwy 52, exit 99A/99B, just s. **Facility:** Meets AAA guest room security requirements. 120 units. 117 one-bedroom standard units. 3 one-bedroom suites. 2 stories (no elevator), interior corridors. *Bath:* combo or shower only. **Parking:** on-site. **Amenities:** video library, high-speed Internet, voice mail, safes (fee), irons, hair dryers. *Some:* DVD players (fee), video games. **Pool(s):** outdoor. **Leisure Activities:** whirlpool, exercise room. *Fee:* game room. **Guest Services:** valet and coin laundry, wireless Internet. **Business Services:** meeting rooms, business center. **Cards:** AX, DC, DS, MC, VI. *(See color ad below)*

S D / SOME UNITS FEE 

▼ See AAA listing above ▼

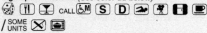

▼ See AAA listing above ▼

(See map and index starting on p. 473)

QUALITY INN EL TUQUE Phone: 787/290-2000 22

Hotel
$90-$193 All Year

Address: Carr 2 KM 220.1, El Tuque **Location:** Just w of town; at Ponce International Speedway Park. **Facility:** Smoke free premises. 99 units. 98 one-bedroom standard units. 1 one-bedroom suite. 1-2 stories (no elevator), exterior corridors. *Bath:* combo or shower only. **Parking:** on-site. **Terms:** 2 night minimum stay - seasonal. **Amenities:** irons, hair dryers. **Pool(s):** outdoor. **Leisure Activities:** playground, basketball. *Fee:* waterslide. **Guest Services:** coin laundry, wireless Internet. **Business Services:** meeting rooms, business center. **Cards:** AX, DC, DS, MC, VI. ***(See color ad below)***

   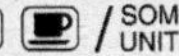  / SOME UNITS 

▼ *See AAA listing above* ▼

(See map and index starting on p. 473)

WHERE TO DINE

LA CAVA RESTAURANT — **Phone:** 787/259-7676 (11)

International
$29-$34

Inside the Hilton resort, this refined restaurant features upscale appointments. Dapper waiters provide attentive service. The restaurant boasts an extensive wine list to complement a creative menu of both complex and simple dishes, including appetizers of escargots, beef carpaccio and duck foie gras and main courses of Australian lamb chops, Kobe beef short ribs, Maine lobster and duck breast. Dressy casual. **Bar:** Full bar. **Reservations:** required. **Hours:** 6:30 pm-10:30 pm. Closed: Sun. **Address:** 1150 Caribe Ave, Suite 201 **Location:** Hwy 52, exit 104B, 1 mi (1.6 km) s on Hwy 12, then 0.5 mi (0.8 km) e; in Hilton Ponce Golf & Casino Resort. **Parking:** on-site (fee) and valet. **Cards:** AX, CB, DC, DS, JC, MC, VI.

MARKS AT THE MELIA — **Phone:** 787/284-6275 (10)

International
$17-$33

The talented chef earns his impeccable local reputation through his deftly prepared dishes, which marry the best attributes of Continental, Puerto Rican and Caribbean cuisine. Inside a downtown hotel, the dining room displays a softly elegant decor. Mofongo, served with either chicken, shrimp or pork, is outstanding. Dressy casual. **Bar:** Full bar. **Reservations:** suggested. **Hours:** noon-3 & 6-10:30 pm, Sun noon-5 pm. Closed: Mon & Tues. **Address:** Calle Cristina 75 **Location:** Across from Plaza Las Delicias and Parque de Bombas; in Melia Hotel. **Parking:** street. **Cards:** AX, MC, VI.

PITO'S SEAFOOD RESTAURANT — **Phone:** 787/841-4977 (12)

Seafood
$18-$35

A longtime favorite among locals, this seaside restaurant offers lovely views and a casual atmosphere. Seafood reigns on a menu that lists varied preparations of lobster, shrimp, red snapper, octopus and calamari. Mofongos and asopaos are Puerto Rican house specialties. Casual dress. **Bar:** Full bar. **Reservations:** accepted. **Hours:** 11 am-11 pm, Fri & Sat-midnight. Closed: Good Friday. **Address:** 218 Carr #2 **Location:** Just w of town; in sector Las Cucharas. **Parking:** on-site. **Cards:** AX, MC, VI.

RINCON pop. 14,767 (See map and index starting on p. 473)

WHERE TO STAY

THE LAZY PARROT INN & RESTAURANT *Book at AAA.com* — **Phone:** (787)823-5654 (7)

Bed & Breakfast
$110-$155 All Year

Address: Rd 413 KM 4.1, Puntas Sector **Location:** On Hwy 413, 2.9 mi (4.6 km) n of downtown, just above El Faro Lighthouse. **Facility:** Smoke free premises. 11 one-bedroom standard units, some with whirlpools. 2 stories (no elevator), interior/exterior corridors. *Bath:* combo or shower only. **Parking:** on-site. **Terms:** office hours 8 am-10 pm, 2 night minimum stay - weekends, 7 day cancellation notice. **Pool(s):** outdoor. **Leisure Activities:** whirlpool. **Guest Services:** wireless Internet. **Cards:** AX, DS, MC, VI.

ASK

▼ See AAA listing p 478 ▼

(See map and index starting on p. 473)

RINCON OF THE SEAS GRAND CARIBBEAN HOTEL Book at AAA.com Phone: (787)823-7500 **8**

Hotel

$190-$495 All Year

Address: Carr 115 KM 12.2 Barrio Pueblo **Location:** Oceanfront. On Hwy 115, 0.7 mi (1.1 km) s of downtown. **Facility:** Meets AAA guest room security requirements. Smoke free premises. 112 units. 109 one-bedroom standard units. 3 one-bedroom suites. 3-5 stories, exterior corridors. *Bath:* combo or shower only. **Parking:** on-site. **Terms:** 1-7 night minimum stay - seasonal and/or weekends, 3 day cancellation notice. **Amenities:** high-speed Internet, voice mail, safes, irons, hair dryers. *Some:* DVD players. **Pool(s):** outdoor. **Leisure Activities:** playground, exercise room. *Fee:* game room. **Guest Services:** valet laundry, wireless Internet. **Business Services:** meeting rooms. **Cards:** AX, MC, VI.

ASK S D / SOME UNITS

RIO GRANDE pop. 52,362 (See map and index starting on p. 473)

WHERE TO STAY

GRAN MELIA PUERTO RICO RESORT & VILLAS Book great rates at AAA.com Phone: (787)657-1026 **2**

Resort Hotel

$194-$354 12/1-4/8
$164-$354 4/9-11/30

Address: 1000 Coco Beach Blvd **Location:** Oceanfront. 18.5 mi (29.6 km) e of Luis Munoz Marin International Airport, 3 mi (4.8 km) n, follow signs. **Facility:** Spacious, attractively appointed guest rooms feature many comforts and extra amenities at this newly built, all-inclusive resort. Meets AAA guest room security requirements. 500 one-bedroom standard units, some with whirlpools. 1-2 stories (no elevator), exterior corridors. **Parking:** on-site (fee) and valet. **Terms:** off-site registration, 3 day cancellation notice-fee imposed. **Amenities:** video games (fee), high-speed Internet, voice mail, safes, irons, hair dryers. *Some:* CD players. **Dining:** 6 restaurants, entertainment. **Pool(s):** 3 outdoor. **Leisure Activities:** whirlpools, paddleboats, sailboats, windsurfing, snorkeling, kayaks, 3 lighted tennis courts, recreation programs, kids club, playground, exercise room, spa, volleyball. *Fee:* saunas, steamrooms, scuba diving, golf-36 holes. **Guest Services:** complimentary laundry, wireless Internet. **Business Services:** conference facilities, business center. **Cards:** AX, DC, DS, MC, VI. *(See color ad p 488)*

FEE 24 S D / SOME UNITS

RIO MAR BEACH RESORT & SPA - A WYNDHAM GRAND RESORT Book great rates at AAA.com Phone: (787)888-6000 **3**

Resort Hotel

$289-$979 All Year

Address: 6000 Rio Mar Blvd **Location:** Oceanfront. 19 mi (30.4 km) e of Luis Munoz Marin International Airport; jct Hwy 3 and 968, 0.8 mi (1.3 km) n on Hwy 968. **Facility:** Extensive beach, tennis and golf facilities are available at this well-equipped resort; built in the mid 1990s, the guest rooms remain well appointed. Meets AAA guest room security requirements. Smoke free premises. 600 units. 584 one-bedroom standard units. 16 one-bedroom suites. 7 stories, interior corridors. *Bath:* combo or shower only. **Parking:** on-site (fee) and valet. **Terms:** check-in 4 pm, 7 day cancellation notice-fee imposed. **Amenities:** dual phone lines, voice mail, safes, irons, hair dryers. *Fee:* video games, high-speed Internet. *Some:* DVD players (fee). **Dining:** 10 restaurants, entertainment. **Pool(s):** 2 outdoor. **Leisure Activities:** saunas, whirlpools, steamrooms, waterslide, lifeguard on duty, beach access, rental boats, rental sailboats, rental sailboards, driving range, golf instruction, tennis instruction, recreation programs, jogging, playground, spa, basketball, volleyball. *Fee:* scuba diving, snorkeling, fishing, charter fishing, personal watercraft, kayaks, parasailing, golf-36 holes, 13 tennis courts (2 lighted), kids club, teens club. **Guest Services:** valet laundry, airport transportation (fee)-Luis Munoz Marin International Airport, area transportation-resort facilities, wireless Internet. **Business Services:** conference facilities, business center. **Cards:** AX, CB, DC, DS, MC, VI. *(See color ad p 489)*

FEE 24 S D / SOME UNITS

▼ See AAA listing p 487 ▼

▼ See AAA listing p 487 ▼

SAN JUAN pop. 434,374 (See map and index starting on p. 477)

WHERE TO STAY

ACACIA BOUTIQUE HOTEL Book great rates at AAA.com **Phone:** (787)725-0668 28

Country Inn
$85-$225 All Year

Address: 8 Taft St **Location:** Just n of corner Taft St and McLeary Ave; in Ocean Park neighborhood. **Facility:** Smoke free premises. 21 one-bedroom standard units. 4 stories (no elevator), interior corridors. *Bath:* shower only. **Parking:** street. **Terms:** office hours 7 am-11 pm, 3 night minimum stay, 10 day cancellation notice. **Amenities:** safes (fee), irons, hair dryers. **Leisure Activities:** whirlpool. **Guest Services:** valet laundry, wireless Internet. **Cards:** AX, DS, MC, VI. **Free Special Amenities: room upgrade (subject to availability with advance reservations).**

   SOME UNITS

AT WIND CHIMES INN Book at AAA.com **Phone:** (787)727-4153 32

Country Inn
$65-$145 All Year

Address: 1750 McLeary Ave **Location:** In Condado; corner of McLeary Ave and Taft St. **Facility:** Smoke free premises. 22 one-bedroom standard units, some with efficiencies. 2 stories (no elevator), interior/exterior corridors. *Bath:* combo or shower only. **Parking:** on-site. **Terms:** 3 night minimum stay, 10 day cancellation notice. **Amenities:** safes (fee). **Pool(s):** outdoor. **Guest Services:** valet laundry, wireless Internet. **Cards:** AX, MC, VI.

    SOME UNITS

BEST WESTERN HOTEL PIERRE **Phone:** (787)721-1200 36

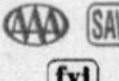

fyi
Hotel
$155-$279 12/1-4/30
$125-$170 5/1-11/30

Under major renovation, scheduled to be completed January 2009. Last rated: **Address:** 105 de Diego Ave **Location:** Near the Condado District; 0.3 mi (0.5 km) n of Hwy 26. **Facility:** 184 one-bedroom standard units. 3-8 stories, interior corridors. *Bath:* combo or shower only. **Parking:** valet. **Terms:** 3 day cancellation notice-fee imposed. **Amenities:** CD players, high-speed Internet, voice mail, safes, irons, hair dryers. *Some:* dual phone lines. **Pool(s):** outdoor. **Leisure Activities:** whirlpool, exercise room. **Guest Services:** valet laundry, wireless Internet. **Business Services:** meeting rooms, PC. **Cards:** AX, DC, DS, MC, VI. **Free Special Amenities: expanded continental breakfast and high-speed Internet.** *(See color ad below)*

AAA Benefit:
Members save up to 20%, plus 10% bonus points with rewards program.

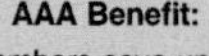

 CALL 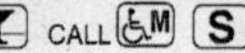    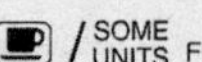  SOME UNITS FEE

BEST WESTERN SAN JUAN AIRPORT HOTEL Book great rates at AAA.com **Phone:** (787)791-1700 50

Hotel
$160-$250 All Year

Address: Airport Rd **Location:** At Luis Munoz Marin International Airport. **Facility:** Originally built in the 1950s, the updated guest units feature contemporary decor, extra amenities and flat-screen televisions. The property is ideal for those who want to stay right at the airport. Meets AAA guest room security requirements. Smoke free premises. 125 one-bedroom standard units. 6 stories, interior corridors. *Bath:* combo or shower only. **Parking:** on-site (fee). **Terms:** cancellation fee imposed. **Amenities:** high-speed Internet, voice mail, safes, irons, hair dryers. **Leisure Activities:** whirlpools, sun deck, billiards, table tennis, exercise room. **Guest Services:** valet and coin laundry, wireless Internet. **Business Services:** meeting rooms, business center. **Cards:** AX, DS, MC, VI.

AAA Benefit:
Members save up to 20%, plus 10% bonus points with rewards program.

(See map and index starting on p. 477)

CARIBE HILTON *Book great rates at AAA.com* **Phone:** (787)721-0303 10

Hotel
$139-$429 All Year

Address: San Geronimo Grounds Calle 1 **Location:** Oceanfront. Between Condado and Old San Juan; off Munoz Rivera Ave. **Facility:** Meets AAA guest room security requirements. Designated smoking area. 812 units. 735 one-bedroom standard units. 66 one-, 6 two- and 5 three-bedroom suites, some with whirlpools. 8-20 stories, interior corridors. *Bath:* combo or shower only. **Parking:** on-site (fee) and valet. **Terms:** check-in 4 pm, 1-30 night minimum stay, cancellation fee imposed. **Amenities:** dual phone lines, voice mail, safes, irons, hair dryers. *Fee:* video games, high-speed Internet. *Some:* CD players. **Dining:** Lemon Grass, Madrid-San Juan, Morton's of Chicago, The Steakhouse, see separate listings. **Pool(s):** 2 outdoor. **Leisure Activities:** whirlpool, lifeguard on duty, snorkeling, 3 lighted tennis courts, recreation programs, playground, spa, basketball, shuffleboard, volleyball, game room. *Fee:* saunas, steamrooms, paddleboats. **Guest Services:** valet laundry, wireless Internet. **Business Services:** conference facilities, business center. **Cards:** AX, DC, DS, MC, VI. ***(See color ad opposite title page & below)***

Hilton

AAA Benefit:

Members save 5% or more everyday!

 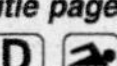  CALL    

▼ ***See AAA listing above*** ▼

(See map and index starting on p. 477)

COMFORT INN SAN JUAN   Book great rates at AAA.com   **Phone:** (787)721-0170   17

Motel
$109-$139 All Year

Address: 6 Clemenceau St **Location:** In Condado; corner of Clemenceau and Mariano Ramirez Bages sts. **Facility:** Meets AAA guest room security requirements. 56 units. 54 one-bedroom standard units. 1 one- and 1 two-bedroom suites. 7 stories, interior corridors. *Bath:* combo or shower only. **Parking:** on-site (fee). **Terms:** cancellation fee imposed. **Amenities:** high-speed Internet, voice mail, safes (fee), irons, hair dryers. **Pool(s):** outdoor. **Guest Services:** wireless Internet. **Business Services:** PC (fee). **Cards:** AX, DC, DS, MC, VI. ***(See color ad below)***

CONDADO PLAZA HOTEL & CASINO   Book great rates at AAA.com   **Phone:** (787)721-1000   14

AAA SAVE

Hotel
$199-$329 12/1-4/30
$169-$329 5/1-11/30

Address: 999 Ashford Ave **Location:** Oceanfront. West end of Ashford Ave. **Facility:** Two mid-rise towers face the ocean and a lagoon at this older property offering facilities including shops and a saltwater pool. Meets AAA guest room security requirements. Smoke free premises. 570 units. 556 one-bedroom standard units. 14 one-bedroom suites, some with whirlpools. 10 stories, interior corridors. *Bath:* combo or shower only. **Parking:** on-site (fee) and valet. **Terms:** check-in 4 pm, 3 day cancellation notice-fee imposed. **Amenities:** high-speed Internet, dual phone lines, voice mail, safes, irons, hair dryers. **Dining:** 4 restaurants, entertainment. **Pool(s):** 3 outdoor. **Leisure Activities:** sauna, whirlpools, steamroom, waterslide, rental paddleboats, rental sailboats, rental sailboards, 2 lighted tennis courts, recreation programs, exercise room, volleyball. *Fee:* snorkeling, kayaks, water sports, massage, game room. **Guest Services:** valet and coin laundry, wireless Internet. **Business Services:** conference facilities, PC. **Cards:** AX, CB, DC, DS, MC, VI. **Free Special Amenities: newspaper and preferred room (subject to availability with advance reservations).** *(See color ad p 493)*

S D / SOME UNITS

CORAL PRINCESS INN   Book at AAA.com   **Phone:** (787)977-7700   18

Bed & Breakfast
$99-$160 All Year

Address: 1159 Magdalena Ave **Location:** In Condado. **Facility:** Smoke free premises. 25 one-bedroom standard units, some with whirlpools. 3 stories, interior/exterior corridors. *Bath:* combo or shower only. **Parking:** on-site (fee). **Terms:** 2 night minimum stay - seasonal and/or weekends, 9 day cancellation notice-fee imposed. **Amenities:** high-speed Internet, hair dryers. *Some:* safes. **Pool(s):** outdoor. **Guest Services:** coin laundry. **Cards:** AX, DS, MC, VI.

D

▼ *See AAA listing above* ▼

▼ See AAA listing p 492 ▼

(See map and index starting on p. 477)

COURTYARD BY MARRIOTT-ISLA VERDE BEACH RESORT Book great rates at AAA.com **Phone:** (787)791-0404 52

Hotel
$216-$319 All Year

AAA Benefit: Members save a minimum 5% off the best available rate.

Address: 7012 Boca de Cangrejos Ave **Location:** Oceanfront. Just e of jct Hwy 187 and 37; east end of Isla Verde. **Facility:** This popular, award-winning hotel is located on a very attractive stretch of beach; guest units are upscale and spacious with extra amenities. Meets AAA guest room security requirements. Smoke free premises. 260 units. 250 one-bedroom standard units, some with whirlpools. 10 one-bedroom suites with whirlpools. 12 stories, interior corridors. *Bath:* combo or shower only. **Parking:** on-site (fee) and valet. **Terms:** 3 day cancellation notice-fee imposed. **Amenities:** DVD players, CD players, high-speed Internet, dual phone lines, voice mail, safes, irons, hair dryers. **Dining:** 4 restaurants, entertainment. **Pool(s):** 2 outdoor. **Leisure Activities:** whirlpool, kids club, playground, exercise room, volleyball, game room. *Fee:* massage. **Guest Services:** valet and coin laundry, wireless Internet. **Business Services:** meeting rooms, business center. **Cards:** AX, CB, DC, DS, MC, VI. *(See color ad below)*

CALL S D

COURTYARD BY MARRIOTT SAN JUAN MIRAMAR Book great rates at AAA.com **Phone:** (787)721-7400 22

Hotel
$153-$227 All Year

AAA Benefit: Members save a minimum 5% off the best available rate.

Address: 801 Ponce de Leon Ave **Location:** 5 mi (8 km) w of airport; Ponce de Leon and Calle Trigo. **Facility:** Meets AAA guest room security requirements. Smoke free premises. 134 units. 124 one-bedroom standard units. 10 one-bedroom suites. 10 stories, interior corridors. *Bath:* combo or shower only. **Parking:** valet. **Terms:** cancellation fee imposed. **Amenities:** video games (fee), high-speed Internet, dual phone lines, voice mail, safes, irons, hair dryers. **Dining:** Augusto's Cuisine, see separate listing. **Pool(s):** outdoor. **Leisure Activities:** exercise room. **Guest Services:** valet and coin laundry, wireless Internet. **Business Services:** meeting rooms, business center. **Cards:** AX, MC, VI.
(See color ad p 495)

S D

(See map and index starting on p. 477)

EL CANARIO BY THE LAGOON Book great rates at AAA.com Phone: (787)722-5058 20

Motel
$120-$165 12/1-4/30
$90-$165 5/1-11/30

Address: 4 Calle Clemenceau **Location:** Just s of Ashford Ave at Joffrey St; overlooking Condado Lagoon. **Facility:** Meets AAA guest room security requirements. Smoke free premises. 44 units. 40 one-bedroom standard units. 4 one-bedroom suites. 5 stories, interior corridors. *Bath:* shower only. **Parking:** on-site. **Terms:** 4 day cancellation notice-fee imposed. **Amenities:** high-speed Internet, voice mail, safes (fee). *Some:* irons. **Guest Services:** coin laundry, wireless Internet. **Cards:** AX, DC, DS, MC, VI. **Free Special Amenities: expanded continental breakfast and newspaper.** *(See color ad below)*

 / SOME UNITS 

▼ See AAA listing p 494 ▼

▼ See AAA listing above ▼

▼ See AAA listing p 479 ▼

(See map and index starting on p. 477)

EL SAN JUAN HOTEL & CASINO Book great rates at AAA.com **Phone:** (787)791-1000 

Hotel
$189-$505 All Year

Address: 6063 Isla Verde Ave **Location:** Oceanfront. 2 mi (3.2 km) nw of airport; in Isla Verde. **Facility:** This centerpiece of Isla Verde features an extravagant world-class lobby, lagoon-style pool, rooftop restaurants and several guest room categories. 382 units. 371 one-bedroom standard units, some with whirlpools. 11 one-bedroom suites, some with kitchens and/or whirlpools. 2-10 stories, interior/exterior corridors. *Bath:* combo or shower only. **Parking:** on-site (fee) and valet. **Terms:** check-in 4 pm, 3 day cancellation notice-fee imposed. **Amenities:** high-speed Internet, voice mail, safes, honor bars, irons, hair dryers. *Some:* DVD players, CD players. **Dining:** 7 restaurants, nightclub, entertainment. **Pool(s):** 3 outdoor. **Leisure Activities:** whirlpools, recreation programs, exercise room, spa, volleyball. *Fee:* lighted tennis court. **Guest Services:** valet and coin laundry, wireless Internet. **Business Services:** conference facilities, business center. **Cards:** AX, CB, DS, MC, VI. **Free Special Amenities: newspaper and preferred room (subject to availability with advance reservations).** *(See color ad p 498)*

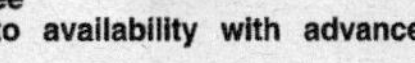

 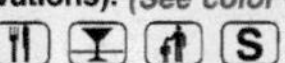 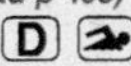  / SOME UNITS 

EMBASSY SUITES HOTEL & CASINO SAN JUAN Book great rates at AAA.com **Phone:** (787)791-0505 

Hotel
$180-$360 All Year

Address: 8000 Tartak St, Isla Verde **Location:** Jct Isla Verde Ave, just s; Hwy 187, exit Tartak St. Located in a commercial area. **Facility:** Recent top-to-bottom renovations at this upscale, modern hotel include spacious guest suites ideal for families or corporate travelers. Meets AAA guest room security requirements. 299 one-bedroom suites. 8 stories, interior corridors. *Bath:* combo or shower only. **Parking:** on-site (fee) and valet. **Terms:** check-in 4 pm, 3 day cancellation notice-fee imposed. **Amenities:** video games (fee), high-speed Internet, dual phone lines, voice mail, safes, irons, hair dryers. **Dining:** 2 restaurants. **Pool(s):** outdoor. **Leisure Activities:** whirlpool, exercise room, game room. **Guest Services:** valet and coin laundry, wireless Internet. **Business Services:** conference facilities, business center. **Cards:** AX, DC, DS, MC, VI.
(See color ad p 499)

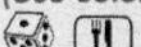      / SOME UNITS 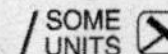

EMBASSY SUITES HOTELS
AAA Benefit:
Members save 5% or more everyday!

HAMPTON INN & SUITES-SAN JUAN Book great rates at AAA.com **Phone:** (787)791-8777 

Hotel
$144-$279 All Year

Address: 6530 Isla Verde Ave **Location:** 2 mi (3.2 km) nw of airport; in Isla Verde area, close to intersection with Hwy 187. Located on the edge of busy commercial area. **Facility:** Meets AAA guest room security requirements. 201 units. 148 one-bedroom standard units. 53 one-bedroom suites. 4-5 stories, interior corridors. *Bath:* combo or shower only. **Parking:** on-site (fee). **Terms:** 1-30 night minimum stay, cancellation fee imposed. **Amenities:** high-speed Internet, voice mail, safes, irons, hair dryers. **Pool(s):** outdoor. **Leisure Activities:** whirlpool, limited exercise equipment. **Guest Services:** valet and coin laundry, wireless Internet. **Business Services:** meeting rooms, business center. **Cards:** AX, DC, DS, MC, VI.

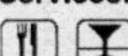    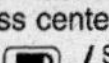 / SOME UNITS  

AAA Benefit:
Members save up to 10% everyday!

▼ See AAA listing p 497 ▼

(See map and index starting on p. 477)

HOLIDAY INN EXPRESS Book great rates at AAA.com **Phone:** (787)724-4160 

Motel

$140-$199 12/1-4/30
$105-$179 5/1-11/30

Address: 1 Mariano Ramirez Bages St **Location:** In Condado; corner of Mariano Ramirez Bages and Clemenceau sts. **Facility:** Meets AAA guest room security requirements. 115 units. 113 one-bedroom standard units. 2 one-bedroom suites. 7 stories, interior corridors. *Bath:* combo or shower only. **Parking:** on-site (fee). **Terms:** 3 day cancellation notice-fee imposed. **Amenities:** high-speed Internet, voice mail, safes (fee), irons, hair dryers. **Pool(s):** outdoor. **Leisure Activities:** whirlpool, limited exercise equipment. **Guest Services:** valet laundry, wireless Internet. **Business Services:** PC. **Cards:** AX, DC, DS, MC, VI. **Free Special Amenities: expanded continental breakfast and high-speed Internet.** *(See color ad p 501)*

D / SOME UNITS

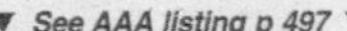
▼ See AAA listing p 497 ▼

(See map and index starting on p. 477)

HOLIDAY INN SAN JUAN Book great rates at AAA.com **Phone:** (787)253-9000 48

Hotel
$195-$320 All Year

Address: 8020 Tartak St **Location:** Jct of Isla Verde Ave, just s; 1.6 mi (2.5 km) w of airport at Tartak St exit, off Hwy 187. **Facility:** Meets AAA guest room security requirements. Smoke free premises. 222 one-bedroom standard units. 3-8 stories, interior corridors. *Bath:* combo or shower only. **Parking:** on-site (fee) and valet. **Terms:** 3 day cancellation notice. **Amenities:** CD players, high-speed Internet, voice mail, safes, irons, hair dryers. **Dining:** 3 restaurants. **Pool(s):** outdoor. **Leisure Activities:** whirlpool, water spray park, limited exercise equipment, game room. **Guest Services:** valet laundry, wireless Internet. **Business Services:** conference facilities, business center. **Cards:** AX, CB, DC, DS, MC, VI. **Free Special Amenities: newspaper and high-speed Internet.** *(See color ad p 502)*

▼ See AAA listing p 499 ▼

▼ See AAA listing p 502 ▼

(See map and index starting on p. 477)

HOTEL EL CONVENTO Phone: (787)723-9020 **1**

AAA SAVE fyi
Historic Hotel
$235-$425 All Year

Under major renovation, scheduled to be completed December 2008. Last rated: ♦♦♦♦ **Address:** 100 Calle Cristo **Location:** Center of Old San Juan; across from San Juan Cathedral. **Facility:** Built in 1651 as a Carmelite convent, this now-elegant small inn offers distinctive, cozy accommodations and a large courtyard. Designated smoking area. 71 units. 66 one-bedroom standard units. 5 one-bedroom suites. 5 stories, interior corridors. **Parking:** valet. **Terms:** 2 night minimum stay - weekends, 3 day cancellation notice-fee imposed. **Amenities:** CD players, high-speed Internet, dual phone lines, voice mail, safes, irons, hair dryers. **Dining:** 4 restaurants. **Pool(s):** outdoor. **Leisure Activities:** exercise room. **Guest Services:** valet laundry, wireless Internet. **Business Services:** meeting rooms, PC. **Cards:** AX, CB, DC, DS, MC, VI. **Free Special Amenities: high-speed Internet.** *(See color ad p 501)*

▼ See AAA listing p 504 ▼

(See map and index starting on p. 477)

INTERCONTINENTAL SAN JUAN RESORT & CASINO Book great rates at AAA.com **Phone:** (787)791-6100 40

Hotel
$199-$659 All Year

Address: 5961 Isla Verde Ave **Location:** Oceanfront. 2.1 mi (3.3 km) e of airport. **Facility:** Situated in lively Isla Verde, the hotel has undergone a multi-million dollar transformation and now offers comfort, style and a host of amenities. Meets AAA guest room security requirements. 402 units. 380 one-bedroom standard units. 22 one-bedroom suites, some with whirlpools. 2-16 stories, interior corridors. *Bath:* combo or shower only. **Parking:** on-site (fee) and valet. **Terms:** check-in 4 pm, cancellation fee imposed. **Amenities:** video games (fee), high-speed Internet, dual phone lines, voice mail, safes, honor bars, irons, hair dryers. *Some:* DVD players. **Dining:** 4 restaurants, also, Momoyama, Ruth's Chris Steak House, see separate listings, entertainment. **Pool(s):** outdoor. **Leisure Activities:** sauna, whirlpools, steamroom, beach access, spa. **Guest Services:** valet laundry, wireless Internet. **Business Services:** conference facilities, business center. **Cards:** AX, CB, DC, DS, JC, MC, VI. *(See color ad p 503)*

LA CONCHA - A RENAISSANCE RESORT **Phone:** (787)721-7500 19

fyi
Hotel
$239-$369 All Year

Under major renovation, scheduled to be completed January 2009. **Address:** 1077 Ashford Ave **Location:** Oceanfront. Center of Condado. **Facility:** Meets AAA guest room security requirements. Smoke free premises. 246 one-bedroom standard units. 12 stories, exterior corridors. *Bath:* shower only. **Parking:** on-site (fee) and valet. **Terms:** check-in 4 pm, cancellation fee imposed. **Amenities:** DVD players, CD players, high-speed Internet, voice mail, safes, irons, hair dryers. **Pool(s):** 2 outdoor. **Leisure Activities:** whirlpools, exercise room. **Guest Services:** valet laundry, wireless Internet. **Business Services:** meeting rooms, business center. **Cards:** AX, CB, DC, DS, MC, VI. ***(See color ad p 505)***

AAA Benefit:
Members save a minimum 5% off the best available rate.

LE CONSULAT - A CLARION COLLECTION HOTEL Book at AAA.com **Phone:** (787)289-9191 33

Hotel
$120-$165 All Year

Address: 1149 Magdalena Ave **Location:** Center of Condado. **Facility:** Smoke free premises. 20 one-bedroom standard units. 3 stories, interior corridors. *Bath:* shower only. **Parking:** on-site (fee). **Terms:** 3 day cancellation notice. **Amenities:** CD players, safes (fee), irons, hair dryers. **Pool(s):** outdoor. **Leisure Activities:** whirlpool. **Guest Services:** wireless Internet. **Cards:** AX, MC, VI.

NORMANDIE HOTEL Book great rates at AAA.com **Phone:** (787)729-2929 7

Hotel
$190-$300 All Year

Address: 499 Munoz Rivera Ave **Location:** Between Condado and Old San Juan; adjacent to New Millennium Park. **Facility:** Meets AAA guest room security requirements. 159 one-bedroom standard units. 7 stories, interior corridors. *Bath:* combo or shower only. **Parking:** on-site (fee) and valet. **Terms:** cancellation fee imposed. **Amenities:** CD players, high-speed Internet, dual phone lines, voice mail, safes, irons, hair dryers. **Dining:** 2 restaurants. **Pool(s):** outdoor. **Leisure Activities:** exercise room, spa. **Guest Services:** valet and coin laundry, wireless Internet. **Business Services:** conference facilities, business center. **Cards:** AX, DC, DS, MC, VI. **Free Special Amenities: local telephone calls and high-speed Internet.** *(See color ad p 506)*

/ SOME UNITS

QUALITY INN EL PORTAL Book great rates at AAA.com **Phone:** (787)721-9010 30

Motel
$116-$129 All Year

Address: 76 Condado Ave **Location:** At entrance to Condado Central. **Facility:** Smoke free premises. 47 one-bedroom standard units. 6 stories, interior corridors. *Bath:* shower only. **Parking:** on-site and street. **Amenities:** high-speed Internet, voice mail, safes, irons, hair dryers. **Guest Services:** valet laundry, wireless Internet. **Cards:** AX, MC, VI. ***(See color ad p 507)***

▼ See AAA listing p 504 ▼

▼ See AAA listing p 504 ▼

▼ See AAA listing p 507 ▼

(See map and index starting on p. 477)

RADISSON AMBASSADOR PLAZA HOTEL & CASINO Book great rates at AAA.com **Phone:** (787)721-7300 

Hotel

$239-$279 All Year

Address: 1369 Ashford Ave **Location:** Center of Condado. **Facility:** Located in the Condado area, this older casino-hotel's informal atmosphere is popular with locals and tourists alike. Some minor recent renovations. Meets AAA guest room security requirements. Designated smoking area. 233 units. 146 one-bedroom standard units. 87 one-bedroom suites, some with whirlpools. 8 stories, interior corridors. *Bath:* combo or shower only. **Parking:** on-site (fee) and valet. **Amenities:** video games (fee), high-speed Internet, dual phone lines, voice mail, safes, irons, hair dryers. **Pool(s):** outdoor. **Leisure Activities:** exercise room. *Fee:* massage, game room. **Guest Services:** valet laundry, beauty salon, wireless Internet. **Business Services:** meeting rooms, business center. **Cards:** AX, DC, DS, MC, VI. ***(See color ad p 506)***

ASK CALL S D / SOME UNITS

▼ *See AAA listing p 504* ▼

(See map and index starting on p. 477)

THE RITZ-CARLTON SAN JUAN HOTEL, SPA & CASINO Book at AAA.com

Phone: (787)253-1700 44

Resort Hotel

$249-$579 All Year

Address: 6961 Avenue of the Governors **Location:** Oceanfront. 1 mi (1.6 km) n of Luis Munoz Marin International Airport; on Isla Verde Ave (Hwy 187). **Facility:** This service-oriented hotel is the epitome of luxury, featuring upscale spa facilities and well-landscaped grounds and pool area. Smoke free premises. 416 units. 405 one-bedroom standard units. 11 one-bedroom suites, some with whirlpools. 10 stories, interior corridors. *Bath:* combo or shower only. **Parking:** on-site (fee) and valet. **Terms:** check-in 4 pm. **Amenities:** video library, video games (fee), CD players, high-speed Internet, dual phone lines, voice mail, safes, honor bars, irons, hair dryers. *Some:* DVD players. **Dining:** BLT Steak, see separate listing. **Pool(s):** outdoor. **Leisure Activities:** sauna, whirlpools, steamrooms, paddleboats, sailboats, windsurfing, snorkeling, 2 lighted tennis courts, recreation programs, spa, volleyball, game room. *Fee:* scuba diving, charter fishing. **Guest Services:** valet laundry, area transportation (fee). **Business Services:** conference facilities, business center. **Cards:** AX, CB, DC, DS, JC, MC, VI.

FEE S D / SOME UNITS FEE

SAN JUAN MARRIOTT RESORT & STELLARIS CASINO Book great rates at AAA.com

Phone: (787)722-7000 24

AAA SAVE

Resort Hotel

$211-$345 All Year

Address: 1309 Ashford Ave **Location:** Oceanfront. In Condado; corner of Calle Caribe and Ashford Ave. **Facility:** A high-rise in the Condado area, this resort offers luxury services, many ocean-facing units and an upscale lobby. Popular with locals. Meets AAA guest room security requirements. Smoke free premises. 525 units. 510 one-bedroom standard units. 15 one-bedroom suites, some with whirlpools. 9-21 stories, interior corridors. *Bath:* combo or shower only. **Parking:** on-site (fee) and valet. **Terms:** check-in 4 pm, cancellation fee imposed. **Amenities:** high-speed Internet, dual phone lines, voice mail, safes, irons, hair dryers. *Some:* CD players. **Dining:** 4 restaurants, entertainment. **Pool(s):** 2 outdoor. **Leisure Activities:** saunas, whirlpool, waterslide, 2 lighted tennis courts, recreation programs, spa, volleyball. **Guest Services:** valet and coin laundry, wireless Internet. **Business Services:** conference facilities, business center. **Cards:** AX, CB, DC, DS, MC, VI.
(See color ad p 509)

Marriott HOTELS & RESORTS

AAA Benefit:

Members save a minimum 5% off the best available rate.

CALL S D

▼ See AAA listing p 508 ▼

(See map and index starting on p. 477)

SAN JUAN WATER & BEACH CLUB HOTEL *Book at AAA.com* **Phone:** (787)728-3666 42

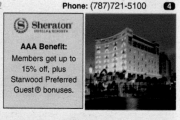

Hotel
$149-$695 All Year

Address: 2 Tartak St **Location:** Oceanfront. In Isla Verde; 3.2 mi (5.1 km) e of airport. **Facility:** 78 units. 74 one-bedroom standard units. 4 one-bedroom suites. 11 stories, interior corridors. *Bath:* shower only. **Parking:** valet. **Terms:** check-in 4 pm, 3 day cancellation notice. **Amenities:** CD players, high-speed Internet, voice mail, safes, honor bars, irons, hair dryers. **Dining:** Tangerine, see separate listing. **Pool(s):** outdoor. **Leisure Activities:** exercise room. *Fee:* massage. **Guest Services:** valet laundry, wireless Internet. **Business Services:** meeting rooms, PC. **Cards:** AX, MC, VI.

ASK S D / SOME UNITS

SHERATON OLD SAN JUAN HOTEL *Book great rates at AAA.com* **Phone:** (787)721-5100 4

Hotel
$149-$449 All Year

Address: 100 Brumbaugh St **Location:** In Old San Juan. Located adjacent to the cruise ship terminal. **Facility:** This recently renovated hotel overlooks cruise-ship terminals in Old San Juan and is convenient to shops and restaurants. Meets AAA guest room security requirements. 240 units. 200 one-bedroom standard units. 40 one-bedroom suites. 9 stories, interior corridors. *Bath:* combo or shower only. **Parking:** valet. **Amenities:** dual phone lines, voice mail, safes, irons, hair dryers. *Fee:* video games, high-speed Internet. *Some:* CD players. **Dining:** 2 restaurants, entertainment. **Pool(s):** outdoor. **Leisure Activities:** whirlpool, exercise room. *Fee:* massage. **Guest Services:** valet laundry, wireless Internet. **Business Services:** conference facilities, business center. **Cards:** AX, CB, DC, DS, JC, MC, VI. *(See color ad below)*

Sheraton Hotels & Resorts

AAA Benefit:
Members get up to 15% off, plus Starwood Preferred Guest® bonuses.

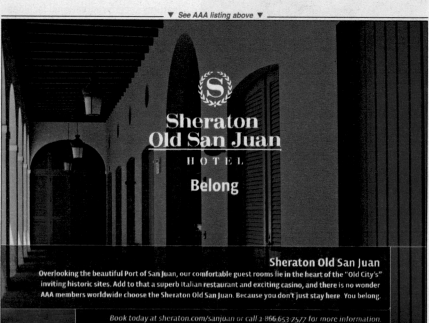

CALL S D / SOME UNITS

▼ See AAA listing above ▼

(See map and index starting on p. 477)

WHERE TO DINE

AGUAVIVA SEASIDE LATINO CUISINE **Phone:** 787/722-0665 (16)

Seafood
$16-$35

One of the newest hot spots on the block in the trendy SOFO area of old San Juan. The vivacity and conviviality among the diners and staff set the mood to enjoy the total Latino inspired seafood. Snuggle up to the ceviche bar to enjoy the marinated pulpo, shrimp, scallops and bacalao. The Spanglish menu offers a sea of opportunity to enjoy flavorful scallops con paella and chorizo or the seared dorado with coconut poached yuca and smoky shrimp salsa. Dressy casual. **Bar:** Full bar. **Hours:** 6 pm-11 pm, Thurs-Sat to midnight, Sun 4 pm-10 pm. Closed: 1/1, 11/26, 12/24, 12/25; also Three Kings Day. **Address:** 363 Calle Fortaleza **Location:** Center of Old San Juan; just n of cruise ship docks. **Parking:** street. **Cards:** AX, MC, VI. **Historic**

AL DENTE RISTORANTE AND WINE BAR **Phone:** 787/723-7303 (24)

Italian
$15-$35

This charming restaurant presents a menu of varied pasta dishes, including gnocchi. Among other entrees are Italian-inspired preparations of fresh fish, lamb and veal. Any of the tempting homemade desserts, such as creme brulee and tiramisu complete a fine meal. Dressy casual. **Bar:** Full bar. **Reservations:** suggested. **Hours:** noon-11 pm. Closed: 1/1, 12/25; also Sun. **Address:** 309 Recinto Sur **Location:** Center of Old San Juan; near cruise ship docks; across from Dona Fela parking garage. **Parking:** on-site (fee). **Cards:** AX, MC, VI. **Historic**

ALLEGRO RISTORANTE **Phone:** 787/273-9055

Regional Italian
$18-$35

The proprietor, a Puerto Rican chef, makes annual treks to Italy bringing back the secrets of Italian cuisine to San Juan. A bit off the typical tourist route, diners will delight in the extensive menu offerings and crisp, attentive service here. Pastas range from spaghetti Bolognese to rigatoni alla vodka and ravioli aurora. At least six different veal and chicken preparations reflect the chef's skills. A large selection of wines and an array of in-house prepared desserts complement the meal. Dressy casual. **Bar:** Full bar. **Reservations:** suggested. **Hours:** Open 12/1-12/22 & 1/21-11/30; noon-3 & 6-10 pm, Sat from 6 pm, Sun noon-5 pm. Closed: 11/26; also Mon, Good Friday & 7/24-7/29. **Address:** 1350 Roosevelt Ave **Location:** Between De Diego Ave and Matadero St; 1.5 mi (2.4 km) w of Plaza Las Americas. **Parking:** valet. **Cards:** AX, MC, VI.

AL SALEM RESTAURANT **Phone:** 787/751-6296 (70)

Arabic
$12-$24

Charming Middle Eastern decor sets the mood. Guests can sample many items from their choice of four combination meals, while additional items include several salads, such as tabbouleh, as well as lamb, beef and three preparations of red snapper. The staff is well groomed. Belly dancers perform on the weekend. Casual dress. Entertainment. **Bar:** Full bar. **Reservations:** suggested, weekends. **Hours:** noon-10 pm, Fri & Sat-11 pm. **Address:** Ave Roosvelt #150 **Location:** 1.1 mi (1.8 km) e of Plaza Las Americas; in Hato Rey. **Parking:** valet. **Cards:** AX, MC, VI.

AUGUSTO'S CUISINE **Phone:** 787/725-7700 (44)

Continental
$24-$45

International, classical cuisine exhibits regional influences. Among menu favorites are foie gras terrine, wild salmon tartar with wasabi flying fish roe, Colorado lamb duo, crispy Muscovy duck breast and Angus filet mignon with black truffle sauce. For dessert, try the chocolate souffle with Grand Marnier anglaise sauce. Because the restaurants caters to an adult crowd, children under 12 are not allowed. Dressy casual. Entertainment. **Bar:** Full bar. **Reservations:** suggested. **Hours:** Open 12/1-7/23 & 8/8-11/30; noon-2 & 7-10 pm, Sat from 7 pm. Closed major holidays; also Sun & Mon. **Address:** 801 Ponce de Leon Ave **Location:** 5 mi (8 km) w of airport; Ponce de Leon and Calle Trigo; in Courtyard by Marriott San Juan Miramar. **Parking:** valet. **Cards:** AX, MC, VI.

BLT STEAK **Phone:** 787/253-1700 (63)

Steak
$28-$48

A recent addition to San Juan's dining scene, this cutting-edge steaks, chops and seafood restaurant from New York City provides flawless service in a refined yet lively atmosphere. Lining the menu are West Coast/East Coast oysters, Alaskan king crab, Kobe and Black Angus beef, Dover sole and Maine lobster. To end a memorable dining experience here, many indulge in American artisan cheese, warm coconut bread pudding with rum raisin ice cream or peanut butter mousse pie with banana ice cream. Dressy casual. **Bar:** Full bar. **Reservations:** required. **Hours:** 6:45 pm-11 pm. Closed: Mon. **Address:** 6961 Ave of the Governors **Location:** In Isla Verde; 1 mi (1.6 km) n of Luis Munoz Marin International Airport; in The Ritz-Carlton San Juan Hotel, Spa & Casino. **Cards:** AX, MC, VI.

BUENOS AYRES BAR & GRILL **Phone:** 787/725-1818 (52)

Argentine
$17-$33

This attractive corner neighborhood churrascaria offers quick friendly service in a relaxed ambience. Grilled beef, pork, chicken and seafood like lobster and fish line the menu. The large pictures of sangria are great for sharing. The tres leches cake is a must order. Casual dress. **Bar:** Full bar. **Reservations:** accepted. **Hours:** 11 am-midnight, Fri & Sat noon-2 am. Closed: 11/26, 12/25; also Good Friday. **Address:** 56 Condado Ave **Location:** Corner of Condado and Magdalena aves; in Condado just s of Ashford Ave. **Parking:** valet. **Cards:** AX, MC, VI.

CAFE' BOHEMIO **Phone:** 787/723-9200 (3)

Caribbean
$8-$15

Adjacent to El Convento, the casual eatery has mostly terrace seating and a small interior dining area. The menu features a lengthy list of appetizers that are great for sharing, as well as international and Puerto Rican dishes along the lines of mofongo (mashed plantains with garlic and lardons), pork loin with spicy barbecue sauce and grilled skirt steak with chimichurri sauce. Casual dress. **Bar:** Full bar. **Reservations:** accepted. **Hours:** 11 am-11 pm. Closed: Wed. **Address:** 100 Calle Cristo **Location:** Center of Old San Juan; in Hotel El Convento. **Parking:** on-site (fee) and street. **Cards:** AX, DS, MC, VI.

CHAYOTE RESTAURANT **Phone:** 787/722-9385 (42)

International
$12-$35

Don't be fooled by the exterior of this non-descript building, located in the historic Miramar neighborhood, because a stylish, chic interior is revealed within. The smartly dressed servers provide conscientious service. Chayote, a type of squash, is featured in several dishes. Dressy casual. **Bar:** Full bar. **Reservations:** required. **Hours:** 11:30 am-2:30 & 6:30-10:30 pm, Sat from 6:30 pm. Closed major holidays; also Sun, Mon & Easter week. **Address:** 603 Miramar Ave **Location:** Just s of Ave Ponce de Leon in Miramar; adjacent to Hotel Olimpio Court. **Parking:** valet. **Cards:** AX, MC, VI.

(See map and index starting on p. 477)

CHE'S RESTAURANT ARGENTINO **Phone:** 787/726-7202 (50)

Argentine
$12-$25

Locals frequent the modestly decorated restaurant for snappy service and simply presented meals with good flavor. Entrees range from steak, veal and pork to chicken and pasta dishes. Good starters include several soups, salad or flaky empanadas. Flan or a dish of ice cream is a sweet finish. Casual dress. **Bar:** Full bar. **Reservations:** accepted. **Hours:** 11:30 am-10:45 pm, Fri & Sat-midnight. Closed: 1/1, 11/26, 12/25; also Good Friday. **Address:** 35 Coaba St **Location:** Jct Laural St and Isla Verde Ave; between Isla Verde and Condado aves; at Punta Las Marias. **Parking:** valet. **Cards:** AX, DC, DS, MC, VI.

DRAGONFLY **Phone:** 787/977-3886 (15)

New Latin American
$12-$25

Along the SoFo restaurant row of Old San Juan is the cozy eatery specializing in Asian-Latino cuisine. Patrons sit at communal tables while enjoying the chef's adventurous creations. Service comes with hip pizzazz. Dressy casual. **Bar:** Full bar. **Hours:** 6 pm-11 pm, Thurs-Sat to midnight. Closed: 1/1, 11/26, 12/24, 12/25; also Sun, Good Friday & Three Kings Day. **Address:** 364 Fortaleza St **Location:** Center Old San Juan; just n of cruise ship docks. **Parking:** street. **Cards:** AX, MC, VI. **Historic**

EL ALCAZAR MARISQUERIA Y TASCA ESPANOLA **Phone:** 787/707-0102 (20)

Spanish
$15-$33

Authentic Spanish restaurant with dapper, attentive servers. The rustically rich decor is very comfortable. Paellas are worth the wait; other entrees ranging from beef, chicken and fish are also very satisfying. The flan de coco is a popular dessert. Dressy casual. **Bar:** Full bar. **Reservations:** suggested. **Hours:** 11 am-10 pm. Closed: 11/26. **Address:** 1013 Roosevelt Ave **Location:** In Puerto Nuevo; just w of Plaza Las Americas. **Parking:** valet. **Cards:** AX, MC, VI.

EL MARIACHI RESTAURANTE **Phone:** 787/724-0420 (57)

Mexican
$10-$26

While the service is a bit barebone the menu offers a nice selection of entrees including churrasco skirt steak, mahi mahi, calamari and pork tenderloin as well as the usual Mexican standards of burritos, fajitas and enchiladas. Mirror walls, sombreros and live cacti help define the casual setting. Casual dress. Entertainment. **Bar:** Full bar. **Reservations:** accepted. **Hours:** 11 am-midnight, Thurs-Sat to 2 am, Sun 2 pm-10 pm. **Address:** 1105 Ave Magdalena **Location:** Center of Condado; across from post office. **Parking:** on-site and valet. **Cards:** AX, MC, VI.

EL ZIPPERLE RESTAURANTE **Phone:** 787/763-1636 (72)

International
$17-$32

With chalet-style decor, murals on the wall and decorative sconce lighting, the dining room evokes the ambience of yesteryear fine dining. The menu lists an interesting mix of German, Spanish and Puerto Rican cuisine. Decision-making can be arduous due to the dizzying array of choices, including nine soups and salads, paella, lobster prepared five ways and Chateaubriand for two. The tableside arrival of the dessert trolley marks the meal's finale. Dressy casual. **Bar:** Full bar. **Reservations:** required. **Hours:** 11 am-midnight. **Address:** Ave Roosvelt #352 **Location:** In Hato Rey; just w of Plaza Las Americas. **Parking:** valet. **Cards:** AX, CB, DC, DS, JC, MC, VI.

FACCIO PIZZA **Phone:** 787/755-5415 (76)

Italian
$6-$18

Family owned and operated for many decades, this popular eatery serves outstanding thin crust pizza and a variety of pastas and other Italian dishes. All moderately priced, it is difficult to choose from the varied menu selections including lasagna, ravioli, manicotti and seafood. Casual dress. **Bar:** Full bar. **Hours:** 10:30 am-11 pm, Fri-Sun to midnight. Closed: 11/26, 12/25. **Address:** Carretera 176 **Location:** Urb. Sagrado Corazon. **Parking:** on-site. **Cards:** AX, DC, DS, MC, VI.

FACCIO PIZZA **Phone:** 787/268-7755 (80)

Italian
$6-$18

Family owned and operated for many decades, this popular eatery serves outstanding thin crust pizza and a variety of pastas and other Italian dishes. All moderately priced, it is difficult to choose from the varied menu selections including lasagna, ravioli, manicotti and seafood. Casual dress. **Bar:** Full bar. **Hours:** 10:30 am-11 pm, Fri-Sun to midnight. Closed: 11/26, 12/25. **Address:** 4820 Ave Isla Verde **Location:** In Isla Verde; in Howard Johnson Hotel. **Parking:** on-site (fee). **Cards:** AX, DC, DS, MC, VI.

FRATELLI RISTORANTE **Phone:** 787/721-6265 (17)

Italian
$17-$29

Upscale decor, including wall murals and decorative ambient lighting, adds character to the historic building, while background music further sets the mood. The Italy-inspired menu features at least four salads, such as spinach and caprese, as well as osso buco, lamb chops, halibut, tuna loin and an assortment of gourmet pasta dishes. Dressy casual. **Bar:** Full bar. **Reservations:** suggested. **Hours:** 6 pm-11 pm, Fri & Sat-midnight. Closed: 1/1, 12/25; also Sun 7/1-9/30. **Address:** Calle Fortaleza 310 **Location:** Just n of cruise ship docks. **Parking:** on-site (fee). **Cards:** AX, MC, VI.

IL MULINO **Phone:** 787/791-8632 (87)

Italian
$24-$65

The famous New York eatery comes to San Juan, bringing its tradition of fine Italian cuisine with fresh pasta, seafood, lamb and more into a cozy, bustling dining room. Dressy casual. **Bar:** Full bar. **Reservations:** suggested. **Hours:** 6 pm-10:30 pm, Thurs-Sat to 11 pm, Sun-10 pm. **Address:** 6961 Ave of the Governors **Location:** 1 mi (1.7 km) n of Luis Munoz Marin International Airport; in The Ritz-Carlton San Juan Hotel, Spa & Casino. **Parking:** on-site (fee) and valet. **Cards:** AX, MC, VI.

JOSE JOSE RESTAURANT **Phone:** 787/725-8496 (38)

International
$30-$46

The slightly hidden gem is well worth the effort to find. Classically decorated dining rooms reflect an elegant atmosphere. Dapper, poised servers provide refined help. The extensive menu often features specialty dishes of ostrich, rabbit, goat and suckling pig. Whole baked red snapper is satisfying, and duck a l'Orange is succulently sweet. Save room for a decadent souffle. The comprehensive wine list includes a good concentration of Spanish wines. Dressy casual. **Bar:** Full bar. **Reservations:** required. **Hours:** noon-3 & 6-10 pm, Sat from 6 pm, Sun noon-6 pm. Closed: 12/25; also Mon. **Address:** 1110 Magdalena Ave **Location:** Just e of jct Ashford and Magdalena aves; in center of Condado section; next to post office. **Parking:** valet. **Cards:** AX, MC, VI.

LA CASONA RESTAURANTE **Phone:** 787/727-2717 (64)

Spanish
$19-$37

The chef/owner, originally from Spain, brings the techniques and recipes of Spanish cuisine to commingle with some Puerto Rican criollo specialties. An Andalusia guitarist has been entertaining guests here for the past 26 years. Dressy casual. Entertainment. **Bar:** Full bar. **Reservations:** required. **Hours:** Open 12/1-6/30 & 8/1-11/30; noon-3 & 6-11 pm, Sat from 6 pm. Closed: 1/1, 12/25; also Sun. **Address:** 609 San Jorge St **Location:** In Santurce; corner of San Jorge St and Ave Fernandez Juncos. **Parking:** valet. **Cards:** AX, CB, DC, DS, JC, MC, VI.

(See map and index starting on p. 477)

LA PICCOLA FONTANA — **Phone:** 787/791-1000 (84)

Italian
$22-$35

Diners enjoy the bustling atmosphere in this cozy yet elegant dining room, where tuxedo-clad staff members whisk by them throughout the night. Lending to the fine European decor are hand-painted murals and lovely chandeliers. The menu lists a good mix of sophisticated Italian fare, including a wide range of freshly prepared pasta, veal, meat and seafood offerings. Semi-formal attire. **Bar:** Full bar. **Reservations:** suggested. **Hours:** 6 pm-11 pm. **Address:** 6063 Isla Verde Ave **Location:** 2 mi (3.2 km) nw of airport; in Isla Verde; in El San Juan Hotel & Casino. **Parking:** valet. **Cards:** AX, DS, MC, VI.

LATIN STAR RESTAURANT — **Phone:** 787/724-8141 (56)

Caribbean
$9-$32

The proximity of nightlife hot spots and casinos contributes to this 24-hour eatery staying busy at all hours. Specializing in Latin and Puerto Rican comfort food, the huge menu features everything from lechon (pork), filet mignon, T-bone steaks, churrasco and pork chops to seafood, including conch, lobster, shrimp and octopus. Local favorites include goat stew, asopao, rice-like gruel with a choice of meat and mofongo made with mashed plantains. Casual dress. **Bar:** Full bar. **Hours:** 24 hours. **Address:** 1128 Ashford Ave **Location:** In Condado. **Parking:** on-site. **Cards:** AX, MC, VI.

LEMON GRASS — **Phone:** 787/724-5888 (34)

New Asian
$18-$36

On the grounds of the nostalgic Caribe Hilton Hotel, this upscale and refined restaurant puts forth a Pacific Island-Polynesian motif. Team-style service is attentive and engaging. Fusion dishes combine the best techniques and ingredients of both Latino and Asian cuisine in an avant-garde style, with healthful aspects in mind. Menu items are sized to encourage grazing, sampling and sharing. Dressy casual. **Bar:** Full bar. **Reservations:** required. **Hours:** 5:30 pm-10:30 pm. Closed: Sun. **Address:** San Geronimo Fort, Los Rosales St **Location:** Between Condado and Old San Juan; just n off Munoz Rivera Ave; in Caribe Hilton. **Parking:** on-site (fee) and valet. **Cards:** AX, MC, VI.

MADRID-SAN JUAN — **Phone:** 787/729-7171 (31)

Spanish
$14-$34

The restaurant offers mainly a tapas menu with such house specialties as alcapurrias, gallego soup, cod fritters and octopus salad. Enjoy dining in refined surroundings with a large, well appointed bar, great for nursing a cognac or glass of wine. Dressy casual. **Bar:** Full bar. **Reservations:** suggested. **Hours:** noon-11:30 pm, Sat 6 pm-11 pm. **Address:** Calle San Geronimo 1 **Location:** Between Condado and Old San Juan; off Munez Rivera Ave; in Caribe Hilton. **Parking:** on-site (fee). **Cards:** AX, CB, DC, DS, MC, VI.

MAKARIOS ARABIAN CUISINE & BAR — **Phone:** 787/723-8653 (21)

Arabic
$10-$24

The genuinely amiable wait staff are attentive. The menu features many Greek and Middle Eastern favorites like stewed lamb, kibbeh, tabouli, cous cous, hummus and stuffed grape leaves. There is a selection of Greek-style pizzas and inspired pastas as well. Casual dress. **Bar:** Full bar. **Reservations:** suggested, weekends. **Hours:** noon-11 pm, Fri & Sat-midnight. Closed: 1/1, 12/24, 12/25; also 12/31. **Address:** 361 Calle Tetuan **Location:** In Old San Juan; between Plaza de Colon and cruise ship docks. **Parking:** on-site (fee). **Cards:** AX, DS, MC, VI. **Historic**

METROPOL RESTAURANT — **Phone:** 787/791-5585 (86)

Cuban
$11-$27

The well-attired staff provides matter-of-fact service at the diner-style restaurant, which is popular with locals and tourists alike. Varied items are freshly prepared, and most come with rice, beans and plantains. Casual dress. **Bar:** Full bar. **Reservations:** accepted, Sun-Thurs. **Hours:** 11:30 am-11 pm. Closed: 12/24, 12/25. **Address:** Boca Cangrejos Rd **Location:** 2 mi (3.2 km) nw of airport; just w of jct Hwy 187; off Isla Verde Ave. **Parking:** on-site. **Cards:** AX, DS, MC, VI.

MIGAS INNOVATIVE CUISINE — **Phone:** 787/721-5991 (58)

International
$18-$30

In a small shopping plaza, this relatively new restaurant may slip with its service but it makes up for it with well-prepared food, including several cuts of beef and several types of fish, and a stylishly enhanced dining room. Dressy casual. **Bar:** Full bar. **Reservations:** suggested. **Hours:** Open 12/1-7/1 & 8/1-11/30; 6 pm-11 pm, Thurs-Sat to midnight. Closed: 1/1, 11/26, 12/24, 12/25; also Good Friday. **Address:** 1400 Magdalena Ave **Location:** East end of Condado. **Parking:** valet. **Cards:** AX, MC, VI.

MOFONGO CRIOLLO CUISINE & BAR — **Phone:** 787/725-6680 (25)

Puerto Rican
$15-$25

Across from the cruise ship docks is this combination bar-restaurant, which serves well-prepared and attractively presented Puerto Rican cuisine. The restaurant's name—Mofongo—points to one of its most popular choices, a national dish of mashed plantains with lardons and garlic filled with seafood, meat or chicken. Diners also can pick from a selection of fresh fish, churrasco steak and asaopas, a hearty stew served with rice. Casual dress. **Bar:** Full bar. **Reservations:** accepted. **Hours:** 9 am-10 pm. Closed: Good Friday. **Address:** 111 Concepcion de Garcia **Location:** In Old San Juan; across from cruise ship terminal; in Sheraton Plaza, adjacent to the Sheraton Hotel & Casino. **Parking:** on-site. **Cards:** AX, CB, DC, DS, JC, MC, VI.

MOMOYAMA — **Phone:** 787/791-8883 (81)

Japanese
$13-$36

Japanese chefs design beautifully presented sushi and sashimi platters, and waitresses in traditional dress serve them. Less adventuresome diners might try teriyaki or tempura dishes. Dressy casual. **Bar:** Full bar. **Reservations:** suggested. **Hours:** noon-3 & 5:30-11:30 pm, Fri-midnight, Sat 5:30 pm-midnight, Sun 1 pm-11:30 pm. **Address:** 5961 Isla Verde Ave **Location:** 2.1 mi (3.3 km) e of airport; in InterContinental San Juan Resort & Casino. **Parking:** on-site (fee) and valet. **Cards:** AX, MC, VI.

MORTON'S OF CHICAGO, THE STEAKHOUSE — **Phone:** 787/977-6262 (30)

Steak
$29-$50

Patrons should make sure to reserve ahead for the popular, well-known steak house. Large portions, including huge cuts of fine beef and plentiful seafood, are the norm. Even the vegetables are oversized, with baked potatoes big enough for sharing. Dressy casual. **Bar:** Full bar. **Reservations:** suggested. **Hours:** 5:30 pm-11 pm, Sun 5 pm-10 pm. Closed major holidays; also Three Kings Day. **Address:** 1 Calle San Geronimo Grounds **Location:** Between Condado and Old San Juan; off Munoz Rivera Ave; in Caribe Hilton. **Parking:** on-site (fee) and valet. **Cards:** AX, DC, MC, VI.

(See map and index starting on p. 477)

OLD HARBOR BREWERY STEAK & LOBSTER HOUSE — **Phone:** 787/721-2100 (6)

International
$12-$38

The only known microbrewery in Puerto Rico, this place boasts a casual side and a more refined side with an exhibition kitchen in the same setting. The varied menu includes salmon, several pasta dishes, escargot, gourmet burgers, Kobe and Angus beef and live Caribbean lobsters plucked straight from the tank. Casual dress. Entertainment. **Bar:** Full bar. **Reservations:** suggested. **Hours:** 11:30 am-1 am. **Address:** 202 Tizol St **Location:** In Old San Juan; corner of Tizol and Recinto Sur sts. **Parking:** on-site (fee). **Cards:** AX, CB, DC, DS, JC, MC, VI.

PANZA RESTAURANT AT CHATEAU CERVANTES — **Phone:** 787/289-8900 (28)

International
$25-$49

Located in the discreet and chic boutique Chateau Cervantes, this restaurant is sure to please. The creative chef blends the best ingredients and techniques of many cultures to create his own signature cuisine. A nice ending is the artisan cheese and fruit plate. Dressy casual. **Bar:** Full bar. **Reservations:** suggested. **Hours:** noon-3 & 6-11 pm. **Address:** 329 Recinto Sur **Location:** Center; Old San Juan. **Parking:** street. **Cards:** AX, MC, VI. **Historic**

THE PARROT CLUB — **Phone:** 787/725-7370 (9)

New Latin American
$12-$36

This ever popular hot spot is a place of continual celebrations in an island vibrant, urban hip atmosphere, and is always brimming with diners. Specializing in Nuevo Latino cuisine, the meals are fun, tasty and creative. Begin with one of the many designer martinis. Enjoy one of the ceviches as an appetizer. Try the tamarind glazed baby back ribs, sashimi grade tuna or smoked chicken for a main course. All meals are served with side accompaniments like plantains and yucca. Dressy casual. Entertainment. **Bar:** Full bar. **Hours:** 11:30 am-3 & 6-11 pm, Thurs-Sat to midnight; Saturday & Sunday brunch noon-4 pm. Closed: 1/1, 11/26, 12/24, 12/25; also Three Kings Day. **Address:** 363 Fortaleza St **Location:** Center of Old San Juan; just n of cruise ship docks. **Parking:** street. **Cards:** AX, DC, MC, VI. **Historic**

PIKAYO — **Phone:** 787/721-6194 (60)

International
$21-$60

The celebrity chef's excellent, imaginative dishes treat diners to a fusion of Puerto Rican, French and Californian flavors. Attentive servers circulate through the stylish dining room, which is set in a museum surrounded by world-class art. Dressy casual. **Bar:** Full bar. **Reservations:** required. **Hours:** noon-3 & 6-11 pm, Sun-3 pm. Closed: 1/1, 12/25; also Mon. **Address:** 299 De Diego Ave **Location:** In Museum of Art of Puerto Rico. **Parking:** on-site (fee) and valet. **Cards:** AX, CB, DC, DS, JC, MC, VI.

PLATOS RESTAURANT — **Phone:** 787/791-7474 (85)

Caribbean
$18-$45

This casual eatery features a contemporary decor and a creative menu of freshly prepared cuisine. Rich sauces and fresh island ingredients enhance the bold flavor and texture in the extensive selection of choices, which make up hearty courses ideal for sharing. Starters such as fried cheese with coconut dipping sauce lead up to entrees of fresh seafood, in addition to meats and pork cooked in varied ways. Even the desserts, such as the excellent guava cheesecake, reflect an island influence. Casual dress. **Bar:** Full bar. **Reservations:** accepted. **Hours:** 5 pm-11 pm. Closed major holidays; also Wed. **Address:** Calle Rosa #2, Isla Verde **Location:** 2 mi (3.2 km) nw of airport in Isla Verde area; close to intersection with Hwy 187. **Parking:** no self-parking. **Cards:** AX, MC, VI.

RESTAURANT AJILI-MOJILI — **Phone:** 787/725-9195 (39)

Caribbean
$16-$28

Puerto Rican cuisine is prepared in a stately mansion in the trendy neighborhood. Specialties include asopao, a chicken or seafood soup; mofongos, mashed fried plantain dough with garlic, meat or seafood; pork chops in tamarind sauce; Angus steaks; grilled lobster; Cornish hens stuffed with mofongo; and white yam fritters. Guests can expect friendly, attentive service. Dressy casual. **Bar:** Full bar. **Reservations:** required. **Hours:** 11:45 am-3 & 6-10 pm, Sat noon-3:30 & 6-11 pm, Sun noon-4 & 6-11 pm. Closed: 1/1; also 12/31, Good Friday, for dinner 12/24 & for lunch 12/25. **Address:** 1006 Ashford Ave **Location:** In Condado. **Parking:** valet. **Cards:** AX, DS, MC, VI.

RESTAURANT ANTONIO — **Phone:** 787/721-2139 (54)

International
$12-$36

Situated in the Condado area, this restaurant features refined surroundings, a dapper staff and an international menu with Italian, Spanish and Mediterranean influences. Dressy casual. **Bar:** Full bar. **Reservations:** suggested. **Hours:** noon-10:30 pm, Sat-6 pm. Closed: 1/1, 12/25; also Sun. **Address:** 1406 Ave Magdalena **Location:** In Condado; just w of corner of Washington and Ave Magdalena. **Parking:** valet. **Cards:** AX, MC, VI.

RESTAURANT COMPOSTELA — **Phone:** 787/724-6088 (62)

Spanish
$14-$38

A popular lunch and dinner spot; the crisply, formerly attired waiters work in teams to provide attentive service. The menu is lined with Spanish and International dishes with a few Puerto Rican selections. Dressy casual. **Bar:** Full bar. **Reservations:** required. **Hours:** Open 12/1-6/30 & 8/1-11/30; noon-2:30 & 6-10 pm, Sat from 6:30 pm. Closed: 1/1, 11/26, 12/25; also Sun & Easter week. **Address:** 106 Condado Ave **Location:** Jct Calle Labra and Condado Ave; just s of Hwy 26, in Santurce. **Parking:** valet. **Cards:** AX, MC, VI.

RESTAURANTE ESCAMBRON BEACH CLUB — **Phone:** 787/724-3344 (32)

Caribbean
$10-$21

When the weather permits, diners enjoy great views of the beach and water from the large outdoor patio, which is well lit at night, or air-conditioned comfort from the casual yet contemporary indoor dining area. A distinctive Puerto Rican flair punctuates the creative island menu, which focuses on fresh local fare, including a section dedicated exclusively to stuffed mashed plantains. Other popular items include local fish and other seafood and grilled meats. Casual dress. **Bar:** Full bar. **Hours:** 11 am-11 pm. **Address:** Ave Munoz Rivera **Location:** At Parque del Tercer Milenio. **Parking:** on-site. **Cards:** AX, MC, VI.

RESTAURANTE LOS CHAVALES — **Phone:** 787/767-5017 (66)

Spanish
$14-$37

Paella is the house favorite while other well-prepared dishes include hearts of palm salad, a hearty Spanish soup called caldo gallego and escargots; the extensive entree menu features lamb osso bucco, sea bass, shrimp empanadas and beef Wellington. Dressy casual. **Bar:** Full bar. **Reservations:** suggested. **Hours:** noon-11 pm. Closed: Sun. **Address:** 253 Ave F.D. Roosevelt **Location:** In Hato Rey; 0.4 mi (0.6 km) e of Plaza Las Americas. **Parking:** valet. **Cards:** AX, MC, VI.

(See map and index starting on p. 477)

RISTORANTE IL PERUGINO — **Phone:** 787/722-5481 (2)

Northern Italian
$28-$40

In a vintage building in the city's heart, the quaint, elegant restaurant has high ceilings and a romantic atmosphere. The owner/chef prepares such imaginative cuisine as warm salad of sea scallops and mushrooms, rigatoni with a rustic bacon tomato sauce and beef medallions in a balsamic vinegar sauce. The strictly Italian wine lists boasts 200 selections. Dressy casual. **Bar:** Full bar. **Reservations:** required. **Hours:** Open 12/1-10/1 & 11/1-11/30; 6:30 pm-11 pm, Tues, Fri & Sat also noon-3 pm. Closed: 1/1, 11/26, 12/25, 12/26; also 12/31, Three Kings Day & Good Friday. **Address:** 105 Calle Cristo **Location:** In Old San Juan; just n of San Juan Cathedral; corner of Calle Luna and Calle Cristo. **Parking:** street. **Cards:** DS, MC, VI. **Historic**

ROPA VIEJA GRILL — **Phone:** 787/725-2665 (46)

Cuban
$16-$32

Part of the pulse of the Condado area is the designer eatery, which whips up some tasty Cuban Criollo fare. Lechon and mofongo are favorites. For a lighter dish, try steamed bacalao, a type of cod. Indulge in one of the refreshing Mojito cocktails. Save space to try one of the silky smooth flans; several flavors are available. Casual dress. Entertainment. **Bar:** Full bar. **Reservations:** suggested. **Hours:** 10:30 am-10:30 pm, Thurs-11 pm, Fri-midnight, Sat 6 pm-midnight. Closed: 1/1, 12/25. **Address:** 1025 Ashford Ave **Location:** In Condado; west end of Ashford Ave. **Parking:** valet. **Cards:** AX, MC, VI.

RUTH'S CHRIS STEAK HOUSE — **Phone:** 787/253-1717 (82)

Steak
$27-$43

The main fare is steak, which is prepared from several cuts of prime beef and cooked to perfection, but the menu also lists lamb, chicken and seafood dishes. Guests should come hungry because the side dishes, which are among the a la carte offerings, could make a meal in themselves. Dressy casual. **Bar:** Full bar. **Reservations:** required. **Hours:** 6 pm-10 pm, Fri & Sat-11 pm, Sun noon-10 pm. **Address:** 5961 Isla Verde Ave **Location:** 2.1 mi (3.3 km) e of airport; in InterContinental San Juan Resort & Casino. **Parking:** valet. **Cards:** AX, CB, DC, DS, JC, MC, VI.

SENOR FROG'S — **Phone:** 787/977-4142

Tex-Mex
$10-$23

Part of the chain of Mexican restaurants that also includes Carlos 'n Charlie's, the fun and festive eatery is a great place to eat with the family or rendezvous with friends. The menu is lined with Tex-Mex, American and Mexican favorites, such as Buffalo wings, quesadillas, fajitas and burritos. After hours, a bar atmosphere prevails. Casual dress. **Bar:** Full bar. **Reservations:** accepted. **Hours:** 11:30 am-midnight. Closed: 12/24, 12/25. **Address:** 104 Paseo Portuario **Location:** Just n of cruise ship docks; behind Sheraton Old San Juan Hotel; across from American Parking Building; in commercial parking building. **Parking:** on-site (fee). **Cards:** AX, MC, VI.

SHOGUN JAPANESE RESTAURANT — **Phone:** 787/982-5555 (74)

Japanese
$19-$37

The cozy sushi and sashimi bar is popular with locals. Other tempting choices include teriyaki and tempura dinners. Dressy casual. **Bar:** Full bar. **Reservations:** accepted. **Hours:** noon-2:30 & 5-11 pm, Thurs & Fri-1 am, Sat 5 pm-1 am, Sun 4 pm-10 pm. **Address:** 31 Isla Verde Ave **Location:** West side of Isla Verde; between Isla Verde and Ocean Park/Condado sections. **Parking:** valet. **Cards:** AX, MC, VI.

SOFIA ITALIAN KITCHEN & WINE BAR — **Phone:** 787/721-0396 (8)

Italian
$12-$36

Within the historical walls of this establishment, guest will be pleased with the attentive, pleasant staff and the sumptuous Italian inspired dishes, great wine selection and in-house prepared desserts. Dressy casual. Entertainment. **Bar:** Full bar. **Reservations:** required. **Hours:** 11:30 am-4 & 6-11 pm, Fri & Sat-midnight, Sun noon-10 pm. Closed: 11/26, 12/25; also Three Kings Day. **Address:** 355 Calle San Francisco **Location:** Center of Old San Juan. **Parking:** street. **Cards:** AX, MC, VI. **Historic**

SONNE' AMBIENCE BAR & RESTAURANT — **Phone:** 787/721-0136 (12)

International
$15-$28

Incredible presentations of artfully prepared food are the big draw at the stylish restaurant. Latino-Asian preparations of lamb, duck, ahi tuna, veal and halibut occasionally draw on French influences. Many dishes come in tapas-size portions which allow for plenty of sharing and sampling. The decor's festive, hip quality and the close proximity of tables encourage a convivial atmosphere. Musicians often perform here. Dressy casual. Entertainment. **Bar:** Full bar. **Hours:** 4 pm-11 pm, Sun from 3:30 pm. Closed: 1/1, 12/25. **Address:** 358 Fortaleza St **Location:** Center of Old San Juan; just n of cruise ship docks. **Parking:** on-site (fee). **Cards:** AX, MC, VI.

TANGERINE — **Phone:** 787/728-6699 (83)

International
$24-$36

In one of San Juan's hippest and most chic boutique hotels, this restaurant offers artfully presented Asian-American-Latino cuisine. Creative dishes also bear creative—and sometimes suggestive—names, such as the "juicy bite" and "grab my green banana." The broad array of choices includes soft-shell crab, baby back ribs, halibut, Angus beef, Australian rack of lamb and Maine lobster. Dressy casual. **Bar:** Full bar. **Reservations:** required. **Hours:** 6 pm-10:30 pm. Closed: Sun, Mon 5/1-12/1. **Address:** 2 Tartak St **Location:** In Isla Verde; in San Juan Water & Beach Club Hotel. **Parking:** valet. **Cards:** AX, MC, VI.

TANTRA — **Phone:** 787/977-8141 (14)

Indian
$16-$30

A newcomer to the Old San Juan dining scene, in the evolving SOFO district, is Chef Ramesh Pillai's blend of Indo-Latino cuisine. Starters include ceviche, empanadas and mofongo with curry sauce. Main course temptations, such as masala-crusted lamb chops and spiced duck breast, awaken the senses. The decor has soothing, contemplative qualities and Hindu and Buddhist elements. Exotic belly dancing performances are featured on Friday and Saturday nights. Casual dress. Entertainment. **Bar:** Full bar. **Hours:** noon-midnight. **Address:** 356 Calle Fortaleza **Location:** Center Old San Juan; just n of cruise ship. **Parking:** street. **Cards:** AX, MC, VI. **Historic**

TIERRA DEL FUEGO — **Phone:** 787/294-7018 (68)

Argentine
$12-$26

Lining the menu is practically every cut of beef imaginable as well as pork, chicken and a few fish entrees. The Churrasco or marinated flank steak is a favorite. Another must-have is the hearty mix-grill. Desserts include creme caramel and a variety of flans. Casual dress. **Bar:** Full bar. **Reservations:** accepted. **Hours:** noon-9:30 pm, Fri & Sat-11:30 pm. Closed: 1/1, 11/26, 12/25. **Address:** #604 Tercer Nivel Plaza Las Americas **Location:** Hato Rey; in Plaza Las Americas; 3rd floor. **Parking:** on-site. **Cards:** AX, MC, VI.

(See map and index starting on p. 477)

TIERRA SANTA RESTAURANT

Phone: 787/754-6865 (67)

Arabic
$11-$23

The lunch buffet is very popular and offers a good value, especially at night when there is an array of Middle Eastern dishes including preparations with lamb, chicken, beef or vegetarian; try the sampler platter that explores a variety of tastes. Dressy casual. Entertainment. **Bar:** Full bar. **Reservations:** accepted. **Hours:** noon-2 & 6-10 pm, Thurs noon-10 pm, Fri & Sat noon-11 pm. **Address:** 284 Roosevelt Ave **Location:** In Hato Rey; 0.3 mi (0.5 km) e of Plaza de las Americas. **Parking:** on-site and valet. **Cards:** AX, MC, VI.

TIJUANA'S BAR & GRILL

Phone: 787/723-3939 (55)

Mexican
$10-$24

A popular hole in the wall in the trendy Condado area, the restaurant affords patrons a choice of indoor seating in an area dominated by the bar or outside, where al fresco meals come with plenty of good people-watching. The food is typical Mexican fare: burritos, enchiladas, nachos and quesadillas. Casual dress. Entertainment. **Bar:** Full bar. **Reservations:** accepted. **Hours:** 11 am-11 pm. **Address:** 1512 Ashford Ave **Location:** In Condado. **Parking:** on-site (fee) and valet. **Cards:** AX, MC, VI.

TROIS CENT ONZE

Phone: 787/725-7959 (10)

French
$16-$38

Decorated with modern and classical elements, this casual fine dining establishment is the preferred place out for a romantic evening or for small intimate party of diners looking for a tranquil sophisticated atmosphere. Southern France cuisine is the main emphasis of the menu where delectable preparations of fresh fish, seafood, duck and beef reign. There is an extensive wine list and a separate bar menu for those desiring something to accompany their cocktail. Dressy casual. **Bar:** Full bar. **Reservations:** suggested. **Hours:** Open 12/1-9/1 & 10/1-11/30; noon-2:30 & 6:30-11 pm, Fri-11:30 pm, Sat 6:30 pm-11:30 pm. Closed: 1/1, 12/25; also Sun. **Address:** 311 Fortaleza St **Location:** Center of Old San Juan; just n of cruise ship docks. **Parking:** street. **Cards:** AX, DC, MC, VI.

YUM YUM TREE

Phone: 787/753-7743 (71)

Asian
$12-$25

In a nondescript building, the tastefully decorated restaurant sports an Asian motif. The extensive menu includes many familiar offerings, such as Peking duck and mu shu pork, as well as vegetarian dishes and shrimp prepared a dozen ways. Keeping up with the trends in dining, this place also offers a complete sushi menu. Casual dress. **Bar:** Full bar. **Reservations:** suggested. **Hours:** 11:30 am-10:30 pm, Fri & Sat-11 pm. **Address:** Ave Roosvelt #131 **Location:** 1.1 mi (1.8 km) e of Plaza Las Americas. **Parking:** valet. **Cards:** AX, MC, VI.

ZABO CREATIVE CUISINE

Phone: 787/725-9494 (47)

International
$16-$28

In a converted house, the well-known meeting place is a terrific spot for grazing on the many "little cravings," such as the smoked duck spring roll and guava-glazed spare ribs. Creative entrees include chicken breast stuffed with goat cheese and Italian sausage and grilled tuna over black bean mash. Chef/owner Paul Carroll is passionate about food and has created an ideal atmosphere for lingering and enjoying the cuisine. Dressy casual. **Bar:** Full bar. **Reservations:** suggested. **Hours:** 6 pm-10 pm, Thurs & Fri-11 pm, Sat 7 pm-11 pm, Sun 4 pm-10 pm. Closed: 12/25; also Mon. **Address:** 14 Candina St **Location:** In Condado; corner of Candina St and Ashford Ave. **Parking:** valet. **Cards:** AX, MC, VI. **Historic**

TOA BAJA pop. 94,088

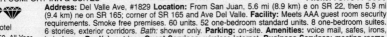

WHERE TO STAY

CAMPOMAR COMFORT INN & SUITES Phone: 787/641-9090

Hotel

$129-$159 All Year

Address: Del Valle Ave, #1829 **Location:** From San Juan, 5.6 mi (8.9 km) e on SR 22, then 5.9 mi (9.4 km) ne on SR 165; corner of SR 165 and Ave Del Valle. **Facility:** Meets AAA guest room security requirements. Smoke free premises. 60 units. 52 one-bedroom standard units. 8 one-bedroom suites. 6 stories, exterior corridors. *Bath:* shower only. **Parking:** on-site. **Amenities:** voice mail, safes, irons, hair dryers. **Pool(s):** outdoor. **Guest Services:** wireless Internet. **Business Services:** meeting rooms. **Cards:** AX, DS, MC, VI. ***(See color ad below)***

    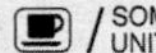   / SOME UNITS FEE

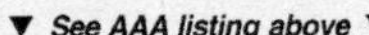

▼ *See AAA listing above* ▼

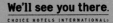

VIEQUES pop. 9,106 (See map and index starting on p. 473)

WHERE TO STAY

HACIENDA TAMARINDO

Bed & Breakfast
$135-$325 All Year

Phone: (787)741-8525 30

Address: Rt 996, 4.5 KM **Location:** 5 mi (8 km) s of airport; 0.8 mi (1.3 km) w of Esperanza. **Facility:** A large tamarind tree rises through the center of the lobby atrium of this charming inn. Each room is creatively decorated and tastefully appointed. Smoke free premises. 17 units. 13 one-bedroom standard units. 3 one-bedroom suites, some with whirlpools. 1 house. 2 stories (no elevator), interior/exterior corridors. *Bath:* combo or shower only. **Parking:** on-site. **Terms:** office hours 8 am-7 pm, age restrictions may apply, 30 day cancellation notice-fee imposed. **Amenities:** hair dryers. **Pool(s):** outdoor. **Leisure Activities:** *Fee:* massage. **Guest Services:** valet laundry, wireless Internet. **Business Services:** PC. **Cards:** AX, DS, MC, VI.

D / SOME UNITS

INN ON THE BLUE HORIZON

Country Inn
$130-$400 All Year

Phone: 787/741-3318 29

Address: SR 996, KM 4.3 **Location:** 5 mi (8 km) s of airport; 0.8 mi (1.3 km) w of Esperanza. **Facility:** The guest rooms at this quaint property vary in size. The decor features many antiques and tasteful appointments. Smoke free premises. 10 one-bedroom standard units. 1 story, exterior corridors. *Bath:* shower only. **Parking:** on-site. **Terms:** office hours 7 am-7 pm, age restrictions may apply, 30 day cancellation notice-fee imposed. **Amenities:** safes, irons, hair dryers. **Pool(s):** outdoor. **Leisure Activities:** 2 lighted tennis courts, exercise room, volleyball. **Guest Services:** valet laundry, wireless Internet. **Cards:** AX, MC, VI.

D / SOME UNITS FEE

ST. BARTHELEMY

This index helps you "spot" where approved lodgings and restaurants are located on the corresponding detailed maps. Lodging daily rate range is for comparison only and show the property's high season. Restaurant rate range is a combination of lunch and/or dinner. Turn to the listing page for more detailed rate information and consult display ads for special promotions.

ANSE DES FLAMANDS

Map Page	OA	Lodging	Diamond Rated	High Season	Page
1 / p. 520		Hotel St. Barth Isle de France	♦♦♦♦	$732-$3907	520

ANSE DES CAYES

Map Page	OA	Lodging	Diamond Rated	High Season	Page
2 / p. 520		Hotel Manapany Cottages and Spa	♦♦♦	$353-$2800	520

Map Page	OA	Restaurant	Diamond Rated	Cuisine	Meal Range	Page
3 / p. 520		Fellini	♦♦♦	Italian	$22-$52	520

GRAND CUL-DE-SAC

Map Page	OA	Lodgings	Diamond Rated	High Season	Page
5 / p. 520	AAA	**Hotel Guanahani & Spa**	♦♦♦♦	$493-$7612 SAVE	521
6 / p. 520	AAA	**Le Sereno** - see color ad p 521	♦♦♦♦	$748-$2074 SAVE	521

LORIENT

Map Page	OA	Lodging	Diamond Rated	High Season	Page
7 / p. 520		La Banane	♦♦♦	$548-$1412	522

Map Page	OA	Restaurant	Diamond Rated	Cuisine	Meal Range	Page
6 / p. 520		K'fe Massi	♦♦♦	International	$30-$45	522

GUSTAVIA

Map Page	OA	Lodging	Diamond Rated	High Season	Page
9 / p. 520		Hotel Carl Gustaf	♦♦♦♦	$1111-$3224	521

Map Page	OA	Restaurants	Diamond Rated	Cuisine	Meal Range	Page
7 / p. 520	AAA	**Pipiri Palace**	♦♦	Creole	$33-$46	522
8 / p. 520	AAA	**Carl Gustaf Restaurant**	♦♦♦♦	French	$22-$68	522
9 / p. 520		La Marine	♦♦♦	Seafood	$38-$69	522
11 / p. 520		Do Brazil	♦♦	International	$16-$34	522
12 / p. 520		Le Repaire des Rebelles et des Emigres	♦♦	Creole	$12-$31	522

TOINY

Map Page	OA	Lodging	Diamond Rated	High Season	Page
11 / p. 520		Le Toiny	♦♦♦♦	$717-$4567	523

Map Page	OA	Restaurant	Diamond Rated	Cuisine	Meal Range	Page
16 / p. 520		Le Gaiac	♦♦♦♦	French	$23-$68	523

ST. JEAN

Map Page	OA	Lodgings	Diamond Rated	High Season	Page
13 / p. 520		Hotel Le Village Saint Jean	♦♦	$180-$630	523
14 / p. 520		Eden Rock Hotel	♦♦♦♦	Rates not provided	523

Map Page	OA	Restaurants	Diamond Rated	Cuisine	Meal Range	Page
18 / p. 520		Le Zanzibarth	♦♦♦	International	$27-$47	523
20 / p. 520		On the Rocks	♦♦♦♦	French	$56-$70	523

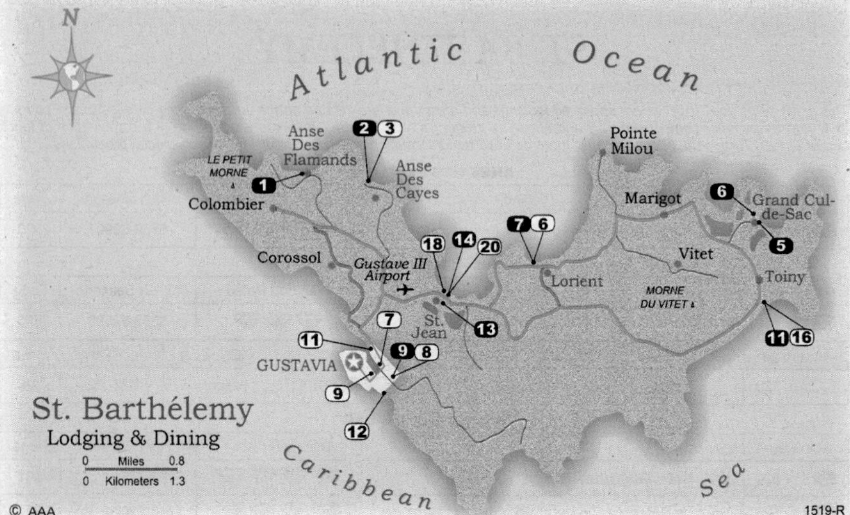

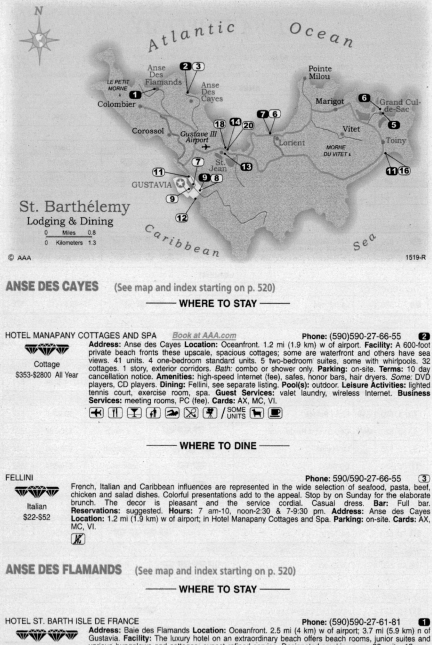

ANSE DES CAYES (See map and index starting on p. 520)

WHERE TO STAY

HOTEL MANAPANY COTTAGES AND SPA Book at AAA.com Phone: (590)590-27-66-55 2

Cottage
$353-$2800 All Year

Address: Anse des Cayes **Location:** Oceanfront. 1.2 mi (1.9 km) w of airport. **Facility:** A 600-foot private beach fronts these upscale, spacious cottages; some are waterfront and others have sea views. 41 units. 4 one-bedroom standard units. 5 two-bedroom suites, some with whirlpools. 32 cottages. 1 story, exterior corridors. *Bath:* combo or shower only. **Parking:** on-site. **Terms:** 10 day cancellation notice. **Amenities:** high-speed Internet (fee), safes, honor bars, hair dryers. *Some:* DVD players, CD players. **Dining:** Fellini, see separate listing. **Pool(s):** outdoor. **Leisure Activities:** lighted tennis court, exercise room, spa. **Guest Services:** valet laundry, wireless Internet. **Business Services:** meeting rooms, PC (fee). **Cards:** AX, MC, VI.

/ SOME UNITS

WHERE TO DINE

FELLINI Phone: 590/590-27-66-55 3

Italian
$22-$52

French, Italian and Caribbean influences are represented in the wide selection of seafood, pasta, beef, chicken and salad dishes. Colorful presentations add to the appeal. Stop by on Sunday for the elaborate brunch. The decor is pleasant and the service cordial. Casual dress. **Bar:** Full bar. **Reservations:** suggested. **Hours:** 7 am-10, noon-2:30 & 7-9:30 pm. **Address:** Anse des Cayes **Location:** 1.2 mi (1.9 km) w of airport; in Hotel Manapany Cottages and Spa. **Parking:** on-site. **Cards:** AX, MC, VI.

AC

ANSE DES FLAMANDS (See map and index starting on p. 520)

WHERE TO STAY

HOTEL ST. BARTH ISLE DE FRANCE Phone: (590)590-27-61-81 1

Cottage
$732-$3907 All Year

Address: Baie des Flamands **Location:** Oceanfront. 2.5 mi (4 km) w of airport; 3.7 mi (5.9 km) n of Gustavia. **Facility:** The luxury hotel on an extraordinary beach offers beach rooms, junior suites and various bungalows and cottages; expect refined service. Designated smoking area. 33 units. 12 one-bedroom standard units. 1 one- and 3 two-bedroom suites with whirlpools. 17 cottages. 1-2 stories, exterior corridors. **Parking:** on-site. **Terms:** age restrictions may apply, 60 day cancellation notice, 30 day off season-fee imposed. **Amenities:** video library, DVD players, CD players, high-speed Internet, safes, honor bars, hair dryers. **Pool(s):** 2 outdoor. **Leisure Activities:** snorkeling, lighted tennis court, exercise room, spa. **Guest Services:** valet laundry, wireless Internet. **Business Services:** business center. **Cards:** AX, MC, VI.

ASK 24 / SOME UNITS

GRAND CUL-DE-SAC (See map and index starting on p. 520)

WHERE TO STAY

HOTEL GUANAHANI & SPA Book great rates at AAA.com **Phone:** (590)590-27-66-60 5

AAA SAVE

Resort Hotel

$493-$7612 All Year

Address: Marigot Bay **Location:** Oceanfront. 5 mi (8.1 km) ne of Gustavia; 3.8 mi (6.1 km) ne of airport. **Facility:** On a 16-acre peninsula, upgraded property offers eight room categories ranging from 290 to 540 square feet. 68 units. 45 one-bedroom standard units. 17 one-, 4 two- and 2 three-bedroom suites, some with kitchens and/or whirlpools. 1 story, exterior corridors. *Bath:* combo or shower only. **Parking:** on-site. **Terms:** 3 night minimum stay, 30 day cancellation notice-fee imposed. **Amenities:** video library, DVD players, CD players, high-speed Internet, dual phone lines, voice mail, safes, honor bars, hair dryers. **Dining:** 2 restaurants. **Pool(s):** 2 outdoor. **Leisure Activities:** whirlpool, steamroom, canoeing, paddleboats, sailboats, windsurfing, snorkeling, kayaks, 2 lighted tennis courts, recreation programs, kids club, exercise room, spa, volleyball. *Fee:* waterskiing, scuba diving, personal watercraft, tennis instructions. **Guest Services:** valet laundry, area transportation-Gustavia Harbour, wireless Internet. **Business Services:** meeting rooms, PC. **Cards:** AX, CB, MC, VI. **Free Special Amenities: continental breakfast.**

/ SOME UNITS

LE SERENO **Phone:** (590)590-29-83-00 6

AAA SAVE

Hotel

$748-$2074 12/1-8/31
$720-$1700 11/1-11/30

Address: Grand Cul-de-Sac Beach Main Rd **Location:** Oceanfront. 5 mi (8 km) ne of Gustavia; 3.7 mi (5.9 km) e of airport. **Facility:** The hotel offers cozy rooms with private patios amid tropical gardens. 37 units. 33 one-bedroom standard units. 3 one-bedroom suites, some with whirlpools. 1 house. 1 story, exterior corridors. *Bath:* combo or shower only. **Parking:** on-site. **Terms:** open 12/1-8/31 & 11/1-11/30, 15 day cancellation notice, 30 day in season-fee imposed. **Amenities:** video library, DVD players, CD players, high-speed Internet, voice mail, safes, honor bars, hair dryers. **Pool(s):** outdoor. **Leisure Activities:** snorkeling, kayak, 2 lighted tennis courts, exercise room. *Fee:* fishing, massage. **Guest Services:** valet laundry, area transportation-Gustavia Ferry Dock, wireless Internet. **Business Services:** PC. **Cards:** AX, DC, MC, VI. *(See color ad below)*

/ SOME UNITS

GUSTAVIA pop. 6,825 (See map and index starting on p. 520)

WHERE TO STAY

HOTEL CARL GUSTAF Book at AAA.com **Phone:** (590)590-29-79-00 9

Hotel

$1111-$3224 12/1-9/1 & 10/13-11/30

Address: Rue des Normands **Location:** Just n of downtown. **Facility:** Upscale cottage suites, each with a plunge pool and personal computer, are perched above Gustavia with tremendous views; the staff is multilingual. 14 units. 1 one-bedroom standard unit with efficiency and whirlpool. 6 one- and 7 two-bedroom suites with efficiencies. 1 story, exterior corridors. *Bath:* shower only. **Parking:** on-site. **Terms:** open 12/1-9/1 & 10/13-11/30, 30 day cancellation notice, 15 day off season-fee imposed. **Amenities:** video library, DVD players, CD players, high-speed Internet, dual phone lines, voice mail, safes, honor bars, irons, hair dryers. **Dining:** Carl Gustaf Restaurant, see separate listing. **Pool(s):** outdoor. **Leisure Activities:** sauna, snorkeling, exercise room. *Fee:* boats, massage. **Guest Services:** valet laundry, area transportation, wireless Internet. **Business Services:** meeting rooms, PC. **Cards:** AX, MC, VI. Affiliated with A Preferred Hotel.

ASK / SOME UNITS

(See map and index starting on p. 520)

WHERE TO DINE

CARL GUSTAF RESTAURANT Phone: 590/590-29-79-00 (8)

French
$22-$68

Overlooking the port, the elegant, open-terrace dining room pampers diners. The menu changes frequently to take advantage of the freshest market ingredients. Examples of the culinary creations include herb-crusted rack of lamb in truffle sauce, pan-roasted foie gras, poached red snapper in banana puree, roasted lobster in aged rum sauce and duckling with morels and sweet potatoes. A comprehensive wine list comprises 400 selections, including 14 champagnes. Dressy casual. Entertainment. **Bar:** Full bar. **Reservations:** required. **Hours:** Open 12/1-9/1 & 10/5-11/30; noon-2 & 7-10:30 pm. **Address:** Rue des Normands **Location:** 0.3 mi (0.5 km) s towards Mt Lurin; in Hotel Carl Gustaf. **Parking:** on-site. **Cards:** AX, MC, VI.

DO BRAZIL Phone: 590/590-29-06-66 (11)

International
$16-$34

Owned by renowned musicians Boubou and Yannick, the beachfront restaurant affords a fantastic view of Shell Beach. Creative, well-prepared dishes blend French, Asian and Creole techniques and ingredients. Casual dress. **Bar:** Full bar. **Reservations:** suggested. **Hours:** Open 12/1-9/1 & 11/1-11/30; noon-3:30 & 7-10 pm. **Address:** Shell Beach **Location:** Just se of downtown. **Parking:** on-site. **Cards:** AX, MC, VI.

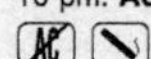

LA MARINE Phone: 590/590-27-68-91 (9)

Seafood
$38-$69

Overlooking the marina, the chic contemporary restaurant offers Caribbean buffets on some nights, with a la minute grilled lobsters, barbecue ribs and chicken, as well as a selection of side dishes. A fine ending to a meal here is the chocolate fondant with a warm liquid chocolate center. Casual dress. **Bar:** Full bar. **Reservations:** suggested. **Hours:** noon-2:30 & 7-midnight. Closed: Mon. **Address:** Gustavia Harbor-La Pointe **Location:** At Harbor Town Centre. **Parking:** street. **Cards:** MC, VI.

LE REPAIRE DES REBELLES ET DES EMIGRES Phone: 590/590-27-72-48 (12)

Creole
$12-$31

Downtown on the waterfront, the restaurant presents an extensive menu of French bistro-style cuisine. Ever-changing daily specials will not disappoint. Plentiful portions appeal to big appetites. Casual dress. **Bar:** Full bar. **Reservations:** suggested. **Hours:** 8 am-11 & noon-10:30 pm. Closed: Sun. **Address:** Rue de la Republique **Location:** Center of downtown waterfront. **Parking:** street. **Cards:** MC, VI.

PIPIRI PALACE Phone: 590/590-27-53-20 (7)

Creole
$33-$46

A truly talented chef deftly combines choice flavors and ingredients into scintillating meals within a Creole-style house verandah. Such soups as gazpacho, cold watermelon with prosciutto, onion au gratin and lobster bisque line the menu. Warm walnut-crusted goat cheese salad, crab cake and fish carpaccio are appetizers to whet the appetite. For an unforgettable seafood dish, try the skate. Meat preparations range from duck and lamb to baby back ribs and fillet of beef flambe with cognac. Casual dress. **Bar:** Full bar. **Reservations:** accepted. **Hours:** Open 12/1-6/30 & 8/1-11/30; 6:30 pm-10 pm. **Address:** Rue du General de Gaulle **Location:** Center; just n of Gustavia Harbour. **Parking:** street. **Cards:** MC, VI.

LORIENT

(See map and index starting on p. 520)

WHERE TO STAY

LA BANANE Book at AAA.com Phone: (590)590-52-03-00 (7)

Cottage
$548-$1412 12/1-8/31
$548-$769 10/20-11/30

Address: Baie de Lorient **Location:** 2 mi (3.2 km) ne of airport; 3 mi (4.8 km) ne of Gustavia. **Facility:** A hip and chic intimate hotel. Guest rooms feature high quality fabrics and splashes of Creole colors. Open air garden bathroom and shower. 9 cottages. 1 story, exterior corridors. *Bath:* shower only. **Parking:** on-site. **Terms:** open 12/1-8/31 & 10/20-11/30, office hours 7 am-9 pm, 21 day cancellation notice-fee imposed. **Amenities:** video library, DVD players, CD players, high-speed Internet, safes, honor bars, hair dryers. **Pool(s):** 2 outdoor. **Leisure Activities:** snorkeling. *Fee:* massage. **Guest Services:** valet laundry, area transportation, wireless Internet. **Business Services:** PC. **Cards:** AX, MC, VI.

ASK / SOME UNITS

WHERE TO DINE

K'FE MASSI Phone: 590/590-29-76-78 (6)

International
$30-$45

This chic restaurant with African overtones is one of the must-dine places on the island. The multi-course gourmet meals are offered in a prixe fixe fashion with different pricing platforms. The skillful chef deftly and artistically prepares each creative minded course with attention to details in the presentation. Enjoy efficient service by a knowledgeable staff and a wide selection of wine and other beverages. Casual dress. **Bar:** Full bar. **Reservations:** suggested. **Hours:** Open 12/1-9/3 & 10/18-11/30; 7 pm-10:30 pm. **Address:** Centre Commercial de l'Oasis **Location:** 2 mi (3.2 km) ne of airport; 3 mi (4.8 km) ne of Gustavia. **Parking:** on-site. **Cards:** MC, VI.

ST. JEAN (See map and index starting on p. 520)

WHERE TO STAY

EDEN ROCK HOTEL Book at AAA.com **Phone:** 590/590-29-79-99 (14)

Hotel
Rates not provided

Address: Baie de St. Jean **Location:** Oceanfront. 0.9 mi (1.4 km) e of airport; on St. Jean Bay; center. **Facility:** Situated along St. Jean Beach; select from well-appointed, stylish guest rooms with oversized bathrooms, each sporting a unique theme decor. 32 units. 12 one-bedroom standard units. 15 one-bedroom suites. 5 houses. 1-2 stories (no elevator), exterior corridors. *Bath:* combo or shower only. **Parking:** on-site. **Terms:** open 12/1-9/1 & 10/16-11/30. **Amenities:** video library, DVD players, CD players, safes, hair dryers. **Dining:** On the Rocks, see separate listing. **Leisure Activities:** sailboats, snorkeling, exercise room. *Fee:* massage. **Guest Services:** valet laundry, area transportation, wireless Internet. **Business Services:** business center.

/ SOME UNITS

HOTEL LE VILLAGE SAINT JEAN **Phone:** 590/590-27-61-39 (13)

Cottage
$180-$630 All Year

Address: St. Jean **Location:** Center; just above St. Jean Bay; 1 mi (1.6 km) e of airport. **Facility:** 27 units. 4 one-bedroom standard units. 3 houses and 20 cottages. 1 story, exterior corridors. *Bath:* shower only. **Parking:** on-site. **Terms:** office hours 7:30 am-8 pm, 45 day cancellation notice, 30 day off season-fee imposed. **Amenities:** CD players, voice mail, safes, hair dryers. **Pool(s):** outdoor. **Leisure Activities:** whirlpool, exercise room. *Fee:* massage. **Guest Services:** TV in common area, valet laundry, wireless Internet. **Business Services:** PC (fee). **Cards:** MC, VI.

ASK / SOME UNITS

WHERE TO DINE

LE ZANZIBARTH **Phone:** 590/590-27-53-00 (18)

International
$27-$47

An innovative setting and upscale contemporary design characterize both the lounge and dining area of this covered open-air eatery. Subtle lighting enhances the romantic atmosphere. French and Caribbean dishes commingle on a menu of international fare. Extensive a la carte choices provide alternatives to the full chef's tasting menu. The highlight here is the dessert offering, which comprises delightful made-to-order indulgences. Casual dress. **Bar:** Full bar. **Reservations:** suggested. **Hours:** 7 pm-11 pm. **Address:** Rt de Saline **Location:** Centre; 1 mi (1.6 km) e of airport. **Parking:** street. **Cards:** MC, VI.

AC

ON THE ROCKS **Phone:** 590/590-29-79-99 (20)

French
$56-$70

Dramatically positioned on a precipice jutting over the ocean, this multitiered dining room breathes a tropical essence. The staff provides solid team service to the lively and well-heeled clientele. Chefs fuse Asian and French ingredients and techniques to create scintillating flavors. Some favorites include shrimp ravioli and sauteed sweetbreads with trumpet mushroom sauce, monkfish and seared foie gras with roasted fig. Dressy casual. **Bar:** Full bar. **Reservations:** required. **Hours:** 7 pm-10:30 pm. **Address:** Baie de St. Jean **Location:** 0.9 mi (1.4 km) e of airport; center on St. Jean Bay; in Eden Rock Hotel. **Parking:** on-site. **Cards:** AX, MC, VI.

AC

TOINY (See map and index starting on p. 520)

WHERE TO STAY

LE TOINY Book at AAA.com **Phone:** (590)590-27-88-88 (11)

Cottage
$717-$4567 All Year

Address: Anse de Toiny **Location:** 4.4 mi (7 km) e of airport; 5.5 mi (8.8 km) ne from downtown Gustavia. **Facility:** A true refuge from the rest of the world; each lavishly decorated and exceptionally equipped cottage has a private pool. 15 cottages. 1 story, exterior corridors. **Parking:** on-site. **Terms:** office hours 7 am-11 pm, 30 day cancellation notice-fee imposed. **Amenities:** video library, DVD players, CD players, high-speed Internet, dual phone lines, voice mail, fax, safes, honor bars, irons, hair dryers. **Dining:** Le Gaiac, see separate listing. **Pool(s):** outdoor. **Leisure Activities:** snorkeling, 2 lighted tennis courts, in-room exercise equipment. *Fee:* massage. **Guest Services:** valet laundry, area transportation, wireless Internet. **Business Services:** PC. **Cards:** AX, DC, MC, VI.

/ SOME UNITS

WHERE TO DINE

LE GAIAC **Phone:** 590/590-29-77-47 (16)

French
$23-$68

Perched on a hillside overlooking the nearby sea and alongside the infinity pools, the alfresco dining room sustains a romantic ambience. A young, friendly and unpretentious wait staff hails mostly from France. The changing menu is a showcase for the chef's skill and knowledge of blending fine ingredients into superb dishes. Lamb is always a favorite, as is the local seafood. Save room for one of the decadent souffles. Dressy casual. Entertainment. **Bar:** Full bar. **Reservations:** required, for dinner. **Hours:** Open 12/1-9/1 & 10/22-11/30; noon-2:30 & 7-10 pm; Sunday brunch two seatings 11 am-11:30 & 1-1:30 pm. Closed: Mon 6/1-9/1. **Address:** Anse de Toiny **Location:** 4.4 mi (7 km) e of airport; 5.5 mi (8.8 km) ne from downtown Gustavia; in Le Toiny. **Parking:** on-site. **Cards:** AX, DC, MC, VI.

AC

ST. EUSTATIUS AND SABA

Saba

This index helps you "spot" where approved lodgings and restaurants are located on the corresponding detailed maps. Lodging daily rate range is for comparison only and show the property's high season. Restaurant rate range is a combination of lunch and/or dinner. Turn to the listing page for more detailed rate information and consult display ads for special promotions.

WINDWARDSIDE (SABA)

Map Page	OA	Lodging	Diamond Rated	High Season	Page
❶ / p. 525		Juliana's Hotel	◆	$110-$135	526

Map Page	OA	Restaurants	Diamond Rated	Cuisine	Meal Range	Page
③ / p. 525		Scout's Place Restaurant & Bar	◆	International	$10-$29	526
④ / p. 525		Swinging Doors	◆	American	$10-$18	526

THE BOTTOM (SABA)

Map Page	OA	Lodging	Diamond Rated	High Season	Page
❸ / p. 525		Queen's Gardens Resort - A Hampshire Classic	◆◆◆	$250-$475	525

Map Page	OA	Restaurant	Diamond Rated	Cuisine	Meal Range	Page
⑤ / p. 525		The King's Crown Restaurant	◆◆	International	$12-$38	525

ORANJESTAD (ST. EUSTATIUS)

Map Page	OA	Restaurants	Diamond Rated	Cuisine	Meal Range	Page
⑦ / p. 525		Golden Era Restaurant	◆	International	$9-$28	527
⑨ / p. 525		Smoke-Alley Bar & Grille	◆	International	$9-$28	527

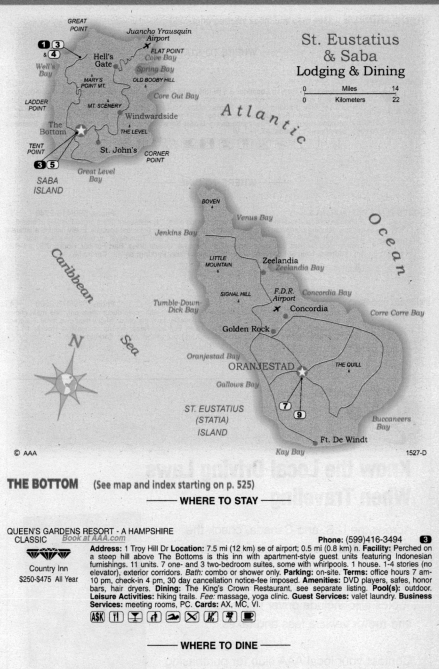

St. Eustatius & Saba
Lodging & Dining

0 Miles 14
0 Kilometers 22

GREAT POINT
Juancho Yrausquin Airport
FLAT POINT
Cove Bay
Well's Bay
Hell's Gate
Spring Bay
MARY'S POINT MT.
OLD BOOBY HILL
Cove Gut Bay
LADDER POINT
MT. SCENERY
Windwardside
The Bottom
THE LEVEL
TENT POINT
St. John's
CORNER POINT
Great Level Bay
SABA ISLAND
Atlantic Ocean
Caribbean Sea
BOVEN
Venus Bay
Jenkins Bay
LITTLE MOUNTAIN
Zeelandia
Zeelandia Bay
SIGNAL HILL
F.D.R. Airport
Concordia Bay
Tumble-Down-Dick Bay
Concordia
Corre Corre Bay
Golden Rock
Oranjestad Bay
ORANJESTAD
THE QUILL
Gallows Bay
ST. EUSTATIUS (STATIA) ISLAND
Buccaneers Bay
Ft. De Windt
Kay Bay
N

1527-D

THE BOTTOM (See map and index starting on p. 525)

WHERE TO STAY

QUEEN'S GARDENS RESORT - A HAMPSHIRE CLASSIC Book at AAA.com **Phone:** (599)416-3494 3

Country Inn
$250-$475 All Year

Address: 1 Troy Hill Dr **Location:** 7.5 mi (12 km) se of airport; 0.5 mi (0.8 km) n. **Facility:** Perched on a steep hill above The Bottoms is this inn with apartment-style guest units featuring Indonesian furnishings. 11 units. 7 one- and 3 two-bedroom suites, some with whirlpools. 1 house. 1-4 stories (no elevator), exterior corridors. *Bath:* combo or shower only. **Parking:** on-site. **Terms:** office hours 7 am-10 pm, check-in 4 pm, 30 day cancellation notice-fee imposed. **Amenities:** DVD players, safes, honor bars, hair dryers. **Dining:** The King's Crown Restaurant, see separate listing. **Pool(s):** outdoor. **Leisure Activities:** hiking trails. *Fee:* massage, yoga clinic. **Guest Services:** valet laundry. **Business Services:** meeting rooms, PC. **Cards:** AX, MC, VI.

ASK

WHERE TO DINE

THE KING'S CROWN RESTAURANT **Phone:** 599/416-3494 5

International
$12-$38

Perched high in the hills of Saba, the restaurant offers panoramic views. The menu reflects West Indies and Italian influences. Goat cheese salad is a tasty way to start off a meal. Creole-style snapper is loaded with a spicy tomato sauce. Casual dress. **Bar:** Full bar. **Reservations:** accepted. **Hours:** 7 am-10, noon-2 & 6-9 pm. Closed: for dinner Tues. **Address:** 1 Troy Hill Dr **Location:** 7.5 mi (12 km) se of airport; 0.5 mi (0.8 km) n; in Queen's Gardens Resort - Hampshire Classic. **Parking:** on-site. **Cards:** AX, CB, DC, DS, JC, MC, VI.

AC

WINDWARDSIDE (See map and index starting on p. 525)

WHERE TO STAY

JULIANA'S HOTEL — **Phone:** 599/416-2269 **1**

Bed & Breakfast
$110-$135 12/1-4/16
$85-$120 4/17-11/30

Address: Z/N Park Ln **Location:** 3.5 mi (5.6 km) s of airport; center. **Facility:** 12 units. 9 one-bedroom standard units. 1 one-bedroom suite with efficiency. 2 cottages. 2 stories, exterior corridors. *Bath:* shower only. **Parking:** on-site. **Terms:** office hours 7 am-6 pm, 30 day cancellation notice-fee imposed. **Amenities:** CD players. *Some:* DVD players, irons. **Pool(s):** outdoor. **Leisure Activities:** whirlpool, hiking trails. *Fee:* scuba diving. **Guest Services:** valet laundry, wireless Internet. **Business Services:** PC. **Cards:** AX, MC, VI.

ASK / SOME UNITS

WHERE TO DINE

SCOUT'S PLACE RESTAURANT & BAR — **Phone:** 599/416-2740 **3**

International
$10-$29

A popular spot for the diving, tourist and local crowds alike, the restaurant offers a good variety of breakfast options including European, American, French or Spanish style breakfast specials. Every night is a different theme night including fajita Mondays, chicken Tuesdays and Thursdays, gyro Wednesdays, soul food Fridays, local cuisines Saturdays and seafood Sundays. Casual dress. **Bar:** Full bar. **Hours:** 7:30 am-8:30 pm. **Address:** Main St **Location:** Center; in Scouts Place. **Parking:** on-site. **Cards:** MC, VI.

SWINGING DOORS — **Phone:** 599/416-2506 **4**

American
$10-$18

In the center of town, the Texas western-themed restaurant with rustic decor offers only one meat choice and one vegetarian platter per night. Some nights, guests have the option to grill their own meat. No credit cards are accepted - cash only. Casual dress. **Bar:** Full bar. **Reservations:** suggested. **Hours:** 10 am-midnight. **Address:** Main St **Location:** 3.7 mi (5.9 km) s of airport; center. **Parking:** street.

St. Eustatius

ORANJESTAD (See map and index starting on p. 525)

WHERE TO DINE

GOLDEN ERA RESTAURANT — **Phone:** 599/318-2455 (7)

International
$9-$28

Uninspired decor does not detract from the oceanfront setting, and nor does the no-nonsense service. Patrons make themselves comfortable on the wood deck to enjoy mostly West Indian- and Italian-inspired preparations of goat and seafood, including fresh local fish. Among menu highlights are lobster, pork cordon bleu, shrimp brochette and chicken piccata. Casual dress. **Bar:** Full bar. **Reservations:** suggested. **Hours:** 7 am-10, noon-2 & 6:30-10 pm. **Address:** Oranjebaai **Location:** 2.5 mi (4 km) sw of airport; in Lower Town; at Golden Era Hotel. **Parking:** street. **Cards:** AX, MC, VI.

SMOKE-ALLEY BAR & GRILLE — **Phone:** 599/318-2002 (9)

International
$9-$28

The waterfront eatery carries out a thin nautical theme. The menu is lined with a range of familiar items, such as fajitas, fish and chips, tacos, New York strip steak and shrimp scampi. Various toppings flavor the wide variety of hamburgers. Check the daily specials and soup du jour. Casual dress. **Bar:** Full bar. **Reservations:** accepted. **Hours:** Open 12/1-9/30 & 10/5-11/30; 11 am-2:30 & 6-10 pm. Closed: 12/25, 12/26; also Sun. **Address:** Lower Town **Location:** 2.2 mi (3.5 km) sw of airport; in Lower Town. **Parking:** on-site. **Cards:** DS, MC, VI.

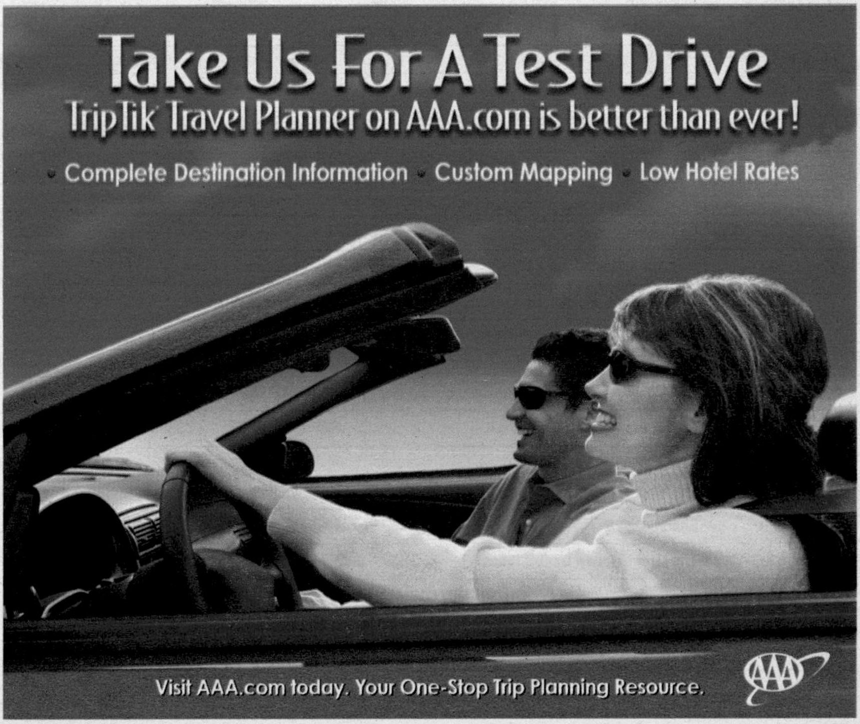

ST. KITTS AND NEVIS

Airport Accommodations

Map Page	OA	ROBERT L BRADSHAW INTERNATIONAL AIRPORT	Diamond Rated	High Season	Page
3 / p. 530		Sugar Bay Club, 2.4 mi (3.8 km) e of airport	◆◆	$185-$300	536

St. Kitts and Nevis

This index helps you "spot" where approved lodgings and restaurants are located on the corresponding detailed maps. Lodging daily rate range is for comparison only and show the property's high season. Restaurant rate range is a combination of lunch and/or dinner. Turn to the listing page for more detailed rate information and consult display ads for special promotions.

BASSETERRE (ST. KITTS)

Map Page	OA	Lodging	Diamond Rated	High Season	Page
1 / p. 530		Ocean Terrace Inn	◆◆	$195-$460	535

Map Page	OA	Restaurants	Diamond Rated	Cuisine	Meal Range	Page
1 / p. 530	AAA	**Serendipity Restaurant & Lounge Bar**	◆◆◆	International	$10-$33	535
4 / p. 530		The Ballahoo	◆	International	$5-$29	535
5 / p. 530		Bambu's	◆	American	$12-$22	535
6 / p. 530	AAA	**Fisherman's Wharf**	◆	Seafood	$24-$34	535
7 / p. 530		Star of India	◆	Indian	$9-$24	535
8 / p. 530		Waterfalls Restaurant	◆◆◆	International	$20-$33	536
9 / p. 530		Circus Grill	◆	Caribbean	$10-$28	535

FRIGATE BAY (ST. KITTS)

Map Page	OA	Lodgings	Diamond Rated	High Season	Page
3 / p. 530		Sugar Bay Club	◆◆	$185-$300	536
6 / p. 530	AAA	**St. Kitts Marriott Resort & Royal Beach Casino** - see color ad p 537, on insert	◆◆◆◆	$164-$318 SAVE	536

Map Page	OA	Restaurants	Diamond Rated	Cuisine	Meal Range	Page
10 / p. 530	AAA	**Marshall's**	◆◆◆	International	$24-$35	538
11 / p. 530	AAA	**La Cucina**	◆◆◆	Italian	$18-$32	538
12 / p. 530		PJ's Bar & Restaurant	◆	Italian	$13-$24	538
14 / p. 530		Monkey Bar & Restaurant	◆	Seafood	$12-$31	538

NEWCASTLE (NEVIS)

Map Page	OA	Lodgings	Diamond Rated	High Season	Page
7 / p. 530		The Mount Nevis Hotel & Beach Club	◆◆◆	$250-$400	534
8 / p. 530	AAA	**Nisbet Plantation Beach Club**	◆◆◆◆	$350-$795 SAVE	534

Map Page	OA	Restaurants	Diamond Rated	Cuisine	Meal Range	Page
26 / p. 530		The Mount Nevis Restaurant	◆◆◆	International	$15-$60	534
27 / p. 530		Seabreeze	◆◆	Caribbean	$10-$17	534
28 / p. 530	AAA	**The Great House Dining Room**	◆◆◆◆	Continental	$60-$65	534

CHARLESTOWN (NEVIS)

Map Page	OA	Lodging	Diamond Rated	High Season	Page
10 / p. 530	AAA	**Four Seasons Resort Nevis**	◆◆◆◆◆	$335-$995 SAVE	531

Map Page	OA	Restaurants	Diamond Rated	Cuisine	Meal Range	Page
16 / p. 530		Downtown Cybercafe	1	International	$10-$15	531
19 / p. 530	AAA	**Sunshines Bar & Grill**	1	Caribbean	$12-$25	531
20 / p. 530		The Dining Room	4	International	$26-$47	531

OUALIE BAY (NEVIS)

Map Page	OA	Lodging	Diamond Rated	High Season	Page
11 / p. 530		Hurricane Cove Bungalows	2	$165-$685	534

GINGERLAND (NEVIS)

Map Page	OA	Lodgings	Diamond Rated	High Season	Page
12 / p. 530		The Hermitage Plantation Inn	2	$180-$450	532
13 / p. 530	AAA	**Montpelier Plantation Inn**	4	$290-$535 SAVE	532
14 / p. 530		Old Manor Estate & Hotel	2	$180-$380	532
15 / p. 530		Golden Rock Plantation Inn	2	$160-$285	531

Map Page	OA	Restaurants	Diamond Rated	Cuisine	Meal Range	Page
21 / p. 530		The Cooperage Restaurant	2	Continental	$10-$33	532
22 / p. 530		Golden Rock Dining Room	2	Caribbean	$12-$42	533
23 / p. 530		Martha's in the Garden Restaurant	2	Caribbean	$8-$17	533
24 / p. 530	AAA	**The Terrace at Montpelier Plantation Inn**	4	International	$20-$60	533

COTTON GROUND (NEVIS)

Map Page	OA	Restaurant	Diamond Rated	Cuisine	Meal Range	Page
30 / p. 530		Coconut Grove Restaurant and Wine Lounge	3	International	$21-$25	531

JONES BAY (NEVIS)

Map Page	OA	Restaurants	Diamond Rated	Cuisine	Meal Range	Page
32 / p. 530	AAA	**Gallipot**	2	Seafood	$12-$22	533
33 / p. 530		Miss June's Cuisine	3	International	$75	534

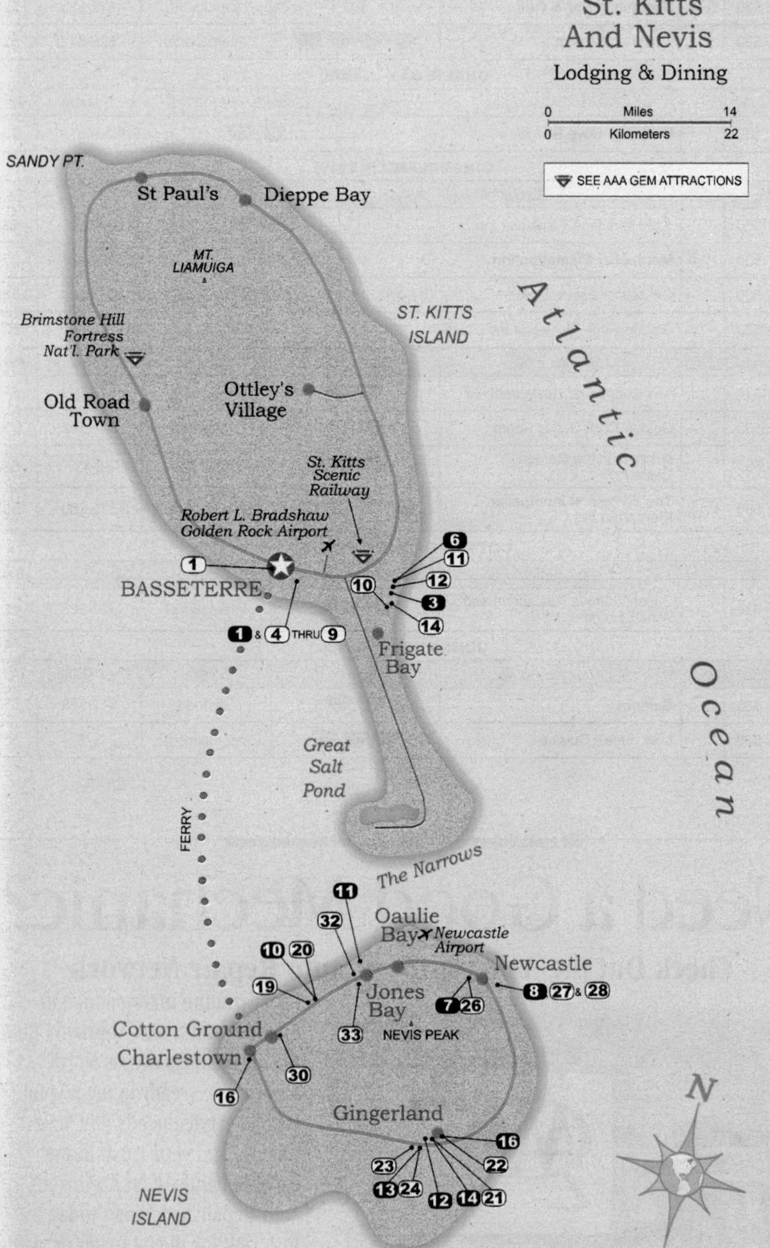
St. Kitts
And Nevis
Lodging & Dining
0 Miles 14
0 Kilometers 22
SEE AAA GEM ATTRACTIONS
SANDY PT.
St Paul's
Dieppe Bay
MT. LIAMUIGA
Brimstone Hill Fortress Nat'l. Park
ST. KITTS ISLAND
Atlantic
Ottley's Village
Old Road Town
St. Kitts Scenic Railway
Robert L. Bradshaw Golden Rock Airport
1
6
11
12
10
3
14
BASSETERRE
1 & 4 THRU 9
Frigate Bay
Ocean
Great Salt Pond
FERRY
The Narrows
11
32
Oaulie Bay
Newcastle Airport
10 20
Newcastle
19
8 27 & 28
Jones Bay
7 26
33
NEVIS PEAK
Cotton Ground
Charlestown
30
16
Gingerland
16
22
23
13 24
12
14 21
NEVIS ISLAND
N
© AAA
1520-D

Nevis

CHARLESTOWN pop. 1,820 (See map and index starting on p. 530)

WHERE TO STAY

FOUR SEASONS RESORT NEVIS **Phone:** (869)469-1111 10

SAVE

Resort Hotel

$335-$995 All Year

Address: Pinney's Beach **Location:** Pinney's Beach; transportation via van and water launch from St. Kitts Regional Airport. **Facility:** Set between the beach and a championship golf course, the world-class resort offers refined service and upscale accommodations in an island setting. 196 units. 179 one-bedroom standard units. 17 one-bedroom suites. 2 stories (no elevator), exterior corridors. **Parking:** on-site and valet. **Terms:** off-site registration, 30 day cancellation notice-fee imposed. **Amenities:** video library, DVD players, CD players, high-speed Internet (fee), dual phone lines, voice mail, safes, honor bars, irons, hair dryers. **Dining:** 4 restaurants, also, The Dining Room, see separate listing, entertainment. **Pool(s):** 3 outdoor. **Leisure Activities:** whirlpool, steamrooms, sailboats, windsurfing, snorkeling, lap lanes, sea kayaks, catamarans, driving range, recreation programs, billiards, croquet, hiking trails, jogging, playground, spa, basketball, horseshoes, shuffleboard, volleyball, game room. *Fee:* boats, waterskiing, scuba diving, fishing, charter fishing, golf-18 holes, 10 tennis courts (5 lighted), clay & hard surface tennis courts. **Guest Services:** valet and coin laundry, wireless Internet. **Business Services:** conference facilities, business center. **Cards:** AX, DC, DS, MC, VI.

D / SOME UNITS

WHERE TO DINE

THE DINING ROOM **Phone:** 869/469-1111 20

International

$26-$47

The restaurant treats diners to an innovative mix of Continental and Caribbean cuisine. Exotic dishes on the ever-changing menu blend fresh local and regional ingredients. Dinner is served in the large, elegant dining room, which sustains an Old World atmosphere, or on the screened patio, which overlooks the ocean. Both areas offer romantic ambience, with candlelit tables and the peaceful sound of the ocean breeze. Dressy casual. **Bar:** Full bar. **Reservations:** suggested. **Hours:** 6 pm-10 pm. **Address:** Pinney's Beach **Location:** Pinney's Beach; transportation via van and water launch from St. Kitts Regional Airport; in Four Seasons Resort Nevis. **Parking:** on-site and valet. **Cards:** AX, CB, DC, DS, JC, MC, VI.

DOWNTOWN CYBERCAFE **Phone:** 869/469-1981 16

International

$10-$15

Check your e-mail or make a phone call and get a healthy homemade lunch at the same time; deli sandwiches, rice and peas, curry chicken, plus vegetarian selections are included in the menu selections. Casual dress. **Hours:** 9 am-4 pm. Closed: 1/1, 11/26, 12/25; also Sun. **Address:** Main St **Location:** Jct Low St; downtown. **Parking:** street.

SUNSHINES BAR & GRILL **Phone:** 869/469-5817 19

Caribbean

$12-$25

Locals and tourists alike flock to this happening beachside eatery to mingle with the owner, Sunshine, who is known for his hospitality, his barbecue and his specialty drink: the Killer Bee. Casual dress. **Bar:** Full bar. **Hours:** noon-3:30 & 6:30-9 pm. **Address:** Pinney's Beach **Location:** Pinney's Beach; just e of Four Seasons Resort Nevis. **Parking:** on-site.

COTTON GROUND (See map and index starting on p. 530)

WHERE TO DINE

COCONUT GROVE RESTAURANT AND WINE LOUNGE **Phone:** 869/469-1020 30

International

$21-$25

One of the area's newer restaurants, the distinctively designed open-air spot abuts a comfortable wine bar. The continually evolving menu comprises classic dishes made from the freshest ingredients and incorporating Asian and Caribbean influences. Gary, the affable host and owner, provides the savoir faire and attention to detail expected at a fine-dining establishment. Dressy casual. **Bar:** Full bar. **Reservations:** suggested. **Hours:** Open 12/1-9/7 & 9/22-11/30; 6:30 pm-10:30 pm. Closed: Mon. **Address:** Main Island Rd **Location:** Just e of town; at Cotton Ground, Clifton Estate. **Parking:** on-site. **Cards:** MC, VI.

GINGERLAND (See map and index starting on p. 530)

WHERE TO STAY

GOLDEN ROCK PLANTATION INN **Phone:** (869)469-3346 16

Country Inn

$160-$285 12/1-8/15

$160-$195 10/15-11/30

Address: Gingerland **Location:** 13.1 mi (21 km) s of Newcastle Airport; 5.5 mi (8.8 km) e of Charlestown. **Facility:** Designated smoking area. 12 units. 1 two-bedroom suite. 11 cottages. 1-2 stories (no elevator), exterior corridors. *Bath:* shower only. **Parking:** on-site. **Terms:** open 12/1-8/15 & 10/15-11/30, office hours 7:30 am-10 pm, 3 night minimum stay - seasonal, 21 day cancellation notice-fee imposed. **Amenities:** hair dryers. **Dining:** Golden Rock Dining Room, see separate listing. **Pool(s):** outdoor. **Leisure Activities:** hiking trails. **Guest Services:** TV in common area, valet laundry, area transportation. **Business Services:** PC. **Cards:** AX, MC, VI.

ASK

(See map and index starting on p. 530)

THE HERMITAGE PLANTATION INN **Phone:** (869)469-3477 **12**

Country Inn
$180-$450 All Year

Address: Gingerland **Location:** 4 mi (6.4 km) e of Charlestown. **Facility:** 15 units. 8 one-bedroom standard units. 1 house and 6 cottages. 1-2 stories, exterior corridors. *Bath:* combo or shower only. **Parking:** on-site. **Terms:** office hours 8 am-10 pm, 21 day cancellation notice-fee imposed. **Amenities:** video library, CD players, safes, irons, hair dryers. *Some:* DVD players. **Pool(s):** outdoor. **Leisure Activities:** sailboats, snorkeling, tennis court, hiking trails. *Fee:* horseback riding, massage. **Guest Services:** coin laundry, wireless Internet. **Business Services:** PC, fax (fee). **Cards:** AX, DS, MC, VI.

/ SOME UNITS

MONTPELIER PLANTATION INN **Phone:** (869)469-3462 **13**

SAVE

Country Inn
$290-$535 All Year

Address: Cole Hill **Location:** 3.5 mi (5.6 km) e of Charlestown; 1 mi (1.6 km) s, follow signs. **Facility:** On 60 acres set 750 feet above sea level, this restored 17th-century sugar plantation evokes the charm of days gone by. Designated smoking area. 18 units. 16 one-bedroom standard units. 1 one- and 1 two-bedroom suites. 1 story, exterior corridors. **Parking:** on-site. **Terms:** office hours 8 am-7 pm, age restrictions may apply, 30 day cancellation notice-fee imposed. **Amenities:** safes, irons, hair dryers. *Some:* CD players. **Dining:** The Terrace at Montpelier Plantation Inn, see separate listing. **Pool(s):** outdoor. **Leisure Activities:** snorkeling, tennis court, croquet. *Fee:* massage. **Guest Services:** TV in common area, valet laundry, area transportation-beach, wireless Internet. **Business Services:** PC. **Cards:** AX, MC, VI. **Free Special Amenities: full breakfast and high-speed Internet.**

OLD MANOR ESTATE & HOTEL **Phone:** (869)469-3445 **14**

Historic Country Inn
$180-$380 All Year

Address: Mount Nevis **Location:** 12.1 mi (19.4 km) s of Newcastle Airport; 4.5 mi (7.2 km) e of Charlestown. **Facility:** Housed in several buildings reconstructed from an 18th-century sugar plantation, this country inn offers a restful ambience. 14 units. 13 one-bedroom standard units. 1 cottage. 2 stories (no elevator), exterior corridors. *Bath:* combo or shower only. **Parking:** on-site. **Terms:** office hours 8 am-6 pm, 14 day cancellation notice-fee imposed. **Amenities:** honor bars, irons, hair dryers. **Dining:** The Cooperage Restaurant, see separate listing. **Pool(s):** outdoor. **Leisure Activities:** whirlpool. **Guest Services:** TV in common area, complimentary laundry, wireless Internet. **Business Services:** meeting rooms, PC. **Cards:** AX, MC, VI.

ASK / SOME UNITS

WHERE TO DINE

THE COOPERAGE RESTAURANT **Phone:** 869/469-3445 **21**

Continental
$10-$33

The menu at this casual open-air dining room changes every three months and features something for everyone. The American and Caribbean fare includes pasta, steaks, seafood and some local dishes. Dressy casual. **Bar:** Full bar. **Reservations:** suggested. **Hours:** Open 12/1-8/30 & 10/15-11/30; 8-10 am, 11:30-2:30 & 6:30-9:30 pm. **Address:** Gingerland **Location:** 12.1 mi (19.4 km) s of Newcastle Airport; 4.5 mi (7.2 km) e of Charlestown; in Old Manor Estate & Hotel. **Parking:** on-site. **Cards:** AX, MC, VI.

(See map and index starting on p. 530)

GOLDEN ROCK DINING ROOM **Phone:** 869/469-3346 (22)

Caribbean
$12-$42

Casual dining is the mode at the restored 1815 sugar plantation. Diners can choose from outdoor terrace seating at lunch and candlelit indoor dining at dinner. Lunch features some lighter fare, such as soups, salads and sandwiches, in addition to full meals. The ever-changing, three-course prix fixe dinner menu centers on fresh local fare. Dressy casual. **Bar:** Full bar. **Reservations:** required, for dinner. **Hours:** Open 12/1-8/31 & 10/1-11/30; 8:15 am-10 & noon-2:30 pm; dinner seating 7:30 pm. **Address:** Gingerland **Location:** 5.5 mi (8.8 km) e of Newcastle Airport; 5.5 mi (8.8 km) e of Charlestown; in Golden Rock Plantation Inn. **Parking:** on-site. **Cards:** AX, MC, VI.

MARTHA'S IN THE GARDEN RESTAURANT **Phone:** 869/469-3399 (23)

Caribbean
$8-$17

Located on the grounds of the Nevis Botanical Gardens, this intimate dining spot is a jewel in the crown. Take a seat outdoors on the second story balcony and peruse the flowers and the majesty of the tropical environment. For your dining pleasure, the menu encompasses a variety of both light and heavier dishes with an abundant variety of drinks including tea selections and smoothies. Casual dress. **Bar:** Full bar. **Reservations:** accepted. **Hours:** Open 12/1-8/15 & 10/15-11/30; 11:30 am-3 pm. Closed major holidays; also Sat & Sun. **Address:** Botanical Gardens of Nevis **Location:** 4 mi (6.4 km) e of Charlestown, follow signs. **Parking:** on-site. **Cards:** AX, MC, VI.

THE TERRACE AT MONTPELIER PLANTATION INN **Phone:** 869/469-3462 (24)

AAA

International
$20-$60

Dinner begins with drinks, canapes and conversation in the Great Room. Guests then adjourn at their whim to the terrace, overlooking floodlit gardens, to enjoy a leisurely three-course, prix fixe choice menu. Caribbean influences are woven into the menu of classical cuisine and the wine list features 74 wines from seven countries. A fish barbecue is offered Friday nights accompanied by soup, an assortment of fresh salads and tasty desserts. Dressy casual. **Bar:** Full bar. **Reservations:** required. **Hours:** Open 12/1-8/16 & 10/7-11/30; 8:15 am-10 & noon-2:30 pm; dinner seating 7:30 pm-8:30 pm. **Location:** 3.5 mi (5.6 km) e of Charlestown; 1 mi (1.6 km) s, follow signs; in Montpelier Plantation Inn. **Parking:** on-site. **Cards:** AX, MC, VI.

JONES BAY (See map and index starting on p. 530)

WHERE TO DINE

GALLIPOT **Phone:** 869/469-8230 (32)

AAA

Seafood
$12-$22

Frequented by locals and the sailing crowd, the restaurant features meals that are hearty and laced with the succulent flavors of the Caribbean. The native Nevis owner/chef prepares curry chicken as well as a surf-and turf selection to include local seafood and imported fine cuts of beef. The pleasant backdrop of a postcard-perfect harbor makes for a lingering and memorable evening. Casual dress. **Bar:** Full bar. **Reservations:** suggested. **Hours:** Open 12/1-7/1 & 11/1-11/30; noon-2:30 & 6-9 pm, Sun 12:30 pm-2:30 pm. Closed: 1/1, 12/25; also Mon-Wed. **Address:** Tamarind Bay **Location:** 1.5 mi (2.4 km) w of airport. **Parking:** on-site. **Cards:** AX, DS, MC, VI.

(See map and index starting on p. 530)

MISS JUNE'S CUISINE — Phone: 869/469-5330 (33)

International
$75

Here diners enjoy a distinctive event as the Trinidadian hostess/chef welcomes guests into her home in a dinner party atmosphere. The six-course meal is partially a buffet of Asian and West Indian specialties. The price includes service, tax and all beverages. Dressy casual. **Bar:** Full bar. **Reservations:** required. **Hours:** Open 12/1-8/1 & 10/15-11/30; Wed seating 7 pm; by appointment only. Closed major holidays. **Address:** Jones Bay **Location:** 4 mi (6.4 km) nw of Charlestown. **Parking:** on-site. **Cards:** MC, VI.

NEWCASTLE (See map and index starting on p. 530)

WHERE TO STAY

THE MOUNT NEVIS HOTEL & BEACH CLUB — Book at AAA.com — **Phone:** (869)469-9373 (7)

Hotel
$250-$400 All Year

Address: Shaws Rd **Location:** 6.7 mi (10.7 km) ne of Charlestown; just n, then 1 mi (1.6 km) e of airport, follow signs. **Facility:** 28 one-bedroom standard units, some with kitchens and/or whirlpools. 2 stories (no elevator), exterior corridors. *Bath:* shower only. **Parking:** on-site. **Terms:** office hours 8 am-7 pm, 7 night minimum stay - seasonal, 14 day cancellation notice, 28 day in winter-fee imposed. **Amenities:** video library (fee), safes, irons, hair dryers. *Some:* DVD players, CD players. **Dining:** The Mount Nevis Restaurant, see separate listing. **Pool(s):** outdoor. **Leisure Activities:** exercise room. **Guest Services:** valet laundry, area transportation, wireless Internet. **Business Services:** meeting rooms, PC. **Cards:** AX, DS, MC, VI.

D VCR / SOME UNITS

NISBET PLANTATION BEACH CLUB — Book great rates at AAA.com — **Phone:** (869)469-9325 (8)

AAA SAVE

Cottage
$350-$795 All Year

Address: Nisbet Beach, St James Parish **Location:** Oceanfront. 1 mi (1.6 km) e of Newcastle Airport; 7.6 mi (12.2 km) ne of Charlestown. **Facility:** Set amid coconut palms and fringed by a long stretch of beach, this 1778 sugar plantation offers a retreat like atmosphere. Refined service prevails. 36 cottages. 1-2 stories (no elevator), exterior corridors. *Bath:* combo or shower only. **Parking:** on-site. **Terms:** office hours 6 am-10 pm, 28 day cancellation notice-fee imposed. **Amenities:** safes, honor bars, irons, hair dryers. **Dining:** The Great House Dining Room, Seabreeze, see separate listings, entertainment. **Pool(s):** outdoor. **Leisure Activities:** whirlpool, snorkeling, tennis court, croquet, library, bocci, exercise room, spa, horseshoes. **Guest Services:** TV in common area, valet laundry, wireless Internet. **Business Services:** PC. **Cards:** AX, MC, VI. **Free Special Amenities: full breakfast and early check-in/late check-out.**

WHERE TO DINE

THE GREAT HOUSE DINING ROOM — **Phone:** 869/469-9325 (28)

AAA

Continental
$60-$65

Elegant candlelight dining in a historic plantation home make this a popular favorite. Island influences punctuate offerings of Continental food. Reserve well ahead for the popular Thursday night beachfront barbecue, a lively and casual event capped by music from a band. Dressy casual. **Bar:** Full bar. **Reservations:** required. **Hours:** Open 12/1-8/24 & 10/7-11/30; 6:30 pm-8:30 pm; 7 pm-8 pm (last seating). Closed: Thurs. **Address:** St. James Parish **Location:** 1 mi (1.6 km) e of Newcastle Airport; 7.6 mi (12.1 km) ne of Charlestown; in Nisbet Plantation Beach Club. **Parking:** on-site. **Cards:** AX, MC, VI. **Historic**

THE MOUNT NEVIS RESTAURANT — **Phone:** 869/469-9373 (26)

International
$15-$60

The locals frequent the open-air restaurant, set high on a hill and offering spectacular views of the mountains, ocean and tropical countryside. Chefs pride themselves in an ever-changing Continental menu that takes regular theme nights into account. The elegant tropical oasis captures the spirit of the islands. Dressy casual. **Bar:** Full bar. **Reservations:** required. **Hours:** Open 12/1-8/1 & 10/1-11/30; 8 am-10:30 & 11:30-2 pm; last seating 6:30 pm-8:30 pm. **Address:** Shaws Rd **Location:** 6.7 mi (10.7 km) ne of Charlestown; just n, then 1 mi (1.6 km) e of airport, follow signs; in The Mount Nevis Hotel & Beach Club. **Parking:** on-site. **Cards:** AX, MC, VI.

SEABREEZE — **Phone:** 869/469-9325 (27)

Caribbean
$10-$17

This restaurant is found right on the beach, where you will be mesmerized by postcard perfect views and island cooking. Enjoy finger foods or a gourmet meal. Sit next to the beach and let the sand tickle your toes or pull up a chair under the covered bar area. Casual dress. **Bar:** Full bar. **Reservations:** accepted. **Hours:** Open 12/1-8/15 & 10/17-11/30; 10 am-6 pm. **Address:** St James Parish **Location:** 1 mi (1.6 km) e of Newcastle Airport; 7.6 mi (12.2 km) ne of Charlestown; in Nisbet Plantation Beach Club. **Parking:** on-site. **Cards:** AX, MC, VI.

OUALIE BAY (See map and index starting on p. 530)

WHERE TO STAY

HURRICANE COVE BUNGALOWS — **Phone:** 781/267-7985 (11)

Cottage
$165-$685 All Year

Address: Oualie Bay **Location:** Just above Oualie Bay, follow signs. **Facility:** 12 cottages. 1 story, exterior corridors. *Bath:* shower only. **Parking:** on-site. **Terms:** check-in 4 pm, 3-7 night minimum stay - seasonal, 90 day cancellation notice-fee imposed. **Amenities:** safes. *Some:* CD players, voice mail, irons. **Pool(s):** outdoor. **Leisure Activities:** limited beach access, snorkeling. **Cards:** MC, VI.

/ SOME UNITS

St. Kitts

BASSETERRE pop. 13,220 (See map and index starting on p. 530)

WHERE TO STAY

OCEAN TERRACE INN Book at AAA.com **Phone:** (869)465-2754 1

Hotel

$195-$460 12/1-4/14
$165-$400 4/15-11/30

Address: Wigley Ave **Location:** At west end of town, 3.7 mi (6 km) ne of Robert L Bradshaw International Airport; at Fortlands. **Facility:** 71 units. 63 one-bedroom standard units, some with efficiencies, kitchens and/or whirlpools. 8 one-bedroom suites. 2-3 stories (no elevator), exterior corridors. *Bath:* combo or shower only. **Parking:** street. **Terms:** 3 day cancellation notice-fee imposed. **Amenities:** voice mail, irons, hair dryers. *Some:* safes. **Dining:** Fisherman's Wharf, Waterfalls Restaurant, see separate listings. **Pool(s):** 3 outdoor. **Leisure Activities:** whirlpools, exercise room. *Fee:* scuba diving, snorkeling, massage. **Guest Services:** valet laundry, area transportation, wireless Internet. **Business Services:** meeting rooms, PC (fee). **Cards:** AX, MC, VI.

WHERE TO DINE

THE BALLAHOO **Phone:** 869/465-4197 4

International
$5-$29

Splashed in bright, tropical decor, the second-story, open-air dining room overlooks the town center. On the menu is a good selection of appetizers, as well as burgers, chicken, pasta, salads, fish, lobster and traditional Caribbean fare. Casual dress. **Bar:** Full bar. **Reservations:** accepted. **Hours:** 8 am-10 pm. Closed: 12/25; also Sun, Good Friday, Whit Monday, Easter Monday & St. Kitts public holidays. **Address:** The Circus **Location:** Town center; at The Circus overlooking the clock tower. **Parking:** street. **Cards:** MC, VI.

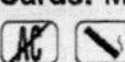

BAMBU'S **Phone:** 869/466-5280 5

American
$12-$22

In the heart of town is this rustic eatery with bamboo walls. Guests can stop by for a beer in the bar and catch up on the latest sports scores. The varied menu lists pizzas, burgers and fried fish, as well as more healthy salads, including Caesar, spinach and Greek. A refreshing sorbet or slice of apple pie or cheesecake will satisfy a sweet tooth. Service is island-friendly. Casual dress. **Bar:** Full bar. **Reservations:** accepted. **Hours:** 8 am-10 pm, Mon & Fri-11 pm; from 10 am 4/1-10/31. Closed major holidays; also Sun. **Address:** Bank St **Location:** Center of downtown; just off The Circus Clock Tower. **Parking:** street. **Cards:** MC, VI.

CIRCUS GRILL **Phone:** 869/465-0143 9

Caribbean
$10-$28

In the hub of Basseterre activity, the second-story open-air restaurant presents a varied menu with a focus on West Indies cuisine. Notable choices include roti, curried goat and the well-seasoned fresh local fish, which taste great after a delicious beginning of callaloo soup or crab back. Guests can sit at the large verandah bar to watch the world go by. Casual dress. **Bar:** Full bar. **Reservations:** accepted. **Hours:** 11 am-10 pm. Closed major holidays; also Sun. **Address:** The Circus **Location:** Center; at The Circus, overlooking the clock tower. **Parking:** street. **Cards:** AX, DS, MC, VI. **Historic**

FISHERMAN'S WHARF **Phone:** 869/465-2754 6

AAA

Seafood
$24-$34

The rustic, nautical-themed restaurant was built over the water. At least six types of fish are cooked according to specifications. The Caribbean-style buffet of fixings that accompanies each meal includes eggplant casserole, peas and rice, potatoes au gratin and such steamed vegetables as broccoli, carrots, cauliflower and chayote. Casual dress. **Bar:** Full bar. **Reservations:** accepted. **Hours:** 6 pm-10:30 pm. Closed: 12/25. **Address:** Wigley Ave **Location:** At west end; 1.8 mi (2.9 km) w of downtown; at Fortlands; just below Ocean Terrace Inn. **Parking:** on-site. **Cards:** AX, MC, VI.

SERENDIPITY RESTAURANT & LOUNGE BAR **Phone:** 869/465-9999 1

AAA

International
$10-$33

A newer restaurant on the St. Kitts gourmet dining scene, this place occupies a converted house and offers inside and terrace dining. Chef Alexander prepares savory, creatively inspired and eye-appealing dishes that may include lamb loin, duck and such favorite fish as grouper and red snapper. Casual dress. **Bar:** Full bar. **Reservations:** required. **Hours:** Open 12/1-8/20 & 9/25-11/30; noon-3 & 6-10 pm. Closed major holidays. **Address:** 3 Wigley Ave **Location:** Just w of downtown; at Fortlands. **Parking:** street. **Cards:** AX, DS, MC, VI.

STAR OF INDIA **Phone:** 869/466-1537 7

Indian
$9-$24

The family-owned-and-operated downtown restaurant presents a menu of Indian food. Begin the meal with pappadams and chutneys or one of the many flavorful naans. Entrees include tandoor chicken, fish, beef and lamb, as well as red, yellow and green curries. Casual dress. **Bar:** Full bar. **Reservations:** accepted. **Hours:** 11 am-10 pm. Closed major holidays; also Sun & for lunch on public holidays. **Address:** Victoria St **Location:** Downtown; just n of The Circus Clock Tower; corner of Victoria and Lozac sts. **Parking:** street. **Cards:** AX, MC, VI.

(See map and index starting on p. 530)

WATERFALLS RESTAURANT **Phone:** 869/465-2754 (8)

International
$20-$33

A tropical waterfall and interesting hand-painted murals depicting local scenes and wildlife greet diners on entry to the dining room. There is a choice of seating on the elegant covered open-air patio or in the sophisticated dining room with upscale artwork. The chef's extensive and innovative international menu offers traditional fine cuisine as well as options with a distinct Caribbean flair. The decadent Sunday buffet brunch has a loyal following. Casual dress. **Bar:** Full bar. **Reservations:** suggested. **Hours:** 7 am-10:30, noon-2 & 7-10 pm. Closed: for lunch Sat. **Address:** Wigley Ave **Location:** At west end of town; 3.7 mi (6 km) ne of Robert L. Bradshaw International Airport; in Ocean Terrace Inn. **Parking:** street. **Cards:** AX, MC, VI.

FRIGATE BAY (See map and index starting on p. 530)

WHERE TO STAY

ST. KITTS MARRIOTT RESORT & ROYAL BEACH CASINO *Book great rates at AAA.com* **Phone:** (869)466-1200 (6)

Resort Hotel
$164-$318 All Year

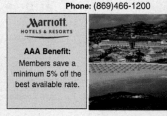

Address: 858 Frigate Bay Rd **Location:** Oceanfront. 2.5 mi (4 km) se of Robert L Bradshaw International Airport; at Frigate Bay. **Facility:** Said to be the largest resort in St. Kitts, this property has earned a reputation for upscale comfort and refined, personalized service. Meets AAA guest room security requirements. Smoke free premises. 513 units. 443 one-bedroom standard units. 60 one- and 10 two-bedroom suites with whirlpools. 3-5 stories, interior/exterior corridors. **Parking:** on-site and valet. **Terms:** check-in 4 pm, 3 day cancellation notice-fee imposed. **Amenities:** CD players, high-speed Internet, dual phone lines, voice mail, safes, irons, hair dryers. **Dining:** 5 restaurants, also, La Cucina, see separate listing, nightclub, entertainment. **Pool(s):** 3 outdoor. **Leisure Activities:** saunas, whirlpools, steamrooms, driving range, 4 lighted tennis courts, recreation programs, kids club, spa, volleyball, game room. *Fee:* paddleboats, scuba diving, snorkeling, kayaks, golf-18 holes. **Guest Services:** valet laundry, wireless Internet. **Business Services:** conference facilities, business center. **Cards:** AX, CB, DC, DS, MC, VI. ***(See color ad p 537 & on insert)***

AAA Benefit:
Members save a minimum 5% off the best available rate.

SUGAR BAY CLUB *Book great rates at AAA.com* **Phone:** (869)465-8037 (3)

Hotel
$185-$300 12/1-3/31
$130-$245 4/1-11/30

Address: Frigate Bay **Location:** Oceanfront. 2.4 mi (5.1 km) se of Robert L Bradshaw International Airport. **Facility:** 94 units. 82 one-bedroom standard units, some with efficiencies. 12 one-bedroom suites, some with efficiencies. 1-2 stories (no elevator), exterior corridors. **Parking:** on-site. **Terms:** 14 day cancellation notice-fee imposed. **Amenities:** *Some:* safes. **Pool(s):** 2 outdoor. **Leisure Activities:** exercise room. *Fee:* lighted tennis court. **Guest Services:** valet laundry, wireless Internet. **Business Services:** PC. **Cards:** AX, MC, VI.

ASK / SOME UNITS

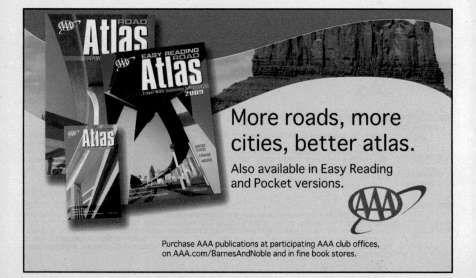

▼ See AAA listing p 536 ▼

(See map and index starting on p. 530)

WHERE TO DINE

LA CUCINA **Phone:** 869/466-1200 (11)

Italian
$18-$32

Relax in the casually elegant dining room while enjoying traditional Italian cuisine. Specialties include osso buco and chicken parmesan, as well as pasta and risotto dishes. An extensive wine list is featured, as is an antipasta buffet. Casual dress. **Bar:** Full bar. **Hours:** 5:30 pm-10 pm. **Address:** 858 Frigate Bay Rd **Location:** 2.5 mi (4 km) se of Robert L. Bradshaw International Airport; in St. Kitts Marriott Resort & Royal Beach Casino. **Parking:** on-site and valet. **Cards:** AX, DC, DS, MC, VI.

MARSHALL'S *Menu on AAA.com* **Phone:** 869/466-8245 (10)

International
$24-$35

The highly reputable restaurant goes to great lengths to provide refined and gracious service. The constant trade winds cool the al fresco dining area. Some highlights of the menu include preparations of Angus beef, lobster, Chilean sea bass, seafood coquilles and duck. The chef uses spices and culinary techniques that span the globe. Dressy casual. **Bar:** Full bar. **Reservations:** required, till 9 pm. **Hours:** 6 pm-10 pm. Closed major holidays; also Sun. **Address:** Frigate Bay **Location:** On hill above Frigate Bay; at Horizons Villa Resort; Fort Tyson Rise. **Parking:** on-site. **Cards:** AX, DS, MC, VI.

MONKEY BAR & RESTAURANT **Phone:** 869/465-8050 (14)

Seafood
$12-$31

Locals frequent the small stool bar, but the beachside al fresco restaurant also offers seating at candlelit tables. The limited menu focuses on grilled meat and fish but also lists appetizers, salads and desserts. Smartly attired servers make an effort to exhibit consistent finesse. Casual dress. **Bar:** Full bar. **Reservations:** suggested. **Hours:** 11 am-11 pm. **Address:** Frigate Bay **Location:** 3 mi (4.8 km) se of Robert L. Bradshaw International Airport. **Parking:** on-site. **Cards:** MC, VI.

PJ'S BAR & RESTAURANT **Phone:** 869/465-8373 (12)

Italian
$13-$24

A favorite local and tourist hangout for the past 17 years, the restaurant is well known for pizza and calzones. Sharing menu space are some familiar Italian entrees, such as eggplant parmigiana, lasagna, spaghetti and meatballs and fettuccine Alfredo. Casual dress. **Bar:** Full bar. **Hours:** Open 12/1-8/1 & 9/1-11/30; 5:30 pm-10 pm. Closed: 1/1, 12/25; also Mon. **Address:** Frigate Bay **Location:** 2.3 mi (3.2 km) se of downtown. **Parking:** on-site. **Cards:** AX, MC, VI.

ST. LUCIA

Airport Accommodations

Map Page	OA	GEORGE F.L. CHARLES AIRPORT	Diamond Rated	High Season	Page
15 / p. 541		Almond Morgan Bay, 2 mi (3.2 km) n of airport	◆◆◆	$413-$875	542
19 / p. 541		Cara Suites Hotel & Conference Centre, 1.5 mi (2.4 km) n of airport	◆◆	$90-$120	542
16 / p. 541		Villa Beach Cottages, 2.4 mi (3.8 km) n of airport	◆◆	$190-$240	542

Airport Accommodations

Map Page	OA	HEWANORRA INTERNATIONAL AIRPORT	Diamond Rated	High Season	Page
36 / p. 541	AAA	**Coconut Bay Beach Resort & Spa, 0.3 mi (0.5 km) of airport**	◆◆◆	$310-$610 SAVE	549

St. Lucia

This index helps you "spot" where approved lodgings and restaurants are located on the corresponding detailed maps. Lodging daily rate range is for comparison only and show the property's high season. Restaurant rate range is a combination of lunch and/or dinner. Turn to the listing page for more detailed rate information and consult display ads for special promotions.

RODNEY BAY

Map Page	OA	Lodgings	Diamond Rated	High Season	Page
1 / p. 541		Harmony Suites	◆◆	$120-$175	545
3 / p. 541		Bay Gardens Hotel	◆◆	$120-$280	544
4 / p. 541		St. Lucian by Rex Resorts	◆◆	$189-$420	545
5 / p. 541		Ginger Lily Hotel	◆◆	$135-$220	545
6 / p. 541		Bay Gardens Beach Resort	◆◆◆	$157-$430	544
7 / p. 541		Coco Kreole	◆◆	$100-$125	544
8 / p. 541	AAA	**The Village Inn & Spa** - see color ad p 544	◆◆	$135-$350 SAVE	545
9 / p. 541		Coco Palm	◆◆◆	Rates not provided	545

Map Page	OA	Restaurants	Diamond Rated	Cuisine	Meal Range	Page
4 / p. 541		Key Largo	◆	Pizza	$9-$15	546
5 / p. 541		Memories of Hong Kong	◆◆	Chinese	$15-$24	546
6 / p. 541		Charthouse Restaurant & Bar	◆◆	Steak & Seafood	$20-$44	546
8 / p. 541		Razmataz Tandoori Restaurant & Bar	◆◆	Indian	$14-$23	546
9 / p. 541	AAA	**Buzz Seafood & Grill**	◆◆	International	$17-$35	545
10 / p. 541		Ku De Ta	◆◆◆	Thai	$14-$26	546
11 / p. 541		Cafe Claude	◆◆	International	$9-$32	545
15 / p. 541		The Edge	◆◆◆	International	$12-$33	546
16 / p. 541		Red Snapper Seafood Restaurant & Bar	◆◆	Seafood	$15-$28	546
17 / p. 541		La Trattoria del Mare	◆◆	Italian	$16-$32	546

GROS ISLET

Map Page	OA	Lodgings	Diamond Rated	High Season	Page
12 / p. 541		Habitat Terrace	◆◆	$90-$230	543

GROS ISLET (cont'd)

Map Page	OA	Lodgings (cont'd)	Diamond Rated	High Season	Page
13 / p. 541	AAA	**Windjammer Landing Villa Beach Resort & Spa** - see color ad p 542	◆◆◆	$175-$1800 SAVE	543

Map Page	OA	Restaurant	Diamond Rated	Cuisine	Meal Range	Page
2 / p. 541	AAA	**Tao Restaurant**	◆◆◆	Asian	$20-$32	543

CASTRIES

Map Page	OA	Lodgings	Diamond Rated	High Season	Page
15 / p. 541		Almond Morgan Bay	◆◆◆	$413-$875	542
16 / p. 541		Villa Beach Cottages	◆◆	$190-$240	542
17 / p. 541		East Winds Inn	◆◆◆	$570-$885	542
19 / p. 541		Cara Suites Hotel & Conference Centre	◆◆	$90-$120	542

Map Page	OA	Restaurants	Diamond Rated	Cuisine	Meal Range	Page
22 / p. 541		Coal Pot Restaurant	◆◆	Creole	$10-$30	543
23 / p. 541		Jacques Waterfront Dining	◆◆	French	$17-$36	543

MARIGOT BAY

Map Page	OA	Lodgings	Diamond Rated	High Season	Page
24 / p. 541	AAA	**Discovery at Marigot Bay**	◆◆◆◆	$350-$2950 SAVE	543
25 / p. 541		The Inn On The Bay	◆◆	$150-$175	544

Map Page	OA	Restaurant	Diamond Rated	Cuisine	Meal Range	Page
25 / p. 541		Chateau Mygo	◆◆	Creole	$12-$28	544

SOUFRIERE

Map Page	OA	Lodgings	Diamond Rated	High Season	Page
28 / p. 541	AAA	**Ladera Resort** - see color ad p 548	◆◆◆◆	$380-$1330 SAVE	549
29 / p. 541	AAA	**Anse Chastanet Resort** - see color ad p 547	◆◆◆◆	$280-$965 SAVE	547
31 / p. 541		Stonefield Estate Villa Resort	◆◆◆	$200-$880	549
34 / p. 541		The Jalousie Plantation	◆◆◆	$225-$900	549

VIEUX FORT

Map Page	OA	Lodging	Diamond Rated	High Season	Page
36 / p. 541	AAA	**Coconut Bay Beach Resort & Spa**	◆◆◆	$310-$610 SAVE	549

ANSE LA RAYE

Map Page	OA	Lodging	Diamond Rated	High Season	Page
37 / p. 541		Ti Kaye Village	◆◆◆	$225-$425	542

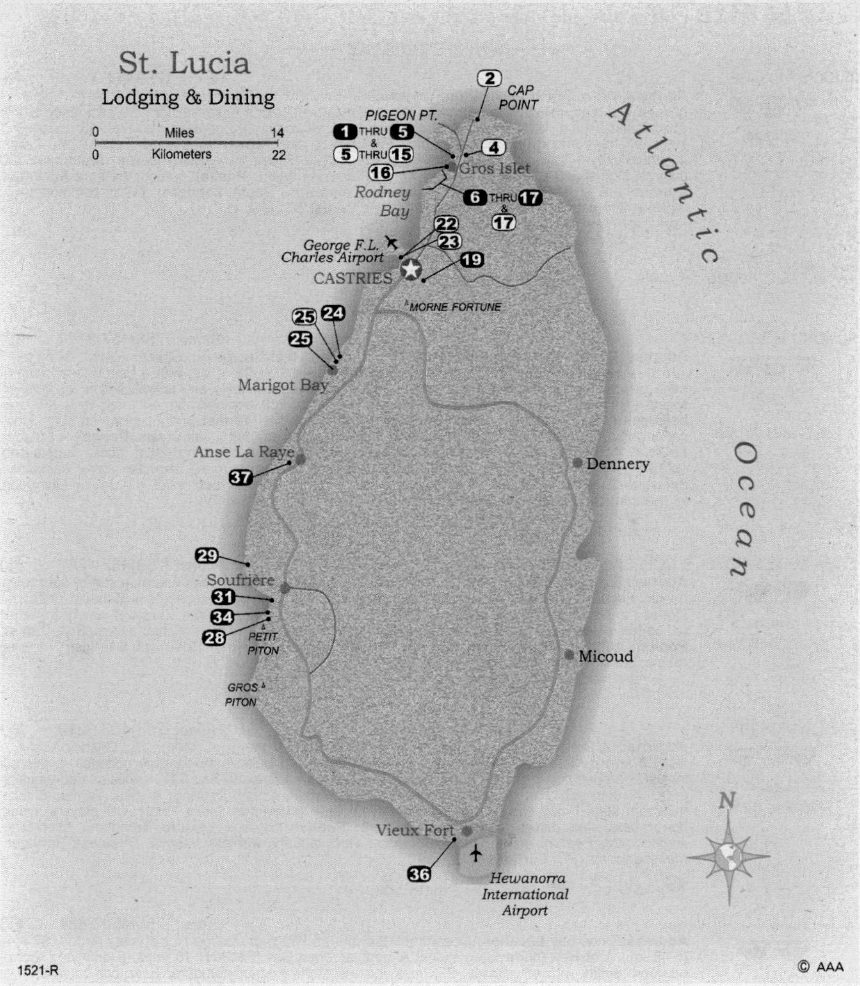

St. Lucia
Lodging & Dining

0 Miles 14
0 Kilometers 22

CAP POINT
PIGEON PT.
2
1 THRU 5 & 5 THRU 15
4
16
Gros Islet
Rodney Bay
6 THRU 17 & 17
22
23
George F.L. Charles Airport
19
CASTRIES
MORNE FORTUNE
25 24
25
Marigot Bay
Anse La Raye
37
29
Soufrière
31
34
28
PETIT PITON
GROS PITON
Dennery
Micoud
Vieux Fort
36
Hewanorra International Airport
Atlantic Ocean
N

1521-R

© AAA

ANSE LA RAYE (See map and index starting on p. 541)

WHERE TO STAY

TI KAYE VILLAGE **Phone:** (758)456-8101 37

Cottage
$225-$425 All Year

Address: Anse Conchon **Location:** Oceanfront. 2 mi (3.2 km) s of town, then 1.9 mi (3 km) w on unimproved road, follow signs. **Facility:** On a hillside overlooking Anse Cochon, the mini-resort is in a spectacular setting; West Indies-style cottages have verandas and open-air showers. 33 cottages. 1 story, exterior corridors. *Bath:* shower only. **Parking:** on-site. **Terms:** office hours 7 am-10 pm, 4 night minimum stay - seasonal, age restrictions may apply, 7 day cancellation notice. **Amenities:** CD players, high-speed Internet, voice mail, safes, irons, hair dryers. **Pool(s):** outdoor. **Leisure Activities:** exercise room. *Fee:* scuba diving, snorkeling, massage. **Guest Services:** TV in common area, wireless Internet. **Business Services:** PC (fee). **Cards:** DS, MC, VI.

CASTRIES pop. 64,344 (See map and index starting on p. 541)

WHERE TO STAY

ALMOND MORGAN BAY **Phone:** (758)457-3700 15

Resort Hotel
$413-$875 All Year

Address: Choc Bay **Location:** Oceanfront. 2 mi (3.2 km) n of George F.L. Charles Airport; 37 mi (59.2 km) n of Hewanorra International Airport. **Facility:** Nestled on 22 acres, with a palm-fringed, sugar-sand beach, this all-inclusive resort offers contemporary guest units and is well suited for families. Meets AAA guest room security requirements. 300 units. 230 one-bedroom standard units. 70 one-bedroom suites. 3 stories, exterior corridors. **Parking:** on-site. **Terms:** 3 night minimum stay, 3 day cancellation notice-fee imposed. **Amenities:** voice mail, safes, irons, hair dryers. **Pool(s):** 4 outdoor. **Leisure Activities:** beach access, paddleboats, sailboats, windsurfing, boat dock, waterskiing, snorkeling, 4 tennis courts (2 lighted), recreation programs, playground, exercise room, basketball, horseshoes, game room. *Fee:* scuba diving, massage. **Guest Services:** valet laundry, beauty salon, wireless Internet. **Business Services:** PC (fee). **Cards:** AX, DS, MC, VI.

/ SOME UNITS

CARA SUITES HOTEL & CONFERENCE CENTRE **Phone:** (758)452-4767 19

Hotel
$90-$120 All Year

Address: La Pansee **Location:** 1.5 mi (2.4 km) se of George F.L. Charles Airport; just e of downtown; center. **Facility:** Meets AAA guest room security requirements. 54 one-bedroom standard units. 1-4 stories (no elevator), exterior corridors. *Bath:* shower only. **Parking:** on-site. **Terms:** 7 day cancellation notice-fee imposed. **Amenities:** high-speed Internet, dual phone lines, irons, hair dryers. *Some:* safes. **Pool(s):** outdoor. **Guest Services:** valet laundry, wireless Internet. **Business Services:** meeting rooms, business center. **Cards:** AX, DC, MC, VI.

EAST WINDS INN **Phone:** (758)452-8212 17

Cottage
$570-$885 All Year

Address: La Brelotte Bay **Location:** Oceanfront. 2.3 mi (3.7 km) n of George F.L. Charles Airport, 1 mi (1.6 km) w via signs. **Facility:** Find tastefully furnished units in single-story cottages at this all-inclusive property on eight acres of tropical gardens on La Brelotte Bay Beach. Designated smoking area. 30 cottages. 1 story, exterior corridors. *Bath:* shower only. **Parking:** on-site. **Terms:** 6 night minimum stay, 7 day cancellation notice-fee imposed. **Amenities:** video library, CD players, safes, honor bars, hair dryers. *Some:* DVD players. **Pool(s):** outdoor. **Leisure Activities:** snorkeling, shuffleboard. *Fee:* massage. **Guest Services:** valet laundry, wireless Internet. **Business Services:** meeting rooms, PC. **Cards:** AX, MC, VI.

/ SOME UNITS

VILLA BEACH COTTAGES **Phone:** (758)450-2884 16

Motel
$190-$240 All Year

Address: Choc Bay **Location:** Oceanfront. 2.4 mi (3.8 km) n of George F.L. Charles Airport; 37.4 mi (59.8 km) n of Hewanorra International Airport; at Choc Bay. **Facility:** 10 units. 8 one- and 2 two-bedroom suites with efficiencies. 2 stories (no elevator), exterior corridors. *Bath:* combo or shower only. **Parking:** on-site. **Terms:** office hours 7 am-10 pm, 3 night minimum stay, 21 day cancellation notice-fee imposed. **Amenities:** safes, irons, hair dryers. **Leisure Activities:** snorkeling. **Guest Services:** valet laundry, wireless Internet. **Business Services:** PC. **Cards:** AX, DS, MC, VI.

▼ See AAA listing p 543 ▼

(See map and index starting on p. 541)

WHERE TO DINE

COAL POT RESTAURANT **Phone:** 758/452-5566 (22)

Creole

$10-$30

A longstanding favorite on Castries Bay, the idyllic open-air waterfront setting in rustic surroundings sets a calm mood for relaxation. The talented chef combines West Indies cuisine with a dash of French influence. Included in the large fish selection are such offerings as tuna, salmon, red snapper, kingfish and bar. Stuffed crab back is a tasty treat to whet the appetite. Diners can expect casual, easygoing service. Dressy casual. **Bar:** Full bar. **Reservations:** suggested. **Hours:** Open 12/1-9/1 & 10/2-11/30; noon-2:30 & 6:30-9 pm, Sat from 6:30 pm. Closed major holidays; also Sun. **Address:** Vigie Marina **Location:** At Vigie Cove; across from airport. **Parking:** on-site. **Cards:** AX, MC, VI.

JACQUES WATERFRONT DINING **Phone:** 758/458-1900 (23)

French

$17-$36

Chef Jacques creates a fusion of Caribbean and French cuisine at the waterfront restaurant. Appetizers include mussels cooked in white wine and garlic and baked herb-crusted crab back. Chilled tomato and green peppercorn soup is refreshing. Deftly prepared entrees range from lamb chops to pan-seared scallops to duck breast in honey, lime and ginger sauce. Desserts—such as lime meringue pie, baked banana pie and coconut creme brulee—are too tempting to pass up. Dressy casual. **Bar:** Full bar. **Reservations:** required. **Hours:** Open 12/1-7/29 & 9/3-11/30; 11:30 am-2:30 & 7-8:30 pm. Closed: 1/1, 12/25; also Sun & public holidays. **Address:** Vigie Cove **Location:** Access road opposite airport; just w of John Compton Hwy, follow sign. **Parking:** on-site. **Cards:** AX, DS, MC, VI.

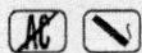

GROS ISLET pop. 20,872 (See map and index starting on p. 541)

WHERE TO STAY

HABITAT TERRACE *Book at AAA.com* **Phone:** (758)452-0822 (12)

Bed & Breakfast

$90-$230 All Year

Address: Old Military Rd & Habitat Dr **Location:** Just n of Rodney Bay, just e on Old Military Rd. **Facility:** Smoke free premises. 11 units. 9 one-bedroom standard units. 2 two-bedroom suites with kitchens. 2 stories (no elevator), interior/exterior corridors. *Bath:* shower only. **Parking:** on-site. **Terms:** age restrictions may apply. **Amenities:** voice mail, safes, hair dryers. *Some:* irons. **Pool(s):** outdoor. **Guest Services:** coin laundry, wireless Internet. **Cards:** AX, DS, MC, VI.

/ SOME UNITS

WINDJAMMER LANDING VILLA BEACH RESORT & SPA *Book great rates at AAA.com* **Phone:** (758)456-9000 (13)

AAA SAVE

Resort Hotel

$175-$1800 All Year

Address: Labrelotte Bay **Location:** Oceanfront. 2.5 mi (4 km) n of George F.L. Charles Airport, 1 mi (1.6 km) w via signs; 38 mi (60.8 km) n of Hewanorra International Airport. Located in a secluded area. **Facility:** Casually sophisticated, this village resort boasts 55 acres and a 1,000-foot stretch of beach; varied rooms, many with private plunge pool. 198 units. 99 one-bedroom standard units. 28 one- and 6 two-bedroom suites with kitchens. 65 houses. 2 stories (no elevator), exterior corridors. *Bath:* combo or shower only. **Parking:** on-site. **Terms:** 3 night minimum stay, 14 day cancellation notice-fee imposed. **Amenities:** DVD players, voice mail, safes, irons, hair dryers. *Fee:* video library, high-speed Internet. **Dining:** 5 restaurants, entertainment. **Pool(s):** 4 outdoor. **Leisure Activities:** whirlpool, steamroom, paddleboats, sailboats, windsurfing, boat dock, 2 lighted tennis courts, recreation programs, Kids club, playground, exercise room, spa, basketball, volleyball, game room. *Fee:* waterskiing, scuba diving, snorkeling. **Guest Services:** valet laundry, wireless Internet. **Business Services:** meeting rooms, PC (fee). **Cards:** AX, MC, VI. **Free Special Amenities: early check-in/late check-out.** *(See color ad p 542)*

FEE / SOME UNITS

WHERE TO DINE

TAO RESTAURANT **Phone:** 758/457-7800 (2)

Asian

$20-$32

The award-winning restaurant occupies an open-air verandah in a health spa. Attentive servers bring out exquisite cuisine that blends the culinary traditions and ingredients of East and West. For starters, gazpacho soup refreshes and the distinctive foie gras bursts with flavor. Entrees run the gamut from char-sui salmon and banga mary (a local fish) to lamb, twice-cooked duck and tandoori chicken. **Bar:** Full bar. **Reservations:** required. **Hours:** 7 pm-11 pm. **Address:** Cariblue Beach **Location:** 9.5 mi (15.2 km) n of Castries; Cap Estates. **Parking:** on-site. **Cards:** MC, VI.

MARIGOT BAY (See map and index starting on p. 541)

WHERE TO STAY

DISCOVERY AT MARIGOT BAY *Book great rates at AAA.com* **Phone:** (758)458-5300 (24)

AAA SAVE

Hotel

$350-$2950 All Year

Address: Marigot Bay **Location:** Oceanfront. At Marigot Bay. **Facility:** The outstandingly appointed units are spacious with all the expected comforts and amenities. Well regarded fine dining restaurant and a complete spa area round out the resort. Meets AAA guest room security requirements. Designated smoking area. 124 units. 67 one-bedroom standard units, some with whirlpools. 57 one-bedroom suites with kitchens, some with whirlpools. 2-4 stories (no elevator), exterior corridors. *Bath:* combo or shower only. **Parking:** on-site. **Terms:** check-in 4 pm, 14 day cancellation notice-fee imposed. **Amenities:** video library, DVD players, CD players, high-speed Internet, voice mail, safes, honor bars, irons, hair dryers. **Dining:** 2 restaurants. **Pool(s):** 2 outdoor. **Leisure Activities:** paddleboats, snorkeling, kayaks, exercise room, spa. **Guest Services:** valet laundry, wireless Internet. **Business Services:** meeting rooms, PC. **Cards:** AX, DS, MC, VI.

(See map and index starting on p. 541)

THE INN ON THE BAY *Book at AAA.com* **Phone:** (758)451-4260 25

Bed & Breakfast
$150-$175 12/1-5/31
$125 6/1-11/30

Address: Seaview Ave **Location:** on Marigot Bay. **Facility:** 5 one-bedroom standard units. 2 stories (no elevator), exterior corridors. *Bath:* combo or shower only. **Parking:** on-site. **Terms:** office hours 8 am-11 pm, check-in 4 pm, age restrictions may apply, 45 day cancellation notice-fee imposed. **Amenities:** hair dryers. **Pool(s):** outdoor. **Leisure Activities:** snorkeling. **Guest Services:** area transportation, wireless Internet. **Business Services:** PC (fee). **Cards:** MC, VI.

WHERE TO DINE

CHATEAU MYGO **Phone:** 758/451-4772 25

Creole
$12-$28

Patrons look out over Marigot Bay from the eatery's open-air dining deck. The varied menu combines West Indies cuisine with Creole family recipes. In addition to pizza and barbecue pork chops, it lists curried lamb, fish with mango-raisin sauce, roast duck with plum sauce and local lobster. Casual dress. **Bar:** Full bar. **Reservations:** accepted. **Hours:** noon-10 pm. **Address:** Main Rd Marigot Bay **Location:** Waterfront Marigot Bay. **Parking:** on-site. **Cards:** MC, VI.

RODNEY BAY (See map and index starting on p. 541)

WHERE TO STAY

BAY GARDENS BEACH RESORT **Phone:** (758)457-8500 6

Hotel
$157-$430 All Year

Address: Reduit Beach **Location:** Oceanfront. 6.3 mi (10.1 km) n of George F.L. Charles Airport; 41.8 mi (66.9 km) n of Hewanorra International Airport. **Facility:** Meets AAA guest room security requirements. 72 units. 36 one-bedroom standard units. 36 one-bedroom suites with kitchens. 3 stories (no elevator), exterior corridors. *Bath:* combo or shower only. **Parking:** on-site. **Terms:** 14 day cancellation notice. **Amenities:** DVD players, safes, irons, hair dryers. *Some:* high-speed Internet, dual phone lines. **Pool(s):** outdoor. **Leisure Activities:** *Fee:* boats, windsurfing, scuba diving, snorkeling. **Guest Services:** coin laundry, wireless Internet. **Business Services:** meeting rooms, business center. **Cards:** AX, DS, MC, VI.

/ SOME UNITS

BAY GARDENS HOTEL *Book at AAA.com* **Phone:** (758)452-8060 3

Hotel
$120-$280 All Year

Address: Rodney Bay Village **Location:** 5.5 mi (8.8 km) n of George F.L. Charles Airport; 41 mi (65.6 km) n of Hewanorra International Airport. **Facility:** 86 units. 78 one-bedroom standard units, some with efficiencies and/or whirlpools. 8 two-bedroom suites with efficiencies. 2 stories (no elevator), exterior corridors. *Bath:* combo or shower only. **Parking:** on-site. **Terms:** 3 day cancellation notice-fee imposed. **Amenities:** voice mail, safes (fee). *Some:* DVD players, CD players, irons, hair dryers. **Pool(s):** 2 outdoor. **Guest Services:** coin laundry, wireless Internet. **Business Services:** meeting rooms, PC. **Cards:** AX, DS, MC, VI.

/ SOME UNITS

COCO KREOLE **Phone:** 758/456-2800 7

Motel
$100-$125 All Year

Address: Rodney Bay Village **Location:** 5 mi (8 km) n of George F.L. Charles Airport. **Facility:** 20 one-bedroom standard units. 2 stories (no elevator), interior corridors. *Bath:* combo or shower only. **Parking:** on-site. **Terms:** office hours 6 am-11 pm, 21 day cancellation notice-fee imposed. **Amenities:** video library (fee), CD players, voice mail, safes, irons, hair dryers. **Pool(s):** outdoor. **Leisure Activities:** *Fee:* massage. **Guest Services:** valet laundry, wireless Internet. **Business Services:** PC. **Cards:** AX, MC, VI.

VCR / SOME UNITS

▼ *See AAA listing p 545* ▼

(See map and index starting on p. 541)

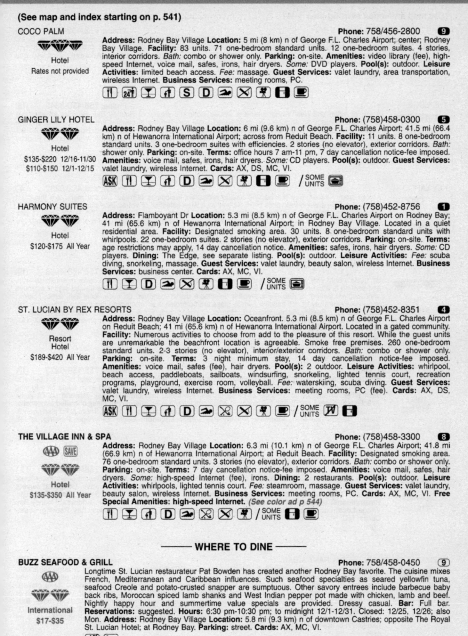

COCO PALM — Phone: 758/456-2800 — 9

Hotel

Rates not provided

Address: Rodney Bay Village **Location:** 5 mi (8 km) n of George F.L. Charles Airport; center; Rodney Bay Village. **Facility:** 83 units. 71 one-bedroom standard units. 12 one-bedroom suites. 4 stories, interior corridors. *Bath:* combo or shower only. **Parking:** on-site. **Amenities:** video library (fee), high-speed Internet, voice mail, safes, irons, hair dryers. *Some:* DVD players. **Pool(s):** outdoor. **Leisure Activities:** limited beach access. *Fee:* massage. **Guest Services:** valet laundry, area transportation, wireless Internet. **Business Services:** meeting rooms, PC.

GINGER LILY HOTEL — Phone: (758)458-0300 — 5

Hotel

$135-$220 12/16-11/30
$110-$150 12/1-12/15

Address: Rodney Bay Village **Location:** 6 mi (9.6 km) n of George F.L. Charles Airport; 41.5 mi (66.4 km) n of Hewanorra International Airport; across from Reduit Beach. **Facility:** 11 units. 8 one-bedroom standard units. 3 one-bedroom suites with efficiencies. 2 stories (no elevator), exterior corridors. *Bath:* shower only. **Parking:** on-site. **Terms:** office hours 7 am-11 pm, 7 day cancellation notice-fee imposed. **Amenities:** voice mail, safes, irons, hair dryers. *Some:* CD players. **Pool(s):** outdoor. **Guest Services:** valet laundry, wireless Internet. **Cards:** AX, DS, MC, VI.

ASK / SOME UNITS

HARMONY SUITES — Phone: (758)452-8756 — 1

Hotel

$120-$175 All Year

Address: Flamboyant Dr **Location:** 5.3 mi (8.5 km) n of George F.L. Charles Airport on Rodney Bay; 41 mi (65.6 km) n of Hewanorra International Airport; in Rodney Bay Village. Located in a quiet residential area. **Facility:** Designated smoking area. 30 units. 8 one-bedroom standard units with whirlpools. 22 one-bedroom suites. 2 stories (no elevator), exterior corridors. **Parking:** on-site. **Terms:** age restrictions may apply, 14 day cancellation notice. **Amenities:** safes, irons, hair dryers. *Some:* CD players. **Dining:** The Edge, see separate listing. **Pool(s):** outdoor. **Leisure Activities:** *Fee:* scuba diving, snorkeling, massage. **Guest Services:** valet laundry, beauty salon, wireless Internet. **Business Services:** business center. **Cards:** AX, MC, VI.

/ SOME UNITS

ST. LUCIAN BY REX RESORTS — Phone: (758)452-8351 — 4

Resort Hotel

$189-$420 All Year

Address: Rodney Bay Village **Location:** Oceanfront. 5.3 mi (8.5 km) n of George F.L. Charles Airport on Reduit Beach; 41 mi (65.6 km) n of Hewanorra International Airport. Located in a gated community. **Facility:** Numerous activities to choose from add to the pleasure of this resort. While the guest units are unremarkable the beachfront location is agreeable. Smoke free premises. 260 one-bedroom standard units. 2-3 stories (no elevator), interior/exterior corridors. *Bath:* combo or shower only. **Parking:** on-site. **Terms:** 3 night minimum stay, 14 day cancellation notice-fee imposed. **Amenities:** voice mail, safes (fee), hair dryers. **Pool(s):** 2 outdoor. **Leisure Activities:** whirlpool, beach access, paddleboats, sailboats, windsurfing, snorkeling, lighted tennis court, recreation programs, playground, exercise room, volleyball. *Fee:* waterskiing, scuba diving. **Guest Services:** valet laundry, wireless Internet. **Business Services:** meeting rooms, PC (fee). **Cards:** AX, DS, MC, VI.

ASK / SOME UNITS

THE VILLAGE INN & SPA — Phone: (758)458-3300 — 8

Hotel

$135-$350 All Year

Address: Rodney Bay Village **Location:** 6.3 mi (10.1 km) n of George F.L. Charles Airport; 41.8 mi (66.9 km) n of Hewanorra International Airport; at Reduit Beach. **Facility:** Designated smoking area. 76 one-bedroom standard units. 3 stories (no elevator), exterior corridors. *Bath:* combo or shower only. **Parking:** on-site. **Terms:** 7 day cancellation notice-fee imposed. **Amenities:** voice mail, safes, hair dryers. *Some:* high-speed Internet (fee), irons. **Dining:** 2 restaurants. **Pool(s):** outdoor. **Leisure Activities:** whirlpools, lighted tennis court. *Fee:* steamroom, massage. **Guest Services:** valet laundry, beauty salon, wireless Internet. **Business Services:** meeting rooms, PC. **Cards:** AX, MC, VI. **Free Special Amenities: high-speed Internet.** *(See color ad p 544)*

/ SOME UNITS

WHERE TO DINE

BUZZ SEAFOOD & GRILL — Phone: 758/458-0450 — 9

International

$17-$35

Longtime St. Lucian restaurateur Pat Bowden has created another Rodney Bay favorite. The cuisine mixes French, Mediterranean and Caribbean influences. Such seafood specialties as seared yellowfin tuna, seafood Creole and potato-crusted snapper are sumptuous. Other savory entrees include barbecue baby back ribs, Moroccan spiced lamb shanks and West Indian pepper pot made with chicken, lamb and beef. Nightly happy hour and summertime value specials are provided. Dressy casual. **Bar:** Full bar. **Reservations:** suggested. **Hours:** 6:30 pm-10:30 pm; to midnight 12/1-12/31. Closed: 12/25, 12/26; also Mon. **Address:** Rodney Bay Village **Location:** 5.8 mi (9.3 km) n of downtown Castries; opposite The Royal St. Lucian Hotel; at Rodney Bay. **Parking:** street. **Cards:** AX, MC, VI.

CAFE CLAUDE — Phone: 758/458-0847 — 11

International

$9-$32

A replicated Creole shack houses the distinctively furnished restaurant. Offerings include a large variety of appetizers and soups, as well as an extensive drink menu and at least eight by-the-glass wines. Panini sandwiches, barbecue ribs, steak au poivre and lasagna are just a sampling of the many available choices. Casual dress. **Bar:** Full bar. **Reservations:** accepted. **Hours:** Open 12/1-9/1 & 10/1-11/30; 7 am-11 pm. Closed: 1/1, 12/25; also Good Friday. **Address:** Rodney Bay Village **Location:** 5 mi (8 km) n of Castries; near entrance to Rodney Bay area. **Parking:** on-site. **Cards:** DS, MC, VI.

(See map and index starting on p. 541)

CHARTHOUSE RESTAURANT & BAR **Phone:** 758/452-8115 (6)

Steak & Seafood
$20-$44

On Rodney Bay, the restaurant has deck seating that overlooks the waterfront. Specialties include steak, ribs and seafood. The humongous lobster will satisfy any appetite. Dressy casual. **Bar:** Full bar. **Reservations:** required. **Hours:** 6 pm-10:30 pm. Closed: 1/1, 12/25. **Address:** Rodney Bay **Location:** Center; Rodney Bay Village. **Parking:** on-site. **Cards:** AX, MC, VI.

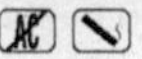

THE EDGE **Phone:** 758/450-3343 (15)

International
$12-$33

A mix of Asian and New World cuisine is served along the shores of Rodney Bay. Besides an attractive dining area there is an enclosed, air conditioned sushi bar. The trio of ceviche are a great starter and the tuna is cooked to perfection. Dressy casual. **Bar:** Full bar. **Reservations:** suggested. **Hours:** Open 12/1-9/1 & 10/1-11/30; 7 am-11, noon-3 & 6:30-10:30 pm. **Address:** Flamboyant Dr **Location:** Waterfront on Rodney Bay; in Harmony Suites. **Parking:** on-site. **Cards:** AX, DS, MC, VI.

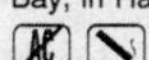

KEY LARGO **Phone:** 758/452-0282 (4)

Pizza
$9-$15

Across from Rodney Bay Marina, the casual restaurant welcomes families. On the menu are thin-crust pizzas baked in a wood-fired brick oven, as well as a wide selection of entree-size salads and pasta dishes. Casual dress. **Bar:** Full bar. **Reservations:** accepted. **Hours:** Open 12/1-6/18 & 7/5-11/30; noon-11 pm. Closed: 12/25; also Tues & Good Friday. **Address:** Gros Islet Hwy **Location:** Just n of town. **Parking:** on-site. **Cards:** AX, MC, VI.

KU DE TA **Phone:** 758/458-4968 (10)

Thai
$14-$26

St. Lucia's only Thai restaurant affords a fine-dining experience. The professional decor is artfully tasteful, and seating is offered in an air-conditioned section or around the herb garden. The trained staff is attentive and accommodating. Skilled chefs prepare delectable dishes centered on duck, local fish, lamb, chicken and pork in an array of rich sauces. Lemon grass creme brulee is an interesting indulgence. Dressy casual. **Bar:** Full bar. **Reservations:** required. **Hours:** 6 pm-10 pm, Fri & Sat-11 pm. **Address:** Reduit Dr **Location:** 5 mi (8 km) n of Castries; near entrance to Rodney Bay area. **Parking:** on-site. **Cards:** AX, DC, MC, VI.

LA TRATTORIA DEL MARE **Phone:** 758/458-0333 (17)

Italian
$16-$32

Beside a nightclub in the heart of Rodney, the Italian eatery employs a congenial staff of eager servers. Chef Antonio, who hails from Sicily, takes great pride in preparing each dish and even takes time to visit each table. In addition to a range of pasta dishes, the menu lists chicken, veal, fish and USDA steak selections prepared with Italian influences. A nice complement is an after-dinner glass of chilled lemoncello. Casual dress. **Bar:** Full bar. **Reservations:** suggested. **Hours:** 6:30 pm-10:30 pm, Thurs & Fri also noon-3. Closed: 12/25; also Mon. **Address:** Rodney Bay Village **Location:** Center of village. **Parking:** street. **Cards:** AX, DC, DS, MC, VI.

MEMORIES OF HONG KONG **Phone:** 758/452-8218 (5)

Chinese
$15-$24

Brightly decorated in Chinese fashion complete with a Pagoda-style roof, this restaurant offers exceptional fare. Fresh seafood, beef, chicken and pork dishes are prepared in a myriad of ways. Congenial servers and an extensive cocktail menu round out the experience. Casual dress. **Bar:** Full bar. **Reservations:** suggested. **Hours:** 5 pm-10:30 pm. Closed: 12/25, 12/26; also Sun. **Address:** Rodney Bay Village **Location:** Across from Reduit Beach; 5.5 mi (8.8 km) n of Castries; at Rodney Bay. **Parking:** street. **Cards:** MC, VI.

RAZMATAZ TANDOORI RESTAURANT & BAR **Phone:** 758/452-9800 (8)

Indian
$14-$23

Authentic Indian cuisine is served in the airiness of a Caribbean-style house with a large verandah. Specializing in Tandoori and Balti cuisine, the menu offers such appetizers as samosas, papadums, and shish kebab. Fragrant and exotic spices are used to flavor such entree dishes as vindaloo, tikka masala, rogan josh and tandoori, most of which can be prepared with either chicken, lamb, beef, vegetable, fish or shrimp. A bevy of side dishes, rice preparations and various naan complete the meal. Casual dress. **Bar:** Full bar. **Reservations:** accepted. **Hours:** Open 12/1-8/30 & 10/1-11/30; 5 pm-10:15 pm. Closed: 1/1, 12/25, 12/26; also Tues. **Address:** Reduit Dr **Location:** At Rodney Bay, across from Reduit Beach; 6 mi (9.6 km) n of downtown Castries. **Parking:** street. **Cards:** MC, VI.

RED SNAPPER SEAFOOD RESTAURANT & BAR **Phone:** 758/466-8377 (16)

Seafood
$15-$28

Guests visit the centrally located restaurant for open verandah dining with nautical and West Indies enhancements. Specialties of fresh fish can be blackened, curried or grilled. Also on the menu are steaks, chicken and a few pasta dishes. Casual dress. **Bar:** Full bar. **Reservations:** accepted. **Hours:** 6 pm-10:30 pm. **Address:** Rodney Bay Village **Location:** 5.1 mi (8.1 km) n of George F.L. Charles Airport, take Rodney Bay turnoff. **Parking:** street. **Cards:** AX, MC, VI.

SOUFRIERE pop. 7,656 (See map and index starting on p. 541)

WHERE TO STAY

ANSE CHASTANET RESORT *Book great rates at AAA.com* **Phone:** (758)459-7000 29

AAA SAVE

Resort Cottage
$280-$965 All Year

Address: Old French Rd **Location:** 2 mi (3.2 km) n of town; 30 mi (48 km) s of Castries via West Coast Rd; 20 mi (32 km) n of Hewanorra International Airport. Located in a secluded area. **Facility:** This is a distinctive resort of cottages scattered throughout 500 lushly landscaped acres extending from the beach to up a steep hillside. 49 cottages. 1 story, exterior corridors. *Bath:* shower only. **Parking:** on-site. **Terms:** office hours 7 am-11 pm, 3 night minimum stay - seasonal, age restrictions may apply, cancellation fee imposed. **Amenities:** safes, irons, hair dryers. **Dining:** 4 restaurants, entertainment. **Leisure Activities:** beach access, sailboats, windsurfing, boat dock, snorkeling, kayaks, tennis court, recreation programs, library, hiking trails, jogging, spa. *Fee:* scuba diving, charter fishing, yacht sailing trips, bicycles. **Guest Services:** valet laundry, area transportation-water taxi, wireless Internet. **Business Services:** PC. **Cards:** AX, DC, DS, JC, MC, VI. **Free Special Amenities: room upgrade (subject to availability with advance reservations).**
(See color ad below)

▼ See AAA listing above ▼

▼ See AAA listing p 549 ▼

(See map and index starting on p. 541)

THE JALOUSIE PLANTATION **Phone:** 758/456-8000 34

Resort Hotel

$225-$900 All Year

Address: Forbidden Beach, Eden Bay **Location:** Oceanfront. Just s of town center, then just w; follow signs. **Facility:** Between the two Piton peaks, this full-service resort encompasses more than 325 acres of lush grounds; find cottage-style units with plunge pools. 112 units. 100 one-bedroom standard units. 12 one-bedroom suites. 1-2 stories (no elevator), exterior corridors. **Parking:** on-site. **Terms:** 30 day cancellation notice-fee imposed. **Amenities:** video library, voice mail, safes, irons, hair dryers. *Some:* DVD players. **Pool(s):** outdoor. **Leisure Activities:** sauna, whirlpools, beach access, golf-3 holes, 3 lighted tennis courts, recreation programs, jogging, exercise room, spa, volleyball. *Fee:* paddleboats, sailboats, windsurfing, scuba diving, snorkeling. **Guest Services:** valet laundry, beauty salon, wireless Internet. **Business Services:** meeting rooms, PC (fee). **Cards:** AX, MC, VI.

LADERA RESORT **Phone:** 758/459-7323 28

Cottage

$380-$1330 12/1-9/7 & 10/4-11/30

Address: Rabot Estate **Location:** 2 mi (3.2 km) s of town; 32 mi (51.2 km) s of Castries via West Coast Rd; 18 mi (28.8 km) n of Hewanorra International Airport. **Facility:** Unique, intimate resort of villas located high atop a mountain ridge nestled between the Pitons and surrounded by a rain forest. All units without afourth wall while retaining total privacy affording spectacular views of Caribbean Sea and the Pitons and either a swimming pool or a plunge pool. 32 cottages. 1-2 stories (no elevator), exterior corridors. *Bath:* shower only. **Parking:** on-site. **Terms:** open 12/1-9/7 & 10/4-11/30, office hours 7 am-11 pm, 3 night minimum stay - seasonal, age restrictions may apply, 21 day cancellation notice-fee imposed. **Amenities:** video library, safes, irons, hair dryers. *Some:* DVD players. **Dining:** entertainment. **Pool(s):** outdoor. **Leisure Activities:** snorkeling, exercise room, spa. **Guest Services:** valet laundry, area transportation-boat to beaches. **Business Services:** business center. **Cards:** AX, DS, MC, VI. ***(See color ad p 548)***

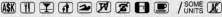

STONEFIELD ESTATE VILLA RESORT **Phone:** 758/459-7037 31

Cottage

$200-$880 All Year

Address: Stonefield Estate Rd **Location:** Just s of town, then just w; follow signs. **Facility:** Thoughtful appointments and fully equipped conveniences make this villa resort ideal for the independent traveling family or couple. 18 cottages. 1 story, exterior corridors. *Bath:* shower only. **Parking:** on-site. **Terms:** office hours 7 am-10 pm, 3 night minimum stay - seasonal, age restrictions may apply, 30 day cancellation notice-fee imposed. **Amenities:** CD players, safes, irons, hair dryers. **Pool(s):** outdoor. **Guest Services:** valet laundry, area transportation, wireless Internet. **Business Services:** PC. **Cards:** MC, VI.

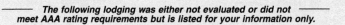

ASK / SOME UNITS

The following lodging was either not evaluated or did not meet AAA rating requirements but is listed for your information only.

HUMMINGBIRD BEACH RESORT **Phone:** 758/459-7232

fyi

Not evaluated. **Address:** Anse Chastanet Rd **Location:** Oceanfront. Just n of town center. Facilities, services, and decor characterize an economy property.

VIEUX FORT pop. 14,754 (See map and index starting on p. 541)

WHERE TO STAY

COCONUT BAY BEACH RESORT & SPA **Phone:** (758)459-6000 36

AAA SAVE

Resort Hotel

$310-$610 All Year

Address: Bean Field **Location:** Oceanfront. Just s of Hewanorra International Airport. **Facility:** Recently renovated guest rooms at this oceanfront, all-inclusive resort are nestled around a waterslide, a full-service spa, tennis courts and pools. 254 one-bedroom standard units. 4 stories, exterior corridors. *Bath:* shower only. **Parking:** on-site. **Terms:** 3 day cancellation notice-fee imposed. **Amenities:** voice mail, safes, irons, hair dryers. **Dining:** 4 restaurants, entertainment. **Pool(s):** 3 outdoor. **Leisure Activities:** whirlpool, waterslide, 4 lighted tennis courts, recreation programs, playground, exercise room, spa, basketball, volleyball, game room. *Fee:* saunas, steamrooms, paintball arena. **Guest Services:** valet and coin laundry, airport transportation-Hewanorra International Airport, wireless Internet. **Business Services:** meeting rooms, PC (fee). **Cards:** AX, DC, DS, MC, VI.

 / SOME UNITS

ST. MARTIN/ST. MAARTEN

This index helps you "spot" where approved lodgings and restaurants are located on the corresponding detailed maps. Lodging daily rate range is for comparison only and show the property's high season. Restaurant rate range is a combination of lunch and/or dinner. Turn to the listing page for more detailed rate information and consult display ads for special promotions.

GRAND CASE (ST. MARTIN)

Map Page	OA	Lodgings	Diamond Rated	High Season	Page
1 / p. 552		Hotel L'Esplanade	◆◆◆	$245-$495	560
5 / p. 552		Le Petit Hotel	◆◆	$360-$520	560

Map Page	OA	Restaurants	Diamond Rated	Cuisine	Meal Range	Page
3 / p. 552		Le Tastevin	◆◆◆	French	$26-$56	560
4 / p. 552		Fish Pot Village Cafe	◆◆◆	French	$15-$40	560
5 / p. 552		Il Nettuno	◆◆	Italian	$23-$38	560
7 / p. 552		L'Auberge Gourmande	◆◆◆	French	$22-$34	560
8 / p. 552		L'Escapade	◆◆	French	$33-$39	560
9 / p. 552		La California	◆◆	French	$24-$30	560
13 / p. 552		Le Pressoir	◆◆◆	French	$34-$46	560
14 / p. 552		Restaurant du Soleil	◆◆	French	$31-$39	561

ORIENT BAY (ST. MARTIN)

Map Page	OA	Lodgings	Diamond Rated	High Season	Page
13 / p. 552		Esmeralda Resort	◆◆◆	$240-$3960	563
14 / p. 552		Alamanda Resort	◆◆◆	$348-$1109	563
15 / p. 552		La Plantation	◆◆◆	$185-$670	563
16 / p. 552		Cap Caraibes-Caribbean Princess Hotel Resort	◆◆	$220-$460	563
17 / p. 552		Palm Court Hotel	◆◆	$255-$380	563

MARIGOT (ST. MARTIN)

Map Page	OA	Lodgings	Diamond Rated	High Season	Page
18 / p. 552	AAA	**Hotel La Samanna**	◆◆◆◆	$475-$2050 SAVE	561
19 / p. 552		Mercure Simson Beach	◆◆	$244-$616	561
20 / p. 552		Le Flamboyant Hotel & Resort	◆◆	$265-$341	561

Map Page	OA	Restaurants	Diamond Rated	Cuisine	Meal Range	Page
21 / p. 552		La Bar de la Mer	◆	French	$14-$32	561
22 / p. 552		La Main a la Pate	◆◆	French	$18-$29	561
23 / p. 552		Don Camillo Restaurant	◆◆◆	Italian	$22-$37	561
24 / p. 552		Le Saint-Severin	◆◆◆	French	$18-$38	562
25 / p. 552		Le Gaiac	◆◆◆◆	French	$48-$70	562
26 / p. 552		Mario's Bistro	◆◆◆	French	$30-$43	562
27 / p. 552		Thai Garden	◆◆	Asian	$19-$26	563
28 / p. 552		L'Oizeau Rare	◆◆	French	$20-$32	562
29 / p. 552	AAA	**Le Santal by the Sea**	◆◆◆◆	French	$39-$66	562
31 / p. 552	AAA	**The Restaurant at La Samanna**	◆◆◆◆	International	$36-$60	562
33 / p. 552		Le Saint Germain	◆◆	French	$10-$30	562
34 / p. 552		L'Arhawak Bar & Restaurant	◆◆	Barbecue	$14-$28	562
35 / p. 552		Le Chanteclair	◆◆◆	French	$32-$39	562
39 / p. 552		Restaurant Les Boucaniers	◆◆	Creole	$15-$28	563

OYSTER POND (ST. MARTIN) (ST. MARTIN)

Map Page	OA	Lodging	Diamond Rated	High Season	Page
26 / p. 552		Captain Oliver's Resort	2 diamonds	$110-$275	564

Map Page	OA	Restaurant	Diamond Rated	Cuisine	Meal Range	Page
44 / p. 552		Captain Oliver's	2 diamonds	Seafood	$12-$27	564

OYSTER POND (ST. MAARTEN) (ST. MAARTEN)

Map Page	OA	Lodgings	Diamond Rated	High Season	Page
27 / p. 552	AAA	**The Westin St. Maarten Dawn Beach Resort & Spa** - see color ad on insert, p 555	4 diamonds	$397-$667 SAVE	554
28 / p. 552		Oyster Bay Beach Resort	3 diamonds	Rates not provided	554

Map Page	OA	Restaurant	Diamond Rated	Cuisine	Meal Range	Page
42 / p. 552	AAA	**Aura**	4 diamonds	French	$35-$49	556

LITTLE BAY (ST. MAARTEN)

Map Page	OA	Lodgings	Diamond Rated	High Season	Page
30 / p. 552		Belair Beach Hotel	2 diamonds	$259-$429	553
31 / p. 552	AAA	**Divi Little Bay Beach Resort** - see color ad p 553	fyi	$208-$812 SAVE	553

MAHO BAY (ST. MAARTEN)

Map Page	OA	Lodging	Diamond Rated	High Season	Page
34 / p. 552		Sonesta Maho Beach Resort & Casino	3 diamonds	$190-$700	553

ANSE MARCEL (ST. MARTIN)

Map Page	OA	Lodging	Diamond Rated	High Season	Page
38 / p. 552		Hotel Marquis Resort & Spa	3 diamonds	$285-$995	558

CUPECOY (ST. MAARTEN)

Map Page	OA	Restaurants	Diamond Rated	Cuisine	Meal Range	Page
50 / p. 552		Dare to be..Rare	3 diamonds	Steak	$26-$54	552
52 / p. 552		Le Montmartre	3 diamonds	French	$31-$55	553
54 / p. 552		La Gondola Ristorante	3 diamonds	Italian	$18-$34	552

PHILIPSBURG (ST. MAARTEN)

Map Page	OA	Restaurants	Diamond Rated	Cuisine	Meal Range	Page
75 / p. 552		Antoine by the Sea	2 diamonds	International	$7-$33	556
76 / p. 552		Pasanggrahan Restaurant	1 diamond	International	$10-$26	556
77 / p. 552		Shiv Sagar Bar & Restaurant	2 diamonds	Indian	$10-$22	556
78 / p. 552		The Greenhouse Bar and Restaurant	2 diamonds	International	$9-$28	556

SIMPSON BAY (ST. MAARTEN)

Map Page	OA	Restaurants	Diamond Rated	Cuisine	Meal Range	Page
80 / p. 552		Skip Jack's Seafood Grill, Bar & Fish Market	2 diamonds	Seafood	$17-$28	556
85 / p. 552		Top Carrot	1 diamond	Vegetarian	$8-$13	556

COLE BAY (ST. MAARTEN)

Map Page	OA	Restaurant	Diamond Rated	Cuisine	Meal Range	Page
81 / p. 552		Los Gauchos Argentine Grill	2 diamonds	Argentine	$18-$30	552

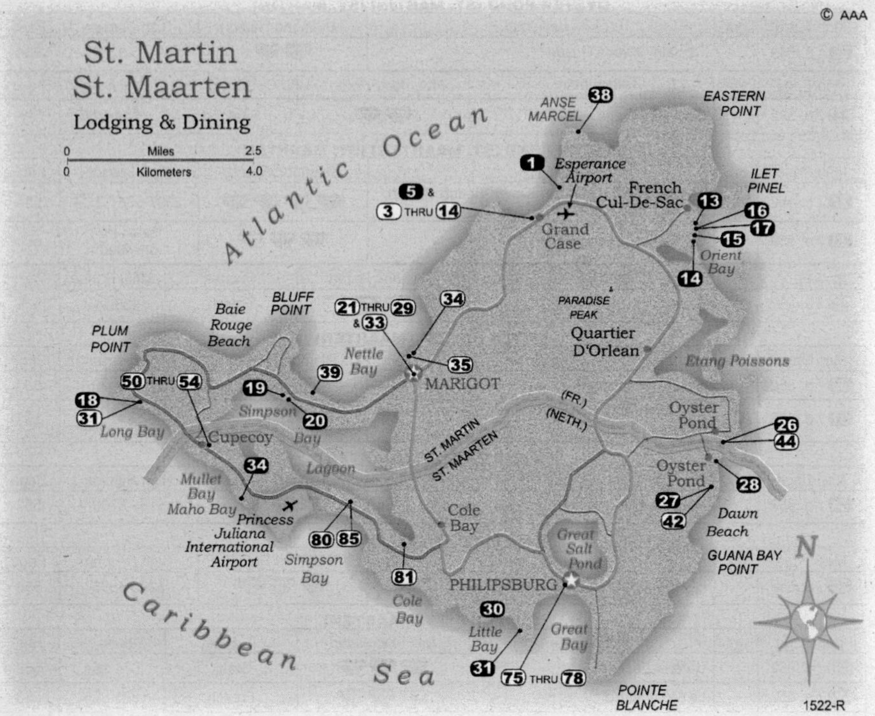

St. Martin
St. Maarten
Lodging & Dining

1522-R

St. Maarten

COLE BAY (See map and index starting on p. 552)

WHERE TO DINE

LOS GAUCHOS ARGENTINE GRILL — **Phone:** 599/544-4084 (81)

Argentine
$18-$30

This place reflects the Pampas region of Argentina in its decor. Flavorful and tender imported grilled meats go into the house specialty churrasco. Diners with hearty appetites might try the parrillada Pampas, an assortment of various cuts of beef. Also on the menu are fish, pasta and chicken dishes. Casual dress. **Bar:** Full bar. **Reservations:** suggested. **Hours:** 11 am-11 pm. Closed: Mon. **Address:** Billy Folly Rd **Location:** On Lay Bay; in Pelican Resort; 1.4 mi (2.2 km) e of Princess Juliana International Airport. **Parking:** on-site. **Cards:** MC, VI.

CUPECOY (See map and index starting on p. 552)

WHERE TO DINE

DARE TO BE..RARE — **Phone:** 599/545-5714 (50)

Steak
$26-$54

One of the latest restaurants to emerge in the St. Maarten dining scene, the sleek, urban and hip spot is the brainchild of local celebrity chef Dino Jagtiani. Several cuts of wet- and dry-aged beef, Kobe beef and veal prove to be most popular. Tantalizing sauces accompany most steaks, and the selection of martinis is extensive. The staff provides superlative service. Dressy casual. **Bar:** Full bar. **Reservations:** suggested. **Hours:** 6:30 pm-10:30 pm. Closed: 1/1, 12/25; also Mon. **Address:** 103 Rhine Rd **Location:** West side of island; just w of Mullet Bay Golf Course; at Atlantis World Casino. **Parking:** on-site. **Cards:** AX, CB, DC, DS, JC, MC, VI.

LA GONDOLA RISTORANTE — **Phone:** 599/545-3938 (54)

Italian
$18-$34

Dine in the air-conditioned intimacy of the dining room or enjoy the air on the small street-side patio at this Italian bistro. Homemade pasta and other traditional fare are on the menu, including lobster ravioli or beef tenderloin in a light Gorgonzola sauce. Dressy casual. **Bar:** Full bar. **Reservations:** suggested. **Hours:** Open 12/1-6/1 & 7/16-11/30; 6 pm-10:30 pm. Closed: 1/1, 12/25; also Tues. **Address:** The Lowlands **Location:** Just w of Mullet Bay Golf Course; at Atlantis World Casino. **Parking:** on-site and valet. **Cards:** AX, MC, VI.

(See map and index starting on p. 552)

LE MONTMARTRE **Phone:** 599/545-3939 (52)

French
$31-$55

Patrons can splurge on a real slice of French ambience and cuisine on the Dutch side of the island. Servers deftly perform filleting. The chefs prepare such temptations as sea bass with Provencal sauce. Fresh, artistic presentations of delectable tiramisu, creme brulee and profiteroles complete a memorable meal. Dressy casual. **Bar:** Full bar. **Reservations:** required. **Hours:** 6 pm-11 pm. **Address:** Atlantis World Casino **Location:** Southwest corner of the island; just e of the French/Dutch border; at Atlantis World Casino. **Parking:** on-site. **Cards:** AX, DS, MC, VI.

LITTLE BAY (See map and index starting on p. 552)

WHERE TO STAY

BELAIR BEACH HOTEL **Phone:** (599)542-3362 (30)

Condominium
$259-$429 All Year

Address: Welgelen Rd **Location:** Oceanfront. 3 mi (4.8 km) w of Philipsburg; 4.5 mi (7.2 km) e of airport, 3.1 mi (5 km) se. **Facility:** Meets AAA guest room security requirements. 68 two-bedroom suites with kitchens. 4 stories, exterior corridors. **Parking:** on-site. **Terms:** check-in 4 pm, 3 day cancellation notice-fee imposed. **Amenities:** video library (fee), voice mail, safes, hair dryers. *Some:* DVD players. **Pool(s):** outdoor. **Leisure Activities:** rental paddleboats, rental sailboards, tennis court. *Fee:* waterskiing, massage. **Guest Services:** valet and coin laundry, wireless Internet. **Business Services:** PC (fee). **Cards:** AX, DC, DS, MC, VI.

ASK D VCR

DIVI LITTLE BAY BEACH RESORT **Phone:** (599)542-2333 (31)

AAA SAVE
fyi

Resort Hotel
$208-$812 All Year

Under major renovation, scheduled to be completed December 2008. Last rated: **Address:** Little Bay Rd **Location:** Oceanfront. 2.7 mi (4.3 km) w of Philipsburg. **Facility:** With hotel and condo-style guest units, the resort is superbly located on a peninsula surrounded by white sand beach and views of Philipsburg. 210 units. 166 one-bedroom standard units. 40 one- and 4 two-bedroom suites with kitchens. 2-3 stories (no elevator), exterior corridors. **Parking:** on-site. **Terms:** check-in 4 pm, 3 night minimum stay, 7 day cancellation notice. **Amenities:** safes, irons, hair dryers. *Some:* DVD players. **Dining:** 3 restaurants, entertainment. **Pool(s):** 3 outdoor. **Leisure Activities:** whirlpools, rental boats, rental canoes, lighted tennis court, recreation programs, exercise room, spa, volleyball. *Fee:* scuba diving, snorkeling, personal watercraft, glass bottom boat. **Guest Services:** valet and coin laundry, wireless Internet. **Business Services:** meeting rooms, PC (fee). **Cards:** AX, DS, MC, VI. *(See color ad below)*

D / SOME UNITS VCR

MAHO BAY (See map and index starting on p. 552)

WHERE TO STAY

SONESTA MAHO BEACH RESORT & CASINO *Book at AAA.com* **Phone:** (599)545-2115 (34)

Resort Hotel
$190-$700 All Year

Address: Maho Bay **Location:** Oceanfront. 0.4 mi (0.6 km) w of Princess Juliana International Airport. **Facility:** A very popular resort in the hub of dining and nightlife activities, the property has several room types that vary in size and decor. 537 units. 512 one-bedroom standard units. 18 one- and 7 two-bedroom suites with whirlpools. 6-10 stories, interior corridors. *Bath:* combo or shower only. **Parking:** on-site (fee). **Terms:** 8 day cancellation notice-fee imposed. **Amenities:** high-speed Internet, voice mail, safes, irons, hair dryers. **Pool(s):** 2 outdoor. **Leisure Activities:** snorkeling, 4 lighted tennis courts, recreation programs, spa, volleyball. **Guest Services:** valet laundry, wireless Internet. **Business Services:** conference facilities, PC (fee). **Cards:** AX, DC, MC, VI.

ASK D / SOME UNITS

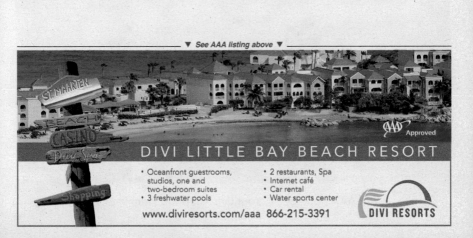

▼ See AAA listing above ▼

OYSTER POND (ST. MAARTEN) (See map and index starting on p. 552)

WHERE TO STAY

OYSTER BAY BEACH RESORT — Phone: 599/543-6040 28

Condominium
Rates not provided

Address: Emerald Merit Rd #10 **Location:** Oceanfront. 5.6 mi (9 km) ne of Princess Juliana International Airport. **Facility:** Set on an eight-acre peninsula between Oyster Pond and Dawn Beach, the property offers original hotel-style units as well as newer condo-style units. Meets AAA guest room security requirements. 151 units. 67 one-bedroom standard units. 54 one- and 30 two-bedroom suites with kitchens. 3 stories (no elevator), exterior corridors. *Bath:* combo or shower only. **Parking:** on-site. **Amenities:** DVD players, CD players, voice mail, safes, irons, hair dryers. **Pool(s):** outdoor. **Leisure Activities:** whirlpool, snorkeling, recreation programs in season, exercise room. *Fee:* charter fishing, massage. **Guest Services:** coin laundry, wireless Internet. **Business Services:** PC (fee).

D / SOME UNITS

THE WESTIN ST. MAARTEN DAWN BEACH RESORT & SPA — Book great rates at AAA.com — Phone: (599)543-6700 27

AAA SAVE
Hotel
$397-$667 All Year

WESTIN HOTELS & RESORTS
AAA Benefit:
Enjoy up to 15% off your next stay, plus Starwood Preferred Guest® bonuses.

Address: 144 Oyster Pond Rd **Location:** Oceanfront. 5.9 mi (9.4 km) e of Princess Juliana International Airport. **Facility:** Situated on Dawn Beach, this new resort features luxurious accommodations and attentive service. Meets AAA guest room security requirements. Smoke free premises. 317 units. 311 one-bedroom standard units. 3 one- and 3 two-bedroom suites. 3 stories, interior corridors. *Bath:* combo or shower only. **Parking:** on-site and valet. **Terms:** 15 day cancellation notice. **Amenities:** high-speed Internet (fee), voice mail, safes, honor bars, irons, hair dryers. *Some:* DVD players (fee), CD players. **Dining:** 2 restaurants, also, Aura, see separate listing. **Pool(s):** outdoor. **Leisure Activities:** whirlpool, kids club, spa, volleyball. *Fee:* saunas, steamrooms, scuba diving, snorkeling, kayaks. **Guest Services:** valet laundry, wireless Internet. **Business Services:** conference facilities, business center. **Cards:** AX, MC, VI.
(See color ad on insert & p 555)

▼ See AAA listing p 554 ▼

(See map and index starting on p. 552)

WHERE TO DINE

AURA — **Phone:** 599/543-6700 (42)

French
$35-$49

The menu presents many chef surprises from the kitchen to whet the appetite. The foie gras or chilled English pea soup are great starters. For entrees, favorites are the rack of lamb or Long Island duck. The desserts and souffles are heavenly. Dressy casual. **Bar:** Full bar. **Reservations:** required. **Hours:** 6:30 pm-10 pm. Closed: Wed. **Address:** 144 Oyster Pond Rd **Location:** 5.9 mi (9.4 km) e of Princess Juliana International Airport; In The Westin St. Maarten Dawn Beach Resort & Spa. **Parking:** on-site. **Cards:** AX, CB, DC, DS, JC, MC, VI.

PHILIPSBURG (See map and index starting on p. 552)

WHERE TO DINE

ANTOINE BY THE SEA — **Phone:** 599/542-2964 (75)

International
$7-$33

The restaurant has been impressing patrons since 1978. Chef Jean-Pierre combines traditional French cuisine with some Italian influences. Escargots, homemade pate and vichyssoise are great beginnings. Seafood specialties include red snapper, tuna steak, baked salmon and shrimp scampi, and duck Montmorency is another rich and flavorful choice. The attractively priced three-course menu also is worth a look. Casual dress. **Bar:** Full bar. **Reservations:** accepted. **Hours:** 11 am-10 pm. **Address:** 119 Front St **Location:** Downtown; on the waterfront; center; on Great Bay. **Parking:** valet and street. **Cards:** MC, VI.

AC

THE GREENHOUSE BAR AND RESTAURANT — **Phone:** 599/542-2941 (78)

International
$9-$28

For over 20 years this restaurant has been a consistent favorite among island visitors and locals alike. Located at Bobby's Marina with views of Great Bay, the casual eatery has a fun loving staff offering an array of whimsically named drinks. The varied menu includes conch fritters, nachos, chicken wings and jalapeno poppers for starters. Main entrees include a variety of entree size salads, sandwiches like the classic Reuben and Philly cheesesteak or steaks, ribs, pasta and seafood. Casual dress. Entertainment. **Bar:** Full bar. **Reservations:** accepted. **Hours:** 11 am-10 pm. **Address:** Bobby's Marina **Location:** Just e of downtown; on boardwalk; at Bobby's Marina, Great Bay. **Parking:** on-site. **Cards:** AX, CB, DC, DS, JC, MC, VI.

AC

PASANGGRAHAN RESTAURANT — **Phone:** 599/542-2743 (76)

International
$10-$26

In a charming inn that dates to 1906, the longtime favorite sits on the city's recently renovated boardwalk. The broad menu lists simple Caribbean, Indonesian and American favorites, including entree salads, lamb, seafood and curry dishes. Unhurried service allows time for reflection. Casual dress. **Bar:** Full bar. **Reservations:** accepted. **Hours:** 7 am-3 & 6-10 pm. **Address:** 19 Front St **Location:** Center of downtown; on waterfront. **Parking:** street. **Cards:** MC, VI. **Historic**

AC

SHIV SAGAR BAR & RESTAURANT — **Phone:** 599/542-2299 (77)

Indian
$10-$22

Just upstairs from the hustle and bustle of the shops on Front Street is an oasis for fine Indian dining. Pleasant uniformed staffers offer many suggestions from the extensive menu, including well-prepared and exotically spiced dishes, curries and tandoori selections. Dressy casual. **Bar:** Full bar. **Reservations:** accepted. **Hours:** 11:30 am-3 & 6:30-10:30 pm, Sun-3 pm. Closed major holidays. **Address:** 20 Front St **Location:** Center of downtown. **Parking:** street. **Cards:** AX, MC, VI.

SIMPSON BAY (See map and index starting on p. 552)

WHERE TO DINE

SKIP JACK'S SEAFOOD GRILL, BAR & FISH MARKET — **Phone:** 599/544-2313 (80)

Seafood
$17-$28

The popular restaurant prepares numerous grilled and seared cuts of meat and fish. The superb lunch spot serves gourmet burgers and entree-size salads. Diners might start a meal with peel-and-eat shrimp or crab cakes or enjoy a libation in the sunken bar area designed to resemble a boat. The good-humored staff provides island-friendly and mostly efficient service. Casual dress. **Bar:** Full bar. **Reservations:** suggested. **Hours:** 11:30 am-3 & 5:30-10 pm, Sun from 5:30 pm. **Address:** Airport Rd **Location:** 0.4 mi (0.6 km) e of Princess Juliana International Airport. **Parking:** on-site. **Cards:** MC, VI.

AC

TOP CARROT — **Phone:** 599/544-3381 (85)

Vegetarian
$8-$13

A good place for a quick breakfast or lunch, the eatery focuses on vegetarian and Middle East-inspired sandwiches and dishes. Popular as well are nutrition drinks that blend such ingredients as carrot juice, wheatgrass and ginger. Ethnic craft displays lend to the decor. Casual dress. **Hours:** 7:30 am-6 pm. **Address:** Airport Rd **Location:** 1.2 mi (1.9 km) of Princess Juliana International Airport; in Plaza del Lago. **Parking:** on-site. **Cards:** MC, VI.

St. Martin

ANSE MARCEL (See map and index starting on p. 552)

WHERE TO STAY

HOTEL MARQUIS RESORT & SPA — **Phone:** 590/590-29-42-30

Hotel
$285-$995 All Year

Address: Pigeon Pea Hill **Location:** Above Anse Marcel Beach, follow signs; north coast of island. **Facility:** 17 units. 15 one-bedroom standard units. 2 one-bedroom suites. 2 stories (no elevator), exterior corridors. **Parking:** on-site. **Terms:** check-in 4 pm. **Amenities:** CD players, voice mail, safes, honor bars, hair dryers. **Pool(s):** outdoor. **Leisure Activities:** 4 lighted tennis courts. **Guest Services:** valet laundry, area transportation, wireless Internet. **Business Services:** PC.

/ SOME UNITS

RADISSON ST MARTIN RESORT, MARINA & SPA — **Phone:** 590/590-87-67-09

fyi
Resort Hotel
$295-$1765 All Year

Too new to rate, opening scheduled for August 2008. **Address:** BP 581 Anse Marcel 97056 St Martin CEDEX **Location:** North coast of island. **Amenities:** 252 units, restaurant, coffeemakers, microwaves, refrigerators, pool. **Terms:** 15 day cancellation notice-fee imposed. **Cards:** AX, DC, DS, JC, MC, VI. ***(See color ad p 559)***

▼ See AAA listing p 558 ▼

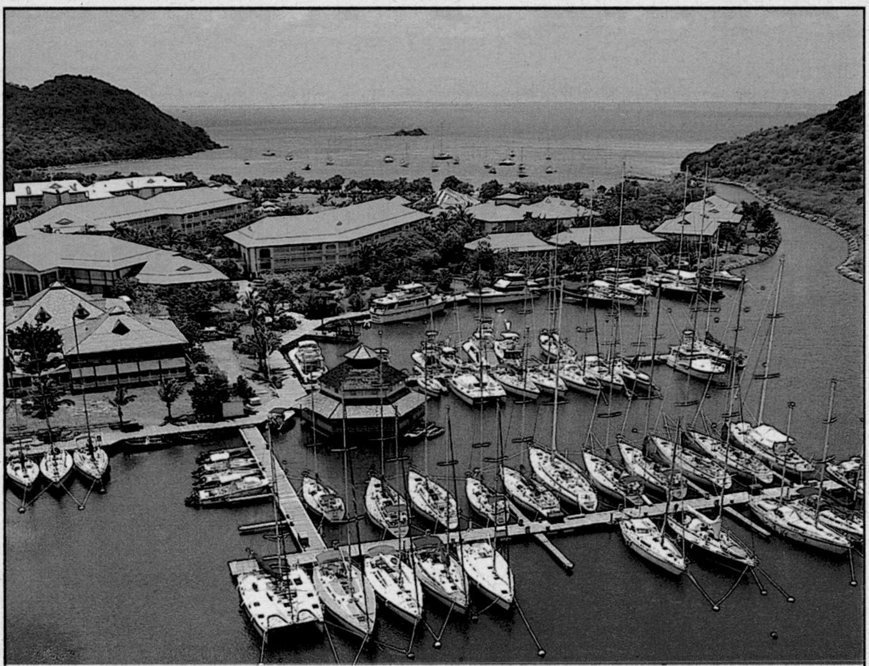

GRAND CASE (See map and index starting on p. 552)

WHERE TO STAY

HOTEL L'ESPLANADE — **Phone:** (590)590-87-06-55 (1)

Motel
$245-$495 All Year

Address: On the Hill **Location:** Just ne of downtown; just n of Grand Case Airport. **Facility:** Designated smoking area. 24 units. 8 one-bedroom standard units with kitchens. 16 one-bedroom suites with kitchens. 2 stories, exterior corridors. *Bath:* combo or shower only. **Parking:** on-site. **Terms:** office hours 7:30 am-9 pm, check-in 4 pm, 45 day cancellation notice, 21 day off season. **Amenities:** DVD players, CD players, safes, irons, hair dryers. **Pool(s):** outdoor. **Leisure Activities:** limited beach access. *Fee:* massage. **Guest Services:** valet laundry, wireless Internet. **Business Services:** PC. **Cards:** AX, MC, VI.

/ SOME UNITS

LE PETIT HOTEL — **Phone:** (590)590-29-09-65 (5)

Motel
$360-$520 12/20-11/30
$260-$370 12/1-12/19

Address: 248 Blvd de Grand Case **Location:** Oceanfront. 0.9 mi (1.5 km) from Grand Case Airport; 9.7 mi (15.5 km) from Princess Juliana International Airport; west end of Grand Case Village. **Facility:** Designated smoking area. 10 units. 9 one-bedroom standard units with efficiencies. 1 one-bedroom suite with efficiency. 3 stories (no elevator), exterior corridors. *Bath:* combo or shower only. **Parking:** on-site. **Terms:** office hours 9 am-5 pm, 45 day cancellation notice, 21 day off season. **Amenities:** video library, DVD players, CD players, high-speed Internet, safes, irons, hair dryers. **Guest Services:** valet laundry, wireless Internet. **Business Services:** PC. **Cards:** AX, MC, VI.

WHERE TO DINE

FISH POT VILLAGE CAFE — **Phone:** 590/590-87-50-88 (4)

French
$15-$40

Classical French cuisine reflects tropical influences. Guests are treated to elegant, open-air, waterfront dining by candlelight. Casual dress. **Bar:** Full bar. **Reservations:** required, for dinner. **Hours:** Open 12/1-9/1 & 11/1-11/30; noon-2:30 & 6-10 pm. Closed: Mon 5/1-9/1. **Address:** 82 Blvd de Grand Case **Location:** Center of village. **Parking:** street. **Cards:** AX, DS, MC, VI.

IL NETTUNO — **Phone:** 590/590-87-77-38 (5)

Italian
$23-$38

Open-air tables offer a view of the waterfront on Grand Case Bay. A good wine list accompanies such fine quality and attractively presented dishes as the house specialty linguine frutti di mare. Servers are knowledgeable and personable. Dressy casual. Entertainment. **Bar:** Full bar. **Reservations:** required. **Hours:** Open 12/1-9/1 & 10/1-11/30; noon-2:30 & 6-10:30 pm. Closed: for lunch 4/1-11/30. **Address:** 70 Blvd de Grand Case **Location:** Center of village. **Parking:** on-site. **Cards:** AX, DS, MC, VI.

LA CALIFORNIA — **Phone:** 590/590-87-55-57 (9)

French
$24-$30

On the waterfront of the former fishing village of Grand Case, the gourmet restaurant presents a menu of exquisitely prepared meals, including frog's legs, crab cakes and foie gras pate appetizers and such popular entrees as lamb chops with baked goat cheese, pork tenderloin with fig sauce, gourmet pizzas and delicately prepared seafood. Casual dress. **Bar:** Full bar. **Reservations:** suggested. **Hours:** Open 12/1-9/24 & 10/25-11/30; 11 am-10:30 pm. Closed: Mon 5/1-11/30. **Address:** Blvd de Grand Case **Location:** Center of village. **Parking:** street. **Cards:** MC, VI.

L'AUBERGE GOURMANDE — **Phone:** 590/590-87-73-37 (7)

French
$22-$34

In a historic Creole home with a street view, the small, candlelit dining room is a cozy, charmingly decorated spot for classic French cuisine. Homemade desserts are excellent, and the wine selection is good. Flavorful cuisine takes into account texture and color. Service is formal yet friendly. Casual dress. **Bar:** Full bar. **Reservations:** suggested. **Hours:** Open 12/1-9/1 & 10/15-11/30; 6 pm-10 pm. **Address:** 89 Blvd de Grand Case **Location:** Center of village. **Parking:** street. **Cards:** AX, MC, VI.

LE PRESSOIR — **Phone:** 590/590-87-76-62 (13)

French
$34-$46

The highly regarded restaurant in the "gourmet capital" of the Caribbean occupies a restored Creole cottage dating back to 1886. The chef shows his talents in lovingly preparing inspired dishes with exquisite sauces, specialized ingredients and artistic presentations. The suave wait staff complement the romantic dining experience with a casual elegance. Dressy casual. **Bar:** Full bar. **Reservations:** suggested. **Hours:** Open 12/1-9/1 & 10/1-11/30; 6 pm-10 pm. Closed: Sun. **Address:** 30 Blvd de Grand Case **Location:** Center of village. **Parking:** on-site. **Cards:** MC, VI. **Historic**

L'ESCAPADE — **Phone:** 590/590-87-75-04 (8)

French
$33-$39

In a French-Creole-style home, the restaurant prepares sumptuous fare for the discriminating palate. Among favorite dishes are Anguillan lobster, tuna tartare, veal sweetbreads, rack of lamb and mussels risotto. Service is casual. Casual dress. **Bar:** Full bar. **Reservations:** required. **Hours:** 11:30 am-10:30 pm; 5:30 pm-10 pm 4/15-12/20. **Address:** 94 Blvd de Grand Case **Location:** On waterfront; center of downtown. **Parking:** on-site (fee). **Cards:** DS, MC, VI.

LE TASTEVIN — **Phone:** 590/590-87-55-45 (3)

French
$26-$56

Diners can unwind on the open-balcony dining room on the bay while sampling lobster and other seafood specialties. Nouvelle creations are the kitchen's hallmark. The dining room sustains a relaxed, country-tropical charm. Lunches are moderately priced. Dressy casual. **Bar:** Full bar. **Reservations:** required, for dinner. **Hours:** noon-2:30 & 6-10 pm; to 10:30 pm 12/22-4/15. Closed: 12/25. **Address:** 86 Blvd de Grand Case **Location:** Center of village. **Parking:** street. **Cards:** AX, MC, VI. **Historic**

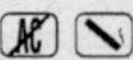

(See map and index starting on p. 552)

RESTAURANT DU SOLEIL **Phone:** 590/590-87-92-32 (14)

French
$31-$39

On the Grand Case waterfront, the refreshingly bright and cheery restaurant offers attractive prices in which one dollar equals one Euro for those who pay cash. Hosts Cedric and Frederic serve sumptuous cuisine that may include such gourmet dishes as rabbit and prune terrine, lobster bisque or monkfish and shrimp in creamy lobster sauce. Casual dress. **Bar:** Full bar. **Reservations:** accepted. **Hours:** 11:30 am-3 & 5:30-10:30 pm. Closed: for lunch 5/1-11/30. **Address:** 60 Blvd de Grand Case **Location:** Center of village. **Parking:** on-site (fee). **Cards:** MC, VI.

MARIGOT pop. 29,078 (See map and index starting on p. 552)

WHERE TO STAY

HOTEL LA SAMANNA **Phone:** (590)590-87-64-00 (18)

AAA SAVE

Resort Hotel
$475-$2050 12/1-9/1 & 11/1-11/30

Address: Baie Longue, Lowlands **Location:** Oceanfront. On Long Bay. **Facility:** An outstanding white-sand beach fronts this upscale property, where lodgings include individual Mediterranean-style cottages or charming hotel rooms. 81 units. 30 one-bedroom standard units. 42 one- and 9 two-bedroom suites, some with efficiencies. 2-4 stories (no elevator), interior/exterior corridors. **Parking:** on-site. **Terms:** open 12/1-9/1 & 11/1-11/30, 30 day cancellation notice. **Amenities:** video library, DVD players, voice mail, safes, irons, hair dryers. *Some:* CD players. **Dining:** 2 restaurants, also, The Restaurant at La Samanna, see separate listing, entertainment. **Pool(s):** 2 outdoor. **Leisure Activities:** sailboats, windsurfing, snorkeling, kayaks, 3 lighted tennis courts, tennis clinic, recreation programs, yoga, exercise room, spa, basketball. *Fee:* waterskiing, scuba diving, personal watercraft, sunset cruises, exercise instructor, Pilates. **Guest Services:** valet laundry, wireless Internet. **Business Services:** meeting rooms, business center. **Cards:** AX, DC, MC, VI. **Free Special Amenities: full breakfast.**

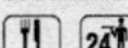   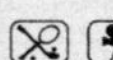  / SOME UNITS 

LE FLAMBOYANT HOTEL & RESORT **Phone:** (590)590-87-60-00 (20)

Resort Hotel
$265-$341 12/1-4/14
$207-$341 4/15-11/30

Address: Baie Nettle **Location:** In Nettle Bay; 1.8 mi (2.9 km) w from center. **Facility:** This 17-year-old, full-service property on landscaped grounds provides good-size guest units with modern amenities and resort-style facilities. 250 units. 185 one-bedroom standard units with kitchens. 60 one- and 5 two-bedroom suites with kitchens. 2-3 stories (no elevator), exterior corridors. *Bath:* combo or shower only. **Parking:** on-site. **Terms:** cancellation fee imposed. **Amenities:** voice mail, safes, hair dryers. **Pool(s):** 2 outdoor. **Leisure Activities:** whirlpool, rental boats, paddleboats, sailboats, windsurfing, boat dock, snorkeling, lighted tennis court, recreation programs, playground, exercise room, volleyball. *Fee:* waterskiing, scuba diving, massage. **Guest Services:** valet laundry, area transportation, wireless Internet. **Business Services:** meeting rooms, PC (fee). **Cards:** AX, MC, VI.

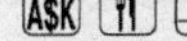  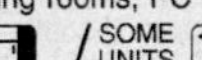 / SOME UNITS

MERCURE SIMSON BEACH *Book at AAA.com* **Phone:** (590)590-87-54-54 (19)

Hotel
$244-$616 All Year

Address: Baie Nettle **Location:** At Baie Nettle-Simson Beach; just s of downtown. **Facility:** 169 units. 125 one-bedroom standard units. 44 one-bedroom suites. 3 stories (no elevator), exterior corridors. *Bath:* shower only. **Parking:** on-site. **Amenities:** safes, hair dryers. **Pool(s):** outdoor. **Leisure Activities:** lighted tennis court, recreation programs, volleyball. *Fee:* paddleboats, scuba diving, snorkeling, massage. **Guest Services:** valet laundry, wireless Internet. **Business Services:** meeting rooms. **Cards:** AX, MC, VI.

 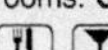 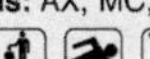 / SOME UNITS FEE 

WHERE TO DINE

DON CAMILLO RESTAURANT **Phone:** 590/590-87-52-88 (23)

Italian
$22-$37

For more than 25 years, the restaurant has received rave reviews from diners, many of whom return year after year. Italian-Mediterranean cuisine focuses on the freshest available ingredients, including fish, lobster, calamari, octopus, beef, chicken, pork and shrimp. Dishes display the presentation and preparation skills of the chef. The waiter, John, shows true finesse in providing refined, detail-oriented service. Dressy casual. **Bar:** Full bar. **Reservations:** suggested. **Hours:** Open 12/1-9/1 & 10/14-11/30; 6 pm-11 pm. Closed: Tues 4/15-11/30. **Address:** 68 La Frigate **Location:** At Marina Port La Royale. **Parking:** street. **Cards:** MC, VI.

LA BAR DE LA MER **Phone:** 590/590-29-57-44 (21)

French
$14-$32

A projection screen shows music videos at the lively cafe, where patrons sit at sidewalk tables and can watch the activity in the lobster tank. Service is casual and deliberate, and the cuisine is the hallmark. The varied menu lists entree-size salads, gourmet pizzas, bouillabaisse, rib steak and pork ribs, as well as paninis, burgers and sandwiches. Casual dress. **Bar:** Full bar. **Reservations:** accepted. **Hours:** 7 pm-11 pm. **Address:** Blvd de France Philippe Laude **Location:** Front de la Mer; waterfront center. **Parking:** street. **Cards:** MC, VI.

LA MAIN A LA PATE **Phone:** 590/590-87-71-19 (22)

French
$18-$29

In the Marigot Marina, where al fresco eateries abound, is this special gem. Gregarious servers are an appealing aspect, as is the menu, which lists gourmet pizzas, varied pasta dishes and nearly a dozen entree-size salads. Tempting desserts include creme brulee and tiramisu. Casual dress. **Bar:** Full bar. **Reservations:** suggested. **Hours:** 10:30 am-11 pm; 10:30 am-3 & 5:30-10:30 pm 4/15-10/20. **Address:** Marina Port La Royale **Location:** Center; at Marina Port La Royale. **Parking:** on-site. **Cards:** MC, VI.

(See map and index starting on p. 552)

L'ARHAWAK BAR & RESTAURANT **Phone:** 590/590-87-99-67 (34)

Barbecue
$14-$28

The popular sidewalk eatery's amazing menu lists many gourmet items, as well as the grilled and barbecue dishes for which it's known. Light service is brisk. An ideal spot for people-watching, the setting provides nice views of the waterfront. Casual dress. **Bar:** Full bar. **Reservations:** accepted. **Hours:** noon-11 pm. **Address:** Front de Mer **Location:** On the waterfront. **Parking:** street. **Cards:** MC, VI.

LE CHANTECLAIR **Phone:** 590/590-87-94-60 (35)

French
$32-$39

Award-winning chef Cecile Briaud-Richard displays talent and virtuosity in preparing find and original French cuisine. Many daily specials employ the freshest specialty and seasonal ingredients. Offerings include foie gras preparations, lamb, duck and Caribbean shrimp. Not-to-be-missed desserts include stewed pineapple and fresh custard, as well as the famous "no name" dessert. Bon appetit! Dressy casual. **Bar:** Full bar. **Reservations:** suggested. **Hours:** Open 12/1-9/15 & 10/15-11/30; 6 pm-10:30 pm. **Address:** 19 Marina Port La Royale **Location:** Center; at Marina Port La Royale. **Parking:** on-site. **Cards:** MC, VI.

LE GAIAC **Phone:** 590/590-51-97-66 (25)

French
$48-$70

On the terrace of the West Indies Mall is one of the finest gourmet restaurants in St. Martin. The cuisine is decidedly French, but the chef innovatively incorporates local flavor and ingredients into the dishes. Wild sea bass grilled with Szechuan peppers and served with vegetables bouillabaisse and anchovy butter is a favorite. The trio of game, which includes pheasant, rabbit and venison, also is sure to be applauded. It's an absolute must to save room for a dessert souffle. Dressy casual. **Bar:** Full bar. **Reservations:** suggested. **Hours:** Open 12/1-8/15 & 10/15-11/30; 6:30 pm-10 pm. Closed: Sun. **Address:** Front de Mer **Location:** On the waterfront; 2nd floor of Le West Indies Mall. **Parking:** on-site. **Cards:** AX, MC, VI.

LE SAINT GERMAIN **Phone:** 590/590-87-92-87 (33)

French
$10-$30

Waterfront views can be appreciated from inside or on the terrace. Well known for crepes, the restaurant also prepares flavorful fish and beef dishes. Service is crisp. Casual dress. **Bar:** Full bar. **Reservations:** accepted. **Hours:** 11 am-11 pm; from 8 am 10/16-4/30. **Address:** Auberge de Mer **Location:** At Marina Port la Royale; center of downtown. **Parking:** on-site. **Cards:** AX, CB, DC, DS, JC, MC, VI.

LE SAINT-SEVERIN **Phone:** 590/590-87-97-00 (24)

French
$18-$38

The chef's passion for employing Southern French and Mediterranean cooking techniques and ingredients shines through in impressive preparations of duck, Dover sole, red mullet, crayfish, veal, French country farm chicken and seafood, some of which is flown in from France. For starters, try foie gras or calamari. Those with hearty appetites might try traditionally prepared paella. The restaurant's unassuming exterior gives no indication of the good food and pleasant service that await within. Dressy casual. **Bar:** Full bar. **Reservations:** required. **Hours:** Open 12/1-5/1 & 6/1-11/30; noon-3 & 6:30-10:30 pm. Closed: Sun & Mon. **Address:** Rue de St. James **Location:** South side of Marigot; in Bellevue section; Les Portes de St. Martin. **Parking:** on-site. **Cards:** AX, CB, DC, DS, JC, MC, VI.

LE SANTAL BY THE SEA **Phone:** 590/590-87-53-48 (29)

French
$39-$66

The award-winning, long-established oceanfront restaurant pampers guests with refined, well-honed service in a romantic atmosphere. Exquisitely prepared cuisine is artistically presented. Among courses prepared tableside are Chateaubriand and flambeed dishes. The marriage of tantalizing flavors and complex cooking techniques showcases the chef's talents. Heavenly souffles in four flavors are a fine finish to an extraordinary dining experience. Dressy casual. **Bar:** Full bar. **Reservations:** required. **Hours:** 6 pm-9:30 pm. **Address:** 40 rue Lady Fish **Location:** At Sandy Ground. **Parking:** on-site and valet. **Cards:** AX, CB, DC, DS, JC, MC, VI.

L'OIZEAU RARE **Phone:** 590/590-87-56-38 (28)

French
$20-$32

Adjacent to the West Indies Mall, this "rare bird" serves as a fine oasis for a relaxing lunch or dinner. The blackboard menu changes frequently, but the fine culinary standards remain the same. Combining French and Creole ingredients and cooking techniques, the flavorful cuisine is sure to please. Guests might begin with carpaccio, foie gras or salad before moving on to entrees of duck, beef and local fish. Casual dress. **Bar:** Full bar. **Reservations:** suggested. **Hours:** Open 12/1-5/6 & 6/15-11/30; 11:30 am-3 & 6:30-10:30 pm. Closed: Sun. **Address:** Front de Mer **Location:** Center of waterfront; adjacent to West Indies Mall; base of the hill of Fort Saint Louis. **Parking:** on-site. **Cards:** AX, MC, VI.

MARIO'S BISTRO **Phone:** 590/590-87-06-36 (26)

French
$30-$43

Outstanding contemporary French cuisine reflects global and regional influences. The bright, colorful, open-air dining room overlooks the water. Service is well-executed, and dishes are prepared with quality ingredients and presented in an aesthetically attractive manner. Casual dress. **Bar:** Full bar. **Reservations:** required. **Hours:** Open 12/1-8/1 & 10/1-11/30; 6:30 pm-10 pm. Closed: 12/24, 12/25; also Sun, Mon 6/1-7/30. **Address:** Sandy Ground Bridge 44 Mornerond **Location:** Just w of Sandy Ground Bridge, 0.6 mi (1 km) w of center. **Parking:** on-site. **Cards:** DS, MC, VI.

THE RESTAURANT AT LA SAMANNA **Phone:** 590/590-87-64-00 (31)

International
$36-$60

Enjoy a memorable lunch or dinner in the elegant open-air dining room overlooking beautiful Baie Longue. The cuisine is a fusion of French and Creole, with Asian influences adding additional flair. The wine cellar boasts an extensive collection. Dressy casual. **Bar:** Full bar. **Reservations:** required. **Hours:** Open 12/1-8/31 & 11/1-11/30; 7 pm-10 pm. **Address:** Baie Longue, Lowlands **Location:** 5 mi (8 km) w on Long Bay; 1.5 mi (2.4 km) e of Princess Juliana International Airport; in Hotel La Samanna. **Parking:** on-site. **Cards:** AX, DC, MC, VI.

(See map and index starting on p. 552)

RESTAURANT LES BOUCANIERS — **Phone:** 590/590-29-21-75 (39)

Creole
$15-$28

The husband and wife duo managing the restaurant exude warm hospitality in the dining room and talent in the kitchen. The chef, formerly of Le Chanteclair, excels in delivering original French and Creole cuisine. For starters try the "boudins Creole" or the "salade de la Mer." Besides nightly specials the menu features fish, seafood, duck and pork. Casual dress. **Bar:** Full bar. **Reservations:** accepted. **Hours:** Open 12/1-9/15 & 10/15-11/30; noon-2:30 & 6:30-10:30 pm. Closed: Mon. **Address:** Lot 51 Nettle Bay Beach Club **Location:** 1.6 mi (2.5 km) w from Marigot Center; across from Baie Nettle. **Parking:** on-site. **Cards:** DC, DS, MC, VI.

THAI GARDEN — **Phone:** 590/590-87-88-44 (27)

Asian
$19-$26

Although the focus of the extensive menu is on Thai cuisine, sushi, sashimi and yakitori also are available. Contributing to the Asian decor are authentic carvings and calligraphy. Uniformed servers are prompt and pleasant. Casual dress. **Bar:** Full bar. **Reservations:** suggested. **Hours:** Open 12/1-9/1 & 10/5-11/30; 6:30 pm-10:30 pm. Closed: Sun. **Address:** Sandy Ground Bridge, Lowlands Rd **Location:** 0.4 mi (0.6 km) w of Sandy Ground Bridge, 1 mi (1.6 km) w of town center. **Parking:** on-site. **Cards:** MC, VI.

ORIENT BAY (See map and index starting on p. 552)

— WHERE TO STAY —

ALAMANDA RESORT — *Book at AAA.com* — **Phone:** (590)590-52-87-40 (14)

Hotel
$348-$1109 All Year

Address: Orient Bay **Location:** Oceanfront. 2.1 mi (3.3 km) se of Grand Case Airport; 9.3 (14.9 km) ne of Princess Juliana International Airport. **Facility:** 42 units. 40 one-bedroom standard units with efficiencies. 2 one-bedroom suites with efficiencies. 2 stories (no elevator), interior/exterior corridors. *Bath:* combo or shower only. **Parking:** on-site. **Terms:** 1-7 night minimum stay - seasonal, 3 day cancellation notice. **Amenities:** safes, hair dryers. **Pool(s):** outdoor. **Leisure Activities:** use of facilities at Esmeralda Resort. **Guest Services:** valet laundry, wireless Internet. **Business Services:** PC (fee). **Cards:** AX, MC, VI.

/ SOME UNITS

CAP CARAIBES-CARIBBEAN PRINCESS HOTEL RESORT — **Phone:** (590)590-52-94-94 (16)

Hotel
$220-$460 All Year

Address: Parc de la Baie Oriental **Location:** Oceanfront. Northeast corner of island. **Facility:** Designated smoking area. 45 units. 35 one-bedroom standard units with efficiencies. 9 two- and 1 three-bedroom suites with kitchens. 2-3 stories (no elevator), exterior corridors. *Bath:* shower only. **Parking:** on-site. **Terms:** office hours 8:30 am-7:30 pm, 60 day cancellation notice-fee imposed. **Amenities:** voice mail, safes, hair dryers. *Some:* irons. **Pool(s):** 2 outdoor. **Business Services:** PC. **Cards:** MC, VI.

ASK / SOME UNITS

ESMERALDA RESORT — **Phone:** (590)590-87-36-36 (13)

Hotel
$240-$3960 12/1-8/26
$240-$1520 10/1-11/30

Address: Baie Orientale **Location:** Oceanfront. At Orient Beach; 1.8 mi (2.9 km) se of Grand Case Airport; 9 mi (14.4 km) ne of Princess Juliana International Airport. **Facility:** 65 units. 49 one-bedroom standard units with efficiencies. 8 one- and 8 two-bedroom suites with kitchens. 1 story, exterior corridors. *Bath:* combo or shower only. **Parking:** on-site. **Terms:** open 12/1-8/26 & 10/1-11/30, 7 night minimum stay - seasonal, 3 day cancellation notice. **Amenities:** safes, hair dryers. *Some:* CD players, irons. **Pool(s):** outdoor. **Leisure Activities:** 2 lighted tennis courts. **Guest Services:** valet laundry, wireless Internet. **Business Services:** PC (fee). **Cards:** AX, MC, VI.

FEE / SOME UNITS

LA PLANTATION — **Phone:** (590)590-29-58-00 (15)

Hotel
$185-$670 12/1-4/12
$200-$355 4/13-11/30

Address: C5 Orient Bay **Location:** Northeast corner of island at Orient Bay. **Facility:** 52 units. 35 one-bedroom standard units with efficiencies. 17 one-bedroom suites with kitchens. 1 story, exterior corridors. *Bath:* shower only. **Parking:** on-site. **Terms:** office hours 8 am-9 pm, 30 day cancellation notice-fee imposed. **Amenities:** safes, irons, hair dryers. *Some:* CD players. **Pool(s):** outdoor. **Leisure Activities:** rental boats, rental sailboats, rental sailboards, exercise room. *Fee:* scuba diving, snorkeling, charter fishing, 2 lighted tennis courts, massage. **Guest Services:** valet laundry. **Business Services:** PC (fee). **Cards:** CB, DS, MC, VI.

ASK / SOME UNITS

PALM COURT HOTEL — **Phone:** 590/590-87-41-94 (17)

Motel
$255-$380 All Year

Address: C5 Orient Beach **Location:** Northeast corner of island; at Orient Beach. **Facility:** Designated smoking area. 24 one-bedroom standard units with efficiencies. 3 stories (no elevator), exterior corridors. *Bath:* shower only. **Parking:** on-site. **Terms:** office hours 9 am-7 pm, 30 day cancellation notice-fee imposed. **Amenities:** safes, hair dryers. **Pool(s):** outdoor. **Guest Services:** wireless Internet. **Cards:** MC, VI.

ASK / SOME UNITS

OYSTER POND (ST. MARTIN) (See map and index starting on p. 552)

WHERE TO STAY

CAPTAIN OLIVER'S RESORT **Phone:** (590)590-87-40-26 26

Hotel
$110-$275 All Year

Address: Oyster Pond **Location:** Oceanfront. 7.5 mi (12 km) e of Princess Juliana International Airport. **Facility:** 50 one-bedroom standard units. 1 story, exterior corridors. *Bath:* combo or shower only. **Parking:** on-site. **Terms:** office hours 7 am-11 pm, 3 night minimum stay - seasonal, 14 day cancellation notice, 7 day off season. **Amenities:** safes, honor bars, hair dryers. **Dining:** Captain Oliver's, see separate listing. **Pool(s):** outdoor. **Leisure Activities:** rental boats, rental sailboats, marina. *Fee:* scuba diving, snorkeling, charter fishing. **Guest Services:** valet laundry, area transportation, beauty salon, wireless Internet. **Business Services:** meeting rooms, PC. **Cards:** AX, MC, VI. Affiliated with A Preferred Hotel.

WHERE TO DINE

CAPTAIN OLIVER'S **Phone:** 590/590-87-30-00 44

Seafood
$12-$27

The deck, which overlooks Oyster Pond and the marina, is a cozy spot for sampling fresh seafood with French and Creole influences. Other good choices include offerings from the barbecue grill. Live entertainment is offered six nights a week, and from November to mid-June, the Saturday lobster buffet is a big draw. Casual dress. Entertainment. **Bar:** Full bar. **Reservations:** suggested. **Hours:** Open 12/1-9/3 & 9/21-11/30; 7-10:30 am, 11:30-5 & 6:30-10 pm. **Address:** Oyster Pond **Location:** 7.5 mi (11.2 km) e of Princess Juliana International Airport; in Captain Oliver's Resort. **Parking:** on-site. **Cards:** AX, DS, MC, VI.

ST. VINCENT AND THE GRENADINES

This index helps you "spot" where approved lodgings and restaurants are located on the corresponding detailed maps. Lodging daily rate range is for comparison only and show the property's high season. Restaurant rate range is a combination of lunch and/or dinner. Turn to the listing page for more detailed rate information and consult display ads for special promotions.

ARNOS VALE

Map Page	OA	Lodging	Diamond Rated	High Season	Page
1 / p. 566		Villa Lodge Hotel	♦♦	$130-$150	567

YOUNG ISLAND

Map Page	OA	Lodging	Diamond Rated	High Season	Page
3 / p. 566		Young Island Resort	♦♦♦	$448-$1222	569

VILLA

Map Page	OA	Lodging	Diamond Rated	High Season	Page
4 / p. 566		Beachcombers Hotel and Restaurant	♦	$75-$275	569

Map Page	OA	Restaurant	Diamond Rated	Cuisine	Meal Range	Page
(4) / p. 566		Lime N' Pub	♦♦	International	$16-$37	569

BEQUIA

Map Page	OA	Lodgings	Diamond Rated	High Season	Page
6 / p. 566		Firefly Bequia	♦♦♦	$525-$575	567
7 / p. 566		Sugar Apple Inn	♦♦	$85-$110	567

CANOUAN

Map Page	OA	Lodgings	Diamond Rated	High Season	Page
8 / p. 566		Raffles Resort Canouan Island	♦♦♦♦	$815-$1420	568
9 / p. 566		Tamarind Beach Hotel & Yacht Club	♦♦	$210-$730	568

PALM ISLAND

Map Page	OA	Lodging	Diamond Rated	High Season	Page
12 / p. 566	AAA	**Palm Island Resort** - see color ad p 568	♦♦♦	Rates not provided SAVE	568

KINGSTOWN

Map Page	OA	Restaurant	Diamond Rated	Cuisine	Meal Range	Page
(2) / p. 566		Basil's Bar & Restaurant	♦	International	$10-$26	568

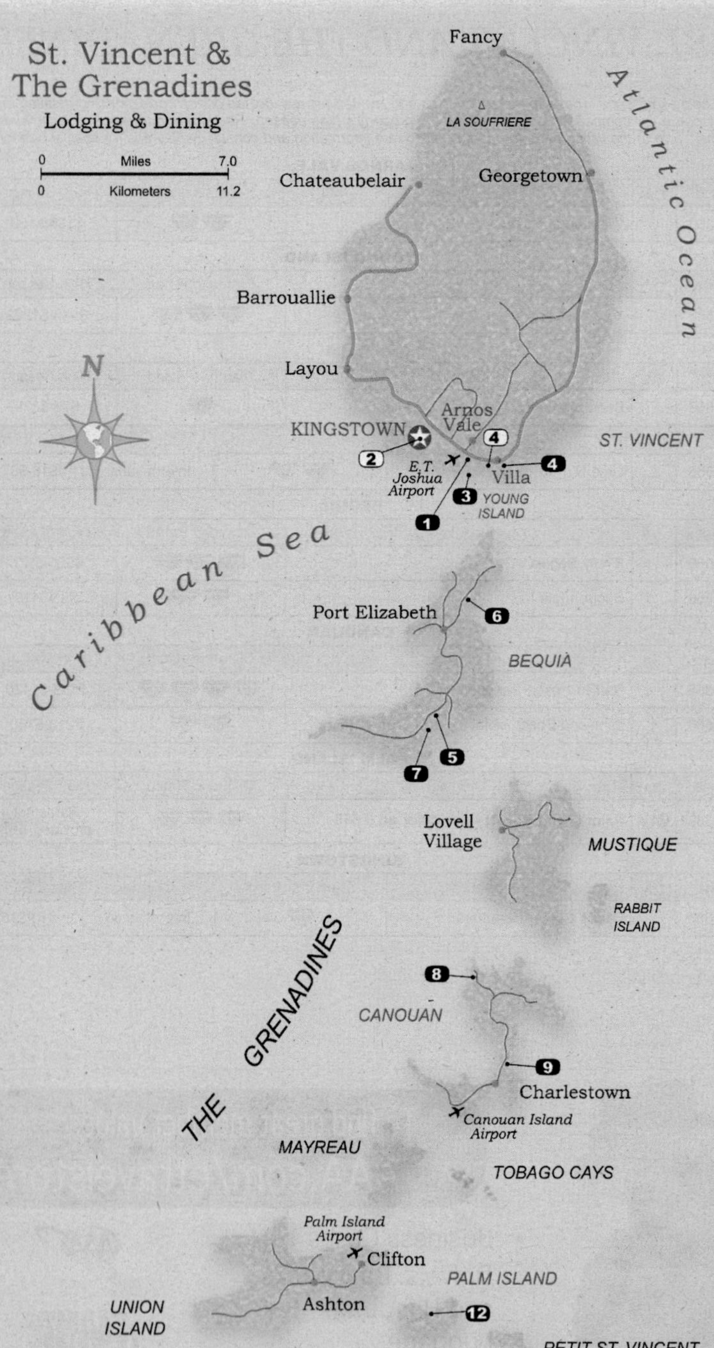
St. Vincent &
The Grenadines
Lodging & Dining
0 Miles 7.0
0 Kilometers 11.2
N
Fancy
LA SOUFRIERE
Atlantic Ocean
Chateaubelair
Georgetown
Barrouallie
Layou
Arnos Vale
KINGSTOWN
ST. VINCENT
2
4
4
E.T. Joshua Airport
Villa
3
YOUNG ISLAND
1
Caribbean Sea
Port Elizabeth
6
BEQUIA
5
7
Lovell Village
MUSTIQUE
RABBIT ISLAND
THE GRENADINES
8
CANOUAN
9
Charlestown
Canouan Island Airport
MAYREAU
TOBAGO CAYS
Palm Island Airport
Clifton
PALM ISLAND
UNION ISLAND
Ashton
12
PETIT ST. VINCENT
1523-E

ARNOS VALE

(See map and index starting on p. 566)

WHERE TO STAY

VILLA LODGE HOTEL

Country Inn

$130-$150 12/1-4/30

$115-$135 5/1-11/30

Book at AAA.com **Phone:** (784)458-4641 **1**

Address: Indian Bay **Location:** 3 mi (4.8 km) se of airport. **Facility:** Designated smoking area. 18 units. 10 one-bedroom standard units. 7 one- and 1 two-bedroom suites with efficiencies. 2 stories (no elevator), interior/exterior corridors. **Parking:** on-site. **Terms:** office hours 7 am-11 pm, 14 day cancellation notice. **Amenities:** safes, irons, hair dryers. **Pool(s):** outdoor. **Guest Services:** valet laundry, wireless Internet. **Business Services:** PC (fee). **Cards:** AX, DS, MC, VI.

ASK D

BEQUIA

(See map and index starting on p. 566)

WHERE TO STAY

FIREFLY BEQUIA

Hotel

$525-$575 All Year

Phone: 784/458-3414 **6**

Address: Spring Bay Rd **Location:** 1 mi (1.6 km) e of airport. **Facility:** 6 one-bedroom standard units. 1-2 stories, exterior corridors. *Bath:* shower only. **Parking:** on-site. **Terms:** age restrictions may apply, 45 day cancellation notice-fee imposed. **Amenities:** CD players, safes, honor bars, hair dryers. **Pool(s):** outdoor. **Leisure Activities:** snorkeling. *Fee:* massage. **Guest Services:** complimentary laundry, wireless Internet. **Cards:** AX, MC, VI.

SUGAR APPLE INN

Motel

$85-$110 All Year

Phone: 784/457-3148 **7**

Address: Friendship Bay Rd **Location:** 1.5 mi (2.4 km) s of airport; 1.5 mi (2.4 km) e of ferry dock; at Frienship Bay. **Facility:** Designated smoking area. 8 one-bedroom standard units with kitchens. 2 stories (no elevator), exterior corridors. *Bath:* shower only. **Parking:** on-site. **Terms:** 2 night minimum stay, 30 day cancellation notice. **Amenities:** DVD players, hair dryers. **Pool(s):** outdoor. **Guest Services:** wireless Internet. **Cards:** MC, VI.

CANOUAN (See map and index starting on p. 566)

WHERE TO STAY

RAFFLES RESORT CANOUAN ISLAND — **Phone:** 784/458-8000 — 8

Resort Hotel
$815-$1420 All Year

Address: Canouan, The Grenadines **Location:** Oceanfront. North side of island. **Facility:** On a secluded island, this world-class resort features two beaches, a golf course, 17th-century church, spa, fine dining restaurants and a casino. 156 units. 47 one-bedroom standard units. 63 one-, 45 two- and 1 three-bedroom suites. 1-2 stories, exterior corridors. **Parking:** no self-parking. **Amenities:** video library, CD players, high-speed Internet, dual phone lines, safes, honor bars, irons, hair dryers. *Some:* DVD players. **Pool(s):** outdoor. **Leisure Activities:** lifeguard on duty, paddleboats, sailboats, windsurfing, 4 lighted tennis courts, recreation programs, bicycles, playground, spa, volleyball. *Fee:* golf-18 holes. **Guest Services:** valet laundry, area transportation (fee), wireless Internet. **Business Services:** conference facilities, PC.

TAMARIND BEACH HOTEL & YACHT CLUB — **Phone:** 784/458-8044 — 9

Hotel
$210-$730 All Year

Address: Main Rd **Location:** Oceanfront. Just n of Grand Bay. **Facility:** 39 units. 31 one-bedroom standard units. 8 one-bedroom suites. 2 stories (no elevator), exterior corridors. *Bath:* combo or shower only. **Parking:** on-site. **Amenities:** safes, honor bars, hair dryers. **Guest Services:** valet laundry. **Business Services:** PC (fee). **Cards:** AX, CB, DC, DS, JC, MC, VI.

/ SOME UNITS

KINGSTOWN pop. 13,212 (See map and index starting on p. 566)

WHERE TO DINE

BASIL'S BAR & RESTAURANT — **Phone:** 784/457-2713 — 2

International
$10-$26

Convenient to businesses, shopping and the ferry dock, the downtown restaurant is in the historic Cobblestone Inn. Guests can stop in for the daily lunch buffet. Regional dishes reflect international influences. Casual dress. **Bar:** Full bar. **Reservations:** accepted. **Hours:** 8 am-10 pm. Closed major holidays; also Sun, except Carnival. **Address:** Upper Bay St **Location:** Downtown; at Cobblestone Inn. **Parking:** street. **Cards:** AX, MC, VI.

PALM ISLAND (See map and index starting on p. 566)

WHERE TO STAY

PALM ISLAND RESORT *Book great rates at AAA.com* — **Phone:** 784/458-8824 — 12

AAA SAVE

Resort Cottage
Rates not provided

Address: Palm Island **Location:** Oceanfront. 1 mi (1.6 km) e of Union Island, accessed via property boat launch. **Facility:** This cabana-village resort on a secluded private tropical island boasts a beautiful white sand beach; cottages feature private indoor/outdoor showers. 41 units. 5 one-bedroom standard units. 4 one-bedroom suites. 32 cottages. 1 story, exterior corridors. *Bath:* combo or shower only. **Parking:** no self-parking. **Terms:** age restrictions may apply. **Amenities:** safes, honor bars, irons, hair dryers. **Dining:** 2 restaurants, entertainment. **Pool(s):** outdoor. **Leisure Activities:** beach access, sailboats, windsurfing, boat dock, snorkeling, fishing, tennis court, croquet, bicycles, hiking trails, limited exercise equipment, horseshoes. *Fee:* charter fishing, yacht, massage. **Guest Services:** TV in common area. **Business Services:** PC. **Free Special Amenities: early check-in/late check-out.** ***(See color ad below)***

VILLA (See map and index starting on p. 566)

WHERE TO STAY

BEACHCOMBERS HOTEL AND RESTAURANT — **Phone:** 784/458-4283 — 4

Hotel
$75-$275 All Year

Address: Villa Main Rd **Location:** 3.5 mi (5.6 km) s of airport; center. **Facility:** Designated smoking area. 28 units. 27 one-bedroom standard units, some with whirlpools. 1 one-bedroom suite. 1-3 stories (no elevator), exterior corridors. *Bath:* shower only. **Parking:** on-site. **Terms:** office hours 7 am-10:30 pm, 14 day cancellation notice. **Amenities:** *Some:* DVD players, CD players, safes, irons, hair dryers. **Pool(s):** outdoor. **Leisure Activities:** sauna. **Guest Services:** valet laundry, wireless Internet. **Business Services:** PC (fee). **Cards:** AX, DS, MC, VI.

/ SOME UNITS

WHERE TO DINE

LIME N' PUB — **Phone:** 784/458-4227 — 4

International
$16-$37

Diners come from the street, dock or Villa Beach to enjoy casual, waterfront, alfresco dining. The menu includes a mix of West Indian and Continental cuisine. House specialties center on fresh seafood. Many coffee specialty drinks are available. Casual dress. **Bar:** Full bar. **Reservations:** suggested. **Hours:** 9 am-11 pm. Closed: 12/25. **Address:** Villa Harbour Landing **Location:** 4 mi (6.4 km) s of airport; adjacent to Young Island Ferry Landing; at Villa Harbour. **Parking:** on-site. **Cards:** AX, MC, VI.

YOUNG ISLAND (See map and index starting on p. 566)

WHERE TO STAY

YOUNG ISLAND RESORT — **Phone:** (784)458-4826 — 3

Cottage
$448-$1222 All Year

Address: South Coast **Location:** Oceanfront. 4 mi (6.4 km) s of airport to Young Island Ferry Landing; call box at landing. Located on private island just off the coast of St. Vincent. **Facility:** A 35-acre private island is the setting for this property offering cottages with ceiling fans, louvered windows, balconies and indoor/outdoor showers. 29 cottages. 1 story, exterior corridors. *Bath:* shower only. **Parking:** no self-parking. **Terms:** office hours 6:30 am-10 pm, 30 day cancellation notice-fee imposed. **Amenities:** safes, hair dryers. *Some:* high-speed Internet (fee). **Pool(s):** outdoor. **Leisure Activities:** paddleboats, sailboats, windsurfing, boat dock, snorkeling, lighted tennis court. *Fee:* massage. **Guest Services:** valet laundry, area transportation, wireless Internet. **Business Services:** business center. **Cards:** AX, MC, VI.

ASK FEE / SOME UNITS

TRINIDAD AND TOBAGO

Airport Accommodations

Map Page	OA	PIARCO INTERNATIONAL AIRPORT	Diamond Rated	High Season	Page
18 / p. 572		Holiday Inn Express Hotel & Suites Trincity Trinidad Airport, 1 mi (1.5 km) n	3 diamonds	$190-$300	576

Airport Accommodations

Map Page	OA	TOBAGO CROWN POINT AIRPORT	Diamond Rated	High Season	Page
8 / p. 572		Coco Reef Resort & Spa, 0.5 mi (0.8 km) n of terminal	3 diamonds	$310-$3646	573
9 / p. 572		Kariwak Village Hotel, just e of terminal	2 diamonds	$125	573
6 / p. 572		Rovanels Resort, 1.3 mi (2.1 km)	2 diamonds	$175-$265	573

Trinidad and Tobago

This index helps you "spot" where approved lodgings and restaurants are located on the corresponding detailed maps. Lodging daily rate range is for comparison only and show the property's high season. Restaurant rate range is a combination of lunch and/or dinner. Turn to the listing page for more detailed rate information and consult display ads for special promotions.

BLACK ROCK (TOBAGO)

Map Page	OA	Lodging	Diamond Rated	High Season	Page
4 / p. 572	AAA	**Plantation Beach Villas**	3 diamonds	$465-$735 SAVE	573

CROWN POINT (TOBAGO)

Map Page	OA	Lodgings	Diamond Rated	High Season	Page
6 / p. 572		Rovanels Resort	2 diamonds	$175-$265	573
8 / p. 572		Coco Reef Resort & Spa	3 diamonds	$310-$3646	573
9 / p. 572		Kariwak Village Hotel	2 diamonds	$125	573

Map Page	OA	Restaurants	Diamond Rated	Cuisine	Meal Range	Page
18 / p. 572		Kariwak Village Restaurant	2 diamonds	Caribbean	$12-$41	574
19 / p. 572		Cafe' Iguana	1 diamond	International	$10-$26	573
20 / p. 572		Cafe Coco	2 diamonds	International	$10-$25	573
21 / p. 572		Dillon's Seafood Restaurant	1 diamond	Seafood	$12-$24	573

PORT OF SPAIN (TRINIDAD)

Map Page	OA	Lodgings	Diamond Rated	High Season	Page
13 / p. 572	AAA	**Courtyard by Marriott Port of Spain**	3 diamonds	$216-$288 SAVE	574
14 / p. 572		Hilton Trinidad & Conference Centre - see color ad opposite title page	fyi	$235-$365	575
15 / p. 572		Kapok Hotel	2 diamonds	$175-$266	575
16 / p. 572		Crowne Plaza Trinidad	3 diamonds	$260	575

Map Page	OA	Restaurants	Diamond Rated	Cuisine	Meal Range	Page
3 / p. 572		Apsara	2 diamonds	Indian	$15-$31	575
5 / p. 572		Il Colosseo Restaurant	3 diamonds	Italian	$12-$35	576

Map Page	OA	Restaurants (cont'd)	Diamond Rated	Cuisine	Meal Range	Page
6 / p. 572		Solimar	♦♦♦	International	$16-$33	576
7 / p. 572		Joseph's	♦♦♦	International	$17-$38	576
8 / p. 572		Melange Restaurant	♦♦♦	International	$20-$40	576
9 / p. 572		Battimamzelle Restaurant	♦♦♦	International	$17-$42	576

TRINCITY (TRINIDAD)

Map Page	OA	Lodging	Diamond Rated	High Season	Page
18 / p. 572		Holiday Inn Express Hotel & Suites Trincity Trinidad Airport	♦♦♦	$190-$300	576

Map Page	OA	Restaurant	Diamond Rated	Cuisine	Meal Range	Page
10 / p. 572		Muscovado Restaurant	♦♦	International	$10-$25	576

MOUNT PLEASANT (TOBAGO)

Map Page	OA	Restaurants	Diamond Rated	Cuisine	Meal Range	Page
11 / p. 572		Cafe Melange	♦♦	Creole	$21-$30	574
12 / p. 572		Shirvan Watermill	♦♦♦	International	$19-$37	574
13 / p. 572		MeShells	♦♦	Steak & Seafood	$19-$47	574
14 / p. 572		Patino's Restaurant	♦♦	International	$22-$41	574

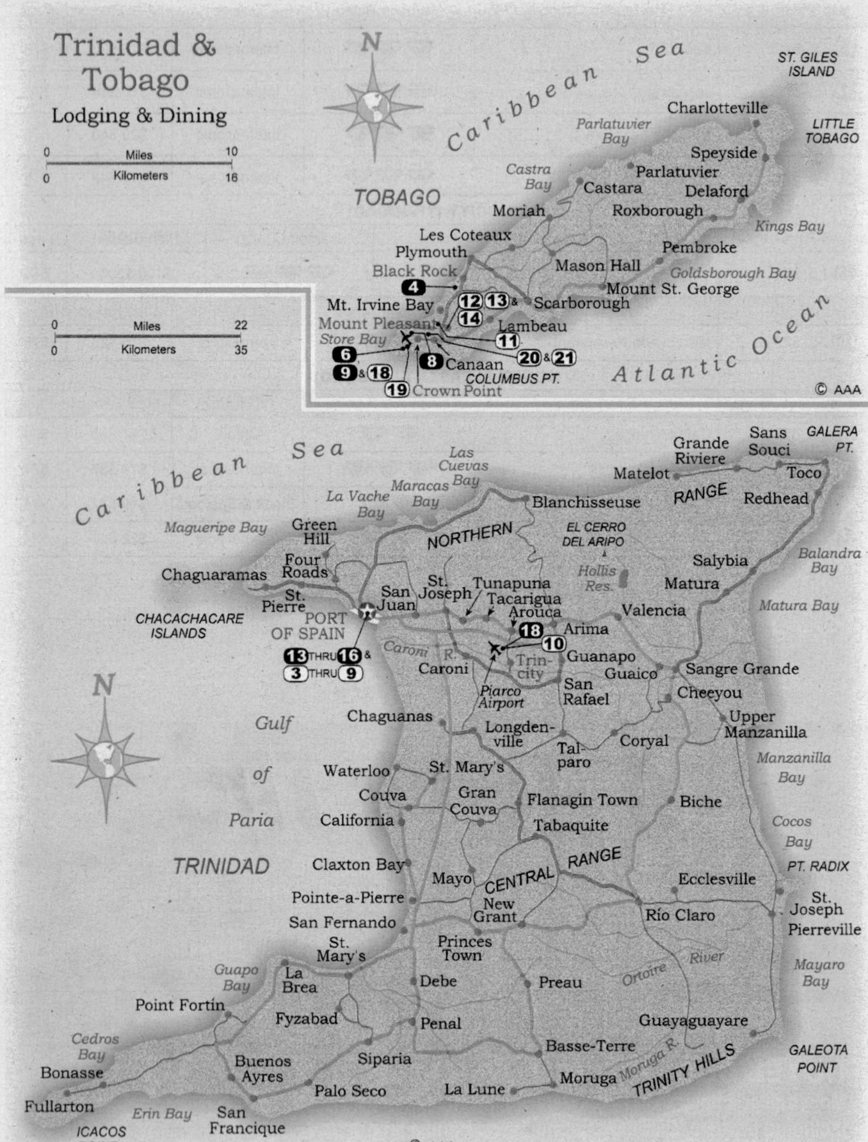
Trinidad & Tobago
Lodging & Dining
0 Miles 10
0 Kilometers 16
TOBAGO
Caribbean Sea
Atlantic Ocean
ST. GILES ISLAND
LITTLE TOBAGO
Charlotteville
Speyside
Parlatuvier Bay
Parlatuvier
Castra Bay
Castara
Delaford
Moriah
Roxborough
Kings Bay
Les Coteaux
Plymouth
Pembroke
Black Rock
Mason Hall
Goldsborough Bay
Mount St. George
Mt. Irvine Bay
Scarborough
Mount Pleasant
Lambeau
Store Bay
Canaan
COLUMBUS PT.
Crown Point
© AAA
0 Miles 22
0 Kilometers 35
Caribbean Sea
Las Cuevas Bay
Maracas Bay
La Vache Bay
Magueripe Bay
Green Hill
Four Roads
Chaguaramas
St. Pierre
CHACACHACARE ISLANDS
PORT OF SPAIN
San Juan
St. Joseph
Tunapuna
Tacarigua
Arouca
Arima
Blanchisseuse
NORTHERN RANGE
EL CERRO DEL ARIPO
Hollis Res.
Matelot
Grande Riviere
Sans Souci
GALERA PT.
Toco
Redhead
Salybia
Balandra Bay
Matura
Matura Bay
Valencia
Caroni R.
Caroni
Piarco Airport
Trincity
Guanapo
Guaico
San Rafael
Sangre Grande
Cheeyou
Upper Manzanilla
Manzanilla Bay
Gulf of Paria
TRINIDAD
Chaguanas
Longdenville
Talparo
Coryal
Waterloo
St. Mary's
Couva
Gran Couva
Flanagin Town
Biche
California
Tabaquite
Cocos Bay
Claxton Bay
Mayo
CENTRAL RANGE
Ecclesville
PT. RADIX
Pointe-a-Pierre
New Grant
Rio Claro
St. Joseph
Pierreville
San Fernando
St. Mary's
Princes Town
Ortoire River
Mayaro Bay
Guapo Bay
La Brea
Debe
Preau
Point Fortin
Fyzabad
Penal
Guayaguayare
Cedros Bay
Buenos Ayres
Siparia
Basse-Terre
Moruga R.
Moruga
TRINITY HILLS
GALEOTA POINT
Bonasse
Palo Seco
La Lune
Fullarton
Erin Bay
San Francique
ICACOS POINT
© AAA
1524-R

Tobago

BLACK ROCK (See map and index starting on p. 572)

WHERE TO STAY

PLANTATION BEACH VILLAS Phone: (868)639-9377 4

AAA SAVE

Vacation Rental House
$465-$735 All Year

Location: 7.5 mi (12 km) n of airport; on west coast. **Facility:** On a hill across a street from the beach, three-bedroom, three-bath villas offer large verandas with ocean views; only bedrooms have air-conditioning. 6 houses. 2 stories (no elevator), exterior corridors. *Bath:* shower only. **Parking:** on-site. **Terms:** office hours 8 am-6 pm, 3 night minimum stay, 45 day cancellation notice. **Amenities:** CD players, safes, irons, hair dryers. *Some:* DVD players. **Leisure Activities:** table tennis, volleyball. *Fee:* massage. **Guest Services:** complimentary laundry, wireless Internet. **Cards:** AX, MC, VI. **Free Special Amenities: early check-in/late check-out and high-speed Internet.**

CROWN POINT (See map and index starting on p. 572)

WHERE TO STAY

COCO REEF RESORT & SPA *Book at AAA.com* Phone: (868)639-8571 8

Resort Hotel
$310-$3646 All Year

Address: Lower Milford Rd **Location:** Oceanfront. 0.5 mi (0.8 km) e of Crown Point Airport; on Coconut Bay. **Facility:** Lush tropical foliage and a sugar-sand beach envelope this award-winning resort, where an attentive staff offers warm, Tobagonian hospitality. Designated smoking area. 135 units. 125 one-bedroom standard units. 6 one- and 4 two-bedroom suites, some with kitchens. 2-3 stories (no elevator), interior/exterior corridors. *Bath:* combo or shower only. **Parking:** on-site. **Terms:** 7 night minimum stay - seasonal, 14 day cancellation notice-fee imposed. **Amenities:** video library, honor bars, hair dryers. *Some:* DVD players, CD players, irons. **Pool(s):** outdoor. **Leisure Activities:** sauna, canoeing, paddleboats, sailboats, windsurfing, snorkeling, 2 lighted tennis courts, recreation programs, exercise room. *Fee:* scuba diving, bicycles, massage. **Guest Services:** valet laundry. **Business Services:** meeting rooms, business center. **Cards:** AX, MC, VI.

SOME UNITS

KARIWAK VILLAGE HOTEL Phone: (868)639-8442 9

Cottage
$125 12/1-4/14
$90 4/15-11/30

Address: Store Bay Local Rd **Location:** Just e of town. **Facility:** Meets AAA guest room security requirements. 24 units. 9 one-bedroom standard units. 15 cottages. 1 story, exterior corridors. *Bath:* shower only. **Parking:** on-site. **Terms:** office hours 7 am-10 pm, 14 day cancellation notice-fee imposed. **Amenities:** safes, irons, hair dryers. **Dining:** restaurant, see separate listing. **Pool(s):** outdoor. **Leisure Activities:** whirlpool, Tai Chai, yoga. *Fee:* massage. **Guest Services:** TV in common area, valet laundry, area transportation. **Business Services:** meeting rooms. **Cards:** AX, MC, VI.

ROVANELS RESORT Phone: 868/639-9666 6

Hotel
$175-$265 All Year

Address: Store Bay Local Rd **Location:** In Store Bay; 1.3 mi (2.1 km) e of airport. **Facility:** Designated smoking area. 62 one-bedroom standard units, some with kitchens and/or whirlpools. 1-2 stories (no elevator), exterior corridors. **Parking:** on-site. **Terms:** office hours 6:30 am-11 am, 14 day cancellation notice-fee imposed. **Amenities:** voice mail, irons, hair dryers. **Pool(s):** outdoor. **Guest Services:** valet laundry. **Business Services:** meeting rooms. **Cards:** AX, DS, MC, VI.

FEE

WHERE TO DINE

CAFE COCO Phone: 868/639-0996 20

International
$10-$25

Fun Caribbean atmosphere offering open air dining in modern art gallery type setting. Unique table tops are a centerpiece on their own. Good menu variety featuring a spicy blend of Island, Mexican and vegetarian specialties. Fresh ingredients. Casual dress. **Bar:** Full bar. **Reservations:** suggested. **Hours:** 4 pm-10:30 pm. **Address:** Pigeon Point Rd **Location:** 0.8 mi (1.3 km) e of Crown Point Airport. **Parking:** street. **Cards:** AX, MC, VI.

CAFE' IGUANA Phone: 868/631-8205 19

International
$10-$26

Adjacent to the airport and the center of Crown Point, this al fresco eatery carries out a bluesy jazz theme in its decor. The menu consists of many local favorites, including fish, baked chicken and curried dishes. Casual dress. Entertainment. **Bar:** Full bar. **Reservations:** accepted. **Hours:** Open 12/1-5/1 & 5/22-11/30; 8 am-10 pm, Fri & Sat-10:30 pm. Closed: Wed. **Address:** Store Bay Local Rd **Location:** Just e of Crown Point Airport. **Parking:** street. **Cards:** AX, MC, VI.

DILLON'S SEAFOOD RESTAURANT Phone: 868/639-8765 21

Seafood
$12-$24

Plain exterior, attractive dining room offering friendly and attentive service. A favorite with the locals. Excellent selection of fresh seafood offered daily. Casual, relaxed atmosphere. Casual dress. **Bar:** Full bar. **Reservations:** suggested. **Hours:** 6 pm-10 pm. Closed: Sun. **Address:** Main Rd **Location:** Center. **Parking:** street. **Cards:** MC, VI.

(See map and index starting on p. 572)

KARIWAK VILLAGE RESTAURANT Phone: 868/639-8442 (18)

Caribbean
$12-$41

Well-prepared and presented West Indian cuisine is served amid attractive island decor. The accent is on fresh, grown-on-the-premises herbs. Open-air seating contributes to the relaxing tropical atmosphere. Full-course set meals are offered at dinner, while the lunch menu centers on lighter selections, such as salads and sandwiches. Dressy casual. **Bar:** Full bar. **Reservations:** suggested. **Hours:** 7:30-10 am, 12:30-2:30 & 7:15-9:30 pm. **Address:** Store Bay Local Rd **Location:** Just outside Crown Point Airport; in Kariwak Village Hotel. **Parking:** on-site. **Cards:** AX, MC, VI.

MOUNT PLEASANT (See map and index starting on p. 572)

WHERE TO DINE

CAFE MELANGE Phone: 868/631-0121 (11)

Creole
$21-$30

In a Creole-style house, the casual restaurant exhibits some hints of fine dining. Seating is mostly al fresco on the expanded porch. The eclectic menu is a showcase for the chef's talents and versatility. Live music—jazz on Tuesdays, Happy and the Pleasant Pirates on Thursday, steelpan on Saturdays and Tobago folk on Sundays—perks up the atmosphere most nights. Casual dress. **Bar:** Full bar. **Reservations:** required. **Hours:** 6:30 pm-10:30 pm. Closed: Sun. **Address:** 133 Shirvan Rd **Location:** 3.8 mi (6.1 km) ne of Crown Point Airport. **Parking:** on-site. **Cards:** MC, VI.

MESHELLS Phone: 868/631-0353 (13)

Steak & Seafood
$19-$47

With a name like MeShells most diners expect a seafood-only menu but, while seafood does steal center stage, there are steaks, pork chops and salads available. Dressy casual. **Bar:** Full bar. **Reservations:** suggested. **Hours:** 6:30 pm-10 pm. Closed: 12/25. **Address:** Old Buccoo Rd **Location:** Corner of Shirvan and Buccoo rds. **Parking:** on-site. **Cards:** MC, VI.

PATINO'S RESTAURANT Phone: 868/639-9481 (14)

International
$22-$41

Offering a refreshing menu served in a garden-like ambiance, this restaurant is fast becoming a tourist and local favorite. Steaks, seafood, fish and a few pasta dishes are well prepared. Casual dress. **Bar:** Full bar. **Reservations:** suggested. **Hours:** Open 12/1-8/30 & 10/15-11/30; 6:30 pm-10 pm. Closed: 12/25; also Tues. **Address:** 198-202 Shirvan Rd **Location:** Corner of Shirvan and Buccoo rds; **Parking:** on-site. **Cards:** AX, MC, VI.

SHIRVAN WATERMILL Phone: 868/639-0000 (12)

International
$19-$37

In a restored sugar mill, the restaurant fills a peaceful, open-air setting. Candlelit tables, an attractive fountain and a fish pond lend to an elegant, yet relaxed, atmosphere. Creative regional selections center on seafood, duck, chicken and beef. Dressy casual. **Bar:** Full bar. **Reservations:** suggested, in season. **Hours:** 5 pm-10:30 pm. Closed: 12/25. **Address:** Shirvan Rd **Location:** 3.5 mi (5.6 km) e of Crown Point Airport, just n. **Parking:** on-site. **Cards:** MC, VI.

Trinidad

PORT OF SPAIN pop. 49,031 (See map and index starting on p. 572)

WHERE TO STAY

COURTYARD BY MARRIOTT PORT OF SPAIN Phone: 868/627-5555 (13)

SAVE

Hotel
$216-$288 All Year

Address: Audrey Jeffers Hwy **Location:** At Invaders Bay; 1.7 mi (2.7 km) n of downtown; across from H Crawford Stadium and adjacent to Movie Town. **Facility:** Meets AAA guest room security requirements. Smoke free premises. 119 units. 116 one-bedroom standard units, some with whirlpools. 3 one-bedroom suites with whirlpools. 4 stories, interior corridors. **Parking:** on-site. **Terms:** cancellation fee imposed. **Amenities:** high-speed Internet, dual phone lines, voice mail, safes, irons, hair dryers. *Some:* DVD players, CD players. **Pool(s):** outdoor. **Leisure Activities:** exercise room. **Guest Services:** valet and coin laundry, wireless Internet. **Business Services:** meeting rooms, business center. **Cards:** AX, MC, VI. **Free Special Amenities: newspaper and high-speed Internet.**

AAA Benefit:
Members save a minimum 5% off the best available rate.

(See map and index starting on p. 572)

CROWNE PLAZA TRINIDAD Book at AAA.com Phone: (868)625-3366 16

Hotel
$260 All Year

Address: Wrightson Rd **Location:** Center of downtown; 15 mi (24.1 km) nw of Piarco International Airport. **Facility:** Meets AAA guest room security requirements. 243 units. 227 one-bedroom standard units. 16 one-bedroom suites. 15 stories, interior corridors. *Bath:* combo or shower only. **Parking:** on-site. **Amenities:** CD players, high-speed Internet, dual phone lines, voice mail, safes, irons, hair dryers. **Pool(s):** outdoor. **Leisure Activities:** exercise room. *Fee:* massage. **Guest Services:** valet laundry, beauty salon, wireless Internet. **Business Services:** conference facilities, business center. **Cards:** AX, MC, VI.

/ SOME UNITS

HILTON TRINIDAD & CONFERENCE CENTRE Phone: (868)624-3211 14

fyi
Hotel
$235-$365 All Year

Under major renovation, scheduled to be completed March 2009. **Last rated:** **Address:** Lady Young Rd **Location:** On Belmont Hill; off Lady Young and Circular rds overlooking Queen's Park Savannah. **Facility:** 412 units. 385 one-bedroom standard units. 27 one-bedroom suites, some with kitchens and/or whirlpools. 6-9 stories, interior corridors. *Bath:* combo or shower only. **Parking:** on-site. **Terms:** 1-30 night minimum stay, cancellation fee imposed. **Amenities:** high-speed Internet, voice mail, safes, honor bars, irons, hair dryers. *Some:* DVD players, CD players. **Pool(s):** outdoor. **Leisure Activities:** sauna, 2 lighted tennis courts, exercise room. *Fee:* massage. **Guest Services:** valet laundry, wireless Internet. **Business Services:** conference facilities, business center. **Cards:** AX, DC, MC, VI. ***(See color ad opposite title page)***

/ SOME UNITS

KAPOK HOTEL Book at AAA.com Phone: (868)622-5765 15

Hotel
$175-$266 All Year

Address: 16-18 Cotton Hill, St. Clair **Location:** Just n of jct Circular and Maraval rds; north end of Queen's Park Savannah. **Facility:** 94 units. 82 one-bedroom standard units, some with efficiencies. 12 one-bedroom suites, some with kitchens. 10 stories, interior corridors. *Bath:* combo or shower only. **Parking:** on-site. **Terms:** 3 day cancellation notice-fee imposed. **Amenities:** high-speed Internet (fee), voice mail, safes, irons, hair dryers. **Pool(s):** outdoor. **Leisure Activities:** exercise room. **Guest Services:** valet and coin laundry, wireless Internet. **Business Services:** meeting rooms, business center. **Cards:** AX, MC, VI.

/ SOME UNITS

WHERE TO DINE

APSARA Phone: 868/627-7364 3

Indian
$15-$31

In one of the mansions that grace the streets of Queen's Savannah, the fine Indian restaurant prepares curries, tandoori and a variety of naans that please the palate. Servers in authentic Indian attire grace the well-appointed dining room. Dressy casual. **Bar:** Full bar. **Reservations:** required. **Hours:** 11 am-3 & 6-11 pm. Closed: 1/1, 12/25; also 12/26, Sun, Boxing Day, Good Friday & for lunch on public holidays. **Address:** 13 Queen's Park E **Location:** Downtown; east side of Queen's Park Savannah. **Parking:** on-site and valet. **Cards:** AX, CB, DC, DS, JC, MC, VI. **Historic**

(See map and index starting on p. 572)

BATTIMAMZELLE RESTAURANT **Phone:** 868/621-0541 (9)

International
$17-$42

An intimate dining area, with the choice of indoor or outdoor garden seating, offers detailed service and an award winning wine list. The cuisine is nouvelle West Indian crated by a locally well-known celebrity chef. Dressy casual. **Bar:** Full bar. **Reservations:** required. **Hours:** Open 12/1-12/2 & 1/2-11/30; 11 am-3 & 6-11 pm. Closed: Sun & for lunch on public holidays. **Address:** 44 Coblentz Ave **Location:** In Cascade section of downtown. **Parking:** on-site. **Cards:** AX, MC, VI.

IL COLOSSEO RESTAURANT **Phone:** 868/628-1494 (5)

Italian
$12-$35

Elegantly upscale decor and polished, refined service enrich the dining experience. The broad menu lists Southern and Northern Italian preparations of veal, beef, chicken, fresh fish and other seafood, as well as a range of skillfully prepared pasta dishes. To finish the evening meal, take a look at the dessert trolley, which is a showcase for no fewer than 10 sweet treats. Dressy casual. Entertainment. **Bar:** Full bar. **Reservations:** required. **Hours:** 11:30 am-2:30 & 6:30-10:15 pm, Sat from 6:30 pm. Closed major holidays; also 12/24, 12/26, Sun, Easter Monday, Good Friday & Carnival. **Address:** 16 Rust St **Location:** Downtown; in St. Clair sector. **Parking:** on-site. **Cards:** AX, MC, VI.

JOSEPH'S **Phone:** 868/622-5557 (7)

International
$17-$38

A romantic mood blooms in the refined garden setting, where live music occasionally enhances the atmosphere. The cuisine ranges from Continental and West Indies to Middle Eastern. Some items to consider include escargots, tabbouleh, frog's legs, kibbeh and lamb specialties. Dressy casual. **Bar:** Full bar. **Reservations:** suggested. **Hours:** 11:30 am-2:30 & 6:30-10:30 pm, Sat from 6:30 pm. Closed: Sun & for lunch on public holidays. **Address:** 3A Rookery Nook Ave **Location:** Maravel section of Port of Spain; in Rookery Nook. **Parking:** on-site. **Cards:** AX, CB, DC, DS, JC, MC, VI.

MELANGE RESTAURANT **Phone:** 868/628-8687 (8)

International
$20-$40

Chef/proprietor Moses Reuben has created a dream restaurant in a former stately house. The varied menu features items such as lobster bisque, roasted rack of lamb, surf and turf and shrimp Santa Fe. Dapper servers are attentive and congenial. Those inclined to lunch can partake of an ever-changing four-course lunch buffet served with a complimentary glass of wine. Dressy casual. **Bar:** Full bar. **Reservations:** suggested. **Hours:** 11:30 am-2:30 & 7-10:30 pm, Mon-2:30 pm. Closed: Sun & for lunch on public holidays. **Address:** 40 Ariapita Ave **Location:** Corner of Ariapita Ave and Cornelio St; in Woodbrook. **Parking:** street. **Cards:** AX, CB, DC, DS, JC, MC, VI.

SOLIMAR **Phone:** 868/624-6267 (6)

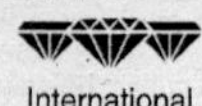

International
$16-$33

First-timers shouldn't be prejudiced by the rustic, subtly unremarkable decor. Joe Brown is one of the most respected chefs in Trinidad, and meals that come from his kitchen are legendary. He searches for the finest ingredients to use in such dishes as the uncommonly good callaloo soup with crabmeat. Lamb loin and swordfish are two favorite entrees. Joe bakes bread daily and prepares an array of desserts, including creme brulee flambeed tableside with sambuca. Dapper servers exhibit finesse. Dressy casual. **Bar:** Full bar. **Reservations:** required. **Hours:** 6 pm-10:30 pm, Fri also 11:30 am-2 pm. Closed major holidays; also 12/24, Sun & Good Friday. **Address:** 6 Nook Ave **Location:** Center of downtown; in St. Anns sector; just off Queens Park Savannah. **Parking:** valet. **Cards:** AX, MC, VI.

TRINCITY (See map and index starting on p. 572)

WHERE TO STAY

HOLIDAY INN EXPRESS HOTEL & SUITES TRINCITY TRINIDAD AIRPORT *Book at AAA.com* **Phone:** (868)669-6209 (18)

Hotel
$190-$300 All Year

Address: 1 Exposition Dr **Location:** 1 mi (1.5 km) n of airport. **Facility:** 82 one-bedroom standard units. 3 stories, interior corridors. *Bath:* combo or shower only. **Parking:** on-site. **Amenities:** high-speed Internet, voice mail, safes, irons, hair dryers. **Pool(s):** outdoor. **Leisure Activities:** exercise room. **Guest Services:** area transportation, wireless Internet. **Business Services:** meeting rooms, business center. **Cards:** AX, MC, VI.

S D / SOME UNITS

WHERE TO DINE

MUSCOVADO RESTAURANT **Phone:** 868/640-9259 (10)

International
$10-$25

Part of a country club golf course that's open to the public, this refined eatery employs a young, eager staff that serves international and West Indies cuisine. Grilled fish, meats and curries line the menu. Dressy casual. **Bar:** Full bar. **Reservations:** suggested. **Hours:** 11 am-10 pm. **Address:** Sunrise Loop Rd **Location:** At Millennium Lakes Golf & Country Club. **Parking:** on-site. **Cards:** AX, MC, VI.

TURKS AND CAICOS ISLANDS

This index helps you "spot" where approved lodgings and restaurants are located on the corresponding detailed maps. Lodging daily rate range is for comparison only and show the property's high season. Restaurant rate range is a combination of lunch and/or dinner. Turn to the listing page for more detailed rate information and consult display ads for special promotions.

NORTH CAICOS

Map Page	OA	Lodging	Diamond Rated	High Season	Page
1 / p. 578		Parrot Cay Resort & Como Shambhala Retreat	♦♦♦♦	$315-$950	579

PROVIDENCIALES

Map Page	OA	Lodgings	Diamond Rated	High Season	Page
5 / p. 578		The Tuscany	♦♦♦	$525-$1300	581
6 / p. 578		Grace Bay Club	♦♦♦♦	$501-$1208	580
7 / p. 578		Ocean Club Resorts Ocean Club and Ocean Club West	♦♦♦	$180-$910	580
8 / p. 578		Royal West Indies Resort	♦♦♦	$180-$845	581
10 / p. 578		Caribbean Paradise Inn	♦♦	$140-$235	579
11 / p. 578	AAA	**Villa Renaissance**	♦♦♦	$295-$1595 SAVE	583
12 / p. 578		Le Vele	♦♦♦	$348-$1484	580
13 / p. 578	AAA	**Point Grace**	♦♦♦♦	$425-$3281 SAVE	580
15 / p. 578		Sibonne Beach Hotel	♦♦	$110-$395	581
16 / p. 578	AAA	**The Regent Palms Turks and Caicos - see color ad p 582**	♦♦♦♦	$325-$2300 SAVE	581
17 / p. 578	AAA	**Comfort Suites-Turks and Caicos - see color ad p 579**	♦♦	$145-$180 SAVE	580
19 / p. 578	AAA	**Trade Winds Condotel**	♦♦	$235-$365 SAVE	581
21 / p. 578	AAA	**The Reef Residences on Grace Bay - see color ad p 581**	♦♦♦	$250-$1325 SAVE	580

Map Page	OA	Restaurants	Diamond Rated	Cuisine	Meal Range	Page
5 / p. 578		Mango Reef Restaurant	♦♦	Caribbean	$7-$29	585
6 / p. 578		Calico Jacks Bar and Restaurant	♦♦	International	$9-$22	584
7 / p. 578		Anacaona	♦♦♦	Mediterranean	$10-$41	583
8 / p. 578	AAA	**Grace's Cottage**	♦♦♦	International	$43-$54	584
9 / p. 578		Hemingway's on the Beach	♦♦	International	$9-$28	584
10 / p. 578		Bay Bistro	♦♦♦	International	$12-$30	583
11 / p. 578		Parallel23	♦♦♦	International	$25-$37	585
13 / p. 578		Caicos Cafe	♦♦	Seafood	$10-$34	584
17 / p. 578		Bella Luna Ristorante	♦♦♦	Regional Italian	$16-$32	584
18 / p. 578		Danny Buoys Irish Pub and Restaurant	♦♦	Irish	$10-$25	584
20 / p. 578		Saltmills Cafe	♦	International	$10-$16	585
21 / p. 578		Iguana Provo's First Seafood and Steakhouse	♦♦♦	Steak & Seafood	$18-$30	584
23 / p. 578		Simba	♦♦♦	Asian	$18-$46	585
24 / p. 578		Magnolia Wine Bar & Restaurant	♦♦♦	International	$22-$31	585
27 / p. 578		Coyaba	♦♦♦	New Caribbean	$32-$50	584
28 / p. 578		Baci Ristorante	♦♦	Italian	$12-$28	583
29 / p. 578		The Beach Cafe	♦♦	Continental	$9-$27	584
30 / p. 578		The Tiki Hut-Cabana Bar and Grill	♦♦	International	$10-$29	585

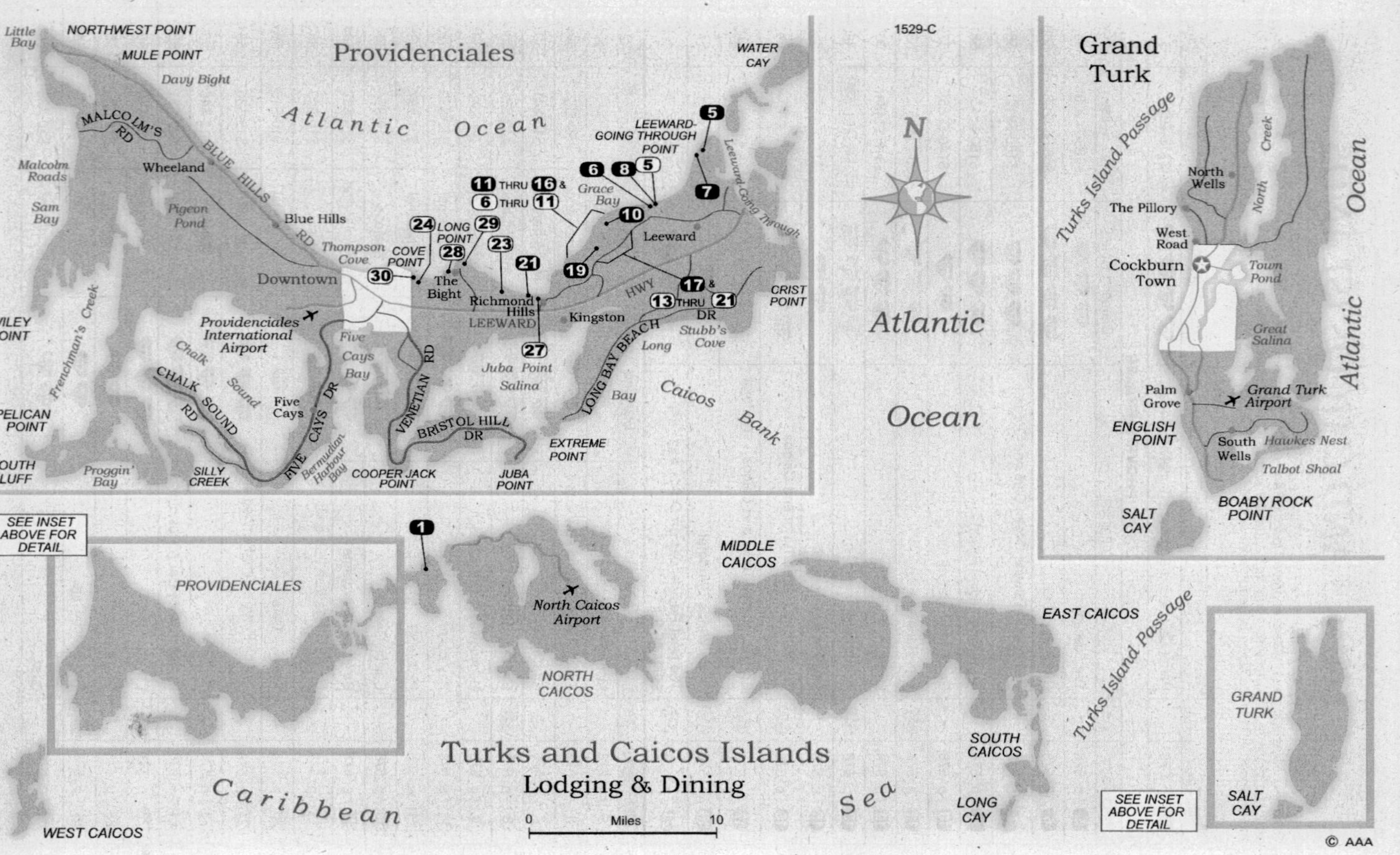
Turks and Caicos Islands
Lodging & Dining
Grand Turk
Providenciales
Atlantic Ocean
Caribbean Sea
Turks Island Passage
Caicos Bank
1529-C
Miles
0
10
SEE INSET ABOVE FOR DETAIL
© AAA
WEST CAICOS
PROVIDENCIALES
NORTH CAICOS
North Caicos Airport
MIDDLE CAICOS
EAST CAICOS
SOUTH CAICOS
LONG CAY
GRAND TURK
SALT CAY
Cockburn Town
The Pillory
West Road
North Wells
North Creek
Town Pond
Great Salina
Grand Turk Airport
Palm Grove
South Wells
Hawkes Nest
Talbot Shoal
ENGLISH POINT
BOABY ROCK POINT
NORTHWEST POINT
MULE POINT
Davy Bight
Little Bay
Malcolm Roads
Sam Bay
WILEY POINT
PELICAN POINT
SOUTH BLUFF
Proggin' Bay
Frenchman's Creek
MALCOLM'S RD
Wheeland
Pigeon Pond
BLUE HILLS RD
Blue Hills
Downtown
Thompson Cove
Providenciales International Airport
Chalk Sound
CHALK SOUND RD
SILLY CREEK
Five Cays
FIVE CAYS DR
Bermudian Harbour Bay
Five Cays Bay
COOPER JACK POINT
VENETIAN RD
BRISTOL HILL DR
JUBA POINT
Juba Point Salina
COVE POINT
LONG POINT
The Bight
Richmond Hills
LEEWARD
Kingston
EXTREME POINT
LONG BAY BEACH DR
Long Bay
Stubb's Cove
CRIST POINT
Leeward
Leeward-Going Through
LEEWARD-GOING THROUGH POINT
WATER CAY
Grace Bay
HWY
11 THRU 16 &
6 THRU 11
13 THRU 17 & 21
1
5
6
7
8
10
19
21
23
24
27
28
29
30

NORTH CAICOS

(See map and index starting on p. 578)

WHERE TO STAY

PARROT CAY RESORT & COMO SHAMBHALA RETREAT

Resort Hotel
$315-$950 All Year

Phone: 649/946-7788 **1**

Address: Parrot Cay **Location:** Oceanfront. Private island off northwest coast of North Caicos Island; between Providenciales and North Caicos. **Facility:** The world-renowned, award-winning resort is set on a private island and offers large units with upscale amenities, a luxury spa and attentive service. Meets AAA guest room security requirements. 65 units. 44 one-bedroom standard units. 13 one-, 2 two- and 6 three-bedroom suites, some with efficiencies or kitchens. 1-2 stories (no elevator), exterior corridors. **Parking:** no self-parking. **Terms:** 3 night minimum stay, 30 day cancellation notice. **Amenities:** video library, DVD players, CD players, voice mail, safes, honor bars, hair dryers. *Some:* high-speed Internet. **Pool(s):** 2 outdoor. **Leisure Activities:** saunas, whirlpools, steamrooms, canoeing, sailboats, windsurfing, 2 lighted tennis courts, exercise room, spa, pilates, yoga. *Fee:* snorkeling. **Guest Services:** valet laundry. **Business Services:** PC. **Cards:** AX, MC, VI.

D / SOME UNITS

PROVIDENCIALES pop. 15,000

(See map and index starting on p. 578)

WHERE TO STAY

CARIBBEAN PARADISE INN

Hotel
$140-$235 All Year

Phone: (649)946-5020 **10**

Address: Grace Bay Rd **Location:** North coast at Grace Bay; 9 mi (14.4 km) e of airport. **Facility:** 16 one-bedroom standard units. 2 stories (no elevator), exterior corridors. *Bath:* shower only. **Parking:** on-site. **Terms:** office hours 9 am-8 pm, 21 day cancellation notice-fee imposed. **Amenities:** voice mail, safes, irons, hair dryers. **Dining:** Coyaba, see separate listing. **Pool(s):** outdoor. **Guest Services:** wireless Internet. **Cards:** AX, MC, VI.

▼ See AAA listing p 580 ▼

COMFORT SUITES-TURKS AND CAICOS — **Phone:** 649/946-8888 **17**

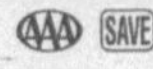

Motel
$145-$180 All Year

Address: Grace Bay Rd **Location:** North coast at Grace Bay; 8 mi (12.8 km) from airport. Located adjacent to the Ports of Call Shopping and Dining Complex. **Facility:** Meets AAA guest room security requirements. Smoke free premises. 98 one-bedroom standard units. 3 stories (no elevator), interior/exterior corridors. **Parking:** on-site. **Terms:** 14 day cancellation notice-fee imposed. **Amenities:** voice mail, safes, hair dryers. **Pool(s):** outdoor. **Leisure Activities:** slot machines. **Guest Services:** wireless Internet. **Business Services:** PC. **Cards:** AX, DC, DS, MC, VI. **Free Special Amenities: continental breakfast and high-speed Internet.** *(See color ad p 579)*

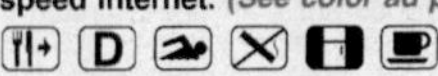

GRACE BAY CLUB — **Phone:** 649/946-5050 **6**

Hotel
$501-$1208 All Year

Address: Inner Grace Bay Cir **Location:** Grace Bay; 8.7 mi (13.9 km) e of airport. **Facility:** On Grace Bay, this oceanfront property offers spacious one-room units to three-bedroom condominiums, adult and family-friendly pools and a spa. 118 units. 59 one-bedroom standard units. 59 two-bedroom suites with kitchens. 3 stories, exterior corridors. **Parking:** on-site. **Terms:** office hours 7 am-11 pm, 30 day cancellation notice. **Amenities:** video library, DVD players, CD players, voice mail, safes, irons, hair dryers. **Dining:** Anacaona, see separate listing. **Pool(s):** 2 outdoor. **Leisure Activities:** whirlpools, sailboats, windsurfing, snorkeling, 2 lighted tennis courts, bicycles, exercise room, spa. **Guest Services:** area transportation, wireless Internet. **Business Services:** meeting rooms, business center. **Cards:** AX, DC, DS, MC, VI.

/ SOME UNITS

LE VELE — **Phone:** (649)941-8800 **12**

Condominium
$348-$1484 All Year

Address: Grace Bay Rd **Location:** Oceanfront. Grace Bay; 6 mi (9.9 km) e of airport. Located in Princess Alexander Park. **Facility:** An Italian-inspired design, spacious guest units with solid wood furniture and 30-foot balconies identify this condo-hotel with views of Grace Bay. Meets AAA guest room security requirements. Designated smoking area. 13 units. 3 one-bedroom standard units with efficiencies. 4 one-, 4 two- and 2 three-bedroom suites with kitchens. 5 stories, interior/exterior corridors. **Parking:** on-site. **Terms:** 21 day cancellation notice-fee imposed. **Amenities:** video library, DVD players, CD players, voice mail, safes, hair dryers. *Some:* irons. **Pool(s):** outdoor. **Leisure Activities:** bicycles, exercise room. **Guest Services:** valet and coin laundry, wireless Internet. **Business Services:** PC. **Cards:** AX, DS, MC, VI.

OCEAN CLUB RESORTS OCEAN CLUB AND OCEAN CLUB WEST — **Phone:** 649/946-5880 **7**

Condominium
$180-$910 All Year

Address: Grace Bay Rd **Location:** Oceanfront. North coast at Grace Bay; 9.7 mi (15.5 km) e of airport. **Facility:** These two different properties one mile apart offer varied studio and one-, two- and three-bedroom, condominium-style units. Meets AAA guest room security requirements. 164 condominiums. 3 stories (no elevator), interior/exterior corridors. **Parking:** on-site. **Terms:** office hours 6 am-11 pm, check-in 4 pm, 21 day cancellation notice-fee imposed. **Amenities:** video library, voice mail, safes, irons, hair dryers. *Some:* DVD players, CD players. **Pool(s):** 3 outdoor. **Leisure Activities:** rental boats, rental canoes, rental sailboats, rental sailboards, fishing, 3 lighted tennis courts, bicycles, exercise room. *Fee:* scuba diving, snorkeling, charter fishing, massage. **Guest Services:** complimentary laundry, area transportation, wireless Internet. **Business Services:** meeting rooms, PC. **Cards:** AX, DS, MC, VI.

/ SOME UNITS

POINT GRACE *Book great rates at AAA.com* — **Phone:** (649)946-5096 **13**

Hotel
$425-$3281 All Year

Address: Grace Bay **Location:** Oceanfront. 7.6 mi (12.1 km) e of airport; Grace Bay. Located in Princess Alexander Park, a marine reserve. **Facility:** Exquisite property for those with discriminating tastes; the spacious, equipped to the hilt suites feature Indonesian furniture and exotic fabrics. 28 units. 11 one-, 13 two- and 4 three-bedroom suites with kitchens, some with whirlpools. 4 stories, exterior corridors. **Parking:** on-site. **Terms:** age restrictions may apply, 30 day cancellation notice-fee imposed. **Amenities:** video library, DVD players, CD players, voice mail, safes, irons, hair dryers. *Some:* fax. **Dining:** Grace's Cottage, see separate listing. **Pool(s):** outdoor. **Leisure Activities:** whirlpool, sailboats, windsurfing, snorkeling, kayaks, bicycles, spa. *Fee:* scuba diving. **Guest Services:** valet and coin laundry, airport transportation-Providenciales International Airport, area transportation-golf course, fitness center, tennis facilities, wireless Internet. **Business Services:** PC. **Cards:** AX, MC, VI. **Free Special Amenities: continental breakfast and newspaper.**

/ SOME UNITS

THE REEF RESIDENCES ON GRACE BAY — **Phone:** (649)941-3713 **21**

Hotel
$250-$1325 All Year

Address: Penns Rd **Location:** Oceanfront. Grace Bay; 6.2 mi (9.9 km) e of airport. **Facility:** 49 units. 4 one-bedroom standard units. 38 one- and 7 two-bedroom suites with kitchens, some with whirlpools. 3 stories (no elevator), exterior corridors. *Bath:* some combo or shower only. **Parking:** on-site. **Terms:** office hours 7 am-10 pm, 14 day cancellation notice-fee imposed. **Amenities:** video library (fee), high-speed Internet, voice mail, safes, irons, hair dryers. *Some:* DVD players, CD players. **Dining:** The Beach Cafe, see separate listing. **Pool(s):** 2 outdoor. **Leisure Activities:** snorkeling & rental equipment, exercise room, spa. *Fee:* scuba diving. **Guest Services:** valet and coin laundry, wireless Internet. **Business Services:** PC. **Cards:** AX, MC, VI. *(See color ad p 581)*

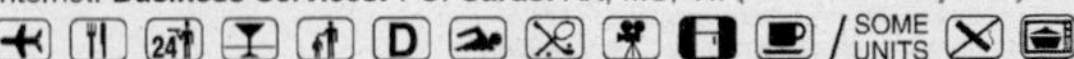

THE REGENT PALMS TURKS AND CAICOS *Book great rates at AAA.com* **Phone:** (649)946-8666 

Resort Hotel
$325-$2300 All Year

Address: Grace Bay Rd **Location:** Oceanfront. Grace Bay; 6.9 mi (11.1 km) e of airport. **Facility:** One of the newest upscale resort hotels on the island, The Palms promises attentive service and spacious units in island-style, refined surroundings. Meets AAA guest room security requirements. Designated smoking area. 164 units. 52 one-bedroom standard units. 52 one-, 52 two- and 8 three-bedroom suites with kitchens, some with whirlpools. 5 stories, interior corridors. **Parking:** on-site. **Terms:** 21 day cancellation notice-fee imposed. **Amenities:** video library, DVD players, CD players, high-speed Internet, voice mail, safes, irons, hair dryers. **Dining:** Parallel23, see separate listing. **Pool(s):** outdoor. **Leisure Activities:** saunas, whirlpool, steamrooms, sailboats, windsurfing, snorkeling, kayaks, personal watercraft, lighted tennis court, spa. *Fee:* charter fishing. **Guest Services:** valet laundry, wireless Internet. **Business Services:** meeting rooms, PC. **Cards:** AX, MC, VI. *(See color ad p 582)*

ROYAL WEST INDIES RESORT **Phone:** (649)946-5004 8

Condominium
$180-$845 All Year

Address: Grace Bay Rd **Location:** Oceanfront. 8.8 mi (14.1 km) e of airport. **Facility:** Well landscaped grounds buffet the gorgeous strand of beach. The rooms are smartly designed and handsomely decorated in colonial Caribbean decor. Designated smoking area. 92 units. 60 one-bedroom standard units with efficiencies. 31 one- and 1 two-bedroom suites with kitchens. 3 stories (no elevator), exterior corridors. *Bath:* combo or shower only. **Parking:** on-site. **Terms:** 3-5 night minimum stay - seasonal, 21 day cancellation notice. **Amenities:** DVD players, CD players, voice mail, safes, irons, hair dryers. **Dining:** Mango Reef Restaurant, see separate listing. **Pool(s):** 2 outdoor. **Leisure Activities:** whirlpool, sailboats, snorkeling, bicycles. *Fee:* massage. **Guest Services:** complimentary laundry, wireless Internet. **Business Services:** PC. **Cards:** AX, MC, VI.

ASK

SIBONNE BEACH HOTEL **Phone:** (649)946-5547 15

Hotel
$110-$395 All Year

Address: The Bight **Location:** Oceanfront. Northeast coast at Grace Bay; 7.1 mi (11.4 km) e of airport. **Facility:** Designated smoking area. 30 units. 29 one-bedroom standard units. 1 one-bedroom suite with kitchen. 2 stories (no elevator), exterior corridors. *Bath:* shower only. **Parking:** on-site. **Terms:** office hours 8 am-10 pm, 21 day cancellation notice-fee imposed. **Amenities:** voice mail, safes, irons, hair dryers. **Dining:** Bay Bistro, see separate listing. **Pool(s):** outdoor. **Guest Services:** valet laundry. **Cards:** AX, MC, VI.

/ SOME UNITS

TRADE WINDS CONDOTEL *Book great rates at AAA.com* **Phone:** (649)946-5194 19

Condominium
$235-$365 All Year

Address: Grace Bay Rd **Location:** 6.2 mi (9.9 km) e of airport. **Facility:** 18 one-bedroom suites with kitchens. 3 stories (no elevator), exterior corridors. *Bath:* shower only. **Parking:** on-site. **Terms:** office hours 7:30 am-6 pm, 30 day cancellation notice. **Amenities:** voice mail, safes, irons, hair dryers. *Some:* DVD players, CD players. **Pool(s):** outdoor. **Leisure Activities:** barbecue grills, bicycles. **Guest Services:** valet and coin laundry, wireless Internet. **Business Services:** PC. **Cards:** AX, CB, DC, DS, MC, VI. **Free Special Amenities: early check-in/late check-out and high-speed Internet.**

THE TUSCANY **Phone:** (649)941-4667 5

Condominium
$525-$1300 All Year

Address: Grace Bay **Location:** Oceanfront. North Coast at Grace Bay, 9.5 mi (15.2 km) from airport. **Facility:** An ultra-upscale design and decor provides the ultimate in luxurious comfort; a cell phone, with island-wide coverage, is provided with each unit. Smoke free premises. 11 condominiums. 5 stories, exterior corridors. **Parking:** on-site. **Terms:** office hours 9 am-5 pm, 30 day cancellation notice-fee imposed. **Amenities:** video library, DVD players, CD players, voice mail, safes, irons, hair dryers. **Pool(s):** outdoor. **Leisure Activities:** whirlpool, lighted tennis court, bicycles, exercise room. **Guest Services:** complimentary laundry, wireless Internet. **Business Services:** PC. **Cards:** AX, MC, VI.

▼ See AAA listing p 580 ▼

▼ See AAA listing p 581 ▼

VILLA RENAISSANCE **Phone:** (649)941-5300 (11)

Condominium
$295-$1595 All Year

Address: Ventura Dr, Grace Bay **Location:** Oceanfront. 8 mi (12.9 km) e of airport; Grace Bay. **Facility:** One of the newest condo properties on Grace Bay; exquisitely appointed spacious units feature marble floors and British Colonial style furnishings. Meets AAA guest room security requirements. Smoke free premises. 21 condominiums. 4 stories, interior/exterior corridors. **Parking:** on-site. **Terms:** office hours 8 am-10 pm, 21 day cancellation notice-fee imposed. **Amenities:** video library, DVD players, CD players, voice mail, safes, irons, hair dryers. **Pool(s):** outdoor. **Leisure Activities:** whirlpool, lighted tennis court, bicycles, exercise room. *Fee:* massage. **Guest Services:** complimentary laundry, wireless Internet. **Cards:** AX, DS, MC, VI.

The following lodging was either not evaluated or did not meet AAA rating requirements but is listed for your information only.

AMANYARA **Phone:** 649/941-8133

fyi

Not evaluated. **Address:** Northwest Point **Location:** On the western shore of Northwest Point bordering the Northwest Point Marine National Park. Facilities, services, and decor characterize an upscale property.

WHERE TO DINE

ANACAONA **Phone:** 649/946-5050 (7)

Mediterranean
$10-$41

Regarded as one of the top spots in Provo for the cuisine and location, the restaurant's al fresco dining room, under a huge bohio, is in one of Grace Bay's most elegant hotels. The talented chef uses high-quality ingredients such as rack of lamb, grouper, ahi tuna, veal tenderloin and local rock lobster and prepares tantalizing dishes with flair. A good beginning is with one of the chilled soups or bisques. The adjacent bar is great for reflecting before or after dinner. Dressy casual. Entertainment. **Bar:** Full bar. **Reservations:** required. **Hours:** 6:30 pm-9 pm. **Address:** Inner Grace Bay Circle **Location:** Grace Bay; 8.7 mi (13.9 km) e of airport; at Grace Bay Club. **Parking:** on-site. **Cards:** AX, CB, DC, DS, JC, MC, VI.

BACI RISTORANTE **Phone:** 649/941-3044 (28)

Italian
$12-$28

At Turtle Cove, this delightful eatery features both indoor and outdoor patio seating. Patrons unwind amid the casual European atmosphere for a meal of Italian fare, including daily lunch specials, entree-size salads, hearty pasta dishes and pizza baked in a brick oven. Casual dress. **Bar:** Full bar. **Reservations:** suggested. **Hours:** Open 12/1-10/1 & 11/1-11/30; noon-2 & 6-10 pm, Sat & Sun from 6 pm. **Address:** Harbour Towne at Turtle Cove **Location:** Harbour Towne at Turtle Cove. **Parking:** on-site. **Cards:** AX, MC, VI.

BAY BISTRO **Phone:** 649/946-5396 (10)

International
$12-$30

In a boutique-style hotel, the recently refurbished restaurant employs servers who make an extra effort to ensure an enjoyable evening. The menu centers on seafood, including creative preparations of tuna, grouper, lobster and snapper. In addition to seafood, diners can order lamb, steaks and a few vegetarian dishes. All desserts are made in-house. Dressy casual. **Bar:** Full bar. **Reservations:** suggested. **Hours:** Open 12/1-8/26 & 10/4-11/30; 7 am-10 pm, Mon-3 pm. **Address:** The Bight **Location:** Northeast coast at Grace Bay; 7 mi (11.2 km) e of airport; in Sibonne Beach Hotel. **Parking:** on-site. **Cards:** AX, MC, VI.

THE BEACH CAFE — **Phone:** 649/941-3713 (29)

Continental
$9-$27

Sea breezes cool the beachfront eatery, which is casual by day and romantic by night. On the menu are hearty breakfasts, casual luncheon fare and a carefully planned dinner menu featuring a small selection of tasty, fresh and well-seasoned seafood, beef and vegetarian selections. Casual dress. **Bar:** Full bar. **Reservations:** accepted. **Hours:** 7:30 am-10 pm. **Address:** Penns Rd **Location:** Grace Bay; 6.2 mi (9.9 km) e of airport; in The Reef Residences on Grace Bay. **Parking:** on-site. **Cards:** AX, MC, VI.

BELLA LUNA RISTORANTE — **Phone:** 649/946-5214 (17)

Regional Italian
$16-$32

An open, elevated deck and indoor dining area with colorful wall and ceiling murals invite diners to relax. The creative menu incorporates selections of fresh pasta and seafood blanketed in rich, tasty sauces. Portions are ample. Children under 10 are not permitted. Dressy casual. **Bar:** Full bar. **Reservations:** required. **Hours:** Open 12/1-9/1 & 10/1-11/30; 6 pm-9 pm; 6 pm-10 pm 11/15-4/30. Closed: Sun 5/1-11/14. **Address:** Grace Bay Rd **Location:** North coast at Grace Bay; 7.5 mi (12 km) e of airport; in Glass House. **Parking:** on-site. **Cards:** AX, MC, VI.

CAICOS CAFE — **Phone:** 649/946-5278 (13)

Seafood
$10-$34

Listed on the daily changing menu are grilled fresh seafood and meat prepared with Caribbean and French influences. The atmosphere is friendly and laid-back. Casual dress. **Bar:** Full bar. **Reservations:** required. **Hours:** Open 12/1-9/1 & 10/9-11/30; noon-2:30 & 6-10 pm, Mon from 6 pm. Closed: Sun. **Address:** Gouvernor Rd **Location:** North coast at Grace Bay; 8 mi (12.8 km) e of airport. **Parking:** on-site. **Cards:** AX, CB, DC, DS, MC, VI.

CALICO JACKS BAR AND RESTAURANT — **Phone:** 649/946-5129 (6)

International
$9-$22

Both locals and tourists enjoy the casual spot, where tasty fare includes tempting finger foods along the lines of wings, conch fritters and rings, as well as hearty burgers, fish and chips, pasta and grilled meats. The feel on the patio is relaxed. Casual dress. **Bar:** Full bar. **Hours:** noon-10 pm, Sun from 5 pm; Mon-Sat from 4 pm 4/15-11/15. Closed: 12/24, 12/25. **Address:** Grace Bay Rd **Location:** In Ports of Call Shopping Plaza. **Parking:** on-site. **Cards:** AX, DS, MC, VI.

COYABA — **Phone:** 649/946-5186 (27)

New Caribbean
$32-$50

At the alfresco dining room, set in a lush tropical garden, the chef comes to the table to explain all that he has created. Some signature dishes include pan-fried fillet of grouper with an ackee and callaloo souffle and rack of lamb with sun-dried tomato pesto and rosemary jus. Each evening features an array of specials. True gourmands favor the sumptuous seven-course tasting menu. Dressy casual. **Bar:** Full bar. **Reservations:** required. **Hours:** Open 12/1-9/1 & 10/16-11/30; 6 pm-10 pm. Closed: Tues. **Address:** Penn's Rd **Location:** North Coast at Grace Bay; 9 mi (14.4) e of airport; in Caribbean Paradise Inn. **Parking:** on-site. **Cards:** AX, DS, MC, VI.

DANNY BUOYS IRISH PUB AND RESTAURANT — **Phone:** 649/946-5921 (18)

Irish
$10-$25

One of the newest area restaurants is a great watering hole for locals, divers and tourist alike. Guests can watch sporting events on large-screen satellite TVs in the handsome bar area. Among the many menu options are such Irish favorites as fish and chips, chicken pot pie and potato-leek soup. Some other house specialties include pot of nachos, buffalo wings and bacon-wrapped scallops. Brunch is served from 10 am-4 pm on weekends. Casual dress. **Bar:** Full bar. **Reservations:** accepted. **Hours:** noon-10 pm, Sat & Sun from 8 am. Closed: 12/25. **Address:** Grace Bay Rd **Location:** Grace Bay; across from Regent Grand; adjacent to The Saltmills. **Parking:** on-site. **Cards:** MC, VI.

GRACE'S COTTAGE — **Phone:** 649/946-5096 (8)

AAA

International
$43-$54

Romantically set al fresco around a gingerbread-style cottage. The chef visits each table to explain the frequently changing menu in great detail, which may feature starters like red snapper ceviche and entrees like grilled wahoo with pineapple salsa or braised lamb shank with rosemary risotto. Dessert is the piece de resistance with choices like mango souffle, tempura bananas with rum butter scotch sauce and roasted pumpkin ginger cheesecake with whiskey and walnut sauce. Dressy casual. **Bar:** Full bar. **Reservations:** required. **Hours:** 6:30 pm-9 pm. **Address:** Grace Bay Rd **Location:** 6 mi (9.6 km) e of airport; Grace Bay; in Point Grace. **Parking:** on-site. **Cards:** AX, MC, VI.

HEMINGWAY'S ON THE BEACH — **Phone:** 649/941-8408 (9)

International
$9-$28

The casual restaurant allows for oceanfront dining in a covered area or on a patio terrace overlooking the sea. Candlelit tables set the scene for a romantic evening. The varied menu blends light finger foods and sandwiches at lunch with full meat, seafood and pasta specialties at dinner. Casual dress. Entertainment. **Bar:** Full bar. **Reservations:** suggested. **Hours:** 8 am-10 pm. **Address:** Grace Bay Rd **Location:** North coast at Grace Bay; 7.5 mi (12 km) e of airport; in The Sands at Grace Bay. **Parking:** on-site. **Cards:** AX, MC, VI.

IGUANA PROVO'S FIRST SEAFOOD AND STEAKHOUSE — **Phone:** 649/941-8145 (21)

Steak & Seafood
$18-$30

At the Salt Mills Plaza, this restaurant blends contemporary decor and innovative style. Steak and seafood selections prepared with an island flair can be savored with accompaniments of coconut rice and mango salsa. Diners can enjoy a pre- or post-dinner cocktail in the upscale lounge and request their preference for indoor or patio seating. Dressy casual. **Bar:** Full bar. **Reservations:** suggested. **Hours:** 6 pm-10 pm. Closed: 12/25. **Address:** Salt Mills, Grace Bay Rd **Location:** Grace Bay Rd; at The Saltmills. **Parking:** on-site. **Cards:** AX, CB, DC, DS, JC, MC, VI.

MAGNOLIA WINE BAR & RESTAURANT **Phone:** 649/941-5108 (24)

International

$22-$31

On a hill, the refined and romantic restaurant offers views of the ocean and marina. Well-attired servers are quick to make recommendations from the varied menu, which includes escargots, tempura shrimp and tuna tartare as appetizers. Main course choices range from seafood bouillabaisse to black Angus beef to rack of lamb with mint-rosemary jus. Molten chocolate cake served warm is luscious. The wine bar is a popular spot for sunsets. Dressy casual. **Bar:** Full bar. **Reservations:** suggested. **Hours:** Open 12/1-8/26 & 10/3-11/30; 6 pm-9:30 pm. Closed: 12/25; also Mon. **Address:** Miramar Resort **Location:** At Miramar Resort; just sw of Turtle Cove Marina; overlooking the marina. **Parking:** on-site. **Cards:** AX, MC, VI.

MANGO REEF RESTAURANT **Phone:** 649/946-8200 (5)

Caribbean

$7-$29

Diners can choose seating indoors or outside on the porch. The Caribbean staff is cheerful. Pineapple and conch fritters with chipotle mayonnaise and rock shrimp tostada are popular choices. Entree-size salads can be topped with seared tuna, jerk chicken or coconut shrimp. Caribbean flavors burst forth from such entrees as island ribs with guava glaze and red snapper Caribe. For lunch, there is a selection of gourmet burgers and sandwiches, including panini. Casual dress. **Bar:** Full bar. **Reservations:** accepted. **Hours:** 7:30 am-10 pm. **Address:** Grace Bay Rd **Location:** 8.8 mi (14.1 km) e of airport; in Royal West Indies Resort. **Parking:** on-site. **Cards:** AX, DS, MC, VI.

PARALLEL23 **Phone:** 649/946-8666 (11)

International

$25-$37

The sophisticated restaurant's gourmet menu combines the best of culinary techniques and ingredients from the East and West. Starters include grouper tostada, beef yakitori and salad of citrus-cured duck confit. For entrees, the chef prepares such items as wood-roasted pork chop, roasted organic chicken, cote du boeuf and poached reef snapper. The attentive islander staff presents dishes with flair. Dressy casual. **Bar:** Full bar. **Reservations:** required. **Hours:** 6 am-11 & 6-11 pm. **Address:** Grace Bay Rd **Location:** 6.9 mi (11.1 km) e of airport; in The Regent Palms Turks and Caicos. **Parking:** on-site. **Cards:** AX, MC, VI.

SALTMILLS CAFE **Phone:** 649/941-8148 (20)

International

$10-$16

One of the area's newest family-owned-and-operated breakfast and lunch spots offers an affordable alternative. Submarine sandwiches, panini sandwiches, pizza and pasta dishes are served in al fresco seating across from Grace Bay. Casual dress. **Bar:** Full bar. **Hours:** 7:30 am-4 pm. Closed: 1/1, 12/25, 12/26; also Sun. **Address:** Grace Bay Rd **Location:** At The Saltmills across from Grace Bay. **Parking:** on-site. **Cards:** MC, VI.

SIMBA **Phone:** 649/946-5800 (23)

Asian

$18-$46

The cozy, intimate setting incorporates an African motif. Executive chef Sebastien creates mouthwatering and eye-appealing dishes that blend Caribbean and Asian flavors. For starters, Mandarin conch seviche and snow crab Asian ravioli are favorites. Among choice entrees are rare seared sesame-encrusted tuna with tropical fruit chutney, curry-and-coconut island snapper and roasted rack of lamb. Dessert selections change frequently. Casual dress. **Bar:** Full bar. **Reservations:** suggested. **Hours:** Open 12/1-9/1 & 10/1-11/30; 7:30 am-10, noon-2:30 & 6-10 pm, Wed-2:30 pm. **Address:** Lower Bight Rd **Location:** 5.9 mi (9.4 km) e of airport; Grace Bay; in Turks & Caicos Club. **Parking:** on-site. **Cards:** AX, MC, VI.

THE TIKI HUT-CABANA BAR AND GRILL **Phone:** 649/941-5341 (30)

International

$10-$29

A local hangout at Turtle Cove Marina, the bustling eatery nurtures a relaxed island atmosphere. Guests can sit in the covered open-air dining room or at the large casual bar. The menu lists a mix of great island and American dishes. Lending to the ambience are friendly servers who often can be heard singing. Casual dress. **Bar:** Full bar. **Hours:** 11 am-10 pm, Fri-11 pm, Sat & Sun 7 am-11 pm. **Address:** Turtle Cove Marina **Location:** At Turtle Cove Marina. **Parking:** on-site. **Cards:** AX, DS, MC, VI.

VIRGIN ISLANDS, BRITISH

This index helps you "spot" where approved lodgings and restaurants are located on the corresponding detailed maps. Lodging daily rate range is for comparison only and show the property's high season. Restaurant rate range is a combination of lunch and/or dinner. Turn to the listing page for more detailed rate information and consult display ads for special promotions.

VIRGIN GORDA ISLAND

Map Page	OA	Lodgings	Diamond Rated	High Season	Page
3 / p. 587		Mango Bay Resort	◆◆	$109-$490	590
4 / p. 587		Olde Yard Village	◆◆◆	$180-$535	590

Map Page	OA	Restaurants	Diamond Rated	Cuisine	Meal Range	Page
1 / p. 587		The Rock Cafe	◆◆	Italian	$15-$30	590
2 / p. 587		Mad Dog	◆	American	$8-$13	590

TORTOLA ISLAND

Map Page	OA	Lodgings	Diamond Rated	High Season	Page
7 / p. 587		Sugar Mill Hotel	◆◆◆	$255-$585	588
8 / p. 587	AAA	**Long Bay Beach Resort** - see color ad p 588	◆◆◆	$145-$915 SAVE	588
9 / p. 587		Fort Recovery Beachfront Villa Hotel & Resort - see color ad p 588	◆◆◆	$290-$380	587
10 / p. 587		Treasure Isle Hotel	◆◆	$250-$350	589

Map Page	OA	Restaurants	Diamond Rated	Cuisine	Meal Range	Page
4 / p. 587		Pusser's Landing	◆◆	International	$15-$32	590
5 / p. 587		Sugar Mill Restaurant	◆◆◆	International	$27-$32	590
7 / p. 587	AAA	**The Jolly Roger Inn**	◆	International	$10-$22	589
8 / p. 587		Capriccio di Mare	◆	Italian	$7-$14	589
9 / p. 587		Brandywine Bay	◆◆◆	International	$22-$60	589
10 / p. 587		Pusser's Road Town Pub & Company Store	◆◆	Caribbean	$10-$21	590
12 / p. 587		Myett's Garden & Grille Restaurant	◆◆	International	$12-$28	589
14 / p. 587		Fat Cat Thai Restaurant	◆◆	Thai	$16-$26	589
16 / p. 587		Kong Ming Asian Terrace	◆◆	Chinese	$9-$22	589
17 / p. 587		Fat Hog Bob's	◆	International	$8-$29	589

PETER ISLAND

Map Page	OA	Lodging	Diamond Rated	High Season	Page
12 / p. 587	AAA	**Peter Island Resort**	◆◆◆◆	$575-$1550 SAVE	587

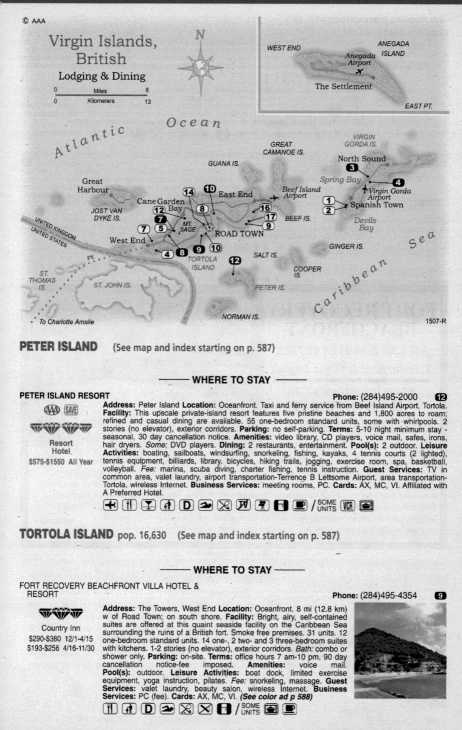

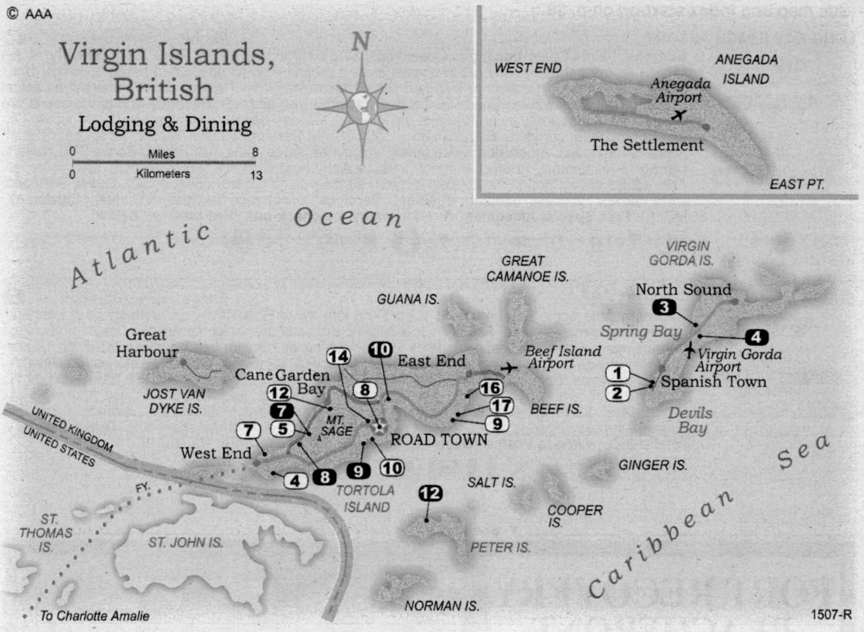

Virgin Islands, British
Lodging & Dining

0 Miles 8
0 Kilometers 13

N

WEST END
ANEGADA ISLAND
Anegada Airport
The Settlement
EAST PT.

Atlantic Ocean
GREAT CAMANOE IS.
VIRGIN GORDA IS.
North Sound
GUANA IS.
Spring Bay
Great Harbour
East End
Beef Island Airport
Virgin Gorda Airport
Cane Garden Bay
Spanish Town
JOST VAN DYKE IS.
BEEF IS.
Devils Bay
UNITED KINGDOM
UNITED STATES
MT. SAGE
ROAD TOWN
West End
GINGER IS.
Caribbean Sea
TORTOLA ISLAND
SALT IS.
FY.
COOPER IS.
ST. THOMAS IS.
ST. JOHN IS.
PETER IS.
NORMAN IS.
To Charlotte Amalie
1507-R

PETER ISLAND

(See map and index starting on p. 587)

WHERE TO STAY

PETER ISLAND RESORT — Phone: (284)495-2000 — 12

AAA SAVE

Resort Hotel

$575-$1550 All Year

Address: Peter Island **Location:** Oceanfront. Taxi and ferry service from Beef Island Airport, Tortola. **Facility:** This upscale private-island resort features five pristine beaches and 1,800 acres to roam; refined and casual dining are available. 55 one-bedroom standard units, some with whirlpools. 2 stories (no elevator), exterior corridors. **Parking:** no self-parking. **Terms:** 5-10 night minimum stay - seasonal, 30 day cancellation notice. **Amenities:** video library, CD players, voice mail, safes, irons, hair dryers. *Some:* DVD players. **Dining:** 2 restaurants, entertainment. **Pool(s):** 2 outdoor. **Leisure Activities:** boating, sailboats, windsurfing, snorkeling, fishing, kayaks, 4 tennis courts (2 lighted), tennis equipment, billiards, library, bicycles, hiking trails, jogging, exercise room, spa, basketball, volleyball. *Fee:* marina, scuba diving, charter fishing, tennis instruction. **Guest Services:** TV in common area, valet laundry, airport transportation-Terrence B Lettsome Airport, area transportation-Tortola, wireless Internet. **Business Services:** meeting rooms, PC. **Cards:** AX, MC, VI. Affiliated with A Preferred Hotel.

D / SOME UNITS VCR

TORTOLA ISLAND pop. 16,630

(See map and index starting on p. 587)

WHERE TO STAY

FORT RECOVERY BEACHFRONT VILLA HOTEL & RESORT — Phone: (284)495-4354 — 9

Country Inn

$290-$380 12/1-4/15
$193-$256 4/16-11/30

Address: The Towers, West End **Location:** Oceanfront. 8 mi (12.8 km) w of Road Town; on south shore. **Facility:** Bright, airy, self-contained suites are offered at this quaint seaside facility on the Caribbean Sea surrounding the ruins of a British fort. Smoke free premises. 31 units. 12 one-bedroom standard units. 14 one-, 2 two- and 3 three-bedroom suites with kitchens. 1-2 stories (no elevator), exterior corridors. *Bath:* combo or shower only. **Parking:** on-site. **Terms:** office hours 7 am-10 pm, 90 day cancellation notice-fee imposed. **Amenities:** voice mail. **Pool(s):** outdoor. **Leisure Activities:** boat dock, limited exercise equipment, yoga instruction, pilates. *Fee:* snorkeling, massage. **Guest Services:** valet laundry, beauty salon, wireless Internet. **Business Services:** PC (fee). **Cards:** AX, MC, VI. ***(See color ad p 588)***

D / SOME UNITS

(See map and index starting on p. 587)

LONG BAY BEACH RESORT — Phone: (284)495-4252 **8**

AAA SAVE

Resort Hotel

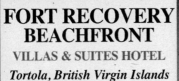

$145-$915 All Year

Address: North Coast **Location:** Oceanfront. 11 mi (17.6 km) nw of Road Town. **Facility:** A full service resort that has been built in phases around a central green space and public buildings. Units range from deluxe beachfront to standard hillside units. Many have a view of the water but an actual sunning beach is a ways away so the property provides free shuttles. The pools and tennis courts are close to the guest units, as are the two restaurants. 159 one-bedroom standard units. 2-3 stories (no elevator), exterior corridors. *Bath:* combo or shower only. **Parking:** on-site. **Terms:** 14 day cancellation notice-fee imposed. **Amenities:** video library, voice mail, safes, irons, hair dryers. *Some:* DVD players. **Dining:** 3 restaurants. **Pool(s):** outdoor. **Leisure Activities:** whirlpool, exercise room, spa, volleyball. *Fee:* scuba diving, snorkeling, boogie boards, surfboards, 2 lighted tennis courts. **Guest Services:** valet laundry, wireless Internet. **Business Services:** conference facilities, PC (fee). **Cards:** AX, MC, VI. **Free Special Amenities: early check-in/late check-out.** *(See color ad below)*

D / SOME UNITS

SUGAR MILL HOTEL — Book at AAA.com — Phone: (284)495-4355 **7**

Country Inn

$255-$585 12/1-7/28 & 10/1-11/30

Address: Little Apple Bay **Location:** 11 mi (17.6 km) nw of Road Town; on north shore in west end. Located in a secluded area. **Facility:** On a hillside, the hotel overlooks the Atlantic Ocean; units range from compact with austere appointments to spacious suites. Smoke free premises. 23 units. 18 one-bedroom standard units. 4 one- and 1 two-bedroom suites, some with kitchens. 2 stories (no elevator), exterior corridors. *Bath:* combo or shower only. **Parking:** on-site. **Terms:** open 12/1-7/28 & 10/1-11/30, office hours 7 am-11 pm, 3 night minimum stay - seasonal, age restrictions may apply, 30 day cancellation notice-fee imposed. **Amenities:** voice mail, irons, hair dryers. **Dining:** Sugar Mill Restaurant, see separate listing. **Pool(s):** outdoor. **Leisure Activities:** snorkeling. **Guest Services:** valet laundry, wireless Internet. **Business Services:** PC (fee). **Cards:** AX, MC, VI.

/ SOME UNITS VCR

(See map and index starting on p. 587)

TREASURE ISLE HOTEL — Phone: (284)494-2501 (10)

Hotel

$250-$350 All Year

Address: Pasea Estate **Location:** 0.5 mi (0.8 km) e of Road Town. **Facility:** Smoke free premises. 24 one-bedroom standard units. 2 stories, exterior corridors. *Bath:* shower only. **Parking:** on-site. **Terms:** office hours 7 am-11 pm, 14 day cancellation notice. **Amenities:** high-speed Internet, irons, hair dryers. **Pool(s):** outdoor. **Guest Services:** valet laundry, wireless Internet. **Business Services:** meeting rooms. **Cards:** AX, MC, VI.

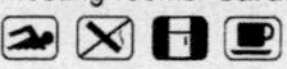

WHERE TO DINE

BRANDYWINE BAY — **Phone:** 284/495-2301 (9)

International

$22-$60

On a breeze-swept hillside overlooking the sea, this historic gunnery's open-air stone terrace makes for an intriguing dining spot. The Italian-born owner creates a daily-changing menu of creative and traditional dishes. House specials include homemade pasta, roast duck and whole fish. Dressy casual. **Bar:** Full bar. **Reservations:** suggested. **Hours:** Open 12/1-7/31 & 11/1-11/30; 6:30 pm-9 pm. Closed major holidays. **Address:** Brandywine Estate **Location:** 3 mi (4.8 km) e of Road Town. **Parking:** on-site. **Cards:** AX, MC, VI.

CAPRICCIO DI MARE — **Phone:** 284/494-5369 (8)

Italian

$7-$14

On a covered sidewalk patio, the casual setting invites diners to unwind while noshing on gourmet pizza, pasta, large salads and panini sandwiches. Also tempting are the great desserts, cappuccino and espresso. Casual dress. **Bar:** Full bar. **Hours:** 8 am-9 pm, Fri & Sat-9:30 pm. Closed major holidays; also Sun, Sat 9/1-10/1. **Address:** Abbot Bldg, Waterfront Dr **Location:** Center Road Town; near ferry terminal. **Parking:** street. **Cards:** MC, VI.

FAT CAT THAI RESTAURANT — **Phone:** 284/494-2615 (14)

Thai

$16-$26

There's not much in the way of authentic Thai fare on Tortola Island, which makes this place a real draw for yellow, green and red curry dishes prepared with chicken, duck, beef and tofu. Lemon grass sorbet is a soothing treat. Casual dress. **Bar:** Full bar. **Reservations:** suggested. **Hours:** 6 pm-10 pm. Closed major holidays. **Address:** Main Rd **Location:** Just w of Road Town Center; in Hotel Castle Maria. **Parking:** street. **Cards:** MC, VI.

FAT HOG BOB'S — **Phone:** 284/495-1010 (17)

International

$8-$29

This eatery offers more than just barbecue. The menu also branches out into dishes such as macadamia-crusted shrimp, blackened grouper, porterhouse steak and pasta preparations. Although the waterfront view from the large porch over Hodges Bay is the big draw, guests also can sit inside. Large portions help compensate for the somewhat uninspired service. Casual dress. **Bar:** Full bar. **Reservations:** suggested. **Hours:** 7 am-10 pm. **Address:** Hodges Creek **Location:** 4.7 mi (7.5 km) e of Road Town; at Hodges Creek east end. **Parking:** on-site. **Cards:** AX, MC, VI.

THE JOLLY ROGER INN — **Phone:** 284/495-4559 (7)

International

$10-$22

The casual menu lists seafood, signature pizzas, rotis and burgers. The weathered surroundings are popular with boaters. Barbecue is the focus of Friday and Saturday specials. The waterfront deck offers nice views. Casual dress. **Bar:** Full bar. **Reservations:** suggested. **Hours:** Open 12/1-8/1 & 10/1-11/30; 8 am-10 pm; to 11 pm in season. **Address:** Soper's Hole Rd **Location:** In West End; just w of ferry dock. **Parking:** on-site. **Cards:** AX, DS, MC, VI.

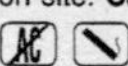

KONG MING ASIAN TERRACE — **Phone:** 284/495-1174 (16)

Chinese

$9-$22

Patrons enjoy upstairs views on the verandah or air-conditioned comfort in the Asia-themed interior dining room. The typically broad Chinese menu lists many soups, as well as entrees centered on ingredients ranging from duck, lamb and spare ribs to prawns and fish. Two popular methods of preparation are Manchurian and Szechuan style. Casual dress. **Bar:** Full bar. **Reservations:** suggested. **Hours:** 11 am-10 pm. Closed: Mon. **Address:** Harbour View Marina **Location:** 6.5 mi (10.5 km) e of Road Town; at Harbor View Marina. **Parking:** on-site. **Cards:** DS, MC, VI.

MYETT'S GARDEN & GRILLE RESTAURANT — **Phone:** 284/495-9649 (12)

International

$12-$28

Chef Stone from Jamaica prepares Caribbean-inspired cuisine at this spot, where patrons soak up the garden atmosphere as they take in partial views of the beach and ocean. Al fresco meals center on steaks, the catch of the day, jerk chicken, roasted duck with tamarind glaze and grilled rack of lamb, as well as more than half a dozen pasta dishes. Favorite starters are conch chowder or pepperpot soup. Dessert temptations include mango cheesecake, Key lime pie and chocolate ecstasy cake. Casual dress. Entertainment. **Bar:** Full bar. **Reservations:** required. **Hours:** 8 am-3 & 6:30-10 pm. **Address:** Cane Garden Bay Rd **Location:** In Cane Garden Bay; oceanside. **Parking:** on-site. **Cards:** AX, MC, VI.

(See map and index starting on p. 587)

PUSSER'S LANDING **Phone:** 284/495-4554 (4)

International
$15-$32

The eatery's ideal marina location attracts a varied crowd of locals, seafaring folks and land-excursion tourists. Nautical and whimsical appointments foster a casual mood that recalls Jimmy Buffett songs. Among well-prepared favorites are baby back ribs, jerk chicken and fish—either escabeche or with coconut curry sauce. Mouthwatering starters include peel-and-eat shrimp, crab cakes and Prince Edward Island mussels. Tempting desserts and creative libations also merit strong consideration. Casual dress. **Bar:** Full bar. **Reservations:** suggested. **Hours:** 11 am-10 pm. **Address:** Soper's Hole Marina **Location:** At Soper's Hole Marina; west end. **Parking:** on-site. **Cards:** AX, MC, VI.

PUSSER'S ROAD TOWN PUB & COMPANY STORE **Phone:** 284/494-3897 (10)

Caribbean
$10-$21

Enjoy a wide variety of Caribbean, English and American fare in this popular gathering spot overlooking the harbor. The menu includes jerk pork and chicken, sherpherd's pie and fish and chips, as well as burgers, sandwiches, salads and pizza. Dine on the porch or inside the air-conditioned Victorian bar. Casual dress. **Bar:** Full bar. **Hours:** 11 am-10 pm. **Address:** Waterfront Rd **Location:** In Road Town; across from ferry dock. **Parking:** on-site. **Cards:** AX, MC, VI.

SUGAR MILL RESTAURANT **Phone:** 284/495-4355 (5)

International
$27-$32

Plentiful artwork by the owner adorns the walls of the rustic setting. Award-winning four-course dinners reflect local and international influences. Although the service has a formal edge, the atmosphere remains casual. Dressy casual. **Bar:** Full bar. **Reservations:** required. **Hours:** Open 12/1-7/30 & 10/1-11/30; 7 pm-8 pm; 7 pm-8:30 pm 11/1-4/30. **Address:** Little Apple Bay **Location:** 11 mi (17.6 km) nw of Road Town; on north shore in west end; in Sugar Mill Hotel. **Parking:** on-site. **Cards:** AX, MC, VI. **Historic**

VIRGIN GORDA ISLAND pop. 3,063 (See map and index starting on p. 587)

— WHERE TO STAY —

MANGO BAY RESORT **Phone:** (284)495-5672 (3)

Cottage
$109-$490 All Year

Address: Plum Tree Rd **Location:** Oceanfront. 2.2 mi (3.5 km) n of ferry dock and airport, follow signs. **Facility:** 22 units. 5 one-bedroom standard units with efficiencies. 10 one- and 5 two-bedroom suites with kitchens, some with whirlpools. 2 cottages. 1-2 stories (no elevator), exterior corridors. *Bath:* combo or shower only. **Parking:** on-site. **Terms:** office hours 9 am-5 pm, 3-5 night minimum stay - seasonal, 45 day cancellation notice-fee imposed. **Amenities:** voice mail. *Some:* hair dryers. **Leisure Activities:** snorkeling. **Business Services:** PC. **Cards:** MC, VI.

OLDE YARD VILLAGE Book at AAA.com **Phone:** (284)495-5544 (4)

Condominium
$180-$535 All Year

Address: The Valley **Location:** 0.5 mi (0.8 km) n of ferry dock and airport. **Facility:** Townhouses and apartments are spread out over 10 landscaped acres; ample on-site leisure and recreational options are near numerous beaches. Smoke free premises. 30 units. 1 one-bedroom standard unit with efficiency. 5 one-, 19 two- and 5 three-bedroom suites, some with efficiencies or kitchens. 3 stories (no elevator), exterior corridors. *Bath:* combo or shower only. **Parking:** on-site. **Terms:** office hours 8 am-5 pm, 3 night minimum stay - seasonal, 60 day cancellation notice, 30 day in summer-fee imposed. **Amenities:** DVD players, safes, irons, hair dryers. **Pool(s):** outdoor. **Leisure Activities:** whirlpool, exercise room, spa. *Fee:* 2 lighted tennis courts. **Guest Services:** valet and coin laundry, beauty salon, wireless Internet. **Business Services:** meeting rooms, PC. **Cards:** AX, DS, MC, VI.

VCR / SOME UNITS

— WHERE TO DINE —

MAD DOG **Phone:** 284/495-5830 (2)

American
$8-$13

It does not get any better than this. Kick back on the wraparound verandah of this plantation house and enjoy the wonderful view and breeze with your new friends: the staff and customers. Choose from a variety of sandwiches and drinks made to order. Casual dress. **Bar:** Full bar. **Hours:** 9 am-7 pm. **Address:** The Baths **Location:** Next to The Baths. **Parking:** on-site.

THE ROCK CAFE **Phone:** 284/495-5482 (1)

Italian
$15-$30

The restaurant is popular for its food, setting and tequila bar. Conch fritters make great munchies before moving on to such pasta dishes as penne Caprese or one of the many local fish dishes. The al fresco dining area is built around boulders and rock outcroppings. Creme caramel has a rich, creamy texture. Casual dress. Entertainment. **Bar:** Full bar. **Reservations:** required. **Hours:** 6 pm-10 pm. **Address:** Tower Rd **Location:** Just s of Spanish Town; between The Baths and Spanish Town; at The Valley. **Parking:** on-site. **Cards:** AX, MC, VI.

VIRGIN ISLANDS, U.S.

Airport Accommodations

Map Page	OA	ST THOMAS - CYRIL E KING INTERNATIONAL	Diamond Rated	High Season	Page
2 / p. 593	AAA	**Best Western Emerald Beach Resort, 0.6 mi (1 km) s of terminal**		$99-$309 SAVE	601

Virgin Islands, U.S.

This index helps you "spot" where approved lodgings and restaurants are located on the corresponding detailed maps. Lodging daily rate range is for comparison only and show the property's high season. Restaurant rate range is a combination of lunch and/or dinner. Turn to the listing page for more detailed rate information and consult display ads for special promotions.

CHARLOTTE AMALIE (ST. THOMAS ISLAND)

Map Page	OA	Lodging	Diamond Rated	High Season	Page
2 / p. 593	AAA	**Best Western Emerald Beach Resort** - see color ad p 602		$99-$309 SAVE	601

Map Page	OA	Restaurants	Diamond Rated	Cuisine	Meal Range	Page
1 / p. 593		The Greenhouse Bar and Restaurant		International	$11-$28	603
2 / p. 593		Hook, Line, & Sinker Bar and Restaurant		American	$7-$26	603
3 / p. 593		Sib's on the Mountain		American	$13-$23	603
5 / p. 593	AAA	**Herve Restaurant & Wine Bar**		International	$10-$35	603
6 / p. 593		Cuzzin's Caribbean Restaurant		Caribbean	$11-$21	603
8 / p. 593		Victor's New Hide Out		Caribbean	$13-$30	603

FRENCHMAN BAY (ST. THOMAS ISLAND)

Map Page	OA	Lodging	Diamond Rated	High Season	Page
5 / p. 593	AAA	**Frenchman's Reef & Morning Star Marriott Beach Resort** - see color ad p 601, on insert		$367-$543 SAVE	604

Map Page	OA	Restaurant	Diamond Rated	Cuisine	Meal Range	Page
9 / p. 593		Havana Blue		Latin American	$28-$48	604

RED HOOK (ST. THOMAS ISLAND)

Map Page	OA	Lodgings	Diamond Rated	High Season	Page
11 / p. 593	AAA	**Secret Harbour Beach Resort** - see color ad p 605		$185-$725 SAVE	605
13 / p. 593		The Ritz-Carlton, St. Thomas		$479-$1690	605

Map Page	OA	Restaurants	Diamond Rated	Cuisine	Meal Range	Page
10 / p. 593		Molly Molones		Irish	$9-$27	606
11 / p. 593		Duffy's Love Shack		International	$9-$17	606
13 / p. 593		The Agave Terrace		International	$24-$45	605
18 / p. 593		Buddha Sushi Lounge & Grill		Sushi	$17-$28	605

SMITH BAY (ST. THOMAS ISLAND)

Map Page	OA	Lodgings	Diamond Rated	High Season	Page
15 / p. 593		Wyndham Sugar Bay Resort & Spa		$187-$646	606
16 / p. 593		Pavilions and Pools Hotel		$260-$360	606

Map Page	OA	Restaurant	Diamond Rated	Cuisine	Meal Range	Page
15 / p. 593		Romano's		Northern Italian	$21-$32	606

VIRGIN ISLANDS NATIONAL PARK (ST. JOHN ISLAND)

Map Page	OA	Lodging	Diamond Rated	High Season	Page
25 / p. 593		Caneel Bay-A Rosewood Resort	◆◆◆◆	$450-$1600	600

CRUZ BAY (ST. JOHN ISLAND)

Map Page	OA	Lodgings	Diamond Rated	High Season	Page
28 / p. 593		Gallows Point Resort	◆◆	$225-$625	599
29 / p. 593	AAA	**The Westin St. John Resort & Villas** - see color ad on insert, inside front cover	◆◆◆	$209-$1079 SAVE	599

Map Page	OA	Restaurants	Diamond Rated	Cuisine	Meal Range	Page
16 / p. 593		Morgan's Mango	◆◆	International	$12-$27	600
17 / p. 593		Asolare	◆◆◆	Regional Specialty	$22-$38	600

CHRISTIANSTED (ST. CROIX ISLAND)

Map Page	OA	Lodgings	Diamond Rated	High Season	Page
31 / p. 593		The Buccaneer - see color ad p 594	◆◆◆	$265-$995	594
32 / p. 593	AAA	**Chenay Bay Beach Resort** - see color ad p 595	◆◆	$309-$799 SAVE	595
33 / p. 593	AAA	**Hotel Caravelle**	◆	$120-$165 SAVE	596
34 / p. 593	AAA	**Holger Danske Hotel** - see color ad p 596	◆◆	$122-$162 SAVE	596
35 / p. 593	AAA	**Divi Carina Bay Resort & Casino** - see color ad p 596	◆◆◆	$210-$626 SAVE	595
38 / p. 593	AAA	**Tamarind Reef Hotel**	◆◆	$300-$400 SAVE	597

Map Page	OA	Restaurants	Diamond Rated	Cuisine	Meal Range	Page
19 / p. 593		Cheeseburgers in America's Paradise	◆	American	$11-$24	597
20 / p. 593		Kendricks	◆◆	International	$20-$32	598
21 / p. 593		Fort Christian Brew Pub	◆	American	$10-$27	597
22 / p. 593		Bacchus	◆◆◆	American	$22-$36	597
23 / p. 593		Tutto Bene	◆◆	Italian	$16-$31	598
24 / p. 593		RumRunners	◆◆	American	$9-$26	598

FREDERIKSTED (ST. CROIX ISLAND)

Map Page	OA	Lodging	Diamond Rated	High Season	Page
37 / p. 593		Sand Castle on the Beach Hotel & Restaurant	◆◆	$89-$279	598

Map Page	OA	Restaurant	Diamond Rated	Cuisine	Meal Range	Page
25 / p. 593		Beachside Cafe	◆◆	International	$9-$30	598

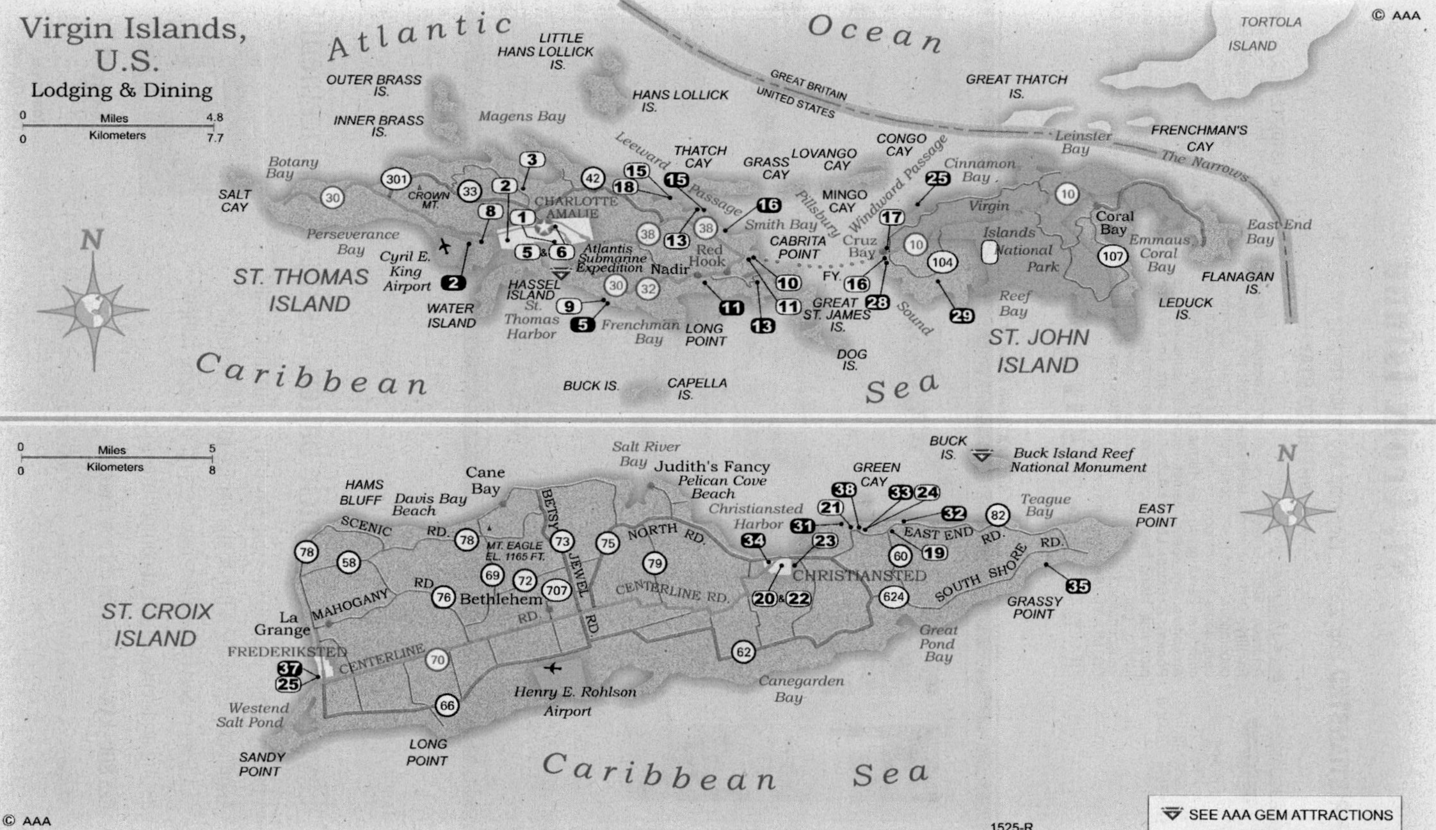
Virgin Islands, U.S.
Lodging & Dining
Miles 0 4.8
Kilometers 0 7.7
Atlantic Ocean
Caribbean Sea
ST. THOMAS ISLAND
ST. JOHN ISLAND
CHARLOTTE AMALIE
TORTOLA ISLAND
GREAT BRITAIN
UNITED STATES
LITTLE HANS LOLLICK IS.
HANS LOLLICK IS.
OUTER BRASS IS.
INNER BRASS IS.
Magens Bay
Botany Bay
SALT CAY
CROWN MT.
Perseverance Bay
Cyril E. King Airport
WATER ISLAND
HASSEL ISLAND
St. Thomas Harbor
Atlantis Submarine Expedition
Nadir
Red Hook
Frenchman Bay
LONG POINT
BUCK IS.
CAPELLA IS.
Leeward Passage
THATCH CAY
GRASS CAY
LOVANGO CAY
CONGO CAY
MINGO CAY
Smith Bay
Pillsbury Sound
CABRITA POINT
Windward Passage
Cruz Bay
FY.
GREAT ST. JAMES IS.
DOG IS.
Sound
Cinnamon Bay
Virgin Islands National Park
Reef Bay
Coral Bay
Emmaus Coral Bay
East End Bay
Leinster Bay
The Narrows
GREAT THATCH IS.
FRENCHMAN'S CAY
FLANAGAN IS.
LEDUCK IS.
© AAA
Miles 0 5
Kilometers 0 8
ST. CROIX ISLAND
FREDERIKSTED
La Grange
HAMS BLUFF
Davis Bay Beach
Cane Bay
SCENIC RD.
MT. EAGLE EL. 1165 FT.
BETSY JEWEL RD.
MAHOGANY RD.
Bethlehem
CENTERLINE RD.
NORTH RD.
Salt River Bay
Judith's Fancy
Pelican Cove Beach
Christiansted Harbor
CHRISTIANSTED
GREEN CAY
BUCK IS.
Buck Island Reef National Monument
EAST END RD.
Teague Bay
EAST POINT
SOUTH SHORE RD.
GRASSY POINT
Great Pond Bay
Canegarden Bay
Henry E. Rohlson Airport
Westend Salt Pond
SANDY POINT
LONG POINT
Caribbean Sea
© AAA
1525-R
SEE AAA GEM ATTRACTIONS

St. Croix Island

CHRISTIANSTED pop. 2,637 (See map and index starting on p. 593)

WHERE TO STAY

THE BUCCANEER

Resort Hotel

$265-$995 12/1-4/2
$280-$695 4/3-11/30

Book great rates at AAA.com — **Phone:** (340)712-2100 — 31

Address: 5007 Estate Shoys Lot, #7 **Location:** Oceanfront. 1.8 mi (2.9 km) e of downtown. **Facility:** Golf and tennis facilities enhance this sprawling resort that has been family-owned for generations; most guest rooms have luxurious appointments. 138 units. 133 one-bedroom standard units, some with whirlpools. 4 one- and 1 two-bedroom suites. 1-2 stories (no elevator), interior/exterior corridors. **Parking:** on-site. **Terms:** 21 day cancellation notice, 7 day in summer-fee imposed. **Amenities:** high-speed Internet, voice mail, safes, irons, hair dryers. *Some:* DVD players, CD players. **Pool(s):** 2 outdoor. **Leisure Activities:** sauna, limited beach access, boat dock, snorkeling, recreation programs, hiking trails, jogging, exercise room, spa, basketball, volleyball. *Fee:* scuba diving, charter fishing, golf-18 holes, 8 tennis courts (2 lighted). **Guest Services:** valet and coin laundry, area transportation (fee), wireless Internet. **Business Services:** conference facilities, PC. **Cards:** AX, CB, DS, MC, VI. ***(See color ad below)***

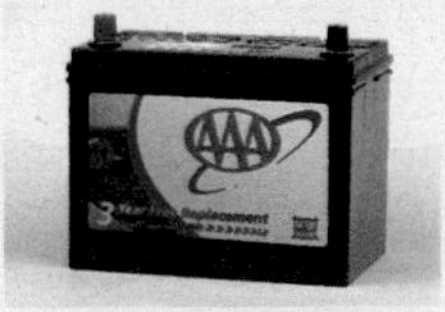

/ SOME UNITS

▼ See AAA listing above ▼

(See map and index starting on p. 593)

CHENAY BAY BEACH RESORT *Book great rates at AAA.com* **Phone:** (340)773-2918 32

Cottage
$309-$799 All Year

Address: #82 East End Quarter, Estate Green Cay **Location:** Oceanfront. 3.6 mi (5.7 km) e of downtown. **Facility:** 50 cottages. 1 story, exterior corridors. *Bath:* combo or shower only. **Parking:** on-site. **Terms:** office hours 8 am-10 pm, 21 day cancellation notice-fee imposed. **Amenities:** voice mail, irons, hair dryers. *Some:* DVD players, CD players. **Dining:** entertainment. **Pool(s):** outdoor. **Leisure Activities:** whirlpool, beach access, paddleboats, sailboats, snorkeling, kayaks, 2 tennis courts, playground, basketball, volleyball. *Fee:* scuba diving. **Guest Services:** coin laundry, wireless Internet. **Business Services:** PC. **Cards:** AX, DC, DS, MC, VI.
(See color ad below)

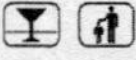 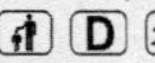   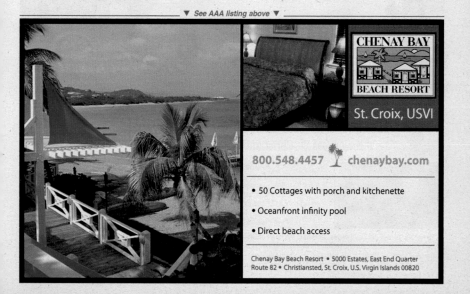 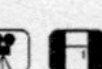 

DIVI CARINA BAY RESORT & CASINO *Book great rates at AAA.com* **Phone:** (340)773-9700 35

Resort Hotel
$210-$626 All Year

Address: 25 Estate Turner Hole **Location:** Oceanfront. 10.4 mi (16.6 km) se of downtown from either north side road or south shore road. **Facility:** In a somewhat remote area, the resort has recently expanded to include a spa and more guest units: Choose from oceanfront rooms or one-bedroom villas. Meets AAA guest room security requirements. 200 units. 178 one-bedroom standard units. 22 one-bedroom suites with whirlpools. 3 stories, exterior corridors. *Bath:* combo or shower only. **Parking:** on-site. **Terms:** 3-7 night minimum stay - seasonal, 7 day cancellation notice-fee imposed. **Amenities:** video library (fee), high-speed Internet, voice mail, safes, irons, hair dryers. *Some:* DVD players (fee). **Dining:** 2 restaurants, entertainment. **Pool(s):** 2 outdoor. **Leisure Activities:** whirlpools, rental paddleboats, rental sailboats, rental sailboards, snorkeling equipment rental, 2 lighted tennis courts, recreation programs, badminton, exercise room, spa, horseshoes, shuffleboard, volleyball, game room. *Fee:* scuba diving, kayaks. **Guest Services:** valet and coin laundry, wireless Internet. **Business Services:** conference facilities, PC. **Cards:** AX, DS, MC, VI.
(See color ad p 596)

     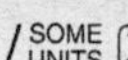 / SOME UNITS

(See map and index starting on p. 593)

HOLGER DANSKE HOTEL Book great rates at AAA.com  

Phone: (340)773-3600 34

Motel

$122-$162 12/1-4/14
$92-$138 4/15-11/30

Address: 1200 King Cross St **Location:** Oceanfront. Historic downtown. **Facility:** Meets AAA guest room security requirements. 39 one-bedroom standard units, some with efficiencies (no utensils). 3 stories (no elevator), exterior corridors. **Parking:** on-site. **Amenities:** high-speed Internet, voice mail, irons, hair dryers. **Pool(s):** outdoor. **Guest Services:** wireless Internet. **Cards:** AX, CB, DC, DS, MC, VI. **Free Special Amenities: local telephone calls and high-speed Internet.** *(See color ad below)*

   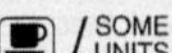 / SOME UNITS 

HOTEL CARAVELLE Book great rates at AAA.com

Phone: (340)773-0687 33

Hotel

$120-$165 All Year

Address: 44A Queen Cross St **Location:** Historic downtown; on waterfront. **Facility:** 44 units. 43 one-bedroom standard units. 1 one-bedroom suite. 3 stories (no elevator), exterior corridors. *Bath:* shower only. **Parking:** on-site. **Terms:** 21 day cancellation notice, 7 day in summer-fee imposed. **Amenities:** voice mail, irons. **Dining:** RumRunners, see separate listing. **Pool(s):** outdoor. **Leisure Activities:** *Fee:* scuba diving. **Guest Services:** valet laundry. **Cards:** AX, CB, DC, DS, MC, VI. **Free Special Amenities: local telephone calls and high-speed Internet.**

/ SOME UNITS

▼ See AAA listing p 595 ▼

▼ See AAA listing above ▼

(See map and index starting on p. 593)

TAMARIND REEF HOTEL Phone: 340/773-4455 38

Hotel

$300-$400 12/1-4/30
$200-$300 5/1-11/30

Address: 5001 Tamarind Reef **Location:** Oceanfront. Just e of town. **Facility:** Meets AAA guest room security requirements. 39 one-bedroom standard units. 2 stories (no elevator), exterior corridors. *Bath:* shower only. **Parking:** on-site. **Terms:** 21 day cancellation notice-fee imposed. **Amenities:** video library (fee), voice mail, safes, irons, hair dryers. *Some:* DVD players (fee). **Dining:** 2 restaurants. **Pool(s):** outdoor. **Leisure Activities:** snorkeling, kayaks, 2 lighted tennis courts. **Guest Services:** coin laundry. **Cards:** AX, DC, MC, VI.

/ SOME UNITS

WHERE TO DINE

BACCHUS Phone: 340/692-9922 22

American
$22-$36

This bistro-style eatery is owned and operated by a young, talented chef. Food is served in the cozy atmosphere of a historic townhouse by gregarious servers. For starters try the roasted beets and gorgonzola or the smoked duck chili. Entrees range from pork prime rib to beef stroganoff to the seafood stew, which is a savory meal of mussels, clams, scallops, shrimp and fish simmered in a white wine herb broth served over spaghetti. Award-winning wine list and very tempting dessert offerings. Dressy casual. **Bar:** Full bar. **Reservations:** required, in season. **Hours:** Open 12/1-9/1 & 10/1-11/30; 6 pm-10 pm. Closed: 4/12, 11/26; also Mon, Sun 4/15-11/1 & Super Bowl Sun. **Address:** 52 Queen Cross St **Location:** Between Strand and King sts; downtown Christiansted. **Parking:** street. **Cards:** AX, DC, DS, MC, VI.

CHEESEBURGERS IN AMERICA'S PARADISE Phone: 340/773-1119 19

American
$11-$24

Under a tent tarp, the fun, open-air spot mostly serves burgers, burritos, nachos and daily specials. Live entertainment is offered Thursday through Sunday. Casual dress. Entertainment. **Bar:** Full bar. **Hours:** 11 am-10 pm. Closed: 11/26, 12/25. **Address:** East End Rd (Rt 82) **Location:** 3.5 mi (5.6 km) e of town. **Parking:** on-site. **Cards:** MC, VI.

FORT CHRISTIAN BREW PUB Phone: 340/713-9820 21

American
$10-$27

In a lovely setting overlooking the town boardwalk and waterfront, this open-air eatery presents a mixed menu of tasty fare. On the menu is a good selection of hearty appetizers, such as wings and nachos, as well as burgers, salads, pasta dishes, steaks and seafood, which go down easily with choices of microbrewed beers, tasty island cocktails and wines. Casual dress. **Bar:** Full bar. **Hours:** 11 am-10 pm, Sun-9 pm. **Address:** 57A Kings Alley **Location:** On the Christiansted boardwalk. **Parking:** no self-parking. **Cards:** MC, VI.

(See map and index starting on p. 593)

KENDRICKS **Phone:** 340/773-9199 (20)

International

$20-$32

The family-owned restaurant's courtyard setting is charming and inviting. French influences are evident in some selections of creatively prepared traditional dishes and pasta. Daily seafood specials are popular. Dressy casual. **Bar:** Full bar. **Reservations:** suggested. **Hours:** 6 pm-10 pm; to 9 pm 6/1-6/30 & 9/1-11/1. Closed: 1/1, 12/25; also Sun, Mon 5/1-6/30 & 9/1-11/30. **Address:** 2132 Company St **Location:** Downtown; jct Company and King Cross sts. **Parking:** street. **Cards:** AX, DS, MC, VI.

RUMRUNNERS **Phone:** 340/773-6585 (24)

American

$9-$26

This open-air restaurant features a relaxed setting directly overlooking the town boardwalk and waterfront. Diners can choose from a wide selection of tasty lighter fare, well-prepared full entrees and daily specials of fresh local seafood, all served with a distinct island flair. All dishes are prepared to order, and the desserts are homemade. Casual dress. **Bar:** Full bar. **Reservations:** accepted. **Hours:** 7-10:30 am, 11:30-3 & 5:30-10 pm, Sun 8 am-2 & 5:30-10 pm. **Address:** 44A Queen Cross St **Location:** Historic district; on waterfront at Hotel Caravelle. **Parking:** no self-parking. **Cards:** MC, VI.

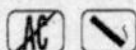

TUTTO BENE **Phone:** 340/773-5229 (23)

Italian

$16-$31

Now in a new, more spacious location, the restaurant continues to live up to its well-earned reputation for excellent Italian cuisine and skilled service. In addition to an array of pasta dishes, the menu lists entrees of salmon, veal, rack of lamb and filet mignon. Casual dress. **Bar:** Full bar. **Reservations:** suggested. **Hours:** 6 pm-10 pm. Closed: 11/26, 12/25. **Address:** 2006 Eastern Suburb, Suite One **Location:** Just e of town. **Parking:** on-site. **Cards:** AX, MC, VI.

FREDERIKSTED pop. 732 (See map and index starting on p. 593)

WHERE TO STAY

SAND CASTLE ON THE BEACH HOTEL & RESTAURANT Book at AAA.com **Phone:** (340)772-1205 (37)

Hotel

$89-$279 All Year

Address: 127 Estate Smithfield **Location:** Oceanfront. 0.5 mi (0.8 km) s of Frederiksted. **Facility:** Meets AAA guest room security requirements. 22 units. 9 one-bedroom standard units. 10 one- and 3 two-bedroom suites, some with efficiencies. 1-2 stories (no elevator), exterior corridors. *Bath:* shower only. **Parking:** on-site. **Terms:** office hours 9 am-9 pm, 60 day cancellation notice-fee imposed. **Amenities:** video library, safes, irons, hair dryers. *Some:* DVD players, CD players. **Dining:** Beachside Cafe, see separate listing. **Pool(s):** 2 outdoor. **Leisure Activities:** beach access, exercise room. *Fee:* snorkeling, massage. **Guest Services:** valet and coin laundry. **Cards:** AX, MC, VI.

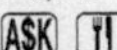     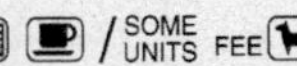 / SOME UNITS FEE 

WHERE TO DINE

BEACHSIDE CAFE **Phone:** 340/772-1266 (25)

International

$9-$30

Enjoy oceanfront dining in an al fresco restaurant with captivating sunsets, nightly specials and ever-changing soups du jour. Lining the menu are curry dishes, steaks, scallops and duck breast. Once a month the restaurant features jazz weekends that are steadfastly gaining in popularity. Casual dress. **Bar:** Full bar. **Reservations:** suggested. **Hours:** Open 12/1-9/18 & 10/6-11/30; 11:30 am-2:30 & 6-9 pm, Sun 10 am-3 & 6-9 pm. Closed: Tues; Wed 4/15-11/30. **Address:** 127 Estate Smithfield **Location:** 0.5 mi (0.8 km) s of Frederiksted; in Sand Castle on the Beach Hotel & Restaurant. **Parking:** on-site. **Cards:** AX, MC, VI.

St. John Island

CRUZ BAY pop. 2,743 (See map and index starting on p. 593)

WHERE TO STAY

GALLOWS POINT RESORT — **Phone:** (340)776-6434 **28**

Condominium

$225-$625 All Year

Address: 3AAA Gallows Point Rd **Location:** Oceanfront. 0.3 mi (0.5 km) s of ferry dock. **Facility:** Meets AAA guest room security requirements. Smoke free premises. 50 one-bedroom suites with kitchens. 2 stories, exterior corridors. *Bath:* shower only. **Parking:** on-site. **Terms:** 3 night minimum stay, age restrictions may apply, 30 day cancellation notice-fee imposed. **Amenities:** video library (fee), CD players, voice mail, safes, irons, hair dryers. *Some:* DVD players. **Pool(s):** outdoor. **Leisure Activities:** whirlpool. *Fee:* snorkeling. **Guest Services:** coin laundry, area transportation, wireless Internet. **Business Services:** PC. **Cards:** AX, MC, VI.

THE WESTIN ST. JOHN RESORT & VILLAS — Book great rates at AAA.com — **Phone:** (340)693-8000 **29**

AAA SAVE

Resort Hotel

$209-$1079 All Year

Address: Great Cruz Bay **Location:** Oceanfront. 2 mi (3.2 km) se of town on Hwy 104. **Facility:** The sprawling resort with a large pool area and sugar-sand beach offers fully-equipped, condo-style units as well as hotel rooms. Meets AAA guest room security requirements. Smoke free premises. 325 units. 175 one-bedroom standard units. 150 condominiums. 2-3 stories (no elevator), exterior corridors. **Parking:** on-site. **Amenities:** video games, high-speed Internet, dual phone lines, voice mail, safes, irons, hair dryers. *Some:* DVD players, CD players, honor bars. **Dining:** 4 restaurants, entertainment. **Pool(s):** 3 outdoor. **Leisure Activities:** saunas, whirlpools, beach access, rental boats, paddleboats, sailboats, windsurfing, boat dock, kayaks, 6 lighted tennis courts, recreation programs, bocci, croquet, kids club & teen center, jogging, playground, spa, basketball, volleyball, game room. *Fee:* scuba diving, snorkeling, charter fishing, personal watercraft. **Guest Services:** valet laundry, airport transportation (fee)-St. Thomas Airport, wireless Internet. **Business Services:** conference facilities, business center. **Cards:** AX, CB, DC, DS, JC, MC, VI. *(See color ad on insert & inside front cover)*

> **WESTIN** HOTELS & RESORTS
>
> **AAA Benefit:**
>
> Enjoy up to 15% off your next stay, plus Starwood Preferred Guest® bonuses.

FEE        / SOME UNITS

The following lodging was either not evaluated or did not meet AAA rating requirements but is listed for your information only.

ESTATE LINDHOLM — **Phone:** 340/776-6121

fyi

Not evaluated. **Address:** Parcel 6 Estate Caneel Bay **Location:** 0.5 mi (0.8 km) n of town. Facilities, services, and decor characterize a mid-scale property.

(See map and index starting on p. 593)

WHERE TO DINE

ASOLARE — **Phone:** 340/779-4747 (17)

Regional Specialty
$22-$38

The terrace of this old stone home above Cruz Bay affords sweeping views of breathtaking sunsets. Imaginative dishes use fresh ingredients and blend Asian and tropical influences. Dressy casual. **Bar:** Full bar. **Reservations:** suggested. **Hours:** 5:30 pm-8:45 pm. Closed: Super Bowl Sun. **Address:** Northshore Rd **Location:** Just n of town. **Parking:** on-site. **Cards:** AX, MC, VI.

MORGAN'S MANGO — **Phone:** 340/693-8141 (16)

International
$12-$27

On the second floor of a West Indies-style verandah is the lively restaurant with a boisterous atmosphere most nights due to the popularity with locals and tourists alike. The menu is a trip around the Caribbean with signature dishes from many of the islands, a few of the favorites being the Voodoo snapper, the seafood brochette and the flying fish. The brie quesadilla or the lobster cakes are savory appetizers to whet the appetite. Casual dress. Entertainment. **Bar:** Full bar. **Reservations:** suggested. **Hours:** Open 12/1-9/20 & 10/1-11/30; 5:30 pm-10 pm. Closed: 1/1, 12/25. **Location:** Center; near ferry dock; across from National Park Visitors Center. **Parking:** street. **Cards:** MC, VI.

VIRGIN ISLANDS NATIONAL PARK

(See map and index starting on p. 593)

WHERE TO STAY

CANEEL BAY-A ROSEWOOD RESORT — Book great rates at AAA.com — **Phone:** (340)776-6111 (25)

Resort Hotel
$450-$1600 12/1-4/30
$395-$1200 5/1-11/30

Address: North Shore Dr **Location:** Oceanfront. On Caneel Bay; reached by ferry from Charlotte Amalie Waterfront. Located in Virgin Islands National Park. **Facility:** This resort, on 170 acres of an old sugar plantation, is surrounded by a national park; widely dispersed lodgings add to the feeling of seclusion. 166 one-bedroom standard units. 1-2 stories (no elevator), exterior corridors. *Bath:* combo or shower only. **Parking:** on-site. **Terms:** office hours 7 am-11 pm, 28 day cancellation notice. **Amenities:** safes, honor bars, irons, hair dryers. **Pool(s):** outdoor. **Leisure Activities:** boating, sailboats, windsurfing, boat dock, snorkeling, 11 tennis courts, recreation programs, hiking trails, playground. *Fee:* scuba diving, charter fishing, massage. **Guest Services:** TV in common area, valet laundry, area transportation (fee), wireless Internet. **Business Services:** meeting rooms, business center. **Cards:** AX, DC, DS, MC, VI.

FEE

St. Thomas Island

CHARLOTTE AMALIE pop. 11,004 (See map and index starting on p. 593)

— WHERE TO STAY —

BEST WESTERN EMERALD BEACH RESORT *Book great rates at AAA.com* **Phone:** (340)777-8800 **2**

AAA SAVE

Hotel

$99-$309 12/1-5/31

$159-$209 6/1-11/30

Address: 8070 Lindbergh Bay **Location:** Oceanfront. 2.5 mi (4 km) w of town, on Lindbergh Bay; 0.6 mi (1 km) from airport. **Facility:** Meets AAA guest room security requirements. 90 one-bedroom standard units. 3 stories (no elevator), exterior corridors. **Parking:** on-site. **Terms:** check-in 4 pm, 3 day cancellation notice-fee imposed. **Amenities:** DVD players, high-speed Internet, voice mail, safes (fee), irons, hair dryers. **Pool(s):** outdoor. **Leisure Activities:** limited beach access, snorkeling, tennis court, limited exercise equipment. *Fee:* sailboats, windsurfing, scuba diving, kayaks. **Guest Services:** valet laundry, wireless Internet. **Business Services:** meeting rooms, PC (fee). **Cards:** AX, CB, DC, DS, MC, VI.
(See color ad p 602)

     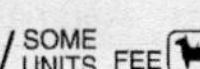 / SOME UNITS FEE

AAA Benefit:
Members save up to 20%, plus 10% bonus points with rewards program.

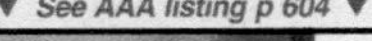
▼ See AAA listing p 604 ▼

▼ See AAA listing p 601 ▼

(See map and index starting on p. 593)

WHERE TO DINE

CUZZIN'S CARIBBEAN RESTAURANT — **Phone:** 340/777-4711 (6)

Caribbean $11-$21

In the heart of Charlotte Amalie's bustling shopping district is the ever-popular restaurant, which offers West Indian fare. On the menu are preparations of fresh local fish and conch, curry dishes and traditional sides such as fungi, a familiar island favorite similar to polenta. Casual dress. **Bar:** Full bar. **Reservations:** suggested, for dinner. **Hours:** Open 12/1-9/14 & 10/7-11/30; 11 am-9:30 pm, Mon-4 pm. Closed major holidays; also Sun. **Address:** 7 Back St **Location:** Jct Trompeter Gade; downtown. **Parking:** street. **Cards:** AX, DC, DS, MC, VI.

THE GREENHOUSE BAR AND RESTAURANT — **Phone:** 340/774-7998 (1)

International $11-$28

Popular with locals and tourists like, the island-centric restaurant, which schedules dining and entertainment theme nights, overlooks the harbor. Entree-size salads, mouthwatering steaks and fresh seafood line the menu. Casual dress. **Bar:** Full bar. **Hours:** 11 am-10 pm. Closed: 12/25. **Address:** Veterans Dr **Location:** Jct Veterans Dr and Storetvaer Gade. **Parking:** street. **Cards:** AX, DS, MC, VI.

HERVE RESTAURANT & WINE BAR Menu on AAA.com — **Phone:** 340/777-9703 (5)

International $10-$35

Excellent French-American cuisine reflects a Caribbean flair and pairs nicely with selections from the extensive wine list. The historic building's terrace offers panoramic views of the town and harbor. Dressy casual. **Bar:** Full bar. **Reservations:** required. **Hours:** Open 12/1-9/8 & 10/9-11/30; 11 am-2:30 & 6-10 pm, Sat & Sun from 6 pm. **Address:** Government Hill **Location:** On Government Hill. **Parking:** street. **Cards:** AX, MC, VI.

HOOK, LINE, & SINKER BAR AND RESTAURANT — **Phone:** 340/776-9708 (2)

American $7-$26

Located at the marina, the casual eatery features a menu of burgers, sandwiches, fresh seafood and pasta dishes. Casual dress. **Bar:** Full bar. **Reservations:** accepted. **Hours:** Open 12/1-9/1 & 9/17-11/30; 7 am-11 pm, Sun 10 am-2:30 pm. Closed major holidays. **Address:** 6200 Honduras **Location:** SR 30 at Frenchtown Yacht Harbor. **Parking:** on-site. **Cards:** AX, MC, VI.

SIB'S ON THE MOUNTAIN — **Phone:** 340/774-8967 (3)

American $13-$23

Perched on the side of the mountain, this longtime local favorite features chicken and seafood dishes, as well as pasta, stir-fries, sandwiches and wraps. Guests can opt to dine in the modest, air-conditioned dining room or outside among the exotic trees of the garden. Casual dress. **Bar:** Full bar. **Hours:** 5 pm-10 pm. Closed major holidays. **Address:** 33-5 Estate Elizabeth **Location:** North of town, halfway up Crown Mountain; at Estate Elizabeth. **Parking:** street. **Cards:** AX, MC, VI.

VICTOR'S NEW HIDE OUT — **Phone:** 340/776-9379 (8)

Caribbean $13-$30

Diners appreciate a panoramic view of Crown Bay Harbor from the large, airy dining room. Native Caribbean dishes and seafood—such as old wife fish, fried plantains, Creoles and curry—are well-prepared and tasty. Casual dress. **Bar:** Full bar. **Reservations:** accepted. **Hours:** 11:30 am-10 pm, Sun from 4 pm. **Address:** 103 Sub Base **Location:** Between airport and center of town; on top of hill just e of airport, follow signs from SR 30. **Parking:** on-site. **Cards:** AX, CB, DC, DS, JC, MC, VI.

FRENCHMAN BAY (See map and index starting on p. 593)

WHERE TO STAY

FRENCHMAN'S REEF & MORNING STAR MARRIOTT BEACH RESORT Book great rates at AAA.com

Phone: (340)776-8500 **5**

Resort Hotel

$367-$543 All Year

Marriott HOTELS & RESORTS

AAA Benefit: Members save a minimum 5% off the best available rate.

Address: 5 Estate Bakkeroe **Location:** Oceanfront. 1 mi (1.6 km) e of town on Frenchman's Bay Rd. **Facility:** This resort sits on the edge of a cliff overlooking the water; one side is decidedly more upscale while the other side is suited for families. Smoke free premises. 478 units. 451 one-bedroom standard units. 27 one-bedroom suites with whirlpools. 2-8 stories, interior/exterior corridors. *Bath:* combo or shower only. **Parking:** on-site. **Terms:** check-in 4 pm, 7 day cancellation notice-fee imposed. **Amenities:** high-speed Internet (fee), voice mail, safes, irons, hair dryers. *Some:* dual phone lines. **Dining:** 4 restaurants, also, Havana Blue, see separate listing, entertainment. **Pool(s):** 3 outdoor. **Leisure Activities:** rental boats, rental sailboats, rental sailboards, boat dock, snorkeling equipment rental, 2 lighted tennis courts, recreation programs, spa, volleyball. *Fee:* sea kayaks, tennis instruction, helipad. **Guest Services:** valet laundry, area transportation (fee)-water taxi to Charlotte Amalie, beauty salon, wireless Internet. **Business Services:** conference facilities, business center. **Cards:** AX, CB, DC, DS, JC, MC, VI. *(See color ad p 601 & on insert)*

CALL   / SOME UNITS

WHERE TO DINE

HAVANA BLUE

Phone: 340/715-2583 **9**

Latin American

$28-$48

The latest trendy restaurant on the island to receive rave reviews has a chic dining room with suave decor reminiscent of South Beach. Inspired young servers energize the floor. Tastefully presented dishes of Angus beef, duck breast, lamb and seafood integrate Caribbean, Cuban and Asian culinary influences. Designer cocktails are especially tempting. Dressy casual. **Bar:** Full bar. **Reservations:** suggested. **Hours:** 5:30 pm-10 pm. **Address:** Estate Bakkeroe **Location:** 1 mi (1.6 km) e of town on Frenchman's Bay Rd; in Frenchman's Reef & Morning Star Marriott Beach Resort. **Parking:** on-site. **Cards:** AX, MC, VI.

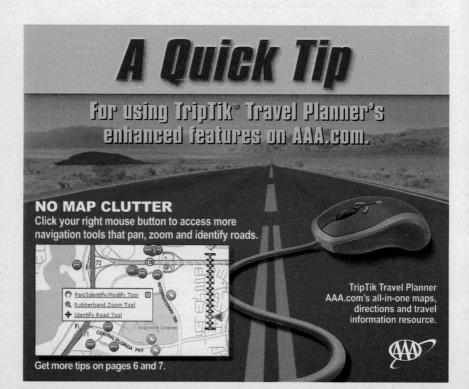

RED HOOK (See map and index starting on p. 593)

WHERE TO STAY

THE RITZ-CARLTON, ST. THOMAS Book at AAA.com Phone: (340)775-3333 13

Resort Hotel
$479-$1690 All Year

Address: 6900 Great Bay **Location:** Oceanfront. 3 mi (4.8 km) e of Charlotte Amalie; Hwy 38 to jct Hwy 32, 3.5 mi (5.6 km) e to jct Hwy 322, 2 mi (3.2 km) se. **Facility:** The resort's main building resembles an Italian-Mediterranean villa with an open-air courtyard; a newly built extension also is featured. Meets AAA guest room security requirements. Smoke free premises. 180 units. 154 one-bedroom standard units. 26 one-bedroom suites. 3-5 stories, exterior corridors. *Bath:* combo or shower only. **Parking:** on-site and valet. **Terms:** 14 day cancellation notice-fee imposed. **Amenities:** video games (fee), CD players, high-speed Internet, dual phone lines, voice mail, safes, honor bars, irons, hair dryers. **Pool(s):** 2 outdoor. **Leisure Activities:** whirlpools, boating, sailboats, windsurfing, snorkeling, 2 lighted tennis courts, recreation programs, spa, volleyball. *Fee:* scuba diving. **Guest Services:** valet laundry, beauty salon. **Business Services:** conference facilities, PC (fee). **Cards:** AX, MC, VI.

24 S D / SOME UNITS FEE FEE

SECRET HARBOUR BEACH RESORT Book great rates at AAA.com Phone: (340)775-6550 11

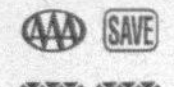

Condominium
$185-$725 All Year

Address: 6280 Estate Nazareth **Location:** Oceanfront. 3 mi (4.8 km) e of Charlotte Amalie; on Hwy 38 to jct Hwy 32, 3.5 mi (5.6 km) e to jct Hwy 322, 1 mi (1.6 km) se. **Facility:** Meets AAA guest room security requirements. 60 units. 15 one-bedroom standard units, some with kitchens. 36 one- and 9 two-bedroom suites, some with kitchens. 3 stories (no elevator), exterior corridors. **Parking:** on-site. **Terms:** 7 day cancellation notice, 14 day in winter, 30 day in season-fee imposed. **Amenities:** video library (fee), DVD players, CD players, high-speed Internet, voice mail, safes, irons, hair dryers. **Pool(s):** outdoor. **Leisure Activities:** boat dock, 3 tennis courts, exercise room. *Fee:* scuba diving, snorkeling, kayaks, pedal boats, massage. **Guest Services:** valet and coin laundry, wireless Internet. **Business Services:** meeting rooms, PC. **Cards:** AX, MC, VI. **Free Special Amenities: local telephone calls.**
(See color ad below)

CALL D VCR / SOME UNITS

WHERE TO DINE

THE AGAVE TERRACE Phone: 340/775-4142 13

International
$24-$45

Situated on a cliff, the open-air dining room offers breathtaking views of the sea and neighboring islands. On the menu are distinctive preparations of the freshest local seafood and lobster. A steel band performs Tuesday and Thursday. Dressy casual. **Bar:** Full bar. **Reservations:** suggested. **Hours:** 6 pm-10 pm. **Address:** 6600 Estate Smith Bay, #4 **Location:** 8 mi (12.8 km) e of Charlotte Amalie; on north coast Hwy 38; in Point Pleasant Resort and Villas. **Parking:** on-site. **Cards:** AX, DS, MC, VI.

AC

BUDDHA SUSHI LOUNGE & GRILL Phone: 340/714-3474 18

Sushi
$17-$28

Do not be fooled by the ordinary exterior because within the Japanese motif offers a pleasant ambiance at this complete sushi bar, the only authentic one in St. Thomas; menu selections include a wide assortment of sushi and sashimi, teriyaki dishes, tempura and grilled fish or meat. Casual dress. **Bar:** Full bar. **Reservations:** suggested. **Hours:** Open 12/1-9/15 & 10/15-11/30; 5 pm-10 pm, Fri & Sat-11 pm. Closed: 12/25. **Address:** East End Rd **Location:** Center; southeast side of island. **Parking:** on-site. **Cards:** MC, VI.

▼ See AAA listing above ▼

(See map and index starting on p. 593)

DUFFY'S LOVE SHACK **Phone:** 340/779-2080 (11)

International
$9-$17

The small open-air spot is known for its nightlife and fun. Most nights are theme nights, such as "King Crab Monday," "Taco Tuesday," "Phat in the Hat Wednesday" and "Lobster Lunacy Thursday." The interesting eclectic menu incorporates Asian, Mexican and Caribbean specialties. Many of the outrageous tropical drinks come in souvenir glasses. Casual dress. **Bar:** Full bar. **Hours:** 11:30 am-midnight. **Address:** 6500 Red Hook Plaza **Location:** East end in Red Hook Plaza; opposite St. John Ferry Dock. **Parking:** on-site.

MOLLY MOLONES **Phone:** 340/775-1270 (10)

Irish
$9-$27

Guests find a bit of Ireland in this pub-style eatery not far from the ferry docks. Lunch options include thick delicatessen sandwiches, gourmet burgers and "Philly" cheese steaks, while the full dinner menu is lined with starters such as wings and conch fritters and entrees such as shepherd's pie, Irish stew, Angus steaks and fresh catches of the day. Casual dress. **Bar:** Full bar. **Hours:** 7 am-11 pm, Fri & Sat-midnight; Saturday & Sunday brunch. **Address:** 6100 Red Hooks Quarters **Location:** Center; at American Yacht Harbour. **Parking:** on-site. **Cards:** AX, MC, VI.

SMITH BAY (See map and index starting on p. 593)

WHERE TO STAY

PAVILIONS AND POOLS HOTEL **Phone:** (340)775-6110 (16)

Cottage
$260-$360 12/1-4/15
$200-$275 4/16-11/30

Address: 6400 Estate Smith Bay **Location:** 7.3 mi (11.7 km) e of Charlotte Amalie; on northeast coast Hwy 38. **Facility:** Smoke free premises. 25 cottages. 1 story, exterior corridors. *Bath:* shower only. **Parking:** on-site. **Terms:** office hours 8 am-9 pm, 21 day cancellation notice. **Amenities:** safes, irons, hair dryers. *Some:* DVD players, CD players. **Guest Services:** coin laundry, wireless Internet. **Business Services:** PC. **Cards:** AX, MC, VI.

ASK / SOME UNITS VCR

WYNDHAM SUGAR BAY RESORT & SPA *Book great rates at AAA.com* **Phone:** (340)777-7100 (15)

Resort Hotel
$187-$646 All Year

Address: 6500 Estate Smith Bay **Location:** Oceanfront. 8.5 mi (13.6 km) e of Charlotte Amalie; on Hwy 38. **Facility:** The resort is on a bluff and all units feature patios with sweeping views of Smith Bay or St. John; a variety of activities are available. Meets AAA guest room security requirements. 295 units. 288 one-bedroom standard units. 7 one-bedroom suites. 3-4 stories, exterior corridors. **Parking:** on-site. **Terms:** 3-7 night minimum stay, 7 day cancellation notice-fee imposed. **Amenities:** voice mail, safes, irons, hair dryers. *Fee:* video games, high-speed Internet. *Some:* CD players. **Pool(s):** 3 outdoor. **Leisure Activities:** saunas, whirlpools, steamrooms, beach access, sailboats, windsurfing, snorkeling, 4 lighted tennis courts, recreation programs, jogging, spa, basketball, volleyball. *Fee:* scuba diving, miniature golf, game room. **Guest Services:** valet laundry, wireless Internet. **Business Services:** conference facilities, PC (fee). **Cards:** AX, DC, DS, MC, VI.

ASK S D / SOME UNITS

WHERE TO DINE

ROMANO'S **Phone:** 340/775-0045 (15)

Northern Italian
$21-$32

Original local art decorates the cozy dining room, where guests taste pasta, seafood and veal prepared in a nouvelle Italian fashion. Nightly specials are worth a try, as are the sinful raspberry or banana Napoleons. Dressy casual. **Bar:** Full bar. **Reservations:** suggested. **Hours:** Open 12/1-8/30 & 11/1-11/30; 6 pm-10:30 pm. Closed major holidays; also Sun, 12/24-12/29 & Carnival. **Address:** 6697 Smith Bay **Location:** On Coral World Rd, just n of jct Hwy 38. **Parking:** on-site. **Cards:** AX, MC, VI.

Caribbean Club Contacts

AAA Auto Club South has an office in San Juan, Puerto Rico, to serve visiting AAA/CAA members. The branch office provides auto travel services, including maps, TourBooks and on-demand Triptiks, as well as travel agency services. The office is at 654 Avenida Muñoz Rivera, Lobby Level, Suites 103-1119, approximately 6 miles from Old San Juan's cruise ship piers in the suburb of Hato Rey. Office hours are Monday through Friday 9-6 (Atlantic Standard Time). For more information, phone (787) 620-7805.

Language Tips

ON THE FOLLOWING PAGES are listed some of the words and phrases that are most useful to English-speaking travelers in the Caribbean. Expressions are given in Dutch, French and Spanish, the three languages most commonly spoken in addition to English.

Although not essential, knowledge of basic terms—particularly "please" and "thank you"—is helpful. Most islanders who deal with tourists speak at least some English, and those who don't will be only too glad to assist you in your attempts at a foreign language.

General Expressions

Dutch

Please .... Alstublief
Thank you .... Dank u zeer
Excuse me .... Neemt u mij niet kwalijk
Yes .... Ja
No .... Neen
Good day (hello) .... Goedendag
Good evening .... Goedenavond
Good night .... Goedenacht
Good-bye .... Tot ziens
Do you speak English? .... Spreekt u Engels?
I do not understand .... Ik begrijp niet
Please repeat .... Zegt u het nog eens
Sir .... Mijnheer
Madam .... Mevrouw
Miss .... Juffrouw

French

Please .... S'il vous plaît
Thank you .... Merci
Excuse me .... Excusez-moi
Yes .... Oui
No .... Non
Good day (hello) .... Bonjour
Good evening .... Bonsoir
Good night .... Bonne nuit
Good-bye .... Au revoir
Do you speak English? .... Parlez-vous anglais?
I do not understand .... Je ne comprends pas
Please repeat .... Répétez, s'il vous plaît
Sir .... Monsieur
Madam .... Madame
Miss .... Mademoiselle

Spanish

Please .... Por favor
Thank you .... Gracias
Excuse me .... Discúlpeme usted
Yes .... Si
No .... No
Good day (hello) .... Buenos días
Good evening .... Buenas tardes
Good night .... Buenas noches
Good-bye .... Adiós
Do you speak English? .... ¿Habla usted inglés?
I do not understand .... No entiendo
Please repeat .... Repita, por favor
Sir .... Señor
Madam .... Señora
Miss .... Señorita

On The Road

English

1. Please show me the road to ____.
2. I want to go to ____.
3. Are we far from ____?
4. Where are we?
5. May I park here?
6. Go straight ahead.
7. To the right.
8. To the left.
9. How far is
   a. a garage?
   b. a gas station?
   c. a doctor?
   d. a police station?
   e. a telephone?
   f. a post office?
   g. a hotel?
   h. a restaurant?

Dutch

1. Wilt u mij de weg naar ____wijzen.
2. Ik wil naar ____.
3. Zijn we ver van ____?
4. Waar zijn we?

5. Mag ik hier stoppen?
6. Rijdt u rechtdoor?
7. Rechts.
8. Links.
9. Hoe ver hier vandaan is
   a. een garage?
   b. een benzinestation?
   c. een doktor?
   d. een politie-bureau?
   e. een telefooncel?
   f. een postkantoor?
   g. een hotel?
   h. een restaurant?

French

1. Veuillez m'indiquer la route a ____.
2. Je desire aller a
3. Sommes-nous loins de ____?
4. Ou sommes nous?
5. Puis-je m'arreter ici?
6. Roulez tout droit.
7. À droit
8. À gauche
9. À quelle distance se trouve
   a. un garage?
   b. un poste a essence?
   c. un medecin?
   d. un poste de police?
   e. une cabine?
   f. la poste?
   g. un hotel?
   h. un restaurant?

Spanish

1. Sirvase indicarme el camino para ____.
2. Quiero ir a ____?
3. ¿Estamos lejos de ____?
4. ¿Dónde estamos?
5. ¿Puedo detenerme aquí?
6. Síga el camino recto.
7. A la derecha
8. A la izquierda
9. ¿A que distancia está
   a. un garaje?
   b. una estación de gasolina?
   c. un médico?
   d. una estación de policia?
   e. una cabina telefónica?
   f. la oficina de correos?
   g. un hotel?
   h. un restaurante?

At The Restaurant

Dutch

Water .... Water
Coffee .... Koffie
Tea .... Thee
Milk .... Melk
Beer .... Bier
Wine .... Wijn
Cider .... Appelwijn
Lemonade .... Citroenlimonade
Hors d'oeuvres .... Hors d'oeuvres
Bread .... Brood
Soup .... Soep
Eggs .... Eiren
Fish .... Vis
Lobster .... Kreeftesla
Meat .... Vlees
Beef .... Rundvlees
Beefsteak .... Biefstuk
Pork .... Varkenvlees
Ham .... Ham
Mutton .... Schapevlees
Venison .... Wild
Veal .... Kalfvlees
Chicken .... Kip
Rice .... Rijst
Potatoes .... Aardappelen
Vegetables .... Groenten
Salad .... Salade
Tomatoes .... Tomaten
Cabbage .... Kool
Green peas .... Doperwten
Green beans .... Princesseboontjes
Cauliflower .... Bloemkool
Mushrooms .... Champignons
Cheese .... Kaas
Fruit .... Fruit
Pastries .... Gebak
Ice cream .... Ijs
Cookies .... Beschult
Orange .... Sinaasappel
Apple .... Appel
Banana .... Banaan
Grapes .... Druiven
Pear .... Peer
Cherries .... Kersen
Strawberries .... Aardbeien
Sugar .... Suiker
Cream .... Room
Salt .... Zout
Pepper .... Peper
Oil .... Olie
Vinegar .... Azijn
Mustard .... Mosterd
Garlic .... Knoflook
Butter .... Boter
Jam .... Jam
Knife .... Mes
Fork .... Vork
Spoon .... Lepel
Bottle .... Fles
Glass .... Glas
Cup .... Kopje
Plate .... Bord
Napkin .... Servet
Rare .... Half rauw
Medium .... Gaar
Well done .... Gebakken
Warm .... Warm
Iced, cold .... Gekoeld
Give me the menu .... Geeft u mij het menu
I should like .... Ik sou willen.
How much is the meal? .... Hoeveel kost de maaltijd?
Is service included? .... Is de bediening inbegrepen?
The bill, please. .... De rekening, alstublift.
Breakfast .... Ontbijt
Lunch .... Lunch
Dinner .... Diner

French

Water .... Eau
Coffee .... Cafe
Tea .... The
Milk .... Lait
Beer .... Biere
Wine .... Vin
Cider .... Cidre
Lemonade .... Citronnade
Hors d'oeuvres .... Hors d'oeuvres
Bread .... Pain
Soup .... Soupe
Egg .... Oeuf
Omelette .... Omelette
Fish .... Poisson

Lobster .... Homard
Shrimp .... Crevette
Oyster .... Huitre
Clam .... Moule
Meat .... Viande
Beef .... Boeuf
Beefsteak .... Bifteck
Pork .... Porc
Ham .... Jambon
Mutton .... Mouton
Lamb .... Agneau
Veal .... Veau
Chicken .... Poulet
Rice .... Riz
Potatoes .... Pommes de terre
Vegetables .... Legumes
Salad .... Salade
Tomatoes .... Tomates
Lettuce .... Laitue
Green peas .... Petits pois
Beans .... Haricots
Asparagus .... Asperges
Carrots .... Carottes
Mushrooms .... Champignons
Cheeses .... Fromages
Fruits .... Fruits
Pastries .... Patisseries
Ice cream .... Glace
Cookies .... Biscuits
Orange .... Orange
Apple .... Pomme
Banana .... Banane
Strawberries .... Fraises
Sugar .... Sucre
Cream .... Creme
Salt .... Sel
Pepper .... Poivre
Butter .... Beurre
Oil .... Huile
Vinegar .... Vinaigre
Mustard .... Moutarde
Gravy, sauce .... Sauce
Garlic .... Ail
Jam .... Confiture
Knife .... Couteau
Fork .... Fourchette
Spoon .... Cuiller
Bottle .... Bouteille
Glass .... Verre
Cup .... Tasse
Plate .... Assiette
Napkin .... Serviette
Roasted .... Roti
Fried .... Frit
Rare .... Saignant
Medium .... A point
Well done .... Cuit
Warm .... Chaud
Iced .... Glace
Show me the menu .... Montrez-moi le menu.
I should like .... Je voudrais.
What is the price of the meal? .... Quel est le prix du repas?
Is service included? .... Le service est-il compris?
The bill, please .... L'addition, s'il vous plaît.
Breakfast .... Petit dejeuner
Lunch .... Dejeuner
Dinner .... Diner

Spanish

Water .... Agua
Coffee .... Café
Tea .... Té
Milk .... Leche
Beer .... Cerveza
Wine .... Vino
Cider .... Sidra
Lemonade .... Limonada
Hors d'oeuvres .... Entremeses
Bread .... Pan
Soup .... Sopa
Eggs .... Huevos
Omelette .... Tortilla
Fish .... Pescado
Lobster .... Langosta
Shrimp, prawn .... Langostino
Oyster .... Ostra
Clam .... Almeja
Meat .... Carne
Beef .... Vaca
Beefsteak .... Bistec
Pork .... Cerdo
Ham .... Jamón
Mutton .... Cordero
Lamb .... Cordero
Veal .... Ternera
Chicken .... Pollo
Rice .... Arroz
Potatoes .... Papas
Vegetables .... Legumbres
Salad .... Ensalada
Tomatoes .... Tomates
Lettuce .... Lechuga
Peas .... Guisantes
Beans .... Habichuelas
Asparagus .... Esparrago
Carrots .... Zanahorias
Mushrooms .... Hongos
Cheese .... Queso
Fruits .... Frutas
Pastries .... Pastelería
Ice cream .... Helados
Cookies .... Galletas
Orange .... Naranja
Apple .... Manzana
Banana .... Güineo
Strawberries .... Fresas
Sugar .... Azúcar
Cream .... Crema
Salt .... Sal
Pepper .... Pimienta
Butter .... Mantequilla
Oil .... Aceite
Vinegar .... Vinagre
Mustard .... Mostaza
Sauce, gravy .... Salsa
Garlic .... Ajo
Jelly .... Jalea
Knife .... Cuchillo
Fork .... Tenedor
Spoon .... Cuchara
Bottle .... Botella
Glass .... Vaso
Cup .... Taza
Plate .... Plato
Napkin .... Servilleta
Roasted .... Asado
Fried .... Frito
Rare .... Poco cocido
Medium .... A punto
Well done .... Bien cocido
Warm .... Tibio
Frozen .... Congelado
Show me the menu .... Muestreme el menú.
I want .... Yo quiero.
How much is the meal? .... Cuánto cuesta la comida?
Is service included? .... Está incluido el servicio?
The bill, please .... La cuenta, por favor.
Breakfast .... Desayuno
Lunch .... Almuerzo
Dinner .... Cena

Metric Equivalents Chart

TEMPERATURE

To convert Fahrenheit to Celsius, subtract 32 from the Fahrenheit temperature, multiply by 5 and divide by 9. To convert Celsius to Fahrenheit, multipy by 9, divide by 5 and add 32.

Celsius °		Fahrenheit °
100	**BOILING**	**212**
37		100
35		95
32		90
29		85
27		80
24		75
21		70
18		65
16		60
13		55
10		50
7		45
4		40
2		35
0	**FREEZING**	**32**
-4		25
-7		20
-9		15
-12		10
-15		5
-18		0
-21		-5
-24		-10
-27		-15

ACRES

1 acre = 0.4 hectare (ha)   1 hectare = 2.47 acres

MILES AND KILOMETRES

Note: A kilometre is approximately 5/8 or 0.6 of a mile. To convert kilometres to miles multiply by 0.6.

Miles/Kilometres		Kilometres/Miles	
15	24.1	30	18.6
20	32.2	35	21.7
25	40.2	40	24.8
30	48.3	45	27.9
35	56.3	50	31.0
40	64.4	55	34.1
45	72.4	60	37.2
50	80.5	65	40.3
55	88.5	70	43.4
60	96.6	75	46.6
65	104.6	80	49.7
70	112.7	85	52.8
75	120.7	90	55.9
80	128.7	95	59.0
85	136.8	100	62.1
90	144.8	105	65.2
95	152.9	110	68.3
100	160.9	115	71.4

LINEAR MEASURE

Customary	Metric
1 inch = 2.54 centimetres	1 centimetre = 0.4 inches
1 foot = 30 centimetres	1 metre = 3.3 feet
1 yard = 0.91 metres	1 metre = 1.09 yards
1 mile = 1.6 kilometres	1 kilometre = .62 miles

LIQUID MEASURE

Customary	Metric
1 fluid ounce = 30 millilitres	1 millilitre = .03 fluid ounces
1 cup = .24 litres	1 litre = 2.1 pints
1 pint = .47 litres	1 litre = 1.06 quarts
1 quart = .95 litres	1 litre = .26 gallons
1 gallon = 3.8 litres	

WEIGHT

If You Know:	Multiply By:	To Find:
Ounces	28.000	Grams
Pounds	0.450	Kilograms
Grams	0.035	Ounces
Kilograms	2.200	Pounds

PRESSURE

Air pressure in automobile tires is expressed in kilopascals. Multiply pound-force per square inch (psi) by 6.89 to find kilopascals (kPa).

24 psi = 165 kPa   28 psi = 193 kPa
26 psi = 179 kPa   30 psi = 207 kPa

GALLON AND LITRES

Gallons/Litres				Litres/Gallons			
5	19.0	12	45.6	10	2.6	40	10.4
6	22.8	14	53.2	15	3.9	50	13.0
7	26.6	16	60.8	20	5.2	60	15.6
8	30.4	18	68.4	25	6.5	70	18.2
9	34.2	20	76.0	30	7.8	80	20.8
10	38.0	25	95.0	35	9.1	90	23.4

Caribbean Customs Information

Each Caribbean nation has its own immigration requirements; these are summarized in the *Fast Facts* boxes. The U.S. Dept. of Homeland Security requires all citizens traveling by air between the United States and the Caribbean to present a valid passport, Air NEXUS card or U.S. Coast Guard Merchant Mariner document to reenter the United States. Citizens traveling by land or sea also are required to present a valid passport or other documents. AAA recommends carrying a passport when traveling anywhere outside the United States, both to expedite your way through customs and to provide identification in case of an emergency. AAA travel agents can assist you with the passport application procedure.

Before you leave, make two color copies of your passport's identification page, keeping one at home and carrying the other with you separately. Should you lose your passport, go to the nearest American Embassy or Consulate, or contact the National Passport Information Center at (877) 487-2778 or TTY (888) 874-7793 for information about obtaining an emergency passport. A U.S. driver's license and a copy of the original passport will save time in applying for a replacement.

Pets taken to the islands are subject to each island's public health department's regulations, and pets taken out of the United States are subject to U.S. Public Health and Department of Agriculture requirements on return. Also check with state, county and municipal authorities about restrictions on importing pets, and make arrangements well in advance. Consult the Pets and Wildlife publication (# 0000-0509) online at www.cbp.gov or by writing to U.S. Customs and Border Protection, 1300 Pennsylvania Ave. NW, Washington, D.C. 20229; phone (202) 354-1000 or (877) 227-5511.

If you plan to carry more than $10,000 in currency or negotiable instruments in or out of the United States, you must file a Currency Reporting Form (FinCen Form 105) with Customs and Border Protection (CBP) at the port of exit or at the port of entry. Forms are available online or from your local CBP office. They also can be obtained at U.S. international airports and all other ports of entry.

Note: Due to heightened security, travel regulations may change without notice. For the most current information about passports, duties and taxes and federal restrictions, contact U.S. Customs and Border Protection at (202) 354-1000 or (877) 227-5511, or visit their web site at www.cbp.gov. The brochure "Know Before You Go" (publication 0000-00512) provides comprehensive information for U.S. citizens traveling abroad.

RETURNING TO THE UNITED STATES

EXEMPTIONS: Any articles you acquire abroad and bring back to the United States must be declared. This requirement includes any repairs made to articles taken abroad and any gifts, such as wedding or birthday presents, you received while abroad.

It is wise to register foreign-made possessions—such as laptop computers, cameras, watches and CD players—at any CBP office *before* leaving the United States in order to avoid being charged duty on them when you return. Only items with serial numbers or other clearly identifiable marks may be registered. If you are traveling with unnumbered items such as expensive jewelry, a sales receipt, insurance policy or appraisal will be sufficient proof that the items were in your possession before you left the U.S. You may register items at the airport prior to departure or take them to a CBP office in advance. Inspectors must *see* the items being registered; keep your documentation for future trips.

Returning U.S. residents are allowed a duty-free exemption for articles they carry with them. If you are arriving from anywhere other than a U.S. insular possession (the U.S. Virgin Islands, American Samoa or Guam), your personal exemption is $800; there are limits on the amount of alcohol, cigarettes, cigars and other tobacco products you may include *(see Alcoholic Beverages and Tobacco Products)*. If you travel to the U.S. Virgin Islands, your duty-free allowance is $1,600, of which no more than $800 may have been acquired elsewhere in the Caribbean.

To receive the duty-free exemption, you must have been out of the country a minimum of 48 hours and have not used the exemption within the preceding 30-day period. The 48-hour minimum does not apply to U.S. residents returning from the U.S. Virgin Islands.

The exemption, based on fair retail value, applies to articles for your personal or household use or intended to be given as bona fide gifts *(see Gifts)*. Returning residents who do not meet the 48-hour or 30-day time requirements may bring back up to $200 worth of items for personal or household use free of duty and tax. Antiques at least 100 years old and fine art may enter the country duty-free.

High-quality merchandise from all over the world is usually featured in most duty-free shops. Prices are generally about the same as you would expect to pay in the country of origin. Do not be misled, however, by the words "duty free." This simply means that the local merchant has been exempted from his own country's taxes. All duty-free goods that return with you to the United States must be declared and are subject to U.S. import duties if you exceed your personal exemption.

DUTIES: A flat rate duty of 3 percent is applied to the next $1,000 worth of merchandise in excess of the maximum customs duty-free exemption. Items purchased in the U.S. Virgin Islands are assessed at a rate of 1.5 percent. The flat-rate provision and duty-free exemptions may not be exercised more than once every 30 days. Assessment of merchandise is based on the fair retail value in the country of origin; remember to retain sales slips for proof of value. Keeping purchases and sales slips in a carry-on bag speeds the customs declaration procedure.

Members of a family residing in the same household and traveling together can make a joint declaration, combining their individual articles for application of the flat-rate duty. Any merchandise that exceeds the flat-rate duty on $1,000 worth of goods is dutiable at the various rates that apply to particular articles.

The United States and the following countries have entered into an agreement called the Caribbean Basin Initiative (CBI). These countries include Antigua and Barbuda, Aruba, The Bahamas, Barbados, the British Virgin Islands, Dominica, the Dominican Republic, Grenada, Jamaica, Montserrat, the Netherlands Antilles, St. Kitts and Nevis, St. Lucia, St. Vincent and the Grenadines, and Trinidad and Tobago. Some articles made in and purchased in these countries are accorded a free rate of duty and are not counted against your exemption or flat rate.

Articles acquired abroad and sent home by you or by the store where you purchased them do not qualify as accompanied baggage and are subject to duty and taxes. You do not have to declare these items, as they cannot be included on the customs exemption; duty may be waived on articles not exceeding $200 in total value.

However, articles you purchase and send home from CBI countries or the U.S. Virgin Islands may be duty-free under your personal exemption if the items are properly declared and processed. The CBP form 255 (Declaration of Unaccompanied Articles) must be affixed to each mailed package; merchants can usually supply this form. All shipped items should be indicated on your customs declaration form.

If requested, you must present all sales receipts to Customs upon returning to the United States. *Do not* accept the friendly shopkeeper's offer to give you a sales slip showing a price lower than that actually paid. Customs inspectors are experts at spotting fraudulent receipts. If you understate an article's value or misrepresent an article on your declaration, you might have to pay a penalty in addition to the duty. Under certain circumstances the article might be seized and forfeited. Keep a record of what you spend for merchandise as you spend it.

If you owe duty, it must be paid when you arrive in the United States. Acceptable forms of payment include U.S. currency, personal checks, money orders, travelers checks (value not exceeding $50 of the amount due), and in some locations, MasterCard or Visa.

GIFTS: Gifts worth up to $100 in total fair retail value where acquired may be sent duty free to friends and relatives in the United States, provided only one such package is received by the same person in one day. The dollar value for gifts sent from the U.S. Virgin Islands increases to $200. Gifts for more than one person may be mailed in the same package, provided each gift is individually wrapped and labeled with the name of the recipient. If any article in the consolidated gift package is subject to duty and tax, or if the total value of all articles exceeds the gift allowance, no article will be exempt from duty and tax. Duty cannot be prepaid; it is collected by the United States Postal Service when the package is delivered.

You may not send gifts to yourself, nor may persons traveling together send gifts to each other. The gift allowance does not include alcoholic beverages, tobacco products or perfume valued at more than $5 if it contains alcohol. All parcels must be marked *Unsolicited Gift,* and the nature of the gift and its estimated fair retail value must be noted on the outside wrapper.

RESTRICTED ARTICLES: To prevent the introduction of plant and animal pests and diseases into the United States, an agricultural quarantine bans importation of most fruits, vegetables, plants, livestock, poultry and meats. For details refer to the Department of Agriculture's Animal Products and Fruit and Vegetable manuals online at www.aphis.usda.gov.

Endangered animal or plant species, and products made from them, generally cannot be exported or imported. This includes products made from elephant ivory, although articles made from antique ivory may be imported, provided they can be documented as being at least 100 years old. If you wish to purchase and bring back to the United States any articles made from whalebone, ivory, tortoise shell, animal skins or fur, or products manufactured wholly or in part of any type of wildlife, contact the U.S. Fish and Wildlife Service at (800) 358-2104 to make sure items are admissible.

Certain articles considered injurious or detrimental to the United States also are prohibited; these include absinthe, firearms, biological specimens, meat products and narcotics. There are stringent import restrictions on firearms and ammunition as well; consult the Bureau of Tobacco and Firearms. Products originating in Angola, Iran, Liberia, Myanmar, North Korea, Serbia and Montenegro, Sudan and Cuba—and all items containing Cuban components—are subject to restriction and require a license. Cuban cigars are expressly forbidden. For further information consult the Office of Foreign Assets Control, Department of the Treasury, 1500 Pennsylvania Ave. N.W., Washington, DC 20220, phone (800) 540-6322, or visit their web site at www.treas.gov/ofac.

If you require medicines containing habit-forming drugs or narcotics, keep them in their original containers and bring an authorizing prescription to avoid potential customs problems upon return to the United States. It is wise to pack medicines in your carry-on luggage.

The distribution rights for many trademarked items are protected by law, and those items may not be brought into the U.S. by unlicensed entities. Residents returning with foreign-made articles bearing a protected trademark are allowed one exemption per type of article; for example, one Chanel handbag and one Polo shirt. The goods must be intended for personal use and must not be sold within 1 year of importation. Articles bearing a counterfeit mark or an inappropriately used federally registered trademark are subject to seizure and forfeiture.

ALCOHOL AND TOBACCO: A returning resident 21 years or older entitled to the $800 duty-free exemption may include 2 liters of alcoholic beverages—provided 1 liter was produced in a CBI country. Additional quantities are subject to duty and taxes. Travelers 21 years and older returning from the U.S. Virgin Islands may bring back 5 liters of alcoholic beverages, provided that 1 liter was produced there. Liquor cannot be mailed to the United States.

There are no federal age restrictions for persons returning with tobacco products. However, the laws of each state where an entry port is located are enforced, and tobacco products may be confiscated if the holder is under the state's minimum age for purchase of tobacco. Persons who meet age requirements may bring back up to 100 cigars and 200 cigarettes. Travelers returning from the U.S. Virgin Islands also may include in their exemption 1,000 cigarettes, provided no more than 200 were acquired elsewhere, and 100 cigars. It is illegal to bring cigars and tobacco products of Cuban origin into the United States.

Travelers may import previously exported tobacco products in quantities not exceeding their eligible exemptions. These items are usually stamped "Tax Exempt: For Use Outside the United States." Amounts exceeding your exemption will be seized and destroyed. Under this regulation, you may bring home 200 previously exported cigarettes plus an additional quantity of foreign-made cigarettes, paying duty and taxes only on the second group.

Laws concerning the importation of cigarettes and alcohol vary from state to state; check the importation requirements of your state of residence, as well as the state of entry.

AUTOMOBILES: Automobiles taken out of the country may be brought back duty free as long as they accompany you upon your return and meet EPA standards. Unleaded fuel is sometimes not available in the Caribbean; if leaded fuel is used, catalytic converters on late-model cars will become inoperative and in most cases will fail to meet emission standards, requiring replacement in order to obtain entry back into the United States. For details visit the EPA's website at www.epa.gov/otaq/imports or contact the agency directly: Environmental Protection Agency, Ariel Ross Bldg., Investigation/Import Section, 1200 Pennsylvania Ave. N.W., Washington, DC 20460; phone (202) 564-2057 or (734) 214-4100.

Points of Interest Index

AIRPORTS

AMPHITHEATERS

ANTIQUES

AQUARIUMS

Index Legend

NB................................national battlefield
NBP...........................national battlefield park
NC................................national cemetery
NF..................................national forest
NHM....................national historic(al) monument
NHP.........................national historic(al) park
NHS..........................national historic(al) site
NL................................national lakeshore
NME..............................national memorial
NMO...........................national monument
NMP...........................national military park
NP...................................national park
NRA.........................national recreation area
NR...................................national river
NS..............................national seashore
NWR.......................national wildlife refuge
PHP.......................provincial historic(al) park
PHS........................provincial historic(al) site
PP...................................provincial park
SF.....................................state forest
SHM.....................state historic(al) monument
SHP...........................state historic(al) park
SHS...........................state historic(al) site
SME..............................state memorial
SP.......................................state park
SRA.........................state recreation area

GEM: Points of Interest Offering a *Great Experience for Members*®

BIRTHPLACES & CHILDHOOD HOMES

EXHIBITS & COLLECTIONS-INDIAN

EXHIBITS & COLLECTIONS-MUSIC

EXHIBITS & COLLECTIONS-RELIGIOUS ITEMS

EXHIBITS & COLLECTIONS-REVOLUTIONARY WAR

EXHIBITS & COLLECTIONS-SCIENCE

EXHIBITS & COLLECTIONS-WARS

EXHIBITS & COLLECTIONS-WEAPONS

EXPERIMENTAL FARMS & STATIONS

FARMS

FERRY SERVICES—BOATS & AIRCRAFT

FISH HATCHERIES

FORESTS

FORESTS, NATIONAL; STATE

FORTS & MILITARY INSTALLATIONS

GAMBLING ESTABLISHMENTS

GARDENS

GEOLOGICAL FORMATIONS

GRAVES & TOMBS

HISTORIC BUILDINGS & HOUSES

HISTORIC DOCUMENTS, MANUSCRIPTS & RARE BOOKS

HISTORIC SITES

HORSE FARMS & RIDING STABLES

INDIAN MOUNDS, REMAINS & RUINS

INDIAN BURIAL GROUNDS

INDUSTRIAL TOURS

JAILS

LAKES, PONDS & RESERVOIRS

LIBRARIES, ARCHIVES

MUSIC HALLS & OPERA HOUSES

NATURAL BRIDGES

NATURAL PHENOMENA

NATURE CENTERS

NATURE TRAILS

NAUTICAL TOURS

OBSERVATORIES

PARKS, CITY; STATE; PROVINCIAL

PARKS, NATIONAL

PERFORMING ARTS ORGANIZATIONS

Bed & Breakfast Lodgings Index

Some bed and breakfasts listed below might have historical significance.
Those properties are also referenced in the Historical index.

Country Inns Index

Some of the following country inns can also be considered as bed-and-breakfast operations.

Historical Lodgings & Restaurants Index

Some of the following historical lodgings can also be considered as bed-and-breakfast operations.

Historical Lodgings & Restaurants (cont'd)

Resorts Index

Many establishments are located in resort areas; however, the following places have extensive on-premises recreational facilities:

Resorts (cont'd)

Comprehensive City Index

Here is an alphabetical list of all cities appearing in this TourBook® guide. Cities are presented by state/province. Page numbers under the POI column indicate where points of interest text begins. Page numbers under the L&R column indicate where lodging and restaurant listings begin.

Comprehensive City Index (cont'd)